TEXAS
HANDBOOK
THIRD EDITION

JOE CUMMINGS

MOON
PUBLICATIONS INC.

TEXAS HANDBOOK
THIRD EDITION

Published by
Moon Publications, Inc.
P.O. Box 3040
Chico, California 95927-3040, USA

Printed by
Colorcraft Ltd., Hong Kong

ISBN: 1-56691-063-3
ISSN: 1078-5418

Editor: Kevin Jeys
Copy Editor: Deana Corbitt Shields
Production & Design: David Hurst, Carey Wilson
Cartographers: Bob Race, Brian Bardwell
Index: Valerie Sellers Blanton

Front cover photo: Tim Thompson
All photos by Joe Cummings unless otherwise noted.

Distributed in the U.S.A. by Publishers Group West
Printed in Hong Kong

Although the author and publisher have made every effort to ensure that the information was correct at
the time of going to press, the author and publisher do not assume and hereby disclaim any liability to any
party for any loss or damage caused by errors, omissions, or any potential travel disruption due to labor or
financial difficulty, whether such errors or omissions result from negligence, accident, or any other cause.

Please send all comments,
corrections, additions,
amendments, and critiques to:

**TEXAS HANDBOOK
MOON PUBLICATIONS, INC.
P.O. BOX 3040
CHICO, CA 95927-3040, USA
e-mail: travel@moon.com**

Printing History
1st edition — August 1990
2nd edition — September 1992
3rd edition — January 1996

CONTENTS

MAPS

CHARTS

SPECIAL TOPICS

ABBREVIATIONS

a/c—air-conditioned
B&B—bed and breakfast
CVB—convention and visitors bureau
d—double occupancy
DFW—Dallas-Fort Worth
FM—"Farm-to-Market," or Farm Road
I—interstate highway
LP—liquefied petroleum
mph—miles per hour
NPS—National Park Service

pp—per person
RM—"Ranch-to-Market," or Ranch Road
  (also RR)
RV—recreation vehicle
s—single occupancy
t—triple occupancy
TCP—Texas Conservation Passport
TPWD—Texas Parks and Wildlife
  Department
w/e—water and electricity

MAP SYMBOLS

FREEWAY	
MAIN HIGHWAY	
SECONDARY ROAD	
UNPAVED RD.	
FOOT TRAIL	
TUNNEL	
RAILROAD	
BRIDGE	
REGIONAL BORDER	
COUNTY BORDER	
STATE BORDER	
INTERNATIONAL BORDER	

N.R.A. NATIONAL RECREATION AREA

S.R.A. STATE RECREATION AREA

N.W.R. NATIONAL WILDLIFE REFUGE

N.P. NATIONAL PARK

✈ AIRPORT

● HOTEL/ACCOMMODATION

INTERSTATE HIGHWAY
U.S. HIGHWAY
STATE HIGHWAY
OTHER NUMBERED ROAD
MEXICAN HIGHWAY
O LARGE CITY
o TOWN
■ POINT OF INTEREST
⌐⌐ GATE
WATER
▲ MOUNTAIN

IS THIS BOOK OUT OF DATE?

Between the time this book went to press and the time it reached the shelves, motels have closed, restaurants have changed hands, and prices have no doubt increased. All prices herein should therefore be regarded as approximations, and are not guaranteed by the publisher or author. Because keeping this book accurate and timely means compiling and printing later editions, we would appreciate hearing about any errors or omissions you may encounter in *Texas Handbook*. Also, if you have any noteworthy experiences— good or bad—with establishments listed in this book, please pass them along. If an attraction is out of place on a map, tell us; if the best restaurant in town is not included, we'd like to know. All contributions will be deeply appreciated and properly acknowledged. Address your letters to:

> Joe Cummings
> *Texas Handbook*
> c/o Moon Publications
> P.O. Box 3040, Chico, CA 95927
> E-mail: travel@moon.com

ACKNOWLEDGMENTS

The following folks were of considerable assistance during the updating process for the third edition of *Texas Handbook*:

Carol Ann Anderson, Kimberly Baker, Carolyn and Riley Binford, Terri Bortness, Marion Szurek Bottomley, Deborah Britton, Elsa Cantu, Phillip Coker, Donna Benevento, Katricia Cochran, John T. Davis, Heidi Dobrott, Soraya Canavati, Suzanne Chapman, Sharon Eason, Deb Freeman and the Texas Music Office, Sal Garza, Barbara B. Grove, Jimmy James, Regina Hill, Vel Anne Howel, Lynette Lancaster, Ernest Loeffler, Jr., Mary K. Manning, Tracie J. Martin and Southwest Airlines, Janice Matte, Shirley McVittie, Patricia Moore, George Myers, Mike Nelson, Eric O'Keefe, Joe Nick Patoski, Lew Perin, Genora B. Prewit, Diane Probst, Penny Reeh, Sabal Palm Grove Sanctuary, Geneva Sapp, Jane Satel and La Mansón del Río, Marty Snortum, Charles Stephens, and Dana Stephens.

Thanks also to talented and energetic research assistants Chris Humphrey and Melissa Rivers, and to editor Kevin Jeys.

My parents, Will Joe and Mary Cummings, provided ongoing research assistance, for which I'm very grateful.

BOB RACE

INTRODUCTION

Texas *is* big. And along with its awe-inspiring size comes an incomparable diversity of people, flora, fauna, arts, and culture. In no other state can you experience as much change, both geographic and cultural, as when you travel from one end of Texas to another. Despite the ho-mogenizing influences of television and chain restaurants, which threaten to create a unified American way of life throughout the U.S., Texas remains a proudly different state, an area with strong roots and uncommon perspective.

THE LAND

Naturalist Richard Phelan has noted that Texas is blessed with "nearly every kind of land except tundra and tropical rainforest." In Texas you can't separate the land from the culture, especially when there is so much more land than people. The state contains 267,300 square miles of faults, folds, extrusions, intrusions, high and low plains, canyons, mountains, valleys, forests, islands, rivers, lakes, and bay-ous—a lot for a geographer to work with. A drive from Laredo on the Mexican border to Wichita Falls on the Oklahoma border will take you through four or five obviously different terrains. Texans are fond of mentioning that it's farther from Texarkana to El Paso than it is from Chicago to New York (or from El Paso to Los Angeles). But few people today recall that when the government of the Republic of Texas signed the treaty annexing their sovereign nation to the United States in 1845, they reserved the right in perpetuity to subdivide the new state into as many as five smaller states. Few Texans have advocated such a course of action in recent years, but in topographical variety as well as size, Texas easily lends itself to that kind of thinking.

Talk to six different Texana experts about how best to divide the state into physiographic regions and you'll hear six different plans. Geography forms climate, and climate in turn influences wildlife and the human population, which make their own contributions to ongoing topographical changes. The task of classification is especially difficult in Texas, which forms the intersection of four major American physiographic regions—the Great Plains, the Interior Lowlands, the Rocky Mountain System, and the Basin and Range Province. But if you synthesize descriptions of Texas from the fields of geology, biology, and meteorology, you'll find they agree on eight basic geographic sections: the **Llano Estacado** (also called High Plains), the **Prairies and Cross Timbers** (or Low Plains), the **Trans-Pecos**, the **Edwards Plateau**, the **Llano Uplift**, the **Rio Grande Plain**, the **Gulf Coast**, and the **East Texas Forests**.

Llano Estacado

One of the myths about Texas is that it's flat and dry. This notion is most likely propagated by people who've driven cross-country via Interstate 40, which cuts across the Texas Panhandle through Amarillo and miles of seemingly unending flat territory. Spanish explorers called this area the Llano Estacado, or "Staked Plain," but no one is sure why. Maybe it was because they had to drive stakes in the earth for navigation purposes since there were few natural landmarks. Or perhaps it was because the western edge (in New Mexico) and eastern edge (in Texas) dropped so suddenly, like a stockade wall—*estacado* can also mean "stockaded."

Geographically speaking, this area represents the southernmost tip of the Great Plains,

which stretch from the Panhandle all the way north to Canada. In Texas, the Llano Estacado covers mostly the western part of the Panhandle as far south as Odessa. A few miles east of Lubbock it's separated from the Low Plains by the Caprock Escarpment, where the hard layer of caliche, marl, chalk, and gravel (the caprock) that underlies the Llano crumbles away. Caliche is a cement-like substance that forms when water evaporates from limestone mixed with soil, leaving behind a calcified "hardpan." You don't see that much caliche naturally exposed on the High Plains, but once you descend the Caprock Escarpment, it becomes a fairly common feature of Central Texas. When Texans say they live "up on the Caprock," they mean in the Llano Estacado area of the Panhandle.

The Caprock slows the erosion of topsoil from the High Plains, and this vast layer of topsoil at one time supported uninterrupted grasslands. Huge herds of buffalo once grazed here, and the Comanche who lived off the herds managed to keep European settlers out of the Llano Estacado until the late 19th century. While neither the Texas Rangers nor the U.S. Army could defeat the Comanches in battle, white buffalo hunters and other Amerindians—often supplied with ammunition by the Army—managed to deplete the buffalo herds to such an extent that many Comanches were forced to move on to Oklahoma. At that point cattle ranchers from farther south in Texas moved in and overstocked the land, destroying the natural grasslands in less than a hundred years.

Today, the grasslands have returned to some degree in the form of large grain farms that grow oats, corn, and sorghum. Many of these farms are irrigated by windmills that pump water from deep below the Caprock. The windmill has become a symbol of Texas farming and on the Llano Estacado many families erect mock Texas windmills in front of their homes, one for each child. The last remaining American windmill manufacturer is located in San Angelo, Texas, at the southernmost edge of the Llano. Ironically, the larger cattle ranches, such as the XIT in Lubbock, have split up, and ranchers must now grow, or purchase, their own feed to supplement grazing.

The table-top flatness of the Llano Estacado is interrupted by two rivers. The Canadian runs east to west across the top portion of the Panhandle, cutting a 20-mile-wide trough known as The Breaks. The Breaks expose layers of gypsum, petrified wood, and a type of flint once highly prized by North American Indians. On a bluff near what is today Lake Meredith are the remains of the Alibates Flint Quarries, where, 12,000 years ago, Indians obtained flint for spear points and arrowheads that were traded throughout the Plains. The Canadian is also known for its quicksand areas and was thus one of the trickier rivers to cross in the days when cattlemen drove stock north to Kansas.

The Prairie Dog Town Fork of the Red River and smaller tributaries have formed the technicolor Palo Duro Canyon south of Amarillo. Charles Goodnight established the first ranch on the Llano in 1876 right in Palo Duro Canyon; he stayed for 53 years.

Trans-Pecos

For many people, the Trans-Pecos region is the most compellingly beautiful of Texas landscapes, an inspiring combination of mountains, desert, mesas, and endless blue skies—in short, what most people think of as classic Southwestern scenery. This area is part of a geologic phenomenon called the Basin and Range Province. Centered in Nevada, it encompasses the Colorado Plateau to include parts of Colorado and Utah, and extends across New Mexico and into Texas for thousands of square miles before butting up against the Texas High Plains. Trans-Pecos means, of course, "across the Pecos River," but in Texas the area actually begins a bit northeast of the Pecos River at the southwestern edge of the High Plains.

The 70-foot sand dunes of the Monahans Sandhills in the eastern Trans-Pecos were once part of the floor of a Permian sea. Although they shimmer in the midday summer heat, at night the dunes make a good campsite—as long as you stay within sight of a road or other stationary landmarks. Smaller dunes feature shinnery oaks, which are only about three feet high but have a root system that reaches as far as 90 feet underground. Mesquite, hardy grasses, and wildflowers also appear occasionally, interrupting the sandy landscape. The lower part of the Trans-Pecos belongs to the great Chihuahuan Desert, which stretches far

THE TRANS-PECOS

The Pecos River is the nominal eastern boundary for the Trans-Pecos region, but geographically this area also includes the Monahan Sandhills, located northeast of the river. For many people, the Trans-Pecos region is the most compellingly beautiful landscape in Texas, with its deep canyons, orange-tinged mesas, flowering cacti, and sparkling arroyos.

The Trans-Pecos once presented a set of formidable barriers to riders, drovers, or wagon trains seeking to travel due west from Central Texas. First was the Pecos River itself, with its sheer chasms and turbulent waters. Then came the long stretches of alluring but unforgiving Chihuahuan Desert, broken only by the equally formidable Glass, Davis, and Guadalupe mountains.

In the 1850s, the U.S. Army imported camels from the Middle East and maintained a Camel Corps for the exploration of the Trans-Pecos. Even until fairly recently, most people drove through the Trans-Pecos with canvas water bags strapped to their radiators. Today Interstate 10 provides a relatively safe and speedy transit across this part of West Texas, if getting to El Paso as quickly as possible is your objective. But a sparse network of good U.S. highways, state highways, and farm/ranch roads makes it fairly easy to explore the scenic Upper Rio Grande, the sandhills, the major mountain ranges, and stunning Big Bend National Park.

When people speak today of the old "Law West of the Pecos," they tend to forget this referred not simply to the vast remoteness of the area, but to the most lawless area of what was generally known as a lawless state. In the 19th and early 20th centuries, you had to be rough to get here, and you had to be rough to survive. Even today, law enforcement is scarce between Del Rio and El Paso; local residents claim they like it that way, that they prefer to take care of disputes on their own.

south into the Mexican state of Chihuahua, from which it gets its name.

Dividing the Mexican part of the desert from the American is, of course, the Rio Grande, which has its source in Colorado. The river flows north-south through New Mexico, then along the Texas-Mexico border until it empties into the Gulf of Mexico. The Upper Rio Grande Valley near El Paso is the oldest irrigated region in the state and the oldest continually cultivated area in the country. Water from the river is so heavily diverted for agricultural use here that the Rio Grande just about comes to a halt until it is joined farther down by Mexico's Rio Conchos at Presidio, Texas. Then, for 100 miles or so, the Rio Grande follows the southern boundary of Big Bend National Park, flowing through three successive canyons: the Santa Eleña, the Mariscal, and the Boquillas.

Texans like saying that their state has 90 mountains over a mile high, but they seldom mention that every one of them is found in the Trans-Pecos area. There are 30 named mountain ranges here and all are "fault-block" ranges, large chunks of the earth's crust that have broken loose and tilted like a broken sidewalk. All the mountain ranges of the Basin and Range Province, including the Rockies, are of this type. The Guadalupe Mountains, straddling the New Mexico border, are the state's highest range (Guadalupe Peak, 8,749 feet), followed by the Davis Mountains (Mount Livermore, 8,382 feet) and the Chisos Mountains of Big Bend (Emory Peak, 7,835 feet).

In places, the Trans-Pecos mountain ranges surround large drainage basins called *bolsones,* Spanish for "bags" or "large purses." These basins hold rainwater that flows down the sides of the mountains; during times of sparse precipitation, this is the only source of surface water. Since the Trans-Pecos receives only about nine inches of rain per annum, yet averages nine *feet* of evaporation in that same time period, minerals distilled from the water tend to collect in the lowest points of a *bolson*. Salt is one of the primary distillates, so salt flats (locally called *playas*) are common among the basin areas, especially at the base of the Guadalupe Mountains. Until quite recently, commercial salt was collected from the *playas* in the Diablo Plateau area.

When rain falls into these basins, it forms lakes and pools of extremely salty water, which compounds the problem of scarce drinking water for humans, animals, and plants. Fortunately for animate life, natural cisterns called *huecos* (Spanish for "hole") occur in rock formations throughout certain parts of the Trans-Pecos, some of which shelter pools of pure rainwater year round. Hueco Tanks State Park, 32 miles east of El Paso, features a high concentration of these pools and is the site of one of the state's largest collections of Indian pictographs. Apaches, Comanches, and Kiowas made Hueco Tanks a regular stop in their travels through West Texas, as did the Butterfield Overland Mail stagecoach line.

Big Bend country, where the Rio Grande forms a deep loop through the Chisos Mountains, is one of the more spectacular places in the Trans-Pecos, or indeed in the entire United States. Big Bend National Park itself is the best-preserved portion of the Chihuahuan Desert in either the U.S. or Mexico. See "Big Bend National Park" in the West Texas chapter for a complete description.

Edwards Plateau

Just south of Abilene lies the Callahan Divide, a series of gaps where the Texas High Plains give way to the lower Edwards Plateau. Large herds of buffalo once migrated through these gaps to warmer and greener pastures during harsh winters. But the soil of the Edwards Plateau is much thinner than that of the High Plains, and grasslands here were overgrazed by cattle even more quickly than on the Llano Estacado.

Below the thin layer of topsoil is a giant slab of limestone that reaches a thickness of 10,000 feet in places. Many old homes, courthouses, and banks in the region feature blocks of this limestone, locally called "tufa" or "tufa limestone." Unpaved roads in Central Texas are usually laid with caliche, a limestone gravel that resists water-soaking. Domesticated animals far outnumber the people in this area and many counties have only one town, the county seat.

Deer and other cloven-hoofed creatures thrive on the rocky terrain; the Edwards Plateau is the world's leading area for the raising of Angora goats for mohair. Even cattle ranchers on the plateau breed goats and sheep to supplement their income from cattle auctions. In many ways the terrain strongly resembles the high plains

Fate Bell Rock Shelter, on the edge of the Edwards Plateau

of East Africa—a few ranches here specialize in exotic breeds from Asia and Africa, including giraffe, rhinoceros, aoudad, and wildebeest.

The plateau stands 1,500 to 3,000 feet above sea level and stretches southward from the Callahan Divide until it begins to crumble away into the Rio Grande and Gulf Coast Plains at a large fault zone called the Balcones Escarpment. The Balcones, so named by Spanish settlers because of its resemblance to a series of balconies when viewed from the plains below, cuts a steep curve east from Del Rio over to San Antonio and then northeast from there past San Marcos, New Braunfels, Austin, and farther northward to Waco. Cracks in the limestone shell allow water to spring forth from underground aquifers all along the fault, forming streams and rivers. Towns developed along the fault zone because of the easy access to water. During the state's Cattle Kingdom era the main trunk of the Chisholm Trail—today Interstate 35—ran parallel to the Balcones Escarpment.

The area of the Edwards Plateau along the fault zone is usually called the Hill Country and is highly prized as a recreation area because of its mild climate and abundant streams. During the height of the summer, nights are dry, cool, and often breezy, while winters are sunny and temperate.

Hundreds of streams pour down from the plateau, through the Hill Country, and over the Balcones onto the Gulf Coast Plains. Chief among them are the Guadalupe, Frio, Sabinal, Nueces, and Pedernales. The south end of the Pecos River also passes through the Edwards Plateau, joining the Rio Grande at Lake Amistad. At the top of the plateau, streams run northward and empty into the Colorado River. South of the town of Junction, at the foot of the Hill Country, is an area called Seven Hundred Springs because of the wealth of springs bubbling up through the limestone.

All this water and limestone naturally results in outstanding caves and cave formations. In Val Verde County, between the Rio Grande and the Pecos, dozens of shallow caves contain ancient Indian pictographs. Farther inside the plateau are much larger caves, like the world-famous Caverns of Sonora and the Devil's Sinkhole. So far, speleologists have counted over 2,000 caves of substantial size in the vicinity, many as yet totally unexplored.

Llano Uplift

The Llano Uplift is a very large, high valley, about 70 miles wide and 1,000 feet high, surrounded by rugged hills. It's actually a huge "bump" in the earth's crust where an upsurge of magma pushed against the crust but never quite erupted into a volcano. Over time, the magma cooled and turned to granite. As you drive north onto the uplift from the Edwards Plateau, the gravel along the side of the road actually turns from white (limestone) to pink (granite). Quarries in the Llano Uplift mine high-quality granite, talc, and graphite, but the mainstay of the local economy is cattle ranching.

The area is named for the Llano River, which runs off the Edwards Plateau from Junction to the town of Llano, and from there to a string of lakes northwest of Austin that were once part of the Colorado River. Called the Highland Lakes, they were created by damming the Colorado River in several places.

The area surrounding the lakes is fast becoming a resort area for Central Texas residents. The recent transformation has been great for Central Texans, but not so good for the dwindling wildlife and plants on the Colorado River floodplains. The dams supply electricity to the area and income for developers, but also provide flood control in an area once plagued by disastrous floods.

Critics claim Nature has its own way of practicing flood control—growing heavy vegetation that traps water and allows it to soak into the water table in flood-prone areas, more effective than damming a river and wiping out protective vegetation. However, natural flood control along this section of the Colorado had already been severely hampered by local farming and ranching practices. The only apparent alternative to erecting the dams would have been abandoning the area—which is what people would have been forced to do during the torrential rains of 1957, when floodwaters threatened to carry off half of Central and South Texas into the Gulf of Mexico. The dams allowed the municipal water authorities to siphon floodwaters systematically from level to level until they reached the coastal plains where the water could be accommodated.

Rio Grande Plain

The South Texas region wedged between the Balcones Escarpment to the north, the lower Rio Grande to the southwest, and the Gulf of Mexico to the southeast is a subtropical zone of seemingly endless chaparral that fades into sand at the Gulf, and palm trees and citrus plantations at the Rio Grande. The town of Southmost, Texas, in the Rio Grande delta (often called the Rio Grande Valley) is only 169 miles north of the Tropic of Cancer. South Texas is the only place in the U.S. that you'll find tropical flora and fauna native to North America (Florida's tropical wildlife comes from the Caribbean).

The Rio Grande Plain is basically the intersection of the Gulf Coast and the northern Mexico plains. The geography, climate, and wildlife are relatively similar from San Antonio all the way to Mexico's Sierra Madre Oriental beyond Monterrey. Much of it consists of the famous "Brush Country" of South Texas and northern Mexico. Brush or chaparral is a rather recent phenomenon, a natural result of the overgrazing

THE RIO GRANDE

The fifth longest river in North America, second longest in the U.S., the Rio Grande—called Río Bravo in Mexico—begins 12,000 feet above sea level in Colorado's Rocky Mountains. From there it flows southeast through Colorado and New Mexico, then along the Texas-Mexico border for more than half its length until it empties into the Gulf of Mexico, for a total distance of 1,896 miles. Its principal tributaries include the Pecos, Devil, Chama, and Puerco rivers in the U.S. and the Salado, San Juan, and Conchos rivers in Mexico. All are important sources of water in a region that generally receives little rainfall. The major portion of the river's volume is provided by Mexican tributaries; the only U.S. affluent of significance is the Pecos River in Texas.

Archaeological evidence indicates Amerindian groups inhabited rock shelters along the river for 10,000-12,000 years before the Spanish *entrada*. Still-visible Coahuiltecan pictographs on the walls of Seminole Canyon near Ciudad Acuña are at least 4,000 years old. The Upper Rio Grande Valley near Ciudad Juárez is the oldest irrigated region in Mexico and the oldest continually cultivated area in North America. The Patarabueyes, a Pueblo Indian group, had been tilling the floodplains since at least A.D. 1200 when the Spanish arrived at La Junta in the 1600s.

The Spanish first explored the river, which they originally called Rio de las Palmas, in the 1500s, settling on the riverbanks in the 17th and 18th centuries. By the mid-19th century steamboat traffic extended northwestward from the Gulf of Mexico as far as Rio Grande City, roughly 105 miles upriver.

Nowadays water from the river is so heavily diverted for agricultural use on both sides of the border near Ciudad Juárez-El Paso that the Rio Grande nearly trickles to a halt until it's joined by Mexico's

Rio Conchos at Ojinaga, Chihuahua. Then, for 93 miles or so, the Rio Grande follows the southern boundary of Big Bend National Park, flowing through three high-walled canyons—the Santa Eleña, the Mariscal, and the Boquillas—that are a favorite destination for river runners.

One of the most pristine sections of the lower Rio Grande is a 70-mile stretch between the Mexican village of Guerrero and the Colombia Bridge north of Laredo. A *San Antonio Express-News* reporter who recently spent four days kayaking this reach wrote that he was amazed by the variety of indigenous wildlife, including great blue and white herons, snowy and cattle egrets, owls, four-foot alligator gars, carp, catfish, bass, white-tailed deer, javelinas, and mountain lions—almost everything native to South Texas except humans.

Major cities along the course of the Rio Grande include Albuquerque, El Paso, and Brownsville in the U.S., and Ciudad Juárez, Nuevo Laredo, Reynosa, and Matamoros in Mexico. Two major international dams, Lake Amistad near Del Rio and Falcon Reservoir near Laredo, have been built along the river to provide water storage through protracted dry periods and to prevent flooding downriver during heavy rains.

Albuquerque, New Mexico, is the only U.S. city that dumps sewage into the river as a matter of standard practice; many Mexican municipalities do. According to the U.S. Environmental Protection Agency, all the major human centers along the river —except, surprisingly, Ciudad Juárez-El Paso— have sewage problems of varying degrees.

Since the passage of NAFTA, the Mexican and U.S. governments have promised to share the US$35 million tab for a new water treatment plant in Nuevo Laredo, Mexico. Similar projects are planned for Matamoros, Ciudad Acuña, and Reynosa.

of cattle that occurred throughout the Great Plains. At one time this area featured extensive savanna or grasslands, but as the grass thinned, the brush took over.

"Brush" is a mixture of tenacious plants, mostly thorny ones: cactus, mesquite, dwarf oak, black bush, yucca, huisache, huajillo, and other wild shrubs. Often it grows in tangled clumps, some of them up to 20 feet in height. Spanish *vaqueros* taught their Anglo counterparts the

skill of "brush-popping," or riding through the brush at top speed in pursuit of stray cattle. This kind of riding required special leather leggings (*chaparrera*) for protection from the brush. Texas cowboys or "buckaroos" (from *vaqueros*) called them "chaps"—a shortening of *chaparrera*.

Cattle ranching is still big on the Rio Grande Plain—this is where it all started—but as on the Edwards Plateau, many ranchers now raise sheep and goats as well. Cloven-hoofed animals like deer, sheep, and goats do well in brush country, since they browse rather than graze—they prefer twigs and leaves to grass. A few South Texas ranches stock Australian and African breeds like ostrich and rhinoceros. Down toward the Rio Grande delta, vegetable and citrus cultivation are important industries.

Gulf Coast

The Texas Gulf Coast is an extension of the coastal plains that reach all the way from the Atlantic Ocean to the Rio Grande. They're bounded at the northwest by the Balcones Escarpment, at the north by the East Texas Forests, and on the southwest by the Rio Grande Plain. The Gulf of Mexico coast, of course, forms the southeast boundary, stretching for over 600 miles. The Gulf, the world's largest body of water by that name, is really a tropical sea in itself, with coral reefs, underwater mountains, and submarine canyons. The well-known Gulf Stream runs clockwise around the Gulf (the "Loop Current") and then into the Atlantic, where it warms East Coast beaches. Near Texas, the water temperature varies from 52° to 85°, depending on the time of year.

Parallel to the coastline are the long, sandy barrier islands of North and South Padre, Mustang, and Matagorda, as well as the vibrant salt-marshes of Galveston Island and the Bolivar Peninsula. Saltmarshes produce the greatest biomass of any environment on the planet—that is, the highest concentration of living organisms per square mile. In the Bolivar Peninsula's saltmarshes you'll see everything from gnats to alligators.

A large underground supply of geothermal energy lies untapped beneath the Texas coast in the form of very hot (320°) water. Geothermal engineers are still deliberating on how best to utilize the energy. The water is fresh, not salty, which makes it a potential source of drinking water once it's cooled.

East Texas Forests

The East Texas Forests are the westernmost extension of the Southern Appalachian Woodland. If the Trans-Pecos belongs to the American Southwest, East Texas belongs to the American Southeast. The forests here can be divided into the Pine Belt (farthest east), the Big Thicket

(south of the Pine Belt), and the Post Oak Belt (west of both).

Timber has been the main long-term industry in the Pine Belt. In addition to pine, hundreds of other tree species grow in the Pine Belt. Because of heavy annual rainfall (up to 60 inches a year), growth is profuse and forest fires rarely a problem. High humidity and the morning fog, common throughout the East Texas woodlands, keep the forest moist. Huge oil and gas fields have also yielded local revenue; cotton and cattle have become increasingly important as well.

Before the 1800s, most of East Texas was almost entirely virgin forest inhabited only by a small group of Caddo Indians. Farming and cattle ranching later turned vast tracts of land into prairie, but the establishment of four national forests as well as a national preserve offers some protection to over a million acres of woodlands.

One of these, Big Thicket National Preserve, is said to be among the most magnificent and complex forests in the world. Part of the reason is its proximity to the Gulf Coast, with which it shares a thick layer of sand just under the topsoil. Roots flourish in the sand, penetrating deeply and easily; sand is also an efficient water repository. This sandy layer, together with the mild combination of subtropic and temperate climates and the lack of forest fires, means trees grow to great size and age. For more detail on this forest wonder, see "Big Thicket National Preserve" in the East Texas chapter

Between Caddo Lake, which straddles the Texas-Louisiana border near Shreveport, and the Sabine River to the south are several classic bayous. The Sabine River flows into the Toledo Bend Reservoir, also on the Louisiana border. If this lake were entirely within Texas, it would form the largest body of water in the state.

The Piney Woods begin to fade out as they move west into the Post Oak Belt. The tall pines give way to sturdy post oaks, which have become fewer and farther between since there are no national forests here to preserve them from farming and ranching interests. Clay, lignite, and other minerals in this area are mined for commercial use. Though based on the same kind of sandy soil, the Post Oak Belt is very much a transition area between the East Texas Forests and the Prairies and Cross Timbers farther west.

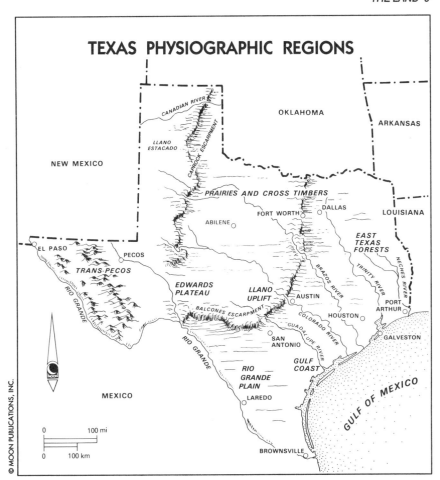

TEXAS PHYSIOGRAPHIC REGIONS

Prairies and Cross Timbers

Between the Caprock Escarpment just east of Abilene and the Post Oak Belt east of Dallas are the Prairies and Cross Timbers, an area consisting of smaller plains, prairies, and former woodlands running in north-south strips toward the Colorado River. Proceeding east to west, they include the fertile Blackland Prairie, the Eastern Cross Timbers, the Grand Prairie, the Western Cross Timbers, and the Rolling Plains. In the same direction, the underlying geology alternates sand, limestone, and red Permian to account for these differing topographies.

The Chisholm Cattle Trail, the Western (Dodge City) Cattle Trail, and the Butterfield Overland Mail stagecoach line all intersected in this part of Texas, which encompasses about a quarter of the state. As the cities of Dallas, Fort Worth, Wichita Falls, and Austin grew along these 19th-century routes (today Interstates 35 and 20), intensive land use blurred the lines between discrete geological entities to form more or less one topographical region: a patchwork of similar-looking farms, cities, towns, and suburbs.

If you look closely, though, as you drive from Dallas to Abilene, you'll notice some variation. The Grand Prairie is dairy country, rolling and grassy. Add the occasional tree to this scene and you've got the Blackland Prairie, one of the most agriculturally rich areas in the state. Toward Abilene, wayward mesas begin to rise among the gently rolling hills, signaling the crumbly red earth of the Permian Basin. The Rolling Plains near Abilene are the last land contours to be seen before they're literally rolled up in the Great Plains of the Panhandle.

CLIMATE

Meteorologists love Texas weather because the state has so much of it. It's said that if you don't like the weather in Texas, just stick around a couple of minutes and it'll change. While this isn't always so, it is true that if you don't like the weather in one part of the state, you can always drive to another part for an entirely different climate.

WET AND DRY

Texas rainfall varies mostly from east to west rather than north to south, though North Central Texas does get a few more inches of rain each year than South Texas. The driest part of Texas is the Trans-Pecos region between Big Bend and El Paso, where the average annual precipitation is eight to 12 inches. The Davis Mountains of the Trans-Pecos get a bit more, up to 18 inches a year.

The wettest places are in East Texas, ranging from 52 inches a year in the Houston area to 56 inches a year on the lower Louisiana border. In areas between far West Texas and far East Texas, rainfall averages 25-28 inches a year.

Time of year is just as important to average precipitation as longitude. The Trans-Pecos receives more rainfall in summer and fall than in winter or spring. In East Texas, on the other hand, it rains most in the spring. In Central Texas, the fall months see the most rain.

HOT AND COLD

Several factors affect the state's average temperatures: latitude, longitude, elevation, and proximity to the Gulf of Mexico. As in most of the U.S., the lowest average temperatures occur between December and February, the highest between June and August.

In January, the average low temperatures vary from 28° F in Wichita Falls to 51° F in Brownsville. The average highs in January for these same cities are 52° F and 70° F respectively.

July temperatures range from average lows of 66° F in Amarillo and 76° F in Corpus Christi to average highs of 95° F in El Paso and 99° F in Laredo.

But averages are only averages—actual temperatures may zoom up and down the thermometer. Furthermore, perceived temperatures can diverge from actual temperatures due to wind velocity and humidity. Eighty-five degrees Fahrenheit is perceived as 80° F at 0% humidity, 86° F at 50% humidity, and 101° F at 100%

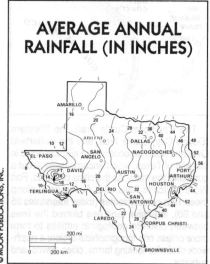

AVERAGE ANNUAL
RAINFALL (IN INCHES)

© MOON PUBLICATIONS, INC.

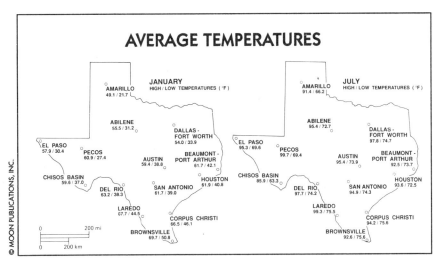

AVERAGE TEMPERATURES

JANUARY HIGH / LOW TEMPERATURES (°F)

AMARILLO 49.1 / 21.7
ABILENE 55.5 / 31.2
EL PASO 57.9 / 30.4
PECOS 60.9 / 27.4
DALLAS - FORT WORTH 54.0 / 33.9
AUSTIN 59.4 / 38.8
BEAUMONT - PORT ARTHUR 61.7 / 42.1
CHISOS BASIN 59.6 / 37.0
DEL RIO 63.2 / 38.3
SAN ANTONIO 61.7 / 39.0
HOUSTON 61.9 / 40.8
LAREDO 67.7 / 44.5
CORPUS CHRISTI 66.5 / 46.1
BROWNSVILLE 69.7 / 50.8

0   200 mi
0   200 km

JULY HIGH / LOW TEMPERATURES (°F)

AMARILLO 91.4 / 66.2
ABILENE 95.4 / 72.7
EL PASO 95.3 / 69.6
PECOS 99.7 / 69.4
DALLAS - FORT WORTH 97.8 / 74.7
AUSTIN 95.4 / 73.9
BEAUMONT - PORT ARTHUR 92.5 / 73.7
CHISOS BASIN 85.9 / 63.3
DEL RIO 97.7 / 74.2
SAN ANTONIO 94.9 / 74.3
HOUSTON 93.6 / 72.5
LAREDO 99.3 / 75.5
CORPUS CHRISTI 94.2 / 75.6
BROWNSVILLE 92.6 / 75.6

© MOON PUBLICATIONS, INC.

humidity. While the Texas coast is more humid than most inland areas, breezes off the Gulf keep temperatures lower. South Central and East Texas, however, are humid year round, ranging from 52% to 93% depending on the time of day—mornings and evenings are the most humid.

In general, the hottest days during the summer months are in the upper Rio Grande plains. The small town of Presidio, for example, often records daily high temperatures in excess of 100° F during June, July, and August. Because of the desert climate, however, nighttime temperatures at Presidio average a relatively cool 70-72° F during these same months. In the mountains of West Texas, temperatures are much more moderate during the summer, e.g., at Chisos Basin the daily average high is 63-73° F.

One climate feature of note is what Texans call a "norther," a cold front that moves in suddenly from a northerly direction. In the fall and winter months, these can arrive so rapidly that temperatures may drop as much as 50 degrees Fahrenheit in a half hour. Sometimes you can actually see the cold front on the distant northern horizon—a steel-blue bank of high clouds floating over clear blue skies. Texans call this a "blue norther," a front that tends to come in fast and hard.

BEST SEASONS FOR TRAVEL

The best months for statewide Texas travel are usually late October through November, March and April, and late May and early June. A pan-Texas tour during these periods would avoid the state's highest and lowest average temperatures as well as the most intense periods of rainfall. Of course not every year is the same.

Texas has no real peak tourist season; the state as a whole tends to receive roughly the same numbers of visitors year round. South Texas, however, is more heavily traveled in the winter due to the influx of "Winter Texans" from the midwestern United States.

For regional travel, optimum months vary according to Texas geography.

Trans-Pecos and Big Bend

October to December and March to May are generally good weather months in the Trans-Pecos and Big Bend area. The summer months, June to August, are usually too hot for the average visitor—daytime temperatures reach the high 90s and low 100s. The mountains are quite temperate this time of year; just stay away from desert hikes. For Rio Grande river running, the fall is best for water action while spring is superior for birdwatching and wildflowers.

along the River Road, Trans-Pecos

Northwest Texas

Upper West Texas and the Panhandle can be rather blustery during the winter months and hot during the summer. Since rainfall is moderate year round, these areas are visited frequently in both spring and fall.

North Central Texas

The area around Dallas, Fort Worth, and Waco features a climate that's a sort of cross between the weather in East Texas and South Central Texas. Heavy rains and the occasional tornado arrive in the late spring (April-May), but the rest of the year the weather is fairly moderate. Summers are hot, but not as hot as farther south or east.

South and South Central Texas

South Texas is fairly seasonable year round, though temperatures in the high 90s are common June to August. During these months, high temperatures coupled with high humidity make parts of South Central Texas quite sticky in the daytime.

Near the Mexican border the humidity is significantly lower, so some people find the lower Rio Grande more comfortable than South Central Texas during the summer, in spite of slightly higher temperatures. The Hill Country makes a good escape from San Antonio or Austin when temperature and humidity rise too high. Temperatures tend to be four or five degrees lower, and, because of the elevation, the air is drier and there's usually a breeze.

During the winter, the weather in the lower Rio Grande valley is prime—as evidenced by the snowbirds who drive down here from the midwestern U.S. to escape plunging temperatures.

East Texas

East Texas is best visited in the fall, when temperatures and rainfall are moderate. During the summer months, high temperatures and humidity slow most visitors down. Spring in East Texas is also comfortable if you can put up with occasional thundershowers.

HEAVY WEATHER

Tornadoes

Texas is famous for tornadoes and, to a much lesser extent, hurricanes. Tornadoes, often called "twisters," evolve from large, heavy thunderstorms in which a combination of atmospheric conditions produces a poorly understood set of spinning air currents. These currents spin faster and faster as they move toward the center.

Texas reports an average of just over 100 tornadoes a year, most occurring during the tornado season, March to May. Most afflict a north-south corridor called "Tornado Alley," which stretches from the North Texas plains through Oklahoma, Kansas, and Nebraska. Tornado warnings are fairly common during the tornado season as national and state meteorologists keep a close watch on storms and air currents that show twister potential.

It's highly unlikely you'll be faced with a twister unless you happen to be traveling through Tornado Alley during peak season. If one is headed your way (you'll know—you'll see a dark funnel cloud undulating on the horizon), repair to the lowest place you can find. A cellar or basement of a building is best, but if you're caught outdoors, look for a ditch or any depression in the ground—twisters tend to skip over such low spots. Don't try to outrun a tornado by car or on foot; experts say, in fact, you'll fare better outside a vehicle, lying flat on the ground if necessary, rather than remaining in an exposed car. Wind speeds at the rotating center of a tornado have been clocked at 280 miles per hour; tornadoes have been known to lift entire cars and houses dozens of feet into the air before they come crashing to the ground.

Hurricanes

Hurricanes are fairly common on the Gulf of Mexico in August and September, less frequently in June, July, and October. The name comes from the Spanish for tropical cyclone, *huracán,* which is itself a corruption of the Mayan word for their storm god, Hunraken or Huraken. By definition, a hurricane or tropical cyclone is a "highly advanced tropical storm"; the effective difference between a tropical storm and a hurricane is force and potential for damage.

Between 1871 and 1982, an average of 41 hurricanes a year entered the state of Texas, most directly from the Gulf. The vast majority caused little or no damage to either the coastal or inland areas of the state. Cities and towns always take the precaution of alerting residents and evacuating areas in advance of a storm's arrival. Oftentimes a hurricane will lose momentum or change direction before hitting the coast, even when severe warnings have been issued. Nonetheless, visitors should definitely avoid the sea whenever there's a hurricane warning.

The most famous Texas hurricane was the Great Galveston Storm of September 8-9, 1900, which has been called the worst natural disaster in U.S. history. Peak wind velocity was estimated at 120 miles per hour and the entire island of Galveston was inundated by 15-foot tides. Somewhere between 6,000 and 8,000 people lost their lives, most by drowning.

FLORA AND FAUNA

Texas features a fascinating variety of flora and fauna, with many species found nowhere else in the United States. Five hundred forty bird species have been identified as well as 142 species of animals. Plant species are virtually uncountable because of the state's wide variety of geographical niches. A certain amount of native vegetation and wildlife is easily visible along the wide expanses of rural Texas, accessible by public farm and ranch roads throughout the state. Thousands of acres have also been set aside by the U.S. and the state of Texas especially for the preservation of Texas plants and animals; most of these admit human visitors as well.

Besides some of the better city zoos in the nation, botanical gardens, and other artificial venues for the viewing of plant and animal life, Texas has 12 National Park Service facilities, 136 state parks, four national forests, 13 national wildlife refuges and 28 state wildlife areas. Many of these are listed in this book by destination.

VEGETATION

Physiographically, the vegetational zones of Texas run the gamut from both the arid and humid lower Sonoran Zones to Canadian Zones. Before the arrival of European settlers, Texas was about 80% grasslands. The remaining 20% of the state consisted of the deserts and mountains of the Trans-Pecos region and the forests of East Texas. Cattle were introduced to the region in the 17th and 18th centuries by the Spanish; by the middle of the 19th century, overgrazing had begun to take its toll on Texas grasslands.

An 1898 U.S. Department of Agriculture report recorded a cattlemen's meeting wherein an attending botanist tried to explain the complex relationship between grazers and grasses. Before the botanist completed his explanation, a rancher interrupted with the following resolution, which was unanimously adopted by the cattlemen: "Resolved, that none of us know, or care to know, anything about grasses, native or otherwise, outside of the fact that for the present there are lots of them, the best on record, and we are after getting the most out of them while they last."

Although this conspicuously ignorant attitude resulted in the thinning or elimination of grasslands throughout Texas (and in the Plains states from Kansas to Montana, too, where the same attitude prevailed), the benefit to nature lovers was that this process allowed many other species to develop and proliferate. The complex "brush" considered a nuisance by ranchers has developed a fascinating ecosystem all its own.

Over 100 million acres of Texas is still considered "range," or land most suitable for grazing, which remains the single largest land use in the state. Rangelands are a vital part of the regional ecosystem; they provide watershed for springs, streams, and lakes, food and shelter for wildlife, and forage for domestic livestock, as well as resources for human recreation—not to mention their prominent role in Texas mythology. The one native grass that still appears throughout most of the state is **sideoats grama,** identifiable by its scimitar-shaped seed tops. **Buffalo grass, Texas grama,** and **Indian grass** are also common across several zones.

Texas in the post-Cattle Kingdom era can be divided into 10 vegetational zones, each discussed below.

Trans-Pecos, Mountains and Basins
Despite the fact this area receives an average of less than 10 inches of rain a year, far West Texas has perhaps the most interesting flora in the state. Texas boasts 106 species of cacti, more than the other 49 states combined, and most are found in this area. The flowering **prickly pear cactus** alone comes in a splendid variety of shapes, sizes, colors, and number of spines. **Agave, yucca,** and **sotol** are ubiquitous here. **Peyote,** a hallucinogenic cactus sought after by certain Indian groups for religious purposes, is native to the Chihuahuan Desert but is difficult to spot because it grows so

century plant

LOUISE FOOTE

low to the ground. Two endangered cactus species, **Nellie cory cactus** and **Chisos Mountain hedgehog cactus,** both threatened by cactus poachers who covet their brilliant flowers, grow only in South and West Texas.

Other common plants include the **cenizo bush,** also called purple sage; the **creosote bush,** which emits a bittersweet "desert" smell after a rain; and the slender **ocotillo,** or coachwhip. In the Big Bend area, the **candelilla** is collected illegally by Mexicans who render wax from the plant. The **guayule** or rubber plant is found in the extreme west portion of the Trans-Pecos.

On the mountain slopes you'll find Rocky Mountain grasses not native to Texas as well as the native **ponderosa pine, madrone, juniper,** and **piñon pine.** Wildflowers appear occasionally in basin areas that receive enough water. In the basins of the Chisos Mountains flourishes the **Chisos bluebonnet.** Mexicans call this plant *el conejo,* the rabbit, because of the resemblance of its white tip to a rabbit's tail.

High Plains
About the only vegetation native to the High Plains is a variety of grasses. With the thinning of the grasslands, "brush" moved in—**mesquite, sagebrush, yucca**—plants common throughout much of Texas. Most of the trees you see in the High Plains were introduced by Texas residents, though the native **cottonwood** grows in Palo Duro Canyon and **sand shinnery oak** is common in certain areas.

On the "sandyland" parts of the High Plains, **little bluestem, switch grass, Indian grass,** and **western wheatgrass** are the principal grasses. On the "hardlands" **buffalo grass** and **blue grama** are common, both excellent for grazing.

Rolling Plains
This area has the same grasses as the High Plains, with the addition of **red love grass, tumble grass, Texas winter grass, sideoats, wild ryes, big** and **sand bluestems,** and **tobosa grass.**

TEXAS IRONWOOD

Texas ranchers often consider the mesquite tree "brush"—problematic vegetation that encroaches on grasslands when native grasses become depleted. They commonly believe there's more mesquite in Texas now than a hundred years ago, and that it has "migrated" from Mexico. In actual fact, the mesquite tree is native to Texas and northern Mexico; in centuries past there were many more of these trees than now, concentrated in large mesquite woodlands scattered throughout the state. Much of the original mesquite was cut down by settlers in the 19th century; the plant is only now coming back due to an overall decline in the use of mesquite as a source of lumber and fuel.

The name for the tree comes from the Aztec *mizquitl;* the Aztecs and other Indian groups have used the trunk, roots, leaves, beans, and bark for hundreds of years for a variety of purposes. The Aztecs combined ground mesquite leaves and water to form a balm for sore eyes—a remedy still used by *curanderos* in rural Mexico. Comanches chewed the leaves to relieve toothaches. Mesquite gum has also been used by various tribes as a balm for wounds, a ceramic glue, a dye, and a digestive.

Indians used the mesquite beans—which grow from mesquite branches in long slender pods—as a source of nutrition as well. A ripe bean pod grows as long as nine inches, contains roughly 30% glucose, and is high in protein. Many animals and birds savor the beans—if allowed to, horses will eat them until they're sick. Rural Mexicans grind the dried pods into a flour with which they make bread and a kind of beer. Today many people in Texas and Mexico enjoy the bean pods straight from the tree, or boiled, dried, and crushed to make jellies, wine, and bread.

Early Texas ranchers used mesquite wood for fenceposts, wagon wheels, fuel, and furniture. Before the Aztec name for the tree became popular, it was known as "Texas ironwood." San Antonio's Houston Street was once entirely paved with mesquite blocks, as were early streets in Brownsville. Mesquite makes an excellent woodcrafting material since it's extremely durable and resistant to rot. Woodworkers in the Southwest have rediscovered the pleasures and profits of working with mesquite— a finely crafted mesquite rocking chair fetches as much as $2500 in Texas today.

But mesquite's most famous use nowadays is as a fuel for barbecue pits and grills as well as for smoking meat, poultry, and fish. The wood is especially well suited to cooking because it yields a hot flame when burned; smoke is sparse and aromatic, imparting a savory flavor to foods cooked over it. Even coffee brewed over a mesquite fire is said to taste better. A tip: to give mesquite-grilled foods an even more pronounced mesquite flavor, throw a few mesquite pods on the coals before cooking.

Mesquite woodlands now make up about half the Rolling Plains, and are considered a big problem by local ranchers. As fast as they can chop it up and send it to Southwestern grills and barbecue houses, the tenacious mesquite grows back.

Edwards Plateau

Sturdy trees have colonized the rocky Edwards Plateau area from the Hill Country on the Balcones Escarpment to the Stockton Plateau, adjacent to the Trans-Pecos. The **bald cypress** is isolated from its native habitat, the bayous of Deep East Texas and southwestern Louisiana, but grows quite well along streams in the Hill Country. Hanging in the cypress is the occasional **ball moss,** a close relative of the Spanish moss commonly seen on cypress and oaks in Deep East Texas. Actually, neither of these species is a true moss—they're flowering plants of the bromeliad family. And, contrary to myth, they aren't parasitic.

Common trees throughout the Edwards Plateau include the omnipresent **mesquite, shinnery oak, pecan,** and **live oak,** as well as **mountain cedar,** a tree that provides the Hill Country with its characteristic fragrance. Along the Balcones Escarpment you'll find a thorny shrub called **huajillo** (also guajillo), especially in the Uvalde area. The white flowers of the huajillo produce Uvalde honey, which honey connoisseurs claim is among the world's best.

Between the trees and brush, the plateau sprouts many of the same grasses as the High and Rolling plains to the north.

South Texas Plains

The area south of San Antonio is a subtropical dryland zone in which smaller trees, shrubs, cacti, and hardy grasses thrive—a mixture of vegetation usually called "brush" or "chaparral." Since this zone has many plants in common with the chaparral of northern Mexico, Spanish names are common. Parts of the South Texas plains are said to resemble Africa's Zambezi Valley, and at least one ranch here is successfully breeding rhinoceros, which thrive on the omnipresent huisache shrub, a close relative of the African acacia.

The most typical brush country inhabitants are **small live oak, mesquite, post oak, prickly pear cactus, catclaw, rat-tail cactus, black chaparral** (black bush), **acacia, granjeño, retama, yucca, cenizo, huisache,** and **huajillo.** Beneath the brush canopy are what remains of the original **bunch grasses,** plus **Arizona cottontop, curly mesquite, buffalo grass,** and various Texas **gramas.**

Toward the Gulf Coast, the sandy soils produce **tanglehead, sandbur, windmill grass, seacoast bluestem, bristle grass,** and **paspalum.** Where the soil is particularly saline, **seashore salt grass, gulf cord grass,** and **alkali sacaton** are the dominant grasses. Along the coast in the Rockport-Fulton area are striking **coastal oaks,** with windswept branches uniformly pointing inland.

At the southernmost reaches of the Rio Grande plains grow the only tropical species in the U.S. native to North America. Of the many palm trees in the area, most are imported royal and California palms, but one belongs to Texas: the *Sabal texana* or **Texas palm.** Look for a straight trunk crowned by palm leaves extending in all directions, like a sphere rather than an umbrella. The fruit of the Texas palm is edible and is occasionally sold in Brownsville and Matamoros markets. The Sabal Palm Grove Sanctuary, a preserve on the Rio Grande near Brownsville, protects a small but significant part of the native palm forest once common throughout the lower Rio Grande delta.

Citrus plantations are now common in tropical South Texas, but the species cultivated there were introduced from other climes.

Prairies and Cross Timbers

This North Central Texas area is a mixture of

small woodlands alternating with prairies. Trees native to the area include **post, live, shinnery,** and **blackjack oak.** Mesquite and juniper are present as well, opportunistically moving in as the grasses were depleted by grazing. Prairie grasses here are similar to those in the westward High and Rolling plains—various **gramas, bluestems, Indian grass,** and **buffalo grass.**

Blackland Prairie

The narrow Blackland Prairie extends for some 400 miles from the Red River south to near San Antonio and has the most fertile topsoil in Texas. The rich, black soil runs deep, and Blackland farms are coveted like gold mines. Hence, most of the land here is under cultivation.

Some of the classic Texas trees are found in the Blacklands. Although farming interests have cleared much of the timberland that once existed here, various species still stand untouched along rivers and streams. A variety of oaks predominate, along with **pecan, elm,** and **bois d'arc** (horse-apple). The bois d'arc was a favorite tree of the Indian bow-makers of East Texas.

Post Oak Savannah

As its name suggests, this was originally grassland with a canopy of hardwoods, predominantly **post oaks.** Post oaks are still characteristic of the area, along with **blackjack oak, pecan, walnut,** and **elm** trees.

Native grasses include the usual gramas, bluestems, switch grass, and Indian grass, plus **longleaf wood oats, spike wood oats,** and **red love grass.** As elsewhere in the state, brush has entered the savannah—**mesquite, oak brush, greenbriar,** and **yaupon** are typical of the area.

Piney Woods

In the space available here, it would be impossible to do justice to the wide variety of vegetation in the East Texas Forests collectively called the Piney Woods. In the Big Thicket alone there are six forest layers and eight separate plant communities extending from the upland forests to the cypress bogs. Plant species you'd never expect to find in Texas, including 40 species of wild orchids and nine carnivorous plants, grow in abundance.

Common trees in the Big Thicket include **loblolly pine, beech, hornbeam, magnolia, sweet gum, black gum, walnut, hickory, white oak, red oak, ash, tupelo, dogwood, hawthorn,** and **mulberry.** Along the forest floor are various ferns and mosses, **partridgeberry, Virginia willow, corkwood, blueberry, holly,** and **swamp honeysuckle.**

The four national forests north of the Big Thicket contain a predominance of pines, plus maples, oaks, beeches, gums, and bois d'arc. Many smaller trees used by the Caddo Indians for food and medicine are also common in the Piney Woods: **persimmon, chinquapin, pawpaw, witch hazel,** and **sassafras.**

On sandier soils toward the coast grow **palmettos,** small semitropical shrubs that resemble dwarf palm trees.

Gulf Marshes and Coast

At one time there were many marshes at river mouths on the mainland shore but a good number have been dredged, filled, or destroyed by dams upriver that deprived them of fresh water and minerals. Today, most of the existing Gulf Marshes are located along the inside of the Gulf Coast barrier islands and Bolivar Peninsula, facing tidal basins. In certain spots along the Bolivar Peninsula and Galveston Island, thriving marshes extend completely across the islands to face the Gulf.

Marshlands vary from wet to dry and fresh to salty, depending on the level of the underlying land and proximity to river mouths. Marsh plants and animals have adapted to various combinations along these continuums, so there is great variety. Because of this extensive variation, salt-marshes represent the most concentrated biomass on the planet, exceeding even tropical rainforests.

The tall grasses growing over the marshlands are generally called "salt grass," though there are actually several different species present. Some grow as high as eight feet, dwarfing the flat-bottomed boats that scoot along the canals, which serve as the preferred method of transport in the marshes. Other vegetation in the Gulf Marshes includes **bullrush, sedge, smooth** and **marshhay cord grasses, maidencane,** and **marsh millet.** On sandy beach areas you may spot a few grasses resistant to saline environments, such as **seashore salt grass.**

One of the more interesting plants occasionally seen along Gulf Coast beaches is the **sargassum weed.** It doesn't grow on the coast, nor does it grow on the sea bottom like other seaweeds. Instead, it floats along on top of the sea, supported by a system of air bladders. Specially adapted tiny animals live and nest in sargassum weed and depend on it for food; some can't swim, and if they lose their hold on sargassum they sink and die. Sargassum is not very common along the Gulf Coast except when severe tropical storms force it ashore. Then it not only litters the beach but after a while begins to stink—the smell comes from the dying organisms clinging to the sargassum.

WILDLIFE

The animals and birds of Texas cannot be as easily confined to geographic areas as Texas plants. While there are definite favored habitats, there's no stopping most critters when they decide to fly, walk, run, hop, or crawl.

While Texas wildlife is easily viewed in national and state parks, forests, and recreation areas, you'll find the most concentrated populations in the 13 national wildlife refuges and 28 state wildlife areas. Though devoted to the preservation of wildlife, many of these areas are open to nature study, hiking, and camping.

In addition, most state wildlife areas are open to hunting and fishing during regulated seasons. The Texas Parks and Wildlife Department issues state hunting and fishing licenses.

Mammals

Probably the most famous Texas animal is the **armadillo,** found virtually all over the state. The standard Texas issue is the nine-banded armadillo (*Dasypus novemcinctus linnaeus*), an armored relative of the opossum. Mesoamerica's Mayans believed that when vultures died they shed their wings and metamorphosed into 'dillos. During the Depression, the animals became a popular food supplement—Texans called them "Texas turkeys" or "Hoover hogs." Stuffed armadillos and armadillo shells are favored curios among residents and visitors alike. Armadillo chili is supposed to be good. It's illegal to harm an armadillo, however; only 'dillos that have died of natural causes can be taken. "Natural causes" includes auto collisions—a common cause of death.

In the caves of Central Texas, the **Brazilian bat, Mexican freetail bat,** and **cave myotis bat** are quite common. In fact, Texas boasts 33 of the 43 bat species known in the U.S.; the world's largest bat colony lives in Bracken Cave near San Antonio. **Eckert James River Bat Cave Preserve,** 18 miles southwest of Mason on FM 385 in the Hill Country, offers bat-watching tours Thurs.-Sun. from mid May through mid October, when the cave contains up to eight million bats. Austin's Congress Avenue bridge offers the nation's best urban bat-watching April to October.

The **black bear,** once seen throughout the state, is now confined to the mountains of the Trans-Pecos and the riverbottoms of East Texas. **Cougars** are still fairly common in places on the Edwards Plateau, in the Trans-Pecos, and in the brush country of South Texas. The **ocelot** and **jaguarundi,** once present throughout South Texas, are now mostly confined to the Laguna Atascosa and Santa Ana National Wildlife Refuges and along the Rio Grande. Smaller cats such as the **bobcat** are common throughout the state. **Coyotes** are found all over Texas, but especially in the brush country of South Texas. They're also a protected species on the Muleshoe National Wildlife Refuge in the Panhandle.

Deer are prolific in Texas, their numbers estimated at well over three million. The most common, the **white-tailed deer,** thrives in the Hill Country and Edwards Plateau, while a smaller cousin, the **Sierra del Carmen white-tailed deer,** lives in the Big Bend area of West Texas. The state's largest deer is the **mule deer,** found in the Trans-Pecos, the Llano Estacado, and to a lesser extent in South Texas. The elegant **pronghorn,** a type of antelope, lives primarily on the Texas plains in the Panhandle and in the Trans-Pecos region. The **Texas bighorn** mountain sheep is native to the Trans-Pecos but has become increasingly hard to find. Many nonnative varieties of deer, antelope, mountain sheep, goats, and even giraffes have been introduced with great success to "exotic game ranches" on the Edwards Plateau. Some of these species, like the **aoudad sheep,** now proliferate in wild herds outside ranchlands in parts of West Texas.

The **javelina** or **collared peccary** (or, occasionally, "muskhog") is a wild, tusked creature similar to a pig (though zoologically unrelated) that's common in South Texas's brush country. Another strange creature in the brush country is the **coatimundi,** a lithe relative of the raccoon.

Texas harbors more **feral hogs** than any other state, over a million. They flourish in many rural areas of the state but are most concentrated in East, South, and Central Texas. Many are descended from pigs brought to the region by early European visitors, while others may be traced to a general release in the 1940s for hunting income. Such is the wild hog's nuisance factor that to this day Texas has no size or bag limits on the hunting or trapping of swine.

The Trans-Pecos area is about the only place you'll find the famed **kangaroo rat.** If you're lucky, you'll see one hopping across your headlight beams while driving at night—they're rarely seen during the day.

The **black-tailed prairie dog** was once ubiquitous throughout the plains and prairies of Texas but has been so nearly eradicated that you now have to go out of your way to see one. Three "prairie dog towns" are preserved in the Panhandle at Mackenzie State Park in Lubbock, Muleshoe National Wildlife Refuge, and Buffalo Lake National Wildlife Refuge.

At one time there were many types of wolves in Texas, but ranchers just about exterminated them. One type which survives in small numbers is the handsome **red wolf,** whose primary habitat now is the Anahuac National Wildlife

Refuge on the Texas coast. There may also be a few **gray wolves** left in the mountains of the Trans-Pecos. The large **Mexican black bear,** once thought to be extinct on the Texas side of the border, has returned to Big Bend National Park in significant, year round numbers and is now a common sight there.

Texas claims a number of resident waterborne mammals, including the **bottlenose dolphin** and the **manatee.** Both are native to the Gulf, but the manatee is occasionally seen in Texas bays and rivers. During the winter, they migrate south toward Mexico's Yucatán Peninsula. Other marine mammals seen on a seasonal, visiting basis along the Gulf of Mexico coast include **Clymene dolphin** (helmet dolphin), **spinning dolphin, Atlantic spotted dolphin, saddle-backed dolphin, Risso's dolphin, dense-beaked whale, right whale, Minke whale,** and the threatened **dwarf sperm whale.**

Reptiles

The largest reptile in Texas, the **American alligator,** is commonly found in the bayous of East Texas and the saltmarshes along the Gulf Coast.

Over a hundred species of snakes call Texas their home, but only 16 species and subspecies are considered poisonous to humans. Of these, three are **copperheads**—the Trans-Pecos, found in the Big Bend area; the broadbanded, inhabiting North and South Central Texas; and the southern, seen in East Texas. The Trans-Pecos copperhead is fairly rare, so hikers in Big Bend country should consider the risk of encounter very low.

Only one water snake in Texas is poisonous, the **western cottonmouth.** The cottonmouth is actually semiaquatic and lives in a variety of habitats near water. Its domain covers the entire eastern half of the state, starting as far west as the Hill Country. The cottonmouth is most common, however, in the coastal marshes of Southeast Texas and along the streams and rivers of East Texas.

Eleven kinds of **rattlesnakes** live in Texas—the western and desert massasauga, found on low plains throughout most of the state; the western pygmy in East Texas; the western diamondback, com-

mon throughout the state except East Texas; the Mojave in far West Texas; the canebrake of East Texas; the mottled rock and banded rock in the mountains of the Trans-Pecos; the black-tailed variety of Central and West Texas; the timber, frequenting the rocky uplands of East Texas; and the prairie rattler in West Texas. Of these, the western diamondback and Mojave rattlesnakes are the most dangerous—the Mojave because it has the most potent venom of any North American snake, the diamondback because it's the second most venomous snake in North America and the most common rattler in Texas.

Finally, Texas boasts one **coral snake,** aptly named the Texas coral snake. It's found in a variety of habitats throughout Central, South, and East Texas. For important information on how to avoid snakebite, see the special topic "Snakebite Prevention and Treatment."

Lizards are common throughout the lower half of the state, especially **geckos** and the large **Texas horned lizard,** often called "horny toad." The horned lizard can shoot a stream of blood from its eyes to distances as great as four feet, but no one knows why.

Five of the world's nine species of sea turtle are occasionally seen along the Texas coast. Largest is the **giant leatherback turtle,** which reaches six to seven feet in length and dives as deeply as 3,900 feet—the deepest of all air-breathing animals. Other Texas sea turtles include the **loggerhead, hawksbill, green sea turtle,** and the endangered **Kemp's ridley.**

LOUISE FOOTE

Texas horned lizard

SNAKEBITE PREVENTION AND TREATMENT

The overall risk of being bitten by a poisonous snake while in Texas is quite low, but it's often exaggerated by Texans who're proud of their snake population. According to Texas Department of Health statistics covering a 10-year period between 1968 and 1978, there were only 2.7 deaths per year attributable to snakebite. Compare this with 5.7 for venomous arthropods (insect stings), 8.1 for lightning strikes, 10.1 for hunting accidents, 518.5 for drowning, and 3,511 for auto accidents. Most of the unfortunate people bitten by snakes in Texas are farmers and small children.

Nonetheless, anyone spending time in the Texas outdoors, including campers and hikers, would be well advised to follow a few simple precautions.

Prevention

First of all, use caution when placing hands or feet in areas where snakes may lie. These include rocky ledges, holes, and fallen logs. Always look first, and if you must move a rock or log, use a long stick or other instrument. Wear sturdy footwear when walking in possible snake habitats. High-top leather shoes or boots are best.

Most snakes strike only when they feel threatened. Naturally, if you step on or next to a snake, it is likely to strike. If you see a venomous snake—or, in the case of a rattlesnake, hear one—remain still until the snake moves away. Sudden movements may cause a snake to strike; snakes rarely strike a stationary target. Also, none of the venomous snakes found in Texas can strike a target that is farther away than three-fourths of its body length. Use this rough measure to judge when it may be safe to move away from a snake, leaving plenty of room for error.

If you'll be hiking in wilderness areas far from professional medical treatment, by all means carry an elastic bandage or two, the type used for sprains. The old "slice and suck" method of treating snakebite has been discredited by most medical experts.

Treatment

If bitten by a snake, it's important to remain calm in order to slow the spread of venom in your body and follow the necessary steps for treatment.

First, immediately following the bite, try to identify the snake. At the very least, memorize the markings and physical characteristics so a physician can administer the most appropriate antivenin. If you can kill the snake and bring it to the nearest treatment center, do it. Just remember, this could expose you or your fellow hikers to the risk of another bite.

Second, examine the bite for teeth marks. A successful bite by a poisonous pit viper will leave one or two large fang punctures in addition to smaller teeth marks; a bite by a nonpoisonous snake will not feature fang punctures. A coral snake bite will usually feature a series of small, closely spaced punctures made by the "chewing" motion of smaller fangs—coral snakes have to chew or bite their victims' flesh repeatedly in order to inject sufficient quantities of venom. In general, nonpoisonous bites cause relatively small, shallow marks or scratches.

If you suspect the bite is poisonous, immobilize the affected limb and wrap it tightly in an elastic bandage. This will slow the spread of venom through the lymph system and mitigate swelling. Make sure the bandage isn't wrapped so tightly it cuts off circulation—you should be able to insert a finger under it without difficulty. Keep the limb below the level of the heart. Avoid all physical activity, since increased circulation accelerates the absorption of the venom. For this same reason, avoid aspirin, sedatives, and alcohol. Do not apply cold therapy — ice packs, cold compresses, and so on—to the bite area or to any other part of the victim's body.

Get the victim to a hospital or physician if possible. Where feasible, carry the victim to restrict physical exertion. Even when wrapping the limb appears successful in preventing symptoms, the bite will need medical attention and a physician may decide antivenin treatment is necessary.

It's possible for a poisonous snake to bite without injecting any venom; up to 20% of reported bites are "dry bites."

Snakebite victims who require antivenin treatment usually receive the broad-spectrum North American Anti-snakebite Serum for pit viper poisoning or a special coral snake anti-venin for coral snake poisoning.

coral snake

LOUISE FOOTE

Birds

Texas harbors more species of birds—close to 600—than any other state, mainly because birds find it a comfortable winter home. The best areas for Texas bird-watching are along the Gulf Coast and in the Rio Grande Valley. Every spring, accommodations along the coast fill up with bird aficionados who come from all over the U.S. to view the variety of birds in the area.

whooping crane

BOB RACE

Late fall is also a popular time for birders. The saltmarshes make especially good spotting grounds for large birds like **egrets, cranes, terns, ducks, geese,** and **herons.**

Perhaps the most famous part-time bird resident in Texas is the **whooping crane,** which commonly has a wingspan of 7.5 feet. In 1941, this huge white bird was on the brink of extinction—only 15 whooping cranes remained in the wild. By 1989, their numbers had swelled to over 100, all spending their winters at the Aransas National Wildlife Refuge on the Texas coast. From November to April, local boats offer cruises devoted to the viewing of the crane.

Another winter resident is the **snow goose,** which nests in saltmarshes along the coast. **Canada geese** are also common among the marshes, as are **blue geese, mottled ducks,** and **ibis.**

Also seen along the coast are a variety of **pelicans, gulls, sandpipers, loons,** and **marsh hawks.** The magnificent and ever present **white pelican** attains wingspans of up to nine feet, and the occasional **frigate bird** reaches seven to eight feet. The pink-feathered **roseate spoonbill,** often mistaken for a flamingo, is another impressive coastal bird.

The Muleshoe National Wildlife Refuge in the Panhandle supports as many as 100,000 **sandhill cranes.** Also in this area are a few remaining **golden eagles.**

The Big Thicket and Piney Woods forests of East Texas are a natural attraction for woodpeckers; several different kinds thrive among the tall pines and oaks. Most impressive is the large, red-crested **pileated woodpecker**—it's not only the largest but the loudest of the woodpeckers, and is sometimes called "peckerwood" by East Texans.

In the Rio Grande plains of South Texas, especially around the Santa Ana National Wildlife Refuge, is the squawking **chachalaca,** also known as a "Mexican turkey," a pheasant-like cross between a wild turkey and a chicken. In brush country throughout South Texas, you'll find lots of **wild turkey, quail, doves,** and **roadrunners.** The latter, as its name suggests, prefers to run rather than fly, and has been clocked at 15 miles per hour. The roadrunner goes by several other names as well—chaparral and paisano are two local names. The endangered **peregrine falcon** and **bald eagle** nest at nearby Laguna Atascosa National Wildlife Refuge.

Fish

Guadalupe bass (the official state fish), **striped bass, spotted bass, largemouth bass, white bass, sunfish, crappie,** and various kinds of **catfish** (channel, blue, and flathead) are freshwater fish of note which are native to Texas. Various other bass have been introduced to lakes and streams with much success, as well as **rainbow trout** and the **saltwater red drum,** which has adapted to freshwater habitats. **Crayfish,** more commonly called crawfish, thrive in the bayous of East Texas.

The Gulf of Mexico is rich with sealife in spite of oil shipping and the commercial fishing industry. Sportfishing is very big in Texas and fishing enthusiasts are part of the conservation effort in the area. Among large Gulf fish are 30 species of **shark,** including the great white shark, which reaches weights of up to 8,000 pounds. Also common are **yellowfin tuna, blue marlin, sailfish, wahoo,** and **tarpon,** as well as various kinds of shellfish, including **shrimp, crabs, clams, oysters,** and **mussels.**

Commercial fishing is big business along the 640-mile Texas coast. Fleets net mostly shrimp

(82% of the weight landed), crabs, and oysters —shellfish, in fact, account for more than 30 times the amount of finfish taken. Among Gulf finfish, the commercial catch includes **black drum, flounder, sheepshead,** and **red snapper.** All are commonly taken by amateur anglers as well. See the Gulf Coast chapter for more information on Gulf sportfishing.

Texas tortise

HISTORY

PREHISTORY

Most of the earliest evidence of human habitation in Texas dates back 10,000-13,000 years. Grinding stones, beads, human skeletons, and pictographs found in several places throughout inland Texas date to this period. These Paleo-Indians were no doubt descendants of Asian groups known to have migrated across the Bering Strait to North America from the Asian continent some 50,000 years ago.

Artifacts spread across the state indicate the Paleo-Indian groups in Texas were nomadic and small in number. They hunted prehistoric bison and small horses. Bison were brought down by flint-headed spears or were driven over cliffs—hunting techniques that persisted through thousands of years of Amerindian history. The first Clovis points were discovered near the Colorado River in Texas in 1924, but weren't named until similar points were found and dated near Clovis, New Mexico, in 1936.

When the Ice Age ended around 5000 B.C., the human population in Texas expanded its hunting cycle to include small as well as large animals. The expanding tool kit included implements for working stone, bone, and wood. They harvested fruits and nuts from the land, and freshwater fish from streams and rivers. Limited trade with other Indian groups commenced, with flint extracted from the Alibates quarry in the Texas Panhandle as a prime unit of barter.

Around the beginning of the 1st century A.D., a Woodland Indian culture developed in East Texas. Pre-Caddoan groups established permanent settlements, erected burial mounds, and made pottery. By the end of the first millennium, a neo-American or late-prehistoric Indian emerged, characterized by a complex culture. The creation of food surpluses by the Caddos of East Texas allowed them to develop social stratification. In addition to hunters and farmers, the Caddos had chiefs, priests, and artisans. A certain gender equality must have existed, since Caddo women as well as men belonged to these latter groups.

Prior to European contact in the 16th century, what is considered "confirmed evidence" about Texas prehistory is rather limited. A number of remaining mysteries have led to some interesting speculations. A series of horizontal and vertical lines engraved on a West Central Texas hillside, for example, are said to be ancient Celtic line writing representative of a Celtiberian language. Epigraphist Barry Fell postulates these

PERIODS OF HUMAN HABITATION IN THE AMERICAN SOUTHWEST

(B.P. = YEARS BEFORE PRESENT)

12,500 B.P.	8500 B.P.	2000 B.P.
Paleo-Indian	Archaic	Ceramic
(Clovis-Folsom-		
Plainview-Firstview)		500 B.P.
		Protohistoric
		350 B.P.
		Historic

Paint Rock pictographs, west of San Angelo

inscriptions are travel instructions left by Celtic explorers who traded in the area long before the arrival of Columbus or the Vikings.

In Big Bend, a plaque bearing an inscription in archaic Libyan was found in the early 1960s. Unfortunately, the plaque was not dated and later was lost. Photos of the undeciphered plaque remain, however, and it's been suggested Africans may have traded with this part of the New World in ancient times. Additional support for this suggestion is available in the Olmec and Toltec statuary of early Mexico, some of which bear Negroid features.

Probably the most mystifying of Texas's prehistoric anomalies are the Malakoff-Trinidad heads. These stone carvings in the shape of human heads were found in Henderson County within an eight-year period overlapping the 1920s and '30s. They were dug from the bottom of a gravel bed that dates 40,000-50,000 years. Assuming they were originally deposited in the stratum in which they were found, this marks a local culture considerably more advanced than that which crossed the Bering Strait at about the same time.

EUROPEAN CONTACT

Spanish Exploration of the New World

Following 700 years of conflict with the Moors over control of the Iberian Peninsula, Spain in the 15th century emerged as the most powerful nation in Europe. Convinced a Roman Catholic God was destined to rule the world with Spain as His emissary, the Spanish monarchy sent Christopher Columbus in search of a new route to the Far East. His mission was to establish contact with a mythical "Great Khan" to develop an alternate trade route with the Orient, since Arabs controlled the overland route through the Middle East. Along the way as many pagans as possible were to be converted to Christianity. Once the Arab trade monopoly was broken, the Holy Land would be returned to Christian control. Pope Alexander VI presented Spain with a papal bull in 1493 which gave the Spanish rights to any new land discovered west of the Azores, as long as the Spanish made "God's name known there." Hence, the Spanish conquest of the New World started as a roundabout extension of the Holy Crusades.

The "discovery" of the West Indies by Columbus was followed by a succession of Spanish expeditions into the Caribbean and Gulf of Mexico. The conquest of Mexico and Central America soon followed. Hernán Cortés subdued the Valley of Mexico Aztecs in three years, and the allegiance of other Aztecs and Mayans followed. At first the Indians were enslaved, but another papal bull issued in 1537 by Pope Paul III discouraged slavery. Spain's policy changed from "conquest" to "pacification"— a policy all too often open to interpretation.

Spanish missionaries debated the best way to effect conversion in conformity with this vaguely worded new policy. A Dominican missionary named Bartoleme de las Casas urged a paternal attitude toward native populations, and from his ideas the mission system was developed. Basically, it worked like this: traveling missionaries offered Indians the protection of Spanish armies in return for a willingness to undergo religious instruction. Those natives who agreed were congregated at a suitable spot and directed to build a mission. The mission in turn became a refuge for the Indians and a place for them to learn European farming and other trades, as well as Catholic ways. Once pacification was complete, the mission became a secularized church community and the missionaries moved on to new areas. The system worked well among the docile Indians of Central Mexico.

The Spanish Push into Texas

As the missions moved north, pacification became increasingly difficult. The nomadic Indians of the north, called *barbaros* by the Spanish, were no more susceptible to Spanish rule than they had been to Aztec rule. The Spanish were intrigued by this new territory, but proceeded cautiously. In 1519, a Spanish captain mapped the coast of Texas under orders from the governor of Jamaica. Two Cortés expeditions also slipped across the Rio Grande in 1528, but returned to Río Pánuco in Mexico that same year.

Then in the 1530s, Alvar Nuñez Cabeza de Vaca, two other Spanish explorers, and a famous Moorish slave named Esteban (considered the first African to arrive in Texas) sailed from Cuba to explore the Gulf Coast. They were shipwrecked somewhere near present-day Galveston and ended up living among a variety of Indian tribes in West Texas and farther west for a number of years. Cabeza de Vaca developed a reputation among Texas Indians as a healer; in his travels he frequently heard tales of great wealth in the "Seven Golden Cities of Cibola," located somewhere to the north.

Esteban stayed on with the Indians, but in 1536 Cabeza de Vaca rejoined his compatriots in Mexico. Tantalized by his stories of gold, the colonial government commissioned Francisco Vasquez de Coronado to explore the Southwest. In the New Mexico area, Pueblo Indians fed Coronado a story about a place with greater riches than even Cibola, called Gran Quivera. Not realizing that accounts of mythical golden cities were simply a way for the Indians to lead the Spanish away from their homelands, Coronado embarked on a search for gold throughout the Texas Panhandle, Oklahoma, and Kansas. He never found any, but along the way he left missionaries in the upper Rio Grande valley to "pacify" the Indians.

The Pueblo Indians of the upper Rio Grande eventually rebelled against the Spanish settlers, and the missionaries retreated to the El Paso area. El Paso del Norte, an opening in the mountains, allowed a trade route to extend between Santa Barbara in Chihuahua and the northern colony. Here the Spanish established the missions of Ysleta del Sur and Socorro del Sur in 1681. Ysleta became part of Texas when the course of the Rio Grande changed and is now the oldest European settlement in the state.

Conflict with the French

Meanwhile the French were conducting their own expeditions in the area. They didn't like the Spanish claims to such a large portion of the New World and in 1682 sent Rene Robert Cavalier, Sieur de la Salle (nowadays shortened to LaSalle) to explore the Mississippi delta area. He claimed the Gulf Coast for France, returned home, then set sail again for the New World with four ships full of potential colonists. On the way he lost two of the ships, finally coming ashore at Lavaca Bay, about halfway between today's Galveston and Corpus Christi. There he established Fort Saint Louis. From here, LaSalle made three exploratory expeditions in the area until he was killed by one of his men while en route to other French colonies along the Mississippi.

In spite of the fact that Fort Saint Louis was subsequently abandoned, France claimed the Rio Grande as the western boundary of the Louisiana Territory. This infuriated the Spanish, who sent five sea expeditions and six land expeditions to explore the Texas coast and interior to learn more about the area and to check French influence.

The Spanish established two unsuccessful missions in East Texas; these expeditions would not be of historic interest except for the Spanish contact with the Caddo Indians. The Caddo were part of a sophisticated native culture en-

Mission San José, San Antonio

compassing a loose federation of settlements throughout East Texas, Arkansas, Oklahoma, and Louisiana. They were anxious to form an alliance with the Spanish when they learned the Spanish were enemies of the French, trading partners with Indian enemies of the Caddo.

They greeted the Spanish missionaries with the Caddo word *taysha* (friend), which the Spanish took to be either the name of the tribe or the name of the territory. Thereafter, the Spanish colonists often referred to the area north of the Rio Grande as Tejas or Texas, Spanish corruptions of *taysha*. Unfortunately, the Spanish missionaries brought with them European diseases which largely decimated the peaceful Caddo. The remaining Caddo blamed the priests' holy water for the fatal illnesses and returned to their traditional religion.

So the missionaries moved out of East Texas and in 1718 established what became the most famous mission in the Southwest, San Antonio de Valero, later nicknamed the Alamo when it was taken over by the military in 1800. Over

the next 13 years, five more missions were established in the San Antonio area.

In 1720 the French diverted their attention from the American colonies to their crumbling economy in France. Trade with the Indians slackened and in response the Indians began attacking French settlements in the Mississippi area. The Spanish took the opportunity to slip into the French territory through the back door, establishing a mission and presidio at Los Adaes, Louisiana. Los Adaes became the capital of the Spanish colonial province of Texas for the next 50 years.

Spanish Expansion in Texas

In the heart of Texas, San Antonio area missions were having a hard time with the pesky Apaches. In fact, the whole area of South Texas right on down to the Sierra Madre Oriental in central Mexico was barely under Spanish control. Few settlers dared make a go of it here and the region became a haven for marauders and renegade Amerindians.

Spain conducted a seven-year search for the "right colonizer" to tame the area. "Good Indians" were brought in from southern Mexico and Central America to serve as role models for the "wayward natives." Colonial descendants from the Canary Islands arrived in 1731 and set up the first civil jurisdiction in San Antonio, the Villa de San Fernando de Bexar. Finally, in 1746, Jose de Escandón, a highly regarded military officer and colonial administrator, received the assignment to survey the area from Mexico's Río Pánuco north to the Nueces River in Texas. The width of the area he surveyed extended from the Gulf Coast to the mountains. In 1747, Escandón began sending colonists into the area, naming it the State of Nuevo Santander after his home province in Spain. By 1753 Texas's first cattle ranch was established on 433,800 acres of land granted to José Vasquez Borrego in what is today Zapata County in South Texas. Many of the wealthy Hispanic landowners living along the Rio Grande today are heirs to these original Spanish land grants.

Although the Spanish colonists had met with hostile Amerindians from time to time, the native population wasn't a major problem until the Spanish introduced horses to the Comanches.

With the increased mobility, the Comanches began moving south onto the Great Plains from the Rocky Mountains in the 17th century. They displaced the Apaches, who moved to the lower Texas plains, displacing in turn the peaceful Jumano and Coahuiltecan tribes. The Jumano and Coahuiltecan both pleaded for help from the Spanish, who turned a deaf ear. The Apaches wreaked havoc throughout the Texas plains and then laid siege to Spanish missions in the El Paso area, though the Spaniards were able to defeat the Apaches on several occasions.

Squeezed between the fierce Comanches to the northwest and the Spanish to the south, the Apaches made peace with the colonizers in the San Antonio area but couldn't gain acceptance in the missions—the other Indians feared and distrusted the warlike Apaches. The mission of San Saba de la Santa Cruz was established in 1757 in an area about 200 miles northwest of San Antonio, but two years later the Comanches destroyed the mission, killing both priests and Indians. A major battle ensued with the Comanches and their Plains Indian allies on one side and the Spanish, Apaches, and various Mexican Indians on the other. The Comanches, using French rifles and field tactics, soundly defeated the Spanish.

The defeat was the most humiliating loss the Spanish had ever suffered against the northern Indians. The more sedentary Indians of Mexico and Central America had been relatively easy to subjugate, but the Plains Indians were a new breed of warrior. Spain's control of the province of Texas began slipping, compounded by France's cession of the Louisiana Territory in 1762 to Spain. This considerably enlarged the Spanish territory and lent a false sense of security to the Spanish colonial administration. The entire province was reorganized to leave East Texas without a defense—no longer needed, it was thought, in the absence of westward pressure from the French. East Texas missions and presidios were closed and moved to Central Texas to defend the area against Indian attacks. For a while this reorganization worked well for the Spanish, and the area from San Antonio west to El Paso was pacified for the last 20 years of the 18th century.

ANGLO-AMERICAN MIGRATION AND MEXICAN RULE

Blurred Borders
By 1803, Spain had returned the Louisiana Territory to France following an alliance with

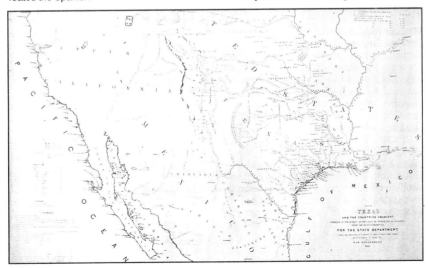

This 1844 U.S. War Department map depicts three nations—Texas, Mexico, and the United States—without international borders.

the losing sides in the French Revolution and the Napoleonic wars. Although Napoleon promised not to turn the territory over to any other power, he sold it to the United States.

United States President Thomas Jefferson at first claimed all the territory extending to the Rio Grande as part of the Louisiana Purchase. Almost immediately, Anglo-Americans began looking toward the undeveloped regions of Texas. Spain maintained a strict immigration policy that barred all non-Hispanics from settling in Texas, but because France and Spain had never agreed on the boundaries between Louisiana and Texas, a sprinkling of Anglo-Americans had settled in East Texas since the 1760s. Without any presidios in East Texas, Spain could hardly enforce its policy. But when Zebulon Pike, commissioned by President Jefferson, arrived in the Spanish-settled upper Rio Grande valley with a survey team, he was arrested by the Spanish and sent back to Washington.

Realizing they'd have to develop Texas to strengthen their claim to it, the Spanish began making plans to send colonists to East Texas, the area receiving the most westward pressure. They offered huge land grants to *empresarios* who'd take on the task of settling large numbers of families in the Texas interior.

Mexican Independence and the New *Empresarios*

By this time, Mexican-born Spanish colonists in Mexico were becoming fed up with the machinations of Spanish rule. In 1810, a revolutionary group of Mexican-born Spanish, *mestizos* (Mexican-Indians), and Indians declared Mexico an independent nation and began 10 years of battle against Spain.

In 1811, Mexican revolutionaries sent an emissary, José Bernardo Gutierrez, to Washington to try to gain support for their cause. The U.S. accorded him a cordial reception but offered no official recognition of the provisional revolutionary government and released no weapons for their armies. What happened next may have seemed odd for the time, but set the trend for U.S.-Mexico-Central America intrigue for the next century. Gutierrez rode to Nachtitoches, Louisiana, and was met there by U.S. agents. Under the leadership of West Point

graduate Augustus Magee, they formed a "Republican Army of the North," which entered Texas in August 1812. After taking Nacogdoches and La Bahia, they occupied San Antonio and declared the "Republic of Texas" in April 1813. The republic was never recognized by any foreign government, and a few months later the Spanish reconquered San Antonio at the Battle of Medina River; over 300 Texas republicans were then executed.

Meanwhile, Spain's Ferdinand VII tried to regain control over Mexico and negotiated a border between Texas and Louisiana with the United States. An attempted punitive invasion of Mexico failed, however, and Spain finally relinquished Mexico in 1821.

In spite of the new Texas-Louisiana border, Anglo-Americans continued to filter across into East Texas, motivated by an unstable U.S. economy. Mexico didn't possess the forces necessary to prevent unregulated and illegal Anglo and Amerindian immigration. So instead they tried to pursue a policy that encouraged Mexicans and Europeans to settle Texas. The idea was to coerce the Anglos to settle in the interior, with non-Anglos putting down roots around the perimeter as a form of containment.

But Europeans and Mexicans didn't seem interested in settling in the remote Texas area, which was part of Coahuila y Texas, the poorest state in Mexico, and few came. The plan to dilute the Anglo presence suffered another blow when Mexico decided to recognize an 1821 land grant Spain had bestowed upon an Anglo-American named Moses Austin. Austin, under the *empresario* plan, was granted the right to settle 300 families in the area between the Brazos and Colorado rivers. Originally Mexico refused to honor the grant, but after Austin spent a year lobbying in Mexico City, they conceded on the condition that Mexican law be strictly adhered to by the new colonists.

Austin turned out to be a successful administrator and he scrupulously followed the terms of the Spanish grant, as well as Mexican policy. The Mexican government remained distrustful of Anglo intentions but admitted Austin's efforts contributed to the development of Texas. The desire to develop Texas as quickly as possible was great, since Mexican leaders wanted a buffer zone between northern Mexico and the

U.S. (and its Plains Indians). In 1825, Mexico authorized Austin to bring 900 more families into Texas, and in 1831 he was contracted to bring in 800 European and Mexican families. By the end of 1831, Austin was responsible for a population of 5,665 among his Texas colonies. Other *empresarios,* both Anglo-American and Mexican, successfully settled new towns as well, though none brought as many immigrants as Austin.

Throughout the early 19th century the new colonists concentrated on establishing themselves. Anglos settling in Central and North Texas tended to come from Missouri, Kentucky, and Tennessee, while those in East Texas usually immigrated from Mississippi, Louisiana, Arkansas, and Alabama. Mexicans gravitated toward South Texas. Cotton farming was the main economic activity, along with the raising of corn and livestock. But distrust between the Mexican government and their Anglo subjects never subsided, and a series of events in the early 1800s caused a growing resentment among the settlers.

Anglo-Mexican Friction

First, the Mexican bank in Texas (Banco Nacional de Texas, in San Antonio) failed because the Mexican government issued Texas bank notes and then refused to redeem them at full face value. Problems with land titles also emerged, mostly due to miscommunication as a result of the Anglo settlers' lack of proficiency in Spanish.

One disgruntled land-losing Anglo organized a group of like-minded individuals and forced Mexican soldiers out of a part of East Texas. They declared a "Republic of Fredonia" and made a pact with the Cherokees to split sovereignty over Texas in return for Cherokee support in battle. The Mexican army, assisted by Anglo colonists who didn't support the "Fredonians," quickly quelled the rebellion.

The failed Fredonian experiment had an immediate effect on Mexican immigration policy. The Mexican government became more anxious than ever about the Anglo presence in Texas and passed a law in 1829 that effectively barred further Anglo-American immigration. The Mexican army then reinforced garrisons in San Antonio, Nacogdoches, La Bahia, and Velasco, establishing five new forts elsewhere in the territory. These measures further alienated the Anglos, who began to feel like they were living under martial law.

Adding to the friction between the two cultures was the lack of religious freedom in Texas (all colonists were required to embrace Roman Catholicism) and the Mexican ban on slavery. Anglo settlers had easily ignored these policies before additional armed forces arrived. With the new military presence religious constraints were still difficult to enforce, but many Texans worried slavery would be eliminated. Even non-slaveholders—the majority of Anglo Texans—supported the right of their fellow colonists to use slaves on their farms.

But the final disillusionment with Mexican rule came about two years after the Mexican election of 1828, when a democratically elected president was overthrown by a losing candidate and Mexico descended into governmental chaos that lasted beyond the remainder of the century. A cycle of coups d'état put a new president into office an average of once every 7.5 months.

THE TEXAN REVOLUTION

Texans Petition Mexico

Although most Texas immigrants arrived with the intention of pledging allegiance to Mexico, they did so with the understanding they would live under a republican form of government, as outlined in the Constitution of 1824. With the overthrow of President Guerrero in 1830 and the installment of dictator General Anastasio Bustamante, the future of republicanism in Mexico looked grim. So the Texans cheered General Antonio López de Santa Anna in Veracruz when he fomented an army revolt in the name of the republican cause and installed himself as president.

Encouraged by Santa Anna's successes, the Texans held a convention in San Felipe to prepare a petition which they hoped to present to the Mexican government. The petition contained requests for several reforms, including the establishment of Texas as a separate Mexican state, a halt to Mexican encroachment on Indian lands, religious freedom, and donation of land for public schools. Mexican officials at the Coahuila y Texas state level condemned the convention and would not accept the petition.

the Alamo, 1994

The Texan response to the government's condemnation was another convention at San Felipe. This time the meeting was led by a more radical faction, though the content of the second petition was essentially the same as the first. A former U.S. senator and Tennessee governor, Sam Houston, chaired the committee that prepared a sample state constitution based on the then-current constitution of Massachusetts.

Stephen Austin went to Mexico City in 1833 and presented the petition to President Santa Anna. Santa Anna agreed with most of the reforms, except for the separation of Coahuila y Texas and the donation of land for schools. Unfortunately, while traveling back to Texas, Austin was arrested in Saltillo for having written a letter from Mexico City to officials in San Antonio requesting they set up a separate Texas state government. The rhetoric contained in the letter was considered treasonous, and Austin was sent to prison in Mexico City in January 1834.

While Austin lay in prison, the Coahuila y Texas state government faithfully began instituting reforms in Texas. Religious freedom was declared, the English language was allowed for official purposes, and a Texas appellate court was established. This seemed promising to the colonists until Santa Anna suddenly exiled his vice president, dissolved the federalist government, repealed the Constitution of 1824, and instituted one-man rule. Soon the Coahuila y Texas government was sapped of all authority and reforms were halted.

Armed Resistance

Austin was never charged or convicted of a crime; and eighteen months after his arrest he was released from prison and returned to Texas. He no longer counseled patience in dealing with the Mexican government, and called for armed struggle to regain the rights Texans had enjoyed under the Mexican Constitution of 1824 and later state reforms. At a convention at Washington-on-the-Brazos, Texans formed a provisional state government with Henry Smith as governor and Austin as commander in chief of the state militia.

The first shots of the Texan Revolution were fired when the Mexican army demanded the return of a six-pound cannon given to the colonists in Gonzales, Texas, for defense against Indian attacks. The Gonzales colonists refused and issued a call for volunteers to help defend the cannon. On October 2, 1835, they flew the famous "Come And Take It" flag over the cannon and repelled a small unit of Mexican troops sent to retrieve it.

The Mexican unit retreated to San Antonio with the Texas volunteers in pursuit. More volunteers joined them and together they laid siege to San Antonio. After five days, the Mexican forces surrendered; the Texans released the survivors after the Mexicans pledged never again to fight against the Constitution of 1824. Texans were also able to gain control of garrisons at Nacogdoches, Goliad, and Anahuac.

By the end of 1835, the Mexican military had been expelled from Texas and the colonists felt they'd won back their rights. The victors were divided, however, about how to use their new-found power. A minority, led by Governor Henry Smith, was in favor of outright independence from Mexico. But most of the state council wanted to throw their support behind Mexican liberals in the restoration of a constitutional Mexican government. Meanwhile, they had to assemble some sort of defense in the event that a non-republican Mexican army tried to retake Texas. There were only about 750 men in the Texan army, nearly all volunteers. Four hundred men were stationed at San Antonio with the rest scattered among the other garrisons throughout the state.

President Santa Anna not only ordered the Mexican army to march on Texas, he led them himself. A force of approximately 6,000 troops left Mexico City in February 1835. At first, the Texans assumed the Mexican army would bypass San Antonio to hit the center of the Anglo colonies in San Felipe. When scouts spotted Santa Anna's front guard and realized San Antonio was the target, it was too late to mount an effective defense.

The legendary battle of the Alamo lasted 12 days. James Bowie, a hard-drinking Indian fighter married to the daughter of Coahuila y Texas's vice governor, was supposed to lead the defense but fell ill the day after the Mexican army lay siege to the Alamo. William Travis took command instead. Santa Anna flew a red flag, the Mexican symbol for "no quarter, no mercy, no surrender" while the colonists flew the Mexican flag, to which they'd added the numeral "1824," the date of the Mexican constitution (the flying of the Mexican flag by the Alamo defenders has naturally been hotly disputed by loyal Texans ever since). Although the defenders, many of whom were of Mexican descent, were outnumbered 40 to 1, the superior marksmanship of the frontiersmen inside the Alamo held off the Mexican troops without a single Texan death until the walls were finally breached on March 6. The Mexican troops killed every one of the defenders and lost about a third of their own.

Independence
Before the Alamo siege ended, the state council convened at Washington-on-the-Brazos and on March 2 declared Texas an independent re-

public. Of the 59 delegates who signed the Texas Declaration, only two were actually born in the state, José Antonio Navarro and Francisco Ruíz. Fifty-three were former U.S. citizens and the remaining four were born in Canada, Scotland, Ireland, and England.

After their victory at the Alamo, Santa Anna's forces regrouped and plunged northward. The remainder of the Texan volunteer army under the command of Sam Houston began retreating in the same direction. Along the way they picked up additional volunteers, including a company of Mexican Texans. No one today seems to know what Houston's intended destination was, but he may well have been heading for Louisiana to seek U.S. assistance. However, Santa Anna's remaining force of 1,100-1,300 somehow got ahead of Houston's battalion on April 21, and while the Mexican troops were enjoying an afternoon siesta at San Jacinto, 800 Texans charged. In less than 20 minutes, the Mexican army surrendered.

Although Santa Anna escaped during the San Jacinto battle, he was captured the next day and held prisoner until he signed treaties which guaranteed the withdrawal of all Mexican troops from Texas and recognized the new Republic of Texas.

THE REPUBLIC OF TEXAS AND U.S. ANNEXATION

The republic lasted 10 years, and throughout its short history it was plagued by difficulties. Most no doubt stemmed from the fact Texans just couldn't govern themselves very well. Perhaps they'd been rebellious citizens of Spain and Mexico too long and couldn't stomach their own authority, perhaps they were simply disorganized. There were many other pressures on the new nation as well: a suffering economy, aggressive Indians, lack of foreign relations, and an unstable government on the southern border.

Sam Houston
Sam Houston, a leading figure before, during, and after the Texas republican period, came forward to guide the fledgling republic. In 1836, he was elected president of the republic and, to-

gether with his vice president Lorenzo de Zavala (born in Yucatán, Mexico), enacted a voter-ratified constitution. Voters also came out overwhelmingly in favor of annexation to the United States. Houston made a formal request for annexation in 1837, but withdrew it when U.S. abolitionists argued against the idea. U.S. President Andrew Jackson formally recognized the republic later that year, just before leaving office.

Under Houston, the Republic of Texas enacted humane Indian policies. Houston had grown up with the neighboring Cherokees in his native Tennessee, and left home to live with a Cherokee tribe for three years when he was 16; the Cherokees called him Co-lon-neh, the "Raven." Long before he arrived in Texas, Houston had been an advocate of Indian rights as governor of Tennessee. During a six-year stint with the Cherokee nation in Arkansas Territory, where he served as a trader, advisor, and special envoy for the tribe on several occasions, he married a Cherokee woman, Tiona Rogers, in a Cherokee ceremony. As president of Texas, his policy toward Texas Indians favored peaceful coexistence wherever possible and he gave land to Indian refugees fleeing persecution in the eastern United States. He was in the process of making peace with the Comanches on the western frontier when his two-year term ended. Under the existing constitution, he could not run for a second consecutive term.

The Lamar Presidency

Mirabeau Lamar succeeded Houston and almost immediately began reversing Houston's Indian policies. In 1838, he forcibly expelled the Cherokees from their new lands in East Texas and killed Cherokee chief Philip Bowles, a close friend of Houston's. Equally disastrous was his 1840 invitation to 12 Comanche chiefs to meet in San Antonio and exchange war prisoners. The Comanches only brought one white prisoner with them, so Texas commissioners tried to hold the chiefs hostage to extract more prisoners captives. The so-called Council House Fight resulted, in which many Indian chiefs and warriors were killed. When the Comanches found out about the treachery, they began a series of raids on Anglo settlements that lasted 35 years.

Texas didn't have the militia to defend western settlements from Indian raids. Instead, ranchers and local communities hired "rangering companies" to guard their interests. The most famous of these were the Texas Rangers. They became known for their skill in fighting the Plains Indians and were paid very well for doing so. Eventually they became a public menace and had to be dissolved as an independent entity, but in the early years of their existence the Rangers played an important role in defending the frontier.

President Lamar fared better in foreign affairs, compelling France to recognize the Republic of Texas in 1839. Holland, Belgium, and Great Britain soon followed. But the economy was on the verge of collapse, so the Texan government reinstated the *empresario* program used by the Mexicans to attract more immigrants. The colonization bill of 1842 awarded Europeans substantial land grants in return for bringing large groups of settlers to Texas. Frenchman Henri Castro brought 600 Alsatians to Texas; his settlement in Central Texas was later named Castroville. Many Germans came over as a result of these land grants as well.

Sam Houston

Overtures to Annexation

When Lamar's term ended, Sam Houston returned to office. Houston immediately took measures to offset the huge budget deficit created by Lamar. He also attempted to bring peace to the Indian frontiers by reopening negotiations with the Comanches and establishing trading posts along the frontier.

But Texas soon had major difficulties with Mexico. In 1842, the Mexican army broke the independence treaty of 1836 and launched guerrilla raids against San Antonio, Goliad, and Victoria. Fourteen hundred Mexican troops occupied San Antonio and declared the reconquest of Texas. The Texas Rangers and a group of 600 Texan volunteers, under the leadership of Captain Jack Hays, were able to expel the Mexicans. Houston was under extreme popular pressure to "punish" Mexico for the assault, but would not order his troops to invade Mexico, an act which would surely have led to a military disaster. The attacks ceased.

Toward the end of Houston's second term, the U.S. began making overtures toward Texas annexation. U.S. leaders were worried Texas was getting too intimate with European nations, especially Great Britain. Already trade between Texas and the U.S. was decreasing while trade with Britain was on the rise. In order to secure trade concessions from Britain, Texas had banned the further importation of slaves. Slavery was a major issue in American politics by this time, and southern Americans were anxious about the future of slavery in Texas. Many feared Texas might become part of the British empire.

In 1844, Texas and the U.S. signed a tentative annexation treaty in which Texas would become a U.S. territory, not a state. However, the treaty was voted down in the U.S. Senate by an unintentional alliance between parties on both sides of the slavery issue. Southern senators who feared the demise of slavery (because of the treaty with Britain) as well as northerners who feared its expansion (because of the reality of slaveholdings in Texas) came out against annexation.

Houston swore he'd never court annexation again. But later that same year, James Polk ran for the U.S. presidency on a Democratic platform of westward expansion, which included the annexation of Texas and occupation of Oregon. Meanwhile, France and Great Britain put pressure on Mexico to lay aside all claims to Texas in hopes an acquiescent Mexico would strengthen Texas independence. They didn't want to see Texas become part of the U.S. and figured that official Mexican recognition would make Texans feel more secure in their status as an independent nation. And so began a short tug-of-war between Europe and the U.S., only a year after the U.S. Congress had refused to ratify annexation.

Polk won the election, but U.S. leadership was so worried about Mexico's decision that before Polk was even inaugurated, the incumbent President Tyler pushed an annexation bill through Congress in February 1845 offering Texas status as a full-fledged state. Great Britain countered by urging Texans to delay acceptance of statehood for at least 90 days while they continued negotiations with Mexico for recognition of the Texas republic. But the Texas government decided in favor of annexation and submitted a state constitution approved by Congress in December 1845.

STATEHOOD, SECESSION, AND CIVIL WAR

War with Mexico

The annexation of Texas to the U.S. sparked the war with Mexico. Mexico hadn't officially recognized Texas as a republic and was slow to accept it as part of the United States. Mexico particularly didn't want to concede the area between the Nueces River and the Rio Grande, in spite of the fact the Mexican military hadn't occupied the territory for many years. The U.S. considered the Rio Grande the southern boundary of Texas, just as the Republic of Texas had. When the U.S. Army moved into the area, Mexico retaliated.

There followed a series of skirmishes along the Rio Grande, during which 200 Texans of Irish descent from San Patricio deserted the U.S. Army and fought for the Mexican army. President Polk then ordered the Army to invade Mexico. Mexico City fell to U.S. forces in March 1847. Mexico signed the Treaty of Guadalupe Hidalgo in 1848, conceding not only the Rio Grande-Nueces River area of Texas but also the territories of Nuevo México and Alta California—which together included the present-day states of Colorado, New Mexico, Nevada, Arizona, California, and parts of Utah and Wyoming. In exchange, Mexico received a payment of US$25 million; the U.S. also assumed responsibility for US$3 million in claims lodged against the Mexican government by citizens of the territories. In retrospect, it is likely the annexation of Texas was part of a U.S. plan to provoke Mexico into declaring war so that the U.S. could gain the entire Southwest.

Population Growth

The state's population began expanding in the middle of the 19th century as new immigrants arrived to take advantage of cheap Texas land. Most of the settlement took place east of the Balcones Escarpment, since the Edwards Plateau and Llano Estacado areas of the Texas High Plains were considered uninhabitable due to the presence of hostile Comanches. The U.S. Army established forts along this line but was unable to push the Amerindians back—no Army unit, whether infantry or cavalry, was a match for mounted Comanches.

John Meusebach led a group of 140 German immigrants onto the edge of the Edwards Plateau, however, and established the town of Fredericksburg in May 1846. Meusebach negotiated a mutually favorable treaty with the Comanches on the San Saba River. This treaty was never broken by either side and gained the distinction of becoming the only successful treaty between whites and any group of Indians in Texas history. Other Germans, seemingly the only immigrant nationality able to do so, moved into the area beyond the Balcones, and by 1850 German Texans outnumbered Mexican Texans.

Between 1850 and 1860 Texas's population exceeded 600,000, nearly triple what it had been 10 years earlier. About a third of Texas farmers at this time held slaves; they were generally the wealthiest and most influential individuals in the state. By 1860, half those holding office at the state and local levels were slaveholders, and Texas was increasingly drawn into the national slavery debate.

Secession

States-rights advocate and Democrat Hardin Runnels was elected governor in 1857 and openly called for the reinstitution of the slave trade, still illegal in Texas. There was talk of joining the growing movement among slave states toward secession from the United States. But Texans had mixed feelings about supporting secession, and when Sam Houston ran again on a strong Unionist platform, he was reelected. Texas also chose two Unionist senators to represent the state in Washington. For the time being, Texas took the Union side against the secessionists.

John Brown's 1860 raid on Harper's Ferry, Virginia and the capture of Brownsville on the Rio Grande by Mexican bandit Juan Cortina changed Texas popular opinion. Secessionists used these incidents as proof of an abolitionist conspiracy to violate state rights and impose authoritarian rule. A siege mentality soon developed and secessionists called for a convention to pass a secession ordinance. Houston maintained his Union stance and refused to approve the convention, so secessionist leaders convened on their own. The ordinance was drafted and issued to Texas counties for a vote. Only 13% of the population participated in the vote; of these, 76% percent—only 61,000, or roughly 10% of the total population—voted for secession.

Houston declared the ordinance unconstitutional since it annexed Texas to a foreign government, the Confederacy. He argued that if Texas were to secede from the Union, it should return to its status as an independent republic. But the secessionists held forth the voter mandate and on March 2, 1861, Texas became a Confederate state.

In a letter to Governor Houston, U.S. President Abraham Lincoln offered to send 50,000 federal troops to aid Houston and the Unionists in putting down the rebellion. But Houston declined, and wrote back saying, "I love Texas too well to bring strife and bloodshed upon her." When he refused to swear allegiance to the Confederacy, Houston was deposed from the governorship. He retired to Huntsville, where he died in 1863.

The Civil War

The interior of Texas saw virtually no action during the Civil War and hence did not suffer the widespread destruction that occurred in the South. The state's main role in the confrontation was as a supplier of cloth and ammunition to the rest of the Confederacy. Eventually, the Union navy barricaded the Gulf Coast to halt the flow of supplies. But shipping continued from the mouth of the Rio Grande since the Union could not block international waters without taking on Mexico. Many of the ships carrying Texas supplies flew under Mexican flags from the Mexican port of Matamoros.

A very few Civil War battles were fought at the perimeters of Texas, most of them at the Louisiana border. Probably the most decisive battle involving Texas occurred at Glorieta Pass, New Mexico, where a Texas supply train was captured on its way to California. Southern California industrial interests supported the Confederacy and had agreed to send gold and lumber to Texas for Confederate use. Once Union soldiers discovered the supply route, they occupied El Paso for the remainder of the war.

By the beginning of 1865, Texan morale was very low. Non-slaveholders, the majority of the state, began to resent the sacrifices they were making on behalf of the wealthy cotton producers. Many were angry when they learned that slaveholders were often exempted from military service. Texan forces rebelled against the Confederacy and raided the state treasury for $5000 in gold. By the time the Confederate army had surrendered at Appomattox in April 1865, the Texas Confederates had disbanded.

The Union occupation of Texas began on June 19, 1865, with the arrival of 1,800 Union soldiers at the port of Galveston. Union General Gordon Granger announced the emancipation of all Texas slaves that same day. June 19 (Emancipation Day) became an annual statewide holiday in Texas and is now an occasion for "Juneteenth" festivals in African-American communities throughout the state.

TEXAS IN TRANSITION

Reconstruction and Frontier Justice

Immediately following the end of the Civil War, Texas entered a period of lawlessness. Local militia were banned by the U.S. as part of "Reconstruction" and the Indian frontier was left defenseless. Federal troops occupied the state but were concentrated along the Rio Grande, so it was difficult to enforce state laws elsewhere in the state. Indian raids increased, gun-dueling became commonplace, and banditry went unchecked. State records registered 1,035 murders between 1865 and 1868, and it is this era in Texas history that earned the state its Wild West reputation. Texas well deserved the distinction: you had to be rough, tough, and quick with a gun to contemplate living on the Texas frontiers. But in the interior towns east of the Balcones Escarpment and north of the Nueces River, life continued as usual.

At first the cotton industry, once the backbone of the Texas economy, suffered a severe labor shortage when the slaves were freed.

BARKER TEXAS HISTORICAL CENTER

Texas Rangers on the banks of the Rio Grande

labor shortage when the slaves were freed. Some blacks elected to stay on as paid laborers or tenant farmers, but most migrated elsewhere. While the East Texas economy declined, the cattle industry in South and West Texas began to develop quickly. During the Civil War, unbranded cattle had proliferated throughout South and West Texas and were available to anyone who took the trouble to round them up. Cattle drives moved hundreds of thousands of cattle northward to Kansas and Missouri, often braving Indian attacks in West Texas and bandits in South Texas.

The greatest trail drive in history moved 700,000 head of cattle from Texas to Kansas in 1871. This helped to offset losses in East Texas and, by 1873, Texas was shipping large amounts of cotton again as new immigration eased the labor shortage. The development of railroads across Texas made it easier to move agricultural products out of state and contributed to a fast-growing economy. Texans contemplated a bright future for themselves and their state.

But the problem of lawlessness remained. In 1874 the state government recommissioned the Texas Rangers to patrol Texas borders. Major L.H. McNelly led a special force of 40 Rangers that patrolled the Rio Grande while Major John Jones was given charge of six units of 75 men each for the Indian frontier. McNelly's brand of ruthless frontier justice soon "pacified" the lower Rio Grande valley, and he moved up the river to Eagle Pass to concentrate on an area plagued by American bandits. An 1876 Texas Ranger report on a cattle thief read "Mean as hell. Had to kill him."

Meanwhile, Rangers on the Indian frontier had their hands full. Spaniards, Mexicans, Texans, and the U.S. Army had spent a century trying to push the Plains Indians out of northwestern Texas, and their efforts had met with overwhelming failure. Some Texas histories claim Major Jones and his battalion of Texas Rangers finally accomplished what the rest could not. They fought what is generally considered to be the last Indian battle on the Texas Plains when they cornered a band of 100 Comanches at Lost Valley in June 1875. The U.S. Cavalry arrived to help the Rangers finish the fight, and from then on the Texas Plains were considered "safe" from Indians. But the truth is that 100 Co-

manches wouldn't have made a bit of difference to the area even 50 years earlier. The Plains Indians had already begun leaving northwest Texas by the latter half of the 19th century because of the lack of buffalo they depended on for survival. White and Amerindian buffalo hunters, not the Texas Rangers, drove the Comanches away by so depleting the migratory herds the Indians had no choice but to move on in search of better hunting grounds.

The Fencing of the Cattle Kingdom

Cattlemen soon moved onto the West Texas plains to take advantage of the grasslands and established huge cattle ranches. They practiced the Spanish tradition of open grazing, whereby cattle were allowed to roam freely most of the time, rounded up only twice a year for branding or trail drives. The introduction of barbed wire, first made on a hand-cranked coffee mill in 1874 by Illinoisan Joe Glidden, revolutionized the cattle industry and divided ranchers into two camps, fencers and open-rangers.

Ranchers who used fences were better able to control the quality of their herds. Farmers (called "nesters" by ranchers) also used barbed wire to keep cattle from trampling their fields. A "Don't Fence Me In" mentality developed among the open-rangers, who called barbed wire "the Devil's hatband," and feelings on both sides provoked a series of small range wars. (In the 20th century, this became a popular premise for B-grade Hollywood Westerns.) Fence-cutting was a favorite activity among open-rangers while fencers would string barbed wire across public roads. In 1883 the state Legislature made it illegal to fence public lands or cut fences other than your own, thus ending the range wars. The barbed wire legacy remains: in West Texas today, often the only sign of human presence on vast tracts of land is a barbed wire fence. Plaques that exhibit varieties of Texas barbed wire (with names like Glidden's Twisted Oval, Briggs's Obvious, Allis's Sawtooth, Scutt's Arrow, or Brinkerhoof's Riveted Splicer) adorn the walls of many West Texas living rooms.

With railroads established, the frontiers tamed, and the cotton and cattle industries booming, Texas by the end of the century was a U.S. leader in commercial agriculture. The standard of living for the average Texan was quite low, however, as most of the money was made by cattle and cotton brokers, not ranch hands and farmers. Railroad monopolies skimmed huge sums of money from the state treasury, until in 1893 the Texas Legislature empowered a public railroad commission to review rates and stock revenues for the first time.

OIL

Long before Europeans arrived, Amerindians in East Texas who found oil seeping from the ground used petroleum for medicinal purposes. Survivors of the DeSoto expedition in 1543 used it to caulk boats near the Sabine Pass. But the first oil well wasn't drilled in Texas until 1866, when Lyne Barret in Nacogdoches County devised the first rotary drill. Oil had only a few uses, then—as a lubricanßt, in road construction (to settle dust), and as a rather expensive cooking or heating fuel. Barret's well, and others drilled in Bexar and Brown counties, produced modest yields.

In 1894, a larger oil reservoir was discovered by accident in Corsicana, which resulted in the first commercial refinery in Texas. The Corsicana refinery developed a locomotive fuel and people became more interested in oil. Yet it was still more expensive than other kinds of fuel, particularly coal and wood.

At the beginning of the 20th century, the Corsicana oil field, at 500,000 barrels a year, was the biggest producer in Texas. Then a 1901 oil strike at Spindletop, near Beaumont, set Texas on its way to becoming the oil capital of the United States. In its first year of production, Spindletop yielded over three million barrels of oil; in 1902 the per annum output climbed above 17 million.

Naturally, the price of oil bottomed out, making petroleum the cheapest fuel available, and new markets soon opened up. Railroads and steamship lines converted from coal to oil and the petroleum industry developed practically overnight. Texaco, Gulf, and Mobil are three present-day oil companies that began at Spindletop.

East and Southeast Texas turned out to be good sources for other large oil deposits because of the presence of huge salt domes

below the earth's surface that created perfect conditions for oil "pooling." Subterranean oil doesn't actually collect in pools but permeates sandstone layers which absorb it like a sponge. Water below the sandstone layers exerts upward pressure on the oil while a thick layer of impermeable Austin chalk above the sandstone holds the oil back. Equally impermeable salt domes form containers around such layers, resulting in higher concentrations of oil. When a drill pierces the layer of Austin chalk that holds the oil back, it spurts forth.

An even bigger oil reservoir than the one at Spindletop was discovered near Kilgore in East Texas in 1930. The East Texas Oil Field covered 200 square miles and yielded 100 million barrels in its first year. Following the East Texas strike, Texas gained a production lead over Oklahoma and California, its previous rivals, and has remained the top U.S. oil producer ever since. Many more large fields have been discovered in Texas since, particularly in the Permian Basin of West Texas, but none were ever as big as the East Texas Oil Field.

INTO THE TWENTIETH CENTURY

Revolution in Mexico

In the early 1900s, Texas was settling down and becoming somewhat civilized. Most of the Rio Grande area had been secured by Texas Rangers, though there were brief skirmishes with bandit-revolutionaries during the Mexican rebellion against a succession of corrupt Mexican presidents between 1911 and 1916. The revolutionaries were initially led by Francisco Madero, an opposition leader who'd been imprisoned by President Porfirio Díaz. Madero fled to Texas and proclaimed himself president of Mexico. His opposition group planned the overthrow of Díaz from San Antonio and Dallas. From their tactical headquarters in El Paso and Juárez, they soon gained control of the northern Mexican states of Sonora and Chihuahua. Thousands of Mexican refugees fled across the border into Texas to escape the violence of the revolution.

Pancho Villa, a cattle rustler and bandit, became an important figure in the Chihuahua takeover. At first the U.S. public was so enam-

Pancho Villa (center) and associates

Gen. Fierro   Gen. Villa   Gen. Ortega

ROCHUN ARCHIVES

ored of his escapades Hollywood film crews accompanied Villa on his raids against local Mexican militia. After he was defeated three times in 1915, however, he turned his attention to border raids on villages in Texas and New Mexico. Whether the raids were a return to his old livelihood or an attempt to draw U.S. forces into military action against Mexico is a matter for continuing debate. At any rate, U.S. President Wilson responded by stationing 100,000 National Guard troops along the border and sending General John Pershing into Mexico in pursuit of Villa in 1916.

Pershing failed to capture Villa, and when the U.S. became involved in World War I in 1917, the Mexican border immediately became a low priority. By 1935, Mexico had steadied its presidential merry-go-round. But the colorful Villa is still remembered by elderly residents in West Texas who love to talk about his movements in Texas—where he had his saddles made, his favorite cantinas, and so on.

A 1919 investigation into the border problems revealed the Texas Rangers played a role in fanning the flames through their vigilante behavior, especially along the lower Rio Grande.

The Rangers were immediately reduced in number from 1,000 men to 76, their activities more closely monitored. One of the last famous Ranger actions was the pursuit and killing of Texas bank robbers Bonnie Parker and Clyde Barrow in the late '20s. Eventually, the Rangers were absorbed by the state highway patrol under the Department of Public Safety.

The Depression and World War II

During the Depression years of the early '30s, Texas managed fairly well, buoyed by the oil boom. Farmers were hit hardest, especially in cotton-growing East Texas where cotton prices bottomed out. New Deal policies eventually pumped $1.5 billion into the Texas economy and revived the agricultural sector. By the end of the decade the economy was back on track and growing at a rate of about four percent per annum.

The World War II years were especially good to the Texas industrial sector. Shipbuilding and aircraft manufacturing became important new industries, and the petroleum companies expanded as fuel demands increased. Between 1940 and 1955, economic growth exceeded nine percent per annum and many Texans moved into urban areas. The development of plastics further fueled the oil boom.

POSTWAR TEXAS

The state's industrial base diversified throughout the '50s and '60s as manufacturing companies moved to the state to take advantage of inexpensive electricity and land. In 1959, Jack Kilby of Texas Instruments developed the first silicon microchip, which put Texas on the high-tech road.

Petroleum continued as the state's principal income-earner and was given a major boost following the Organization of Petroleum Exporting Countries (OPEC) embargo of the United States market. American oil now had no competition from foreign suppliers, so Texas fields went into full production. Oil exploration and speculation moved forward unchecked and Texas soon became the capital of U.S. millionaires, ushering in the privileged lifestyle for a privileged minority depicted in the world-popular soap opera Dallas.

Over the next decade, Texas prospered, upgrading the state university system, sponsoring new arts programs, and attracting Americans from around the country seeking to benefit from the boomtown atmosphere. But in the mid-1980s the economy suffered a shock when oil prices plummeted because of disagreements on production quotas among OPEC members. During a single two-month period in 1986, the price of crude oil dropped from $20 to $10 a barrel. For Texas oil interests, this meant it was no longer profitable to pump oil fields at 100% capacity and petroleum exploration slowed to a near halt.

Cities that were oil dependent, like Houston, suffered the most, turning into partial ghost towns virtually overnight. But the entire state had to face the reality of the situation and admit the economy needed further diversification. Texans have also begun to realize that even if oil prices rise again (as they did in the late '80s), petroleum reserves are running low. Even newly discovered oil fields will probably not be sufficient to compensate for the overall decline in reserves.

Texas has worked vigorously to attract more high-tech interests and to expand the service sector of the economy, including tourism. So far the state has been very successful in bringing in new light industries which benefit from the lower cost of production in Texas (lower wages, energy costs, and real estate). By 1989 Texas had clawed its way back to the employment level attained before the 1986 oil price collapse. Every year since 1990 the state has posted the highest economic growth rate of any U.S. state, buoyed by the continued influx of high-tech, "knowledge-oriented" business, increased trade with Mexico, and the general population shift toward the Southwestern states.

GOVERNMENT

Texas attained its current status as an American state when the Texas Constitution was approved by the U.S. Congress on February 15, 1876 (an earlier 1845 constitution had been nullified by secession in 1860). Amendments to the state constitution are enacted by a two-thirds majority vote in the state legislature, followed by a simple majority of Texas voters at large. The Texas governor does not have veto power over constitutional amendments.

Like the U.S. Congress, the Texas legislature is bicameral—divided into the Senate, consisting of 31 members, and the House of Representatives, with 150 members. At the national level, Texas has two U.S. Senators and 27 members in the U.S. House of Representatives.

Traditionally, Texas has been a bastion of the Democratic Party at both the state and national levels. During the past two decades, however, Republicans have gained strength rapidly. In 1978, William P. Clements Jr. became the first Republican candidate to win the state governorship. He lost to Democrat Mark White Jr. in 1982 but won again in 1986. In 1990 the state elected Austin Democrat Ann W. Richards as governor, the third time in the state's history a woman had been selected for this office; she was defeated for re-election in the Republican landslide four years later.

The state is divided into 254 county jurisdictions with an average county size of 1,000 square miles. Brewster County in West Texas is the largest, with an area of 6,169 square miles but a population density of only 1.3 persons per square mile.

ECONOMY

Contrary to popular belief, petroleum is nowhere near the state's number-one source of revenue. The value of manufactured goods produced in Texas in 1992 totaled a whopping $65 billion, making manufacturing the state's second most important income-earner after services ($75 billion). The next most important contributor to the state GDP is wholesale and retail trade, which accounted for $62 billion in 1992. Finance, insurance, and real estate squeeze in at fourth place, taking in $61 billion for 1992.

Crude oil production in Texas dropped from a peak of 1.3 billion barrels in 1972 to just over 642 million in 1992 (about 25% of total U.S. oil production), earning $11 billion in gross revenues. Obviously, fairly small changes in oil prices can significantly affect oil's rank in the state economy. Natural gas is also an important product, earning over $8.6 billion in '92. Minerals—crushed stone, sulfur, gypsum, talc, and salt—were valued at $1.4 billion that same year.

Texas leads the nation in livestock production and in the number of farms and ranches. Incredibly, the total land area occupied by agricultural and ranching concerns exceeds the combined areas of Maine, New Hampshire, Vermont, Massachusetts, Rhode Island, Connecticut, New York, New Jersey, Pennsylvania, Delaware, Maryland, West Virginia, and Washington, D.C.

Texas livestock far outnumber Texans. At the beginning of 1992, the state's ranches harbored 13.6 million cattle, 2.1 million sheep, 1.9 million goats (1.5 million of which were mohair-producing Angora), 762,000 hogs, and over 18 million chickens. Ranching receipts for 1992 totaled $6.8 billion, more than any other state. Farming follows ranching with a 1992 income of $3.9 billion. The leading crop is cotton, followed by grains (grain sorghum, rice, wheat, corn, barley), vegetables, pecans, peanuts, citrus, and other fruits. Texas leads the nation in cotton and rice production.

Texas weathered the nation's 1990-92 recession better than most states and since 1990 has led the nation in economic growth rates (average 1.9% per annum over this period) and total number of jobs created—of the 382,000 jobs added nationwide 1990-93, 373,000 went to Texas. Although it's providing for the third most populous state in the U.S., the economy is still creating new jobs, due largely to continuing successes in high tech, cinema, and tourism. And thanks in part to NAFTA, Texas now exports more to Mexico, nearly $40 billion annually, than any other state. It's now safe to say Texas has largely accomplished a transition from a commodities-supported economy of the ground to a services-supported economy of the mind.

shrimp trawler, off the South Texas coast

THE PEOPLE

POPULATION

In 1990, the U.S. census estimated the population of Texas at 16,986,500, with an average population growth of about 3.9% per annum; current estimates put the state's population at 17,655,600. Like other states in the Sun Belt, Texas is benefiting—or suffering, depending on your point of view—from the gradual exodus of Americans from the colder and more industrialized northern states. Texas is now the country's second-most populous state, after California, having recently overtaken New York.

The state's four primary metropolitan areas have populations exceeding one million each: Houston (3,301,900), Dallas (2,553,400), San Antonio (1,302,100), and Fort Worth-Arlington (1,332,000). There are 3,885,400 people in the Dallas-Fort Worth area and 3,711,000 in the Houston-Galveston-Brazoria region. When Houston and Dallas residents argue over which city is bigger, they often confuse these two different ways of counting the population. However you slice it, Texas has three of the country's largest 10 cities: Houston ranks fourth nationwide, Dallas eighth, and San Antonio 10th.

Seven metropolitan areas in the state have populations between 250,000 and one million: Austin, Beaumont-Port Arthur, Brownsville-Harlingen, Corpus Christi, El Paso, Killeen-Temple, and McAllen-Edinburg-Mission.

Texas also has hundreds of tiny towns with minute populations. Driving along out-of-the-way farm and ranch roads you might come across places like Acme (pop. 14), Airville (pop. 10), Babyhead (pop. 20), Bug Tussle (pop. 15), Eolian (pop. 9), Grit (pop. 30), Nickel Creek (pop. 16), Rio Frio (pop. 50), and Zorn (pop. 26).

TEXAS FILM

More American motion pictures have been produced with the name "Texas" or "Texan" in the title than all the other 49 states combined. Add to this the number of films either made in Texas or about Texas themes, and the total probably exceeds 1,000.

The first movies filmed here were shot in the early 1900s; French director Gaston Melles actually moved his studio from Brooklyn to San Antonio in 1909 and made a string of Western-genre films, including the first Alamo film, *The Immortal Alamo* (1911), starring John Ford's older brother, Francis Ford.

The first film shot in Texas by a Hollywood studio was *The Warrens of Virginia* (Fox Film Co.) in 1923. Every year since then Hollywood has scheduled location shooting somewhere in the state, usually for several movies simultaneously. Texas now has nine film commissions that court the major studios and provide production assistance: two each in Dallas/Irving and Austin, and one each in Amarillo, Brownsville, El Paso, Houston, and San Antonio. The year 1984 was a watershed for Texas filmmaking, when seven of the top eight Academy Awards went to films made entirely in Texas; in 1991 44 major movies were shot in the state.

Some of the most influential films in American cinematic history have been shot on location in the state, including John Ford's *The Searchers* (1956), Arthur Penn's *Bonnie And Clyde* (1967), Sam Peckinpah's *The Wild Bunch* (1969) and *The Getaway* (1972), Peter Bogdanovich's *The Last Picture Show* (1971, written by Texas writer Larry McMurtry), James Brooks's *Terms Of Endearment* (1983, another McMurtry vehicle), Robert Benton's *Places in the Heart* (1983), Bruce Beresford's *Tender Mercies* (1983, written by Texan Horton Foote), the Coen brothers' *Blood Simple* (1984), David Byrne's *True Stories* (1986), *Lonesome Dove* (1990, McMurtry again), David Lynch's *Wild At Heart* (1990), Oliver Stone's *JFK* (1991), Robert Rodriguez' *El Mariachi* (1992; like the Coen brothers, Rodriguez was a University of Texas film student), Richard Linklater's *Slacker* (1990, another UT film student effort that became a hit), and Steve Martin's *Leap of Faith* (1992).

(CONTINUED ON NEXT PAGE)

A long list of classic horror films have been shot in Texas as well, including *The Giant Gila Monster*, *Killer Shrews*, and *The Texas Chainsaw Massacre*. The state has even spawned its own nationally syndicated movie critic, Grapevine's Joe Bob Briggs, who mixes American social commentary into his reviews of films released for the drive-in market.

But perhaps the two most famous films made in Texas have been *Giant* (1956), starring Elizabeth Taylor, Rock Hudson, and James Dean in his last screen role, and John Wayne's unintentionally comical *The Alamo* (1960). At great personal expense, Wayne produced, directed, and starred in this tribute to the Texan Revolution (which he considered filming in Mexico before a grassroots Texas campaign convinced him to shoot in South Texas), but the resulting box office fizzle all but sank his career. In 1987 *Alamo: The Price of Freedom*, filmed at Wayne's preserved Alamo Village set, became the 16th Alamo film; it now shows daily at the IMAX Theatre in San Antonio. Yet another Alamo film was produced in Texas in 1992. Tentatively entitled *Citizen Wayne*, the as yet unreleased effort is a feature-length documentary of John Wayne's obsession with the *The Alamo*.

Native Texan Tommy Lee Jones, who has a home in San Antonio's Terrell Hills neighborhood and a ranch in San Saba, is the state's biggest cinematic export at the moment. Jones seemed to appear in every other big-budget movie released in 1994; that same year he directed his own movie, *Good Ol' Boys*, in the Trans-Pecos area.

Since 1980 an average of 29 major film projects

James Dean on the set of Giant

COURTESY BIG BEND QUARTERLY

per year have used the state for location and/or studio shooting. In a typical year the motion picture industry employs approximately 19,000 Texas residents and spends around $70 million in Texas. To keep the public informed of cinematic activity, the Texas Film Commission maintains a 24-hour production hotline (512-463-7799) with recorded information on the location and casting agency for every film and television series under current production in the state.

Age

Texas is a young state, demographically speaking. The 1990 U.S. census shows that of the 10 most populous states in the U.S., Texas has the largest percentage (40.6%) of residents under 25 years of age. Of these 10 states, Texas also has the smallest share of those over 45 years.

PEOPLES

Although Texas histories often emphasize the east-to-west movement of the Western frontier, the state's true demographic history involves not a simple line moving west, but a convergence of several migrational lines from all points

of the compass. Most significantly these include the movement of Hispanics northward, Anglos and northern Europeans westward, French Canadians southward, and Asians eastward.

Since the mid-19th century, the majority of Texans have been of European descent. At present, roughly two-thirds of the population is of Anglo or northern European ancestry. About one-fourth is Hispanic, that is, of Spanish, Mexican, or *mestizo* (Mexican-Indian) descent. The third-largest ethnic group, African-Americans, make up about 12% of the state's residents. Of these three groups, the Hispanic populace is increasing the most rapidly and is expected to constitute about one-third of the state by the year 2000. This disproportionate increase is due to a higher overall birthrate along with a steady stream of Mexican immigration.

Asians are one of the newer immigrant groups to make Texas their home and are especially prominent in the Houston and Beaumont-Port Arthur areas. In the major urban areas, many other ethnic groups are represented as well.

Although many have tried to define a "Texan character" or personality, it never really works. This is mainly because Texans are such a diverse people, both historically and presently. In spite of the Anglo majority, cross-influences from many different cultures—Amerindian, European, African, and Hispanic—have made it impossible to identify Texan culture with any one ethnicity. The most that can be said for a traditional "Texas spirit" is that perhaps there is a shared attitude of tenacity in the face of adversity—a "do or die" temperament both courageous and stubborn. This attitude was typical of early residents in many other Western and Southwestern states, but seems to have been best preserved in only a very few—besides Texas, perhaps Montana, Wyoming, and Alaska.

Amerindians

Unfortunately, the "frontier spirit" that is so noble in many ways was responsible for the almost complete demise of the great Indian cultures that existed throughout North America before

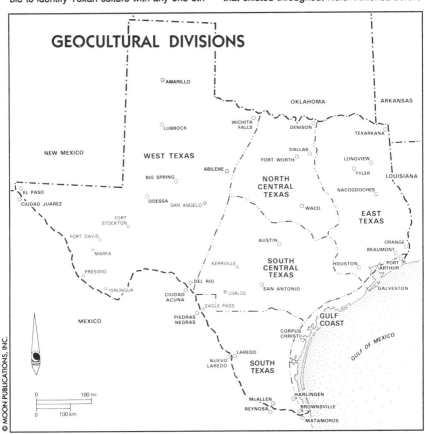

European immigration began 500 years ago. It would be unethical and dishonest for any writer to ignore this basic and unchangeable fact of history.

To be fair, however, it must be noted that when the Spanish first arrived in what is now Texas, the Indian population was fairly small and consisted of mainly nomadic tribes whose residency was somewhat sporadic or seasonal. Later, the Indian population in Texas grew concurrent with Anglo-American immigration, as many of the new Indian arrivals were themselves immigrants fleeing persecution in the eastern states. The Plains Indians that we see in American "Cowboy-and-Indian" movies were not native to Texas but came down from the Rocky Mountains and the Great Plains following the first European settlements in the 17th century.

The groups that can be considered most "native" to Texas—the Caddos (actually a sophisticated confederation of around 25 tribes) of East Texas, the Tonkawas of Central Texas, the Coahuiltecans and Jumanos of South and Southwest Texas, and the Karankawa Indians of the Gulf Coast—are gone today and were all but gone before the Anglo-American push westward. Most died at the hands of the Spanish and French, either by disease or in colonial violence, and the rest were later absorbed by the Mexican colonial population or killed by the more aggressive Plains Indians. By the mid-19th century, virtually all the Indian tribes in Texas were originally from elsewhere—the Plains Indians (Comanche, Apache, Kiowa) from the Rocky Mountains and Great Plains, and the Five Civilized Tribes (Choctaw, Chickasaw, Cherokee, Creek, and Seminole) from the eastern United States.

From the start, the source of friction between the Europeans and Indians was essentially cultural, resting primarily on differing concepts of property—the Europeans believed in the ownership of land, the Indians didn't. Perceiving that Indians didn't lay personal claims to land, Europeans practiced homesteading, and were then surprised when the Indians reacted. This is, admittedly, a gross simplification, since behavior among all groups concerned varied tremendously. But in the end it came down to the fact that the Europeans had more firepower than the Indians, and so their culture prevailed. By the end of the 19th century, most of the Indians living in Texas had been exterminated or assimilated, left on their own, or been forced out of the state in the same way Indians were "removed" by other U.S. states.

Today, there are only two officially recognized tribes, the Tiguas and the Alabama-Coushattas, living in Texas year round; there's one migratory tribe, the Kikapu or Kickapoos, of seasonal residents. The Tiguas, a Pueblo Indian group, can be considered neo-native to Texas, having moved into the El Paso area around 1680. Residing in Ysleta del Sur Pueblo, just outside El Paso, the Tiguas are descendants of an original Spanish mission community. Their most important festival takes place every June 13, the feast day of their patron saint, Saint Anthony.

The only other permanent Indian group maintaining a tribal tradition in Texas are the Alabama-Coushattas, a mix of two closely related Creek Indian tribes originally from Mississippi and Alabama. The Alabama-Coushatta reservation is located in the Big Thicket area of East Texas, on lands given to them by Sam Houston in the 19th century in return for their assistance during the Texan Revolution. The reservation is fairly large and is the site of a yearly national pow-wow.

During certain times of the year, the Kikapu migrate from their home in Nacimiento, Mexico, to a 125-acre residential site on the Rio Grande near Eagle Pass. A U.S.-Mexican agreement gives them the right to travel freely between the two countries and reside in either.

The largest Amerindian populations in Texas nowadays actually live in Dallas and Houston, and consist mainly of Cherokees from Oklahoma and Navajos and Mescalero Apaches from New Mexico who've come in recent years to take advantage of the state's relatively superior economy. These newcomers do not live along tribal lines, but many participate in intertribal community activities.

In spite of the low numbers of Amerindians residing in Texas, an Indian influence on Texas remains in the language (place-names, geographical terms, camping terms), cuisine (much of what is called "Mexican" or "Tex-Mex" cuisine was developed from Amerindian cookery), and folklore of Texas.

San Antonio Gun Club,
early 1900s

BARKER TEXAS HISTORICAL SOCIETY

Western Europeans

Most of the **Anglos** or English-speaking immigrants who came to Spanish and later Mexican Texas in the 19th century were former U.S. citizens seeking new opportunities. They largely set the tone for Texas settlement and assumed positions of leadership in the political events which led to independence and later U.S. annexation. They were joined by small groups of Anglo Europeans, generally Scotch and Irish, who were often fleeing religious or political persecution in their homelands.

Texans of **German** descent make up the state's fourth-largest ethnic group, behind Anglos, Hispanics, and African-Americans. Early German immigrants settled mostly in Central Texas, bringing with them the customs, dialects, and social organization of village Germany. In 1842, a group of Germans residing on the Rhine formed the Mainzer Adelsverein, a "Society for the Protection of German Immigrants to Texas." This organization worked with Texas land-grant *empresarios* to encourage German immigration. The Germans were the first immigrant group to settle successfully along the Indian frontiers in Texas.

Today, German-style beer halls are fairly common in Central Texas, as is the tradition of German sausage-making. Around 17 German "singing societies" are still active in the state, getting together for regular *Sängerfests* or song festivals. Few German descendants in Texas,

however, speak German as their mother tongue, and even during the famous *wurstfests* of Fredericksburg and New Braunfels, the festivities feature rather trivialized representations of German culture—though they're still great fun.

People of **French** ancestry occupy fifth place among the ethnic groups in Texas due to the Acadian French (or Cajun) presence in Southeast Texas. The first French settlement in Texas was LaSalle's Fort Saint Louis at Matagorda Bay, which lasted from 1685 to 1689 before succumbing to famine, disease, and Indian attacks. In 1817, the famous French buccaneer Jean Lafitte established Campeachy, a colony of 1,000 assorted pirates and privateers on Galveston Island, but in 1821 the U.S. Navy forced them to leave the vicinity.

The first established French colony began when Henri Castro received a land grant in 1842 to settle 600 families along the Medina River near San Antonio. By 1848, Castro had brought Texas more than 2,000 French immigrants, most from the province of Alsace. Today, many of the citizens of Castroville, Quihi, Vandenburg, and D'Hanis are descendants of these first colonists. The local language, food, and architecture continue to reflect Alsatian French heritage.

Other French immigrants came in smaller groups in the late 19th century, settled around the state, and were eventually assimilated. The discovery of oil in the early 20th century, however, brought thousands of French-speaking Cajuns and Creoles from Louisiana, most of them settling in Southeast Texas. Cajuns are descendants of a French-Canadian group from Nova Scotia, also known as Acadia, who were forced by the British to leave Canada in the 18th century when they refused to swear allegiance to the British Crown. The Acadians, or Cajuns as they came to be known by Anglos, brought their unique culture with them and have made the Port Arthur-Beaumont-Orange area—sometimes called the Cajun Triangle—a center for Cajun music and food, cultural hallmarks enjoyed by many non-French Texans.

The Creoles are most often said to be of mixed African-American and French descent or *mulâtres*. Actually, many Creoles are non-*mulâtre* descendants of either the slaves of French planters in Louisiana and Haiti or *gens libres de couleur* (free people of color) from the French Caribbean. In New Orleans, people of mixed French and Spanish descent often call themselves Creoles—the term can be applied quite loosely.

Creoles have emigrated in large numbers to the Houston-Galveston area. Fewer Creoles speak French than do the Cajuns nowadays, and they've to a large extent been assimilated by other black populations in Texas, though they still carry on a unique musical tradition.

Central Europeans

Slavic immigration has also made its mark on Texas culture. Communities of Poles, Czechs, and Wends dot Central and East Texas, with Czechs the most numerous group. Thousands of Czechs immigrated to Texas from Bohemia and Moravia in the late 19th and early 20th centuries. The town of Panna Maria (pop. 96) in Karnes County, founded by Poles in 1854, is the oldest Polish settlement in the United States. Currently, the largest rural populations of Czechs in North America are found in Texas.

In the towns of Praha, Fayetteville, and Halletsville, Czech is still a first language for some residents. Czech Texans support two Czech-language periodicals, the weekly *Nasinec* (out of Granger) and monthly *Hospodar* (West), plus one Czech page in Temple's daily *Herald*. Almost every small-town bakery in South Central Texas sells *kolaches*, a traditional Czech pastry.

Country and western music owes a large debt to the polkas and waltzes of Moravia and Bohemia, and the Texas-style dance hall was actually introduced by the Czechs. Moreover, the accordions used in Tex-Mex *conjunto* bands, as well as in the Creole zydeco music of East Texas and southern Louisiana, were introduced by early Czech immigrant musicians (Germans played accordions as well, but not in the style adopted by Mexicans and Creoles).

African-Americans

Black Texas residents live mostly in East Texas, particularly in the Houston-Galveston and Port Arthur-Beaumont areas. For many of their ancestors, immigration to Texas was not voluntary—they came as slaves or indentured servants. Once slavery was abolished in Texas following the Civil War, many former slaves migrated to urban centers outside Texas. Some remained, however, and took advantage of the situation as best they could. As elsewhere in America, blacks didn't receive full civil rights by federal law until the 1960s.

The numerous Creoles of Southeast Texas constitute one African-American group that immigrated to the area voluntarily, either in flight from French plantations in Louisiana and Haiti in the 18th century, or in search of better economic circumstances later in the 19th and 20th centuries.

African-American Texans played an important role in Texas history when they served as the U.S. vanguard, in several all-black infantry and cavalry units, during the Indian Wars of the late 19th century. The Comanches called them "buffalo soldiers," and the famous 9th and 10th cavalries adopted the buffalo as their coat of arms. Black cowboys were fairly common throughout the Cattle Kingdom era, and there is still a strong black cowboy tradition in East Texas. Beaumont was the original venue for the annual Bill Pickett Invitational Rodeo, an all-black event named for the famous African-American rodeo cowboy who invented "bulldogging," the now-standard event in which a steer is wrestled to the ground.

African-Americans have also made undeniably strong contributions to a collective Texan culture, particularly to Texas music. Their influence is present in Texas cuisine as well, especially throughout East Texas, where "homestyle" or "southern" cooking predominates. Even Texas barbecue aficionados are divided between those who favor the "Western" style developed by white and Hispanic chuckwagon cooks and those who prefer the "soul" style developed by African-Americans in East Texas.

Hispanics

Historically, Hispanics have had more influence in Texas than any other group besides Anglo-Americans. The Hispanic influence began, of course, with the arrival of the Spanish in the 16th and 17th centuries and continued through the period when Texas was a Mexican territory. Altogether, Texas was under Spanish or Mexican rule for around 150 years, from the first Spanish colony at Ysleta in 1681 until Texas independence from Mexico in 1836.

Hispanic influences on many phases of Texan life—language, food, architecture, music, and fashion—are so ubiquitous it would take a thick chapter to enumerate and describe them even briefly. Some influences are so deeply woven into the Texan fabric that their origins are vir-

tually indiscernible from what is assumed to be Anglo-American culture.

Practically the entire Texas cowboy mythology, for example, is based on the Spanish *vaquero* tradition, which developed when Spaniards brought cattle to the New World in the 16th century. Many of the words associated with "Western" life come from the Spanish language—ranch (*rancho*), buckaroo (*vaquero*), rodeo, lariat (*la reata*), corral, chaps (*chaparreras*), bronco, and posse are a few well-known borrowings.

Texas architecture has also borrowed much from Spanish and Mexican heritage. In addition to the Spanish cathedrals, missions, and presidios that remain standing in West and South Texas, modern interpretations of these early buildings continue to evolve and provide the state with a distinguishable regional style of architecture.

From margaritas to fajitas, Texas food wouldn't be Texan without the Spanish-Indian influence responsible for many of its tastiest dishes. Almost every Texan has his or her favorite Mexican or Tex-Mex restaurant and is quick to claim that Texas Mexican is better than Arizona or California Mexican. In the "nouvelle Tex" or "Southwestern" cuisines of Dallas and Houston restaurants, the Hispanic influence is always part of the presentation, whether it's a touch of cumin and lime or paste of ancho chiles.

A few descendants of the original Spanish colonists still live along the Rio Grande and in San Antonio, but for the most part, the Hispanics living in Texas now are of Mexican or Mexican-American ancestry. Mexicans continue to migrate to Texas from Mexico, some legally and others as immigrants who cross the border illegally. It's ironic that undocumented Mexican immigrants are considered "illegal aliens" in an area that 150 years ago belonged to Mexico and doubly ironic that many Anglo-Americans were themselves illegal aliens in Texas at that time.

LANGUAGE

Since the annexation of Texas to the U.S. in 1845, English has become the most widely spoken language in the state, with Spanish a distant second. Ironically enough, one of the issues that provoked the Texan rebellion against Mexican rule was the Anglo-American desire for English as an official language alongside the majority language, Spanish; these days, Chicanos struggle for a similar recognition of Spanish.

The majority of Texans, whatever their ethnic background, speak a unique style of English that sets them apart from the residents of other states in the South and Southwest. Stephen Brook, British author of the insightful *Honkytonk Gelato,* enthused thusly about Texas speech:

> *What nourishing mouthfuls of language, flush with redundancy, one can hear in Texas, words stumbling over each other, vowels endlessly elongated into diphthongs like verbal rainbows, containing elements and ghosts of every vowel sound known to the human race, including a few that, like the Big Bend mosquitofish, are unique to Texas.*

In the cities, the language is diluted by cosmopolitan populations into something approximating Standard American English, but in rural areas, the ripe Texas sound is usually quite prominent. Texan English also varies from one part of the state to another, especially from east (very slow rhythms) to west (linguistic minimalism, punctuated by long squints at the horizon).

Texas vocabulary can also vary significantly from Standard American English. For example, the three meals of the day are usually breakfast, dinner, and supper, rather than breakfast, lunch, and dinner. In small towns, people may say a cinema has "refrigerated air" rather than air-conditioning. Many rural Texans like to use two words when one would suffice, as in "big ole" for "big" and "little bitty" (or even "itty bitty") for "little"; in West Texas, you might also hear "t-niny" for "tiny." And, of course, Texans are well known for hyperbole; when talking about their state, it's always

"biggest," "best," or "most"—only true about half the time.

In South and Southwest Texas, Texas-born residents of Mexican descent often speak a unique mixture of Spanish and English that non-Hispanics may call Spanglish or Tex-Mex. It's especially distinctive among older and rural Chicanos who mix a Texas drawl with Spanish vocabulary. Nowadays, many younger, urban Chicanos speak a blend common throughout the Southwest and California, a symbol of the pan-Hispanic social movement among Hispanic Americans. Listen to the local radio stations of San Antonio, Corpus Christi, Brownsville, and Laredo and you'll hear bilingual disc jockeys switching back and forth between Spanish and English as they play an exciting mixture of Tex-Mex *conjunto,* salsa, and swamp music.

Anglos throughout Texas pepper their language with Spanish words and phrases like *arroyo* (dry stream bed) or *Quien sabe?* (Who knows?). The pronunciation of these is very Texan however. Most Spanish words ending in "o" will get an "a" sound instead; likewise an "e" ending is pronounced like a "y" or "i." Pecos becomes Pay-kas, Amarillo is Am-a-rill-a, arroyo is a-roy-a, and Rio Grande is Rio Grand-y.

In a few small towns in Central Texas, European languages are still spoken, most notably Czech, German, Polish, and Alsatian or Belgian French. In Southeast Texas, primarily in the Port Arthur-Beaumont-Orange triangle but also in Houston and Galveston, approximately 50,000 residents speak Cajun or Creole French as a first language. In Port Arthur, about 10% of the population is Vietnamese, so dialects of the Vietnamese language are common.

Body language in Texas can differ significantly from other states as well. West of the Brazos River, men may emphasize a point by grabbing a listener's shoulder briefly or with a quick slap on the back. In South Texas, the *abrazo,* a friendly embrace, is common even among non-Hispanics.

BOB RACE

ON THE ROAD
OUTDOOR RECREATION

ON LAND

**National Parks, Forests,
Recreation Areas, and Preserves**

Texas offers some of the largest and least crowded national outdoor recreation facilities in the United States. The U.S. National Parks Service manages Big Bend National Park, Guadalupe Mountains National Park, Padre Island National Seashore, Rio Grande Wild and Scenic River, Lake Meredith National Recreation Area, Amistad National Recreation Area, and Big Thicket National Preserve. Each of these is described in some detail elsewhere in this book, together with addresses and phone numbers. Depending on the park, preserve, or recreation area, a range of outdoor activities is available, from wilderness hiking and backcountry camping to boating and fishing.

In addition, Texas has several Park Service-operated national monuments, historical sites, and historical parks: Alibates Flint Quarries National Monument, Chamizal National Memorial, Fort Davis National Historic Site, Lyndon B. Johnson National Historical Park, and San Antonio Missions National Historical Parks. None of these feature camping or hiking facilities, but are interesting outdoor attractions nonetheless.

Some NPS-administered sites in Texas charge nominal entry fees—usually $1-3 per person or $3-10 per vehicle. The NPS offers several entrance passes that can reduce total fee expenditures for visitors who plan to visit several NPS sites. Each is available at any fee-operated national site. A **Golden Eagle Pass** costs $25 and allows unlimited admission for one calendar year to all federally operated outdoor recreation areas, including national parks, forests, recreation areas, and wildlife areas. Senior citizens age 62 and over are entitled to a **Golden Age Passport** allowing lifetime entry to all the same facilities for a one-time fee of $10. The **Golden Access Passport,** for blind and disabled people, carries all the same benefits as the Golden Age Passport. Finally, a

Park Pass can be purchased from specific NPS-administered sites for $10-15 and allows unlimited entry to that site for one calendar year. For general information on national parks, preserves, recreation areas, and monuments in Texas, write the National Park Service, Southwest Region, P.O. Box 728, Santa Fe, NM 87504.

State Parks

Lauded as the best state park system in the nation, the Texas Parks and Wildlife Department operates 131 state parks, state historical parks, and state natural areas. There's a state park within a two-hour drive of every metropolitan area in Texas; over half offer camping facilities. More parks and camping facilities are added all the time; the state's objective of establishing a state park within a two-hour drive of every metropolitan area in Texas had been realized as of the end of 1994.

Each state park charges an entry fee that ranges from $2 to $6 per vehicle and $1 to $3 per individual on bicycle, foot, horse, or boat. Senior citizens (65 years or older) and veterans with a 60% or greater VA disability can obtain a State Parklands Permit that exempts them from all entry fees.

Not every state park and recreation area is covered in this book. The State Department of Highways *Official Highway Travel Map* marks every one of them, however. You can order this map from the Texas Department of Highways or from the Texas Tourism Division; see "Services and Information" later in this chapter. Or, for a complete list, contact Texas Parks and Wildlife Department (tel. 512-389-8900 or 800-792-1112), 4200 Smith School Rd., Austin, TX 78744. A *Texas State Parks Guide Map* showing the location of all 131 state parks and listing fees and facilities for each is available from the TPWD for $2.95.

If you plan to visit several Texas state park facilities, invest $25 for the Texas Conservation Passport (TCP), which allows unlimited admission into all state parks. Only one TCP card per vehicle is necessary for all passengers to enter free of charge. The Conservation Passport also provides a $1 discount on overnight facility use fees, secures access to certain park areas closed to non-Passport holders, and allows for participation in periodic guided tours. In addition, TCP holders receive the quarterly *Passport Journal,* which provides current special event schedules, the latest Passport discounts, and assorted state park news. The TCP can be purchased by mail or phone from the Texas Parks and Wildlife Department or in person at any fee-entry state park.

Texas Highways magazine (tel. 800-839-4997) offers a subscription discount for TCP cardholders, and with a paid subscription you receive a "Texas Highways Travel Passport" entitling the holder to 10-15% discounts at around 1,500 non-TPWD facilities around the state, including Fossil Rim Wildlife Center in Glen Rose, the Running 'R' Ranch in Bandera, and a number of hotel and restaurant chains.

Hiking and Backpacking

From desert basins to mountaintops, from saltmarshes to hardwood forests, from creeks to canyons, Texas offers an unsurpassed variety of hiking trails. The state's hundreds of designated trails can be divided into three basic categories: nature trails, which are generally short (one to two hours walk) and require little preparation; day-hiking trails, which can be completed in a day or less and call for some planning in the way of water, food, clothing, and footwear; and backpacking trails that cover distances requiring overnight camping and careful preparation in camping equipment, food supplies, and clothing. Several parks in Texas also have horse trails for use with private and/or hired mounts.

Longer trails can, of course, be broken into a series of shorter hikes. Few people, for example, have hiked the entire length of the 140-mile Lone Star Trail through Sam Houston National Forest. Instead, hikers and backpackers tend to tackle the trail a few days at a time.

Around 800 trail miles are set aside around the state for backcountry hiking and backpacking in state and national parks, national forests, and national preserves. An annotated list of Texas trails is available through Statewide Planning and Research, Texas Parks and Wildlife Dept. (tel. 800-792-1112). You can obtain descriptions and maps of state and national park trails from individual park offices.

Maps of the 14 Woodland Trails in the Piney Woods region of East Texas can be ordered by calling or writing the Texas Forestry Association (tel. 409-632-TREE), P.O. Box 1488, Lufkin, TX 75901. Maps of the Lone Star Trail are distributed by the Forest Supervisor (tel. 409-639-8501), 701 N. First St., Lufkin, TX 75901.

For wilderness backpacking and backcountry camping you may want to bring along an appropriate topographic map. The best available are those researched and published by the Department of Interior's United States Geological Survey (USGS). USGS topo maps are available in several scales; the most detailed is the 1:24,000 scale (one inch = 2,000 feet) primary series. It takes literally hundreds of these 22-inch by 27-inch sheets to cover the entire state—18 sheets to cover Big Bend National Park alone. For most hikers, the 1:100,000 scale (one inch = 1.6 miles) topos will be sufficient. Individual sheets can be ordered directly through USGS Map Sales, P.O. Box 25286, Federal Center, Bldg. 810, Denver, CO 80225 or through any of the Texas map dealers listed in "Tourist Information" in the "Services and Information" section of this chapter. Another USGS map dealer worth checking is Timely Discount Topos (tel. 800-821-7609, 303-469-5022), 9769 W. 119th Dr., Suite 9, Broomfield, CO 80021.

Other information on Texas hiking is available from **West Texas Trail Walkers,** 1100 Wayland Drive, Arlington, TX 76012, which is affiliated with the American Hiking Society and American Volkssport.

Private Recreation Areas

Besides the large, privately owned Texas amusement parks like Six Flags Over Texas, Fiesta Texas, and Astroworld, a variety of active outdoor possibilities are offered around the state by private individuals, families, and small companies.

In the Hill Country, and to a lesser extent in West Texas, are a number of popular "dude ranches." A dude ranch offers city people and other non-ranchers an opportunity to experience ranch life for a few days or weeks. Typical activities include trail rides, outdoor ranch-style dances, fishing, river rafting, barbecues, and nature tours. Dude ranches vary from inexpensive, family-oriented affairs to higher-priced working ranches oriented toward equestrians and sometimes hunters. These last don't like

to be called "dude ranches," but still cater mainly to city folks.

Private campgrounds occasionally offer outdoor activities in conjunction with basic camping facilities. This is especially true for those camping areas located near streams and rivers, where tubing, rafting, canoeing, and fishing gear can often be rented or where guided trips are provided.

Private recreation areas of note are described throughout this book.

Hunting

Hunting is popular in Texas among men and women of all ages. Many state wildlife management areas allow regulated hunting in season, as do licensed private game ranches.

The ethics of hunting for sport is a controversial topic. But it must be recognized that Texas hunters, as a group, play an important role in state wildlife conservation efforts. Several introduced species that are now extinct in Asia and Africa are maintained on Texas game ranches, for example; these same ranches have been known to send U.S.-born animals to their native habitats for breeding in countries where they've been eliminated through excessive hunting.

Whether on state or private grounds, hunting regulations that include bag (size and number) limits are strictly enforced. White-tailed deer, mule deer, and wild turkey are by far the most popular game animals, followed by javelina (collared peccary), elk, squirrel, aoudad sheep, pronghorn, feral hog, prairie chicken, pheasant, chachalaca, rabbit, hare, and smaller game birds. The state permits the hunting of mountain lions without limit on size or number, a legal condition of much controversy in Texas today. Except on game ranches, lion hunting is mostly restricted to protection of livestock.

The best hunting in the state is said to be in South Texas and on the Edwards Plateau, which is also where most game ranches are located. The Texas Parks and Wildlife Department issues 12 different types of licenses, ranging from resident and nonresident basic seasonal hunting licenses ($13 and $200) to licenses for alligator hunters ($35 resident, $300 nonresident) and trappers ($15 resident, $250 nonresident). For detailed information on licenses, seasons, and regulations, write or call the Texas Parks and Wildlife Department (tel. 512-389-8900 or 800-792-1112), 4200 Smith School Rd., Austin, Texas 78744. TPWD publishes an annual *Texas Hunting Guide,* available free by mail.

Birding

With nearly 600 recorded species—over 75% of all bird varieties occurring in the continental U.S.—Texas is one of North America's prime birding destinations. Overall, the best regions for spotting birdlife are the lower Rio Grande corridor, the Gulf Coast, and the Trans-Pecos area. Among the more notable rare species that lure birders from around the world include the whooping crane, golden-cheeked warbler, black-capped vireo, green kingfisher, Attwater's prairie chicken, Lucifer hummingbird, and Colima warbler.

Free birdlists are available at most state and national parks, as well as at various state natural areas, wildlife management areas, national wildlife refuges, and at Padre Island National Seashore. Texas Parks and Wildlife publishes a useful booklet entitled *Birding in Texas,* which is available at many state park facilities or by contacting the TPWD office in Austin. TPWD also publishes *A Checklist of Texas Birds* (Technical Series No. 32), containing both common and Latin names as codified by the American Ornithologists Union. Tourist bureaus in Brownsville, Corpus Christi, and Rockport-Fulton publish and distribute their own regional birdlists.

Chickadee Nature Store (tel. 713-956-2670), 1330-L Wirt Rd., Houston, TX 77055, carries bird checklists for most areas in Texas, plus a number of birding guides and bird-watching paraphernalia. Another suggested stop on the Texas birder's itinerary is the **Dallas Museum of Natural History** (tel. 214-670-8457), P.O. Box 150433, Fair Park, Dallas, TX 75315, which contains permanent exhibits on Texas waterfowl and birds of prey. The museum's gift shop stocks an unusually good selection of books on birding and birding supplies.

The best general book on Texas birding is Ed Kutac's 1989 *Birder's Guide to Texas,* which also contains a complete list of bird clubs around the state. Birding expert Roger Tory Peterson has devoted an entire volume to the Texas aviary, *Field Guide to the Birds of Texas.* Two statewide organizations with copious information

on birdlife are the National Audubon Society's Texas Regional Office (tel. 512-327-1943), 2525 Wallingwood, Suite 1505, Austin, TX 78746, and the Texas Ornithological Society, 326 Live Oak, Ingram, TX 78025.

ON WATER

One of the common myths about Texas is that the entire state is bone dry. While it is true the Trans-Pecos area of far West Texas is mostly desert, elsewhere in the state the facts quickly dispel this myth. According to the annual U.S. Statistical Abstract, Texas is second only to Minnesota in the amount of inland water area within its borders, including over three million acres of lakes, streams, rivers, and springs. Then, of course, the Texas Gulf Coast is the third-longest shoreline in the continental U.S., over 600 miles long. Finally, the legendary Rio Grande, second longest river in the U.S., runs for 1,200 miles along the Texas-Mexico border. East Texas is the wettest part of Texas, where well over 50 inches of yearly rainfall keeps the water level high in lakes, rivers, and bayous.

Thirteen major rivers and over 11,000 named streams, creeks, and bayous run across Texas, mostly in a Gulfward direction. Many were first explored by Spanish colonists and hence have Spanish names. Besides the Rio Grande, some of the more popular rivers for water recreation include the Nueces, Guadalupe, Colorado, Canadian, San Antonio, Brazos, Neches, Sabine, and Red Rivers. Of these the most popular for riparian recreation is the Colorado River, which runs 600 miles from Dawson County in West Texas to Matagorda Bay on the Gulf, forming the Highland Lakes northwest of Austin along the way. Colorado waterways immediately above the lakes and below Austin to the Gulf are navigable; interested paddlers should obtain the Texas Parks and Wildlife Department's free *Recreationist Guide to the Colorado River.*

Over 150 lakes and reservoirs dot the state, all created by the damming of inland waterways to provide drinking water, agricultural irrigation, and hydroelectric power. Virtually all of the state's lakes and reservoirs are open to recreational activities like sailing, canoeing, swimming, and fishing. Many of the larger lakes are suitable for waterskiing and scuba diving as well. Major bodies of water, each over 20,000 acres in surface area, include Amistad Reservoir, Lake Buchanan, Calaveras Lake, Cedar Creek Reservoir, Choke Canyon Reservoir, Lake Conroe, Falcon Reservoir, Lake Fork Reservoir, Livingston Lake, Lake Palestine, Lake Ray Hubbard, Richland Creek Reservoir, Sam Rayburn Reservoir, Lake Tawakoni, Toledo Bend Reservoir, and Lake Wichita.

Fishing

Sportfishing is popular all over the state, from the Red River in the Panhandle to the Gulf Coast. Deep-sea fishing in the Gulf of Mexico is one of the state's most important tourist industries. Surf fishing and flats fishing in the shallow waters of lagoons created by barrier islands are also quite popular. You'll find sportfishing outfits that rent equipment, charter boats, or lead small-group fishing trips from the ports of Galveston, Port Aransas, Port Arthur, Corpus Christi, Port Mansfield, and Port Isabel as well as a few smaller port towns. Bass fishing is excellent on many Texas lakes.

According to the International Game Fish Association, Texas often leads the nation in the number of annual record-breaking saltwater and freshwater catches. By comparison, Florida is usually a distant second, with only about half the number of records for largest fish species. During a typical July-Aug. period (high season for many Gulf fish), Texas boasts 19 saltwater fishing tournaments, Florida only seven; the number of Gulf fishing piers in Texas also exceeds Florida's. Of 10 new all-tackle world records listed in the most recent issue of IGFA's *The International Angler,* three came from Texas, one from Florida and none from any other U.S. state.

As with hunting the Texas Parks and Wildlife Department regulates type, size, and number of gamefish taken from Texas waters. Fishing equipment also comes under detailed regulation (types of lines, traps, and nets that can be used, for example). But unlike hunting, fishing regulations aren't strictly enforced, simply because it's virtually impossible to patrol all the inland and coastal waterways. Nonetheless, fishing licenses are fairly inexpensive and it's best for future sportfishers and fish if everyone cooperates with state efforts to preserve the decreasing marine population.

Sportfishing licenses vary from $13 for a year-long resident license to $20 for a five-day non-resident license. Both are good for all freshwater fishing. The fee is $7 for a saltwater sport-

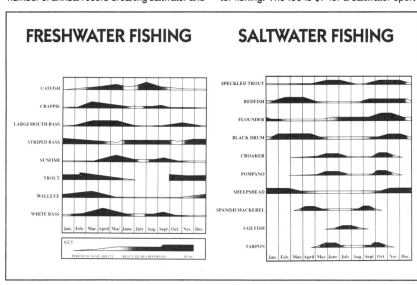

fishing stamp. Special licenses are needed to take shellfish such as shrimp, oyster, clams, and mussels. Crab has no season or number limit, though it's unlawful to take egg-bearing females or crabs less than five inches in body width. Tarpon, the magnificent "silver kings" of the Gulf, have recently made a significant comeback but in Texas waters they're a "catch-and-release" fish only.

For detailed information on sportfishing regulations and licenses, write or call the Texas Parks and Wildlife Department (tel. 800-792-1112, 512-389-4820) 4200 Smith School Rd., Austin, TX 78744. Specific information on local fishing spots is included with destinations listed in this book.

GUIDED TRIPS

Many organizations around the state offer guided outdoor recreation, ranging from trail rides to canoeing and backcountry camping. Guided trips are a great way for novices to learn outdoor skills under the supervision of experienced guides. For experts they're a good way to meet folks interested in similar activities.

The best places to contact guides are in the vicinity of recreational areas. Near Big Bend National Park, for example, several companies lead raft trips through the canyons of the Rio Grande. Along sections of other rivers in the state popular for rafting or canoeing are outfits that rent equipment and/or provide guided trips. **Texas River Expeditions** (tel. 915-371-2633 or 800-839-RAFT), P.O. Box 301152, Houston, TX 77230, arranges one- to three-day guided rafting trips on the Guadalupe River in the Hill Country and along the Big Bend stretch of the Rio Grande.

Wherever there are horse trails in national or state parks, you'll find a stable or two nearby that offer guided trail rides. Outdoor societies such as the Sierra Club arrange regular hiking and camping trips around the state. Some clubs concentrate on a particular kind of activity, such as rockclimbing or canoeing.

Along the coast are dozens of places that lead fishing trips. In many of the same ports are dive shops that organize scuba trips to the Flower Gardens reefs in the Gulf. Inland dive shops also lead dives at Texas quarries, lakes, and reservoirs.

Perhaps some of the best places to find a wide selection of outdoor trips are Texas college and university campuses. Many schools have established outdoor programs that run year round, but most are active primarily in the summer months. Most activities are open to the public and costs are very reasonable.

The University of Texas at Austin, for example, offers a week-long canoe trip on the Rio Grande for around $260 that covers transport, food, group camping equipment, and a guide. The university also has a regular program of one-day nature hikes that run around $7. Uni-

rapids on the Rio Grande, Santa Elena Canyon, Big Bend National Park

versity programs like these offer the best bargains in the state for guided outdoor trips. For a current schedule of UT-sponsored activities, call or write UT Recreational Sports Outdoor Program (tel. 512-471-1093), Gregory Gym 31, Austin, TX 78712.

ARTS AND ENTERTAINMENT

Texas has become a very entertaining place in the late 20th century. In fact, during most of the year and in most of the state (sparsely populated West Texas is the exception), you'd be hard pressed to drive more than 20 miles without coming across a festival, honky-tonk, party, concert, rodeo, or outdoor dance.

If you're looking for something to do in Texas but don't know where to find it, a good place to start is the local newspaper. Don't worry about the general lack of high-quality journalism—with few exceptions, Texas newspapers aren't known for their excellence. Most publish an informative "datebook" or "calendar" on Friday, Saturday, or Sunday which lists local events and ongoing exhibits. Independent arts-oriented weeklies in San Antonio (*Current* and *SA News*), Austin (*Austin Chronicle*), Houston (*Houston Press*), and Dallas (*Dallas Observer*) contain fairly comprehensive activities calendars that are generally superior to the daily papers. These papers, distributed around town free, cover not only the cities in which they're published, but also the surrounding towns.

City Texans are amazingly diverse in their interests, perhaps even more so than their counterparts in other U.S. capitals. Young folks in Texas think nothing of hitting a blues bar on Friday night, a polka festival Saturday afternoon, followed by Saturday night sushi and cowboy punk.

Museum and classical music enthusiasts needn't feel left out either. As an obvious consequence of big oil and high-tech money, some of the most well-endowed public and private museums in the U.S. are located in Texas. Most are in the large urban centers of Dallas, Houston, and San Antonio, but Texas travelers shouldn't neglect the smaller, more remote places like the Cowboy Artists Museum in Kerrville or the Museum of the Pacific War in Fredericksburg.

All the major cities have their own symphonies and dance companies, and some are quite good. In addition, several prestigious music festivals are staged in the state, including the acclaimed San Antonio Festival, the Van Cliburn International Piano Competition in Dallas, and the Round Top Music Festival.

TEXAS MUSIC

The classical music in Texas is fine, but where the state really excels is in American roots music. You can hear good Beethoven in New York or Minneapolis, but Texas offers a combination of uniquely American musical styles, most of which developed in Texas, that no other state can match.

The main reason for the heavy proliferation of musical styles in the state is simple geography —Texas occupies a position in the nation that is impossible to avoid or breeze through quickly

Blind Lemon Jefferson

BARKER TEXAS HISTORICAL CENTER

when traveling east to west along the southern half of the United States. Plus it has the longest international border of any state and curves right up into the Mississippi delta, the birthplace of American music as distinct from European music. A color-coded map of the U.S., in which different colors represent different musical influences, turns Texas into a patchwork quilt.

Scores of bands throughout the state continue to experiment with the many musical styles available, forging new sounds and garnering critical praise. In *Musician* magazine's nationwide "Best Unsigned Bands" contest, as many as four of the 12 winning bands may be from Texas; no other state on the award list has had more than one winner in the same year.

There's only one place where you can hear "Texas radio and the big beat" (Jim Morrison), and that's "down in Texas where the guitars grow" (Steve Miller). If for no other reason, it's worth traveling to Texas to hear roots music—but you have to know where to look for the best.

Blues and R&B
Blues music is probably the oldest popular music form in Texas. The blues, sung by freed black slaves, developed during the post-Civil War years in an area that stretched from Texas to Alabama. Records show collectors were transcribing blues lyrics in Texas as early as 1890. The singing style originated from "field hollers" or "shouts"—that is, a capella work songs—but evolved into a troubadour tradition in the late 19th and early 20th centuries, in which wandering musicians accompanied themselves on guitar or fiddle. Musically, the obvious origins of blues-style melodies and rhythms are African, but lyrically, early black Americans developed their own topics based on the suffering they experienced first as slaves and later in the post-emancipation South.

Wandering musicians were drawn to developing urban areas in the South and Southwest, and Dallas and Houston quickly became blues centers because of their large black migrant populations. The Deep Ellum area of Dallas, at the east end of Elm Street where it meets Central Avenue, was a favorite venue for legendary blues guitarists and singers like Blind Lemon Jefferson and Huddie Ledbetter ("Leadbelly") in the 1910s and 1920s. Virtually all blues players today can trace their

roots back to Blind Lemon, whose mid-1920s recording of "Black Snake Moan" made him the first popular blues performer in the United States. *Jefferson,* a leading European blues magazine published in Sweden, is named after him. Other famous blues musicians who came out of the Deep Ellum tradition include Lonnie Johnson, Texas Alexander, Sam Price, and Mance Lipscomb, who didn't perform there but created his style from watching Blind Lemon play in Deep Ellum.

The electric guitar was invented by San Marcos-Dallas blues and jazz guitarist Eddie Durham (1906-87), who devised a microphone from radio and phonograph amplifiers that fit into the body of his guitar. Earlier he'd developed the first acoustic guitar resonator from a tin plate, and later a vibrato arm from a clothes hanger. When the D'Armand Company developed a factory-built guitar pickup, Durham was among the first to use it. Jazz guitar legend and fellow Texan Charlie Christian learned about the pickup from Durham and also copied Durham's legato playing style. Christian was later hailed as the father of the jazz guitar.

Probably the second-most influential blues artist in American music, after Blind Lemon Jefferson, is T-Bone Walker. T-Bone was born in Linden, Texas, but moved to Dallas while still a boy. There he befriended Jefferson and was introduced to the electric guitar by Charlie Christian. He made his first blues recording in Dallas in 1929 and eventually revolutionized electric guitar playing by bending strings to create a "vocal" sound, thus establishing the guitar as a lead instrument. His influence on the entire blues idiom was tremendous and he's credited with developing the style known as "Texas shuffle blues" or "jump blues," an uptempo form with links to early swing jazz. Out of Texas shuffle evolved early **rock and roll** as composed and performed by Chuck Berry, Jerry Lee Lewis, Elvis Presley, and others.

Another hallmark in Texas blues history occurred when Mississippi-born Robert Johnson made his only known recordings—29 in all—at makeshift studios in a San Antonio hotel room and Dallas warehouse in 1936 and 1937. Johnson's international cult status among modern blues aficionados today borders on the fanatic.

Houston's blues tradition goes back at least

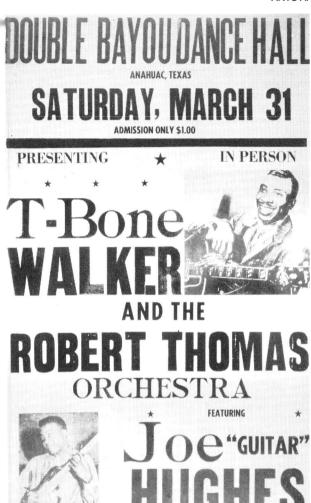

DOUBLE BAYOU DANCE HALL

ANAHUAC, TEXAS

SATURDAY, MARCH 31

ADMISSION ONLY $1.00

PRESENTING ★ IN PERSON

★ ★ ★

T-Bone WALKER

AND THE

ROBERT THOMAS

ORCHESTRA

FEATURING

★ Joe "GUITAR" ★

HUGHES

what are today considered his greatest performances. Lightning was a major influence on such famous rock guitarists as Billy Gibbons of ZZ Top and Jimi Hendrix, as well as on developers of the blues-tinged "swamp sound" like Creedence Clearwater Revival and Omar and the Howlers.

Houston's post-Lightnin' Hopkins blues style includes not only the up-tempo Texas shuffle originally popular in Dallas and Fort Worth but also a slow-to-medium blues with the 6/8 tempo popularized by the Junior Parker and Bobby Blue Bland orchestras. Besides Parker and Bland, other Houston-based blues performers who've achieved international status include Sippie Wallace, Charles "Gatemouth" Brown, Katie Webster, Slim Harpo, Big Mama Thornton, Juke Boy Bonner, and, more recently, Pete Mayes, Johnny Guitar Watson, B.B. King, Johnny Copeland, and Albert Collins.

By the '60s, blues music was commonly played by non-black as well as black musicians. Whites had actually been playing blues since the

as far, but the city didn't develop a blues recording industry until the late '40s. Lightning Hopkins (1901-82) is the earliest blues musician of note who performed regularly in Houston. His style was basically an idiosyncratic interpretation of Jefferson's; Hopkins was also influenced by his older cousin Texas Alexander. From 1947 to 1949 he recorded on Houston's Gold Star label

late 19th century, when black fiddlers and white guitarists played together at white dances, and throughout the '30s and '40s many white swing bands played blues tunes. Blues purists complain that white players watered down the blues during the heyday of white guitar blues in the '60s and '70s, but the fact is most blues musicians, black and white, were branching into other musical areas at the time, including **rhythm and blues,** "soul music," and rock. White Texas artists such as Doug Sahm, Johnny Winter, Janis Joplin, Steve Miller, Boz Scaggs, and Stevie Ray Vaughan, and Texas bands like ZZ Top and the Fabulous Thunderbirds varied in their devotion to the blues, but all were blues-inspired. What promoted the blues most during this period may have been the British blues experiments of groups like the Rolling Stones, Cream, and Led Zeppelin. For most of the British bands at the time, however, playing the blues was just a passing fad and by the mid-'70s the "blues experiment" had ended.

In the '80s, a blues revival spread across the U.S. and more Texas bands than ever swore their allegiance. Today Houston is indisputably the state's blues capital, but you can also hear new and "revived" Texas blues and R&B artists in clubs in Austin, Fort Worth, San Antonio, and Beaumont, as well as in various honky-tonks, roadhouses, and cafes in more rural areas. Look for these artists and bands around the state: T.D. "Little T-Bone" Bell, Erbie Bowser, Henry Qualls, Anson Funderburgh and the Rockets, Marcia Ball, Delbert McClinton, the Arc Angels, Grady Gaines, Delta Blue, Long John Hunter, Super Blues Party, Angela Strehli, the Juke Jumpers, Sue Foley, Jesse Taylor and Tornado Alley, and Steve James.

Jimmie Vaughan, the late Stevie Ray Vaughan's brother, has left the commercially successful Fabulous Thunderbirds for a solo career based on a brilliantly performed repertoire of 1950s-vintage Duke/Peacock-style R&B, Memphis soul, and Texas shuffles. San Antonio's Doug Sahm sometimes travels the U.S. with Texas musicians that include the house band from Antone's, a popular Austin club devoted to American roots music. Sahm and Co. play an assortment of Texas music that includes blues tunes originally performed by T-Bone Walker, Junior Parker, and Bobby Blue Bland. The current favored contender for the Texas blues guitar throne vacated by Stevie Ray Vaughan's tragic 1990 death is Houston's Vince Converse, one-third of the band Sunset Heights, which has recorded a CD called *Texas Tea* for the indie label Victory. Also look for Sue Foley's *Young Girl Blues* on the Antone's label—maybe (gasp) a woman will inherit Stevie's crown.

California cinematographer Les Blank has directed two definitive films about Texas bluesmen, *The Blues Accordin' to Lightnin' Hopkins,* and *A Well Spent Life,* about Mance Lipscomb. These are frequently shown at university campuses and art cinemas around the U.S. and Europe and are available on video from Flower Films & Video (tel. 510-525-0942), 10341 San Pablo Ave., El Cerrito, CA 94530. Both are worth seeing before you come to Texas; the Lipscomb film is the better of the two.

More Texas blues and R&B greats you might find in rare record stores include Frankie Lee Sims, Gene Vell, Big Bo and the Arrows, Little Wilson Pickett and his Fab Rockin' Fenders, and Cal Valentine and the Texas Rockers.

C&W and Folk

The style of country and western music most associated with Texas essentially developed from a meeting between the Anglo-Irish-Scottish fiddle traditions and folk ballads of British descendants and the polkas and dance music of central and eastern Europe, principally Germany, Poland, Bohemia, and Moravia. That's about the extent to which you can generalize about Texas C&W, however, since it covers such a myriad assortment of styles, from the range songs of Gene Autry to the rockabilly of Buddy Holly.

You might say Texas put the "Western" in "country and western." The early country music of Kentucky and Tennessee is traditionally more bluegrass or mountain music oriented, featuring fiddle and banjo as prominent instruments, while Texas country is traditionally supported by fiddle and guitar. In the 1920s, Texas fiddler A.C. Robertson made what is considered the first recording of American country music, "Sally Gooden."

Texas C&W also borrowed a great deal from outside the classic Appalachian sound, starting with the electric instrumentation and jazz stylings that created honky-tonk and Western swing. Ernest Tubb, "the Texas Troubadour," developed the guitar-based honky-tonk tradition that drew heavily from jazz arrangements, most notably in the walking bass lines; Hank Williams and Hank Thompson continued the tradition. The most famous Western swing (also known as "Texas swing") outfit was Bob Wills and His Texas Playboys, a band which assembled in the 1920s and continued to perform into the 1970s. Wills, along with other Texas swing bands like the East Texas Serenaders, Prince Albert Hunt and the Texas Ramblers, the Light Crust Doughboys, Milton Brown and His Musical Brownies, and the Tune Wranglers, performed eclectic dance hall repertoires that pitched blues, country, ragtime, Cajun, and Bohemian melodies against jazz chord changes and rhythms.

Today, Austin's Asleep at the Wheel and San Antonio's George Strait carry on the tradition of Western swing, occasionally bringing in Texas locales, as in Strait's "All My Ex's Live in Texas." Lyle Lovett updates it with a style that's part Western swing, part rhythm and blues. Texas C&W has also incorporated Mexican border influences from *norteño* or Tex-Mex music that now seem right at home in Austin or Nashville.

George Jones, every country singer's first hero, was born in Saratoga, Texas, and recorded his first record ("No Money in this Deal") in a home studio in Beaumont for the Houston-based Starday label. Jones also cut several rockabilly singles under the name "Thumper Jones" for Starday before ascending to international country superstar status. Another East Texas native who walked the yellow brick road to Nashville is singer-picker Mark Chesnutt; he recently scored 11 consecutive top-ten singles on the U.S. country charts.

In the '60s and '70s, the difference between the Austin and Nashville sounds was less a musical split than one of attitude toward the music business—"outlaw" artists versus "commercial" artists. Austin performers Willie Nelson, Waylon Jennings, Billy Joe Shaver, Michael Murphy, and Jerry Jeff Walker embodied outlaw country and influenced changes throughout the C&W scene. They claimed the right to inject modern C&W with nontraditional song topics, and to dress in more "expressive" styles, but the music they played was essentially the same. A strong sense of Texas geography was often present as well, as in Waylon and Willie's "Luckenbach, Texas" single and Jerry Jeff's *Viva Terlingua* and *Viva Luckenbach* albums.

Today, Texas C&W continues to borrow from other sources, most prominently folk and rock and roll. Joe Ely of Lubbock and Steve Earle of San Antonio are two musicians pursuing a raw,

more elemental sound that attracts listeners from disparate audiences nationwide. Other songwriters who've created and continue to create an updated Texas music style using Austin, the Hill Country, and Lubbock as their geographical centers include Townes Van Zandt, Butch Hancock, Jimmie Dale Gilmore, Robert Earl Keen, Jr., James McMurtry, Nanci Griffith, Jimmy LaFave, Michelle Shocked, Guy Clark, Lucinda Williams, Ray Wylie Hubbard, Alejandro Escovedo, Willis Alan Ramsey, and Hal Michael Ketchum. In addition to the classic folk/country themes of working-class angst, lost love, unemployment, travel via trains and trucks and horses, drinking, loneliness, and songs about Texas, these songwriters have branched off into non-traditional topics such as interpersonal relationships and environmental awareness.

Authentic Texas country and western of various styles can be heard in clubs and concert halls in the state's major cities, but is probably best enjoyed in the dance halls, honky-tonks, and roadhouses of small town Texas. In general, you'll find more live music venues in South and West Texas than in the "dry" counties of the north and east. If you draw a line extending from El Paso in the west to Orange in the southeast, you can figure it's honky-tonk territory below the line and churches above, with Lubbock, Amarillo, and Fort Worth as notable exceptions. The Hill Country between Austin and San Antonio is an especially good area, with venues like Gruene Hall in Gruene, Floores Country Store in Helotes, Luckenbach Dance Hall in Luckenbach, the Leon Springs Cafe in Leon Springs, and the Blue Bonnet Palace on the outskirts of San Antonio. Over in East Texas, Cutter's in Beaumont has become especially notorious since local performer Mark Chestnutt hit the big time.

Tex-Mex (*Conjunto*)

Texas-Mexican border music is perhaps the most interesting of all Texas music with regard to the mixture of influences that created it. Because it hasn't received as much nationwide commercial attention as other Texan forms, no record industry publicist has yet written a definitive history for border music, thus providing room for greater speculation among aficionados. They can't even agree on the best name for

ERIK WEBER

Flaco Jiménez

the music—it's been called border music, *norteña, tejano, conjunto,* and Tex-Mex. Texas-Mexican border music and *conjunto* seem to be the terms in current vogue, with "Tex-Mex" receiving the widest publication in English-language media. Hispanics in Texas generally prefer the term *"conjunto* music," while musicians in Mexico call it *norteña.*

The Tex-Mex or *conjunto* sound has been an acknowledged influence for a number of non-Texas performers, including Paul Simon, Ry Cooder, Tom Waits, Los Lobos, and the Talking Heads. Through these and other international recording artists, more music listeners are turning an ear toward San Antonio and the Rio Grande. The Texas Tornados, a band consisting of blues/rock/country/Tex-Mex legends Doug Sahm, Freddy Fender, Flaco Jiménez, and Augie Meyers, offered listeners a rich compendium of Texas music styles with heavy Tex-Mex underpinnings. All four hail from South Texas; their second album, *Zone of Their Own,* earned a 1991 Grammy for Best Mexican-Amer-

ican performance. The band is now "in hiatus" after several successful albums and tours, but future reunions are very likely.

History: Actually, the most descriptive term for this music might be Czech-Mex, since *conjunto* originally developed from accordion music, primarily the waltz, polka, schottische, and mazurka. This sound was introduced to Hispanics in South Texas and northern Mexico by Czech (Bohemian or Moravian) and German immigrants in the late 19th and early 20th centuries. While the Spanish word *conjunto* refers to any musical group, along the Texas-Mexico border—very fluid prior to the 1920s—it has always referred to an ensemble led by an accordion and *bajo sexto,* a large Mexican 12-string guitar. Originally, these two instruments were supported by a string bass and trap drum set only; later, electric bass and guitar were occasionally added, along with alto sax and keyboards. Most *conjunto* bands maintain the traditional accordion, *bajo sexto,* bass, and drums line-up.

The first known *conjunto* recording was made in 1935 by Narciso Martinez of San Benito, Texas, also the birthplace of Baldermar Huerta, better known as Freddy Fender. The music became extremely popular on both sides of the border in the '40s and '50s when singer Lydia Mendoza, known as "La Alondra de la Frontera" ("Lark of the Border"), performed on border-blaster radio stations that reached all over North and Central America. In 1958 Tony De La Rosa of Sarita, Texas, recorded "Atotonilco," the first recording to use the now-standard four-piece ensemble of accordion, *bajo sexto,* bass, and drums. The early 1960s saw a decline in the popularity and performance of *conjunto,* but by the late '60s it was on a roll again and has remained popular ever since. Typical performances by Chicanos (Mexican-Americans) today present a range of songs sung in Spanish that include primarily polkas, *rancheras* (similar to C&W), and *corridos* (Mexican ballads), as well as modern Latin forms like *cumbia* and salsa.

Current Trends: Contemporary Texas *conjunto* stars include accordionists Ramon Ayala, Valerio Longoria, Fred Zimmerle, Flaco Jiménez, Rubén Naranjo, Eva Ybarra, Mingo Saldívar, David Lee Garza, Tony De La Rosa, and Esteban (Steve) Jordán.

Flaco Jiménez has done more to spread *conjunto* around the world than any other Texan or Mexican artist, performing or recording with Willie Nelson, Ry Cooder, Bob Dylan, Buck Owens, Dwight Yoakam, Carlos Santana, the Rolling Stones, and many other internationally known musicians. His current discography lists over 60 LPs and CDs, three of which have earned Grammys since 1986. Steve Jordán, sometimes nicknamed "El Parche" for the eye-patch he wears, is a particularly hot player who blends *conjunto,* salsa, jazz, and blues into a passionate whole. Emilio Navaira y Su Grupo Río Amble perform an updated *conjunto* style, sometimes called progressive *conjunto* or pop polka, mixing in some C&W material and singing in both English and Spanish. This sound is currently very big in Texas. Little Joe y La Familia, seemingly on a perpetual state tour, perform a slightly more plush blend of country and *conjunto* designed to appeal to older listeners. In 1992 San Antonio's Domingo "Mingo" Saldívar made *conjunto* history when he performed at Bill Clinton's presidential inauguration.

Border music has long been popular with Anglo-Texans as well as Hispanics, as performed by enduring Texas artists like Doug Sahm, Augie Meyers, Joe "King" Carrasco, and the Brave Combo, all of whom often sing in a mixture of English and Spanish and play other styles of Texas music together with Tex-Mex. Augie Meyers prefers to call his brand of border music "Mexican rock and roll." Austin's Brave Combo performs an especially engaging mixture of Tex-Mex, polka, and Latin music that explores both the Czech and Latin roots of *conjunto.*

A newer, more commercial form of Texas Hispanic music commonly called *tejano* mixes elements of *conjunto,* rock and roll, pop dance tunes, rap, country, and salsa. Currently the biggest *tejano* groups in Texas include La Mafia, Grupo Mazz, Ram Herrera and the Outlaws, Culturas, Desperadoz, and Selena y los Dinos. Corpus Christi's Selena Quintanilla-Perez (more commonly known simply as "Selena") won top honors at San Antonio's annual Tejano Music Awards the last seven years straight; in 1993 she earned a Grammy for best Mexican-American album for her release *Selena Live!* featuring the hit single "Amor Prohibido." In Mexico

Mingo Saldívar

this release at first sold an average of 2,000 copies a day; sales increased when Selena was shot to death by a disgruntled former employee in 1995. Houston's *cumbia* king Fito Olivares has also made a huge impression on the Latin music scene. Three major record labels, Sony, Capitol/EMI, and Arista, recently established branch offices in San Antonio and Austin to catch the *tejano* wave.

Venues and Resources: *Conjunto*-style performances can be heard throughout Texas, but particularly in the South Texas border towns between Brownsville and Laredo and in San Antonio, where the population is over half Mexican and Chicano. The latest *tejano* sounds are played in clubs all over South Texas and in larger cities elsewhere in the state.

Les Blank, along with Arhoolie Records' Chris Strachwitz, has directed a film on traditional Tex-Mex music called *Chulas Fronteras,* available on video from Flower Films & Video (tel. 415-525-0942), 10341 San Pablo Ave., El Cerrito, CA 94530. The film is a great introduction not only to the music but the *frontera* (border) culture of South Texas. San Antonio's Guadalupe Cultural Arts Center, sponsor of the city's annual **Tejano Conjunto Festival,** distributes a video anthology of live performances by Tony De La Rosa, Flaco Jiménez, David Lee Garza, Steve Jordán, and others at the 1992 festival; to order, call or write the GCAC (tel. 210-271-3151, fax 271-3480), 1300 Guadalupe St., San Antonio, TX 78207.

Joey Records, 6707 W. Commerce St., San Antonio, TX 78227, tel. (512) 432-7893, is the granddaddy of Texas *conjunto* labels, with releases by Valerio Longoria, Flaco Jiménez, Los Tigres del Norte, Los Alegres, and others. Other Texas labels (some now defunct) to look for include Falcón, Ideal, Hacienda, Dina, Zarape, Freddie, Río, Lira, Corona, Alamo, Del Bravo, Sombrero, and Norteño. A Japanese label called El Grito (20-3 Sakaechou Nerima-ku, Tokyo 176, tel. 03-399-1580) also produces *tejano* and *conjunto* recordings.

San Antonio's Martín Macías created the modern *bajo sexto* in the '40s by extending the traditional fingerboard onto the body and adding a neck cutaway, rococo strike plates, and the checkerboard binding now standard on every *bajo.* He also makes a 10-string *bajo quinto,* a smaller version of the *bajo sexto,* and custom string sets for *bajos.* For further information, contact Macías Musical Instruments, (tel. 512-923-0563), 1130 Division Ave., San Antonio, TX 78225.

Cajun and Zydeco

The Louisiana-born Cajun and Texas-born zydeco musical genres (sometimes called "French music" because the lyrics are usually sung in Cajun or Creole French) are very popular in Southeast Texas, particularly in Houston, Galveston, and the Beaumont-Port Arthur-Orange area known as the "Cajun Triangle." About 150,000 Cajuns and Creoles live in this part of the state, at least 50,000 speak Acadian or Creole French as a first language. Texans of non-French descent tend to confuse the two distinct musics, misled by newer bands that play both types.

Cajuns are whites of French descent, and the typical Cajun ensemble features fiddle, guitar, and button accordion. Cajun music is basi-

cally a cross between traditional Acadian dance music and Texas-style country music; it was the Hank Williams hit song "Jambalaya" that first brought Cajun music to national attention. Traveling to Texas in search of a better life is a common theme in Cajun song lyrics. Port Arthur is one of the better places to hear Cajun music in Texas today, as hundreds of Cajuns work at the oil refineries in the Port Arthur area. In spite of the fact that many of the most well-known Cajun bands come from Louisiana, Port Arthur remains the site of the annual Cajun Music Awards.

Zydeco music is most often played by Creoles, people of mixed African-American and French heritage. The name "zydeco" is a Creole French pronunciation of *les haricots,* "the snapbeans," from the song "Les Haricots Sont Pas Salés" ("The Snapbeans Aren't Salted"). The song was first recorded by the legendary Clifton Chenier (1925-1987), who was born in southwestern Louisiana but performed often in Southeast Texas, where this style of music originated. Before Chenier popularized the name zydeco, the music was known as "la la" (slang for *la musique Creole*).

Zydeco (occasionally spelled "zydico" or "zodico") is essentially a fusion of African-Caribbean rhythms, blues, and traditional Cajun song forms created by Creoles living in Houston, Galveston, and Port Arthur during World War II. The pre-zydeco music, or "la la," was played originally in southwestern Louisiana by Creole ensembles featuring button accordion, fiddle, *frottoir* or rub board (a corrugated metal slab used for washing clothes), and "iron angle" (triangle). But in the World War II and postwar era, modern rhythm and blues became an important influence as well, as Creoles moved to the urban areas of Texas and were exposed to R&B for the first time. To accommodate these new influences, the button accordion was replaced by the larger piano accordion, the fiddle and triangle were lost, and instruments typical of urban R&B bands, such as electric guitars, bass, keyboards, and horns, were added. The *frottoir,* however, remains.

Today the biggest zydeco centers are Lake Charles, Louisiana, and Houston, Texas—although Galveston, Beaumont, Port Arthur, and Corpus Christi also support plenty of zydeco bands. Catholic churches in Houston frequently hold zydeco dances, and several Houston clubs—the Continental Zydeco Ballroom, the Silver Slipper Club, the Zydeco Cha-Cha Lounge —feature zydeco music on a regular basis. The word zydeco, in fact, often refers to social gatherings where the music is played.

Zydeco players worth searching out in Southeast Texas include old-timers like Fernest Arceneaux, L.C. Donatello, Anderson Moss, Clarence Garlow, Boozoo Chavis, Lonnie Mitchell, and Vincent Frank, as well as relative newcomers Paul Richard, Wilfred Chavis, and Jabo. Clifton Chenier's heir apparent to the zydeco throne, Stanley "Buckwheat" Dural, is based in Louisiana but often plays clubs elsewhere in Texas as well, such as Antone's in Austin.

The Les Blank film about the late Clifton Chenier, *Hot Pepper,* is a good aural primer for the music.

Rock and Roll

Some would say American rock started rolling in Texas with the music of Lubbock's Buddy Holly, whose stripped-down, hiccuping sound carved out a huge piece of international territory that is still being explored. A contemporary from West Texas, Roy Orbison, added a layer of silk to the early rockabilly movement that eventually led to Sun Studio sessions in Memphis with Elvis Presley, Carl Perkins, and Jerry Lee Lewis; he finished with a collaborative effort called the Traveling Wilburys that also featured Tom Petty, George Harrison, and Bob Dylan. Over in East Texas, Jivin' Gene Bourgeois, Moon Mullican, and Rockin' Dave Allen stoked early rock and roll

TEXAS MUSICAL AMBASSADOR

When asked to name one musical personality who has most exemplified Texas music, many music fans might cite Willie Nelson or perhaps Buddy Holly. For me, however, it's San Antonio native Doug Sahm. Although he has never attained Willie's level of success, Sahm has shown an uncanny ability to survive the harsh realities of the music biz while carrying the state's musical landscape all over the globe. A perfect example of the cross-fertilization of musical styles possible in Texas, Sahm grew up mixing blues, Tex-Mex, country, and swamp rock. He played steel guitar on the Louisiana Hayride before he was 13, scored a top-ten hit ("She's About a Mover") in the mid-'60s with his garage rock band the Sir Douglas Quintet, and moved on to San Francisco, Sweden, and British Columbia in search of *la grande vida* before returning to Texas in the '80s to replenish his roots.

In 1989 he joined Flaco Jiménez, former SDQ member Augie Meyers, and Freddy Fender to form the Texas Tornados, a touring and recording success whose albums could serve as Texas music primers. You never know in which guise Sahm will turn up next: rocking the house backed by Antone's blues band, picking out neat lines on a *bajo sexto,* or crooning 6/8-tempo Huey Meaux jukebox ballads. As a recent *Texas Monthly* accurately described, Sahm "has outlasted the British invasion, psychedelia, progressive and urban country, the blues revival, disco, punk, metal, and every other signifi-

cant trend since 1955." Sahm is as cross-cultural as you can get and still be in Texas, and wherever he plays live he seems to find a new audience.

Doug Sahm

ERIK WEBER

with the swamp beat that pervaded the Texas-Lousiana Gulf Crescent in the late '50s and early '60s.

In the 1960s Texas held off the British invasion with the garage rock of Sam the Sham and the Pharoahs ("Wooly Bully") and the Sir Douglas Quintet ("She's About A Mover"), followed by the psychedelia of Bubble Puppy and 13th Floor Elevators, Austin's answer to Pink Floyd. The Elevators spawned their own mad genius, Roky Erickson, who maintains a cult following to this day. As the decade shifted toward a close, Port Arthur's Janis Joplin moved to San Francisco with a gutful of Texas blues and exploded on the scene with Big Brother and the Holding Company's *Cheap Thrills* before dying of a heroin overdose in 1971. The Steve Miller Band made a similar musical and geographical transition from Texas blues to West Coast psychedelic soul, splintering apart in the process. Former Steve Miller Band sideman and later solo pop star Boz Scaggs now runs a successful San Francisco nightclub called Slim's that books a high proportion of Texas artists.

Houston power trio ZZ Top stuck it out in the Lone Star State and broke through in the '70s with the smash album *Tres Hombres,* which featured the heavily John Lee Hooker-influenced "La Grange," a song about a famous East Texas brothel. ZZ Top, in their trademark shades and beards, continues to climb the charts with every new album release and tour.

Beaumont native Johnny Winter toured with Muddy Waters in the '60s and recorded a couple of straight blues albums, but didn't hit the big time till he went rock and roll with pyrotechnic

DISCOGRAPHY

A small sampling of the best of recorded Texas music:

Asleep at the Wheel—*Asleep at the Wheel* (Epic)

Bobby Blue Bland—*Two Steps From the Blues* (MCA)

Big Brother & the Holding Company (with Janis Joplin)—*Cheap Thrills* (Columbia)

Brave Combo—*Musical Varieties* (Rounder)

Clarence "Gatemouth" Brown—*The Original Peacock Recordings* (Rounder)

Clifton Chenier—*Clifton Chenier: 60 Minutes With the King of Zydeco* (Arhoolie)

Arnett Cobb and Eddie "Cleanhead" Vinson—*Live at Sandy's* (Muse)

Ornette Coleman—*The Shape of Jazz to Come* (Atlantic)

Albert Collins—*Truckin' With Albert Collins* (MCA)

Tony De La Rosa—*Atotonilco* (Arhoolie)

Freddy Fender—*Swamp Gold* (ABC)

Lefty Frizzell—*Lefty Frizzell: American Originals* (Columbia)

Jimmie Dale Gilmore—*After Awhile* (Elektra)

Buddy Holly—*Buddy Holly: From The Original Master Tapes* (MCA)

Lightning Hopkins—*Texas Blues* (Arhoolie)

Blind Lemon Jefferson—*King of the Country Blues* (Yazoo)

George Jones—*Best of George Jones 1955-1967* (Rhino)

Steve Jordán—*The Return of El Parche* (Rounder)

Freddie King—*Freddie King: Just Pickin'* (Modern Blues)

Mance Lipscomb—*Texas Songster* (Arhoolie)

Lyle Lovett—*Lyle Lovett* (MCA)

Willie Nelson—*Red-Headed Stranger* (Columbia)

Emilio Navaira y Su Grupo Río Amble—*Unsung Highways* (Capitol/EMI)

covers of "Jumpin' Jack Flash" and "Rock and Roll Hootchie-Koo" in the '70s. The touring, partying, guitar-hero lifestyle almost did Winter in, and since the 1980s he has retreated to the blues world. Winter and Joplin are emblematic of what sometimes happens when Texas roots music strays too far from home, a message many younger musicians in Texas seem to have taken to heart with the strong, renewed interest in "rootsier" styles like rockabilly, blues, honky-tonk country, Western swing, Cajun, zydeco, polka, and *tejano*. Not that the mold wasn't made to be broken—two of the most innovative bands to come out of the Austin alternative scene in the last decade, the Butthole Surfers and Poi Dog Pondering, eschewed any overt Texas influences; both bands hit high on the college charts.

Jazz and the Texas Tenor

Dallas guitarist Charlie Christian was the state's first jazz legend, but saxophonists dominate the list of successful home-staters. Creators of the hip and honkin' "Texas tenor" sound include James Clay, David "Fathead" Newman, Eddie "Cleanhead" Vinson, and Arnett Cobb. Other saxmen who have made significant contributions to jazz evolution are Wilton Felder of the Jazz Cruzaders (a band out of Texas Southern University) and the extremely influential Ornette Coleman, a Fort Worth native. Guitarist Herb Ellis and bop pianist Red Garland round out the state's historic jazz roll call.

Texas Music Sources

Two stores that carry large selections of LP, cassette tape, and compact disc recordings of

---

Roy Orbison—*The Legends: Roy Orbison* (CBS Special Products)

Junior Parker—*Junior's Blues* (MCA)

Poi Dog Pondering—*Poi Dog Pondering* (Columbia)

Doug Sahm—*Juke Box Music* (Antone's)

Selena y Los Dinos—*Selena Live!* (Capitol/EMI)

Sam the Sham & the Pharoahs—*Pharoahization!* (Rhino)

Frankie Lee Sims—*Frankie Lee Sims: Lucy Mae Blues* (Specialty)

Sir Douglas Quintet—*The Best of Doug Sahm & the Sir Douglas Quintet* (Mercury)

George Strait—*Ocean Front Property* (MCA)

Texas Tornadoes—*Zone of Their Own* (Reprise)

13th Floor Elevators—*13th Floor Elevators* (International Artists)

Hank Thompson—*Hank Thompson: The Country Music Hall of Fame Series* (MCA)

Big Mama Thornton—*Hound Dog: The Peacock Records* (MCA)

Ernest Tubb—*Ernest Tubb: Live 1965* (Rhino)

Townes Van Zandt—*Live & Obscure* (Sugar Hill)

Stevie Ray Vaughan & Double Trouble—*Couldn't Stand the Weather* (Epic)

Jimmie Vaughan—*Strange Pleasure* (Epic)

Jerry Jeff Walker—*Viva Terlingua* (MCA)

T-Bone Walker—*The Complete Imperial Recordings* (EMI)

Katie Webster—*Whooee Sweet Daddy* (Flyright)

Lucinda Williams—*A Sweet Old World* (Chameleon)

Bob Wills & His Texas Playboys—*Tiffany Transcriptions* (Rhino)

Johnny Winter—*Johnny Winter* (Columbia)

Lou Ann Barton, Marcia Ball, Angela Strehli, Toni Price, Sue Foley—*Antone's Women* (Antone's)

Various artists—*Tejano Roots/Raices Tejanas* (Arhoolie)

Various artists—*Texas Music Vols. 1, 2, & 3* (Rhino)

Texas roots music are Antone's Record Store (tel. 512-322-0660), 2928 Guadalupe, Austin, TX 78705, and Roots and Rhythm Music (tel. 510-525-1494), 10341 San Pablo Ave., El Cerrito, CA 94530. Both handle mail and telephone orders.

Another mail-order house specializing in Texas roots music is Home Cooking Records (tel. 713-666-0258, fax 666-1444), P.O. Box 980454, Houston, TX 77098. For *tejano* and *conjunto* your best bet is Del Bravo Record Shop (tel. 210-432-8351, fax 433-1630), 554 Old Hwy. 90 W, San Antonio, TX 78237. Del Bravo does mail orders as well as walk-in retail.

The state-funded **Texas Music Office** (tel. 512-463-6666), P.O. Box 13246, Austin, TX 78711, serves as an information clearing house for clubs, artists, management companies, record labels, and virtually every other state organization related to music.

Radio: Texas radio carries plenty of regional programming. All over South Texas and in urban areas you can pick up local Spanish-language programs playing a blend of *tejano, conjunto, tropicale,* rock, swamp, and/or country. El Paso, Del Rio, Laredo, San Antonio, Brownsville, Houston, and Corpus Christi in particular offer powerful stations commanded by bilingual DJs who switch back and forth between Spanish and English in the blink of an eye—often in the same sentence.

In the vicinity of Shiner, Taylor, Cuero, and Hallettsville in Central Texas you can pick up stations that broadcast polka music for the local Czech/Pole/Wend population, and in the Cajun Triangle of East Texas you'll hear Cajun and zydeco. A couple of stations in the Hill Country specialize in Texas singer-songwriters; one still carries German-language programming.

About half the radio stations in rural Texas play country music, sometimes mixed with gospel or polka. The big four—Dallas, Houston, San Antonio, and Austin—tend to offer commercial radio stations with typical American playlists along with a smaller number of more adventurous college and public radio stations.

RODEO

Rodeo is a huge year round sport in Texas. A *Rodeo Times Calendar* for the month of May alone—not even the height of the rodeo season—lists nearly a hundred rodeo events around the state, from goat roping to full open rodeos. First prize for any single event at a professional rodeo can be as high as $50,000—a huge purse when you consider most rodeo events are over in well under a minute.

Professional rodeo began in the 1800s with impromptu roping and riding contests between cowboys, whether on ranches or on the trail. The oldest rodeo in the U.S. is the annual Pecos Rodeo in Pecos, Texas, which began as an open invitational competition in 1883 and is still held every July 4.

Mesquite Rodeo, Dallas

DALLAS CONVENTION AND VISITORS BUREAU

Nowadays, the Professional Rodeo Cowboys Association sets the standards for competition, from the various professional levels on down to amateur youth, civic, high school, and college rodeo. These standards provide systematic and exacting methods for judging rodeo events, monitoring rodeo safety, and for the welfare of livestock used in competition, as well as regulating cowboy tack (equipment used in the rodeo, such as bronc saddles, spurs, bull rope, and bareback rigging). Rodeo is part of the curriculum at many Texas colleges and universities; Sul Ross State University in Alpine, West Texas, is reputed to have the top rodeo school in the nation.

The rodeo world comes with its own language: "hooey," a half-hitch knot used in calf roping; "pullin' leather" or "grabbin' the apple," referring to touching any part of the saddle with the free hand during the saddle bronc riding event, which is immediate grounds for disqualification; "lap and tap," a cattle-roping event in which cattle are not given the usual 10- to 30-foot head start, used only in small arenas; "piggin' string," a six-foot length of soft rope used in calf roping; "honda," the eye in the end of a rope. As with any sport, to fully appreciate Texas rodeo, it helps to know a bit of the jargon commonly used by announcers and spectators in order to understand the fundamentals of the action.

The roughstock events are the most well-known and dangerous events in rodeo. The basic objective for these three events, **saddle bronc riding, bareback riding,** and **bullriding,** is the same: the rider must stay atop the animal for at least eight seconds, holding on with one hand only. Additional rules govern recoveries from near falls and spurring—no rowels or spiked wheels are allowed, and only certain areas of the animal can be spurred. The rules are generally slanted in favor of the animal; points are scored for the ride as a whole, with half the potential points allotted to the animal and half for the rider.

Rodeo "roughstock" is livestock considered untrainable. The bucking broncs you see in the arena are not wild in the sense of being born away from human society, but are horses who refuse any kind of domestication, and cannot be used in ranching, pleasure riding, racing, or even as pack horses. Owners of such animals approach rodeo stock contractors who give them a tryout to see if they're truly untrainable. Most of the time these ill-tempered animals only buck a few times out of the chute, and then calm down in the hands of professional riders. Only a small percentage of horses are accepted as pro rodeo broncs (from the Spanish *bronco,* "rough"). Prices can go into five figures; a genuine bronc will perform well for up to 20 years.

The harder a horse or bull is to stay on, the more points it scores toward the ride. Bareback broncs are small and quick, and the saddle rigging used has no stirrups, making the bareback event somewhat more difficult than saddle-bronc riding. Bullriding takes exceptional balance and control because of the sheer power of the bull. Once a year the top 30 pro rodeo cowboys select three animals as "bucking stock of the year" for their outstanding performances. In spite of the violent appearance of roughstock events, a cowboy's riding finesse is much more important than strength—it's simply not possible for a 200-pound rider to overpower bucking animals that weigh anywhere from 1,000 pounds to a ton.

Another common rodeo event is **barrel racing,** which involves a slalom-type horseback race through a triangle of three equidistant barrels. Times are measured in hundredths of seconds.

In the **steer wrestling** event, a cowboy rides alongside a running steer, slides from the horse onto the steer, and wrestles it to the ground by a skillful turning of the horns. As in the roughstock events, technique and timing are more important than strength.

Roping competitions are popular among amateur rodeo cowboys because they don't require the apparent daredevil attitude of roughstock and steer wrestling events. In **calf roping** the rider must chase a running calf, lasso the animal, and drop to the ground to quickly tie the calf's legs together with a soft rope. **Team roping** requires two riders, a "header" and a "heeler," to chase a steer and then rope the horns (the header) and hind legs (the heeler). The rider's end of the rope must be given a couple of "dallies" (turns) around the saddle horn as part of the action—a thumb or finger caught between horn and rope is instantly lost.

Less common events may supplement the standard six rodeo events. Goat roping or tying, similar to calf roping, is fairly commonplace in Texas, especially at rodeos in the Edwards Plateau where goats and sheep are raised. The World Championship Goat Roping contest takes place every June in San Angelo. Women compete in rodeos too, and Fort Worth's Stockyards are the site of a National Cowgirl Hall of Fame as well as an annual All Girl Rodeo.

In South Texas, Mexican rodeos or *charreadas* are an exciting alternative to the usual fare. Rules and events for the *charreada* significantly differ from American rodeo and are generally festive occasions as well. Events are sponsored by local *charro* (equestrian) associations, most belonging to the Mexico-based, binational Federación de Charros. Brownsville on the Texas-Mexico border annually holds *charreadas*

during the last week of February, and there are several in San Antonio throughout the year.

The best source of information on Texas rodeo events is the *Rodeo Times*, a monthly newspaper published in San Antonio (2823 Hillcrest, San Antonio, TX 78201, $25 a year)— it's distributed free at rodeos and many Western-wear stores. Texas travelers who don't have the time to seek out periodic local or state rodeos might try the weekly Mesquite Championship Rodeo. This professional rodeo in the town of Mesquite, just west of Dallas, has been a weekly event from April to September for over 30 years. Events are held in the Mesquite Arena every Friday and Saturday night 8-10 p.m.; the entry fee is $8 for adults, $4 for children 12 and under.

HOLIDAYS, FESTIVALS, AND EVENTS

Perhaps due to the cross-cultural blend of peoples and its proximity to Mexico, Texas is an unusually festive state. Besides the usual national and state holidays there's a full range of activities that celebrate ethnic heritage, folklore, ranching, farming, and Texas cuisines. The Tourism Division of the State Department of Commerce publishes a yearly calendar of events that lists and describes such activities across the state. Even more comprehensive is the Department of Highways' quarterly *Texas Events Calendar,* which can be obtained free by writing to Texas Events Calendar, P.O. Box 5064, Austin, TX 78763.

NATIONAL HOLIDAYS

Government offices and some businesses may close on the following national holidays when they fall on weekdays. These closings are not always mentioned in the text, so you may want to call ahead to make sure.

New Year's Day: January 1
Civil Rights Day (Martin Luther King Jr.'s Birthday): January 15; usually observed the third Monday in January
Presidents' Day: third Monday in February
Easter Sunday: late March or early April

Memorial Day: last Monday in May
American Independence Day: July 4
Labor Day: first Monday in September
Columbus Day: second Monday in October
Veterans Day: November 11
Thanksgiving Day: fourth Thursday in November
Christmas Day: December 25

STATE FESTIVALS AND EVENTS

Some of the more memorable yearly events around the state are highlighted below according to month. Some of the festivals and events listed here are in towns that aren't described elsewhere in the text, places worth visiting only during a particular festival. Actual dates may vary from year to year, so check the Texas Highways Department calendar in advance.

January
Cotton Bowl Football Game and Parade, Dallas; New Year's Day. A football classic in which the champion college team of the Southwest Conference plays another regional winner.

Southwestern Exposition Stock Show and Rodeo, Fort Worth; usually the last week of the month. Began in 1918 as the world's first indoor rodeo and has expanded to become one of

COWBOY POLO

If you've never heard of cowboy polo, don't worry—neither have most Americans. Only nine states have member teams in the National Cowboy Polo Association (NCPA)—Texas, California, Colorado, Alabama, New Mexico, Washington, Oregon, Montana, and Arizona. The NCPA was formed in 1959 when cowboy polo split off from its American predecessor, palmetto polo, which is still played in Florida.

If cowboy polo differs from palmetto polo, it's a world away from English polo, though all three sports involve horses, mallets, and balls. To begin with, the playing atmospheres and social backgrounds of English and cowboy polo are very different. While English polo is generally a game of the aristocracy, cowboy polo is a rough-and-tumble working-class game. As one player described the difference: "English polo is tea and crumpets. We're beer and hamburgers."

A cowboy playing field is more compact than the English field, 300 feet by 120 feet. Teams field five players who remain in designated zones, which makes it more difficult to move downfield without a constant jostling for control of the ball. The ball used in cowboy polo is made of rubber and is 13 inches in diameter; the English ball is small and wooden, more like a croquet ball. (Admittedly, this is one area where English polo seems more macho than cowboy polo.)

Until the '70s the only acceptable headgear was a cowboy hat. These days many NCPA players wear helmets, including football helmets or construction hardhats with a heavy wire grill rigged across the face. NCPA rules require jeans and Western-style shirts, and of course only Western saddles are allowed—none of these cowboys would be caught dead on an English saddle anyway. Players wear padded chaps as shin guards.

At the moment, the best team in the NCPA is a Texas club from San Jacinto. The Boston Celtics of cowboy polo, San Jacinto has won the national title 12 times in the last 14 years. Also tops is the San Angelo team from West Texas. Their main rivals are the Colorado and Cal-Zona (a California/Arizona team) clubs, but competition is always hot, regardless of the teams involved. The cowboy polo season starts in March and ends in August with the national title series. Most matches are held in rodeo arenas, sometimes in conjunction with professional rodeos.

---

the largest livestock expositions in the United States.

February
Mardi Gras, Galveston; early February. Several Southeast Texas towns with large Creole and Cajun populations celebrate Mardi Gras, but Galveston started its in 1867; the event is now the state's biggest, with masked balls, coronations, parades, Cajun and Creole cookoffs, and a series of jazz performances that lasts 10 days. For many people, Galveston's Mardi Gras is a satisfying alternative to the currently overcrowded festivities in New Orleans.

Southwestern Livestock Show and Rodeo, El Paso; first week of February. The largest livestock exposition in West Texas, since 1931.

Shakespeare Festival, Odessa; every weekend from mid-February through mid-March. The state's oldest Shakespeare festival, staged at a faithful replica of the original Globe Theatre.

Charro Days, Brownsville; late February.

Three days of Mexican rodeo (*charreada*), balls, street dances, and parades in the Mexican fiesta tradition.

George Washington's Birthday, Laredo; third week in February. As unlikely as it may sound, Laredo celebrates George Washington's Birthday and the signing of the U.S. Constitution in a big way. This is one of the best times to visit Laredo; beauty contest ("Princess Pocahantas"), *tejano* music festival, jalapeño-eating contest, parades, dancing, Mexican food competitions.

March
South by Southwest Music and Media Conference, Austin; second week of March. Over 300 musical groups from throughout the state and beyond perform in some 25 clubs and other venues around town in hopes of being noticed by members of the music industry and press. Other activities include music workshops and award presentations. In recent years, this has

become one of the most important pop music events in the United States.

Rio Grande Valley Livestock Show and Rodeo, Mercedes; third week of March. The Valley's largest event, with all the usual activities.

April

Hill Country Wine and Food Festival, Austin and Lake Buchanan; first week in April. Wine-tastings, seminars, vintner demonstrations, eating, and more eating. Typically features wines and foods of Texas, California, and France.

Fiesta San Antonio, San Antonio; third week in April. A celebration of the city's Hispanic heritage and one of Texas's most impressive festivals. The Fiesta features *charreada,* street food, *conjunto* and mariachi performances, country and western dances, parades, art shows, fashion shows, and lots of flowers.

Buccaneer Days, Corpus Christi; 10 consecutive days in mid-April. Celebrates Alonzo Alvarez Piñeda's landing in Corpus Christi Bay in 1519 with sailing regattas, a music festival, a coronation ball, and fireworks.

May

Polka Festival, Ennis; first full weekend in May. One of the state's premier Czech polka fests, with plenty of dance performances, costumes, and traditional Czech food.

Cinco de Mayo, San Antonio and other towns with significant Hispanic populations; first week in May. This festival commemorates the defeat of an attempted French invasion at Pueblo de los Angelos, Mexico, during the American Civil War. Mexican music, dance, food, and other cultural events.

Texas Wine Country Chili Cookoff, Lakeside or another location near Dallas-Fort Worth; second weekend in May. A North Texas wine-tasting and chili competition. The morning after could be deadly.

Old Fiddlers Reunion, Athens; last weekend in May. A reputable and enduring fiddlers festival sponsored by the Texas Fiddlers Association. The program most prominently features the unique Texas fiddle tradition, but also attracts fiddlers from around the country who play different kinds of American and Irish-Scottish fiddle music and compete for cash prizes. A must for people who like to fiddle around.

Van Cliburn International Piano Competition, Fort Worth; every four years during late May and early June (last competition was in 1993). The most prestigious piano competition in the United States, held in honor of Fort Worth native Van Cliburn. Thirty-five of the world's most gifted pianists are invited to compete.

June

The Lone Star outdoor drama, Galveston; from June through Labor Day in early September. A historical drama written by Pulitzer Prize-winning author Paul Green recounting the events of the Texan Revolution. The show actually alternates nights with a different contemporary Broadway show every year.

Texas: A Historical Musical Drama, Palo Duro Canyon State Park; summer. Another outdoor musical penned by Paul Green, *Texas* has run for over 25 years and puts the awesome canyon setting to good use in enacting the highlights of Texas history. It's a slanted perspective for sure, but the cast of 80 actors and actresses, plus props that include a real, working train, make an enjoyable show.

Fiesta Noche del Rio, San Antonio; every Thursday, Friday, and Saturday from Memorial Day through Labor Day. A variety of Hispanic cultural performances held at the outdoor Arneson River Theater on the San Antonio River.

Chisholm Trail Roundup, Fort Worth; second week in June. Commemorates Fort Worth as the last stop on the Chisholm Trail. Includes traditional trail rides, chili cookoffs, Indian dance competition, street dances, rodeos, and shootouts. Most activities are centered in the Stockyards district.

Texas Water Safari, San Marcos and Seadrift; second weekend in June. A grueling, four-day, 260-mile boat race along the San Marcos and Guadalupe rivers.

Round Top Music Festival, Round Top; mid-June through mid-July. Features high-quality classical musical performances and forums from a variety of repertoires and periods. Special pre- and post-festival programs are also held. For information contact the Festival-Institute at Round Top (tel. 409-249-3129), P.O. Drawer 89, Round Top, TX 78954.

Juneteenth (Emancipation Day), statewide; week of June 19. A commemoration of the an-

from the opening moments of Texas, *the stirring Palo Duro musical drama*

nouncement in Galveston that Texas slaves were freed following the War Between the States. Black civic organizations throughout the state hold festivals of various lengths featuring music, dancing, and food. The biggest Juneteenth festival, on two consecutive weekends, is in Houston, site of the **Juneteenth Blues and Gospel Festivals,** which feature local and national talent.

Watermelon Thump Festival, Luling; last weekend in June. One of the oldest fruit-growing festivals in the state, the Watermelon Thump offers several different kinds of competitions involving watermelons—largest melon, tastiest melon, seed-spitting contest, melon-eating contest, and so on. There's also the coronation of the Watermelon Thump Queen, and lots of barbecue—Luling is the acclaimed capital of Central Texas-style barbecue.

July
Texas Cowboy Reunion, Stamford; week of July 4. The biggest amateur rodeo in Texas.

Only real working cowboys and cowgirls can participate, no rodeo pros allowed.

West of the Pecos Rodeo, Pecos; week of July 4. The oldest ongoing professional rodeo in the country; always features top pro rodeo champs.

Texas Jazz Festival, Corpus Christi; first weekend in July. Jazz performances at Bayfront Park, plus free jazz workshops, jazz cruises in the Gulf, and jazz films.

The Great Texas Mosquito Festival, Clute; last weekend in July. Inane, but true, the little town of Clute pays tribute to the Texas mosquito. Features a mosquito legs lookalike contest, a mosquito-calling contest, as well as other excuses for a good time.

August
XIT Rodeo and Reunion, Dalhart; first weekend in August. An annual homecoming for the remaining XIT ranch hands (the XIT was once the largest ranch in Texas). In addition to the rodeo, activities include dances, pony express races, parades, and storytelling.

Texas Folklife Festival, San Antonio; first weekend in August. A well-attended celebration of the state's ethnic diversity that exhibits a compendium of arts, crafts, music, folklore, and foods from around the world.

All Girl Rodeo, Fort Worth (formerly in Hereford); second week in August. An all-female professional rodeo with all the familiar events.

Prazka Pout, Praha; August 15. Czech homecoming centered around an English and Czech mass at St. Mary's Church. A Czech country bazaar includes traditional Czech games, food, music, and dancing.

Saint Louis Day, Castroville; August 25. An Alsatian and Belgian festival held at Koenig Park on Medina River, celebrating Castroville's Alsatian/Belgian heritage with music, dance, crafts, and food. The food alone is worth a trip from San Antonio.

September
Westfest, West; Labor Day. A Czech and Slavic festival with traditional street dances, costumes, Sokol gymnastics, folk dancing, and a Miss Westfest contest.

National Championship Pow-Wow, Grand Prairie; first weekend after Labor Day. A large

Amerindian gathering that draws participants from throughout the Southwest and the Dakotas, sponsored by the Dallas-Fort Worth Intertribal Association. Indian dancing competitions, arts and crafts shows, and food booths.

Republic of Texas Chilympiad, San Marcos; third weekend in September. Reputedly the largest "bowl o' red" cookoff in the country. Sponsored by the Chili Appreciation Society International (CASI).

Texas International Wine Classic, Lubbock; last weekend in September. The most prestigious of the state's wine festivals, featuring seminars, tastings, and gourmet dinners. Texas's best wineries are in this area and are open for tours.

October

Heart O' Texas Fair and Rodeo, Waco; first weekend in October. One of the largest fairs in Texas (average attendance 300,000), featuring livestock exhibits and a professional rodeo.

Oktoberfest, Fredericksburg; first full weekend in October. Many Central Texas towns hold Oktoberfest celebrations in recognition of the early German immigration to Texas. Since this is the oldest and largest of the early German colonies, the celebration is especially hearty. *Bierhalle*-style entertainment, dance contests, costumes, and lots of sausage and beer.

Texas State Fair, Fair Park, Dallas; first three weeks in October. The largest state fair in the United States, a virtual "mega-fair." Rodeos,

football games (University of Texas versus the University of Oklahoma is the "big game"), livestock shows, theater, and other events.

Lone Star Vegetarian Chili Cookoff, South Padre Island, second Sunday in October. For six consecutive years the Rio Grande Valley Vegetarian Society has attempted to prove you don't have to be carnivore to enjoy chili.

Texas Rose Festival, Tyler; mid-October. A tribute to the unofficial state flower—the bluebonnet is official but probably not as readily identified with Texas as the rose—and the state's rose capital (over half the roses commercially grown in the U.S. are grown here). Rose shows, Rose Parade (with rose-decorated floats), local garden tours, and the coronation of the Rose Queen.

Czhilispiel, Flatonia; third weekend in October. A Czech-German heritage festival and the second-largest chili cookoff in Texas.

November

World Championship Chili Cookoff, Terlingua; first Saturday in November. The first and most famous chili contest in Texas, also called the "Original Frank X. Tolbert/Wick Fowler Memorial Championship Cookoff." The original cookoff has split into two events. See "Terlingua" under "Vicinity of Big Bend National Park" in the West Texas chapter for more details.

Wurstfest, New Braunfels; first full week of November. The state's largest German festival, with sausage-making demonstrations, Ger-

Dickens on The Strand

man music, singing, dancing, contests, and other activities. The best of the "wurst."

December
Jefferson Christmas Candlelight Tour, Jefferson; first weekend in December. Historic homes in Jefferson open their doors to Christmas carolers and out-of-town visitors. Free choral concerts and other Christmas shows.

Dickens Evening on the Strand, Galveston; first weekend in December. Galveston's historic Strand district is transformed into a century-old English street scene à la Dickens. Participants dress in period costume and present street performances; there are Dickens shows on local stages as well.

Christmas at Old Fort Concho, San Angelo; first weekend in December. This four-day celebration centers on the restored frontier garrison of Fort Concho, which is decorated especially for the occasion. Activities vary from year to year but usually include caroling, dancing, and an "Old Fashioned Melodrama" in a tent on the parade grounds. Culminates on Sunday with a cowboy church service.

Las Posadas, San Antonio; second week in December. Dance, drama, music, food, and piñata parties, climaxing in a candlelight procession along the Paseo del Rio in commemoration of the Holy Family's search for lodging. Laredo holds a similar celebration.

ACCOMMODATIONS

Accommodations are available in Texas for every budget and proclivity, including hostels, historic inns, bed and breakfasts, swank international-class hotels, dude ranches, and campgrounds.

HOTELS AND MOTELS

Budget
Hotels and motels in Texas are, generally speaking, reasonably priced when compared with average hotel rates across the United States. In smaller towns they can be downright bargains, averaging about $35 a night for the best place in town (which may be the only place in town—and definitely not a Hilton); in such towns you can also find plenty of places in the $20-30 range. In mid-sized and larger towns, your best bets are the bargain chains like Motel 6, Super 8, or Econo Lodge. Except in South and West Texas you won't find many places anywhere under $20, so if you want to keep accommodation expenses lower than this, see "Hostels" and "Camping."

Moderate
In the $40-65 range, you'll find a wide choice of chain hotels like Best Western, Ramada, and Holiday Inn (though not all Holiday Inns will be this low—the newer ones are moving upscale).

Near urban centers like Houston, Dallas, San Antonio, Beaumont, and Austin, the interstate highways are lined with hotels and motels like these, as well as a few independents in this price category.

Luxury
You'll find truly deluxe accommodations only in Dallas, Houston, El Paso, and San Antonio. Here again, Texas is good value. For a room that would cost $250 in New York or San Francisco, you can get away with paying about $125-150. In any of these cities, you can also find several high-quality hotels in the $75-100 range.

Two Dallas hotels made it onto *Condé Nast Traveler*'s 1994 list of the world's ten best hotels; Crescent Court was ranked number two, the Mansion on Turtle Creek number nine. On the magazine's U.S. list, three of the nation's top ten were in Dallas, making Texas the only state with such representation: Crescent Court, number one; Mansion on Turtle Creek, number two; Four Seasons, number seven.

Historic Inns
With hundreds of 19th-century hostelries still standing throughout the state, the restoration of historic hotels and inns has become a popular Texas undertaking. Historic inns range from the three-room Lickskillet Inn in Fayetteville to the 310-room Warwick in Houston. Those in

smaller towns are usually medium-priced, while those in larger cities mostly fit into the deluxe category. The deluxe historic inns can further be divided into the ones that have attempted a faithful reproduction of the original interiors and those with historic exteriors and lobbies but rooms that are rather the same as any other hotel in this price range.

If you plan to stay in hotels while traveling in Texas, you really owe it to yourself to stay in at least one historic place. Usually the attention to restorative detail carries over to attentive guest service as well, and the traditional Texas architecture, whether it's Mission style, Alsatian, classic Richardson-Romanesque, or Queen Anne Victorian, makes the travel experience so much more satisfying than staying in another nondescript Sheraton or Holiday Inn.

Historic inns of note are mentioned throughout the text. Another source of information is the Historic Hotel Association, which has a membership roster of 50-plus hotels and inns throughout the state. Their membership by no means includes all the historic inns in Texas, but does list places that more appropriately belong in the bed and breakfast category; the brochure is a fair starting point for those interested in seeking out such sites. For information on this organization, call or write Historic Hotel Association (tel. 210-997-3980), 231 W. Main St., Fredericksburg, TX 75226.

A good source of background information on historic inns is Ann Ruff's *A Guide to Historic Texas Inns and Hotels* (Houston: Gulf Publishing, 1985). The book gives a fairly comprehensive, if somewhat dated, account of historic accommodations in Texas, including brief histories and descriptions of each place.

BED AND BREAKFASTS

The bed and breakfast concept has taken full root in Texas. As elsewhere in the U.S. and Europe, Texas bed and breakfast establishments are basically private homes with a few rooms for rent. Rates always include some kind of breakfast and often much more—complimentary tea or coffee in the afternoon, possibly wine in the evening, reading material, attentive service, and sightseeing tips. Bed and breakfast hosts tend to

be gregarious folks, hence, if anonymity is high on your list of accommodations criteria, B&B lodgings might not be your cup of tea. Many solo women travelers report a greater sense of security on the B&B circuit.

Bed and breakfast rates in Texas are very reasonable, starting at around $40 for more modest establishments and topping out at around $150 for accommodations with truly deluxe amenities. In historic districts or towns, the line between "bed and breakfast" and "historic inn" often blurs. Hence, bed and breakfast rates at a home that is a registered state or national landmark may run $100 or more. Old Victorians in historic Galveston or Jefferson are in this higher range as well, due to simple supply and demand; Houston and Dallas residents keep them booked most weekends. Most bed and breakfast inns of this nature, however, will offer discounted rates for weekday guests.

An organization called Bed & Breakfast Texas Style (tel. 800-899-4538, 214-298-8586), 4224 W. Red Bird Lane, Dallas, TX 75237, handles information requests and bookings for many Texas B&Bs but does not cover every place in the state. Many towns with several bed and breakfasts have their own B&B associations; some towns, such as Fredericksburg, support two local booking organizations. Occasionally, in towns with only a few B&Bs, you'll have to book directly through the proprietors.

Names and addresses of individual bed and breakfast inns as well as local B&B associations are listed in the "Accommodations" section for each destination throughout this book. Individual chambers of commerce around the state can usually provide you with updated B&B information as well.

HOSTELS

American Youth Hostels have member hostels in Austin, Houston, Friendswood, San Antonio, El Paso, and Port Aransas. In spite of the name, youth hostels are open to people of all ages, and staying at hostels is a good way to cut costs no matter your income. Conditions vary from hostel to hostel, but generally you can expect clean, quiet accommodations. Regulations include the mandatory use of a sleeping sheet (a regular sheet folded in half and sewn to form a bag; they can be purchased or rented at most hostels for a nominal cost), a curfew of 11 p.m. (though keys for later entry can usually be rented), and minimal participation in hostel maintenance—usually sweeping or dishwashing. Males and females sleep in separate rooms or dormitories; this applies to couples, too.

The rates at Texas hostels vary from $10.25 a night in Houston to $14.85 in San Antonio. Advance reservations are not usually necessary—El Paso and San Antonio are exceptions—but are accepted with one night's deposit. To stay at a hostel, you must be a member of either the Hostelling International (HI) or American Youth Hostels (AYH). A 12-month membership costs $25 for adults (age 18-54), $10 for youths (age 17 and under), and $15 for senior citizens (over 55). There are also special family memberships—write or call AYH for details. A temporary AYH membership, good for one night only, may be purchased for $3 at any hostel. The cost of temporary membership can be applied toward a full membership later if desired.

The address and nightly rate of each Texas hostel are listed in the text under the corresponding destination. For further information on American hosteling, call or write HI/American Youth Hostels (tel. 202-783-6161), 733 15th St., Washington, D.C. 20005. In Canada, contact Hostelling International (tel. 613-748-5638), 1600 James Naismith Dr., Gloucester, ON K1B 5N4.

CAMPING

Sleeping outdoors is one of the best ways to experience the Texan wilderness while cutting accommodation costs dramatically. With over 200 state, federally, or privately owned public campgrounds throughout Texas, there's someplace to camp near virtually every destination worth visiting.

Federal Campgrounds
These include not only campgrounds in Park Service-operated national parks, recreation areas, and forests, but also those along the 20 plus lakes administered by the U.S. Army Corps of Engineers. As with all federal, state, and private campgrounds, fee schedules and regulations vary from one site to the next, depending on facilities and user demand. For details on campground fees and regulations, refer to individual destinations in the text.

People 62 years and older can obtain a lifetime Golden Age Passport for $10 at any national park, forest, or recreation area, or by writing or calling the National Park Service. This permit exempts them from all entry fees and provides a 50% discount on all other federal user fees, including campground fees. The Golden Access Passport offers the same benefits to blind and disabled people. For more information write the National Park Service, Southwest Region, P.O. Box 728, Santa Fe, NM 87504.

State Campgrounds
The extensive state park system manages around 70 parks and recreation areas that permit camping. These parks offer a range of amenities from camping areas where facilities are as yet undeveloped, to parks with full trailer hookups, campsites, and barbecue grills. Nearly all the state parks that permit camping have, at minimum, graded campsites, water, cooking areas, and restrooms, while many also feature electrical hookups. Thirty-one state parks also include cabins or screened shelters suitable for overnight stays.

The rates for state park camping vary according to campsite facilities and whether your stay is on the weekend (Friday or Saturday night) or during the week. A primitive site without water but suitable for tent camping costs $4-8. With running water the rate goes to $6-12; add electrical outlets and it's $9-15; with electrical and sewage hookups (for trailers and other recreational vehicles) rates run $10-16. Screened shelters, available at a few parks, cost $15-20 a night, depending on the park. One vehicle per campsite is admitted free; additional vehicles (small utility or boat trailers don't count) are $2 each. Reservations for campsites or shelters can be made by phone, mail, or in person at any state park up to 90 days in advance, but reservations made more than 10 days in advance require a deposit equal to one day's campsite/shelter fee. Deposits are due within five calendar days of making a reservation.

Since March 1994, a Central Reservations Center number (tel. 512-389-8900), has been available for making facilities reservations anywhere in the state park system. The CRC accepts Visa and MasterCard for payment of reservation deposits.

If you have a Texas Conservation Passport you can save $1 a night on camping fees at selected parks. The TCP card costs $25 and allows unlimited admission into all state parks. You can purchase a TCP at any state park or by phone through the Central Reservations Center.

Most state parks enforce a camping limit of 14 days; some limit stays to seven days. The Texas Department of Highways and Transportation issues a handy booklet called *Texas Public Campgrounds,* which lists all state and national parks with campgrounds and/or trailer facilities, including a list of the facilities, stay limits, and auto directions. Each entry in the booklet is keyed by number to the department's *Official Highway Travel Map;* armed with map and booklet, you'll never have to sleep indoors while in Texas. These free publications may be obtained by writing to the Travel and Information Division, State Department of Highways and Transportation, P.O. Box 5064, Austin, TX 78763.

Private Campgrounds
Roughly half the total number of campgrounds in Texas are privately owned but open to the paying public. Some belong to campground chains like KOA Kampgrounds or Good Sampark. Nearly all private campgrounds cater to RV (recreational vehicle) campers as well as tent campers, and many rent tents as well. Campground facilities range from basic drive-through campsites to trailer parks with spas and shuffleboard.

Private campgrounds tend to be found clustered around major cities; on the outskirts of larger state and national parks; along the Gulf Coast and on the shores of popular lakes, reservoirs, and rivers; and in the "snowbird" retreat area between Brownsville and McAllen (the Rio Grande Valley) in South Texas, near the Mexican border, where retirees from the colder midwestern states migrate during winter.

Rates vary from $5 to $18 a night, depending on facilities and location. Most private campgrounds have lower weekly and monthly rates as well. Rates listed in this guidebook are daily, non-discounted rates; most private campgrounds and RV parks offer discounts for long-term stays and special rates for RV club members. A park that charges $15 per day for a site with full hookups usually drops to $90-100 for a week's stay, or as low as $250-350 per month. Note that if you're tent camping, you'll save as much as $10 a night if you seek out a state park rather than a private campground.

The best list of private campgrounds available is the free *RV and Camping Guide to Texas,* issued annually by the Texas Association of Campground Owners (tel. 512-459-8226), P.O. Box 14055, Austin, TX 78761. TACO is an affiliate of the National Campground Owners Association (NCOA).

Another source of information for RV owners is the Texas Recreational Vehicle Association (tel. 512-327-4514), 3355 Bee Cave Rd., Austin, TX 78746. TRVA will provide a free list of RV parks in Texas upon request. The Texas KOA Kampground Owners Association, 6805 Guadalupe St., Austin, TX 78752, lists 18 member campgrounds around the state.

FOOD AND DRINK

FOOD

Texans love life and they love food. In the cities, you'll find all the latest culinary trends, from Thai to West Coast nouvelle to mesquite-grilled nuevo Southwest, as well as American fast-food chains like McDonald's, Pizza Hut, and Kentucky Fried Chicken. In the smaller towns and hamlets, you can forget about trendy haute cuisine, it's down to two basic choices: the local Dairy Queen or real Texas food.

Real Texas food comes in different varieties, depending on what part of the state you're in. Certain Texas foods may be found almost anywhere in the state but are differentiated by local recipe twists. To appreciate all the subtle variations might require several years of eating and travel. But by the time you're an expert, you'll have gained more than several pounds, as real Texas food is not your typical health food. In fact, it should be taken in measured quantities in order to stave off a premature heart attack. Some say Texas has more opportunities for indigestion than any other state; wise Texans vary their diet in order to live long and fruitful lives.

Barbecue Pits and *Bierhalles*

Basically, what you'll find in Texas are five different styles of regional cooking. In West Texas, the accent is on barbecued brisket, sirloin steaks, spit-roasted chicken, ranch-style salads, barbecue beans, and dessert cobblers. An authentic Texas-style barbecue establishment features oak or mesquite logs piled out back and serves a choice of brisket, ribs, sausage, and either chicken or turkey. In Central Texas, barbecued meats and poultry are also popular but are prepared with different marinades than in West Texas. Also common in Central Texas are "chicken-fried" steak (fried breaded beef or veal with a cream-style gravy), Polish and German sausages, standard Tex-Mex fare like tacos and enchiladas, beans, pickled vegetables, and Dutch apple pie.

Downhome

Over in East Texas are two major culinary divisions. Northeast Texas is known for "downhome," "homestyle," or "southern" cooking, which includes dishes like fried catfish, cornbread, fried chicken, roast ham, cream gravy and biscuits, boiled cabbage, poke salad, and vinegar pie. In Southeast Texas, which has a higher black and Cajun population than the rest of the state, you'll find "soul food" like barbecued ribs, chitterlings (fried tripe), boiled collard greens, candied sweet potatoes, rice, and cornbread, as well as Cajun and Creole dishes like shrimp gumbo, crawfish étouffée, boudin (a rice and pork sausage), French-style rolls, and potato pie.

One chain that serves reliable—but not spectacular—Texas downhome is Luby's, a cafeteria franchise that began in San Antonio in 1946 and now seems to be in every Texas town with a population of 30,000 or greater. Not a single Luby's location is mentioned in this guidebook simply because they're so numerous and so similar descriptions would quickly become redundant. But if you're looking to pile a cafeteria tray with downhome food for a small investment —and don't want to leave a tip—Luby's is always an easy bet.

BITS AND BITES

- As in American cinema, no other U.S. state name shows up in food products as often as "Texas."
- Miller Brewing Co. began embossing a half-inch Texas star just below the neck of its 12-ounce bottles in 1993.
- Pace Foods, famous for "Pace Picante Sauce" and the nation's largest salsa producer, exports to Mexico.
- Texas is the largest U.S. producer and consumer of jalapeño peppers.

Tex-Mex victuals

Tex-Mex

South Texas is the bastion of true Tex-Mex food, as well as a few Mexican dishes of more remote origins that Texans refer to as "interior cooking" (as differentiated from "border cooking"). Almost all Mexican foods are, of course, a blend of Indian and Spanish influences.

But most Americans are familiar with a kind of chain restaurant-style Mexican food that bears little relation to what you'll find in the *frontera* cuisine of South Texas, except for the shared names of some dishes. Tex-Mex cooking, like Tex-Mex music, is a regional style found across a broad area from San Antonio and El Paso to Torreon and Monterrey, Mexico. Tacos and enchiladas are the most common dishes, both made with corn tortillas and filled with various meats and cheeses. Wheat flour tortillas are most often eaten on the side as an accompanying bread in Texas and northern Mexico, rather than as burritos, a Sonoran specialty more typical of Arizona and California Mexican.

One Tex-Mex dish that has become a favorite addition to Mexican menus across the U.S. is fajitas (pronounced fa-HEE-tas), which started out as street vendor's fare—strips of inexpensive skirt steak marinated in lime juice and spices, then grilled over a hot fire and served with flour tortillas and *pico de gallo,* a freshly made salsa (sauce) of tomatoes, onions, and hot chilies. Other typical grilled meats like *cabrito* (roast kid) are also common, served with plenty of tortillas, salsa, and beans—either pinto

beans or black beans. *Carne asada* is the Mexican equivalent of barbecue, while a *barbacoa* is a more elaborate Mexican smorgasbord featuring several dishes. Most Tex-Mex dishes are not inherently hot and chile-laden—individual diners devise their own degree of spiciness at the table by adding from a variety of salsas.

Another typical Tex-Mex dish is the tamal (plural tamales), shredded pork or chicken mixed with Mexican spices, rolled in a thick cornmeal dough, wrapped in a corn husk, and steamed. Most Mexican cafes in South Texas also serve mouthwatering breakfasts like *migas,* eggs scrambled with onions, chiles, and corn tortilla strips; *chilaquiles,* similar to *migas* but with cheese; or *huevos mexicanos,* eggs fried with tomatoes, onions, and chiles.

A word about "nachos," the tortilla-chip appetizers commonplace all over the United States. In most border towns between Del Rio and Brownsville, "nachos" refers to one arrangement only—cheese melted over tortilla chips, with sliced jalapeños on the side. If you add beans to the dish, it becomes *cincos;* add guacamole and it's *pericos.* In Laredo, they also have *ponchos,* nachos with beef.

In general, the most typical and most inexpensive Mexican restaurants in Texas are those with "Bakery" or "Cafe" in the name. "Restaurants" are a bit pricier, though usually quite moderate by restaurant standards, and tend to alter time-tried recipes in search of either middle-America-style Mexican for tourists or "nouvelle

Tex-Mex" for Dallas and Houston urbanites. Noteworthy Texas restaurants and cafes are mentioned throughout the text. If you want to get a lively conversation going among a small crowd of Texans, ask one or both of the following questions: Where's the best barbecue in town? or Where's the best Tex-Mex around these parts?

If you're drooling over the prospect of dining on Tex-Mex right away, drive straight to Texas to whichever of the following is nearest your starting point: Mi Tierra Bakery and Cafe, 218 Produce Row, San Antonio; Avila's, 6232 N. Mesa, El Paso; or Joe T. Garcia Mexican Bakery, 2201 N. Commerce, Fort Worth. These are three of the most dependable and authentic Tex-Mex eateries in the state. But they're not necessarily the best—the best are the little discoveries you make on your own.

Chili

You don't have to think twice to guess the "state dish" of Texas. Chili, from the Texan pronunciation of *chile* (Spanish for the pepper of the Capsicum family; originally from the Nahuatl word *chilli*), is a thoroughly Texan food found on menus throughout the state. It's very possible the word entered the Texan vocabulary before the Spanish linguistic corruption of *chilli* to *chile* was complete, in which case Texans can quite correctly refer to hot peppers as "chilis" (much to the dismay of New Mexican pepper connoisseurs).

Traditional Texas chili is a meat stew in a fiery sauce of chilies, onions, and various Tex-Mex spices. Beef is the customary meat employed in chili, though virtually every other kind of meat appears in modern variations, from armadillo to venison. Texas chili aficionados eschew beans as an ingredient, though they can be served on the side. As the saying goes, "If you know beans about chili, you know chili has no beans."

No one knows for sure when it was created, but mid-1800 accounts of Texas street life seldom fail to mention the "chili queens" of San Antonio, women who sold bowls of chili from impromptu street stands. The dish seems to have been conceived by Texas cowboys in the 1840s, when they began pounding tough, stringy beef with *chilipequins* (called *chiltepines* or *chiles*

pequines in today's Mexico) and ground spices into compressed bricks. The bricks were later boiled in pots along the trail to make a stew; the peppers and spices helped preserve the meat and also masked the taste when it began to go bad.

Somewhere along the middle of the 20th century, chili developed into a Texas cultural symbol. The Chili Appreciation Society International (CASI) was founded by chili fanatics in 1951 and has chapters ("pods") all over the world which indulge in collective chili appreciation. Will Rogers called it "a bowl of blessedness" and Elizabeth Taylor had chili flown to Rome during the filming of *Cleopatra*. Many chili-eaters consider it a potent aphrodisiac; chili is obviously a popular excuse for shedding one's inhibitions, as attendance at any major Texas chili cookoff will surely demonstrate.

Entire books have been written about this humble dish, most notably *A Bowl of Red* by the late *Dallas Morning News* food columnist Frank X. Tolbert. Tolbert organized the first chili cookoff, "The Great Chili Confrontation," between Texas chili cook Wick Fowler and New York journalist H. Allen Smith, who claimed he could prepare better chili than anyone in Texas. The standoff took place at high noon on an October day in 1967, in the abandoned mining town of Terlingua in West Texas. No one won, since the judges declared their taste buds had become paralyzed (some say it was the beans in the New York chili, others say it was the peppers in Wick's). The cookoff became an annual event in Terlingua and chili cookoffs are now part of Texas festival life. See "Terlingua" under "Vicinity of Big Bend National Park" in the West Texas chapter for more information on the annual World Championship Chili Cookoff. Whatever H. Allen Smith's status as a chili cook may have been, he takes the prize for the juiciest chili description: "The chief ingredients of all chili are fiery envy, scalding jealousy, scorching contempt, and sizzling scorn."

In an average year the state hosts some 15 chili competitions per month; this means there's a cookoff somewhere in the state every other day year round. One monthly periodical maintains a running schedule of virtually all Texas chili events: the *Goat Gap Gazette* ("Clarion of the Chili World"—tel. 713-667-4652), 5110 Bayard Ln. #2, Houston, TX 77006.

Sweets

Texas desserts aren't fancy. Pie is the state favorite, especially pecan pie (pecan trees thrive in most of the state) and buttermilk pie. In Central Texas, German and Czech pastries are common, especially the *kolache,* a fluffy star-shaped pastry similar to what most Americans call a "Danish," but not as sweet and sticky.

Ice-cream connoisseurs shouldn't miss tasting the Texas-made Blue Bell brand. This ice cream is made in Brenham and distributed throughout the state—you can only get it in Texas, though an occasional shipment makes it as far as Oklahoma City. Years ago *Time* magazine proclaimed Blue Bell the best ice cream in America.

Pecan pralines, a chewy concoction of buttery caramel and pecans, are another Texan specialty. These vary incredibly from recipe to recipe, but the most savory, as judged by yours truly, are Lamme's Texas Chewies made in Austin. Texans must like sweetened nuts: besides pecan pralines and pecan pie, practically every Texas schoolkid knows the trick of buying a bag of salted peanuts and adding them to a bottle of Dr. Pepper, a soft drink named for the Waco father of the inventor's girlfriend.

DRINK

Texas has liquor laws that make travel there a bit like traveling in India. Fifty-four of the state's 254 counties are "dry," which means no beer, wine, or liquor at all is permitted for sale within county boundaries. Thirty-seven are "wet," which means any alcoholic beverage may be sold. The remaining 153 counties vary in local restrictions; some sell only beer or beer and wine, others sell liquor in bars but not at liquor stores. A legislative "local option" allows 79 counties to have both wet and dry areas within the same jurisdiction—upscale North Dallas, for example, is dry, while other areas of the city are wet. In actual practice, however, booze is everywhere in Texas, since no dry area is ever very far from a wet one.

Beer

Of the several brands of beer brewed in Texas, three are famous as Texas beers: Pearl, Lone Star, and Shiner. Just as Texans argue about the best barbecue and best Tex-Mex food, they differ on which Texas beer is best. All three taste as typically bland as most mass-produced American beer, but every Texan agrees the best container from which to consume the foamy stuff is the longneck bottle. In fact, in Texas, "longneck" is practically synonymous with "beer."

One Texas brew that stands out from the rest is Shiner Bock, a dark variety produced from toasted barley. In many urban Texas bars nowadays this is the only Shiner offered, either on tap or in longnecks. A few microbreweries in Texas are cashing in on the national trend toward pricey "handmade" beer (Celis, a Belgian-style beer label from Austin, is among the best), and a 1993 change in Texas state law finally made it legal to operate brew pubs, where beers are brewed and served at the same location. Brew pubs have already opened in Austin, Dallas, and Fredericksburg—more are sure to spring up over the next few years.

Wine

Twenty years ago, wine made in Texas was strictly a curiosity left on the shelf as a conversation piece. In 1975 there existed only one commercial vintner in the state, Del Rio's Val Verde Winery, originally founded in 1883. Today the state claims around 7,000 acres of vineyards supplying 26 bonded wineries. Some of them produce very good wines, on a par with certain of the better California vintages. The retail value of Texas wines produced in 1990 was over $30 million, which places Texas fifth among wine-producing states. The largest markets for Texas wine are, in descending order, Texas, New Mexico, Oklahoma, Louisiana, and France.

Until Prohibition, Texas was a leader in North American viticulture. Franciscan padres planted the first vinifera (wine grapes) in 1662 in the El Paso area, a century before Junipero Serra began cultivating California's first vines. By the early 1900s, Texas had as many commercial wineries as it does now, but Prohibition forced them all to close. Unlike in California, where winemaking took off in the early '60s, the Texas viticultural renaissance didn't occur until the late '70s.

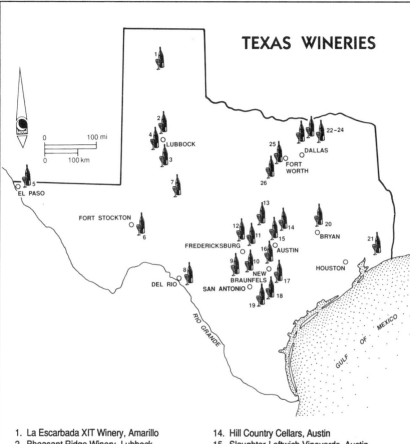

TEXAS WINERIES

1. La Escarbada XIT Winery, Amarillo
2. Pheasant Ridge Winery, Lubbock
3. Llano Estacado Winery, Lubbock
4. Cap Rock Winery, Lubbock
5. Bieganowski Cellars, El Paso
6. Ste. Genevieve Winery, Fort Stockton
7. St. Lawrence Winery, Garden City
8. Val Verde Winery, Del Rio
9. Pedernales Vineyards, Fredericksburg
10. Sister Creek Vineyards, Sisterdale
11. Grape Creek Vineyard, Stonewall
12. Bell Mountain/Oberhellmann Vineyards, Fredericksburg
13. Fall Creek Vineyards, Tow (Austin)
14. Hill Country Cellars, Austin
15. Slaughter-Leftwich Vineyards, Austin
16. Wimberley Valley Wines, Driftwood
17. Guadalupe Valley Winery, New Braunfels
18. Moyer Texas Champagne, New Braunfels
19. Alamo Farms Winery & Vineyards, Adkins
20. Messina Hof Wine Cellars, Bryan
21. Piney Woods Country Wines, Orange
22. Schoppaul Hill Winery, Ivanhoe
23. Homestead Winery, Ivanhoe
24. Preston Trail Winery, Gunter
25. La Buena Vida Vineyards, Fort Worth
26. Sanchez Creek Vineyards, Weatherford

Outside California's Napa and Sonoma valleys, some areas of Texas probably have the best wine-producing conditions in the United States. In fact, according to recognized wine authority Leon Adams, there are more naturally present grape species in Texas than anywhere else in the world. Texas wine country can be divided into four small areas: on the Llano Estacado near Lubbock; just west and north of the Dallas-Fort Worth area; in the Trans-Pecos region near mountainous areas; and in the Hill Country near Austin and San Antonio. There are also a few scattered wineries in East Texas, but this area is really too humid and rainy to produce a world-class or even nationally ranked wine.

The state's top labels are found in the Lubbock area: Llano Estacado Winery, Pheasant Ridge Winery, and the newer Cap Rock Winery. All three have won awards in state and national wine competitions, and two wineries in the Hill Country, Grape Creek Vineyards and Slaughter-Leftwich Vineyards, have also earned national rankings. Many wine critics say Fall Creek Vineyards, on the shore of Lake Buchanan near Austin, makes the nation's finest riesling and carnelian varietals. Val Verde Winery in Del Rio is acclaimed for its port wine.

For information on tours and tastings at these and other wineries, see the appropriate destination in the text. For wine festivals and competitions, see April, May, and September entries under "Holidays, Festivals, and Events." The Texas Department of Agriculture publishes the *Texas Wine Country Tour Guide,* a free 20-page pamphlet pinpointing and describing the state's 26 wineries. Write or call the Texas Department of Agriculture (tel. 512-463-7624), P.O. Box 12847, Austin, TX 78711.

Tequila

This well-known product of the agave cactus is not made in Texas, at least not legally—Jalisco state in Mexico is the only place that produces real tequila. But tequila is probably the most popular alcoholic beverage in the state after beer. The authentic, Mexican way to drink tequila is straight up, chased with water or beer. A popular alternative is to lick a few grains of salt from the back of your hand, down a shot glass of the fiery liquid, and then bite into a wedge of lime and suck out the juice. Ay caramba!

The margarita, a potent concoction of tequila, lime juice, and triple sec served in a salt-rimmed glass, was probably invented on the Texas border, but no one remembers which side. Drink a few of these and you won't care either. The true, classic margarita is served over ice, not blended into a frozen drink like the Cuban daiquiri. Most Texas bars and restaurants serve them in the traditional fashion only, though those oriented toward the tourist trade will offer a choice between frozen and "on the rocks."

Other Spirits

Along the Texas-Mexican border you also may come across a few varieties of "moonshine" or illicit liquor. In the Big Bend area, the fermented juice of the heart of the sotol plant is popular—it's usually called "sotol" after the plant. Less common are pulque, a rough relative of tequila made from agave leaves, and mesquite beer, made from mesquite beans.

RESTAURANT RATING KEY

$	Less than $4 per meal
$$	$4-8 per meal
$$$	$9-16 per meal
$$$$	Over $16 per meal

Ratings are based on
the average price of an entree.

BORDER CROSSINGS

Texas shares borders with four different Mexican states: from east to west, Tamaulipas, Nuevo León, Coahuila, and Chihuahua. Practically every Texan has crossed into Mexico at least once. Many out-of-state visitors take the opportunity to cross over as well, even if just for an hour or two of shopping and dining.

INTO MEXICO

Papers

For visits to Mexican border towns of less than 72 hours, no visa or tourist card is necessary, but you should have identification to show immigration officers when reentering the United States. Visitors who don't have U.S. citizenship or a resident alien card should carry a passport.

To enter Mexico at any of the Texas border crossings for stays of longer than 72 hours, you must possess a tourist card. All you need to receive the card is proof of your identity and citizenship. For U.S. and Canadian citizens, any of the following are acceptable proof of citizenship: birth certificate, passport, voter registration, or notarized affidavit from a U.S. or Canadian government office. For citizens of other countries, only a passport is acceptable.

The tourist card is valid for up to 180 days and must be surrendered upon exiting Mexico. You can obtain the card at any official border crossing, or in advance at Mexican consulates or embassies, Mexican tourist offices, AAA offices, and at most travel agencies and airline offices in Texas.

If you drive a vehicle into Mexico, you can obtain a temporary import permit at the border after your tourist card is stamped, but only if you present proof of ownership (a photocopy of the title will do), an American insurance policy valid for at least two months after the date of entry, and a credit card to pay for the $12 permit fee. This vehicle permit is not required if you're staying less than 72 hours. Keep the paperwork handy if you're driving, as the Mexican police will demand it if you're stopped—12 miles into Mexico, every vehicle without Mexico tags is stopped at border patrol checkpoints. AAA members can have all their paperwork taken care of

ACROSS THE BORDERLINE

The following list includes only those crossings with U.S. and Mexican immigration posts.

• Ciudad Juárez, Chihuahua; bridge, opposite El Paso; there are also three bridge crossings southeast of El Paso near Fabens and Fort Hancock; open 24 hours.

• Ojinaga, Chihuahua; bridge, opposite Presidio; 7:30 a.m.-9 p.m. Mon.-Fri., 8 a.m.-4 p.m. Sat.-Sun.

• Ciudad Acuña, Coahuila; bridge, opposite Del Rio; 24 hours.

• Piedras Negras, Coahuila; bridge, opposite Eagle Pass; 24 hours.

• Nuevo Laredo, Tamaulipas; bridge, opposite Laredo; plus second crossing northeast at Colombia, Tamaulipas; 24 hours.

• Nueva Ciudad Guerrero, Tamaulipas; bridge, opposite Salineno; 7:30 a.m.-9 p.m. Mon.-Fri., 8 a.m.-4 p.m. Sat.-Sun.

• Ciudad Miguel Alemán, Tamaulipas; bridge; opposite Roma; 24 hours.

• Camargo, Tamaulipas; bridge, opposite Rio Grande City; 7:30 a.m.-9 p.m. Mon.-Fri., 8 a.m.-4 p.m. Sat.-Sun.

• Díaz Ordaz, Tamaulipas; ferry, opposite Los Ebanos; bridge to be constructed; 7:30 a.m.-9 p.m. Mon.-Fri., 8 a.m.-4 p.m. Sat.-Sun.

• Reynosa, Tamaulipas; bridge, opposite Hidalgo/McAllen; 24 hours.

• Nuevo Progreso (Río Bravo), Tamaulipas; bridge, opposite Progreso; 7:30 a.m.-9 p.m. Mon.-Fri., 8 a.m.-4 p.m. Sat.-Sun.

• Matamoros, Tamaulipas; bridge, opposite Brownsville; 24 hours.

at selected AAA offices in the U.S. border states.

Mexican auto insurance is highly recommended for all vehicles entering Mexico—U.S. insurance is not valid in Mexico, no matter what your insurance company may tell you. Several agencies maintain offices at the border where insurance can be arranged for a few dollars. Sanborn's is a reliable American company specializing in Mexican auto insurance for short-term visitors to Mexico; the company staffs offices in all the larger border towns as well as in San Antonio.

U.S. Customs

Upon returning from Mexico, you're allowed a $400 exemption on customs duties every 30 days. For tobacco, this includes 100 cigars and 200 cigarettes; for alcoholic beverages, one liter of wine, beer, or liquor.

INTO THE U.S.

Overseas visitors need a passport and visa to enter the United States. Except for diplomats,

students, or refugees, this means a non-immigrant visitor's visa, which must be obtained in advance at a U.S. consulate or embassy abroad. Residents of Western European and Commonwealth countries are usually issued these readily; residents of other countries may have to provide the consulate with proof of "sufficient personal funds" before the visa is issued.

Upon arrival in the U.S., an immigration inspector will decide on the time validity of the visa—the maximum for a temporary visitor's visa (B-1 or B-2) is six months. If you visit Mexico from Texas (or from anywhere else in the U.S.) for stays of 30 days or less, you can reenter the U.S. with the same visa, provided the visa is still valid, by presenting your stamped arrival/departure card (INS form I-94) and passport to a U.S. immigration inspector. If your U.S. visa has expired, you can still enter the country for a stay of 29 days or less on a transit visa—issued at the border—but you may be required to show proof of onward travel, such as an air ticket or ship travel voucher.

MONEY, MEASUREMENTS, AND COMMUNICATIONS

In general, prices in Texas are a bit lower than the U.S. average due to an overall deflationary state economy, which makes it an excellent American travel bargain. Gasoline is less expensive than in most states, hotel rates in Texas cities are lower than in other U.S. cities of comparable size, and food, both in grocery stores and in restaurants, is noticeably cheaper. Most other consumer items cost about the same as in other parts of the continental United States.

Any prices mentioned in this book were current at press time, but prices do change. All Mexican border towns will accept U.S. currency. Texas has a 6.25% sales tax on merchandise as well as a 6% hotel tax. With the addition of city/county levies, these figures can increase to as high as 8.25% and 15% respectively.

COMMUNICATIONS

Time Zones
Most of Texas is in the U.S. central time zone, which is six hours earlier than Greenwich mean time. The exception is the El Paso area, which is

on mountain time, seven hours ahead of Greenwich time. From the last Sunday in April until the last Sunday in October, Texas, like the rest of the U.S., goes on daylight saving time, which advances the clock one hour across all American time zones.

Voltage
Power outlets in the U.S. run on a 117-volt AC system, which means that only appliances of that approximate voltage will run as manufactured. If you bring along a hair dryer or another small appliance that runs on 200 or 220 volts, you'll have to use a transformer or it won't work properly. Transformers, as well as adaptors to make the prongs on foreign appliances fit American outlets, are available in most larger American hardware stores and in many electronic supplies stores. Department stores such as JCPenney or Sears also carry such equipment.

Modern hotels in the larger Texas cities may feature switchable power outlets in the bathroom which allow the use of 200/220 volt appliances, but carrying your own transformer is safer than relying on these—they aren't always there and, when they are, may not work properly.

Postal Service

General U.S. Postal Service (USPS) hours are Mon.-Fri. 8:30 a.m.-5:30 p.m. Many post offices also open for a few hours on Saturday mornings, usually 8:30 a.m.-noon. The main post offices in larger cities often have longer weekday hours; a select few are open as late as 10 p.m. Call ahead to find out.

Visitors can have mail sent to them at any town in Texas c/o General Delivery. A General Delivery letter will only be held by the post office for 10 days before it's returned to sender. You can also rent a post office box in any town where they're available for around $6 a month.

Various privately owned and operated establishments also handle mail, most prominently a nationwide company called Mail Boxes, Etc. These places generally stay open longer hours than USPS offices and handle telegram, facsimile, and UPS parcel services as well. If you need to mail something and can't find an open post office, check the local phone book for one of these private services.

Telephone Services

Texas has nine different area codes; see the "Texas Area Codes" map for locations. Most telephone systems in the U.S. require you enter a "1" before dialing a long-distance number. For directory assistance within the local area code, dial 411; between different area codes, dial the area code plus 555-1212. Many businesses offer toll-free (no charge) long-distance numbers; these are always preceded by "800" rather than an area code.

Business Hours

Most businesses in Texas are open Mon.-Fri. from 8 or 9 a.m. until 5 or 5:30 p.m. Small shops may close for lunch from noon to 1 p.m. or thereabouts. Retail shops usually don't open until 10 or 11 a.m., closing their doors at 5 or 6 p.m. The exception for retail shops is in large shopping malls, where they'll often stay open until 8, 9, or 10 p.m.

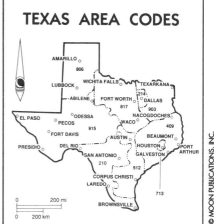

TEXAS AREA CODES

© MOON PUBLICATIONS, INC.

Restaurants and cafes vary widely in the hours they choose to open their doors. It isn't uncommon for restaurants in small and medium-sized towns to close on Sunday; some close on Monday or Tuesday as well. Trying to find a non-chain restaurant open on Sunday in a small Texas town is often futile; your only choice may be the Dairy Queen or the grocery store, and sometimes the grocery stores are closed on Sunday. In general, small-town restaurants close by 9 or 10 p.m., sometimes a bit earlier. In Dallas, Houston, Austin, and San Antonio, however, there's always someplace to eat or drink—any time, day or night.

Banks and museums are among the most restrictive places when it comes to getting inside their doors. Public banking hours are usually confined to a short period between 9-10 a.m. and 3-4 p.m., weekdays only. Many museums are open Wednesday through Saturday only, including even big ones like the Amon Carter in Fort Worth.

Monday and Tuesday, then, are good days to visit parks and outdoor attractions, since many indoor urban attractions may be closed on these days. Also, you'll have almost exclusive use of such facilities since local weekend tourists won't be around.

SERVICES AND INFORMATION

Emergency Services

Emergency medical and police assistance can usually be summoned by dialing 911 from any phone, whether public or private (no charge for the call). If you get no response dialing 911, try the operator (dial "0"). Virtually every town of any size in Texas has a hospital or clinic that provides 24-hour emergency service.

Tourist Information

Texas has an excellent Tourism Division, administered under the State Department of Commerce, which provides fairly extensive information on standard Texas travel. To request information, call or write the Tourism Division (tel. 512-462-9191 or 800-452-9292), Texas Department of Commerce, P.O. Box 12728, Austin, TX 78711, or 900 Congress Ave., Suite 501, Austin, TX 78701.

Another good source of information is the State Department of Highways and Transportation. The department's *Official Highway Travel Map* seems quite accurate and up-to-date, and marks the location of every state and national park, forest, preserve, recreation area, monument, and wildlife refuge. The department also operates 12 travel information centers around the state, mostly in state and international border areas. The bureaus are conveniently located off interstate and U.S. highways, plus one in the State Capitol in Austin. The map is available free of charge at these bureaus, or by mail from the Tourism Division or directly from the department. For further information or to request a map, contact the State Department of Highways and Transportation (tel. 800-452-9292), P.O. Box 5064, Austin, TX 78763.

The State Department of Highways also issues a free quarterly *Texas Events Calendar* that provides up-to-date details on virtually every state celebration, from chili cookoffs to jazz festivals. Each calendar covers only three months and is usually very accurate. They're available from the State Tourist Bureaus or by writing Texas Events Calendar, P.O. Box 5064, Austin, TX 78763.

Many Texas towns also operate their own local tourist offices, sometimes as part of convention and visitors bureaus (CVBs). These are usually headquartered in the local chamber of commerce or very nearby. When a town doesn't have a CVB, you can always get information at the chamber of commerce—every Texas town (well, almost) has something it's proud of, even if this author hasn't yet discovered it.

The Highway Department's state map is more than sufficient for most travel needs, but if you're looking for something more detailed—including hiking maps, topographic maps, or coastal navigation charts—try one of the following map retailers in Texas: Apaches Trading Post (tel. 915-837-5149), P.O. Box 997, Alpine, TX 79831; Ventura Map & Globe (tel. 512-452-2326), 2130 Highland Mall, Austin, TX 78752; One Map Place (tel. 214-241-2680), 212 Webb Chapel Village, Dallas, TX 75220; Key Maps (tel. 713-522-7946), 1411 W. Alabama St., Houston, TX 77006; Ferguson Maps (tel. 210-341-6277), 8131 I-10 West, San Antonio, TX 78230; Treaty Oak (tel. 512-326-4141), P.O. Box 50295, Austin, TX 78763.

Weather Information

If you have any intimation that catastrophic weather—e.g., tornadoes or hurricanes—may be in the vicinity or headed your way, tune in to one of the following AM radio frequencies to receive a continuous state forecast: 162.550 KHz, 162.400 KHz, or 162.475 KHz. Different parts of the state broadcast via one of these three; all you have to do is head for 162.4 KHz on the AM range and make minor adjustments to receive the proper frequency.

Magazines

Of the several Texas magazines with statewide coverage, the best for travel information are *Texas Monthly* (tel. 800-759-2000), P.O. Box 1569, Austin, TX 78767-1569, and *Texas Highways* (tel. 512-483-3689), P.O. Box 5016, Austin, TX 78763-5016. The award-winning *Texas Monthly* offers a variety of well-researched, well-edited features on political and social trends in the state, together with regular columns on music, art, cuisine, sports, and Texana.

Texas Highways, published by the State Department of Highways and Transportation, carries detailed articles on destinations, festivals, people, and cultural events throughout the state, accompanied by mouthwatering photos snapped by the state's top shooters. Readers interested in Texas flora and fauna may want to subscribe to Texas Parks & Wildlife magazine, 4200 Smith School Rd., Austin, TX 78744, which has a format similar to that of Texas Highways—excellent photography, detailed travel information, with an emphasis on wildlife.

GETTING THERE AND AROUND

BY AIR

Texas claims over 1,600 aircraft landing facilities, more than any other state. Three are classified international—Dallas-Fort Worth, Houston, and San Antonio. Several airports in South and West Texas can also be considered international since they offer flights to and from Mexico. You should have no trouble at all finding flights in, out, or around the Lone Star State, since Texas is second only to California in the number of commercial aircraft arrivals/departures per year in the United States.

About 50 air carriers operate out of Texas, including at least 17 commuter airlines. The commuter lines are constantly jockeying for a greater share of the market, keeping intrastate fares relatively low. Though it's always worth checking around for the lowest fare, Southwest Airlines seems to do the best job of keeping fares at a consistently economical level. Baggage service and punctuality are two other areas in which Southwest stands out from most other American airlines.

BY LAND

Driving

For most people, the best way to get around Texas is by car. The state has an excellent highway system, with 300,000 miles of roadway, the most extensive road network in the nation. The best thing about driving in Texas is that—anywhere in the state outside Dallas, San Antonio, and Houston—traffic is relatively light. In West Texas, you can drive for half an hour or more without seeing another vehicle. The longest highway in Texas, and the longest in any state in the U.S., is US 83, which runs 903 miles from Perryton on the Oklahoma border to Brownsville on the Rio Grande.

Always keep an eye on your fuel gauge when traveling long distances in rural areas, particularly in West Texas, as gas stations may be scarce on some stretches of road. When driving in the West Texas desert during the summer months, always carry several gallons of water for radiator mishaps or for drinking should you become stranded. If you do become stranded on a desert road, it's best to stay with the vehicle until a highway patrol car or good Samaritan happens along. If you decide to leave your vehicle to seek assistance elsewhere, leave a note on the vehicle indicating your route and departure time.

The state highway department maintains over a thousand roadside rest stops, some with picnic tables, drinking water, and restrooms, some with tables only. Scenic overlooks may provide just a turnaround area. While camping per se is prohibited at these rest stops, vehicles are allowed to park for rest purposes for periods up to 24 hours—as long as you don't pitch a tent or go over the time limit, you're welcome to sleep in your car, truck, van, or RV at any rest stop.

Auto Rental

All the major American auto rental agencies staff offices in Texas, and most offer airport locations so it's easy to get off a plane and pick up a rental car. The most economic way to rent a vehicle is on a weekly or monthly basis. Most agencies also have special weekend deals featuring three days rental for the price of two. Some agencies provide an extra discount to customers who reserve cars at least a week in advance. With planning, you can rent a small car for as little as $20 a day, or $105 a week.

Motorcycles

Texas is a great state for motorcycle touring—lots of room to stretch out on the highway, and few bothersome cars and trucks. The mountainous parts of the Trans-Pecos, the Hill Country in Central Texas, and the Piney Woods area of East Texas are probably the best areas overall for motorcycle touring.

Only about a third of the Gulf Coast has a road that parallels the shore. This begins in the Brazosport Area at Surfside Beach, then proceeds northeast over Follets Island, by toll bridge to Galveston Island, by ferry to the Bolivar Peninsula, then a final straight shot along the Gulf to Sabine Pass and the Louisiana border.

Other good rides include along the Rio Grande between Eagle Pass and Langtry via State 277 and State 90, between Lajitas and Presidio on Ranch Road 170, and in the Davis Mountains along State 118 and State 166.

Roadways

For the most part, you'll find four different types of roadways in Texas, identified by the symbol enclosing the highway number on roadside signs.

Biggest and best maintained are the interstate highways, indicated by a blue shield. As elsewhere in the U.S., two-digit, even-numbered interstates (e.g., I-10, I-20) run in an east-west direction, while odd-numbered interstates (I-35, I-45) run north-south. This is the way they're designed, anyway; some parts of an interstate may run in a different direction for a number of miles, but the overall direction will conform to the odd-even system of numbering. It helps to know this if you get lost somewhere in the middle of East Texas and are trying to figure out which interstate to take. A three-digit interstate is merely a "beltway" or "loop" (Texans prefer the latter term) that runs around major cities.

The interstates are almost always the fastest way to get from one point to another, but they're not always the most scenic. And they're definitely not the type of road to take if you want to stop in small towns along the way. No sir, if you want to see the Heart of Texas, you'll have to slow down a bit and take the lowlier U.S. highways (red shield), state highways (black circle), or farm/ranch roads (white silhouette of Texas with a black background).

The farm and ranch roads will take you to some of the most inspiring places in Texas. These rural roads were developed by the state beginning early this century to enable ranchers and farmers to transport their livestock and crops to town markets. Hence, their full classification is "Farm-to-Market" or "Ranch-to-Market," which is why the road signs read "FM" or "RM" before the route number; it's surprising how few Texans know what these initials stand for. There's no difference between them except that ranch roads are in areas that are traditional ranch territory while farm roads are in farming areas. In West Texas, you'll occasionally see "RR," which stands for "Ranch Road"—they link ranch areas rather than ranch and urban areas.

Regulations

The maximum speed limit in Texas is 65 miles per hour on interstates in rural parts of the state. Near towns and cities, the interstate speed limit is 55 miles per hour. On state highways, the police sometimes enforce speed limits strictly, especially on the outskirts of small towns where speeding fines may be an important source of municipal funds. A state highway can drop from a 55-mph limit to 25 mph in a very short span.

Texas has the following seatbelt laws: All front-seat occupants of cars and trucks must wear safety belts. Children aged two to four must wear belts no matter where they sit, and infants under two must ride in a federally approved child safety seat. Most rental car agencies will supply customers with a safety seat when requested.

You are permitted to turn right at a red light after coming to a full stop, unless a road sign says otherwise.

Driving Etiquette

Texas drivers are generally courteous. On rural state highways and farm/ranch roads, most Texans will automatically pull onto the shoulder of the road when approached from behind by a faster vehicle. You should do the same if a faster vehicle approaches you from behind. In sparsely populated areas, don't be surprised on a two-lane road if the driver of a vehicle coming toward you from the opposite direction raises a hand or waves. Folks who live hundreds of miles apart in these areas may consider each other neighbors. Wave back: you might need that rancher's help down the road.

Although you won't find much traffic in rural Texas, you're likely to encounter various animals on the road, from armadillos to mule deer. In some areas, carcasses are so common people make "roadkill chili"; the meat ingredient is whatever was flattened out on the road that day. There's even a line of Texas arts and crafts called Road Kill, which designs pieces from bones and feathers found on the roadside. Do keep an eye out for such creatures so that they're less likely to end up in a chili bowl or hanging on a wall.

Buses

Various regional bus companies connect virtually all the towns in Texas. Larger cities are also linked by Greyhound-Trailways Bus Lines. All intercity buses are air-conditioned and equipped with restrooms. Because of the state's size, if you plan to travel by bus, a bus pass may be more economical than single-journey tickets. Outside North America, a Greyhound-Trailways **Ameripass,** which allows unlimited bus travel within specified dates, can be purchased from travel agencies at a discount—a seven-day pass bought outside the U.S. might cost $120; in the U.S., $145.

Within large towns and cities, local bus systems serve the downtown areas and, to a lesser extent, the suburbs. Houston, Dallas, Fort Worth, Austin, Corpus Christi, and San Antonio all have special downtown lines for visitors and shoppers that are handy on weekends, when many bus services are otherwise curtailed.

Trains

Rail is an excellent, if somewhat costly way to travel to Texas. The state's first railroad line, the 32-mile Buffalo Bayou, Brazos & Colorado Railroad (BBB&C), was laid in 1853 and ran between Harrisburg (now part of Houston) and the town of Richmond. Railway development spread quickly in Texas and since 1905 the state has boasted more track than any other state in the nation. Today many of the old regional railways have been replaced by Amtrak, a nationwide passenger service.

Two Amtrak lines run through Texas, the *Texas Eagle* (Chicago to San Antonio, with a Dallas to Houston connection) and the *Sunset Limited* (Los Angeles to Miami). These two trains stop at the following 20 passenger terminals: Alpine, Austin, Beaumont, Cleburne, College Station-Bryan, Corsicana, Dallas, Del Rio, El Paso, Fort Worth, Houston, Longview, Marshall, McGregor, San Antonio, Sanderson, San Marcos, Taylor, Temple, and Texarkana.

Amtrak has special one-way, roundtrip, or excursion fares on occasion—always ask before booking.

Outside North America, a **USA Railpass** can be purchased from travel agencies, allowing unlimited rail travel within specified dates. In the U.S., the All Aboard America Fare allows unlimited travel for up to 45 days with three permitted stopovers. The cost varies according to season and zone of travel from $179 for single-zone, low-season travel to $279 for two-zone, high-season travel. For schedule information or bookings inside the U.S., call (800) 872-7245 (800-USA-RAIL).

Within Texas, several non-Amtrak alternatives are availabe. A steam train, the Texas State Railroad, runs weekend tourist excursions through the Piney Woods between Rusk and Palestine. It's the only state historical park in the nation that's a railway.

Other opportunities for rail travel include these excursion railways: the **Texas State Railroad** (tel. 903-683-5126) Rt. 4, Box 431, Rusk, TX 75785; the **Hill Country Flyer** (tel. 512-477-8468), P.O. Box 1632, Austin, TX 78767; **Texas Limited** (tel. 800-374-7475), 567 T.C. Jester, Houston, TX 77007; the **Tarantula** (tel. 817-625-7245), 140 E. Exchange Ave., Ste. 350A, Fort Worth, TX 76106; and the **Jefferson and Cypress Bayou Railroad** (tel. 903-665-8400), P.O. Drawer A, Jefferson, TX 75657. See the relevant destination chapters for details on each of these excursion lines.

The state's longest excursion line, recently established by Houston-based **DRC Rail Tours** (tel. 713-872-0190 or 800-659-7602), is the deluxe *South Orient Express* between Fort Worth and Presidio on the Mexican border, with stops in San Angelo, Fort Stockton, and Alpine. An optional add-on links passengers by motor-coach with a rail trip from Ojinaga (opposite Presidio) through Mexico's Copper Canyon to Los Mochis on the Sea of Cortez coast. Packages start at $995 per person for the Fort Worth-Presidio tour, up to $2299 for a nine-day Copper Canyon trip, and include all transport, guided sightseeing, hotel accommodation, meals, and non-alcoholic beverages.

The Texas High Speed Rail Authority, using French and North American financing, is developing plans for a 200 mph bullet train that will link San Antonio, Dallas, Fort Worth, and Houston, with stops in San Marcos, Austin, and Waco. The first phase of the proposed $4.4 billion rail system is expected to begin construction by 1998 and will link Houston and Dallas-Fort Worth. When operational, the Dallas-to-Houston run is expected to deliver passengers from one end to the other in 1.5 hours. San Antonio and Austin will be added by 2005, the other cities by 2010. The completed "Texas Triangle" will extend a total of 618 miles, if it happens at all—several communities along the suggested route oppose the railway due to potential noise pollution. The competition from Southwest Airlines, which carries the highest ratio of passengers to population in the country along its Dallas-Houston route, makes it doubtful such a railway could be run profitably.

Bicycles

Texas is a good state for cycling, since the variance in elevation in most of the state is not great. Of course, distances are long, but serious touring cyclists won't find that much of a deterrent.

One of the best areas for cycling is the Hill Country, since it's fairly compact, by Texas standards; most of the roads have wide shoulders; the many small towns are nicely spaced, not so far apart that total self-sufficiency is necessary, nor so close together that one has to keep constant watch for cars or pedestrians. Because of all the university students, Austin is definitely the state cycling capital and hence the best place to seek out bicycle supplies or tricky repairs.

A decent, lightweight touring bike is best for the kind of terrain most of Texas offers. A mountain bike might be better, however, if you plan to do a lot of cycling in Big Bend country, the Davis Mountains, or the Guadalupe Mountains. Inside the national parks, of course, no off-road cycling is allowed.

If you enjoy cycling competitions and/or group touring, check with any Texas bicycle shop for a schedule of current events. Cycling is very popular in the state and there's almost always a cycling event going on. Check the free monthly *Texas Athlete,* 1750 N. Collins Blvd., Suite 209, Richardson, TX 77065, for a partial listing.

BY SEA

You can also sail in and out of one of the Gulf Coast's 29 ports. In fact, you could sail all the way from Florida and down the Texas coast without actually braving Gulf currents, following the Gulf Intracoastal Waterway, which is part canal, part natural waterway formed by barrier islands. You'll have to bring your own boat, however, since there are no commercial passenger lines between Texas and other states.

BOB RACE

WEST TEXAS
EL PASO

To people who haven't been there, the name El Paso evokes images of the quintessential Old West town. The reality is that El Paso possesses a heady mixture of identities making it difficult to classify. Imagine a place caught in a cultural twilight zone between American, Mexican, Indian, Texan, and New Mexican cultures and you'll begin to get an idea of what it's really like.

The dominant cultural presence is Mexican, simply because it's joined by the Rio Grande to Mexico's fourth-largest city, Juárez, home to about 1.2 million people. The Tigua Pueblo Indians who live in greater El Paso's Ysleta, the oldest settlement in Texas, have also brought their influence to bear on modern El Paso. The *maquiladora* or "twin plant" industry, which takes advantage of Third World labor costs and First World management, has drawn people from all over the world, thus adding a thin but expanding cosmopolitan veneer. Tourism also adds to the mix, attracting people to El Paso for shopping and gambling in Juárez or simply for the abundant sunshine that bakes this desert town year round.

El Paso is the largest city on the U.S.-Mexico border and the fourth-largest city in Texas, with a booming population of 600,000. It's the unofficial capital of *la frontera,* the unique third nation created by the meeting of Mexico and the United States that extends from the Gulf of Mexico to the Pacific Ocean. But sitting out on the edge of the Chihuahuan Desert, El Paso is practically in the middle of nowhere. It's just barely in Texas, in fact, tucked away in a remote pocket where Texas, Mexico, and New Mexico meet—the nearest American town to El Paso is Las Cruces, New Mexico. Thus, it's closer to three other state capitals—Santa Fe, Phoenix, and Chihuahua City—than to Austin, and in fact closer to Los Angeles than to Houston. And unlike the rest of Texas, El Paso is in the mountain time zone.

CLIMATE

El Paso sits at an elevation of 3,762 feet and features a desert climate. The average annual rainfall is only 7.7 inches and most of the time the air is extremely dry. The city records maximum temperatures above 90° F an average of 104 days a year, most falling between May and September. Because of the desert environment, nights around El Paso are usually cool, even during the summer. The average low temperature between June and August—the hottest months—is 67-69° F. As long as the temperature isn't greater than 96° or so, summer days are tolerable because of the relatively low humidity. But don't let anyone lead you too far astray on this humidity business; a hundred degrees in the desert feels hot. And, unfortunately, air pollution from the nearby *maquiladoras* sometimes becomes compressed by convection layers over the city, and this phenomenon is worse during the summer months.

Freezing temperatures occur an average of 65 days a year, mostly between November and February; the average low temperature during these months is 32° F. Climate-wise, the best months to visit El Paso are March, April, May, October, and early November, when the temperatures are neither too hot nor cold and the air is usually clear.

HISTORY

The Pass of the North
The first Europeans "discovered" El Paso del Norte ("The Pass of the North") during the Rodriguez-Chamuscado expedition of 1581. The discovery was considered significant because the pass provided access to the north for Spanish colonists in Mexico. Later opportunists coming from the east used the pass to continue westward.

In 1598, Don Juan de Oñate led a group of several hundred conquistadors from Santa Barbara, Mexico across the Chihuahuan Desert to the pass. They were lured by Indian stories of gold in the mountains of New Mexico and far West Texas. Most historians say the Spanish never found any substantial gold deposits, but one commonly recited legend says that Juan

de Oñate cached a vast treasure of gold, silver, and jewels in the Lost Padre Mine somewhere in the Franklin Mountains, on the northern outskirts of El Paso.

Sixty-one years after Don Juan came north, the first Spanish mission was established in what is now Juárez. The mission was named Nuestra Señora de Guadalupe, and the village that grew up around it was called El Paso del Norte. This settlement became an important stop on the Camino Real or "Royal Road," which extended between Chihuahua City and Santa Fe and later became known as the Chihuahua-Santa Fe Trail, the first road in North America.

Anglo-American Settlement
In 1680, El Paso del Norte received an influx of Spanish and Tigua Indian refugees from the Pueblo Indian Revolt in Ysleta, New Mexico. They called their new home Ysleta del Sur ("The Islet of the South"), and the Spanish-Indian settlements thrived for a time. In 1780 the Spanish military garrison of San Elizario was founded near Ysleta del Sur. The first Anglo-Americans began arriving in 1827, and by the late 1840s there were five Anglo settlements north of the Rio Grande. Although Juan María Ponce de León built a hacienda in what is now downtown El Paso, it was the Anglo settlement of Franklin, named for one of the principal settlers, that provided the political anchor for what later became the Texas Republic's El Paso.

The U.S. Army established Fort Bliss in 1848 to defend the area against Apache attacks. When the California Gold Rush of 1849 suddenly increased east-west traffic through the pass, two stagecoach lines were established, including the famous Butterfield Overland Mail (the first Butterfield Overland coach arrived in El Paso in 1858). During the Civil War, Fort Bliss briefly fell into the hands of the Confederacy, but Union troops from California regained control, and so it remained a federal post throughout most of the war.

During this same period, the French invaded Mexico and crowned Maximilian as emperor of Mexico. Mexican President Benito Juárez established a revolutionary government at El Paso del Norte, and following the Mexican defeat of the French in 1866 the city was renamed Juárez in his honor.

The Wild West

The Southern Pacific Railroad finally reached El Paso from California in 1881. The Santa Fe and Mexican Central railroads soon followed suit and El Paso was opened to the world at large. For the next 40 years or so, gunfighters, soldiers of fortune, Texas Rangers, cattle rustlers, banditos, and Mexican revolutionaries gave El Paso its reputation as "Six-Shooter Capital" of the United States. Famous marshalls came and went, among them Wyatt Earp, Bat Masterson, and Pat Garrett, and the fastest gunslinger in the West, John Wesley Hardin, was shot here in 1895.

The end of an era came with General Blackjack Pershing's expedition against Pancho Villa in 1916, which was based at Fort Bliss. Pershing failed to capture Pancho Villa, but the expanded military presence at Fort Bliss brought a measure of law and order to the El Paso area.

ECONOMY

El Paso's economy rests on Fort Bliss, tourism, agriculture, and the *maquiladora* industry, and the manufacture of boots and jeans. This is one of the only areas in the U.S. where long-staple Egyptian cotton is cultivated, along with the famous Mesilla Valley chile and an abundant crop of sweet onions. The growing number of *maquiladoras* on the Juárez side of the river infuses capital into El Paso, while bestowing Juárez with the lowest unemployment rate of any large city in Mexico.

Levi's, Wrangler, and several boot manufacturers operate large plants in El Paso, making the city the world's cowboy boots and jeans capital. Perhaps that's why Cormack McCarthy, author of the massively best-selling *All the Pretty Horses* and *The Crossing,* two postmodern, Western-genre novels, adds to the city's coffers by making the city his home.

SIGHTS

The Mission Trail

The oldest settlements in Texas grew up around Spanish missions and presidios established along the Rio Grande and the Camino Real near what are today El Paso and Juárez. The old Camino Real is now divided into State 20 (Alameda Ave.) and FM 258 (Socorro Dr.). The Mission Trail is marked by signs with mission symbols and mileage between missions, beginning at the Zaragosa exit off I-10, southeast of downtown El Paso, and ending at FM 1110 (Clint-San Elizario Rd.).

A leisurely drive along the eight-mile trail is definitely an El Paso must (tourist brochures often report it at 12 miles, but this includes San Lorenzo Church in Clint, which was neither a mission nor a presidio). As these are the earliest Spanish-Indian monuments in North America, they show more Indian influence than do the missions and presidios of Spanish California or Central Texas. Besides leading to the missions of Ysleta and Socorro and the presidio of San Elizario, the Mission Trail runs through El Paso's oldest Mexican and Indian districts, and there are several good restaurants, craft shops, and antique stores along the way. The Ysleta-Socorro area—unlike most of El Paso—is blessed with lots of trees.

None of the mission or presidio chapels charge admission fees, but donations for continued restoration are always welcome—there's usually a collection box near the entrance.

Tigua Indian Reservation

Two miles along the Mission Trail you'll enter the Tigua Indian Reservation (Ysleta del Sur Pueblo). The focus of the Tigua community for many visitors is the Cultural Center, which is situated in a living replica of a Tigua pueblo. This is the only part of the reservation open to the public and includes pottery, jewelry, woodcarving and weaving workshops, outdoor breadbaking in traditional hive-shaped adobe ovens, and a dance plaza where a variety of Pueblo social dances are occasionally performed for the public.

A new attraction, **Speaking Rock Super Bingo** (tel. 800-860-7724 or 915-870-7777), is a high-stakes bingo casino that charges $1-2 per sheet, with wins starting at $250 and jackpots of $1000-50,000. The casino is open Mon.-Thurs. 7-10 p.m., Fri.-Sat. 6-9 p.m. and 10 p.m.-1 a.m., Sunday 2-5 p.m. and 6-9 p.m.

Ysleta Mission

The original 1681 foundation and some of the

original adobe walls form part of the current mission chapel, which is adjacent to the Tigua Indian Reservation. Much of the mission was destroyed by a flooded Rio Grande in 1740 and again by a fire in 1907. Originally christened as Misión Santisma Sacramento and dedicated to St. Anthony, after it was rebuilt in 1908 the name was changed to Our Lady of Mount Carmel. In a niche over the entrance is a statue of St. Anthony. Next to the altar is a Santo Enterrio or Christ-in-a-coffin dating from 1722 which is used for Easter processions.

Socorro Mission

This mission is two miles east of Ysleta on FM 258 (Socorro Rd.). It's one day younger than Ysleta and was originally built by Piro Indians—like the Tiguas, refugees from the Pueblo Indian Revolt—as Nuestra Señora de los Piros del Socorro. An 1829 flood destroyed the original building and the site was moved to higher ground in 1840.

The Socorro chapel embodies probably the most uniquely Indian mission architecture in the country. The shape of the chapel facade is said to represent the Piro rainstorm deity. Inside, the distinctive hand-carved vigas or roof-beams are the handiwork of the Piros, salvaged from the original chapel. The vigas support latias or lattices of sotol, a desert shrub.

Next to the altar is a hand-carved wooden statue of San Miguel (St. Michael) with a legend attached to it. The story goes that in 1845 it was being transported by cart from Mexico to a church in New Mexico, but the cart miraculously became too heavy to move as it passed Socorro. So the Socorro parish took the statue for its own.

Although the Ysleta mission is one day older, the Socorro parish is considered the oldest active parish in the U.S. since Ysleta was apparently abandoned for a period of time during the 19th century.

THE TIGUA

The Tigua Indians are the oldest identifiable ethnic group in Texas, having lived in Ysleta del Sur (now simply called Ysleta) since 1680. They're a "displaced portion" of the Tiwa Pueblo Indians of New Mexico, and have chosen the Spanish spelling ("Tigua") to distinguish themselves from that group. The original Tiguas were converted to Christianity by Spanish missionaries and took St. Anthony as their patron saint. When a number of them fled the Pueblo Indian Revolt of 1680, they brought their patron saint with them, thus differentiating themselves from the Tiwas who remained behind. The Tiguas, along with a number of Piro Indians (whose community no longer survives), built the Ysleta del Sur mission in 1681 near the banks of the Rio Grande.

In spite of their devotion to St. Anthony, today's Tiguas still practice many of the traditional Pueblo customs practiced before the Spanish arrived, including a basic form of tribal government, some of the original ceremonial dances, the use of herbal medicine, and a pueblo-style living arrangement. Until recently, only tribal elders maintained the Tigua language, but efforts are now being made among the young people to revive Tigua as a means of tribal communication.

The Tiguas were not officially recognized as an Indian tribe by state and federal authorities until the mid-1960s. This came in the nick of time, since many Tigua Indian homelands were being foreclosed and their sense of identity was eroding. A Tribal Roll was established for Tiguas to make voluntary application for tribal membership. Membership must be approved by the Tribal Junta or their representatives, the Tribal Council, after verification of blood lines and blood quantum.

A Tribal Junta is a public meeting that settles all important tribal matters by consensus without any formal constitution or bylaws. The Junta selects members of the Tribal Council, which consists of a *cacique,* generally the oldest man in the tribe, who looks after ceremonial affairs; a war chief, assistant to the *cacique;* a governor and lieutenant governor, who act as administrators; and the *alguacil;* plus two members at large from the tribal community. The Council is authorized to represent the Tigua tribe in dealings with the Texas Indian Commission. Today there are around 600 Tigua Indians living on or near the 37-acre urban reservation.

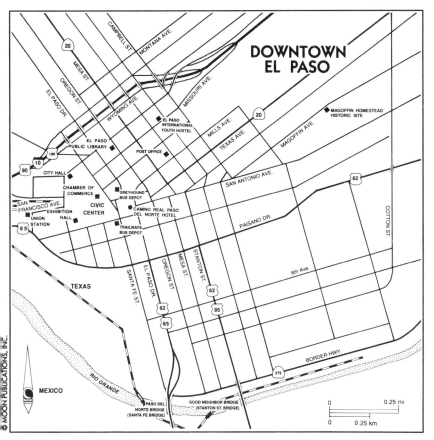

San Elizario Presidio Chapel

Six miles east of Socorro is the site of an old Spanish presidio or garrison. The San Elizario Presidio was originally established in 1774 at a nearby site and was moved to the current site at Hacienda de los Tiburcios in 1780. Following a flood, the chapel was reconstructed in 1877.

In front of the chapel are five state historical markers which detail Spanish expeditions to the area in 1581, 1582-83, and 1598. The impressive bell tower over the chapel supports four bells, and to the left of the entrance is a Virgin Mary shrine. The inside of this still-active chapel is striking, with a painted tin ceiling, stained glass windows, hand-carved wooden pews, and an ancient wooden confessional.

Museums

El Pasoans take great pride in their museums. While there's nothing here to compare with the museums of Dallas and Houston, for a city of half a million they fare pretty well. Entry to all those listed below is free of charge.

The **El Paso Museum of Art** (tel. 915-541-4040) is located in the 1910 home of former Senator W.W. Turney, at 1211 Montana Avenue. The west wing of the museum contains the permanent Kress Collection, which encompasses 59 paintings and sculptures by various European masters. The works of art are displayed in three galleries corresponding to the three classic periods of European art history. In the east wing are two galleries in which 15 to

20 temporary exhibits are presented. The EPMA also offers art classes, free tours, and a reference library for art historians and working artists. Hours are Tues.-Sat. 10 a.m.-5 p.m. and Sunday 1-5 p.m.

The **Americana/Southwestern Museum of Cultural History** (tel. 542-0394) is located in the Convention and Performing Arts Center on Santa Fe Street. Exhibits in this small museum display Pan-American and pre-Columbian art, especially ceramics, in a chronological fashion to recount the cultural history of the Southwest. Hours are Tues.-Sat. 10 a.m.-5 p.m.

Better is the **El Paso Centennial Museum** (tel. 747-5565) on the University of Texas at El Paso (UTEP) campus. The museum was established in 1936 during the state's centennial celebration and exhibits focus on the human and natural history of the region surrounding El Paso. Indian pottery, prehistoric tools, dinosaur remains, as well as local folk art and historical photographs from the late 19th century, are some of the more interesting displays. Open Tues.-Fri. 10 a.m.-4:30 p.m., Sat.-Sun. 1-5 p.m.

The **El Paso Museum of History** exhibits dioramas and period rooms that depict historical life in the El Paso area since the days of Spanish exploration. It was once the Cavalry Museum, so most displays are keyed to "men on horseback"—Indians, conquistadors, *vaqueros,* cowboys, U.S. cavalrymen. The museum is about 15 miles east of downtown off I-10 at the Americas Ave. exit (12901 Gateway West). Open Tues.-Sun. 9 a.m.-4:50 p.m.

The **Wilderness Park Museum** is an indoor-outdoor museum situated on 17 acres at the eastern edge of the Franklin Mountains. It's dedicated to natural and Indian history of the El Paso region, from the Paleo-Indian era to the present. A mile-long nature trail leads visitors through replicas of a Pueblo ruin, kiva (Indian meeting house), and pithouse. Inside the Diorama Hall are life-size dioramas depicting various scenes from Indian life. The Wilderness Park Museum is at 2000 Transmountain Rd. and is open Tues.-Sun. 9 a.m.-5 p.m.

Next to the Wilderness Park Museum at 4315 Transmountain Rd., the **Border Patrol Museum** (tel. 759-6060) displays rotating exhibits drawn from 30,000 pieces of donated memorabilia chronicling the history of the patrol since its 1924 inception. Admission is free; the museum is open Tues.-Sat. 9 a.m.-4:45 p.m.

Magoffin Homestead Historic Site
This adobe hacienda was built by El Paso pioneer Joseph Magoffin in a part of El Paso once known as Magoffinville. Finished in 1875, it's a splendid example of the Southwest Territorial architecture that flourished between 1865 and 1880. The four-foot-thick adobe walls are composed of handmade, sun-dried brick plastered and scored to make the house look as if it were built of stone. All the hand-hewn flooring and woodwork were brought from mountainous Mescalero, a hundred miles distant. The house is decorated in authentic period furnishings and accessories, much of which belonged to the original owners.

Six of the 19 rooms in the Magoffin Homestead are open to the public at 1120 Magoffin Avenue. From I-10 take the Cotton St. exit and follow Cotton St. south to Magoffin Avenue. Hours are Wed.-Sun. 9 a.m.-4 p.m.; admission is $1 adults, 50 cents for children, under six, no charge. Includes a guided tour.

Concordia Cemetery
This famous cemetery was named for the early 1840s settlement of Concordia established by Chihuahua trader Hugh Stephenson. When his wife died in 1856, Stephenson buried her here, and the ground slowly became the cemetery for all El Paso. It was divided into different sections according to various ethnic, religious, or civic divisions, and as you wander around you'll begin to discern how Chinese, Catholic, Jewish, Masonic, military, and other formal designations are clustered together. Many of the town's pioneering families are buried here.

Concordia's most famous resident is John Wesley Hardin, who felled more men than Billy the Kid and Jesse James combined and is said to have been the fastest gun in the West. Legend has it he won 40 gun duels before being shot in the head by lawman John Selman, who is also buried here. There are no signposts to Hardin's grave. To find it look for the entrance to the walled Chinese section of the cemetery; the gunfighter's headstone is just a little northwest of the west entrance to the Chinese section, in the undistinguished "Boot Hill" area for desperadoes who died with their boots on. The stone merely reads "John Wesley Hardin, 1853-1895." Superstitious visitors sometimes leave poker hands, Colt .45 cartridges, or votive candles beside the stone.

The cemetery is just north of I-10 at the Gateway North and US 54 interchange, which locals call the "spaghetti bowl"—you'll know why if you try to get here directly from the freeway. The easiest access to the cemetery is from Yandell Drive, which runs parallel to I-10. Coming west on I-10, take the Copia Street exit, make a right on Stevens and another right on Yandell.

Fort Bliss

The small frontier fort of the 1840s has grown into a 1.2-million-acre facility that is the largest air-defense establishment in the Western world and headquarters for the U.S. Army Air Defense, 11th Brigade. Well over 20,000 American troops are stationed here, including the only stateside armored cavalry regiment. There are also uncounted military personnel from 25 different nations who come to the Air Defense School for training.

Fort Bliss is open to the public and features four museums. The museum of greatest general interest is the **Fort Bliss Museum** (tel. 915-568-4518) at Pershing and Pleasanton, which consists of a group of adobe buildings that are exact replicas of the original fort as it appeared between 1848 and 1868. A 30-star American flag, representing the 30 U.S. states of the period, flies over the museum, the only such flag authorized for public display in the country. Three of the buildings contain displays that chronicle the 100-year history of Fort Bliss from 1848 to 1948—the fort actually had five different locations in and around El Paso. The museum is open daily 9 a.m.-4:30 p.m. and admission is free.

Of interest to military history buffs are these museums: the **Air Defense Artillery Museum** (tel. 568-5412), Building 5000, Pleasanton Rd., open daily 9 a.m.-4:30 p.m., which includes an outdoor display of antiaircraft weapons from around the world; the **Cavalry Museum,** Building 2407, at Forest and Chaffee roads, open Mon.-Fri. 9 a.m.-4:30 p.m., which chronicles the history of the U.S. Cavalry since 1856 with photos, paintings, armored vehicle displays,

and other artifacts; and the **Museum of the Noncommissioned Officer,** Building 11331, 5th and Barksdale, Biggs Army Airfield, open Mon.-Fri. 9 a.m.-4 p.m. and Sat.-Sun. noon-4 p.m., which pays tribute to the evolutionary development of the NCO since the Civil War—Fort Bliss is the home of the U.S. Army Sergeant Majors Academy. Admission to all these museums is free of charge.

Chamizal National Memorial

The Chamizal plains area along the Rio Grande that is now Chamizal National Memorial was once a serious bone of contention between the U.S. and Mexican governments. Because the river occasionally changed course, neither side was able to establish a mutually agreed-upon border. Finally, in 1963, the two governments agreed to build a concrete channel from which the river could not stray. At the time the agreement was reached, this meant an 823-acre gain for Mexico.

Both sides chose to develop their portions of the Chamizal as national parks. The American side encompasses 55 acres, including a visitor's center that contains a border history museum, information desk, art gallery, and 500-seat theater. The grounds are used for picnicking and outdoor performances during the spring, summer, and early fall. The Border Folk Festival is held here in October, the Siglo de Oro Drama Festival in March.

The entrance to the park is off Paisano Dr. (US 62) on San Marcial Street. Hours are daily 8 a.m.-5 p.m., year round; on days when there are outdoor performances, it's open till 11 p.m. Admission is free, though theater performances may occasionally charge admission fees.

The Mexican side, Parque Conmemorativo Chamizal, encompasses 700 acres of well-landscaped grounds, botanical gardens, and an archaeological museum. Access is from Avenida de las Americas, via the Bridge of the Americas (also called Cordova Bridge) from I-10 on the El Paso side.

Paso del Norte Hotel

Now managed by Mexico's Camino Real chain, this historic hotel was erected between 1908 and 1912 by an architect inspired by the great hotels of San Francisco. Pancho Villa, President Taft, and General Blackjack Pershing have all been guests here, and President Johnson and Mexican President Díaz-Ordaz signed the Chamizal agreement in the hotel. During downtown El Paso's postwar decline, the hotel closed for a time and was eventually sold to Mexican interests for $1 million in 1972. In 1981 the Westin chain undertook an extensive, $2 million renovation, and today the place probably looks better than when it first opened.

Even if you're not staying here, you can get a taste of history by visiting the hotel's Dome Bar, which was the original lobby. A Tiffany dome overhangs the round, marble-topped bar and has been insured by Lloyd's of London for a reputed $1.2 million. An incredible array of marble walls, columns, and flooring surround the bar—in cherrystone, black, and pink marble. The building has earned a listing with the U.S. Department of Interior's National Register of Historic Places.

The Camino Real Paso del Norte is located at the junction of El Paso, San Francisco, and Santa Fe streets downtown. For information on rates, see the "El Paso Hotels and Motels" chart.

Sierra del Cristo Rey
At the junction of Texas, New Mexico, and Mexico, atop a 4,756-foot peak, a Cristo Rey or "Christ the King" statue overlooks El Paso, visible from I-10 as you drive west into New Mexico. Sculptor Urbici Soler carved the figure from Cordova cream limestone in 1938; it's identical in style and scale to the Christ on the Cross overlooking Rio de Janeiro in Brazil.

On the last Sunday of October, Sierra del Cristo Rey is the site of an annual procession in which hundreds of worshippers climb two and a half miles along a winding footpath to reach the top via the 14 Stations of the Cross. Hiking to the shrine alone is not advisable due to the potential for robbery in this remote area. Wait for the annual pageant or assemble a small group.

University of Texas at El Paso
UTEP was founded in 1913 as the Texas State School of Mines and Metallurgy. It became Texas Western College in 1949 and was finally brought into the University of Texas system in 1967. The school's strongest departments are still geology and metallurgy, but the curriculum

has broadened to include the liberal arts, of which international relations (especially inter-American relations) and Spanish linguistics enjoy good reputations. Student enrollment averages around 17,000 a year and includes more Mexican students than any other university in the United States.

The most outstanding visual feature of the university is its resemblance to a Himalayan lamasery. The original buildings were designed in this style in 1914 after the first dean's wife saw pictures of Bhutanese lamaseries in an issue of *National Geographic*. The mountain setting of the pictures reminded her of El Paso, so she convinced her husband to build the university following a similar architectural style. The original theme has been preserved in newer buildings as well.

Each December, UTEP's Sun Bowl Stadium is the venue for the nation's second-oldest postseason college football match.

Viewpoints
You can enjoy panoramic views of El Paso and Juárez from aptly named Scenic Drive, which skirts the southern edge of the Franklin Mountains and passes tiny Murchison Park. The park features a parking lot and offers the best view of the area.

The Transmountain Rd. cuts through the Franklin Mountains from west to east and affords impressive views at several points. Most of the road is actually a four-lane highway, with plenty of space to pull off to the side along the way. To get there from the west, take the Transmountain Rd. exit off I-10 at Canutillo; from the east, access from the North-South Freeway (US 54).

ACROSS THE BORDER TO JUAREZ

The fourth-largest city in Mexico, and probably the largest border city in the world, Ciudad Juárez is a bursting metropolis 1,128 meters (3,760 feet) above sea level on the Rio Grande opposite El Paso. The city capitalizes on its location at the junction of three major interstate highways (Mexico 45, I-25, and I-10) and several railways. Rail and truck shipping are major sources of income, along with revenue from 13 industrial parks skirting the city's perimeters.

Juárez also serves as an important regional education center, with four major colleges and universities: Universidad Autónoma de Cd. Juárez, Instituto Tecnológico de Cd. Juárez, Instituto Tecnológico de Monterrey, and Universidad Autónoma de Chihuahua.

If you make it to El Paso, a visit to Juárez is a must. Besides the tourist strips along Avenida Juárez and Avenida Lincoln, the city offers a historic plaza with a classic cathedral and 17th-century mission, great Mexican restaurants, bullfighting, *charreada* (Mexican rodeo), and bargains on handmade goods such as boots and weavings, as well as tobacco and liquor.

Sights

Misión Nuestra Señora de Guadalupe: Facing the west side of Plaza Principal (also called Plaza de Armas) between the Palacio Municipal and Mercado Cuauhtémoc, off Calle Mariscal downtown, is this humble stone church dwarfed by the modern cathedral next door.

To appreciate Guadalupe's historic charm, you must enter the church, walk halfway down the center aisle, and look up to see the superb hand-carved *vigas* (wooden roof beams) and *coro* (choir mezzanine). The church was built between 1668 and 1670 and has been restored numerous times.

Museo Histórico de Cd. Juárez: This INAH-sponsored museum in the recently restored Antigua Aduana (Old Customs) building, on Av. 16 de Septiembre between Av. Juárez and Av. Lerdo, is perhaps the city's most important cultural center. The building's central hall hosts temporary, rotating exhibits on history, archaeology, or anthropology, while rooms surrounding the hall contain the museum's permanent collection.

The first room, Sala 1, begins with Chihuahuan prehistory, including displays on the Conchos, Tobosos, Tepehuanes, Sumas, and Jumanos, while Sala 2 is entirely devoted to the Paquimé culture. Salas 3 and 4 continue with the Spanish conquest, Mexican independence and the Virreinato, followed by the Epoca Nacional and the history of the Chamizal (Sala 5), La Apachería and the Porfiriato (Salas 6, 7, and 8), and the Mexican Revolution (Salas 8 and 9).

American and European film programs are presented twice a week in the museum's auditorium. The museum is open Tues.-Sun. 10 a.m.-6 p.m.; admission is free.

Museo de Arte: Sponsored by the Instituto Nacional de Bellas Artes, this small museum in the former PRONAF center (now called Plaza de las Americas) houses rotating contemporary art exhibits of varying quality. Museum hours are Tues.-Sun. 10 a.m.-6 p.m.; free admission.

The Cine Club Francés screens French films for the public (free admission) at the Museo de Arte every Sunday evening at 7:30 p.m.

Museo de la Revolución: On the second floor of Pueblito Mexicano in Plaza de las Americas, this small commercial operation is devoted to the 1910-20 Mexican Revolution, with a heavy emphasis on local hero Francisco Villa. Displays include weaponry, period clothing, historic photos, and newspapers from the era. Open Tues.-Sun. 10 a.m.-10 p.m.; admission is 50 cents.

Parque Conmemorativo Chamizal: Chamizal is a local favorite for long-distance walkers and joggers who savor its shady trees, neat landscaping, and overall tranquility. Other assets include a huge field of basketball courts near Av. Malecón, a swimming pool, an exposition center, and a soccer stadium used by the Cobras, a first-division pro team since 1987.

The park's **Museo de Antropología e Historia,** open Tues.-Sun. 9 a.m.-7 p.m. (free admission), contains a small collection of artifacts and the usual revolution-era photos, but the museum's real attraction is behind the building itself—a garden with ponds, flowers, trees, and large-scale reproductions of sculpture from ancient Mayan, Aztec, Toltec, Zapotec, Mixtec, Teotihuacan, Olmec, Tarascan, Totonac, and Huastec cultures. Although some of the reproductions are unfortunately deteriorating, a tour of the garden makes a nice stroll.

The park is closed to outside traffic in July, when it's used for Formula 3 racing. Horsecart rides are available in the park year round for US$1.60 per person.

According to the Juárez tourist office, a US$110 million theme park—complete with replicas of Mexico's historical attractions—is planned for some portion of Chamizal in the near future.

EL PASO-JUAREZ

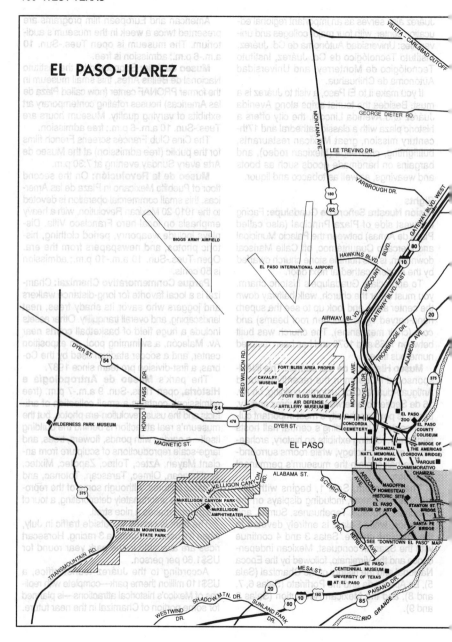

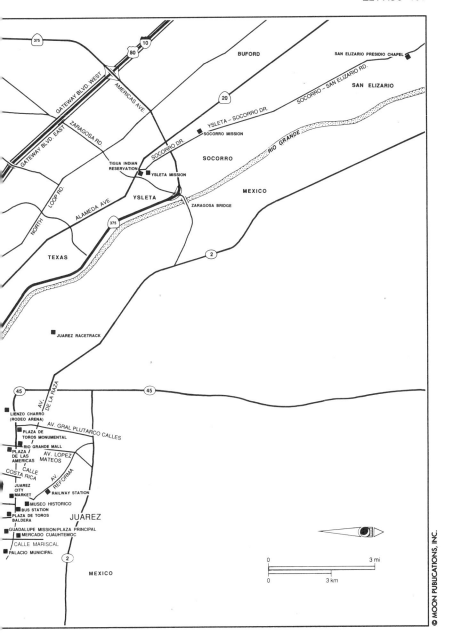

Getting There

On Foot: The easiest way to visit Juárez on day trips is to walk 10 minutes across the Santa Fe Street Bridge (also called Paso del Norte Bridge) from downtown El Paso. You can also drive across this bridge, but the traffic scene is intense. There are several parking lots near the El Paso side of the bridge. The toll for crossing this bridge is 10 cents for pedestrians, 25 cents for cars. To return to El Paso from this part of Juárez, you must take the parallel Stanton Bridge.

Driving: If you're driving, the best way to get to Juárez is via the Cordova Bridge (Bridge of the Americas) on I-10. This takes you past Parque Conmemorativo Chamizal and toward Av. Lincoln, where Plaza de las Armas and the Centro Artesanal are located. To reach the more interesting plaza area of town, you must turn right at Av. 16 de Septiembre and proceed 15 blocks or so till you reach Av. Juárez—then pray for a parking spot!

Yet a fourth bridge crossing is via Zaragosa St. off I-10, near Ysleta. After crossing the bridge, Zaragosa St. meets Federal Mexico Hwy. 2, which, if you turn right, becomes Av. de la Raza, which eventually turns into Av. 16 de Septiembre.

Border Jumper: The **El Paso-Juárez Trolley Co.** (tel. 915-544-0061 in El Paso) operates this trolley-style bus between downtown El Paso and Juárez. The trolley departs from the El Paso Civic Center and makes eight stops along a circular route via the Cordova Bridge, Plaza de las Americas (Pueblito Mexicano), Salón Mexico (bar/restaurant/disco), Chihuahua Charlie's (bar/restaurant), and Mercado Juárez (City Market) before returning to El Paso via the Santa Fe Bridge. The fare is $10 per person roundtrip; trolleys leave hourly 9 a.m.-4 p.m. Nov.-March, 10 a.m.-5 p.m. April-October. A free shuttle service to the Civic Center terminal is available from the following hotels: Camino Real Paso del Norte, Holiday Inn (Sunland Park), El Paso Airport Hilton, Howard Johnson Lodge, Embassy Suites, Radisson Suite Inn.

Border Taxis: A number of taxicab companies on the El Paso side specialize in quick trips across the border, including **Texas Cab** (tel. 562-0033), **Border Taxi** (tel. 565-1440), and **Yellow Cab** (tel. 533-3433). A short trip between downtown El Paso and downtown Cd. Juárez costs US$10-13. The fare from the Mexican side is about the same; there's a taxi stand near the Stanton St. Bridge.

ACCOMMODATIONS

Hotel and Motels

El Paso features hundreds of rooms ranging from around $18 to $130 a night. Most hotels and motels in the city are clustered in the airport/mid-city area and east of town along I-10. To a lesser extent, there are also choices downtown and west of the city. Any location in the city is convenient if you have a car; for those relying on foot and public transit, a downtown location is the most convenient; you can walk to Juárez from downtown.

The accompanying chart is representative of the kinds of places available and also lists some of the choicest spots, like the Camino Real Paso del Norte. The El Paso Convention and Visitors Bureau publishes an *Accommodations and Dining Guide* that lists most of the hotels and motels in El Paso—unfortunately, rates aren't listed. The guide is available at the Bureau office at One Civic Center Plaza and at Texas Information Centers around the state.

Youth Hostel

The **El Paso International Youth Hostel/Gardner Hotel** (tel. 915-532-3661) is located at 311 E. Franklin Ave. in downtown El Paso. The building is on the El Paso Historic Register and John Dillinger purportedly stayed here just before he was captured in Tucson. The location is good; a mile from Juárez, and five to six blocks from the Greyhound-Trailways bus depot.

Room rates are the same for AYH or Hostelling International members and non-members: $17 s, 24 d for a room with bath in the hall, $24 s, $26 d for rooms with shared bath, and $26 s, $30 d for rooms with private bath. The hostel offers discounts for weekly and monthly stays. Dorm rooms are $12 for members, $14 for nonmembers.

Camping

The nearest state park campground is Hueco Tanks State Park, 32 miles east of downtown El

EL PASO HOTELS AND MOTELS

Add 14% hotel tax to all rates. Area code: 915.

DOWNTOWN

Cliff Inn; 1600 Cliff Dr.; tel. 533-6700; $62; pool, tennis, kitchenettes

Park Place; 325 N. Kansas; tel. 533-8241; $89; pool, airport shuttle

TraveLodge City Center; 409 E. Missouri; tel. 544-3333 or (800) 654-2000; $55; heated pool, airport shuttle

Camino Real Paso del Norte; 101 S. El Paso; tel. 534-3000 or (800) 228-3000; $109-145; health club, historic, 50% weekend discount, senior discount; heated pool; airport shuttle

AIRPORT/MID-CITY

Best Western Airport Inn; 7144 Gateway E; tel. 779-7700 or (800) 528-1234; $41-64; heated pool, airport shuttle

Coral Motel; 6420 Montana Ave.; tel. 772-3263; $30-38; pool, senior discount

Econo Lodge; 6363 Montana Ave.; tel. 778-1097; $32-36; small pool, weekly rates, airport shuttle

El Parador; 6400 Montana Ave.; tel. 772-4231; $34-40; pool, airport shuttle

El Paso Airport Hilton; 2027 Airway Blvd.; tel. 778-4241 or (800) HILTONS; $85-95; health club, airport shuttle

El Paso Marriott; 1600 Airway Blvd.; tel. 779-3300 or (800) 228-9290; $64-114; pools, airport shuttle, weekend discounts

Embassy Suites; 5100 Gateway E; tel. 779-6222 or (800) EMBASSY; $98-158; pool, health club, kitchenettes, complimentary breakfast, airport shuttle

Holiday Inn, Airport; I-10 and Airway Blvd.; tel. 778-6411 or (800) HOLIDAY; $59-64; pool, airport shuttle

Holiday Inn Sunland Park; 900 Sunland Park Dr.; tel. 833-2900 or (800) HOLIDAY; $63-72; pool, monthly rates

La Quinta; 7550 Gateway E; tel. 778-9312 or (800) 531-5900; $49-63; heated pool, airport shuttle

Radisson Suite Inn; 1770 Airway Blvd.; tel. 772-3333 or (800) 333-3333; $76-105; pool, health club, kitchenettes, complimentary breakfast, airport shuttle

WEST

Executive Inn; 500 E. Executive Center Blvd.; tel. 532-8981 or (800) 234-8981; $42-47; pool, senior and weekend discounts, complimentary continental breakfast, airport shuttle

La Quinta; 7550 Remcon Circle; tel. 833-2522 or (800) 531-5900; $49-63; pool

Motel 6; 7840 N. Mesa; tel. 584-2129; $24.95 plus $6 each additional person; pool

Warren Inn; 4748 N. Mesa; tel. 544-4494; $28-35; pool, kitchenettes, senior discount

EAST

Comfort Inn; 900 Yarbrough; tel. 594-9111 or (800) 226-5150; $40-44; pool, airport shuttle

Howard Johnson Lodge; 8887 Gateway W; tel. 591-9471; $43-50; pool, airport shuttle, senior discount

Motel 6; 11049 Gateway W; tel. 594-8533; $24.95 plus $6 each additional person; pool

---

Paso along US 62/180 and RM 2775. During the week, the park is virtually deserted—except during rockclimbing season, late October through February—so there are almost always campsites available. A Texas Conservation Passport is a prerequisite for park entry. For information on camping facilities, see "Hueco Tanks State Park," below.

RV Parks
Mission RV Park (tel. 915-859-1133), at I-10

and Americas Ave. (exit 34), is the largest and most modern of the local RV facilities. Each of its 118 drive-through slots goes for $17 a day, with discounts for long-term stays. On the premises are a pool and jacuzzi, tennis and basketball courts, and a recreation hall with shuffleboard, billiards, and table tennis.

Four more RV parks are located about 10-15 miles east of El Paso, off I-10 or US 62/180. All charge around $15 a night for full hookups, with discounts for long-term stays. **Roadrunner**

Travel Trailer Park (tel. 598-4469) is at 1212 Lafayette, about 10 miles east off I-10. **Western Horizon Campground** (tel. 852-3388) and **Samson RV Park** (tel. 859-8383) are both just off I-10 at the Horizon exit. **Cotton Valley RV Park** (tel. 851-2137) is eight miles east of the city at the Clint exit. **Desert Oasis Park** (tel. 855-3366) lies 16 miles east of town on US 62/180, convenient to El Paso and Hueco Tanks.

There's also one RV park just northeast of town near the east edge of the Franklin Mountains—**Starlight Mobile Home Park** (tel. 755-5768) at Dyer (US 54) and Transmountain Road.

FOOD

El Paso fancies itself the Mexican food capital of Texas—of the *world*, if you ask some of the more ambitious residents. And there is indeed a good variety of Mexican restaurants here, most serving good ol' Tex-Mex. The El Paso Convention and Visitors Bureau's *Accommodations and Dining Guide* contains a comprehensive list of reliable eateries, including price ranges. Restaurants across the river in Juárez are especially good value.

Dress for almost all restaurants in El Paso is casual, more so than in Dallas, Houston, or even San Antonio. The more expensive places often require reservations, however, so be sure to call ahead. It's a good idea to call anyway, to make sure a place is open, as restaurant hours change frequently in Texas's fluctuating economy. The following restaurants have either been duly tested by the author or enjoy solid reputations among El Paso residents. Per person price ranges, excluding beverages, are marked $ for inexpensive (under $8), $$ for moderate ($8-15), $$$ for expensive (over $15).

Asian
Several Chinese and Japanese restaurants are located on the east side of town, between I-10 and Montana.
$ to $$ **Shangri-La:** An old, established Cantonese restaurant in Juárez owned by Paco Wong. The menu is extensive and consistent. At 133 Av. de las Americas (tel. 915-546-3837, or in Juárez 13-00-33). Open daily for lunch and dinner.

$ to $$ **Delhi Palace:** A good spot for North Indian dishes. The weekday lunch buffet is a bargain. Near the airport at 1160 Airway (tel. 772-9334); open daily for lunch and dinner.

Barbecue
El Paso, like most sizable Texas towns, features plenty of barbecue joints. In El Paso, they're mostly Central and West Texas style, and none really stand out.
$ to $$ **Buck's Bar-B-Que:** All the usual—brisket, links, and ribs, plus chicken. At 9496 Dyer (tel. 915-755-1356); open daily for breakfast, lunch, and dinner.
$ to $$ **Buffalo Soldiers BBQ:** Vinegar-laced East Texas-style barbecued ribs and brisket amidst memorabilia from the heyday of the state's famous African-American cavalry. Leave room for the sweet potato pie. At 4005 Fort Blvd. (tel. 566-2300). Open Mon.-Thurs. 5-7 p.m., Fri. 5-9 p.m., Sat. 11 a.m.-9 p.m.
$ to $$ **The State Line:** Part of a statewide Texas barbecue chain that originated in Austin. The quality is consistent and the place bakes its own bread—homemade ice cream, too. In addition to the usual barbecue setup, The State Line also serves steaks. At 1222 Sunland Park Dr. (tel. 581-3371). Open daily for lunch and dinner.

Burgers
El Paso features the usual American franchises like McDonald's and Dairy Queen, but with El Paso twists like green-chile cheeseburgers, tacos, and gorditas. Two unusual places for burgers, fries, and shakes are:
$ to $$ **El Paso Surf Club:** A student hangout across from UTEP with a bar, dining room, and outdoor patio. The logo depicts a surfboard propped against a cactus. At 2500 N. Mesa (tel. 915-544-7873); open daily for lunch and dinner.
$ **Hudson's Grill:** Here the theme is 1950s Americana. In addition to the usual burger and fries selection is a daily "blue plate special" that might include chicken-fried steak or other Texas favorites. At 1770 Lee Trevino Dr. (tel. 595-2769), open daily for lunch and dinner.

European
El Paso's not exactly a mecca for connoisseurs of continental cuisine, but there are a handful of restaurants that specialize in European food.

$$-$$$ **Bella Napoli:** Typical middle-America Italian, with Chianti-bottle candleholders on checkered tablecloths. Good, mostly Neapolitan menu. At 6331 N. Mesa (tel. 915-584-3321), open Tues.-Sun. for lunch and dinner.

$$$ **The Dome Grill:** One of El Paso's most refined dining venues, sited in the historic Camino Real Paso del Norte hotel. The kitchen specializes in continental dishes with a sometimes nouvelle approach. Steak and seafood also available. At 101 S. El Paso (tel. 534-3010), open daily for lunch and dinner.

$$ **Günther's Edelweiss:** Serves good Bavarian cuisine in a kitschy German decor. At 11055 Gateway W. (tel. 592-1084), open Tues.-Sun. for lunch and dinner.

Mexican

$ **Avila's:** Probably El Paso's most well-known Mexican restaurant, and deservedly so. The extensive menu is classic Tex-Mex, with no orange cheese, and features unique dishes such as tri-color enchiladas, chile relleno burritos, *chilaquiles,* and an endless assortment of combination plates. All meals are served with fresh sopapillas and/or tortillas. There are two locations, one on the east side and one on the west side—only the east side restaurant serves margaritas, both serve beer. The westside Avila's is at 6232 N. Mesa (tel. 915-584-3621). The east side location is at 10600 Montana (tel. 598-3333). Both open daily for lunch and dinner.

$$ to $$$ **Cafe Central:** Mexican in inspiration only, the ever-changing menu at this tony spot features such marvelous sepcialties as *frutas del mar,* a delicately sauces shellfish extravaganza, and *tacos tres colores,* marinated and grilled lobster, chicken, and beef folded into handmade corn tortillas. Open Mon.-Sat. for lunch and dinner. Live jazz weekend nights. Opposite the Camino Real Paso del Norte Hotel at 1 Texas Court (tel. 545-2233).

$$ to $$$ **Chihuahua Charlie's Bar & Grill:** The northernmost outpost—in Mexico, that is—of the famed Grupo Anderson chain, Charlie's features a menu of original recipes based on such familiar Chihuahua standards as *carne asada* and *queso fundido,* along with homemade tortillas and fresh seafood specialties like tequila shrimp and *huachinango veracruzano.* Open daily 8 a.m.-1 a.m.; live music

Wednesday and Sunday. Located at Paseo Triunfo de la República 2525, Juárez (tel. 13-99-40).

$ **Delicious Mexican Eatery:** Despite the unimaginative name, this casual restaurant is worth seeking out for chiles rellenos and the exemplary *gorditas,* thick pita-like corn tortillas stuffed with your choice of fillings. Two locations: 3314 Fort Blvd. (tel. 566-1396) and 1335 Montwood (tel. 857-1396). Open daily for breakfast, lunch, and dinner.

$ **Forti's Mexican Elder:** Another long-time El Paso favorite. The specialties here include fajitas and *tacos al carbón.* Forti's is located at 321 Chelsea, at the Paisano exit off I-10 (tel. 772-0066). Open daily for lunch and dinner.

$ to $$ **Griggs Gourmet New Mexican Food:** Sometimes called Señor Juan's, Griggs serves food New Mexican or Santa Fe style—not as fiery as Tex-Mex, but still tasty. At 9007 Montana on the west side (tel. 598-3451); second branch at 5800 Doniphan (tel. 584-0451). Open daily for lunch and dinner.

$ **Gussie's Tamales and Mexican Food:** This east side take-out joint at 2200 Piedras (tel. 566-8209) sells tamales by the dozen, *pan dulce* (Mexican pastries), *menudo* and other Mexican-style delicatessen foods. Open daily 8 a.m.-8 p.m.

$ **H&H Car Wash:** Whether or not you go for the $8.50 car wash, the hearty Mexican breakfast at the adjoining diner is fortifying enough for any road trip. The house specialty is *picadillo,* ground beef stir-fried with chilies, onions, and tomatoes. Two locations: 701 E. Yandell at Ochoa (tel. 533-1144) and 8630 Dyer St. (tel. 755-2131). Open Mon.-Sat. for breakfast and lunch.

$ **La Hacienda:** An inexpensive Mexican restaurant located in an 1880s building once part of one of Fort Bliss's former locations, right near the Rio Grande. Combination plates are huge; one of the few Mexican places in El Paso open for breakfast. At 1720 W. Paisano, under the Yandell overpass (tel. 532-5094). Open daily for breakfast, lunch, and dinner.

$ **Julio's Cafe Corona:** Once touted as Juárez's best Mexican eatery, Julio's now has an El Paso location as well. Caldo Tlapeño, a spicy chicken-avocado soup, and Veracruz-style bass are among the highlights here. Other offerings exemplify the El Paso/New Mexico style of cooking, with lots of deep red chile sauces. In Juárez, the restaurant is located at the intersection of Av. de las Americas and Av. 16 de Septiembre (tel. 13-33-97). In El Paso, Julio's is at 8050 Gateway E (tel. 591-7676). Open daily for breakfast, lunch, and dinner.

$ **Leo's:** Very similar to Avila's but a tad cheaper. El Pasoans argue about which is better. The four locations are 2285 Trawood (tel. 591-2511); 5315 Hondo Pass (tel. 757-0505); 5103 Montana (tel. 566-4972); 8001 N. Mesa (tel. 833-1189); and 7872 N. Loop (tel. 593-9025). All open daily for lunch and dinner.

$ **Taco Cabana:** An ever-dependable drive-in open 24 hours. At 1777 Lee Trevino (tel. 595-8898) and 5866 N. Mesa (tel. 833-9337).

$$ **Viva México:** The walls of the large, circular dining room are painted to look like a colonial cityscape in silhouette—kind of corny—but the food is very dependable, very Mexican, and the clientele more local than gringo. The attached Cantina El Atorón serves "Pancho Villas" and *vampiros,* two typical Chihuahuan cocktails. Open Mon.-Thurs. 8 a.m.-2 a.m., Fri.-Sat. 8 a.m.-3 a.m. On the first floor of Pueblito Mexicano, Av. de las Americas, Juárez (tel. 29-01-56).

Seafood

El Paso and Juárez are a good distance from both oceans and the Gulf, so seafood is not an area specialty. Best to stick with freshwater fish (e.g., black bass) caught in nearby lakes or streams.

$$ **Nuevo Martino:** As with Chinese food, Juárez is the place to go for the best seafood in the area. Extensive menu. At Av. Juárez 643 (tel. 12-33-70), within walking distance of downtown El Paso. Open daily for lunch and dinner.

$$ to $$$ **Pelican's:** A good local reputation on the El Paso side. Two locations, on the west side at 130 Shadow Mountain (tel. 915-581-1392) and on the east side at 9077 Gateway W (tel. 591-8139). Open Tues.-Sun. for dinner only.

$ to $$$ **Seafood Galley:** One of the first seafood places ever established in El Paso. Standard American seafood selection, specializing in fried dishes. Fresh oysters available here. At 1130 Geronimo (tel. 779-8388).

Steak

$$ **Cattleman's Steakhouse at Indian Cliffs Ranch:** Though 33 miles southwest of the I-10/US 54 interchange in El Paso, near Fabéns, this is always cited by El Pasoans as the best steak around. *People* magazine even called it the best steak in the United States. Along with steak, house specialities include mesquite-smoked barbecue and pineapple-laced coleslaw. Indian Cliffs Ranch is a great place to take children, as there are all kinds of free recreational opportunities—a small children's zoo, playground, "Fort Apache." Get a window or outdoor table as the desert sunset is beautiful. Free hayrides on Sundays, weather permitting. Take I-10 west to the Fabens exit (28 miles), then north for five miles on FM 793. Open Mon.-Fri. 4:30-10 p.m., Saturday 4-10 p.m., Sunday noon-9 p.m. (tel. 915-544-3200).

$$ to $$$ **Restaurant Nuevo Martino:** In the heart of the Av. Juárez bar/restaurant/disco strip, this venerable establishment is known for steak Milanesa (Mexico's version of chicken-fried steak) and Spanish brochette—skewered chunks of beef, onions, tomatoes, and green peppers served over Spanish rice. Open 11 a.m.-midnight daily; Av. Juárez 643, Juárez (tel. 12-33-70).

ENTERTAINMENT

Clubs and Bars

El Paso's hot spots for C&W dancing are **McGee's** (tel. 915-592-995) at 8750 E. Gateway E, **Dallas** (tel. 598-1309) at 1840 Lee Trevino, and **Pistoleros Saloon & Grill** (tel. 833-9387). All are open nightly but charge a $3-4 cover only on weekends. Pistoleros customers can try their luck at live bullriding Fri.-Sat. nights at 8:30 p.m.

For rock and Top 40, the **El Paso Surf Club** (tel. 544-7873) at 2500 N. Mesa is popular. DJs handle the Sun.-Wed. program while live bands perform Thurs.-Sat., when there's a small cover charge. **Club 101** (tel. 544-2101) is the center for El Paso's alternative music scene; on most nights there's recorded dance music but live acts perform occasionally as well.

The classiest disco in town is **Uptown** in the Paso del Norte Hotel. A cover is collected on weekends.

Juárez: Av. Juárez is lined with bars and small discos, but none really live up to the town's former wild reputation—especially since they close everything down at midnight, purportedly to curb teenage alcoholism in Juárez. Avenida Juárez's real heyday stretched from the Prohibition years through the '50s. A few of the classic bars still hang on, including **El Kentucky Club,** at 629 Av. Juárez in a building that has been a cantina or bar for nearly 150 years, and the amazing **Cavern of Music**—also called Las Glutas Bar—near the intersection of Av. Juárez and Ignacio Mejia. The women's room at Las Glutas has a famous statuette of Adam with movable fig leaf—lift the leaf and flashing lights go on in the bar. Behind the plaza area—in perfect irony, not far from the cathedral—is "Boy's Town," the Juárez redlight district. Warning: a sign that reads "ladies bar" doesn't mean it's a bar for ladies; on the contrary, it's a bar for men looking for ladies.

Just opposite the bridge is a cluster of bars and discos catering almost exclusively to an El Paso crowd, including **XO Laser, Fantasy, Spanky's, Cheers Video Bar,** and **Tequila Derby.** The next couple of streets west of Av. Juárez, particularly Calle Mariscal, are devoted to go-go bars—which do not, as promised by street touts, feature topless or nude dancers but rather young women dressed in bikinis. Topless dancing is illegal in Juárez.

At the southern end of the avenue is a cluster of ranchero bars featuring dancing to live *norteña* music. Although this end of the avenue has a rough reputation, the clubs with cover charges (usually around US$2.50) are generally pretty safe. **El Sinaloense** on Av. Juárez, just north of 16 de Septiembre, usually has the best bands.

Radio

The liveliest FM radio station in El Paso is KBNA ("K-Buena") at FM 97.5. Bilingual DJs on KBNA play a great mix of *conjunto,* South Texas R&B, soul, and other jumpin' music. For more salsa, listen to Juárez's XEWR-AM 1110, where you can hear tunes by Mexican bands like Los Teen Tops and Rebeldes de Rock. El Paso's most popular C&W stations are KHEY-FM 96 and KSET-FM 94.7. The University of Texas at El Paso's FM station (KTEP 88.5) is also quite

good and plays a variety of non-commercial music.

Viva! El Paso Outdoor Pageant

This outdoor musical drama pays tribute to the area's 400-year history with creative sets, period costuming, special effects, dancing, music, and action sequences. It's held from the last week of June through the first week of September at McKelligon Canyon Amphitheater, on McKelligon Canyon off Alabama, Thurs.-Sat. at 8:30 p.m. Tickets are $6-10 for adults; $5-9 for those over 65, active military members, and children 13-17; $3-7 for under 13. Barbecue dinners are available for an extra charge beginning at 6:30 p.m. Call (915) 565-6900 or Ticketmaster for more information.

Racetracks, Off-Track Betting, and Sports Book

The **Juárez Racetrack** (tel. 542-1942), off Av. Vicente Guerrero to the east of Plaza de las Americas, is primarily a *galgodromo* (dog track) and features greyhound racing Wed.-Sat. at 8 p.m. year round; horse races are occasionally held during the summer. Seats in the air-conditioned general admission section cost US50 cents, while the Jockey Club section upstairs runs US$3. The advantages to Jockey Club seating are giant-screen replay and table service for food and beverages. A bar downstairs offers off-track betting and sports book, TV tables for watching several races and sports events, and full food and beverage service. The racetrack operates shuttle buses to and from several of the city's major hotels.

Sunland Park Racetrack (tel. 505-589-8989), across the state border in New Mexico, about five miles west of El Paso via I-10, offers thoroughbred and quarter-horse racing Fri.-Sun. between October and May. Grandstand admission is $1, Turf Club $5; parking $1 Grandstand, $2 Turf Club, and $3 Turf Club valet.

The **Juárez Turf Club,** downtown a block south of the Santa Fe Bridge on the east side of Av. Juárez, allows El Paso residents to walk over Santa Fe Bridge and wager on live horse and greyhound races—as well as a range of televised North American sports events—without going all the way out to the track. Facilities include a full bar, multiscreen TV for off-track betting and sports, and betting counters. Open 10 a.m.-midnight daily.

Bullfights

Each summer, four bullfights are held in Juárez at the **Plaza de Toros Monumental** on Av. 16 de Septiembre, beside Rio Grande Mall a bit east of Plaza de las Americas. Seating up to 17,000, Monumental is the world's fourth-largest bullring and a major stop on the professional *corridas* circuit. The annual season runs April-Sept.; the first *corrida de toros* takes place around Easter and then three more *corridas* are held on four Sundays before Labor Day. These are real Spanish-style bullfights in which the bull may be killed by the matador.

Admission costs US$9-18 depending on the seat, while parking costs US$1; rent cushions for US40 cents. The city's older ring, Plaza Balderas (downtown at Calle F. Villa), is now used only for concerts and other events. Check with the Tourist Information Center (tel. 14-01-23 in Juárez) or the El Paso Convention and Visitors Bureau for the latest scheduling.

Mexican Rodeos (*Charreadas*)

Mexican rodeo cowboys *charros* are quite active in the El Paso-Juárez area. In Juárez, you can attend (*charreadas*) at the **Lienzo Charro Adolfo López Mateos**, about a half mile past the Plaza de Toros Monumental off Av. de 16 Septiembre on Av. del Charro between Av. Hnos. Escobar and Paseo Triunfo de la República. Mexican rodeos are held here most Sundays between April and October at 4 p.m. or so. Admission is about $4.

On the El Paso side, the Emiliano Zapata Charro Association holds *charreadas* most Sunday afternoons at an arena on North Loop (FM 76) about two miles east of Horizon Blvd. in southeast El Paso. *Charreadas* are also held at Chamizal Memorial Park during the Border Folk Festival in October and sometimes during other celebrations.

Baseball

During the summer you can watch the **El Paso Diablos,** a farm team for the Milwaukee Brewers in the Texas League, play at well-designed Cohen Stadium (tel. 915-755-2000), 9700 Gateway North.

EVENTS

February

Southwestern Livestock Show and Rodeo, El Paso County Coliseum, 4200 E. Paisano. This 10-day event is reported to be the oldest livestock show and rodeo in the Southwest. Over 2,800 animals are entered in the show by nearly 1,500 contestants. The rodeo is PRCA-sponsored and features top rodeo performers from all over the U.S. and Canada. Call (915) 532-1401 for information.

March

Siglo de Oro Drama Festival, Chamizal National Memorial Theater. Siglo de Oro roughly translates as "Golden Age" and refers to the zenith of Hispanic drama and literature between the 16th and 18th centuries. Troupes from all over the Hispanic world and the U.S. meet at this two-week festival to perform dramas in English, Spanish, and Portuguese by Miguel de Cervantes and other Spanish master playwrights. For more details, call (915) 532-7273.

Transmountain Run, Transmountain Road, Franklin Mountains. A 10-mile foot race sponsored by the American Heart Association (tel. 833-1231).

May

International Balloon Festival. On Memorial Day weekend, hot-air balloonists from around the U.S. and Mexico meet for a balloon border crossing. Also features music, dancing, food vendors, and fireworks.

June

Feast of St. Anthony, Ysleta Mission, Tigua Indian Reservation. June 13 is St. Anthony's Day, the most important religious holiday for Ysleta's Tigua Indians. The celebration starts with various ceremonies at the mission, followed by feasting and dancing later in the day. Visitors are welcome to attend the festivities.

July

Viva! El Paso Outdoor Pageant, McKelligon Amphitheater. Continues through Labor Day. See "Entertainment," above.

Festival de la Zarazuela El Paso/Ciudad

THE NASHVILLE NETWORK

Don Gay, bull rider

Juárez, Chamizal National Memorial. Another Spanish drama festival with performing troupes from all over the Hispanic world, this one is focusing on Spanish folk opera. For information on scheduled events, call (915) 532-7273 or 591-7283.

September
Diez y Seis, various locations in El Paso and Juárez. The 16th (*dies y seis*) of September is the day Mexico celebrates independence from Spain. Festivities begin on the 15th at Chamizal National Memorial in El Paso with music and a *charreada*. A colorful parade and other events are held in downtown Juárez on the 16th.

October
Amigo Airshow, Biggs Army Airfield, is a major regional airshow that features fancy formation flying, weapons displays, and skydiving. Held the second weekend in October.

During the same weekend is the **Kermezaar Arts and Crafts Festival** at El Paso Convention and Performing Arts Center, which emphasizes Southwestern art and is attended by artisans from all over the Southwest and northern Mexico.

Border Folk Festival, Chamizal National Memorial, is usually held the first weekend of October. This cross-cultural celebration features music and dance from the Anglo and Hispanic worlds, a craft show, ethnic food, and a *charreada*.

November
NARC World Finals Rodeo, El Paso County Coliseum, marks the grand finale of the North American Rodeo Commission's rodeo season. The NARC is the largest international rodeo association in the world, and this event attracts contestants from the U.S., Canada, Mexico, and Australia. The event's location used to rotate from year to year but seems to have found a permanent home in El Paso.

Sun Carnival Parade, on Thanksgiving Day, kicks off a series of sports-related events leading to the John Hancock Sun Bowl on Christmas Day.

December
John Hancock Sun Bowl Football Classic, Sun Bowl, UTEP. A postseason college bowl game.

RECREATION

Indian Cliffs Ranch
Sort of a daytime dude ranch for families, Indian Cliffs covers 23,000 acres of desert with the main facilities set on a hill. Activities include free hayrides, trail rides, a children's petting zoo, a mock frontier fort, and such exotic animals as emus, Barbados sheep, African goats, and Belgian horses. Groups can arrange overnight hayrides to the fort in advance. Admission is free as long as you eat in the restaurant. Call (915) 544-3200 for further details.

El Paso Zoo

This 18-acre zoo has about 400 creatures on display in natural settings, including elephants, bears, large African cats, amphibians, birds, and reptiles. It's located at Evergreen and Paisano, across from the El Paso County Coliseum. Hours are Mon.-Fri. 9:30 a.m.-4 p.m., Sat.-Sun. and holidays 9:30 a.m.-6 p.m. Adult admission is $2, children 3-11 and seniors get in for $1, infants under three are admitted free. Call (915) 544-1928 for further information.

Golf

El Paso has two 18-hole golf courses open to the public; Juárez has one. The lowest green fees in El Paso are at the county course in **Ascarate Park** (tel. 915-772-7381)—only $8 weekdays, $10 weekends. The **Cielo Vista Municipal Golf Course** (tel. 591-4927) is at 1510 Hawkins and charges $10.83 weekdays, $13 weekends. Active or retired military and Department of Defense employees, as well as their dependents and guests, can play at 18-hole **Painted Dunes Desert Golf Course** (tel. 821-2122) at 12000 McCombs Rd., off US 54 near Fort Bliss.

Across the border, the well-kept **Campestre Golf Course** at the Juárez Country Club (tel. 173439 in Juárez, 011-52-16-173439 from El Paso) has green fees of $22 weekdays, $33 weekends.

Horseback Riding

Cowboy Trading Post (tel. 915-581-1984) arranges day and overnight horseback trips into the Franklin Mountains and other sites around El Paso. The Post also rents and sells horses and riding gear if you want to try it on your own. **Blue Sky Outfitters** (tel. 855-3845 or 800-251-RIDE) organizes equestrian trips further afield in the Guadalupe Mountains and southwestern New Mexico.

Hiking the Franklin Mountains

The Franklin Mountains are honeycombed with narrow, faded footpaths—probably worn by people looking for the Lost Padre Mine where Don Juan de Oñate supposedly hid a fortune in gold, silver, and jewelry. **Franklin Mountains State Park** covers a 16,108-acre portion of the mountains; the park is undeveloped and so far only

day use is permitted. Big Bend it's not, but hardy hikers may want to give desert hiking in the Franklins a try.

The only formally constructed trail in the park is the Ron Coleman Trail. It's unmarked but fairly easy to follow—other trails in the Franklins may require some orienteering skills. The Coleman trail starts at Smuggler's Pass, off Transmountain Rd. (Loop 375) 5.3 miles west of the North-South Freeway (US 54). If you're coming from the west side of the mountains, Smuggler's Pass is about six miles east of the Canutillo exit off I-10. There's a turnout at the side of the road where hikers usually park their cars or have accomplices retrieve them. The trailhead is on the south side of the road and is marked by a ruined stone gate. Alternatively, the hike can be attempted from the south end in McKelligon Canyon—just follow the directions backward.

The trail from Smuggler's Pass to McKelligon Canyon is about 3.5 miles. For the seven-mile roundtrip hike figure on four to five hours' hiking time with an elevation change from 5,400 (Smuggler's Pass) to 6,700 (ridge along South Franklin Mountain) to 4,880 feet (McKelligon Canyon). The going is fairly strenuous in the steep parts, but there are also long stretches of easy walking.

About 300 yards down the trail from Smuggler's Pass, you'll come to an old road on the right, which you'll take for another 160 yards or so till the trail branches left. The trail then reaches the crest of a ridge and follows it for another 0.6 mile. When the path seems to fade or branch off, look ahead for where it picks up along the ridge crest. You can see three FAA radio towers from here—head in that direction. As you approach the towers, the trail drops to the left below the jagged crest to the south. At mile 1.6 you'll come to a level area with a good view; here the trail forks into three. Two of the trails go left (east) to the radio towers and the summit of South Franklin Mountain (elev. 6,764 feet) while the one on the right continues south along the Ron Coleman Trail.

From here, the trail is fairly easy to follow as it skirts a small canyon and comes to a meadow at mile 1.8, a good spot for a picnic. Beyond the meadow, the trail drops quickly to the right (west) of the ridge till it arrives at a three-by-five-foot hole in the ridge known as the Keyhole. After this, the trail drops and dissolves across an area of loose rock for 50 yards or so—take care on the descent. Keep the top of the ridge in sight so you can pick up the trail again when it crosses over onto the other side of the ridge at mile 2.2.

By this time, you should be able to see a paved, circular road in McKelligon Canyon—a good landmark to keep in sight as you try to pick out the main trail crisscrossed by several side trails. The trail ends at the parking area off McKelligon Canyon Road. You are now in McKelligon Canyon Municipal Park. If you started from this end, you're finished; if you started at Smuggler's Pass, it's more strenuous on the return since you have to ascend at the Keyhole.

SHOPPING

El Paso-Juárez is the regional trade center for the Southwest and literally hundreds of manufacturers and importers are headquartered here. Hence, selection and bargains abound. Among the better buys are Tarahumara Indian blankets, Casas Grandes pottery, Pueblo Indian jewelry, and cowboy boots. Rustic Southwestern-style furniture made of mission oak and/or ponderosa pine is good value as well. There's also a lot of junk for sale, so it pays to shop around before spending your money. Skip the big shopping malls like Cielo Vista unless you want to go to the movies.

El Paso Saddleblanket

This huge store offers Southwestern pottery, handwoven blankets, leather goods, local antiques, furniture, and just about anything else of Mexican or Indian origin you might expect to find in the El Paso-Juárez area. Most everything comes from Mexico and Central America—whole villages in Guatemala are in the store's employ—and while it's cheaper and more fun to ferret this stuff out in Juárez on your own, if you're short on time and bargaining skills this is a reasonable proxy. As the name suggests, the place is strong on blankets and has probably the largest selection of Indian blankets in the country. At 601 N. Oregon downtown next to the Ramada Inn; open Mon.-Fri. 9 a.m.-5 p.m. and Sat. 10 a.m.-4 p.m.

Ysleta and Socorro

The Mission Trail through Ysleta and Socorro is lined with arts and crafts and antique shops specializing in Mexican and Southwestern goods—most open only on weekends. In Socorro, three of the larger places are the **Bosque Trading Post,** at 10167 Socorro Rd., open Fri.-Sun. 10 a.m.-5:30 p.m.; **El Mercadito,** at 10189, Wed.-Sun. 10 a.m.-5:30 p.m.; and the **Riverside Trading Post,** at 10300, Thurs.-Sun. 10 a.m.-5:30 p.m., all ensconced in 19th-century pueblo-style houses near the river. The jewelry shops here feature good selections. The **Tigua Indian Reservation Cultural Center** specializes, naturally, in Tigua Indian art. Tigua pottery, which features very bold designs, is a definite highlight here.

Boots, Jeans, and Western Gear

More cowboy boots are made in El Paso than anywhere else in the world, and all the major Texas bootmakers maintain factory outlets here. Prices are usually about 20-40% lower than retail, sometimes more on selected boots. Boots on display at these outlets tend to be either "seconds" with flaws or outrageous styles that didn't sell—e.g., pink ostrich-skin boots. Because of this, the range of sizes available also varies erratically—but there's always a chance you'll stumble onto something you like that actually fits. Bootmakers with outlets include: **Justin,** 7100 Gateway E (tel. 915-779-5465); **Tony Lama,** 7176 Gateway E (tel. 772-4327); and **Dan Post and Lucchese,** 6601 Montana (tel. 778-8060).

For the best cowboy footgear in El Paso, stop by **Rocketbuster Boots** (tel. 541-1200) at 115 S. Anthony Street. Custom-designed, handmade boots average $400-750 and blast off to as high as $5000 for the museum or signature series. Many of Rocketbuster's boots are inspired by designs from the 1940s and '50s, including short-topped "peewees" and "shorties," and bear names like "Cool Arrows," "Rose-A-Rita," and "Shadowrider." Recent clients have included Arnold Schwarzenegger, Sly Stallone, Tom Cruise, Goldie Hawn, Emmy Lou Harris, and Pam Tillis. Rocketbuster also sells custom belts and other accessories; browsers are welcome.

For custom-made boots over in Juárez, you might try **Botas Santa Fe** at 738 Av. de las

VIRGIN GUADALUPE

ROCKETBUSTER BOOTS #13

Rocketbuster boots: the makers claim this pair will induce "a religious experience, to say the least."

Americas, near Plaza de las Americas and Av. Lincoln. Santa Fe specializes in exotic skins like python, armadillo, and ostrich. **Botas Arizona** is similar but perhaps lower priced, and is on Av. 16 de Septiembre across from the City Market. There's also **Botas Herradero** at Av. Insurgentes and Saltillo, a little more off the tourist track. At any of these three, you should be able to get a pair of custom-made cowhide boots for under $100, quite low compared to stateside prices. For exotics, you'll have to pay $100-300, depending on the critter who gave up his life for your stylish walking.

Both Levi's and Wrangler have large plants in El Paso, so good buys on these brands abound. **Morris Saddlery** (tel. 859-6705) at 10949 E. Burt sells custom- and ready-made saddles, Western and English riding gear, and Western wear. **Farah** has a factory outlet in El Paso at 8889 Gateway E, but, as all Texans know, real cowboys and cowgirls wear Wrangler Prorodeo 13 MWZ Cowboy Cut jeans.

Another good spot for saddles and tack is

Cowboy Trading Post (tel. 581-1984) at 301 E. Borderland, off I-10 W near Canutillo in El Paso's "Upper Valley." Owner John Middagh has been selling and renting everything to do with horses for nearly 20 years. Ranchers from Mexico and the Trans-Pecos area trade used saddles here, so this is a good place to buy used gear. Local equestrians practice riding maneuvers in an arena on the grounds; the Post also has facilities for boarding horses.

Recorded Music
Music collectors should not miss **Nostalgia Records, Tapes, and CDs** (tel. 915-594-9900) at 1360 N. Lee Trevino, two blocks north of I-10 in Sunpointe Centre. Nostalgia sells collectible recordings, imports, pop, C&W, *tejano,* rock, and just about any other kind of regional roots music, plus books and other materials for music collectors. Open Mon.-Sat. 10 a.m.-9 p.m., Sunday noon-6 p.m.

Sporting Goods
Gardenswartz Sportz (tel. 915-833-9700) at 735 S. Mesa Hills Dr. carries a varied line of sports equipment, including gear for rock-climbers headed to Hueco Tanks State Park.

Food
The **El Paso Chile Company** (tel. 915-544-3434) at 909 Texas Ave. sells everything having to do with the chile, including salsas, powdered capsicum, T-shirts, chile wreaths, *ristras* (strings of dried chiles), and cookbooks. Open Mon.-Fri. 9 a.m.-5 p.m., Saturday 10 a.m.-2 p.m.

Juárez
Two sections of town are the focal points of tourist shopping, one catering to auto traffic (Av. Lincoln and the Plaza de las Americas complex) and one for pedestrians (Av. Juárez). Both areas carry the same variety of arts and crafts, but quality and prices are a bit higher along Av. Lincoln.

Avenida Juárez near the border is mostly Mexican kitsch, but there are bargains available, especially in the sidestreet stores primarily for Mexican shoppers. Untaxed liquor and cigarettes are always reliable deals in either area.

Continue south along Av. Juárez, turn left on Av. 16 de Septiembre, and you'll come to **Mer-**

cado Juárez, heart of the city's older shopping district. This funky, two-story market building is filled with vendors selling handicrafts, fruits, piñatas, clothes, foodstuffs, silver, leather, and Mexican curios (my favorite: chess sets in which the opposing sides represent *federales* vs. revolutionaries or conquistadors vs. Indians). Outside along one side of the building is a half-gentrified section with open-air cafes, restaurants, and ice cream parlors.

More traditional yet is the three-floor **Mercado Cuauhtémoc,** off Calle Mariscal south of the cathedral at the south end of Av. Juárez. The ground floor is home to cheap *loncherías,* fresh meats, and *queso asadero* (similar to mozzarella) from Villa Ahumada. On the upper floors you'll find an assortment of live chickens, doves, parrots, fruits, flowers, medicinal herbs, and lucky buddhas with crosses and other charms inside. East of the market for three or four blocks is an outdoor market consisting mostly of fruit and vegetable vendors, while Calle Minas behind the market is lined with *carnicerías* (butcher shops) and various other *tiendas.*

The government-sponsored **Centro Artesanal,** on Av. Lincoln opposite the Plaza de las Americas, carries an extensive selection of quality ceramics—including some one-of-a-kind pieces—plus clothes, woodcarvings, masks, basketry, and other craft media, all of it handmade. Ample parking is available at Plaza de las Americas opposite; there are several other upscale handicraft shops in the vicinity.

In the **Plaza de las Americas** itself, the newish **Pueblito Mexicano** gathers a collection of small shops—a *farmacía,* a *dulcería* with sweets from all over Mexico, a duty-free *perfumería,* a photo studio where you can pose in antique Mexican clothing, and dozens more that haven't opened yet—all around a simulated, enclosed town plaza offering air-conditioned comfort. More shops are planned for the future. This is a major stop for the daily Border Jumper trolley bus from El Paso.

The U.S. dollar is acceptable currency throughout Juárez. Many shops, hotels, and restaurants quote prices in dollars. If you want to change dollars for Mexican pesos, there are plenty of moneychangers on either side of all four bridges over the Rio Grande.

INFORMATION

Tourist Offices

Out on I-10 at the Texas-New Mexico state line is a Texas Department of Highway information center, where you can get info about El Paso and the rest of Texas. Better for information specific to the El Paso area are the two **El Paso Tourist Information Centers;** one in Civic Center Plaza downtown (tel. 915-534-0653), another at El Paso International Airport. The two in town are open Mon.-Fri. 8 a.m.-5 p.m., while the airport counter is open daily 10 a.m.-6 p.m. The staffs are very helpful, dispensing maps, brochures, and other free publications.

The **El Paso Convention and Visitors Bureau,** also located in Civic Center Plaza, is oriented mostly toward arranging for group tourism and conventions.

In Juárez there's a **Mexico Tourist Information Center** in the Municipal Building just across the border on Av. Colegio Militar between Av. Juárez and Av. Lerdo. It's open Mon.-Fri. 8 a.m.-8 p.m., Sat.-Sun. 8 a.m.-noon. The staff speak English and distribute travel information for Juárez and Mexico. They can also assist if you have a problem, such as theft, while in Juárez.

Ciudad Juárez has a **U.S. consulate** (tel. 13-40-48, after hours 525-6066 in El Paso) at Av. López Mateos 924, just north of the Universidad Autónoma de Cd. Juárez.

Publications

Periodicals: The two main English-language dailies in El Paso are the *El Paso Times* (issued in the morning) and the *El Paso Herald Post* (afternoon). Either is worth reading for the latest information on local cinema and events.

Two Spanish-language dailies are distributed in El Paso, the long-established *El Continental* and the *Diario de Juárez,* which covers Juárez, El Paso, and Las Cruces, New Mexico.

Guidebooks: If you're considering continuing deeper into the Mexican state of Chihuahua to the Copper Canyon or beyond, have a look at Moon's new *Northern Mexico Handbook,* or the all-inclusive *Mexico Handbook,* both written by the same author who created this book.

Maps: *El Paso* from Continental Maps is widely available at El Paso grocery stores and at tourist offices. Better is the AAA El Paso map, available from most AAA offices in Texas. The El Paso AAA office at 1201 Airway Blvd. (tel. 915-778-9521), near the airport, is open Mon.-Fri. 8:30 a.m.-5 p.m. Both maps show portions of Juárez as well.

Mexican Consulate General

The Mexican consulate in El Paso is located at 910 E. San Antonio (tel. 915-533-3644). If you're a U.S. citizen planning to enter Mexico as a tourist, without a private vehicle, for less than 180 days, you don't need to come here at all. Citizens of other countries may need to apply in advance for a visa to enter Mexico. Any non-Mexican citizen who intends to take a car, motorcycle, or other vehicle across the border must apply for the necessary papers at the consulate or at the border; AAA members can take care of the necessary paperwork at the El Paso AAA.

Telephone Service

The area code for El Paso is 915; when calling El Paso, remember it's in the mountain time zone, unlike most of the rest of Texas, which is in the central time zone.

Calling Juárez: The area code for Juárez is 16. If dialing a Juárez number from the U.S. you must precede the area code and phone number with 011-52. Juárez phone numbers should have six digits; if a Juárez listing only shows five digits, add a "1" as the first number (most phone numbers in Juárez begin with a "1," so it's often left off in the listings). For example, if you've located a number for someplace in Juárez that reads 53342 and you're dialing from El Paso, dial 011-52-16-153342.

EL PASO TELEPHONE INFORMATION

Emergency (police, fire, medical): 911
Telephone Directory Assistance: 411
Area Code: 915
Weather Service: 778-9343
Crisis Help Line: 779-1800
Fort Bliss Information: 568-2121
U.S. Customs: 541-6794

GETTING AROUND

City Buses

Sun Metro is the name of the city bus line, which only operates during the day and is really only convenient for the downtown area. Call (915) 533-3333 for schedule information.

Taxi

Two companies operate reliable taxi services in El Paso, **Checker** (tel. 915-532-2626) and **Yellow Cab** (tel. 533-3433). Fares are comparable to taxi services in other American cities. At either side of the several bridges that cross the Rio Grande are fleets of private taxis that ferry passengers back and forth between El Paso and Juárez—the average gringo fare is $13-20.

Tours

Several companies in El Paso conduct bus tours of the area that include half- or full-day sightseeing tours, shopping tours, and tours to the Juárez Racetrack or bullring. Most motels and hotels can arrange the tours, or you can contact one directly: **Around and About Tours** (tel. 915-833-2650); **Golden Tours** (tel. 779-0555); and **Si El Paso Tours** (tel. 581-1122).

HUECO TANKS STATE PARK

History

Hueco Tanks is a unique complex of huge syenite (a granite-like rock) masses in the middle of the Chihuahuan Desert. The formations, created 34 million years ago, are named for the myriad *huecos* (pronounced "WAY-kos") or hollows that are scattered across the rock surfaces, some large, most the size of a fist. Geologists disagree on how the *huecos* were formed, but most likely they're the result of some as yet undocumented weathering process. Most significantly, the *huecos* are a source of stored rainwater, a scarce commodity in the desert. Because of this natural capacity to collect and store water, the area became an important habitat for semi-nomadic Indian tribes as far back as 10,000 years ago. Evidence of an early Paleo-Indian culture has been found at Hueco Tanks in the form of flint tips called Folsom points.

Later, during the Desert Archaic period, the first rock art appeared in the form of pictographs drawn by hunter-gatherers with paints made of ground stone. These groups were succeeded by the Jornada branch of the Mogollon Culture (A.D. 1000-1500), who added classic Pueblo motifs to the growing collection of rock art. In the 19th century, the Apaches, Kiowas, and Comanches created the bulk of the dynamic pictographs and petroglyphs (rock carvings) that are still visible—look in crevices near ground level.

From 1858 to 1859, Hueco Tanks was an important stop for the famous Butterfield Overland Mail, and Butterfield built a stone and adobe stagecoach station here. When an alternate route through Fort Davis offered protection from Indians and highwaymen, the Hueco Tanks station was abandoned; the ruins can still be seen near the entrance of the park.

The latest group to take a liking to Hueco Tanks has been rockclimbers, both technical climbers and scramblers, who have made the park something of an international rockclimbing mecca over the last few years. The large pocked boulders offer some of the most exciting bouldering in the world, complete with sets of complex "problems" climbers must work out step by step.

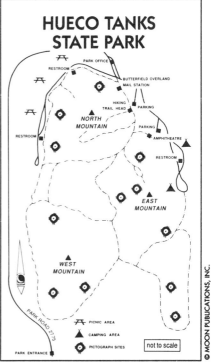

Wildlife

Hueco Tanks State Park encompasses 860 acres, most covered by the three main syenite mountains and interspersed with desertscrub and the park's own unique ecosystem. The *huecos* and *tinajas* (small desert springs) attract an unusually rich combination of flora and fauna, including over 190 verified species of birds—turkey vultures, red-tailed hawks, golden eagles, prairie falcons, cliff swallows—as well as bobcats, gray foxes, and the occasional cougar. The best time for birdwatching is late October through early March, when the native species are supplemented by migrational species. Animals are attracted not only by the water but by the varieties of shrimp found in water-filled *huecos.*

Besides the usual Chihuahuan desertscrub like creosote, mesquite, yucca, agave, and various desert acacias, the areas between the syenite masses support a variety of grasses, sotol, ocotillo, and small trees like the Mexican buckeye, juniper, Arizona oak, hackberry, and Texas mulberry. Wildflowers come out after the late summer rains and as many as 10 species of ferns can be found in wet years.

Rockclimbing

While you can view a number of the estimated 5,000 Indian pictographs at Hueco Tanks from park trails, the best way to see them is to do some bouldering. A backcountry permit is required and can be obtained at the office at the park entrance; rangers can also be quite helpful in suggesting simple hiking and climbing routes. Climbers with permits may climb anywhere they like except on rock art. No bolts, pitons, or other equipment with a potential for damaging the rock faces are allowed.

The main season for rockclimbing is late October to February, though any time of year other than June through August is good. During the summer months the boulders really get too hot to handle, this capacity to store and reflect heat is a definite asset during cold weather.

Experienced rockclimbers will want to take a look at the booklet tethered to the information counter in the park office. Called *Hueco Tanks: A Climber's and Boulderer's Guide,* by Sherman, Crump, Head, and Head (Chalkstone Press, Evergreen, CO), it describes each of the climbing routes in detail. The booklet can usually be purchased at Pete's or Gardenswartz Sportz in El Paso.

Better yet, talk to the climbers who hang out at Pete's, the Quonset hut on the left side of RR 2775 as you approach the park. Pete's is owned and operated for the primary benefit of rockclimbers by Pete Zavala and his wife Queta, who treat climbers like part of the family. Besides providing climbers with a cheap place to camp, Pete sells food, beer, and chalk (to enhance a climber's hand grip), and also keeps a dogeared notebook entitled "New Routes and Register," in which climbers write

rockclimbing, Hueco Tanks State Park

tips and tales of rockclimbing. As you'll soon see from scanning this notebook or the *Indian Heights* guide, Hueco Tanks has an incredible variety of potential climbs that range in difficulty from "Looking For Mars Bars" (5.5 on the Yosemite Decimal System, suitable for accomplished novices) to "The Gunfighter" (5.13, the most difficult).

Other routes have equally creative names like "Do Fries Go With That Shake?" and "Dark Heart." "Center El Murray" on Mushroom Boulder is said to be Hueco Tanks's greatest problem climb—to date, only one climber has accomplished it. Hueco Tanks has even added a term to the climber's technical vocabulary— "hueco pulling."

Park Facilities and Services
The park provides 20 drive-in campsites with electricity and water, a trailer dump station, showers, and restrooms. Camping fees are $8 for sites with water, $11 with water and electricity. For day use, there's a $2 per person entry fee for ages 13 and older. Most of the year the park is very uncrowded although summer weekends see a lot of local families; during the climbing season climbers make their presence known but never really take over the place.

From June through August, park rangers offer guided tours of Hueco Tanks rock art and on Friday and Saturday evenings offer slide shows. The park gates open at 8 a.m. and close at sunset to all except campers. The park office is open daily 8 a.m.-5 p.m. For further information on the park or campsite reservations, contact the Superintendent (tel. 915-857-1135), Hueco Tanks State Park, Rural Route 3, Box 1, El Paso, TX 79935.

Outside the Park
Many climbers don't stay in the park but elect instead to camp at **Pete's,** otherwise known as Hueco Tanks Country Store, (tel. 915-857-1095), Rural Route 3, 611 Hueco Tanks Rd., El Paso, TX 79936, which is on RR 2775 on the way to the park from US 62/180. Pete charges $2 to pitch a tent on his lot—the only amenities a portable toilet. Until he got fed up with the outrageous antics of a few climbers, Pete allowed visitors to sleep on the floor in the upstairs portion of his large Quonset hut.

Mission Espada, San Antonio (Joe Cummings)

1. Mission Concepción, San Antonio;
2. the Alamo (photos by Joe Cummings)

Getting There
To reach Hueco Tanks State Park from El Paso, drive or hitch 26 miles east on US 62/180 till you see the sign for the park, then head north on RR 2775 for another six miles till you come to

the park entrance. Buses between El Paso and Carlsbad, New Mexico will let passengers off at the entrance to RR 2775—make arrangements with the driver in advance—from where you can hike the six miles to the park.

GUADALUPE MOUNTAINS

The Guadalupe Mountain range lies astride the Texas-New Mexico border, rising high above the surrounding Chihuahuan Desert. The north end of the range opens up like the top of a V and descends gradually into New Mexico's Carlsbad Plains, while in the south the range ends abruptly at precipitous cliffs over a huge salt

basin in Texas. You can see the Guadalupes' craggy peaks from at least 50 miles away in any direction, yet the area has long been virtually ignored by the nation that grew up around it. Many cross-country tourists find their way to Carlsbad Caverns on the New Mexico side, but few venture farther south to the 76,000-plus

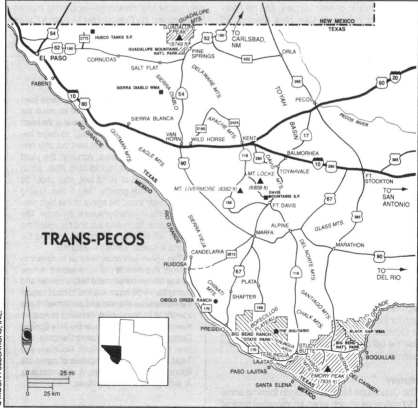

acres of magnificent highlands and canyons over the Texas line that make up Guadalupe Mountains National Park—only 201,000 visitors in 1993, compared with nearly 700,000 next door at Carlsbad Caverns National Park. Fewer still backpack into the 46,850 acres set aside as wilderness, making this one of the least crowded national parks in the United States.

It isn't likely the Guadalupe Mountains will ever get the crowds typical of many other national parks in the west because of a conscious effort on the part of the National Park Service and the locals to keep it as pristine a wilderness as possible. This is partially because the main attractions of the park's interior are simply inaccessible by road, but the policy extends even beyond park boundaries. No hotels or lodges have been built in or near the park, and the nearest motel is in White's City, New Mexico, 35 miles to the north. And neither of the two drive-in campgrounds in the park have RV hookups, though RVs are allowed to park in spaces provided. For a true Southwestern wilderness experience, this national park is unparalleled.

Climate

Temperatures in the Guadalupe Mountains vary from an average high/low of 53°/30° F in January to an average high/low of 88°/63° F in July. High winds can be expected between late fall and late spring. In the highlands, 60-mile-an-hour winds are not uncommon, and velocities in excess of 100 mph have been recorded. Average precipitation is highest in August (3.77 inches) and September (5.22 inches), but it can rain anytime—backpackers shouldn't consider camping in the Guadalupes without a tent. The driest months are November, December, March, and April. Snow is not unusual in the high country during the winter.

October and April are probably the best times to visit the Guadalupes, considering all weather factors. These months are also peak tourist season for the area, but except for the last weekend in October—when hundreds of people come to see the fall change of colors—crowding doesn't seem to be a problem.

History

The Guadalupe Mountains began forming some 250 million years ago when an immense tropical ocean, teeming with life, covered much of what is today Texas and New Mexico. Calcium compounds secreted by marine organisms and precipitated from the ocean water gradually formed a 400-mile horseshoe-shaped reef, later named Capitan Reef by geologists in honor of the peak called El Capitan at the southern tip of the Guadalupe range. Eventually the sea evaporated, leaving a thick sediment that buried the reef for millions of years until lateral compression forced it upward through the sediment, thus exposing what was to become known as the Guadalupe Mountains, part of the world's largest fossil reef. Two other exposed portions make up the Apache Mountains near Van Horn and the Glass Mountains near Alpine.

Archaeological evidence—pictographs, firepits, stone tool remnants—suggests humans first occupied the Guadalupes' McKittrick Canyon some 12,000 years ago. In recorded history, Spanish conquistadors who passed through in

SACRED MESCAL

The Mescalero Apaches got their name from mescal, their most important food source in the Guadalupe Mountains area. Mescal is the heart of the agave or "century plant," so called because it seemed the plant sent out only one bloom every 100 years. Actually, the plant sends up its single reproductive stalk, which reaches heights of 10-15 feet, after about 20 years of normal growth. Then it dies. During that 20-year span, the agave stores high concentrations of carbohydrates in its center. The Mescaleros discovered this and harvested the plants just before they bloomed, roasting the hearts in special earthen mescal pits.

The agave was considered so important to survival that mescal pits were sacred. A new pit was always consecrated before sunrise and during the 24-36 hours required to roast mescal the Mescaleros chanted and performed rituals specific to its preparation. Remains of Apache mescal pits can be seen near the Pine Springs Campground, by the Mescalero Campsite, and near the junction of the Bush Mountain and Tejas hiking trails. Three species of agave still flourish in the Guadalupes, *A. neomexicana, A. lechuguilla,* and *A. gracilipes.*

the 16th century made the first recorded references to Indian habitation in the Guadalupes. While searching for gold in the New World, they found these mountains were the exclusive domain of the Mescalero Apaches, who continued to control the area until the mid-1800s. The Mescaleros used the canyons as shelter from their enemies as well as from the harsh desert climate and lived on native agave, sotol, deer, elk, rabbit, and bison. They also believed their sacred fire god dwelt on Guadalupe Peak (8,749 feet), the tallest mountain in Texas.

Following the 1849 California gold rush, the Butterfield Overland Mail established a stage station called the Pinery along the St. Louis-San Francisco route (now US 62/180); you can see the ruins near Pine Springs Campground. In 1858 the first meeting of transcontinental stagecoaches occurred just west of Guadalupe Pass.

By the 1880s, the Mescaleros had been driven out of the mountains by the U.S. Army, and a few cattle and sheep ranchers and copper and bat guano miners moved into the area. Stories of vast deposits or caches of gold in the Guadalupes have been around since the era of the Spanish conquistadors. Even the Apache chief Geronimo claimed that somewhere in the mountains was the greatest gold mine on earth. One famous prospector, William Sublette, used to ride into West Texas towns with moneybelts full of gold dust and nuggets, claiming

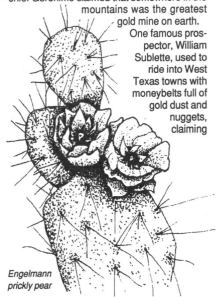

Engelmann prickly pear

he'd pulled the stuff from the Guadalupes. When Sublette ran out of gold, he went back for more, often with would-be miners in pursuit; stories say he knew the mountains so well he always lost his pursuers. Sublette died in 1892 without ever giving up the secret source of his wealth, and no one ever found the cache. It's been theorized he may have stumbled onto a cave that concealed gold taken in a Butterfield stage robbery. This is quite plausible, as Butterfield stagecoaches were held up several times in the area before the route was diverted along the safer Fort Davis route.

In the early 1930s, petroleum geologist William Pratt established a ranch in McKittrick Canyon—named for an earlier canyon resident who lived in a dugout house—that eventually spread for 16,000 acres. In the '50s, Pratt began donating portions of his ranch to the U.S. government for use as a national park and by 1959 he'd given it all away. Pratt's original stone cabin has been preserved in McKittrick Canyon. Additional land (70,000 acres) was later purchased from the J.C. Hunter Ranch and Guadalupe Mountains National Park was officially opened in 1972.

Flora

The Guadalupe Mountains stretch from the southeastern limit of the Rocky Mountains to the northern limit of the Chihuahuan Desert. Because of the rare interaction of desert, canyon, and highland biotic communities, the Guadalupes support an unusually diverse community of plant and animal species.

Along the desert surrounding the Guadalupes and on the floors of the lower canyons are typical Chihuahuan Desert plants and succulents like agave, prickly pear, creosote bush, lechuguilla, yucca, and sotol. With elevation gains, one encounters ponderosa pine, Douglas fir, quaking aspen, chokeberry, and piñon. In sheltered canyons, add big-tooth maple, walnut, chinquapin oak, alligator junipers, and various ferns.

One of the most beautiful and rare trees found in the canyons is the Texas madrone (*Arbutus texana*), which grows only in the mountains of West Texas and on the Edwards Plateau. Outside of the Guadalupes and Big Bend, its numbers are fast dwindling since it thrives only in the wild. The madrone is identified by its smooth,

LOUISE FOOTE

reddish bark and thick, deep-green oval leaves. The leaves don't drop off in the winter, and clusters of small white flowers appear in the spring. In the fall, bright red berries sprout and are an important food source for birds and other native wildlife.

Mammals

Around 58 species of mammals make the Guadalupe Mountains their home. Among the smaller varmints are 14 species of bats (including two free-tail species) and three species of rabbits. Javelinas or collared peccaries, an introduced species, are occasionally seen.

Pronghorn, mule deer, bison, and bighorn sheep were once native to the area, but all except the mule deer had disappeared by the turn of the century. Mule deer are commonly seen throughout the canyons and highlands. Merriam's elk (*Cervus canadensis merriami*) are native to the Guadalupes, but the closely related species seen here now are descendants of a herd of Rocky Mountain elk (*Cervus canadensis*) from South Dakota that J.C. Hunter introduced to the mountains in 1928. About 50 wander all parts of the park and are frequently spotted by hikers.

Other mammals commonly seen include gray foxes, coyotes, raccoons, and porcupines. At night, you can often hear a chorus of coyotes singing the high desert blues. Less common are black bears, bobcats, and mountain lions.

The estimated mountain lion population in the park is 50-60 individuals. Like most felines, lions are nocturnal creatures so your chances of encountering one are very slim unless you like to hike at night. See the special topic "Seeing the Lion" in the "Big Bend National Park" section below to find out how to handle mountain lion encounters.

Birds

The number and variety of bird species in the Guadalupes is fairly remarkable. At last count, 255 species in 44 bird families had been spotted in the park. Among the birds seen year round are wild turkeys, roadrunners, doves, woodpeckers, Montezuma and scaled quail, killdeer, and sharp-shinned, Cooper's, and red-tailed hawks.

Bald eagles occasionally breed here in the summer and may appear in the spring or fall as migrant species. The golden eagle can be seen year round but is most frequently spotted in the winter. Four species of falcon frequent the park— the American kestrel, the merlin, the peregrine, and the prairie. Hummingbird fanciers can thrill to no less than six species, most commonly the magnificent black-chinned and broad-tailed.

Amphibians and Reptiles

Now for the creepy-crawly things. Eight amphibs (frogs, toads, and salamanders) and 42 reptile species (including 19 kinds of lizards and 23 species of snakes) are known to inhabit the Guadalupes. Of the 23 snake species, six are venomous rattlesnakes.

The most commonly encountered rattlesnake in the park is the northern blacktail (*Crotalus molossus*), which is gray-brown or green in color with irregular blotches along its back, and is 2.5 to 4 feet long. The western diamondback (*crotalus atrox*), 2.5 to 6 feet long with diamond-shaped markings, is also fairly common. Both rattlers prefer rocky areas like dry stream beds —never reach or step into a pile of rocks without lifting them first with a stick. Better yet, avoid rockpiles altogether. The other four rattlesnake species in the park are rarely spotted by humans.

Visiting

The **Headquarters Visitor Center** is off US 62/180 east of Guadalupe Pass and is open daily 8 a.m.-4:30 p.m. Besides restrooms and drinking water, the visitor center offers free park brochures and maps, a slide program, various exhibits, and a schedule of ranger-guided walking tours. A ranger on duty will be glad to assist with planning your visit, whether you're a wilderness backpacker or a day hiker. The center also sells books with extensive historical and natural information about the area as well as topographic maps for backpackers.

Information on the park can be obtained in advance by calling or writing Guadalupe Mountains National Park (tel. 915-828-3251), HC 60, Box 400, Salt Flat, TX 79847-9400.

Hiking

It's impossible to appreciate the beauty and grandeur of Guadalupe Mountains National Park without hiking into the interior. Unlike other na-

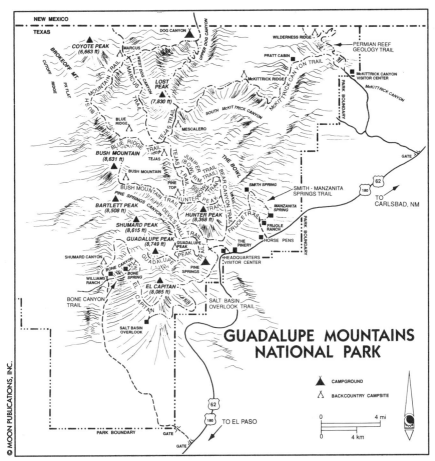

GUADALUPE MOUNTAINS
NATIONAL PARK

▲ CAMPGROUND

Λ BACKCOUNTRY CAMPSITE

0   4 mi

0   4 km

tional parks such as Yosemite or Big Bend, you can't drive up to scenic overlooks. None of the canyons or highlands is accessible by car, though there's now a parking lot at the mouth of McKittrick Canyon: visitors must still walk a minimum of 2.3 miles to really get into the canyon. Fortunately, the park offers 80 miles of trails extending through the length and breadth of the canyons and high country, ranging from the 2.3-mile Devil's Hall Trail from Pine Springs Campground to the 12.3-mile Bush Mountain Trail from the Tejas Trail Junction. If you can spare the time and stamina required for hikes into the

interior, you'll be greatly rewarded by eye-popping vistas and a rich pageant of natural history.

Most hikes in the park involve some elevation gain—anywhere from 400 to 3,000 feet. Inquire at the Headquarters Visitor Center if you have any doubt about your abilities to accomplish a particular trail. You should figure on spending about one hour per mile of hiking, taking into consideration elevation changes and rest stops. Sturdy shoes or hiking boots are a must. Since temperature and precipitation can vary widely from place to place, it's essential to prepare for possible weather changes. In the summer, a hat, sunglasses, sunscreen, and light raingear are essential; in the winter, wear warm, layered clothing.

The only sources of drinking water in the park are at Headquarters Visitor Center, McKittrick Canyon Visitor Center, Pine Springs Campground, and Dog Canyon Campground. You can't count on finding spring water, even in the highlands. Hikers should carry at least a half gallon of water on day hikes (more on hot days); overnight hikes require a minimum of one gallon of water per person.

Backpacking

Two of the park's campgrounds are accessible by car, Pine Springs and Dog Canyon. Beyond these drive-in campgrounds, farther into the interior of the park, are nine designated wilderness camping sites accessible only on foot. Backcountry camping in the Guadalupes requires careful preparation because of the water situation and changeable weather patterns. A no-fee backcountry use permit is also required and can be obtained from the visitor center or at Dog Canyon Campground.

Backpacking essentials include a compass, map, first-aid kit, waterproof matches, knife, flashlight with extra batteries, foul-weather gear, tent or sleeping shelter, a signal device (mirror or whistle), and, of course, ample food and water.

For extensive backpacking trips, a topographic map is highly recommended. A waterproof topographic map of the park, published by Trails Illustrated, is available at the visitor center for $8.50. This detailed map marks the backcountry campsites and established hiking trails, as well as primitive hiking trails, equestrian trails, all trail distances, unpaved roads, intermittent streams, wooded areas, springs, and contour differentials. The giveaway National Park Service map is also quite good, but lacks contour lines, trail distances, and many of the intermittent streams. Remember that you can't count on any of the springs or streams as dependable sources of water—during dry spells, the flow retreats below ground. Another good source of backpacking information is the booklet *Trails of the Guadalupes,* sold at the visitor center for $5. This 55-page publication contains a history of the area and detailed descriptions of many park trails, plus essays on the Guadalupe environment. The maps included are not as detailed as the Trails Illustrated topo map.

True detail hounds with lots of hiking time and energy may want to obtain these four USGS 1:24,000 scale topographical maps: PX Flat, Guadalupe Peak, Patterson Hills, and Guadalupe Pass. Most of the best hiking is covered on the Guadalupe Peak sheet. Individual sheets can be ordered directly through USGS Map Sales, P.O. Box 25286, Federal Center, Bldg. 810, Denver, CO 80225.

The usual minimum-impact camping ethics apply for the Guadalupes: pack out all trash, bury human waste four to six inches down, build no open fires (if you plan to cook, bring a backpacking stove). For the sake of historical preservation, please don't disturb Indian mescal pits or pictographs. Special cave entry permits are required for hikers who wish to explore caves within the park boundaries—apply at the visitor center.

Horseback Riding

Approximately 80% of the park trail system is open to equestrian use, mostly along the north-south ridges that run through the center of the park. Neither the Park Service nor anyone nearby has horses for hire, so all saddle stock must be brought to the park. Riding is not permitted on the following trails: McKittrick Canyon between McKittrick Ridge Campsite and the visitor center, Bear Canyon, the Bowl Loop, Devil's Hall, Smith-Manzanita Spring, and Permian Reef Geology. Riders must obtain a free backcountry use permit from the visitor center before taking their horses on any park trail. During periods of wet weather, trails may be closed to horses until dry enough to prevent tread damage.

You'll find horse pens near Frijole Ranch about a mile east of the Headquarters Visitor Center and a corral at Dog Canyon. Both corrals include water. Riders must stop by one of the visitor centers for a permit before using either facility.

A free "Saddle Stock Access Guide" for the park is available at the visitor center. This guide rates 16 different trail sections according to difficulty, using a three-point scale: 1 = easy, 2 = moderate, 3 = difficult. None of the trails in Guadalupe Mountains National Park are suitable for novice riders or horses unconditioned to mountain trail riding.

McKITTRICK CANYON

Often called "the most beautiful spot in Texas," McKittrick Canyon is also the most popular destination for visitors to Guadalupe Mountains National Park. Of all the canyons in the park, McKittrick has the greatest variety of foliage and is particularly colorful from late October to mid-November, when the leaves of chinquapin oak, big-tooth maple, and walnut trees change color. William Pratt, the geologist who donated his ranch to the Park Service, constructed a cabin of local limestone in 1929 at the west end of the canyon where it splits into North and South McKittrick canyons. The Pratt Cabin still stands and there is now a picnic area nearby.

Next to the parking area at the canyon mouth is the McKittrick Canyon Visitor Center, which features interpretive exhibits, restrooms, and a picnic area. A 0.8-mile interpretive nature trail starts next to the visitor center. You can also get water here before starting out on the McKittrick Canyon Trail. No camping is allowed in McKittrick, but there are backcountry camping sites at McKittrick Ridge, 7.4 miles from the visitor center, and at Wilderness Ridge, 4.1 miles from the visitor center. The canyon is open to visitors daily 8 a.m.-6 p.m. in the summer and 8 a.m.-4:30 p.m. during the winter. Backpackers are permitted to leave their vehicles in the McKittrick parking area overnight while hiking.

Vehicle access to the McKittrick Canyon Visitor Center and trailhead is via a five-mile road off US 62/180 that begins about seven miles northeast of Pine Springs.

Trails
McKittrick Canyon Trail (10.9 miles) begins at the McKittrick Canyon Visitor Center and proceeds 2.3 miles along the canyon floor to the picnic area at Pratt Cabin. From here, it's another 1.1 miles to the Grotto Picnic Area, one of the most scenic areas in McKittrick Canyon proper. For a good view of the canyon and encompassing ridges, continue four more miles to McKittrick Ridge. This section of the trail involves an elevation gain of about 2,300 feet and is fairly demanding. A roundtrip hike to McKittrick Ridge from the trailhead can be accomplished in a full day but is better tackled as an overnight.

The trail continues on another 3.5 miles along the McKittrick Ridge above South McKittrick Canyon, affording good views of Hunter Peak, the Bowl, and the Blue Ridge to the southwest. The McKittrick Canyon Trail ends at a T-junction with the Tejas Trail.

Permian Reef Geology Trail (4.7 miles) begins a few hundred feet from the McKittrick Canyon Visitor Center and forks north along the northern edge of the canyon and then west along Wilderness Ridge. Elevation gain is about 2,000 feet, with views all the way into South McKittrick Canyon. The trail skirts McKittrick Peak (7,064 feet) before reaching the Wilderness Ridge Campsite at mile 4.1. From here the trail veers north again and after 0.6 mile ends at the New Mexico state line. At this point, the established trail gives way to a primitive trail that continues north into New Mexico's Lincoln National Forest. A map of Lincoln National Forest trails can be purchased at any of the visitor centers in Guadalupe Mountains National Park or at the Lincoln National Forest Office in Carlsbad, New Mexico.

At points along the Permian Reef Geology Trail, you can see fossil-ridden segments of the Permian Reef as well as fore-reef and back-reef marine deposits.

PINE SPRINGS

The park's Pine Springs area, just off US 62/180 at Guadalupe Pass, has a long history of human habitation—water was easily available from Lower Pine Spring (the spring was buried following a 1931 earthquake). Numerous mescal pits near the Pine Springs Campground indicate Mescalero Apaches occupied the spot at times. Before and after the Civil War, the U.S. Army camped here during Indian campaigns, and in the 1850s the Butterfield Overland Mail established a stage station at Pine Springs called the Pinery.

Pine Springs Campground
This is the larger of the two drive-in campgrounds in the park, with 19 tentsites and 29 RV sites. Water, restrooms, and tables are available. There are no RV hookups or dump stations and the Park Service has no plans to pro-

view from El Capitan

CHRIS HUMPHREY

vide them in the future. Wood or charcoal fires are not permitted for environmental reasons.

Camper registration at Pine Springs is mandatory and "self-service" via the registration board near the restrooms. Camping fees are $6 per site per night and are collected daily from the fee deposit tube near the registration board. Golden Age and Golden Access Passport holders pay only $3. During the summer, park rangers present interpretive programs every evening at the campground; during the rest of the year these programs are scheduled less regularly. Campground restrooms and campsite number 25 are wheelchair accessible.

The Pinery
The original Butterfield Overland Mail came through Guadalupe Pass and stopped at the Pinery Station, one of 200 stage stations between St. Louis and San Francisco. The Pinery was the only inhabited spot for the 458-mile stretch between Fort Chadborne and El Paso and was the highest stage station (5,543 feet) along the 2,800-mile route.

The station consisted of high limestone walls enclosing a wagon repair shop, blacksmith shop, corral for replacement horses, and three mud-roofed rooms where passengers and crew could rest while coach and team were tended to. Stagecoaches arrived at the Pinery four times a week, but the station was open for business 24 hours a day; it also handled express riders, mule trains, and road crews.

The first Butterfield coach arrived at the Pinery in September 1858 and the last in August 1859, when the Guadalupe route was abandoned for a better-protected route serving Fort Stockton and Fort Davis. Long after the Pinery was abandoned it continued to play host to passing emigrants, desperadoes, and cattle drovers. The ruins of the Pinery Station are the best preserved of any Butterfield station close to a major U.S. highway—in this case, US 62/180, which began as the original Butterfield mail route. The new route became the basis for I-10 farther south. The Pinery ruins are just off the road leading to Pine Springs Campground.

Pine Springs Trails
Tejas Trail (11.9 miles) extends the length of the park between Pine Springs and Dog Canyon and is one of the main access routes to the high country. The first section climbs for 3.8 miles along the base of Pine Springs Canyon and then along a series of steep switchbacks to the top of the north canyon wall, for an elevation gain of about 2,000 feet. The ascent is fairly difficult but affords excellent views of the canyon below as well as Guadalupe, Bartlett, and Shumard peaks. This section makes an excellent day hike for those who wish to return to the Pine Springs Campground before evening. Hikers who want to continue on from this escarpment can change over to the Bush Mountain or Hunter Peak trails; 0.2 miles west along Bush Mountain Trail is Pine Top Campsite.

For those staying with the Tejas Trail, the next section descends north along a short ridge into a stand of pine and Douglas fir. About 1.5 miles from the escarpment is the junction for the Bowl Rim Trail to the east, which leads into the Bowl. After another 1.1 miles, the Tejas Trail meets the **Blue Ridge Trail,** which leads west to the Marcus Trail junction and Blue Ridge Campsite, then on to another section of the Bush Mountain Trail.

From the Blue Ridge Trail junction, the Tejas Trail continues with little elevation change north above the west end of South McKittrick Canyon to Mescalero Campsite. From here, the trail starts climbing to McKittrick Ridge, meeting the terminus of McKittrick Canyon Trail 1.5 miles after the Blue Ridge Trail junction. The trail continues to climb as it crosses the slopes of Lost Peak (7,830 feet), where a side trail leads to the summit and affords views of the overall reef structure to the north.

After Lost Peak, the Tejas Trail begins descending toward Dog Canyon along an old wagon track. West of the trail are the remains of a 1930s cabin built by a copper miner who worked the nearby Texas Calumet Mine. The woods of Dog Canyon are a refreshing sight, and hikers finally reach Dog Canyon Campground 5.5 miles past the Blue Ridge Trail junction.

Guadalupe Peak Trail (4.4 miles) leads to the highest point in Texas, Guadalupe Peak (8,749 feet). This steady upward hike along a well-maintained trail is not as difficult as the peak's elevation might suggest. It's best not to stray from the path, however, since limestone cliffs easily crumble underfoot.

The views from Guadalupe Peak are outstanding. To the north are the park's second- and third-highest points, Bush Mountain and Shumard Peak. To the immediate south is El Capitan, the point of the wedge formed by the Guadalupes, and beyond are vast expanses of the Chihuahuan Desert.

About a mile before the summit is Guadalupe Peak Campsite. In spite of the pine and juniper trees that surround it, the campsite is subject to high winds.

El Capitan is the very impressive cliff peak one sees upon approaching the Guadalupes from the south on US 62/180. **El Capitan Trail** (9.4 miles) doesn't lead to the summit of El Capi-

tan as the name suggests—it would be quite dangerous to attempt such an ascent—but skirts the base and leads to the west side of the Guadalupe Escarpment, then the Williams Ranch. The hike all the way to the ranch is rigorous, mainly due to exposure to southwesterly winds and lack of water at the other end. Most people who want to visit the Williams Ranch area come by four-wheel drive along the unpaved road from US 62/180. Backpackers can also camp at Shumard Canyon Campsite, 0.3 mile north of Williams Ranch.

Hiking the first 3.4 miles of the El Capitan Trail to Guadalupe Canyon or continuing on a bit to the Salt Basin Overlook Trail is perhaps more rewarding than hiking the trail's entire length. This section breaks off from the Guadalupe Peak Trail a short distance from Pine Springs Campground and proceeds through desert savannah, then gradually climbs along the base of El Capitan. At 3.4 miles the trail descends into Guadalupe Canyon and meets a junction where hikers can choose to go south along the Salt Basin Overlook Trail loop, or north along the west side of the escarpment on the main trail. You can follow the main trail along the base of the escarpment until it meets the west junction of the Salt Basin loop at 4.3 miles. At this point the views of the cliffs and the huge salt flat below begin to open up. It's another 5.1 miles to the Williams Ranch, 4.8 to the Shumard Canyon Campsite.

Salt Basin Overlook Trail (3.5 miles) begins in Guadalupe Canyon as described above and heads south into the canyon, then up along steep cliffs till it rejoins the El Capitan Trail. About a half mile before the loop rejoins the El Capitan Trail, a short path leads to the Salt Basin Overlook, which provides an excellent view of the *bolsones* (salt lakes) below. The smooth-surfaced Salt Basin extends for 90 miles along a northwest-southeast axis between the Permian Front Ranges (Guadalupe, Delaware, and Apache mountains) to the east and the Diablo Plateau to the west; this is one of the best vantage points for appreciating its grand scale. Along the way are several views of El Capitan.

If one hikes El Capitan to the first junction with the Salt Basin loop, hikes the loop, then exits at the west junction and returns to the Pine Springs Campground via El Capitan, the entire journey is 11.2 miles.

Bear Canyon Trail (3.3 miles) goes east from the Tejas Trail just beyond the Guadalupe Peak Trail junction, then north into the high country via Upper Pine Spring. The ascent to the top of Bear Canyon is very steep, so this trail is most often used to descend from the high country. The trail, once part of Hunter Ranch, was used to maintain a pipeline system that pumped water from Upper Pine Spring until 1967. The trail passes just above Upper Pine Spring about 1.5 miles from the trailhead. The water source has created an oasis for maple, ash, oak, and madrone.

Just beyond Upper Pine Spring, the Frijole Trail branches off to the east and hooks up with Smith-Manzanita Springs Trail after 1.2 miles. The Bear Canyon Trail continues north along its steepest incline for 1.8 miles until it ends at the Bowl Rim Trail. Just before the terminus, it passes a junction for Hunter Peak Trail to the west.

The Bear Canyon and Bowl trails are joined by **Hunter Peak Trail** (0.9 miles), which extends east-west between them via Hunter Peak (8,368 feet). From Hunter Peak there are good views into Pine Springs Canyon as well as across the entire reef structure.

Devil's Hall Trail (2.3 miles) leads to the upper end of Hiker's Staircase, a canyon formed by Pine Springs. Devil's Hall refers to the narrow, stratified walls at this end. Because of the pools of water that usually collect in the canyon, this is a good hike for viewing wildlife and vegetation. It's also a relatively cool hike on hot days, since the narrow canyon walls shade much of the trail. The trailhead is reached via the Guadalupe Peak Horse Trail; the mileage figure is from Pine Springs Campground.

The Frijole Trail connects Bear Canyon Trail at Upper Pine Spring with the **Smith-Manzanita Springs Trail** and is not very exciting in itself. The Smith-Manzanita Springs Trail is easier to reach from **Frijole Ranch,** about three miles north of the Headquarters Visitor Center. Frijole Ranch was built in 1876 and was supposedly the first permanent residence in the park. It's now a ranger residence.

The Smith-Manzanita Springs Trail forms an easy 2.3-mile loop, and the trailhead is near the ranch. If you take the east fork, you'll come to Manzanita Spring after 0.3 mile. This spot was inhabited by Mescaleros until they were routed out by the U.S. Cavalry in 1878. From here it's another 0.9 mile with a gradual ascent along Smith Canyon to Smith Spring, an oasis for madrone, maple, and juniper. Taking the west half of the loop for the return, hikers will pass the Frijole Trail junction at 0.9 mile from Smith Spring; from there it's 0.2 mile back to the trailhead at Frijole Ranch.

THE BOWL

This large depression in the high country contains a dense Douglas fir and pine forest and is an important source of water for wildlife. Two trails lead into the Bowl, the Bowl Trail and the Bowl Rim Trail; the latter is called the Juniper Trail on the Trails Illustrated topographic map.

The 0.9-mile **Bowl Trail** connects Hunter Peak Trail with the Bowl Rim. The **Bowl Rim Trail** links the Tejas and Bear Canyon trails and passes through the center of the Bowl for a total distance of 2.8 miles. The nearest campsites for Bowl explorations are Pine Top, 0.7 mile from the Bowl Trail, and Mescalero, 0.8 mile from the Juniper/Bowl Rim Trail.

DOG CANYON

This canyon in the north of the park receives runoff from ridges leading to Lost Peak, water that supports a variety of deciduous trees and wildlife. This means Dog Canyon, like McKittrick Canyon, is a good viewing spot for fall foliage. Rocky Mountain elk and mule deer often browse in the canyon as well. Two major trailheads are located near Dog Canyon Campground, the Tejas Trail and Bush Mountain Trail.

Dog Canyon Campground

This is the second drive-in camping facility in Guadalupe Mountains National Park. Because of its 6,300-foot elevation, temperatures tend to be a bit cooler than at the Pine Springs Campground to the south. Since Dog Canyon is also less dry than Pine Springs, cooking grills are provided for charcoal fires. Open fires are not permitted.

Camping facilities include 18 walk-in tentsites and five RV parking spaces. As at Pine Springs, there are no RV hookups or dump stations. A ranger station, picnic area, restrooms, and horse corrals are close at hand. Drinking water for hikers is available.

Vehicle access to Dog Canyon Campground is via New Mexico State Hwy. 137, which runs south off US 285 about 12 miles north of Carlsbad. From this junction it's around 59 miles to the Dog Canyon Campground through private lands and the Lincoln National Forest. It takes about two hours to reach Dog Canyon by vehicle from the park Visitor Center.

Bush Mountain Trail (12.3 miles) is the park's longest single trail, running vaguely parallel to the Tejas Trail from Dog Canyon Campground to the top of Pine Springs Canyon. It also runs as far west into the Guadalupes as established trails will take you, following the western escarpment over Bush Mountain, the second-highest peak in the park. The trail could be hiked starting from either end; the following description begins in Dog Canyon.

The first section of the trail takes you west from the canyon floor, up and over a ridge into West Dog Canyon, meeting the **Marcus Trail** junction at 3.5 miles. The Marcus Trail heads directly south along West Dog Canyon and terminates at the Blue Ridge Trail after 3.8 miles. About 200 yards north of Marcus-Bush Mountain Trail junction is the Marcus Campsite.

From the Marcus Trail junction, Bush Mountain Trail veers southwest, climbing past Cox Tank (part of a former ranch water system) toward Blue Ridge. Once Blue Ridge is attained, hikers can see the Chihuahuan Desert thousands of feet below to the west, as well as Lost Peak to the east. Some 7.4 miles from Dog Canyon Campground—3.9 miles from the Marcus Trail junction in West Dog Canyon—the trail meets the west terminus of Blue Ridge Trail, which leads east to the Blue Ridge Campsite a half mile away and connects Bush Mountain Trail with the central section of the Tejas Trail.

On the ascent toward Bush Mountain you can look west and spot the lush green fields of Dell City, Texas, 20 miles away. About two miles south of the Blue Ridge Trail junction, the trail passes over the slopes of Bush Mountain (8,631

feet), then descends to Bush Mountain Campsite. From here the trail twists east above the upper reaches of Pine Springs Canyon, providing excellent views of the canyon below, Bartlett Peak (8,508 feet) on the other side of the canyon, and Shumard Peak (8,615 feet) to the south. Bush Mountain Trail terminates at the Tejas Trail, 2.9 miles from the Bush Mountain Campsite.

WILLIAMS RANCH

The Williams Ranch lies to the west of the Guadalupe Escarpment amidst a classic shrub desert biome. Originally built in 1900 by Henry Belcher as a longhorn cattle ranch, it was bought by James Adolphus Williams in 1915 and converted to a sheep ranch. A mile east of the ranch house is Bone Canyon, which exposes the oldest layer of limestone reef in the park. Because the west side of the Guadalupes receives the least amount of average precipitation, Bone Canyon is nearly bone-dry, though there is a grassy area near the source of Bone Spring. El Capitan towers above.

You can reach the Williams Ranch area by horse or foot via El Capitan Trail from Pine Springs Campground, 9.4 miles away, or by four-wheel drive via an eight-mile unpaved road off US 62/180, about 8.5 miles south of Guadalupe Pass.

GUADALUPE AREA ACCOMMODATIONS AND FOOD

Guadalupe Mountains National Park has no lodging facilities other than campgrounds, nor are there any grocery stores or gas stations in the park. The nearest tourist motels are in Whites City, New Mexico, 35 miles north on US 62/180, where two Best Westerns (tel. 800-528-1234) offer rooms for $50-80 a night; less expensive accommodations are available in Carlsbad, New Mexico, 20 miles past Whites City. The nearest Texas motels are in Van Horn, 75 miles south of the park at I-10 and State 54.

Thirteen miles west of the park on US 62/180, about seven miles west of the near-ghost town of Salt Flat, the unsigned **Dell Junction Cafe** serves burgers, canned food, soft drinks, and fruit; it also maintains a couple of gas pumps. The woman who does the cooking serves tasty Filipino chicken with rice (is this really West Texas?) and "Shanghai coffee." Cowboys ride in from local cattle drives for the burgers. In Salt Flat, the **Salt Flat Cafe** offers standard diner fare as well as gasoline. These two diners offer the only food and gas services between Cornudas (another 17 miles further west) and Whites City, New Mexico.

The **Cornudas Cafe** in tiny Cornudas, 32 miles west of the park, serves the best breakfasts and green-chile burgers in a 100-mile radius; open daily 8 a.m.-9 p.m. The cafe sponsors "Goose Poop Bingo," in which a goose is turned loose onto a large numbered grid; wherever it leaves a deposit determines the winning number. Next to the cafe is a trucker's motel that is sometimes open, sometimes not.

GETTING THERE

Guadalupe Mountains National Park is 110 miles east of El Paso, 75 miles north of Van Horn, and 55 miles southwest of Carlsbad, New Mexico. Regional Texas and New Mexico bus lines pass the park en route between El Paso and Carlsbad and between Carlsbad and Fort Stockton. Since there's no official bus stop at the park, you must make advance arrangements with the driver to get off; call (806) 765-6641 for more information.

DAVIS MOUNTAINS

The Davis Mountains are unique among West Texas mountain ranges in that they're mostly smooth-topped and grassy. These mountains constitute the northern end of the Tertiary Volcanic Region that lies between the Western Front Ranges of Malone, Quitman, Eagle, and Indio and the Eastern Front Ranges of Sierra del Carmen, Santiago, Del Norte, and Altuda. The Tertiary Volcanic Region, formed by thick accumulations of lava flow, extends from the Davis Mountains in the north to the Bofecillos Mountains on the Texas-Mexico border to the south, just west of Big Bend National Park. The state's fifth-highest peak, **Mt. Livermore** (8,382 feet), is in the southeastern section of the Davis Mountains, in the middle of a loop formed by Texas Highways 166 and 118.

It's no secret in Texas that this area has what many agree is the best year round climate in the state. The cool summers and mild winters are mostly due to the elevation, which averages around 5,000-6,000 feet. Also, unlike most of the Trans-Pecos, the Davis Mountains average over 20 inches of rain a year, more than enough to support wooded grasslands. The air is so clear that when the University of Texas decided to build an observatory, the Davis Mountains were the natural choice.

DAVIS MOUNTAINS STATE PARK

About six miles west of Fort Davis off State 118, this 1,869-acre park is centered around a canyon formed by Limpia Creek. The park features easy to moderate hiking trails, a longhorn herd, a scenic drive with overlooks, and an interpretive center. A trail that starts at the interpretive center proceeds east 4.5 miles to Fort Davis National Historic Site. Between June and August, rangers conduct campfire programs. Fishing and swimming are permitted in Limpia Creek.

Facilities

Separate camping areas feature sites with water only ($8), water and electricity ($11), and full RV hookups ($13). All sites have tables and cooking grills. Hot showers, restrooms, and trailer dump site available. For campsite reservations, contact the Superintendent (tel. 915-426-3337), Davis Mountains State Park, P.O. Box 786, Fort Davis, TX 79734.

The **Indian Lodge** is a 39-room pueblo-style motel in the park built by the Civilian Conservation Corps in the 1930s. The adobe walls of the lodge are 18-22 inches thick and many of the interior furnishings are original. Rooms are basic, but all have TV and air-conditioning; some have beamed adobe ceilings lined with river cane from the banks of the Rio Grande. The lodge has a good restaurant (open daily 7:30 a.m.-9 p.m. except when the lodge is closed) and heated swimming pool. The Indian Lodge is open year round except for two weeks beginning on the second Monday of January, when it's closed for general repairs. Room rates are $40-50 per night.

The park user fee is $4 per person, free for TCP holders. For further information and reservations (accepted up to a year in advance), contact the Indian Lodge Manager (tel. 426-3254), P.O. Box 786, Fort Davis, TX 79734.

FORT DAVIS

The town of Fort Davis (pop. 1,200) is named for a frontier fort founded in 1854 near the intersection of the Chihuahua Trail and the San Antonio-El Paso Trail. The fort closed in 1891 but the town managed to hang on as county seat of first Presidio County and then Jeff Davis County. Today its economy for the most part depends on serving visitors to the Davis Mountains and Fort Davis National Historic Site.

Fort Davis sits at an elevation of 5,050 feet, making it the highest town in the state, at about the same elevation as Denver, Colorado. Temperatures in the summer are a pleasant 70-80° F while in the winter the mercury is stuck in the 30s and 40s.

The main street of Fort Davis has a couple of historic inns and buildings, and a few tourist-oriented shops. To get an idea of the town's real charm, walk or drive the unpaved back streets, with their cozy adobe, wood-frame houses and little country churches.

SIGHTS

Fort Davis National Historic Site

History: Fort Davis was established by the U.S. Army to protect travelers and freight along the San Antonio-El Paso Trail from Apache and Comanche Indian attacks. The first garrison buildings were built in 1854 of pine slabs with thatched roofs and named for then Secretary of War Jefferson Davis. When the Civil War broke out, the Union army abandoned the fort and it was taken over by Confederate troops in 1861. The Confederates held Fort Davis for less than a year; when Union troops took El Paso, the Confederates at Fort Davis joined other Confederate troops along the West Texas frontier in a general retreat to San Antonio.

The fort lay abandoned for five years and was burned to the ground by the Mescalero Apaches. Two years after the end of the Civil War, in 1867, the U.S. Army returned and rebuilt the fort, this time of stone and adobe. Fort Davis became the headquarters for the 9th U.S. Cavalry, one of two black cavalry regiments that earned the nickname "Buffalo Soldiers" from Indians who encountered them in the ensuing Indian Wars. The fort's military function evolved from one of frontier defense to one of outright assault upon area Apache tribes. The last Apache battle in Texas was fought by African-American soldiers from Fort Davis along the Mexican border in 1880. In 1885, the Buffalo Soldiers were transferred to Arizona Territory, where they obtained Geronimo's surrender in the following year. When there were no Indians left to fight, the fort closed in 1891. The National Park Service took over the site in 1961 and eventually restored half of the original 50 structures.

Facilities: The restored site features a visitor center (in a former company barrack) with slide and audio programs, a small museum chronicling the 1854-91 history of the fort, and a self-guiding tour. During the summer, the park staff and volunteers dress in period costume and give free guided tours. An 1875 vintage Retreat

Parade is also reenacted with sound effects (bugles and cavalry hoofbeats) daily at 11 a.m. and 4 p.m. during the summer.

Behind the officers' quarters is the trailhead for the **Tall Grass Nature Trail,** a 1.2-mile loop that takes hikers to a viewpoint in the hills over the site.

The fort is located at the north end of the town of Fort Davis, off State 17. Admission is $2 per person or $4 per carload. People over age 62 holding the Golden Age Passport are admitted free. For additional information, contact the Superintendent (tel. 915-426-3225), Fort Davis National Historic Site, P.O. Box 1456, Fort Davis, TX 79734.

McDonald Observatory

High atop Mount Locke at 6,800 feet, this University of Texas astronomy research center is one of the top 10 observatories in the world. The Davis Mountains are a particularly good location for astronomical viewing because of the lack of light pollution from nearby artificial

107-inch telescope, McDonald Observatory

light sources, the high annual number of cloudless nights, and the concentration of native plants and trees in the vicinity that filter dust and radiation.

When built in 1938, the observatory's 82-inch telescope was the second largest in existence. In 1969, the observatory added a 107-inch telescope under joint contract between the university and NASA. This scope is in heavy demand by research astronomers from around the country for all kinds of research but is best suited for spectroscopic analysis of the light from planets, satellites, stars, and quasars.

McDonald is also the site of a 16-foot millimeter-wave dish for studying gas clouds and particles in the Milky Way, a 30-inch scope responsible for over half the world's records on lunar occultations (which occur when the moon passes in front of a star), and a laser-ranging telescope used for precise lunar calculations of orbit and distance. The $13.5 million Hobby-Eberly Telescope (HET), currently under construction at the observatory, will position 91 hexagonal mirrors over a 36-foot-wide surface to produce the world's largest mirror scope. In a valley below the peak is the Harvard Radio Astronomy Center, which harbors a radio telescope that's part of a worldwide system called Very Long Base Array (VLBA). Radio scopes in this system, a joint University of California-University of Texas-Harvard University project, measure continental drift by base-line vectoring.

The observatory complex lies 19 miles northwest of Fort Davis via State 118 and Spur 78, otherwise known as Skyline Drive (constructed, like Indian Lodge, by the CCC in the 1930s).

Visitor Center: A few hundred yards below the peak is the W.L. Moody, Jr. Visitors' Information Center, where visitors are asked to check in before proceeding to the observatory complex. The exhibits here are quite good and the gift shop carries star charts and other astronomy-related items. Don't miss the Gravity Well. The center is open daily 9 a.m.-5 p.m. except for Thanksgiving, Christmas, and New Year's Day.

Visitor Activities: Only the dome that contains the 107-inch scope is open to the public. Guided tours of the dome and the immediate grounds are conducted daily at 2 p.m. year round, and from June through August at 9:30 a.m. as well. The tours are excellent and last

about an hour, but if you miss the appointed starting times you can take a self-guided walking tour of the facility. The Moody Center distributes maps with step-by-step instructions for the self-guided tour. There is no charge for either type of tour but donations are accepted in the 107-inch telescope dome.

Once a month the observatory allows visitors to view the sky through the big scope—this is the only major observatory in North America with such a program. Admission is $5 for adults, $4 for students and seniors, or $2.50 for children under 12. Tickets and a schedule of the public viewing nights are available from the W.L. Moody, Jr. Visitors' Information Center.

Every Tuesday, Friday, and Sunday evenings, the Moody Center puts on a "Star Party," in which a docent presents a visual tour of the constellations as well as a chance to view heavenly bodies through eight- and 14-inch telescopes. Star parties are free of charge and begin just after sunset outside the center, weather permitting.

Daily at 11 a.m. and 3:30 p.m., the center holds solar viewing sessions in which active sunspots are viewed through a filtered telescope. Lunar spying is also a possibility during these sessions on days when the moon rises early or sets late. For more information call or write McDonald Observatory (tel. 915-426-3640), P.O. Box 1337, Fort Davis, TX 79734.

Star Date: The observatory produces a nationally syndicated two-minute radio program broadcast daily on National Public Radio-affiliated stations throughout the United States. Topics include astronomy, skywatching, and space exploration. A companion bimonthly magazine, *Star Date,* is available with a $15 annual subscription from the University of Texas at Austin (tel. 512-471-5285), 2609 University Ave. #3118, Austin, TX 78712.

Chihuahuan Desert Research Institute
Founded in 1974 by Sul Ross University for the scientific study of the Chihuahuan Desert and for public education, the institute covers 580 acres that include an arboretum, nature trails, and a botanical garden with over 500 regional species. Native plants are for sale—the largest selection is around the last week of April during the institute's annual Native Plant Sale. In late Sep-

tember the CRDI sponsors a symposium on Chihuahuan Desert research. The visitor center lies 3.5 miles south of Fort Davis on State 118. Open April 1 to Labor Day, weekdays 1-5 p.m. and weekends 9 a.m.-5 p.m. No admission charge, though donations are welcome. Call (915) 837-8370 for information.

Scenic Loop

State Highways 166 and 118 form a 74-mile loop through the lower third of the Davis Mountains, circling Mount Livermore and passing Madera Canyon, Mount Locke, and Davis Mountains State Park. Driving west from Fort Davis, the mountains look their prettiest at sunrise or, from the east, at sunset.

ACCOMMODATIONS, FOOD, AND ENTERTAINMENT

Hotels and Motels

The **Old Texas Inn** (tel. 915-426-3118), P.O. Box 785, Fort Davis, TX 79734, above Fort Davis Drug on the town's main drag, has six rooms decorated with country antiques for $40 s plus $5 per each additional guest. Discounts are available for longer stays and you can rent the entire Inn for $200 a night. Across the street is the **Limpia Hotel** (tel. 800-662-5517), P.O. Box 822, Fort Davis, TX 79734, originally built in 1912 and restored in 1978; nine rooms on the

upper floor and eight across the street in "Limpia West." Three suites in the old wing sleep four to eight. Rates are $59 s, $62 d, $68 t; add $5 for suites. During the winter months, Sun.-Thurs. rates are approximately $10 lower; year round there's a 10% senior discount for those 62 years and over.

The **Stone Village Motel** (tel. 426-3941) is the closest lodging to Fort Davis National Historic Site. Simple but well-kept rooms cost $29-41 a night, the best value in town. The nearby **Butterfield's** (tel. 426-3252) has four cottages with jacuzzis and fireplaces for $60 a night. Off the main road in town are a couple of bed and breakfasts: **Wayside Inn** (tel. 426-3535 or 800-582-7510) for $55-77 a night and Victorian-style **Neill Doll Museum** (tel. 426-3969) for $55-65. The doll museum displays over 400 antique dolls.

The new **Fort Davis Motor Inn** (tel. 426-2112 or 800-80-DAVIS), on State 17 N just northeast of the State 118 turnoff, offers typical motel rooms for $59-75.

The **Prude Ranch** (tel. 426-3202 or 800-458-6232), P.O. Box 1431, Fort Davis, TX 79734, 6.5 miles northwest of town off State 118, is a tourist attraction in itself. It started out in 1898 as a cattle ranch; in the '30s cabins were erected on the ranch for workers building the McDonald Observatory. Currently, it's a combination dude ranch, mountain resort, RV park, and campground. Cabins run $49-68, motel rooms $65-75,

Hotel Limpia

full RV hookups $12.50, sites with water and electricity $8.50 for pop-ups and $10 for trailers. Weekly rates are lower. Facilities include tennis courts, indoor swimming pool, and hot tub.

Campgrounds and RV Parks
Tent, trailer, and RV camping are permitted at nearby Davis Mountains State Park.

Stone Village Motel operates **Fontainebleau RV Park,** a block south of the hotel on Old Murphy. Drive-through sites cost $5 for campers, $10 for vans, $12 for full hookups. The park offers laundry and shower facilities.

Food
Good food is available at **Fort Davis Drug** on the town square, but it's only open for breakfast and lunch during the week, and for breakfast, lunch, and dinner on Friday and Saturday. It's no longer a pharmacy, although the original soda fountain has been preserved and the place still offers hand-mixed Cokes and ice-cream floats.

Across the street, the **Hotel Limpia Dining Room** serves good country-style fare for breakfast, lunch, and dinner daily, plus a special breakfast buffet Sat.-Sun. 8-10:30 a.m. The **Bandana Room** upstairs is the only bar in the county. **KC's Country Kitchen,** next to Stone Village Motel, is a popular and inexpensive breakfast spot open Mon.-Sat. 6 a.m.-2 p.m.

Farther north along the main street are several other possibilities, including the popular **Cueva de Leon,** a Tex-Mex place open daily for lunch and dinner (special fajita buffet Saturday nights). The nearby **Desert Rose** offers a simple menu of Texas and Mexican dishes daily 6 a.m.-2 p.m. and 5-9 p.m. Further north, **Poco Mexico** is an inexpensive choice for Mexican lunches; open 11 a.m.-2 p.m. only, closed Thursday.

Raul's Barbecue, on the east side of town at the intersection of State 118 and State 17, serves some of the best brisket in West Texas. Don't look for any neon signs, as the business is operated from a modest frame house. The meat's ready around 11 a.m. and gone by 7 p.m. In addition to the by-the-pound brisket and ribs, Raul sells a barbecue sandwich called the Tejano.

Shopping
Several shops in town sell West Texas souvenirs, including one attached to the Hotel Limpia Dining Room. This shop also carries a good selection of books on Texas.

Fort Davis Astronomical Supply, next to the Stone Village Motel, sells everything for the amateur astronomer including large backyard scopes.

Horseback Riding
Davis Mountains Horseback Tours (tel. 915-426-3022 or 426-3016), P.O. Box 277, Fort Davis, TX 79734, offers guided trail rides ranging from $10 per hour to $90 all day, meals included. Half- and full-day rides require a minimum of three riders; reservations must be made at least eight days in advance.

VICINITY OF FORT DAVIS

Balmorhea
Pronounced "BAL-mo-RAY" and named for three early residents (Balcom, Morrow, and Rhea), this small farming community of 568 is irrigated by San Solomon Springs, an old watering place along the San Antonio-El Paso Trail. The springs pump 26 million gallons of water a day onto 14,000 acres and flow into the country's largest spring-fed swimming pool at Balmorhea State Recreation Area.

Lake Balmorhea, three miles south of town off US 290, is an impoundment of Sandia Creek that covers nearly 600 acres. The lake is stocked with catfish, stripers, bass, and crappie, and fishing is permitted on the lake for $2 a day. RV hookups are available for $7 a night.

Highway 17 between Balmorhea and Fort Davis winds through scenic, mostly unpopulated Davis Mountains countryside, passing several cool running streams, interesting rock formations, and lots of potential picnic spots.

Accommodations and Food: On State 17 through town, **Country Inn** (tel. 915-375-2477), housed in a WW II-era building with a balcony around the entire upper floor, offers rooms for $30-100 depending on size and amenities. It's popular with divers during the summer scuba season.

Opposite the Country Inn on State 17, the **Fillin' Station Cafe** (tel. 375-2233) serves inexpensive burgers and Mexican food Mon.-Fri. 11 a.m.-2 p.m. and 5-9 p.m., weekends 7 a.m.-9 p.m. This is the only place in Balmorhea that sells beer to go. **Dutchover Restaurant** (tel. 375-2567), a quarter mile down the road towards Fort Davis, offers basic Mexican and steaks, plus cheap breakfasts. It's open Tues.-Thurs. 8 a.m.-2 p.m. and Fri.-Sun. 8 a.m.- 9 p.m. during the winter, daily 8 a.m.-9 p.m. during the summer.

Balmorhea State Recreation Area

Four miles southwest of Balmorhea off US 290, near the minuscule town of Toyahvale (pop. 60), is a state park whose claim to fame is a spring-fed pool with a 68,000-square-foot surface. In some places the pool is 30 feet deep, making this a scuba diving center for much of West Texas. The bottom of the pool is a mixture of rock and sand, interspersed with native aquatic plants. The water is Caribbean clear, as the constant flow from San Solomon Springs changes the entire pool volume every six hours. The temperature is a constant 72-76° F. Freshwater fish inhabit the pool, including catfish, crayfish, perch, and the Comanche Springs pupfish, Leon Springs pupfish, and Pecos gambusia (mosquitofish). The pool is open from Memorial Day through Labor Day, with scuba diving restricted to mornings from 8:30 to 11. The non-diving public can stay until sunset when the park closes. The rest of the park is open year round.

Each year the park staff drains the pool for 10 days of cleaning at the end of April or beginning of May.

Facilities: The park has 28 campsites with water ($7 weekdays, $9 weekends) and six with water and electricity ($10/12). No RV hookups are available but there's a dump station, a picnic area with grills, restrooms, showers, and, in the summer only, a snack bar and bathhouse. Rooms at the rustic **San Solomon Springs Court** cost $35 s, plus $5 for each additional adult. Children ages 6-12 are $2 each; add $5 for rooms with kitchen units.

The park day use fee is $5 per vehicle, $2 per person on foot or bike, free for TCP holders. For more information contact the Superintendent (tel. 915-375-2370), Balmorhea State Recreation Area, P.O. Box 15, Toyahvale, TX 79786.

Valentine

Valentine is one of two towns along US 90 that were practically killed off when the construction of I-10 diverted traffic away from the lovely valley between the Sierra Vieja and Davis Mountains. If you happen to be passing through Valentine before February 14, you can stop off here and mail a bundle of Valentine's Day cards from the post office (you can't miss it, there's only one). Why? So your cards will receive postmarks from Valentine, Texas. This post office has a unique service in which the postmaster holds cards so designated until just before February 14, then franks the stamps with a special Valentine's Day cancellation. You can actually get this done from anywhere in the U.S. by sending your bundle of cards in a large envelope, before February 10, to Postmaster, Valentine, TX 79854.

BIG BEND NATIONAL PARK

Big Bend is a corner of Texas where the Rio Grande bends its mighty elbow around an area of extreme geologic confusion. Indians say the Great Spirit placed all the leftover rocks here after creating the Earth. In this massive detour, in which the river interrupts its southeast flow to head northeast, the Rio Grande must cut through three Big Bend mountain ranges, thus creating the Bend's most striking canyons.

The Chihuahuan Desert, resting between the "mother ranges" of the Sierra Madre Oriental and the Sierra Madre Occidental, is the backdrop for a national park that covers nearly a million acres, an area larger than the state of Rhode Island. Some 234 miles of the Rio Grande are administered for recreational and educational use. The desert, North America's largest, covers parts of six states—Texas and New Mexico in the U.S., plus Chihuahua, Coahuila, Durango, and Zacatecas in Mexico; the park encompasses the best-preserved example of native Chihuahuan Desert in the U.S. or Mexico.

Big Bend is one of North America's greatest national parks—one most park aficionados would place in the top five. Yet it receives far fewer visitors than any of its rivals, and is thus one of the least-crowded national parks in the United States. In 1993, for example, Big Bend received 327,000 visitors, while Arizona's Grand Canyon National Park saw 4.9 million, California's Yosemite National Park endured 3.9 million, and Montana's Glacier National Park took in 2.1 million.

Big Bend is not all desert. Besides the very nondesert-like Rio Grande environment that runs along the base of the park through brakes of river cane and tamarisk, there are mountain oases where conifer forests and shaded springs provide startling biotic contrasts—like ferns and cacti living side by side. Unique plant and animal communities thrive on these mountain islands cast in a desert sea, several species of which are found only in the Big Bend area. This uniqueness led UNESCO in 1976 to designate Big Bend as an International Biosphere Reserve, one of only 250 sites in the world.

One of the best descriptions of Big Bend was offered by an unidentified Mexican *vaquero* over a hundred years ago: "Where the rainbows wait for the rain, and the big river is kept in a stone box, and water runs uphill and mountains float in the air, except at night when they go away to play with other mountains . . ."

BIG BEND BLACK BEAR

The increase in black bear sightings in Big Bend National Park has been phenomenal, up from less than 50 in 1992 to 502 in 1993. The actual resident bear population is thought to be around eight to 12 adult bears; the bears have apparently learned to associate human presence with food sources, and are simply making the rounds in search of easy snacks. Although these 200-pound animals can be quite assertive in searching tents and backpacks for food, so far no bear has harmed a visitor. They've been known to crush butane canisters, hence it's imperative that anything that might smell like food be appropriately stored. For hikers, the park service recommends locking any food or beverages not accompanying you in a vehicle trunk; on the trail, don't leave packs or food unattended.

In response to the increased bear-human encounters, park rangers have installed bearproof steel boxes for food storage throughout the Chisos Mountains camping areas. The park service can fine visitors $50 per offense for improper food storage.

The Land

Film buffs might say it's classic Sergio Leone country, but geologists classify Big Bend as part of the Eastern Volcanic Area of the state's Tertiary Volcanic Region. This area extends from the Bofecillos Mountains just west of the park to the Sierra del Carmen along the park's eastern border, and as far north as the Santiago Mountains. The dominant range within the park, and within the entire Eastern Volcanic Area, is the **Chisos Mountains,** a collection of exposed intrusive lava masses and peaks that reach up to 7,835 feet. Other volcanic ranges in the park

Tuff Canyon, Big Bend National Park

include the Sierra de Santa Eleña and the the northern half of the Rosillos Mountains, as well as many singular peaks like Burro Mesa, Tule Mountain, Talley Mountain, Chilicotal Mountain, and Mariscal Mountain.

The volcanos that erupted in this area probably did so after the dinosaurs disappeared, while the American Southwest was pushing its way up through tropical seas, some 29-35 million years ago. At least eight calderas have been identified in Big Bend; their output of lava, volcanic ash, and other debris covered an area of nearly 10,000 square miles with a thickness of about a mile and a half. In the intervening eons, erosion carved peaks and canyons from the layers of volcanic detritus to create Big Bend's topographical majesty.

Over its half-century history, the park's ecosystem has continued to flourish, coming ever closer to its original state before humans intervened—i.e., the Comanches, who trampled it beneath the feet of captured slaves and livestock by making Big Bend the main intersec-

tion for the Comanche War Trail; the Mexicans, who overfarmed and overgrazed it; and the Anglos, whose ranches and mines threatened to turn the area into another El Paso. Recently the park has benefited from the addition of the Rosillos Mountains Preserve (90,000 acres transferred to the Park Service by the Texas Nature Conservancy) to the north; Black Gap Wildlife Management Area (administered by Texas Parks and Wildlife) to the east; and Big Bend Ranch State Park (over 215,000 acres) to the west. These areas provide large, natural buffers for the biomes in Big Bend National Park.

Recently national park officials have re-established discussions with their Mexican counterparts about the possibility of creating an international park extending across the border into Mexico's Sierra del Carmen. On the U.S. side of the border this range is known as the Dead Horse Mountains; the peaks rise in elevation along a southeast axis from Boquillas Canyon. If the international park is established, it will join Glacier-Waterton International Peace Park on the U.S.-Canada border to become North America's second cross-border nature preserve. In preparation, the Mexican government has already set aside 37,000 acres of the Sierra del Carmen as a nature reserve.

Climate
Because of the great variation in elevation within the park (1,800 feet at the Rio Grande to over 7,800 feet in the Chisos Mountains), Big Bend harbors a number of microclimates, ranging from furnace-like summer temperatures at Mesa de Aguila on the park's extreme western edge and the Dead Horse Mountains in the east, to short-lived winter snow in the Chisos. Average

BIG BEND TEMPERATURES		
MONTH	MAX. (° F)	MIN. (° F)
February	66.2	37.8
April	80.7	52.3
June	94.2	65.5
August	91.1	68.3
October	78.8	52.7
December	62.2	36.4

annual precipitation varies from five to eight inches along the desert floor to 15 inches or more in the Chisos. Most of the year, visitors can count on a high percentage of sunshine, even during the wetter months (July to October). The chart accompanying shows average temperatures for selected months, measured at Panther Junction near the park's center. Temperatures in the mountains may run five to 10 degrees Fahrenheit lower than this average, while along the river they may be five to 10 degrees higher.

Overall, the best times to visit Big Bend are October to November and March to April. In March, the park's most crowded month, campsites and lodge rooms are usually full. Fall is best for river running, with water levels reaching about four feet, while spring is best for birding and wildflower viewing. Even in the height of summer the park can be comfortable if you stick to the mountains; in winter stay in the lower elevations. August is the coolest summer month, thanks to afternoon rains.

Flora

People who've never visited a living desert imagine vast tracts of sand dunes with vultures circling above. As they first enter the Chihuahuan Desert, they're awed to see just how beautiful the arid landscape can be. The subtle tapestry of desert plants yields hues of purple, brown, blue, orange, yellow, and green that change with the seasons—definitely not the uniform khaki of cartoon deserts.

One of the most characteristic Big Bend desert plants is the **creosote bush,** a short evergreen with a taproot that goes down as far as 30 feet to obtain underground water. In the spring, after a good rain, it blooms with yellow flowers. After any rainfall, it emits the creosote aroma for which it is named—the smell of the desert. Another common Chihuahuan Desert plant is the **ocotillo** or coachwhip, so called because it looks like a bunch of coachwhips stuck in the ground. After a rain it bursts with tiny green leaves and during dry spells it looks almost dead, with just the bare brown stems waving in the arid breeze.

The "indicator" plant for the Chihuahuan Desert is the **lechuguilla,** Spanish for "little lettuce," a unique succulent which grows only in this desert. The lechuguilla belongs to the genus *Agave,* from the Greek word for "noble," and as such blooms only once in its lifetime of 10-15 years, when it shoots up a 15-foot stalk and then dies. Unlike more typical broad-leaved agaves, the lechuguilla produces clusters of narrow, spiked blades that are a menace to hikers, horses, and deer but perfect for making strong twine—locally called istle or tampico fiber—used in weaving mats, ropes, bags, and other household items. The tradition of istle-making has not been lost in Big Bend; outside the park, where the plant is not protected, you can buy items made from lechuguilla—rope, donkey bridles, cordage, brooms, and sandals—at the Lajitas Trading Co. just west of the park.

If you've come to Big Bend to see cacti you won't be disappointed. No other national park has so many species of cacti, over 70 at last count, nor as many unique species. In the spring, usually in early to mid-April, many cacti produce splendid flowers. They come in two basic groups, those with glochids, the tiny barbed hairs or bristles that sprout around the same areole from which cactus spines emerge, and those without glochids. Most common among the first group, all of which belong to the genus *Opuntia,* are the **chollas** and **prickly pears.** Chollas feature cylindrical stems that branch out and may extend anywhere from a few inches to over five feet tall, while prickly pears produce flattened pads that also branch out but stay closer to the ground, usually under three feet.

Cane cholla is one of the most common chollas in Big Bend—it's the one that looks like twisted rope standing on end. Prickly pears occur in nine commonly seen varieties, including the **blind prickly pear,** which has no spines; the **Chisos prickly pear,** with yellow spines and glochids; and the **purple-tinged prickly pear,** which has very long spines and purplish pads that are most pronounced in winter. The prickly pear cactus is often eaten locally, especially before Christian lent—look for *nopales* or *nopalitos* on menus.

The non-glochid cacti belong to seven different genera—*Echinocactus, Echinocereus, Cereus, Ariocarpus, Mamillaria,* and *Epithelantha*—all of which produce spines, and *Lophophora,* which does not have spines. Some of the most striking include the **southwestern barrel cactus,** with a globular, ribbed stem and hooked spines; and **devil's claw** or "horse crippler," which is a barrel cactus that grows low to the ground but bears thick, heavy spines. One of the most common cacti in Big Bend is the **strawberry cactus,** which forms stem mounds around three feet high and four feet wide, is covered with a profusion of spines, and produces bright red flowers and fruit in the spring and summer. The fruit may be eaten like strawberries, and is especially tasty with honey and milk or cream. The rare **Chisos Mountain hedgehog cactus** puts out a brilliant pink flower which blooms around 8:30 a.m. and withers by noon. Due to poaching, this endangered cactus is thought to number less than 200.

The most famous of the non-glochids in Big Bend is **peyote** (*Lophophora williamsii*), also called "mescal" or "dry whiskey," a cactus that contains a variety of psychoactive alkaloids, principally mescaline. The dried "buttons" of the peyote cactus have been used by various Indian tribes as a hallucinogenic sacrament in important religious ceremonies since pre-Columbian days. Peyote came to prominence among non-Indians in the 1960s and early '70s, together with a series of books by Latin American writer Carlos Castañeda, who supposedly ate peyote in northern Mexico under the tutelage of a Yaqui sorcerer named Don Juan. The cactus is actually very difficult to find, since it grows in small clumps very close to the ground, disappearing beneath the ground altogether during dry periods. After spring and summer rains, small pink flowers appear in the center of the spineless stem. Peyote cacti are rare within the park boundaries, in part because so many would-be Don Juans have dug them up over the years. Remember, it is illegal to remove or cut any part of any plant in the park, and possession of peyote, classified as a harmful drug by most state governments, is illegal in Texas.

In the highlands you'll find thick conifer forests mixed with high desertscrub. The typical Chisos Mountain woodlands are dominated by **piñon, oak,** and **juniper.** Outside Mexico, **drooping juniper**—so called because the tree's foliage appears to sag or droop, even after a good rain—is found only in the Chisos Mountains. Other trees not normally found outside Mexico are the **chinquapin oak** and the **Coahuila scrub oak.** Also growing in the Chisos are **ponderosa pine, Arizona cypress, Douglas fir, bigtooth maple,** and **quaking aspen,** all at the southern or western extremes of their normal ranges. The rare **Texas madrone,** with its shiny evergreen leaves and brilliant red berries, is seen in the Big Bend high country as well. Highland vegetation found only in the park, and nowhere else in the world, includes the **Chisos oak,** seen only in Blue Creek Canyon, and the **Chisos agave.**

The banks of the Rio Grande comprise their own vegetational zone, what might be termed desert riparian. Subtropical river cane grows thickly in many places and is still used locally for ramadas (shade porches) and simple roofing. Salt cedar grows in some abundance along the river.

Fauna

At least 75 species of **mammals** make Big Bend their home. Among the larger mammals are two species of deer, **Sierra del Carmen whitetail,** generally found above 5,000 feet, and **mule deer,** usually below 5,000 feet; two foxes, the **kit fox** and, more commonly, the **gray fox; pronghorn,** on the increase in the park; the **coyote;**

SEEING THE LION

About 95% of all mountain lion sightings since the 1950s have been along park roads, rather than on hiking trails. Furthermore, lions are nocturnal animals, so you're not likely to see them unless you hike at night. At last estimate about two dozen lions lived in the park, most often seen in the Chisos. If you encounter a lion while hiking in the park, the Park Service advises you to "convince the lion that you are not prey and that you may be dangerous yourself." First, do not run from the lion. Do not try to hide or crouch down either, since the lion will have seen you long before you've seen it. If you hold your ground, shout, and wave your hands, the lion will most likely leave the vicinity; if the lion behaves aggressively, throw stones. If you're hiking with children, it's best to pick them up so you and they look larger to the lion.

javelina

the **Mexican black bear;** and the nocturnal **mountain lion,** also called cougar, panther, or puma. Only the mountain lion has been known to attack humans, and then only rarely. There have been only two attacks since 1984; in both cases the attacking lions were killed by park rangers.

A more common nocturnal creature is the **javelina,** or collared peccary. Although the javelina looks like a wild pig, it's actually a member of a very small family of mammals called Tayassuidae, and is more closely related to tapirs and horses than to pigs of any kind. They're common in Big Bend, and if you spend any time in the park campgrounds or near the Chisos Mountain Lodge, you're quite likely to see one or even a small herd when they feed in the early morning or late evening. Because they're very nearsighted and naturally curious, javelinas will occasionally approach people for a few sniffs, but there's no need to be alarmed unless young peccaries are present—that's when the mothers may act unpredictably.

A host of smaller mammals live in the park, including various rabbits, squirrels, bats, raccoons, skunks, badgers, and mice. Of these, perhaps the most distinctive are the huge **black-tailed jackrabbit** and the **kangaroo rat.** Both are uniquely adapted to desert life. The long, upright ears of the jackrabbit enable it to hear sounds from quite a distance, a necessity for an animal that is prey for practically every larger animal (including coyotes, eagles, and bob-

cats) in the park. The ears also act as radiators on hot desert days, allowing the jackrabbit to release excess body heat into the air. The kangaroo rat, which you may see hopping in front of your headlights at night, is built so it doesn't need to drink water, ever. It derives moisture from seeds, from the air deep inside its burrows where the relative humidity is 30-50%, and from condensation in its nasal passages. Its efficient kidneys excrete uric acid in a concentrated paste, rather than in liquid form.

Big Bend is a mecca for **birds** since it's at the southern end of the central flyway and there's such a diversity of habitats. Well over 400 species of birds have been recorded here, more than in any other national park in the U.S. or Canada. Several bird species appear only in Big Bend, specifically in the Chisos Mountains. Others are native to Mexico and Central America and Big Bend is the northern limit of their habitat. Most famous is the **Colima warbler,** a small yellow-and-gray warbler that nests in Boot Canyon and in Laguna Meadow and is most commonly seen May to July. The **Lucifer hummingbird** is another bird whose only American habitat is Big Bend; it's very common around blooming agave plants in the summer. Other birds found in Big Bend include **great blue herons, Mexican mallards, roadrunners** (usually called "paisano" locally), **golden eagles, bald eagles, red-tailed hawks, American kestrels, peregrine falcons, great horned owls, screech owls, white-throated swifts,** and **cactus wrens**—the latter build their nests in cacti. To learn the best seasons to spot these and other species, obtain the *Bird Checklist* published by the Big Bend Natural History Association and distributed by the National Park Service. **Big Bend Birding Expeditions** (tel. 915-371-2356) arranges half-day, one-day, and two-day birdwatching excursions starting at $70 per person.

Big Bend's herpetofauna includes 10 species of **amphibians** and 56 species of **reptiles.** There are 30 snake species, 22 lizard species, and four turtle species. Look for the **Rio Grande leopard frog,** a slim, slimy, spotted green frog found in pools alongside the river and occasionally in springs and *tinajas,* or the uncommon **spiny softshell turtle,** found only in the Rio Grande. Naturally the park has horned lizards ("horny toads") in abundance—there are two species, the **Texas horned lizard,** found in grassy areas of the park's northernmost parts; and the **round-tailed horned lizard,** found in sparse desert flats, often near ant mounds.

Probably the most commonly seen snake is the harmless **coachwhip,** a long pink snake that slithers along very quickly. Most of the other 29 species found in the park are on the shy and secretive side, so you won't see many of them. Five are venomous: the **Trans-Pecos copperhead,** which is nocturnal and lives in cane patches along the river, is occasionally seen in canyons. The mostly nocturnal, aggressive **western diamondback rattlesnake** frequents dry riverbeds, desert flats, grasslands, and canyons—just about any rocky place below 4,500 feet. The **mottled rock rattlesnake** looks like mottled rock and prefers rocky terrain but is somewhat uncommon. The aggressive **Mojave rattlesnake,** also rather uncommon, frequents hot desert flats, especially around creosote bush. The most common Big Bend rattler, the **black-tailed rattlesnake,** is found throughout the park, but mostly in the Chisos Mountains and surrounding foothills. Visitors are very unlikely to be bitten by one of these venomous snakes, but the usual precautions should be followed.

Rio Grande **fishing** is said to be good, especially for anglers who like tasty **blue, channel,** and **flathead catfish.** Other fish large enough for the hook include **longnose gar, carp, small-** **mouth buffalo, river carpsucker,** and **freshwater drum.** Most other fish species in the Rio Grande and in river pools are minnow-like; some of the more Big Bend-specific fishes are the **Mexican stoneroller,** known only in this park and in Arizona's Rucker Canyon, the **Chihuahua shiner,** found only in the park and in a few locations in the Mexican state of Chihuahua, and the **Big Bend gambusia,** found only in a certain pond in the park's Rio Grande Village.

A few poisonous **insects and arachnids** inhabit Big Bend, but most are non-lethal. Yes, the park has **tarantulas,** commonly seen on roadways in the late summer and fall. These large, hirsute spiders have quite a movie reputation for mayhem but are not the least bit dangerous to humans. If handled roughly, they may bite in self-defense, but they aren't poisonous. The **giant desert centipede** is another formidable-looking creature and is worth avoiding. Its poisonous bite is quite painful to humans but not lethal. This centipede prefers darkness and is not commonly seen in daylight. **Millipedes** are often mistaken for centipedes, but their legs are more numerous and they're generally smaller than centipedes. They aren't poisonous and they don't bite. Big Bend harbors around 15 species of **scorpions,** which inject venom by means of a stinger in their tails. None of the scorpions found in the park carry a sting lethal to humans, unless you happen to be allergic to scorpion stings. "Whip scorpions" or **vinegaroons**—named for the vinegar-like odor they emit as a defense mechanism—can reach six inches in length. They look nasty and their pinchers are larger than those of the scorpion, but they have no stinger. The vinegaroon is strictly nonpoisonous.

History
Prehistoric Inhabitants: Seventy-five million years ago Big Bend was inhabited by dinosaurs, including the recently discovered pterosaur, a flying reptile with a 50-foot wingspan—seven feet longer than the wingspan of a F-15A jet fighter. Human habitation in the Big Bend area goes back about 12,000 years, starting with big-game hunters who preyed on mastodon, bison, camels, pronghorns, and horses. During this period, at the end of the Ice Age, the Big Bend country was lush with vegetation thriving on the

volcanic soils. As the earth warmed and the glaciers receded, Big Bend began to dry up, the big-game species perished, and the hunters moved on.

They were followed around 8,000 years ago by groups of nomadic hunter-gatherer Indians. Anthropological evidence shows they hunted desert animals for meat and hides and ate all the classic desert plant foods—yucca, agave hearts, mesquite beans, and prickly pear cactus. They also crafted baskets, mats, sandals, and nets from desert plant fibers, particularly lechuguilla, just as local Mexicans do today. These nomads later either disappeared or were supplanted by Patarabueyes Indians who built pueblos and farmed the alluvial plains to the west, near present-day Presidio, beginning around A.D. 1200. Some historians believe there may have been a trade relationship between the two peoples, but the evidence is very thin.

Chisos and Chisos Apaches: These Puebloans were in the area when the Spanish arrived in the 1500s; the Europeans named them La Junta Indians, because the center of their culture was at the meeting—*la junta*—of the Rio Conchos and the Rio Grande. But neither the Spanish nor the La Junta had much interest in rugged Big Bend, which they called El Despoblado ("The Unpeopled" or "Uninhabited"). So the area was vacant when an Amerindian tribe from north central Mexico began spending their summers in Big Bend a few years later (though some archaeologists maintain the Chisos arrived in Big Bend before the Spanish *entrada*). These were the Chisos, who gave their name to Big Bend's highest mountain range. "Chiso" is probably derived from the Apache word *chishe,* which means "people of the forest"; some historians think the name may come from the Spanish *hechizo,* meaning "magic"—a possible reference to their Chisos Mountains habitat, which the Spanish commonly considered haunted. Spanish conquistadors eventually began kidnapping the Chisos and forcing them to work as slaves in their copper and silver mines, but the Chisos gathered their forces and were able to keep the Spaniards away from Big Bend following a great 1644 battle.

When the Comanches began persecuting the Apaches on the Great Plains to the north, groups of Apaches were forced into Texas. Like dominoes falling, many of the Chisos were then forced out of the Big Bend area by the Apaches. This was the same group of Apaches that came to be known as Mescaleros for their ritual and nutritional dependence on agave hearts or "mescal," but in this area they became known as Chisos Apaches. In their new West Texas homelands, the Mescaleros became fierce guerrilla fighters and supreme desert dwellers, holding off all intruders throughout the 18th century—until the Comanches came to Texas on Spanish horses.

Among the greatest horsemen the world has ever known, the Comanches reigned over the south plains from Oklahoma to Texas like Hell's Angels on hooves and turned Big Bend into a crossroads for the notorious Comanche War Trail. For over a century they came down from the Llano Estacado through Persimmon Gap (now the park's north entrance) every September during the full moon on their way to Mexico. They forded the Rio Grande at Paso Lajitas and then pillaged every village between there and Durango for whatever they needed. On the way back, they brought captive slaves and livestock northward through the Paso de Chisos, just west of Mariscal Canyon. This put them farther away from the Spanish garrison at Presidio to the west of Big Bend, an important consideration during the return trip when they were loaded down with slaves and pillaged goods. For decades after the last Comanches left Big Bend, their War Trail left a mile-wide scar on the land, scraped bare by horses' hooves. People who live in the area still call the September full moon "Comanche Moon."

The Comanches forced the remaining Chisos Apaches deep into Big Bend's interior. In the late 1800s, the westward expansion of Anglo-American settlements put pressure on the Comanches and the raids stopped. The Chisos Apaches were invited to sign a peace treaty with the Mexican government, but when the last Chisos chief, Alsate, took his braves across the river for the signing of the treaty, the Mexicans got them drunk, manacled them, and forced them to march to Chihuahua, where some were killed and others were distributed among the Mexican *rurales* (roughly equivalent to the Texas Rangers) as household slaves. Mexican villagers say Alsate's ghost still appears in the

BIG BEND NATIONAL PARK

TEXAS

MEXICO

RIO GRANDE

TO MARATHON (39 mi)

385

PARK ENTRANCE

SANTIAGO MTS.

DOG CANYON

STILLWELL STORE

BLACK GAP WILDLIFE MANAGEMENT AREA

LA LINDA

ADAMS RANCH

DEAD HORSE MTS.

SIERRA DEL CARMEN

SIERRA DEL CARMEN

PARK BOUNDARY

DAGGER FLAT

OLD ORE RD.

STRAWHOUSE

BOCQUILLAS CANYON

ROSILLOS MTS.

385

FOSSIL BONE EXHIBIT

TELEPHONE CANYON RD.

RIO GRANDE VILLAGE

VISITOR CENTER

BOQUILLAS

GRAPEVINE HILLS

PANTHER JUNCTION VISITOR CENTER

TORNILLO CREEK

DUGOUT WELLS

RIO GRANDE VILLAGE DR.

DANIELS RANCH

SAN VICENTE

PARK BOUNDARY

PAINT GAP HILLS

LOST MINE PEAK (7,550 ft.)

PINE CANYON

CHILICOTAL MT. (4,108 ft.)

JUNIPER CANYON

TALLEY MT. (3,765 ft.)

MARISCAL MT. (3,932 ft.)

CHRISTMAS MTS.

118

SANTA ELENA JUNCTION

PANTHER PASS

THE WINDOW

THE BASIN

CASA GRANDE (7,235 ft.)

CHISOS MTS.

BLACK GAP

MARISCAL MINE

ROSS MAXWELL SCENIC DR.

TERLINGUA RANCH

TULE MOUNTAIN

OLD RANCH

CHISOS BASIN RD.

SOUTH RIM (7,835 ft.)

EMORY PEAK (7,825 ft.)

OUTER MOUNTAIN LOOP (DODSON)

ELEPHANT TUSK (5,249 ft.)

MARISCAL CANYON

MAVERICK RD.

CREEK RANCH

MULE EARS SPRING

SOTOL VISTA

DOMINGUEZ MT. (5,156 ft.)

DOMINGUEZ SPRING

TO ALPINE (58 mi)

STUDY BUTTE

PARK ENTRANCE

LUNA'S JACAL

BURRO MESA POUROFF

CHIMNEYS

TUFF CANYON

MULE EARS PEAK (3,881 ft.)

RIO GRANDE

TERLINGUA GHOST TOWN

TERLINGUA

TERLINGUA CREEK

CASTOLON

TO PRESIDIO (50 mi)

VILLA LA DE MINA

LAJITAS

PARK BOUNDARY

MESA DE AGUILA

SANTA ELENA CANYON OVERLOOK

SANTA ELENA CANYON (RAPIDS)

ROCK SLIDE (RAPIDS)

SIERRA DE SANTA ELENA

170

10 mi

10 km

© MOON PUBLICATIONS, INC.

Sierra del Carmen on the Mexican side of Big Bend from time to time; others identify the mysterious Marfa lights with the last band of Chisos Apaches.

Cinnabar and Candlewax: With the Indian threat removed, Anglos finally began moving into the Big Bend area at the turn of the century. At first their only enterprises were sheep and cattle ranches, but when a red ore called cinnabar was discovered, Big Bend changed almost overnight. Cinnabar had long been used for pictographs and war paint by the Indians. When cinnabar is heated, it produces "quicksilver," or mercury vapor, which can be condensed and collected as liquid mercury. The towns of Terlingua and Study Butte grew up around the cinnabar mines, which were mostly owned by the Chisos Mining Company. For a time this outfit had the second-largest cinnabar mine in the world, producing 100,000 flasks over a 40-year period. Eventually the ore veins were exhausted, and the 2,000 workers who lived in Terlingua and Study Butte drifted away around the start of WW II, leaving ghost towns behind.

Another local industry that thrived for a while was the rendering of wax from the candelilla plant, a Big Bend succulent that coats itself with hard wax during the dry season. Candelilla wax was used in the U.S. for the production of candles, phonograph records, chewing gum, and polishes during the first half of the 20th century; in Mexico, it still is. As the plant became scarcer because of all the wax factories at McKinney Springs and Glenn Springs, and as other methods of wax manufacture became more cost-effective, the candelilla industry waned. Today there are still a few Mexican wax camps along the Rio Grande where candelilla is processed using traditional methods; some of the plants used are gathered illegally in the park. But since the industry is now small-scale and rangers patrol the park for *candelilleras* (wax makers) during the dry seasons, the plant is flourishing once again.

Park Establishment: Everett E. Townsend, a U.S. Customs inspector, Texas Ranger, and Brewster County Sheriff in the early 1900s, lobbied to set aside part of the Big Bend region as a park. The Texas legislature responded to public pressure by establishing a Texas Canyons State Park in May 1933 which included the

Santa Eleña, Mariscal, and Boquillas canyons. A few months later, the Chisos Basin was added and the name was changed to Big Bend State Park. The Civilian Conservation Corps (CCC) developed trails and built stone cabins during the late '30s and early '40s. Meanwhile, concerned Texans began applying pressure in Washington to change Big Bend over to national park status. After the state agreed to donate another 286,000 hectares of land for the prospective park, the federal government made Big Bend the country's 27th national park in June 1944.

Park Access

Two highways lead into the park: US 385 from Marathon through Persimmon Gap to the north along the old Comanche War Trail, and State 118 from Alpine through Study Butte to the west. You can also drive to Big Bend via Marfa and Presidio on US 67 and FM 170, a particularly scenic drive; FM 170 then connects with State 118 at Study Butte. There is no public transport into the park, but buses are available between Alpine and Study Butte, at the west entrance; call (915) 424-3471 for current schedule and fare information.

The park headquarters is at Panther Junction in the north-central area of the park. The main visitor center is here, but there are also ranger stations at Castolon Valley in the southwest quarter of the park, Chisos Basin in the center, Persimmon Gap, and Rio Grande Village in the southeast; the latter is usually closed during summer. The Panther Junction Visitor Center is open daily 8 a.m.-6 p.m. The park entrance fee is $5 per vehicle or $3 per person for cyclists and pedestrians. At the moment, this fee is collected only at Panther Junction and at the Basin, but there's a possibility collection kiosks will be installed at the north and west entrances eventually. Payment of the entrance fee covers one week's visit.

U.S. residents who are 62 years or older are admitted free with a Golden Age Passport, which can be issued on the spot for $10. Disabled U.S. residents can receive the same benefits with the Golden Access Passport. Children under 16 are also admitted free. Adults can purchase a Big Bend Park Pass for $15 that allows unlimited entry into the park for one calendar year.

ACCOMMODATIONS

Chisos Mountains Lodge

The park's only indoor accommodation originated as cabins for CCC workers in the '30s and early '40s. The lodge comp lex, located in the Chisos Basin at 5,400 feet, now consists of a motel unit, a lodge, and several stone cabins, for a total of 34 guest rooms. Rooms in the lodge and motel units are $57 s, $62 d, while the stone cabins sleep three to six persons for $66 t plus $10 for each additional person. Reservations must be made well ahead of time and require payment for one night's lodging in advance. The Lodge Dining Room and Coffee Shop serves a variety of American and Mexican food and is open 7 a.m.-7:30 p.m. in the winter, 7 a.m.-8 p.m. in the summer. Lunch and dinner run $5-12, breakfast less.

For reservations, contact National Parks Concession, Inc. (tel. 915-477-2291), Chisos Mountains Lodge, Big Bend National Park, TX 79834.

Camping

There are three drive-in camping areas in the park. **Chisos Basin Campground,** in the Basin a few hundred feet below the Chisos Mountains Lodge, has 63 sites suitable for tents and campers under 24 feet, along with flush toilets, running water, dump station, tables, cooking grills, and bearproof food storage boxes. The fee is $5 per night per site.

Rio Grande Village in the park's southeast corner on the river has a 25-site RV park with full hookups—the only hookups in the park. A space costs $11 a night per vehicle with two people, plus $1 for each additional person. Also at Rio Grande Village is a Class A campground with 100 sites, flush toilets, running water, tables, and grills; $5 per night per site. An adjacent overflow campground with pit toilets only—no tables or grills—is open only when the Class A campsites are full and also cost $5 a night. Within walking distance of this campground are the river crossing to Boquillas and the functioning ruins of a hot springs spa constructed between 1909 and 1927.

The **Cottonwood Campground** in Castolon Valley along the Rio Grande has 35 sites, pit toilets, water, tables, and grills; $5 per site per night. Except during holiday periods, it's usually less crowded than Rio Grande Village.

Between February 1 and April 15, a 14-day camping limit is in effect for the developed campgrounds and RV park at the Basin, Rio Grande Village, and Cottonwood Campgrounds. During the remainder of the year you may stay up to 28 days with the day-to-day approval of park authorities.

During the summer, mid-May to mid-November, no fees are collected at the Rio Grande Village and Cottonwood campgrounds—if you can stand the heat.

Backcountry campsites are scattered throughout the park and offer no facilities other than a flat area for pitching tents and bearproof food storage boxes. Backcountry permits are required for use of these sites and are available free from any ranger station.

All campgrounds and campsites in the park (except for the Government Springs equestrian site) are assigned on a first-come, first-served basis. Outside the park, there are also campgrounds and RV parks in Terlingua, Study Butte, and Lajitas. See "Vicinity of Big Bend" for more information.

SUPPLIES AND SERVICES

The most complete facilities are in the Basin, where there's a well-stocked grocery and sundries store (open 9 a.m.-8:45 p.m. May 1-Oct. 1 and 9 a.m.-5:30 p.m. Nov. 1-April 30); a gift shop with photographic supplies, crafts, postcards, and souvenirs; a restaurant; post office; and Western Union office accepting incoming wires only. The post office, open the same hours as the grocery store, will take poste restante letters under visitors' names addressed to Big Bend National Park, TX 79834.

A service station at Panther Junction offers gasoline, diesel, auto parts, and minor automotive repairs; open 7:30 a.m.-7 p.m. May 1-Oct. 31, 8 a.m.-6 p.m. Nov. 1-April 30. Gas and oil are also sold at Rio Grande Village; 9 a.m.-6 p.m. June 1-Feb. 28, 9 a.m.-8 p.m. March 1-May 31. The stores in Panther Junction, Castolon, and Rio Grande Village sell groceries, ice, and camping supplies.

Hot showers and a coin-operated laundromat are available at Rio Grande Village. See "Vicinity of Big Bend" for facilities outside the park.

DRIVING IN THE PARK

The park has three kinds of roads suitable for motorcycles, automobiles, and trucks: paved roads, improved dirt roads, and backcountry dirt roads. An ordinary passenger car can handle the first two except during heavy rains when even improved dirt roads may turn to mud (in which case the park staff will close them to all traffic). The backcountry dirt roads are only suitable for high-clearance vehicles; for most of them four-wheel drive isn't required, but the vehicle chassis must be high enough to avoid the large rocks common along these roads. Check with one of the visitor centers for recommendations before embarking on any extensive backcountry drives. No off-road travel is allowed anywhere in the park, even on motorcycles. The maximum speed limit in the park is 45 mph; on some roads it's much lower.

Most RVs can handle the paved and improved dirt roads. Vehicles over 24 feet long should not use Basin Drive due to tight switchbacks. ATVs and trailers are also banned from narrow Hot Springs Road.

Scenic Drives
Recommended drives for the typical passenger car include the **Ross Maxwell Scenic Drive,** 22 miles from Santa Eleña Junction; **Rio Grande Village Drive,** 20 miles from Panther Junction; **Maverick Drive,** 13 miles from Santa Eleña Junction; and **Basin Drive,** nine miles from Panther Junction. If you don't have time for all these, the Ross Maxwell Scenic Drive, which leads west along the Chisos to the historic farming settlement of **Castolon Valley** and to the mouth of **Santa Eleña Canyon,** is the most scenic, offering plenty of mountain, canyon, and desert vistas along the way. Drive-in campgrounds are available at the ends of the Ross Maxwell Scenic Dr. (Cottonwood Campground), Rio Grande Village Dr. (Rio Grande Village Campground), and Basin Dr. (Basin Campground). Recreational vehicles over 24 feet long or autos towing trailers over 20 feet should not attempt to reach the Chisos Basin because of the steep and winding nature of Basin Drive.

High-clearance vehicles have an additional choice of 150 miles of backcountry dirt roads, of which these four are especially recommended: Old Ore Rd., 26.4 miles; Glenn Spring Rd., 15.6 miles; River Rd., 50.6 miles; and Paint Gap Rd., 3.9 miles. River Rd. is the most scenic, beginning at Castolon and proceeding along the bottom edge of the park to the Rio Grande Village Visitor Center. Along the way, you'll pass river vistas, old ranches and mining camps, Mariscal Mountain, arroyos, and salt cedar brakes, as well as over 15 different designated backcountry campsites.

The *Road Guide to Paved and Improved Dirt Roads* and the *Road Guide to Backcountry Dirt Roads* are available at Panther Junction Visitor Center. Each contains detailed route descriptions as well as suggested side trips.

Vehicle Precautions
Whatever type of vehicle you're driving, always be sure to start off with a full tank of gas, since gas is only available at two widely separated points in the park: Panther Junction and Rio Grande Village. Travel with a spare tire, jack, and plenty of water—for yourself as well as for the vehicle's radiator, especially during the summer. For primitive road travel, you should also carry a tire pump, extra fan belts and radiator hoses, and a first-aid kit.

If you get stuck in sand, don't spin the wheels—this will only bury them more deeply. Instead, get out and deflate the tires to around 15 psi and then slowly accelerate out of the sand. If the vehicle breaks down or gets stuck so badly you're unable to extricate it, stay with it until a park ranger or another traveler comes along. If you're anywhere near a telephone, call (915) 477-2251 ext. 9 for towing service.

The park staff recommends you always lock your vehicle when hiking and not leave valuables in sight; petty theft is a problem in the park, particularly along isolated dirt roads near the river.

BIG BEND HIKING AND BACKPACKING

Over 200 miles of developed trails are accessible in the park, with designated lengths from 50 yards to 33 miles, and a range of elevation from 1,800 feet (Boquillas Canyon) to 7,835 feet (Emory Peak in the Chisos). Thirty-six separate hikes are detailed in the highly informative *Hiker's Guide to Trails in Big Bend National Park*, published by the Big Bend Natural History Association and available at all visitor centers within the park. The routes are divided into eight self-guiding trails, 11 developed trails (including the High Chisos Complex, which actually consists of six additional shorter routes), and 17 primitive routes. Each trail is further classified according to difficulty—easy walking, medium difficulty, strenuous day hike, and strenuous backpackers only.

If this hiking guide isn't detailed enough to suit your purposes, obtain USGS map number 29103-C2PF, a 1:100,000-scale (one inch = 1.6 miles) sheet that covers the entire park, plus parts of adjacent areas, with contour lines every 80 feet.

Prerequisites

Always carry plenty of water—a minimum of one gallon per person per full day of walking during hot weather, slightly less in winter. Although there are a few springs and *tinajas* in the park, the water level varies considerably and you shouldn't count on finding sources of water along the way. If you need drinking water from one of these sources, always purify it first by boiling for at least 10 minutes, filtering, or adding iodine. Bring enough food for the duration of your hike.

You can wear sneakers or street shoes for some of the shorter, easier hikes, but for any serious hiking wear sturdy hiking boots. Lug soles are preferable, as they provide protection from sharp rocks and desert plants. Bring along a first-aid kit that includes an elastic bandage for sprains and snakebite treatment and a pair of tweezers for removing thorns and cactus spines. Also bring a flashlight, compass, and, for long hikes on primitive routes, a topographic map.

Recommended Day Hikes

The **Santa Elena Canyon Trail** (1.7 miles roundtrip) begins where Ross Maxwell Scenic Dr. ends at the junction of the Rio Grande and Terlingua Creek. To start the trail, you must wade across the creek; during periods of heavy rain, it may be too swift and too deep to cross. On the other side is a section of concrete steps that will take you up and over a rocky point and into the mouth of the canyon. From here the trail winds around several huge boulders until the canyon wall veers right into the Rio Grande. The canyon scenery is quite impressive, especially since this is one of the narrowest sections of Santa Elena Canyon. Easy, but some climbing involved.

Many repeat visitors say **Window Trail** (5.6 miles roundtrip) is their favorite Big Bend hike because it covers such a variety of terrain and affords great valley and desert views. Starting at the Basin trailhead, the first section involves a rapid descent with distant views of "the Window"—a cleft in the mountain peaks surrounding Chisos Basin. As the trail drops from subalpine topography to canyon floor, piñon pines, oaks, sotol, and grasses give way to oaks, mesquite, prickly pear, and agave. After passing though wooded, spring-fed idylls the trail ends at a clearing where trail riders tie their horses, but you can continue hiking along rock steps to the Window itself. From the Window, a waterfall drops 200 feet to the desert floor below; a second cleft rock formation opposite the Window is known as "the Gunsight," and beyond to the west are the Christmas Mountains. This hike takes three to four hours roundtrip depending on pace and number of stops.

Lost Mine Trail (4.6 miles roundtrip) is an interpretative trail heading west from Panther Pass, off Basin Drive. Elevation gain on the trail is about 1,250 feet as it proceeds along the northern slope of Casa Grande, a volcanic block, to a ridge dividing the Pine and Juniper canyons. A good, fairly short trail for viewing typical Chisos Mountains flora and fauna—figure on about four hours roundtrip. A self-guiding booklet is available at the Panther Pass trailhead; Mexican black bears were frequently encountered along this trail in 1993 and rangers urge all hikers to store food in the bearproof box at the trailhead. Medium difficulty.

Pine Canyon Trail (four miles roundtrip) begins at the end of Pine Canyon Rd., a dirt road off Glenn Spring Rd., which is itself a dirt road off the paved Rio Grande Village Dr., about five miles from Panther Junction. Winding up through Pine Canyon, the trail is one of the park's prettiest, with stands of Mexican piñon, juniper, and oak. Higher up come ponderosa pine, bigtooth maple, Emory and Graves oaks, and Texas madrone. The trail ends at the bottom of a 200-foot cliff that supports a waterfall during the rainy season (July-September). There's a backcountry campsite near the mouth of the canyon. Medium difficulty; high-clearance vehicle necessary to reach the trailhead.

South Rim Loop (13-14.5 miles roundtrip): South Rim refers to the southwestern edge of the Chisos Mountains, about 2,500 feet above the

desert. This loop within the High Chisos Complex offers some of the most stupendous mountain views in the park (or anywhere in the Southwest for that matter), but you'll have to earn them through fairly challenging hiking. It can be done as a strenuous day hike, starting and finishing at the Basin trailhead, or you can take your time and camp along the way. There are 13 backcountry campsites along the South Rim alone, and over two dozen more throughout the Chisos trail complex. On the way up you can choose between the **Pinnacles Trail** (6.4 miles one way) or the **Laguna Meadow Trail** (6.5 miles one-way). Pinnacles is the steeper of the two, and is usually used for the descent from South Rim. Once you make the South Rim, you'll be able to see Mexican peaks that are 80 miles away or more, plus Emory Peak (highest in the Chisos)

CHISOS TRAILS

and Santa Eleña Canyon. On a very clear day, views may extend up to 200 miles. To the east is the Sierra del Carmen range, which starts at the top of the park and crosses some 50 miles into Mexico. Take care descending on scenic Pinnacles, as it's easy to lose traction on the loose rubble. The High Chisos Complex connects with the Juniper Canyon Trail at Boot Canyon, 4.5 miles from the Basin trailhead, and there are backcountry campsites at the intersection of this trail and Outer Mountain Loop, 6.2 miles from Boot Canyon. During the peregrine falcon nesting season (February to mid-July), some parts of the South Rim Loop and connecting trails may be closed to visitors.

Emory Peak Trail (one mile from Pinnacles Pass or 4.5 miles from the Basin trailhead) runs west off the Pinnacles Trail just beyond Pinnacles Pass. Not very difficult, except for the last 15-foot scramble up a sheer rock face. Naturally a great view, since this is the highest point in the park (elevation 7,835 feet). The equipment at the summit is part of Big Bend's solar-powered two-way radio system.

Blue Creek Trail (5.5 miles one way from the South Rim or nine miles from the Basin trailhead) can be attempted from the Blue Creek Ranch Overlook, near Sotol Vista on the Ross Maxwell Scenic Dr., though that means a constant ascent for 5.5 miles. The least strenuous route involves arranging to leave a vehicle parked at the Blue Creek Ranch Overlook and hiking down to it from the South Rim or the Basin. You'll pass through several different terrains, from high woodlands to sotol grasslands, oak and juniper canyon floor, and desert savannah. The desert part of the trail meanders through some of the park's most colorful volcanic formations. Originally developed as a sheepherding trail.

Chimneys Trail (4.8 miles roundtrip) starts from the west side of Ross Maxwell Scenic Dr. about 1.2 miles south of the turnoff for Burro Mesa. It follows an old dirt track to a series of high rock outcroppings ("chimneys") to the west of Kit Mountain. Rare Indian petroglyphs can be seen on the southernmost chimney. This track continues eastward another 4.6 miles past Peña Spring to the Chimneys West backcountry campsite at the base of Peña Mountain.

Backpacking

Preparation: To stay overnight at a backcountry campsite, you must obtain a backcountry use permit in advance from one of the ranger stations or visitor centers. If you're backpacking alone, you should fill out a Solo Hiker Form so the rangers will know where to look if you don't come back when you predict you will. Topographic maps are highly recommended for backcountry hikes and can be purchased at the Panther Junction Visitor Center. During the colder months or summer rainy season, a tent is a good idea. Other essential gear includes a compass, flashlight, knife, and first-aid kit. No open fires are allowed in the park, so bring a backpacking stove if you plan to cook.

Minimal camping supplies are available at the Chisos Basin store or outside the park at the Lajitas Trading Post.

On the Trails: Pack out all trash (including cigarette butts—they take 10-12 years to decompose), bury human waste six inches down, and don't use soap in streams or springs. Be sure to store *all* food (even snacks and dirty dishes) in the bearproof boxes provided at selected campsites.

Backcountry Trails

The following hikes involve primitive trails that either require overnight stops or aren't easily reached by the day hiker.

Cross Canyon Trail (14 miles from the Solis backcountry campsite): Solis is a put-in point for river runners below Mariscal Canyon. The trail starts west of the Solis campsite and leads west over limestone ridges and flats toward the eastern cliffs of Mariscal Mountain. At the cliffs, the trail climbs up and through a break, then follows along the summit ridge until it heads south into Mariscal Canyon, ending at the edge of the river. Directly across the river, you can see a Mexican wax camp. Out in the river is a set of boulders known as Tight Squeeze because of the difficulty boaters experience in navigating between them.

The **Outer Mountain Loop** (31.6 miles) comprises parts of the Dodson, Juniper Canyon, Pinnacles, Laguna Meadows, and Blue Creek trails. The trail can be worked clockwise or counterclockwise beginning at any of three trailheads—Blue Creek Ranch Overlook, the Basin,

1. Monahans Sandhills, West Texas;
2. ocotillo, Big Bend (photos by Joe Cummings)

1. Palo Duro Canyon; **2.** volcanic formations, Big Bend;
3. Santa Eleña Canyon, Big Bend (photos by Joe Cummings)

or Juniper Canyon. Whichever route you choose, this loop will take you through more different kinds of Big Bend terrain and biotic communities than any other hike. The route with the fewest elevation changes is from the Basin up to Laguna Meadow and the South Rim, then down Blue Creek Canyon Trail until it meets the Dodson Trail, then east on the Dodson to the Juniper Canyon Trail and up to Boot Spring, where you take the Pinnacles Trail down to the Basin. The Pinnacle-South Rim-Laguna Meadow sections of the loop are covered under "Recommended Day Hikes."

TEXAS MOUNTAIN RANGES

Texas has 18 major mountain ranges, all located in the Basin and Range region of West Texas. They can be divided into four main groups: the Permian Ranges, the Western Front Ranges, the Eastern Front Ranges, and the Volcanic Region. The list below enumerates the highest peaks in each range.

Permian Ranges
Guadalupe Mountains: Guadalupe Peak, 8,749 feet
Franklin Mountains: North Franklin Peak, 7,192 feet
Cornudas Mountains: San Antonio, 7,031 feet
Hueco Mountains: Cerro Alto, 6,717 feet

Western Front Ranges
Eagle Mountains: Eagle Peak, 7,496 feet
Quitman Mountains: Quitman Peak, 6,505 feet
Van Horn Mountains: High Lonesome, 5,612 feet
Indio Mountains: Squaw Peak, 5,435 feet

Eastern Front Ranges
Altuda Mountains: Bird Peak, 6,140 feet
Glass Mountains: Cathedral Peak, 5,938 feet
Sierra del Carmen: Sue Peak, 5,854 feet
Serrania Highlands: Cupola, 3,988 feet

Volcanic Region
Chisos Mountains: Emory Peak, 7,835 feet
Chinati Mountains: Chinati Peak, 7,721 feet
Davis Mountains: Mt. Livermore, 8,382 feet
Sierra Vieja: Capote Peak, 6,208 feet
Solitario Mountains: Needle Peak, 5,193 feet
Bofecillos Plateau: La Mota, 5,037 feet

The **Dodson Trail** itself is 11.5 miles long and crosses very rugged terrain with lots of ups and downs. The trail is not always distinct, so a 7.5-minute topo map is necessary if you're not familiar with the trail. From the Blue Creek Trail junction, the Dodson Trail is fairly easy to follow until you reach the junction for the Elephant Tusk Trail, about halfway. Keep an eye out for cairns that point the way, since several drainages break up the trail. At around mile six you should reach the remains of the Dodson Place, a ranch that operated between 1919 and 1943. A spring near the old ranch usually has water, but don't count on it and treat the water before drinking if you do find the spring flowing. After the Dodson Place, follow the trail as it parallels an old fence to the south. If you keep the fence on your right, you won't lose the trail as it intersects with several smaller trails. There are also rock cairns along this part of the trail. Going west along Dodson, be careful at the junction of Dodson and Smoky Creek; many hikers miss the cairn here and end up in Smoky Creek.

The **Juniper Canyon Trail** is 6.2 miles from the Dodson Trail junction to Boot Canyon. There's one primitive campsite at the Dodson-Juniper Canyon Trail junction, as well as a primitive dirt road (Juniper Canyon Rd.) that leads southeast to the Glenn Spring Road. The trail is fairly level through Juniper Canyon until you reach Upper Juniper Spring, where it climbs up and over a ridge into Boot Canyon.

Horseback Riding
As of August 1994, Big Bend Park no longer has a stable and riding concession. Riders are permitted to bring their own stock for use on two trails, Laguna Meadow Trail and the Window Trail; see "Recommended Day Hikes" for trail descriptions. The former riding concession used the latter trail for most of its day rides.

The only park facility dedicated to equestrians is a corral at the Government Springs backcountry campsite off Grapevine Hills Road. Reservations for the campsite and corral can be made up to 10 weeks in advance by calling BBNP headquarters.

RUNNING THE RIO GRANDE

The segment of the Rio Grande that wraps around Big Bend wasn't successfully navigated until rather late in the 19th century; it was initially considered impassable. Unlike the upper reaches of the Rio Grande near El Paso, which are fairly tame waters, the river here gains volume and momentum after being joined by Mexico's Rio Conchos near Presidio, 55 miles west of the park. By the time the Rio Grande reaches the canyons of Big Bend, its currents are strong and deep. The Apaches especially feared the high narrow walls of Santa Eleña Canyon, believing anyone who entered would never be seen again. In 1852, the Chandler-Green expedition released an empty boat at the entrance of Santa Eleña; at the other end, nothing but splinters emerged. Several other adventurers unsuccessfully tried to float the river in the latter half of the 19th century. Finally, in 1899, a well-equipped Dr. Robert Hill, with the aid of a local trapper who knew the canyons, completed a successful Rio Grande journey from Presidio to the mouth of the Pecos near Langtry. It took him a month.

Now, nearly a century later, anyone with determination and the assistance of local experts can float down 245 miles of well-preserved Rio Grande wilderness in a couple of weeks. The river forms the southern boundary of Big Bend National Park for 118 miles, running through three major canyons—the Santa Eleña, Mariscal, and Boquillas. The Park Service also has jurisdiction over an additional 127 miles of the river downstream from Boquillas designated as the **Rio Grande Wild and Scenic River.** This section runs through an area called the Lower Canyons that is popular among serious river runners; there are few take-outs along the 83 miles of canyons, so a week is usually necessary to complete this run. Above the park is the Colorado Canyon, with numerous moderately easy rapids. Because of the impressive scenery and whitewater runs they offer, the individual canyons are the focus for most river trips, rather than the entire stretch.

Equipment

The Rio Grande can be navigated by canoe, kayak, or inflatable raft. Unless you're an ex-

perienced whitewater canoeist, canoes should not be taken into the Colorado, Santa Eleña, or Lower canyons because they're unlikely to hold up in collisions with boulders and canyon walls. A sturdy inflatable raft, on the other hand, will bounce off walls and boulders and will stay afloat even if filled with water. Rafts should be made of heavy-duty neoprene or rubberized canvas. Whatever the craft, park regulations require river runners to carry one USCG-approved life jacket per person, one extra paddle or oar per boat, a boat-patching kit, a pump (for inflatable rafts and kayaks), a bailing bucket, and a campstove or fire pan if cooking is planned. Additional gear recommended by the Park Service includes a throw line (a 60-foot length is suggested), cords for lashing gear to the craft, a bow or stern line (40-foot recommended), first-aid kit, tarp, trash bags, signal mirror, and flashlight, plus enough food and water for the planned trip and some extra provisions for unplanned trip extensions.

River use permits (free) must be obtained from ranger stations at Persimmon Gap, Panther Junction, Rio Grande Village, or in Lajitas at the Lajitas Museum.

Rafting equipment can be rented and supplies purchased at Lajitas Trading Post outside the park in Lajitas (open 8 a.m.-9 p.m. daily, tel. 915-424-3234) or through **Rio Grande Outfitters** (tel. 371-2424). Raft rentals start at $15 per person per day. Motors are forbidden on most stretches of the river administered by the park, as well as in any of the canyons during the peregrine nesting season (mid-February to mid-July). To learn the exact locations of these zones, and for further information on river-use regulations, call the information number for the Rio Grande Wild and Scenic River, tel. 477-2251.

Other Considerations

When you pick up a river use permit at one of the ranger stations, the rangers will apprise you of river conditions and can help with route planning if this is your first Big Bend river trip. For the novice river runner, water levels between one and four feet (measured in Boquillas Canyon) are generally navigable with the proper equipment. Levels over four or five feet shouldn't be attempted except by experienced whitewater rafters. During the rainy season, July to October, the river level can be quite high following heavy rains—it's best to wait a few days until the level recedes to a depth you're capable of handling.

If you plan an overnight river run, be sure to set up camp well above the high-water mark due to the possibility of flash floods at any time of year. Stow gear that needs to remain dry (cameras, food, etc.) in watertight containers—ice chests work nicely. Don't attempt the challenging Santa Eleña Canyon or Lower Canyons until you've successfully navigated Mariscal or Boquillas or both. If you see a section of white water or tight boulders ahead that look like more than you can handle, carry the craft around or lead it through from shore with a line.

One major logistical problem that must be worked out in advance is how you'll get back to your vehicle once you reach the end of the run. It's best to have a companion drop you off at the start of the run and meet you at the take-out at a designated time. Or use two vehicles, one parked at the put-in and one at the take-out. Keep in mind that theft is common along the river—leave no valuables in the vehicles. It's also possible to pay someone in Lajitas, Terlingua, or Study Butte to shuttle you back to your put-in—ask around, and don't pay until they've picked you up, of course. **Big Bend Shuttle Service** (tel. 915-371-2523) in Terlingua and **Scott Shuttle Service** (tel. 800-613-5041) in Marathon offer shuttle services; inquire at the park visitor centers for other possibilities.

If you're running the canyons for the first time, it's essential to purchase the relevant copy or copies of the *River Guide* series from one of the ranger stations in the park. These thoroughly researched booklets contain detailed topographic maps that indicate river mileage, whitewater areas, navigation tips, and points of interest along the way.

Colorado Canyon

This canyon is actually west of the park boundary but is often run as a day trip because of its short duration and ease of navigation. Most people make the 10-mile run from the Rancheras Canyon put-in to the Teepees Roadside Park take-out (look for the picnic shelters built to resemble Indian teepees), which is near the boundary of Big Bend Ranch State Park. Both are off FM 170 and easily reached by car.

The Colorado Canyon walls are of interest because they're entirely volcanic, unlike the three major park canyons, which contain layers of limestone. The Rancheras Rapids at the very beginning of the run in Rancheras Canyon are Class II rapids—easy rapids with waves up to three feet and wide clear channels—as are the Closed Canyon, Quarter-Mile, and Panther rapids further on before the Teepees take-out. You could float all the way to Lajitas, a 21-mile trip, but once you're out of the Colorado Canyon the waters aren't very challenging until you reach the mouth of Fresno Creek, 15 miles from Rancheras Canyon, where there are Class III rapids with high, irregular waves capable of swamping a canoe. It's a good idea to scout these from shore first.

Santa Eleña Canyon

This is the classic Big Bend river run, and the most popular run among visitors who choose to take guided trips. Once you're in this high-walled box, there's no turning back. The scenery is stupendous, ranging from feather-leafed salt cedar and river cane along sandy banks to 1,500-foot-high stone walls. For dedicated river runners, Santa Eleña boasts the infamous Rock Slide, a series of swirling Class IV rapids that sling boats between, around, and against house-sized boulders. Not a canyon for novices.

The only put-in for Santa Eleña is near where FM 170 breaks west from Lajitas on the way to Presidio. The put-in is directly opposite Paso Lajitas, a village on the Mexican side of the river. Most rafters take out 20 miles downriver at the mouth of the canyon, just past where Terlingua Creek feeds into the river. The run can be done in a day, but is perhaps better as an overnight trip. The first 11 miles pass through occasional minor rapids until the canyon entrance is reached, where a set of stiff rapids cuts back and forth with the river—kayakers have been known to get caught in rock undercuts along the base of the wall when the river level is down. Most overnighters camp on the left bank just before the river enters the canyon, since this is the approximate halfway point. This also gives you a whole day to run the canyon itself, in case you experience difficulties.

Two miles downstream from the entrance is the Rock Slide, with its tight squeezes, suck-

mouth of Santa Eleña Canyon

CHRIS HUMPHREY

holes, and Class IV rapids. The Rock Slide in Santa Eleña has been responsible for more deaths, injuries, and other boating mishaps than any other feature in the Big Bend section of the river. So by all means pull over to the side and take some time to scout the rapids first. If it looks too rough, you can skirt around them on the Texas side by portage and line, or, during times of extremely high water when the lower Texas side is flooded, portage over the higher Mexican side. If you decide to go for it, make sure your gear is tightly secured.

Two to three miles past the Rock Slide are two side canyons on the Mexican side of the river, Arch and Fern. Organized raft trips sometimes stop for a short hike into narrow Fern Canyon, with its clear spring and atypical ferns growing from crevices. Another mile down on the right is a large dome-like cave variously known as Smuggler's, Sheep, or Cow cave. The canyon ends after another mile at Terlingua Creek.

Mariscal Canyon

The straightforward Mariscal Canyon run from the Talley put-in to the Solis take-out extends only 10 miles, an easy day trip. Mariscal features the Rock Pile, about 100 yards from the canyon entrance, with Class II and III rapids. In another half mile or so is the Tight Squeeze, with Class III rapids that should be scouted first by novices—there's room for a landing on the right just before the rapids. Just over a mile later

is another chute of Class II rapids. The rest of the canyon is peaceful floating, with good canyon scenery—look for great horned owls, canyon wrens, falcons.

The Mariscal run can be combined with the Vicente and Hot Springs Canyon downriver for a 32-mile desert and canyon trip that takes three or more days. There are virtually no rapids in these canyons, but in between you'll pass Mexican villages and Tornillo Creek, site of the old Boquillas Hot Springs Resort.

Boquillas Canyon

The usual run through Boquillas Canyon is 33 miles between the put-in near Rio Grande Village and the take-out at La Linda, Mexico—the Mexican authorities allow river runners to drive vehicles across the bridge here for boat pick-ups and launches. Except for one chute at Arroyo del Veinte (Class II-III), about 3.5 miles before La Linda, there's usually no whitewater, but the scenery is quite good. Boquillas is more eroded than the other park canyons, so colors and shapes of rock formations are more complex. This trip takes at least two days. There are plenty of landings along the way for camping.

Lower Canyons

This trip is absolutely *not* for novice river runners, mainly because it's remote, long (83 miles), and requires extensive preparation. Even seasoned river rats should tackle this one first with someone who's made the Lower Canyons trip before. Or consider going with one of the river out-fitters. Most of the land along this section of the river is privately owned—you're allowed to camp anywhere along the floodplain but go beyond and you may be trespassing. The canyons and scenery are quite rugged—that's why it's called the Rio Grande Wild and Scenic River—and you're virtually guaranteed not to see other humans anywhere along the way.

The usual put-in is at La Linda. You can take boats out at Dryden Crossing (a five-day trip), or, to run the total length of the Lower Canyons, float all the way to Foster's Ranch or Langtry, which will add two or three days to the trip. From La Linda, the Lower Canyons don't really begin for 29 miles. There are several springs near the riverbanks along this first stretch, including a couple of thermal springs, where you can collect drinking water. Just before the mouth of the first canyon (Big Canyon) is a set of Class II rapids. Once you pass through this entrance, you're walled in for the next 43 miles. At 41 miles from La Linda you'll hit Hot Springs Rapids (Class III-IV). After another seven miles are the Palmas Canyon Rapids (Class II-III). Then it's another four miles to the small Complejo del Caballo Rapids, and five more until the Class IV Upper Madison Falls, the most exciting of the Lower Canyons trip. Lower Madison Falls, two miles downriver, are Class III, followed by the Panther Rapids (Class II-III), the San Francisco Rapids (Class II-III), the Sanderson Rapids (Class I-II), and finally, just before Dryden Crossing, the anticlimactic Class II Agua Verde Rapids.

Guided Raft Trips

Visitors without previous whitewater rafting experience, and even experienced river runners who haven't tackled the Big Bend canyons before, might want to consider participating in a guided raft trip. Going with a licensed, experienced outfitter is safer the first time out since the pilots are expert navigators and know practically every inch of these canyons. They can also offer informed commentary about the environment and answer questions about the river and rafting techniques specific to Big Bend. You can also concentrate on enjoying the trip and let the outfitters worry about equipment details and navigation.

The oldest outfitter is **Far Flung Adventures** (tel. 915-371-2489 or 800-359-4138), P.O. Box 377, Terlingua, TX 79852, to the west of the park off FM 170. Far Flung offers 11 different trips in all the canyons, ranging from a one-day Colorado Canyon trip for $81 per person to a seven-day Lower Canyons trip for $650. A two-day Santa Eleña trip is $180 per person. FFA also runs occasional specialty raft trips that focus on music, gourmet cooking, photography, or whitewater rafting instruction. Groups of two or more can charter raft(s) and guide for non-scheduled trips. One-day trips include lunch, overnighters include all meals beginning with

rafting the Rio Grande,
Big Bend National Park

lunch on the first day through lunch on the last. All gear except sleeping bags is provided, including watertight metal boxes for cameras and personal effects. FFA also offers trips that combine river running with horseback riding and/or mountain biking.

Another established local company is **Big Bend River Tours** (tel. 800-545-4240), P.O. Box 317, Lajitas, TX 79852, headquartered at the Lajitas On The Rio Grande complex in Lajitas. The company's itineraries and rates are about the same as those of Far Flung Adventures. Other local river-running outfits include **Outback Expeditions** (tel. 371-2490 or 800-343-1640), P.O. Box 229, Terlingua, TX 79852; **Texas River Expeditions** (tel. 371-2633 or 800-839-RAFT), P.O. Box 301152, Houston, TX 77230; and **Rio Grande Outfitters** (tel. 371-2424), P.O. Box 362, Terlingua, TX 79852. Rio Grande Outfitters also rents rafts and rafting equipment for self-guided trips.

Canoe Trips
Scott Canoe Livery (tel. 800-613-5041), P.O. Box 477, Marathon, TX 79842, specializes in guided canoe trips through the canyons as well as canoe rentals. You can also arrange canoe trips through **Outback Expeditions.**

MEXICAN BORDER VILLAGES

You can easily visit two Mexican villages from the park or while river rafting: Santa Elena, across the river from Castolon, and Boquillas, across from Rio Grande Village. Both are fairly typical representations of rural, rustic Mexico, with border overtones; Santa Elena has electricity and Boquillas may soon receive power lines from an NPS-sponsored, low-impact solar generator on the U.S. side.

Boquillas is the most picturesque, with the Sierra del Carmen range as a backdrop. When you land on the Mexican side of the river, the locals will try to sell you a $3 burro ride for the three-quarter-mile walk into the village—if you've never ridden a burro, here's your chance. Less expensive is the pick-up "taxi" service, which costs $2 per person roundtrip. Or simply walk. The main activity is sitting on the front porch of José Falcón's store, drinking cold *cerveza* and

THE LEGEND OF LOST MINE PEAK

According to Trans-Pecos legend, 16th-century Spanish miners stumbled across a rich gold vein somewhere on Big Bend's Lost Mine Peak and established a profitable mine. Chisos Apaches, forced to work the mine as slaves, eventually rebelled, killed their Spanish captors, and sealed off the shaft from further exploitation. No one has since been able to find any evidence of the gold mine, but according to local folklore, if on Easter morning you stand in the door of the ruined chapel in the Mexican village of San Vicente across the Rio Grande and look toward Lost Mine Peak, you'll be able to see the sun's first rays reflecting off the mine entrance. The peak is accessible via the park's Lost Mine Trail, should you catch that magic glint.

eating hot burritos. A real bar up the street has a pool table and is well-stocked with tequila and other liquors—including fiery *sotol* (US$1 per *probita*). The village also has a few souvenir shops selling dresses, leather goods, blankets, and untaxed liquor. If you happen to be in the park on Christmas Eve, cross over to Boquillas to watch Las Posadas, a candlelight procession in which Mexican Catholics commemorate Joseph and Mary's search for lodging. The candles are made locally from the rendered wax of the candelilla plant. Rowboats ferry residents and visitors back and forth across the Rio Grande near Rio Grande Village for $2 roundtrip; pay on the way back.

Santa Elena is slightly larger than Boquillas and features a small town plaza, a candelilla wax factory, a schoolhouse, and a couple of churches. Residents raise cattle and alfalfa to feed them. Two cafes, **Enedinas** and **María Elena's,** serve simple border-style food. Mexican crafts can be purchased at either village. As at Boquillas, rowboats ferry people back and forth for $2. To find the ferry landing, go past the Castolon store and make a left at the sign reading Santa Elena, Mexico. The road to the crossing closes at 5:30 p.m. daily.

A third village, **Paso Lajitas,** is easily reached from Lajitas on the U.S. side, just beyond the park's southwestern perimeter.

Another village farther into northern Mexico that gringos sometimes visit is **San Carlos,** about 17 miles south of the Rio Grande. An island in the desert, San Carlos sits 4,300 feet above sea level in a green, spring-fed arroyo; temperatures tend to run 15 degrees cooler than in Lajitas. Local guide Kiko Garcia leads all-day GMC Suburban trips to San Carlos from the Lajitas Trading Post for $50 per person (20% discount for seniors) including lunch. Trips leave every Saturday, Sunday, and Monday at 10 a.m., returning at 6:30 p.m. In addition to cruising the town, Kiko leads a hike through Cañon de San Carlos that takes in a hot springs, wax factory, and 150-year-old aqueduct. After lunch the group goes to Cañon de las Pilas to cool off in a waterfall.

PARK INFORMATION

Naturalist Activities
Park staff at Big Bend arrange daily activities that include guided interpretive walks, slide presentations, and occasional special lectures. An up-to-date Naturalist Schedule is posted at all campground bulletin boards and is also available at ranger stations.

Seminars
The Big Bend Natural History Association sponsors annual seminars in the park from mid-April through late August on topics as varied as Trans-Pecos archaeology, mountain lion behavior and ecology, the history of early Big Bend river settlements, wildlife photography, and oil painting. Depending on the seminar, each of which generally lasts two to four days, class meetings may be held at campground amphitheaters, the Panther Junction Visitor Center, or in the wilderness. Varying fees are charged for each seminar, but they include free camping at group sites. For the latest schedule, write to the Seminar Coordinator, Big Bend Natural History Association, P.O. Box 68, Big Bend National Park, TX 79834.

Events
The park sponsors an **International Good Neighbor Day Festival** during the third weekend of October. The festival is held at Rio Grande Village and features Mexican folk dance performances, Texas country dances, and *conjunto* music.

Publications
El Paisano, the "Official Big Bend National Park Newspaper," comes out quarterly and contains up to 12 pages of information on currently scheduled park events, special naturalist features, general park information, and park news. It's distributed free at various points throughout the park. *Big Bend, Handbook No. 119* is a Park Service publication that serves as a combination guidebook and natural history text. It's available for $7.95 at the Panther Junction Visitor Center. The Big Bend Natural History Association publishes a dozen or more free handouts on separate park topics, from mountain lions to wildflowers; they're available at any ranger station or at the visitor center.

General Information
For further information on park features, regulations, or activities, contact the Superintendent (tel. 915-477-2251), Big Bend National Park, TX 79834. The Big Bend Natural History Association, which produces most Big Bend National Park publications and organizes park seminars, can be contacted at (tel. 477-2236), P.O. Box 68, BBNP, TX 89834.

VICINITY OF BIG BEND NATIONAL PARK

The four counties in the crux of Big Bend's elbow—Brewster, Presidio, Jeff Davis, and Pecos—are known in Texas as "Big Bend Country." Geologically speaking, only Presidio, Jeff Davis, and the southern portion of Brewster share the Tertiary Volcanic Region that characterizes Big Bend National Park. The topography of north Brewster, including the Glass, Wood Hollow, and Tinaja mountains, and west Pecos below the Stockton Plateau, are defined by the Marathon Uplift, an area of limestone and sandstone formations.

All four counties are sparsely populated. Brewster County is the largest in the state at 6,169 square miles, larger than Connecticut and Rhode Island combined. But it has only five towns and a total population of 8,681—a density of barely one person per square mile. Only one law enforcement officer—a deputy sheriff and former Texas Ranger whose father, grandfather, and great grandfather all served as Texas Rangers—covers the entire southern half of the county, from Alpine to the Mexican border. Tourism, ranching, and farming are the main sources of income in Big Bend Country.

A good source of current information on Big Bend Country is the *Big Bend Quarterly*, published four times a year by Trans-Pecos Productions (tel. 214-942-4905), P.O. Box 4124, Dallas, TX 75208, which also carries works on the history and folklore of the region. The *BBQ* is distributed free at various locations throughout Big Bend or you can obtain a year's subscription for $10 by writing the above address. Another freebie, *The Lajitas Sun*, is also well worth reading, or you can order a 12-issue annual subscription for $6 from Lajitas On The Rio Grande (tel. 915-424-3471), Star Route 70, Box 400, Terlingua, TX 79852.

LAJITAS

At the extreme southwest corner of Brewster County, wedged between the Presidio-Brewster county line and Big Bend National Park, is the trading post turned desert resort of Lajitas. In the 18th and 19th centuries the Rio Grande crossing here was popular among Indians and traders. In the early 1900s General "Blackjack" Pershing established a cavalry outpost to deal with *bandido*-revolutionary Pancho Villa, who used this crossing for raids on local villages.

Rancher H.W. McGuirk founded a town next to the Rio Grande here in 1899. His only visible legacy is **Mission Santa María y san José**, a small Catholic chapel by the river. Renovations in 1990 included stained-glass windows created by artist Jim Box.

Lajitas Trading Post
Since 1915 the social center for Lajitas has been the Lajitas Trading Post, which still operates from the same adobe building but is now somewhat dwarfed by the Lajitas On The Rio Grande resort that has grown around it. For such a small establishment, the trading post sells an amazing variety of farm and ranch supplies, food, and recreational gear. Mexicans still cross the river from nearby Paso Lajitas to trade here. Occasionally the store holds *conjunto* dances on Saturday night. A goat pen out front contains Clay Henry, Jr., offspring of famous beer-drinking goat Clay Henry, Sr., who passed away in 1992 at the age of 22. Junior carries on the sad tradition of drinking himself silly for the entertainment of passersby.

Barton Warnock Environmental Education Center
Near the entrance to Lajitas on FM 170, toward Terlingua, is a TPWD-operated hacienda-style building containing a regional museum. Exhibits include archaeological and geological displays, photography, and local natural history. The building also houses a gift shop with books and souvenirs, and a small research library. Outside is a four-acre desert garden that showcases Chihuahuan Desert flora as well as fauna (javelinas, burros, tortoises). The facility is open daily 8 a.m.-4:30 p.m. Admission is $2.50 for adults, $1.50 for children under 12, free for children

CHIHUAHUAN DESERT

Deserts are loosely defined as those areas averaging less than 10 inches of rain per year. By this definition, large portions of every U.S. state west of Fort Worth can be classified "desert," although one finds considerable variation in rainfall between one locale and another.

It isn't mere aridity that makes a desert most distinctive but rather the range of biologic responses to aridity. Because periods of rain are so infrequent, resident species must make use of "ephemeral habitats"—those that exist only temporarily—to carry out the breeding and feeding necessary for survival. Only organisms specially adapted to these conditions of desert living can survive as a species; typically desert plants and animals are dormant or torpid between seasons of activity. What distinguishes one desert from another is the range of endemic and/or predominant biological entities present.

The North American desert regions can be divided into four major deserts: the Great Basin, Mojave, Sonoran, and Chihuahuan. The first two are entirely located within U.S. boundaries, while two-thirds of the Sonoran Desert and three-fourths of the Chihuahuan Desert lie in northern Mexico.

The Chihuahuan Desert, largest of the North American deserts, covers approximately 196,000 square miles or 36% of the total desert area. It is a high arid zone where the lower basins average over 2,200 feet above sea level with surrounding areas commonly 4,500-5,000 feet—as high as 7,200 feet at the southern end in Mexico's San Luis Potosí. No other North American Desert reaches comparable heights.

Rainfall is most prominent in the winter months, with secondary rainfall in August and September. Amounts range from just under eight inches a year at lower elevations to 10 inches or more in desert grasslands near mountain ranges. This makes the Chihuahuan Desert one of the the "wetter" North American deserts. Temperature ranges are extreme, varying from 104° F in mid-summer to well below freezing in winter. Citing these weather patterns, desert specialists typically classify the Chihuahuan Desert as a "warm-temperate desertland" along with the Saharan, Arabian, Indian, Mojave, and Iranian deserts.

Most of the Chihuahuan Desert is underpinned by a layer of hard limestone commonly known as caliche, covered by a thin soil that supports over a thousand plant species endemic to this desert, pre-dominantly grasses, yuccas, and agaves. The general topography encompasses alluvial plains, bajadas (outwash plains), and low mountains which variously combine to form three distinct subdivisions: Trans-Pecos, overlapping southern New Mexico, far West Texas, northeastern Chihuahua, and northwestern Coahuila; Mapimian, eastern Chihuahua and western Coahuila; and Saladan, mostly northern San Luis Potosí.

Indicator plants—dominant species which occur only or mostly in the Chihuahuan Desert—include creosote bush, tarpaper bush, whitethorn acacia, lechuguilla, peyote cactus, candelilla, and crucifixion thorn. Although cactus species are common, they tend to be outnumbered by other desertscrub vegetation. There is a noticeable lack of the various columnar cacti normally associated with the Sonoran Desert to the west; locally dominant cacti include prickly pear, cane cholla, and other low-growing varieties. In spite of their low profile, the cacti of the Chihuahuan Desert number some 250 species, more than any other North American desert.

under six. The center (tel. 915-424-3327) also provides information and permits for Big Bend Ranch State Park.

Paso Lajitas

Just across the Rio Grande from Lajitas is the Mexican village of Paso Lajitas. Boatmen waiting at the shore will take visitors across for $1 roundtrip; you pay on the way back. There's not much to do in Paso Lajitas except drink beer and eat good border-style food at **Garcia's** and **Dos Amigos.**

Accommodations and Food

The modern desert resort of **Lajitas On The Rio Grande** (tel. 915-424-3471), State Rt. 70, P.O. Box 400, Terlingua, TX 79852, started out as the Cavalry Post Motel. Built on the foundations of General Jack Pershing's former post, it has grown to include additional lodgings, tennis courts, swimming nine-hole golf course, 4,777-foot airstrip, and various other enterprises catering to Big Bend tourists. At present the resort offers five comfortable lodging choices: the **Badlands Hotel,** with 17 rooms in an old west theme; **La Placita,** with eight village-style rooms; the 18 mission-style rooms of **La Cuesta; Officers Quarters,** featuring 20 rooms in a frontier fort theme; and the original **Cavalry Post,** offering 26 rooms done up in early American style. Rates are about the same in all five hotels/motels—from $59 s, $65 d Feb. 1-June 15 and Sept. 15-Jan. 31; $48 s, $53 d the remainder of the year. Additional guests in the same room pay $6 each. La Placita costs a little less; $47.70 s, $58.30 d including tax. Condos are also available at $100 for a one-bedroom, $157 for a two-bedroom, including tax.

Also on the grounds is the **Lajitas RV Park,** which offers full hookups for $13 a night; tentsites available for $9 a night. Discounts for weekly and monthly stays.

A real estate office in the complex is busy buying up the surrounding desert and reselling it at a premium. Most of the resort is owned by Houstonian Walter Mischer and his Southern Investors Service. The resort has its own 4,777-foot airstrip; pilots can radio ahead on Unicom 122.9 Mhz for a taxi (free with reservations at the Badlands Hotel).

The **Badlands Restaurant** in the Lajitas On The Rio Grande resort serves a range of moderately priced Mexican and Texan dishes. Open

Mon.-Fri. 7 a.m.-2 p.m. and 5-9 p.m., Sat.-Sun. 7 a.m.-9 p.m. Also on the boardwalks is the **Frontier Drug Co.** (open daily 8 a.m.-6 p.m.), good for sandwiches, salads, chili, and ice cream, and **Badlands Bakery,** open Monday and Wed.-Sat. 7 a.m.-3 p.m. You can buy homemade tamales and a few other grocery items at **Lajitas Trading Post.**

Events

Comanche Moon, the September full moon when the Comanches used to ride down the War Trail through Lajitas into Mexico, is sometimes celebrated in these parts. Check the *Lajitas Sun,* published monthly and distributed free in Lajitas, Terlingua, and Big Bend National Park, for scheduled activities.

The **Chihuahuan Desert Challenge,** an international-class, off-road bicycle race, is held yearly in mid-February. Designated a "Classic" by the National Off-Road Bicycle Association, the UCI class C race features 34- and 70-mile loops charted in and adjacent to the Big Bend Ranch State Park. The 1995 event drew a record 700 cyclists who competed for $10,000 in prizes. Non-pros can participate in fun rides to nearby Buena Suerte Ghost Town and San Carlos, Mexico. For information contact the Chihuahuan Desert Riders Mountain Bicycle Club, c/o Far Flung Adventures (tel. 915-371-2489 or 800-359-4138), P.O. Box 377, Terlingua, TX 79852.

Recreation

Lajitas On The Rio Grande offers free tennis courts and a nine-hole golf course available for guests. Nonguests may play golf for a greens fee of $10 weekdays, $14 weekends and holidays; rental clubs and carts are available. The **Lajitas Stables** (tel. 915-424-3238), across from the Lajitas Airfield, offers trail rides that vary in length from one hour ($14) to all day ($60). Those who don't like to straddle horses but who'd nevertheless like to see the desert can take buckboard rides instead. Charges run $7 for one hour, $12 two hours, $20 four hours. Overnight trips can also be arranged.

Big Bend Adventures (tel. 424-3234), operated out of Lajitas Trading Post, offers river raft rentals, raft trips, hikes, San Carlos trips, and just about any Big Bend area adventure you can dream up.

Big Bend River Tours (tel. 800-545-4240), P.O. Box 317, Lajitas, TX 79852, is a licensed river outfitter that features raft trips along the Rio Grande through the canyons of Big Bend National Park and beyond.

Desert Walker (tel. 371-2533) is a small outfit that leads Big Bend hikes emphasizing the natural and human history of the area. Rates average $45 for a half-day hike, $75 for a full day, with discounts available for groups.

TERLINGUA

Terlingua, a few miles west of Big Bend on FM 170, was the center of the Big Bend quicksilver mining industry between the late 1800s and mid-1900s. When the cinnabar ore was played out around the start of WW II, the miners' adobe shacks were abandoned and Terlingua became a ghost town almost overnight. It's still called a ghost town by the media, but the truth is a small number of people began living and working here again in the 1960s, drawn this time by the beauty of the Chihuahuan Desert and the thrills of river running.

The official year round population here is only 25; that number swells to over 7,000 during the Terlingua chili cookoffs in November. The nonprofit Terlingua Foundation is trying to preserve a bit of Terlingua's history and has restored some of the old miners' shacks and the original storefronts.

You'll find the sometimes-poetic town gossip sheet, *Terlingua Moon,* posted on bulletin boards from Lajitas to Study Butte.

Accommodations and Food
Terlingua has nothing on quite so grand a scale as Lajitas On The Rio Grande (yet), but it does offer a couple of choices: **Easter Egg Valley Motel** (tel. 915-371-2254) on FM 170 offers basic rooms for $40-50 a night, as low as $30-40 in the off season. The adjacent **Chisos Mining Co.** (same phone) features tent/trailer/RV sites with w/e for $8.

A couple of miles east along FM 170 on the way to Study Butte, **Big Bend Travel Park** (tel. 371-2250), offers 50 RV spaces with full hookups for $10 a night. Tentsites are also available here for $2 per person. Located next to the famous La

Kiva restaurant/bar. **BJ's RV Park** (tel. 371-2259) nearby on FM 170 is similar.

Terlingua has five eateries. **Terlingua Cafe** (tel. 371-2305), off FM 170 next to Terlingua Trading Co. and Far Flung Adventures, serves breakast and lunch daily 6 a.m.-5 p.m. Prices are moderate to high, with the picture window at one end providing a Chisos view.

Desert Opry Restaurant (tel. 371-2265), attached to Big Bend Art Studio on the north side of FM 170 near a bridge over Terlingua Creek and close to Big Bend Travel Park/La Kiva, is less expensive and includes vegetarian dishes on its menu. Many of the herbs and vegetables served in the Desert Opry are grown by the proprietors. Hours can be erratic, but it tends to be open 7 a.m.-9 p.m. during the fall and early spring, from 9 a.m. till whenever they feel like it the rest of the year.

La Kiva (tel. 371-2250), on the opposite side of FM 170 in the same area as Desert Opry, is more of a nightspot, with excellent margaritas, barbecued chicken, steak, and plenty of atmosphere—it's built into the side of a hill and the bar stools are tree trunks. La Kiva is typically open every day from 5 p.m. until the last customer staggers out.

Another dinner-only spot is the **Starlight Theater** (tel. 371-2316), a rustically restored version of the old Terlingua Opera House; reputable steak dinners nightly, and a mesquite bar that beats La kiva's. The restaurant is open daily 5-9 p.m. while the bar stays open till midnight. The Starlight offers live music almost every night.

On FM 170 between Terlingua and Lajitas is the newish **Long Draw Saloon,** which serves pizza and spaghetti for dinner only.

Events
If you've ever heard of Terlingua, it's probably because of the annual **World Championship Chili Cookoff** first held here in 1967. Frank X. Tolbert and Wick Fowler, two renowned Texas chili experts, competed that year against a New England journalist who claimed he could make better chili than any Texan. Since chili is the national dish of Texas, the challenge had to be met. No one won that first competition, but every year since then chili chefs, chili-eaters, spectators, and assorted hellraisers from

SIERRA DEL CARMEN

This beautiful but little-known, little-explored limestone and volcanic mountain range in Coahuila's northwest corner spills over the U.S.-Mexico border into Big Bend National Park, where it's known as the Dead Horse Mountains. On the Mexican side the highest and most pristine section of the mountain range, an area known as the **Sierra de Maderas del Carmen** (also called Sierra las Maderas or simply Las Maderas) is entirely volcanic, with two peaks over 9,500 feet, at least seven peaks over 8,200 feet, and ten times as much terrain over 5,000 feet as Big Bend's Chisos Mountains.

Although the area was heavily logged in the late '40s and early '50s, dense groves of Douglas fir, Ponderosa pine, aspen, and Arizona cypress can still be seen at higher elevations, along with grassy, flowered meadows and clear streams similar to those in Big Bend's Chisos Mountains. Among the prettiest meadows are those in the high *cañones,* including Cañon Cinco and Cañon del Oso. The area is home to hundreds of animal species, many considered rare. The Sierra del Carmen white-tailed deer, for example, lives only in the Sierra del Carmen and Chisos Mountains.

Park Status

Since the 1930s Mexican and U.S. government officials have talked about establishing an international park that would encompass Big Bend and parts of the Sierra del Carmen, thus protecting over a million acres of pristine "mountain islands in a desert sea." Recent meetings between U.S. National Park Service directors and their Mexican counterparts in Mexico City have been more fruitful than in the past, mainly because proposals covering Mexican lands are finally proceeding according to Mexican terms. Participants are hopeful NAFTA's passage will encourage U.S. technological support for the development of the park—especially in the villages of Boquillas del Carmen and San Vicente on the Río Bravo border. At the moment tariffs on U.S. goods and services are too costly for Mexico to

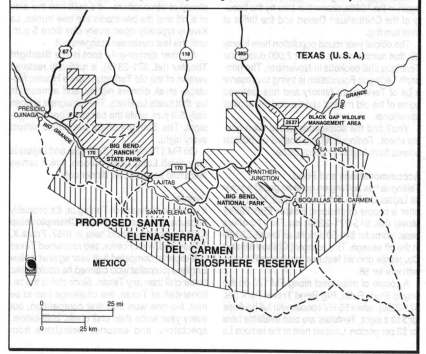

consider such support.

Four years ago the state government of Coahuila was so confident the international park was about to become a reality it affixed "Parque Internacional del Río Bravo" to 1990 state maps (the label was deleted from the map's most recent edition). Weary of waiting for international authorities to come to an agreement, the Coahuila state government has already set aside 37,000 acres of the Sierra del Carmen as a natural sanctuary.

State and federal officals in Mexico are currently developing guidelines for El Proyecto Reserva de la Biósfera Santa Eleña-Sierra del Carmen ("the Santa Eleña-Sierra del Carmen Biosphere Reserve Project," more commonly known on the U.S side simply as "the Santa Eleña Project"). The intention is to establish a 1.5-million acre preserve roughly divided between the states of Chihuahua and Coahuila. If approved, the reserve will extend 200 miles east-ward from a point on the Rio Grande near Redford, Texas, and would coincide with the Texas borders of the Big Bend Ranch State Park, Big Bend National Park, and Black Gap Wildlife Management Area, covering the Sierra del Carmen in Coahuila as well as the Sierra Rica in Chihuahua. The projected reserve would thus protect about 50% more land than the combined territory of the three protected areas on the Texas side. The Mexican plan is then to apply for UNESCO biosphere status in combination with the Big Bend area, forming an international reserve exceeding 2.5 million acres—nearly 4,000 square miles.

Much of the sierra remains in private hands—some choice highlands are owned by a former Coahuila state governor—or is occupied by *ejidos*, agricultural peasant collectives. U.S. park rangers cross the Rio Grande monthly to attend *ejido* meetings to ensure cooperation in the development of a Sierra del Carmen biosphere.

---

around the world have gathered here to practice chili voodoo.

Several years ago, Fowler and Tolbert had a difference of opinion with the Chili Appreciation Society International (CASI) regarding commercial sponsorship. Tolbert and Fowler, the purists, stayed in Terlingua behind the Terlingua store on FM 170; that event is officially called the **Original Terlingua International Frank X. Tolbert/Wick Fowler Memorial Championship Chili Cookoff,** often shortened to "Viva Terlingua." This event attracts fewer chili chefs than **Arriba Terlingua,** the CASI cookoff now held down FM 170 at a new spot called Rancho CASI, about four miles from Terlingua Trading Co. toward Lajitas. The Arriba event typically attracts three times more participants than the funkier "behind-the-store" cookoff. Both events can get pretty rowdy, but because of its size, Arriba has the edge.

Both cookoffs are held the first weekend in November. It's best to arrive a few days early since campgrounds and motels in Terlingua, Lajitas, and Study Butte fill up fast. If you want to avoid the crowds altogether, leave town before the weekend begins, as many locals do.

On the first weekend of February, local residents sponsor a Cookie Chill-Off to lampoon the chili cookoffs and raise money for the Ter-lingua Foundation. It's a semi-serious contest, though—a no-bake dessert competition held in the old ghost town area off FM 170.

Recreation

Far Flung Adventures (tel. 915-371-2489) is the oldest, most established river outfitter in the Big Bend area. It organizes raft trips down the Rio Grande as well as in Arizona, New Mexico, Colorado, and Mexico. The head office is located next to Terlingua Trading Co., just north of FM 170. The hand-drawn map of the Rio Grande on one of the office walls is worth a special trip for those seeking detailed rafting info—it's the best around.

Far Flung also arranges monthly pack-horse trips into Mexico's unspoiled Sierra del Carmen with local outfitter and Big Bend National Park river ranger Marcos Paredes. The five-day trip climbs to nearly 10,000 feet with stops at various canyons and mountain ridges along the way. The cost is $500-600 per person including transport, saddle stock, pack animals, meals, and guide services. Call or write Far Flung for their current schedule; the Sierra del Carmen trips don't operate Dec.-Feb. because of the risk of snowstorms. You can contact Paredes directly by calling 477-2223 or 371-2469.

Guided Hikes

An outfit called **Desert Walker** (tel. 915-371-2533 or 800-545-4240) in Terlingua offers half-day and full-day guided hikes for individuals and groups. Rates vary from $25 per person for a half-day hike (five-person minimum) to $225 per person (up to seven persons) for a two-day, one-night trip that includes a hike over Mesa de Aguila and a raft trip through Santa Eleña Canyon.

Shopping

The **Terlingua Trading Co.** (tel. 915-371-2234) in the original Chisos Mining Co. building off FM 170 sells souvenirs and crafts. In the back of the store is **Quicksilver Jewelry Gallery,** which offers better than average Indian and Mexican jewelry. Another room off the main store contains an excellent selection of books on Texana, Mexican and Southwestern cooking, geology, geography, natural and regional history, Native American and Mexican cultures, and art. The complex is usually open daily 8 a.m.-8 p.m.

Entertainment

Next to Far Flung Adventures and the Terlingua Trading Co., the restored **Starlight Theater** (tel. 915-371-2326) hosts live music on weekends, sometimes during the week.

STUDY BUTTE

Pronounced Stoody Beaut—it's named for miner Will Study, and that's how he said his name—this former ghost town is located at the junction of State 118 and FM 170, near the west entrance to Big Bend National Park. The town, just a cluster of scattered buildings, is well-located for park visits, though traffic in and out of the park detracts.

Accommodations and Food

Big Bend Motor Inn. (tel. 915-371-2218) on State 118 at the FM 170 junction is a modern sort of place with rooms for $60 s, $65 d; efficiencies cost $67 s, $72 d. The attached RV park's rates are $12.50 full hookups, tentsites $8, for two people; additional persons pay $2 each. The motel's cafe serves a first-rate, family recipe chili. A bit farther north on State 118 is the lower-priced **Mission Lodge** (tel. 371-2555, under the same management as Big Bend Motor Inn),

where rooms are $50 s, $55 d a night; Mission Lodge also has an RV park where full hookups cost $12.50, tentsites $8.

Desert Trailer Park (tel. 371-2457), near the Study Butte Store, offers very basic tent/trailer/RV sites in a dirt lot for $4-8.

Terlingua Ranch Hotel (tel. 371-2416) offers rooms in the $30-40 range, tentsites ($3) and RV sites ($6), plus its own 4,800-foot airstrip. Despite its name it's not in Terlingua but 15.5 miles off State 118 via a dirt road; the turnoff is about 18 miles north of Study Butte on the way to Alpine. Also on State 118, about six miles northwest of Study Butte, **Wildhorse Station** (tel. 371-2526) rents furnished cabins starting at $35 for a small cabin, more for a two-bedroom structure or larger party.

The funky **Study Butte Store** sells groceries as well as gasoline, diesel, and propane. Next door, **Roadrunner Deli** serves sandwiches, bagels, omelettes, and take-out picnic lunches; open 7 a.m.-3:30 p.m. daily. Groceries and gas are also available at the **Chevron station** at the State 118 and FM 170 intersection.

Recreation

Turquoise Trailrides (tel. 371-2212) next door to Big Bend Motor Inn arranges horseback trips in the area for $15 one hour, $23 two hours, $41 four hours, $110-125 overnight, depending on the number of people.

Big Bend Touring Society (tel. 915-371-2548) offers guided natural history tours of Big Bend Country and across the border into Mexico. **Texas River Expeditions** and **Outback Expeditions** (see "Guided Raft Trips") each have offices in Study Butte.

Post Office

Outside of Big Bend's Chisos Basin, the only post office for at least 50 miles in any direction is in Study Butte, at State 118 and FM 170. This post office used to be in Terlingua and is still called the "Terlingua Post Office." Hours are Mon.-Fri. 8 a.m.-1 p.m. and 2-4:30 p.m.

BIG BEND RANCH STATE PARK

This 1988 Texas Parks and Wildlife Department acquisition has doubled the size of the state park system. Those who've seen it say it rivals

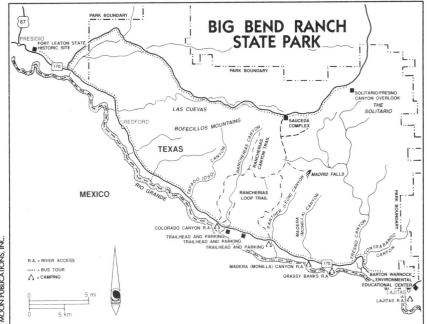

© MOON PUBLICATIONS, INC.

Big Bend National Park for raw scenery and possesses several geographical features the national park doesn't have. One is the **Solitario,** a huge laccolith with a diameter of nine miles. It was formed by a subterranean magma fount that lifted the limestone bedrock like a giant blister and then collapsed, leaving a ragged series of concentric circular mountain ranges. From the air, the Solitario looks like a pond that froze just as a thrown stone ripples through the water.

The other principal feature of the 265,000-acre park is the **Bofecillos Mountains,** a result of the same volcanic forces that shaped the Chisos and Davis mountains. The Bofecillos top out at about 5,000 feet and are honeycombed with canyons and caves. Fresno Canyon's Arroyo Segundo contains the 100-foot Mexicano Falls, one of the three highest in the state. The second highest, the Madrid Falls, is also in Fresno Canyon, at Arroyo Primero. Many of the caves feature Indian pictographs, as well as a diversity of bat species reportedly unparalleled anywhere in the world.

Until it was sold to the TPWD, Big Bend Ranch was operated by the Diamond A Cattle Company and was owned by the chairman of the Atlantic Richfield oil company. Planned recreational use at BBRSP has finally been approved and several kinds of visitor activities are now permitted in the area, including rafting, hiking, camping, hunting (for aoudad and ibex), and bus tours. A herd of longhorns grazes in the park, but rumors say all stock may be removed at some point in the future.

A drive along the River Road from Lajitas to Presidio, which requires no special permits or fees, is probably the best introduction to the area's stunning topography. Rafts or canoes can put in at three points along the river for the Colorado Canyon run.

A movie set at Contrabando Creek was used to film several recent Westerns, including the 1995 CBS mini-series *Streets of Laredo,* a sequel to the hugely successful *Lonesome Dove.* The set has been left standing as a tourist attraction and is accessible from FM 170.

Hikers can choose among three trails open to the public: the Rancherías Loop Trail (21 miles, overnight camping permitted); Rancherías Canyon Trail (9.5 miles); and Closed Canyon Trail (0.7 mile). All are accessible from FM 170; hikers must possess valid backcountry use permits ($3 per person for 24 hours), available at Headquarters Complex opposite Fort Leaton near Presidio or the Barton Warnock Environmental Education Center in Lajitas. For the Rancherías Loop Trail you must also hold a Texas Conservation Passport; for the other trails fees are waived for TCP holders. At the Headquarters Complex you can obtain a good topographical map—along with a compass, a necessity for hiking the longer trails at these facilities.

Primitive camping is permitted at several areas near the Rio Grande and RM 180, including Madera Canyon, Grassy Banks, and Colorado Canyon. There are also two group camping areas at Arenosa and Contrabando ("Movie House"). All of these sites feature composting toilets but not potable water or electricity.

In addition, 10 drive-in sites are available in the interior of the park. None have water, trash containers, or toilets, so campers must come prepared. Rates are $3 a night for TCP holders, $6 for everyone else. Reservations are required and may be obtained in person at the Headquarters Complex opposite Fort Leaton near Presidio, or by calling (915) 229-3416 Mon.-Fri. 8 a.m.-5 p.m.

If you'd like more over your head than tent canvas or a ceiling of stars, sleep in one of the old ranch buildings at the Sauceda Complex, a visitor center in the middle of the park. The **Big House** offers a screened veranda, living room, dining room, kitchen, three bedrooms with fireplaces, and three bathrooms. It sleeps up to 10 for a cost of $40 per person per night; linens and firewood provided. The nearby **Bunkhouse** accommodates 15 men and 15 women in spearate quarters for $15 per person. Along with dining room and kitchen, the Bunkhouse contains a large living room with fireplace and satellite TV. For reservations at either facility, call (915) 229-3416.

Texas Parks and Wildlife naturalists lead twice-monthly interpretive bus tours of BBRSP.

On the first Saturday of the month, the bus leaves from Fort Leaton (tel. 915-229-3613) at 8 a.m., returning at 5 p.m.; on the third Saturday it leaves from the Warnock Center (tel. 424-3327) at 8 a.m., returning at 5:30 p.m. The bus route extends well into the interior of the park, stopping at the Fresno Canyon Overlook for a view of Solitario. The cost is $60 per person, which includes roundtrip transport from Fort Leaton or the Warnock Center, guide service, and a chuck-wagon lunch at the Sauceda Complex. TCP holders receive a $5 discount on the tour fee. These tours are very popular, so reservations should be made far in advance; for a current schedule or other information, write or call the Superintendent, Big Bend Ranch State Park (tel. 229-3416, fax 229-3613), P.O. Box 1180, Presidio, TX 79845.

The TPWD also offers periodic multiday birding and hiking tours in the park for around $245-300 per person. Private tours led by park-trained and park-certified guides can be arranged by calling (915) 371-2548 or 424-3234.

PRESIDIO

Unless you were an aficionado of frontier forts or La Junta, the only reason to come to Presidio used to be the spectacular drive down **River Road** along the Rio Grande between Lajitas and Presidio. Now that the state has established the Big Bend Ranch State Park, the Lajitas-Presidio trip is likely to become more alluring to travelers.

Along with Ojinaja across the river, the town was founded by the Spanish in the 1600s. The original name for the settlement was Nuevo Real Presidio de Nuestra Señora de Betleña y Santiago de Las Amarillas de La Junta de Los Rios Norte y Conchos—"New Royal Presidio [Garrison] of Our Lady of Bethlehem and St. James on the Banks of the Junction of the Rios Grande and Conchos." On the American side, this was later shortened to Presidio del Norte and finally Presidio.

The surrounding floodplains are extremely fertile and are the oldest continually cultivated farmlands in North America. The Patarabueyes Indians, about whom little is known except that they seem to have been a Pueblo Indian group, farmed this land as long ago as A.D. 1200.

When the Spanish arrived in the early 1500s, they were astonished by these "advanced" Indians who lived in adobe houses and cultivated their own food. By the late 1600s, the Patarabueyes had been missionized; due to Spanish mistreatment and pressure from the Mescalero Apaches, they disappeared by the 19th century.

Today Presidio is primarily known as the hottest town in Texas. Visit in midsummer, and you'll be able to confirm this—the *average* high temperature in June is 103° F. The population of 1,800 are predominantly Mexicans and Chicanos who speak a Chihuahuan-inflected Spanish; the town newspaper (*International/Internacionale*) is bilingual and priced in both U.S. and Mexican currency. The surrounding area is famed for its sweet onions and cantaloupes. A sign on the eastern outskirts of town reads Welcome to Presidio—Gateway to the Interior of Mexico and Onion Capital of the World. Local *botánicas* sell traditional herbal medicine made from desert plants.

Fort Leaton, Presidio

In addition to selling books and maps covering Texas and Mexico, **Presidio Information Center and Gift Shop** (tel. 915-229-4478) dispenses free travel information. On US 67 next to the post office; open 9 a.m.-6 p.m. daily.

Mexican vehicle insurance can be obtained at **La Junta Travel** (tel. 915-229-4621 or 800-847-8305) at the junction of US 67 and O'Reilly St. just before crossing the border.

Fort Leaton State Historic Site
Fort Leaton began as a trading post for Ben Leaton, an American formerly employed as an Indian scalphunter for the Mexican government. Leaton built his private adobe fortress in 1848 on the site of an earlier Spanish settlement, El Fortín de San José, which was built in the 1770s and abandoned in 1810. In spite of his former occupation, Leaton traded with the local Apaches and Comanches and is said to have encouraged Indian raids on Mexican villages—which is why local Hispanic residents still refuse to call the settlement Fort Leaton, referring to it instead as El Fortín. Leaton's business also benefited from its location on the San Antonio-Chihuahua Trail, which extended 800 miles from Chihuahua, Mexico to Indianola on the Texas Gulf Coast.

Leaton died in 1851. The adobe fort passed through various hands, with the Texas Parks and Wildlife Department acquiring the property in 1968. It's been fully restored and now contains excellent exhibits on the area's history, including displays on the Patarabueyes Indians. A shaded, sometimes breezy picnic area adjoins the grounds. Open daily 8 a.m.-4:30 p.m. Admission is $2 adults, $1 children 6-12, free under 6.

El Camino del Rio (River Road)
The 50-mile stretch of FM 170 between Presidio and Lajitas parallels a trail used by Spanish explorers over three centuries ago. The San Antonio-Chihuahua Trail passed along here as well until the railroads came through in the 1880s; in the early 1900s Pancho Villa reactivated the trail for his mule trains during the Mexican Revolution. During this era, the road earned the name Muerte del Burro ("Donkey's Death"); paved only 37 years ago, the road still boasts a 15% grade at one point. The scenery along the eastern half of the road is excellent, as the road

winds up, down, and around the volcanic and limestone rock formations of the Bofecillos Mountains, with views of the Rio Grande below. West of the mountains, the road passes through the farming community of **Redford** (pop. 107), a collection of adobe houses, a church, and the Cordera Store, where gas and food are available.

Forty-eight miles west of Presidio the road ends at **Candelaria** (pop. 55). Like Lajitas it was founded as a U.S. Cavalry post in the Pancho Villa era early this century. Mexicans in the larger ranching settlement of San Antonio, Chihuahua, on the opposite bank of the Rio Grande, cross the river to receive their mail at the village general store, **Candelaria Mercantile.** Gas, food, and cold drinks are available at the **End of the Raod Cantina.**

Ojinaga

This Mexican city of 45,000 people is only 142 miles from Chihuahua, capital of the Mexican state of the same name. The Chihuahuan Desert provides material for local cottage industries inherited from the former native inhabitants—rope and twine called istle made from lechuguilla (*Agave lechuguilla*), bootleg liquor from sotol (*Dasylirion wheeleri*), wax from candelilla (*Euphorbia antisyphilitica*), and herbal remedies from a number of other desert plants.

A block off the plaza on Calle Zaragoza, **Panadería La Francesa** ("French Bakery") occupies an old Spanish building that briefly served as Pancho Villa's headquarters during the Revolution. Ojinaga was once notorious as a conduit for contraband drugs coming from the interior of Mexico, but state and local police have largely wiped out the drug trade in recent years and the town is now safe for foreign visitors. The local *transitos* (traffic police) are very helpful to visiting motorists and will even provide free escort services for lost drivers as well as emergency automotive repairs.

The town also provides short- or long-term security parking in a large, fenced lot in the middle of town (at Calle Hidalgo and Calle de la Paz) for motorists wishing to take the bus to Chihuahua or beyond.

About an hour's drive south of Ojinaga via Mexico 16 (the highway to Chihuahua's state capital), the Río Conchos cuts the scenic, 2,000-

foot-deep **Cañon de Peguis** into the high desert floor. Vehicles can be parked at the well-marked *mirador* (viewpoint) at the side of the highway near the canyon. A trail leads from the parking area down to the canyon edge.

Border Formalities: The Presidio-Ojinaga border crossing is open Mon.-Fri. 7:30 a.m.-9 p.m., Sat.-Sun. 8 a.m.-4 p.m. If you're planning to stay more than 72 hours you'll need a tourist card, and if you're planning to drive beyond Cañon de Peguis to Chihuahua you'll need a temporary auto import permit—both are available at the border station. If you're just driving around the Ojinaga area, including the canyon, an auto permit isn't necessary.

Ocotillo Unit Wildlife Management Area

Thirty-six miles upriver along the Rio Grande, the Ocotillo Unit WMA protects 2,000 acres of river plains as a nesting and feeding place for white-winged doves. Dove hunters holding a TPWD hunting permit may pursue the white-wings in season. Call (915) 358-4444 for information.

Accommodations and Food

Three Palms Inn (tel. 915-229-3211) is on the north edge of Presidio off US 67 on the way to Marfa. Clean, basic rooms are $30-38; pool on the premises. Also on US 67 is the six-room **La Siesta Hotel** (tel. 229-3611) with rooms for $22-30.

The Three Palms features a popular coffee shop that serves steaks and good Tex-Mex food. At the FM 170/US 67 intersection in town, the year-old **El Patio** serves inexpensive Mexican daily 6:30 a.m.-10 p.m. In the center of town off FM 170 is **La Pampas** (tel. 299-3552), a Mexican restaurant that also serves a few Argentine and Italian dishes. Owner Gualberto Laperuta played professional soccer in Mexico and Latin America. The restaurant is open daily for breakfast, lunch, and dinner. **La Frontera** is also good for Mexican dishes.

Across the border in Ojinaga, **Restaurant Los Comales,** opposite the city hall at Calle Zaragoza 106, serves Mexican breakfasts, combo platters, and steak from 8 a.m. to midnight. **Chuco's,** at Av. Trasviña y Retes and Calle 13a, is a popular gringo stop for beer and Mexican food and claims to stay open 365 days a year.

About 25 miles north of Presidio off State 67, the sprawling **Cibolo Creek Ranch** recently opened its gates as an elegant, adult-oriented dude ranch for harried urban execs seeking a remote retreat. Once the kingdom of West Texas cattle baron Milton Faver—known by local Hispanics as "Don Meliton"—the ranch features a heavily restored version of El Fortín de Cibolo, Faver's private fortress against Amerindian raids. The one-story structure consists of one- to four-foot thick adobe walls supported by cypress and cottonwood beams around an interior courtyard with round corner towers pierced by gunports and wooden drain spouts. Activities on the 25,000-acre spread include horseback riding and hunting for deer, dove, quail, and javelina; a pool, jacuzzi, and exercise room are also available. Suites, decorated with hand-stitched quilts, antique Mexican furniture, retablos, and Saltillo tile floors, are divided among Hacienda de Cibolo, La Morita, and La Cienega units. Daily tariffs, which include all lodging, meals, and activities, run $325 single and $210-259 per person double occupancy for the Cibolo and La Cienaga units, $495 s/d for La Morita. For reservations or information, contact Cibolo Creek Ranch (tel. 800-525-4800), P.O. Box 44, Shafter, TX 79850.

Getting There

A few years ago a group of Big Bend and Dallas investors bought the rights to a railway route that runs from the Dallas Union Station to Presidio via Fort Stockton and Alpine. They also purchased several Pullman cars and eventually intend to launch a regular passenger service; so far it's only been run as a freight line. If the project reaches fruition, this will not only provide a transport alternative between the Dallas-Fort Worth and Big Bend areas, it will also create an important U.S. rail link with the famous Copper Canyon train from Chihuahua to Los Mochis, Mexico.

Ojinaga-Chihuahua passenger rail service was discontinued some years ago, but the Transportes Chihuahuenses bus line operates eight buses per day to Chihuahua for around $8.

MARFA

This is the Presidio County seat (pop. 2,466), but for most Texans it's famous for just two things: the filming of the James Dean, Elizabeth Taylor, Rock Hudson epic *Giant* and the Marfa Lights—usually referred to in the press as "the mysterious Marfa Lights." Named for the heroine of a Russian novel, Marfa is the second highest town in the state, with an elevation of 4,688 feet. It's a mecca for glider pilots, with air currents that are perfect for long sailplane flights.

The local economy rests on cattle, goat, and sheep ranching, so Marfa has a real "ranch town" feel. Wander some of the side streets for a look at the tidy adobe and wood-frame houses.

James Dean, as oil wildcatter Jet Rink, relaxes in front of the Marfa ranch set for Giant.

Downtown

Highland Ave. is Marfa's main thoroughfare, where you'll find the **El Paisano Hotel,** a refurbished 1929 hotel listed on the National Register of Historic Places. El Paisano has become something of a shrine for James Dean fanatics, not because he stayed here (he didn't) during the filming of his last movie, *Giant,* but because a glass case in the lobby contains autographed pictures of each of the major cast members and newspaper clippings about the production. The 1955 movie was actually filmed on a ranch west of Marfa. The crew stayed at El Paisano, but Jimmy, Rock, and Liz stayed at rented private homes in town. Tangentially, Marfa was the script setting for the 1983 motion picture *Come Back to the Five and Dime, Jimmy Dean* (starring Sandy Dennis, Karen Black, and Cher), a movie about the effect of the *Giant* production on a group of Marfa residents.

More architecturally impressive is the 1886 Presidio County Courthouse at the end of Highland Avenue. There's a good view of the surrounding countryside from its Renaissance-style dome open to the public during office hours.

Marfa Lights

Nobody can figure out the source of these lights—theories include UFOs, Indian ghosts, and atmospheric reflections. Most nights you can easily see them from the Official Marfa Lights Viewing Site, complete with bronze state plaque, off US 90, nine miles east of town. "Ghost lights" were first reported in the 1800s, which is why some people dismiss the common theory they're headlights reflected off atmospheric inversion layers from vehicle's farther down US 90 or nearby US 67.

You can order a 50-page booklet on the phenomena, *Marfa Lights,* from Ocotillo Enterprises, P.O. Box 195, Alpine, TX 79831.

The Chinati Foundation

The Chinati Foundation is a nonprofit organization centered in Marfa that sponsors Big Bend Country artists. At the site of now-defunct Fort Russell, south of Marfa off US 67 near Border Patrol Headquarters, is a collection of concrete sculpture by renowned sculptor Donald Judd. You'll find additional aluminum pieces in the former gun sheds at the old fort.

Foundation artwork is also on display in a former mohair and wool warehouse on Highland St., including a permanent exhibit of John Chamberlain sculpture. The warehouse is open Thurs.-Sat. 1-5 p.m. or by appointment; call (915) 729-4362.

Accommodations and Food

The **Lash-Up Bed & Breakfast** (tel. 915-729-4487) at 215 N. Austin, a block from the county courthouse, is a two-story 1909-vintage house with four country-decorated bedrooms for $50 per room per night, including a full breakfast (lunch and dinner available on request). **El Paisano Hotel** is a time-share now, but when suites are unoccupied the hotel will take walk-in guests for $60-100 a night. The **Thunderbird Hotel** and **Holiday Capri Inn** (tel. 729-4391) on W. US 90 share the same management and offer basic motel rooms for $33 s, $39 d.

There are trailer slots for $10-12 a night at **Apache Pines RV Park** (tel. 729-4326), W. US 90; **Corder Trailer Park** (tel. 729-4576), 816 N. Hill; and **Marfa Overnight Trailer Park** (tel. 729-4405), S. US 67.

The enchiladas at **Mando's** (tel. 729-8170), on W. US 90 just outside Marfa, are famed for miles around. Beer can be consumed on the premises if you bring your own. Another good Tex-Mex spot, especially for breakfast, is **Carmen's Cafe,** on the north side of US 90 just east of the US 67 intersection.

Vicinity of Marfa

Ranch Road 2810 south from Marfa to Riudosa on the Mexican border passes through secluded ranch country with glimpses of burgeoning pronghorn antelope and mule deer herds. While there's nothing to see in Riudosa, this road connects with FM 170 to Presidio and Lajitas.

ALPINE

Alpine is the Brewster County seat and the largest town in the tri-county area (pop. 5,637). At an elevation of 4,481 feet, it's not exactly in the mountains but is set in a geological cul-de-sac formed by the Altuda Mountains and the Paisano Plateau. The town developed as the intersection between two rail lines, the Southern Pacific and the Atchison, Topeka, and Santa Fe. More important nowadays is the fact it's the home of Sul Ross State University, the only institute of higher education in Big Bend Country.

Outside magazine recently named the town in its second-tier top-ten retirement places for the outdoor active. Robert James Waller, author of national bestsellers *The Bridges of Madison County* and *Slow Waltz in Cedar Bend,* recently moved to a 971-acre ranch just east of town in the Del Norte Mountains foothills—perhaps further proof Alpine is beginning to attract some attention. According to the *Dallas Morning News,* when Waller walked into an Alpine real estate office saying he wanted to purchase a big ranch—perhaps a thousand acres, the realtor replied, "Well sir, around here a thousand acres is a little ranch."

Tune in radio station KVLF-AM 1240 if you like big band music. If you need cash, First National Bank at 101 East Ave. E. has a 24-hour ATM that takes Visa, MasterCard, Discover, and most ATM cash cards.

Sul Ross State University

Located on US 90 east of town, Sul Ross reportedly has one of the best range science departments in the country; even the liberal arts departments specialize in what might be termed "West Texas Studies." The **National Intercollegiate Rodeo Association** (NIRA) was founded at Sul Ross in 1948 and the university rodeo team is one of the nation's top collegiate competitors. The NIRA championship competition takes place in the Sul Ross Range Science Arena each October.

Also on campus is the **Museum of the Big Bend** (tel. 915-837-8143), which features exhibits that chronicle Big Bend history from the early Indian settlements and Spanish exploration through the development of American ranching in the area. Open Tues.-Sat. 9 a.m.-5 p.m., Sunday 1-5 p.m., free admission.

In March, the university sponsors a Cowboy Poetry Gathering wherein cowboy poets from California to New York meet for a long weekend of lectures and readings. Not long ago cowboy poetry was a dying art, but a recent revival of interest in Western lyricism has brought it back from the brink of extinction.

Woodward Agate Ranch

This 4,000-acre ranch is a favorite haunt for rock-hunters. For 25 cents a gram, you can collect all the rock specimens you can carry. Over 70 varieties are available, including pom pom agate, red plume, opal, and amethyst. The ranch also features a store where you can purchase rocks. Guided tours of an opal mine on the property are available for $15 per person.

The ranch, about 15 miles south off State 118 toward Big Bend, is always open; there're also a campground and RV park here. Call (915) 364-2271 for more information.

Elephant Mountain Wildlife Management Area

The Texas Parks and Wildlife Department uses this 26,000-acre tract of well-preserved Chihuahuan Desert, 26 miles south of Alpine, for radio telemetry studies of mule deer movement, and as a base for bighorn sheep restoration. Texas Conservation Passport holders can arrange guided tours by calling (915) 364-2228.

Hotels and Motels

Most visitors to Big Bend Country pass through Alpine with plans to stay somewhere in the Davis Mountains or closer to Big Bend National Park. The **Highland Inn** (tel. 915-837-5811), on US 90 E opposite the Sul Ross State campus, costs $36-41 per night and has a pool. Nearby on the same road, **Siesta Country Inn** (tel. 837-2503) offers 15 rooms laid out on one level with a pool and a simple, family-oriented atmosphere for $26-31.

Other motels strung out along US 90 include **Bien Venido** (tel. 837-3454), **Days Inn** (tel. 837-3417), and **Sunday House Motor Inn** (tel. 837-3363), all with rooms in the $25-38 range.

Holland Hotel (tel. 837-3455 or 800-535-8040), at 207 W. Holland on US 90, extends the retro-Western trend begun by the Gage Hotel by offering nine rooms decorated with Texas-Mexican motifs for $40 to $105 a night. The hotel's greatest strength is its atmospheric restaurant.

About 65 miles south of Alpine on State 118 is the new **Longhorn Ranch Motel** (tel. 371-2541, fax 371-2540), where rooms cost $40-50 a night. The Longhorn has a pool and is the first motel in the area to receive AAA approval.

Campgrounds and RV Parks

Just outside Alpine are three RV parks in the $11-15 a night range with full hookups ($7-8 for tents): **Alpine Pecan Grove RV Park** (tel. 915-837-7175), US 90 W; **Danny Boy Camper Park** (tel. 837-7135), US 90 E; and **La Vista 5400 RV Resort** (tel. 364-2293), State 118 S. La Vista has 50-amp electrical service.

Campsites at the **Woodward Agate Ranch** cost $11.50 for RVs, $6 for tents. Showers are available.

Bed and Breakfast

Corner House Bed & Breakfast (tel. 915-837-7161) at 802 East Ave. E (off US 90 near Sul Ross State) offers four attractively decorated, quiet rooms in a two-story wood-frame house for $50 d; rates include a large country-style breakfast. A friendly, well-traveled English couple runs the place.

Food

Alpine dining has improved immensely over the last two years. Attached to the Holland Hotel, **Cinnabar** (tel. 915-837-3455) features a creative, ever-changing menu of haute Tex-Mex and Southwestern dishes, served in a comfortably trendy dining room inspired by Marathon's Gage Hotel; the head chef in fact formerly worked at the Gage. It's open Tues.-Sat. for lunch and dinner, Sunday for brunch and dinner.

Little Mexico Cafe (tel. 837-2855) at 204 W. Murphy serves chiles rellenos, stuffed jalapeños, enchiladas, chicken-fried steak, burritos, burgers, fries, and $3.99 daily specials; open Mon.-Sat. 11 a.m.-9 p.m. **Gallegos Mexican Restaurant** (tel. 837-2416) at 1102 E. Holland (US 90), famous for flat, stacked enchiladas, is open daily except Sunday 11 a.m.-9 p.m. and features a popular all-you-can-eat buffet 11:30 a.m.-1:30 p.m. For steak and barbecue, **Longhorn Cattle Company** (tel. 837-3692), 801 N. 5th St. (State 118), is the eatery of choice, open for lunch and dinner daily except Sunday.

Alpine Bakery, at 302 E. Holland, is a good spot for an early breakfast of coffee, pastries, eggs, and pancakes; open Mon.-Fri. 7 a.m.-4 p.m., Saturday 8 a.m.-3 p.m.

Downtown Brown's (tel. 837-2694) at 203 N. 5th St. serves pit barbecue, fajitas, vegetarian sandwiches, soups, and salads in a relaxed coffeehouse atmosphere surrounded by local art. Open late nightly, with live music on the weekends.

Corner House Cafe, part of Corner House Bed & Breakfast, enjoys local popularity for its fresh-baked bread, healthy menu, and outdoor eating area. Open Tues.-Sat. 11 a.m.-4 p.m.

Entertainment

Railroad Blues, at 504 W. Holland, promotes itself as a "rhythm and blues rock 'n' roll tavern" and offers dancing, darts, and pool tables. Open Mon.-Fri. 4 p.m.-midnight, Saturday 6 p.m. to 1 a.m. **Reata Restaurant and Patio Bar** (tel. 915-837-9232), named for the fictional *Giant* ranch, features live music nightly along with "Texas cowboy cuisine" at 203 N. 5th Street.

Events

On the first weekend of March, Sul Ross State University hosts the **Texas Cowboy Poetry Gathering.** Cowboys from all over the state and beyond meet to share odes to western life. Other activities include a chuckwagon supper and an auction of cowboy gear.

Rockhounds converge at the annual **Gem and Mineral Show,** held the third weekend of April at Alpine Civic Center. Call 915-837-3301 for details.

The biggest event of the year is the **Sul Ross National Intercollegiate Rodeo,** held at the Sul Ross State University Rodeo Arena the first weekend of October. Numerous champions from this rodeo have graduated directly to the pro rodeo circuit. Call SRSU at 837-8200 for more information.

Shopping

Big Bend Saddlery, off US 67 at the north entrance to Alpine, crafts custom leather gear for working cowboys from the tri-county area and as far away as New Mexico, England, and Japan. Big Bend also sells belts, belt buckles, boots, hats, bandannas, and other Western wear, as well as books on ranching and Western lore. The **Apache Trading Post,** in a log cabin off US 90 about a mile west of town, carries souvenirs, Indian crafts (including a good selection of silver and turquoise jewelry), Mexican Indian pottery, books, and a variety of regional maps.

Hook or Crook Books (tel. 915-837-3128), 110 N. 6th St. and **Books Plus** (tel. 837-3360), 608 E. Ave. E, specialize in new, used, and rare books on West Texas. **Ocotillo Enterprises** (tel. 837-5353), 205 N. 5th St., carries books, magazines, craft supplies, audio cassettes, and rocks.

Getting There and Around
Air: Dallas Express Airlines (tel. 800-529-0925) flies between Dallas Love Field and Alpine's Casper Airport once a day Tues.-Fri. and Sunday. The 55-minute flight costs $109 each way.

The next nearest airports with regularly scheduled air services are in Midland, over 180 miles northeast of Alpine, and El Paso, 220 miles west.

Skies of Texas (tel. 837-2290) offers charter air service in the region aboard four- and six-seater Beechcrafts.

Train: Amtrak's *Sunset Limited* stops in Alpine.

Big Bend Shuttles: Sun Runner Tours (tel. 915-364-4205) operates a shuttle to the Study Butte area, adjacent to Big Bend National Park, for $50 per person each way; reservations are necessary and there's a two-person minimum.

Rental Cars: Aerflite (tel. 837-2744 or 837-3009) can arrange rental cars from Alpine's Casper Airport, just three miles outside town.

MARATHON

A retired sea captain who'd sailed the Aegean Sea gave this town its name because the area reminded him of Marathon, Greece. If you're driving to Big Bend from Fort Stockton or Del Rio, you'll pass through Marathon—if it's been a long drive, you might consider dining or staying the night at the historic Gage Hotel. Otherwise, there's little else to see or do in Marathon itself, though the Gage Hotel operates jeep, horseback, and rafting trips in the Big Bend area.

The Marathon Chamber of Commerce distributes an annotated walking tour map of the town that leads visitors to a couple of old churches, the original railroad depot, and various other historic buildings. You can pick up the map in the lobby of the Gage Hotel.

Gage Hotel
Alfred Gage, a banker and cattle baron who once owned a half-million-acre ranch in the area, built this hotel in 1927 to house business acquaintances. He died the year after the hotel opened, but it became a popular resting place for ranchers and cattlemen from all over Texas. In 1978 a Houston interest bought the yellow-brick property and skillfully refurbished it. The bedrooms and common rooms are tastefully decorated with West Texas antiques and artifacts. You'll find Tarahumara pottery in the lobby, and in the bar

Gage Hotel

there's a Yaqui Indian altar and a Chusa game, a sort of Mexican roulette that involves rolling several white marbles on a cowhide board. Guest rooms upstairs are furnished with Mexican colonial and 19th-century Texas ranch furniture, each with a separate theme (e.g., the "Dagger Mesa" room is decorated with Spanish daggers).

From mid-September through mid-April, rates are $70 per room with private bath, $52 with shared bath; subtract $10 the remainder of the year. The motel's new adobe has suites with fireplace and private bath for $125, rooms without fireplace for $80, plus a swimming pool. The restaurant (tel. 915-386-4205) is open daily for breakfast, lunch, and dinner, and specializes in creative Southwestern and Mexican cuisine—including such anomalies as cabrito enchiladas. Located right on US 90 at Avenue C.

Other Accommodations and Food
Marathon Motel & RV Park (tel. 915-386-4241) on W. US 90 has motel rooms for $31-38 a night, full RV hookups for $11.50, and tent sites for $8. RVers can also find full hookups for a bargain $8 ($4 for tents) at **Southern Route RV Park** (tel. 386-4558) on E. US 90.

Stillwell Store & Trailer Park (tel. 376-2244), 46 miles southeast of Marathon off US 385 on FM 2627 near Black Gap Wildlife Management Area, has RV sites with full hookups for $11.50, tent/camper sites with water and electricity for $10.50, and primitive tentsites for $3.50 a night. There's hiking in the immediate area; the Stillwell outfit can also arrange jeep tours of Maravillas Canyon and shuttle service for river trips.

If you follow FM 2627 all the way till it ends at a bridge over the Rio Grande, you'll come to **Heath Canyon Guest Ranch** (tel. 376-2235). A room here costs $35, or you can camp for $3. Facilities include a boat launch and 2,900-foot paved airstrip. The bridge leads to La Linda, Coahuila, on the Mexican side. As the property counts 4,000 feet of Rio Grande frontage and also borders Black Gap Wildlife Management Area, opportunities abound for fishing, birding, rafting, hiking, or just getting away from civilization.

Aside from the Gage Hotel, Marathon has no stellar food attractions. The popular **Phil's Southern Route Diner** (part of Southern Route RV Park) serves solid, reasonably priced Tex-Mex, chicken-fried steak, and brisket daily except Tuesday 11 a.m.-8 p.m. **Gilda's Grill,** in an old gas station on US 90 E, just past the US 385 junction, offers inexpensive breakfast, burgers, hot dogs, and chicken fried steak; open daily 8 a.m.-8 p.m. The **Open Sky Cafe,** at Heath Canyon Guest Ranch, features ranch-style Mexican Wed.-Sun. for dinner only.

Shopping
The growing influx of tourists to Marathon supports a couple of unique shops. **Haley's Trading Post** (no phone), on US 90 east of the Gage Hotel, offers used cowboy gear, cow skulls, and other items favored these days to create Southwestern interiors. **Lovegene's** (tel. 386-4366), at 21 S. 1st St., is a gallery-style shop with ceramics, paintings, jewelry, and photographic lampshades crafted by owner-photographer James Evans.

Black Gap Wildlife Management Area
This 100,000-acre preserve is not open to the general public for recreational use except during state-designated fishing and hunting seasons, nor are there any hiking or camping facilities. FM 2627 passes through the area, however, and visitors are permitted to take "driving nature tours" along the road. Located 55 miles south of Marathon off US 385 and adjacent to Big Bend National Park, it's the largest WMA in Texas and comprises mostly shrub desert plus 25 miles of the Rio Grande. Principal game species include mule deer, javelina, quail, and dove. For Black Gap hunting information, contact Texas Parks and Wildlife, 3407 S. Chadbourne, San Angelo, TX 76904.

FORT STOCKTON

Pecos County seat and home to about 9,000 West Texans, Fort Stockton began as a Spanish mission called St. Gall in the 18th century. The Spanish left when the Comanches came down to water at what later became known as Comanche Springs (the springs were pumped dry in the 1950s following a long drought and never returned). In 1840 the U.S. Army established Camp Stockton at the intersection of the San Antonio-Chihuahua Trail and the Comanche War Trail to protect settlers from Indian attacks. The camp closed at the outbreak of the Civil War but reopened as Fort Stockton in 1867. Around 90% of the troops then garrisoned at the fort were black soldiers from the 9th and 10th Calvary and the 24th, 25th, and 41st Infantry. The Army left again in 1886 but the town retained the name and developed into a prosperous ranching and farming community. When oil and natural gas deposits were discovered in nearby fields in the '20s, the local economy shifted toward the energy industry.

The first thing visitors see when entering Fort Stockton from I-10/US 67 is the Paisano Pete statue, "the world's largest roadrunner" at 10 feet tall and 22 feet long.

First National Bank at 1000 W. Dickinson has an ATM machine; this, along with First National's ATM in Alpine, is the only place to get after-hours cash south of Midland-Odessa between San Antonio and El Paso.

Annie Riggs Memorial Museum

A striking example of "frontier Victorian" or "territorial" adobe architecture, this 1900-vintage building was originally a hotel catering to passengers on the Butterfield Overland Mail coaches. The 14 rooms now contain historical artifacts from the frontier era and local fossils, including the tusks and other remains of a 22,000-year-old mastodon. At 301 S. Main St. (tel. 915-336-2167); open Mon.-Sat. 10 a.m.-noon and 1-5 p.m., Sunday 1:30-5 p.m. between September and May, or Mon.-Sat. 9 a.m.-8 p.m., Sunday 1:30-8 p.m. June through August. Admission is $1 adults, 50 cents children.

Between June and August, the museum presents **Summer on the Patio,** four evenings of live music.

Downtown Historical Tour

This is a self-guided driving tour through town past 16 historical sites—follow the orange arrow. A free map of the route is available at the Annie Riggs Museum. The Old Fort Stockton part of the route can be done as a walking tour, starting at the Guardhouse between 3rd and 4th streets off Rooney Drive. Three of the original 1867-70 Officers Row buildings remain standing near the intersection of 5th and Rooney. A bit north of Officers Row, off Water St., is the old fort cemetery. A look at the headstones shows that most

people died by the age of 40. Sheriff A.J. Royal, who terrorized Pecos County in the late 1800s with ruthless six-shooter justice, is also buried here. Local citizens drew beans to see who would assassinate him, and that's how the headstone reads—"assassinated."

Other notable sights along the route include the **Grey Mule Saloon,** originally built and operated by the infamous Sheriff Royal; the 1885 **county jail;** and the 1875 **St. Joseph's Church.**

Butterfield Overland Mail Stop

A stagecoach "remount stand" has been reconstructed 20 miles east of town at a highway rest stop on I-10/US 290. It was moved here stone by stone from its original location at Tunis Springs (a mile and a half southwest) during the 1936 Texas Centennial to make it more accessible to modern travelers.

Ste. Genevieve Winery

This winery has 7,000 acres of vineyards under cultivation and is a cooperative effort between the University of Texas (which owns the land) and France's Domain Cordier (which supplied the technology and expertise). Almost all the equipment is of French manufacture and French viticulturalists work on site, unusual for an American winery. The Ft. Stockton Chamber of Commerce (tel. 915-336-2264) sponsors tours of the winery and vineyards every Saturday at 10 a.m. for $5 per person, which includes winetasting. Tours leave from the chamber of commerce office at 222 W. Dickinson Boulevard.

Accommodations

Most Ft. Stockton accommodations are on Dickinson Blvd., which is the same as US 67/290, just off I-10. Cheapest motels are the **Economy Inn** (tel. 915-336-2251), 901 E. Dickinson Blvd., with rooms for $18 s, $25 d; **Motel 6** (tel. 336-9737), 3001 W. Dickinson Blvd., with rooms at $23 s, additional adults $6 each; and the **Sands Inn** (tel. 336-2274), 1801 W. Dickinson Blvd. at the Junction of US 285 and US 67/290, at $25 s, $28 d. Near the Motel Six is the **Sunset Inn** (tel. 336-9781), 2601 I-10, exit 257, with $30-36 rooms. All three motels have small pools. Moving up in price, the **Best Western Sunday House** (tel. 336-8521), 3200 W. Dickinson Blvd., I-10 exit 257, has nicer rooms for $38-56 a night.

The **Econo Lodge** (tel. 336-9711) at 800 W. Dickinson Blvd. features satellite TV and a pool with rooms for $38-48 a night. Several other small motels along Dickinson Blvd. offer basic but serviceable rooms for only $15-19 a night, including **Comanche Motel,** E. Dickinson and Gatlin; **El Rancho Motel,** opposite Econo Lodge; **Spanish Trail Lodge,** next to El Rancho; **Deluxe Motor Inn,** opposite the Spanish Trail; **Gateway Lodge; Texan Inn;** and **Town and Country Motel.**

The **KOA Fort Stockton** (tel. 395-2494), 3.5 miles east of town off I-10, has what may be the best commercial RV park and campground in West Texas. It features a well-stocked store with gas, ice, and groceries, as well as a cafe, cactus garden, pool, and 80 acres to wander around. Rates are $17.50 for a tent/camper site with w/e, $19.50 for a full RV hookup, or $24 for a cabin.

Food
The **Comanche Tortilla Factory** (tel. 915-336-3245, 107 S. Nelson), run by the Gallegos family and open Monday through Friday, makes a good take-out food stop if you're continuing east- or westward through Fort Stockton. A dozen homemade jumbo tamales cost under $5; also fresh tortillas and tostados. Go south on Nelson off Dickinson Blvd. at the Big A Auto sign to find this little adobe across from Sarah's. **Sarah's Cafe** (tel. 336-7124), 106 S. Nelson, is the oldest and most famous Mexican restaurant in town. It's open Mon.-Sat. for lunch and dinner; the enchiladas and chile con queso are recommended.

Events
The three-day **Pecos County Fair** is held annually in mid-October at the Fort Stockton Civic Center (Pecos Hwy., near I-10), featuring arts and crafts exhibits, food vendors, games, and a fiddler's competition.

SANDERSON

A center for sheep and cattle ranching, and a major stop along the Southern Pacific Railroad's El Paso-San Antonio run, Sanderson (pop. 1,200) functions as an I-10 supply stop and county seat for Terrell County.

Occasionally leisure motorists heading west toward Marathon and Big Bend underestimate the drive and end up calling it a night in Sanderson. Truckers and Southern Pacific employees also make regular stops here, so there's a good supply of accommodations, food, and gas.

Practicalities
Sunset Siesta Motel (tel. 915-345-2541), on the highway at the eastern edge of town, has economic rooms for $19-27 a night. Next door is the **Western Hills Motel** (tel. 345-2541), with rooms for $26-30, while toward the west end of town on the highway, **Desert Air Motel** (tel. 345-2572) charges $27-38.

DK's Restaurant, opposite the Sunset Siesta Motel, stays open 24 hours and caters to railroaders with basic American fare. The more popular **Kountry Kitchen,** in the center of town on the highway, is open 6 a.m.-9 p.m.

TOYAH-PERMIAN BASINS

"Basin" is a fancy geological term for a low, flat place, and that's about all you get between the Delaware, Apache, and Davis mountains to the west and the edge of the High Plains to the northeast—a wide, low, flat place. The Toyah Basin lies just within the northern perimeter of the Chihuahuan Desert as it slopes down to meet the Pecos River, which cuts the basin in half along a northwest-southeast axis. The alluvial plains of the Pecos River are remarkably fertile considering the overall geographic context, and with canal irrigation the Pecos River Plains have become an important agricultural area.

East of the Pecos River the desert landscape expires in a beautiful series of sand dunes known as the Monahans Sandhills. Beyond the Sandhills begins the Permian Basin, layers of lower Permian strata that contain the largest oil and natural gas deposits in Texas. The towns and counties of the Permian Basin developed along with the petroleum industry beginning in the '20s and have watched their fortunes grow and shrink with the vacillations of the petrol market ever since.

PECOS

One of the city's main claims to fame is that it was the roughest frontier town in the Old West—a short period of time between the 1880s and the early 1900s. Back then, the town's name could be used as a verb; to "pecos" somebody was to shoot him and dump his body in the Pecos River. All that remains of this legacy is the West of the Pecos Museum.

It is also said the first American rodeo was held here, motivated by a saloon argument between cowhands from several local ranches about riding and roping skills. To decide on the best steer ropers and saddle-bronc riders, they held a competition on July 4, 1883, next to the courthouse. The purse was $40 and a thousand spectators showed up to watch the event. The West of the Pecos Rodeo has been held every year since.

A third fame claim is that Pecos cantaloupes are the sweetest in Texas. If you come through Pecos between July and August, cantaloupe season, you'll see 'loupe vendors all along US 285 and elsewhere around town. The surrounding county is also a major producer of watermelons, cotton, onions, alfalfa, and bell peppers.

Seventeen miles north of Pecos along US 285, then 10 miles east on RR 302, lies **Mentone** (pop. 20), the only town in the least populated county in the lower 48, Loving County (pop. 110). Other distinctions: Loving County has had the same sheriff, "Punk" Jones, since 1965, boasts the highest voter turnout (87%) of any county in Texas, and harbors more oil leases (402) than residents. The latter make it the wealthiest county, per capita, in the country, leaving behind such also-rans as Orange County, California, and Westchester County, New York.

West of the Pecos Museum
At Cedar St. (US 285) and 1st St., the museum occupies a former saloon, built in 1896, and 30 rooms of the adjacent Orient Hotel, added in 1904. At one time this hotel was the classiest hostelry between El Paso and Fort Worth, but it stopped

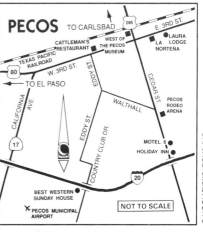

taking guests in the mid '50s and was converted into a museum in the early '60s. The rooms contain a variety of exhibits with a local history focus on railroads, Indians, and ranching, plus one exhibit in the large room downstairs presenting a good geocultural history of the region. The saloon has been restored to its original appearance and features bronze plaques that mark the spots where two men fell dead in a gun duel with one Barney Riggs, a Pecos man, in 1896.

In back of the museum is a collection of local artifacts commemorating the town's Wild West reputation: a hanging tree, a replica of Judge Roy Bean's saloon-courthouse (the original was in Langtry), a jail, and the grave of Clay Allison, "The Gentleman Gunfighter."

The museum is open Mon.-Sat. 9 a.m.-5 p.m., Sunday 2-5 p.m. (2-6 p.m. in the summer); admission is adults $3, senior citizens $2, children 6-12 50 cents, under six free.

Accommodations
Pecos is blessed with a **Motel 6** (tel. 915-445-9034) where single rooms are only $25, plus $4 for each additional person. It's at 3002 S. Cedar (US 285), just north of I-20. **Laura Lodge** (tel. 445-4924) at 1000 E. US 80 (3rd St.) on the honky-tonk strip, costs just $20 s, $25 for up to four people. Also cheap is the **Town & Country Motel** (tel. 445-4946) at 2128 US 80 W, where spartan rooms cost $18 s, $26 d.

The **Best Western Sunday House** (tel. 447-2215 or 800-528-1234) at 900 W. Palmer, east of the State 17 and I-20 junction, is the nicest place in town and costs $36-42 a night. Also off I-20, at US 285, is a **Holiday Inn** (tel. 445-5404 or 800-HOLIDAY), where rooms go for around $40.

Trapark (tel. 447-2137) at 3100 Moore offers RV slots for $12.60 per night.

Food
The Pecos population is 80% Hispanic, so there are plenty of Tex-Mex restaurants in town, especially along 3rd St. (US 80). **La Norteña Tortilla Factory,** on 3rd St. across from La Norteña Ballroom, has inexpensive tamales to go, daytime only. A similarly named Tex-Mex spot, **La Norteña Restaurant** (tel. 915-445-2990) at 802 S. Eddy, has a larger menu and is open Mon.-Sat. 10:30 a.m.-9 p.m.

One of the town's most popular eateries, **Cattleman's Restaurant** (tel. 445-3433), offers reasonably priced steaks, sandwiches, and Mexican food; it's next to the Sonic on W. 3rd and is open daily 6 a.m.-9 p.m.

For a quick breakfast or coffee-and-donut fix, stop by **Ma Wilson's Texas-Sized Donuts** on Cedar St. (US 285), about midway between 1st St. and I-20. A classic car hop on W. 3rd, **Sonic,** does burgers and other fast food. There's also a **Pizza Hut** on Cedar St. near the 3rd St. intersection.

If curiosity gets the best of you and you find yourself in Mentone, Loving County (named for renowned cattle drover Oliver Loving), drop by the venerable **A&G Cafe.**

ROBERT CLAY ALLISON
1840 — 1887

HE NEVER KILLED A MAN
THAT DID NOT NEED KILLING

Pecos headstone

Entertainment and Events

The **West of the Pecos Rodeo** is held annually for four days around the 4th of July at the Pecos Rodeo Arena. The main rodeo events start nightly at 8 p.m. and tickets are $4-7. Other events during the day include rodeo parades, an Old West Pageant (with the coronation of the latest Golden Girl), a Western art show, and the Sheriff's Posse Bar-B-Q. For information on current scheduling, call the Pecos Chamber of Commerce at (915) 445-2406.

On the second weekend of August, all of Pecos turns out for the **Cantaloupe Festival,** held at the Reeves County Civic Center. Activities include music and food competitions. **Diez y Seis** celebrates Mexican Independence Day on the closest weekend to the 16th of September with a parade and festival.

Along 3rd St. (US 80) are several honkytonks and Mexican dance halls, including the **Oasis Lounge** and **La Norteña Ballroom.**

Shopping

Pecos Emporium (tel. 915-445-5822) at 123 S. Eddy carries souvenirs, boots, and Western wear. **Ray's Boot & Shoe Repair** (tel. 447-5015) at 1219 S. Eddy makes custom boots.

MONAHANS SANDHILLS STATE PARK

About halfway between Pecos and Odessa off I-20, this 3,840-acre park protects a huge complex of sand dunes, some of which reach 70 feet high. The entire dune field stretches for some 200 miles northwest into New Mexico. Many of the dunes are still active—that is, drifting—while some are stabilized by rooted vegetation such as the **shin oak** (*Quercus havardii*), also known as the dwarf shinnery oak or Havard oak, which at full maturity reaches only four feet. The shin oak produces an abundance of acorns, which various nomadic Indian groups used as an important food source. Shin oaks also signal where to find water among the dunes, and the Apaches and Comanches often battled here over water and acorns. They weren't the first to know of the dunes; the Spanish explorer Cabeza de Vaca encountered Jumano Indians here in 1535.

Other vegetation growing among the dunes includes tasajilla or "Christmas cactus," mesquite, yucca, prickly pear, sand sagebrush, and several varieties of "desert morning glory," including the white-flowered **bindweed.** Hiking is permitted throughout the park; the dunes form pristine hills and valleys of sand that can be explored for hours The park office rents out sandsurfing discs for $1 for use in sliding down the dune slopes. The dunes are highest in the summer.

Facilities

The park visitor center contains interpretive exhibits that explain the geological, historical, and botanical features of the sandhills. Next to the center is a quarter-mile nature trail where examples of native vegetation are on display. During the summer, a concession stand is open in a former railroad section house near the campground.

The park has 24 tent/camper sites, 19 of which offer w/e for $9 a night; the remaining five have water nearby and are $6 a night. A dump station is available, as are flush toilets, showers, grills, and tables. The park entry fee is the standard $3 per vehicle, $1 for cyclists and pedestrians. For further information, contact the Superintendent (tel. 915-943-2092), Monahans Sandhills State Park, P.O. Box 1738, Monahans, TX 79756.

ODESSA

Originally Odessa was merely a way station on the Texas & Pacific Railroad, named by Russian rail workers for its resemblance to the Ukrainian town of the same name (it's as flat as the Steppes). After the large Permian Basin oil and gas discoveries in the late '20s, it became an oil town practically overnight. Neither Odessa nor its next-door neighbor Midland are places you'd want to drive out of your way to see—Odessa once made Rand McNally's list of the 10 worst places to live in the U.S.—but if you happen to stop here on a cross-Texas trip via I-20, you'll find a city of around 100,000 and the nation's largest inland petrochemical complex.

In an all-out effort to make the town more attractive to visitors and potential residents, civic leaders have promoted the establishment of several cultural and performing arts centers, so visiting Odessa doesn't have to be as bleak as the barren landscape might suggest. The second-largest meteor crater in the U.S., the sixth largest in the world, is just southwest of the city.

Odessa Meteor Crater

A large nickel-iron meteorite shower made a series of craters over a two-square-mile area here 20,000 years ago. One particularly large meteor, estimated to weigh 1,000 tons, penetrated deep into the surrounding bedrock and exploded, leaving a crater 550 feet in diameter. Smaller craters in the area have diameters of 15-70 feet. Over the eons, the largest crater has filled to within six feet of its top with accumulated sediments, so what remains is not dramatically deep. Exploratory trenches and shafts—which are still in place—were dug into the main crater in the late '30s and early '40s, and have brought to the surface portions of "rock flour," an extremely fine, powdered rock formed by shock waves through the bedrock below the earth's surface. A nature trail leads across the center of the crater and along one side of the crater rim.

To get to the Odessa Meteor Crater, drive west from Odessa on US 80/I-20 until you see signs for the crater about 5.5 miles from town. An access road goes south for two miles to the crater. Admission is free.

The Globe Theatre

This is a replica of England's Globe Theatre, and like the original it's designed specifically for performances of William Shakespeare's dramas. A Shakespeare Festival is held here annually February-March, and during the rest of the year there are other theatrical performances. The Globe is on the Odessa College campus on Shakespeare Rd., just west of US 385. Free tours of the theater are offered Mon.-Fri. 9 a.m.-noon and 1-5 p.m. For performance schedules and other information, call (915) 332-1586.

Presidential Museum

A museum dedicated to the office of the U.S. presidency, with campaign memorabilia, presidential medals, inaugural gowns, and other relics. Fascinating to some, the height of boredom for others. Located at 622 N. Lee at 7th Street. Open Tues.-Sat. 10 a.m.-5 p.m.; free admission.

Art Institute for the Permian Basin

The three galleries contain all the art that oil money can buy, with an emphasis on contemporary artists. The institute also offers a varied series of films and concerts. At 4909 E. University between Loop 338 and Parkway Blvd., not far from the Odessa Hilton. Open Tues.-Sat. 10 a.m.-5 p.m., Sunday 2-5 p.m.; free admission. Call (915) 368-7222 for further information.

Accommodations

The **Villa West Inn** (tel. 915-335-5055) on I-20 at exit 116 has rooms for $19-28. **Motel 6** has two locations, one at exit 116 (tel. 333-4025) and one at 2925 E. 2nd St. (tel. 332-2600); room rates at both are $23 s, $4 for each additional adult.

Nearby **Classic Suites Hotel** (tel. 333-9678), 3031 E. 2nd, has rooms with kitchenettes for a reasonable $30-40. **La Quinta Motor Inn** (tel. 333-2820), at 5001 E. 2nd (exit 116 off I-20) has well-kept rooms for $48 s, $55 d. Top digs in Odessa is the **Odessa Hilton** (tel. 368-5885) at 5200 E. University. Rooms at the Hilton cost $75-89.

Food

The **Barn Door** (tel. 915-337-4142) at 2140 Grant St. (Andrews Hwy.) is a moderately priced local favorite for steaks, seafood, and Tex-Mex.

Open Mon.-Sat. for lunch and dinner. Next door under the same management is the **Pecos Depot Lounge,** an 1892 train depot moved here from Pecos. Along Andrews Hwy. are tons of other restaurants, mostly fast-food places, including all the usual chain restaurants.

Odessa's oldest restaurant is **Manuel's** (tel. 333-2751) at 1404 E. 2nd, which started out as a tortilla factory but now serves a full range of Mexican, steak, chicken, and seafood dishes. The tortillas now come from down the street. Open Tues.-Sun. for lunch and dinner. For inexpensive, buffet-style Tex-Mex, **Rosa's Café and Tortilla Factory** (tel. 332-6648) at 1810 E. 8th St. can't be beat. Tortillas are made fresh here throughout the day, and their salsa bar has an extensive selection. Open daily for lunch and dinner. There's a second location at 3760 Andrews Hwy. (tel. 366-8144).

Unique **Dos Amigos** (tel. 368-7556) at 47th St. and Golder Ave. offers a mostly Tex-Mex menu Tues.-Sat. 11 a.m. till late, with a cook-your-own-steak special on Tuesday evening and by-the-pound boiled shrimp and fried catfish Thursday night. Seating arrangements are rather unusual; see "Entertainment" below for a description of the restaurant's main attraction.

Dumplin's Home Cookin' at US 385 (Andrews Hwy.) and W. 46th specializes in inexpensive, downhome breakfasts and homemade pies. Open Mon.-Sat. 6 a.m.-2:30 p.m.

Entertainment

An open courtyard at **Dos Amigos Restaurant** contains a professional bullriding arena where jackpot events are staged every other Sunday March-Oct., 2-8 p.m. When not filled with snorting, bucking bulls, the arena may be used as a volleyball court or live concert stage—Jerry Jeff Walker and Joe Ely have both performed here.

Dena's (tel. 915-335-8839) at 8th and Grandview Ave. is an urban country dance hall open Mon.-Sat. till 2 a.m. There's a happy hour buffet Mon.-Fri. 4-8 p.m., when free food goes with the drinks. **Texas Rock Saloon** (tel. 981-6033) at 8206 W. 18th hosts live rock and blues bands Wed.-Saturday.

Blues fan should keep an eye peeled for performances by guitar legend Long John Hunter, who paid his dues in the El Paso-Juárez area in the '50s and '60s and is now based in Odessa.

MIDLAND

Midland (pop. 97,000) got its name because it was midway between Fort Worth and El Paso on the Texas & Pacific Railroad line in the 1880s. It was just a small farming community until the Permian Basin oil discoveries of the '20s. Even though Midland County itself wasn't a site for major oil strikes, the town somehow maneuvered itself into becoming the West Texas capital for petrobusiness. This means that, like its neighbor Odessa, the local economy swings up and down with international oil prices.

Permian Basin Petroleum Museum

Everything you ever wanted to know about the history of oil exploration and oil technology is covered in this museum, probably the largest in the world devoted exclusively to the petroleum industry. It's all very well executed, with many audiovisual and hands-on exhibits. A "Time Trip" tunnel-like diorama takes visitors through a facsimile of the reef bottom of the 230-million-year-old Permian Ocean. Antique drilling machinery is displayed outside in the "Oil Patch." Open Mon.-Sat. 9 a.m.-5 p.m., Sunday 2-5 p.m. Admission is $4 adults, $2 for children 6-11, under six free. Wheelchairs and baby strollers available. Off I-20 at State 349.

Museum of the Southwest

This museum houses permanent and rotating collections of Southwestern art, as well as archaeological artifacts, in a 1934 mansion designed by Anton Korn. One of the permanent exhibits is the Hogan Collection, which includes works by the founding members of the Taos Society of Artists. The mansion itself covers an entire city block, with an interior of carved wooden friezes and handpainted tilework. At 1705 W. Missouri at J St., a block south of US 80. Open Tues.-Sat. 10 a.m.-5 p.m., Sunday 2-5 p.m.; free admission.

Confederate Air Force and American Airpower Flying Museum

The Confederate Air Force (tel. 915-563-1000) is a nonprofit organization, headquartered at the airport, whose members collect and restore military aircraft used during WW II. The CAF

nose art, Confederate Air Force Museum

now has over 140 craft representing 61 different models from the U.S. Army Air Force, Royal Air Force, German Luftwaffe, and Imperial Japanese Navy. Many are the only flyable planes of their kind in existence; examples include the A-20 Havoc, A6M2 Zero, SB2C Helldiver, F-82 Twin Mustang, and B-29 Superfortress. Members of the CAF are called "colonels," and there are CAF "wings" and "squadrons" in 25 countries. Neither a pilot's license nor veteran status is required for membership. There's even an "officers' club" on site. Ask a member why it's called the "Confederate" Air Force and you'll get a funny look. Every October there's a four-day air show featuring the Ghost Squadron.

Visitors may view about a third of the planes on the CAF ramp or in the hangar at any given time—other aircraft may be on tour to air shows or other CAF wings/squadrons, or busy in Hollywood film production. On the interior walls of the hangar is a collection of classic nose art—pinup-style paintings of scantily clad sirens with labels like Night Mission, Flamin' Mamie, and Miss Yourlovin'. An indoor museum contains detailed exhibits which display the uniforms of the Allied and Axis powers, WW II memorabilia, propaganda posters, and various bits of war machinery. A rather moldy but informative 30-minute movie at the officers' club chronicles the history of the Ghost Squadron. At the entrance to the museum is a souvenir shop that sells historic military patches and flight jackets, including exact reproductions of the classic Cooper B-2 USAAF leather jacket.

The CAF Flying Museum is open Mon.-Sat. 9 a.m.-5 p.m., Sunday and holidays noon-5 p.m. Admission is $5 adults, $4 teens and seniors, $2 children 6-12.

Accommodations and Food

Most hotels and motels in Midland are clustered around the intersection of Midkiff and Wall St. off I-20 (exit 134). **Motel 6** (tel. 915-697-3197) at 1000 S. Midkiff between I-20 and W. Wall St. costs $24-27 for the usual spartan rooms. Nearby **Lexington Hotel Suites** (tel. 697-3155) at 1003 S. Midkiff has rooms with kitchenettes for $38-45. **La Quinta Motor Inn** (tel. 697-9900) at 4130 W. Wall St. has comfortable rooms for $48-61. Another choice for those on a budget, **Royal Inn** (tel. 694-8821), has rooms for $27-31 at 3601 W. Wall Street in the same vicinity.

A step up is the **Ramada Hotel** (tel. 699-4144), 3100 W. Wall St., where rooms run $42-56. At the top is the **Midland Hilton** (tel. 683-6131), downtown at Wall and Lorraine, with rooms for $78-108.

For campers, there's the **Midessa KOA** (tel. 563-2368) off I-20 at exit 126, between Odessa and Midland. Tentsites with w/e cost a steep $18, full hookups are $20, and Kamping Kabins are $27 d; $2 for additional people.

Midland restaurants are a little more upscale than those in Odessa. **Luigi's** (tel. 683-6363) at 111 N. Big Spring is a small, moderately priced trattoria that's been serving reputable Italian food for over 25 years. Open Mon.-Sat. for lunch and dinner, Sunday for dinner only. The **Wall Street Bar & Grill** (tel. 684-8686) downtown at 115 E. Wall St. has a grand 1867 bar and embossed tin ceiling, and specializes in seafood and steaks. Open Mon.-Sat. for lunch and dinner, Sunday for brunch only.

Doña Anita's (tel. 683-6727) at 305 W. Florida on the south side of town serves Midland's best norteña-style Mexican food. House specialities are *tacos al carbón* (grilled skirt steak wrapped in corn or flour tortillas) and chiles rellenos.

Entertainment
The **Granada Club** (tel. 915-697-4138) at 3312 W. Wall St. is a venerable country dance hall that's open every night except Sunday. No cover charge.

BIG SPRING

Big Spring sits on the southern edge of the Caprock Escarpment as it gives way to the Edwards Plateau below. This geological intersection brought significant springs to the surface in several areas, which is how the town got its name. The Comanches and Shawnees used to fight over the water, travelers stopped here to fill their water containers, and finally in 1881 the railroad came through. Still, Big Spring wasn't much of a town until oil was discovered nearby. Cotton is also big in these parts; you'll see large cotton fields along the highway. During the fall harvest, huge container-sized bales of harvested cotton lie in the fields awaiting pickup.

The downtown area features a few historic buildings, and the hilly environment lends the sort of charm to the town that is absent from most stopovers along I-20. The **Heritage Museum of Big Spring** (tel. 915-267-7501) at S. Scurry and W. 5th St. contains collections of pioneer and Indian artifacts from the area. Open Tues.-Fri. 9 a.m.-5 p.m., Saturday 10 a.m.-5 p.m.; $2 admission. The **Potton House** at 2nd and Gregg streets is a 1901 sandstone Victorian listed with the National Register of Historic Places. Tours are free with paid admission to the Heritage Museum.

Record collectors should not miss **The Record Shop** (tel. 267-7501) at 211 Main St., which has been in continuous operation since

1934 and offers some 8,000 vintage 33s, 45s, and 78s as well as new titles. Some of the 78s go back to the early 1900s.

A mile north of town off State 350 stands **The Stampede** (tel. 267-2060), a warehouse-like dance hall built by Western swing star Hoyle Nix for his West Texas Cowboys in 1954. Hoyle, best known for his hit "Big Balls in Cowtown," died in 1985, but his son Jody opens the place for dancing on Saturday night when his own band isn't playing somewhere else.

Accommodations and Food
There's a **Motel 6** (tel. 915-267-1695) just off I-20 at US 87, with typical rooms for $25. Nearby is the **Best Western Mid-Continent Inn** (tel. 267-1601 or 800-528-1234) with room rates of $39-45. The **Ponderosa Motor Inn** (tel. 267-5237) at 27000 S. Gregg (US 87 S) has rooms for $23-30.

Off I-20 at exit 179, the town's westernmost exit, are two other motels: **Days Inn** (tel. 263-7621), with uninspiring rooms for $40-50, and the smaller but nicer **Great Western Motel** (tel. 267-4553), with rooms for $26-33.

Tent/camper/RV sites are $10-14 a night at the **Whip In Campground** (tel. 393-5242), seven miles east of town at the junction of I-20 and Moss Lake Road.

La Posada at 206 W. 4th serves fresh tortillas and Tex-Mex Tues.-Sun. for lunch and dinner. For tamales and menudo, **Josie's** (tel. 267-9135) at 1009 E. FM 350 is your best choice; it's open Tues.-Sat. 6 a.m.-2 p.m. and 5 p.m.-10 p.m., Sun.-Mon. 7 a.m.- 2 p.m. **Big John's Feed Lot** (tel. 263-3178) at 802 W. 3rd is a rustic barbecue place with the menus written on paper sacks. Open Mon.-Sat. for lunch only. For steaks, **K-C Steakhouse** (tel. 263-1651), on a hillside off I-20 (exit 176), is the top choice. It's open Mon.-Sat. for dinner only.

Events
Big Spring is the site for the annual **Rattlesnake Roundup** held in the Howard County Fairgrounds every March. A ton and a half of rattlesnakes are rounded up for the occasion; then they're milked, skinned, eaten, and made into belts and hatbands. Whether it's herpetophobia or herpetophilia, it's definitely a one-of-a-kind event.

AMARILLO

Amarillo is the unofficial Panhandle capital by simple virtue of being the largest city (pop. 162,000) and because it's an important trans-shipment point for goods carried by truck across the southern half of the nation. It started out as a buffalo-hide tent camp for railroad workers in 1887, and within a few years was the nation's largest shipping point for northward-bound cattle. Wildcatters struck the vast Panhandle Oil and Gas Field in 1916; this remained the world's largest single petroleum deposit until the Arabian oil fields were discovered in 1930. In 1929, helium was extracted from gas in Amarillo for the first time, and the area is now the source for 90% of the world's helium, used in aerospace technology, welding, cryogenics, and as a prime leak detector.

CLIMATE

Summers in Amarillo are warm during the day and cool at night. Late fall, winter, and early spring are blustery. Because of the mostly flat terrain, winds can sweep across the plains with considerable momentum, so wind chill often alters the perceived temperature. Rainfall averages 20 inches a year; the wettest months are May, June, and August, with around three inches a month during each. During the winter, snow is not uncommon.

SIGHTS

Amarillo Livestock Auction

Every Tuesday beginning at 9 a.m., what may be the world's largest weekly cattle auction is held at Amarillo's Western Stockyards, S. Manhattan at 3rd Street. Annually, the stockyards sell off around a half-million head of cattle. Visitors are welcome to attend, with no obligation to bid on livestock and no admission charge. On other days of the week, there are occasional smaller, special auctions. Call (806) 373-7464 for more information or look for the *Amarillo Livestock Reporter,* a weekly featuring livestock industry news.

Amarillo Museum of Art

This three-building complex, designed by architect Edward Stone, serves as the cultural and fine arts center for West Texas. The permanent collection focuses on 20th-century art, including works by Georgia O'Keeffe, Fritz Scholder, Franz Kline, Jack Boynton, and Elaine de Koonig. Rotating exhibits bring in everything from cowboy art to Rembrandt. In addition to the six galleries, there is also a theater, sculpture court, outdoor amphitheater, and several rooms for art classes, seminars, and other periodic cultural events. Located on the main campus of Amarillo College, 2200 S. Van Buren. Galleries are open Tues.-Fri. 10 a.m.-5 p.m., Sat.-Sun. 1-5 p.m., plus Wednesday evening 7-9:30 p.m. Free admission, donations accepted. Call (806) 371-5050 for information.

American Quarter Horse Heritage Center and Museum

"Dedicated to America's favorite mount," this facility adjacent to the American Quarter Horse Association headquarters contains hands-on displays, laser-movie presentations, a library and research archives, and works of art focusing on quarterhorses. Outside, a demonstration arena allows visitors to observe occasional special riding programs. Attached to the museum is **Quarter Horse Outfitters,** a store selling leather tack, Southwestern jewelry, books, art prints, and toys. At 2601 I-40 E (tel. 806-376-5181), the museum is open May 1-Aug. 31 daily 9 a.m.-6 p.m.,

AMARILLO TEMPERATURES		
MONTH	**MAX. (° F)**	**MIN. (° F)**
January	50	24
March	62	33
May	80	53
July	94	67
September	85	58
November	60	32

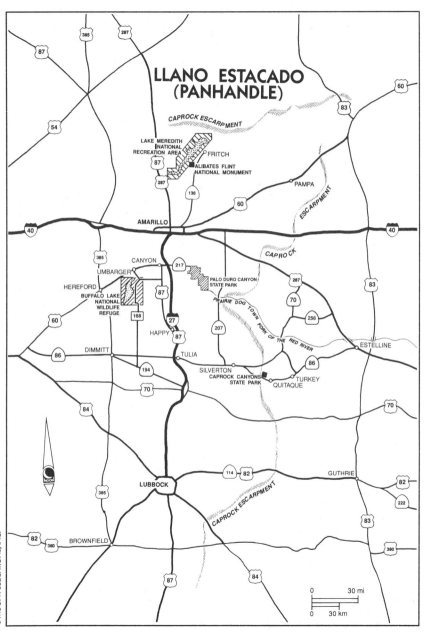

LLANO ESTACADO (PANHANDLE)

CAPROCK ESCARPMENT

Lake Meredith National Recreation Area

FRITCH

ALIBATES FLINT NATIONAL MONUMENT

PAMPA

ESCARPMENT

CAPROCK

AMARILLO

CANYON

UMBARGER

HEREFORD

Buffalo Lake National Wildlife Refuge

PALO DURO CANYON STATE PARK

PRAIRIE DOG TOWN FORK OF THE RED RIVER

HAPPY

DIMMITT

TULIA

SILVERTON

CAPROCK CANYONS STATE PARK

QUITAQUE

TURKEY

ESTELLINE

LUBBOCK

GUTHRIE

CAPROCK ESCARPMENT

BROWNFIELD

| 0 | 30 mi |
| 0 | 30 km |

© MOON PUBLICATIONS, INC.

*Cadillac Ranch,
Amarillo*

Sept. 1-April 30 Mon.-Sat. 10 a.m.-5 p.m., Sunday noon-5 p.m.; admission is $4 adults, $3.50 seniors, $2.50 children 6-18. AQHA members receive a $1 discount.

Cadillac Ranch

Ten 1949-63 model Cadillacs buried nose-down in a field at the same angle used for the Cheops pyramids—what could it mean? Could be a tribute to the time when Route 66 reigned supreme as the country's main east-west artery and fins were hot; could be a poke at the Texas oilman's proclivity for Cadillacs; or it could be a simple testament to the eccentricity of helium tycoon Stanley Marsh III (his ranch bears the very un-Texan name of "Toad Hall"), who put them here in 1974 in collaboration with a San Francisco design collective known as the Ant Farm. It's worth the short drive west of Amarillo just to check out the graffiti on these rusting hulks. To reach the monoliths, drive west on I-40 about five miles; take the Hope Rd. exit, then turn onto the frontage road that heads east back toward Amarillo (like most frontage roads in Texas, it's one-way); Cadillac Ranch will be on your right before the Soncy Rd. onramp. A worn path in the field leads straight to the Caddies.

FOOD

Since Amarillo is a livestock center, the local emphasis is on steak. But there are also barbecue, Tex-Mex, downhome, Asian, continental, and nouvelle restaurants in town. And all along

I-40 through town is a string of the usual fast-food and chain restaurants. For one-of-a-kind eating, try the following.

Artsy

In its own category, the **OHMS (On Her Majesty's Service) Gallery Café** is both a power-lunch scene and a gathering place for Amarillo's artists and musicians. Food is served buffet-style and includes pasta, stews, salads, light sautés, and other wholesome dishes. Paintings by local artists decorate the walls, while folksingers, cowboy poets, and bongo players do their thing—when it's open (Mon.-Fri. 11:30 a.m.-1:30 p.m., Sat.-Sun. 6:30-9 p.m.). Prices are moderate. At 619 S. Tyler in the Atrium (tel. 806-373-3233).

Asian

$ **Blackstone Café:** An unpretentious diner featuring American breakfasts and unique Thai and Chinese dishes for lunch (Mon.-Fri.) and dinner (Thurs.-Sat.). At 202 W. 10th St. downtown (tel. 806-372-7700).

$ **Hong Kong Restaurant:** Out on Amarillo's honkytonk strip is this classic American-Cantonese joint with great egg rolls and egg fu yung. At 3011 E. Amarillo Blvd. (tel. 383-4304); open daily for lunch and dinner.

Barbecue

$ to $$ **Sutphen's:** The traditional Amarillo favorite, catering to the *Texas* outdoor drama at Palo Duro in the summer. At 7101 I-40 W (tel. 806-355-9025); open daily 11 a.m.-8 p.m. Expect

to wait for a table during peak dining hours.
$ to $$ **Cattle Call:** Preferred by younger Amarilloans, if for no other reason than to avoid the long lines at Sutphen's. At Westgate Mall, off I-40 W (tel. 353-1227); open Mon.-Sat. 11 a.m.-9 p.m., Sunday 11 a.m.-6 p.m.

$ **Van Dyke's Bar-B-Q:** More than a barbecue place, though it does serve the usual brisket and links. Country-style breakfasts are huge, and come with Van Dyke's famous sourdough biscuits. Lunch features ham and beef stew as well as barbecue. Customers order at the counter and bus their own tables. At 210 W. 6th (tel. 373-1441); open for breakfast and lunch daily except Sunday.

Burgers and Sandwiches

$$ **Barnaby's Beanery:** Specializes in burgers, sandwiches, and chili. According to the menu, the restaurant was "created due to a lack of places in Amarillo with good food." No arguments

here. At 3809 W. 6th, near the San Jacinto district (tel. 806-359-1141); open Monday 11 a.m.-3 p.m., Tues.-Sat. 11 a.m.-9 p.m.

$ **Doodles:** The best burger joint in town because you can make them yourself. Great fries and dessert cobbler. At 3701 Olsen Blvd. (tel. 355-0064).

$$ **York Street Pub:** Burgers, sandwiches, beer, and large-screen TV for sports fans. At 2626 Paramount; open Thurs.-Sat. 11 a.m.-11 p.m., Sun.-Wed. 10 a.m.-11 p.m.

Mexican

$ **The Plaza:** A large, airy place with a fountain in the middle of the dining room. Plates are huge and come with tortillas or sopapillas, El Paso-style. Extensive menu. Located in a shopping center at 3415 Bell St. (tel. 806-358-4897); open Mon.-Sun. for lunch and dinner.

$ to $$ **Restaurant Los Insurgentes:** The real thing, including interior cooking like *mole*

AMARILLO ACCOMMODATIONS

Add 13% hotel tax to all rates. Area code: 806.

HOTELS AND MOTELS

Best Western Amarillo Inn; 1610 Coulter; tel. 358-7861 or (800) 528-1234; $62-75; indoor heated pool, coin laundry

Big Texan Motel; 7701 I-40 E (exit 75); tel. 372-5000; $35-43; heated pool, Old-West decor, coin laundry

Comfort Inn-Airport; I-40 (Ross-Osage exit); tel. 376-9993; $45-60; heated pool

Comfort Inn-West; 2100 S. Coulter; tel. 358-6141; $45-60; heated pool, coin laundry, refrigerators

Coronado Motel; 701 S. Pierce (downtown); tel. 372-8501; $19 s plus $5 for each additional person; pool

Econo Lodge; 2801 I-40 W; tel. 355-9171; $34-44; pool

Fifth Season Inn-East; 2500 I-40 E; tel. 379-6555 or (800) 245-5525; $60-80; spa, pool

Fifth Season Inn-West; 6801 I-40 E (Coulter St. exit); tel. 358-7881 or (800) 245-5525; $60-150; heated pool, airport shuttle

Harvey Hotel; 3100 I-40 W at Georgia; tel. 358-6161; $80-100; heated pool, health club, airport shuttle

Holiday Inn-Holidome I-40; I-40 E at Ross; tel. 372-8741; $70-80; heated pool, airport shuttle

La Quinta Inn; 1708 I-40 E (Ross-Osage exit); tel. 373-7486; $42-55; heated pool

Motel 6 (Central); 2032 Paramount (I-40 exit 68-A); tel. 355-6554; $26; small pool

Motel 6 (East); 3930 I-40 (exit 72-B); tel. 374-6444; $26; small pool

TraveLodge-East; 3205 I-40 E; tel. 372-8171; $40-55; pool, coin laundry

Westar Hotel; 6800 I-40 (Bell St. exit); tel. 358-7943; $60-90; heated pool, kitchenettes

BED AND BREAKFASTS

Galbraith House; 1710 S. Polk; tel. 374-0237; $60-75; 1912 house, 5 rooms, private bath, full breakfast

Parkview House; 1311 S. Jefferson; tel. 373-9464; $50-75; 1909 house, 3 rooms, shared bath, continental breakfast

CAMPGROUNDS

Amarillo KOA; off US 60, 3 miles east of town; tel. 335-1792; $16 tents, $21 RVs, $26 cabins

Overnight Trailer Inn; off I-40 east; tel. 373-1431; $18 RVs

poblano as well as classic Tex-Mex dishes like fajitas, *cabrito,* and menudo. At 3521 W. 15th (tel. 353-5361); open daily except Sunday for lunch and dinner.

Steak

$ to $$$ The Big Texan: Could also be called "The Big Tourist Trap," except that even the locals like to come here once in a while. You can't miss the billboards on all highways leading to Amarillo that advertise a free 72-oz. steak (4.5 pounds) if you can eat the entire thing; what they don't mention is that you have to eat all the side dishes as well—shrimp cocktail, baked potato, salad, and roll—and eat it all within one hour. If you don't make it, the price of the meal is $30. Over 200,000 have tried and about 20% succeeded. Big Texan also offers smaller steaks, barbecue, chicken, seafood, and such West Texas specialties as jackrabbit, rattlesnake, buffalo burgers, and "calf fries" (bovine testicles).

The restaurant's latest deal, the "Big Opry Breakfast," is a reservation-only affair that includes an all-you-can-eat breakfast buffet accompanied by live country music. Off I-40 E (tel.

806-372-7000 or 800-657-7177 outside Amarillo); open daily 10:30 a.m.-10:30 p.m.

ENTERTAINMENT

Clubs

The Caravan (tel. 806-359-5436), one of several huge country dance clubs by the same name in Texas and New Mexico, features live music Tues.-Sunday. Men must check cowboy hats at the door. At 3601 Olsen Blvd.; open every night. **Sneakers** (tel. 355-0811), at 2600 Paramount, is the type of country rock club found only in the Panhandle—for urban cowboys who like their country music with some extra sizzle. More rock bands are playing here these days. The **Western Horseman Club** (tel. 379-6555), at the Fifth Season Inn off I-40 (Nelson St. exit), caters to an older country disco crowd. For more of a honky-tonk atmosphere, try the **Rodeo** at 2700 S. Georgia.

The *real* honky-tonk strip is E. Amarillo Blvd., along former Route 66, where cross-country truckers hang out; if you've never been honky-tonkin' before, start easy with **The Other Place**

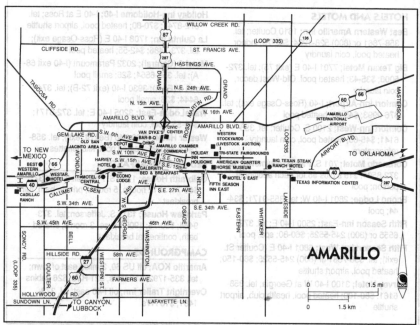

AMARILLO

0   1.5 mi

0   1.5 km

© MOON PUBLICATIONS, INC.

LS Ranch range boss addresses the boys around the chuckwagon, 1908

(tel. 383-9000) at 5625 E. Amarillo Blvd., where live country bands play on weekends only.

Amarillo has its share of rock music clubs, too, but they're notoriously temporary. **S.R.O. Club** (tel. 358-8163) at 34371 I-40 W tends toward recorded techno and hip-hop, while **Bangers** (tel. 356-0387) at 607 S. Independence St. offers live, straight-ahead rock.

Ponderosa Ballroom (tel. 698-2101), at 3881 Vine, is a no-frills, Texas-style dance hall that hosts live country music, especially Western swing, on weekends and recorded country other nights of the week.

Amusement Parks

Kids will like **Wonderland Park** (tel. 806-383-4712), with the Texas Tornado, a double-loop roller coaster, and the Rattlesnake River Raft Ride. It's in Thompson Park, north of town off US 87/287, and is open from 1 p.m. weekends mid-March through September; May through Labor Day it's also open weekdays from 7 p.m. Admission is $1 per person plus separate fees per ride or you can get an all-rides ticket for $8.95 during the week, $12.95 weekends.

EVENTS

June-August

The *Texas Outdoor Musical Drama* is held in Palo Duro Canyon. See the "Palo Duro Canyon State Park" listing under "Vicinity of Amarillo" for details.

September

The **Tri-State Fair** attracts participants from New Mexico, Texas, and Oklahoma for a week-long series of activities including the usual farming and ranching exhibits, arts and crafts vendors, rodeo and livestock competitions, and a carnival. Held at the fairgrounds, Bell and 10th St.; usually begins the third Monday in September.

November

The **National Old-Timers Rodeo** is the U.S. finals competition for rodeo cowboys over the age of 40. Usually held four days in early November at the Civic Center, Buchanan and 3rd Street.

Tours

Old West Tours, in conjunction with the Amarillo Convention and Visitors Bureau, offers a range of tours of Amarillo and the vicinity for individuals as well as groups. A guided city tour costs $20 an hour.

The most popular tour is **Cowboy Morning** at Tom Christian's Figure 3 Ranch on the rim of Palo Duro Canyon. Visitors ride in a mule-drawn wagon to a canyon overlook and then eat a huge "cowboy breakfast" that includes cowboy coffee, scrambled eggs, country sausage, skillet gravy, orange juice, and sour-dough biscuits served from the chuck wagon. Breakfast is followed by roping and branding demonstrations. To join the Cowboy Morning tour, you must drive 27 miles to the ranch in time for the 8:30 a.m. chuckwagon departure—or cadge a ride from the Amarillo CVB. This activity costs $19 for adults, $14.50 for children 4-12. The Figure 3 also operates a similar **Cowboy Evening** program (times vary according to season) for those who can't make the morning program. Evening meals include ribeye steak, salad, red beans, sourdough biscuits, campfire cobbler, and cowboy coffee, and cost $22.50 for adults, $14.50 children 4-12. Reservations must be made in advance by contacting Old West Tours, P.O. Box 9480, Amarillo, TX 79105 (tel. 800-692-1338 in Texas, 800-654-1902 outside Texas) or by contacting the Figure 3 Ranch directly at (806) 944-5562 or (800) 658-2613 (call after 5 p.m. or on weekends only). To get there, take I-40 east to the Pullman Rd. exit, then head south on FM 1258 to the Figure 3 Ranch.

SHOPPING

Old San Jacinto

There's a string of antique and craft shops along W. 6th St. between Western and Georgia in what used to be a streetcar suburb. Some specialize in furniture and accessories, others sell records, coins, used books, and just about any other aged item. **Precision Gunsmithing** still does custom gunsmithing and repairs. The unique **Tecovas Creek Traders** deals in historical frontier clothing and accessories.

Boot and Saddle Shops

Hilltop Boot and Saddle (tel. 806-383-0501), at 4624 River Rd. north of Thompson Park off US 87/287, offers custom-made boots (prices start at around $300), belts, wallets, and other leather work. Hilltop's saddles are ready-mades. **Bob Marrs Stockman's Saddle Shop** (tel. 372-8439), at 2710 E. 3rd at Nelson, near the stockyards, makes saddles for working cowboys throughout the country, as well as leather tack and chaps. Marrs's work is in high demand—you

may have to wait as long as a year for a custom-made saddle. **Oliver Bros. Saddle Shop** (tel. 372-7562), at 3016 Plains, between Western and Georgia, also does custom saddle and leather work, and their customers include pro rodeo cowboys and other professional equestrians in addition to working cowboys. Oliver Bros. makes English as well as Western gear and has one of the largest selections of tack in the state.

Western Wear

Several shops and department stores in Amarillo offer Western wear, but the best prices and selection are found at **Boots 'n' Jeans** (tel. 806-353-4368) at 2225 S. Georgia downtown. A pair of Wrangler Prorodeo 13 MWZ Cowboy Cut Jeans is a bargain $15 here. Boots start at around $55 for Ropers.

INFORMATION

Tourist Offices

The **Amarillo Convention and Visitors Bureau** (tel. 806-374-1497 or 800-654-1902) is headquartered in the historic Bivins Home at 1000 S. Polk downtown (zip code 79101). The staff is happy to assist individuals or groups and can provide all manner of brochures and maps on the city and area, as well as information on Old West Tours. Open Mon.-Fri. 8 a.m.-5 p.m. The city also maintains an information booth at Amarillo International Airport.

There's a **Texas Information Center** (tel. 335-1179) just off I-40 at the Airport exit where you can get information on Amarillo as well as

---

AMARILLO TELEPHONE INFORMATION

Emergency (police, fire, medical): 911
Telephone Directory Assistance: 411
Area Code: 806
Weather Service: 335-1684
AAA Emergency Road Service: 376-5821
Texas State Highway Patrol: 359-4751
Road Conditions: 358-6300

the rest of the state. Open daily 8 a.m.-5 p.m.

Publications

Accent West Amarillo is a monthly magazine that covers local events and culture; available at newsstands and bookstores. The Amarillo CVB issues a bimonthly *Amarillo Entertainment Guide* that contains a comprehensive, up-to-date calendar of events for each two-month period; available at the CVB at 1000 Polk Street.

Detailed maps of the city are available free from any of the three tourist offices mentioned above.

Telephone and Post

The area code for Amarillo and vicinity is 806. Like most of Texas, Amarillo is in the central time zone. The main post office is at 2300 Ross St., Amarillo, TX 79120. Western Union has an office at 2403 W. 3rd. Supplementary mail services, including packing and shipping, are available at **The Mail Man,** 5701 S.W. 45th, and at **Pack-N-Mail,** 2514 Paramount.

GETTING THERE AND AROUND

Amarillo International Airport

Three airlines use the Amarillo airport: American (tel. 800-433-7300), Continental (tel. 800-525-0280), and Southwest (tel. 800-435-9792). The airport information number is 335-1671.

Buses

For city bus information, call **Amarillo City Transit** at (806) 378-3094. The **Greyhound Trailways** bus terminal, for long-distance buses, is centrally located at 700 S. Tyler. Regional bus lines to New Mexico and Oklahoma stop at 117 S. Johnson. Shuttles to the *Texas Outdoor Musical Drama* at Palo Duro are available through **Amarillo Tours,** tel. 655-9637.

Taxis

Three cab companies do business in Amarillo: **Bob's Taxi Service** (tel. 806-373-1171), **Checker Cab** (tel. 376-8211), and **Dependable Cab** (tel. 372-5500).

VICINITY OF AMARILLO

PALO DURO CANYON STATE PARK

A gem of the Texas state park system, this 120-mile-long canyon drops 1,200 feet from rim to floor. You can drive past millions of years of geologic time on a park road that winds through the canyon along the Prairie Dog Fork of the Red River. Other activities include camping, hiking, horseback riding, picnicking, riding the Sad Monkey Railroad, and, in the summer, watching the outdoor historical-musical drama *Texas*. The park is 22 miles southeast of Amarillo, via I-27 S and State 217 E.

History

Four major geologic periods are exposed by the canyon walls. The lowermost strata are from the Permian period (230-250 million years ago) when this area was under the Permian Sea. The layers left behind consist of dark red shale and mudstone with veins of white gypsum. Next up are the red, gray, yellow, and lavender shales and sandstones of the Triassic period, which form blocky ledges and cliffs undercut by erosion. Fossils in this layer show the area was once covered by swamp and inhabited by 12-foot-long, crocodile-like amphibians. The Trias-

sic layers are topped by the pink and tan Ogallala caliche of the Tertiary period, which is in turn covered by the Pleistocene sands and pond deposits of the Quaternary period.

Because of the shelter provided by the canyon walls and the availability of water from springs and perennial waterways, the canyon vegetation is quite lush in places, especially in comparison with the surrounding plains. Rocky Mountain and juniper woodlands along the canyon floor gave Palo Duro its name (Palo Duro is Spanish for "hard wood"), and riparian species thrive along the Prairie Dog Fork of the Red River. Even the upper parts of the canyon display brush-covered slopes and grasslands.

Humans apparently didn't make use of this plains oasis until 10,000-12,000 years ago when Folsom man and Clovis man hunted mastodon and giant bison in the area, using flint weapons that were quarried at nearby Alibates. Later came the hunting and foraging Archaic Indians (8,000-10,000 years ago) who utilized the plants and animals of the canyon environment to support minor settlements. They were followed by a High Plains pueblo culture in the 13th-15th centuries A.D.

The first Europeans to set eyes on the canyon were Spanish conquistador Francisco Coronado and his men, who found winter shelter here in

Prairie Dog Fork of the Red River, Palo Duro Canyon

LLANO ESTACADO

The "Staked Plain" or Llano (pronounced YAH-no) Estacado is the southernmost extension of the Great Plains, a broad, flat area of limestone caprock that finally gives way at the Caprock Escarpment at Big Spring. Texans sometimes call it "the Panhandle" because most of the Llano Estacado juts above the rest of Texas on U.S. maps, like the handle of a pan. The term "panhandle" is terribly imprecise, though, and people argue over where the handle ends and the pan begins.

It's not entirely flat, either. The flatness is interrupted in several places by low hills and deep canyons, most notably Palo Duro Canyon just below Amarillo. But the mainly flat plain is the most memorable feature of the Llano Estacado; when George Lucas sought a perfectly flat landscape for the final scenes of the film *Indiana Jones and the Last Crusade,* he chose a ranch at the edge of Palo Duro.

Oil and helium are the big income earners here, along with ranching and agriculture (cotton, wheat, sorghum, vegetables, and sunflowers). Wineries in the Lubbock area have garnered international acclaim for the excellent wines they produce.

Texas: A Musical Romance of Panhandle History

From mid-June through late August every year since 1966, a cast of 80 has performed this musical drama at the outdoor Pioneer Amphitheater, with 600-foot canyon cliffs as a backdrop. The drama was penned by Pulitzer Prize-winner Paul Green, a native of North Carolina who also wrote *The Lost Colony.* Although it sounds very hokey, the whole performance actually succeeds as a heartwarming piece of Americana. The story centers on seven main characters who collaborate to establish a railroad through the Panhandle and eventually develop the first Panhandle town.

The show starts at 8:30 p.m. Tickets cost $6-14 for adults, $3-14 for children under 12, depending on seating, and are available by mail from Texas, P.O. Box 268, Canyon, TX 79015, or at the Pioneer Amphitheater box office between 6 and 7 p.m. Telephone reservations are accepted at (806) 655-2181, Mon.-Sat. 8:30 a.m.-4:30 p.m.

Parking for the performance is free. An added bonus: if you enter Palo Duro Canyon after 5:30 p.m., you don't have to pay the $2 park admission. Come early and watch the sun set over the canyon. Sutphen's Barbecue of Amarillo caters a barbecue meal in the park starting at 6:30 p.m.; about $5 a plate. Shuttle buses to the performance are available from virtually any hotel or motel in Amarillo for a nominal cost.

Visitor Center

About a quarter mile past the park entrance is the visitor center, where interpretative exhibits explain the area's geology, history, flora, and fauna. An overlook next to the center affords a good view of the widest part of the canyon. A trail next to the parking lot leads to lower sets of cliffs where side canyons can be viewed.

Sad Monkey Train

If you don't plan to hike along the canyon floor, the miniature Sad Monkey Railroad is a good

---

1541 while searching for the Seven Cities of Cibola. Over the next two centuries, several Plains Indian tribes, including the Apache, Cheyenne, Arapaho, and Kiowa, began using the canyon intermittently as shelter from the fierce High Plains winters and to take advantage of the abundance of game. As elsewhere in the Southwest, they displaced the more peaceful Pueblo Indians they encountered. But by the beginning of the 19th century, Comanches, the most aggressive of Plains Indians, dominated the canyon.

As the 19th century came to a close, Palo Duro Canyon was the last Texas holdout for the Comanches until they were driven out in the 1874 Battle of Palo Duro, when a unit of Texas Rangers cornered them in the canyon and captured their horses. The Comanches retreated to Oklahoma on foot and never came back. Two years later, ex-Texas Ranger Charles Goodnight started the first commercial ranch in the Panhandle when he drove 1,600 head of cattle into the canyon. He and his English partner John Adair established the J.A. Ranch in the canyon, which grew to a peak of nearly a million acres and 100,000 head of cattle. In 1933, 16,000 acres of the canyon were acquired by Texas Parks and Wildlife for development into a state park.

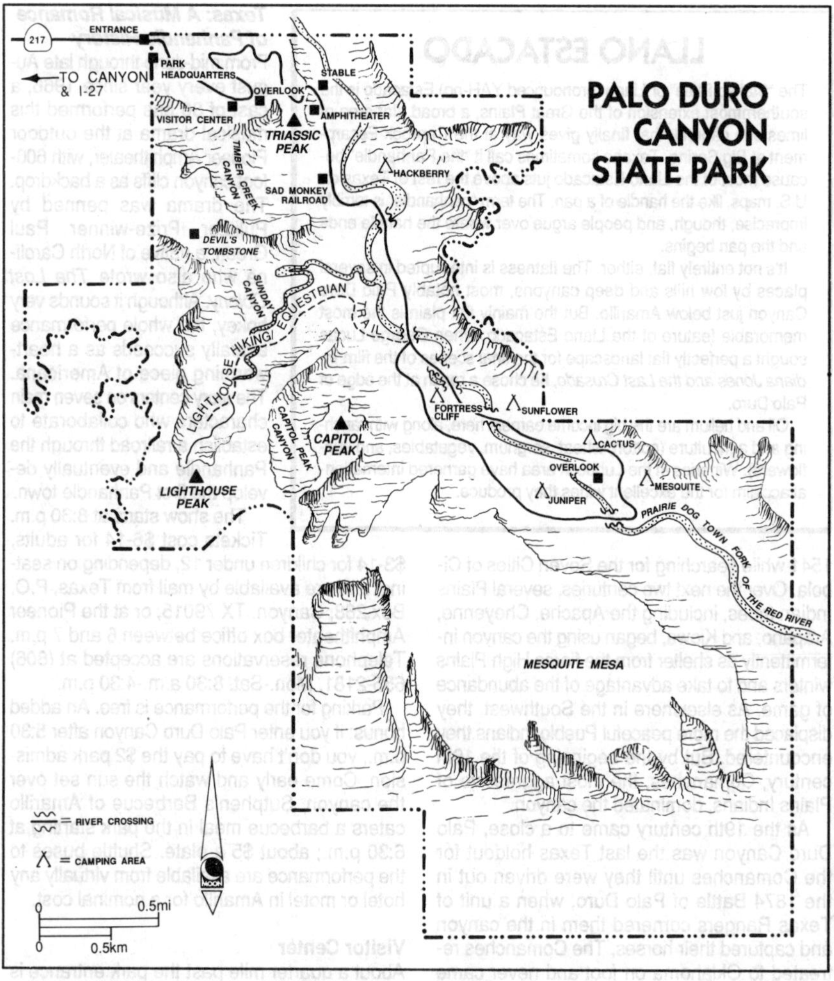

PALO DURO CANYON STATE PARK

© MOON PUBLICATIONS, INC.

≈ = RIVER CROSSING

Λ = CAMPING AREA

0   0.5mi

0   0.5km

way to get closer to some of the canyon's colorful rock formations, since the park road only passes a few. The two-mile train ride lasts about 20 minutes. A guide provides an ongoing narrative of the history and geology of the canyon as the train passes the formations of Santana's Face, Triassic Peak, Sad Monkey Rock, Spanish Skirts, and Catarina Cave, as well as Indian petroglyphs. Fare is $3 per person, children under five free.

Trails

The park has few developed trails, but visitors are free to wander anywhere along the Prairie Dog Fork of the Red River, which is particularly scenic in late October when the leaves are turning, or in April when the wildflowers are out. The other option is to explore the side canyons, which can be quite challenging since a bit of rockclimbing is usually required. Don't get too close to cliff edges, as the limestone, mudstone, and sandstone can easily crumble. An official hiking and equestrian trail (the "Lighthouse Trail") leads south from where the park road forks and into Sunday Canyon, past a promontory called Sleeping Indian, and ends at the foot of Lighthouse Peak, the rock and mudstone tower that is the "symbol" of Palo Duro; it's about three miles roundtrip (allow three hours on foot). During periods of heavy rain (rare) the trail may be closed because of the danger of flash floods.

Horses and riding equipment can be hired at the park stables, located next to Goodnight Trading Post.

The new **Capitol Peak Mountain Biking Trail** runs along a four-mile loop through the park—ask at the Visitor Center for a map. The charge for using this trail is $5 June-Aug., $3 the remainder of the year. Annual $25 permits allow unlimited usage.

Facilities

Camping: The park features six camping areas, with a total of 116 sites. Each camping area is off the main park road, which crosses the river six times; during high-water periods, some areas may be temporarily closed. The first sites you come to as you enter the lower canyon are part of the **Hackberry Camping Area,** which contains multi-use sites with drinking water, showers, and electricity ($12). About a half mile further, the road splits; the left fork leads to the **Fortress Cliff Camping Area,** which has tentsites with drinking water only ($8). Next is the **Sunflower Camping Area,** with tentsites, drinking water, and showers ($9); this is followed by the **Cactus Camping Area,** with tentsites and drinking water only ($8). As the road curves around, you'll come to **Mesquite Camping Area,** offering trailer sites with showers, water, and electricity ($12). Then the road makes the last river crossing, beyond which is **Juniper Camping Area,** with the same facilities as Mesquite. None of the trailer sites has sewage hookups, but there are dump stations near the Hackberry and Mesquite camping areas. Campsite reservations may be made by calling (806) 488-2227 daily 8 a.m.-5 p.m. or by writing Palo Duro Canyon State Park, Route 2, Box 285, Canyon, TX 79051.

Food and Supplies: The Goodnight Trading Post opposite Pioneer Amphitheater sells gas, groceries, and camping supplies. An attached restaurant is open daily for breakfast, lunch, and dinner. The snack bar at the Sad Monkey Railroad terminal serves fast food during the day.

CANYON

Panhandle-Plains Historical Museum

A 1933 Art Deco building in the small town of Canyon (pop. 12,000), 15 miles south of Amarillo off I-27/US 87, contains the oldest and largest state-supported museum in Texas. The ambitious aim of the museum is to cover Panhandle history all the way back to the Jurassic period, 160 million years ago. Exhibits encompass two million artifacts, collected and preserved since the 1921 formation of the Panhandle-Plains Historical Society. They're spread over 300,000 square feet divided into paleontology, Indian history, ranching, pioneer town-building, the discovery of oil and gas, transportation, fashions, natural history, and art. The three art galleries, focusing on American, European, and Texan art, represent one of the finest collections in the Southwest.

A research library, open to the public, contains publications and manuscripts related to Panhandle history, genealogy, art, and archaeology. Just northeast of the museum annex is the oldest intact building in the Panhandle—the former headquarters of the T Anchor Ranch, built in 1877.

The museum (tel. 806-656-2244) is open Mon.-Sat. 9 a.m.-5 p.m. from Labor Day to Memorial Day, till 6 p.m. the remainder of the year, and Sunday 1-6 p.m. No admission charge; donations requested.

West Texas A&M University

This 6,500-student campus, until 1993 called West Texas State University, supports six schools and colleges in the arts and sciences, fine arts, agriculture, business, and education. Among the more unusual course offerings—not really so unusual when you consider the surrounding community—are saddlemaking and horsemanship. Many of the students in the dance and drama departments become members of the *Texas* cast at Palo Duro Canyon.

BUFFALO LAKE NATIONAL WILDLIFE REFUGE

Approximately 30 miles southwest of Amarillo off US 60, this wildlife refuge was established by the U.S. Fish and Wildlife Service in 1958 to protect 7,664 acres of prairie and marshlands. Twenty years earlier, the construction of Umbarger Dam impounded Tierra Blanca Creek and created Buffalo Lake for recreational purposes. After heavy rains in 1978, engineers declared the dam unsafe and the lake was drained.

Today a system of shallow, natural lakes called *playas* (Spanish for sandy depression or beach) serve as an important watering site for a wide variety of birds and mammals, including herons, pelicans, swans, bald eagles, peregrine falcons, quail, pheasant, owls, mule deer, coyotes, pocket gophers, and prairie dogs; thousands of ducks and geese from Canada spend their winters here. The playas predate Buffalo Lake; theories on how they formed range from UFO visitations to meteor landings to long-term wind action. At the southern end of the main lake lies large Stewart Marsh.

An interpretive auto tour road extends along the west side of the lake, terminating at an observation deck that provides a view of the entire refuge. On the east side of the lake is a prairie dog town with an interpretive walking trail. A birding trail through Cottonwood Canyon at the northern end of the lake affords visitors glimpses of resident and migrating bird species; pick up a bird checklist at the visitor center.

The refuge is open to the public daily 8 a.m.-10 p.m. Facilities include no-fee campsites, fire rings, grills, picnic tables, restrooms, and water. Entry to the refuge costs $2 per vehicle. For further information, contact the Refuge Manager (tel. 806-499-9382), P.O. Box 228, Umbarger, TX 79091.

HEREFORD

Ever heard of Deaf Smith wheat? Hereford, 45 miles southwest of Amarillo at the intersec-

tion of US 60 and US 385, is the seat for Deaf Smith County, one of the state's top grain producers. The county's named for the head scout at the Battle of San Jacinto, in which Texas gained independence from Mexico. Cattle is also an important industry in Deaf Smith, with the county feed lots servicing nearly a million head per year on average.

National Cowgirl Hall of Fame
Founded in 1975, the female counterpart to the National Cowboy Hall of Fame inducts honorees during the annual Rhinestone Roundup in June. Most of the women honored have been professional rodeo performers, but other women who've been inducted because of their significant contributions to Western heritage include yodeling country singer Patsy Montana, Nocona bootmaker Enid Justin, and rancher Mamie Burns. The Hall of Fame displays memorabilia associated with individual inductees, including riding costumes, saddles, photos, trophies, and the like; it also houses a gallery of Western art and a small research library.

To reach the Hall of Fame from Amarillo, enter Hereford via US 60 from the northeast, turn right on US 385 to the north, then right on 15th Street. The Hall of Fame is about a half mile down 15th Street. Open Mon.-Fri. 9 a.m.-5 p.m. Admission is $3 adults and children 12 and over, children under 12 free. For information, call (806) 364-5252.

Unfortunately for Hereford and Deaf Smith County, the National Cowgirl Hall of Fame will soon move to Fort Worth's Stockyard District. Call the Fort Worth Convention and Visitors Bureau to verify the move before heading all the way out to Hereford.

All Girl Rodeo
The National Cowgirl Hall of Fame sponsors this rodeo every August. One of the largest women's rodeos in the country, it lasts for several days and includes bareback bronc riding, calf roping, barrel racing, goat tying, bullriding, and team roping. It's held at the Riders Club Arena on US 60, southeast of town. Call the Hall of Fame at (806) 364-5252 or the Hereford Chamber of Commerce (tel. 364-3333) for current information.

CAPROCK CANYONS STATE PARK AND VICINITY

The area around the small towns of Turkey and Quitaque, roughly 100 miles southeast of Amarillo via State 86, attracts two major groups: canyoneers and Western swing fans. Hunters also frequent the area seasonally for quail, mule deer, and wild hog.

Caprock Canyons State Park and Trailway

Fifteen thousand acres of rugged plains and canyonlands fill this state park, which is three miles north of Quitaque (pop. 600). Notable wildlife includes wild aoudad sheep, mule deer, pronghorn, mountain lion, feral hog, golden eagles, and a small herd of buffalo. Fishing and swimming are permitted at the park's 100-acre Lake Theo, which is stocked with large and smallmouth bass, bluegill, perch, crappie, catfish, and rainbow trout.

The 64.5-mile Caprock Canyons State Park Trailway, extending along a former Burlington Northern railbed between the Panhandle towns of South Plains and Estelline, can be enjoyed on foot, horseback, and mountain bike. Only about 25 miles of the trailway are now open; as renovations continue, the remainder will open by the end of the decade. The trailway intersects High Plains farmlands and passes through a 700-foot former railway tunnel before dropping into the Caprock Canyons, formed by the Caprock Escarpment. If you don't have your own stock, horses can be hired at **Quitaque Riding Stables** (tel. 806-455-1208) in nearby Quitaque for $8.50 per hour (two-hour minimum).

Admission to the park costs $5; a separate $2 fee is collected for use of the trailway. Primitive campsites are available for $8 a night "premium primitive" sites with picnic tables, grills, and restrooms cost $9; sites with water run $10; and drive-in sites with w/e are $12. For further information on the park and trailway, contact the Superintendent, Caprock Canyons State Park (tel. 455-1492), P.O. Box 204, Quitaque, TX 79255.

Turkey

This small ranch town of 516 residents was the birthplace of Bob Wills, creator of a unique Texas music genre called Western swing, which is characterized by country music melodies played against early (1920s-1940s) jazz rhythms. Born in 1905, Wills played fiddle and led the world-famous Texas Playboys, a seminal ensemble formed in the 1920s that continued to perform into the 1970s. He died in 1975, leaving millions of fans around the world.

Turkey's **Bob Wills Museum,** at 6th and Lyles, displays memorabilia from the bandleader's life, including fiddles, clothing, and historical photos. It's open Mon.-Tues. 9-11:30 a.m. and 1-5 p.m., Wed.-Fri. 8-11 a.m. and 1-5 p.m.; admission is free. Tours can be arranged during other hours by calling Turkey City Hall at (806) 423-1033.

Over 10,000 Western swingers turn out for the annual **Bob Wills Days,** a festival held in Turkey on the last weekend in April. Activities include Western swing performances, a fiddlers' contest, parade, arts and crafts, and plenty of Texas food, including barbecued turkey legs. For information contact the Bob Wills Foundation (tel. 423-1033), P.O. Box 415, Turkey, TX 79261.

A memorial obelisk dedicated to Bob Wills and surmounted by a pair of sculpted, over-sized fiddles stands at the west end of Main Street.

Practicalities: To paraphrase an old Singapore hand, "stay in Turkey, but feed and entertain in Quitaque." **Hotel Turkey** (tel. 800-657-7110), P.O. Box 37, Turkey, TX 79261, a restored 1927-vintage building, offers moderately priced rooms, RV hookups, tent camping, and horse-boarding facilities. It fills up fast for Bob Wills Days in April, so be sure to make reservations far in advance if you plan to attend this event.

The only places to stay in Quitaque are hunter-oriented: **Rail to Trails Sports and Hunting Lodge** (tel. 455-1344) and **Quitaque Quail Lodge** (tel. 455-1261).

Ranchers gather for mid-morning coffee most weekdays at **Caprock Cafe,** a good spot for breakfast. Check out the **Sportsman Cafe** on Fri.-Sat. nights for the all-you-can-eat burgers and fajitas buffet, accompanied by live country music in a family atmosphere. Both cafes are open Mon.-Sat. 6 a.m.-10 p.m. On Sunday Caprock Cafe is open 11 a.m.-3 p.m. while the Sportsman Cafe opens in the morning 6 a.m.-11 p.m. and again in the afternoon 2:30 p.m.-10 p.m. Quitaque is about 12 miles west of Turkey at the edge of Caprock Canyons State Park.

FRITCH AND LAKE MEREDITH

This town of 2,000, 38 miles northeast of Amarillo via State 136, is the gateway for Lake Meredith and the Alibates Flint Quarries National Monument.

Lake Meredith National Recreation Area

The only lake in the Panhandle didn't exist until 1964 when the Canadian River was dammed. Now it draws over a million visitors a year in search of water recreation. The nonstop Panhandle winds attract sailors and windsurfers. In the summer there are at least six sailboat regattas, and both the Lake Meredith Yacht Club and the Amarillo Yacht Club are quite active on the lake.

Fishing is also big, since the lake is stocked with walleye; smallmouth and largemouth bass; yellow perch; blue, channel, and flathead catfish; crappie; bluegill; carp; and sunfish. A Walleye Tournament is held each Memorial Day. In season, Lake Meredith opens public hunting land with white-tailed and mule deer, wild turkey, quail, dove, geese, and ducks.

The National Park Service administers eight public-use areas around the lake that make up the Lake Meredith National Recreation Area. Facilities at these shore areas include picnic tables, grills, restrooms, undeveloped campgrounds (seven in all, no fee), and boat launches. There are also a few commercial facilities, like the **Lake Meredith**

Marina, just west of the dam, which offers 212 boat slips for rent; a ship's store, with gas and bait as well as sailing gear; a heated fish house; and a fishing pier.

The Park Service headquarters (tel. 806-857-3151) is at 419 E. Broadway (State 136) in Fritch.

Alibates Flint Quarries National Monument

About six miles south of Fritch off State 136 is an 800-acre area protected by the National Park Service that features a series of ancient Indian flint quarries. Over thousands of years, from the time of the prehistoric game hunters until iron was introduced to the Plains Indians in the 19th century, Indian groups mined flint here. Alibates flint (named for Ali Bates, a cowboy who once lived here) is equal in hardness to the hardest of steels and was highly valued because of its brilliant color variations. One Indian tribe, possibly Pawnees, settled in the area for 250 years, trading the flint with other Indians far and wide; tools made of Alibates flint have been found throughout the U.S. as a result.

The Park Service leads free one-mile tours through the quarries and Indian ruins daily during the summer at 10 and 2, on weekends only in spring and fall. The tour ends with a flint-chipping demonstration. During the winter, tours can be arranged by calling the local Park Service office at (806) 857-3151.

LUBBOCK

Lubbock was established in 1890 as a ranching center for the South Plains area of the Panhandle. Some of the state's largest ranches developed in north Lubbock County, including the three-million-acre XIT. By the early 1920s, farming began competing with the livestock industry and today agriculture is the second-greatest economic producer locally, primarily generating cotton, grain sorghum, and wheat. Number one is Texas Tech University (and the Texas Tech Health Sciences Center), one of the state's four major universities, which makes Lubbock very much a university town. About 13% of the city's 190,000 population consists of TTU students. Nearby Reese Air Force Base, a training center for jet pilots, is the third most important economic force in Lubbock. Lubbock area vineyards have also achieved some esteem due to the award-winning efforts of three local vintners.

One aspect of Lubbock's heritage, however, seemingly overshadows all the others. It's world famous as the birthplace of singer-songwriter Buddy Holly, a major figure in the early development of rock 'n' roll. Fans from all over the world come to Lubbock to pay homage to Holly at his memorial statue and grave. Lubbock is still very much a music town, though it seems most talented local musicians end up going elsewhere to "make it."

SIGHTS

Buddy Holly Monuments
Holly was born in Lubbock in 1936 and became an international star when his song "That'll Be the Day" broke in 1957. In February 1959 he died in a plane crash in Iowa with singers Ritchie Valens and The Big Bopper (J.P. Richardson). His rockabilly-style music lived on and has been an acknowledged major influence on many noted performers, including the Beatles (whose name paid tribute to Holly's band, the Crickets), Linda Ronstadt, Marshall Crenshaw, Elvis Costello, Blondie, and the Cranberries.

In 1979, Holly's hometown unveiled a **Buddy Holly statue** to coincide with the release of the motion picture *The Buddy Holly Story*. The 8.5-foot bronze statue stands at the corner of 8th and Ave. Q near the Lubbock Civic Center. A **Walk of Fame** has been established around the base of the statue to honor other Lubbock area musicians who succeeded in the music business, with bronze plaques commemorating the likes of Sonny Curtis (one of the original Crickets), Roy Orbison, Waylon Jennings, Mac Davis, Bobby Keys, and Joe Ely. Each year another plaque is added during the Lubbock Music Festival in August.

Buddy Holly's grave is in the Lubbock Cemetery at the east end of 31st Street. After entering the cemetery, take the right fork and you'll find the grave on the left not far from the

favorite son

1909 ranch house,
Ranching Heritage
Center

entrance. The original headstone was stolen and has been replaced by a newer one, with engraved guitar and musical notes; the spelling "Buddy Holley" preserves the singer's birth name. You may notice triangular pieces of plastic on the grave—along with flowers, fans often leave guitar picks.

Anyone interested in Holly and the early West Texas rockabilly scene may want to look into the magazine *Rockin' 50s* (P.O. Box 6123, Lubbock, TX 79493), produced locally by Holly expert Bill Griggs.

Texas Tech University

Yes, the official name is Texas Tech University, or Texas Tech for short (or locally, just Tech). The university was chartered in 1923 and now has over 25,000 students in seven colleges covering 115 majors, a graduate school (with 104 majors), and a law school. TTU shares an attractive 1,800-acre campus in the center of town with the Texas Tech University Health Sciences Center, which includes one of the state's major schools of medicine.

One of Tech's most outstanding features is **The Museum of Texas Tech University,** which includes the main museum, the Ranching Heritage Center, the Moody Planetarium, the Lubbock Lake Landmark, and two research-oriented museums not open to the general public: the Natural Science Research Center and the Val Verde County Research Site.

The Museum: The main museum building at Texas Tech is located on campus at 4th and Indiana. Temporary and permanent exhibits cover various topics in the natural and social sciences as well as the visual arts. Permanent exhibits worth seeing include the Heritage of the Llano Estacado, the Taos/Southwest Art Gallery, and the Early Texas Cultures Hall. You'll also come across small, well-curated displays on Asian, African, and Central American art. Open Tues.-Sat. 10 a.m.-5 p.m. (Thursday till 8:30 p.m.) and Sunday 1-5 p.m. Admission is free. For further information, call (806) 742-2490.

Ranching Heritage Center: This is a mostly outdoor attraction, consisting of 33 ranching structures relocated to the center from around the state. The 14-acre grounds are adjacent to the main museum building on the Texas Tech campus; a free map guides visitors along a trail through the center. Among the most interesting structures are four different kinds of windmills from the turn of the century, an 1838 log cabin, a 1918 railway depot complete with steam locomotive and cattle shipping pens, an 1877 horse barn, an 1880 bunkhouse, an 1886 house from the XIT Ranch, an 1890s schoolhouse, and a huge 1909 Victorian ranch house.

An indoor portion of the center contains a gallery that displays ranching tools and other artifacts of Southwestern ranch life, including

LUBBOCK

TO AMARILLO

LUBBOCK INTERNATIONAL AIRPORT

LUBBOCK LAKE LANDMARK STATE HISTORICAL PARK

CORONADO INN

CLOVIS RD.

EL TEJAS MOTEL

MUNICIPAL DR.

LOOP 289

82

62

PRAIRIE DOG TOWN

TO REESE AFB

4th ST.

MUSEUM AND RANCHING HERITAGE CENTER

TEXAS TECH. UNIV. HEALTH SCIENCES CENTER

TEXAS TECH UNIVERSITY

SUPER 8
SHERATON

BUDDY HOLLY STATUE AND WALK OF FAME

MacKENZIE STATE PARK

PARKWAY DR.

SOUTH PLAINS FAIRGROUND

8th ST.

LUBBOCK MEMORIAL CIVIC CENTER

BROADWAY

LA QUINTA HOLIDAY INN

19th ST.

POST OFFICE

DEPOT RESTAURANT

IDALOU RD.

GUAVA AVE.

MOON

LUBBOCK CHRISTIAN UNIVERSITY

LUBBOCK CONVENTION AND VISITORS BUREAU

STUBB'S BAR-B-Q

PARAGON HOTEL

LONE STAR OYSTER BAR

AVE. H

AVE. A

QUIRT AVE.

BUDDY HOLLY'S GRAVE

LOOP 289

82

62

QUAKER AVE.

INDIANA AVE.

34th ST.

UNIVERSITY AVE.

AVE. Q

84

87

SOUTHEAST DR.

50th ST.

KOKO INN

SLIDE RD.

66th ST.

BEST WESTERN LUBBOCK REGENCY

SLATON RD.

FRANKFORD AVE.

BARCELONA COURT HOTEL

LOOP 289

LUBBOCK PLAZA HOTEL

MIDNIGHT RODEO

TO WINERIES

84

ABUELO'S

RESIDENCE INN BY MARRIOTT

87

82nd ST.

© MOON PUBLICATIONS, INC.

0   2 mi
0   2 km

collections of spurs, saddles, and firearms. The center is open Mon.-Sat. 10 a.m.-5 p.m., Sunday 1-5 p.m. Free admission.

Lubbock Lake Landmark State Historical Park

A watering place for humans and animals for at least 12,000 years, Lubbock Lake has yielded a cultural and geologic record of the Clovis period, North America's earliest human culture, plus evidence of archaic, ceramic, proto-historic and historic occupation of the area. Two boys digging in the leftover mud from a 1939 WPA-sponsored dredging project found the first Amerindian artifacts in the area; to date only around three percent of the identified archaeological sites have been excavated.

The Nash Interpretive Center on the site contains exhibits on the discoveries and work of the archaeologists as well as a children's educational center and gift shop. There is also a picnic area, self-guided interpretive trail, and four-mile nature trail.

The park is located at the northwest edge of the city; from the junction of US 84 and Loop 289 follow the signs to Landmark Drive. It's open Tues.-Sat. 9 a.m.-5 p.m., Sunday 1-5 p.m.; admission is $2 adults, $1 children and seniors. For more information, call (806) 765-0737.

Science Spectrum
and Omnimax Theater

The Omnimax Theater uses a film format 10 times larger than common 35mm to present science- and nature-oriented films on a massive, 80-foot dome screen backed with 72 huge speakers pumping six-track digital sound. Films show continuously, Mon.-Tues. 1-5 p.m., Wed.-Thurs. 1-8 p.m., Friday 1-10 p.m., Saturday 11 a.m.-10 p.m., and Sunday 1-8 p.m.

The Science Spectrum offers permanent, hands-on exhibits demonstrating scientific principles, plus traveling and temporary displays on science and technology. A current exhibit on space exploration is a big hit with kids. It's open Mon.-Fri. 10 a.m.-5:30 p.m., Saturday 10 a.m.-6 p.m., Sunday 1-5:30 p.m.; admission is $5.50 adults, $4.50 students and seniors.

Admission to both museum and theater costs $8.50 adults, $6.50 students and seniors. Both facilities are at 2579 S. Loop 289 (between University and Indiana).

Wineries

Viticulture has become so important to Lubbock that the chamber of commerce city logo now features a bunch of grapes dangling across the "O." Three of the major vintners, Llano Estacado, Cap Rock, and Pheasant Ridge, have won awards in statewide and national competitions. All three produce the standard appellations made popular by California winemakers: cabernet sauvignon, chardonnay, Johannisberg riesling, chenin blanc, and gewürztraminer, as well as various red and white blends. For all Lubbock area wineries, however, the gewürztraminer seems particularly well-suited to the soil and climate. Two of these wineries are open daily for free tours and tasting and are close enough together they can be visited in an afternoon.

Llano Estacado: This winery has the best overall reputation and distribution in Texas, has won the most awards (300 since 1987), and was the first "modern" (Napa Valley-style) vintner in Texas, founded in 1976. The company ships to 35 states and seven countries, and became the first U.S. winery to sell in Russia. The winery gift shops sells wines and wine-serving paraphernalia. To get there, drive south of Lubbock on US 87 to FM 1585, about four miles south of Loop 289, and then east 3.2 miles. The winery (tel. 806-745-

2258) is open for tours and tasting Mon.-Sat. 10 a.m.-5 p.m.and Sunday noon-5 p.m.

Cap Rock Winery: This state-of-the-art winery opened in 1988 as Teysha Cellars; at a cost of $6 million, it's the most expensive winemaking facility ever built. The main building, which contains the tasting room, is a striking example of new Southwestern architecture. Cap Rock's first-tier wines include a reserve chardonnay, reserve cabernet sauvignon, and methode champenoise sparkling wine; the latter has won several gold medals in recent U.S. competitions. "Tapestry," a unique third-tier wine, blends sauvignon blanc, semillon, and melon. The winery (tel. 863-2704 or 800-546-WINE) is open for tours and tasting Mon.-Sat. 10 a.m.-5 p.m., Sunday noon-5 p.m.

Prairie Dog Town

This is one of only two prairie dog towns left in the state—these rodents proved such pests early this century farmers practically wiped them out. They look like giant, tan squirrels without tails. It's hard to believe the little retaining wall around this colony actually keeps them from colonizing local fields. If you have binoculars, bring them, as sometimes the prairie dogs stay close to their burrows and don't come near the wall, and visitors aren't allowed inside. Other times they seem to be all over the place. PD Town is in MacKenzie State Park in the northeast corner of Lubbock; the entrance is at Ave. A and E. Broadway. Free.

FOOD

Any visitor looking to buy beer, wine, or liquor in Lubbock will quickly learn it's a "dry" town where such evils are permitted only in restaurants or bars. A collection of liquor stores known as the "Strip" sits on US 87 south of town, right at the city limits.

American

$$ **The Depot:** A 1928 railroad depot converted to a very popular restaurant that specializes in prime rib, steak, and seafood. Great salad bar and outdoor beer garden. At 19th and Ave. G (tel. 806-747-1646); open Mon.-Fri. for lunch and dinner, Sat.-Sun. dinner only.

LUBBOCK HOTELS AND MOTELS

Add 13% hotel tax to all rates. Area code: 806.

Barcelona Court; 5215 S. Loop 289; tel. 794-5353; $70-100; atrium, heated pool, kitchens, coin laundry, airport shuttle, senior discount

Best Western Lubbock Regency; 6624 Ave. H; tel. 745-2208 or (800) 528-1234; $55-88; heated pool, coin laundry, airport shuttle

Coronado Inn; 501 Amarillo Hwy. (north of town near the airport); tel. 763-6441; $20-32; pool, kitchenette

Days Inn; 2401 4th; tel. 747-7111; $35-60; pool

El Tejas Motel; 1000 N. Ave. Q; tel. 763-9343; $35-50; pool

GuestHouse Inn; 3812 21st St.; tel. 791-0433; $43-50; laundry, covered parking

Holiday Inn Civic Center; 801 Ave. Q; tel. 763-1200; $67; heated pool, coin laundry, refrigerators available, airport shuttle

Holiday Inn South; 3201 S. Loop 289; tel. (800) HOLIDAY; $67-80; heated pool, health club privileges, airport shuttle

KoKo Inn; 5201 Ave. Q; tel. 747-2591; $37-46; heated pool, airport shuttle

La Quinta Motor Inn; 601 Ave. Q; tel. 763-9441; $53-63; pool, airport shuttle

Lubbock Inn; 3901 19th St.; tel. 792-5181 or (800) 545-8226; $48-72; pool, kitchenettes available, airport shuttle

Motel 6; 909 66th; tel. 745-5541; $35-45; small pool

Paragon Hotel; 4115 Brownfield Hwy.; tel. 792-0065 or (800) 333-1146; $55-80; pool, refrigerators available

Residence Inn Marriott; 251 S. Loop 289; tel. 745-1963; $41-95; heated pool, spa, fireplace, kitchens, coin laundry

Sheraton Inn Lubbock; 505 Ave. Q (near 4th); tel. 747-0171; $62-150; heated pool, airport shuttle

Stadium Motel; 405 University; tel. 763-5779; $18-38

Super 8 Motel; 501 Ave. Q; tel. 762-8726; $35-45; pool

Village Inn; 4925 Brownfield Hwy.; tel. 795-5821; $34-44; heated pool, coin laundry, senior discount

Villa Inn; 5401 Ave. Q; tel. 747-3525; $43-52; atrium, indoor pool

---

$$ Grapevine Cafe and Wine Bar: Strong in salads and seafood, with Gulf Coast influences. Earned a check mark from tony *Texas Monthly* magazine for "restaurant of very good quality for the city in which it is located." At 2407-B 19th (tel. 744-8246); open Monday 11 a.m.-2 p.m., Tues.-Sun. 11 a.m.-11 p.m.

$$ The Greenery: Offers a wide variety of American dishes, but is especially good for daily breakfasts and Sunday brunch, with made-to-order omelettes and cheese blintzes. At 801 Ave. Q (tel. 763-1200); open daily 6 a.m.-10 p.m.; Sunday brunch served 10 a.m.-2 p.m.

$ Old Town Cafe: Owned by a demolitions expert, the Old Town is renowned for hearty, homestyle breakfast and lunch buffets, plus dinner on weekends. Packed with entertaining, kitschy memorabilia—old boots, signs, photos, posters. BYOB. At 2402 Ave. J (tel. 762-4768); open Mon.-Thurs. 6 a.m.-3 p.m., Fri.-Sat. 6 a.m.-9 p.m.

$ to $$ Schlotzsky's: Part of a Texas chain that serves good deli-style sandwiches. Four locations: 3719 19th St. (tel. 793-5542), 5204 Slide Rd. (tel. 793-1233), 8101 Indiana Ave. (tel. 792-3396), and 1200 Main St. (tel. 744-3803). Open daily for lunch and dinner.

Asian

$ to $$ Great Wall: Hunan and Szechwan cuisine, plus all-you-can-eat Mongolian barbecue. At 1625 University Ave. (tel. 806-747-1264); open Sun.-Fri. for lunch and dinner, Saturday dinner only.

$ Thai Thai Restaurant: Good selection of curries, noodles, and Thai-style salads at low prices. Could be called Tex-Thai, since the Thai food here accommodates local tastes without losing its essential Thainess—the innovative "Thai Thai" is a chicken-potato eggroll. At 5105 Quaker Ave. (tel. 791-0024); open daily except Tuesday 11:30 a.m.-9 p.m.

Barbecue

$ to $$ Bigham's Smokehouse: The local favorite, at two locations: 4302 19th St, (tel. 806-793-6880) and 3310 82nd St. (tel. 797-9241). Open daily for lunch and dinner.

$ to $$ The County Line: Part of a statewide chain that started in Austin. Always reliable, with a basic menu of ribs, brisket, sausage, and chicken, served with cole slaw, potato salad, and beans. Occasional "blue plate specials" include smoked duck, grilled fish, and other non-typical selections. The Lubbock branch (tel. 763-6001) is situated next to a stream frequented by ducks, on FM 2641 a half mile west of I-27/US 87 north. Open daily for dinner.

$ J&J Bar-B-Q: Lubbock's most traditional barbecue house serves lean and flavorful brisket, ham, and sausage. Old-fashioned fountain Cokes available. At 1306 Texas (tel. 744-1325). Open Mon.-Fri. 11 a.m.-3 p.m., or until the barbecue sells out.

$ Mesquite's BBQ & Steaks: Besides barbecue, specialties here include homemade onion rings and Mexican food. At 2419 Broadway (tel. 763-1159); open daily for breakfast, lunch, and dinner.

$ to $$ Stubb's Bar-B-Q: After sojourns in Austin and Dallas, Stubb has returned home to provide pit-cooked barbecue ribs, pork, beef, sausage, and chicken, along with smokin' roots music—jukebox by day, live by night. At 19th and I-27 (tel. 747-4777); open Mon.-Wed. 11 a.m.-11 p.m., Thurs.-Sun. 11 a.m.-2 a.m.

Health Food and Vegetarian

$ to $$ Tenanga: Focuses on African food, especially fish and curry dishes, along with a few vegetarian entrees. At 2411 Main St., opposite the main entrance for Texas Tech (tel. 806-763-6633); open Sun.-Fri. 11 a.m.-11 p.m., Saturday 3-11 p.m.

$ Well Body Natural Foods: The eclectic, health-oriented menu features dishes like spinach lasagna and walnut broccoli stir-fry cooked with light oils and using all-natural ingredients. Chicken and seafood dishes. No smoking is allowed in the dining room—unusual for Texas. At 3651 34th (tel. 793-1015); open Mon.-Fri. 7 a.m.-8 p.m., Saturday 8 a.m.-6 p.m.

Italian

$ Giorgio's Pizza: Good pizza by the slice or by the pie. At Broadway and Ave. J downtown (tel. 806-765-9330); open Mon.-Fri. 11 a.m.-6 p.m.only.

$$ Olive Garden Restaurant: This local favorite specializes in traditional Italian cuisine. Near South Plains Mall at 5702 Slide Rd. (tel. 791-3575). Open daily for lunch and dinner.

$ to $$ Orlando's: Features huge portions of pasta, veal dishes, pizza, and other Italian meals. At 2402 Ave. Q (tel. 747-5998) and 6951 Indiana (tel. 797-8646); open Mon.-Sat. for lunch and dinner, Sunday dinner only.

Mexican

$$ Abuelo's: The outdoor courtyard at Lubbock's most upscale Mexican eatery makes this a good choice during periods of pleasant weather. At 4401 82nd and Quaker (tel. 806-794-1752); open daily 11 a.m.-10 p.m.

$ Jimenez Bakery and Restaurant: Offers classic Tex-Mex and Mexican pastries at 1219 Ave. G (tel. 744-2685). The restaurant is open daily except Saturday 7 a.m.-3 p.m. only; the bakery is open daily 6 a.m.-6 p.m.

$$ Santa Fe: Southwestern-style Mexican along with a few downhome dishes like chicken-fried steak. At 4th and Ave. Q (tel. 763-6114); open daily for lunch and dinner.

$$ Texas Café and Bar: Specializes in Tex-Mex, but also serves steak, barbecue, and downhome dishes. At 3604 50th St. (tel. 792-8544); open daily 11 a.m.-2 a.m.

Seafood

$$ Lone Star Oyster Bar: A popular seafood place that specializes in fresh oysters (on the half shell, baked, or fried), gumbo, and catfish. Two locations: 34th and Flint (tel. 806-796-0101) and 5116-C 58th (58th and Slide, tel. 797-3773). Open daily for lunch and dinner.

ENTERTAINMENT

Lubbock, like Amarillo, is a town where live bands tend to play a mixture of rock and country, in the spirit of Buddy Holly. Local groups perform original as well as cover tunes, and singer-songwriters are plentiful. If you're lucky, you may get to see Jimmie Dale Gilmore, Joe Ely, Butch Hancock, or Jesse Taylor perform here in their hometown, although they usually stay close to Austin these days, where the recording studios are. Cover charges are quite reasonable at Lubbock clubs, usually under $5.

The **Texas Café and Bar** brings in progressive country (or, as some call it locally, "aggressive country") and Western swing. More traditional C&W is the fare at the **Westernaire Club** (tel. 806-747-5763), 4801 Ave. Q, a longtime favorite of the Western swing crowd. The **Villa Club** (tel. 744-8026), 5401 Ave. Q, is another established country dance hall. For more of a honky-tonk atmosphere, complete with pool tables and raised wooden dance floor, try **Midnight Rodeo** (tel. 745-2813), 7301 University Avenue. **Jiggers Up** (tel. 744-5061), 4802 Ave. Q, hosts country jam sessions on Sunday evening, as does the **Silver Bullet** (tel. 799-9166), 5145 Aberdeen.

For Texas singer-songwriters, **Stubb's** is the place—Joe Ely and several other Lubbock musicians got a boost at a previous Stubb's location. Stubb's features live music nightly but only charges a cover Thurs.-Sat. nights. The **Main Street Saloon** (tel. 762-0940), 2417 Main St., showcases live rock 'n' roll and blues bands; on Sunday nights it hosts an open jam session. **Tracks** (tel. 797-0220), 5203 34th St., hosts country and *tejano*, live on Friday nights, recorded the remainder of the week.

Popular spots for techno, hip-hop, and other dance music are **Club Berlin** (tel. 744-1928), 1928 Ave. H, and **The Tunnel,** 2211 4th. **Depot 10th Street Warehouse** (tel. 747-6156), 1824 Ave. G, offers recorded rock and dance tracks, plus live rock in the attached Beer Garden.

EVENTS

Most of the major events in Lubbock seem to take place in September and October—it's too hot in the summer, too cold in the winter, and spring is tornado season.

National Cowboy Symposium and Celebration
People interested in cowboy culture from around the nation and beyond descend on Lubbock for this five-day event in early to mid-September. Activities include a trail ride, rodeo, chuckwagon and chili cookoffs, country dances, and performances by cowboy poets, musicians, and storytellers. Venues are divided among the Civic Center, South Plains Fairgrounds, and V-8 Ranch (off FM 835 about five miles southeast of town). For details, contact the Lubbock Convention and Visitors Bureau.

Fiestas del Llano
This is the local version of Diez y Seis, Mexican Independence Day. Held at the Lubbock Memo-

rodeo Lubbock style

rial Civic Center (6th St.) for three days around September 16, the celebration features plenty of Mexican food, music, and dancing. Call (806) 745-2855 for information.

Buddy Holly's Birthday
Holly was born September 7, 1936, so this event is held the first week of September. The main purpose of the celebration is to display, trade, buy, and sell Buddy Holly memorabilia—records, autographs, musical instruments. For information on location and scheduling, call Bill Griggs at (806) 799-4299.

Texas International Wine Classic
An event that takes place one weekend in late September or early October, the Wine Classic features tastings and competition among local, national, and international wines, plus wine seminars, lectures, and gourmet meals. Held in the Lubbock Memorial Civic Center. Call (806) 763-4666 for details.

Panhandle South Plains Fair
Held in late September or early October at the Fair Park and Fair Park Coliseum, 105 E. Broadway. Includes all the usual fair events: carnival, midway, horse and livestock shows, agricultural and industrial exhibits, contests, games, and music by top country performers.

SHOPPING

Lubbock has the usual malls and chain department stores. One unique spot is the **Antique Mall** (tel. 806-796-2166) at 7907 W. 19th St. (about three miles west of Loop 289), where around 50 antique and collectibles dealers rent booths. A map of the mall is available from the Lubbock Convention and Visitors Bureau. Another is **Cactus Alley** at 2610 Salem, where shops around a courtyard are devoted to such whimsical items as balloons, spices, clocks, stuffed bears, costumes, and art. One store specializes in eggshell art and items shaped like eggs.

LUBBOCK TELEPHONE INFORMATION

Emergency (police, fire, medical): 911
Telephone Directory Assistance: 411
Area Code: 806
Weather Service: 762-0141
Texas Tech University: 742-3610
Chamber of Commerce: 763-4666

INFORMATION

Tourist Office
The **Lubbock Convention and Visitors Bureau** is oriented toward group tourism and conventions but the staff is happy to answer questions from individuals. The office distributes a number of helpful maps and brochures that may be of interest to the casual visitor. At Ave. K and 14th St., tel. (806) 763-4666 or (800) 692-4035.

GETTING THERE AND AROUND

Lubbock International Airport
The four commercial passenger airlines that fly into Lubbock are America West (tel. 800-247-5692, in Texas), American (tel. 806-763-0675 or, in Texas, 800-334-7400), Delta (tel. 800-221-1212), and Southwest (tel. 800-435-9792).

Buses
For city bus information, call **Citibus** at (806) 762-0111. The bus terminal for the **Texas, New Mexico, and Oklahoma** line, a subsidiary of Greyhound, is at 1313 13th St. (southeast corner of 13th and Ave. M) downtown. Call 765-6644 for TNM&O information.

Taxis
There are two cab companies in Lubbock: **City Cab** (tel. 806-765-7474) and **Yellow Cab** (tel. 765-7777).

THE PRAIRIES

Wedged between Oklahoma to the north, the Llano Estacado to the west, the Edwards Plateau to the south, and the Cross Timbers to the east is an area of rolling, grassy hills known as the Prairies. Because there are only two cities of size here, Abilene and Wichita Falls, the area is often lumped together with the Panhandle.

The area was a favorite buffalo-hunting ground for the nomadic South Plains Indians during the winter, when buffalo herds migrated here to avoid colder weather on the High Plains. Buffalo Gap, near present-day Abilene, was one of the first areas on the Prairies to be settled; white and Creek Indian buffalo hunters began coming here in the 1870s when they discovered what the Plains Indians knew all along—that huge buffalo herds always used this gap in the Callahan Divide on their way south in the late fall and north in the early spring. As the demand for buffalo hide increased in the eastern U.S., a wholesale slaughter ensued: buffalo hunters shot hundreds of animals daily, followed by skinners who skinned the buffalo where they fell and stacked the hides on the ground to be collected later by traders. This forced the Comanches, who depended on the buffalo as a source of food, clothing, household tools, and shelter, to move on, leaving the area open for farms, ranches, and railroads—the taming of the Wild West.

ABILENE

Once the Comanches were out of the area, the Texas & Pacific Railroad established a railhead in 1881 at milepost 407 along the telegraph line between Marshall and El Paso. The town founders named it after Abilene, Kansas, in hopes the new town would soon become as prosperous as its namesake.

Abilene's economy rests on ranching, agriculture, oil, and the military at Dyess Air Force Base. Early on, the town became a stronghold for circuit preachers, forerunners of today's Christian fundamentalists; the town has been called "the buckle of the Bible Belt." The three universities here are religious institutions: Abilene Christian University (Church of Christ, established 1906, 4,600 students), Hardins-Simmons University (Baptist, established 1891, 2,000 students), and McMurray University (Methodist, established 1923, 1,600 students).

Downtown Abilene is undergoing a slow but steady cultural renaissance, especially along historic Cypress Street.

Grace Cultural Center/Museums of Abilene
Housed in the 1909-vintage former Grace Hotel at 102 Cypress St. downtown, the GCC brings together three museums. The Historical Museum presents an excellent series of displays on Abilene history, with a surprising amount of detail on local church growth, the Ku Klux Klan, and other controversial themes, while the Children's Museum features hands-on science and arts exhibits. The Art Museum contains changing and permanent exhibits of regional, contemporary, and folk art; a recent display included a fine selection of Thomas Hart Benton lithos.

Several of the hotel rooms have been renovated in typical period detail. A restored ballroom on the first floor hosts local social events.

The museums are open Tuesday, Wednesday, Friday, and Saturday 10 a.m.-5 p.m., Thursday 10 a.m.-8:30 p.m., and Sunday 1-5 p.m.; admission is $2 adults, $1 children 12 and under, free for all on Thursday 5-8:30 p.m.

Center for Contemporary Arts
A nonprofit arts association, the CCA operates two galleries—one dedicated to photography, the other to painting—at 220 Cypress. Upstairs are artist studios and a small research library. The CCA organizes "art walks" through downtown Abilene once a month when a new exhibit starts up. At least one exhibitor each month is a local artist. Open Tues.-Fri. 11 a.m.-5 p.m., Sat.-Sun. 1-4 p.m.; call (915) 677-8389 for more information.

Buffalo Gap

Ten miles southwest of Abilene off FM 89 (Buffalo Gap Rd.) is a little town that's hardly changed since the turn of the century, except that now it caters to tourists rather than frontierspeople. Many of the 397 residents are ranchers; the rest work in Abilene. The Buffalo Gap Volunteer Fire Department has an all-woman staff since most men are out riding herd—or commuting—during the day. The main tourist attraction is **Buffalo Gap Historic Village,** a collection of hundred-year-old buildings.

The original Taylor County Courthouse and Jail, built in 1879 of sandstone blocks and Civil War cannonballs, still stands solidly. The building now houses a museum with local artifacts from that era. Other buildings include a chapel, railroad depot, print shop, post office, wagon barn, and several mercantile stores. Open to visitors daily 10 a.m.-6 p.m.March 15-Nov. 15, or on Fri.-Sat. 10 a.m.-5 p.m.and Sunday noon-5 p.m.Nov.16 -March 14. Admission is $4 adults, seniors $3, children $1.75.

Several small country restaurants and cafes in Buffalo Gap include the **Bar-B-Que Barn** (barbecue), **Judy's Gathering Place** (Mexican), **Perini Ranch** (ranch food), and **Dutchlander Garden** (catfish and steaks).

Abilene Zoo

This 13-acre zoo is the only zoo between Fort Worth and El Paso. It's divided into three habitats—the Texas Plains, the African Veldt, and the Herpetarium. The Texas Plains exhibit is of particular note since it houses animals native to upper West Texas that you might not otherwise get a chance to see, including bison, pronghorn, javelina, coyote, wild turkey, prairie dogs, and roadrunners.

The zoo's 10,300-square-foot **Discovery Center** is a self-contained facility consisting of four climatized biomes that compare habitats in the American Southwest and Mexico with similar areas in East Africa and Madagascar. The "Aquatic Adventure" section, for example, draws parallels between Lake Amistad in Texas and Africa's Lake Tanganyika, as well as the Rio Grande and the Zambesi River. The zoo is located in Nelson Park, off US 80 just inside Loop 322. From Memorial Day to Labor Day, hours are weekdays 9 a.m.-5 p.m., weekends and holidays 9 a.m.-7 p.m., and the rest of the year daily 9 a.m.-5 p.m. Admission is $2 adults, $1 seniors and children. Call (915) 672-9771 for further information.

Fort Phantom Hill

This was one of four U.S. Army infantry forts established in the early 1850s to protect the westward-expanding Texas frontier. It was never

Buffalo Gap
Historic Village

ABILENE CONVENTION AND VISITORS BUREAU

Fort Phantom Hill

officially named, however, and was known only as the Post on the Clear Fork of the Brazos. The five infantry companies based here were of little use against the mounted Comanches. The current name probably originated after the fort closed in 1854, either in reference to its abandoned condition or because the hill it rests on seems to recede as one approaches it. In 1858 it was turned into a way station (No. 54) for the Butterfield Overland Mail, but was again abandoned upon the outbreak of the Civil War. During the war, a Confederate Frontier Battalion occasionally used the abandoned fort as a base, and in the 1870s it became a sub-post for nearby Fort Griffin in the last of the Indian Wars.

The ruins consist of three half-standing buildings and over a dozen chimneys, all of locally quarried stone. They're on privately owned land 14 miles north of Abilene on FM 600, but are open to the public at no charge.

Four miles south of the ruins is **Lake Fort Phantom Hill,** a 4,200-acre reservoir that's a popular local fishing spot for walleye and crappie. Lake facilities include marinas, public boat ramps, free campsites, and picnic areas.

Abilene State Park
Once a Comanche rest stop, this scenic, 621-acre park runs along Cedar Creek near Lake Abilene. A spring-fed swimming pool is open to the public daily noon-9 p.m. between Memorial Day and Labor Day. There are also nature trails, picnic areas, campsites, and screened shelters. To get there from Abilene, take FM 89 southeast 14.5 miles to Park Rd. 32. Admission is $3 per vehicle or 50 cents per person for pedestrians and cyclists, free for TCP holders.

Dyess Air Force Base
Abilene AFB (changed to Dyess AFB in 1956) was established as a Strategic Air Command (SAC) base during the Korean War in 1952. Today the base is the headquarters for the 7th Wing, which flies B1-B bombers and C-130 transport planes. During WW II, the 7th Wing bombed Japanese supply lines in Southeast Asia, including the famous Bridge over the River Kwai.

A collection of 25 restored military aircraft from WW II and the Korean and Vietnam wars is on display at the Linear Air Park (tel. 915-696-2196) on base. Admission is free; stop at the main base entrance for a pass.

Hotels and Motels
Rooms at Abilene's **Motel 6** (tel. 915-672-8462), 4951 W. Stamford St., exit 282 off I-20, are $22-34. The **Kiva Inn** (tel. 695-2150), 5403 S. 1st, is good middle-range value, with well-kept rooms

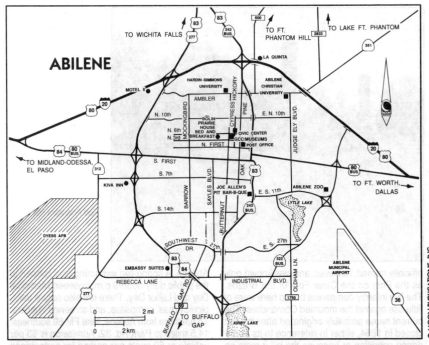

ABILENE

for $39 s, $46-59 d—and it has a heated indoor pool, whirlpool, and saunas. The **Embassy Suites Hotel** (tel. 698-1234), at 4250 Ridgemont Dr., across from the Mall of Abilene, has efficiencies for $77-88. **La Quinta** (tel. 676-1676 or 800-531-5900) has good rooms for $47-50 per night including continental breakfast.

Bed and Breakfasts
Bolin Prairie House Bed & Breakfast (tel. 915-675-5855) at 508 Mulberry (just west of downtown, within walking distance) offers four antique-furnished rooms in a 1902 home set in a quiet neighborhood for $50-60.

Campgrounds and RV Parks
Abilene has plenty of nearby camping options, including two city parks that allow free camping for up to three days. At **Seabee Park,** 3.2 miles north of I-20 on FM 600, on Elm Creek, camping is permitted over a 40-acre area, but only four sites are developed. **Johnson Park** at

Lake Phantom Hill, 6.6 miles north of I-20 on FM 600, has a 37-acre camping area, with five developed sites. Both parks feature flush toilets but no drinking water; call (915) 676-6218 for information.

You can also camp at **Abilene State Park** (tel. 572-3204), choosing drive-in sites with water for $6, with w/e for $9, or screened shelters for $10-12. Toilets and showers on the premises; a snack bar is open during the summer. The park sits alongside Lake Abilene; take FM 89 (off US 84) 14.5 miles south to Park Rd. 32 and follow signs to the park entrance.

Abilene RV Park (tel. 672-0657), on I-20 at exit 292-B, has full hookups for $15. There is a **KOA Kampground** (tel. 672-3681) off I-20 West, a half mile west of US 277 (exit 282 for Shirley Rd.). Tent/camper sites with w/e are $18 a night while a full hookup is $20. Discounts are available for weekly and monthly stays and a snack bar serves breakfast and dinner during nonwinter months.

Further west out I-20, at exit 278, **Tye RV Park** (tel. 691-5700) and **West of Dallas RV Park** (tel. 691-5700) offer full hookups for $13 and $9 a night respectively.

Food

This is steak country and the most popular steak place in town is **John Zentner's Daughter Steak House** (tel. 915-695-4290) at 4358 Sayles Blvd. at Danville; open daily for lunch and dinner. For barbecue, **Joe Allen's Pit Bar-B-Que** (tel. 672-6082), 1233 S. Treadaway, is the local favorite; open Mon.-Sat. for lunch and dinner. The **Perini Ranch** (tel. 572-3339) in Buffalo Gap serves a highly acclaimed ranch roast as well as ribs, chicken, red snapper, and unique side dishes like superb Mexican hominy. It's open for dinner every day except Monday. **Judy's Gathering Place** (tel. 572-3731) in Buffalo Gap specializes in New Mexican-style Mexican for lunch daily except Monday.

Back in town the inexpensive **Dos Amigos** (tel. 672-2992) at 3650 N. 6th St. specializes in Sonoran dishes and is open Mon.-Sat. for lunch and dinner. Dos Amigos also has cantina dancing in the evenings—one of the few dance venues in town. For fresh take-out tamales, **Pompa's** at 1326 Butternut can't be beat—it's been supplying Abilene with fresh tortillas since 1954.

House of Hunan (tel. 695-9282) has a menu that goes on forever and includes rice dishes, noodles, seafood, all the usual beef, poultry, and pork dishes, plus a long list of house specialties. This Chinese oasis is at 3106 S. Clack St. and is open daily for lunch and dinner. Several chain restaurants along Clack St. include Red Lobster, Arby's, and Casa Olé.

Moving upmarket a bit, Cypress Street Station (tel. 676-3463) at 158 Cypress St. downtown, next to the Paramount Theater, serves well-prepared pasta, pizza, seafood, duck, and rack of lamb; open Tues.-Sat. for lunch and dinner, Sun.-Mon. lunch only. Espresso Europa (tel. 675-6806) is the town's hippest little hangout, with a range of coffee drinks, pastries, chessboards, art, and live music on weekends; open Mon.-Fri. 8 a.m.-midnight, Sat.-Sun. 4 p.m.-midnight (sometimes later).

Entertainment

Although Abilene is working hard to revitalize its downtown district and cultural life, it's still a fairly conservative town. So don't go looking for honky-tonks—the usual Texas nightlife is virtually nil.

The **Paramount Theater,** a beautifully restored 1930 Southwest Deco/Spanish/Moorish theater at 352 Cypress, hosts live theater, films, and concerts throughout the year under a faux canopy of drifting clouds and winking stars, rimmed by arches and twin-domed turrets. Listed on the National Registry of Historic Places, the theater was taken over by a private, non-profit group and restored in 1986. In May the theater sponsors the West Texas Film Festival. Self-guided tours are permitted Mon.-Fri. 1-5 p.m. Call (915) 676-9620 for a current schedule of performances.

Events

Two annual events draw people to Abilene. The first is the **Western Heritage Classic,** a real ranch rodeo that brings in working cowboys from 12 West Texas ranches, including the famous Pitchfork Ranch, for a May weekend of ranch-style celebrating. Rodeo events include bronc riding, team branding, team roping, cutting, wild cow milking, and a barrel race. The Classic also includes two cookoffs, one for chuckwagon meals cooked on open fires (the International Championship Campfire Cookoff) and one for barbecue (the Son-of-a-Gun Brisket Cookoff). Other activities include the Australian Shepherd Working Trials (a contest among ranch dogs), a mounted parade, and a longhorn steer trail drive. A Western art show, Western literature review, and Saturday night dance round out the weekend. All events are held in the Taylor County Expo Center on State 36. For scheduling information, call the Abilene Convention and Visitors Council at (915) 677-7241, or Taylor County Expo (tel. 677-4376).

A smaller, more local event is the **Chili Superbowl** that's held each Labor Day weekend at the Perini Ranch in Buffalo Gap. All proceeds from this event benefit the Ben Richey Boys Ranch. Call (915) 677-2781 for more information.

Shopping

Two shops in Abilene specialize in outfitting working cowboys with handmade goods. **James Leddy Boots** (tel. 915-677-7811) at 926 Ambler is a member of the famous bootmaking Leddy family; his custom-made boots start at $300 for basic cowhide and go over $2000 for something in exotic skins with extra hand-tooling. Leddy accepts visitors who just want to look around the shop. At nearby **Art Reed Custom Saddles** (tel. 677-4572), 904 Ambler, Art Reed makes saddles, tack, chaps, and belts. Reed even makes his own saddle trees (the wooden frame the saddle is sewn onto)—a rare skill among custom saddlemakers these days.

Under One Roof collects 35 antique vendors together at 244 Pine under, you bet, one roof. It's open Mon.-Sat. only. You'll also find antiques for sale in a cluster of old homes on Hickory Street's 500 to 700 blocks, a stretch known as **Historic Hickory Street.**

Information

The **Abilene Convention and Visitors Council** (tel. 915-677-7241), housed in the well-restored Texas & Pacific Railroad depot at 1101 N. 1st St., can provide information on sights, accommodations, dining, and activities in Abilene and the surrounding area. It's open Mon.-Fri. 8:30 a.m.-5 p.m., Saturday 10 a.m.-5 p.m., Sunday 1-5 p.m. Abilene's area code is 915.

WICHITA FALLS

Like Abilene, Wichita Falls grew up around a rail stop in the 1880s, but somehow the circuit preachers that came through town didn't stay on as they did in Abilene. Instead of churches, Wichita Falls raised saloons, and soon became known as "Whiskeytaw Falls." Today you can still get a "red draw" (a local invention consisting of beer and tomato juice) at any drinking establishment in town. The Wichita Falls economy is based on oil, wheat, and manufacturing, with the accent on oil. Sheppard Air Force Base, north of town, also contributes to city revenues.

There isn't much to see in Wichita Falls itself; for most Texas visitors, it's just a brief stop upon entering the state via I-44 from Oklahoma City. The waterfall that gave the town its name was destroyed by an 1886 flood, but in 1987 an artificial waterfall was constructed along the Wichita River to take its place (too many visitors were asking "Where's the falls?"). The new falls are 54 feet high, supposedly 10 times taller than the original.

Wichita Falls Railroad Museum
At the former Union Station site on 7th St. downtown is the nation's largest collection of rolling stock from the Missouri, Kansas & Texas Railroad, commonly known as "the Katy" in its heyday. Also on display are various other rail artifacts and memorabilia. The museum is open Saturday noon-4 p.m.or by appointment. Free admission. For further information, call (817) 322-2294.

Lake Arrowhead State Park
Lake Arrowhead is a Little Wichita River impoundment that covers 16,000 acres of what used to be an oil field. Folks around here like the oil business so much they've left oil derricks in the middle of the lake as ornamentation (anglers also say the fishing is best around the old derricks). Boating, swimming, waterskiing, picnicking, and camping are popular activities in the park, and there are a few nature trails as well. Forty-eight campsites with water and electricity are $9 a night; 19 sites with water only are $6 a night. Entry fee is $3 for vehicles, $1 for pedestrians and cyclists. Call (817) 528-2211 for campsite reservations or information.

Accommodations and Food
The **Best Western Towne Crest Inn** (tel. 817-322-1182 or 800-528-1234), 1601 8th St. two blocks west of US 82 S, has rooms for $30 s, $35-36 d. The trusty **Motel 6** (tel. 322-8817) is off I-44 at 1812 Maurine St. (Maurine exit) and costs $28 s, plus $4 per additional adult. The nearby **Days Inn** (tel. 723-5541), 1211 Central Fwy., Maurine exit I-44, has rooms for $36 s, $42-48 d. Also on Central Fwy., at No. 100 (Texas Tourist Bureau exit off I-44), is the **Wichita Falls Sheraton** (tel. 761-6000), where rooms are $59-72, the most expensive in town. Senior discounts available.

There's a **KOA Kampground** (tel. 569-3081) 15 miles north of town off I-44 (E. 3rd St. exit) where tent/camper sites are $14 a night, full hookups $17. **Wichita Bend RV Park** (tel. 761-7490), north of the Sheraton off I-44, offers two-way hookups (dump station available) for only $5 a night. **Shady Park RV and Travel** (tel. 723-1532), 2944 5th St. off US 277 west, has shaded spaces with full hookups and cable TV for $12-14 a night.

All the usual fast-food joints line up along I-44. **Hacienda Hernandez** (tel. 767-5932), 1105 Broadway, serves inexpensive Tex-Mex and American; open Mon.-Sat. for lunch and dinner. The **McBride Land & Cattle Co.** (tel. 692-2462), 501 Scott, has mesquite-grilled steaks and frog legs at moderate prices; open weekdays for lunch and dinner, weekends dinner only.

Events
Two large events held every August are the **Hotter 'n Hell One Hundred,** the largest 100-mile bicycle race in the U.S., and the **Texas Ranch Roundup,** in which ranch hands from around the state compete in events that display working-ranch skills, including saddle-bronc riding, horseshoeing, chuckwagon cooking, even fiddling and guitar-picking. The ranch team that accumulates the most points is awarded the title "Best Ranch in Texas."

Information
The Wichita County Heritage Society (tel. 817-723-0623), 900 Bluff St., distributes *A Drive Through History,* an annotated map of historical landmarks in the city that includes many buildings built around the turn of the century.

One of the Texas Highway Department's 12 tourist bureaus is on I-44 at the edge of town. A wealth of maps, brochures, newspapers, and information on Texas travel is available here seven days a week, 8 a.m.-5 p.m. The Wichita Falls area code is 817.

SAN ANGELO

One might think that a town of 90,000 out in the middle of central West Texas wouldn't have much to offer. But it's almost a secret that San Angelo (pronounced "sin-EN-jala" in local dialect) is in fact one of the most inhabitable towns north of the Hill Country. Unlike its counterparts to the west (Odessa and Midland) and to the north (Abilene and Wichita Falls), it's a vibrant city, mainly due to the fact the local economy isn't dependent on oil. Geography has been San Angelo's main savior; while some oil has been discovered in the area, the rocky Edwards Plateau environment is perfect for raising goats and sheep, and the town has become the U.S. wool and mohair capital. Four scenic rivers join here, the Main Concho, the North Concho, the South Concho, and the Middle Concho, and there are lakes on three sides of the city. The locals almost regard themselves as living on an island, not because of the surrounding rivers and lakes but because this is the only town of any size between Lubbock and San Antonio, a distance of 400 miles.

Anyone cutting diagonally across the state on US 87, which extends over 600 miles from Amarillo to the Gulf Coast, might consider spending a night or two here. Western history buffs shouldn't miss old Fort Concho, said to be the most well-preserved Western fort in the U.S., and Paint Rock, the country's largest Indian pictograph site. Concho Street, the town's original thoroughfare, serves as a focus for San Angelo tourism with restored architecture and shopping. The city is also famous for Concho River pearls, striking natural pearls found in mussels that live in the Concho River.

Climate

San Angelo has hot summers and short, fairly mild winters. June and July are the hottest months, with daytime high temperatures in the 90s and occasionally over 100 degrees. From December to February, average low temperatures are in the 30s and 40s (with an average of 42 days a year below freezing), average highs in the 50s and 60s. Precipitation runs roughly 24 inches per year, with showers most frequently occurring in the spring and late summer. As a San Angelo Convention and Visitors Bureau brochure states, "Contrary to fact, not all of West Texas is dry."

History

Although El Paso's Ysleta district is considered the oldest continually inhabited European settlement in Texas, Spanish missionaries settled San Angelo first. Franciscans established a Jumano Indian mission along the Main Concho River in 1632, but it lasted only six months. In 1650 the Spanish explorers Hernán Martín and Diego del Castillo traded with local Indians for Concho River pearls, some of which eventually found their way into the crown jewels of Spain. The name for the river, in fact, comes from the Spanish for "shell," *concho*. In the 18th century, Plains Indians came down from the north and made this part of the Edwards Plateau uninhabitable for Europeans until Fort Concho arrived on the scene in 1867. The fort was built at the junction of the Concho and Middle Concho rivers to protect mail routes and escort cattle drives.

San Angelo cowboys, 1887

FORT CONCHO HISTORICAL LANDMARK

The first sheep ranchers arrived in the area in 1877 and found the fort a ready market for wool. Around this time, pioneer Bart DeWitt planned a town to service the comings and goings of the military. The town, which DeWitt apparently named after his deceased wife Angela de la Garza, grew up across the North Concho from the fort. Records disagree as to whether it was originally called Saint Angela or Santa Angela but somehow people started calling the town San Angela; in the 1880s, postal authorities objected to the Spanish gender clash and changed the name to San Angelo.

In 1882 the U.S. Army's 16th Infantry headquarters were moved to Fort Concho, further increasing the fort's significance, and by 1884 there was a local building boom. Five years later, Fort Concho was abandoned as the Indian Wars came to a close, but by then San Angelo was well-established as a rough-and-ready ranching town.

SIGHTS

Fort Concho National Historic Landmark

An active frontier fort from 1867 to 1889, Fort

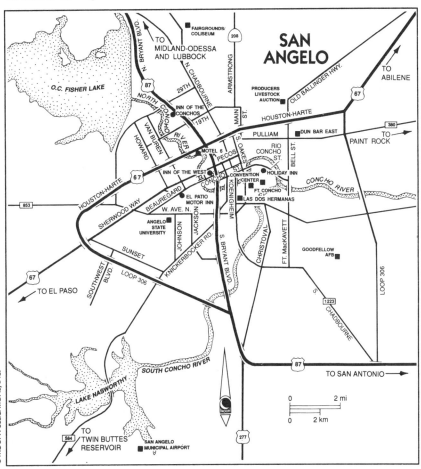

Concho housed eight companies in 40 buildings made of locally quarried limestone. Though abandoned over a century ago, the fort is still very much a center of San Angelo life. The townspeople have been painstakingly restoring the fort ever since the 1930s, and at this writing at least 25 buildings have been renovated. Members of the Fort Concho Museum Association hold on-site events throughout the year and publish the monthly *Fort Concho Members' Dispatch* as well as the *Concho River Review,* a journal of Texas and Southwestern literature, and the *Fort Concho and the South Plains Journal,* a historical journal and update of the national landmark's master plan.

Visitor facilities at the 20-acre fort, between Oakes and Burgess streets and avenues C and D, include the **San Angelo Museum of Fine Arts,** housed in the former quartermaster storehouse. The museum features rotating exhibits of historic and contemporary works of art, a lecture series, and a museum shop that sells crafts, books, cards, and unique children's toys. The museum is open Tues.-Sat. 10 a.m.-4 p.m.and Sunday 1-4 p.m. Admission is 75 cents adults, 25 cents children six to 17, free for children under six. For more information, call (915) 658-4084.

In Officers' Quarters No. 4, the new **E.H. Danner Museum of Telephony** contains a display of early phones and phone directories that chronicle the history of the telephone. Included in the collection are New York's first Bell Telephone list of subscribers (only one page long) and one of only two examples in existence of the original five models of the Gallows Frame Telephone designed by Alexander Graham Bell. The museum is open Tues.-Sat. 10 a.m.-5 p.m.and Sunday 1-5 p.m.; closed Monday. Admission is free.

Other buildings open to the public are collectively known as the **Fort Concho Museum** and include a restored infantry barracks, officers' quarters, hospital, and mess hall. Open Tues.-Sat. 10 a.m.-5 p.m., Sunday 1-5 p.m.; admission is $1.25 adults, 75 cents for active military and students, free for children under six. For more information, call 657-4444.

The **Fort Concho Living History Program** has enlisted around 60 San Angelo volunteers who recreate frontier military life at Fort Concho events as well as elsewhere in the state. The 60 men belong to four historic Fort Concho units: the 11th and 16th Infantry Regiments, the 4th Cavalry Regiment, and the Buffalo Soldiers or 10th Cavalry Regiment, an all-black unit. The program is dedicated to an authentic appearance, including uniforms and gear as well as training maneuvers.

Yearly Fort Concho events include Black History Month (February); Sabers, Saddles, and

*lowering the flag,
Fort Concho*

FORT CONCHO HISTORICAL LANDMARK

Spurs (May); Frontier Day (part of Fiesta del Concho in June); U.S. Independence Day (July 4); Fiestas Patrias (Mexican Independence Day, September 16); and Christmas at Old Fort Concho (December).

Miss Hattie's Bordello Museum

Around the turn of the century, Concho St. was a strip of saloons and bordellos, or "parlor houses." Miss Hattie's was established in 1896 and stayed in business until 1946 when Texas Rangers shut it down. During its time, Miss Hattie's was one of many bordellos in San Angelo, but was considered the most elegant. Miss Mona's Chicken Ranch in La Grange (East Texas), immortalized as "The Best Little Whorehouse in Texas," wasn't nearly as swank an establishment—Miss Hattie's even had an underground tunnel to the bank next door. Once the place closed, it was boarded up and abandoned until a local woman bought the building in 1976 and found that all the period furnishings were still there. It's now a museum, and you can wander through the front parlor of velvet and lace and into the 10 bedrooms where the women plied their trade amidst oak-and-brass beds, satin sheets, and Oriental rugs. The largest room belonged to a blonde prostitute named Goldie, who was the highest draw and charged a steep $2. Miss Hattie herself lived on in San Angelo until she passed away in 1982 at the age of 104.

The museum is at 18 E. Concho and is open Tues.-Sat. 9:30 a.m.-4 p.m. Admission is $2.

Concho River Walk

A well-maintained, 4.5-mile walking/jogging trail parallels the Concho River and passes by several hotels, shady pecan trees, the convention center, the River Stage (outdoor entertainment), and Sunken Garden Park, a small botanical garden. The highlight of the River Walk is a 1.5-mile section between Concho St. and the 1st St. dam, where there's a series of brick plazas, fountains, falls, and walkways that incorporate native stone. The newest attractions on the River Walk are the **Celebration Bridge,** a footbridge linking the downtown area with the historic fort district and dedicated to the people of San Angelo, and "The Pearl of the Concho," a sculpture of a mermaid holding a Concho pearl shell. A few fortunate residents have large, his-

San Angelo stockyards

toric houses overlooking the river—all future residential construction has been banned.

Producers Livestock Auction

San Angelo has the second-largest cattle auction in Texas and the largest sheep and goat auction in the United States. Sheep and goats are auctioned weekly on Tuesday starting around 9 a.m., while cattle sales take place Thursday at the same time. Visitors are welcome to sit at the indoor auction ring and watch, or walk along the catwalks above the outdoor pens. The stockyards are at the north end of Bell St. just after it forks left from Old Ballinger Highway.

Civic League Park

The water lily display at this park at the corner of Harris Ave. and Park St. features lilies from all over the world, including several rare and endangered species. The Victoria, the world's largest water lily, develops pads reaching up to eight feet in diameter; this amazing lily blooms daily at dusk. Most of the lily varieties here reach their floral peak between March and September. According to the San Angelo Convention and Visitors Bureau, the best viewing time is 10:30 a.m.-2:30 p.m.

Aermotor Windmill

San Angelo is the home of the last American windmill manufacturer, Aermotor; there aren't more than three windmill manufacturers left in the world. The first Aermotor windmill was the final result of over 5,000 steel windmill experiments conducted by Thomas Perry in Chicago in the 1880s. His wheel was 87% more efficient than the best wooden wheels in use at that time, but he sold only 45 units in 1888, the first year it was on the market. By 1892, the Aermotor was the definitive "mathematical windmill," as windmills became a popular way to pump water on farms and ranches all over the United States and in the world. The company made a considerable fortune until the 1960s when windmills fell out of fashion, so in 1969 the company moved to Argentina, where demand remained high. Ten years later it was purchased by another company and moved to Arkansas, where it stayed until 1986 when another group of investors bought the company and moved the factory to San Angelo. Aermotor now makes six sizes of windmills, ranging in diameter from six to 16 feet. The plant is located at 4277 Dan Hanks Lane; visitors are welcome to tour the plant if they call ahead (tel. 915-651-4951).

Paint Rock

Thirty miles west of San Angelo, close to the north banks of the Concho River, is a long set of limestone cliffs that are a virtual Indian art gallery. For thousands of years the site was a favorite camping area for nomadic tribes, since the river provided water, game was plentiful, and the cliffs could be used not only as shelter but as a bison run-off, in which Indians would chase herds of bison over the cliffs. The cliffs also provided the perfect stone canvas for Indian pictographs as well as the materials for making paint. Their palette consisted of red, made from a mixture of bear or buffalo fat and powdered hematite; yellow, from geodes and ochers; and black, from charcoal and manganese oxide. An estimated 1,500 images decorate the site, including such standouts as winged serpents, Indian shields, shamanic figures, comets, a propellered sun, running bison, and Spanish missionaries.

The land surrounding the pictograph site is owned by Kay Campbell, whose grandparents settled at Paint Rock in the 1880s. Her small tour operation, **Paint Rock Excursions,** has an office in the little town of Paint Rock, at the intersection of FM 380/180 and US 83. To view the pictographs, you must take a guided tour with her or a member of her family. The tour takes about an hour and proceeds along a trail about 50 feet below the bluff. Kay usually provides a paint-making demonstration before or after the tour, grinding hematite to a powder with flint and then mixing it with oil in an Indian paint pot (river stones with eroded depressions or holes). Tours are available during the summer Mon.-Sat. 9 a.m.-4 p.m., Sunday 1-5 p.m., on weekends only from April to May and Labor Day to Thanksgiving at the same times. For information or reservations, call (915) 732-4418 on weekends, 721-4376 on weekdays.

Angelo State University

Around 6,400 students are enrolled in the undergraduate and graduate programs here. ASU has been listed in *US News and World Report*'s guide to the country's best colleges as one of a few "up and comers." The planetarium is said to be one of the best in the state. Off Ave. N between Johnson and Rosemont.

Goodfellow Air Force Base

Southeast of town, Goodfellow is headquarters for U.S. Air Force Intelligence, a training site for other military espionage branches, and a major local employer. Not open to the public (naturally).

ACCOMMODATIONS

Hotels and Motels

Three places near the river include **Motel 6** (tel. 915-658-8061), 311 N. Bryant Blvd., $26-32; the **Best Western Inn of the West** (tel. 653-2995), 415 W. Beauregard, $41-47; and the **Holiday Inn Convention Center** (tel. 658-2828), 441 Rio Concho Dr., $55-75.

The clean and comfortable **El Patio Motor Inn** (tel. 655-5711), at 1901 W. Beauregard, has large rooms for $31 s, $35 d. Another good value, the friendly **Inn of the Conchos** (tel. 658-2811 or 800-621-6041), offers very sharp rooms for $36-42. For something less expensive, try the centrally located **Corner Inn** (tel. 653-1351) at 402 W. Beauregard, where basic but clean rooms cost $20-25.

Bed and Breakfasts

Two moderately priced B&Bs in the Paint Rock area offer rooms for $35-45 a night including breakfast. **Chaparral Ranch Bed & Breakfast** (tel. 915-732-4225), RR 1, Box 20, San Angelo, TX 76866, is near the Concho River and two creeks; rooms in a large ranch house with a fireplace and rock floor cost $40-45. **Lipan Ranch Bed & Breakfast** (tel. 468-2571), RR 1, Box 21C, San Angelo, TX 76866, offers rooms with TV and kitchenettes for $35 s plus $10 for each additional guest. Nonsmoking rooms are available at Lipan Ranch.

Camping

Twin Buttes Marina (tel. 915-949-2651), four miles west of town off US 67, has a campground where full hookups are $12.50; other facilities include boat ramps, marina, and dumpsite. **Spring Creek Marina** (tel. 944-3850) at 45 Fisherman's Rd. on Lake Nasworthy has full hookups plus cable TV for $15 a night. The San Angelo **KOA Kampground** (tel. 949-3242) is off Knickerbocker Rd. (FM 584) three miles west of Loop 306. Tentsites are $11, RV sites are $15.50 without hookups, $16.50 with w/e, $15.50 with full hookup.

FOOD

Like most of upper West Texas, steak is king in San Angelo. Locals say the best steak is served at **Twin Mountain Steakhouse** (tel. 915-949-4239), two miles west of town on US 67 (Mertzon Hwy.). The specialty here is "scraps"—called "tenders" on the menu—small choice cuts of steak. Twin Mountain also serves chicken and seafood. Open for dinner nightly except Sunday. A competitor for best local steakhouse is **Zentner's Daughter Steak House** (tel. 949-

2821) at 1901 Knickerbocker across from the San Angelo Stadium. Open daily except Sunday for lunch and dinner.

The hot spot for Tex-Mex is the inexpensive **Mejor Que Nada** ("Better Than Nothing") at 1911 S. Bryant (tel. 655-3553), in a former gas station. Open daily except Sunday for lunch and dinner. A personal favorite, and even cheaper, is **Las Dos Hermanas** (tel. 655-6057) at 1406 S. Chadbourne, open daily 7 a.m.-10 p.m.—great *desayuno* (Mexican breakfast) for under $3. On Sunday Hermanas serves *caldo* and menudo. Also good for Mexican is the diner-style **Fuente's Cafe** (tel. 658-2430), at 101 S. Chadbourne and Broadway downtown. Open daily except Sunday 10 a.m.-10 p.m.

Mexican and steaks are what San Angelo restaurants do best, but there is also an excellent downhome-style place near the Producers Livestock Auction called **Dun Bar East** (tel. 655-8780), 1728 Pulliam. Catfish, chicken-fried steak, and liver and onions are the specialties of the house, along with delicious homemade pies and cornbread. Open Tues.-Sun. 6 a.m.-10 p.m.; on auction days the lunch crowd gets pretty thick.

A Taste of Italy (tel. 944-3290), 3520 Knickerbocker, Southwest Plaza, serves good Italian food weekdays for lunch and dinner, Saturday dinner only. Closed Sunday.

ENTERTAINMENT

For over a hundred years, San Angelo has enjoyed a reputation as a wide-open town; an early sheepman once wrote it was "overrun with drink saloons, gambling dens, and dance houses of the lowest class." It still has an unusually large number of clubs for a town its size, from little honky-tonk bars to huge dance halls. The big rockin' cowboy spots are **Texas,** at 4611 S. Jackson, and the **Little River Club,** at 2502 Loop 306. These two feature mostly "aggressive country" crossover bands.

Caraway's, in "Block One" on historic E. Concho St., is a popular piano bar that's not as formal as the term implies—it's more New Orleans than New York. Caraway's is housed in the former San Angelo National Bank building, the bank that had the tunnel to Miss Hattie's bordello. **Tierra Linda** (tel. 915-653-8235) at 2401

N. Chadbourne hosts live *conjunto, tropicale,* and *tejano* bands.

Santa Fe Junction (tel. 658-5068) at 1524 S. Bryant offers straight-ahead rock—recorded during the week, live on weekends. **Maxx 2000** (tel. 949-6766) at 3520 Knickerbocker Rd. is a popular dance club for recorded top 40 and rock 'n' roll Thurs.-Sat. nights.

EVENTS

March
The **San Angelo Stock Show and Rodeo** features a PRCA-sponsored rodeo, livestock shows, country music, and arts and crafts at the Coliseum Fairgrounds (tel. 915-942-1900).

May
Sabers, Saddles, and Spurs focuses on the Fort Concho Equestrian Review, featuring polo, cavalry drills, and displays of horsemanship. The San Angelo Saddle Club has one of the best polo teams in the state. Held on the Fort Concho parade grounds (tel. 915-658-4084).

June
Fiesta del Concho is the city's biggest festival and is centered on the Concho River from the second weekend in June through the third weekend. Activities include barge rides, arts and crafts, food vendors, armadillo races, a parade, and a Western dance. On the second Saturday, Frontier Day is held at Fort Concho with the Living History Program in full swing. Call (915) 655-4136 for more information.

September
Fiestas Patrias Celebrates Mexican independence during the second week of September at Fort Concho. Parades, Mexican food, music, and dance.

December
Christmas at Old Fort Concho is a community-wide effort that always takes place the first weekend in December. The officers' quarters are decorated according to themes in Fort Concho's cultural history, e.g., Victorian House, Early Texas House, Mexican House, German House, Czech House, Arc Light Saloon, and an "Officer's Christ-

mas." Each house is candlelit and staffed by volunteers in period costume; food is served, too, with the Czech House usually providing the greatest bounty. Other events include a children's tea party, a "Christmas Comida," caroling, a historical pageant on the parade grounds, a melodrama matinee, a live nativity, and Sunday Christmas dinner. A huge tent is erected on the parade grounds for the weekend to house craft demonstrations and food vendors.

RECREATION

The main sources of outdoor activity in San Angelo are the three lakes within 30 minutes' drive of town. **O.C. Fisher Reservoir** (tel. 915-949-4757) is three miles northwest of town off FM 2288 (Mercedes St.) and is sometimes called Lake San Angelo or North Concho Lake. It's a 12,700-acre impoundment of the North Concho River, built and maintained by the U.S. Army Corps of Engineers. There are 20 boat launches along the south shore and the lake is well-fished for walleye; crappie; sunfish; white and black bass; smallmouth; and channel, flathead, and yellow catfish. Swimming and picnicking are popular activities in the warmer months. Boat rentals are available at Spring Creek Marina. The four camping areas around the lake are Dry Creek Park ($7 tent, $9 w/e), Grandview Park (primitive, free), Highland Range Park (primitive, free), and Red Arroyo Park ($7 tent, $9 w/e). All campsites have a 14-day limit.

Lake Nasworthy (tel. 944-3850) is six miles southwest of town off FM 584 (Knickerbocker Rd.) and covers 1,500 acres, fed by the South Concho River. The black bass fishing here is very good. Two camping areas: Spring Creek Marina Park (full hookups available, $12) and Middle Concho (primitive sites, no fee).

Twin Buttes Reservoir is actually two lakes totaling 10,000 acres connected by a canal, just south of Lake Nasworthy off US 67. The larger northern section is fed by Spring Creek and the Middle Concho River while the smaller southern section is fed by the South Concho River. Hybrid striped bass and blue catfish are big here. Recreational facilities are more developed than at either of the other two area lakes. Primitive tentsites are $2 a night, $5 with electricity. See

"Accommodations" for details on the Twin Buttes Marina campground.

SHOPPING

Concho Pearls
The rare Concho pearl is found only in the Concho River complex of West Texas, most especially in the "sweetwater" vicinity of San Angelo. It's a product of a native river mussel that was once an Indian food staple; there are 12 or more mussel species in the Concho system, but only one, *Cyrtonaias tampicoenis,* produces pearls. In the 17th century, Spanish explorers traded with local Indians for the Concho pearls, which vary in color from a soft pink to a deep lavender. Today's Texans find the huge, leathery mussels unpalatable, but the pearls are more highly prized than ever. Size varies from a couple of millimeters to around 6.5 mm. Several jewelry shops in town carry the pearls loose, in strands, and in gold settings. One shop that specializes in Concho pearls is **Bart Mann Originals** (tel. 915-653-2902) at 105 S. Irving. All jewelry designed and crafted on the premises.

Boots
Famous bootmaker M.L. Leddy came to San Angelo in 1936, purchased Mercer Boot Co., and enjoyed much local success. Generations later, there are three boot shops that claim to be direct descendants of the original: **M.L. Leddy Boots & Saddles** (tel. 915-942-7655), 2200 W. Beauregard, in the Village Shopping Center; **J.L. Mercer & Son Boots** (tel. 658-7634), 224 S. Chadbourne; and **Rusty Franklin Boot Co.** (tel. 655-7784), 3275 Arden Road. All make custom boots that start at around $350.

Saddles and Saddleblankets
M.L. Leddy's custom saddles start at the customary $1000. The most venerable saddlery in town is the **R.E. Donaho Saddle Shop** (tel. 915-655-3270), which has been doing a steady business since 1890—Pancho Villa had his saddle work done here. Donaho's most famous model is the Concho Saddle, a cross between Mexican and Western styles. Prices start at $1000 for a basic working saddle. At 8 E. Concho, near Miss Hattie's.

Since San Angelo is a wool center, saddleblankets are a popular item. Probably the best selection is at **Ingrid's** (tel. 732-4370 or 800-752-8004) in Paint Rock at the intersection of FM 380/180 and US 83. Custom floor rugs and wallhangings as well. Ingrid Haas also maintains a branch San Angelo shop, **Haas Hand-Weaving,** at 242 E. Main in an 1888 building that housed the White Elephant Saloon till 1917.

Antiques
Most of the town's antique stores are clustered on E. Concho, including **Adobe Red Antiques** at no.

R.E. Donaho saddle shop

33, and **Concho Confetti** (also a tea room) at no. 42. North Chadbourne St. is another area of antique shops, with **Sunshine Place** at no. 226, **Doris' Den of Antiquities** at no. 1901, **Concho Rarities** at no. 1911, **The White Elephant** at no. 2613, and **S&R Trading Post** at no. 4736.

Art

The **Chicken Farm Art Center** (tel. 915-653-4936) is a chicken farm that's been converted into artists' studios and galleries. Visitors are welcome to watch local artists at work or peruse works of art for sale. At 2505 Martin Luther King off US 87 N; take 23rd St. east to Martin Luther King.

Jalapeños

At **Sam Lewis and Assoc.** (tel. 915-658-1432) you can stock up on jalapeño-flavored lollipops, jalapeño-stuffed olives, jalapeño peanut brittle, and many other food items made with the fiery pepper. Owner "Jalapeño Sam" also serves as president of the World Armadillo Breeding and Racing Association; if he's around the shop, chances are good you'll have a chance to pet a live armadillo. At 420 N. Van Buren.

INFORMATION

Tourist Office

The **San Angelo Convention and Visitors Bureau** (tel. 915-655-1206 or 800-375-1206) is at 500 Rio Concho Dr. and is open Mon.-Fri. 8:30

a.m.-5 p.m. Staff hand out plenty of free brochures and maps for visitors and can also arrange tours. The **San Angelo Chamber of Commerce** office is in the same building. On weekends, visitor information is available at the Fort Concho Museum.

Telephone

San Angelo has a 915 area code.

VICINITY OF SAN ANGELO

Fort McKavett State Historic Site

Old Fort McKavett is about 75 miles southeast of San Angelo in Menard County. The fort was established in 1852 as the "Camp on the San Saba" by five companies of the 8th Infantry, named in honor of an 8th Infantry colonel killed in the War with Mexico's Battle of Monterrey. As with Fort Concho and other West Texas forts, Fort McKavett served as a first line of de-

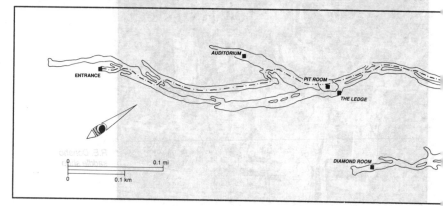

fense against Indian raids along the Texas frontier and provided protection for travelers along the Upper San Antonio-El Paso Trail. Later in the 1850s, the 8th Infantry was joined by the 2nd Dragoons and the 1st Infantry, but when area Indian activity declined, the fort was temporarily abandoned in 1859.

In 1868 the post was reestablished by the 4th Cavalry after local residents lobbied for Army protection against renewed Indian attacks. The 4th Cavalry was soon replaced by a company of black troops, the 38th Infantry, and out of that unit and the 41st, the famous 24th Infantry was organized at McKavett in 1869. All four of the Army's black units, whose members came to be known as "Buffalo Soldiers" by the Indians, eventually served at McKavett, including the 9th and 10th cavalries. Of all the frontier forts, McKavett is said to have had the best site—built high on a hill on the banks of the San Saba River in the shade of oak and pecan groves. Soldiers were able to supplement the basic Army diet of beans and salt pork by fishing in the river and cultivating vegetables in the river's floodplain. As at Fort Concho, a settlement of camp followers established itself on the opposite bank of the river, known at Fort McKavett as "Scabtown."

The fort was abandoned at the end of the Indian Wars in 1883 and civilians took over the buildings. Because the fort structures have been in continuous use since the 1850s, they're in better condition than most. Fourteen buildings of the original 40 have been restored, including the officers' quarters, barracks, hospital, school,

bakery, and post headquarters. Seven other buildings are in ruins, and the rest are gone. The hospital ward serves as a visitor center and contains interpretive exhibits that explain the natural and military history of the area. A nature trail leads to the old fort kiln and the "Government Springs."

The fort sponsors two events each year: on the third Saturday in February is a reenactment of 1870s civilian life at the fort, complete with saloon and stores. while the third Saturday in March is devoted to a reenactment of 19th-century military life.

To approach the fort from San Angelo, take US 277 43 miles south to US 190, then east 30 miles to FM 864, then southwest about six miles on FM 864 to the small town of Fort McKavett (pop. 105, many of them retirees who take advantage of the excellent San Saba fishing).

Fort McKavett (tel. 915-396-2358) is open Wed.-Sun. 8 a.m.-5 p.m. from Labor Day to Memorial Day, then daily 9 a.m.-6 p.m. the remainder of the year. Admission is $2 for adults, $1 for children 6-12, children under six free.

The Caverns of Sonora
This cave is among many in the Lower Cretaceous Edwards Limestone found throughout the Edwards Plateau region, but nothing compares with the speleological beauty found here. The cave was in fact kept secret for several years after its discovery in 1955 by Dallas spelunkers who feared the cave would be overrun. The founder of the American Speleological So-

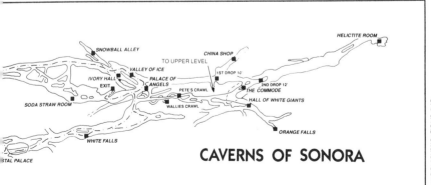

CAVERNS OF SONORA

© MOON PUBLICATIONS, INC.

ciety has said the Sonora caverns are "the most indescribably beautiful caverns in the world. Their beauty can't possibly be exaggerated—even by Texans."

The cave is one of the state's longest, with nearly eight miles (an estimate, since mapping isn't yet complete) of passages through seven levels. The lower levels are the most striking, since they're still actively producing cave formations; these formations run the gamut of all known types, including some found nowhere else. Some are luminous and phosphorescent, some are crystalline and transparent, and all have shape-inspired names like "The Mummy," "The Passing Quarterback," and "The Ice Cream Cone." Some passages contain solid flowstone that covers the walls, floor, and ceiling, a rarity. Long "soda straws" or tubular stalactites up to six feet long but only a quarter inch in diameter are common in some passages. In the "Christmas Tree Room" are stalagmite formations known as coral trees. One of the most amazing rooms is full of helictites, bursting star-like formations formed by a water flow that's so slow gravity doesn't affect the random shape, as the crystals emanate outward in all directions. Looking around, it's hard not to imagine you're standing in a world made of rock candy.

Tours through the cave are managed by a private enterprise, which means you have to put up with a somewhat tacky entrance and souvenir shop on the way in. The tour takes visitors through a mile and a half of the cave, a 1.5 to two-hour walk. The temperature in the cave is a constant 70° F with 98% relative humidity, so even in winter it can be a bit clammy. The lowest point on the walk is 150 feet and the highest is 2,230 feet, so the walk involves some elevation change. Tours are led from the souvenir shop seven days a week about every half hour, 8 a.m.-6 p.m. May-Sept., 9 a.m.-5 p.m. the rest of the year. Admission is $8 per adult, $6 children 6-11, under six free. A covered wagon dinner theater is held Fri.-Sat. nights from mid-June through mid-August.

Outside the cave are picnic and camping areas. Overnight fee for tent campers is $6; for RVs it's $13. For more information contact Caverns of Sonora (tel. 915-387-3105 or 387-6507), Box 213, Sonora, TX 76950. Sonora is 65 miles south of San Angelo via US 277; to reach the caverns head west eight miles from Sonora along I-10 and exit at RR 1989, then follow the signs eight more miles to the entrance.

Accommodations and Food: You can put up at the two-story **Devil's River Inn** (tel. 915-387-9928) on I-10 (exit 400). Tidy rooms with cable TV and free local calls cost $45-60; there's a pool and coin laundry on the premises.

DEL RIO

Texans will argue over whether Del Rio is in West Texas or South Texas. The truth is it's a little of both. The Pecos River is less than an hour's drive west of town; terrain-wise, the Edwards Plateau meets the eastern edge of the Chihuahuan Desert here; it's at the same latitude as San Antonio (South Central Texas) yet west of San Angelo (usually considered West Texas). One thing's for sure, it's a long way from anywhere else—the nearest towns of any size are San Angelo (150 miles), Laredo (180 miles), and San Antonio (153 miles).

For many visitors to Texas, it's just a stopover on US 90 between San Antonio and Big Bend. Savvy Texans, however, know that Acuña, Amistad National Recreation Area, and Seminole Canyon make Del Rio a worthwhile destination in its own right. Nearby Brackettville and Langtry are worthy side trips, too. "Winter Texans" have also discovered the Del Rio area, and an increasing number are coming here to avoid the winter crowds in Harlingen-Brownsville and McAllen.

Once away from the new developments along the highway, Del Rio boasts a pleasant selection of shady, tree-lined streets and older residential and downtown architecture.

Climate

July and August are the hottest months, with average high temperatures in the mid-90s and overnight lows in the 70s. Coolest months are December and January, when average lows are around 40° F. Average annual precipitation for the area is 23 inches, with spring and late summer months receiving the most rain.

History

Del Rio was originally settled by Spanish missionaries who arrived on St. Philip's Day in 1635 and named their mission San Felipe del Rio. Archaeological evidence suggests the area around Del Rio, in particular the canyons of the Rio Grande and Pecos River, have been inhabited for at least 12,000 years. Indian pictographs that remain on canyon walls are 4,000-8,000 years old.

The Indians who resided in the area when the Spanish arrived were probably Coahuiltecans; whoever they were, they didn't submit to missionization and the San Felipe mission was short-lived. The Coahuiltecans mysteriously disappeared sometime during the 18th century and the area was abandoned until the 1850s when Fort Clark was established in nearby Brackettville to protect the San Antonio-El Paso Trail. As the area became "pacified," Anglo-American speculators became interested in the land around San Felipe Springs, which then, as now, pumped around 90 million gallons of water a day from the rocky ground. The springs were an important water stop for stagecoaches on the San Antonio-San Diego route (which connected with the Chihuahua Trail as well) and for the U.S. Camel Corps during their Big Bend surveys. In 1869, five men formed an irrigation company, sold shares, and established

rancher in wool chaps, circa 1890

COURTESY FORT CONCHO MUSEUM.

farming homesteads. By the mid 1870s, San Felipe del Rio was still nothing more than a collection of adobe huts with thatched roofs; building materials were difficult to bring in since the town was in the middle of a burgeoning haven for Comanches and Mexican bandits.

A Fort Clark cavalry outpost called Camp del Rio was established nearby in 1876 and by the mid-1880s was abandoned as the Indian Wars came to a close. But what contributed most to the town's development was the meeting of the Southern Pacific and the Galveston, Harrisburg, and San Antonio railroads in 1883 at a nearby junction. After the commemorative silver spike was driven into the rails, Del Rio was connected to the outside world and began prospering almost immediately. Irrigated farming expanded; the post office shortened the town name to Del Rio, so as not to confuse it with another Texas town, San Felipe de Austin.

As Del Rio is on the edge of the Edwards Plateau—an environment perfect for cloven-hoofed livestock—sheep and goat ranches moved in and the town has become a major contender for the national "wool and mohair capital" title along with San Angelo farther north. Another boon to Del Rio development was the impounding of the Rio Grande, Pecos, and Devils rivers behind Amistad International Dam in the 1960s, which created one of the largest lakes in the United States. This not only added to the availability of water for irrigation, hydroelectric, and other utilitarian purposes, it made Del Rio and Acuña recreational centers on both sides of the border; the lake was nearly a thousand miles of shoreline.

The latest development has been the establishment of *maquiladoras* or "twin plants," American-owned factories located in or near Acuña on the Mexican side, which have helped to expand Del Rio's population to its current 35,000. Acuña has about three times as many people.

Another claim to fame for Del Rio-Acuña is that two famous radio figures broadcast their shows from a "pirate" radio station, XER, on the Mexican side of the border. The first was Dr. John R. Brinkley, the infamous goat gland surgeon of the '30s; the second was rock 'n' roll DJ Wolfman Jack in the late '50s and early '60s. The facility was set up so announcers could operate out of a Del Rio studio while the 500,000-watt transmitter—with a signal that reached all the way to Canada—was actually located in Acuña, thus circumventing FCC licensing. Mexican radio still rules the airwaves in this part of Texas.

SIGHTS

Historic Buildings
Del Rio has an unusually high percentage of buildings still standing from the late 1800s, some built by Italian stonemasons. The Gothic-style **Sacred Heart Church,** at 310 Mill St. downtown, was built in 1892. Nearby at 400 Pecan St. is the **Val Verde County Courthouse,** a huge Victorian built in 1887 of native limestone. At 1901 S. Main is the **Chris Qualia Home,** an 1898 Victorian with gingerbread and cupolas.

South of Canal St. is a residential area lined with historic old homes, including the **Second Taini Home** at 1100 S. Main, which Taini built for his family in 1904. The **Taylor-Rivers House** at 100 Hudson Dr. was built in 1870 of adobe and is the oldest existing house in Del Rio.

The **Brinkley Mansion** on Qualia Dr., past the Val Verde Winery, is not so old—it was built in 1929—but is an impressive monument to probably the biggest medical fraud ever perpetrated in North America. "Dr." Brinkley (none of his claimed medical degrees were ever recognized by the AMA) built an empire on the "Brinkley operation," goat gland transplants for men that were supposed to preserve or restore virility. Woodrow Wilson supposedly asked to have one performed in secret. In the '30s, the city allowed Brinkley to establish a clinic in the Hotel Roswell downtown. Del Rio civic leaders still won't admit they harbored a fraud and a fugitive (fleeing indictments in Kansas and California), because they're still trying to save face and because they're grateful for his local philanthropy, which included donations to hospitals and schools. And of course, what would have become of the late Wolfman Jack (and rock 'n' roll) if Brinkley hadn't established the most powerful radio station on the continent?

San Felipe District
Across the Old San Felipe Canal to the south is the traditionally Mexican district of San Felipe; drive through here and you may think you've crossed the border. This is also one of the oldest parts of town; **Brown Plaza,** at Cantu and Cis-

neros, was a favorite gathering place for Mexican residents at the turn of the century. Nowadays it's been co-opted by the community for local celebrations of all types.

Val Verde Winery

Established in 1883 by Italian immigrant Frank Qualia and still run by the Qualia family, Val Verde is the oldest winery in Texas. During Prohibition it was one of the only licensed wineries in the country. The 18-inch-thick adobe walls provide a cave-like atmosphere for the aging process, accomplished in French white-oak barrels; total output is around 7,000 gallons a year. The first vinifera the Qualias planted, a "Lenoir" variety from Madeira, is still the the winery's mainstay. The lenoir is a smooth, dry table red, similar to other Spanish varietals. Val Verde also produces a ruby cabernet (doesn't quite compare with the cabernets from Texas's Llano Estacado region or from Northern California), a dry and a semisweet herbemont (light and nutty), an ehrenfelser (okay), a Texas blush (okay), and an award-winning tawny port (good). Wine prices are quite reasonable. The winery offers free tours and winetasting Mon.-Sat. 9 a.m.-5 p.m. at 100 Qualia Dr. (tel. 210-775-9714).

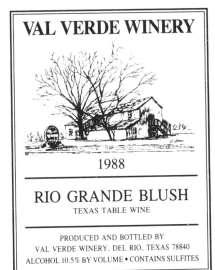

VAL VERDE WINERY

1988

RIO GRANDE BLUSH
TEXAS TABLE WINE

PRODUCED AND BOTTLED BY
VAL VERDE WINERY, DEL RIO, TEXAS 78840
ALCOHOL 10.5% BY VOLUME • CONTAINS SULFITES

Whitehead Memorial Museum

The Whiteheads are a local ranching family who bought the old 1870s Perry Store to preserve it from demolition in the early '60s. They turned it into a museum that now encompasses several buildings on the same lot, including an Indian chapel, a log cabin, a barn, the Hal Patton Labor Office, and yet another replica of Judge Roy Bean's Jersey Lilly Saloon (which makes three—one each in Pecos and Del Rio, plus the original in Langtry). The judge himself and his son Sam are buried on the museum grounds. Each of the nine museum buildings contains exhibits related to area history; probably the most interesting is the exhibit on the Black Seminoles in the Patton building, along with the Indian religious art in the chapel.

The recently added **Cadena Nativity,** a Mexican-style *nacimiento* created by local craftsperson Beatrice Cadena, extends 32 feet and contains nearly 1,900 individually fashioned elements (including 605 figurines), running streams, and campfires. At 1308 S. Main St., tel. (210) 774-7568. Open Tues.-Sat. 9 a.m.-4:30 p.m.; admission $2 adults, 50 cents children.

The Firehouse

This 1932 building at 120 E. Garfield was originally a combination city hall, jail, and firehouse. Today it's headquarters for the Del Rio Council for the Arts (tel. 210-775-0888 or 774-5454), which provides gallery space for regional artists and offers classes in fine arts, crafts, Spanish, dance, and music. The gallery features rotating exhibits including a Western art show in May associated with the annual bullriding competition.

Ciudad Acuña

Across the Rio Grande from Del Rio via Spur 277 (Garfield/Las Vacas) is one of the Texas-Mexico border's least spoiled and cleanest towns. Acuña (Ciudad means "City") is just large enough (100,000) to be of varied interest to the casual visitor, yet small and remote enough to have escaped the Nuevo Laredo-Juárez "fleece-the-gringo" syndrome. Founded as a military encampment in 1877, the town is named for revolutionary Mexican poet Manuel Acuña and belongs to the Mexican state of Coahuila, which was itself once part of the larger Mexican state Coahuila y Texas. Perhaps because of this

DEL RIO-CIUDAD ACUÑA

TO
LAKE
AMISTAD

NATIONAL PARKS
SERVICE OFFICE

377
277
90

MOTEL 6
RAMADA INN
LA QUINTA
BEST WESTERN LA SIESTA
DESERT HILLS MOTEL

CHAMBER OF COMMERCE/
CONVENTION AND VISITORS BUREAU

VAL VERDE COUNTY FAIRGROUNDS/
VAL VERDE DOWNS RACETRACK

SAN FELIPE CREEK

SAN FELIPE
SPRINGS

SAN FELIPE
SPRINGS RD.

TO
SAN
ANTONIO

17th ST.
14th ST.
9th ST.

AVE. H
AVE. F
BEDELL AVE.
N. MAIN ST.
AVE. G
AVE. Q

BEST WESTERN INN
OF DEL RIO

DEL RIO
INTERNATIONAL
AIRPORT

90

E. RODRIQUEZ

GARFIELD

MARGARITE AVE.

277

FIRE HOUSE
(DEL RIO COUNCIL
FOR THE ARTS)

3RD ST.

GIBBS
OGDEN
BROADWAY
GRINER
NICHOLSON
FARLEY LN.
CIENEGAS RD.

S. MAIN ST.

MEMO'S

CANTU
PECAN
RODRIQUEZ

BROADBENT AVE.

TO
EAGLE
PASS

DEL RIO

BROWN PLAZA

WHITEHEAD
MEMORIAL
MUSEUM

VAL VERDE
WINERY

HUDSON DR.

239
277

QUALIA DR.

BRINKLEY
MANSION

TO AMISTAD DAM

LOOP RD.

CARRETERA
PRESA AMISTAD

HIDALGO
MADERO
GALEANA
VICTORIA

CROSBY'S RESTAURANT
& BAR

PLAZA CANALES

MATAMOROS
MORELOS
BLVD. GUERRERO

CIUDAD ACUÑA

MEXICO

RIO GRANDE

TEXAS

1988

0   1 mi
0   1 km

© MOON PUBLICATIONS, INC.

shared past, Acuña and Del Rio seem particularly compatible border sisters. Former UT student Robert Rodríguez chose Acuña for the location shooting of his film *El Mariachi*, a cult favorite produced for a budget of $7000.

The town's social center is shady Plaza Benjamin Canales, named after another revolutionary hero and located just on the other side of the International Bridge. On warm evenings, the streets come alive with food vendors and evening strollers. On Sunday there are sometimes band concerts at the plaza's gazebo. *Calandrias* or horse carriages take visitors around the old part of the city for around $5 an hour. Though not especially geared toward gringo shoppers, there are several *artesanías* and liquor stores along Av. Hidalgo near the bridge. Street touts don't hound gringos as in Juárez and sales pressure in the shops is low. Prices are also low: a liter bottle of Cuervo Especial tequila is only $4.50. Acuña has a bullring, **Plaza de Toros La Macarena**, on Libramiento Oriente (West Bypass), not far from the International Bridge, as well as a *charro* ring, **Lienzo Charro El Potrero**, in the northwest corner of town on Calle California off Blvd. López Mateos. Check with the tourist office for a current schedule of *charreadas* and *corridas de toros*.

It's not that easy to walk across the border to Acuña—from city limit to city limit it's three miles—which is another reason the city isn't inundated with tourists. Instead, visitors can drive, catch public buses, or take taxis from downtown Del Rio. You shouldn't drive, though, unless you have Mexican insurance. There are parking lots on Las Vacas St. in Del Rio (closest point to the crossing) where you can park a car all day for $2. Buses pass regularly on the way into Acuña and cost 40 cents each way—get off at the plaza once you've crossed the bridge. A taxi from Del Rio (Las Vacas) is $7 one-way; taxis coming the opposite way will ask for more, but you shouldn't pay over $8. Cab companies on the Del Rio side provide free parking if you hire one of their taxis.

Arreola's Insurance (tel. 210-775-3252), near the bridge on Spur 239, can arrange Mexican auto insurance for longer journeys south of the border. The Coahuila state **tourist office** (tel. 2-40-70) at the border station (opposite the offices of immigration and customs) has in-

formative, annotated maps of the region and state.

The Cd. Acuña crossing is open 24 hours. For Americans and Canadians, no immigration or vehicle papers are necessary for visits of less than 72 hours.

ACCOMMODATIONS

Hotels and Motels

The main hotel/motel strip in Del Rio is Ave. F (US 277 N/US 90 W). Here you'll find the inexpensive **Desert Hills** (tel. 210-775-3548) at no. 1912, with rooms for $22.50-27 (senior and long-term stay discounts available); the two-story, well-maintained **Del Rio Motor Lodge** (tel. 775-2486) at no. 1300 for $22-30; and the **Motel 6** (tel. 774-2115) for $25 s, plus $6 for each additional adult. The moderately priced **Best Western Inn of Del Rio** (tel. 775-7511 or 800-528-1234) is at no. 810 and has rooms for $48 s, $56 d; it also offers complimentary breakfasts and cocktail hour, a pool, hot tub, laundry, and fax service. Rooms with additional amenities are available at the **Ramada Inn** (tel. 775-1511) at 2101 Ave. F, $58-71; the **Best Western La Siesta** (tel. 775-6323 or 800-528-1234), 2000 Ave. F, $56-65 with complimentary breakfast and cocktails; and the new **La Quinta Inn** (tel. 775-7591) at 2005 Ave. F, $58-66. All three have spacious guest rooms and pools.

Acuña has few hotels that cater to gringos. One that belongs to the Del Rio Chamber of Commerce is **Hotel San Antonio** (tel. 2-55-35) on Calle Hidalgo at Calle Lerdo. It's well located and the $36-40 room rates are decent value for a/c, satellite TV, and off-street parking. The less expensive **Hotel San Jorge** (tel. 2-20-70), also conveniently located downtown at Calle Hidalgo 165 (at Av. V. Guerrero, two blocks form Plaza Canales), offers rooms with carpet, phones, and private baths for US$18-20 s/d.

Out at Lake Amistad are several hotels and motels—see "Amistad National Recreation Area" under "Vicinity of Del Rio" for details.

Camping

Yucca Trailer Village (tel. 210-775-6707) on US 90 W toward Lake Amistad has shaded full hookups for $10 a night; weekly and monthly discounts available. **Fisherman's Headquarters** (tel. 774-4172) is located north of town where US 90 and US 277 split. Full hookup sites are $11 per night; other facilities include barbecue pits, convenience store, dump station, and propane delivery; hunting/fishing guides can be arranged. Other campgrounds are available on the lake.

FOOD

The Mexican presence in Del Rio is strong, so Tex-Mex restaurants far outnumber any other kind. One of the best is **Memo's** (tel. 210-775-8104) at 804 E. Losoya on the banks of San Felipe Creek. The same family has operated the restaurant since 1936, turning out dependable *chalupas,* fajitas, and enchiladas as well as steaks for moderate prices. A bonus is that one of the family members is "Blondie" Calderon, the pianist for C&W singer Ray Price's band. Whenever he's not on the road, Blondie gets a band together for a jam session at Memo's to entertain diners. Regular live music nights are Tuesday and Thursday. Open Mon.-Sat. for lunch and dinner, Sunday for dinner only.

For cheap, gutbucket Tex-Mex, you might try **Mi Casa** at 1912 Ave. F (attached to the Desert Hills Motel), which is open 24 hours and has all the usual border specialties.

Of course, you could cross the river for Mexican food, with Mexico for atmosphere. The favorite hangout for gringo border-hoppers is **Crosby's Restaurant & Bar** (tel. 2-20-20) at Av. Hidalgo 195, just a few blocks from the International Bridge. Since the 1930s Crosby's has drawn a curious mix of Coahuilan cowboys, Texas ranchers, and tourists. House specialties include *cabrito,* Portuguese-style chicken, frog legs, roast quail, and the usual border platters. Open daily 9 a.m.-midnight. Another outstanding choice is **Asadero La Posta** at 350 Allende St., left off Hidalgo eight blocks from the bridge, which specializes in fajitas, *queso con chile, queso fundido,* and *carne asada.* On weekends, the upstairs room occasionally hosts live *conjunto* music. La Posta is open daily 8 a.m.-11 p.m.

For American food, the favorite local spot is the **Cripple Creek Saloon** (tel. 775-0153) at US 90 W just after it splits from US 277. The saloon specializes in mesquite-grilled steaks, swordfish, frog legs, prime rib, catfish, lobster, and shrimp; open Mon.-Sat. for dinner only.

EVENTS

May
George Paul Memorial Bull Riding Competition, usually held the first Sunday in May, is followed by a week of other PRCA rodeo events, art shows, and country dances. Contestants in the event, formerly called Super Bull, are top-rated professional bull riders who compete here for the largest bullriding purse in the world, around $60,000 in prize money and a 14-karat-gold belt buckle studded with rubies. At the Val Verde County Fairgrounds on N. Main Street.

Cinco de Mayo commemorates the Mexican defeat of a French naval invasion at Puebla on May 5 with music, dancing, and food at Brown Plaza in the San Felipe District.

September
Diez y Seis: Mexican independence celebration on September 16, with fiestas in Del Rio and Acuña, including food, music, and dancing.

October
Fiesta Amistad is Del Rio's biggest annual event, held in cooperation with Ciudad Acuña to commemorate U.S.-Mexico relations. The festival has been held yearly since October 24, 1960, when U.S. President Dwight Eisenhower and Mexican President Adolfo López Mateos agreed to build a dam across the Rio Grande for the benefit of both countries. The schedule of events lasts nine to 10 days and features Señorita Amistad and Miss Del Rio beauty pageants, an international parade from Del Rio to Acuña, a Battle of the Bands, professional rodeo, foot and bike races, an arts and crafts show, an open house at nearby Laughlin Air Force Base, rodeos, and an *abrazo* or friendly embrace between U.S. and Mexican dignitaries on the Amistad Dam.

December
On the second Saturday of the month, local and visiting sailors parade illuminated boats of all shapes and sizes along the lake's south shore for the **Festival of Lights.**

INFORMATION

The Del Rio Chamber of Commerce (tel. 210-775-3551 or 800-889-8149) at 1915 Ave. F distributes maps and brochures related to the Del Rio area. The area code for Del Rio is 210. To call Acuña telephone numbers from Del Rio, dial 011-52-877 plus the number.

Del Rio's Mexican consulate (tel. 774-5031) at 1010 Main St. can handle most documentation for short- and long-term visits to Mexico.

VICINITY OF DEL RIO, LOWER PECOS

AMISTAD NATIONAL RECREATION AREA

Lake Amistad (*amistad* means "friendship" in Spanish) came about after the governments of the U.S. and Mexico, through the International Boundary and Water Commission (IBWC), agreed to build the Amistad Dam across the Rio Grande, or the Río Bravo as it's known in Mexico. Del Rio-Acuña was chosen as the best possible site since it's just below the confluence of the Rio Grande, the Pecos River, and Devils River—allowing control over three rivers at once. The primary functions of the dam are water conservation, flood control, hydroelectric power, and recreation (swimming, boating, camping, fishing, hunting, and scuba diving). The surface area of the reservoir varies between 65,000 and 89,000 acres and the shoreline is 800-1,000 miles (with over half on the U.S. side), which makes it one of the largest artificial lakes in the United States. The National Park Service administers nine sites along the American side of the lake, while Texas Parks and Wildlife manages those areas not under specific Park Service jurisdiction. As a national recreational site, it's probably the most undeveloped and noncommercial of any Park Service-supervised lake, although 1.5 million visits were recorded in 1993. Of all the state's 106 major reservoirs, Amistad measures second best in underwater visibility.

Boating
Sailors enjoy Amistad because it's large, uncrowded, and surrounded by side canyons; the three rivers that feed into the lake also offer opportunities for exploration. An added bonus is that some of the river canyons contain 4,000- to 8,000-year-old Indian pictographs that can only be seen by boat. Some of the most spectacular canyons run along Devils River, which also happens to pass through Indian Head Ranch, an exotic game preserve—sometimes the odd impala or wildebeest is visible along the cliffs from the river.

There are three marinas and eight boat launches on the American side. You can rent boats from the **Lake Amistad Resort & Marina** (tel. 210-774-4157) and **Forever Resorts** (tel. 774-4157 or 800-255-5561) at the Diablo East Marina, from the **Creek Boat Rental** (tel. 774-3334) at Rough Canyon, and from the **Rough Canyon Inn & Country Store** (tel. 774-6366) in Rough Canyon. A 16-foot bass boat or a 19-foot runabout with a 90 hp engine typically costs $90-100 a day, an 18-foot deck boat with a 165 hp engine goes for $150 a day, a 24-foot pontoon boat that sleeps 10-12 costs $175 for 24 hours. Other configurations are available; the cheapest deal is a 16-foot bass boat with 55 hp engine from Rough Canyon Inn for $65 a day. Lake Amistad Resort rents 50-foot houseboats for around $1000 a week. Water-skis are also available for rent. Discounts on all rentals are available in the off season (Oct.-May).

The other two marinas on the Del Rio side are the Park Service-administered Rough Canyon Marina to the north and the U.S. Air Force Marina near the dam. The USAF Marina is open only to the military and their families. A marina on the Mexican side is accessible by boat or by driving six miles across the dam into Mexico.

Fishing
Amistad is open to anglers year round. The lake is stocked with walleye, smallmouth, striped bass, striped hybrid bass, white bass, Florida

bass, six species of sunfish, two species of crappie, Rio Grande and African perch, freshwater drum, northern pike, buffalo, four species of gar, and five species of catfish. Anglers should keep an eye on the IBWC buoys that divide U.S. from Mexican waters; a Mexican fishing license is required to fish the Mexican side, easily available from the U.S. marinas or bait shops in Del Rio.

Swimming

Shore swimming is permitted at all of the designated camping areas and at the three designated swimming beaches at Governor's Landing, Rough Canyon, and Old 277 North. On the Mexican side you can swim just about anywhere; there's a designated Mexican swimming beach, with picnic ramadas, near the west end of the dam.

Hunting

Only certain shore areas, mostly to the east, are designated by Texas Parks and Wildlife for hunting. Hunting is allowed only in season, and game animals—white-tailed deer and javelina—may be taken only with bow and arrow. Details on seasons and bag limits are available at the Diablo East and Rough Canyon ranger stations.

Scuba Diving

Best underwater visibility is 25-30 feet, Nov.-April. Algae growth during the warmer months can cut visibility by five to 10 feet. The most popular dive site is at Diablo East, where a cove near the View Point Cliffs has been marked off for diving and swimming only. The depth exceeds 100 feet at the outer edge of the cove; a dive platform is anchored at 40 feet and there's a boat wreck for divers to explore. Other good spots include Castle Canyon, the US 90 bridge, the cliffs area in Cow Creek Canyon, and Indian Springs, 6.5 miles up the Devils River via Rough Canyon. Spearfishing is permitted (a valid fishing license is required), but only for "rough" fish, including gar, drum, buffalo carp, and African perch. You must register at park headquarters before setting off on a dive.

Camping

Primitive drive-in campsites are available at Governor's Landing (17 sites), San Pedro Flats (12 sites), Old 277 North (eight sites), Old 277 South (four sites), and Spur 406 (12 sites). All designated camping areas provide chemical toilets and cooking grills but no drinking water or showers. Camping is also permitted anywhere along the shore below contour 1,144.3 feet except next to marinas and in posted noncamping areas. There are no camping fees, but campers are limited to 14 days in a calendar year.

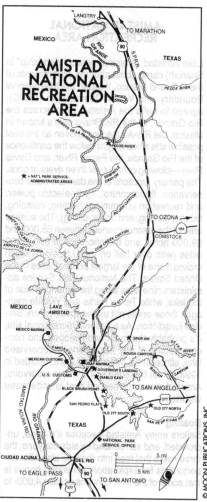

© MOON PUBLICATIONS, INC.

Near the Diablo East Marina are three commercial campgrounds, **American RV Resort Campground** (tel. 210-755-6484) with RV/tent sites for $14.75; the shady **Amistad RV Park** (tel. 775-6491) with RV sites for $12, tentsites for $8; and **Holiday Trav-L Park** (tel. 775-7275), $14 for RVs or $10 for tents. Near the Rough Canyon Marina is the **Rough Canyon Trailer Park/Campground** (tel. 775-6707), where sites are $10 a night. Yet another option is **Fisherman's Headquarters** (tel. 774-4172) at the junction of US 277 and US 90, where full hookups cost $10.50 a night. All commercial campgrounds at the lake offer discounts for weekly and monthly stays.

Motels

Amistad Lodge (tel. 210-775-8591) overlooks the lake off US 90 W between Black Brush Point and Diablo East; rooms for $32-43, pool. The nearby **Angler's Lodge** (tel. 775-1586) features rooms with kitchenettes for $27-36. Both are clean, well-maintained inns; both can arrange hunting and fishing guides. Farther down US 90 W toward the dam is the **Lakeview Inn** (tel. 775-9521), which is closer to the marina but farther from Del Rio; room rates are $33-41. Over at Rough Canyon off US 277 is the more expensive **Laguna Diablo Resort** (tel. 774-2422), where rooms start at $62.50. Also at Rough Canyon, the **Rough Canyon Inn** (tel. 774-6266) has rooms with kitchenettes for $24-

32. There are also plenty of motel accommodations in Del Rio itself.

Information

Park headquarters is at the US 90/277 split, where you can pick up a map of the lake as well as handouts on fishing, boating, hunting, and park-use regulations. At the mouth of the Pecos River, 44 miles west of park headquarters off US 90, is a quarter-mile, self-guiding nature trail that exhibits native regional plants. The Big Bend Natural History Association offers publications at the trailhead. For further information on Lake Amistad, contact the Superintendent (tel. 210-775-7491), Amistad National Recreation Area, P.O. Box 420367, Del Rio, TX 78842.

SEMINOLE CANYON STATE HISTORICAL PARK

Seminole Canyon, named for the Seminole Indians who frequented the area at the time of Anglo-American expansion in the mid-19th century, is one of the larger river canyons that runs north of the Rio Grande. At least 200 Indian rock-art sites have been discovered in these canyons and elsewhere in the Lower Pecos region. As many as a hundred were submerged following the construction of the Amistad Dam, including 10 major sites; three of the most striking, Parida Cave, Panther Cave, and the Fate

Seminole Canyon

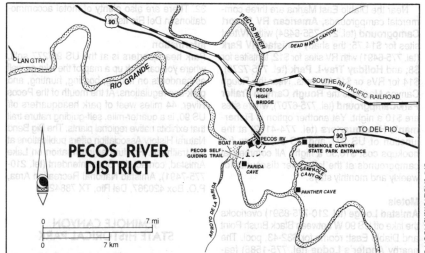

PECOS RIVER DISTRICT

© MOON PUBLICATIONS, INC.

Bell Shelter, are above the high-water mark and can still be seen today.

History

The first North American Indians, big-game hunters who followed herds of camel, mammoth, and bison, began living along the Rio Grande and in the Pecos and Devils river valleys 10,000-12,000 years ago. By around 8,000 years ago, they'd been replaced by, or perhaps evolved into, groups of peaceful foragers who lived on the plants and small animals of the intersecting desert and chaparral terrains. By 4,000 years ago, and perhaps earlier, groups of Indians had begun painting on the rock walls of the canyon caves, and they continued to add to the collection for another 2,800 years or so. The resulting pictographs cover a wide range of subjects and designs, most of which can be identified with regional phenomena, though some are completely open to conjecture.

As elsewhere in Texas, the Indians made paint by grinding various minerals—ocher, iron oxide, manganese oxide, and clay—into powder and then mixing the powders with animal fat. They used parts of local plants or their hands and fingers for brushes. Anthropologists who've analyzed the paintings can discern different art periods, distinguished by a move from realism to

abstraction, and from one set of colors to another (the Red Monochrome Period, for example, occurred between A.D. 600 and 1000). In some areas of the canyon, the artists painted layer upon layer of pictographs, without regard for "posterity"; this is one reason the function of the paintings is thought to be ceremonial. In the early historic period (beginning in the 16th century), it's known that Coahuiltecans lived in the canyons, but whether they were descended from the earlier canyon-dwellers hasn't been ascertained. By the time Anglo-Americans established Fort Clark in nearby Brackettville in the 1850s, only Comanches frequented the area. The Seminoles arrived later, at the invitation of the Mexican government.

Visiting the Park

Seminole Canyon is 45 miles west of Del Rio. The park covers 2,173 acres in and around the canyon and protects a combination of flora and fauna that represents a meeting of Tamaulipan Thorn Scrub, Edwards Plateau, and Chihuahuan Desert terrains. Two trails have been established for exploring the area, and these lead to the canyon's two main pictograph sites.

The short trail to **Fate Bell Shelter** is open only to those accompanied by a park ranger. Fate Bell is a major Indian site, with a long series of painted cave shelters beneath a semicircular canyon ledge. The cave bottom has a 13-foot layer of debris accumulated over 6,000 years of continuous habitation, including intact thatched mats, sandals, and stone tools. Several levels of pictographs have been covered by this layering. The main rock-art period visible here is the Pecos River Style, marked by stick-like figures carrying *atlatls* (spear throwers) and pouches made from prickly pear cactus. Guided tours along this trail are led Wed.-Sun. at 10 a.m. and 3 p.m. year round.

The other trail is a six-mile roundtrip self-guiding path that leads down to a Rio Grande overlook opposite Panther Cave. This is a worthwhile hike for enjoying the Lower Pecos environment, but to get a good look at the Panther Cave pictographs, you really need to go by boat via the Rio Grande. Biking is permitted along this trail.

The visitor center is open Wed.-Sun. 8 a.m.- 5 p.m. and contains excellent interpretive exhibits that depict daily life in the Archaic Indian period, including a life-size diorama that demonstrates hunting and foraging techniques. The staff can also answer questions about the pictograph sites and about area activities. Those interested in a general tour of the area should pick up a copy of the *Pecos River District Self-Guided Tour* pamphlet.

The park entry fee is $3 per vehicle or $1 for pedestrians and cyclists.

Camping

The park camping area has 31 drive-in sites, $6 a night with water and $9 a night with w/e. Restrooms have flush toilets and hot showers.

Accommodations Outside the Park

The privately run **Pecos RV** (tel. 915-292-4460), near the east end of the Pecos High Bridge, offers sites with full hookups for $11, tent/camper sites for $6.

In nearby Comstock you'll find **Desert Hills RV Park** ($8 RV or tent) and **The Owl's Nest RV Park** ($7.50 RV or tent). Also in Comstock, **Casa Blanca Motel** (tel. 292-4431) on the highway has basic rooms for $20-26.

Boat Tours

By boat, visitors can explore the Pecos-Rio Grande River area in the vicinity of Seminole Canyon and see pictograph sites that aren't accessible on foot. Chief among these are Parida Cave and Panther Cave. **Parida Cave** is a few miles north of Seminole Canyon just below the mouth of the Pecos River. In 1987, the Park Service constructed a boat dock and rock-trail system with interpretive signs so the general public could easily visit the cave by boat. Like the Fate Bell Shelter in Seminole Canyon, Parida was inhabited continuously for thousands of years, starting around 3000 B.C. and ending about 500 years ago. Hundreds of pictographs and a burnt rock midden have been left behind. When the Southern Pacific Railroad came through in 1883, Parida became the Painted Caves Station, where passengers rested while the train was serviced. The remains of the station are now 50 feet below the surface of Lake Amistad.

Panther Cave is near the mouth of Seminole Canyon and is the model by which all other Pecos River pictographs are judged in terms of period, style, and color. The Sistine Chapel of painted caves, the shelter features pictographs covering the walls and part of the ceiling 12 feet above the floor. The cave got its name from a panther painting that's over 15 feet long. Because the cave is so popular, a chain-link fence has been erected across the shelter to prevent vandalism, but there are camera portholes built into the fence. As at Parida, a Park Service dock allows visitors to approach by boat.

Another popular sightseeing stop for boaters is the **Pecos High Bridge,** about five miles up the Pecos River from the Rio Grande junction. The construction of the original span in 1882 was a significant event in the completion of the country's second transcontinental rail line and required a crew of 8,000, who cut two 1,500-foot tunnels through solid rock on either side of the river. The second version in 1891 was the highest bridge in the world when built—321 feet high—and its completion shortened the rail route by 13 miles. This bridge was replaced in 1944 by another of about the same height, which is still used by transcontinental trains. The 1891 bridge was disassembled and sold to Venezuela and is reportedly still in use there.

If you don't have your own boat, you can rent one at Lake Amistad or join a guided boat tour. Only four experienced tour operators are licensed to lead tours in the Pecos-Rio Grande-

Devils River area. Manuel and Inez Hardwick of **High Bridge Adventures** (tel. 915-292-4495), P.O. Box 816 Comstock, TX 78837, lead boat tours from the Pecos River Boat Ramp. Their three-hour tours visit Parida and Panther caves, several lesser-known pictograph sites, and the Pecos High Bridge for $25 per person. **American Watersports** (tel. 775-6484 or 800-LAKE-FUN), at Lake Amistad's Diablo East Marina, offers two different river/pictograph tours. One takes in the Pecos River area, the other the lesser known Devils River; either tour costs $45 per hour for up to six people. A third outfit, **Lake Amistad Tours** (tel. 775-7100), arranges similar tours or can customize a two-hour to two-day tour to fit your schedule and needs.

Jim Zintgraff, a professional photographer who's documented the Lower Pecos pictographs for nearly 40 years, leads boat tours from the Diablo East Marina on Lake Amistad. Tours all the way to the Pecos cost as much as $45 a person and take the better part of a day. Jim can be contacted by calling (210) 525-9907 in San Antonio.

Information
For more information, contact the Superintendent (tel. 915-292-4464), Seminole Canyon State Historical Park, P.O. Box 820, Comstock, TX 78837.

The **Rock Art Foundation** (tel. 210-525-9907), 3861 Fredericksburg Rd., San Antonio, TX 78212, promotes the study and preservation of Lower Pecos rock art sites.

LANGTRY

Langtry was established in the 1880s when the Southern Pacific and the Galveston, Harrisburg, and San Antonio railroads were joined at nearby Dead Man's Gulch. At the time, the only settlement in the area was a tent city named Vinegaroon with a reputation for extreme lawlessness. The railroad and the Texas Rangers commissioned Vinegaroon store owner Roy Bean to serve as justice of the peace at a new town site next to the rail line. Judge Roy Bean christened the town Langtry, after his idol Lillie Langtry, a famous English actress of the period, and opened a saloon called the Jersey Lily (her international title, which Bean misspelled as "Lilly") that also served as his courtroom. The rest, as they say, is history. With a volume of the 1879 Revised Statutes of Texas and a six-shooter, the judge declared himself the "law west of the Pecos," often fining defendants by ordering a round of drinks for the house. In 1896, Bean defied Texas and Mexico law by staging the Maher-Fitzsimmons championship prizefight on a sandbar in the middle of the Rio Grande (at the time, professional boxing was illegal on both sides of the river). Bean died in 1904. In 1972, director

Jersey Lilly Saloon, Langtry

John Huston filmed Bean's story in *The Life and Times of Judge Roy Bean,* starring Paul Newman.

Judge Roy Bean Visitor Center

The visitor center itself is one of the State Highway Department's 12 tourist bureaus and distributes information on travel throughout the state. Behind the center is the restored Jersey Lilly saloon, which is open to touring (free). Next to the center is a nature trail through a well-planned Chihuahuan Desert garden in which the plants are labeled with their scientific names and the medicinal and utilitarian uses of each.

Food

Bud's Place Barbecue and Beer, a block south of the information center, is open daily for lunch and dinner. Not bad considering the lack of competition.

BRACKETTVILLE

Brackettville (pop. 1,844), 32 miles east of Del Rio on US 90, grew up around Fort Clark, a frontier fort that opened in the 1850s and didn't close until 1946. It's the county seat for Kinney County, which is larger than the state of Rhode Island but has only one other town (Spofford, pop. 77, 10 miles south of Brackettville). It's mostly a ranching (cattle, sheep, goats) and farming community that is also a popular hunting area for deer, javelina, wild turkey, quail, and dove. Brackettville has two claims to fame: Fort Clark, home of the renowned Black Seminole Scouts, and Alamo Village.

Seminole Indian Scout Cemetery

This unassuming cemetery, about five miles south of Brackettville on FM 3348, is the only monument to a remarkable group of people with a remarkable history. Buried here along with some of their descendants are around a hundred Black Seminoles who served as Army scouts at nearby Fort Clark. Their history goes back to the early 1800s when a group of slaves ran away from Georgia and South Carolina to Florida, where they became sharecroppers for Seminole Indians. In Florida, the blacks and the Seminoles intermarried and fought the U.S. Army

together. In the 1840s several bands of black and Seminole warriors were captured by the army and sent to a Cherokee reservation in Oklahoma. From here they escaped across Texas to northern Mexico, where they were employed by the Mexican government to keep the Apaches and Comanches at bay, thus earning a reputation as fearless Indian fighters. In exchange for their services, Mexico gave them land at Naciamente, below Piedras Negras.

Throughout the 1850s and 1860s, the mixed band of blacks and Seminoles kept to themselves and began to merge toward a single ethnicity that featured a mixture of Indian and African dialects (it's thought that most of the Africans originated from North Africa's Barbary Coast). As the Civil War came to a close, the U.S. Army approached the Black Seminoles for help in ridding the Fort Clark area of Comanches. Lieutenant John "Thunderbolt" Bullis led the Seminole-Negro Indian Scouts, as they were officially called, in 26 successful Indian campaigns between 1871 and 1881. Three Seminole scouts earned Medals of Honor; a fourth was awarded the Medal of Honor during a campaign with MacKenzie's Raiders. All four have grave markers in the cemetery.

The Seminole Indian Scouts disbanded in 1914. Around 50 of their descendants live in Brackettville and another hundred or so in Naciamente, Mexico. Others live in Del Rio, Fort Davis, San Antonio, and farther afield. The last scout to be buried in the cemetery was Curly Jefferson, who died in the 1950s. Black Seminoles living in Brackettville maintain the cemetery and occasionally hold barbecues to raise funds for grounds improvement.

Fort Clark Springs

Fort Clark is the only frontier fort in Texas that has been turned into a resort, complete with golf course, swimming pool, motel, bar, and RV park. Some of the original buildings have been restored—the 1872 barracks is now the motel—and you can tour the grounds during the day. It's on the east edge of town off US 90.

Alamo Village

This replica of the 19th-century Alamo Mission is the largest movie set ever built outside Hollywood. It took 5,000 men two years (1957-59) to build, using the original Spanish plans and adobe bricks made on-site by adobemakers from Mexico—all to be used for John Wayne's epic film The Alamo. The 1959 film cost $12 million to produce, the highest budget Hollywood had then ever seen. After the film was completed, the set was expanded to include an Old West town that has been used by production companies in making nearly 40 feature films and hundreds of TV shows (including the perennial hit Lonesome Dove) and commercials. One end of town is said to represent 1880s San Antonio and the other Fort Worth.

Every Labor Day the Cowboy Horse Races are held here; riders race through the town for distances of 200, 250, 300, 350, and 440 yards. The final race is a tribute to the original quarter-horse races, which were named after the quarter mile (440 yards) that made up the main streets of most Old West towns.

The complex is located on the Shahan HV Ranch, six miles north of Brackettville on RR 674. It's open to visitors daily 9 a.m.-6 p.m., May 15-Sept. 15, 10 a.m.-5 p.m. the remainder of the year except December 21-26, when it's closed. During the summer months there's live entertainment, including music and simulated gun duels. Admission is $6 adults, $3 ages 6-11 from Memorial Day to Labor Day, $5 and $2.50 the remainder of the year.

BOB RACE

NORTH CENTRAL TEXAS
DALLAS

Dallas tries to be all things to all people: Manhattan of the Southwest, cowboy capital, temple of consumerism, arts center, church center, Sun Belt suburbia. To a certain degree, the city succeeds: it ranks third in the U.S. as headquarters for Fortune 500 companies; is one of only two cities in Texas with a weekly rodeo; has more shopping centers and more retail space per capita than any other U.S. city; 60 downtown acres are set aside as an arts district; it harbors the two largest Methodist and Baptist churches in the world; and is encircled by planned suburban communities.

The one million residents of Dallas are secure in feeling superior to other Texas cities, calling Dallas the "Cadillac of Texas towns," yet insecure about their status in relation to other U.S. metropolitan centers. They've gone from the city that shot J.F.K. to the city that shot J.R. (J.R. Ewing, the sleazy billionaire on TV's *Dallas*); the convention and visitors bureau has even used the slogan "If you like the show, you'll

love the city," which probably made average Dallasites cringe. It's virtually impossible to arrive in Dallas for the first time without a bundle of preconceived images; in spite of this tendency—or perhaps because of it—most visitors seem surprised by how much they like Dallas. It's a city that invites parody, yet no one who spends any time there can deny that it's an extremely vibrant place.

The Land
Of course, you can't achieve the "bright lights, big city" effect without cutting down a few trees and leveling a few hills. The terrain around Dallas used to be a series of wooded prairies collectively called the Cross Timbers. As the city grew from "Dallas" to "Greater Dallas" to the "Metroplex" (a linking of Dallas, Arlington, Fort Worth, and several smaller towns by spaghetti freeways), virtually all characteristics that distinguished the Cross Timbers from the Prairies were erased or covered over. Which is not to say

DALLAS-FORT WORTH

© MOON PUBLICATIONS, INC.

there aren't plenty of greenbelts in and around Dallas—but these are artificial oases.

Climate
Dallas weather is fairly moderate most of the year, thanks to its position between the chilly High Plains to the west and the muggy lowlands to the east. Average humidity is 50-60% year round. Average temperatures range from 36-56° F in January to 74-95° F in July. Average annual rainfall is 39 inches, with April, May, and September the wettest months (three to four inches per month).

History
Dallas started as one log cabin in 1840, when John Neely Bryan came from Tennessee and established a small trading post on the Trinity River. Other settlers joined him, including his Arkansas neighbor Joe Dallas, for whom Bryan named the town. In 1855, around 350 French colonists from La Réunion moved to Dallas following the dissolution of their Texas colony, thus expanding the settlement. As with many Western towns, it was the coming of the railroads that really put Dallas on the map. Two rail lines came through: the Houston and Texas Central in 1872 and the Texas & Pacific in 1873.

Although a certain amount of ranching and farming was established in the Dallas area, the city stayed close to its trading-post roots—instead of riding herd or planting cotton, Dallas interests preferred buying and selling Texas assets. When oil was discovered elsewhere in the state, this is where the oilmen kept their money. After World War II, Dallas became a banking and insurance headquarters as the high tech, communications, aviation, medicine, conventions, film, and fashion industries joined oil, livestock, and agriculture in boosting the economy. Since the city financiers were fairly diversified, the oil recession of the '80s affected Dallas little.

Costs
For its comparative size, Dallas enjoys a reasonable cost of living. Nonetheless, it's the state's most expensive city, especially if you're staying or eating downtown. To save money, you might consider choosing a place to stay east or west of the city. There's not much avail- able to the south, and north Dallas is just as expensive as central Dallas. Shopping at the Farmer's Market off Pearl Expressway is a good way to cut costs; fresh fruits and vegetables are sold daily from dawn to dusk.

SIGHTS

Downtown Architecture
Of the many buildings that make up the city's Manhattan-like skyline, three distinguish it from other urban profiles. The structure that looks like a shiny sphere at the end of a 50-story shaft is the **Reunion Tower,** linked to the Hyatt Regency Hotel, the Union railway station, and the Reunion Arena, home to the Dallas Mavericks basketball team and Dallas Stars hockey team. The view from the tower is probably the best city view accessible to the public, especially at night. An elevator ride to the observation deck costs $2 adults, $1 for children under 12 and senior citizens. Or you can ride an elevator to the

Reunion Tower, Dallas

Top of the Dome Club bar, two floors higher than the observation deck, for free.

The **Renaissance Tower** is the 56-story glass-and-steel building that's illuminated at night with elongated double Xs. It's shown around the world on reruns of the TV show *Dallas* as J.R. Ewing's offices, but it actually belongs to Prudential Insurance. Another Dallas landmark is the red neon Pegasus flying over the much shorter **Mobil Building.** The corporate logo of the Magnolia Petroleum Co., it was originally erected in honor of the 1945 American Petroleum Institute, the first major convention held in the city (Dallas is now the number-two convention city in the U.S.). The tallest highrise in Dallas is the 72-story Nations Bank tower, which is outlined at night by two miles of green argon tubing.

Dallas Arts District

This ambitious project involves 60 acres of prime downtown real estate, developed by a mixture of private and public investment. The district is bounded on the north by Woodall Rodgers Freeway, on the west by St. Paul, on the east by Routh, and on the south by Ross. Existing facilities include the Dallas Arts Magnet High School, the Dallas Museum of Art, the Dallas Theater Center, the Meyerson Symphony Center, and the Trammel Crow Center. The latter is a multi-use building that often houses traveling folk art exhibits from the Smithsonian and other American museums. It also features a sculpture garden that displays 22 French bronzes, including works by Rodin. Several historic buildings have been preserved within the district: the Greek Revival-style Belo Mansion, St. Paul United Methodist Church, and Catedral Santuario de Guadalupe.

Museums

The **Dallas Museum of Art** (tel. 214-922-1200) is the centerpiece of the Arts District. A modern, state-of-the-art facility, it houses an average of 10,000 items ranging from prehistoric art to contemporary painting and sculpture. Permanent gallery exhibits include pre-Cortesian, African, 19th-century and early modern European, and 18th-century to post-WW II American collections. A Decorative Arts Wing features a re-created Mediterranean villa housing the Hoblitzelle Collection of silver and the Wendy and Emery Reves Collection of European furniture, impressionist paintings, and Chinese porcelain. The Museum of the Americas, a new wing added in 1993, showcases North, Central, and South American art from pre-Hispanic times through the mid-20th century. The museum is at 1717 N. Harwood. Free museum tours are given Tuesday, Wednesday, and Friday at 11:30 a.m.; Thursday at 7 p.m.; and Saturday and Sunday at 2 p.m.; all starting at the Visitors Service Desk. General museum hours are Tues.-Wed. 11 a.m.-4 p.m., Thurs.-Fri. 11 a.m.-9 p.m., and Sat.-Sun. 11 a.m.-5 p.m. Admission to most of the galleries is free; there's a $3 admission to the Reves Collection, and special temporary exhibits may also charge.

The **Age of Steam Railroad Museum** (tel. 428-0101) at the Fair Park (Washington and Perry) is a must for railroad buffs. Here you'll find the world's largest steam locomotive; a 1903 depot; a 1930s passenger train complete with dining car, sleepers, and several cabooses; and an authentic whistle tree. Open Thurs.-Fri. 10 a.m.-3 p.m., Sat.-Sun. 11 a.m.-5 p.m. Admission is $3 adults, $1.50 ages 12 and under.

Even non-Christians might be interested in the **Biblical Arts Center** (tel. 691-4661), a nondenominational museum devoted to world art evoking the early biblical era. The main work on display is the "Miracle at Pentecost" mural, which measures 124 feet by 20 feet; it took Dallas artists Torger Thompson and Alvin Barnes three years to paint it. Every half hour, when the museum is open, the mural is the focus of a sound and light presentation. Two other galleries within the center house traveling exhibits and occasional performing arts. The center is at 7500 Park Lane at Boedeker, six miles north of downtown Dallas off the Central Expressway (US 75). Open Tues.-Sat. 10 a.m.-5 p.m., Sunday 1-5 p.m. Admission to most exhibits is free, but the sound and light show costs $3.75 adults, $3 seniors, $2 children 6-12.

The **Dallas Memorial Center for Holocaust Studies** (tel. 750-4654) houses a library, memorial, and museum dedicated to the WW II-era Jewish experience in Europe. The center's entry stairwell features changing exhibits of Jewish art, and at the bottom of the stairs is a National Belgian Railway boxcar once used to transport people to Nazi death camps. Permanent exhibits begin with European Jewish life before WW II and document the rise of Nazism, ghettos, and liberation through films, photos, and various other memorabilia. One enters the somber Memorial Room through cast-iron "Gates of Fire" symbolizing the burning of the Torah and Jewish prayer books by the Nazis. In the center of the room a large granite slab is surrounded by 12 marble pillars representing the 12 camps where survivors now residing in Dallas were interned. A sculpted hand extending from flames is at the top of the stone. Three of the surrounding walls bear plaques inscribed with survivor names—the fourth is blank in memory of the generations lost in the Holocaust. Located at 7900 Northhaven, Royal Lane exit off US 75. Open Mon.-Fri. 10 a.m.-4 p.m., Sunday noon-4 p.m.; free admission.

The **Museum of African-American Culture** (tel. 565-9026) has moved from Bishop College to the WRR Building at Fair Park (1515 First Ave.). It features collections of African and African-American art and artifacts from pre-slavery Africa through modern times. Admission varies according to the exhibit.

Southern Methodist University (SMU) is the site for the **Meadows Museum** (tel. 768-1675), a portion of a $35 million endowment made by oil tycoon Alger Meadows. The museum specializes in Spanish art and houses a permanent collection of works by Spanish masters Goya, Picasso, Murillo, Valázquez, Miró, and others. In the Owens Fine Art Center, SMU campus, at Bishop and Binkley. Open Mon.-Tues. and Fri.-Sat. 10 a.m.-5 p.m., Thursday 10 a.m.-8 p.m., Sunday 1-5 p.m.; admission free.

The **Sixth Floor** (tel. 653-6666) calls itself a "permanent educational exhibition examining the life, death, and legacy of John F. Kennedy within the context of American history." Formerly part of the Texas School Book Depository, this is the floor from which Lee Harvey Oswald allegedly shot JFK as he drove through Dealey Plaza on November 22, 1963. The window area Oswald used as a vantage point is protected behind a glass wall, and has been restored to the way it was on the day of the assassination. Other exhibits evoke American life in the Kennedy era. The building now contains offices of Dallas County government and is located at 411 Elm Street. The Kennedy exhibit is open Sun.-Fri. 10 a.m.-6 p.m., Saturday 10 a.m.-7 p.m. Admission is $6 adult, $5 senior; an audio tour is available.

Dallas County Historical Plaza

This area, bounded by Elm, Market, Commerce, and Houston, is actually divided in two: Founder's Plaza, with a reconstruction of John Neely Bryan's original log cabin, and Kennedy Memorial Plaza, which contains a bizarre structure of concrete walls surrounding a small monument dedicated to Kennedy. Although

"Old Red"—the Dallas County Courthouse

Kennedy's limousine passed by here that fateful day in 1963, he was actually shot west of Houston St., in Dealey Plaza. On the west edge of Kennedy Memorial Plaza stands "Old Red," the huge Romanesque-style Dallas County Courthouse, built in 1891 of dark-red Pecos sandstone.

Old City Park

This re-created early Dallas village features 36 restored North Central Texas structures from 1840-1910, including the antebellum Millermore home, a general store, bank, post office, train depot, dentist's office, school, church, smokehouse, barbershop, Indian teepee, and various small houses and cabins. The 13-acre grounds have picnic areas and trails. The entrance is at 1717 Gano, just south of downtown at I-30 and Harwood. Open Tues.- Sat. 10 a.m.-4 p.m., Sunday noon-4 p.m. Admission is $5 adults, $4 seniors, $2 children 3-12.

Dallas Arboretum and Botanical Gardens

The scenic 66-acre grounds of the former De-Golyer and Camp estates on White Rock Lake are the setting for this series of floral, herbal, and vegetable gardens. The best time of year for a visit is spring, when everything's blooming. The Spanish colonial-style DeGolyer mansion has been turned into a museum that contains 17th- to 18th-century European art and furnishings. Open daily 10 a.m.-6 p.m. Admission is free Friday 3-6 p.m.; other times it's $6 adults, $5 seniors, $3 children 6-12. Call (214) 327-8263 for more information.

Dallas Zoo

This zoo features over 1,600 animals in 20 environments, including a tropical rainforest. The Wilds of Africa exhibit displays six distinct habitats and is the first such exhibit in the country to cover every major habitat of an entire continent; nature trails and a monorail traverse the 25-acre exhibit. A train also circles the entire zoo every 15 minutes. A schedule of feedings is available. In the summer, there's a children's petting zoo with goats, sheep, and rabbits. In Marsalis Park, 621 E. Clarendon Drive. Open daily Oct.-March 9 a.m.-5 p.m. and April-Sept. 9 a.m.-6 p.m.; admission $5 adults, $1 children 3-11 and seniors.

Fair Park

Besides serving as the site of the enormous Texas state fair every October, Fair Park contains several science-oriented exhibitions year round. The **Dallas Aquarium** (tel. 214-670-8441) is the nation's largest inland aquarium, with over 340 species of marine, tropical, and freshwater fish. It's open daily 9 a.m.-4:30 p.m. and costs $1 for adults and children over three. The **Museum of Natural History** (tel. 670-8457) houses permanent exhibits on the plants and animals of Texas and the Southwest, including 50 dioramas and a fossil hall. The museum's Earth Science Hall contains a 32-foot reconstructed mosasaur, one of the world's largest prehistoric sea serpents, as well as a 15-foot mammoth from nearby Trinity River. Open Mon.-Sat. 9 a.m.-5 p.m., Sunday noon-5 p.m.; admission free.

The **Science Place** (tel. 428-5555) hosts traveling science exhibits, recently including movie special effects, robot dinosaurs, and music, as well as a permanent collection of exhibits on medicine and physics. It's open Mon.-Sat. 9:30 a.m.-5:30 p.m., Sunday noon-5:30 p.m.; admission is $6 adults, $3 children 3-16 and seniors. The **Science Place Planetarium** next door features a star show and hands-on exhibits like the Shadow Room, where bursts of light transpose visitors' silhouettes onto phosphorescent walls. Open Mon.-Sat. 9:30 a.m.-5:30 p.m., Sunday noon-5:30 p.m.; to gain admission to the planetarium show you must pay for a regular Science Place ticket plus $1.

Fair Park is also home to the **Texas Star,** the largest Ferris wheel in the U.S. and second largest in the world.

Union Station

This huge, beaux arts-style railway depot was built in 1914, but it decayed along with the importance of railway passenger travel over the next 60 years. In 1974 it was restored to its former glory and now contains restaurants, shops, and a small Amtrak depot. Amtrak still stops here. At 400 S. Houston, across from the Hyatt Regency; open 24 hours a day.

Dallas Farmer's Market

In the early 1900s, farmers came daily to Pearl and Cadiz streets to sell fresh produce to wholesale distributors. Traffic jams increased and city

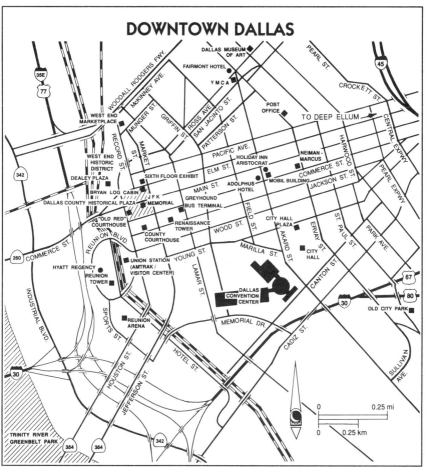

DOWNTOWN DALLAS

DALLAS MUSEUM OF ART

FAIRMONT HOTEL

YMCA

POST OFFICE

TO DEEP ELLUM

WEST END MARKETPLACE

WEST END HISTORIC DISTRICT

DEALEY PLAZA

SIXTH FLOOR EXHIBIT

HOLIDAY INN ARISTOCRAT

NEIMAN-MARCUS

BRYAN LOG CABIN

JFK MEMORIAL

ADOLPHUS HOTEL

MOBIL BUILDING

DALLAS COUNTY HISTORICAL PLAZA

GREYHOUND BUS TERMINAL

"OLD RED" COURTHOUSE

RENAISSANCE TOWER

CITY HALL PLAZA

COUNTY COURTHOUSE

CITY HALL

UNION STATION (AMTRAK / VISITOR CENTER)

HYATT REGENCY

REUNION TOWER

DALLAS CONVENTION CENTER

OLD CITY PARK

REUNION ARENA

MEMORIAL DR.

TRINITY RIVER GREENBELT PARK

0   0.25 mi

0   0.25 km

residents complained, but instead of barring the produce markets, the city built a farmer's market shed in the late '30s, just south of downtown. They added three more sheds in 1946, 1954, and 1982, plus a fifth in 1994, so that it's now among the largest urban farmer's markets in the country. Over a thousand farmers sell fresh fruits and vegetables at the market daily; floral vendors participate March to December as well. The market sheds are on either side of the Pearl Expressway between Harwood St. and the Central Expressway (US 75). Open daily, sunrise to sunset.

Adolphus Hotel

When it was built in 1912 by beer magnate Adolphus Busch, the Adolphus Hotel was said to be the most beautiful building west of Venice, Italy. Following its restoration and reopening in 1981, it's probably more impressive than it was then— 21 stories of ornate brick and granite in the French Renaissance style on the outside, all marble and wood paneling on the inside. Common rooms are furnished with antiques and objets d'art like the 1805 Doré crystal chandelier and huge 1661 Brussels tapestries hanging in the lobby. The hotel's restaurants are just as posh; the French Room features a 59-color carpet that was custom-designed in Hong Kong as well as Italian hand-blown glass chandeliers. Many historic hotel restoration projects subdivide guest rooms to increase occupancy, but at the Adolphus they combined 800 rooms to make 439 larger rooms. All rooms are decorated with Chippendale- and Queen Anne-style furniture and Williamsburg paneling. At 1321 Commerce St. downtown. See "Dallas Hotels and Motels" chart for rates.

Southfork Ranch

The TV home of J.R., Sue Ellen, Bobby, and Miss Ellie was once a real ranch owned by another J.R., but only the exterior was used in the TV show. It's now a *Dallas* museum that features memorabilia from the cast and show, including the gun that shot J.R. and an 18-story oil rig. To get here, take US 75 north to Parker Rd. (exit 30), then go east six miles and make a right at FM 2551, then left at the Southfork sign. Winter hours are 9 a.m.-5 p.m., summer hours 9 a.m.-6 p.m. Admission, which includes a guided tour, is $6 adults, $5 seniors, $4 children 4-12. Parking costs an additional $2 per vehicle. Call (800) 989-7800 or (214) 442-6536 for more information.

The Studios at Las Colinas

When it comes to attracting cinematic projects to Texas, one of the state's most important assets is this film production complex in Irving, just outside the city's northwestern city limits.

The Studios offers tours of soundstages where interiors for *Silkwood, Talk Radio, Robo-Cop, Born on the Fourth of July, JFK, True Stories, The Trip to the Bountiful, Wayne's World, Leap of Faith,* and many other movies were shot. The admission price of $9.95 for adults, $7.95 for ages 65 and above, and $4.95 for ages 4-12 includes entrance to the adjacent **National Museum of Communications.** At 6301 N. O'Connor Rd. in Irving, northwest of Dallas via I-635, then two miles north of the Las Colimas horse sculptures. For further information call (214) 869-FILM.

ACCOMMODATIONS

Dallas has all the usual chain hotels but unfortunately very little in the budget category. Although Hostelling International/American Youth Hostels maintains an affiliate North Texas Council (tel. 214-350-4294), 3530 Forest Lane, no. 127, Dallas, TX 75234, there is as yet no hostel in Dallas—or anywhere north of Austin for that matter. The Council intends to establish something in the DFW area within the near future, so call in advance of arrival if hosteling fits your travel style.

Visiting royalty need not rough it. The city's top hotels continue to receive high critical acclaim for lavish service. *Condé Nast Traveler*

home of the stars,
Southfork Ranch

DALLAS CONVENTION AND VISITORS BUREAU

2

1. Cadillac Ranch, Amarillo; **2.** boots, Cadillac Jack Boot Co., Austin (photos by Joe Cummings)

1. longhorn steer; **2.** End of the line in the beef industry;
3. Y.O. Ranch entrance, Mountain Home (photos by Joe Cummings)

DALLAS HOTELS AND MOTELS

Add 13% hotel tax to all rates. Area code: 214.

DOWNTOWN

The Adolphus; 1321 Commerce; tel. 742-8200 or (800) 221-9083; $156-295; historic, refrigerators, weekend discounts

Crescent Court; 400 Crescent Ct.; tel. 871-3200 or (800) 527-654-6541; $230-320; near McKinney Ave. entertainment district, heated pool, spa

Dallas Grand Hotel; 1914 Commerce; tel. 747-7000; $59-125; weekend and senior discounts

Fairmont Hotel; 1717 N. Akard St.; tel. 720-2020 or (800) 527-4727; $120-215; Arts District location, heated pool

Holiday Inn Aristocrat; 1933 Main; tel. 741-7700 or (800) HOLIDAY; $99-133; historic, refrigerators, weekend discounts

Hotel St. Germain; 2516 Maple Ave.; tel. 871-2516; $200-600; historic, near McKinney Ave., jacuzzi, fireplaces

Howard Johnson; 1015 Elm; tel. 748-9951; $78-88; pool

Hyatt Regency; 300 Reunion; tel. 651-1234 or (800) 233-1234; $150-175; pool, tennis courts

Ramada Inn; 1011 S. Akard; tel. 421-1083 or (800) 272-6232; $45-55; near Convention Center, heated pool, airport shuttle

Southland Center Hotel; 400 N. Olive; tel. 922-8000 or (800) 227-6884; $60-165; art gallery, exercise room

DALLAS-FORT WORTH AIRPORT

Airport Marriott; 8440 Freeport Pkwy.; tel. 929-8800 or (800) 228-9290; $129-145; pool, airport shuttle, coin laundry, weekend discounts

Crowne Sterling Suites; 4650 W. Airport Frwy.; tel. 790-0093; $99-110; heated pool, airport shuttle, coin laundry, complimentary full breakfast, evening cocktails, weekend discounts

Comfort Inn (Airport); 825 Esters Blvd.; tel. 929-0066 or (800) 221-2222; $39-51; pool, airport shuttle, complimentary breakfast

Four Seasons Resort and Club; 4550 N. MacArthur Blvd., Irving; tel. (214) 717-0700, fax 717-2550; $140-265; refrigerators, golf course, tennis courts, racquetball, squash, three pools (one heated), sauna, business center

Harvey Hotel (Airport); 4545 John Carpenter Frwy.; tel. 929-4500; $95-130; heated pool, airport shuttle, weekend discounts

La Quinta Motor Inn; 4105 W. Airport Frwy.; tel. 252-6546 or (800) 531-5900; $49-57; pool, airport shuttle

Red Roof (Airport); 8150 Esters Blvd.; tel. 929-0020 or (800) 843-7663; $35-48; airport shuttle

Sheraton Grand Hotel; 4440 W. John Carpenter Frwy.; tel. 929-8400 or (800) 325-3535; $102-153; heated pool, airport shuttle, weekend discounts

NORTH DALLAS (OFF THE LBJ FREEWAY)

Comfort Inn; 3536 W. Kingsley; tel. 340-3501 or (800) 221-2222; $44-48; heated pool

Courtyard by Marriott; 2930 Forest; tel. 620-8000 or (800) 228-9290; $49-85; pool, weekend discounts

Dallas Parkway Hilton; 4801 LBJ Frwy.; tel. 661-3600 or (800) 445-8667; $85-125; heated pool, shuttle to Galleria, weekend discounts

Econo Lodge; 9356 LBJ Frwy.; tel. 690-1220; $42-48; pool, coin laundry, senior discounts

Grand Kempinski; 15201 Dallas Pkwy.; tel. 386-6000 or (800) 426-3135; $145-185; indoor/outdoor pool, health club, weekend discounts

Motel 6; 2753 Forest Lane; tel. 620-2828; $28-35; pool

The Westin Hotel Galleria; 13340 Dallas Pkwy.; tel. 934-9494 or (800) 228-3000; $149-169; pool, refrigerators, jogging track, linked to Galleria

NORTHWEST (INCLUDING MARKET CENTER)

Best Western Market Center; 2023 Market Ctr.; tel. 741-9000 or (800) 528-1234; $45-87; pool, complimentary evening beverage, complimentary breakfast

The Clarion Hotel; 1241 W. Mockingbird; tel. 630-7000 or (800) 221-2222; $89-99; pool, coin laundry

(CONTINUED ON NEXT PAGE)

DALLAS HOTELS AND MOTELS (CONT.)

Add 13% hotel tax to all rates. Area code: 214.

Days Inn Texas Stadium; 2200 E. Airport Frwy.; tel. 438-6666 or (800) 325-2525; $40-46; pool, coin laundry, complimentary breakfast

Embassy Suites Market Center; 2727 Stemmons Frwy.; tel. 630-5332 or (800) EMBASSY; $109-119; heated pool, coin laundry, complimentary evening beverage

Executive Hotel; 3232 W. Mockingbird; tel. 357-5601; $49-72; near Love Field, pool, airport shuttle

Feature Holiday Market Center; 1955 Market Center; tel. 747-9551; $55-65; pool

Mansion on Turtle Creek; 2821 Turtle Creek Blvd.; tel. (214) 559-2100, fax 528-4187; $270-370; heated pool, health club, secretarial services

Ramada Hotel Market Center; 1055 Regal Row; tel. 634-8550 or (800) 346-8782; $59-99; pool, tennis courts, airport shuttle

Red Roof MC; 1550 Empire Central; tel. 638-5151 or (800) 843-7663; $35-45

TraveLodge MC; 4500 Harry Hines; tel. 522-6650; $54-76; seasonal and senior discounts

EAST

Days Inn Dallas; 6222 Belt Line; tel. 226-7621 or (800) 325-2525; $32-37; pool, complimentary breakfast

La Quinta Motor Inn East; 8303 E. Thornton Frwy.; tel. 324-3731 or (800) 531-5900; $45-58; pool

Motel 6; 3629 I-30 and Belt Line; tel. 226-7140; $28-35; pool

Motel 6—Mesquite; 3629 US 80; tel. 613-1662; $26 plus $5 each additional person; pool

Red Roof Inn Dallas East; 8108 E. Thorton Frwy.; tel. 388-8741 or (800) 843-7663; $42-51

---

magazine has ranked the **Mansion on Turtle Creek** among the top 10 hotels in the world for several years running. Two other Dallas hotels, **Crescent Court** and **Four Seasons**, have consistently made Condé Nast's top 10 U.S. list.

Another luxury hotel worth admiring is the 1906-vintage, French boutique-style **Hotel St. Germain** (tel. 871-2516), 2516 Maple Ave., which offers just seven guest suites. The St. Germain is cherished for such Gallic touches as Bastille Day winetastings for guests; if you have to ask the room rates, you definitely cannot afford them—$200-600, including a sumptuous breakfast. Another Maple Ave. European-style luxury inn is the 1924 **Stoneleigh Hotel** (tel. 871-7111), 2927 Maple Ave., with rates of $115-190.

See the "Dallas Hotels and Motels" chart for more specific information on hotel/motel accommodations throughout the city.

Campgrounds
KOA Kampgrounds Dallas (tel. 214-497-3353) in Denton, 30 miles northwest off I-35 E (Corinth Exit 460), offers tent/camper sites for $18, full hookups $23, and cabins $25; there's a pool on the premises. Closer to the city is the **Dallas Hi-Ho Campground** (tel. 223-4834), 18 miles south off I-35 E at Bear Creek Rd. (exit 412); full hookups are around $20. There are also several RV parks near Fort Worth.

Bed and Breakfasts
Bed & Breakfast Texas Style (tel. 800-899-4538 or 214-298-8586) is the largest B&B registry in the state, covering not only Dallas but most of the rest of the state. To book a B&B in North Central Texas, contact director Ruth Wilson, 4224 W. Red Bird Lane, Dallas, TX 75237.

FOOD

As you would expect for a city its size, Dallas offers food for virtually every taste and budget. It's definitely the state's gourmet capital, even if many of the big name places are corporate-owned. Meal prices tend to be on the high side if there's anything Southwestern on the menu.

American/Southwestern

$$$ Baby Routh: An offspring of the once highly acclaimed Routh Street Cafe of Stephan Pyles. This restaurant is spread across a pair of Victorian houses and is now the Dallas headquarters for Texas-style Southwestern cuisine. Like its progenitor, Baby Routh features an artful blend of international inspirations culled from culinary voyages through such disparate corners of the world as Japan, New Mexico, the Middle East, and the Deep South). At 2708 Routh downtown (tel. 214-871-2345); open Mon.-Sat. for lunch and dinner, Sunday for brunch and dinner.

$$$+ Dakota's: Nouveau Southwestern, with an emphasis on mesquite-grilled items served amidst a marble-floored, wood-paneled atmosphere. Great key lime pie. At 600 N. Akard downtown (tel. 740-4001); open Mon.-Fri. for lunch and dinner, Sat.-Sun. dinner only.

$$ to $$$ Deep Ellum Café: Serves a creative variety of Texas-American dishes, from Southwestern to Tex-Mex to Cajun to downhome. Very chic Deep Ellum location at 2704 Elm (tel. 741-9012); open Mon.-Fri. for lunch and dinner, Sat.-Sun. brunch and dinner.

$ 8.0: The ultra-chic, eclectic, health-oriented menu features such memorable dishes as "Ecraser dans la Rue (the Roadkill Platter)." Popular *après-soir* hangout—the CD jukebox has over 1,500 selections. At 2800 Routh (tel. 979-0880); open Mon.-Wed. 11 a.m.-1 a.m., Thurs.-Sat. 11 a.m.-2 a.m., Sunday 10 a.m.-midnight.

$$$+ Mansion on Turtle Creek: Where Dallas's rich and famous eat to be seen. The menu is always changing but is, as usual in Dallas, first-class Southwestern. Recent samplings have included barbecued veal and quail quesadillas, cheese-filled squash blossoms with grilled jicama, and tomato-pozole salad with roasted garlic-jalapeño dressing. Consistently chosen by the nation's food critics for lists of America's "top ten" or "top 50" restaurants. At 2821 Turtle Creek (tel. 526-2121); open daily for lunch and dinner.

$$$ Star Canyon: Here superstar chef Stephan Pyles offers up New Southwestern with a stronger emphasis on Texas roots than his previous endeavors. This means larger portions, plenty of Mexican elements—corn, beans, squash—and wood-roasted meats. Don't miss the house cocktail, a chile-infused rum concoc-tion known as *piña diabla.* Glitz-casual, Southern California atmosphere. At 3102 Oak Lawn at Cedar Springs (tel. 520-7827); open Sun.-Thurs. 6-10 p.m., Fri.-Sat. 6-11 p.m.

Asian

$ First Chinese B-B-Q: In spite of the name, this restaurant caters to a primarily Chinese clientele. Good Chinese-style barbecued pork ribs, marinated chicken, plus a few Vietnamese dishes. At 111 S. Greenville, Richardson (tel. 214-680-8216); open daily for lunch and dinner.

$ to $$ Han-Chu: Excellent northern Chinese menu. At 9100 N. Central (tel. 691-0900); open daily for lunch and dinner.

$ to $$ New Big Wong: A primarily Cantonese place with lots of fresh seafood selections. Another favorite late night spot. At 2121 Greenville (tel. 821-4198); open daily for lunch and dinner till 3 a.m.

$ to $$ Taiwan Restaurant: Probably the best Chinese restaurant in Dallas, featuring a range of regional cuisines. At 4890 Belt Line (tel. 387-2333); open daily for lunch and dinner.

$ Tong's House: Good Szechwan and Cantonese menu, very reasonable prices. At 1910 Promenade Center, Richardson (tel. 231-8858); open Mon.-Fri. for lunch only, Saturday for lunch and dinner.

$$ to $$$ Uncle Tai's Hunan Yuan: A branch of the famous Hunan restaurant of the same name in New York; the menu includes unusual dishes like venison in chile sauce. Elegant atmosphere. In the Galleria, north Dallas (tel. 934-9998); open daily for lunch and dinner.

$ Thai Lanna: All the usual noodle and curry dishes. At 4315 Bryan St. (tel. 827-6478); open Mon.-Sat. for lunch and dinner, Sunday dinner only.

Barbecue

$$ Clark's Outpost: Would you drive 128 miles roundtrip just to eat barbecue? Many Dallasites do, along with a number of the state's prominent chefs. Plain blue-checkered tablecloths, vinyl-backed chairs—by looking at it you'd never guess Clark's Outpost is a culinary mecca. The small but steady stream of celebrities, whose photos line the walls, is fairly recent; since 1974, Clark's has mostly served ranchers and their families from the Tioga area.

Owner-chef Warren Clark smokes ribs, brisket, and turkey breast over smoldering pecan, oak, and hickory for three days to achieve the silky smoothness for which his barbecue is famous. Other house specialties include quail legs, Idaho trout, calf fries, and tamales. Take a close look at the cowboy camp mural on one wall; the faces of the campers bear a close resemblance to those of chefs Dean Fearing (Mansion on Turtle Creek), Stephan Pyles (Star Canyon, Dallas), Robert Del Grande (Cafe Annie, Houston), and Clark himself.

The Outpost is at the intersection of US 377 and RM 922, 26 miles northeast of Denton, which is 38 miles north of Dallas via I-35 (tel. 817-437-2414); open Mon.-Thurs. 11 a.m.-9 p.m., Fri.-Sat. 11 a.m.-9:30 p.m., Sunday 11 a.m.-8:30 p.m.

$ **Sonny Bryan's Smokehouse:** Most Dallasites say Sonny's has the best barbecue in town—it's so popular the meat often sells out by 2 p.m. The quirky interior features chintzy Americana-like car-hood tables and school-desk chairs. At 2202 Inwood (tel. 357-7120); open Mon.-Fri. 10 a.m.-5 p.m. (or until they run out of barbecue), Saturday 11 a.m.-3 p.m. (ditto). Also in the West End at 302 N. Market (tel. 744-1610).

$ **Two Podners Bar-B-Q:** Smoked chicken is the star here, along with catfish, ribs, and a good variety of vegetable sides, cornbread, and cobbler. Take-out available. At 1441 Robert B. Cullum in downscale South Dallas (tel. 421-5387); open Tues.-Sun. for lunch until it's all gone.

$ **Ziggy's BBQ:** Picture servings of barbecue and chicken-fried steak in an ultramodern glass-and-steel setting and you've got Ziggy's pegged. In Plaza of the Americas at 600 N. Pearl (tel. 969-0953); open weekdays for lunch only.

Burgers

$ to $$ **Hard Rock Cafe:** Corporate rock 'n' roll America with burgers, pig sandwiches, fajitas, and rock memorabilia. At 2601 McKinney (tel. 214-855-0007); open daily 11 a.m.-1 a.m.

$ **Joe Willy's Market & Grill:** Big, do-it-yourself burgers with homemade fries and onion rings. At 7033 Greenville (tel. 691-8930); open daily for lunch and dinner.

$ **Prince of Hamburgers:** A locally famous, pre-McDonald's drive-in with curb service that's been serving burgers, fries, and shakes since 1927. At 5200 Lemmon Ave. in the Oak Lawn district (tel. 526-9081); open daily for lunch and dinner.

Cajun/Creole/Caribbean

$$ **Café Margaux:** Serves a mixture of Cajun and Creole dishes, with the accent on the latter. Good oysters Bienville and sautéed veal in Creole sauce. At 4527 Travis (tel. 214-520-1985); open Mon.-Sat. for lunch and dinner.

$ **Crescent City Café:** Great variety of inexpensive New Orleans dishes—po'boys, muffalettas, red beans and rice, étouffée—even café au lait and beignets. In the Deep Ellum district at 2615 Commerce (tel. 745-1900); open Mon.-Sat. for lunch and dinner, till 1 a.m. Friday and Saturday.

$ **Elaine's Kitchen:** An authentically Jamaican menu features jerk chicken, curried goat, and a host of other stews and curries. At 1912 Martin Luther King, Jr. in the up-and-coming South Dallas cheap gourmet ghetto (tel. 565-1008); open daily for lunch and dinner.

$$ **Pappadeaux Seafood Kitchen:** A boisterous branch of Houston's highly reputed Greek-owned Cajun seafood restaurant. All seafood is fresh and expertly prepared; house specialties include oysters Pappadeaux, boudin, and bread pudding. At 3520 Oak Lawn (tel. 521-4700); open daily for lunch and dinner.

Coffee

$ **City Java:** A popular Deep Ellum coffeehouse with high-quality, strong, dark-roasted coffees and espressos, pastries, homemade pizza, and rich desserts. Wednesday night poetry sessions adhere to the theme. At 2639-C Elm (tel. 214-742-JAVA); open Tues.-Thurs. 11:45 a.m.-midnight, Fri.-Sat. 1 p.m.-2 a.m., Sunday 1-6 p.m.

Downhome

$ **Bubba's:** All the classics—fried chicken, catfish, biscuits and cream gravy, chicken-fried steak. At 6617 Hillcrest (tel. 214-373-6527); open daily 6:30 a.m.-10 p.m.

$ **Celebration:** Offers downhome cooking served in a converted home. Adds middle-America fare like pot roast and meatloaf to the usual southern-style menu. At 4503 W. Lovers Lane (tel. 358-0612); open daily for lunch and dinner.

$ **Mama's Daughters' Diner:** A very popular breakfast and lunch spot with superb cornbread, yeast rolls, mashed taters, and fried chicken, plus thick, homemade pies. At 2014 Irving Blvd. (tel. 742-8646); open Mon.-Fri. 6 a.m.-3 p.m.

European

$$$+ **Juniper:** Foie gras, shaved black truffle, veal medallions with artichokes, and other selections prepared in the French country style at this local favorite. At 2917 Fairmount in northwest Dallas (tel. 214-855-0700); open Tues.-Sat. for dinner only.

$$ **L'Ancestral:** This family-owned, bistro-style restaurant serves country French cuisine. At 4514 Travis (tel. 528-1081); open Mon.-Sat. for lunch and dinner.

$ to $$ **Momo's Italian Specialties:** Probably the most authentic Italian food in town; also the best calzones and pizza. At 9191 Forest Lane (tel. 234-6800) and 8300 Preston (tel. 987-2082); open Mon.-Fri. for lunch and dinner, Sat.-Sun. dinner only.

$$$+ **The Riviera:** This chic Mediterranean-style dining room is highly acclaimed for Provençal-inspired offerings like mussels and scallops in saffron sauce, pepper-edged rack of lamb or duck, mixed grill of smoke quail, and pheasant sausage with polenta and sage. On Mimi Sheraton's list of the best 50 restaurants in America. At 7709 Inwood Rd. (tel. 351-0094); open daily for dinner only.

$$ **White Swan Cafe:** With far ranging selections like fajitas, lasagna, grilled rack of lamb, Cuban tapas, and coconut shrimp, it's hard to categorize the menu at this new spot in swank Turtle Creek Village. Count on a spicy, romantic evening. At 3888 Oak Lawn at Blackburn (tel. 528-7028) and at 6334 La Vista in northwest and northeast Dallas respectively; open Mon.-Sat. 11 a.m.-2 p.m., Sun.-Thurs. 5-10 p.m., Fri.-Sat. 5-11 p.m., Sunday brunch 10 a.m.-2 p.m.

Indian

All the Indian restaurants in Dallas serve a similar, North Indian, tandoor-based cuisine—South Indian restaurants apparently haven't made it this far south yet. Good bets are:

$$ **Bombay Cricket Club:** A cut above the others when it comes to service and atmosphere. At 2508 Maple Ave. (tel. 214-871-1333); open daily for lunch and dinner.

$ **India Palace:** Open daily for lunch and dinner at 13360 Preston (tel. 392-0190).

$ **Kebab-N-Kurry:** A good lunch buffet on weekdays. At 401 N. Central, Ste. 300 (tel. 231-5556); open daily for lunch and dinner.

$ **Taj Mahal:** Open Mon.-Fri. for lunch and dinner, Sat.-Sun. dinner only; at 9100 N. Central (tel. 692-0535).

Mexican

$ **Taco Cabaña:** Best Mexican take-out in the city. At 3923 Lemmon (tel. 214-522-3770); open 24 hours.

$ **Casa Rosa:** Among the most popular of the city's Mexican restaurants, with trendy specialties like blue corn enchiladas with fajitas and other Texas standbys. At 165 Inwood Rd. at Lovers Lane (tel. 350-5227); open daily for lunch and dinner.

$ **La Suprema Tortillería:** Specializes in no-lard, organic-grain tortillas and all-natural meats. At 7630 Military Pkwy. in Urbandale (tel. 388-1244); open Fri.-Sun. for lunch and dinner, Tues.-Thurs. lunch only.

$ to $$ **Mario's Chiquita:** Tasty, upscale Tex-Mex menu that includes ceviche, *tacos al carbón,* and *carne asada.* At 4514 Travis, Ste. 105 (tel. 521-0721); open daily for lunch and dinner.

$ **Martinez Café:** Solid, inexpensive Tex-Mex. At 3011 Routh (tel. 964-7898); open daily for lunch and dinner.

$ **Mia's:** A family-run place with the best chiles rellenos in town—expect long lines during peak dining hours. Where the Dallas Cowboys like to fatten up. At 4322 Lemmon (tel. 526-1020); open Mon.-Sat. for lunch and dinner.

$ to $$ **El Ranchito:** One of the only places in Dallas that serves *cabrito* (barbecued kid), albeit in the sanitized style required by state law rather than true *al pastor.* Mariachis nightly. At 610 W. Jefferson (tel. 946-4238); open daily for lunch and dinner.

Seafood

$$ **Daddy Jack's:** A casual spot with huge fresh seafood plates, convenient to Greenville

nightlife. At 1916 Greenville (tel. 214-826-4910); open daily for dinner only.

$ Dinger's Catfish Café: Excellent mesquite-smoked catfish in lime sauce and seafood salad; funky atmosphere, reasonable prices. At 8989 Forest (tel. 235-3251); open Mon.-Sat. for lunch and dinner.

$ to $$ S&D Oyster Company: The reliable kitchen specializes in fresh Gulf seafood, raw, boiled, or fried. At 2701 McKinney (tel. 880-0111); open Mon.-Sat. for lunch and dinner.

Steak

$$ to $$$ The Butcher Shop: A grill-it-yourself steak place; add $2 and have it cooked for you. At 808 Munger at Lamar (tel. 214-720-1032); open daily for dinner only.

$$$ Del Frisco's Double Eagle Steak House: Often cited as the city's best steakhouse; cuts are huge. Seafood selections also available. At 4300 Lemmon (tel. 526-9811); open Mon.-Sat. dinner only.

$$$+ Morton's of Chicago: A branch of Chicago's famous surf 'n' turf place. In the basement of a restored West End building at 501 Elm (tel. 741-2277); open daily for dinner.

$$ to $$$ Ruth's Chris Steak House: Famous nationwide for custom-aged, handcut, USDA prime beef; seafood also available. At 5922 Cedar Springs Rd. (tel. 902-8080); open daily for dinner only.

Vegetarian

$ Cosmic Cup: Hippie-Indian-style veggie dishes and great smoothies served in a converted Oak Lawn house. At 2912 Oak Lawn (tel. 214-521-6865); open Sun.-Thurs. 11 a.m.-10 p.m., Fri.-Sat. till midnight.

$ Kalachandji's: Pure Indian vegetarian (no eggs), served buffet-style by Hare Krishna followers without any obvious attempts to proselytize. Cheap and easy. At 5430 Gurley Ave. in the northeast part of the city (tel. 821-1048); open daily for lunch and dinner.

$$ Planet Cafe: "Eat globally, dine locally" is the motto at this smoke-free restaurant serving creative, tasty vegetarian dishes like tofu fajitas and veggie burgers made with ground broccoli, peas, and squash. At 6106 Luther Lane at Preston Center (tel. 368-2456); open Mon.-Sat. for lunch and dinner.

ENTERTAINMENT

Clubs and Bars

Dallas is a good town for club- and pub-crawling, with something for every predilection. As elsewhere, names come and go with astonishing regularity, so it's best to read the local papers for what's happening. The *Dallas Morning News* "Guide" section, published every Friday, is an excellent source of information since clubs are listed by category. Another good source, though not as meticulously organized, is the *Dallas Observer,* published every Thursday and emphasizing local music, art, and film criticism. Most clubs close at 2 a.m.

Several Dallas clubs specialize in satisfying "polkaholics," including the hot **Czech Club** (tel. 214-381-9072) at 4930 Military Pkwy., Saturday nights only. Other roots/ethnic dancing places include the Afro-Caribbean **Tropical Cove** at 1820 West Mockingbird (tel. 630-5822). Don't miss the Saturday night Trinidad-style chicken curry with potato-and-chickpea-stuffed roti. The **Royal Rack Reggae Pool Hall** (tel. 824-9733), 1906 Greenville, features live performances on weekends, and the Celtic-style **Tipperary Inn** (tel. 823-7167), 5815 Live Oak at Skillman, offers live music Thurs.-Sunday.

One of the most popular urban cowboy-type dance halls in Dallas is the **Country Connection** (tel. 869-9922), 2051 W. Northwest Hwy., which is generally open Tues.-Sunday. **Palms Danceland** (tel. 388-1922), 4906 Military Pkwy., used to be a daytime dance hall where housewives and truckers got together; in its latest incarnation, it's open Mon.-Sat. nights. The Palms gives lessons in two-step, schottische, and other country dances on Monday evenings. The **Top Rail** (tel. 556-9099), 2110 W. Northwest Hwy., has live country nightly, and gives lessons on Sunday and Monday evenings. At the **Pocket Sandwich Theatre** (tel. 821-1860), 5400 E. Mockingbird Lane, you can sometimes catch the Light Crust Doughboys, one of the greatest Western swing bands of all time. House band the Original Debonaires sends boots scootin' at **Debonair Danceland Westernplace** (tel. 826-5890) at 2810 Samuell in East Dallas.

Deep Ellum is the district for new rock and experimental music. Some of the clubs here aren't even labeled with signs—people just cruise the area and gather in Soho-style ware-houses for a night of light and sound pulsations. **Deep Ellum Live** (tel. 748-6222), 2727 Canton at Crowdus, draws national names in an eclectic nightly schedule of funk, rock, world beat, and alternative. The **Club Dada** (tel. 744-3232), 2720 Elm St., features a similar mix on a more local level. **Club Clearview** (tel. 283-5358), 2806 Elm, presents a harder-edged sound ranging from roots rock to punk funk. In the same warehouse on Elm is **The Video Lounge**, where patrons dance to the latest rock videos, including quite a few that never make it on MTV. You can hear more live music loosely labeled "alternative" at Deep Ellum's **Loose Change** (tel. 651-8988), 2807 Elm; **The Orbit Room** (tel. 748-5399), 2809 Commerce; **The Bone** (tel. 744-BONE), 2724 Elm; **Trees** (tel. 748-5009), 2709 Elm; and **The Terminal** (tel. 761-0040), 2610 Elm.

At the other end of the dance spectrum is the Top 40-ish **Dallas Alley** (tel. 988-WEST) in the West End district, where a complex of five dance clubs is frequented mostly by tourists and conventioneers. The **Hard Rock Cafe** (tel. 855-0007), 2601 McKinney, features the occasional eclectic lineup of live music, again geared more to tourists than locals.

Jazz fans will find several Dallas havens, including the **Collateral Club** (tel. 241-1969), 11407 Emerald, live music on Fridays; **Dream Café** (tel. 954-0486), 2800 Routh, live music Wed.-Sun.; and **Strictly Tabu** (tel. 528-5200), 1 Lomo Alto, nightly.

For blues, try **Ernie's** (tel. 233-8855), 5100 Belt Line #502, nightly; **RJ's Sho-Nuff** (tel. 528-5230), 3910 Maple, weekends; **Blue Cat Blues Club** (tel. 744-2293), 2617 Commerce, Wed.-Sun.; or **Schooner's** (tel. 821-1934), 1212 Skillman, Thurs.-Sunday. The Bone hosts a blues jam every Tuesday evening and often has blues bands on Wednesday and Thursday as well. For the latest blues happenings, call the Dallas Blues Society's recorded hotline at 521-BLUE.

Folk-music lovers can seek satisfaction at **Poor David's Pub** (tel. 821-9891), 1924 Greenville, live music Thurs.-Sun.; and **Barley House** (tel. 824-0306), 2916 N. Henderson, weekends. Texas singer-songwriters like Ray Wiley Hubbard, Mary Cutrufello, and Alejandro

Escovedo are often featured at the **Ozona Westex Grill** (tel. 265-1283), 4615 Greenville Ave., Thurs.-Saturday.

The Dallas branch of the statewide chain **Tejano Rodeo** (tel. 740-9967), 1815 N. Griffin St., hosts live *tejano* and *conjunto* bands.

If all else fails, simply wander down Greenville (the 1900 and 2000 blocks are "pub crawl central") and you'll be sure to come across something funky.

Cinema
Among the usual assortment of moviehouses large and small, one Dallas cinema stands out—way out. The 85,000 square-foot **AMC Grand** (tel. 350-7488) at I-35 and Northwest Hwy. boasts two dozen screens, and is the lagest movie theater in the country. The plush screening rooms feature seats with retractable armrests, 48 inches of legroom, and state-of-the-art sound. Trams shuttle moviegoers around the 13-acre parking lot; just don't forget where you parked.

Radio
KERA-FM 90.1, the city's primary public radio station, carries NPR and APR news along with eclectic programs of Texas singer-songwriter material, jazz, folk, blues, classic, alternative, and world music. Other non-traditional stations of interest: KAAM-AM 1310, big band, nostalgia; KNON-FM 89.3, *tejano,* R&B, folk, reggae; KOAI-FM 107.5 jazz; KPLX-FM 99.5 country; and WRR-FM 101.1, classical.

Amusement Parks
Six Flags Over Texas is a monster attraction located in Arlington—see "Vicinity of Dallas-Fort Worth."

EVENTS

January
Cotton Bowl: This nationally televised, college postseason football game on New Year's Day is a Texas athletic tradition. The halftime show often features the famous Kilgore Texas Rangerettes.

Greater Southwest Guitar Show: Once a year, usually the last weekend in January, some 8,000 musicians, dealers, and guitar collectors from around the globe attend the world's largest guitar show to wheel and deal on new and vintage instruments. Occasionally there are impromptu "superstar" jam sessions. At the Dallas Convention Center (tel. 214-243-4201), 650 S. Griffin.

April
Prairie Dog Chili Cookoff and Pickled Quail Egg-Eating World Championship: The oldest and largest chili cookoff in the Metroplex area. There aren't any prairie dogs in the chili, but the pickled quail eggs are for real. At Traders Village, 2602 Mayfield Rd., Grand Prairie. Usually the first weekend in April.

May
Cinco de Mayo: A Mexican holiday celebrated with zest at Fair Park in Dallas and at Traders Village, 2602 Mayfield Rd., Grand Prairie, with music, dancing, and food.

June-July
Shakespeare Festival of Dallas: Takes place at Samuel Grand Park (off E. Grand) Tues.-Sun. from mid-June through July. Two plays per season are presented, beginning at 8 p.m. Admission is free, but if you don't get there by 7 p.m., you probably won't get a seat. Concessions sell food, beer, and wine for picnics. Call (214) 559-2778 for more information.

Fourth of July: Freedom Fest at Fair Park features an array of musical acts and one of the largest fireworks displays in the Southwest. Call 670-8400 for details.

The **Mesquite Balloon Festival,** usually held in early July, attracts almost a hundred colorful competitors for a hot-air balloon rally. Call 285-0211 for location and dates.

September-October
National Championship Pow-Wow: Indian tribes from all over the U.S. come to Traders Village (Grand Prairie) the first weekend after Labor Day to celebrate Amerindian culture. Activities include an Indian dance competition with 11 different categories, archery contests, an arts and crafts show, and Indian food concessions. Sponsored by the Dallas-Fort Worth Intertribal Association (tel. 214-647-2331).

Texas State Fair: This combination livestock show, fireworks display, country music festival,

rodeo, and fashion show is over a hundred years old and is the largest state fair in the country. Held mid-September to late October; average attendance is around three million. At the Fair Park, where it's always been.

December
Candlelight Tour: The grounds and historic structures of the Old City Park are decorated for Christmas, and during the first or second week of the month, Dallas residents gather for caroling, storytelling, square dancing, and a candlelight promenade.

SPORTS AND RECREATION

Rodeo
Every Friday and Saturday night from the first week in April through the last week in September, the **Mesquite Championship Rodeo** is held in Mesquite Arena, about 15 minutes southeast of Dallas. This professional event has been a tradition since 1958; nowadays a "skybox" at the covered arena leases for up to $9000 a season, and the rodeo is broadcast weekly on the Nashville Network. The show is very well executed—if you've never been to a rodeo this is a good one to start with, since the excitement level here rivals that of a professional football game. The two-hour rodeo starts at 8 p.m., but gates open at 6:30 p.m. The Barbecue Pavilion serves barbecue plates for $8 adult portion, $5 childrens.

The rodeo arena is off LBJ Freeway (South) at the Military Parkway exit. Grandstand seating is $8 adults, $7 seniors 59+, $4 children 12 and under; reserved boxes $12. For information and reservations, call (800) 833-9339 or (214) 285-8777.

Baseball
The **Texas Rangers** American League team plays in the Ballpark in nearby Arlington from mid-April to early October. See the "Arlington" section under "Vicinity of Dallas-Fort Worth" for details.

Basketball
The **Dallas Mavericks** is a relatively young basketball team, but it's already getting into the playoffs every year. The team plays at Reunion Arena in the Reunion district between

November and April. Call (214) 658-7068 for ticket information.

Football
The **Dallas Cowboys** play from late August through mid-December (later, if they make it to the playoffs) at Texas Stadium off E. Airport Freeway.

Guided tours of the stadium cost $4 and include a walk down the field, a ride in the coaches' elevator, and a tour of the press box. Tours depart at 10 a.m. and 2 p.m. on weekdays, 11 a.m. and 12:30 p.m. on weekends. Call (214) 579-5000 for tour, game, or ticket information.

Hockey
The **Dallas Stars** professional hockey team plays at Reunion Arena from October to mid-April. Call (214) GO-STARS for game dates and ticket information. The **Dallas Freeze** of the Central Hockey League plays Nov.-April at Fair Park Coliseum. Call 631-PUCK for information.

Polo
The **Willow Bend Polo and Hunt Club** is headquartered in Plano, north of Dallas. The season runs May-June and Sept.-November. Many of the matches pit international teams against the Texans. For information, call (214) 248-6298.

The **Dallas Dragoons** play cowboy polo year round at the **Bear Creek Polo Ranch** in Red Oak, 25 minutes south of downtown Dallas. Admission to their games on Tuesday, Thursday, Saturday, and Sunday is $10 and includes a barbecue at the ranch. Call 979-0300 for more information.

Nature Trails
The **Mountain View College Nature Trail** winds through 40 acres of the northern section of this campus, off W. Illinois Ave. southwest of Dallas near Grand Prairie. Open daily; free admission. In southwest Dallas the **Dallas Nature Center,** a preserve of wooded hills and rolling prairies, is a living example of how the whole area once appeared. It's at 7575 Wheatland (tel. 214-296-1955); admission is $1 adults, 50 cents children; open daily 9 a.m.-5 p.m. The **L.B. Houston Nature Trail** is part of L.B. Houston Park, a large nature preserve maintained by Dallas Parks and Recreation, just north of the University of Dallas on the west edge of the city limits. Open daily; free admission.

Wet 'n' Wild
This water park is northeast of Dallas in the satellite city of Garland. It features the usual water fun: a Surf Lagoon wave pool, Hydramaniac and Blue Niagara water rides, plus swimming pools and food concessions. At the intersection of LBJ Frwy. and Northwest Highway. Open weekends in May, daily from Memorial Day through mid-August, then weekends again till mid-September. Admission is $19 adults, $15 children 3-9, and $9.50 seniors (55+). Parking is free. Call (214) 840-0600 for additional information.

Texas Stadium, Dallas

SHOPPING

Dallas boasts 630 shopping centers, more per capita than anywhere else in the United States. Most are just like shopping centers anywhere else, rows of chain stores or trendy boutiques. Also, if you're looking for bargains, this isn't the place—try Fort Worth, or better yet, El Paso. That said, there are a few shopping places worth visiting as attractions in themselves.

The **Galleria** (tel. 214-702-7100), Dallas Pkwy. at LBJ Frwy. in north Dallas, is a "supermall" with an attached Westin Hotel, four-star restaurants, five-theater cinema, year round ice rink, and 195 stores, including Tiffany & Co., Gucci, Louis Vuitton, Saks Fifth Ave., the American Museum of Historical Documents, FAO Schwarz, and many other ritzy names. **Highland Park Village** (tel. 559-2740), Preston and Mockingbird in central Dallas, claims to be the first shopping center in Texas (est. 1931). It's situated on the line between two fashionable neighborhoods,

the Galleria

Highland Park and University Park. The parking lot is full of German cars; stores in this Rodeo Drive wannabe include Polo-Ralph Lauren, Chanel of Paris, and Guy Laroche.

Back on earth, there's **Olla Podrida** (tel. 934-3603), with over 60 arts, crafts, and antique specialty shops. At 12215 Coit Rd., south of the LBJ Frwy. in north Dallas. For bargains, try **Traders Village** (tel. 647-2331), a 106-acre flea market that attracts an average of 1,600 vendors every weekend (Sat.-Sun. 8 a.m. to dusk). It's at 2602 Mayfield Rd. in Grand Prairie, west of Dallas off State 360; no admission charge, but parking costs $2.

The **West End MarketPlace** (tel. 954-4350) in the historic West End district features around 100 retail shops intermixed with restaurants. Then, across town at Main and Ervay, there's the original **Neiman-Marcus** (tel. 741-6911), the department store that started the American craze for expensive gifts. When Stanley Marcus sent out his first mail-order catalog in 1959, he advertised a Black Angus steer, delivered alive or in steaks. A more recent catalog offered pairs of Shar-Pei puppies ($4000) and Private Reserve Barbecue Sauce ($14).

An eclectic collection of shops has moved into the Elm St. warehouses of **Deep Ellum** (tel. 747-DEEP), including Arrangement, Southwest-style furniture; Elluments, ceramics and other decorative pieces; O.G.'s Funk, retro furniture; D'Gallery, art; Two Women Boxing, stationery and packing supplies; LA Street Beat, music; Blue Suede Shoe, used, new, and custom-made cowboy boots; and the Mozzarella Company, fresh cheeses.

INFORMATION

Tourist Offices
The **Dallas Visitors Information Center** at the front entrance of the West End Marketplace (tel. 214-880-0405), 603 Munger Ave., carries a large selection of maps and brochures on Dallas and North Central Texas. Open Mon.-Sat. 11 a.m.-8 p.m., Sunday noon-8 p.m. Another branch of the visitor center occupies 1303 Commerce St. downtown. The **Dallas Convention and Visitors Bureau** (tel. 746-6677) is headquartered in Renaissance Towers at 1201 Elm St. in the offices

---

DALLAS TELEPHONE INFORMATION

Emergency (police, fire, medical): 911
Telephone Directory Assistance: 411
Area Code: 214
Weather Service: 787-1111
Time/Temperature: 844-4444
Amtrak: (800) 872-7245
DART: 979-1111
Road Conditions: 374-4100

---

of the chamber of commerce. Open Mon.-Thurs. 7:30 a.m.-7 p.m., Friday 7:30 a.m.-5 p.m., Saturday 9 a.m.-noon. For up to the minute information on Dallas happenings, call the Bureau's 24-hour Special Events Hotline at 746-6679.

Publications

The *Dallas Observer* is a free weekly newspaper with plenty of information on local events, arts, music, cinema, and restaurants. It's distributed mostly in restaurants and clubs, and in some shops. *D Magazine* is a monthly focusing on a mix of local politics, civic happenings, fashions, and personalities. *D* is available at local newsstands. The daily *Dallas Times Herald* carries reviews of local restaurant and entertainment, as well as a listing of current events and museum exhibits.

Maps

The AAA Dallas map is quite good and is available free to AAA members from the office at 4425 N. Central Expwy. (tel. 214-526-7911). It's open Mon.-Fri. 8:30 a.m.-5 p.m., Saturday 9 a.m.-1 p.m. Serious map users will want to obtain the Mapsco Dallas set of maps ($22), which are revised annually. Contact Mapsco, Inc., (tel. 521-2131), 5308 Maple Ave., Dallas, TX 75235.

Telephone

The area code for Dallas is 214.

GETTING THERE AND AROUND

Airports

Dallas-Fort Worth International Airport (tel. 214-574-3197) is the world's second-busiest airport and the largest U.S. airport. Around 20 airlines offer daily service to 167 U.S. and 62 international destinations. The airport is 18 miles northeast of Dallas; allow 30 to 45 minutes' driving time from the downtown area ($20-25 by taxi, $8-10 by airport shuttle). DFW is practically a self-contained city, enhanced by the attached Hyatt Regency DFW (Terminal 3). The Hyatt's health club, golf course, and tennis and racquetball courts are open to airport travelers, as is the 24-hour Business Communication Center for faxes, copying, and the like. The DFW Airport Assistance Center at Terminal 2W, Gate 4, is also open 24 hours. Snacks, meals, and beverages to suit virtually every craving are available from the airport's 37 restaurants and food outlets.

Should you have time to kill while waiting at DFW, skip over to the **American Airlines C.R. Smith Museum** (tel. 817-967-1560), four miles southwest of the airport off State 360 South. The 25,000-square-foot, $8.7-million facility opened in 1993, features a fully restored DC-3, scale models of various American Airlines aircraft, several aircraft engines, and over 1,000 other aviation artifacts. Also of interest is a flight lab containing wind tunnels, test equipment, and flight simulators; a theater furnished with first-class airplane seats presents the large-screen film *Dream of Flight* in surround-sound stereo.

Love Field is a commuter airport seven miles northwest of town (taxi $12-15, shuttle $8-10, city bus to the Arts District 25 cents). The main user of Love Field is Southwest Airlines.

Super Shuttle offers van service to both airports and Dallas. The airport terminals have designated waiting zones; from Dallas, you must call for a reservation (tel. 817-329-2000).

City Buses

Dallas Area Rapid Transit (DART) has bus routes through town as well as to DFW International Airport and Love Field. One very useful service is the three "Hop A Bus" high-frequency routes (look for the buses painted like rabbits, kangaroos, and frogs) that circulate downtown through the Arts District, Deep Ellum, the Core, West End, and Reunion areas. These cost 25 cents one-way with unlimited transfers on any one route in one direction. Depending on the route, the Hop A Bus runs every five to 12 minutes from 6:30 a.m. till 6:30 p.m. A Hop A Bus route map is available at the Dallas Visitors Center, or you can call (214) 979-1111 for schedule information.

Also useful for exploring the McKinney Ave. dining and shopping area is the "McKinney Ave. Trolley," which plies a 2.8-mile, 23-stop route along McKinney Ave. Operating hours are 10 a.m.-10 p.m. Sun.-Thurs., till midnight Friday and Saturday; fares are 75 cents one-way or $3 for an all-day pass for adults, 50 cents one-way for children 2-12. Three-day and monthly passes also available.

Taxis
Two taxi services in Dallas include **Lone Star Cab** (tel. 214-821-6310) and **Yellow Checker Cab** (tel. 426-6262 or 800-749-9422).

Tours
D-Tours (tel. 214-241-7729) offers custom, escorted sightseeing of Dallas and vicinity to individuals and groups. Bilingual and multilingual guides available on request. **Dallas Gray Line Tours** (tel. 824-2424) has several prearranged itineraries covering the city's main attractions that range from $20 for a three-hour tour to $32 all day.

FORT WORTH

"Cowtown, U.S.A." is the smaller brother to Dallas in the double heart of the Metroplex. It's been said that while Dallas is yuppie, Fort Worth is just "yup" (cowboyese for "yes"), but in several respects the city is more sophisticated than Dallas will ever be. Despite the fact that its population (475,000) is less than half that of the Big D's, its art museums are as good or better than anything found in Dallas, it has a modern music/theater/dance center that's a world treasure, and its liquor laws are much more liberal. A recent survey found one tavern for every 26 people, compared with one per 3,500 in Dallas. City planning is, for the most part, exemplary; the park network is second in total acreage only to Chicago. Several national publications have named Fort Worth on their "America's Best Places to Live and Work" top 10 lists.

But the city really shouldn't be compared to Dallas. Since the early 1900s, it's been the pet project of a succession of local millionaires, from publisher Amon Carter to the financier Bass brothers, who've taken it upon themselves to make Fort Worth a livable city. Examples: a Bass private security force patrols the downtown area; the city subway is owned by the Tandy Corporation. If you ask city residents how they feel about this patronization, most say they prefer a well-run monarchy to a potholed democracy. One thing's for certain: there's not another town anything like it in the United States.

Climate
Fort Worth's weather is virtually the same as in Dallas, ranging from 36-56° F in January to 74-95° F in July. Precipitation most frequently occurs April-May and September.

History
Fort Worth began when the U.S. Army's Company F, Second Dragoons, established Camp Worth, named for Major General W.J. Worth, a hero of the War of 1812 and the just-completed War with Mexico. The camp was built on a bluff overlooking the Trinity River; in the 1850s, a settlement grew up around the camp and it was upgraded to Fort Worth. Following the Civil War, the great Texas cattle drives flourished; it's estimated that between 1866 and the mid-1880s around 10 million head of Texas cattle were driven north along the Chisholm, Dodge City, and Loving-Goodnight trails. The Chisholm Trail, named for Texas cattleman Jesse Chisholm, ran right through Fort Worth, which soon became known as "Cowtown." This was the last major outpost along the trail before it continued

FORT WORTH CONVENTION AND VISITORS BUREAU

Fort Worth

CATTLE TRAILS

to Abilene, Kansas, so cattle drovers always stopped here for supplies and last minute revelry; on the way back from delivering beeves, it was the first stop where they could spend their earnings. Hence, the town quickly grew into an assemblage of saloons, casinos, and brothels. The wildest part of town was Hell's Half Acre, where the Convention Center and Water Gardens are now situated. This was a favorite hiding place for George Parker and Harry Longabaugh, better known as Butch Cassidy and the Sundance Kid.

When the railroad came to town in 1876, Fort Worth was transformed from a place where cattle drives started to a spot where they ended—livestock continued northward by rail. By the turn of the century, Armour and Swift had established meat-packing plants at the Fort Worth Stockyards so fewer live cattle had to be transported. By the mid-20th century trucking had entered the picture, which meant meat and livestock could be moved northward more quickly and in smaller units. This resulted in the gradual decline of the stockyards, since the need for thousands of pens, feed lots, water facilities, and yard-hand personnel was greatly reduced.

In the post-WW II era, Fort Worth's fortune waxed and waned with livestock and agriculture, but in recent years the city has been aggressive in attracting high-tech interests to the area, including defense and aerospace contractors. The Tandy Corporation, owner of the nationwide Radio Shack chain, is a major local employer, as are American Airlines, Lockheed Fort Worth, Burlington Northern Railroad, Pier 1 Imports, and Bell Helicopter. The city is also home to one of the major U.S. currency plants outside of Washington, D.C.

SIGHTS

Fort Worth Stockyards National Historic District

In the early part of the century, the Fort Worth stockyards were the largest in the world. Their size and importance declined with the advent of the trucking industry, but in 1976 the U.S. Department of the Interior added the entire district to the National Register of Historic Places, thereby saving the area from further modification. The yards still play a very active role in the Texas livestock industry and are host to 42 livestock commission companies who participate in weekly auctions. Around 50 restaurants, saloons, dance halls, art galleries, and Western-wear shops in the district add to the daily and nightly activity.

The center of the Stockyards is the **Livestock Exchange** at 131 E. Exchange Ave., an immense mission-style structure built in 1902. In addition to livestock commission offices, the complex houses the offices of a number of Fort Worth attorneys and architects, the **North Fort Worth Historical Society,** and art galleries. Behind the exchange are the stock holding pens and the auction arena. Weekly cattle auctions are held every Wednesday at 2 p.m. and transmitted by satellite to buyers all over the country; the public is welcome to attend. Hog auctions take place Mon.-Tues. at 9 a.m., and special auctions occur the last Thursday of every month. Next door is the **Cowtown Coliseum** (tel. 817-625-1025), built in 1907-08 to house the annual Southwestern Exposition and Stock Show. This was the site of the first indoor rodeo in 1918.

The **Fort Worth Visitor Information Center** occupies a small building opposite the Livestock Exchange Building. Across the street from the Coliseum are mule barns built in 1911, which serve as the new home of the **National Cowgirl Hall of Fame.** On the next block east from the Coliseum is the **Stockyards Hotel** (Thannisch Building), constructed in 1906-07 and restored in 1984. Bonnie and Clyde once stayed here; the "Bonnie and Clyde Room" is one of several Texas theme rooms offered to guests. On the first floor of the hotel is **Booger Red's Saloon & Restaurant** and the **Stockyards Drugstore,** both in continuous operation since 1913. Other buildings along N. Main and Exchange vary in age, with most dating from 1910-22.

The Stockyards really come alive during Pioneer Days in September, the Chisholm Trail Roundup in June, and the Southwestern Exposition Stock Show and Rodeo in January. On Sunday mornings during these events you can visit the interdenominational **Cowboy Church** in a dirt corral behind the auction arena. Practically everybody who attends—mostly rodeo cowboys, livestock traders, and ranchers—will be wearing Resistols and Wranglers, including the pastor.

The Stockyards District is approximately 2.5 miles north of downtown Fort Worth via N. Main. Turn right on E. Exchange to reach the Coliseum, Livestock Exchange, and visitor center. A guided walking tour of the Stockyards can be arranged through the visitor center on E. Exchange Avenue.

Fort Worth Cultural District

If you're keeping score, note that Fort Worth has four museums in its arts district while Dallas has only one. None of the museums described below charges admission except for occasional special exhibits. Foremost is the **Kimbell Art Museum** at the intersection of Arch Adams St. and Camp Bowie Boulevard. Fort Worth industrialist Kay Kimbell left his art collection and his entire fortune to the Kimbell Art Foundation, which opened the museum in 1972. The building was designed by architect Louis Kahn and is an optimal combination of vaulted ceilings and natural light sources. The permanent collection includes works by Picasso, Tinteretto, Murillo, Van Dyck, El Greco, Rembrandt, Monet, Cézanne, and other big names, as well as collections of Greek, pre-Cortesian, Asian, and African art. This museum is said to have the second-highest acquisition budget in the U.S., and since it's a fairly young institution, new acquisitions are still accumulating. A recent purchase was Matisse's $1 million L'Asie. The Kimbell also regularly hosts traveling exhibits, art seminars, lectures, films, and musical performances. Open Tues.-Fri. 10 a.m.-5 p.m., Saturday noon-8 p.m., and Sunday noon-5 p.m.; admission is free. Call (817) 332-8451 for information.

The **Amon Carter Museum** (tel. 738-1933) is off Camp Bowie Blvd. between Lancaster and Montgomery. Amon Carter, the founder of the Fort Worth Star-Telegram, left his collection of Western art by Frederic Remington and Charles Russell, as well as a considerable sum of money to the city for the establishment of a museum devoted to American art and photography. Other artists whose works are on display include Georgia O'Keeffe, Winslow Homer, Laura Gilpin, Ansel Adams, Grant Wood, Martin Johnson Heade, and William Michael Harnett. Open Tues.-Sat. 10 a.m.-5 p.m. and Sunday 1-5:30 p.m. Admission is free.

The **Modern Art Museum of Fort Worth** (tel. 738-9215) lies across Lancaster St. from the Amon Carter. This was the city's first museum, originally occupying the second floor of the Carnegie Library downtown starting in 1901. The new location houses the best collection of modern art in the Southwest, including works by Picasso, David Hockney, Mark Rothko, Frank Stella, Andy Warhol, and Jackson Pollock. Open Tues.-Sat. 10 a.m.-5 p.m., Sunday 1-5 p.m. Free admission.

At Montgomery and Crestline is the **Museum of Science and History**, which includes the **Noble Planetarium** and the **Omni Theater.** At the Omni, a six-foot, one-ton film projector projects 70 mm images on a tilted dome screen 80 feet in diameter. Together with a 72-speaker, six-track sound system, the theater's science presentations are guaranteed to keep you awake. Hours are Mon. 9 a.m.-5 p.m., Tues.-Thurs. 9 a.m.-8 p.m., Fri.-Sat. 9 a.m.-9 p.m., Sunday noon-8 p.m. General museum admission is $3 adults, $1 seniors and children. Omni shows cost $5.50 adults, $3.50 seniors and children under 12. Planetarium admission is $3. Call 732-1631 for program information.

Other Museums

The **Cattleman's Museum** (tel. 817-332-7064), at 1301 W. 7th on the first floor of the Texas and Southwestern Cattle Raisers Foundation, is a small collection of exhibits that chronicle the development of the ranching and cattle industry. Open Mon.-Fri. 8:30 a.m.-4:30 p.m.; free admission.

Seven restored Texas log cabins make up the **Log Cabin Village** (tel. 926-5881) off University Dr. (2100 Log Cabin Village Lane) near Texas Christian University. Each was once owned by a different Tarrant County pioneer family; one belonged to the uncle of Cynthia Ann Parker, a young girl who became famous when she was kidnapped by Comanches. Years after her capture, she was rescued but couldn't reaccustom herself to Anglo culture; she eventually married Chief Nocona and gave birth to Quanah Parker, the last Comanche war chief. During tours of the cabins, there are demonstrations of candledipping, weaving, spinning, quilting, and flour-milling. Open Mon.-Fri. 9 a.m.-5 p.m., Saturday 11 a.m.-5 p.m., and

Sunday 1-4:30 p.m. Admission is $1.50 adults, $1.25 for children under eight. Guided tours are available for $2.

Sundance Square

Named for the Sundance Kid, who used to hole up in Fort Worth between bank robberies, this downtown district preserves some of the city's turn-of-the-century architecture. It covers eight historic city blocks, separated by redbrick streets. At the north end of the square is the massive Tarrant County Courthouse, built around 1895 of pink granite and marble in the Renaissance Revival style.

The oldest building in the square is the **Knights of Pythias Hall** at 317 Main. On the National Register of Historic Places, the turreted building was erected in 1881 as the world's first Pythian Temple by Justus H. Rathbone, the fraternal order's founder. Haltom's Jewelers on the bottom floor has been in business since 1893. The top floor is now home to Casa Mañana On the Square, with year round live-theater performances. The **Plaza Hotel,** at 301 Main, was built in 1908 and was one of the town's last working brothels before it was restored in 1982 as an office building with the urbane Prego Pasta House Restaurant on the bottom floor.

The unnamed building at 309 Main was erected in 1895 and now houses the **Sid Richardson Collection of Western Art,** an assortment of 60 paintings by Frederic Remington and Charles Russell. Other buildings of historic interest include the Weber Building (1880-1915) at 302 Main, the Conn Building (1906) at 310 Main, the Jetts Building (1907) at 400 Main (with Richard Haas's trompe l'oeil mural *The Chisholm Trail*), the City National Bank Building (1886), and Fire Station No. 1 (1907), which houses an interpretive exhibit recounting Fort Worth history.

Caravan of Dreams

The hard-to-classify Caravan of Dreams experiment could be placed under several different headings, but as much as anything else belongs alongside museums and historic buildings as one of Fort Worth's unique attractions. Backed by billionaire "ecopreneur" Ed Bass, the Caravan's location at the west edge of Sundance Square supports a live theater, multitrack and MIDI recording studio, rooftop grotto and desert garden, multicultural mural group, and nightclub/restaurant. It's one of various Bass ventures found throughout the world, including Synergetic Press and Biosphere II in Arizona, and the October Galleries in London and Kathmandu. Jazz musicians often claim the Caravan is at the top of their list of places to play in the world; seminal alto saxophonist/composer Ornette Coleman has recorded several albums on the Caravan's label. The center's Texas Stage, formerly the more imaginatively named "Theater of All Possibilities," presents every-

theater mural, Caravan of Dreams

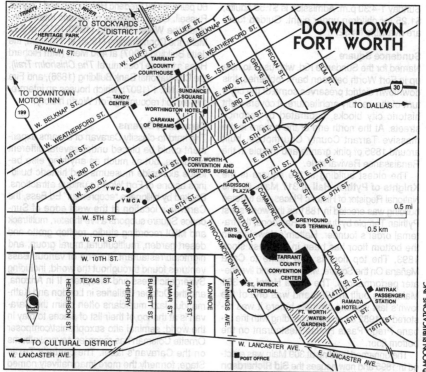

DOWNTOWN FORT WORTH

© MOON PUBLICATIONS, INC.

thing from Greek tragedies to Asian classical drama to experimental theater.

The landmark geodesic dome on the roof contains a controlled biosphere for some 300 varieties of cacti and succulents, including rare species like the Malagasy thorn forest's *Didierea trolii.* Inside the building are several murals created by Caravan artists Zara Kriegstein, Flash Allen, Corinna MacNeice, and Felipe Cabeza de Vaca. Two jazz murals cover a total of 720 square feet and recount the history and development of jazz from the arrival of African slave ships to its ascension as a world art. A gift shop in the lobby sells Caravan souvenirs. It's at 312 Houston (tel. 817-429-4000) and is open to the public Mon.-Fri. from 11 a.m., Sat.-Sun. at 4 p.m. For an excellent account of Ed Bass's multiple interests, read "The Long, Strange Trip of Ed Bass" in the June 1986 *Texas Monthly.*

Fort Worth Water Gardens

Architect Philip Johnson designed this descending series of terraces and water sculptures, built in 1974. The park covers four city blocks in an area known as "Hell's Half Acre" during the Wild West era. Now it's a quiet place to get away from the downtown summer heat. Between Houston and Commerce streets near the Convention Center.

Fort Worth Zoo

Once again, Fort Worth outdoes Dallas. Established in 1909, this 35-acre zoo holds nearly 5,000 animals of 948 different species, including the largest collection of reptiles in the country. Recently it was rated one of the top five zoos in the country by *Family Life* magazine, among the top 12 by the *Los Angeles Times.*

The James R. Record Aquarium features an extensive selection of fresh- and saltwater fish, and the elephant grounds is one of the most successful in the U.S. for Asian elephant breeding. In the Asian Falls section, the new Asian Rhino Ridge offers a boardwalk stroll past rare one-horned Asian rhinos, Asian cranes, Axis deer, and blackbuck antelope.

The World of Primates exhibit—the only such exhibit in the nation to feature all four great ape species—allows visitors to observe endangered lowland gorillas, bonobos, and orangutans in an indoor, climate-controlled tropical rainforest. The new Raptor Canyon highlights birds of prey. Near Texas Christian University at 1989 Colonial Parkway off University Dr.; open Mon.-Fri. 10 a.m.-5 p.m., Sat.-Sun. 10 a.m.-6 p.m. Admission is $5 adults, $2.50 seniors over 65 and children 3-12; half-price admission for all every Wednesday. Call (817) 871-7000 for more information.

Thistle Hill Cattle Baron Mansion

Originally built in 1903 on the city's southern edge, this handsome Georgian Revival mansion recalls the Fort Worth cattle boom that created a new Western aristocracy around the turn of the century. Listed on the National Register of Historic Places, the home is completely furnished with fine period antiques.

Thistle Hill is open for hourly guided tours Mon.-Fri. 10 a.m.-3 p.m., Sunday 1-4 p.m. Admission is $4 adults, $2 seniors and children 7-12. At 1509 Pennsylvania Ave.; call (817) 336-1212 for information.

Tarantula Steam Train

Named for an early railroad map of Fort Worth that showed spider-like rail lines radiating in all directions, this excursion train is operated the by Fort Worth & Western Railroad, a regional freight line. Southern Pacific engine No. 2248, used on the Texas State Railroad until the passenger load became too great, steams a 1.5-hour, 10-mile roundtrip route from the Eighth Avenue Depot downtown at 2318 S. 8th Ave., across the Trinity River, to the Stockyards Station at 140 E. Exchange Avenue. At the Stockyards the train slides onto a 1920s-vintage Union Pacific turntable before heading back in the opposite direction.

The Tarantula makes three runs daily, except Thanksgiving and Christmas, at 12:15, 2:30, and 4:45 p.m. A half-hour stopover at the Stockyards Station, housed in a former sheep and hog pen, allows for an examination of feed bins, animal loading ramps, and other artifacts left behind after the closing of the Swift and Armour meat-packing plants 30 years ago. In the return direction the train departs at 1:15, 3:30, and 5:45 p.m. Roundtrip fares are $10 for adults, $8 over 55, $3 ages 3-12; one-way tickets cost $6, $5, and $3 respectively.

ACCOMMODATIONS

See the accompanying chart for hotel and motel information.

Campgrounds and RV Parks

The U.S. Army Corps of Engineers administers six public campgrounds on Benbrook Lake, six miles southwest of town off Loop 820 at US 377. Five feature drive-in sites with water only for $8-10 a night, w/e for $10-14: **South Holiday, Bear Creek Park, Mustang Point Park, Rocky Creek Park,** and **Westcreek Circle.** Mustang Point Park is closed October 1 to March 31. The remaining campground, **Mustang Creek Park,** is a no-fee, three-acre primitive site without water. All campsites have a 14-day limit; call (817) 292-2400 or (800) 284-2267 for more information.

Sunset RV Park (tel. 800-238-0567 or 738-0567) at 4921 White Settlement Rd., off the I-820 Loop (exit 4) east of downtown Fort Worth, has full hookups for $15-17 a night, plus a laundry room and clubroom with shower. Farther west, **Cowtown RV Park** (tel. 441-RVRV) is in Aledo off I-20 W (between the Farmer Rd. and Willow Park Rd. exits) about a 20-minute drive from Fort Worth. Facilities include convenience store, pool, laundry room, and full hookups for $16.25-18 a night.

Bed and Breakfasts

Miss Molly's Bed & Breakfast (Miss Molly's Hotel) (tel. 817-626-1522), once a "bawdy house" run by Madam Josie, now has eight guest rooms themed to the personalities of prior occupants—cowboys, gunslingers, cattle barons,

FORT WORTH HOTELS AND MOTELS

Add 13% hotel tax to all rates. Area code: 817.

DOWNTOWN

Days Inn Convention Center; 1010 Houston; tel. 336-2011 or (800) 325-2525; $30-65; pool, monthly rates

Downtown Motor Inn; 600 N. Henderson; tel. 332-6187 or (800) 221-4049; $30; pool, coin laundry

Radisson Plaza; 815 Main; tel. 870-2100 or (800) 333-3333; $50-153; heated pool, sauna

Ramada Hotel; 1701 Commerce; tel. 335-7000 or (800) 272-6232; $73-89; coin laundry

The Remington; 600 Commerce; tel. 332-6900; $61-103; sauna, exercise room, coin laundry, senior discount, weekly and monthly rates

The Worthington; 200 Main; tel. 870-1000 or (800) 433-5677; $109-170; historic, heated pool, sauna, tennis courts

WEST

Best Western W. Branch Inn; 7301 W. Freeway; tel. 244-7444 or (800) 528-1234; $39-60; laundry, senior discount, refrigerator on request

Caravan Motor Hotel; 2601 Jacksboro Hwy.; tel. 626-1951; $28-42; pool

Days Inn West; I-30 at Las Vegas Trail; tel. 246-4961 or (800) 325-2525; $32-47; senior discount

Deluxe Inn; 3800 US 377 S; $28-34

Green Oaks Inn; 6901 W. Freeway; tel. 738-7311 or (800) 433-2174; $59-98; pool, tennis courts

La Quinta Motor Inn Fort Worth; 7888 I-30 (Cherry Rd. exit); tel. 485-2750 or (800) 531-5900; $48-56; kitchenettes, monthly rates, complimentary evening beverage

Motel 6; I-30 at Las Vegas Trail; tel. 244-9740; $22.95 plus $6 each additional person; pool

Ramada Inn; 1401 S. University; tel. 336-9311 or (800) 272-6232; $50-65; pool, coin laundry

NORTH-NORTHEAST (NEAR MEACHAM FIELD)

Best Western Mid-Cities; junction of Loop 820 and State 10; tel. 284-9461 or (800) 528-1234; $50-55; pool, airport shuttle, senior discount, complimentary evening beverage

Downtown Motor Inn; 600 N. Henderson; tel. 332-6187; $31-37; coin laundry

Holiday Inn Conference Center; 2540 Meacham; tel. 625-9911 or (800) HOLIDAY; $60-90; heated pool, sauna, tennis courts

La Quinta Inn; 7920 Bedford-Euless; tel. 485-2750 or (800) 531-5900; $48-56; pool, airport shuttle

Sandpiper Inn; 4000 N. Main; tel. 625-5531; $40-60; heated pool, coin laundry, weekly rates

Stockyards Hotel; 109 E. Exchange St.; tel. 625-6427 or (800) 423-8471; $75-105; historical district

railroad men. Located at 109 W. Exchange Ave. within walking distance of the Stockyards, rooms here run $68-125 s or d, including breakfast. For other B&B suggestions, contact the Fort Worth Convention and Visitors Bureau (tel. 800-433-5747).

FOOD

As you would expect from a livestock and meat-packing center, in Cowtown restaurants the emphasis is on meat, from burgers to barbecue. Chili is also a local favorite, with many area restaurants serving bowls o' red during the winter.

American

$ to $$ Booger Red's Restaurant & Saloon: In business since 1907; the bar has saddles for stools. The varied menu includes chicken-fried steak, veal, duck, calf fries, seafood, burgers, barbecue, omelettes, and sandwiches. In the Stockyards Hotel, Stockyards District (tel. 817-625-6427); open daily for breakfast, lunch, and dinner.

$ to $$ Hubba Hubba's Great American Diner: '50s decor with burgers, steaks, chicken, seafood, some Tex-Mex, and biscuits and gravy. At 8320 State 80 W (tel. 560-2930); open daily for lunch and dinner, bar open till midnight.

$ to $$ Vance Godbey's: A local institution that serves roast beef, ham, barbecue, chicken (fried, barbecued, or roasted), and other American dishes cafeteria-style. All-you-can-eat deals are $8.95 Thurs.-Sat., $6.95 Sunday. At 8601 Jacksboro Hwy. (tel. 237-2218); open Thurs.-Sat. for dinner, Sunday for lunch and dinner.

$$ to $$$ **Michael's:** Call it *nouvelle Americaine,* call it "contemporary ranch," the cooking here packs two dining rooms with Fort Worthians seeking the excitement of dishes like cornbreaded rack of lamb, grilled eggplant and radicchio salad, pheasant sausage in honey-bourbon sauce, and linguine with salmon in dill sauce. The menu is cleverly divided into "Small Plates" and "Big Plates" to cater to varying appetites. At 3413 W. 7th (tel. 877-3413); open Mon.-Fri. for lunch and dinner, Saturday for dinner only.

Asian

$ to $$ **Autumn Moon:** Hunan and Szechwan dishes; lunch buffet daily. At 5516 Brentwood Stair Rd. (tel. 817-496-6633); open daily for lunch and dinner.

$ to $$ At **China Jade Restaurant:** The extensive menu features several regional cuisines. At 5274 Hulen St. (tel. 292-1611); open daily for lunch and dinner.

$$ **Szechwan:** As the name of the restaurant suggests, spicy Szechwan specialties hold sway on the moderately priced Chinese menu here. At 5712 Locke Ave. (tel. 738-7300); open daily for lunch and dinner.

Barbecue

$ **Angelo's Barbecue:** This local legend serves standard Texas barbecue fare, plus ham, braunschweiger, and draft beer. At 2533 White Settlement Rd. (tel. 817-332-0357); open Mon.-Sat. for lunch and dinner.

$ **Jim Riscky Grocery:** The 18-spice "Riscky dust" that Jim puts in his barbecue has a cult following. Although he now has several locations throughout Fort Worth, this grocery (tel. 624-8662) is where it all started. At 2314 Azle Ave. (FM 1220), south of Ephriham Ave. (State 183), east of the Stockyards District; open Mon.-Sat. for breakfast, lunch, and dinner.

Burgers

$ **B.J. Keefer's:** A build-your-own burger place where the beef is ground on the premises.

Makes its own hamburger buns. At 909 W. Magnolia (tel. 817-921-0889); open Mon.-Sat. for lunch and dinner.

$ **Charles Kincaid Grocery & Market:** Selected by 400 food critics around the country as purveyor of the best burgers in America. Besides burgers, Kincaid's offers chicken and dumplings, plate lunches with fresh vegetables, and chicken-fried steak. At 4901 Camp Bowie Blvd. (tel. 732-2881); open Mon.-Sat. for lunch and dinner.

Downhome

$ **Celebration:** A branch of the Dallas restaurant that serves the usual downhome dishes plus pot roast and broiled fish. At 4600 Dexter, at Camp Bowie and Hulen (tel. 817-731-6272); open daily for lunch and dinner.

$ **Paris Coffee Shop:** This friendly, classic coffee shop in south Fort Worth has served huge, Texas-style breakfasts and lunches with lots of biscuits and gravy since the 1930s. At 700 W. Magnolia (tel. 335-2041); open Mon.-Fri. 6 a.m.-3 p.m., Saturday 6-11 a.m.

European

$$ **Bella Italia West:** Innovative northern Italian cuisine, featuring fresh seafood, quail, veal with shrimp, and calamari with walnuts and pink peppercorns. At 5139 White Settlement Rd. (tel. 817-738-1700); open Mon.-Sat. for dinner only.

$$ **Edelweiss:** A Bavarian-style *bierhalle* with all the German standards, including schnitzel, sauerkraut, sauerbraten, and Black Forest cake, as well as marinated herring and Shashlik Caucasian ("steak on a stick"). Live German music and dancing nightly. At 3801A Southwest Blvd. off Loop 820 (tel. 738-5934); open Tues.-Sat. dinner only.

$$$ **Saint Emilion:** Country French cuisine in a country atmosphere. A la carte menu and two prix-fixe menus ($16-22), daily lunch buffet. At 3617 W. 7th (tel. 737-2781); open Tues.-Fri. for lunch and dinner, Monday and Sat.-Sun. dinner only.

Indian

$ to $$ **Maharaja:** Northern Indian tandoor and curry dishes. All-you-can-eat buffet weekdays. At 6308 Hulen Bend Blvd. (tel. 817-263-7156); open daily for lunch and dinner.

Lebanese

$ to $$ Hedary's Lebanese Restaurant: Good selection of shish kebabs, *sfiha* or "Lebanese pizza," baked chicken, and broiled lamb, all prepared with fresh ingredients. At 3308 Fairfield Ave. (tel. 817-731-7961); open Tues.-Sat. for lunch and dinner, Sunday dinner only.

Mexican

$ Joe T. Garcia's Mexican Bakery: The place to get away from the gringo lunch crowds at Joe T's larger branch. Great Mexican breakfasts—*chilaquiles, migas,* huevos rancheros. Too bad the dining room isn't open at night. At 1109 Hemphill St. (tel. 817-332-2848); kitchen open daily 6:30 a.m.-5:30 p.m.

$ to $$ Joe T. Garcia's Mexican Dishes: In business since 1935, Joe T's is often named as one of the best Tex-Mex restaurants in the state. It's a huge, plaza-style place (part of the building looks like it's about to fall over), and there are no menus; the choice is the regular dinner, which consists of nachos, two tacos, two enchiladas, rice, beans, guacamole, tostaditos, and salsa, or chicken or beef fajitas with beans, tortillas, *pico de gallo,* and guacamole. At lunch the place usually offers tamales, chiles rellenos, *flautas,* and steak ranchero as well. At 2201 N. Commerce (tel. 626-4356 or 429-5166); open daily for lunch and dinner.

$ Taco Cabaña: A classic, all-night Tex-Mex drive-in and outdoor patio with great fajitas and *frijoles borrachos,* "drunken beans." Beer and margaritas, too. At 6600 Camp Bowie Blvd.; open 24 hours.

Seafood

$ to $$ Catfish & Co.: Specializes in fresh, farm-raised catfish (all you can eat for $10), and oysters on the half shell. At 4004 White Settlement Rd. (tel. 817-738-8833); open daily for lunch and dinner.

$ to $$ J&J Oyster Bar: New Orleans-style seafood, featuring oysters (raw, fried, barbecued), catfish, crawfish (in season), and gumbo. At 929 University Dr. (tel. 335-2756); open daily for lunch and dinner.

Steaks

$$ to $$$ Cattleman's Steak House: A rustic Stockyards institution (established 1947) with a wide variety of charbroiled steaks, as well as barbecue, chicken, and seafood. At 2458 N. Main St. (tel. 817-624-3945); open Mon.-Sat. for lunch and dinner, Sunday dinner only.

$$-$$$ Risky's Sirloin Inn: This steakhouse in the heart of the Stockyards serves every cut of beef imaginable, but it's the "calf fries"—also known as Rocky Mountain Oysters—that generate the most attention, not to mention questions. At 120 E. Exchange Ave. (tel. 624-4800); open Tues.-Sun. for lunch and dinner.

$ Star Café: An 80-year-old Stockyards District cafe with the least expensive steaks in town, offered two ways: grilled in lemon butter or chicken-fried. The chili here is also a big draw. At 111 W. Exchange Ave. (tel. 624-8701); open Mon.-Sat. for lunch and dinner.

ENTERTAINMENT

Caravan of Dreams Performing Arts Center

The Caravan's well-designed nightclub features live music—mostly national and international jazz, fusion, folk, and new music artists or ensembles—Wed.-Sun. nights. Most shows start at 8 p.m. The equally well-designed theater hosts dance and drama performances from a wide variety of traditions. Most events have cover charges. The **Rooftop Grotto Bar** is open nightly from 4 p.m. till 1:30 a.m. The center is on Sundance Square at 312 Houston St.; for more information call (817) 429-4000.

Stockyards District

At least a dozen saloons and dance halls grace the Stockyards District, some dating from the turn of the century. All are within walking distance of each other, along E. and W. Exchange or N. Main. One of the more famous is **Billy Bob's Texas** (tel. 817-624-7117) at 2520 Rodeo Plaza. Billed as "the world's largest honkytonk," it's got to be seen to be believed—100,000 square feet with 42 bar stations, a restaurant, and a bullring for live bullriding (Friday and Saturday only). Live music on weekends at Billy Bob's tends toward urban-cowboy country crossover, featuring big-name acts like Joe Ely, Jerry Jeff Walker, and Highway 101. Very commercial. It's open Mon.-Sat. 11 a.m-1 a.m., Sunday noon-1 a.m.

At the other end of the Stockyards spectrum is the **White Elephant Saloon** (tel. 624-1887), which has been around since 1887 and features traditional C&W and country swing nightly. Cover charge only on weekends. At 106 E. Exchange; open Mon.-Sat. till 2 a.m., Sunday till midnight. *Esquire* magazine listed the White Elephant in its "100 Best Bars in America." The saloon has been expanded to include **Upstairs at the White Elephant,** a cabaret theater, and the open-air **White Elephant Beer Garden** next door, which is open for country dancing April-October.

Another popular Stockyards spot for country music is the **Longhorn Saloon** (tel. 624-4242) at 121 W. Exchange.

Pawnee Bill's Wild West Show

From April to mid-September, the Cowtown Coliseum is the site of Pawnee Bill's Wild West Show, a rootin' tootin' roundup of trick riders, Indian dancers, singing cowboys, bulldogging, and stagecoach holdups in the grand Buffalo Bill tradition. Tickets cost $8 adults, $5 seniors and children 3-12. Call (817) 654-1148 for further information.

Country, Folk, Blues, and Rock

Country and western music is Fort Worth's main strength when it comes to live music venues. In addition to those mentioned earlier these include **Cheyenne Cattle Co.** (tel. 817-370-2662), 4759 Bryant Irvin Rd.; **Johnnie High Country Music Revue** (tel. 481-4518), 3120 Carson St; **Stagecoach Ballroom** (tel. 831-2261), 2516 Belknap; and **Rockin' Rodeo** (tel. 922-9131), Fort Worth Town Center, I-35 at Seminary Drive.

The **Pig and Whistle** (tel. 731-4938), 5731 Locke Ave., showcases live folk and pub rock nightly. The city has one club that regularly features blues and R&B, **J&J Blues Bar** (tel. 870-2337), 937 Woodward. Live bands booked Wed.-Saturday.

The **Crossing** (tel. 332-2767), 224 E. Vickery; **The Hop** (tel. 921-0075), 2905 W. Berry St.; and **Mad Hatter's** (tel. 335-6349), 1514 W. Magnolia, offer the latest rock and alternative bands from around the area Thurs.-Sat. nights.

EVENTS

January
Southwestern Exposition Stock Show and Rodeo: Begun in 1896, this is one of the largest events of its kind in Texas. The highlight of the 17-day show is the all-Western parade (no motor vehicles allowed) that starts at the corner of W. Weatherford and Houston, then proceeds south on Houston to 9th, east to Main, and north again to the Tarrant County Courthouse. In 1994 a record 18,351 animals participated; as many as 2,000 horses ride in the parade. Rodeos nightly as well as rodeo matinees on weekends. Usually held the last week of January and first week of February, with most events taking place at the Will Rogers Memorial Coliseum on W. Lancaster. For more information call (817) 877-2400.

February
The Last Great Gunfight: In 1887, Luke Short, the owner of the White Elephant Saloon, outdrew ex-Fort Worth Marshall Jim "Longhair" Courtright in front of the saloon. This was supposedly the last gunfight of significance in the town, and every year the duel is reenacted in mock gunfights on Exchange Ave., in front of the White Elephant. Usually the first weekend in February. More information is available by calling (817) 624-9712.

April
Main Street Fort Worth Arts Festival: A street festival held on Main St. between the Convention Center and the County Courthouse. Features arts and crafts shows, food vendors, and outdoor concerts. Usually the second weekend of the month.

May-June
Every four years, the prestigious **Van Cliburn International Piano Competition** is held over a two-week period in Fort Worth, with preliminaries at Landreth Auditorium, Texas Christian University, finals at the Tarrant County Convention Center Theater. Van Cliburn is a Fort Worth native who won the Tchaikovsky International Piano

Competition in Moscow in 1958. The Van Cliburn competition is now among the top three such contests in the world. The next competitions are scheduled for 1997 and 2001. Contact the Fort Worth Convention and Visitors Bureau (tel. 817-336-8791) for more information.

June
Chisholm Trail Roundup: A three-day event usually held the second weekend in June, featuring barbecue and chili cookoffs, chuckwagon races, mock gunfights, street dances, armadillo races, livestock shows, an Indian dance competition, a Western writers workshop, mariachi competitions, C&W concerts, and the Chisholm Trail Ride. A high point of the weekend is the Texas Old Time Fiddlers Contest, which attracts the cream of the Texas fiddle tradition. All events except the trail ride are held within the Stockyards District—at the Cowtown Coliseum, the Mule Barns, or on Exchange Avenue. Call (817) 625-7005 for more information.

    Juneteenth Heritage and Jazz Festival: A three-day jazz, blues, and gospel music festival held around June 19th at the Convention Center (Friday evening) and Rolling Hills Parks (Saturday and Sunday daytime). Stanley Turrentine, David "Fathead" Newman, Gil-Scott Heron, Wynton Marsalis, and other name artists have been featured in recent years. Food vendors serve Cajun catfish, barbecued goat ribs, fried chicken, and a variety of other dishes. Tickets are usually $10-15.

September
Pioneer Days: A three-day celebration during the third weekend in September that pays tribute to early Fort Worth settlers. Events include a fajitas cookoff, music and dancing, and the annual Police Rodeo. At the Stockyards (tel. 817-626-7921).

October
Sponsored by the Texas Agricultural Extension Service during the third weekend in October, the annual **Red Steagall Cowboy Gathering** presents cowboy poetry, ranch rodeo, chuckwagon camping, and Western swing. Steagall is considered the living master of Western swing. Events are held around the Stockyards District. Call (817) 884-1945 for more information.

November-December
National Cutting Horse World Futurity: Sponsored by the National Cutting Horse Association, this event is a trial for three-year-old cutters (horses used to separate herds of cattle). The action is simple: a cowboy and his horse cut a calf from the herd, then the rider loosens the reins to allow the horse to keep the calf from rejoining the other cows. The most skilled horses win as much as $2 million for their owners. Held at Will Rogers Memorial Coliseum.

SPORTS AND RECREATION

Fort Worth Championship Rodeo
The Stockyards' Cowtown Coliseum was the site of the first indoor rodeo in 1917. The tradition continues every Saturday in a year round series of PRCA-sponsored contests. Rodeo events begin at 8 p.m. and last about two hours. Special amateur competitions are occasionally held during the season, such as the Texas High School Rodeo Finals in early June and the Chisholm Trail Roundup Rodeo in mid-June. Regular admission is $8 adults, $5 seniors, $3 children 3-12. Call (817) 626-2228 for information.

Trinity Meadows
First opened in May '91, this pari-mutuel racetrack nine miles west of town off I-20 (exit 418) holds horse races Thurs.-Mon. throughout the year except January and February. General admission is $5 including parking. Post times vary; call (817) 441-9240 for information.

Parks and Gardens
The **Fort Worth Botanic Gardens** covers 114 acres and contains thousands of varieties of flowers, plants, and trees. Of note are the Rose Garden, with over 3,500 rosebushes, and the Fragrance Garden, designed for the blind. The gardens are at 3220 Botanic Garden Dr. off University Dr. west of downtown. Open daily from 8 a.m. till dusk; free admission. The gardens also contain a Conservatory for tropical flora; hours are Mon.-Fri. 10 a.m.-9 p.m., Saturday 10 a.m.-6 p.m., Sunday 1-6 p.m. Admission is $1 adults, 50 cents children 4-12. Call (817) 871-7686 for more information.

BOOTS AND BOOTMAKERS

Western-wear shops are popular destinations for many Texas visitors. Cowboy hats, yoked Western shirts with mother-of-pearl buttons, and *bolos* (rawhide Mexican ties) are all favorite purchases. But of all classic cowboy gear, boots probably hold the most allure for Texans and non-Texans alike.

Texas produces more boots than anyplace else in the world, though most come from factories rather than individual bootmakers. A century ago, an estimated 600 bootmakers plied their craft in Texas. Now there are only 60 or 70; the best are descendants of Mexican craftsmen who inherited their trade from the Spanish. The best-quality boots are totally handmade, handcut and handstitched in small shops.

When boots became a popular part of mass American culture in the 1960s, many bootmakers began using machines to keep up with the demand. Older cowboy boots (pre-1970) generally feature the favored "X-toe," a sharply pointed toe, rather than a rounded toe. The rounded toe can be stitched by machine; the X-toe cannot.

The classic cowboy boot is designed for Western riding and ranching (not for propping up on guitar cases). The pointed toe makes it easy to slip the front of the boot through the stirrup, while the arch and heel hold it in place. The tall sleeve or upper part of the boot protects the wearer from brush, snakes, and the friction of the stirrup strap. Modern ranchers prefer a medium rounded toe for reasons of comfort; the most popular boot in Texas today is the practical Justin Roper, a round-toed, thick-soled, mid-calf boot introduced in the 1950s.

The Justin Boot Company of Fort Worth was the first bootmaker to use lasts (forms in the shape of the foot) on which to craft boots; it also introduced the steel shank between the heel and sole, which adds a large degree of support and comfort to bootwear. Founded in the 1870s, the company no longer makes boots by hand (Justin's annual output now tops three million pairs), but offers a good quality off-the-shelf Texas boot, as do Tony Lama of El Paso and Lucchese of San Antonio. Of the three, Lucchese—until the early '70s a custom bootery—probably makes the best-looking boot.

For the ultimate, you need to have a bootmaker to measure your feet, create custom-made lasts, and cut and sew a pair of boots by hand. Handmade boots will feature small wooden pegs holding the outer sole to the shank, rather than nails. Nails rust and fall out while pegs hold their position until removed by a bootmaker or repairman. A good boot, in fact, will last a lifetime with periodic resoling. Although custom-made boots start at a rock-bottom $175-300 a pair, you can sometimes find good used boots in pawn shops or shoe and boot repair shops for as little as $30-50. Cadillac Jack in Austin (tel. 512-452-4428), 6623 N. Lamar, is one shop that specializes in used boots and other Western wear. The latest trend favors vintage "peewees," short 1940s-style boots with lots of color and detail. El Paso's Rocketbuster Boots (tel. 915-541-1200) specializes in re-creating such vintage styles.

Austin has become something of a Texas boot capital because of the local music industry. Austin's most famous bootmaker, Charlie Dunn, passed
(CONTINUED ON NEXT PAGE)

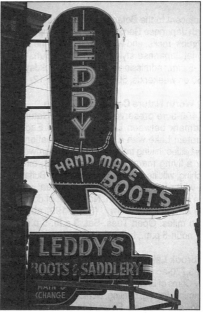

BOOTS AND BOOTMAKERS (CONT.)

away in 1993, but a former apprentice of his, Lee Miller (tel. 512-443-4447, by appointment only), designs boots in the Charlie Dunn tradition. Another highly reputable bootmaker in Austin is Noel Escobar Jr. of Texas Custom Boots (tel. 512-892-6321), 6616 US 290 West.

Some of the best bootmakers live in South Texas near the Mexican border, carrying on the Mexican tradition of fine bootmaking. Armando Duarte maintains a shop in Raymondville called Armando's Boot Company (tel. 512-689-3521). Raymondville has a couple of other custom-boot shops, as does nearby Mercedes.

Other well-known Texas bootmakers include the M.L. Leddy Company and J.L. Mercer & Son Boots, both in San Angelo in West Texas; Henry Leopold in Garland, north of Dallas; and Dave Little in San Antonio.

Whether you buy a pair of boots off the shelf or

have them custom-made, here are a few pointers in assuring a good fit. **Heel:** The heel of a new boot should slip a bit. This is because the sole is still stiff; once the ball of your foot wears in the boot enough so the sole flexes normally, heel slippage will disappear. No heel slippage in a new boot means it's too tight and will cause blisters and other foot problems. **Instep:** Should be fairly snug, even hard to slip on at first. If the instep is loose or the boot slides on easily, the instep is probably too large and you should try for a narrower size. **Ball and Toe:** The widest part of the boot should line up with the ball of the foot. If the ball of your foot sits forward of the widest part, it's too small, and the toes will be crammed into the toe box; if the ball sits much behind the widest part of the boot, the boot is too large and will chafe your foot mercilessly when you walk. **Arch:** The boot shank should be wide enough and long enough to cover your entire arch.

(CONTINUED ON NEXT PAGE)

Adjacent to the Botanic Gardens is the **Fort Worth Japanese Garden,** a 7.5-acre compound of shrubs, rocks, and water arranged in the traditional Japanese style. Open Tues.-Sun. 10 a.m.-5 p.m.; admission $1 adults on weekdays, $1.50 on weekends, 50 cents children 4-12.

Fort Worth Nature Center and Refuge
A 3,400-acre preserve and National Natural Landmark between Lake Worth and Eagle Mountain Lake with a variety of recreational possibilities: hiking trails (including a boardwalk over a living marsh), equestrian trails, birdwatching, wildlife viewing, and picnicking. Buffalo and white-tailed deer wander the area, and there's a prairie dog town. Northwest of downtown off Jacksboro Hwy. (State 199) about seven miles. Open Tues.-Sat. 9 a.m.-5 p.m., Sun. noon-5 p.m.; free admission.

Benbrook Lake
This 3,770-acre lake, administered by the U.S. Army Corps of Engineers, is a favorite local spot for swimming, fishing, boating, picnicking, trail riding, hiking, and camping. Recreation areas around the lake offer varying facilities—campsites, picnic areas, trails, boat ramps, fishing piers. A stable

at Dutch Brand Park rents horses for trail riding. Admission to the various parks is free. See "Accommodations" for camping information. The lake is about 12 miles southwest of downtown Fort Worth off US 377. For further information, contact the manager (tel. 817-292-2400), Benbrook Lake, P.O. Box 26619, Fort Worth, TX 76126.

SHOPPING

Western Wear
Williams Western Tailors (tel. 817-625-2401) designs, cuts, and sews Western-style shirts for Texas celebrities, including country music stars, prorodeo cowboys, and the cast of *Dallas.* Williams also tailors Western suits and just about anything else made of cloth. Figure around $50 for a basic shirt. At 1104 N.W. 28th, northwest of the Stockyards. For readymades, try **Luskey's Western Wear** (tel. 335-5833) at 101 Houston St., which has served Fort Worth cowboys and cowgirls since 1919.

Boots and Saddles
Two shops in the Stockyards District make custom boots. **M.L. Leddy's Boots and Saddlery** (tel.

817-624-3149) is at 2455 N. Main. Boots here start at around $400, saddles from $1400. The shop also sells used saddles, tack, and Western wear. **Ryon's Saddle and Ranch** (tel. 625-2391) is just up the street at no. 2601. Boots cost about the same as at Leddy's, saddles a bit less.

The **Justin Boot Co. Factory Outlet** (tel. 654-3103) at W. Vickery Blvd. and Lipscomb sells readymade factory seconds or overstocks at 40-50% below retail.

Antiques

Central Antiques (tel. 817-332-5981) offers two floors of antiques and collectibles. In back is a barn where estate auctions are occasionally held. At 401 S. Freeway (I-35 W).

Antique Connection (tel. 429-0922) specializes in European and early American antique furniture and collectibles. At 7429 E. Lancaster.

INFORMATION

Tourist Offices

The **Fort Worth Visitor Information Center** (tel. 817-624-4741) is opposite the Livestock Exchange in the Stockyards District. Downtown in Sundance Square, at 415 Throckmorton, is the **Fort Worth Convention and Visitors Bureau** (tel. 800-433-5747 or 336-8791). Both offices distribute useful brochures on local attractions (including a map of the Cultural District), dining, and accommodations.

Publications

On Friday, the *Fort Worth Star-Telegram* publishes "Star Time," a detailed datebook con-

---

FORT WORTH TELEPHONE INFORMATION

Emergency (police, fire, medical): 911

Telephone Directory Assistance: 411

Area Code: 817

Weather Service: 787-1111

Amtrak: (800) 872-7245

Texas State Highway Patrol: 359-4751

Road Conditions: 335-4222

---

taining information on dining and entertainment. The free weekly *Dallas Observer* also covers Fort Worth happenings, as does the *Dallas/Fort Worth Area Official Visitor Guide,* published by the Dallas-Fort Worth Area Tourism Council.

Maps

The chamber of commerce distributes a free, detailed street map of Fort Worth at the Stockyards visitor center. Somewhat better is the AAA map, which can be obtained at the Fort Worth AAA office (tel. 817-370-2503) at 5431 S. Hulen St.; it's open Mon.-Fri. 8:30 a.m.-5 p.m., Sat. 9 a.m.-1 p.m.

Telephone

The area code for Fort Worth is 817.

GETTING THERE AND AROUND

Dallas-Fort Worth Airport

DFW is equidistant between Fort Worth and Dallas. **Super Shuttle** (tel. 817-329-2000) provides pickup van service between the airport and town. For more details, see "Getting There and Around" under "Dallas."

Downtown

Fort Worth has made it easy for visitors to get around downtown without a car or even bus fare. The Fort Worth Transit Authority bus system (the "T") is free downtown along Throckmorton (northward) and Houston (southward). Elsewhere in Fort Worth, the "T" costs 75 cents. Two-day Visi-Tour bus passes allow visitors unlimited use of the bus system for $3 per person. For schedule information, call (817) 870-6200.

There's also a free subway from the Tandy Center at the north end of Throckmorton out to the free Trinity Riverside parking lot, so you can park outside the downtown area and take free public transport.

Yellow Checker Cab can be reached at 534-5555.

Tours

Gray Line (tel. 817-625-5887) offers a standard tour of the Stockyards, cultural district, historical buildings, and downtown for $39 per adult, $20 children.

VICINITY OF DALLAS-FORT WORTH

ARLINGTON

Arlington began back in 1876 as a midpoint station between Dallas and Fort Worth on the Texas & Pacific Railroad route west. The city is now nicknamed the "Midway of the Metroplex," not only for it's central location 15 miles west of Dallas and 15 miles east of Fort Worth, but because of its carnival midway atmosphere and amazing array of entertainment and dining options. The city's primary sights—baseball and amusement parks—are found in the Magic Mile Entertainment District lining both sides of I-30, the main artery linking Dallas and Fort Worth.

Texas Rangers and
the Ballpark in Arlington

The Arlington-based Texas Rangers professional baseball team now plays home games in season at the Ballpark in Arlington, about 15 miles east of downtown Fort Worth at 1000 Ballpark Way, I-30 at State 157, just south of the Arlington Convention and Visitors Bureau.

Modeled after great open-air parks like Wrigley Field, the Ballpark opened in April 1994 to replace the old Arlington Stadium and has since become a tourist attraction in itself. The ex-

terior of the $190 million complex is decorated with relief sculptures depicting Texas scenes—oil wells, longhorn cattle, Texas Ranger lawmen, the Alamo, cattle drives—wrapped around 49,292 seats overlooking a natural grass ballfield. The concourse features a river walk of retail shops and restaurants, anchored by a baseball hall of fame museum on the southwest corner. **Sports Legacy**, a 3,600-square-foot art gallery, sells posters, prints, and original art by famous sports artists. A picnic area, a youth ballpark, and jogging and biking trails are also part of the 270-acre entertainment complex; two six-acre lakes and an amphitheater were added in 1995. Contact the Texas Rangers Ticket Office (tel. 817-273-5100) for game schedules and ticket prices. Tours of the Ballpark can be arranged by calling 273-5222.

Amusement Parks

Every kid in Texas has to make a pilgrimage to **Six Flags Over Texas** at least once in his or her life. Newest among the 100 plus rides and shows are the 143-foot-tall Texas Giant, a rival to the infamous Rattler at San Antonio's Fiesta Park for title of "largest, fastest wooden rollercoaster in the world." There's also the heartstopping Flashback, in which cars drop forward

the Judge Roy Scream rollercoaster, Six Flags Over Texas

COURTESY SIX FLAGS OVER TEXAS

from a 125-foot tower through three loops, then backward to the starting point. Other stars of the show include Looney Tunes Land for the little ones, the Batman Stunt Show, and more thriller rides—Shockwave, Cliffhanger, Avalanche Bobsled, and Splashwater Falls, this last a boat ride over a five-story falls.

Six Flags is next door to the Ballpark off I-30 and is open early March through November from 10 a.m. Closing time varies from week to week. Admission fees are $26 adults, $20 seniors over age 55 and children under 48 inches tall. A ticket for two consecutive days costs a bargain $33 for adults, $26 for seniors and children. Parking is $2 additional. Call (817) 640-8900 for information.

Across the highway from Six Flags at 1800 E. Lamar Blvd. is **Wet 'n' Wild** (tel. 265-3356), a 47-acre amusement park devoted to water recreation, including a wave pool, water tunnels, waterslides (the Kamikaze and Blue Niagara, each with a 300-foot drop), and Lazy River, an artificial river for rafting. Open daily May through Labor Day, weekends only in May and mid-August to mid-September. Admission is $19 adults, $15 children 3-9, and $9.50 seniors over 55. Parking is free.

Connected to the Wet 'n Wild Complex is **FunSphere,** a pay-as-you-play amusement park with video arcade games, miniature golf courses, batting cages, mini-race car tracks, and bumper cars and boats. In the new LaserTron you and your teammates try to destroy an enemy base using mock weapons that emit harmless laser beams. Hours are the same as for Wet 'n' Wild; admission is free but games range $1-5 per play. Call 265-3356 for the current price information.

For something completely different, visit the **Air Combat School** (tel. 640-1886) at 921 Six Flags Dr., Suite 117, where you'll go through ground school, dress in pilot's gear, and experience a vertigo simulator and ejection seat before climbing into a jet fighter simulator to outmaneuver enemy pilots and become "top gun" for a day. Open daily 9 a.m.-5 p.m. by appointment only; the school charges $35 per hour.

Accommodations

The popular **Lexington Hotel Suites** (tel. 817-640-4444 or 800-950-5066) at 1607 N. Watson Rd. offers rooms, many with kitchenettes, for $59-79 s and $79-89 d, rates which include a complimentary breakfast buffet and airport shuttle transportation. Slightly closer to the major attractions, the new **Fairfield by Marriott** (tel. 800-228-2800) at 2500 E. Lamar charges $60 s, $68 d including complimentary breakfast. Falling in the middle price range is the **Inn Towne Lodge** (tel. 649-0993 or 800-441-1651) at 1181 N. Watson Rd., where rooms with kitchenettes run $39 s, $39-45 d.

Of the budget properties in town, **Value Inn** (tel. 640-5151) at 820 N. Watson and **Motel 6** (tel. 649-0147) at 2626 E. Randoll Mill Rd. are closest to the attractions; rates at each are around $26-28 s, $32-35 d.

Food

The **Key West Grill** (tel. 817-640-3157) serves grilled coconut shrimp, conch fritters, tropical salads, and, of course, the original "Cheeseburger In Paradise," made famous by Key West's favorite son, Jimmy Buffet. At 919 Six Flags Dr., just before the entrance to Six Flags, it's a moderately priced alternative to the somewhat expensive fast food served in the park. Open daily for lunch and dinner.

If your tastes run toward farmed catfish, head to **Catfish Sam's** (tel. 275-9631), 2735 W. Division, where the spiny fish comes cornmeal-breaded and fried, broiled in lemon pepper, or blackened. Charbroiled chicken and steak also available. Meals here are bountiful, since the main course is accompanied by coleslaw, potato or fries, pickles, green tomato relish, pinto beans, hush puppies, and rolls. Open Mon.-Fri. for lunch and dinner, Saturday for dinner only.

If the ever-present crowd of locals and consistently overflowing parking lot are any indication, **Pappadeaux** (tel. 543-0544) is the most popular restaurant in Arlington. Cajun is the emphasis here, with boudin, po'boy sandwiches, crawfish, gumbo, blackened fish, and étouffée drawing rave reviews. Near the Ballpark at 1304 Copeland Rd.; open daily for lunch and dinner.

For shrimp, chicken, or ribs seared on the barbie, Aussie chips, Botany Bay fish o' the day, and other down-under delicacies, check out the **Outback Steakhouse** (tel. 265-9381) at 2101 N. Collins Ave. No worries, mate, it's open daily for lunch and dinner.

When all the deep-fried Texas carnival food gets to be too much and you're ready to seek out the city's more elegant—and expensive—eateries, consider **Cacharel** (tel. 640-9981) at 2221 E. Lamar. High-brow *nouvelle Americaine* has put the dining room on *Condé Nast Traveler's* "best 50 restaurants in America" list. Highlights include the perfect Caesar salad, honey-ginger duck breast, and soft-shelled crab in pesto butter. Prix fixe, multicourse meals are available at $12 for lunch, $28 for dinner. Open Mon.-Fri. for lunch and dinner, Saturday dinner only.

Information

The **Arlington Convention and Visitors Bureau** (tel. 817-265-7721 or 800-433-5374) at 1250 E. Copeland Rd., Suite 650, and the **Visitor Information Center** (tel. 640-0252 or 800-342-4305) at 921 Six Flags Dr., distribute maps and colorful brochures on virtually everything in the city.

Getting There

Arlington is centrally located 15 miles west of Dallas and 15 miles east of Fort Worth via I-30.

GLEN ROSE

The county seat of diminutive Somervell County sits at the confluence of the Brazos and Paluxy Rivers, 52 miles southwest of Fort Worth via US 377 and State 144. In recent years the town's historic homes, quaint B&Bs, dinosaur park, and wildlife center have made it a favorite weekend retreat for people from Dallas and Fort Worth.

Sights

Depending on the Paluxy River's current water level, numerous 100-million-year-old dinosaur tracks are clearly visible in the limestone riverbeds of 1,247-acre **Dinosaur Valley State Park** (tel. 817-897-4588). Tracks of the sauropod, a 60-foot, 30-ton vegetarian, were first discovered here; other rare footprints include those of the theropod and duck-billed dinosaurs. Full-size fiberglass models of the reptiles and various track impressions are on display in the park and at the visitor center. Along with camping and picnicking facilities, the park maintains trails suit-able for hiking, biking, and horseback riding. From US 67 in Glen Rose, take FM 205 west 2.8 miles to Park Road 59, then go north one mile to park headquarters. The park is open daily 8 a.m.-5 p.m.; drive-through admission is $5.

Exhibits at the nuclear-powered **Comanche Peak Electric Station** explain in detail how nuclear fusion creates electrical energy. Interactive displays include a Geiger counter and computerized energy quiz; there is also an observation area where you can watch reactor operators training in a control room simulator. The plant's visitor center (tel. 897-5554) is about a mile inside Comanche Peak's front gate off FM 56 north of Glen Rose. Open Mon.-Sat. 9 a.m.-4 p.m.; admission is free.

Fossil Rim Wildlife Center

This unique enterprise dedicates 3,000 acres of North Central Texas grasslands to the protection and breeding of exotic and endangered species from around the planet. The only privately owned wildlife park in the nation accredited by the American Association of Zoological Parks and Aquariums, the center is also a participant in the association's Species Survival Plan (SSP). The program's objective is to breed severely threatened animal species and reintroduce them to their natural habitats.

In numerical terms, the emphasis at Fossil Rim is on African species, including white rhinoceros, scimitar-horned oryx (currently extinct in its native North Africa), reticulated giraffes, cheetah, dama gazelles, Grevy's zebra, and addax.

Visitors may observe some of the nearly 11,000 animals protected by the facility by taking the 9.5-mile drive-through tour. Facilities along the drive include an education center, petting pasture, restaurant, self-guiding nature trail, nature store, playground, and picnic areas. The drive-through is open daily (except Thanksgiving and Christmas) from 9 a.m. until two hours before sunset from Labor Day to Memorial Day, from 8 a.m. the remainder of the year. Admission is $12.95 adults, $11.95 seniors, $9.95 children 4-11.

Naturalists on staff lead guided tours in open vehicles to explain the natural behavior and history of the 23-plus species seen along the scenic drive. The tour lasts about two hours and costs $25 adults, $18 children; tour times vary with the season, so call ahead for reservations. Visi-

PHYLLIS STAFF

Mexican gray wolf,
Fossil Rim

tors with a keen interest in the work of the center may want to take the "behind-the-scenes" tour for $25 adults, $18 children. This includes a visit to the white rhino breeding facility and the Intensive Management Area, where such rarities as the Mexican gray wolf, red wolf, and Atwater's prairie chicken are bred in captivity.

The Fossil Rim Wildlife Center is located three miles southwest of Glen Rose off US 67. Glen Rose is 70 miles northwest of Waco, 58 miles southwest of Fort Worth, and 75 miles southwest of Dallas. For more information on Fossil Rim activities, call (817) 897-2960.

Foothills Safari Camp
Another way to experience Fossil Rim is by signing on for a three- to five-day stay at the Safari Camp. During the day, participants are guided on jeep and horseback animal-watching tours, nature hikes, and fossil hunts. Evenings feature gourmet meals served by the camp chef, after which guests may gather around a bonfire or gaze at the stars through the camp's telescope. Guests stay in safari-style tents (air-conditioned in summer, heated in winter) with private baths.

Rates for a two-night/three-day safari are $375 Tues.-Thurs., $450 Fri.-Sun.; children ages 2-6 accompanying their parents are charged $300/375, children two and under are free. Included in the price are accommodations, meals, activities, lectures, and guided tours. Longer safaris are avail-

able by special arrangement. For further information, call (817) 897-3398 or (800) 245-0771.

Accommodations
In addition to the extraordinary Safari Camp at Fossil Rim Wildlife Center, there is now an elegant **Lodge at Fossil Rim** (tel. 817-897-7452). Once the home of a playboy oilman, this cedar and stone structure features five romantic rooms (some with jacuzzi baths, some with fireplaces), an airy living room with cathedral ceiling, pub/game room, sunny breakfast room, and broad deck overlooking a spring-fed swimming pool and the preserve's largest pasture. Rooms cost $125-185 double occupancy, full breakfast included. Dinners are available on the weekends, and guests can arrange for a private, early-morning game tour with the innkeepers for a behind-the-scenes look at the preserve.

Of the numerous B&Bs in town, the nicest is the **Inn on the River** (tel. 897-2101) at 205 S.W. Barnard Street. This plush country inn was at one time a sanatorium for tuberculosis patients, but has been completely renovated and outfitted with period furnishings, down comforters, and lace curtains that frame windows looking out over charming gardens, a pool, or the Paluxy River. Rooms run $78-155 s or d, suites $125-145; breakfast is included in the tariff.

The newer **Hummingbird Lodge** (tel. 897-2787, fax 897-3459), P.O. Box 128, Glen Rose, TX 76043, features six guest rooms on 144 acres, 1.7 miles south of US 67 west of Glen Rose. Rates for rooms with private bath are $79 a night while rooms with shared baths are $74. Continental breakfast is included and there's a hot tub on the grounds.

The Hideaway (tel. 823-6606, fax 823-6612), Rt. 2, Box 148, Bluffdale, TX 76433, offers two log cabins on 150 wooded acres about 15 miles west of Glen Rose off US 67. Exact directions are released only after you've made a reservation. Both cabins offer full kitchens, outdoor grills, private spas, and picnic tables for $62-72 without breakfast, $70-80 including continental breakfast.

At the ranch-style **Popejoy Haus Bed and Breakfast** (tel. 897-3521), P.O. Box 2023, Glen Rose, TX 76043, the proprietors speak German and serve full German breakfasts. A room with sitting area and private bath costs US$75 a night. Located northwest of town via State 365 and CR 321. The **Glen Rose Motor Inn** (tel. 897-2940) on US 67 at FM 56 offers simple rooms for $42 s or $46 d Sun.-Thurs., $52 s or $56 d Fri.-Saturday.

Campgrounds and RV Parks

Dinosaur Valley State Park offers primitive campsites for $7 weekdays, $8 weekends, drive-in sites with water for $7/10, and full-hookup sites for $14/16.

Tres Rios (tel. 817-897-4253) off FM 312 has tent camping for $10-11, full hookups for $14, teepees for $20-50, treehouses for $25, and cabins for $50-80 per night. This large campground also presents chuckwagon dinners with an old west stage show and spring and fall Bluegrass Festivals. Call ahead for schedule and reservations.

Food

The policy at **Hammonds Bar-B-Q** (tel. 817-897-3321) on US 67 is to serve heaping platters of barbecue generous enough to satisfy the owner, obviously a man with a healthy appetite. The result is huge mounds of meat and whatever trimmings you select—fries, potato salad, slaw, beans—piled on a plate that would satisfy two, maybe three, normal appetites. The restaurant is open Wednesday, Thursday, and Sunday 11 a.m.-2 p.m., Fri.-Sat. 11 a.m.-8 p.m., but they shut the doors when they run out of food, so don't count on this place for dinner on the weekends.

Chachi's Mexican Food (tel. 897-7504), also on US 67, doesn't look like much but serves good Tex-Mex, chicken-fried steak, grilled fish and shrimp, and burgers, and is open daily for lunch and dinner.

An interesting weekend alternative is a chuckwagon meal served at the **McNeill Ranch** (tel. 897-2221) off FM 144 not quite three miles east of Glen Rose. From mid-May through mid-October, the place serves a Cowboy Breakfast (scrambled eggs, campfire coffee, sausage, and dutch-oven biscuits) on Saturday and Sunday at 8:30 a.m., and a Sunset Cookout (steak, beans, potatoes, dutch-oven biscuits, cobbler, ice cream, and campfire coffee or tea) on Friday and Saturday at 6:30 p.m.

Information

The **Glen Rose Chamber of Commerce** (tel. 817-897-2286) on Vine St. in downtown Glen Rose can provide maps as well as lists of B&Bs, campgrounds, local museums, shops, and restaurants.

WAXAHACHIE

The rich blackland prairies of Waxahachie (an Indian name meaning "Buffalo Creek") attracted farmers beginning in the early 19th century. One of the oldest towns in North Central Texas, it was incorporated as the Ellis County seat in 1850 and by 1900 was a prosperous cotton center. The early cotton kings built lots of Victorian homes, earning Waxahachie the nickname "Gingerbread City." Filmmakers have found the town to be the perfect backdrop for Texan Americana—*Bonnie and Clyde, Tender Mercies, On Valentine's Day, Places in the Heart,* and *A Trip to Bountiful* were all filmed here.

Long dependent on farming and ranching, this city of 20,000 recently began courting tourism. A tour of local sites that have appeared on celluloid is available through the Waxahachie Chamber of Commerce, 3700 Hogge Rd. (tel. 214-937-2390 or 800-989-7800).

Historic Buildings

Over 225 properties in town are listed on the National Register of Historic Places. Street signs indicate the way to the major sites. The chamber

1. McDonald Observatory, Fort Davis; **2.** cactus garden, Caravan of Dreams, Fort Worth; **3.** Sabal Palm Grove Sanctuary, Brownsville (photos by Joe Cummings)

1. Dallas skyline (Dallas Convention and Visitors Bureau); **2.** Cowboy Artists of America Museum, Kerrville (Joe Cummings); **3.** Fiesta Noche del Rio, San Antonio (San Antonio Convention and Visitors Bureau); **4.** Houston by night (Tracey Maurer); **5.** Zydeco Creole Dust Fest, Beaumont (Joe Cummings)

of commerce distributes *Historic Waxahachie Downtown Walking Tour* and *Driving Tour* brochures, available at the chamber (tel. 214-937-2390), 102 YMCA Dr., off US 277, at the Ellis County Historical Museum; or at the Mahoney-Thompson House. Some of the historic downtown houses now contain antique and craft shops, like **Briarpatch** at 404 W. Main.

The 1895 **Ellis County Courthouse** at Main and College is the most spectacular courthouse in Texas—and Texas has a lot of spectacular courthouses. Its elaborate arches, balconies, turrets, carved faces, and clock tower make it look more like a medieval castle than a government building. Like many of the larger turn-of-the-century courthouses in the state, it was designed by architect J. Reily Gordon and built of granite and sandstone by Italian stonemasons. The building is open to the public Mon.-Fri. 8 a.m.-5 p.m.; free admission.

The **Mahoney-Thompson House** at 604 W. Main was built in the Greek Revival style in 1904 and now belongs to the Ellis County Historical Museum. It's been redecorated in period furnishings and is open for tours Saturday 10 a.m.-5 p.m., Sunday 1-5 p.m., or by appointment. A $2 donation is requested for admission.

The **Ellis County Historical Museum** is housed in a restored 1889 Masonic Temple built in the Romanesque Revival style. Exhibits feature artifacts from Waxahachie's late 1800s heyday, including a rare fan collection. Open Tues.-Sat. 10 a.m.-5 p.m., Sun. 1-5 p.m. Admission is free.

Gingerbread Trail
During the first weekend of June every year, several privately owned Victorians, the county museum, the Mahoney-Thompson House, and the courthouse are open to the public for touring. Other activities include a street dance, performances on the square and at Getzendaner Park, and an arts and crafts show. Tickets are $10 adults, $4 children. Ticket gazebos are set up at all town entry points. There's a 20% discount for advance ticket purchases. Call (214) 937-2390 for information.

Scarborough Faire
A recreation of an English Renaissance-period country fair, with jugglers, jesters, wizards, jousting, music, food, and arts and crafts. The event

takes place over seven weekends April-June at a site on FM 66, two miles west of I-35 E. For information call (214) 938-1888.

Getting There
Waxahachie is 35 miles south of downtown Dallas off I-35 E.

HAGERMAN NATIONAL WILDLIFE REFUGE AND LAKE TEXOMA

This 11,230-acre preserve straddles the Big Mineral arm of Lake Texoma on the Texas-Oklahoma border, around 60 miles north of Dallas via US 75.

Wildlife
About 3,000 acres of the refuge are marsh and wetlands, the rest uplands and farmlands cultivated for waterfowl feed—milo, corn, and green wheat. Hagerman is home to a variety of native mammals, including **white-tailed deer, bobcat, beaver,** and **raccoon.** But the most honored residents are the thousands of waterfowl that spend portions of fall, winter, and spring on the wetlands and marshes. Over 3,000 **Canada geese** winter at Hagerman, along with **white-front** and **snow geese.** Duck varieties include **mallards, pintail, green-winged teal, blue-winged teal, shovelers, redheads, canvasbacks, scaup,** and **ringbacks.** Other birds who reside at the refuge include **bobwhite quail, mourning doves,** and various other songbirds.

Visitor Activities
Sightseeing: A four-mile auto tour route winds through the refuge; maps are available at the refuge headquarters. Several nature trails and field roads are open to hiking and are equipped with footbridges and photography blinds. Fall and winter are the best times of year for bird-watching; if you visit during the summer, bring insect repellent.

Fishing and Hunting: Daytime shoreline fishing is permitted year round. Boats are allowed on the lake April 1-Sept. 30 only and there are three boat ramps available. Hunting is permitted during announced "special hunts." Contact the refuge staff for the latest information.

Camping is not permitted in the refuge, but there are Corps of Engineers-administered campgrounds north of the refuge boundary along Lake Texoma's substantial shoreline. Primitive, no-fee camping is permitted at 125-acre **Paradise Cove Camp** (FM 120 off US 69/75), where facilities include pit toilets, grills, and boat ramp; you must supply your own water. Before camping at Paradise Cove, obtain a permit from the project office on Park Road 2 off US 69/75.

Dozens of other campgrounds along Lake Texoma shores are available for drive-in campers for fees of $6-12 a night, including **Flowing Wells Resort, Mill Creek Resort, Preston Bend Recreation Area,** and **Lighthouse Resort and Marina,** all with w/e, boat ramps, and toilets. Call (800) 284-2267 or (903) 465-4990 for current fees and reservations.

Information
Contact the Refuge Manager (tel. 903-786-2826), Hagerman National Wildlife Refuge, Route 3, Box 123, Sherman, TX 75090.

Lake Texoma
One of the largest reservoirs in the world, this impoundment of the Red River covers 89,000 acres of Texas and Oklahoma and offers 580 miles of shoreline for public recreational use. Rod and reel can take trophy-size, native largemouth bass, Florida bass, Kentucky spotted bass, crappie, blue cat, flathead catfish, and white (sand) bass. The latter, known locally as "sandies," are a popular catch, even though they only reach two to three pounds in weight. Every June brings the week-long National Sand Bass Festival.

WACO

History

Waco (pronounced WAY-co) was named for the Waco Indian tribe, a subgroup of the Tawakonis, who once lived in the area along the Brazos River. The town grew up around a ferry service that carried westward immigrants across the river in the mid-19th century. In 1870, the ambitious townspeople substituted a toll bridge for the ferry. At the time it was the longest suspension bridge in the U.S. and second longest in the world. When the railroad arrived in 1872, the town became an important transportation crossroads; early this century the hobo slums along Bridge St. on the Brazos River's

right bank were known as "Rat Row." As at Waxahachie to the north, cotton was, and still is, an important part of the local economy, but Waco took further advantage of its geographic position to become an intermediate trading center between San Antonio and Dallas. In 1886 Baylor University, the largest Baptist university in the world, was moved here from Independence.

The Waco business community continued to diversify in the 20th century, managing to attract dozens of manufacturing interests. Two soft drinks were born here—Dr. Pepper and the all-time Texas favorite, Big Red. Today Waco is a half-college, half-industrial town of around

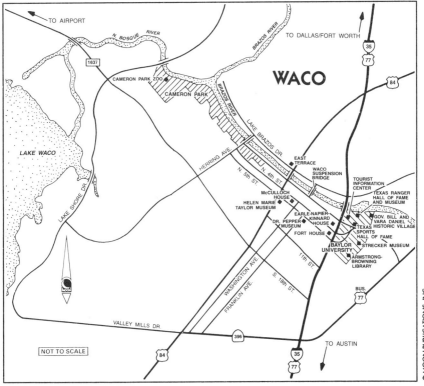

100,000. Celebrity claims to fame: local band Hank Thompson and the Brazos Valley Boys put Waco on the map with their hit "Six Pack to Go," and comedian Steve Martin was born here.

SIGHTS

Waco Suspension Bridge

Waco's most famous landmark was erected in 1870 as a toll bridge along the Chisholm Cattle Trail. Once the largest suspension bridge in the U.S., and a model for New York's Brooklyn Bridge, the twin-towered span was reconstructed in 1913-14 and finally closed to vehicles in 1971. Today it serves as a scenic pedestrian bridge linking public parks on both sides of the Waco River.

Texas Ranger Hall of Fame and Museum

The Rangers are an integral part of Texas frontier legend. They began as privately hired "rangering companies" that provided security for land *empresarios* along the Indian frontier in West Texas; Stephen F. Austin hired the first 10 Texas Rangers in 1823. They played a significant role in the Texan Revolution against Mexico, and eventually developed into a state paramilitary force that fought Indians and patrolled the Mexican border with virtually no supervision. It was said that a Ranger could "ride like a Mexican, trail like an Indian, shoot like a Tennessean, and fight like the devil." But not all their activities were heroic, and in 1935 the state government reigned them in under the jurisdiction of the Department of Public Safety as a special investigative unit; currently, there are only about 100 active Rangers in the state. Texans prefer to remember them fondly as an elite and noble police force. An oft-told story describes the Ranger who steps down from a train in a riot-torn town and is asked, "You mean they sent only one Ranger?" to which he stoically replies, "You only got one riot, don't you?"

The museum and hall of fame are part of a 35-acre park built around a replica of the Texas Rangers' Fort Fisher. This temporary Ranger outpost was originally established in 1837 and is now the active headquarters of Ranger Company F. The museum features a number of exhibits chronicling the history of the Rangers, including dioramas, audiovisual presentations, paintings, memorabilia, a library, and impressive gun collections. The Colt display traces the development of the pistol that won the west. The Hall of Fame honors 26 Rangers considered exemplary figures.

Fort Fisher Park is off I-35 at University Parks Dr. (exit 335B). Open daily 9 a.m.-5 p.m.; admission is $3.50 adults, $2.50 children 6-12. For additional information, contact the Texas Ranger Hall of Fame (tel. 817-750-5986), P.O. Box 2570, Waco, TX 76702.

Mount Carmel

Waco gained unwanted international media attention in 1993 when the U.S. government's war on David Koresh (the "Wacko from Waco") and the Branch Davidian sect came to a fiery head during an April 19 fire in which the Mount Carmel compound burned to the ground. There is little left of the compound; tank tracks and huge piles of rubble are surrounded by 12-foot barbed-wire-topped contamination fences. Yet many who witnessed the tragedy on television are drawn to Mount Carmel when they visit Waco. The Visitors Information Center at Fort Fisher provides a detailed map of the convoluted route to the compound, located 14 miles northeast of Waco, as well as a brochure listing some of the recorded historical facts that led to what is to date the largest armed conflict between the government of America and its citizens since the Civil War.

Helen Marie Taylor Museum

Exhibits of mild interest at this new regional museum include historical items used to interpret the city's founding and subsequent development, the growth of the cotton industry, and an in-depth look at the freedoms guaranteed under the U.S. Constitution. Of more interest to the casual visitor, perhaps, is the historical retrospective put together by Baylor University students to answer some of the many questions surrounding the Mount Carmel incident. The exhibit displays a mock-up of the compound and a collection of photos depicting the Branch Davidian siege.

The museum (tel. 817-752-4774) is at 701 Jefferson Ave. and is open Tues.-Sat. 10 a.m.-4 p.m., Sunday 1-4 p.m. Admission is $2 adults, $1.50 seniors, $1 students.

THE REAL THING

If you develop a thirst in the vicinity of Dublin, Texas (on US 67/377 between Comanche and Stephenville, about 90 miles southwest of Fort Worth), consider dropping by the only Dr. Pepper bottling plant in the world that still follows the soft drink's original formula. The 102-year-old plant's bottling machinery cranks out just 36 bottles a minute—12 times slower than a modern Dr. Pepper factory—and can only accept 6.5-ounce bottles, a rare commodity these days. Once the small bottles stop coming back—most plants have discontinued their use—the Dublin plant may be out of business since the original molds don't exist anymore.

Regular customers—who hail from as far away as California and Canada—swear by the Imperial sugar recipe (other plants substituted less expensive corn syrup long ago) even though it retails at over $15 for a case of 24, including an $8 deposit for the precious bottles.

The plant, and a small museum on the premises, is open for touring Mon.-Fri. 9:30 a.m.-noon and 1:30-5 p.m. A soda fountain on site dispenses original formula Dr. Pepper. For further information, contact the Dr. Pepper Bottling Company (tel. 817-445-3466), 221 South Patrick, P.O. Box 307, Dublin, TX 76446.

Dr. Pepper Museum

Originally formulated at Waco's Old Corner Drug Store in 1885, Dr. Pepper became the pet project of chemist R.S. Lazenby, who perfected the recipe and named the beverage after his girlfriend's father. The original 1906 Dr. Pepper bottling plant, a Richardson Romanesque structure built around an artesian well that once supplied the water for all bottled Dr. Pepper, now houses a museum chronicling the history of this and other Texas soft drinks, including the infamous Big Red. The building also contains an authentic 1945 soda fountain where the staff can "shoot" you a soda or prepare tempting floats, shakes, and sundaes the old-fashioned way. At 300 S. 5th St. (tel. 817-757-1024); open Mon.-Sat. 10 a.m.-4 p.m., Sunday noon-4 p.m. Admission to the museum is $3 adults, $2.50 seniors, $1 students. No admission fee for soda fountain visits.

Baylor University

Founded in 1845 and moved here from Independence in 1886, this is the state's oldest institution of higher learning and the largest Baptist-sponsored university in the world, with some 11,000 students. The 425-acre campus is worth visiting for a look at the **Armstrong-Browning Library** (tel. 817-755-3566), which contains the most extensive collection of Robert and Elizabeth Barrett Browning material in the world. The library includes all the poets' first editions, thousands of their letters and manuscripts, and just about everything ever written about the Brownings in the English language. The building itself was constructed in the 18th-century Italian Renaissance style and features 54 stained-glass windows, each depicting a different Browning poem. Ten of their poems are illustrated on the bronze-paneled entrance doors. The library is open to the public Mon.-Fri. 9 a.m.-noon and 2-4 p.m., Saturday 9 a.m.-noon. Free admission.

Also on campus is the **Strecker Museum** in the Sid Richardson Science Building (tel. 755-1110), which contains natural history exhibits in the fields of geology, biology, Indian lore, anthropology, and archaeology. Outside the hall is a reconstructed town that is supposed to represent life along Texas waterways in the 19th century. Open Tuesday, Wednesday, and Friday 9 a.m.-4 p.m., Thursday 9 a.m.-8 p.m., Saturday 10 a.m.-4 p.m., Sunday 2-5 p.m. Free admission.

The campus also encompasses the **Governor Bill and Vara Daniel Historic Village** (tel. 755-1160), a spread of more than 20 wood-frame buildings along the banks of the Brazos River. Representing life in an 1890s Texas cotton-farming community, the structures include a cotton gin, school, livery stable, church, hotel, saloon, and various other buildings typical of the era. The village is open Tues.-Fri. 10 a.m.-4 p.m., Sat.-Sun. 1-5 p.m.; admission is $3 adults, $2 seniors, $1 students.

Baylor's main entrance is near Fort Fisher Park off University Parks Dr. (I-35 exit 335B). A free trolley shuttles students and visitors around campus.

Texas Sports Hall of Fame

Opened in 1993 next to Baylor University and Fort Fisher Park, this facility contains exactly what you'd expect it to contain: memorabilia from famous Texas athletes, including George

Foreman, Lee Trevino, Babe Didrikson Zaharias, Nolan Ryan, and Byron Nelson, along with displays on notable high school and collegiate sports around the state. Relive the video glory of the Dallas Cowboys in the Tom Landry Theater. At 1109 University Parks Dr.; open daily 10 a.m.-5 p.m. Admission is $4 adults, $3.50 seniors and students, $1.75 children.

Cameron Park Zoo

Opened in July 1993, this natural habitat zoo features an African savannah with elephants, rhinos, giraffe, zebra, and antelope, an island of gibbons, and a treetop village. Exhibits currently under construction include a reptile compound and open areas for longhorn, bison, and red wolves. At 1600 N. 4th St. (tel. 817-750-8400), the zoo is open weekdays 9 a.m.-5 p.m., weekends 9 a.m.-6 p.m.; admission is $4 adults, $3.50 seniors, $2 children 4-12.

Historic Homes

Typical of cotton towns in North Central and Northeast Texas, Waco sports a number of 19th-century homes in the Antebellum, Greek Revival, and Italianate Villa styles. The **Historic Waco Foundation** has restored four of these and filled them with authentic period furniture and decorative art: **Fort House**, 503 S. 4th St.; **East Terrace**, 100 Mill St.; **Earle-Napier-Kinnard House**, 814 S. 4th St.; and **McCulloch House**, 407 Columbus Avenue. At each of these a $2 admission fee is collected. The foundation (tel. 817-753-5166) has its office at 810 S. 4th St.; stop by for more information or to pick up a map to the homes.

Lake Waco

This 7,260-acre lake is the largest in Texas inside city limits. Facilities for swimming, boating, fishing, waterskiing, and picnicking are available at seven parks along 60 miles of shoreline. As at many dam-built lakes, the recreation areas are administered by the Corps of Engineers (tel. 817-756-5359). The easiest access to the lake is via State 6 W from I-35 S.

ACCOMMODATIONS AND FOOD

Accommodations

The cheapest rooms in town are at the **Viking Inn** (tel. 799-2414), 1300 New Dallas Hwy.—

$20 s, $25 d, with efficiencies on request. The rates of the nearby **Motel 6** (tel. 817-799-4957), 1509 Hogan Lane, Behrens Circle exit off I-35, are $22 s, $26 d. For two or more, the nearby The popular **Best Western Old Main Lodge** (tel. 800-528-1234 or 753-0316) at 215 Dutton, I-35 exit 335A, has rooms for $49 s, $55 d, with complimentary continental breakfast. The **Howard Johnson Riverplace Inn** (tel. 800-792-3257 or 752-8222) at 101 I-35 N, exit 335C, is on the Brazos River; some rooms overlook the water. Rates are $31-39; continental breakfasts are on the house. Top drawer is the **Waco Hilton** (tel. 800-792-3267 or 754-8484), 113 S. University Parks Dr., where rooms are $65-85.

Camping

Fort Fisher Park (tel. 817-750-5989 or 800-922-6386) offers a campground along the Brazos River with facilities for both tent ($10) and RV camping ($12), as well as screened shelters ($12).

Around Lake Waco are six camping areas maintained by the U.S. Army Corps of Engineers: **Airport Park, Speegleville Park I**, and **Speegleville Park III** have basic drive-in sites for $8 a night, or with w/e for $12 a night, plus hot showers on site; **Speegleville Park II** is a 575-acre primitive camping area with dump station, pit toilets, and grills for $8; **Midway Park** and **Flat Rock** have primitive, free camping areas with pit toilets and a nearby snack bar. For Lake Waco information or reservations, call the Corps of Engineers at 756-5359.

KOA Waco North (tel. 826-3869), about 17 miles north of Waco near the Czech town of West off I-35 (exit 355, look for signs), has the usual pricey KOA facilities on large, shaded grounds.

Food

The famous **Elite Café** ("Where the Elite Meet to Eat") serves classic Texas diner food, including the house specialty, chicken-fried steak. It's at 2132 S. Valley Mills at I-35 (tel. 817-754-4941) and is open daily for breakfast, lunch, and dinner. **Nick's** (tel. 772-7790), 4508 W. Waco Dr., is a Greek-American restaurant that's served dependable *souvlaki* and *dolmathes* to wacky Waco for three generations. Besides Greek dishes, it also offers steak and seafood; open Mon.-Fri. for lunch and dinner, Saturday dinner only. For real Tex-Mex, try **El Conquistador** (tel. 799-

6655) at 901 N. Loop 340. House specialties include *tacos al carbón* and *carne guisada.*

The traditional Baylor student hangout for the last 50 years has been **George's** (tel. 753-1421) at 1525 Circle Road. Chicken-fried steak is a favorite here, along with the "Big O," a huge, frosted globe of beer; open Mon.-Sat. 7 a.m.-11 p.m. You'll also find all the usual fast-food joints along I-35 near Baylor University.

SHOPPING

Southwest Outlet Center, 35 miles north of Waco via I-35 in Hillsboro, offers impressive discounts among its 56 outlet stores (mostly clothing and accessories), including upscale Eddie Bauer.

INFORMATION

The **Waco Convention and Visitors Bureau** (tel. 800-321-9226 or 817-750-5810) maintains a **Visitors Information Center** (tel. 800-922-6386 or 750-5996) at Fort Fisher Park, off I-35 at University Parks Dr. (exit 335B).

GETTING THERE AND AROUND

Waco is off I-35, around 90 miles south of Dallas-Fort Worth and 100 miles north of Austin.

Around town, the **Brazos Trolley** (tel. 817-753-0113) plies a very useful weekend route along University Parks Dr. and N. 5th St., passing many of the city's major sites, including the Texas Ranger and Texas Sports halls of fame, Fort Fisher, Baylor University, Strecker Museum, the Dr. Pepper Museum, Waco Suspension Bridge, several historic homes, and the Cameron Park Zoo. The trolley costs 50 cents per person and operates 10 a.m.-6 p.m., weekends only.

Waco Regional Airport is served by **Atlantic Southwest Airline (tel. 800-282-3423),** American Eagle (tel. 800-433-7300), and **Dallas Express** (tel. 753-1757).

BOB RACE

SOUTH CENTRAL TEXAS

Many visitors find this the most culturally interesting region of Texas. Because of the abundance of water and the relatively mild climate, South Central Texas was the area of choice for land *empresarios* who obtained land grants from Spain and later Mexico for their private colonies. Many of the towns that dot the area were started in the early 19th century by European immigrants—Czechs, Poles, Germans, French, and Belgians—and most of these show discernible traces of their origins. While the frontierspeople who settled other parts of Texas were usually looking for cheap land, the *empresario* colonists often fled some degree of political or economic oppression; hence, their descendants have tended to sympathize with social causes. During the Civil

War, South Central Texas was the largest stronghold of Union supporters in the state. Today, Austin and San Antonio are the state's most politically progressive cities, largely because of this early immigrant heritage.

The unique topography of South Central Texas is determined by the falling away of the Edwards Plateau as it meets the coastal plains of South Texas. This drop, the Balcones Escarpment, extends all the way from San Antonio to just below Dallas but is most conspicuous in the Hill Country and the Llano Uplift west of Austin and San Antonio. The hilly terrain and the springs, creeks, rivers, and 150-mile chain of Highland Lakes attract visitors from all over the state and beyond.

AUSTIN

Austin presents a combination state capital, university town, and high-tech center. You'd think this might result in a big, busy city, but it doesn't; within the city limits are less than 500,000 people. Austin residents are proud of their city's

reputation for both a small-town atmosphere and urban sophistication.

The total Austin metro area, however, contains a sizable 870,000 residents, many of whom arrived during the city's recent economic boom.

In 1992 *Money* magazine ranked Austin the third best place to live in the nation, while the following year *Fortune* placed the city fifth on the magazine's list of the nation's top 10 "best cities for business." That same year *Men's Journal* dubbed the city the "Soul of the New Southwest." Has the fuss gone to Austin's head? *Esquire*, in its own survey, concluded it was America's most overrated city—a conclusion for the most part motivated by the city's high level of self-conceit. Still, if you can tolerate a little excess pridefulness, you'll find Austin an amazing blend of the vibrant and laidback, the slick and downhome, all wrapped in an attractive package of historic and modern architecture, venerable oaks, rolling hills, and clear lakes.

CLIMATE

Austin has mild winters with occasional cold snaps. Summers are hot and humid, averaging 64% relative humidity in July. August can be oppressively hot, with daily highs exceeding 98° F. The average annual precipitation for the area is 31 inches, with most rain falling in May and September.

AUSTIN TEMPERATURES		
MONTH	MAX. (° F)	MIN. (° F)
January	60	41
March	71	49
May	85	65
July	95	75
September	90	69
November	70	48

HISTORY

Spanish priests from San Antonio established a short-lived mission at Barton Springs in 1730, but apparently the local Tickanwatic Indians didn't take to missionizing—the priests gave up after a year. In 1838 trader Jake Harrell set up camp at a spot that later became the center of downtown Austin; he was soon joined by a sprinkling of other settlers, who built log cabins and a stockade. They called the settlement Waterloo. Republic of Texas Vice President M.B. Lamar, an acquaintance of Harrell's, joined him for a buffalo shoot in Waterloo that same year. When Lamar succeeded Sam Houston as president, he decided to establish the national capital at Waterloo and began construction in 1839. Perhaps because of the unfortunate associations of the name "Waterloo" (Lamar's middle name was Bonaparte), the capital was soon named Austin, after land *empresario* Stephen F. Austin. The resulting polity became one of only three cities, along with Washington, D.C., and Brazil's Brasilia, carved from the surrounding wilderness to serve as national capitals.

By 1860, at which time it had been demoted from national to state capital, Austin claimed a population of around 3,500. City residents, along with those of surrounding Travis County, voted against secession from the Union in 1861. The Civil War had little effect on the state capital, except for the year the Confederacy fell (1865), when a unit of renegade Texas Confederates raided the State Treasury for gold and silver coins. The University of Texas opened in 1883, establishing Austin as a town of scholars and bureaucrats. Around 27% of the city's population today works for the government.

Austin remained a college and government town until the Tracor electronics company arrived in the 1960s. Texas Instruments, which developed the first silicon microchip in 1959, eventually moved here and has since been followed by Motorola, IBM, Dell, Applied Materials, 3M, Apple, Hewlett Packard, Digital Equipment, Advance Micro Devices, NCR, Sematech, and many other electronics companies. Since 1986 alone over 180 high-tech companies have moved into or expanded in Austin, attracted by the relatively low cost of living and the high-quality work force. An estimated 30.7% of the population holdS college degrees, resulting in the most highly educated American city with over 250,000 people.

Music is another important Austin industry, pumping around $400 million a year into the area local economy. Within the last 25 years, Austin has become the pop-music world's Third Coast, joining Nashville, New York, and Los Angeles as a seminal performance and recording center.

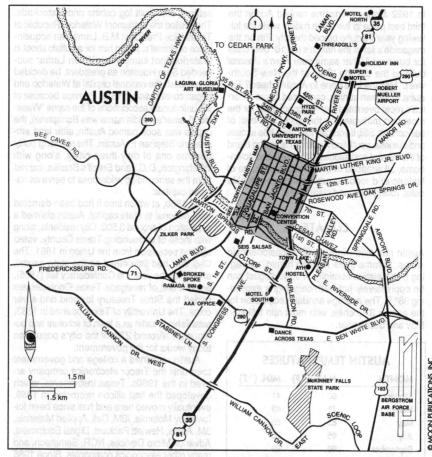

AUSTIN

CENTRAL AUSTIN MAP

SEE "CENTRAL AUSTIN" MAP

TO CEDAR PARK

COLORADO RIVER

CAPITOL OF TEXAS HWY.

LAGUNA GLORIA ART MUSEUM

LAKE AUSTIN BLVD.

BEE CAVES RD.

MOTEL 6 NORTH

THREADGILL'S

HOLIDAY INN

SUPER 8 MOTEL

KOENIG LN.

ROBERT MUELLER AIRPORT

MEDICAL PKWY.

BURNET RD.

LAMAR BLVD.

RED RIVER ST.

MANOR RD.

HYDE PARK

45th ST.

38th ST.

36th ST.

34th ST.

31st ST.

ANTONE'S

UNIVERSITY OF TEXAS

MARTIN LUTHER KING JR. BLVD.

E. 12th ST.

ROSEWOOD AVE. OAK SPRINGS DR.

GUADALUPE ST.

LITTLE ST.

SAN JACINTO BLVD.

7th ST.

CONVENTION CENTER

CESAR CHAVEZ (1st) ST.

SPRINGDALE RD.

AIRPORT BLVD.

VALLEY RD.

BARTON SPRINGS RD.

ZILKER PARK

SEIS SALSAS

OLTORF ST.

TOWN LAKE

AYH HOSTEL

LAMAR BLVD.

FREDERICKSBURG RD.

71

BROKEN SPOKE

RAMADA INN

S. 1st ST.

S. CONGRESS AVE.

MOTEL 6 SOUTH

BURLESON RD.

E. RIVERSIDE DR.

PLEASANT VALLEY RD.

AAA OFFICE

290

STASSNEY LN.

WILLIAM CANNON DR. WEST

DANCE ACROSS TEXAS

E. BEN WHITE BLVD.

MOON

1.5 mi

0   1.5 km

McKINNEY FALLS STATE PARK

183

BERGSTROM AIR FORCE BASE

WILLIAM CANNON DR.

SCENIC LOOP

EAST

35

81

© MOON PUBLICATIONS, INC.

SIGHTS

Historic District

Ever mindful of preserving its 19th-century architectural history, Austin has thus far designated nine different historic districts, three well-developed enough to warrant the publication of free walking tour map/pamphlets by the Austin Visitors Center. For two of these districts, the city sponsors free guided walking tours—highly recommended for those interested in regional architecture and local history.

Congress Avenue and East Sixth Street: These streets have been the center of Austin's downtown life since the mid-1800s. Congress Ave. once formed the city's main north-south artery, leading to the magnificent State Capitol, while E. Pecan Street (which became E. 6th) led east to Houston. The original buildings along the two streets date between 1854 and 1909, with most built in the 1870s and 1880s. They feature a combination of Victorian and Renaissance Revival styles, in brick and native stones (limestone and pink granite). The Austin Visitor Information Center at 201 E. 2nd St. distributes the excellent *Congress Ave. and Sixth Street Historic Walking Tour* pamphlet, which guides visitors along a 10-block section of Congress and nine-block section of E. 6th St. and offers descriptions of historic buildings encountered along the way.

Office staff lead free guided walking tours of the area Thurs.-Sat. at 9 a.m. and Sunday at 2 p.m. starting from the south entrance of the State Capitol (weather permitting).

East Sixth Street itself has been designated a National Historic District. As Pecan St., it was the town center in the 1870s and early 1880s; the name was changed to E. 6th in 1884. Most of the two- and three-story buildings are former mercantile houses of Victorian design. The street's respectability has been somewhat suspect ever since the 1888 completion of the State Capitol shifted the downtown emphasis to Congress Avenue. Short-story writer O. Henry, who lived in Austin during the 1890s as editor of the original *Rolling Stone,* wrote that E. 6th St. was "bold, bad, and hard to curry." By the 1960s, it was something of a skid row.

A neighborhood renaissance began in the late '60s, as local entrepreneurs started restoring historic E. 6th St. structures. As the Austin music scene burgeoned in the '70s, E. 6th St. developed into a popular live music venue. By 1980 it was a nightly street party; when the Texas legislature raised the drinking age from 18 to 21 things calmed down a bit. An older crowd began patronizing the district and E. 6th St. grew up. More recently the city has slapped a downtown 10 p.m.-6 a.m. curfew on those under 17. This is still Austin's primary entertainment district, dotted with live-music clubs and restaurants—"Austin's Bourbon St.," as journalists are wont to say, though it's a lot less touristy than the street in New Orleans. During the last weekend in September the street is blockaded off for the Old Pecan Street Arts and Crafts Festival.

Bremond Block: Bounded by 7th St., 8th St., Guadalupe St., and San Antonio St., this large city block serves as a platform for 11 restored mid-19th-century homes in Greek Revival and Victorian styles. All were built by the union of two merchant families, the Bremonds and Robinsons. The pièce de résistance, the two-story, Second Empire-style **John Bremond, Jr. House** at 700 Guadalupe St., receives almost as many sightseers as the State Capitol. Completed in 1887, this was the first residence in Austin to contain an indoor toilet. None of these homes are open to the public—you'll have to be satisfied with exterior views.

The *Bremond Block Historic Walking Tour* pamphlet, available from the Austin Visitor Information Center, will guide you through the district; or you can turn up at the **Texas Governor's Mansion** at 1010 Colorado St. any Saturday or Sunday morning at 11 a.m. for a free guided walking tour, weather permitting.

Hyde Park: Austin's first "suburb," this residential district founded in 1891 was originally linked to downtown Austin by its own tramway. Bounded by 43rd St., Ave. B, 40th St., and Ave. G, the district today exhibits a raffish hodgepodge of one-story late Victorian and California Craftsman bungalows, Tudor revival homes, and bold stone experiments such as sculptor Elisabet Ney's castle-like studio. As usual, the Austin Visitor Information Center distributes a well-annotated pamphlet and map suitable for self-guided walking tours.

State Capitol

Standing seven feet taller than the U.S. Capitol in Washington, D.C., this is the largest state capitol building in the country—truly Texas size. At the time of its completion in 1888, it was believed to be the seventh-largest building in the world, with 8.5 acres of floor space on three acres of land. Like many of the grander government buildings built in Texas in the late 1800s, it was designed in the Renaissance Revival or neoclassic style—although this is one of the more sober-looking interpretations of that style in the state; county courthouse fans may be disappointed. It took 15,000 railroad cars full of pink granite, quarried at Marble Falls, to complete the cruciform exterior. The cornerstone alone weighs eight tons. Eighty-five thousand square feet of copper cover the roof. No expense was spared for the interior, either, which contains seven miles of oak, pine, cherry, cedar, ash, walnut, and mahogany wainscoting. The 500 doors and 900 windows are framed in oak, pine, and cherry.

The impressive rotunda interior displays the usual paintings of Texas statespersons and historic documents, including the Texas Declaration

State Capitol, Austin

of Independence and Ordinance of Secession. Free tours of the Capitol are given daily between 8:30 a.m. and 4:30 p.m., starting at the visitor center in the south foyer. The entrance foyer and rotunda are open 24 hours, however, so you can come by anytime for a self-guided tour.

Art Museums
The **Laguna Gloria Art Museum** is housed in a 1915 Spanish-style villa built as a "winter retreat" by the founder and publisher of the *Austin American* on 28 acres overlooking Lake Austin. The galleries host traveling exhibits of 20th-century American painting and photography; about half the works come from local/regional people, half from nationally and internationally known artists. The museum also offers films, lectures, and music, as well as art classes. Perhaps the best part of the museum is the palm- and pecan-shaded grounds, natural relief from Austin's summer heat. Laguna Gloris is located at the end of W. 35th St. (tel. 512-458-8191); open Tues.-Sat. 10 a.m.-5 p.m. (Thurs. till 9 p.m.), Sunday 1-5 p.m. Admission is $2 adults, $1 seniors and

students, children under 16 free.

German sculptress Elisabet Ney, the first woman ever admitted to the Munich Art Academy, built a home/studio in Austin in 1892. After she died in 1907 it was turned into the **Elisabet Ney Museum**, one of only four intact 19th-century sculptor's studios in the country. It's now a designated National Historic Site. In Europe, Ney sculpted such legends as Schopenhauer, the Bismarck, and King Ludwig; after moving to Texas she switched from sculpting Old World satin to New World buckskin, creating state-commissioned sculptures of Sam Houston (now in the U.S. Capitol), Stephen Austin (in the Texas Capitol), and other Texas figures. Ney's sculptures and the tools of her trade are on display, and the building itself is an artful design of stonemasonry with cast-iron fittings and wood flooring. A spiral staircase leads to a loft containing several interpretive exhibits on Ney's life and work. The museum also offers art classes. It's located at 304 E. 44th Ave. (at Ave. H) in the historic Hyde Park district; call 458-2255 for further information. Open Wed.-Sat. 10 a.m.-5 p.m., Sunday noon-5 p.m.; free admission.

The **Mexic-Arte Museum** (tel. 480-9373) at 419 Congress Ave. houses a permanent display of Mexican art, as well as changing exhibits in several visual media. Open Mon.-Sat. 10 a.m.-6 p.m.; free admission.

At the **Umlauf Sculpture Garden and Museum** (tel. 445-5582), just east of Zilker Park at 605 Robert E. Lee Rd., visitors can view over 130 works by renowned Austin sculptor Charles Umlauf. Open Friday 10 a.m.-4:30 p.m., Thursday, Saturday, and Sunday 1-4:30 p.m.; admission $2 general, $1 students.

Art Galleries: At last count Austin harbored 26 small galleries tucked away in downtown warehouses and other low-rent districts. Some are run by art co-ops, others by solo artists. They tend to come and go with great frequency—check the "Art" section in the back of the weekly *Austin Chronicle* for a complete and current list. One unique gallery that's been around for a while is singer-songwriter Butch Hancock's **Lubbock or Leave It** (tel. 478-1688), 406 Brazos downtown, which showcases the singer's visual and audio work; a small recording studio adjoins the gallery. Open Tues.-Fri. 11 a.m.-6 p.m., Saturday noon-6 p.m.

Other Museums

Another artist who lived in Austin in the late 19th century was American writer William Sydney Porter, better known by his pen name "O. Henry." While residing in Austin (1885-95), Porter worked as a bank clerk and was editor and publisher of an Austin weekly called *Rolling Stone*. A small collection of Porter memorabilia, along with original and period furnishings, is kept in his Victorian cottage at 409 E. 5th St. (at Neches St.), now called the **O. Henry Museum** (tel. 512-472-1903). In May the museum sponsors an annual O. Henry Pun-Off. Open Wed.-Sun., noon-5 p.m.; free admission.

The **George Washington Carver Museum** (tel. 472-4809) contains artifacts, photos, videos, and other archival material devoted to African-American history in Texas. At 1165 Angelina St., it's open Tues.-Thurs. 10 a.m.-6 p.m., Fri.-Sat. noon-5 p.m.; free admission.

Other museums of note in Austin can be found on the UT campus.

Driskill Hotel

Cattleman Jesse Lincoln Driskill built this striking, Richardson Romanesque-style hotel on Pecan St. (now E. 6th) in 1886. A bust of Driskill sits atop the south facade facing E. 6th St., and busts of his sons A.W. and J.W. decorate the other entrances. While the state legislature was waiting for the Capitol to be completed (1888), Driskill let them use the hotel for meetings and official sessions. Governor Sul Ross established an Austin tradition by holding the first gubernatorial inaugural ball here in 1887. Lyndon B. Johnson used the hotel as headquarters for his first Senate campaign, as well as his successful bid for the presidency in 1964. The hotel now has its own curator who looks after the governors' memorabilia on display in the first-floor hallway between the lobby and the Lobby Bar.

There have been several different owners since Driskill died in 1890. The most recent management completed a full restoration in 1989, elevating the facilities to first-class standards while preserving the historical ambience. Among the 15 terraced suites are the Governor's Suite and the LBJ Suite.

University of Texas at Austin

Since its inception in 1883, UT has grown to encompass a 357-acre campus with an enrollment of 50,000—over 10% of Austin's municipal population. The on-campus student population is so large that one residence hall, Jester Center, represents two voting precincts and has its own zip code.

Academic headquarters for the entire UT system, with 14 institutions statewide, the Austin campus boasts three graduate programs ranked in the U.S. top five (botany, linguistics, and Spanish) and five more (Germanic languages, civil engineering, classics, zoology, and computer science) among the top 10. The Austin campus

the Driskill Hotel

also has the sixth-largest university library in the country, with nearly six million volumes.

It takes money to achieve these kinds of rankings, and UT has one of the largest public endowments of any educational institution in the world. The state legislature gave the university two million acres of West Texas desert during the latter half of the 19th century, which might not have amounted to much except that oil was discovered on the land in 1921. Royalties from drilling rights led to the establishment of the Permanent University Fund, and it's been fat city ever since. Of course now that oil prices are in the doldrums, the fund may turn out to be not so permanent.

Austin's best museums are located on the UT campus. The **Harry Ransom Humanities Research Center** (tel. 512-471-9111), housed in the Harry Ransom Center and the Academic Center, is comprised of the Leeds Gallery, featuring rare books and manuscripts; the Photography Collection, with over five million prints and negatives, including the world's first photograph and 3,000 pieces of antique photographic equipment; the Iconography Collection, consisting of iconographic artwork spanning four centuries; and several other smaller humanities-oriented collections. One of five existing Gutenberg Bibles is displayed on the first floor of the Ransom Center. Other rare birds in the Center's stupendous book collection include a 1450 edition of *The Canterbury Tales;* William Blake's earliest published poetry (*Poetical Sketches*, 1783) plus one of 11 existing hand-colored copies of Blake's greatest work, *Songs of Innocence;* the Vander-Poel Collection of Charles Dickens; extensive manuscript holdings from Edgar Allan Poe, Mark Twain, Ernest Hemingway, Walt Whitman, and Henry Miller; and the complete working libraries of James Joyce, Evelyn Waugh, and e.e. cummings. Both buildings are located at the west edge of campus, on W. 21st and Guadalupe. Hours are Mon.-Fri. 9 a.m.-4:30 p.m.; free admission.

The **Archer M. Huntington Art Gallery** (tel. 471-7324) is housed in two halls, the Ransom Center and the Art Building. The permanent exhibits include collections of 19th- and 20th-century North American and contemporary Latin American art, Greco-Roman art, and 2,000 other works of various provenance. Traveling exhibits

are also on display. The Art Building is at E. 23rd and San Jacinto. Hours for both halls are Mon.-Fri. 9 a.m.-5 p.m., Sunday 1-5 p.m.; free admission.

The **Texas Memorial Museum** (tel. 471-1604) is a collection of research exhibits in the sciences, including the fields of geology, paleontology, anthropology, archaeology, and natural history. At 2400 Trinity; open Mon.-Fri. 9 a.m.-5 p.m., Sat.-Sun. 10 a.m.-5 p.m. Free admission.

The first presidential museum built on a university campus, the **Lyndon Baines Johnson Library and Museum,** displays LBJ memorabilia, four stories filled with presidential manuscripts, and a replica of the Oval Office during the LBJ administration. There is also a general exhibit of presidential campaign memorabilia covering the George Washington era to the present. The "First Lady Theater" presents a short film on the life and work of Lady Bird Johnson. At 2313 Red River; open daily except Christmas 9 a.m.-5 p.m. Free admission.

The **Frank C. Erwin Jr. Special Events Center** at 1701 Red River is an 18,000-seat arena that hosts everything from UT basketball games to big-name rock concerts. The center's monthly *Applause* magazine contains details on upcoming events; call 477-6060 for ticket information. The general information number for the university is 471-3434.

French Legation

France was the first country to recognize Republic of Texas sovereignty, and in 1840 the French sent chargé d'affaires Alphonse Dubois de Saligny to Austin to establish a foreign-service outpost. In 1841 Dubois constructed a Louisiana Bayou-style house of Bastrop pine that surpassed in elegance every house in town but the president's. All the window glass and furniture was imported from France, all the hardware (brass hinges, locks, keys) from England. Because of a dispute with a local hotelier over unpaid bills, Dubois left town before he'd completed a year's residence, and the house passed into the hands of a bishop and later a doctor. The state purchased the home in 1948 and allowed the Daughters of the Republic of Texas to restore it for public viewing. It now stands as probably the best example of French colonial style in the U.S. outside Louisiana; the free-standing kitchen is said to be the only fully restored early French kitchen in the country. At 8th and San Marcos (tel. 512-472-8180); open Tues.-Sun. 1-5 p.m. Admission $2 adults, $1 ages 10-18, 50 cents ages 5-9.

Wineries and Breweries

Owned by a former general partner in Lubbock's Llano Estacado Winery, **Slaughter-Leftwich Vineyards** cultivated one of the state's first vinifera vineyards near Lubbock in 1979. S-L's grapes still hail from the Panhandle wine country, but the winery itself—where all the crushing, aging, and bottling takes place—sits on a hillside west of town near Lake Travis. For wine lovers it's worth a special trip to taste S-L's Texas chardonnay, which earned a double gold medal at the 1984 San Francisco Fair and since 1986 has been the most awarded chardonnay in the state. The winery's cabernet sauvignon, sauvignon blanc, and chenin blanc have also garnered acclaim at wine competitions.

The winery is located on Eck Lane, off RM 620 about six miles north of the US 71/RM 620 junction at Bee Cave. Tours of the winery are offered Sept.-May, Sat-.Sun. 1-5 p.m. and June-Aug. Thurs.-Sat. 1-5 p.m. Open for tastings and sales daily 1-5 p.m. year round. For further information call (512) 266-3331.

Celis Brewery produces a very well-received Belgian-style line of beers and ales, including a popular pale bock and a wheat beer ("white beer" in Belgian parlance) spiced with orange peel and coriander. The latter is a two-time gold medal winner at the Great American Beer Festival. The Celis Grand Cru is a weighty ale that contains 7.2% alcohol; a raspberry-flavored *framboise* will soon be released. Opened in 1992, Celis claims to be the fastest-growing microbrewery in the nation. Free 20-minute tours, offered Tues.-Sat. at 2 and 4 p.m., cover background history of the Belgian-owned and -built facility; a look at the brewing process, including the impressive 1938-vintage, hand-hammered copper brewing kettles; and a complimentary tasting. At 2431 Forbes Drive (tel. 835-0884).

Tiny newcomer **Hill Country Brewing and Bottling Company** (tel. 512-385-9111), at 730 Shady Lane in southeast Austin, so far brews two ales, "Balcones Fault Pale Malt" and "Bal-

cones Fault Red Granite," both of which are sold only in the Austin-Hill County area. Tours of the microbrewery are available by appointment.

Further afield, another winery worth visiting is Fall Creek Vineyards near Lake Buchanan; see the "Highland Lakes" under "Vicinity of Austin" for details.

ACCOMMODATIONS

Hotels and Motels

Austin offers hotel and motel lodgings to fit every budget. Conveniently located a few blocks south of Town Lake, a quick bus hop from the downtown area, the **Austin Motel** (tel. 512-441-1157), 1220 S. Congress, has simple but clean rooms for $28-48 with weekly discounts available. The motel features a pool and video rental library. Farther south along S. Congress, **State Motel** (tel. 442-2778), 2500 S. Congress, features similar rooms for $26-32.

Other choices on the economical end are clustered around the junction of I-35 and US 290 E and include the **Country Inn** (tel. 452-1177), $35 s/d plus $4 each additional person; **Friendship Inn** (tel. 458-4759), $34-44 s/d plus $4 each additional person; **Austin Motor Inn** (tel. 835-0333), $22-24; and **Super 8 Motel** (tel. 467-8163), $42-45 s/d plus $3 each additional person.

Near the university at 2900 I-35 N (exit 235B), the **Rodeway Inn at University** (tel. 477-6395) has good rooms for $38-50 s/d plus $5 each additional person.

At the upper end of the scale, Austin's best hotel—and one of the best hotels in the state—is the elegant, 292-room **Four Seasons Hotel** (tel. 478-4500 or 800-332-3442; fax 478-3117) at 98 San Jacinto Blvd. on Town Lake. Almost every room at the Four Seasons comes with a lake view and the hotel's restaurants are among the city's most celebrated. Rates run $133-195 s/d a night. Other highly rated luxury hotels include **Sheraton Austin Hotel, Driskill Hotel,** the **Hyatt Regency Austin,** and the **Stouffer Austin Hotel,** all in the $110-185 range during the week. Weekend discounts at the more expensive hotels slice as much as 40% off these rates; during the week be sure to inquire about corporate rates if you're traveling on business. See the "Austin Hotels and Motels" chart for details on these and other lodgings around the city.

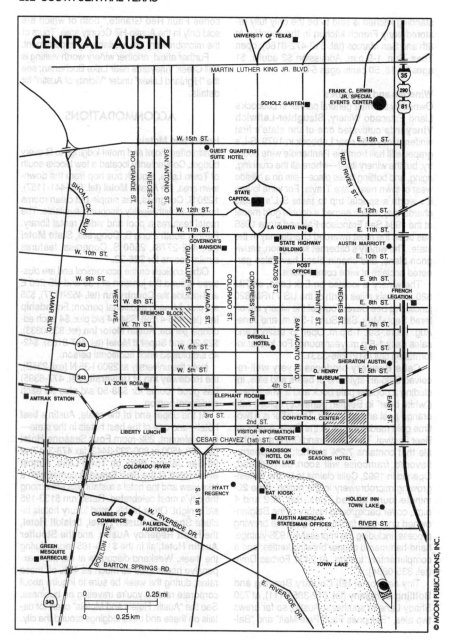

CENTRAL AUSTIN

UNIVERSITY OF TEXAS

MARTIN LUTHER KING JR. BLVD.

FRANK C. ERWIN JR. SPECIAL EVENTS CENTER

SCHOLZ GARTEN

W. 15th ST.   E. 15th ST.

GUEST QUARTERS SUITE HOTEL

RIO GRANDE ST.
SAN ANTONIO ST.
NUECES ST.

SHOAL CK. BLVD.

STATE CAPITOL

RED RIVER ST.

W. 12th ST.   E. 12th ST.

LA QUINTA INN

W. 11th ST.   E. 11th ST.

GOVERNOR'S MANSION

STATE HIGHWAY BUILDING

AUSTIN MARRIOTT

W. 10th ST.   E. 10th ST.

W. 9th ST.

GUADALUPE ST.

COLORADO ST.

CONGRESS AVE.

BRAZOS ST.

POST OFFICE

E. 9th ST.

WEST AVE.

LAVACA ST.

TRINITY ST.

NECHES ST.

FRENCH LEGATION

W. 8th ST.   E. 8th ST.

BREMOND BLOCK

W. 7th ST.   E. 7th ST.

SAN JACINTO BLVD.

DRISKILL HOTEL

W. 6th ST.   E. 6th ST.

LAMAR BLVD.

W. 5th ST.   E. 5th ST.

SHERATON AUSTIN

O. HENRY MUSEUM

LA ZONA ROSA

4th ST.

AMTRAK STATION

ELEPHANT ROOM

3rd ST.

EAST ST.

CONVENTION CENTER

2nd ST.

LIBERTY LUNCH

VISITOR INFORMATION CENTER

CESAR CHAVEZ (1st) ST.

COLORADO RIVER

RADISSON HOTEL ON TOWN LAKE

FOUR SEASONS HOTEL

HYATT REGENCY

BAT KIOSK

HOLIDAY INN TOWN LAKE

S. 1st ST.

W. RIVERSIDE DR.

CHAMBER OF COMMERCE

PALMER AUDITORIUM

AUSTIN AMERICAN-STATESMAN OFFICES

RIVER ST.

GREEN MESQUITE BARBECUE

BOULDIN AVE.

BARTON SPRINGS RD.

TOWN LAKE

E. RIVERSIDE DR.

0   0.25 mi

0   0.25 km

© MOON PUBLICATIONS, INC.

AUSTIN HOTELS AND MOTELS

Add 13% hotel tax to all rates. Area code: 512.

NORTH (INCLUDING THE AIRPORT)

Austin Hilton & Towers; 6000 Middle Fiskville Rd. (off I-35); tel. 451-5757 or (800) 347-0330; $84-105; pool, airport shuttle

Austin Motor Inn; 11400 I-35 N; tel. 835-0333; $22-24; pool

Best Western Chariot Inn; 7300 I-35 N; tel. 452-9371 or (800) 528-1234; $38-52; pool, airport shuttle, complimentary continental breakfast

Budget Host Inn of Austin; 820 E. Anderson (off I-35 N at US 183); tel. 835-4311; $29-39

Country Inn; 5656 I-35 N; tel. 452-1177; $35; pool

Days Inn North; 8210 I-35 N; tel. 835-2200; $33-45; pool, airport shuttle

Friendship Inn; 6201 US 290 E; tel. 458-4759; $34-44; pool

Heritage Inn; 9121 I-35 N; tel. 836-0079; $40-44; pool, airport shuttle

Holiday Inn-Airport; 6911 I-35 N; tel. 459-4251 or (800) HOLIDAY; $53-64; pool, coin laundry, airport shuttle

Holiday Inn Northwest Plaza; 8901 Business Park (US 183 and Loop 1); tel. 343-0888 or (800) HOLIDAY; $75-80; heated pool, airport shuttle, weekly rates

La Quinta Motor Inn-North; 7100 I-35 N; tel. 452-9401 or (800) 531-5900; $50-65; pool, airport shuttle

Motel 6 Airport; 5330 I-35 N (exit 238A); tel. 467-9111; $26-27; pool

Motel 6 North; 9420 I-35 N; tel. 339-6161; $22.95 plus $6 each additional person; pool

Red Lion Hotel Airport; 6121 I-35 N; tel. 328-5466; $80-131; pool, sauna, coin laundry, airport shuttle, weekend discount

Rodeway Inn Airport; 5526 I-35 N; tel. 451-7001; $38-48; pool, airport shuttle

Super 8 Motel; 6000 Middle Fiskville Rd.; tel. 467-8163, $42-45; coin laundry

CENTRAL

Austin Motel; 1220 S. Congress; tel. 441-1157; $28-48; pool, video rental library; weekly rates

Austin Marriott at the Capitol; 701 E. 11th; tel. 478-1111 or (800) 347-0330; $105-145; heated pool, saunas, airport transportation, weekend discount

Budget Inn Capitol; 1201 I-35 N; tel. 472-8331; $30-40; pool, weekly rates

Driskill Hotel; 604 Brazos at E. 6th; tel. 474-5911; $109-119; historic, valet parking, airport shuttle, weekend discount

Embassy Suites Downtown; 300 S. Congress; tel. 469-9000 or (800) EMBASSY; $99-129; heated pool, sauna, airport shuttle, weekend discount, complimentary evening beverage, many rooms with kitchenettes

Four Seasons Hotel Austin; 98 San Jacinto, on Town Lake; tel. 478-4500 or (800) 332-3442; $132-195; heated pool, saunas, health club, airport shuttle, most rooms with Town Lake view

Guest Quarters Suite Hotel Austin; 303 W. 15th; tel. 478-7000 or (800) 424-2900; $135-155; 1-2 bedroom apartments with kitchens, pool, coin laundry, airport shuttle, weekend discount

Hyatt Regency Austin; 208 Barton Springs; tel. 477-1234; $119-150; some rooms overlook river, heated pool, airport shuttle, weekend discount

Kensington Motor Lodge; 3300 Manor (west off I-35); tel. 478-5959; $30-42; kitchens in all units, weekly rates

La Quinta Inn Capitol; 300 E. 11th; tel. 476-7151; $61-73; pool, airport shuttle

Motel 6 Central; 8010 I-35 N; tel. 837-9890; $21-27; airport shuttle

Radisson Hotel on Town Lake; 111 E. 1st and Congress; tel. 478-9611 or (800) 333-3333; $65-125; pool, airport shuttle

Rodeway Inn at University; 2900 I-35 N; tel. 477-6395; $38-50; pool, senior discount, weekly and monthly rates

Sheraton Austin Hotel; 500 I-35 N; tel. 480-8181 or (800) 325-3535; $124-134; pool, sauna, exercise room, airport shuttle, weekend discounts

State Motel; 2500 S. Congress; tel. 442-2778; $26-32; weekly rates

(CONTINUED ON NEXT PAGE)

AUSTIN HOTELS AND MOTELS (CONT.)

Stouffer Austin Hotel; 9721 Arboretum; tel. 343-2626 or (800) 468-3571; $146-186; heated pool, sauna, health club, nine-story atrium, valet parking, airport shuttle

SOUTH

Best Western Seville Plaza; 4323 I-35 S; tel. 447-5511 or (800) 528-1234; $40-55; pool, coin laundry, weekly rates

Best Western South; 3909 I-35 S; tel. 444-0531 or (800) 528-1234; $39-54; pool, coin laundry, airport shuttle

Capitol Motor Inn; 2525 I-35 S; tel. 441-0143; $29-37; pool, senior discount, weekly rates

Exel Inn of Austin; 2711 I-35 S (exit 231); tel. 462-9201; $39-59; pool, weekend discounts

La Quinta Inn Ben White; 4200 I-35 S; tel. 443-1774 or (800) 531-5900; $52-64; pool

Motel 6 South; 2707 I-35 S (exit 231/232A); tel. 444-5882; $26-31; pool

Ramada Inn South; 1212 W. Ben White (off US 290); tel. 447-0151; $52-68; pool

Bed and Breakfasts

Austin's B&Bs continue to multiply, offering both leisure and business visitors individualized comfort and security. Many are housed in historic turn-of-the-century homes; you're best off choosing by first deciding where in the city you wish to sleep.

Ziller House (tel. 512-462-0100 or 800-949-5446; fax 462-3922) at 800 Edgecliff Terrace is near the downtown area and has a view of Town Lake. Tastefully decorated rooms with private baths cost $95-110 including a fix-it-yourself breakfast.

Seven blocks west of the University of Texas in a 1936-vintage house, **The Wildflower Inn** (tel. 477-9639), 1200 W. 22 1/2 St., offers country-furnished rooms for $54-69 a night including continental breakfast.

The 1897-vintage, late Victorian **Governor's Inn** (tel. 477-0711) at 611 W. 22nd St., west of the UT campus, rents antique-furnished rooms with private baths for $45-89

weekdays, $55-99 weekends including a full breakfast. Another late Victorian (1907) in a similar neighborhood is **The McCallum House** (tel. 451-6744) at 613 W. 32nd St., where rooms range from $55 s on weekdays to $95 d on weekends including a full breakfast. Most rooms come with kitchens; monthly rates of $1200-1500 are available.

Southwest of campus at 1900 David St., **Carrington's Bluff** (tel. 479-0638) is run by a Texan-British couple who let rooms in their 1877 farmhouse for $55-68 per night, including continental breakfast.

In the historic Hyde Park district, not far from the Elisabet Ney Museum, the two-story, 1900-vintage **Woodburn House** (tel. 458-4335) at 4401 Ave. D offers period-furnished rooms for a reasonable $55-78 per night with complete breakfast. Corporate and monthly rates available.

Southard House (tel. 474-4731), a two-story, 1890 Greek Revival home at 908 Blanco between W. 9th and W. 10th, lies near Austin's eclectic antique shop/gallery district. Large rooms with wooden floors and high ceilings start at $68 including continental breakfast.

Bed & Breakfast Texas Style (tel. 800-899-4538 or 214-298-8586), 4224 W. Red Bird Lane, Dallas, TX 75237, can handle reservations for the above B&Bs or suggest others in the Austin area.

AYH Hostel

Austin International AYH Hostel (tel. 512-444-2294) is housed in the renovated Old Rowing Club Boathouse on Town Lake, 2200 S. Lakeshore Boulevard. The no-curfew hostel has a fully equipped self-service kitchen and a large, 24-hour common room overlooking Town Lake. Dormitory beds cost $12 a night for AYH members; $3 additional for a temporary membership card. There's a couples room with a king-size waterbed for the same per-person rate. Reservations recommended.

To reach the hostel by city bus, take Capital Metro bus no. 26 or no. 27 from downtown to Pleasant Valley and S. Lakeshore, or a no. 7 from the Greyhound station to Riverside and S. Lakeshore. By private vehicle, take the Riverside Dr. exit and head east, then turn left onto S. Lakeshore Blvd.

Austin Area Campgrounds and RV Parks

Austin has an abundance of campgrounds and RV parks. The **Austin KOA** (tel. 512-444-6322) is the most expensive in the state at $22 for a tentsite, $25 full hookup, with weekly and monthly discounts available. Cabins are $32-42. There's a pool and a lounge with fireplace, but otherwise it isn't worth more than any other KOA. Located south of Austin off I-35 at the Wm. Cannon Dr. exit (exit 228).

At nearby **McKinney Falls State Park** (tel. 243-1643) off US 183 S at the southeast edge of town, drive-in sites with water are $6, with w/e $9; screened shelters are $18. Dump stations available. Also off US 183 S, at US 71 near Bergstrom AFB, is the **Royal Palm Mobile Home and RV Community** (tel. 385-2211), oriented toward long-term residents but accepting RVs for $15 a night.

The **Shady Grove RV Park** (tel. 499-8432) lies within the city limits and is very close to downtown Austin at 1600 Barton Springs Rd., near Zilker Park. Rates are $15 per site per day. Nearby at 1518 Barton Springs is the similar **Pecan Grove RV Park** (tel. 472-1067), where RV sites are also $15.

Northwest of town at **Emma Long Metropolitan Park** (tel. 346-1831) are $6 tentsites; drive-in sites with w/e are $10. One-time $3 entry fee Friday through Sunday.

The following Highland Lakes offer campgrounds on their shores: Lake Travis, Lake Marble Falls, Lake LBJ, Inks Lake, Lake Buchanan, and Lake Bastrop. See the "Highland Lakes Camping" chart under "Vicinity of Austin" for details.

FOOD

There are probably more restaurants per capita in Austin than in any other Texas town. Quantity doesn't mean quality, though, and this is especially the case in a college town—students will eat anything. The restaurants listed below are all safe bets.

American

$$$ **The Café at the Four Seasons:** Austin's toniest restaurant offers innovative dishes with impeccable service and Town Lake views. The menu includes pork tenderloin in a foccacia dijon crust with citrus butter, buffalo mozzarella, and roasted peppers; smoked salmon in a basil crepe, and roasted free-range chicken with garlic mashed potatoes and rosemary au jus. Pastry carts laden with temptations like crème brûlée and lemon ginger soufflé roll by at dessert time. Vast wine selection. Located in the Four Seasons Hotel, 98 San Jacinto Blvd. (tel. 512-478-4500, ext. 6158); open daily for breakfast 6:30-11 a.m., lunch 11 a.m.-2 p.m., and dinner 6-11 p.m.

$$ **City Grill:** Specializes in mesquite-grilled beef and seafood, including fresh tuna, redfish, and swordfish, served in a renovated warehouse overlooking Waller Creek. At 401 Sabine (tel. 479-0817); open daily for dinner only.

$ to $$ **Good Eats Café:** A fairly successful attempt at updating the classic Texas cafe, adding seafood to a meatloaf and barbecue menu. Country breakfasts, local art on display. At 1530 Barton Springs Rd. (tel. 476-8141) and 680 Burnet (tel. 451-2560); open daily for breakfast, lunch, and dinner.

$$$+   **Hudson's on the Bend:** Hunting-lodge decor with a variety of local cuisines, including Southwest and German, with an emphasis on fresh, pecan-smoked game. On Mimi Sheraton's list of top 50 restaurants in the United States. At 3509 RM 620 near Lake Travis (tel. 266-1369); open Tues.-Sun. for dinner only.

$$$ **Jeffrey's:** Nouvelle cuisine that borders on French. Long lines, good food. At 1204 W. Lynn (tel. 477-5584); open Mon.-Sat. for dinner only.

$ **Magnolia Café:** Good pancake breakfasts, breakfast tacos, and vegetarian dishes. At 1920 S. Congress (tel. 478-8645) and 2304 Lake Austin Blvd. (tel. 478-8645); open 24 hours.

$ **Scholz Garten:** A beer garden founded by August Scholz in 1862, with the Saengerrunde Hall next door. Serves an American hybrid of German, Texan, Italian, and Cajun dishes, plus over 50 brands of beer. An Austin institution. At 17th and San Jacinto (tel. 477-4171); open Mon.-Sat. for lunch and dinner.

$ to $$ **Threadgill's:** This legendary, diner-style downhome restaurant features such classics as chicken-fried steak, Texas caviar (marinated black-eyed peas), fried okra, "bronzed catfish," and the best pecan pie in Texas. Free seconds offered on all 23 vegetable dishes, listed on the menu under "Victory for Vegetables" and available in any combination. *Gourmet* magazine profiled Threadgill's in 1994; local regulars hope it won't ruin the place. Janis Joplin got her start here in the early '60s; nowadays music is provided by a free jukebox containing vintage Texas records by Bob Wills, Freddy Fender, Janis, and the late Ken Threadgill himself yodeling "St. Louis Blues." Occasional live music Wednesday evenings. At 6416 N. Lamar (tel. 451-4550); open daily (even Christmas and New Year's Day) 11 a.m.-10 p.m.

Asian

$$ Azuma: Traditional Japanese cuisine, including sushi and *teishokus* (set dinners). Sushi happy hour 5:30-7 p.m. and after 8 p.m. At 11906 Research Blvd. (tel. 512-258-3780); open Mon.-Sat. for lunch and dinner.

$$ Beijing Imperium: A semiformal restaurant specializing in Hunan and Szechwan cuisine. At 10000 Research Blvd. in the Arboretum Center (tel. 343-2944); open daily for lunch and dinner.

$$ China Palace: A huge, popular place with a long menu that features everything from dim sum to hotpots. At 6605 Airport (tel. 451-7104); open daily for lunch and dinner.

$ Kim Phung: The menu features a range of Vietnamese and Chinese dishes, but the house specialty is large, economic bowls of Vietnamese beef noodle soup. At 7601 N. Lamar (tel. 451-2464); open Tues.-Sat. for lunch and dinner.

$$ Kyoto: Standard Japanese fare and sushi bar. At 315 Congress (tel. 482-9010); open Mon.-Fri. for lunch and dinner, Saturday dinner only.

$ to $$ Satay: Food from countries on the South China Sea (Thailand, Malaysia, Indonesia), including the restaurant's namesake—small, marinated meat kebabs served with peanut sauce. Vegetarian dishes available. All-you-can-eat Sunday buffet. At 3202 W. Anderson Lane, Shoal Creek Plaza (tel. 467-6731); open Mon.-Sat. for lunch and dinner, Sunday noon-3 p.m. and 5-11 p.m.

$ Say Hi: No doubt the name means something (hopefully something good) in some Chinese dialect. The friendly humor extends to the menu, which focuses on roll-your-own spring rolls. At 5249 Burnet Rd. (tel. 453-1411); open Mon.-Sat. 10 a.m.-7 p.m.

$$ Thai Kitchen: Good, standard Thai (no mean feat in Austin); above-standard service. At 803A E. William Cannon (tel. 445-4844); open Mon.-Sat. for lunch and dinner.

Barbecue

$ to $$ County Line On The Hill: Offers a Hill Country view and great, lean barbecue, including smoked turkey and duck, and blue-plate specials. At 6500 Bee Caves Rd. (tel. 512-327-1742), with a second location, **County Line On The Lake**, at 5204 RM 2222 on Lake Austin (tel. 246-3664); open daily for lunch and dinner.

$ to $$ Green Mesquite Barbecue: Another Austin classic; standard barbecue plus smoked turkey and homemade peach cobbler. Live music nightly. At 1400 Barton Springs Rd. (tel. 479-0485); open daily for lunch and dinner.

$ to $$ Ruby's BBQ: An updated, "clean" barbecue, with USDA-certified, hormone-free beef. Black beans instead of the same old pintos, and a choice of creamy or vinaigrette slaw. Great chicken. Convenient location next to Antone's, 512 W. 29th at Guadalupe (tel. 477-1651). Open daily Sun.-Thurs. 11 a.m.-midnight, Fri.-Sat. till 4 a.m.

Belgian and French

$$ Belgian Restaurant L'Estro Armonico: The menu changes daily and features dishes strong on Belgian sauces—fish in soubise (puree of onions and rice) or potatoes in béchamel, for example. Good value considering all the work that goes into the cuisine. At 3520 Bee Cave Rd. (tel. 512-328-0580); open Tues.-Sun. for dinner only.

$$ Chez Nous: Run by an expatriate Frenchman and popular with visiting Europeans, this transplanted bistro offers a fixed-price French menu du jour that includes soup, salad or appetizer, entree, and dessert for around $16. At 510 Neches (tel. 473-2413); open Tues.-Fri. for lunch 11:45 a.m.-2 p.m., and Tues.-Sun. for dinner 6-10:30 p.m.

Brew Pubs

Austin's new brew pubs—finally permitted through a breakthrough state law—had just opened as we went to press. I didn't have a

THE BARBECUE TRIANGLE

Good barbecue can be found in Austin and throughout most of the rest of the state, but many brisket fans swear the best sizzles slowly in the smoky brick, iron, and stone pits of the "Barbecue Triangle" south and east of Austin. Roughly delineated by the towns of Taylor, Luling, and Giddings, this haven of smoked meats and spicy-cured sausages—called "hot guts" in these parts—also encompasses Elgin, Bastrop, Smithville, and Lockhart. All share a basic pit-cooking technology in which fresh cuts are cooked in giant oak-fired ovens designed to draw smoke and heat across the meat without exposing it to flames.

Each of the following offers a variety of pit-barbecued ribs, brisket, pork, chicken, and/or sausages, along with side dishes such as potato and/or macaroni salad, beans, coleslaw, and homemade pies. Elgin, where Czech, Polish, and German immigrants and their descendants have been stoking the fires since 1882, produces the best hot guts. Elgin sausage—made from secret recipes handed down from generation to generation—typically sells for around $4 a pound.

Unless otherwise noted, the barbecue joints listed below are in the 512 area code. Finding these places should be easy since all but two of the barbecue triangle towns sport populations of less than 5,000; Lockhart (9,000) and Taylor (11,000) are the exceptions. The friendly townsfolk will be glad to provide directions if needed.

Southside Market and BBQ, 1212 US 290 W, Elgin (tel. 285-3407)

Crosstown BBQ, 211 Central Ave., Elgin (tel. 285-9308)

Louie Mueller BBQ, 206 W. 2nd St., Taylor (tel. 352-6206)

Rudy Mikeska Bar-B-Q, 300 W. 2nd St., Taylor (tel. 352-5561)

Bastrop Bar-B-Q and Meat Market, 19 Main St., Bastrop (tel. 321-7719)

Bastrop Pit Barbecue, State 71 W, Bastrop (tel. 321-4344)

Zimmerhanzel's Barbeque, State 95 at the Colorado River bridge, Smithville (tel. 237-4244)

City Market, 633 Davis, Luling (tel. 210-875-9019)

Kreutz Market, 208 S. Commerce St., Lockhart (tel. 398-2361)

City Market, 101 W. Austin, Giddings (tel. 409-542-2740)

---

chance to sample all the beers but a quick tour of each pub was very promising.

Armadillo Brewing Co. (tel. 512-322-0039), in the heart of the E. Sixth Street bar strip at No. 419 E. 6th St., serves a decent range of beers and ales from behind an imposing wooden bar backed by copper brewing vats. The simple menu features salads, soups, sandwiches, and pizza. **Waterloo Brewing Co. and American Grill** (tel. 477-1836) at 401 Guadalupe offers a good variety of brews, including a refreshing raspberry beer, served with reasonably priced Texan and Tex-Mex food. Tap offerings at the **Bitter End** (tel. 478-2337), 311 Colorado St., were a bit thin and bland. All are open daily 11 a.m.-2 a.m.

Chili
$ **Texas Chili Parlor:** The only place in town that specializes in chili, and in every possible permutation—in bowls, in chili pie, on hot dogs, in flour tortillas. You choose the degree of hotness—X, XX, or XXX. At 1409 Lavaca (tel. 512-472-2828); open daily 11 a.m.-2 a.m.

German
$$ **Gunther's Restaurant:** Authentic Bavarian cuisine, including *schweinshaxe* (pork joint) and jaegerschnitzel (veal cutlet in mushroom and wine sauce). Spaten beer on tap, served in the half-liter as in Germany. At 11606 I-35 N (tel. 512-834-0474); open Tues.-Fri. for lunch and Tues.-Sun. for dinner.

Health
$ to $$ **Mother's Café and Garden:** Austin's best vegetarian food, including health-conscious Tex-Mex. At 4215 Duval (tel. 512-451-3994); open Mon.-Sat. for lunch and dinner, and for Sunday brunch.

$ High Time Tea Bar & Brain Gym: Austin's only no-booze, no-smoke bar serves a few snacks and nutrient-rich drinks. At 314 S. Congress; open 1 p.m.-2 a.m. daily.

$ Mr. Natural: A bakery and juice bar with light buffets and takeout, all vegetarian. At 1901 E. Cesar Chavez (1st St.) (tel. 477-5228); open Mon.-Sat. 8 a.m.-6 p.m.

Italian and Mediterranean

$$$ Basil's: This innovative Italian kitchen uses only fresh herbs and homemade pasta, with an emphasis on seafood; make reservations to avoid the line. At 10th and Lamar (tel. 512-477-5576); open daily for dinner only.

$ to $$ The Brick Oven Restaurant: Chicken, lasagna, stromboli, and Austin's best pizza—all baked in an 1890 wood-fired brick oven. At 1209 Red River (tel. 477-7006); open Mon.-Sat. lunch and dinner, Sunday dinner only. Second location at 10710 Research Blvd. (tel. 345-6181); same hours.

$$ Caffé Azzurro: Bistro-style ambience and an eclectic menu that includes a variety of *tapas* and light Mediterranean fare. Located in a historic limestone building at 918 Congress (tel. 477-6969); open for lunch Sun.-Fri., dinner Tues.-Saturday.

$$ Hill Country Pasta House: For my money there's no better pasta in the Austin area than that draping the plate at this converted home near Lake Travis. In addition to fresh pastas and delicious foccacia, the menu features brick-oven pizzas. Makes a good stop on the way to or from Slaughter-Leftwich Vineyards, which is just up the road. At 3519 RM 620 S (tel. 266-9445); open for lunch Sun.-Fri., dinner daily.

Mexican

Austin is very strong in Tex-Mex, rivaling its more Hispanic neighbor to the south, San Antonio.

$ to $$ Chuy's: A popular place with trendy dishes like blue corn tortilla enchiladas as well as traditional chiles rellenos. Good margaritas and amusing Mexican kitsch decor, including an Elvis shrine and Hubcap Room. At 1728 Barton Springs Rd. (tel. 512-474-4452); open daily for lunch and dinner.

$ Cisco's: This place has been going strong since 1949; LBJ used to eat here, and Longhorn (UT team) fans fill the place on weekends for breakfasts of *migas* or huevos rancheros—the kind they made before Tex-Mex became trendy, with thick sauces. Rumor says Cisco's is for sale, so it may change when owner Rudy Cisneros relinquishes control. Catfish on Friday. At 1511 E. 6th (tel. 478-2420); open daily for breakfast and lunch.

$ to $$ Fonda San Miguel: A contender for best Mexican in Austin, this vibrantly painted restaurant specializes in dishes from Yucatán, Veracruz, and Oaxaca. Owner-chef Miguel Ravago has laid out Mexican menus for the Mexican embassy in Washington, D.C., Maxim's, and the James Beard House in New York. Heart-stopping 11:30 a.m.-2 p.m. Sunday buffet includes a creative array of regional dishes. At 2330 W. North Loop (tel. 459-4121); open daily for lunch and dinner.

$ to $$ La Zona Rosa: In a town of great Mexican restaurants, this trendy place wouldn't rate except for the chili—which, of course, isn't really Mexican. The owner, Gordon Fowler, is the son of the late Wick Fowler of "Two-Alarm Chili" fame. At 612 W. 4th St. (tel. 482-0662); open daily for lunch, dinner till late.

$ Las Manitas Avenue Café: The best Mexican breakfasts in town, including *migas especiales con hongos* (eggs scrambled with corn tortilla strips and mushrooms), served with black beans. Different lunch specials every day, from *caldo azteca* to *tamal vegetariano;* Saturdays feature menudo and *barbacoa.* Walk through the kitchen to reach the patio out back. *Conjunto* music on occasional Friday evenings in the summer. At 211 Congress (tel. 472-9357); open Mon.-Fri. 7 a.m.-4 p.m., Sat.-Sun. 7 a.m.-2:30 p.m.

$$ Matt's El Rancho: An Austin favorite since 1952, Matt's serves a consistent range of Tex-Mex and authentic Mexican from basic *enchiladas verdes* to fancier chiles rellenos topped with raisins and pecans to button-popping Shrimp a la Matt Martinez, a platter of barbecued shrimp flanked by bean and cheese flautas. Matt's isn't the only place in town serving corn tortillas made from scratch, but it's probably the only one where the corn meal is actually ground on the premises. With the friendly, efficient service, it's difficult to have a bad meal experience here, though weekend nights can be very crowded. Outdoor dining on the terrace during good weather. At 2613 S. Lamar Blvd. (tel. 462-9333); open Wed.-Mon.

for lunch and dinner. Closed Tuesday so Matt, a former Golden Gloves champ, can watch amateur boxing in San Antonio.

$ to $$ México Típico: Another cafe-style place with great breakfasts, serving *migas* with fried potatoes, just like on the border, plus great *licuados* (Mexican fresh-fruit smoothies). At 1707 E. 6th (tel. 472-3222); open daily for breakfast, lunch, and dinner.

$ Seis Salsas: "Six Salsas" is what you'll find on the table: *tomatillo, chile arbol, serrano, chipotle, pico de gallo*, and *ranchera*. Fresh handmade tortillas and consistent, traditional Tex-Mex, including *carne guisada* and killer breakfast tacos. At 2004 Cesar Chavez (1st St.) (tel. 445-5050); open daily for breakfast, lunch, and dinner.

Seafood

$ to $$ Maceo's Seafood Co: Basic surf-and-turf menu, with an all-you-can-eat catfish special for lunch Friday. At 3-4 W. 4th St. (tel. 512-477-0970); open Mon.-Fri. for lunch and dinner, Saturday dinner only.

$$ Pearl's Oyster Bar: A mostly Cajun-Creole menu, including blackened redfish and fresh Gulf oysters. At 9033 Research Blvd. (tel. 339-7444); open daily for lunch and dinner.

$$ South Point Seafood: Fresh fish prepared in several ways—fried, steamed, baked, or grilled—and served with baskets of hush puppies. Next door to a fish market. At 2330 S. Lamar (tel. 442-6077); open Mon.-Fri. for lunch and dinner, Sat.-Sun. dinner only.

Steak

$ to $$ Dan McKlusky's: Considered by many to have the best steaks in town; the waiters bring the raw meat to your table for inspection before grilling. Chicken and seafood also available. At 419 E. 6th (tel. 512-472-8924); open Mon.-Fri. for lunch and dinner, Sat.-Sun. dinner only. Second location at 1000 Research, Arboretum Center (tel. 346-0780); same hours.

$$ Night Hawk: An Austin institution for over 50 years, as well as a favorite Longhorn hangout. The menu extends beyond steaks (a rival for McKlusky's) to catfish and oysters. Children's menu available. Two locations—the "Frisco Shop" at 5819 Burnet Rd. (tel. 459-6279), open daily for breakfast, lunch, and dinner; and "The Steakhouse" at 6007 N. I-35 at US 290 (tel. 452-0296), open daily for lunch and dinner.

$$ to $$$ Ruth's Chris Steakhouse: Another Austin contender for best steak title. Serves only U.S. prime cuts, chicken and seafood also available. At 3010 Guadalupe (tel. 477-7884); open daily for dinner only.

ENTERTAINMENT

Austin residents are fond of mentioning the fact (over and over) that Austin has more musicians and more music venues per capita than any place in the country. It's true, and what's more, there's an incredible variety of bands, definitely a wider spectrum than in most Texas cities. For out-of-staters in search of unique, regional styles, Austin is offering more of what American music lovers hanker for—blues, swamp music, Tex-Mex, zydeco—than anytime since the '60s. During the '80s, Austinians seemed embarassed about their roots and embraced all that was modern and trendy; nowadays thrash, country, and blues co-exist peacefully.

Live Music

If you're serious about hearing live music in "The Big Twang," you need to consult the right publications. Amateurs can get by with the latest issue of the *Austin Chronicle* weekly, distributed free from streetcorner stands downtown and in many restaurants and bars. The *Chronicle* lists all the acts at the major venues and many of the minor ones. The *Austin American-Statesman's* "Onward" section, printed on Thursday, also details current musical happenings. Pros should seek out the *Chronicle's* semi-annual *Austin Music Industry Guide*, which lists over 100 live music venues (not bad for a city of less than half a million), 68 major and independent record labels, plus extensive listings of recording studios, engineers, music attorneys, musicians' organizations, and so on. The guide is usually published once yearly in May or June; to obtain a back issue ($3), call or stop by the *Chronicle* office at 4000 I-35 (at 40th St. off I-35) (tel. 512-454-5766); the mailing address is P.O. Box 49066, Austin, TX 78765.

At the Austin Convention and Visitors Bureau you can pick up a copy of the useful brochure *Austin Music Live*, which contains a listing of live music venues around the city together with maps showing their location.

Most live music clubs are in the E. 6th area; a few are concentrated along "the Drag," the section of Guadalupe ("GWAD-a-loop") next to the UT campus. Here are some of the best:

Antone's: (tel. 474-5314) 2915 Guadalupe. Calls itself "Austin's Home of the Blues," but it's more like the Texas roots music headquarters for the entire state, one of the few places in Austin that books zydeco acts. The Fabulous Thunderbirds, the late Stevie Ray Vaughan, and other national names got a leg up here. Live music Mon.-Saturday.

Austin Outhouse: (tel. 451-2266) 3510 Guadalupe. Blues, folk, country, and rock, every night. Honky-tonk atmosphere.

SUSAN ANTONE

Babe's: (tel. 473-2262) 208 E. 6th. Showcases blues, R&B, and roots. Live music Tues.-Saturday.

Back Room: (tel. 441-5838) 2015 E. Riverside. Hard rock and metal, including some touring acts. Live music Tues.-Saturday.

Black Cat Lounge: (no phone) 309 E. 6th. Eclectic, mostly roots music. Live music nightly.

Broken Spoke: (tel. 442-6189) 3101 S. Lamar. Classic country dance hall, with cafe in front. Mostly traditional C&W and Western swing—look for Alvin Crow and the Pleasant Valley Boys or Johnny Bush and the Bandeleros. Live music Wed.-Saturday.

Cafe Brazil: (tel. 476-0254) 1806 Barton Springs Road. Live Latin and *tejano* music nightly.

Chez Fred Crossroads: (tel. 451-6494) 9070 Research Boulevard. Live jazz on weekends (mostly local acts, nothing too lively).

Chicago House: (tel. 473-2542) 607 Trinity. A theater-style place just off E. 6th featuring live folk music.

Club Palmeras: (tel. 473-0798) 217 Congress. Books Latin and Caribbean acts Mon.-Saturday.

The **Continental Club:** (tel. 441-2444) 1315 S. Congress. Home to roots rock, blues, and zydeco, with some touring acts. Live music Tues.-Sunday.

Dance Across Texas: (tel. 441-9101) 2202 Ben White Boulevard. Classic Texas dance hall with live music Wed.-Saturday.

Donn's Depot: (tel. 478-0336) 1600 W. 5th. Live country Tues.-Saturday

El Columpio: (tel. 479-0421) 1912 E. 7th. Live Latin and *tejano* music on weekends.

Electric Lounge: (tel. 476-3873) 302 Bowie. Live folk and alternative five nights a week.

Elephant Room: (tel. 473-2279) 315 Congress Avenue. Only a real music town could support live jazz nightly.

Emo's: (tel. 477-EMOS) 603 Red River. An eclectic line-up of semi-major names leaning toward alternative. Live music Thurs.-Sunday.

Fat Tuesday's: 508 E. 6th. A daiquiri bar with live blues, roots, and rock Fri.-Sunday.

Flamingo Cantina: (tel. 474-9336) 515 E. 6th. Roots, rock, reggae, and world beat. Live music Wed.-Saturday.

Green Mesquite: (tel. 479-0485) 1400 Barton Springs. A mix of rock, country, blues, and jazz. In the summer, outdoor performances in the beer garden. Live music every night.

Headliner's East: (tel. 478-3488) 406 E. 6th. Mostly blues, R&B, and rockabilly nightly.

Hole in the Wall: (tel. 472-5599) 2538 Guadalupe. A classic Austin venue with mostly roots rock, some country and folk. Live music every night.

Hondo's Cafe & Saloon: (tel. 472-7785) 407 E. 6th. Live music Wed.-Saturday.

Jazz On 6th: (tel. 479-0474) 212 E. 6th. Live jazz Wed.-Saturday.

Joe's Generic Bar: (tel. 480-0171) 315 E. 6th Street. Home to blues and R&B nightly.

Las Manitas Avenue Café: (tel. 477-6007) 211 Congress Street. Hosts "Ramon's Ice House" on several Friday evenings during the summer (6-8 p.m.); *conjunto* and Latin American music performances in support of La Peña, a nonprofit Latino arts organization. Politically correct fun.

La Zona Rosa: (tel. 482-0662) 612 W. 4th Street. Behind this Tex-Elec restaurant stretches a semi-outdoor venue for Texas singer-songwriters and touring R&B acts; Fri.-Sun. evenings only.

Liberty Lunch: (tel. 477-0461). A reincarnation of Armadillo World Headquarters. This semi-outdoor venue books the best of roots, reggae, and world beat, Wed.-Saturday.

Lumberyard: (tel. 255-9622) 16511 Bratton. Large venue emphasizing local and touring progressive country acts. Live music Mon.-Saturday.

Maggie Mae's: (tel. 478-8541) 323 E. 6th. Three stages: downstairs, upstairs, and in back ("old side"). Mostly pop and funk, occasional acoustic acts. Live music Mon.-Saturday.

Old Santa Fe Saloon: (tel. 476-4296) 505 E. 6th. Live country Tues.-Saturday.

Saxon Pub: (tel. 448-2552) 1320 S. Lamar. Hosts country and Texas singer-songwriters nightly.

Steamboat: (tel. 478-2912) 403 E. 6th. Local roots and alternative rock venue with live music nightly.

Threadgill's: (tel. 451-5440) 6416 N. Lamar. Acoustic folk or country acts Wednesday night— usually someone good. Janis Joplin used to sing here when she was a UT student, as recalled in a plaque mounted next to the jukebox.

311 Club: (tel. 477-1630) 311 6th. Local and Texas acts—mostly roots rock—nightly.

Wylie's: (tel. 472-3712) 400 E. 6th. Offers a varied menu, including roots rock, Brazilian, pop, and reggae. Live music Thurs.-Saturday.

Dance Clubs (Discos)

These clubs feature canned music—usually modern rock, hip-hop, and techno—and state-of-the-art sound systems, plus the usual flashing lights. Many are found in the vicinity of the Sixth Street entertainment district. Most are open Mon.-Sat. nights, some Thurs.-Sat. only.

Abratto's: (tel. 477-1641) 318 E. 5th.

Buffalo Club: (tel. 476-8828) 405 E. 7th.

Chances: (tel. 472-8273) 900 Red River.

Chaindrive: (tel. 480-9017) 504 Willow.

Escape Club: (tel. 444-8452) Congress and Riverside.

Infinity: (tel. 472-2711) 600 E. 6th.

Mirage: (tel. 474-7531) 222 E. 6th.

New West: (tel. 467-6134) 7934 Great Northern Blvd.

OHMS: (tel. 472-7136) 611 E. 7th.

Paradox: (tel. 469-7615) 311 E. 6th.

Phaces: (tel. 472-8008) 709 E. 6th.

Spirit's: (tel. 473-3707) 422 E. 6th.

Television Shows

Austin City Limits premiered in 1975 and has been broadcast by over 280 public TV stations since. Featured bands cover the American folk music spectrum: country, bluegrass, folk, zydeco, *conjunto,* and Western swing. The shows are taped at KLRU studios on the UT campus, weekday nights only. Tickets are free but must be picked up a day or two in advance at KLRU. To find out about upcoming performances, call the Austin City Limits Hotline at (512) 471-4811. Once you've got the ticket, be sure to arrive at the studios at least a half hour in advance, since seating is first-come, first-served, and a ticket doesn't guarantee a seat. Free beer served before the performance. *The Texas Connection* is taped weekly for the cable Nashville Network at the same studios; information on these shows is available by calling the same number.

Austin Community Television (ACTV) broadcasts several live music programs each week on cable channels 10, 11, and 13, including *Citizens Live* cable channel 10, Saturday at 8 p.m., featuring 90 minutes of local performances.

Radio

There are 29 AM and FM radio stations in the Austin area. Some of the more interesting include KASE-FM 101 (progressive country), KAZI-FM 88.7 (community radio emphasizing R&B, gospel, blues, and jazz), KELG-AM 1440 (Hispanic music, including local artists), KKLB-FM 92.5 (*tejano*), KFAN 107.9 ("Texas Rebel Radio," mostly Texas music), KLBJ-FM 94 (album-oriented rock, some local music), KGSR 107.1 FM (eclectic mix of folk, blues, alternative, R&B, and Austin artists), KMFA-FM 89.5 (100% classical), KTXZ-AM 1560 (bilingual programming, Tex-Mex), KUT-FM 90.5 (UT station, eclectic), and KVET-AM 1300 (traditional country, some local music).

Polka fans should tune in KTAE-AM 1260 (from nearby Taylor) to hear *Polka Time*, Mon.-Sat. 11 a.m.-noon, Sunday 1-2 p.m. Features traditional Bohemian polkas with one 15-minute break for classified ads. KTAE also spins country and Tex-Mex.

Comedy Clubs

Three long-running clubs support local and touring comedians.

Esther's Follies (tel. 512-320-0553) at 525 E. 6th is a 16-year musical comedy revue running Thurs.-Sat. featuring a series of evolving ensemble skits, sometimes involving the participation of a local or touring stand-up comic.

The Laff Stop (tel. 467-2333), 8120 Research Blvd., offers local and touring stand-up acts Tues.-Sunday.

The Velveeta Room (tel. 320-0553), 521 E. 6th, next door to Esther's Follies. Thursday is open-mike night, Friday and Saturday feature local and touring stand-up comedy.

EVENTS

January

Red-Eye Regatta: Over 50 first-class keel boat crews compete in this New Year's Day race on Lake Travis. Spectators gather at the Austin Yacht Club (tel. 512-266-1336).

March

Jerry Jeff Walker's Birthday Celebration: This three-day celebration of Austin's greatest musical spokesman features dances, rodeo events, footraces, and a Saturday night Jerry Jeff performance at the Paramount Theater.

South by Southwest Music and Media Conference (SXSW): Staged for the benefit of music writers and record company people, who converge on Austin in droves for this event, but the whole town profits from a week of free concerts and general craziness. Bands play their best, hoping they'll be picked up by a national label. Call (512) 467-7979 for details.

Spamarama: Annually for 15 years, this cooking festival has lifted the ignoble luncheon meat to new heights. Anyone for Spambalaya, Spamuccini Alfredo, or Moo Goo Gai Spam? Don't miss the musical Spam Jam. Usually held the last weekend of the month. For information contact Whole Hog Productions (tel. 280-7961).

March-April

Austin-Travis County Livestock Show and Rodeo: Ten days in late March or April devoted to livestock exhibits, auctions, live C&W music, a barbecue cookoff, and the rodeo. At the Texas Exposition and Heritage Center, 7311 Decker Lane (tel. 512-928-3710).

Highland Lakes Bluebonnet Trail: The "trail" is an auto route from Austin through Marble Falls, Burnet, Llano, and Kingsland, where hordes of Texas bluebonnets are in peak bloom this time of year. On weekends, each of these towns hosts small arts and crafts fairs and other events. Best place in the state for bluebonnet viewing.

Austin Downtown Conjunto Festival: This relatively new event celebrates Texas-Mexican border culture with two days of live *conjunto* music, centered at Mexic-Arte Gallery, 5th and Congress.

May

Cinco de Mayo: The 5th of May sees a celebration of Mexican culture commemorating the defeat of the French navy at Puebla, Mexico, on May 5, 1862. Activities include music, dance, arts and crafts exhibits, and a menudo cookoff. At Fiesta Gardens, 2101 Bergman.

Fiesta Laguna Gloria: An event held as a fundraiser for the Laguna Gloria Art Museum, usually the third weekend in May. Features a huge, very well-juried art show (one of the best in the country), food vendors, street performers, and an art auction. At the museum, 3809 W. 35th (tel. 458-8191).

Old Pecan Street Spring Arts & Crafts Festival: Sixth Street is blocked off from vehicle traffic while over 400 vendors purvey ceramics, weavings, paintings, sculpture, and other visual art media. With plenty of food and beverages. Call (512) 448-1797 for information.

June
Green Mesquite Rhythm & Blues Festival: First weekend in June at Green Mesquite Barbecue (tel. 512-479-0485). A strictly local festival featuring homegrown blues acts.

Clarksville/West End Jazz and Arts Festival: A cultural festival dedicated to the celebration of Austin's West End, a predominantly African-American neighborhood. Features local jazz, Brazilian, and African talent. On W. 6th St. and other West End venues. Call 477-9438 for scheduling information.

Hyde Park Historic Homes Tours: On Father's Day each year a number of turn-of-the-century Hyde Park homes open their doors to public viewing. Call 458-4319 for further information.

July
Freedom Festival: Around 50,000 people turn out for this annual Fourth of July celebration at Zilker Park. Live musical performances, food and beer vendors, and an impressive fireworks/laser presentation.

Bastille Day at the French Legation: The historic French Legation celebrates French independence day with food, wine, French pastries, fashion shows, French music, and dancing matches. At 8th and San Marcos (tel. 512-472-8180).

August
Austin Aquafest: A series of events held over the last weekend in July and the first two weekends in August to distract residents from the heat. Events include a waterskiing exhibition, music and dance festivals, a softball classic, fishing tournaments, and a nighttime water parade at Town Lake's Auditorium Shores.

September
Diez y Seis: Hispanics and Mexico enthusiasts celebrate Mexican independence for six days beginning September 16. Activities include folk dancing, *tejano* and *conjunto* music, mariachi bands, a Fiesta Patrias Queen pageant, and plenty of Mexican food. Call (512) 482-0175 for details.

October
Halloween on Sixth Street: As many as 60,000 costumed revelers roil about during this seven-block street party—Austin's answer to Mardi Gras.

November
Día de los Muertos: The Mexican Day of the Dead is celebrated on the first two days of November with a downtown parade of skeletons and various Latino art exhibits.

December
Several public events throughout the city celebrate Christmas, foremost among them the **Zilker Park Tree Lighting, Christmas at the French Legation,** and the **West End Christmas Walk.** Contact the Austin Convention and Bureau Center for scheduling information.

RECREATION

Ballooning
Somehow hot-air ballooning has taken hold in Austin. Most trips include aerial views of the city, Hill Country, and/or the Highland Lakes followed by post-flight refreshments (dawn flights are the most popular). Rates start at around $150 for an hour's flight. **Austin Aeronauts** (tel. 512-440-1492) and **Balloonport of Austin** (tel. 835-6058) offer federally licensed pilots and federally inspected equipment.

Rockclimbing
Limestone cliffs and rock formations in the Hill Country west of Austin offer virtually endless rockclimbing opportunities—the sport has a large Austin following.

In the city you can both learn and practice at **Pseudo Rock** (tel. 512-474-4376), 2nd St. and San Jacinto. Pseudo Rock provides an indoor 5,000-square-foot climbing wall with everything from novice to expert surfaces. You can climb all day for an $8 admission fee, plus $5 for rental gear if you don't bring your own. Beginners are welcome and the staff offers free instruction as needed. Long-term discount passes available for frequent climbers.

Those seeking to purchase or repair rock-climbing gear will find support at **REI** (tel. 474-2393), 1112 N. Lamar, and the **Whole Earth Provision Co.** (tel. 444-9974), 4006 S. Lamar Boulevard.

Cycling

Austin maintains 30 miles of interconnected, paved hike-and-bike trails throughout the city, plus the 7.5-mile unpaved **Barton Creek Greenbelt** along Barton Creek.

The Veloway (tel. 512-480-3032 or 480-9821) at 4103 Slaughter Lane winds 3.1 miles through meadows and woods at Slaughter Creek Metropolitan Park. The 23-foot-wide asphalt track is open daily dawn to dusk and is open to bicycles only.

Several local cycling clubs, including the **Austin Cycling Association** (tel. 837-3666) and **Austin Ridge Riders** (tel. 454-3949), sponsor group rides on weekends.

The **Bicycle Sport Shop** (tel. 477-3472) at 1426 Toomey offers cycling equipment, repairs, and rentals.

Bat Watching

Bat Conservation International claims Austin is home to the largest urban bat population in the world. Between April and October bat lovers gather on the Congress Ave. bridge over the Colorado River (Town Lake) at sunset to watch up to 750,000 Mexican free-tail bats emerge in search of an evening meal. It's estimated the bats eat as many as 30,000 pounds of bugs a night. In October or November the bats head to Mexico for the winter.

On the north bank of the river, just east of the bridge, stands a special bat-watching kiosk built by Bat Conservation International, which is headquartered in Austin. Another observation kiosk, donated by the *Austin American-Statesman*, sits on the opposite bank. If you'd rather watch the evening bat flight from more elegant surroundings, try The Cafe or the Shoreline Grill in the Four Seasons Hotel, where waiters announce

bat flights as they pass the hotel. The exact flight times vary with the seasons and weather conditions, from an hour before sunset to an hour after—usually earlier during hot, dry weather and later during cool, rainy weather.

For more information on bat watching in Austin and surrounding areas, contact BCI (tel. 512-327-9721), P.O. Box 162603, Austin, TX 78716.

UT Outdoor Program

UT Recreational Sports (tel. 512-471-1093), Gregory Gym, UT campus, has an excellent Sept.-May roster of guided outdoor trips throughout the state that are open to the public. Prices are low, even lower for UT students. Programs vary in length from a day ("Rafting the Guadalupe") to 10 days ("Canoeing the Rio Grande"). Other programs include "Snorkel the San Marcos," "Backpack Big Bend," "Hike Seminole Canyon State Park," "Rockclimb Clinic at Lake Travis," and "Kayak the Salt River."

Parks

Town Lake Park is a series of small parks along a section of the Colorado River between Tom Miller Dam to the west and Longhorn Dam to the east. An 8.5-mile walking-jogging-biking trail runs through the parks and there are several picnic areas. Fishing and boating (no motors) are allowed, but swimming is prohibited. These parks lie along the south edge of town; when Austin residents refer to "the river," they mean Town Lake (which is, of course, an impounded section of the Colorado River).

Zilker Park is the site of Barton Springs, a 1,000- by 125-foot natural swimming pool extremely popular during the hot summer months. The clean, limestone-filtered water stays a constant 68° F; lap-swimmers hit the springs every morning before 9 a.m., when lifeguards come on duty and admission is charged (mid-March through October only). The park's Zilker Botanical Garden encompasses the Taniguchi Oriental Garden, Xeriscape Garden, Mabel Rose Garden, Blachly Butterfly Trail, an herb and fragrance garden, and a cactus and succulent garden. Other facilities scattered throughout the 400-acre park include ballfields, picnic areas, playgrounds, and boat ramps along Town Lake. Off Barton Springs Rd. to the southwest of the city center.

Emma Long Metro Park, the town's oldest park, is usually called City Park. The park runs along three miles of Lake Austin shoreline with cliffs, beaches, and boat ramps. Boats and canoes can be rented on-site.

McKinney Falls State Park

The park is named for Thomas F. McKinney, one of Stephen Austin's original colonists, who settled next to Onion Creek in the 1850s and bred racehorses. You can see the ruins of his stables and homestead in the park. The creek is the park's centerpiece, winding 1.7 miles with scenic pools and two waterfalls. Flora along the creek include bald cypress, Texas oak, pecan, elm, sycamore, and other water-loving trees, while the uplands of the 640-acre park are characterized by mesquite, cedar, live oak, cacti, and various grasses. The Smith Rockshelter Trail is an interpretive trail with labeled flora. Fauna you spot in the park include white-tailed deer, raccoons, armadillos, wild turkey, and various songbirds.

The park contains several picnic sites, playgrounds, and a paved hike/bike trail, as well as 84 campsites. Under construction are a new mountain bike trail under the auspices of REI and an artificial sport-climbing wall. You can reach the park via US 183 south to FM 812 west, seven miles southeast of the city center. For more information, contact the Superintendent (tel. 512-243-1643), McKinney Falls State Park, 7102 Scenic Loop Rd., Austin, TX 78744.

Horse Racing

Pari-mutuel betting has become a reality in Texas. **Manor Downs** (US 290 and Manor, tel. 272-5581) hosts races monthly except in December.

SHOPPING

Austin isn't a big shopping mecca, offering just the usual assortment of shopping malls and unimpressive antique/junk stores. Several places are worth mentioning, however.

Markets

Austin Country Fleaworld at 9500 US 290 E spreads across 130 acres; 360 covered stalls offer everything from antiques to fresh produce.

The **People's Renaissance Market** at W. 23rd and Guadalupe is a throwback to the '60s when arts and crafts street vendors set up along the Drag. Today they're confined to one block, but the merchandise is still occasionally innovative.

At the **Travis County Farmers Market** (tel. 512-451-3802), 6701 Burnet Rd., you'll find trucked-in produce at great prices (open April-October, Saturday only). On the last weekend in August, the Farmers Market hosts North America's largest salsa competition, with entries in restaurant, commercial, and homemade categories. Admission is free, as are the endless samples.

Unique

One-of-a-kind shops in town include the **Eclectic Ethnographic Gallery** (tel. 512-477-1863) at W. 12th and Lamar, which offers a collection of ethnic arts, crafts, jewelry, and clothing from all over the Third World.

Electric Ladyland (tel. 444-2002) at 1306 S. Congress carries vintage American clothing (men's and women's) as well as Halloween costumes. Bob Dylan has made purchases here. Another vintage clothing shop, **Blue Velvet** (tel. 474-5147), at 500 W. 17th St., purveys self-sloganed "Cheap clothes for sleazy people." **Zoom** (tel. 472-3316) at 512 W. 12th has it all: T-shirts, used clothing, jewelry, jeans, tattoos, and body piercings.

Out of Africa focuses on African crafts, with locations at 2901 S. Capital of Texas Hwy. (tel. 480-8149) and 606 Blanco (tel. 480-8149). **Tesoros Trading Co.,** 2095 Congress Ave. (next door to Las Manitas Restaurant) sells Latin American folk art.

If you're looking for a vintage guitar or want to sell one, check out **Workhorse Guitars** (tel. 458-6505) at 5531 Burnet. In addition to buying and selling used axes, Workhorse also sells, rents, and repairs amps, accessories, and sound systems.

TravelFest (tel. 418-1515) at 9503 Research Blvd. carries a complete collection of travel guidebooks and supplies. Open daily 9 a.m.-11 p.m., the shop also offers currency exchange, plane tickets, and language classes.

Boots

Cadillac Jack Boot Co. (tel. 512-452-4428) at 6623 N. Lamar sells reconditioned cowboy boots from before the decline of handmade boots (pre-1970s), plus other vintage Western wear. Used boots start at around $40 a pair in the bargain bin, more for collector quality. Owner Jimmy James keeps a row of colorful boots behind the counter that are part of his private collection—they're not for sale, but you can look for free.

If you've come to Austin looking for bootmaker Charlie Dunn of Jerry Jeff Walker song fame, you're too late—he passed away in 1993 after a lifetime of fashioning boots of the highest quality. Lee Miller of **Texas Traditions** (tel. 443-4447), 2222 College, has taken over for Charlie and is now considered one of the best bootmakers in the state. **Capitol Saddlery** (tel. 478-9309), 1614 Lavaca, is where Dunn began, and the place still makes custom boots as well as other leather cowboy gear. Noel Escobar, Jr. of **Texas Custom Boots** also comes highly recommended. Escobar's shop (tel. 327-7969) is in nearby Oak Hill on the southwest edge of Austin at 3654 Bee Cave Road. At any of these custom shops, a pair of boots runs a minimum of $500-600.

Hats
Although it's in Buda, around 15 miles south of the city via I-35, **Texas Hatters** (more commonly known as "Manny's") probably sells more hats to Austin residents than anyone else in the state. With the motto "big or small, we top them all," owner Manny Gammage blocks every hat by hand. He's fashioned hats for a long list of U.S. presidents, movie stars, and musical celebrities. Hatting materials include Panama straw, beaver, and exotics; each hat is customsized. Prices run $150-250.

For a catalog containing representative styles, call or write Texas Hatters (tel. 512-295-4287; 441-4287 in Austin), P.O. Box 100, Buda, TX 78610. Manny's workshop is found at 5003 Overpass, just off the highway in Buda (exit 220, east side of the highway), about halfway between San Marcos and Austin.

INFORMATION

Tourist Offices
The **Austin Convention and Visitors Bureau** (tel. 512-474-5171 or 800-926-2282) maintains

a very helpful information center at 201 E. 2nd Street, open Mon.-Fri. 8:30 a.m.-5 p.m. The **State Department of Highways** maintains a visitor center in the State Capitol at 11th and Congress. The staff distributes travel information on Austin as well as the rest of Texas; open daily 8 a.m.-5 p.m.

Yet another source of tourist information is the hospitality desk at the **Old Bakery and Emporium** (tel. 477-5961) at 1006 Congress. The usual selection of maps and brochures as well as specific information for senior citizen services and activities; open Mon.-Fri. 9 a.m.-4 p.m. For info on the University of Texas, visit the **University of Texas Visitors Center** (tel. 471-1420) at UT's Little Campus (Martin Luther King and I-35); open Mon.-Fri. 8 a.m.-4:30 p.m.

Publications
The weekly *Austin Chronicle,* published every Friday, is distributed free throughout the city and contains up-to-date information on Austin recreation, dining, music, and local politics. For local business news and occasional general-interest features, check the chamber of commerce's monthly *Austin,* which maintains an up-to-date calendar of events and list of restaurants. Austin's one daily paper is the *Austin American-Statesman.*

The free tourist magazine *Experience Austin,* issued monthly, contains lots of good ideas of things to do in the Austin area, plus extensive listings of hotels, restaurants, entertainment venues, and recreational facilities.

Maps
At least five maps of Austin are available. The Austin CVB's giveaway map is sketchy but useful for general orientation. The Old San Francisco Steak House's cute and colorful map, also distributed by the CVB, helps pinpoint landmark attractions in and around town, but its distorted scale undermines its usefulness as a streetfinder. Rand McNally's map lacks color contrast and is hard to read, while the Continental Map is too densely saturated with color, and also hard to read. Try instead the accurate and easy to read AAA map. AAA's Austin office (tel. 512-444-4757) is at 321 W. Ben White Blvd., Suite 205; open Mon.-Fri. 8:30 a.m.-5 p.m., Saturday 9 a.m.-1 p.m.

AUSTIN TELEPHONE INFORMATION

Emergency (police, fire, medical): 911
National Weather Service: 476-1700
Area Code: 512
Telephone Directory Assistance: 411
Crisis Intervention Hotline: 472-4357
University of Texas Information: 471-3434

Telephone
The area code for Austin and the surrounding area is 512; 915 for Kingsland.

GETTING THERE AND AROUND

Robert Mueller Municipal Airport
Austin's small airport is only three miles from the city center. Around 20 airlines provide daily service to Mueller Municipal, mostly from other cities in Texas. Taxis between the airport and downtown charge around $8 a trip. Capitol Metro bus no. 20 goes to the airport from downtown Austin for 50 cents.

Hill Country Flyer
Southern Pacific steam engine No. 786 pulls five 72-passenger coaches and two first-class parlor cars through stunning Hill Country scenery every weekend from March through December. The track, originally laid in the 1880s for hauling granite blocks to build the State Capitol, threads Short Creek Canyon and the San Gabriel and Colorado river valleys.

The train runs every Sat.-Sun. at 10 a.m. from Cedar Park (15 miles north of Austin on US 183 and FM 1431) to Burnet and back, a 66-mile, five-hour roundtrip excursion that returns at 5:30 p.m. This leaves three hours for dining, shopping, and wandering around Burnet. Fares are $24 per adult or $10 for children 13 and under in ordinary class, $38 in first class. No age discounts. First-class fares include air-conditioned coaches and complimentary snacks and beverages; snacks are available for purchase in ordinary class.

An evening, first-class-only version of the train, the *Twilight Flyer,* rolls out of Cedar Park at 7 p.m., returning at 8:45 p.m. with no layover in Burnet. Tickets cost $26 per individual or $50 per couple, including snacks and beverages. For more information, contact the Austin Steam Train Association (tel. 512-477-8468 or 477-6377), P.O. Box 1632, Austin, TX 78767.

City Buses
Austin is blessed with one of the better city bus systems in the state, Capital Metro. There are over 50 neighborhood routes, 11 express and feeder routes, and three special downtown routes nicknamed 'Dillos (Armadillo Express).

The Congress/Capitol 'Dillo (Blue Line 'Dillo) runs from the Park & Ride lot at the City Coliseum and Palmer Auditorium (south of Town Lake) and Barton Springs Rd., via Congress Ave., 11th St., Lavaca St., 12th St., and Guadalupe; the bus operates 6:30 a.m.-7 p.m. weekdays. The ACC/Lavaca 'Dillo (Green Line 'Dillo) also starts at the Park & Ride lot and runs north-south along Guadalupe and Lavaca all the way to 21st St. via 15th St. and Speedway, returning via Guadalupe and Rio Grande; hours of operation are 6:45 a.m.-10:15 p.m. weekdays. Parking at the Park & Ride lot and at the State Parking Garages along San Jacinto and Trinity is free. The Convention Center/UT 'Dillo (Red Line 'Dillo) starts from the same spot and follows a more complicated route along Cesar Chavez (1st), Trinity, Brazos, 11th, 15th, and Congress, returning via the same streets, except San Jacinto is substituted for Brazos and 2nd St. for Cesar Chavez. It runs 6:30 a.m.-7 p.m. weekdays, 11 a.m.-7 p.m. Saturdays.

Even if you're driving an auto, riding the Capital Metro can save *mucho dinero* on parking fees during the day. Capital Metro fares are 50 cents for adults, 25 cents for students with ID, and free for seniors. 'Dillo rides are free—that's right, no charge. Express buses cost $1 adults, 50 cents students. A $10 monthly Metro Pass ($5 for students) entitles the bearer to unlimited ridership on all Metro routes. Passengers ages 65 or older and those with mobility impairments can pick up a special $3 pass that entitles them to free ridership throughout the Capital Metro system; these are available at Passport Express, 1107 Rio Grande, or at the Capital Metro office. The latter, located at 2910 E. 5th St., offers Metro schedules and route maps, or you can call Capital Metro at (512) 474-1200 for information.

Taxis
Two established cab companies offer 24-hour taxi service: **American Cab** (tel. 512-452-9999) and **Yellow Cab** (tel. 472-1111).

Tours
Gray Line (tel. 512-345-6789) offers a four-hour city tour for $16 ($8 ages 5-11) that visits the State Capitol, LBJ Library, Governor's Mansion, UT, Barton Springs, Town Lake, E. 6th St., the O. Henry Museum, and historic buildings.

VICINITY OF AUSTIN

HIGHLAND LAKES

After a series of catastrophic floods, Austin persuaded the state to dam the Colorado River in several places northwest of the city. This Colorado, incidentally, is not the river in Colorado; this one starts and ends in Texas. The impoundment system is today administered by the Lower Colorado River Authority (LCRA). Ecologists lament the fact it destroyed the ecosystem of the surrounding flood plain, but most Austin residents love the fact they can now enjoy a weekend playground of seven artificial lakes. From north to south, the lakes are Buchanan, Inks, LBJ, Marble Falls, Travis, Austin, and Town. Of these seven, only Buchanan, LBJ, and Travis are of any significant size; Lake Austin and Town Lake are within or adjacent to the city.

The LCRA, in conjunction with Travis County, operates a number of free or very inexpensive

lakeshore campgrounds in the lake country; see the "Highland Lakes Camping" chart for details.

The "capital" of the Highland Lakes area is **Burnet** (pronounced BURN-it), 62 miles northwest of Austin. Although the Highland Lakes Tourist Association mailing address is in Austin (P.O. Box 1967, Austin, TX 78767), you can receive the same information from the Burnet Chamber of Commerce (tel. 512-756-4297), 705 Buchanan Dr., about a mile west of US 281. One of the best times to visit the lake country is in April, when the bluebonnets are in bloom. Burnet holds a **Bluebonnet Festival** the second weekend in April in the town square, featuring a parade, arts and crafts fair, footraces, and a street dance.

Lake Travis
Travis, the second-largest Highland Lake, has an average surface area of 18,900 acres. It's impounded by Mansfield Dam, built in 1941.

skimming over Lake Travis

Because it's large and relatively close to Austin, Travis is heavily used by boaters, anglers, water-skiiers, and scuba divers. Besides an assortment of private facilities, there are six public parks on the shores with camping, plus one day-use park.

Recreation: McGregor/Hippie Hollow Park (off RM 620 east of Mansfield Dam) is a longtime Austin favorite for swimming and hiking; restrooms are the only facilities. **Windy Point County Park,** 1.5 miles past Hippie Hollow off RM 620, receives a steady year round breeze and is popular for windsurfing, swimming, diving, and picnicking.

Sailing lessons and bareboat and captained charters are available at **Texas Sailing Academy and Commander's Point Yacht Basin** (tel. 512-266-2333), 4600 Commander's Point Dr., just off RM 620 near Mansfield Dam. **Emerald Point Marina** boasts a state of the art, 500-slip marina with heated fishing pier, boat rentals and sales, and a beach. You can also arrange boat rentals at Lake Travis Marina, Dodd Street Marina, Paradise Cove Marina, Eagle Ridge Marina, Yacht Harbor Marina, Skip's Boat Rentals, and several other docking areas around the lake. The Austin Yacht Club hosts two sailing regattas per year in fall and spring.

HIGHLAND LAKES CAMPING

Campgrounds listed with phone numbers 473-4083 or 473-9437 (area code 512) are Lower Colorado River/Travis County facilities; stays are limited to 14 days in a 30-day period. Travis County sells a $50 yearly pass that entitles the holder to free park entry and 50% off camping rates.

CAMPGROUND/RV PARK; PHONE; LOCATION; DAILY RATES; FACILITIES

LAKE TRAVIS (AREA CODE 512)

Arkansas Bend; tel. 320-7435; near Lago Vista off Lohman's Ford; $10; tentsites, boat ramp

At the Park; tel. 264-1395; FM 2322 near Pace Bend Park; $6-10; w/e, full hookups, senior discount

Cypress Creek; tel. 473-4083; FM 2769 and Old Anderson Mill; $10; tentsites, boat ramp

Hudson Bend Camper Resort; tel. 266-1562; Hudson Bend near Mansfield Dam; $12-15; full hookups

Krause Springs; tel. 210-693-4181; northwest shore near Spicewood, off FM 71; $8-12

Mansfield Dam Park; tel. 473-4083; FM 620 at Mansfield Dam; $10; tentsites

Pace Bend Park; tel. 473-4083; FM 2322, 4.6 miles east of US 71; $10; tentsites, full hookups, boat ramp

Sandy Creek Park; tel. 473-4083; Lime Creek near FM 1431; $5; primitive

Windy Point/Bob Wentz Park; tel. 473-4083; near Mansfield Dam; $10; tentsites, boat ramp

LAKE MARBLE FALLS (AREA CODE 210)

Kampers Korner; tel. 693-2291; S. Marble Falls; $14; full hookups

River View RV Park; tel. 693-3910; S. Marble Falls; $16.75; full hookups

LAKE LBJ (AREA CODE 915)

Kingsland Lodge; tel. 388-4830; Kingsland; $15 campsites, $50-60 cabins; full hookups, boat slips

LA-Z-L RV Park; tel. 388-3473; Kingsland; $15; full hookups, boat ramp, fish dock

Longhorn Resort; tel. 388-4343; Kingsland; $8-12 RV, $42-70 cabins; full hookups, cabins, marina

Plainsmen Lodge; tel. 388-4344; Kingsland; $15 campsites, $60 d cabins, plus $5 each additional person; full hookups, boat dock

Rio Vista Resort; tel. 388-6331; Kingsland; $8, $12; tentsites, full hookups, boat/fishing docks, laundry, boat slips

INKS LAKE (AREA CODE 512)

Inks Lake State Park; tel. 793-2223; Park Rd. 4 off US 29; $6, $9, $12; boat ramp, tentsites, w/screen shelter

Rock-A-Way Park; $15; tel. 793-2314; tentsites, boat ramp, fishing dock

Shady Oaks; tel. 793-2718; near Inks Dam; $8 tent, $15 RV; tentsites

LAKE BUCHANAN (AREA CODE 512)

Black Rock Park; tel. 473-4083; FM 261, 4 miles north of US 20; $3; primitive, boat ramp

Cedar Lodge; tel. 793-2820; US 261; $10-13 RV, $50-90 cabins; w/e, full hookups, cottages

Colorado Bend State Park; RR 501, Bend; $5; primitive

Crystal Cove Resort; tel. 793-6861; US 261; $11, $47; full hookups, cabins

Poppy's Point; tel. 793-2819; US 261; $12; full hookups, boat ramp

Shaw Island; tel. 473-4083; 4.2 miles off US 261; $3; primitive

Silver Creek RV Park; tel. 756-2381; RR 2341; $12; full hookups

Hurst Harbor (tel. 512-266-1069 or 800-342-3242), off RM 620 north of Bee Cave, rents 50-foot and 54-foot furnished houseboats for $895-995 per weekend or four days during the week, $1295-1495 per week. Each houseboat sleeps up to 10 persons and comes with air-conditioning and heating, full kitchen with utensils, barbecue grill, one bathroom, TV with VCR, stereo system, swim platform, and boating supplies.

Divers explore the lake's several sunken boat wrecks and a barred section of Mansfield Dam. **Scuba International** (tel. 219-9484), 6808 RM 620 N, and **Pisces Scuba** (tel. 258-6646), 11401 RM 2222, offer diving equipment rental, certification courses, and boat dives.

Lake LBJ

This is a medium-sized lake of 6,375 surface acres formed by the Alvin Wirtz Dam. The fishing is good here because of the many caves and coves among the limestone cliffs. It's also popular among waterskiing enthusiasts because it's protected from high winds. There are several resorts and private campgrounds around LBJ, but no free public campgrounds.

Lake Buchanan

Buchanan Dam, built in 1937, created this 23,060-acre body of water, the largest in the Highland Lakes system. A number of public and private facilities along its shores support fishing, boating, swimming, and other water recreation.

One of the highlights of Lake Buchanan is the **Vanishing Texas River Cruise,** which takes visitors in search of bald eagles. The American bald eagle is extremely rare these days, but a population of 18-30 (including both varieties, the northern and the southern) spends winters at the lake. The cruises run daily between mid-November and late March at 11 a.m.; peak eagle-watching times are January and February. During the 2.5-hour trip, other birds—great blue herons, egrets, terns, cormorants, pelicans—are commonly sighted. Rugged cliffs surround the lake, and the cruise passes 50-foot Fall Creek Falls. The boat leaves from the northeast shore off FM 2341, and has a heated cabin and food galley serving coffee and hot chocolate. Rates are $15 adults; $13 seniors, students, and military; $10 children 6-

12. Contact Vanishing Texas River Cruise for reservations (required) (tel. 512-756-6986), P.O. Box 901, Burnet, TX 78611.

Fall Creek Vineyards (tel. 915-379-5361) can be found off FM 2241 near the northwestern shore of Lake Buchanan. Many wine critics agree Fall Creek makes some of the state's finest wines. The winery's 65 acres of vinifera produce award-winning sauvignon blanc, emerald reisling, chardonnay, cabernet sauvignon, carnelian, and zinfandel. Open for tastings and sales Monday, Wednesday, and Friday 11 a.m.-2 p.m. or for tours and tastings each Saturday noon-5 p.m. For reservations contact the Fall Creek Vineyards office at 1111 Guadalupe St. (tel. 512-476-4477) in Austin.

The lake is surrounded by a variety of private and public campgrounds and lodges. The quickest way to the lake from Austin is via I-35 N to Georgetown, then west on State 29, about 75 miles total. A more scenic route is US 290 west to State 71, then west to US 281, north to State 29 at Burnet.

Longhorn Cavern State Park

This is the only cave in Texas administered by the park system, although a local concession handles day-to-day operations. A long limestone cave formed by ancient underground streams, Longhorn was used by early Indian tribes as temporary shelter, as evidenced by bones and arrow tips found on the cavern floor. During the Civil War, Confederate troops manufactured gunpowder here. In the early 1900s, Burnet and Llano County residents used the cave as a social center for dancing and dining during the hot summer months; the interior temperature is a constant 64° F. Various chambers in the cave are named for their shapes or the predominant formations contained therein: Frozen Waterfall, Crystal City, Hall of Gems, Queen's Throne, Viking's Prow.

Facilities in the 634-acre park include picnic areas, a snack bar, hiking and nature trails, and a gift shop. Cavern tours last about an hour and a half for a 1.25-mile roundtrip walk. During the summer (Memorial Day through Labor Day) two-hour tours are scheduled hourly 10 a.m.-6 p.m., seven days a week; Labor Day through February tours leave at 10:30 a.m., 1 p.m., and 3 p.m. Mon.-Fri., and hourly 10 a.m.-5 p.m. on weekends. From March to May tours leave hourly 10 a.m.-4 p.m. Mon.-Fri., 10 a.m.-5 p.m. Sat.-Sunday. The cave is off US 281 between Burnet and Marble Falls, 12 miles southwest of Burnet not far from Lake LBJ. Admission costs $6.50 adults, $4 children 5-12, TCP holders free. For further information contact Longhorn Cavern State Park (tel. 512-756-6976), Route 2, Box 23, Burnet, TX 78611.

WASHINGTON COUNTY

Because it's roughly halfway between Austin and Houston along US 290, the town of Brenham and surrounding Washington County have long been popular stops for road travelers. The county terrain of rolling hills and oaks is particularly scenic during the spring wildflower bloom.

Brenham

Founded by German settlers in the 1860s, Brenham (pop. 12,400) serves as the county seat and boasts a number of historic buildings. Probably the single most famous tourist attraction is the **Blue Bell Creameries** (tel. 800-327-8135), two miles southeast of town center on Horton Street (FM 577). Blue Bell ice cream, often cited as "America's best"—*Time* magazine went so far as to call Blue Bell the "the best ice cream in the world"—has been made here since 1907. The creamery offers tours Mon.-Fri. at 10 a.m. and 1 p.m.; the Blue Bell Country Store sells ice cream and souvenirs Mon.-Fri. 8 a.m.-5 p.m., Saturday 9 a.m.-3 p.m.

Nine miles northeast of town via State 105, the Franciscan nuns of the **Monastery of St. Clare** (tel. 409-836-6011) raise miniature horses. Visitors are welcome to tour the barns and corrals daily 2-4 p.m. A gift shop on the premises sells ceramics and other crafts made by the nuns.

Accommodations and Camping: The **Hilltop Motor Inn** (tel. 836-7915), 2413 S. Day, and **Roadrunner Motor Inn** (tel. 830-0030), US 290 W, offer rooms in the $30-45 range. Both motels have pools. **The Brenham Inn** (tel. 836-1300 or 800-256-0167), 2217 S. Market, and **Preference Inn** (tel. 830-1110), 201 US 290 Loop East, cater to business travelers with slightly nicer rooms in the $45-60 range. Several historic homes in and around Brenham have been converted to bed and breakfast inns; these can be booked through the **Bed and Breakfast Registry** (tel. 836-3695).

RV sites at **Artesian Park RV Campground** (tel. 836-0680), seven miles west of town on US 290, cost $15 a night. Primitive campsites ($10) and back-in camper sites with w/e ($12) are available at **Somerville Lake**, about 13 miles north of town off State 36, at the U.S. Army Corps of Engineers-administered Big Creek Park, Overlook Park, Rocky Creek Park, and Yegua Creek Park (same number for all parks: tel. 596-1622).

Food: Brenham's **Fluff Top Roll** (tel. 836-9441) at 210 E. Alamo specializes in homestyle soups, stews, chili, hearty breakfasts, and "fluff-top rolls." It's open Mon.-Sat. 5:45 a.m.-2 p.m., Sunday 7 a.m.-2 p.m. **Patio's Bistro & Biergarten** (tel. 830-8536), on historic Ant St., features sandwiches on fresh baked breads, salads, soups, and a large selection of beers; in addition to horseshoes and darts, the restaurant hosts live music on weekends. Open daily for lunch and dinner.

Farther east along US 290 in the town of Chappell Hill, **Bevers Kitchen** (tel. 836-4178) on Main St. serves downhome food in a converted historic home. It's open Mon.-Thurs. for lunch only, Fri.-Sat. for lunch and dinner.

Radio: Washington County residents, many of whom are descendants of German, Czech, Polish, and Wend settlers, listen to country and polka broadcasts on KWHI-AM 1280 from Brenham and KLVG-AM 1570 from La Grange.

Washington

Originally known as Washington-on-the-Brazos, this small town of 265 inhabitants calls itself "the birthplace of Texas," since the Texas declaration of independence from Mexico was signed here in 1836. Washington-on-the-Brazos served as the capital of the Republic of Texas from 1842 to 1846.

The **Star of the Republic Museum** (tel. 409-878-2461) stands on the site where the declaration was signed. Various exhibits—some of them audiovisual—chronicle the town's four-year term as Texas capital. The museum is open March-Aug. daily 10 a.m.-5 p.m., the remainder of the year Wed.-Sun. 10 a.m.-5 p.m. Admission is free.

The 154-acre **Washington-on-the-Brazos State Historical Park** (tel. 409-878-2214), on FM 1155 off State 105 south of town, preserves a portion of the original town site as well as an outdoor amphitheater, a picnic area, and a reconstruction of Independence Hall, the building where the famous declaration was signed. The park is open daily 8 a.m. till dusk; Independence Hall is open 10 a.m.-5 p.m.

Accommodations and Camping: Dreams Comin' True (tel. 836-6999 or 800-836-6999), a ranch bed-and-breakfast on FM 390 N west of Washington off US 290, offers seven rooms for $50-65 including a big country breakfast. Rustic camping is possible at nearby Peaceable Kingdom School.

Peaceable Kingdom School: Founded in 1972, this educational farm near the junction of the Brazos and Navasota Rivers features the largest organic ornamental garden in Texas, plus 152 acres of mixed woodlands and meadows. Among the plants cultivated here are rare native and wild strains of cotton and corn lost to most of the world. A two-story barn on the grounds won architectural awards in Texas and Japan soon after its 1974 construction. The school offers periodic classes on organic gardening, herbs, cooking, and nature appreciation. Guided tours of the gardens, turkey and chicken pens, greenhouse, and "pig palace" cost $2 per person; fresh produce available for sale.

Facilities for picnicking and camping are available, along with three rental cabins for $25 (sleeps two), $40 (sleeps five), and $50 (sleeps six) per night. A camping shelter (there's only one) that sleeps four goes for $15, while tentsites cost $5 per person. The shelter and campsites share a solar shower, coldwater sink, and outhouse. Each Saturday 11 a.m.-2 p.m. the school offers "gourmet herbal home-cooked" lunches at the PKS Dining Porch.

On the Saturday before Labor Day, the school sponsors a well-attended Fall Food Festival. The Kingdom's quarterly newsletter on organic farming costs $15 a year, $10 for senior citizens and students. The entrance to Peaceable Kingdom is on Mt. Fall School Rd., off Pickens Rd., north of State 105 between Navasota and Brenham. Call or write Peaceable Kingdom

School (tel. 409-878-2353), P.O. Box 313, Washington, TX 77880, for further information.

GEORGETOWN

Originally a stop for cattle drovers along the Chisholm Trail, then a railhead for the shipping of local cotton, Georgetown languished for decades after cotton prices bottomed out during the Depression. A 1982-83 restoration of its quaint Victorian square turned the town of 15,000 into one of Austin's favorite weekend playgrounds. A growing number of people who work in Austin choose to commute from Georgetown, which is 26 miles north of the state capital via I-35.

The late 18th century buildings that line the square contain restaurants, art galleries, antique shops, and other tourist-oriented ventures. In addition to the town square, Georgetown boasts two residential districts on the National Historic Register. Stop by the **History and Visitors Information Center** at 101 W. 7th St. for pamphlets that outline suggested walking or driving tours through historic districts. For further information, contact the Georgetown Convention and Visitors Bureau (tel. 512-869-3545), P.O. Box 409, Georgetown, TX 78627.

Nearby **Lake Georgetown,** maintained by the U.S. Corps of Engineers, offers three shoreline recreational sites with boat ramps, picnic areas, and restroom/shower facilities: Cedar Breaks Park, Russell Park, and Jim Hogg Park.

Accommodations

The following hotels offer rooms in the $45-55 range: **Comfort Inn** (tel. 512-863-7504), 1005 Leander Rd.; **Georgetown Inn** (tel. 863-5572), I-35 N; and **Ramada Inn** (tel. 869-2541), 333 I-35 N. **Bed & Breakfast Texas Style** (tel. 214-298-8586) can arrange stays at local Victorian B&Bs for $40-80 including breakfast.

SAN MARCOS

San Marcos is on the far eastern edge of the Hill Country, 26 miles south of Austin via I-35. The town (pop. 36,000) takes its name from the

San Marcos River, named by 18th century Spanish explorers who "discovered" it on St. Mark's Day. The Spaniards attempted to missionize the area several times without success. It was finally settled by Anglo-Americans in the 1840s.

Long before Europeans laid eyes on the San Marcos River it was an important source of water for Indian tribes. The river's constant temperature (about 71° F) and crystal clarity sustain two globally rare fish species, as well as the world's only known stands of Texas wild rice (Zizania texana).

Evidence found in the bottom of Aquarena Springs, source of the San Marcos, shows that Indians inhabited the area 12,000 years ago. This may, in fact, be one of the oldest Indian sites in North America. The Texas Nature Conservancy has recently undertaken a San Marcos River project to try and protect the riparian system from further encroachment by city and county development.

Texas visitors flock to San Marcos for the huge selection of factory outlet shops on the outskirts of town.

Aquarena Springs

The headwaters of the San Marcos River form Spring Lake, site of this water-oriented nature park. Visitors can view aquatic plant varieties, schools of fish, bubbling spring sources, and underwater ballet while riding in a glass-bottom boat, or from the Submarine Theatre, which is lowered beneath the water for a 30-minute aquatic show that features Ralph the Swimming Pig (yes, the one and only) and his human cohorts. The Sky Spiral lifts a revolving dome 250 feet above the park for a panoramic view of San Marcos and the surrounding hills, while the Swiss Sky Ride crosses over the springs to the Hanging Gardens. Also on the grounds are the remains of a 1753 Spanish mission and a replica frontier village.

Aquarena Springs (tel. 512-396-8900 or 800-999-9767) is just off I-35 (exit 206) and is open Memorial Day to Labor Day daily 10 a.m.-8 p.m. and the remaining months till 5 p.m. Admission is $14.95 adults, $12.95 seniors, $11.95 children 4-15. Single attraction tickets are available for $5.95 ($4.95 children) each, or you can wander the grounds for just $3. Parking is free.

Wonder World

This large cave was formed by a prehistoric earthquake along the Balcones Escarpment, rather than by the erosive processes common in most limestone caves. The 45-minute cave tour exits the cave via an elevator ride to the top of a 146-foot observation tower; from the tower visitors can clearly see the Escarpment where the Edwards Plateau ends and the coastal plains begin. Other attractions include an anti-gravity house and a train ride through a wildlife park. You can purchase separate tickets for each attraction, or buy an all-inclusive ticket for $11.95 adults, $9.95 seniors and children 4-11. Open March 1- Oct. 31 8 a.m.-8 p.m., the rest of the year 9 a.m.-6 p.m. Call (512) 392-3760 for further information.

Accommodations and Camping

On weekends between April and October, when San Marcos becomes very popular among outlet shoppers, it's best to reserve a hotel or motel room in advance.

Motel 6 (tel. 512-396-8705) has single rooms for $24-30 at 1321 I-35 N (exit 206). Next least expensive is Executive House Hotel (tel. 353-7770) at the junction of I-35 and Loop 82, which charges as low as $30 per room on winter weekdays, up to $45-65 d on summer weekends. Another fairly economical possibility includes the Days Inn (tel. 353-5050) at 1005 I-35 N (exit 204B or 205), where standard rooms cost $45-55 s, $55-75 d mid-March to mid-October, $38-45 s, $40-58 d the remainder of the year.

At the Friendship Inn (tel. 396-6060) at 1507 I-35 N (exit 206), rooms go for $55 s, $65 d June-Sept., $5 less the rest of the year. The 1929-vintage Aquarena Springs Inn (tel. 396-8901), on the grounds of the Aquarena Springs amusement park, has rooms for $59 s or d with one bed, up to $99 with two beds, continental breakfast included.

The Holiday Inn is at the junction of I-35 and Loop 82; $52-62 s/d June-Sept., $47-57 s/d the rest of the year.

The Crystal River Inn (tel. 396-3739) is a bed and breakfast housed in a restored 1883 Greek Revival-style home in San Marcos's historic downtown (326 W. Hopkins). Rooms are $60-90 a night, including a full breakfast. Open to the public on weekends for brunch.

Near the main cluster of highway motels, **United Campground** (tel. 353-5959) at 1610 I-35 N (exit 206) offers 100 shaded sites with full hookups (30/50 amps) and a swimming pool for $15 a night. Good Sam discounts available. A couple of miles east of San Marcos off State 80 in Martindale, **Shady Grove** (tel. 357-6113), FM 1919 crossing, and **Pecan Retreat** (tel. 393-6171), on the San Marcos River, have family-oriented campsites with w/e for $10-12 a night. A bit further east along State 80 in nearby Fentress, **Leisure Camp and RV Park** (tel. 488-2563), County Road 125, has shaded sites with w/e for $12.

Food

San Marcos features all the usual fast-food joints along I-35, mostly clustered around exit 205. For a little atmosphere, try the **Katy Station Restaurant** (tel. 512-353-5888) at 400 Cheatham, off Allen Parkway. The building is a former "Katy" (Missouri, Kansas, & Texas) railroad depot, built in 1890. A variety of steak, chicken, and seafood dishes are served. Open Mon.-Sat. for lunch and dinner. **Pepper's at the Falls** (tel. 396-5255) is a popular family restaurant serving American food at 100 Sessom Dr. (I-35 exit 206) on the river. Open daily 11 a.m.-11 p.m. **Capers on the Lake** (tel. 392-5929), inside Aquarena Springs (no admission required), features a very reasonably priced menu of pastas, salads, seafood, and Mexican; open daily for lunch and dinner.

Reliable, inexpensive Mexican is dispensed 24 hours a day at the **Taco Cabana** at 135 Long. For Central Texas-style, slow-smoked, pit-cooked barbecue, try **Woody's Meat Market** (tel. 392-1199) at 2601 Hunter Rd., or **Fuschak's Pit Bar-B-Q** (tel. 353-2712) at 920 State 80.

Events

On the second Saturday in June, San Marcos is the starting point for the **Texas Water Safari**, a grueling marathon canoe race along 260 miles of the San Marcos and Guadalupe rivers to the Gulf of Mexico. Billed as "the world's toughest boat race," crews must paddle and portage non-stop through rough water, log jams, dams, and other hazards to arrive in Seadrift on the coast within a 100-hour time limit. For information on the race, call (512) 357-6113.

The **Republic of Texas Chilympiad** is the world's largest CASI-sanctioned chili cookoff. It usually convenes for three days beginning the third weekend in September and attracts as many as 500 teams from around the world. Spectators are invited to taste, though it always pays to ask what's in the pot first; rattlesnake and armadillo aren't unknown. Other activities include music performances, nightly dances, and an arts and crafts show. Held at the Hays County Civic Center (I-35 exit 201).

Canoeing and Tubing the San Marcos

The clear San Marcos River, fringed by cypress and elephant ears, draws canoeists and kayakers from San Marcos, Austin, and San Antonio. Equipment can be rented from **Spencer Canoes** (tel. 512-357-6113) at 360 S. LBJ Dr. and **T.G. Canoes** (tel. 353-3846) on State 80.

The local **Lions Club** (tel. 392-8255) rents large inner tubes for floating the river between May and September. Rates are a reasonable $3 a day (plus $10 deposit). From the City Park on Bugg Lane, tubers can float all the way to Rio Vista Park where a Lions Club vehicle will shuttle them back to the start for $1.25 per person.

Skydiving

Sky Dive San Marcos (tel. 512-488-2214) takes first-timers on tandem jumps that include a 30-second freefall and five-minute parachute drop into a private 128-acre air park for $135. Experienced USPA jumpers can hitch a ride to 9,500 feet for $12, or exit from as high as 12,500 feet for $17. A bunkhouse that sleeps up to six is available free of charge. The air park is located 13 miles east of town on State 80. Skydiving has become tremendously popular in the area over the last few years.

Shopping

The largest factory outlet complex in the state, **San Marcos Factory Shops** on I-35 contains around 70 outlet stores—including upscale names like Brooks Brothers and Donna Karan—selling clothing, accessories, and housewares in a sprawling, modern mall. Discounts average around 25-30%, but occasionally drop as much as 75%. Nearby on I-35 (exit 200), **Tanger Factory Outlet Center** offers another 30 outlet stores, including a **Sarah Lee Bakery Outlet**.

WIMBERLEY

During the latter half of the 19th century, Cypress Creek provided the power for a succession of mill owners who supplied nearby Austin and San Marcos with flour, molasses, shingles, and sawn lumber. The last of the mills closed down in 1925, and the town almost faded away before Austin urbanites began using it as a weekend getaway. Historic structures include the **Wimberley Mill, John Henry Saunders Homestead, Wimberley Cemetery,** and **Pyland Blacksmith Shop.** But the real draw for most visitors are the town's antique shops, bed and breakfasts, and restaurants. Many Austinites have weekend homes in the area.

Wimberley is 15 miles west of San Marcos via RR 12, 40 miles southwest of Austin via I-35 and RR 12. Traffic along the two-lane RR 12 through town can become a little intense on weekends.

Accommodations and Food

Wimberley Lodging (tel. 800-460-3909) arranges bed and breakfast and guesthouse stays; most are modest limestone or wood cottages in the $50-80 range while a few of the larger, historic units go for $100 and over. At **The Blue Hole** (tel. 512-847-9127), tent and RV sites with w/e are available for $9-12.

Casa Blanca Cafe (tel. 847-1320) serves 20 kinds of breakfast tacos Tues.-Sat. 8 -11 a.m., plus standard enchiladas, tacos, and chiles rellenos for lunch and dinner.

HILL COUNTRY

Practically every person living in South Central Texas suggests different borders for the Hill Country. The Texas Hill Country Association, an organization of businesses in 23 South Central Texas counties, would have you believe that towns as distant as Uvalde, San Antonio, San Marcos, and Austin all belong to it. The Highland Lakes area is also often included because it's hilly. But for purposes of this book, we're considering only the hills formed where the southeastern edge of the Edwards Plateau meets the Balcones Escarpment, not the geologically separate rise formed by the Llano Uplift around Austin. Coverage predominantly includes the counties of Real, Bandera, Gillespie, Kerr, Kendall, Comal, northern Uvalde, northern Medina, and northwestern Bexar.

Everyone tries to crowd under the Hill Country banner because the moniker is a significant tourist draw for this part of the state, especially for elevation-starved South and East Texans. And these aren't alpine heights either—1,400-1,700 feet is the high norm. In the heat of a South Texas summer, however, the Hill Country breezes and relatively low humidity can make it feel like Eden rediscovered. Beyond the mild climate, there's also a seductive Hill Country culture of sorts, a combination of small town quaintness and Texas self-sufficiency. It's been called the state's "heartland," like England's Lake District, France's Provence, or Germany's Black Forest. Most of the towns date to the mid-1800s and were settled by Europeans of German, Polish, and Czech descent. Historic buildings are constructed of cream-colored, locally quarried tufa limestone. Many people find the scenery beautiful, but you really have to seek out the beauty, since much of the Hill Country is like South Texas—lots of cacti, mesquite, and caliche—with added hills. The most scenic areas are along the Hill Country rivers, most notably the Frio, Sabinal, Guadalupe, Medina, and Pedernales. Many a Texan's dream is to retire with a little rancho along one of these rivers.

San Antonio is a popular jumping-off point for Hill Country road tours, whether by car or bicycle—be warned that public transportation is virtually nonexistent in these parts. Hill Country aficionados often make a loop via State 16 northwest to Bandera and Kerrville, then west on scenic FM 337 or State 39 to the Frio Canyon area of Leakey, Rio Frio, and Concan, then back to San Antonio via US 90, taking in the non-Hill Country towns Uvalde and Castroville along the way. This general route offers a good sampling of the area's best without running into hordes of tourists; the approximately 200 road miles could take anywhere from two days to a week, depending on how long you stop over along the way. Recommended side trips off the loop include the pleasantly named Comfort, near Kerrville, and Utopia, near Frio Canyon. There are lots of other "itty-bitty" towns—and bigger towns like Fredericksburg—off this circuit worth visiting as well.

All phone numbers in this section are in the 210 area code unless otherwise noted.

BANDERA

The first settlers in the Bandera area were woodcutters who came in the 1840s to make shingles from the bald cypress growing along the Medina River. They were followed by a Mormon contingent and later by Polish immigrants; the Polish built the town that became modern Bandera.

The U.S. Army also contributed to the development of Bandera by establishing nearby **Camp Verde.** Troops stationed at Camp Verde called it "Little Egypt" since it was the headquarters for the short-lived U.S. Army Camel Corps, a unit that played a significant role in the exploration of the Big Bend region of far West Texas.

Billing itself as the "Cowboy Capital of the World," Bandera today (pop. 1,000) is more of a weekend-cowboy destination than a true ranch town—"Dude Ranch Capital" would in fact be more accurate. The town claims more rodeo champions than any Texas town of comparable size. Local legends Toots Mansfield, Scooter Fries, Clay Billings, and others are commemorated by a plaque in front of the 1890 Renaissance Revival-style courthouse, constructed of locally quarried limestone. Other buildings in the Main St. area are typical 1880s ranch-style clapboard or stucco, some with intact boardwalks out front.

Main St. businesses include a honky-tonk, several restaurants, and a couple of Western-wear stores. Horse-and-buggy tours are available on weekends, when the town fills up with racetrack enthusiasts and visitors from San Antonio.

Frontier Times Museum

This is the kind of museum you find only in small town America. It's basically a collection of everything the townsfolk have thought was memorable since the museum was established in 1927. The 40,000 objects on display include an impossibly eclectic range of old photos, artwork, bells from around the world, plates, and unique items like a two-headed goat, a South American shrunken head, a baby incubator, and a camelhair pillow from Camp Verde. At 506 13th St. (tel. 210-796-3864); open Mon.-Sat. 10 a.m.-4:30 p.m., Sunday 1-4:30 p.m. Admission is $2 for adults, 25 cents for students 6-18.

Historic Sites

Polish immigrants built **Saint Stanislaus Catholic Church,** at 7th and Cypress, of tufa limestone in 1876; after the one in Panna Maria, it's the second-oldest Polish church in Texas. Behind the church is the **St. Joseph's Convent Parish Museum,** built in 1874. The nearby **Catholic Cemetery** on Cypress between 7th and 8th was established by the first 16 Polish families who arrived in 1855. Many of the headstones date to the mid-19th century and are inscribed in Polish. The limestone **Old Bandera Courthouse and Jail** on 12th and Cypress were constructed in 1868 and 1881 respectively.

Look for Jeannie Park and her horse Comet clomping down Main street or standing in front of the Old Bandera Courthouse. Together they lead a **carriage tour** around Bandera for a reasonable $5 per person. For reservations or information, call (210) 235-4685.

Camp Verde

Camp Verde's camel corps imported the beasts, along with camel handlers, from North Africa by boat via the now-defunct port of Indianola, Texas. The camels made very successful pack animals for the Army's Trans-Pecos explorations. They didn't consume as much water as horses or mules and were more sure-footed in rough terrain. Also, Indians wouldn't steal them; they were apparently afraid of the odd-looking creatures. The outbreak of the Civil War ended the camel experiment—when Confederate troops took over Camp Verde they set some of the 80 animals loose and killed others. Today there are no physical remains of Camp Verde, just a historical marker narrating a short history of the post at the former site of the camel pens. But you could stop at the **Old Camp Verde General Store and Post Office** on State 173, 11 miles north of Bandera, which sells food, souvenirs, and Texana. The store has been in continuous operation since 1857. Across the road is a picnic area.

Spurs

Stop by **Sims Spur Co.** (tel. 210-796-3716) on Main Street for a look at the amazing spur designs by the state's oldest and world's largest crafter of spurs and bits. Tours of the factory can be arranged.

Dude Ranches

There are eight dude ranches in the Bandera vicinity, all oriented toward family vacations for urbanites seeking a "ranch experience." Lodging is generally in rustic cabins and meals are "ranch-style." Common Bandera dude ranch activities include trail rides, hay rides, outdoor barbecues, and Medina River recreation. Guests are not obliged to participate in any group activities and can choose instead to make use of the facilities on their own. Kids love these places, so there are always lots of them around; a guest ranch more suitable for adults traveling without children is the Y.O. Ranch near Kerrville, though couples without children are welcome at those listed below as well.

The most renowned of the Bandera bunch is the **Mayan Ranch,** off Pecan St. about 1.5 miles west of Bandera's Main Street. The Mayan's 326 wooded acres abut the Medina River, so the scenery is especially pleasant. Rates include lodging, all meals (with optional "cowboy breakfast" served on an early morning trail ride), swimming and tubing on the Medina River, horseback riding, hiking, tennis, country dance lessons, and various other activities the Hicks family dreams up on the spot. Rates are $95 a day for adults, $60 per day for teens, and $40 daily for children. Rates are $5 per day less for weekly stays. For reservations, call or write Don and Judy Hicks (tel. 210-796-3312), P.O. Box 577, Bandera, TX 78003.

The **Dixie Dude Ranch** has been a working ranch since 1901 and offers perhaps the most authentic ranch experience. The 711-acre spread has plenty of room for experienced equestrians but also offers trail rides for the less experienced. Rates are $70-90 per adult and $25-55 per child under 16 per night, depending on the cabin and season. Activities include horseback riding, hayrides, swimming, bonfires, cookouts, and live entertainment. Owner Clay Conoly plays the fiddle. The Dixie is nine miles southwest of Bandera on FM 1077. Contact Clay Conoly (tel. 796-7771 or 800-375-9255), P.O. Box 548, Bandera, TX 78003.

Just a bit farther on FM 1077 is the **Silver Spur Dude Ranch** (tel. 796-3037 or 796-3639), P.O. Box 1657, Bandera, TX 78003, a 275-acre, family-owned guest ranch built in 1980 on dry, hilly rangeland. Accommodations include modern cabins with color TV. All the usual activities, including a large swimming pool; $75 for adults, $24-55 for children a night, $20 for day use only.

Other Bandera guest ranches include: **Flying L Guest Ranch** (tel. 796-3001 or 800-292-5134), P.O. Box 1376, Bandera, TX 78003; **LH7 Ranch Resort** (tel. 796-4314), P.O. Box 1474; **Lost Valley Resort Ranch** (tel. 460-7958), P.O. Box 2170, Bandera, TX 78003; **Diamond H Ranch** (tel./fax 796-4820), HCO-2, Box 39C; and **Twin Elm Guest Ranch** (tel. 796-3628), P.O. Box 117. Each charges around $75 a day for adults, $45-55 for children and teens.

Bridging the gap between B&B and guest ranch, **Lightning Ranch** (tel. 535-4096), Rt. 1, Box 1015, Pipe Creek, TX 78063, offers one- and two-bedroom guesthouses with full kitchen, TV, a/c, heating, and private porch for $70-80 a night. Each kitchen is stocked with all the ingredients for a do-it-yourself full breakfast. Horseback rides can be arranged for $16 an hour, $60 for a half day. Lightning Ranch is less than a mile east of Pipe Creek Junction on FM 1283.

Hotels, Motels, and Condos

The **Bandera Lodge** (tel. 210-796-3093) at 1900 State 16 S has rooms for $49-58 and a pool. Senior discounts available. The **River Front Motel** (tel. 796-3690), facing the Medina River at 1004 Maple, has individual cottages for $40-45 a night. The **Frontier Hotel** (tel. 796-4100) on State 16 and Cherry St. in town costs $40 s/d with one bed, $50 d with two beds. Similar rates are available at **River Oak Inn** (tel. 796-7751), 1105 Main Street.

*cowboys come
in all sizes*

Three miles north of town on State 173 is the small, wooden **Horseshoe Inn** (tel. 796-3105 or 800-352-3810), where seven simply furnished but charming rooms with private baths run $40 d during the week, $50 d on weekends. Rates include a full breakfast and the use of tubes for floating on the nearby Medina River.

As incongruous as it may seem, condos have arrived in Bandera, mainly for the use of weekend gamblers playing the horses at Bandera Downs. **Bandera Homestead** (tel. 796-3051) at 150 River Ranch Drive, 2.5 miles from the racetrack, has one- and two-bedrooms units on the Medina River for $95 and $106 a night respectively.

Bed and Breakfasts
Hackberry Lodge (tel. 210-460-7134), 1005 Hackberry, a charming, two-story 1890 native stone house in town, offers two-bedroom suites with fireplaces and kitchens for $135 a night, including continental breakfast. A similarly historic carriage house on the 4.7-acre property features two one-bedroom suites, each with private entrance, for $85 a night. Two more modern, one-bedroom efficiency units are available at the same rate. All accommodations are air-conditioned and include cable TV. Long-term discounted rates can be arranged.

Bandera Creek Bed & Breakfast (tel. 796-3517 or 796-3518), southeast of town on State 16 near Bandera Downs, has two rooms with air-conditioning, TV, and shared bath for $85 including continental breakfast.

Campgrounds and RV Parks
Each of the RV parks in and around Bandera charges a moderate $10 a night for full-hookup sites, even less for long-term stays. **Bandera Beverage Barn and RV Park** (tel. 210-796-8153) has 30 sites overlooking the river at 1503 Main St. in Bandera. **Skyline Ranch RV Park** (tel. 796-4958) is a mile west of town on State 16 and features full hookups, cable TV, lounge, and pavilion. The family-oriented **Yogi Bear's Jellystone Park** (tel. 796-3751) is on the river near the River Front Motel. In addition to full hookups, the park has a swimming pool and facilities for canoeing and tubing. **LH7 Ranch Resort** (see "Dude Ranches") offers RV hookups as well.

Cowboy Capitol Campground (tel. 535-4840) offers spacious, shaded RV, camper, and tentsites 5.5 miles east of town off State 16. **The Farm** (tel. 589-2276), 7.5 miles northwest of Bandera off FM 2828 on the river, features tent camping for $7 a night in addition to RV sites. Free primitive camping is permitted at the **Hill Country State Natural Area.**

Food
Locals enjoy the **O.S.T. Restaurant** (tel. 210-796-3836) at 305 Main, which serves time-warp Tex-Mex, like enchiladas served with a thick tomato sauce and chili, and downhome fare like homemade soups, chicken-fried steaks and biscuits. The acronym stands for Old Spanish Trail, which once passed through Bandera. The restaurant also serves Mexican or American breakfasts at any hour—a real plus. Open Sun.-Thurs. 6 a.m.-11 p.m., Fri.-Sat. 6 a.m.-midnight. **Harvey's Old Bank Steakhouse** at 309 Main offers hearty breakfasts, steak, and other Texas dishes. A pleasant outdoor eating area is open in good weather. Open daily 6:30 a.m.-2 p.m. and 5-10 p.m.

Rustic **Busbee's Bar-B-Q** at 319 Main has barbecued beef, sausage, chicken, and ribs weekdays 10:30 a.m.-8 p.m., weekends till 9 p.m. or until sold out. Tiny **El Jacalito** at 304 11th, one block west of Main, turns out respectable Tex-Mex.

North of Bandera on State 16 is **Thuy's** (tel. 796-8496), a Vietnamese restaurant open Fri.-Sat. 4-9 p.m. only. Nearby is the best local Mexican place, **Un Taco Mas, Etc.** (tel. 796-7257), which serves enchiladas, tacos, chalupas, menudo, and breakfast tacos daily 9 a.m.-2 a.m.

One place most tourists don't know about is the incomparable **Pipe Creek Junction Café** (tel. 535-4742), which is about 12 miles east of Bandera at the junction of State 16 and FM 1283. It looks like a country store from the outside, but the eye-popping menu inside includes farm-raised catfish (all you can eat Wednesday and Friday), Gulf shrimp (Tuesday and Thursday), frog legs, rabbit, catfish-fried chicken livers, grilled teriyaki chicken, and homemade breads, plus daily specials listed on a chalkboard. Also breakfast tacos and incredible buttermilk pie. Open Tues.-Sun. 6 a.m.-11 p.m.

PIPE CREEK JUNCTION CAFE BUTTERMILK PIE

3 eggs, beaten
1 tsp. vanilla
1/2 cup melted butter or margarine
2 cups sugar
1/2 cup flour
3/4 cup buttermilk
1 deep-dish pie shell

Mix all ingredients except buttermilk in a large bowl. Add buttermilk and stir well. Pour mixture into pie shell and bake in preheated 325° oven until "set"—about 1 hour and 15 minutes.

Dance Halls

Can't have a cowboy capital without a couple of honky-tonks. The **Cabaret Dance Hall** (tel. 210-796-3095), at 801 Main, has been a big draw for over 50 years. Hank Williams and Bob Wills rattled the walls in the early days of country music; Billy Joe Shaver and Willie Nelson filmed performances here more recently. Nowadays Texas names like Johnny Bush and the Bandeleros and Hank Thompson play on weekends. Open Fri.-Sun. till 2 a.m. A bit funkier is **Arkey Blue's Silver Dollar** (tel. 796-8826) at 308 Main, where Arkey Blue and the Blue Cowboys motivate boot heels on a sawdust dance floor Friday and Saturday nights; Dusty Britches performs Wednesday night.

Bandera Downs

At this racetrack founded in 1990, horses run Fri.-Sun. from February to September; exact dates vary from year to year. General admission is $3 including parking; other seating options include Grandstand ($5), Turf Club ($7), and air-conditioned Jockey Club ($10-12). For further information or ticket reservations, call (210) 796-7781 or (800) 572-2332.

Rodeos

From Memorial Day through Labor Day each year, open non-PRCA rodeos alternate between Mansfield Park on Tuesday and Friday and Twin Elm Guest Ranch on Saturday. Barrel racing events at Mansfield Park run the remainder of the year.

On Labor Day weekend the Cowboy Capital Rodeo Association sponsors a PRCA-sanctioned rodeo at Mansfield Park.

River Recreation

You can rent tubes, canoes, and kayaks for floating or paddling the Medina River at **Bandera Beverage Barn,** State 16 N; **Fred Collins Workshop,** State 16 N; and **Yogi Bear's Jellystone Park,** State 173 S. The same establishments can arrange shuttle service.

Hill Country State Natural Area

This 5,400-acre park, 10.5 miles southwest of Bandera via FM 681 and FM 1077, preserves a chunk of the Hill Country in its natural, undeveloped state. The varied terrain encompasses Bandera Creek bottom, grassland meadows, upland woods, and craggy limestone hills.

Thirty-four miles of multi-use trails are available for hiking, horseback riding, and all-terrain cycling. Horseback trail rides can be arranged through Bandera's **Running 'R' Ranch** (tel. 210-796-3984), Rt. 1, Box 590, Bandera, TX 78003, the only outfit with a concession to lead trail rides in the park.

There are three swimming holes along West Verde Creek; fishing for catfish, largemouth bass, and perch is permitted. Camping—free for hikers or $4 per vehicle—is permitted at 10 walk-in tent campsites with toilets about 75 yards from parking, or at three hike-in sites without toilets 1.5-3.5 miles from parking. Water is supplied at park headquarters; fires are permitted within designated fire rings only. Near park headquarters is a special horse camp with trailer parking, barn, 10 horse stalls, and toilet facilities.

The park is open to day use 8 a.m.-5 p.m. Thurs.-Mon. only; entry is $3 per vehicle. No overnight camping is permitted Monday nights. For further information, contact the manager (tel. 796-4413), HCSNA, Rt. 1, Box 601, Bandera, TX 78003.

Medina Lake

The floor of 5,575-acre Medina Lake was once the site of Mountain Valley, an early Mormon colony destroyed by a 1900 flood. Unlike many Texas dams that are state or federally funded, the Medina Dam was built, in 1912, by private interests. Before it was dammed, the Medina River valley was probably the most beautiful in the Hill Country. The wooded bluffs that ringed the dramatic valley, now filled with water, still lend an added beauty to the lake. The dam and the entire lakeshore are still privately owned, though there are public facilities at a few commercial campgrounds and marinas. Many San Antonio families own weekend homes here. The lake is very popular for boating, waterskiing, swimming, and fishing.

Medina Lake is 22 miles from Bandera, via State 16 east to Pipe Creek, then FM 1283 south to Park Road 37. Two small, unincorporated communities, Mico and Lakehills (sometimes spelled Lake Hills), offer minimal grocery and gas facilities.

Lake Facilities: There are four RV parks in Lakehills, all with sites for $10 a night; long-term discounts available. **Goat Hill Camp** (tel. 210-751-2072) has 14 lakeshore acres at the end of 19th St. (Goat Hill Rd.) off Park 37; full hookups, cabins, a boat ramp, and boat rentals available. **Bob's Cove** (tel. 751-9923) is off a dirt road that starts where Park Road 37 ends; $8 w/e only, $10 with sewer, tents allowed, marina available. **Lakehills Mobile Home & RV Park** (tel. 751-3030) is off Park Road 37 next to the EMS barn; full hookups. The **Hitching Post** (tel. 751-3222) is on Park Road 37 a mile west of FM 1283; full hookups. **Pop's Place** (tel. 535-4366), off FM 1283 south of Pipe Creek, has been around for 30 years and features full-hookup RV spaces and a marina. **Thousand Trails** (tel. 751-2406) in Lakehills on Medina Lake is a membership-only campground that costs just $5 a night for members.

Cedar Point Landing (tel. 751-3115) on Medina Dam Rd. (just off FM 1283) features a boat ramp open to the paying public.

Spiritual Retreats

Northwest of town off State 16, **Venture Inward** arranges group and individual retreats in various genres of spiritual growth, including yoga and meditation, on 43 acres of riverfront land. Spiritually minded, self-contained campers may stay on the property for $5 a night by prior arrangement only. For further information and a schedule of retreat events, call Beth Hodges at (210) 796-8473.

Horseback Riding

Bandera's guest ranches offer horseback riding activities in conjunction with their daily programs. Independent stables in the area will arrange horseback rides by the hour, day, or overnight. Try **Heartland Stables** (tel. 210-589-2587), **Lightning Ranch** (tel. 535-4096), **Luna Creek Livery** (tel. 796-3291), **Running 'R' Ranch** (tel. 796-3984), and **Wagon Wheel Riding Stables** (tel. 966-3678).

Horse Country (tel. 535-4212) in Pipe Creek stocks 2,000 videos and books on the breeding, training, and care of horses. For saddles and tack, trot over to **Clark Saddlery** (tel. 796-7661), across from Bandera Downs on State 16.

Information and Services

The friendly **Bandera County Convention and Visitors Bureau** (tel. 800-364-3833) at 1206 Cypress distributes a number of useful brochures and maps, and can answer tourist inquiries.

First State Bank on Main St. sports a 24-hour ATM, one of the only cash machines in this part of the Hill Country. **USA Postal** (tel. 210-796-381) at 805-C Main St. provides parcel and packing services, mailbox rentals, 24-hour fax service, and mail forwarding.

KERRVILLE

This town of 18,000 has grown beyond its quaint Hill Country roots into an arts center of sorts. The town itself is not much of an attraction except at the end of May, when the Kerrville Folk Festival and Texas State Arts and Crafts Fair take place, and during September's Jimmie Rodgers Jubilee. The surrounding area is dotted with youth camps and ranches.

For historic architecture, cruise the area around Main and Earl Garrett Streets, where you'll find a number of turn-of-the-century limestone block buildings.

Cowboy Artists of America Museum

The Cowboy Artists of America is an organization founded in 1965 consisting of around 25 active artists, plus eight emeritus members, from the school of Western American Realism. The museum features rotating exhibits by mem-

*from the Cowboy Artists of America
Museum, Kerrville*

ber artists and occasionally by nonmembers. The facility, built in 1985, is quite large and includes a research library, auditorium, and museum store. An artist in residence sometimes paints or sculpts in public view in a studio off one of the galleries. The museum also regularly sponsors workshops for aspiring Western artists. The works themselves are always a bit of history, meticulously researched down to the last spur and Indian feather, mixed with romanticism. Member Bill Owens has said it's important "to show the public who the true cowboy is, and what he does. In some ways, he doesn't fit into a mold, but there are some things about him that are very characteristic. There is a code, an unspoken etiquette, that the cowboy has that separates him from other people." Even if you don't buy that statement, you'll probably enjoy the exhibits for the sheer technique involved—these guys are good.

The museum (tel. 210-896-2553) is at 1550 Bandera Hwy. (State 173) east off State 16; open Tues.-Sat. 9 a.m.-5 p.m., Sunday 1-5 p.m. June through August it's also open Monday 9 a.m.-5 p.m. Admission is $2.50 adults, $2 seniors, $1 12 and under.

Hill Country Museum

This turreted limestone mansion was originally the home of cattle baron and ex-Texas Ranger Charles Schreiner. Then, for a while, it was a Masonic temple. It now contains exhibits interpreting the history of the Schreiner family and Kerr County. The house itself is the most interesting exhibit, with a parquet floor made of 10 kinds of wood and other flourishes. At 216 E. Garrett; open Tues.-Sat. 9:30 a.m.-noon and 1:30-4:30 p.m. Admission is $2.50 adults, $1 children 6-12.

Y.O. Ranch

Texas Ranger Captain Charles Schreiner, a native of Alsace Lorraine, founded this ranch in 1880 after making his fortune by driving 300,000 head of longhorn cattle to Dodge City, Kansas. Schreiner bought the Y.O. brand from another rancher; it stood for Young-Olsten at the time. Over the years, the ranch has shrunk from 550,000 to 40,000 acres but is still quite a spread. Charles Schreiner III ("Charlie III") brought the longhorn breed back from near extinction in the 1950s and the Y.O. now has the largest quality registered herd in the country. Charlie III has also bred "exotic" game on the ranch for the last 30 years, one of the first Texans to do so.

Some of the species bred on the ranch are endangered in their native countries; the blackbuck antelope had been completely wiped out in Pakistan before they began importing from the Y.O. in recent years. Other cloven-hoofed creatures inhabiting the ranch include axis and sika deer; mouflon, red, and aoudad sheep; addax; Persian ibex; barasingha; oryx; and eland. The ranch also breeds emu, ostrich, rhea, giraffe, and zebra—a virtual zoo of African and Australasian animals. The game species are hunted when the herds get too big—the ranch claims only five percent are taken by strictly regulated hunting, less than the percentage that would die of natural attrition in the wild.

Most of the visitors to the Y.O. are nonhunters who come for the ranch tour or to spend a day or two in the antique-furnished, century-old guest cottages that are listed in the National Register of Historic Places. A half-day tour takes visitors through the wildlife areas and includes a large ranch-style lunch in the cowboy mess. The cost is $23 adults, $12 children 10 and under. Overnight stays cost around $75-85, depending on the cottage, including three meals a day. Facilities include horse stables, swimming pool, guest lodge, tennis court, and hot tub.

On Memorial Day weekend in late May the ranch runs a three-day **Y.O. Ranch Longhorn Cattle Drive** across the ranch. Besides herding longhorn, activities include campfire entertainment and chuckwagon cookouts. The cost is $175 per person if you bring your own horse, additional fees if you have to rent one.

For more information, contact the Y.O. Ranch (tel. 210-640-3222), Mountain Home, TX 78058. To reach the ranch, take I-10 west from Kerrville 18 miles to Mountain Home, then State 41 south another 14 miles till you see the Y.O. sign.

Accommodations

The **Inn of the Hills River Resort** (tel. 210-895-5000 or 800-292-5690), 1001 Junction Hwy. (State 27), has basic rooms for $50 s, $60 d, plus more expensive rooms and condos with a river view starting at $110. The **Sands Motel** (tel. 896-5000 or 800-292-5690) on State 27 and the **Save Inn Motel** (tel. 896-8200 or 800-225-1374) on State 16 each have rooms for $25-45. Also on State 16 is the **Best Western Sunday House Motor Inn** (tel. 896-1313 or 800-677-9477), which features rooms for $59-76 s, $68-98 d.

Two moderately priced places on State 16 (also known as Sidney Baker St.) are the **Econo Lodge** (tel. 896-1711 or 800-225-1374) and **Hill Country Inn** (tel. 896-1511 or 800-274-2111), both with rooms in the $36-40 range, $10 more for the Econo Lodge on weekends.

The **Y.O. Ranch Holiday Inn** (tel. 257-4440), 2033 Sidney Baker St., is Kerrville's poshest digs and features a hunting lodge atmosphere. September through March rooms are $65-75 s, $75-95 d. The rest of the year, add $5 to all rates.

Guest Ranch

Lazy Hills Guest Ranch, eight miles northwest of town via State 27, offers a typical Hill Country

guest ranch program of horseback riding, hayrides, and cookouts, plus facilities for swimming and tennis. Daily rates including three meals per day are $85 per person single occupancy, $65 per person double, or $58 per person triple for adults, and $20-35 per child. Three-day minimum; weekly rates are available. For more information contact Lazy Hills Guest Ranch (tel. 210-367-5600 or 800-880-0632), Box G, Ingram, TX 78205.

RV Parks, Cabins, and Camping

Guadalupe River RV Resort (tel. 210-367-5676 or 800-582-1916) has 120 pull-through sites on the Guadalupe River with full hookups, cable TV, phone, picnic facilities, clubhouse, swimming pool, spa, exercise room, and 6,000-square-foot pavilion—in short, a fully developed resort for the onwardly mobile. RV slots cost $19.50 a night, less for long-term stays. Ten furnished, two-bedroom cottages with full kitchens are available for $75 d, plus $4 per each additional person. Located at 2605 Junction Hwy. (State 27) northwest of town.

AmeriCamp Leisure Resort (tel. 896-6052), a half mile west of the State 16 and I-10 junction on Benson Rd., charges $8 for tentsites, $13 for full hookups.

Kerrville KOA (tel. 895-1665 or 800-874-1665) on FM 1338 a half mile south of I-10 (exit 501) has full hookups for $18 per couple per night. **Take-It-Easy RV Park** (tel. 800-828-6984) offers similar rates.

Tent and RV camping is also permitted at Kerrville-Schreiner State Park.

Food

Beyond the fast-food chains crowding the State 27 and State 16 junction, there isn't a huge selection of places to eat. **Annemarie's** (tel. 210-257-8282) at 1001 Junction Hwy. offers various schnitzels and sausage platters, as well as American standbys like steak and fried chicken. Open daily for breakfast, lunch, and dinner. More down-home cooking is available at **Joe's Jefferson Street Cafe** (tel. 257-2929), housed in a 100-year-old building at 1001 Jefferson Street. The menu includes homemade breads and pastries, chicken-fried steak, seafood, and steaks. **Bill's Barbecue** (tel. 895-5733) at 1909 Junction Hwy. (State 27), serves brisket, links, ribs, chicken, and, on occasion, *cabrito.* Open Tues.-Sat. 11 a.m.-3 p.m., or until the meat runs out.

Like its sister restaurant by the same name in Bandera, **El Jacalito** (tel. 257-7767) serves good Tex-Mex. Specials change daily and include various enchiladas, *chalupas,* Mexican-style stuffed bell peppers, fajitas, *chimichangas,* tamales, and *flautas.* It's next to the Hill Country Inn on Sidney Baker St. (State 16). Senior citizens receive 15% discounts across the board. At 1718 Sidney Baker St. (State 16), the **Acapulco Restaurant** (tel. 895-2232) serves border food like *carne guisada, tacos al carbón,* and *chalupas.* Open daily for lunch and dinner.

Entertainment

In the past, Kerrville's music scene dried up as soon as the Folk Festival ended each year. No longer. Opened in 1994 at 1701 Junction Hwy. (State 27) between Kerrville and Ingram, **Cross Creek Roadhouse** (tel. 210-895-5090) hosts live country dance music Wed.-Sat. throughout the year.

Events

May-June: The **Kerrville Folk Festival** is an 18-day event with live music every day and night from late May to early June, held annually for 20 years. "Folk" in this case means just about any original music performed at below 120 decibels. A more appropriate name might be "Kerrville Songwriting Festival" since it not only showcases the best Texas songwriting talent but offers songwriting workshops. The 1994 lineup included Jimmy LaFave, Tom Paxton, Pele Juju, Sara Hickman, Tish Hinojosa, Gary P. Nunn, Butch Hancock, Ray Wylie Hubbard, Christine Albert, Peter Yarrow, Carolyn Hester, Mumbo Gumbo, and many more. A typical festival format includes 11 six-hour evening concerts, 11 two-hour sundown concerts, song-sharing sessions beneath "the Ballad Tree," the annual New Folk competition for emerging songwriters, plus lots of handicraft, record/CD, and food booths. The festival is held at Quiet Valley Ranch, nine miles south of Kerrville on State 16. Advance single-day tickets cost $8 weekdays, $10 Sat.-Sun. (add $2 if bought at the door); multiple-day tickets range from $24 for three days to $125 for all 18 days. Camping is free for multiple-day ticket holders, $3 a day for others.

The **Texas State Arts and Crafts Fair** runs concurrently with the Folk Festival, over the last weekend in May and first weekend of June. The number of exhibitors at this fair is limited to 250 and they're carefully selected for quality. In addition to the exhibits, there are also performances of music and cowboy poetry. The fair is held on the Schreiner College campus. Tickets are $5 a day adults, $1 children 6-12. For more information, contact TSACF, P.O. Box 1527, Kerrville, TX 78209.

As if there weren't enough events in May already, the Y.O. Ranch hosts a three-day longhorn commemorative cattle drive. See "Y.O. Ranch," above, for details.

July: In nearby Medina, the self-proclaimed "apple capital of Texas," the **Texas International Apple Festival** celebrates the annual apple harvest on the last Saturday of July with oceans of cold apple cider, live music, arts and crafts, and booths with every imaginable apple culinary presentation, from apple pie to apple pizza. Call (210) 589-7224 for more information.

September: Jimmie Rodgers, the "Blue Yodeler," was born in Mississippi in 1897, contracted tuberculosis in 1924 while working on southern railroads, and was forced to take up another line of work. He began performing, became a recording star in 1927, and moved to Kerrville in 1929 hoping that the clear air and mild climate would mitigate his TB. A white singer who learned to sing the blues from black railway workers, he forged his own style of country blues by adding a yodeling technique to the melodic lines. He continued to perform in Texas and had his own radio show in San Antonio, but died in a New York hotel room in 1933 after attending a recording session. In his memory, Kerrville holds a **Jimmie Rodgers Jubilee** during the last weekend in September. Blue yodelers from around the region meet at the jubilee for performance competitions, which are held at **Schreiner College.** Rodgers sang a lot of hobo songs, so on Saturday there's a hobo stew cookoff. For information on upcoming jubilees, contact the Kerrville Chamber of Commerce (tel. 800-221-7958), 1700 Sidney Baker (State 16), Kerrville, TX 78028.

Kerrville-Schreiner State Park

This 517-acre facility begins 2.5 miles south of town on State 173 and runs along the Guadalupe

River. There are facilities for swimming, boating, fishing, picnicking, and camping, as well as hiking trails with scenic views. Tent/camper sites with water only are $4 on weekdays; $6 a night on weekends; RV/camper sites with w/e are $9/11, and RV sites with full hookups are $10/12. There are also 23 screened shelters for $15/16 a night. Contact the Superintendent (tel. 210-257-5392), Kerrville-Schreiner State Park, 2385 Bandera Hwy., Kerrville, TX 78208.

COMFORT

German immigrants founded Comfort in 1854, appending the name because it was the first "comfortable" spot they came to after a hard journey from New Braunfels. Like many European immigrants they fled political and religious persecution in the Old World, but unlike other German groups who migrated to Texas the Comfort settlers weren't particularly religious; not a single church was built in Comfort for 40 years after its founding. They also held strong pro-Union and antislavery views, a stance that brought them Confederate persecution.

Today, Comfort remains a small, unincorporated town of around 1,500 without a single traffic light. Ten blocks of pre-1900 buildings in the downtown area are listed on the National Register of Historic Places. Most are in the characteristic Central Texas style—creamy limestone cubes. A few are wooden Victorians. The chamber of commerce office (tel. 210-995-3131) at 7th and High distributes a free *Tour Through Comfort History* booklet that details the location and history of structures within the Comfort Historic District.

If you're traveling the San Antonio-Kerrville-Frio Canyon loop, you'll have to make an 18-mile detour east on State 27 from Kerrville to find the little town of Comfort.

Truer der Union Monument

A simple obelisk on High St. between 3rd and 4th, erected in 1865, commemorates 68 local Union sympathizers assaulted by Confederate troops during the Civil War. Persecuted for refusing to sign a Confederate oath of allegiance, these men, mostly Germans, attempted to flee to Mexico in 1862. While camped on the Nueces

River near Brackettville, only about 35 miles from the Rio Grande, a Confederate cavalry unit caught up with them. Nineteen were killed in the ensuing battle, 15 were captured and later executed, and the remainder made it to Mexico or back to the Comfort vicinity. Comfort residents later gathered the remains of the slain (who were left unburied) and interred them in a community grave beneath the 1865 "True to the Union" marker. A 1991 congressional declaration added the monument to a list of only six historic sites in the nation where the U.S. flag may be flown at half mast in perpetuity.

Ingenhuett Store

Built in 1867, this is one of the oldest continuously operating general stores in the state, run by the same German-American family for four generations. They carry everything from work clothes to parts for a 1920 Lavelle cream separator, fresh meat, and single bolts or nails. At 830 High St. (tel. 210-995-2149).

Antiques

Around a dozen antique shops line High St. and 7th St. off High. One of the better selections is at **Comfort Common**, 818 High, which is on the bottom floor of the restored 1880 Faust Hotel (now a bed and breakfast), originally designed by noted architect Alfred Giles.

Perfect for the toy town of Comfort is the **Little People Car Co.** (tel. 210-995-2905) on High near 6th Street. Housed in a former blacksmith shop, this father-and-son enterprise rebuilds antique pedal cars, the kind that were a popular children's toy in the '20s and '30s. Little People also makes all-new pedal cars based on the same specifications of the classic models. It's the only company in the country that still manufactures and restores the little cars, most bought by collectors. An average car costs $300-400; highly collectible restored models (e.g., a 1928 Cadillac) are priced much higher.

Accommodations and Food

The **bed and breakfast** above the Comfort Common (tel. 210-995-3030) features three suites and a cottage that cost $55-90 a night for two people, including coupons for breakfast at the **Café on High Street** next door. Additional guests are charged $12 a night, and there's a discount for stays of two or more consecutive nights. The Comfort Common staff can also arrange B&B stays in local homes for $50-90 a night.

Aside from the breakfasts served to Comfort Common guests, the **Café on High Street** (tel. 995-3470) serves soups, salads, and sandwiches to the public Thurs.-Sun. 11 a.m.-4 p.m. **Arlene's Cafe,** also on High St., has similar hours and menu.

Out on State 27, the **Cypress Creek Inn** has been serving downhome meals for over 40 years. It's open Tues.-Sat. for lunch and dinner, Sunday for lunch only, and offers a variety of daily specials. Cypress Creek Inn packs in the regulars for the popular Wednesday special of smothered pork chops and creamed cabbage. Also worth trying on State 27 are **Los Jarritos** for family-style Mexican and the **Service Station Grill** for burgers, pizzas, and fajitas served amidst automotive decor.

FREDERICKSBURG

The Society for the Protection of German Immigrants (Mainzer Adelsverein) in Texas founded its second colony here in 1846, a year after the founding of New Braunfels. Baron Ottfried Hans von Meusebach (who dropped his title and changed his name to John O. Meusebach the day he sailed for Texas) led 120 Germans to this spot in the middle of Comanche territory and named it for Prince Frederick of Prussia. Meusebach managed to negotiate a treaty that allowed the colonists to stay, the treaty becoming the only agreement between Indians and whites in Texas never to be violated by either side. Like many South Central Texas colonies, the citizens of Fredericksburg and surrounding Gillespie County voted overwhelmingly against Texas secession from the Union prior to the Civil War.

Many of the descendants of the first settlers still live in Fredericksburg, which has a current population of around 7,000. Some of the older generation speak German as a first language, and one town church still holds services in German. As in New Braunfels there are occasional German festivals. The downtown architecture hasn't changed much since the turn of the century and displays its German heritage in mansard roofs, *fachwerk* (half-wooden) walls,

and lacy storefronts. On weekends, Main St. is filled with daytrippers from Austin and San Antonio (it's more or less equidistant between the two), so if you want to avoid the crowds, it's best to visit Fredericksburg on a weekday.

Admiral Nimitz Museum
And Historical Center

World War II buffs will want to visit this unique complex at 340 E. Main. Fleet Admiral Chester Nimitz was born in Fredericksburg of German parents in 1885; his grandfather opened the Nimitz Hotel, which now houses the museum, in the 1850s. After building modifications assumed a nautical form in the 1880s, it became known as the "Steamboat Hotel." Among the guests listed on the hotel's earliest registers are Rutherford B. Hayes, Robert E. Lee, Ulysses S. Grant, Jesse James (under the alias "C.C. Howard"), and Elisabet Ney.

Well-researched, often moving exhibits chronicle events in the war's Pacific theater as well as the life and naval career of the admiral. Four hotel rooms off the second floor have been restored as an exhibit on the building's history as a hotel. On display in the uppermost room, corresponding to the "bridge" in the building's vague steamboat shape, is a scale model of the famous aircraft carrier USS *Nimitz.*

Behind the former hotel is the **Japanese Garden of Peace,** a gift from the Japanese government, which contains replicas of Admiral Togo's office and teahouse, a bamboo spring, pool, and stream. Each summer Japanese middle school students come to work in the garden. Two blocks east is the **History Walk of the Pacific,** a four-acre outdoor exhibit of war machinery used in Pacific battles. A $4 million addition at an adjacent site will house a large interactive exhibit reenacting the battle of Henderson Field on Guadalcanal with a high-tech sound-and-light show. A small bookstore on the premises stocks hundreds of titles on WW II themes; a museum ticket isn't necessary for book-browsing. Open daily 8 a.m.-5 p.m.; admission $3 adults, $1.50 children 6-12. For further information call (210) 997-4379.

Other Museums
The octagonal **Vereins Kirche Museum** (tel. 210-997-7832) is off W. Main in the old town

square—more commonly known as Marktplatz—opposite the County Courthouse. Originally built in 1847, Vereins Kirche, German for "Society Church," was one of the first public buildings erected in the new colony. The current structure is a 1936 replica built for the Texas Centennial. It now houses the Gillespie County Archives as well as a small historical collection of photos, documents, and other local artifacts. Open Mon.-Fri. 10 a.m.-2 p.m.; admission is $1 per person over age 12.

The **Pioneer Museum Complex** (tel. 997-2835), 309 W. Main, is a collection of 19th-century structures with period furnishings, including the 1849 Kammlah House, the 1870s Fassel House, the 1855 First Methodist Church, a barn, smokehouse, log cabin, and "Sunday house." Farmers built one-room Sunday houses with sleeping lofts in town so that when they came in on Sunday for church and shopping, they'd have a place to stay. Open March through mid-December, Mon.-Sat. 10 a.m.-5 p.m. (closed Tuesday), Sunday 1-5 p.m.; the rest of the year, Sat. 10 a.m.-5 p.m., Sun. 1-5 p.m.

Motels

The **Dietzel Motel** (tel. 210-997-3330) is on US 290 at US 87, a mile west of the town center. Simple, well-maintained rooms cost $31-39 s, $39-44 d. South of Main St. at 908 S. Adams (State 16) is the **Comfort Inn** (tel. 997-9811 or 800-221-2222), which has rooms for $54 s, $59 d. At 501 E. Main is the **Best Western Sunday House Inn** (tel. 997-4484 or 800-528-1234), the biggest place in town with rooms for $59 s, $65 d. The new **Econo Lodge** (tel. 997-3437) at 810 S. Adams offers modern rooms for $40-55 a night. All four motels have swimming pools.

Less expensive accommodations in town can be found at the **Budget Host Deluxe Inn** (tel. 997-3344) at 901 E. Main. Motel-style rooms, some with kitchenettes, cost $28-48 s, $32-55 d. **Comfort Inn** (tel. 997-9811 or 800-221-2222) at 908 S. Adams (State 16 S) has rooms for $49-54 including complimentary coffee and pastries each morning.

Bed and Breakfasts

Fredericksburg claims to be the first town in Texas to establish B&B-type lodging. These days three different agencies book over 150 B&Bs as well as "guesthouses," similar to B&Bs except there are no breakfasts and no hosts. The typical Fredericksburg guesthouse or B&B is housed either in a historic home/cottage in town or in a rustic cabin on the outskirts. The town's largest agency, **Gästhaus Schmidt** (tel. 210-997-5612), 231 W. Main, Fredericksburg, TX 78624, lists around 90 different properties with rates of $60-100 a night. A booklet with descriptions of each is available at the Gästhaus Schmidt office. **Bed And Breakfast Of Fredericksburg** (tel. 997-4712), 102 S. Cherry, Fredericksburg, TX 78624) now has a list of around 25 private homes that take guests at rates from $45 to $100 a night. **Be My Guest** (tel. 997-4712), 402 W. Main, offers a similar number of properties. The Fredericksburg Convention and Visitors Bureau at 106 N. Adams (tel. 997-6523) also distributes a list of B&B/guest house accommodations.

Many B&Bs and guesthouses will take bookings directly. **Country Cottage Inn** (tel. 997-8549), across from the Nimitz Museum on Main St., is housed in the town's first two-story stone residence, built circa 1850. **Baron's Creek Inn** (tel. 997-9398), 110 E. Creek, Fredericksburg, TX 78624, is a 1911 German house with a grape arbor and windmill. The **Delforge Place** (tel. 997-7042), 710 Ettie, is an 1848 home decorated with antiques and mementos passed down among several generations of sea captains; the breakfasts served here have been praised in *Gourmet* magazine.

Stay above the Fredericksburg Brewing Co. at the new **Bed & Brew** (tel. 997-1646), at 345 E. Main, and you won't have far to walk for a beer; rooms cost $79-89. The inn's 12 rooms, decorated with furniture and accessories from local boutiques, cost $79-89.

Nine miles northeast of town off FM 1631 is the quiet, secluded **Landhaus** (tel. 997-4916 or 997-9624), an 1887-vintage B&B on 50 acres of land.

Camping

At **Lady Bird Johnson Municipal Park** (tel. 210-997-4202), three miles southwest on State 16 on the Pedernales (Purd-NAL-lez) River, tent/camper sites with w/e are $6 a night and full hookups including cable TV cost $13. Facilities include boat ramp, fishing, tennis and volleyball courts, and an 18-hole, par-72 golf course.

Oakwood RV Park (tel. 997-9817), two miles south of town off State 16 S, offers 116 drive-throughs with full hookups for $16.60 a day, $89 a week, or $180 a month. Sites with w/e go for $13 a day. Facilities include large swimming pool, laundry, cable TV, and basketball court. **Hill Country Travel Park** (tel. 997-2072), on US 290 E next to Wal-Mart, has 43 pull-throughs starting at $13 a night. In the opposite direction on US 290, the simpler **Frontier Inn Mobile Home Park** (tel. 997-4389) charges $12 a night for full hookups. Comfort Inn permits RVers to park overnight for a nominal fee.

Six miles east of town on US 290 is the **Fredericksburg KOA** (tel. 997-4796), where tentsites are $12.50, full hookups $15.75, Kamping Kabins $27.50. A swimming pool is open in the summer.

Food

Fredericksburg has an incredible number of restaurants for a town its size. Many are owned and operated by German-Americans and feature attached beer gardens. One of the best German restaurants is **Der Lindenbaum** (tel. 210-997-9126) at 312 E. Main. House specialties include *königsberger klopse* (pork and beef meatballs in caper sauce), *käse schnitzel* (breaded steak with cheese), locally made sausages and kraut, a large selection of draft and bottled German beers, and home-baked German desserts. It's open daily 10:30 a.m.-10 p.m.; an attached biergarten features live music on weekends. **Friedhelm's Bavärian Restaurant & Bar** (tel. 997-6300), at 905 W. Main, serves authentic Bavarian-style cuisine; the jaegerschnitzel, potato dumplings, and imported sauerkraut are tops. Open Tues.-Sun. for lunch and dinner.

The **Altdorf Biergarten and Restaurant** (tel. 997-7774), in an 1860 tufa limestone building at 301 W. Main, has German cuisine as well as steaks and Tex-Mex. Open Mon.-Sat. for lunch and dinner, Sunday lunch only. An 1850s wagon house at 312 W. Main, **The Plateau Cafe** (tel. 997-1853), features yet more German food, plus other continental dishes, steak, and seafood. During winter, the fireplace is a definite plus.

Eleven miles northwest of town on Mason Hwy. (US 87), the **Hill Top Cafe** (tel. 997-8922) serves a Greek/Texan/Cajun menu that includes shrimp mytilini, crab au gratin, crawfish tails,

Fredericksburg biergarten

spanokopitas, roast leg of lamb, boudin, tiropitas, and chicken-fried steak. It's open Wed.-Sat. for lunch and dinner, Sunday for brunch (9:30 a.m.-1 p.m.).

Bakeries: Established in 1876 (at 312 Main, now a bank), **Dietz Bakery** at 218 E. Main is the oldest bakery in town. Everything in the shop is made fresh daily, including country-style breads and pastries. Across the street at no. 141, **Fredericksburg Bakery** has been in operation since 1923 (the building was erected in 1889) and offers more delicious breads and pastries, plus ice cream. At both bakeries, the best bread selection is early in the morning (they open at 8 a.m.); by afternoon, there may not be much left. **Fredericksburg Fudge** at 234 W. Main sells a couple dozen varieties of chocolate concoctions, some from traditional German recipes, some local creations. **The Cookie Jar & Muffin Mania** at 106 E. Main is a good morning spot for coffee and pastries; open Mon.-Sat. 8 a.m.-5 p.m.

Cured Meats: Sausage fans should tour **Opa's Smoked Meats** at 410 S. Washington, a third-generation smokehouse with fresh and dried sausages, ham, turkey, bacon, pork and beef jerky, and other smoked meats; open Mon.-Saturday. **Sunday Haus Cafe** at 122 E. Main is another smokehouse, this one known for its smoked turkey—whole birds, turkey sausage, legs, thighs, wings, and breasts.

Another local favorite is **Rabke's Table Ready Meats** (tel. 685-3266), a deli market, deer-processing facility, and dining room 13 miles north of town via State 16, then right at the Eckert Rd. turnoff and four miles along a signed, narrow road. Rabke's offers all the smoked standards including whole smoked turkeys, plus tamales, beef-and-pork sausage, venison of all kinds, and, for the health-minded, turkey jerky—a tender, spicy alternative to beef jerky. Open daily 7 a.m.-7 p.m.

Peaches: At 100-acre **Hallford's Pick Your Own Orchard** (210-997-3064 or 800-880-4041), on FM 1631 a mile northeast of E. Main, visitors are welcome to gather 12 varieties of peaches, three varieties of nectarines, Oriental persimmons, plums, blackberries, and tomatoes—paying by the box. Peaches of some kind or another are ripening from mid-May through mid-October, persimmons Oct.-December. If you can't make it out to the orchard, buy from **The Peach Basket** at 334 W. Main in town.

A list of other peach orchards around Gillespie County is available from the Fredericksburg Convention and Visitors Bureau; most are in the immediate vicinity of town but several others can be found near Stonewall to the east and along US 290 between the two towns. In Stonewall the best place to buy peaches and other local fruit is the **Gillespie Co. Fruit Growers Co-op,** on US 290 near the FM 1623 junction. It's open daily 8:30 a.m.-7 p.m.

Entertainment

Local/regional bands play blues and roots music on weekend nights at the **Hill Top Cafe** and **Gould's Station** (tel. 210-997-0349), both on Mason Hwy. (US 87 N). Hill Top owner Johnny Nicholas, proficient on guitar, piano, mandolin, and harmonica, has played with many blues greats as well as Austin's Asleep at the Wheel. A live CD, *Thrill on the Hill,* was recorded live at

the restaurant in 1995. Closer to town, the **Black Forest Bier Garten** (tel. 997-7828) on US 290 W hosts live music on Saturday nights.

The new **Fredericksburg Brewing Co.** (tel. 210-997-1646), in a beautifully restored 1926-vintage building at 245 E. Main, takes advantage of the state's new laws permitting beer brewing on the premises.

Local radio station KFAN-FM 107.9 plays Texas music of all genres, including ample doses of blues, country, rock, and Western swing. KNAF-AM 910 broadcasts a mix of country, polka, and German programming.

Events

April: The **Easter Fires Pageant** lights up the night before Easter Sunday at Gillespie Fairgrounds. A 600-plus cast re-creates the history of Fredericksburg's founding and the signing of the peace treaty with the Comanches. During the mid-1800s, parents told their children that the Indian fires burning in the hills were set by the Easter Bunny for boiling Easter eggs. Call the Fredericksburg Convention and Visitors Bureau (tel. 210-997-6523) for information.

June: During the summer, Fredericksburg is awash in peaches, since three quarters of the peaches sold in Texas are grown here. Local restaurants often feature peach cobbler and fresh peach ice cream. On the third weekend of June, the nearby town of Stonewall (16 miles east on US 290) holds the **Stonewall Peach Jamboree** in the Stonewall Rodeo Arena. Events include a rodeo, parade, fiddler's contest, peach pie-baking contest, and country dancing on Friday and Saturday nights.

July: Night In Old Fredericksburg serves as the town's summer version of Oktoberfest. It's held for two nights on the second weekend of July at the Gillespie County Fairgrounds. Many townsfolk wear German attire to enjoy the lineup of polka bands, German food, and beer. Parimutuel horse races are held on Saturday and Sunday at 1 p.m.

August: The century-old **Gillespie County Fair** is held at the County Fairgrounds, three miles south of town on State 16. All the usual county fair activities, including livestock and agricultural exhibits, arts and crafts, a carnival, music, and horse races. Held the fourth weekend in August.

October: One of the biggest events of the year in this German-Texan town is of course **Oktoberfest,** held on the first weekend in October. Activities are centered on the old town square (Marktplatz), with German music and dancing, sausage eating, and lots of beer drinking. Everyone dresses in variations of traditional German clothing.

Fredericksburg Food and Wine Fest: Since 1991, the restaurants, B&Bs, and vintners of the area have come together annually for a celebration of Fredericksburg's culinary heritage. Activities include food seminars, arts and crafts, an auction of Texas wines and gourmet foods, wine and food tastings, and live music. A single admission of $10 ($5 under 21) allows visitors five wine tastings and unlimited food samples. On the third Saturday of October at the Marktplatz (Market Square).

December: At the annual **Kristkindl Markt,** held the second weekend of December at the Marktplatz, the Fredericksburg Shopkeepers Guild offers a special array of locally made Christmas gifts. The Guild also sponsors wandering minstrels and carolers, creating an especially festive air. Call 997-8515 for details.

Shopping

As many people come to Fredericksburg to shop as to tour the historic sites. All along Main St. dozens of shops sell antiques, souvenirs, arts and crafts, and home decorating accessories. The more intriguing shops include **Room No. 5,** French country- and art nouveau-style bedroom furniture and accessories; **Homestead,** country decor and antiques; **Rancho No Tengo,** ranch-style and Southwestern interior decorating; **Early Texas,** antique reproduction furniture; **American Higgledy-Piggledy,** eclectic collections of country, French, and ranch; **Idle Hours,** creative garden items; **The Dulcimer Factory,** dulcimers and other folk music instruments; **Rustic Style,** Texan, Mexican, Southwestern, Amerindian, and American Lodge furniture and accessories; and **Texas Jack's,** retro Western wear.

Dooley's 5-10-25-Cent Store, at 131 E. Main, offers a huge storeful of inexpensive bargains (such as three straw hats for $2) packed between aged wooden floors and pressed tin ceilings. **Main Book Shop** (tel. 210-997-2375) at 143 E. Main carries a good selection of reading

materials, including a well-stocked section on Texana.

Bicycles

Baron's Creek Bike Club (tel. 210-997-8898) will deliver rental bikes (Fuji, Mongoose, Schwinn) anywhere in Fredericksburg.

Information

The **Fredericksburg Convention and Visitors Bureau** (tel. 210-997-6523) at 106 N. Adams distributes useful brochures and maps. During the spring and summer, the *Fredericksburg Standard/Radio Post* newspaper publishes a thick "Visitors Guide" available free from various sources around town.

VICINITY OF FREDERICKSBURG

Scenic Drives

Almost any road out of town turns into a scenic drive after a few miles. Milam Rd. (RR 965) heads north out of Fredericksburg, then bends northeast to meet State 16 N, bisecting 26 miles of classic Hill Country scenery. Along the way this road passes **Enchanted Rock State Natural Area** and **Crabapple,** a minuscule village that appears on very few Texas maps. Two buildings make up urban Crabapple, an old Lutheran Church and a stone-walled community center where around 25 people meet on the first Sunday of each month to play the domino games of Moon, 42, Nello, and Lowboy. Once you meet State 16, you can turn right (south) and follow the highway straight back to Fredericksburg.

A more ambitious loop drive might include a drive west along US 290 to the town of Harper, then 14 miles north on RR 783 to Doss, then east 12 miles on RR 648 to US 87, which heads southeast back to Fredericksburg. Or continue north on RR 783 another 15 miles till the road meets US 87, then wheel south back to Fredericksburg. There are no major sights along this loop, just rolling, limestone-encrusted hills, ranches, and older farmhouses.

Wineries

Three wineries near Fredericksburg are open to the public. **Bell Mountain/Oberhellmann Vineyards** (tel. 210-685-3297), 14 miles north of town on State 16, makes the best wine in the area, including a delicious semillon (with just a hint of a jalapeño flavor, though at no time in the process are jalapeños actually introduced), reisling, chardonnay, cabernet sauvignon, pinot noir, and fumé blanc. Tours and tastings in the Bavarian-style winemaker's house on Saturday at 11 a.m., 1 p.m., and 3 p.m. from the first Saturday in March through the second Saturday in December.

Grape Creek Vineyard, in nearby Stonewall off US 290, produces awardwinning wines from 16 acres of vinifera grapes along South Grape Creek. Varietals currently in production include fumé blanc, cabernet blanc, cabernet sauvignon, and cabernet trois (a three-grape cabernet blend) aged in French or American oak racked in an underground cellar. Tours and tastings are hosted Tues.-Sat. 10 a.m.-6 p.m., Sunday noon-6 p.m. Visitors may also enjoy the adjacent six-acre **Grape Creek Gardens,** a small farm growing fruits and vegetables (including Stonewall's famous peaches). Bring along some food, buy a bottle of wine, and enjoy a picnic in the winery's pecan grove on South Grape Creek. If you really like the place, spend the night at the **Inn on Grape Creek,** a B&B overlooking the vineyard. For more information contact **Grape Creek Vineyard** (tel. 644-2710 or 800-950-7392), P.O. Box 102, Stonewall, TX 78671.

Pedernales Vineyards (tel. 210-997-8326), 5.4 miles south of Fredericksburg on State 16, is open for tours and tasting Mon.-Sat. 9 a.m.-5 p.m.

Enchanted Rock State Natural Area

Enchanted Rock is a massive, pink granite dome. In geologic terms, it's a batholith, the second largest in the country. It stands 70 acres across, rising 325 feet from its exposed bottom—a much larger portion remains underground. As part of the Llano Uplift formed in the Precambrian era, it's also one of the oldest exposed rock surfaces in the state.

The Enchantment of the Rock: Amerindian sites at Enchanted Rock show evidence of human habitation 8,000 years ago. Indians from Late Prehistoric and early Historic eras also inhabited the area, and evidence shows Enchanted Rock was sacred to the latter. Legend has it the Comanches held human sacrifices upon boul-

Buzzard's Roost, Enchanted Rock

ders at the base of the rock. An 1883 *New York Mirror* reported that Comanches performed annual ceremonies known as *paynim* here, but failed to describe the ritual. Most anthropologists agree the Indians held the rock in fearful veneration and believed it to be haunted. At night, the rock fills the air with spooky creaks and groans, probably from the contraction of the granite as it cools. Under a full moon, the surface sparkles and glistens—partly from minute reflections in the granite itself, partly from small *huecos* or rock hollows where water collects. Today, New Agers occasionally gather at Enchanted Rock on full-moon nights, believing it to be a source of spiritual power.

The park is listed as an "archaeological district" on the National Register of Historic Places.

Flora and Fauna: Around the base of the dome run two creeks, Sandy and Walnut Spring. Some of the park's vegetation is typical of the Edwards Plateau—live oak, mesquite, Texas persimmon, Mexican buckeye, prickly pear, and various grasses. Other species not usually found in the Hill Country grow well here, such as blackjack oak, hickory, and post oak. Atop the rock itself are fragile patches of vegetation called "vernal pools" or "gnammas," rock depressions where a thin layer of soil supports bluestem grasses, live oak, and other plantlife. The native animals are more typically Hill Country—jackrabbits, wild turkey, armadillos, and white-tailed deer.

Facilities: A four-mile loop trail winds through the four major rock outcroppings in the 1,643-acre park, and one moderately difficult trail leads to the dome's crest (nice view). Rock climbing and rappelling are permitted and Enchanted Rock is one of the country's great challenges, especially the pinnacle known as Buzzard's Roost in the northeast sector of the park.

Walk-in tentsites with water are available for $9 a night on weekdays, $8 on weekends, and flush toilets and showers are available. Primitive sites without water are $7. No RVs. Fires are permitted only in fire rings and grills in the tent camping area; you can purchase firewood at the park headquarters. The park entry fee is $5 per vehicle, $2 for pedestrians or cyclists, free for TCP holders. For further information or campsite reservations, contact the Superintendent (tel. 915-247-3903), Enchanted Rock State Natural Area, Rt. 4, Box 170, Fredericksburg, TX 78624.

Getting There: Enchanted Rock is 18 miles north of Fredericksburg on RR 965.

Luckenbach

In the song that made this little town famous, Waylon Jennings and Willie Nelson sang ". . . in Luckenbach, Texas, ain't nobody feelin' no pain." With a population optimistically set at 25, there's hardly anyone here to feel anything. Before Waylon and Willie's song put Luckenbach on the map in the '70s, luring country music pilgrims from all over who just wanted to say they'd been here, it was a place known only to Austinians—and fans of Jerry Jeff Walker's classic *Viva Terlingua!,* an album recorded in Luckenbach.

The ramshackle, 1880-vintage **Luckenbach Dance Hall** (tel. 210-997-3224) occasionally holds Saturday night dances with such performers as Gary P. Nunn, Robert Earl Keen Jr., and Monte Montgomery. On the first Saturday of October there's a ladies-only chili cookoff. In the summer of 1993, Jerry Jeff Walker celebrated the 20th anniversary of *Viva Terlingua!* with the live dance hall recording of *Viva Luckenbach,* a work well-received by the country music press.

The late owner of the dance hall and adjacent general store/post office was humorist Hondo Crouch, who was really the main draw in town. There's a bust of Hondo in front of the store, and his spirit lives on in the homespun *Luckenbach Moon* newspaper. A small bar in back of the store/post office sells beer and sou-

Luckenbach pilgrims Jerry Jeff Walker and the Gonzo Compadres.

venirs; regulars come here to play dominoes. When the weather's decent, there are usually a couple of guitar-pickers out back playing music and sipping longnecks under the shady oaks.

Getting There: It's easy to drive right past Luckenbach without knowing it, since souvenir-seekers perpetually steal the city limits signs on either side of town. From Fredericksburg, go east on US 290 toward Austin about six miles to FM 1376, then south another 4.5 miles to Luckenbach. Take the second left posted "Luckenbach Road." Coming from the north along FM 1376, take the first signposted right.

Lyndon B. Johnson State and National Historical Parks

LBJ's legacy in the Hill Country reaches almost sacred proportions, and this complex of attractions in and around the town named for him serve as a shrine for devotees and the curious. In Johnson City the NPS-managed **Johnson Settlement,** a cluster of buildings built by LBJ's forbears, and the tiny, L-shaped **Boyhood Home,** where he grew up are open to the public daily 9 a.m.-5 p.m. (no admission). A marked walking trail connects the two.

Fourteen miles west of Johnson City on the way to Fredericksburg via US 290 is a second section of the LBJ National Historical Park, more commonly known as the LBJ Ranch. On the north bank of the Pedernales River is the **LBJ Ranch House,** which Johnson built after he became a successful state legislator; the reconstructed **LBJ Birthplace,** where he was born; and the **Johnson Family Cemetery,** where the former U.S. president was buried in 1973. To see these structures visitors must take a 1.5-hour NPS bus tour. Buses leave frequently daily 10 a.m.-4 p.m. from the Visitor Center at **LBJ State Historical Park** on the south bank of the river, just off US 290. The Visitor Center contains a number of exhibits chronicling Johnson's life and interpreting local wildlife; it's open daily 8 a.m.-5 p.m. and entry is free. Also on the state park premises are a swimming pool and the **Sauer-Beckman Farm** (open daily 8 a.m.-4:30 p.m.), a "living history" display in which produce, poultry, hogs, and other livestock are raised and processed using early 1900s methods.

For information on LBJ Ranch bus tours, call (210) 644-2241.

Pedernales Falls State Park

One of the prettiest parks in Central Texas, Pedernales Falls State Park covers 5,211 acres of prime riparian Hill Country terrain eight miles east of Johnson City (38 miles west of Austin) via US 290 and RR 3232. The falls themselves tumble over a 3,000-foot section of limestone boulders. Bass and catfish angling in this section of the Pedernales River is reportedly good. Canoeists and kayakers can put in at the park for a 40-mile paddle to Lake Travis (take-out at the State 71 bridge), a pristine stretch crossed by only three roads.

Nearby **Westcave Preserve** and **Hamilton Pool Preserve** feature idyllic, fern-adorned limestone grottoes; the latter contains more than enough water for a refreshing swim on either side of the Pedernales River off RR 3238 (Hamilton Pool Rd.). You can visit Westcave only in the company of a park ranger—call in advance.

Horseback trail rides in the park can be arranged at the park stables (tel. 512-479-9443) for $15 an hour. Most Saturday mornings rangers lead free guided nature hikes; on Sunday bird-watching tours are offered for $5 per person. Multi-use campgrounds with w/e cost $7; primitive sites $7; reservations suggested. Entry costs $6 per vehicle, $1 per pedestrian/cyclist, $2 per horse. For further information, contact the Superintendent, Pedernales Falls State Park (tel. 210-825-3442), General Delivery, Round Mountain, TX 78663.

FRIO AND SABINAL CANYONS

The Frio River forms stunning reaches of shallow river valley and diminutive canyonlands between Leakey to the north and Concan to the south. The river runs clear and cold year round (*frio* is Spanish for "cold") and is lined with cypress, pecan, live oak, cedar, walnut, wild cherry, piñon, and mountain laurel. Some areas also feature bigtooth maple and sycamore, a major tourist attraction in the late fall when the leaves turn color. US 83 parallels the river and you'll find a dozen or more camps and lodges between the highway and the river, the latter a popular spot for fishing and tubing. About 15 miles east of the Frio is the equally beautiful Sabinal River, which runs along the same north-south axis. The drive between the two rivers on FM 337 (and on the same road farther west to a third river, the Nueces) is one of the most scenic in the state, as it winds gently through high limestone cliffs and spare forests of piñon, madrone, and oak.

Leakey

Pronounced LAY-key, this small community of 500 is the Real County seat. It was founded by

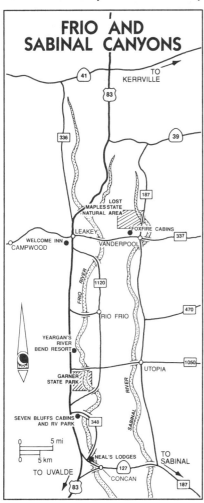

FRIO AND SABINAL CANYONS

TO KERRVILLE
41
83
336
39
187
LOST MAPLES STATE NATURAL AREA
FOXFIRE CABINS
LEAKEY
337
WELCOME INN
CAMPWOOD
VANDERPOOL
FRIO RIVER
1120
RIO FRIO
470
YEARGAN'S RIVER BEND RESORT
GARNER STATE PARK
UTOPIA
1050
SABINAL RIVER
SEVEN BLUFFS CABINS AND RV PARK
348
0   5 mi
0   5 km
NEAL'S LODGES
TO SABINAL
TO UVALDE
127
CONCAN
83
187

© MOON PUBLICATIONS, INC.

John and Mary Leakey in the mid-1800s; many early limestone buildings still stand. There's not much to do in Leakey, but if you're looking for a place to stay near Lost Maples State Natural Area, this is among the closest. The tin-roofed, wooden-sided **Welcome Inn Motor Hotel** (tel. 210-232-5246) on State 83 at 7th St. has motel rooms and cabins starting at $42. There's also an RV park on the grounds where full hookups are $12 a night. If the Welcome Inn is full or doesn't suit you, try the **Sunset Inn** (tel. 232-6077) near the junction of US 83 and FM 336 at the north end of town. You can buy groceries at **D&D Supermarket** on US 83 in the middle of town; open Mon.-Sat. 7:30 a.m.-6 p.m. At the **Frio Canyon Cafe, Feed Store, and Exxon** in town you can grab a bite, feed your horse, and gas up the hog.

Off FM 337 in Vanderpool (pop. 20), next to the Sabinal River, **Foxfire Cabins** offers white-pine interiors, full kitchens, woodburning stoves in some units, and barbecue grills. The cabins rent for $63-68 d a night on weekdays, $70-85 d weekends. For reservations, call or write Foxfire Cabins (tel. 210-966-2200), HC01 Box 142, Vanderpool, TX 78885. Similar accommodations are available just east of here on the Frio River at **Paradise** (tel. 232-6351), P.O. Box 520, Leakey, TX 78873. Other lodgings along the Frio River between Leakey and Vanderpool include **Clearwater Ranch** (tel. 232-6686), P.O. Box 1101, Leakey, TX 78873 and **River Haven Cabins** (tel. 232-5400), P.O. Box 510, Leakey, TX 78873, both in the $50-60 range.

Campland (tel. 966-2323) offers w/e hookups ($12) and tent camping ($6) a half mile from Lost Maples on FM 187. On the premises are a swimming pool, showers, restrooms, fire rings, and hiking trails.

Rio Frio

This flyspeck of a town sports a population of 50 and the largest live oak in Texas. The centuries-old tree is in LeAnn Walker's front yard off FM 1120 on the east side of the Frio River—you can't miss it. LeAnn keeps a pet deer and has a dog named Hunter that likes to climb the big oak. And that's it for Rio Frio entertainment. But the river is nearby and it's a very peaceful spot to unwind unknown to most San Antonio residents.

Frio River, Concan

LeAnn's **Rio Frio Bed & Breakfast** (tel. 210-232-6633) offers eight furnished cottages for $45-120 a night.

Garner State Park
This 1,420-acre facility offers 1.5 miles of frontage along the Frio River and is a very popular local spot for swimming, canoeing, and fishing. Bald cypress, oak, elm, and pecan trees line the river, while the hills feature cedar, cherry, persimmon, and the rare Texas madrone, which grows only in Frio Canyon, Big Bend, and the Guadalupe Mountains. There are a few short hiking trails, plus a miniature golf course, paddleboat rentals, and a dance terrace. The latter is the social center for Frio Canyon summers, since it has a free jukebox stocked with Johnny Cash, George Strait, and Jimmie Rodgers records. In May there's a "dance reunion" with live music. Summers can get crowded, especially on weekends.

Facilities: Garner offers every type of overnight facility in the state park system except for a hotel: campsites with water only ($10-12), with w/e ($15-17), screened shelters ($20-22), and cabins ($35 for two people, plus $5 each additional adult, $2 each additional child 6-12). Entry is $6 per vehicle, $1 for cyclists and pedestrians. For a summer cabin reserve early, up to 90 days in advance.

For further information or reservations, contact the Superintendent (tel. 210-232-6132), Garner State Park, Concan, TX 78838.

Getting There: The park is a mile south of the US 83 and FM 1050 junction, nine miles south of Leakey.

Concan
Outside Lost Maples and Garner state parks, this is the prettiest part of Frio Canyon. River vistas in the Concan area are particularly stunning, with the crystal-clear Frio River winding around smooth-topped boulders banked by tall stands of pecan and oak. As with Garner State Park, summer is the local season and lodgings may then be full, especially on weekends.

Nobody knows for sure how the town got its name but everyone likes to speculate. At one time it was spelled Con Can, but an 1885 postmaster changed it to one word. "Concan" or "Con Can" may have been a Mexican game of chance played by Mexicans in tent camps on the banks of the Frio—that's the most reported story, though today no one knows anything about the game.

Accommodations and Food: Among the better places off US 83 in Concan is **Yeargan's River Bend Resort** (tel. 210-232-6616 or 232-6190), HCT 70, Box 616, Concan, TX 78838, which sits on the west bank of the Frio River off US 83 north of Garner State Park. It's open year round and offers several kinds of overnight facilities with rates depending on the number of people and time of year. Motel rooms with kitchenette cost $60 for one to four people, while cottages go for $75 for up to four people, $82 for larger units that sleep eight. Camping rates start at $15 for tent/camper sites with w/e, $18 for full hookups. A screened shelter costs $20 a night. Camping rates are fairly reasonable for small groups, since one fee admits two vehicles and up to eight people. Rates in the "low season" (March 1-May 1 and Oct. 1-Jan. 1, excluding holidays) are a bit lower.

A longtime Texas favorite among Concan accommodations is **Neal's Lodges** (tel. 232-6118), established in 1926. Neal's features 60 cabins, nine RV hookups, and tentsites on the river, plus a grocery store, restaurant, and laundromat. The cabins are $40-150 a day for four people, depending on the cabin; all but four have kitchenettes. All feature either "refrigerated air" (air-conditioning) or evaporative coolers. Rates are 30-40% lower in the winter. RV hookups run $17 a night for one to four people, plus $3 for each additional person. There are 25-30 campsites on the river, depending on tent size; rates are $15 per vehicle with up to four people, $3 each additional person. No reservations are taken for campsites.

Neal's rents inner tubes for river floating ($3 a day, $2 for shuttle service up the river), and also leads horseback trail rides for $10 a person and sunset hayrides for $3 a person. For further information or cabin reservations, contact Neal's Lodges, P.O. Box 165, Concan, TX 78838.

Caliche-surfaced County Road 348 leads 1.2 miles east off US 83 to **Seven Bluffs Cabins and RV Park** (tel. 210-232-5260), P.O. Box 184, Concan, TX 78838, an idyllic spot under a tall limestone cliff with spacious, shady grounds and barbecue grills. Campsites with full hookups cost $15 for two people ($2.50 for each additional person), $68 for cabins that sleep up to four, $87 for cabins sleeping seven, and $95 for an eight-bed cabin. The turnoff for CR 348 is 3.2 miles north of the US 83/State 127 junction. Just south of Seven Bluffs along the west bank of the Frio River, **Concan Cabin Rentals** (tel. 232-6068), HCR 70, Box 409, Concan, TX 78838, and **Frio Country Campsites & Cabins** (tel. 232-6625), P.O. Box 254, Concan, TX 78838, offer cabins in the $65-75 range and campsites for $8-13.

You can stock up on supplies at Concan's **Happy Hollow Grocery** near the US 83/State 127 junction. **Ken's Restaurant** nearby offers homestyle meals.

Getting There: Concan is 17 miles south of Leakey on US 83.

UTOPIA

As you enter town a sign reads Welcome to Utopia—Let's Keep It Nice. You might think the town was named for the mild climate, clean air, and clean water, but it could have been named by frontier circuit preachers who found it a heavenly place to hold camp meetings and save souls. Though Utopia has a population of only 360, there are seven churches in town.

The **Sabinal Canyon Museum** on Utopia's main street displays local arts and crafts, including antique handmade quilts, historic photos, farm implements, arrowheads, spurs, and other artifacts that outline Bandera County history. It's open Saturday 10 a.m.-4 p.m., Sunday 1-4 p.m. or by appointment (tel. 210-966-2326 or 966-3474).

Specialty Shops

Huajillo honey is a local specialty and there's no better place to buy a jar than the **Utopia Honey House** on FM 187, which is the main drag running through town. The Honey House is also the official dispenser of tourist information for Utopia and vicinity. **Utopia Organic Gardening** on the same road sells fruits and vegetables grown without the use of chemical pesticides or fertilizers.

Accommodations

Two miles south of town on FM 187 is the turnoff for **Utopia on the River** (tel. 210-966-2444), a large inn built of native stone and cedar. Each of the 12 rooms has a microwave and refrigerator. In back of the inn are a sauna, small pool, and jacuzzi, plus a 2.5-mile trail along the Sabinal. A large cypress near the river is an estimated 750-800 years old. The proprietors allow deer and turkey hunting on the 650-acre property, for guests only. Room rates are $74 d including a full country breakfast of pancakes, sausage, eggs, bacon, and hashbrowns.

The **Bluebird Bed & Breakfast Inn** (tel. 966-3525 or 966-2320), 10 miles west of Utopia on FM 1050, features stone and wood cabins for $70 a night, including a full breakfast.

Off FM 187, the family-owned **Good Shepherd Campground** (tel. 966-2325 or 966-2402), P.O. Box 457, Utopia, TX 78884, offers tent space ($10, with yours, $20 with a Good Shepherd tent), RV sites with full hookups ($15), and apartments ($45). All rates are discounted for stays of two or more nights.

Food
There are a couple of restaurants in the center of town on FM 187. The **Lost Maples Inn** serves breakfasts, sandwiches, and Tex-Mex daily 7:30 a.m.-10 p.m.

Recreation
You can rent inner tubes for floating the Sabinal at the Good Shepherd Campground for $2 a day. The campground also rents canoes for $4 an hour or $10 a day, 10% off if you rent two canoes, 20% off for four canoes.

Another place that rents tubes is **Conrad's Trading Post** at 544 Main (FM 187). About three miles north of Utopia off FM 187 to the east is **Wagon Wheel Riding Stable** (tel. 210-966-3678), which rents horses by the hour.

Getting There
Utopia is located at the junction of FM 187 and FM 1050. From Leakey, it's 24 miles via US 83 south and FM 1050 east. You could also come here directly from Bandera by following FM 470 west (off State 16) through Tarpley for 29 miles till it terminates at FM 187; turn south on FM 197 two miles to Utopia.

Lost Maples State Natural Area
The hundreds of "lost maples" here are leftovers from the Pleistocene epoch when the region was wetter and cooler. High canyon walls along the Sabinal River continue to protect the park's flora from dry winds and high summer temperatures. Other trees in the canyon bottoms include sycamore, various oaks, pecan, hackberry, and walnut. Even more rare than the bigtooth maples are American smoke tree, Canada moonseed, and witch hazel, all of which grow here hundreds of miles from their native habitats. On the densely wooded upper slopes you'll find lacey oak, Texas oak, live oak, Texas ash, and Ashe juniper. Still higher are upland plateaus with mostly live oak and Texas madrone.

Notable birdlife includes canyon wrens, golden-cheeked warblers, black-capped vireos, the green kingfisher, and, in the winter, golden and bald eagles. The 2,208-acre park is also home to three unique amphibians—the rare barking frog, the Texas salamander, and the Texas cliff frog. Animals living in the park include white-tailed deer, armadillo, gray fox, Russian boar, javelina, bobcat, opossum, raccoon, and mountain lion.

Fall Color Changes: The bigtooth maples usually hit their peak colors of brilliant red, yellow, and orange sometime during the last two weeks of October and the first two weeks of November. During this four-week period, it gets quite crowded Saturday and Sunday; if you can, visit the park during the week instead. The timing and brilliance of the color depends on environmental factors such as rainfall and temperature over the previous months. The park maintains a "Maple Hotline" (tel. 800-792-1112, in Texas only) after October 1 that offers a recorded color forecast to help color-crazy visitors time their visits.

Trails: The park has 10.5 miles of hiking trails with elevations between 1,500 and 2,400 feet. Contour maps are available free from park headquarters The most popular hike is the easy Maple Trail (half a mile roundtrip), which starts at the designated picnic area and leads along the Sabinal River through stands of maple, pecan, sycamore, and walnut. If you cross the river (there are stones and shallow places), you can connect with the 4.2-mile (one-way) **East Trail.** This trail proceeds north along the river, then crosses west to Primitive Camping Area A at mile 1.5, then down along a steep ridge to an overlook and along Can Creek back to the overflow parking lot near the visitor center. The **West Trail,** a large, 3.4-mile half-loop between the top of Can Creek and one of the park residences, passes through steep Mystic Canyon. There are three primitive camping areas along this trail, and two more on a 1.8-mile side loop northwest of the trail.

Facilities: The visitor center features interpretive exhibits on local natural and cultural history and is open daily 8:30 a.m.-5 p.m. The main campground has drive-in sites with w/e for $9 a night plus the entry fee. There are also eight primitive camping areas throughout the park near hiking trails; these cost $4 a night. There's a $4 entry fee per vehicle, $1 for pedestrians or cyclists. For further information, contact the Superintendent (tel. 210-966-3413), Lost Maples State Natural Area, HC01, Box 156, Vanderpool, TX 78885.

Getting There: The park entrance is about four miles north of Vanderpool off FM 187. Vanderpool is 17 miles east of Leakey on FM 337.

SAN ANTONIO

San Antonio is every Texan's favorite town. It's also quite popular with out-of-state tourists, over a third of whom make it to Alamo City during their Texas travels, more than any other place in the state. Year in and year out San Antonio tops the list in tourist surveys of best places to visit in Texas. It is also home to four of the state's top 10 attractions—the Alamo, the River Walk, the San Antonio missions, and Sea World. More recently the city made *Condé Nast Traveler* magazine's coveted top 10 lists for both U.S. (ranked number two after San Francisco) and world (number nine) destinations.

If you're the type of traveler who usually avoids hordes of tourists, rest assured this city of nearly a million—10th-largest in the U.S.—absorbs them rather well. With the relaxed attitude of the locals, it's not always easy to tell who's on vacation and who's not.

What makes San Antonio so popular? To be sure, the Alamo is an American pilgrimage point, like the Grand Canyon and the Empire State Building. But most folks find the Alamo a rather puny monument when sized up against their imagination—you'd think word would get around. It's more likely the strong historical and cultural appeal, which led Will Rogers to call San Antonio "one of four unique cities in America" (Boston, New Orleans, and San Francisco were the other three). First and foremost, it's a "Texican" town, a bicultural blend of Old World and New World and the largest city in the U.S. with a Hispanic majority (56%). It's also one of the state's most progressive cities. Things are relaxed; while even in laidback Fort Worth just about every man walking around downtown on a midweek afternoon is wearing a tie, in San Antonio you're more likely to see *guayaberas,* short-sleeved, open-at-the-neck shirts worn in tropical capitals from Mexico City to Manila. Long lunch breaks are common, a custom dating to the pre-air-conditioning era when summer temperatures and humidity mandated a two-hour siesta.

The city's cultural keynote is not the stereotypical *mañana* attitude sometimes associated with Mexico, but rather a social ethic in which people are encouraged to live and work with a festive outlook. It's hard not to be festive in a city that holds fiestas or celebrations of some sort every month of the year. Even going to church can be an occasion for exuberance, if you happen to be attending Mission San José's mariachi mass on Sunday. It's a city that looks as festive as it acts: flower gardens are everywhere, from the barrios of the West Side to the mansions of Alamo Heights. Most of the buildings downtown were built before 1930, many before 1900, producing a historic cityscape that adds to the city's overall visual romanticism.

The Land

San Antone (some locals hate the term "San Antone," but like the nickname "Frisco" for San Francisco, its use predates the lives of current residents—lots of Texans pronounce it "San 'Tone") is uniquely positioned between the Edwards Plateau to the north and the brush country of the Coastal Plains to the south. Hence, it's a mixture of hilly and flat—mostly the latter. The San Antonio River bisects the city along a north-south axis, with a 2.5-mile horseshoe-shaped section that runs through six downtown blocks, developed as the Paseo del Rio or River Walk. Other notable waterways include San

SAN ANTONIO TEMPERATURES		
MONTH	MAX. (° F)	MIN. (° F)
January	62	42
March	72	50
May	85	65
July	94	74
September	89	69
November	70	49

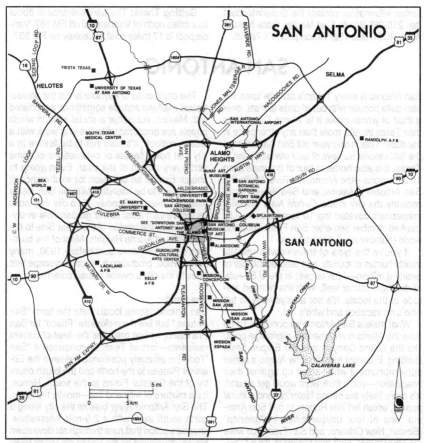

© MOON PUBLICATIONS, INC.

Pedro and Salado creeks, both of which feed into the river.

Climate

With an average relative humidity of 66%—as high as 87% on July mornings—and an average temperature of 60° F, the city borders on subtropical. Optimum months weatherwise are October-November and March through early June. June through September are hot and muggy (Septembers are often rainy), and December-January can be on the cool side, with maybe a week's worth of intermittent freezing weather. Average annual precipitation is 29 inches, with the most frequent rains in May, June, and September—over three inches, on average, in each of these months. Overall, the city has clear skies 60% of the time, from 48% in January to 75% in July.

History

The Founding of the Alamo: Dominga Terán de los Ríos, governor of the Spanish colonial province of Texas, arrived at what's now south San Antonio in 1691 and encountered a hospitable group of Coahuiltecan Indians. They were living on the banks of a river whose curves inspired them to call it "drunken old man going home at night." The date happened to be Saint Anthony's Day, so the governor named the spot San Antonio. Word spread that the Coahuiltecans at San Antonio were "friendly" (i.e., easily dominated), and in 1718 a Franciscan priest established a mission there called San Antonio de Valero (Valero was the viceroy of Mexico at the time). A military contingent founded a presidio at San Antonio that same year and by 1731 a civilian settlement called Villa de Bexar had established itself. In order to boost the non-Indian population at Villa de Bexar, Spain allowed 55 colonists to immigrate here from North Africa's Canary Islands; their modern-day descendants still proudly declare their roots. Four other missions were established in the intervening years—San José, Concepción, San Juan, and Espada.

By 1794, as San Antonio grew and became the capital of Spanish Texas, the heathen-converting function of the missions became less important to the Spaniards. One by one, beginning with San Antonio de Valero, the missions were secularized. By 1801, Misión San Antonio had been turned into a garrison for a cavalry unit from Alamo de Parras in northern Mexico. The name for the place was commonly shortened to Alamo ("cottonwood" in Spanish), a word eventually applied to the garrison as well.

Revolution and Resettlement: Following the Mexican Revolution of 1821, San Antonio became part of the Republic of Mexico. That same year, Stephen F. Austin came to the war-torn town and negotiated a land grant from Mexico which allowed him to bring 300 Anglo-American colonists into Texas. By 1836, San Antonio had an Anglo population of 3,500. When General Antonio López de Santa Anna seized the Mexican presidency and abolished the 1824 Mexican constitution, many Texans, including most Hispanics, refused to recognize his dictatorship. This led to the famous Battle of the Alamo in March 1836 in which every Texan defender was killed. In the midst of the Alamo siege, Texas leaders declared independence from Mexico, which they later won at the Battle of San Jacinto.

Immediately following the Alamo siege, the city was more or less abandoned by non-Hispanics until German settlers began arriving in the 1840s. They established the historic King William district (named for King Wilhelm of Prussia) and erected trilingual street signs in German, English, and Spanish. After the Republic of Texas was annexed to the U.S. in 1845, other groups began moving to San Antonio; the population had grown from 800 to 8,000 by 1860. The Civil War stifled growth again, but in the 1870s the city developed into a ranching center as it became the starting point for the Chisholm Trail cattle drives to Kansas. The railroad arrived in 1877, and within 10 years the city had telephones and electricity.

Economy

San Antonio's military heritage began with the arrival of Spanish conquistadors in 1718 and continued with the occupation of the missions by various Spanish, Mexican, and Texan army

San Antonio Plaza, late 1800s

units. Because it was the crossroads of important north-south (Chisholm Trail) and east-west (San Antonio-El Paso-Chihuahua Trail) trade routes, it was naturally viewed as a strategic area. Fort Sam Houston was founded in 1876 and is still in business. In 1898, Teddy Roosevelt came here to recruit his Rough Riders for the war with Spain in Cuba; he found them in San Antonio saloons and outfitted them at Fort Sam. The U.S. Army post was soon joined by four Air Force bases: Brooks and Kelly in 1917, Randolph in 1930, and Lackland in 1941. Needless to say, these five bases comprise one of the linchpins of San Antonio's economy, bringing in billions in federal funds and creating thousands of jobs.

Another key contributor is tourism, since San Antonio is the number-one tourist destination in the number-two state. The fact that the city wants to preserve its share of tourism explains why it's so anxious to create projects like Sea World and the Alamodome. Education, another legacy of the Spanish missions, is also important. Saint Mary's University (1852), Trinity University (1869), Incarnate Word College (1881), and Our Lady of the Lake College (1911) established the city as an educational center, followed by the University of Texas at San Antonio and eight other institutions of higher learning, including a branch of the University of Mexico, two medical research centers, a theology school, and the largest junior college in the state, San Antonio College. A variety of regional manufacturing interests round out the picture, such as Pace Foods (which buys its chilies directly from the *chileros* of Mexico's Jalapa, as in jalapeño, and is the largest producer of salsas in the U.S) and two Texas beers, Pearl and Lone Star.

Even more so than in the 19th century, the city is a major transportation crossroads. The Chisholm Trail has become I-35, joining Laredo with Kansas City and extending all the way to Duluth, Minnesota on the banks of Lake Superior. The San Antonio-El Paso Trail has been buried by I-10, which now connects the Atlantic (Jacksonville) and Pacific (Los Angeles). One of the biggest interstate loops in the country, Loop 410, keeps tractor trailers from plowing through downtown San Antone. Five other U.S. highways converge on the city as well, which makes for some interesting traffic configurations.

The population within the city limits is currently estimated at 972,000; if measured as a standard metropolitan statistical area the figure rises to 1.3 million.

SIGHTS

San Antonio Missions National Historical Park

San Antonio is the only city in the U.S. with five Spanish missions within its city limits. All were built along the San Antonio River, establishing a pattern around which the modern city developed. The Alamo was the first, established in 1718, but is a separate state historic site. The other four were established as missions between 1720 and 1731, although the stone chapels that stand today were begun in the 1740s and 1750s. Three of the missions, San Juan, Espada, and Concepción, were moved from earlier sites in East Texas because of French and Indian pressures. In East Texas, they attempted to missionize Caddo Indians, who eventually revolted; in San Antonio it was the more docile Coahuiltecans. The fourth, San José, is considered the "queen of the missions" because of its historic success and because it's the most impressive architecturally. All four mission chapels are active Roman Catholic parishes serving the surrounding communities. They're administered cooperatively by the National Park Service, the state of Texas, and the local Catholic archdiocese.

You can visit each of the four missions along a 5.5-mile Mission Trail that runs south of I-10 from the downtown area. If you start from the Alamo, add another 2.5 miles, and follow Alamo St. to S. St. Mary's, which eventually becomes Mission Parkway. All four missions are worth a visit, but if you're pressed for time San José is the most extensively restored and ornate. The historical park also includes a Spanish dam and aqueduct near the San Juan and Espada missions. These 250-year-old waterworks are still a functioning part of the local irrigation system.

The park facilities are open to the public daily 8 a.m.-5 p.m. central standard time and 9 a.m.-6 p.m. central daylight saving time. Admission is free, but donations are gratefully accepted in the chapels.

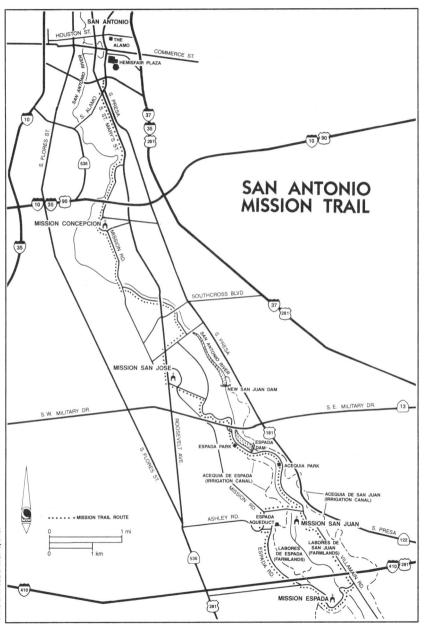

Worship services are held on Sunday morning and religious holidays, so these times may not be the best for visits unless you would like to attend a service. For further information, contact the Superintendent (tel. 210-229-5701), San Antonio Missions National Historical Park, 2202 Roosevelt Ave., San Antonio, TX 78210.

Mission Concepción: Established as Misión Nuestra Señora de la Purísima Concepción de Acuña in 1731, this is the oldest unrestored stone Catholic church in the country. One reason it's so well preserved is that it was constructed on bedrock, so the earth's movements have had little effect on the building. The chapel design includes the typical twin bell towers and cupola, with simple, carved-stone embellishments around the doorway. Some of the original interior frescoes remain. In the front of the chapel is an original *noria* (well). By 1772, the church, *convento* (convent), *labores* (farmlands), and ranch at Mission Concepción were self-sufficient. Between 1794 and 1824, the mission underwent secularization but in 1855 the Catholic Church regained the mission. On the first Sunday in August the mission holds a **parish festival** featuring Latino music, food vendors, and other festivities. The mission is at 807 Mission Rd. at Felisa (tel. 210-532-3158).

Mission San José: Founded in 1720, two years after the Alamo, by Fray Antonio Margil de Jesús as Misión San José y San Miguel de Aguayo, this important Texas mission settlement was moved along the San Antonio River several times before settling at its present site in 1740. The chapel/sacristy was designed and built between 1768 and 1782 in the Churrigueresque, late Spanish Renaissance style and is considered one of the finest examples of Spanish mission architecture in the United States. When Spain sent Fray Juan Augustín Morfi on a tour of frontier missions in 1777, he reported: "[San José] is in truth the first mission in America, not in point of time, but in point of beauty, plan, and strength, so that there is not a presidio along the entire frontier line that can compare with it."

Today, it is the most well restored of the San Antonio missions and serves as headquarters for the entire historical park. The surrounding compound has been restored so that visitors may view the Indian quarters, granary, mill,

Mission San Juan

kilns, *convento,* and Spanish residence. An *horno*—a small dome-shaped oven made of tufa limestone—stands in the courtyard. The mission-dwellers burned wood inside until the oven was hot, then the coals were raked out, food inserted, and the *horno* sealed until the food was cooked.

The chapel's asymmetrical front features a bell tower on one side and a flat-topped, ventilated facade on the other. In the middle of the lengthy roof behind is a large dome which makes that section of the church taller than the building's entire length. The lavishly sculptured entryway is said to have been carved by descendants of the original artisans at Spain's Alcazar. On the south side of the building, in the sacristy, is "Rosa's Window," bordered by stone scrolls and foliage that have made it a San Antonio mission highlight. At least two stories offer an explanation for the window's name: that the sculptor worked on it for five years while mourning the death of his wife Rosa, or that it was somehow associated with St. Rose's Day.

The Park Service has established several interpretive exhibits in parts of the Indian quarters near the main entrance to the complex, including a six-minute audiovisual presentation on the mission's history. At noon on Sunday, there is mariachi mass at the church. Annual events at Mission San José include El Día de las Misiones on August 6, which commemorates the founding of the mission and kicks off the Semana de las Misiones, a weeklong celebration at all five of San Antonio's missions. At 2200 Roosevelt Ave. and Mission Rd. (tel. 229-4770).

Mission San Juan: This outpost is thought to have been established at or near the spot that was first claimed as San Antonio by the Spanish in 1691. Originally called Misión San Juan Capistrano (est. 1731), it was smaller than either Concepción or San José. For the first few years it consisted only of a friary and granary. In 1756, a small church was built, which has since been reduced to its foundation; a larger church was started on adjacent grounds in the 1760s (these ruins are also still visible) but was never completed before secularization began in 1792. The current church is actually a former granary that was transformed by the addition of Moorish arches in the early 1900s, when the Catholic diocese regained the parish. Inside and out, the building is quite simple; altars inside display rare Christ and Virgin figures of cornstalk pith.

The *convento* is today a small museum with good exhibits on mission archaeology and the Coahuiltecan Indians. Much of San Juan's charm is its location in a quiet, relatively rural area. A daily mass is performed at 7 p.m. San Juan holds its **parish festival** on the last Sunday in May (Memorial Day weekend), beginning with an outdoor mass. At 9101 Graf Rd. (tel. 532-5840).

Mission Espada: The most remote of the five missions, Misión San Francisco de la Espada is still encircled by *labores* (farmlands) owned by descendants of the original mission community. Like San Juan and Concepción, the Espada missionaries had moved from an earlier site in East Texas, in this case the oldest of the three, San Francisco de los Tejas (established 1690). The original adobe church no longer stands. A larger limestone church, begun in 1756, was never finished, though the sacristy for this larger structure was completed and became part of the current church in the late 1800s. Double-tiered Moorish arches support three bells over the church's simple stone facade. The interior is well cared for, and the St. Francis figure at the front is believed to date from the 1780 completion of the original sacristy.

Mission Espada was falling apart by 1858, when Franciscan Father Francois Bouchu moved into the mission and began a painstaking restoration that lasted 40 years. Father Bouchu restored the chapel and added the current choir

*interior of
Mission Espada*

loft, wooden floor, and pews. His renovations continued up until a week before his death.

Next to the chapel is a *noria* similar to the one at Mission Concepción. The restored *convento* is closed to the public since it's now the church rectory. The Park Service information center is at the southeast corner of the compound in rooms adjoining the only remaining bastion. Various other walls and ruins encircle the courtyard. Espada's **parish festival** is held in late September or early October. At 10040 Espada Rd. (tel. 627-2021).

Espada Aqueduct: Between 1719 and 1740, the Spanish constructed a sophisticated *acequia* for irrigating cultivated lands around San Antonio. Espada Dam, part of the system and the oldest existing dam in the U.S., is unique in that it slants downstream toward the stream's flow. Much of the system is still in use to the south of the city and there are even a few *acequias* or canals remaining in downtown San Antonio. Of the several engineering feats the mis-

sionaries accomplished, perhaps the most impressive is the aqueduct built over Piedras Creek, about a mile and a half northwest of Mission Espada. This arched stone structure has carried water over the creek to Espada fields by force of gravity for two and a half centuries, making it the oldest Spanish water system in the country. In 1965 it was declared a national historic landmark, and the small **Aqueduct Park,** now a favorite local picnic spot, was laid out next to it.

The Alamo State Historic Site

This big chunk of limestone in the middle of downtown San Antonio has become a national icon, symbolic of America's one-time frontier spirit and a willingness to die for independence. How many died here in the Battle of the Alamo is still a matter of debate but the figure on the defenders' side was probably 187 or 188 (including 10 Hispanics), who fought a Mexican force of 5,000, around 1,600 of whom were also slain in

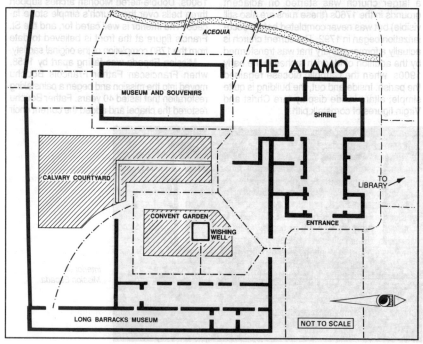

THE SECOND BATTLE OF THE ALAMO

Recently the Daughters of the Republic of Texas, a society of women who claim to be descendants of Texans who defended the Alamo during the infamous 1836 siege, has come under unrelenting attack for the society's overall administration of the Alamo Historical Site and more specifically for the history lessons it presents. Recent painstaking research, for example, shows the DRT's official list of Alamo heroes contains as many as 40 names that should be removed. And a building erected as a convent is labeled the "long barracks" simply because it functioned as such during the 12-day (or was it 13?) siege.

Different interest groups resent different aspects of the DRT's "official history" but all agree that using the Alamo to commemorate one particular battle—and recognize only one point of view on that battle—reduces rather than enhances the Alamo's ultimate historical significance. Some groups would like to see the Alamo restored to its original mission shape, much like the four missions to the south along the Mission Trail; others would have Amerindian burial grounds beneath Alamo Plaza uncovered and memorialized; still others would be

satisfied to halt commercial exploitation in the immediate vicinity (two hamburger chains, a couple of entertainment complexes, and the Hyatt garage stand on the block opposite the chapel). The DRT has so far resisted all revisionist proposals, pointing out quite correctly that if it hadn't been for their stewardship, the monument would never have been preserved in the first place.

For the most part the city is unanimous in recognizing the importance of the Alamo as a city and state symbol, and as a major tourist draw. A series of San Antonio Express-News articles published in 1994 presented the many issues involved and proposed an elegant solution in which the area surrounding the complex would be transformed into a city park presenting all historical phases of the mission. Such a solution would require a compromise between the divergent interests fighting for their respective turfs, including the DRT and commercial developers on the fringe of the Alamo Plaza. The latter have the most to lose from any Alamo expansion that affects the plaza, unless the city or state can provide satisfactory financial compensation.

the heated battle. Alamo lore remains a sacred subject among a very small group of Texans who haven't yet figured out Texas is no longer a republic. One fellow has even fueled the fire by publishing the provocatively titled *Forget the Alamo!* which, despite its title, is a perfect example of the subculture.

History: What tends to get lost, even among the site's historical exhibits, is the history of the Alamo as Misión San Antonio de Valero, its original name. Had it not been for the founding of this mission in 1718, the city of San Antonio wouldn't exist. The Spaniards established San Antonio as a halfway point between northern Mexico and their short-lived East Texas missions (the route they plied became known as El Camino Real, "the Royal Road," which Anglo settlers later called the Old San Antonio Road). The mission started out on the San Antonio River's west bank, at its junction with San Pedro Creek, but was moved upriver to its current site in the 1720s. The chapel made famous by countless postcards was erected in 1744. By

the mid-1700s, it was a thriving mission community with *acequia*-irrigated farmlands, a cattle ranch, granary, chapel, and *convento*, as well as blacksmith, carpenter, and textile shops. As the Texas missions began declining in the late 18th century because of problems with migrating Apaches, the Catholic Church secularized Mission San Antonio and distributed the farmlands among the mission Indians. The church leased the abandoned mission grounds and buildings to a Spanish cavalry unit from northern Mexico's Alamo de Parras in the early 1800s, and the compound gained the nickname "El Alamo."

The famous Alamo fight took place in 1836; afterwards the Alamo was again abandoned. Beginning in 1845, a succession of other tenants leased the buildings from the Catholic Church, including the U.S. Army, the Confederate army, and a couple of mercantile interests who used the chapel as a warehouse. The state bought the chapel from the Catholic Church in 1883. In 1903 the Daughters of the Republic of Texas (DRT) bought the "long barracks" (originally a *convento*), and the state turned over the remainder of the property to the DRT shortly thereafter.

Exhibits and Facilities: The heavily restored chapel and convent—labeled "Long Barracks" by the DRT—are the only buildings remaining from the original mission compound. The Museum/Souvenir Shop, the DRT Research Library, the walls, and other limestone structures on the grounds are 20th-century additions carefully designed to blend with the original architecture. The grounds are well kept and flower-filled in the spring; behind the chapel you can see the original San Antonio *acequia.*

The modest displays in the chapel itself are mostly oriented around the 1836 battle, including a miniature three-dimensional model of the compound as it looked at the time. The information desk at the front distributes self-guiding tour pamphlets, or you can take one of the free 30-minute tours that leave periodically. The DRT has removed the large, tacky painting from the north interior wall which featured Davy Crockett swinging his flintlock at a mob of Mexican soldiers—the figure's face was unmistakably John Wayne's.

Tourist traffic through the chapel is channeled so you end up leaving by a rear door to the left, where a path leads directly to the Museum/Souvenir Shop. Unfortunately, this means many visitors miss the Long Barracks Museum, which is well to the left of the exit, against the front wall of the compound. In this latter museum are two automated slide shows, one on the battle, one on the mission's overall history. The remainder of the exhibits are again battle-oriented. In the Museum/Souvenir Shop are exhibits of Sam Houston memorabilia, an early gun collection, and piles of Alamo souvenirs, from imitation coonskin caps to Remember The Alamo bumper stickers. And of course a dozen or more versions of Alamo postcards.

Visitors sometimes have trouble finding the Alamo among all the taller buildings which surrounding it; it's on Alamo St. between E. Houston and E. Crockett, on Alamo Plaza. Admission to the complex is free. Hours are Mon.-Sat. 9 a.m.-5:30 p.m., Sunday 10 a.m.-5:30 p.m. Go just after it opens or just before it closes to avoid the crowds. Sunday is usually less crowded, since fewer conventions are in town that day. For further information call (210) 225-1391.

SAMA Museums

The **San Antonio Museum Association** operates two museums; paying the admission fee ($4 adults, $2 seniors, $1.75 children 4-11) to either one grants the purchaser a 50% discount on admission to the other. The hours for each are the same: Mon.-Sat. 10 a.m.-5 p.m. (till 6 p.m. June-August), Sunday noon-5 p.m. On Tuesday they're open till 9 and admission is free 3-9.

The Association's **San Antonio Museum of Art** (tel. 210-829-7262) is housed in a former Anheuser-Busch brewery at 200 W. Jones, off Broadway, and has only been open since 1983. There are nine galleries total in the tastefully renovated building, four in each of two towers plus one in the hall that connects them. The museum is strong in Latin American art as well as folk art from a variety of cultures. Permanent collections include the excellent pre-Columbian and Spanish Colonial exhibit, which features sculpture and ceramics from the Colima, Nayarit, Jalisco, Olmec, and Mayan cultures. The equally splendid Mexican Folk Art gallery contains 2,500 pieces from the Nelson Rockefeller Collection as well as 2,000-2,500 other pieces collected by SAMA.

Another gallery displays ancient Greco-Roman art, including rare Greek urns and sculpture from the 3rd-5th centuries B.C. The Asian art gallery has a fairly standard collection of ceramics, sculpture, jewelry, and painting, as do the historical American and European galleries. Remaining galleries contain rotating displays of contemporary American art and other traveling exhibits. The museum also hosts various lecture series; SAMA's Friends of Folk Art organization, for example, presents lectures on topics such as "Tradition and Symbolism of Indian Textiles in Guatemala,""Caribbean Folk Art and Festivals,"and "Indigenous Arts of Rural India."

The **Witte Museum** (tel. 978-8100) in Brackenridge Park off Broadway has long been popular among children—some of the exhibits invite visitor participation, with an emphasis on science and natural history. An exhibit called "Texas Wild: Ecology Illustrated" explores the state's ecological diversity. Another exhibit is devoted to the dinosaurs that once roamed the Texas plains, while a third chronicles the daily life of the Southwest's Archaic Indians of 8,000 years ago.

Other Museums and Galleries

The **Marion Koogler McNay Art Museum** (tel. 210-824-5368) is at 6000 N. New Braunfels in the upscale northeast section of the city. A blend of Mediterranean and Southwest architectural styles, the building, courtyard, and gardens of the McNay make up one of the most pleasant art facilities in the Southwest, with 10 galleries and 10,200 square feet of support space in all. Formerly the residence of oil heir Marion McNay, it opened as an art museum in 1954 and houses a variety of collections. The Oppenheimer Collection includes medieval and Gothic wood and stone sculptures, stained glass, tapestries, and panel paintings. In other collections, the emphasis is on modern European and American paintings of the late 19th and early 20th centuries, with works by Monet, Gauguin, Van Gogh, Klee, Degas, Pissarro, Matisse, Renoir, Cézanne, O'Keeffe, and Picasso, as well as the graphic art of Toulouse-Lautrec, Goya, Jasper Johns, Willem de Kooning, and Robert Rauschenberg. The Tobin Collection of Theater Arts displays rare books and sketches on theater architecture, set and costume designs, and stage models.

The McNay also offers a year round calendar of activities, including receptions, teas, musical performances, lectures, and art classes (as part of the museum's San Antonio Art Institute). Open Tues.-Sat. 10 a.m.-5 p.m., Sunday noon-5 p.m.; admission is free, with donations accepted.

The University of Texas sponsors the **Institute of Texan Cultures** (tel. 226-7651) at 801 S. Bowie in HemisFair Park. The Institute is a center for the study of some 25 different cultural groups who've contributed to Texan history. Besides the research facilities, there are several galleries with revolving exhibits, so it's worth revisiting if you've been here before. The *Faces and Places of Texas* film presentation in the Dome Theater offers a good multicultural overview. Occasional special presentations by visiting experts on Texas culture include slide shows and lectures. A gift shop features a wide selection of books on Texana as well as folk crafts. In August the Institute sponsors the four-day Texas Folklife Festival. The galleries and gift shop are open Tues.-Sun. 9 a.m.-5 p.m.; free admission, with parking $2 a day.

The **Mexican Cultural Institute (Instituto Cultural Mexicano)** (tel. 227-0123), also at HemisFair Plaza, is sponsored by the University of Mexico and is devoted to Mexican history and culture. The galleries host traveling art exhibits, films, lectures, workshops, and concerts. Gallery hours are Tues.-Fri. 9 a.m.-5:30 p.m., Sat.-Sun. 11 a.m.-5 p.m. Free admission.

The **Hertzberg Circus Collection** (tel. 299-7810), housed in an art deco-style former public library at 210 W. Market, is a unique museum devoted to the circus world. The centerpiece of the exhibit is a miniature model of a traditional three-ring circus, complete with big top, side show, animal stables, and dining tents. There are over 20,000 other pieces of circus memorabilia on display, including circus posters and literature, costumes, and various rarities such as an 1843 carriage built for 40-inch Tom Thumb. A hands-on area for children offers experiments in changing facial expressions through masks, mirrors, and computers. Traveling exhibits have included such themes as "The Folk Art of Tattooing." From Memorial Day through Labor Day, the museum is open Mon.-Sat. 9 a.m.-5 p.m., Sunday and holidays 1-5 p.m.; the remainder of the year it's open Mon.-Sat. 9 a.m.-5 p.m. only. Admission runs $2 for ages 13-63, $1 ages 3-12.

The **Blue Star Arts Complex,** at the south end of the River Walk just beyond the King William Historic District (1400 block of S. Alamo), brings together a number of small art galleries, studios, and performance spaces under the aegis of a loosely organized, nonprofit artists collective. The artist-operated, retail-oriented **Milagros Contemporary Art, Martin-Rathburn Gallery,** and **Primary Object Gallery** display rotating exhibits of contemporary, regional art. One complex objective is to involve the local community through a strong hands-on, educational component. Open to the public Wed.-Sun. noon-6 p.m.

Paseo del Rio (River Walk)

One of the biggest tourist attractions in San Antonio, the River Walk is a set of cobblestone and flagstone paths extending for 21 blocks (2.8 miles) along the San Antonio River from the Municipal Auditorium on the north end to the King William Historic District at the south. The river itself is below street level, so one descends

*Paseo del Rio,
the River Walk*

LA MANSIÓN DEL RÍO HOTEL

stone stairways at various intersections to arrive on the paths. Designed by local architect Robert Hugman under an urban park plan called "The Shops of Aragon and Romula," the River Walk's entwining paths, 35 bridges, and 31 stairways were built by WPA crews between 1935 and 1941. Following completion, the area lay all but neglected until the 1968 HemisFair, when the city allowed commercial development.

Today the River Walk or Paseo del Rio is the center of downtown life. The city maintains a selection of lush flora along the river, including 75 species of trees (predominantly the native bald cypress, pond cypress, and crepe myrtle), subtropical plants, and flowers. Scenic arched bridges span the river at intervals. A variety of indoor/outdoor restaurants, cafes, bars, hotels, boutiques, and the Rivercenter shopping mall now line the River Walk. Barges (for groups) and river taxis (for individuals) carry visitors up and down the river—there are even nighttime dinner cruises on the flat-bottomed boats. Where the river curves by La Villita, the Arneson River Theater features live theatrical and musical performances during the warmer months. The River Walk is also an important focus for many of the city's festivals. The latest development along the River Walk is a project called South Bank, three side-by-side buildings designed in late 1800s period style that contain dining and entertainment establishments including Hard Rock Cafe, Fat Tuesday's, Starbuck's, County Line Barbecue, Paesano's, and Planet Hollywood.

In spite of the groomed look of the River Walk, the San Antonio River is a natural, spring-fed, dirt-bottom river (except for the horseshoe extension along the River Walk with a concrete channel) that starts just outside the city limits and flows 180 miles to the Guadalupe River near the Gulf Coast. Chief tributaries include the Medina River and Cibolo Creek. Every year following New Year's Day, the River Walk area is drained for general cleaning. To keep the River Walk tourist traffic from grinding to a halt, the city sponsors a Mud Festival in celebration of the empty riverbed.

See "Getting There and Around," below, for details on charter boats, tour boats, and river shuttle services.

La Villita National Historic District
"The Little Town" developed as a Spanish squatters' settlement along the east bank of the San Antonio River, next to the original Mission San Antonio de Valero, in the mid- to late 18th century. In the mid-19th century, Anglo and European immigrants began arriving, La Villita's adobe huts were replaced by sturdier limestone buildings, and the district became the town center. In the

PASEO DEL RIO WALKING TOUR

This route begins at the Fourth Street Bridge at the north end of the River Walk and ends at the King William Historic District, a distance of about 2.5 miles. Along the way you'll observe aspects of the San Antonio River that most visitors—who tend to limit themselves to the short east end of the horseshoe bend between Crockett and Villita—have never seen. Even at a slow pace, this walk is easily accomplished in 45 minutes if you can manage to run the gauntlet of restaurants and cafes without stopping for a drink or a bite to eat. An hour or so before sunset is probably the best time of day, since most businesses along the river are open, people are getting off work, and the general mood is festive.

Addresses refer to street level entrances.

Fourth St. Bridge: Thirty-five different bridges span the San Antonio River along the River Walk. The U.S. cavalry tested the predecessor to this 1926 bridge by filling it with mounted horses.

Richmond St. Bridge: Look for the fine multi-hued tilework along the railings.

Southwest Craft Center, at 300 Augusta: A unique example of French frontier architecture, built as a convent girls school in 1851.

Augusta St. Bridge: Constructed in 1890 by the Berlin Bridge and Iron Works of East Berlin, Connecticut, this is one of only three original iron-and-wood bridges left in the city. Stand below the bridge to watch how it flexes as vehicles pass over.

Milam Building, at 115 E. Travis: Built in 1928, this art deco skyscraper became the world's first air-conditioned high-rise. At one time every big oil company in Texas kept an office here; today the building's Milam Diner perfectly preserves 1950s linoleum-and-vinyl Americana.

Texas Theater, at 175 E. Houston: A cornerstone of the 1928 Southwestern Bell Corporation Headquarters building, the splendid Southwest Deco facade of this defunct theater was saved from wrecking crews by San Antonio mayor Henry Cisneros in 1981.

Houston St. Bridge: The four colorful lampposts on this span were added during the 1980s—each post features handpainted tilework commemorating one of the four missions along San Antonio's Mission Trail. At this point the river's concrete bottom begins, and the waterway deepens from two feet (at Fourth St. Bridge) to 22 feet.

Ben Milam Cypress Tree: On the river's left bank, just around the bend from the Holiday Inn, stands the River Walk's oldest tree. Named for a Texan killed during the Bexar Siege of 1835, the old cypress concealed a Mexican sniper who reportedly shot Milam while he stood on the opposite bank in front of Veramendi House. The latter belonged to James Bowie's father-in-law, the vice governor of Coahuila y Texas.

Floodgate No. 3: The original River Walk architect, Robert Hugman, designed this floodgate to tame the waters of the San Antonio River and produce the horseshoe bend that now serves as the River Walk's main tourist center. Before a system of flood control was established, the downtown area was regularly inundated with high water during the rainier months.

The Esquire Bar, at 155 E. Commerce: The only bar on the river that doesn't openly cater to the tourist trade, The Esquire was founded in 1933 and continues to bring in a loyal, if somewhat rough-and-tumble, local clientele. The original 76-foot wooden bar still stands.

La Mansión del Río, at 112 College: The river's oldest and most distinctive hotel. (See "Accommodations" for more.) Opposite La Mansión, the new South Bank complex houses two major dining/entertainment attractions, **Hard Rock Cafe** and **Planet Hollywood.**

Nix Medical Center, at 414 Navarro: This 24-story, 1929-vintage building boasts the city's finest terracotta, gargoyle-studded facade.

Riverside Building, at 517 N. Presa: The Argonne Hotel occupied this building when it opened in 1929, and the first Luby's Cafeteria (now a statewide chain) occupied a ground floor location 1946-1979. On the river level, **The Bayous Restaurant** serves good Creole-style seafood.

Hyatt Regency, at 123 Losoya: Designed by renowned local architect O'Neil Ford in 1979, the 16-story Hyatt encloses one of the nation's largest atrium lobbies. The hotel's public thoroughfare, Paseo del Alamo, provides a quick shortcut from the River Walk to the Alamo. On the river level, **The Landing** is the Southwest's top venue for traditional jazz. Cornetist Jim Cullum first opened The Landing at a nearby site in 1963, when the only other business on the river was Casa Rio Mexican Restaurant; it's been a smash success ever since. The music starts

(CONTINUED ON NEXT PAGE)

PASEO DEL RIO WALKING TOUR (CONT.)

at 9 p.m. nightly. Four or five Saturday evening performances per year are broadcast live via KSTX-FM 89.1 radio and syndicated on 150 radio stations throughout the country.

Restaurant Row: This section of the River Walk between Crockett and Commerce street bridges is lined on both sides with restaurants and cafes. Best of the lot: Rio Rio Cantina (Mexican), Paesano's (Italian), Boudro's (Southwest/Gulf Crescent), and Zuni Grill (nouvelle Texan).

Clifford Building, 423 E. Commerce: A classic example of turn-of-the-century San Antonio architecture, this four-story Richardson Romanesque building opened in 1893 and serves as one of the area's most distinctive landmarks due to the powerful tower design facing E. Commerce Street. The architect was James Reily Gordon, a noted designer of Texas county courthouses. River Walk visionary Robert Hugman maintained his architectural offices here during the WPA project; look for the plaque honoring him as "Father of the River." Today the building is occupied by the Royalty Coin Shop.

Commerce St. Bridge: San Antonio's first bridge, made of wood, spanned the river here in 1736. An iron bridge that replaced it in 1880 has been moved to Johnson St. in the King William Historic District. Before it was moved, a sign on the bridge read Walk Your Horse Over This Bridge, Or You Will Be Fined, in English, German, and Spanish.

HemisFair Extension: This artificial eastern section of the river was added in 1968 to allow boat traffic to reach the HemisFair. Portugal presented the statue of **San Antonio de Padua,** the city's patron saint, on the extension's left bank. The canal also provides access to the **Rivercenter Mall** shopping complex and two Marriott hotels.

Hilton Palacio del Rio Hotel, 200 S. Alamo: Built for the 1968 HemisFair, this 21-story, 500-room hotel was the first modularly constructed hotel in the world. Guestrooms were assembled in a factory south of the city and transported by truck to the building site, where a crane lifted them floor by floor; a huge fan fashioned from helicopter blades

blew the rooms into their proper positions.

Arneson River Theater: Part of the original WPA project, this ingeniously designed amphitheater uses the San Antonio River to separate the stone-and-grass seating area from the stage. The five mission-style bells over the stage were installed during a 1978 ceremony honoring architect Robert Hugman for his River Walk design. After being fired by the city in 1940 because he wouldn't hire a friend of the mayor's, Hugman worked in relative obscurity at Randolph Air Force Base until the early '70s. The nearby 1890-built Presa St. Bridge is the city's oldest iron bridge still in its original location.

La Villita: San Antonio mission soldiers lived here in the 1700s. Restored in 1939 by the WPA, the cobbled village is now a touristy complex of shops.

Bowen's Island: A Philadelphian named John Bowen built a farm on this small peninsula in 1845 after living seven years in Venezuela. Before flood controls were established, the peninsula became an island during high water periods. Up at street level on St. Mary's St. is the 1928-vintage, art deco **Tower Life Building,** where Dwight D. Eisenhower once served as commanding officer for the U.S. 3rd Army.

Old San Antonio Public Library: The former library's most unique feature is the basement marina where barges and river patrol boats dock. The river's horseshoe bend ends ahead; turn left to continue to the end of the walking tour.

King William Historic District: The river stretch between the end of the horseshoe bend and plush King William Historic District is relatively quiet and undeveloped except for a couple of bed and breakfast establishments. See "Sights" for a complete description of the district.

Blue Star Arts Complex, 116 Blue Star: By this point the river is four times as wide as when you started out at the Fourth St. Bridge. The BSAC, a group of warehouses occupied by a nonprofit artists collective since 1986, hosts art workshops, artist studios, a performance theater, and small galleries with changing art exhibits.

---

early 20th century, it declined into a virtual slum until artists and other "bohemian" elements moved in during the '40s and '50s and renovated the old structures. As often happens when artists take up residence and make improvements in a

low-rent area, the city decided it would make a good tourist attraction; following a major renovation in the early '80s, it became a showcase for middle-of-the-road artists and craftspeople. Many of the crafts now come from Mexico and

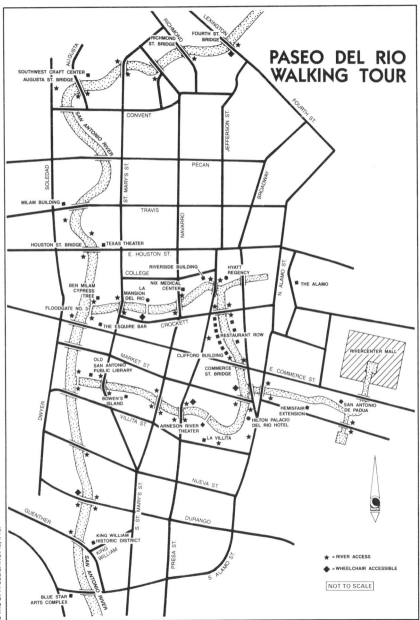

PASEO DEL RIO
WALKING TOUR

★ = RIVER ACCESS

◆ = WHEELCHAIR ACCESSIBLE

NOT TO SCALE

© MOON PUBLICATIONS, INC.

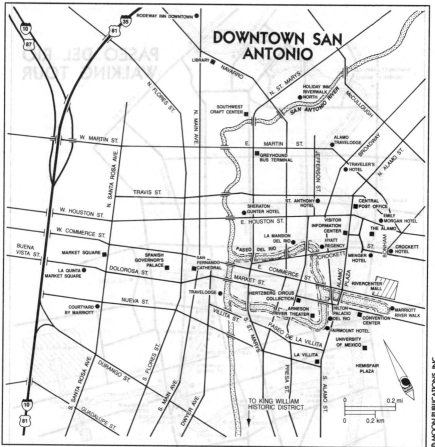

DOWNTOWN SAN ANTONIO

Central America, including pottery, weavings, jewelry, and clothing.

Among the small district's historic attractions are the 19th-century "Little Church," a frequently chosen site for wedding ceremonies, and the Arneson River Theater. Several festivals schedule all or part of their customary events at La Villita.

Market Square

West of the downtown area at Commerce and San Saba, just off I-35, this restored market plaza is surrounded by buildings that date from as early as 1840. A farmer's market, Mexican restaurants, and a large Mexican-style market building—the largest outside Mexico—have made this another important tourist attraction. The **Centro de Artes del Mercado,** housed in a renovated 1922 building on the square, offers art exhibits as well as music and dance performances; it also serves as a meeting place for civic and social functions. The city plans to use the Centro to house permanent art and historical exhibits in the future.

Overlooking Market Square is a statue of St. Cecilia, the patron saint of musicians, and there's always live Mexican music somewhere in the square. During the summer, music and dance performances are usually presented around noon in the center of the square (Mariachi

Plaza). Mi Tierra Café and Bakery usually features a few *trovadores* (singing guitarists) strolling around the restaurant, and twice a year (August and November) the square is the site of a Trovadores Festival that draws wandering Mexican guitarists from near and far.

San Fernando Cathedral

Canary Islanders laid the original cornerstone for the nation's oldest cathedral in 1738, completing the cathedral in time for a visit by the Bishop of Guadalajara 20 years later. At the time, the domed, mission-style structure could be seen from miles around and the city was called Villa de San Fernando in honor of the church's patron saint. Most of the original church was replaced—stone by stone, brick by brick—with a larger Gothic-style cathedral in 1872, without an interruption in services. Remnants of the original sanctuary walls stand behind the altar.

Hallmarks of the handsome interior include an interment of Alamo defenders in the inside left alcove and a votive altar beneath a black Christ (a replica of a renowned 1595 figure in Esquipulas, Guatemala) flanked by photos of people whose prayers have been answered. The cathedral is still attended by descendants of the original Canary Islander parish, along with other San Antonio Catholics, who were honored with a papal visit in September 1987. Every March 8 a special mass commemorates the 1731 arrival of the islanders.

The cathedral dome serves as the city's geographical center, from whence all distances to and from the city are measured. At 115 Main Plaza.

St. Joseph's Catholic Church

Often referred to as "St. Joske's" because it was flanked by Joske's department store (now Dillard's), this church was built by the German community in 1868. The male choir group San Antonio Liederkranz sings German music during mass on the last Sunday of every month.

Spanish Governor's Palace

This simple building (tel. 210-224-0601), built in 1749 as a residence for the Spanish governor of Texas province, is one of the most evocative of all colonial structures still standing in San Antonio. The San Antonio Conservation Society has lovingly restored the building and fitted it with period furnishings. The fountain and foliage in the garden patio, at the back of the house, make a welcome oasis from summer heat. Open Mon.-Sat. 9 a.m.-5 p.m., Sunday 10 a.m.-5 p.m.; admission is $1 adults, 50 cents children 7-13.

Southwest Craft Center (Ursuline Academy)

This complex of mid-19th-century, French-designed, limestone-and-rammed-earth buildings at 300 Augusta at Navarro once housed the first girls school in San Antonio, the Ursuline Academy (now in a different location). Founded by Catholic nuns in 1847, the Gothic-style convent, courtyards, and school buildings are now owned by the **Southwest Craft Center** (tel. 210-224-1848), which offers a variety of arts and crafts classes (woodworking, pottery, weaving), workshops, exhibits (two galleries, one for visiting artists and one for staff and students), and the Copper Kitchen restaurant (open Mon.-Fri. for lunch). There are usually a few artists or craftspersons working on the premises; crafts are for sale as well. Open Mon.-Sat. 10 a.m.-4 p.m.; free admission.

Attached to the center are the serene **Convent Gardens.** At the garden's souheast corner, the acoustically perfect **Elizabeth Huth Maddox Chapel** features original cypress woodwork and stained glass. Chapel and garden are a popular site for weddings.

San Antonio Public Library

Prominent Mexican architect Ricardo Legorreta designed San Antonio's vibrant new downtown library, a striking stack of interlocking cubes, grids, and spheres that opened to the public in May 1995. The six-story building's deep terracotta hue was designated "enchilada red" in a *San Antonio Express-News* name-that-color contest. It contrasts boldly with the limestone whites and granite grays of the surrounding downtown buildings.

With a capacity of 750,000 volumes, collection space measures ten times that of the old library, which is now used for city offices. A new computer cataloging system provides remote access from home computers. Other features include an indoor-outdoor children's area, media center, retail shop, and restaurant. The library's Texana collection preserves materials dating to the era of the Texas Republic in a special room floored with oiled mesquite blocks.

The new library also promises to become a significant contemporary art venue. For the south foyer famed San Antonio muralist Jesse Treviño painted a 36-foot by 10-foot fresco depicting a downtown San Antonio street scene circa the 1940s. Patrons enter the library through a western foyer filled with blue neon light, an art installation designed by New York artist Stephen Antonakos to provide a transition from bustling street life to the tranquility of the library.

At 600 Soledad St. at Navarro; open Mon.-Thurs. 9 a.m.-9 p.m., Fri.-Sat. 9 a.m.-5 p.m., Sun. 1-5 p.m.

King William Historic District

German settlers established this 25-block district on the east bank of the river (now south of downtown) in the late 1800s and named it after Prussia's King Wilhelm I. At the time it was the most elegant neighborhood in San Antonio. Over the years it decayed, but many of the distinctive homes built between the 1850s and 1920s in the Victorian, Creole Colonial, and Richardson Romanesque styles have been restored to their former glory. King William St. itself has the most striking set of homes—the media often describe it as the most beautiful residential street in the state.

The highly active San Antonio Conservation Society (tel. 210-224-6163) has its headquarters at 107 King William; staff distribute a free brochure map describing a walking tour of the district. The society bought and renovated one house now open to the public: the **Steves Home** (tel. 225-5924) at 509 King William. The restoration includes period furnishings and a period kitchen. Open daily 10 a.m.-5 p.m.; admission is $2 adults, free for children under 12. Look also for **Kalteyer House** at 425 King William St., one of the only surviving residential structures created by James Reily Gordon, a noted designer of Texas county courthouses.

San Antonio Zoological Gardens and Aquarium

This widely acclaimed zoo (tel. 210-734-7183) is nicely situated among the rock cliffs of an old limestone quarry in Brackenridge Park, off Broadway and Hildebrand north of downtown. The zoo was established in 1929, and some of the exhibits, like the Barless Bear Pits, have served well ever since; other sections have been upgraded and expanded. There are now over 3,600 animals from over 670 species on 50 acres of well-kept grounds. The setting and weather must agree with the animals here, since the zoo has a national reputation for captive breeding; it was the first to hatch a flamingo and the first to deliver a white rhino. The impressive bird collection exhibits everything from penguins to an endangered whooping crane, and the African antelope collection is one of the most extensive in the world. The cat exhibit includes

Steves Home

the rare jaguarundi, a feline species native to South Texas, Mexico, and Central America. The monkey and ape collection is also outstanding. The Children's Zoo features a boat ride past an Everglades exhibit, a petting zoo, and an educational Rain Forest exhibit. Camera loans are available at the zoo entrance. Open daily 9:30 a.m.-5 p.m., summer till 6:30 p.m. Admission is $6 adults, $4 children 3-11 and seniors.

Alamodome

Built at a cost of $187 million, financed by a half-cent city sales tax, and opened in May 1993, this impressive monument to sports and entertainment technology adds a huge, mosque-like profile to San Antonio's city skyline. A short walk from downtown, the 18-acre Alamodome can seat up to 77,000 for 24 kinds of events, from trade shows to Superbowls and, of course, home games for the San Antonio Spurs basketball team. Four 400-foot masts contain a bridge cabling system which supports the 175-foot-tall, nine-acre dome roof. Beneath the dome lie two permanent ice-skating rinks, 12,000 retractable seats, and 16,000 square feet of exhibit space.

Informative guided tours of the facility leave daily from the Alamodome's south entrance at 10 a.m., 1 p.m., and 3 p.m., except when pre-empted by dome events. The tours last about 45 minutes and cost $3. The Alamodome is located just off I-37 on Montana Street; call (210) 207-3663 for further information.

Westside

Although San Antonio's largest Hispanic neighborhoods are found in both the west and south sides of the city, "Westside" is considered the city's Hispanic cultural heart. One of the largest Hispanic art institutes in the country, the **Guadalupe Cultural Arts Center** (tel. 210-271-3151), at 1300 Guadalupe northwest of downtown, focuses on Chicano art. Besides changing visual art exhibits, the center offers art classes, films, and music and dance performances. One of the highlights of the yearly calendar is the Tejano Conjunto Festival.

Also on Guadalupe, near the Guadalupe Cultural Arts Center, is a public market that has taken over the functions formerly provided to the Hispanic community by Market Square. Several other food and handicraft shops in the vicinity are contributing to a slow cultural renaissance in the neighborhood under the auspices of the **Avenida Guadalupe Association** (tel. 223-3151), 1327 Guadalupe Road.

The **Union Stockyards** (tel. 223-6331) between San Marcos and Brazos about 10 blocks south of Guadalupe (next to the intersection of two railway lines) have been in business since 1889. A system of catwalks over the feed lots allows visitors an opportunity to view penned livestock from above. Visitors are also welcome in the auction house, where animals are bought and sold every Monday and Wednesday beginning at 9 a.m. The restaurant in the Livestock Exchange Building serves very inexpensive breakfasts and lunches Mon.-Saturday.

Off Zarzamora St. near the Laredo St. intersection, the **Produce Terminal** processes and wholesales around $75-100 million worth of fruits and vegetables from around the country each year. You can walk around the terminal as long as you don't enter the processing areas; some companies sell produce to the public, but usually by the box only.

Breweries

Four breweries in San Antonio produce beer for local and regional consumption. Neither of the city's two largest breweries, Lone Star and Pearl, gives tours anymore, but each has a visitors center where you may buy items emblazoned with beer logos. Lone Star Brewery also features the **Buckhorn Hall of Horns, Fins, and Feathers** (tel. 210-270-9467) at 600 Lone Star Blvd. downtown. The original Buckhorn Bar was an elegant saloon built in 1881 and distinguished by its collections of animal horns and antlers. This collection was expanded and later moved to the Hall of Horns, which now displays over 3,500 specimens of horned game animal trophies from all over the globe. The Hall of Fins and Hall of Feathers contain—what else—fish and bird trophies. Buckhorn Hall is supposedly the second-most-visited attraction in the city after the Alamo. Adjacent to the hall stands the **O. Henry House,** a two-room stone cottage where the famous short-story writer once resided. Open daily 9:30 a.m.-5 p.m.; admission is $4 adults, $3.50 seniors and military, $1.75 children 6-11. Complimentary beer served in the replica Buckhorn Bar.

Founded by a German brewmaster in 1886, **Pearl Brewery** (tel. 226-0231) stands north of downtown at 312 Pearl Pkwy. and Ave. A—you can't miss the towering yellow Victorian.

The city's first—and the state's smallest—microbrewery is **Yellow Rose Brewery** (tel. 210-496-6669) at 17201 San Pedro Avenue. Yellow Rose produces three Engish-style ales (Honcho Grande Brown Ale, Cactus Queen Ale, Yellow Rose Pale Ale), a lager (Bubba Dog Beer), a porter (Vigilante), and a stout (Wildcatter's Crude). Tours are available by appointment only the first and third Saturdays of each month.

Frio Brewery (tel. 210-225-8222) makes and bottles crisp, hoppy Frio Lager at 1905 N. St. Mary's. Tours of the facility and beer tastings are available Mon.-Fri. 9 a.m.-6 p.m.

Sea World of Texas

This is the largest of the four Sea Worlds in the U.S. and one of San Antonio's top tourist spots. The 250-acre park (tel. 210-523-3611) is 16 miles northwest of the city center off State 151, between Loop 1604 and Loop 410 West. The central attraction is Shamu Stadium, the largest facility for the presentation of marine animals in the world, with 4,500 seats and seven million gallons of water. Killer whales Shamu, Namu, Kandu, and the 1988-born Baby Shamu thrill audiences here with their aquabatic skills, while the smaller New Friends Stadium presents four other species of dolphins and whales.

Other venues feature trick waterskiing; a penguin exhibit in a simulated Antarctic environment, complete with snow; a 450,000-gallon shark tank; and a 300,000-gallon Indo-Pacific reef aquarium. The 12-acre Cypress Gardens offers paths winding through a display of native Texas flora; *doncellas,* young women in traditional Spanish gowns, are stationed amid the gardens to answer questions and pose for pictures. The usual assortment of restaurants, ice-cream parlors, and gift shops (with Shamu caps and T-shirts) are on hand, plus a four-acre playground with a nautical theme and a carnival midway. Recent additions include the Texas Splashdown, a six-minute flume ride; Rio Loco, a simulation of Central Texas river tubing; and the five-acre Lost Lagoon, complete with sand beach and gently rolling waves—perfect for cooling off during summer visits. Open daily at 10 a.m.,

Shamu and son steal the show

with closing hours varying from 6 to 10 p.m. depending on the time of year. Admission is $25.95 adults, $17.95 children 3-11, seniors $22.06; group discounts, two-day passes, and season passes available; tax is not included

Sea World has a downtown information center across from the Alamo that offers a free film preview of the park, a miniature 3-D model of the layout, and information on express buses to the park.

Getting There: VIA Metro bus no. 63, Sea World Express, goes directly to Sea World from downtown San Antonio. If you're driving, take Loop 410 to the Hwy. 151 W exit and follow the signs; from downtown, take US 90 west to the Hwy. 151 W exit. There's a fee for parking.

Fiesta Texas

Opened in 1992, this unique theme park joins Sea World as one of the San Antonio area's top attractions. The 200-acre facility, partially surrounded by the 100-foot cliffs of a former limestone quarry, contains five Texas theme areas, each offering an array of musical entertainment, rides, and food. **Los Festivales** represents the state's Hispanic heritage and features two performance venues, the 2,000-seat, air-conditioned Zaragoza Theater, with Mexican folkloric performances and the *Heart of Texas* historic show; and the 746-seat, open-air Teatro Fiesta, featuring *conjunto* and *tejano* music. A large restaurant and a couple of cafes serve Mexican and Tex-Mex foods.

A Western theme dominates **Crackaxle Canyon,** constructed to resemble a 1920s Texas boomtown and featuring 4,000-seat Lonestar Lil's, hosting a choreographed music/ dance production based on the West Texas oil-boom era; and the 1,500-seat Sundance Theater, with country music and comedy performances. This section of the park also contains what has become Fiesta Texas's biggest draw, The Rattler—the world's tallest (180 feet, six inches), fastest (73 mph top speed), and steepest (61.4-degree angle on the first drop) wooden rollercoaster. The Rattler winds 5,080 feet over and *through* the natural limestone canyon surrounding the park. In 1993, following complaints from riders who found the rollercoaster "too intimidating and aggressive," Fiesta Texas tamed The Rattler somewhat by altering the length of the first drop. But take my word for it, this is still one terrifying ride. Crackaxle Canyon also features the Gully Washer, a simulated whitewater rapids

tube ride, and the Ol' Waterin' Hole, a complex of other water rides, slides, and pools. Old Blues Bar-B-Que offers West Texas-style barbecue ribs, chicken, brisket, steaks, and sausage with the usual accompaniments.

The theme of the Rockville section of the park is 1950s-era small-town Texas. So far the park's favorite musical show seems to be the 45-minute Broadway-style musical performed in the realistic, 1,000-seat Rockville High School auditorium. Called *Rockin' at Rockville High,* the performance weaves a humorous storyline around a collection of top-10 '50s teen anthems. Rockabilly and '50-60s oldies bands play at a smaller open-air theater next door. Rides in Rockville include the Power Surge, in which a large boat plunges down a 100-foot waterfall to a tremendous splashdown at the bottom, and the Motorama, a track with scaled-down, electric-powered models of classic '50s American cars, complete with car radios playing vintage rock 'n' roll.

The fourth theme section is the German-inspired **Spassburg** ("Fun Town"), centered around the 1,000-seat Sangerfest Halle. This combination beer garden, theater, and restaurant presents a menu of German specialties along with live tuba, accordion, and German choir ensembles. The rides at Spassburg are tamer than those in the rest of the park and include an early 1900s-style German carousel, a Bavarian swing ride, and various other mild thrills mostly oriented towards children.

The Rattler,
Fiesta Texas

Added in 1994, the new Fiesta Bay Boardwalk section features a 90-foot Ferris wheel, miniature golf, bumper cars, arcade games, and other attractions reminiscent of a 1950s beach town.

Depending on the time of year, Fiesta Texas opens at 10 a.m., 2 p.m., or 4 p.m. and closes after sunset following a spectacular laser and fireworks show. Admission prices, not including 8.25% sales tax, are $24.95 for ages 12-54, $17.95 for ages 4-11 and over 55. USAA members are offered a $5 discount on admission rates at a special ticket window near the entrance. Discounted group and two-day passes are available to the general public. For further information call (210) 697-5050 or (800) 473-4378.

Getting There: Take I-10 west from downtown San Antonio and go north at Loop 1604 (exit 555).

Splashtown

This 18-acre water park offers a dozen aquatic amusement rides, from the slow-paced Siesta del Rio, which approximates a lazy river rafting experience, to StarFlight, which pitches riders through a fast, double-tube configuration ending in a pool. Surfriders can enjoy the largest wave pool in South Texas. Open June-Aug. daily 11 a.m.-9 p.m., May and September weekends only; admission $14 for adults, $11 for children under four feet tall, seniors over 65 and children under three admitted free. Call (210) 227-1400 for further information.

Splashtown is off I-35 north of downtown at 3600 North Pan Am Expressway.

Fort Sam Houston

Commonly called "Fort Sam," this military base founded in 1876 today serves as headquarters for the 5th U.S. Army. Brooke Army Medical Center, famed for its state-of-the-art burn treatment center, is one of the world's largest military medical facilities. The post's Academy of Health Sciences supervises all U.S. Army medical training nationwide.

The "Quadrangle," a park-like square that dates to Fort Sam's original founding, is worth visiting to see the small, free-running menagerie of white-tailed deer, ducks, rabbits, geese, and exotic varieties of chickens. Fort Sam Houston Museum, housed in Building 123, contains exhibits chronicling the history of the fort; it's open Wed.-Sun. 10 a.m.-4 p.m. and admission is free. At Grayson St. and New Braunfels Ave. (tel. 210-536-2203).

Universities

San Antonio boasts 11 colleges and universities, 12 if you count the Health Science Center separately. The **University of Texas at San Antonio** (tel. 210-691-4011) has an enrollment of 13,000 in Bachelor's and Master's degree programs in liberal arts, fine arts, and engineering on a 600-acre campus northwest of town (Loop 1604). The UT Health Science Center (tel. 210-567-7000), nearby at 7703 Floyd Curl, enrolls around 2,300 students in medical, dental, nursing, biomedical sciences, and allied health sciences.

Trinity University (tel. 736-7011), on Stadium and Hildebrand near Brackenridge Park, was founded by the Presbyterian Church in 1869. It is one of the city's most attractive universities, situated on a hill overlooking San Antonio. It's small (3,000 students) and expensive, with a fair academic reputation—education and communications are among its strongest departments. The tennis team has won several national championships; the university hosts the Houston Oilers training camp each summer.

San Antonio boasts four Catholic universities and colleges. **St. Mary's University** (tel. 436-3011) at Camino Santa Maria and Cincinnati is the city's oldest, founded by the French order Society of Mary in 1853. The school has an enrollment of about 3,200 and is known most for its law and business programs. Dwight Eisenhower coached football here in 1916. The other Catholic university is **Our Lady of the Lake University** (tel. 434-6711) at 411 S.W. 24th at Commerce. Founded in 1911, OLLU emphasizes programs for lower-income students and Hispanics. Enrollment is around 1,700. The Sacred Heart Chapel on campus, built in 1896, is a splendid structure of carved wood, marble, gold leaf, and stained glass. Smaller Catholic institutions include **Incarnate Word College** (tel. 829-6000), at 4301 Broadway; **Oblate School of Theology** (tel. 341-1366), 285 Oblate Dr.; and **St. Philip's College** (tel. 531-3200), 1801 Martin Luther King.

The largest institute of higher education in the city is **San Antonio College** (tel. 734-7311), which also happens to be the largest two-year college in Texas, with an enrollment of 22,000. Its urban campus, at San Pedro and Dewey just north of downtown, was established in 1925. The college **planetarium** (tel. 733-2910) offers free shows on Sunday at 5, 6:30, and 8 p.m. Also on campus is the **Koehler Cultural Center,** a Victorian built by Pearl brewmaster Otto Koehler that now features art and cultural exhibits and is jointly administered by the San Antonio Art League. The **Autonomous National University of Mexico** (tel. 222-8626) has a small branch at 600 HemisFair Park. It serves mainly as a Mexican cultural center (no degree programs here); courses offered include four levels of Spanish as well as Latin American art, history, and anthropology. The Spanish courses are offered on a regular semester basis or as summer intensives, and all instructors are from Mexico.

ACCOMMODATIONS

Hotels and Motels

The city has a range of places to stay to fit any budget. Most are clustered in four areas: downtown, off N.E. Loop 410, near the airport, and off N.W. Loop 410. There are also a few places west of the city near Sea World and Lackland AFB. Downtown hotels are the most expensive, but are within walking distance of the River Walk, the Alamo, La Villita, Market Square, and other attractions.

Historic Hotels: San Antonio has more open and operating historic hotels than any other city in Texas. The oldest is the **Menger Hotel,** built by brewer W.A. Menger in 1859 to serve the surrounding trade district; at the time, it was said to be one of the finest hostelries west of the Mississippi. Famous guests have included short-story writer O. Henry, poet Sidney Lanier, Ulysses S. Grant, General Robert E. Lee, Dwight D. Eisenhower, Oscar Wilde, Sarah Bernhardt, Mae West, and Teddy Roosevelt. The original limestone and ironwork edifice still stands next to the Alamo and offers period rooms as well as newer rooms in the "motor hotel" addition. The old Rotunda lobby is worth a visit even if you're not staying here. Likewise for the Menger Bar, sometimes called the Roosevelt Bar, which was originally built as a replica

of a pub in London's House of Lords. Teddy Roosevelt is supposed to have recruited some portion of his Rough Riders at this bar for the Spanish-American War.

The **St. Anthony** at 300 E. Travis was erected in 1909 and certainly gave the Menger a run for its money as one of the best hotels of its time in the Southwest. Now owned by Hong Kong's Park Lane Hotels International, it has been completely restored and remains a favorite among hotel patrons who wouldn't dream of staying at a chain hotel. No two rooms here are alike. Another well-renovated 1909 hotel is the **Sheraton Gunter Hotel** at 205 E. Houston. Blues legend Robert Johnson recorded 16 songs for Paramount's Vocalion label in one of the Gunter's original rooms in November 1936. The Sheraton group is the current owner and has made the Gunter one of the city's top-drawer places to stay, with lots of wood and brass in the public areas.

Yet a third place built in 1909 is the **Crockett Hotel** at Bonham and Crockett. Similar on the outside to other buildings made of native stone, the inside is decorated in a tasteful, modern Southwest style rather than in period style. Best Western now manages the hotel.

In 1910, rooms at the **Fairmount Hotel** were 75 cents a night. In 1985, investors moved the building from its original location on E. Commerce to S. Alamo; now rooms are 200 times the original tariff. It's listed in the *Guinness Book of World Records* under "world's largest building move"—it took six days to move the Italianate Victorian structure six blocks, using 38 specially designed hydraulic dollies. Another venerated San Antonio hotel is **La Mansión del Río,** housed in a multi-story, mission-style edifice on the river, with a street entrance on College between Navarro and St. Mary's as well as a river entry. The core building was originally constructed in 1852 as a Catholic boys school, which later became St. Mary's College and then St. Mary's University of Law. Since 1967, when it was transformed into a hotel, it has had the same owner—unusual in the fast-paced world of hotel deals in which Sheraton, Radisson, and Hyatt swap luxury properties with regularity. Because of its location on a quiet, out-of-the-way corner of the River Walk, La Mansión is a favorite among visiting entertainers and dignitaries.

SAN ANTONIO HOTELS AND MOTELS

Add 13% hotel tax to all rates. Area code: 210.

DOWNTOWN

Alamo Inn Motel; 2203 E. Commerce; tel. 227-2203; $35-45; close to Alamodome

Alamo Travelodge; 405 Broadway; tel. 222-9401 or (800) 578-7878; $60-110; close to Municipal Auditorium, north end of River Walk

Best Western Crockett Hotel; 320 Bonham; tel. 225-6500 or (800) 528-1234; $85-140; historic, pool, weekly rates

Elmira Motor Inn; 1126 E. Elmira; 222-9463 or (800) 584-0800; $33; close to N. St. Mary's club district

Fairmount Hotel; 401 S. Alamo; tel. 224-8800; $145-185; health club privileges, famous restaurant (Polo's)

Hilton Palacio del Rio; 200 S. Alamo; tel. 222-1400; $163-215; on River Walk, some rooms with river views, pool, refrigerator

Holiday Inn Market Square; 318 W. Durango; tel. 225-3211; $73-103; pool, coin laundry

Holiday Inn River Walk; 217 N. St. Mary's; tel. 224-2500; $125-135; heated pool

Hyatt Regency; 123 Losoya; tel. 222-1234; $125-190; River Walk, some rooms with views, pool, weekend discount

La Mansión del Río; 112 College; tel. 225-2581 or (800) 531-7208; $190-260; River Walk, many rooms with views, pool, refrigerator, weekend discount

La Quinta Motor Inn Convention Center; 1001 E. Commerce; tel. 222-9181 or (800) 531-5900; $85-95; opposite HemisFair Park, pool

La Quinta Motor Inn Market Square; 900 Dolorosa; tel. 271-0001 or (800) 531-5900; $76-83; pool

Marriott Rivercenter; 101 Bowie; tel. 223-1000 or (800) 228-9290; $160-180; heated pool, saunas

Marriott River Walk; 711 E. River Walk; tel. 224-4555 or (800) 228-9290; $130-170; many rooms with views, heated pool, saunas

Menger Hotel; 204 Alamo Plaza; tel. 223-4361 or (800) 345-9285; $122-138; historic, next to the Alamo, pool, spa, fitness center

Motel 6 Downtown; 211 N. Pecos; tel. 225-1111; $38-44; near Market Square, pool

Navarro Hotel; 116 Navarro; tel. 224-0255; $25-40

Plaza San Antonio Hotel; 555 S. Alamo; tel. 229-1000; $160-180; heated pool, saunas, tennis courts, weekly rates

Ramada Emily Morgan at Alamo Plaza; 705 E. Houston; tel. 225-8486 or (800) 824-6674; $89-99; historic, near Alamo, heated pool, saunas, refrigerator on request

Rodeway Inn Downtown; 900 N. Main; tel. 223-2951; $82-88; pool

Rodeway Inn Laredo St.; 1500 I-35 S (at Laredo); tel. 271-3334; $82-88; pool, airport shuttle, free shuttle to Market Square

St. Anthony Hotel; 300 E. Travis; tel. 227-4392 or (800) 338-1338; $124-144; historic, heated pool, airport shuttle

Sheraton Gunter Hotel; 205 E. Houston; tel. 227-4392 or (800) 222-4276; $130-155; historic, heated pool

TraveLodge on the River; 100 Villita; tel. 226-2271; $109-119; on River Walk, some rooms with views, pool

Traveler's Hotel; 220 N. Broadway; tel. 226-4381; $22-46; near Alamo and River Walk, weekly and monthly rates available

NORTHWEST

Amerisuites Fiesta Park; 10950 Laureate (off US 281 N); tel. 342-4800; $79-89; 1 bedroom suites with kitchenettes, pool, coin laundry, airport shuttle

Fontana Motel; 3414 Fredericksburg Rd.; tel. 736-4444; $35-40

Holiday Inn Northwest; 3233 N.W. Loop 410 (I-10 Junction); tel. 377-3900 or (800) HOLIDAY; $92-105; pool, health club privileges, coin laundry, airport shuttle

Hyatt Regency Hill Country Resort; 9800 Hyatt Resort Dr. (off State 151 between Loop 410 and Loop 1604, close to Sea World); tel. 647-1234 or (800) 233-1234; $145-220; regional architecture; wooded setting, health club, four-acre water park with waterfalls, swimming pools, and tubing, tennis courts, 18-hole golf course, cycling and jogging paths, airport shuttle, package rates available

La Quinta Motor Inn/Vance Jackson; 5922 . N.W. Expressway (Vance Jackson exit); tel. 734-7931 or (800) 531-5900; $52-72; pool, senior discount

La Quinta Motor Inn/Wurzbach; 9542 I-10 W (Wurzbach Exit); tel. 690-8810 or (800) 531-5900; $56-80; pool, senior discount

Lexington Hotel Suites; 4934 N.W. Loop 410 (exit 13B); tel. 680-3351; $59-79; suites, pool, coin laundry, airport shuttle

Motel 6/Northwest; 9400 Wurzbach; tel. 593-0013; $36 plus $6 each additional person; pool

Oak Hills Motor Inn; 7401 Wurzbach; tel. 696-9900 or (800) 468-3507; $65-75; opposite S. Texas Medical Center, pool, airport shuttle

San Pedro Motor Hotel; 6231 San Pedro; tel. 340-2238; $20-30

Siesta Motel; 4441 Fredericksburg; tel. 733-7154; $29-37; pool, weekly rates

Wyndham Hotel San Antonio; 9821 Colonnade (off I-10 Wurzbach exit); tel. 691-8888; $139-160; heated pool, sauna, airport shuttle

NORTHEAST

Aloha Motel; 1435 Austin Hwy.; tel. 828-0933; $35-42, $45-85; one- and two-bedroom units with full kitchens; pool, coin laundry, weekly and monthly rates, senior discount, airport shuttle

Best Western Continental Inn; 9735 I-35 N (exit 166/167A); tel. 655-3510 or (800) 528-1234; $44-70; pool, coin laundry

Chevy Chase Apartments; 1422 N.E. Loop 410; tel. 828-2801; $35; kitchens

Days Inn Northeast; 3433 I-35 N (Coliseum exit); tel. 225-4521 or (800) 325-2525; $50-60; pool, weekly rates

Holiday Inn/Northeast; 3855 N. Pan American Expressway; tel. 226-4361 or (800) HOLIDAY; $60-66; pool, coin laundry, senior discount

Motel 6; 9503 I-35 N (exit 167); tel. 650-4419; $36 plus $6 each additional person; pool

Oak Motor Lodge; 150 Humphreys off Broadway and US 81; tel. 826-6368; $28-50; pool, kitchen on request (add $5), weekly rates

Silver Dollar; 1125 Austin Hwy.; tel. 826-3859; $26-45

Skyline Motel; 1401 Austin Hwy.; tel. 824-2305; $40-50

AIRPORT

Best Western Town House Motel; 942 N.E. Loop 410 (Broadway exit); tel. 826-6311; $49-56; pool, airport shuttle

Courtyard by Marriott Airport; 8615 Broadway; tel. 828-7200 or (800) 321-2211; $72-82; pool, coin laundry, airport shuttle, senior discount

Drury Inn Airport; 143 N.E. Loop 410 (airport exit); tel. 366-4300 or (800) 325-8300; $66-83; pool, coin laundry, airport shuttle, complimentary evening beverage

Embassy Suites Hotel/Airport; 10110 US 281 N (Jones Maltsberger exit); tel. 525-9999 or (800) EMBASSY; $149-169; refrigerator, suites, heated pool, sauna, airport shuttle, monthly rates, complimentary beverage

Hilton/Airport; 611 N.W. Loop 410 (San Pedro exit); tel. 340-6060 or (800) 333-3333; $109-135; heated pool, saunas, health club privileges, airport shuttle

Holiday Inn/Airport; 77 N.E. Loop 410 (airport exit); tel. 349-9900 or (800) HOLIDAY; $95-145; pool, coin laundry, airport shuttle, senior discount

La Quinta Motor Inn/Airport East; 333 N.E. Loop 410 (airport exit); tel. 828-0781 or (800) 531-5900; $63-80; pool, airport shuttle, senior discount

Ramada Hotel Airport; 1111 N.E. Loop 410 (Nacogdoches exit); tel. 828-9031 or (800) 288-9031; $59-95; (seasonal) pool, health club privileges, airport shuttle

Sheraton Fiesta San Antonio; 37 N.E. Loop 410 (McCullough exit); tel. 366-2424 or (800) 325-3535; $115-155; suites, pool, airport shuttle, senior discount

WEST/SOUTH

Best Western Lackland Lodge; 6815 State 90 W (1.5 miles east of Loop 410); tel. 675-9690; $50-57; pool

Casa Manana Hotel; 6500 Old US 90; tel. 674-1511; $25-50

Commerce Inn Motel; 2607 W. Commerce; tel. 212-6319; $23-30

Dunes Motel West; 6301 Old US 90; tel. 673-1616; $30-35

El Camino Hotel; 6543 Old US 90; tel. 674-7760; $25-50

La Quinta Motor Inn/Ingram Park; 7134 N.W. Loop 410 (Culebra exit); tel. 680-8883 or (800) 531-5900; $54-78; pool, senior discount

La Quinta Motor Inn/Lackland; 6511 Military W; tel. 674-3200 or (800) 531-5900; $53-64; heated pool

(CONTINUED ON NEXT PAGE)

**SAN ANTONIO
HOTELS AND MOTELS (CONT.)**

La Quinta Motor Inn South; 7202 I-35 and S.W. Military; tel. 922-2111; $52-68; pool

Mission Inn; 3760 Roosevelt; tel. 923-2361; $30-52

Motel 6; 2185 S.W. Loop 410 (exit 7); tel. 673-9020; $36 plus $6 each additional person; near Sea World and Fiesta Park, pool

Travelers Inn; 6861 US 90 W at Military; tel. 675-4120 or (800) 433-8300; $32-42; pool, senior discount

---

Budget Hotels: Two downtown hotels within walking distance of the Alamo, the River Walk, and other sights provide simple but secure rooms in the $25-50 range: **Navarro Hotel** at 116 Navarro (tel. 210-224-0255), and **Traveler's Hotel** at 220 N. Broadway, (tel. 226-4381).

For complete addresses, phone numbers, and room rates, see the "San Antonio Hotels and Motels" chart.

Bed and Breakfasts

At last count, the city had around 25 publicly listed bed and breakfast inns with rates varying from $50 to $140 a night. King William Historic District has the greatest concentration of B&Bs by far, with 17, and is within a two-mile River Walk stroll of most downtown attractions. If you're traveling with children or pets, be sure to ask whether they're permitted before making a reservation.

The Royal Swan (tel. 210-223-3776), 236 Madison, is a turn-of-the-century King William Victorian with an antebellum interior and five rooms with private baths and TV for $80-125 a night including full breakfasts. One of the showpieces of King William B&Bs is the 1857 **Oge House** (tel. 223-2353 or 800-242-2770), 209 Washington St., where 10 rooms filled with fine antiques go for $125-195. Another one high on the list of the district's best B&Bs is the **San Antonio Yellow Rose** (tel. 229-9903), 229 Madison, with three often-booked rooms furnished with antiques for $85-125 including full breakfast.

One of the less expensive King William spots is Victorian-style **Gatlin House** (tel. 223-6618),

123 Cedar St., where three antique-furnished rooms with private porches cost $50-75 a night with full breakfast.

Near Fort Sam Houston, **Terrell Castle Bed & Breakfast** (tel. 271-9145), 950 E. Grayson, offers 26 rooms in a large, turreted, 1894 Richardson Revival-style mansion designed by Alfred Giles for a former U.S. ambassador to Belgium. Spacious rooms cost $75-85 a night including a full breakfast served till noon. Other registered San Antonio B&Bs include **Adams House** (tel. 224-4791 or 800-666-4810), 231 Adams St., $70-75; **Beauregard House** (tel. 222-1198), 215 Beauregard, $75-95; **Beckman Inn and Carriage House** (tel. 229-1449 or 800-945-1449), 222 E. Guenther, $80-120; **Bed & Breakfast on the River** (tel. 225-6333), 129 Woodward, $99-139; **Belle of Monte Vista** (tel. 732-4006), 505 Belknap Place, $50-60; **Brookhaven Manor** (tel. 733-3939 or 800-851-3555), 128 W. Mistletoe, $65-85; **Cash's Cottage** (tel. 227-5773), 206 Madison, $60-80; **Chabot-Reed House** (tel. 223-8697), 403 Madison, $125; **Classic Charms** (tel. 272-7171 or 800-209-7171), 302 King William, $65-95; **Falling Pines** (tel. 733-1998), 300 W. French Place, $67-97; **Joske House** (tel. 271-0706), 241 King William, $75-95; **La Posada Marquesa** (tel. 490-3135), 201 N. St. Mary's, $125-150; **Linden House** (tel. 224-8902), 315 Howard, $54-68; **Norton Brackenridge House** (tel. 271-3442 or 800-221-1412), 230 Madison, $75-95; **Pancoast Carriage House** (tel. 225-4045), 102 Turner St., $90-115; **River Haus** (tel. 225-7555), 107 Woodward Place, $99; **Summit Haus I & II** (tel. 736-6272), 427 W. Summit, $58-150; **Victorian Lady Inn** (tel. 224-2524), 421 Howard, $80-90. These and other B&Bs can be booked through **Bed & Breakfast Hosts of San Antonio** (tel. 824-8036), 166 Rockhill, San Antonio, TX 78209.

AYH Hostel

The **Bullis House Inn/San Antonio International Hostel** (tel. 210-223-9426), P.O. Box 8059, San Antonio, TX 78208, is located opposite Fort Sam Houston at 621 Pierce Street. The historic, Greek Revival-style mansion was built in 1906-09 for General John L. Bullis, a former Union army officer who came to Texas after the Civil War to serve in the Indian Wars and led the famous Seminole Indian Scouts of

DAN NOLAN

Bullis House Inn

Brackettville. The house is divided into two sections, a bed and breakfast inn and gender-segregated hostel dormitories. Rooms in the B&B section vary, depending on room size, from $41 for a single with breakfast and shared bath to $69 for a large double with private bath and breakfast. Extra people in a room are $10 with breakfast, $6 without.

Dorm beds are $12.62 for AYH members, $15.62 for nonmembers; weekly rates (members only) are $70 per person. Private rooms are also available for $30-51. Facilities include a swimming pool, rental linens, kitchen lockers, baggage storage, and on-site parking. Reservations suggested July-August.

Bus no. 11 and no. 15 run from near the Bullis House to downtown San Antonio (Houston St.). To get here by car, take the New Braunfels/Fort Sam Houston exit off I-35 N, then drive New Braunfels St. north to Grayson and make a left (west), then another left (south) on Pierce Street.

Campgrounds and RV Parks

Northeast of the airport at Jones-Maltsberger and Buckhorn, the 856-acre **McAllister Park** (tel. 210-821-3000) has a tent-camping area that's $6 a night on weekdays, $12 on weekends.

The camping/RV facility nearest to downtown San Antonio is **Dixie Campground** (tel. 337-6501 or 800-759-5267, CB channel 4) at 1011 Gembler Rd.—go three miles east of downtown

on I-35, then a half mile south on Coliseum to Gembler, then follow the signs. Shaded tentsites cost $12, full hookups are $15, and cabins go for $14.95 s, $28.75 d. Facilities include pool, jacuzzi, camp store, and nearby city bus service. **San Antonio KOA Kampground** (tel. 224-9296 or 800-833-KAMP) is nearby at 602 Gembler Rd. KOA is next to a small lake and Salado Creek, so there's fishing and other water recreation, plus a heated pool and 18-hole golf course. Tent/camper sites are $13.75 a night; add $2 for w/e. Full hookups are $18.75 a night for two adults, plus $2 for each additional adult. Cabins are available for $26-37.

Travelers World RV Park (tel. 532-8310) is at 2617 Roosevelt Ave., three miles south of the city off Military Dr., then another mile or so on Roosevelt. RV sites are $18 a night for two, plus $1 per person for additional adults. Weekly and monthly rates available.

Large, 240-site **Admiralty Park** (tel. 800-999-7872) lies west of the city near Sea World and Fiesta Texas at 1485 N. Ellison Dr. (Military Dr. exit off Loop 410). RV sites are $15.50 a night plus $2 for additional adults; four-day, weekly, and monthly rates available. Admiralty Park provides free shuttle service to Sea World. Other services and facilities include a/c, laundry room, store, large pool, and free movies. Also near Sea World is the 184-site **Tejas Valley RV Park & Campground** (tel. 679-7715 or 800-729-7275) at 13080 Portranco Rd. (FM 1957,

2.3 miles off Loop 1604). Rates start at $16 a day for full hookups; among the facilities are a laundry room, recreation hall, restaurant, pool, and store.

Greentree Village North RV Park (tel. 655-3331) is about 12 miles north of the city off I-35 at the 12015 O'Conner Rd. (O'Conner Rd. exit). RV/camper sites cost $15 for two persons, plus $1 for each additional adult, $17 for full hookups. Weekly and monthly rates available.

FOOD

Ever since the chili queens served bowls of red on the streets of 19th-century San Antonio, the city has been regarded as something of a culinary adventureland. Restaurants here tend to be more moderately priced than in Dallas and Houston, so gastronomic experiments needn't eat up your savings. More restaurants here seem to be open on Sunday, too. A lot of the better restaurants are north of the city center on and off Broadway. The River Walk establishments aren't known for culinary excellence since the steady flow of tourists and conventioneers assures a profit for any restaurateur who can get space there, but in recent years the overall quality has improved. Local connoisseurs agree that The Bayous, Boudro's, Zuni Grill, Paisano's, and Rio Rio Cantina are the best River Walk eateries. These and several other riverside restaurants can arrange barge dinner cruises along the river with a few days notice; there's usually a minimum group size but occasionally there's extra room for small groups.

Does San Antonio have the best Mexican food in Texas? Maybe—at the very least, it has the largest number and largest variety of Mexican and Tex-Mex places of any city in the state. A bit of trivia: Fritos were invented here in 1942.

American/Texan

$ Alamo Cafe: Among the most popular restaurants in San Antonio and recently ranked fifth statewide by *Texas Highways* readers, the two Alamo Cafes offer state-of-the-art Tex-Mex food (all tortillas made on the premises), chicken-fried steak, huge salads, creative desserts (especially good are coffee-flavored flan and lime margarita pie), and reasonable prices. At

9714 San Pedro (tel. 210-341-4526) and 10060 I-10 W (tel. 691-8827). Both locations are open daily for lunch and dinner.

$$ to $$$ BIGA: Another original by San Antonio's premier chef, ex-Londoner Bruce Auden (who earned his national reputation in the Fairmount Hotel's kitchens), this casual, moderate-to-expensive restaurant serves such creations as poblano bisque, sautéed soft-shell crab with cilantro lime on angel hair pasta, and oak-fired pizza topped with spicy chicken, basil, and fontina cheese. The menu changes daily but perennials include onion rings served with habanero ketchup and Debra Auden's "rustic breads." The restaurant's name comes from the sourdough starter used in many of the baked-on-the-premises breads and pastries; Auden grows most of the herbs used in the kitchen in an adjacent garden. At 206 E. Locust, in an old house on the corner of Locust and McCullough St. (tel. 225-0722), at the edge of the Monte Vista Historical District; open Tues.-Fri. for lunch and dinner, Monday and Saturday for dinner only.

$$ LocuStreet Bakery: In the back of the same building, open Mon.-Sat. (tel. 225-0723), sells muffins, scones, cookies, and other pastries, along with coffees, teas, and juice, from 7 a.m. till sellout and breads from 11 a.m. till sellout.

$$ Cappy's: A renovated lumber warehouse. Serves everything from salad and seafood to burgers, including a few low-fat, low-cholesterol dishes. At 5011 Broadway (tel. 828-9669); open daily for lunch and dinner.

$ to $$ Earl Abel's: A classic, day-and-night American eatery with fried chicken, steak and fries, and other meat-and-potatoes fare. At Broadway and Hildebrand (tel. 822-3358); open 6:30 a.m. to 1 a.m. daily.

$$ Farm to Market: This popular market and bakery has a kitchen in a converted railroad car that turns out daily specials like sweet potato vichyssoise, cilantro soup, smoked chicken and brown rice salad, and red pozole stew. At 1133 Austin Hwy. (tel. 822-4450); open Mon.-Sat. 8:30 a.m.-8 p.m.

$$ Hard Rock Cafe: This link in the chain has swept into the River Walk's new South Bank project with the usual collection of rock memorabilia, recorded pop tunes, and above-average burgers, steaks, fresh seafood, and salads. The busy, three-floor restaurant features a guitar-shaped bar on the river level, sports monitors, and occasional live music. At 111 Crockett (tel. 224-7625); open daily 11 a.m.-2 a.m.

$$ **Liberty Bar:** An exceptionally good, moderately priced restaurant housed in an ancient, former general store/brothel. The rootsy, *nouvelle-Americaine* menu changes regularly but specializes in mesquite-grilled meats, fresh-sautéed vegetables, homemade bread, and desserts. At 328 E. Josephine (tel. 227-1187); open daily for lunch and dinner, plus Sunday brunch.

$ **Luby's:** There are 17 other Luby's cafeterias in San Antonio, plus a zillion others around the state. This is the oldest but not the original, which was in the 1920s-vintage Riverside Building on N. Presa until 1979. Zing your tray down gleaming rails past heavily cooked vegetables, chicken-fried steak, roast ham, corned beef, biscuits and gravy, pies, cakes, and just about anything else from the Texas culinary mainstream. At 911 N. Main downtown (tel. 223-1911); open Sun.-Sat. 10:45 a.m.-8 p.m.

$$ **Mama's:** A friendly restaurant with the most American menu in town—meatloaf to chocolate cake. At 9907 San Pedro (tel. 349-5662); open 7 a.m.-11 p.m. Sun.-Thurs., 8 a.m.-1 a.m. Fri.-Saturday.

$$$+ **Polo's Restaurant:** Extremely chic restaurant in the historic Fairmount Hotel. Chefs come and go here, but the dishes are always avant-garde Texas; e.g., wok-charred lamb in peanut sauce, braised blackbuck antelope, boudin-stuffed quail, prawns in pineapple salsa, and my favorite dish title: fricassee of Texas rabbit with roast peppers and *nopalitos*. At 401 S. Alamo (tel. 224-8800); open daily for breakfast, lunch, and dinner.

$ **Twin Sisters Bakery & Café:** Popular Alamo Heights breakfast-and-lunch place with good omelettes, soups, homemade breads, sandwiches, and baked desserts (cookies and muffins). Decent coffee, too. At 6322 N. New Braunfels (tel. 822-2265); open Monday 7:30 a.m.-3 p.m., Tues.-Sat. 7:30 a.m.-9 p.m.

$$ **Zuni Grill:** Under the same ownership as Paesano's and Rio Rio, this daring Texan/Southwestern cafe turns out the most inventive dishes of any restaurant on the River Walk; e.g., pecan-crusted chicken with mixed greens, and Texas goat cheese with spinach in chile vinaigrette. Also vegetarian enchiladas, duck nachos, and a variety of quesadillas and flautas. Next to La Paloma del Rio at 511 River Walk (tel. 227-0864); open daily for breakfast, lunch, and dinner.

Asian

$$ to $$$ **Chinatown Café:** Features a nouveau Asian menu, mixing Hunan ("General Tao's Chicken") and Thai ("Tai Pepper Basil Shrimp") dishes. At Broadway and Nacogdoches (tel. 210-822-3522); open daily for lunch and dinner.

$ to $$ **Hung Fong:** The oldest Chinese restaurant in the city (est. 1939)—full of Chinatown kitsch, like the pair of neon flags on the ceiling (one U.S., one Taiwan). Mostly Cantonese dishes, large portions. At 3624 Broadway (tel. 822-9211); open daily for lunch and dinner.

$ to $$ **Dang's Thai:** Good standard Thai dishes, plus some northern-style Thai and Vietnamese. At 1146 Austin Hwy. (tel. 829-7345); open Mon.-Sat. for lunch and dinner.

$$ to $$$ **Niki's Tokyo Inn:** Choice of Western and Japanese seating, plus a sushi bar. Best sushi in town. At 819 W. Hildebrand (tel. 736-5471); open Tues.-Sat. for dinner.

$ **Vietnam Restaurant:** A neighborhood favorite for the low prices and tasty lemongrass chicken, crab noodles, and crab rolls. At 3244 Broadway (tel. 822-7461); open daily for lunch and dinner.

Barbecue

$ to $$ **Clubhouse Pit Bar-B-Q:** Brisket, beef and pork ribs, chicken, and Texas sausage are slow-cooked in a brick pit. All-you-can-eat deals offered Tuesday and Friday evenings; live music Friday evening. At 2218 Broadway (tel. 210-229-9945); open Mon.-Sat. 6:30 a.m.-9 p.m.

$$ **The County Line:** Another link in the state's best barbecue chain. Features all the standards plus smoked duck, chicken, pork ribs, steaks, and fish. At 606 W. Afton Oaks Blvd. (tel. 496-0011); open Mon.-Sat. for dinner, Sunday for lunch and dinner. A second branch recently opened on the River Walk at 111 W. Crockett (tel. 229-1941); open daily 11 a.m.-11 p.m.

$ **Miller's Barbecue:** East Texas or "southern-style" barbecue cooked over oak in a rustic, pre-World War II atmosphere. Great prices. West central district, at 1020 Morales (no phone); open Mon.-Sat. for lunch or until the barbecue runs out.

$ Pig Stand: The city's oldest continually operating restaurant and a classic '50s-style take-out barbecue, including their famous "pig sandwich," co-opted by Hard Rock Cafes all over the world. The management claims to be the first in the U.S. to feature curb service, too. At 1508 Broadway (tel. 222-2794); open 24 hours.

Chili

San Antonio's hometown dish is found on many menus, mostly in inexpensive diners and cafes. Among the better bowls of red are those served at the **Lone Star Café** at 237 Losoya, **Luther's Café** at 1325 N. Main, and **Republic of Texas** at 429 E. Commerce (on the River Walk). **Chili's Southwest Grill & Bar** (tel. 340-1906) at 9938 San Pedro began in San Antonio and is now a national chain.

French

$$$+ Chez Ardid: Classic French dishes like coquilles Saint-Jacques served in an elegant, early 1900s home. At 1919 San Pedro at Woodlawn (tel. 210-732-3203); open Mon.-Fri. for lunch and dinner, Saturday dinner only.

$$$ La Louisiane: A San Antonio institution that serves classic French Creole dishes like red snapper Pontchartrain and chicken Marengo. At 2632 Broadway (tel. 225-7984); open Mon.-Sat. for lunch and dinner.

$$ to $$$ L'êtoile: A rare find—top-drawer French cuisine at reasonable prices. Outdoor tables are available during warm weather. At 6106 Broadway (tel. 826-4551); open Mon.-Sat. for lunch and dinner, Sunday for dinner only.

German

$$ Edelweiss: The Swiss-German menu here leans heavily on veal and pork, including the reliable jaegerschnitzel and Zurich-style veal cutlets. The German beer and wine list, along with the friendly service, brings in the crowds. At 4400 Rittiman (tel. 210-829-5552); open Tues.-Fri. for lunch and dinner, Saturday dinner only. Live German music Fri.-Sat. nights.

$$ Karla's Restaurant & Gaststube: Standard Bavarian specialties and decor. At 5512 FM 78 (tel. 661-7617); open Mon.-Fri. for lunch and dinner.

$ to $$ Schilo's: A German/American-style deli with sausage, cold cuts, hot plates, sandwiches, sauerkraut, and homemade root beer; a downtown institution. At 424 E. Commerce (tel. 223-6692); open Mon.-Sat. 7 a.m.-8:30 p.m.

Italian and Mediterranean

$$ to $$$ Babylon Grill: Trendy, foccacia-and-olive-oil-on-every-table Mediterranean cuisine has arrived in San Antonio. While the decor at Babylon Grill outshines the entrees, the *tapas* and salads are quite good. At 910 S. Alamo (tel. 210-229-9335) at the edge of the King William Historic District. Open Mon.-Sat. for lunch and dinner, Sunday 11 a.m.-3 p.m.

$$ to $$$ Nona's Homemade Pasta: Specializes in pizzas baked in a woodburning oven with unusual toppings (jalapeños and sausage, cream cheese and caviar, fresh fruit), as well as fresh, homemade pastas and *schiacciatine,* flat bread baked with olive oil, herbs, and cheese. During the week, a jazz ensemble performs for diners; on weekends there's belly dancing. Casual atmosphere at 2809 N. St. Mary's (tel. 736-9896); open Mon.-Thurs. 11 a.m.-11 p.m., Friday till midnight, Saturday 3 p.m.-midnight.

$$ to $$$ Paesano's: The city's most popular Italian restaurant specializes in artfully prepared and filling appetizers, salads, and entrees. The most famous house specialty is shrimp Paesano, sautéed in a savory wine, lemon, and garlic sauce; this dish can be ordered as an appetizer or entree. Other good bets are baked trout, grilled salmon, pastas, and, a personal favorite, honey-roasted quail stuffed with figs and pinenuts, served with a creamy risotto. Service is friendly and efficient. At 1715 McCullough (tel. 226-9541); open Tues.-Fri. for lunch and dinner, Saturday dinner only. A second branch, **Ristorante Paesano's River Walk** (tel. 227-2782) recently opened with an artsy but comfortable decor in the new South Bank building on the River Walk at 111 W. Crockett; open daily 11 a.m.-11 p.m.

Mexican

Listing all the *good* Mexican places in San Antonio would take up way too much space, so here are the simply *great.*

$ to $$ Aldaco's Mexican Cuisine: This friendly, modest little spot in St. Paul's Square serves authentic *chilaquiles,* tostadas, quesadillas, *cal-*

dos, Mexican breakfasts, and combo plates at very reasonable prices. The San Antonio Amtrak station is nearby—hanging out at Aldaco's beats sitting around at the spooky station. At 1141 E. Commerce (tel. 210-222-0561); open 7 a.m.-8 p.m. Monday, till 9 p.m. on Tuesday, till 10 p.m. Wed.-Sat.; closed Sunday.

$ Big Ern's Taco Palace: This popular taco joint opposite La Mansión del Río Hotel is famous for its *chilaquiles* and puffy chicken tacos. Half the fun is hearing Big Ern call out the orders in his operatic tenor. At 203 College (tel. 227-1830); open 7 a.m.-2 p.m. daily.

$$ El Jarro de Arturo: Reliable border food, including fajitas, chiles rellenos, flautas, and chicken *fundido.* At 13421 San Pedro at Bitters (tel. 494-5084); open daily for lunch and dinner.

$ El Mirador: Inexpensive Mexican and Tex-Mex with an especially good *almuerzo* (Mexican brunch) menu. Saturday morning the place is jammed with Mexican soup devotees. Specialties are *sopa Azteca,* spicy tomato broth with chicken, avocado, spinach, chilies, cheese, and tortilla strips; *caldo xochitl,* chicken broth with lime, vegetables, cilantro, and rice; and *sopa tarasco,* bean soup. Convenient downtown location at 722 St. Mary's (tel. 225-9444); open Mon.-Sat. 6:30 a.m.-4 p.m.

$$ Los Barrios: I include this place only because it's such a San Antonio favorite. Although in the middle of a mostly Hispanic neighborhood, the clientele is 90% gringo and the table sauce tastes like something from the supermarket. The restaurant's reputation has long outlived the quality of the *cocina,* which goes to show that even San Antonio natives don't always know where to find the best Mexican food. At 4223 Blanco (tel. 732-6017); open daily for lunch and dinner.

$ to $$ La Calesa: A converted, tastefully decorated home serving traditional Yucatecan specialties, including *cochinita pibil* (pit-cooked pork) and *pollo en escabeche* (marinated chicken). At 2103 Hildebrand (tel. 822-4475); open daily for lunch and dinner.

$ to $$ La Fonda: This San Antonio institution doesn't have the most daring Mexican kitchen in town, but the consistent quality and warm, friendly service enjoy a loyal following. Extensive, traditional Tex-Mex menu. At 2415 N. Main (tel.

733-0621); open daily for lunch and dinner.

$ to $$ Mi Tierra Café & Bakery: Owned and operated by the Cortez family since 1941, Mi Tierra is a San Antonio institution right on Market Square. The continually expanding restaurant receives a steady stream of tourists during the day, but slide in after midnight and it's a different crowd altogether. Classic border cuisine, with exemplary enchiladas and chiles rellenos. The *panadería* offers a large selection of Mexican baked goods. There are strolling guitarists during prime-time dining hours. One of the dining rooms contains a huge color relief fresco executed by Tamaulipan muralist Jesús Díaz Garza in 1991; the mural depicts the history of America's Latinization. At 218 Produce Row (tel. 225-1262); open 24 hours.

$ Johnny's Mexican Restaurant: Inexpensive Tex-Mex joint near Fort Sam Houston with the best *cabrito* (barbecued goat) in town. At 1808 N. New Braunfels (tel. 225-9015); open daily for lunch and dinner.

$$ Rio Rio Cantina: This casual bar/restaurant serves the most consistent Mexican food on the River Walk. The varied menu offers all the Tex-Mex standards—fajitas, chiles rellenos, enchiladas—plus regional dishes like *pollo en mole,* all prepared with the freshest ingredients. Great margaritas, too. At 421 E. Commerce St., with a River Walk entrance (tel. 226-8462); open daily for lunch and dinner.

$ to $$ Rosario's: According to the *New York Times,* this is the most authentic interior-style cuisine in San Antone (most San Antonio diners couldn't care less). Dishes from North Central and Gulf Coast Mexico predominate, including savory black bean soup, *camarones al mojo de ajo* (shrimp in garlic sauce), lobster tacos, crab enchiladas, and *rajas con queso blanco* (*chile poblano* strips in melted cheese). At 1014 S. Alamo (tel. 223-1806) in the King William Historic District; open daily for lunch and dinner. Live Latin music on weekends.

$ Taco Cabana: You can find take-out taco chains all over Texas, but San Antonio has the best. This one started as a small family-run joint at San Pedro and Hildebrand and has expanded to eight or more locations. Reliable fajitas, breakfast tacos served anytime, *chalupas,* and enchiladas. Locations: all over the city; open 24 hours.

Natural Foods

$ Adelante: Features an inexpensive, health-oriented Tex-Mex menu with lard-free beans and natural meats. The veggie combo plate allows vegetarians entry into the Tex-Mex world. Opposite the Bookstop and very casual—no one minds if you sit and read long after you finish eating. At 21 Brees, off Austin Hwy. (tel. 210-822-7681); open Mon.-Fri. 7:30 a.m.-8:30 p.m., Saturday 8 a.m.-5:30 p.m.

$ to $$ Gini's Homecooking & Bakery: Low-fat, low-cholesterol, and vegetarian American dishes, strong on homemade breads, soups, and salads. At 7214 Blanco at Loop 410 (tel. 342-2768); open daily for breakfast, lunch, and dinner.

Seafood

$$ to $$$ The Bayous: Cajun/Creole seafood, including gumbo, crawfish (in season), oysters, and shrimp. Operated by the Cace family, who made Johnny Cace's in Longview famous, this is one of the more reliable River Walk restaurants. On the River Walk off N. Presa (tel. 223-6403); open Mon.-Sat. for lunch and dinner, Sunday dinner only.

$$ to $$$ Ernesto's: Chef Ernest Torres combines regional, French, and Mexican flavors to produce a rich, saucy, and creative selection of fish and shellfish entrees. At 2559 Jackson Keller at Vance Jackson (tel. 344-1248); open Mon.-Sat. for dinner only.

$$ Landry's Seafood: Another place with a Cajun/Creole emphasis. The menu offers an assortment of gumbos, and the snapper Pontchartrain gives La Louisiane a run for its money. At 600 E. Market (tel. 229-1010); open daily for lunch and dinner.

$$ Water Street Oyster Bar: Branch of the popular Corpus Christi eatery. Fresh seafood specials daily, plus a variety of oysters—raw, baked, steamed, or grilled. Oyster happy hour 5-7 p.m. daily. At 999 E. Busse, off Broadway (tel. 829-4853); open daily for lunch and dinner.

Steaks

$$ The Barn Door: Friendly, high-volume steakhouse with 10 cuts of prime beef, plus all the fixin's. At 8400 N. New Braunfels (tel. 210-824-0116); open Mon.-Thurs. for lunch and dinner, Fri.-Sat. dinner only.

$$ to $$$ The Grey Moss Inn: Grilled steaks, including pepper steak, served in a romantic, old stone house with outdoor patio. Seafood (charcoal-grilled snapper is a good bet) and chicken also served. About 12 miles northwest of the city on Scenic Loop Rd., between State 16 and I-10 (tel. 695-8301); open daily for dinner only.

$$$+ Little Rhein Steakhouse: This 1847 stone house on the River Walk is the oldest two-story structure in the city. The steaks are 100% USDA center-cut prime, the best and most expensive San Antonio has to offer. Seafood available also. At 231 S. Alamo (tel. 225-2111); open daily for dinner.

$$$ Ruth's Chris Steak House: A statewide chain that uses only aged U.S. prime beef, chicken and seafood also available. At 7720 Jones Maltsberger, Concord Plaza shopping center (tel. 821-5051); open nightly from 5 p.m.

ENTERTAINMENT

Live Music

San Antonio may have the most authentically regional music scene in Texas. Whether it's country, blues, swamp, *conjunto*, or German polkas, the city has it. To find out who's playing where, study the *San Antonio Express-News* "Weekender" section, published every Friday. The club listings are comprehensive and up-to-date, and the "Night Lights" column will help separate wheat from chaff. The *San Antonio Light* publishes a similar music column in its weekend section, published on Thursday. *Current* is a free biweekly that lists upcoming musical performances, but not as comprehensively as the Weekender. The free monthly *SA News* is somewhat better about music listings, including weekday as well as weekend performances, though it only lists the better-known clubs.

The most fertile part of town for music is the N. St. Mary's club strip, which is similar to Austin's E. 6th St. scene except that it's smaller, funkier, and less touristy. Stretching between Josephine and Magnolia streets, near both San Antonio College and Trinity University, you'll find live music of several varieties most nights of the week. It's convenient to the downtown area and cover charges run a reasonable $2-6, with sometimes no cover during the week.

Below is a list of San Antonio's better live music venues. Most have bands Thurs.-Sun. nights only; on other nights of the week they may be open but you should call first to find out whether live music is scheduled.

Acapulco Sam's: (tel. 210-522-1707) 4903 N.W. Loop 410. Rock, world music.

Billy Blue's Barbecue & Grill: (tel. 225-7409) 330 E. Grayson Street. Blues and R&B.

Blue Bonnet Palace: (tel. 651-6702) 16845 I-35 north of Selma, exit 174B. Urban cowboy dance hall with live country music and indoor bullriding; open Fri.-Sat. nights only.

Boardwalk Bistro: (tel. 824-0100) 4011 Broadway. Jazz, folk.

Cameo Theatre: (tel. 226-7055) 1123 E. Commerce Street. Rock, alternative.

Cibolo Creek Country Club: (tel. 651-6652) 8640 Evans Road. Roots rock, zydeco, blues, R&B, country, folk.

Country on the Rocks: (tel. 656-6463) 8024 Cross Creek. C&W and country rock.

Dallas: (tel. 349-6946) 2335 N.W. Military Highway. Country.

Desperado: (tel. 680-7225) 6844 Ingram Road. *Tejano.*

El Fandango: (tel. 532-0377) 114 W. Caroline. *Conjunto,* some *tejano.*

Eva's Cozy Spot: (tel. 732-4538) 2217 Blanco Road. *Conjunto,* some *tejano* pop.

Farmer's Daughter: (tel. 333-7391) 542 N.W. White Road. Classic country dance hall decorated with old photos of country stars like Jimmie Rodgers. Western swing pioneers Adolph Hofner and His Texans still play here regularly.

Fiasco: (tel. 490-2651) 2250 Thousand Oaks. Blues, roots rock, country.

Floore Country Store: (tel. 697-8827) Old Bandera Rd. (State 16), Helotes (two miles west of Loop 1604). A country classic since 1942; C&W, Texas singer/songwriters.

Hacienda Salas: (tel. 923-1879) 3127 Mission Rd. *Conjunto, tejano.*

Hangin' Tree Saloon: (tel. 651-7391) 18425 2nd Street. Country.

Hippodrome: (tel. 340-4523) 258 Central Park Mall. Blues, jazz, rock, reggae.

Jack's: (tel. 494-2309) 2950 Thousand Oaks. Blues, roots rock, country, folk, jazz.

Jim McCullum's The Landing: (tel. 223-7266) Hyatt Regency, River Walk. Traditional jazz nightly since 1963, live radio shows around twice a month.

Leon Springs Cafe: (tel. 698-3338) Boerne Stage Rd., Leon Springs. Major singer/songwriter venue; also blues and bluegrass.

Leon Springs Dance Hall: (tel. 698-7070) Leon Springs, 12 miles north of San Antonio off I-10. Country.

Lerma's: (tel. 732-0477) 1602 N. Zaragoza Avenue. *Conjunto.*

Los Mesquites: (tel. 628-1259) 9901 N. Zarzamora Avenue. *Tejano,* weekends only.

Main Street: (tel. 490-3038) 13477 Wetmore. Blues.

Floore Country Store

Midnight Rodeo: (tel. 655-9300) 12260 Nacogdoches. Country.

Riverbend Saloon: (tel. 229-9696) Hyatt Regency, River Walk. Country.

Rock Island: (tel. 641-6877) 8779 Wurzbach Road. Rock and R&B.

Rosario's: (tel. 223-1806) 1014 S. Alamo. Salsa and other Latin sounds.

R&R Bar & Grill: (tel. 532-5688) 306 E. Mitchell. *Tejano.*

Saluté International Bar: 2801 N. St. Mary's. Rock, blues, *conjunto.*

Sneakers: (tel. 653-9176) 11431 Perrin-Beitel Road. San Antonio's premier hard rock club, with local and touring acts.

Taco Land: (tel. 223-8406). Modern rock, alternative.

Tejano Rodeo: (tel. 822-5483) 8585 Broadway. Part of a statewide chain; *tejano.*

Tejano Rose: (tel. 654-8737) 2803 N.E. Loop 410. *Tejano.*

Texas South: (tel. 281-8700) State 97 (west of Pleasanton). Country, *conjunto, tejano.*

T Town: (tel. 340-8026) 7011 San Pedro. *Tejano.*

Tropical Drink Co.: (tel. 271-0396) 126 Losoya. Rock, R&B, Caribbean.

Tycoon Flats: (tel. 737-1929) 2926 N. St. Mary's Street. Rock, eclectic.

Wacky's Kantina: (tel. 732-7684) 2718 N. St. Mary's Street. Rock, alternative.

Yosemite Sam's: (tel. 558-488) 5999 De Zavala Road. Rock, blues, R&B.

If you're just looking for a good bar and don't care about live music, try the **Menger Bar** (tel. 223-4361) in the Menger Hotel, next door to the Alamo. Well over a hundred years old, the bar is reputed to have been a recruitment site for Teddy Roosevelt's Rough Riders. At **The Esquire** (tel. 222-2521), at 115 E. Commerce off the River Walk, the jukebox—and the clientele—is mostly *tejano.* Like any good Texas bar, it only serves beer in longnecks. In 1988 the bar celebrated its 50th anniversary with a contest in which patrons guessed how many longnecks could fit on the 76-foot-long wooden bar. Answer: 4,392. Another place with some history is **Durty Nelly's Irish Pub.** On the River Walk, it's a big favorite with both locals and tourists. Guinness on tap, peanut shells on the floor, and piano players who urge the crowd to sing along

(and hand out lyric sheets for this purpose) add to the charm.

German and Classical

Beethoven Mænnerchor Halle und Garten, 422 Pereida St., presents monthly garden concerts of the Beethoven Mænnerchor between Maifest (mid-May) and Oktoberfest (early October) every year. Around 30% of the 230 Beethoven Halle members are native German speakers. Friday evening performances are held outdoors at 7 p.m.; German food, beer, and wine are served at wooden picnic tables. During festival times, the schedule includes lively German band performances as well. There's a small entry fee for nonmembers.

The **Majestic Performing Arts Center** (tel. 210-226-2626), 212 E. Houston, is a magnificent restoration of the 1929 Majestic Theatre, one of the few vaudeville theaters in the country designed by celebrated architect John Eberson. The theater's first performer was blue yodeler Jimmie Rodgers. It's now primarily a performance venue for the San Antonio Symphony, but other musical and theatrical performances are held here as well. It's worth attending an event here at least once just to view the breathtaking interior—the domed ceiling features a twilight sky, complete with twinkling stars, birds, and swirling clouds. The renovation of the smaller Renaissance Revival-style **Empire Theatre** (opened in 1914) at 226 N. St. Mary's, when complete, will add another live performance venue to the city's newly designated Cultural Arts District downtown.

Radio and Television

Music pilgrims might try KONO-AM 860, which emphasizes music born in South and Southeast Texas, such as the Sir Douglas Quintet, Augie Meyers, Charlie and the Jives, and Rudy and the Reno Bops. KENS-AM 1160 also features Texas music programming (mixed with a news talk format), with an emphasis on newer artists in the country, folk, and *conjunto* genres.

For *tejano/conjunto* sounds, tune in KXTN-FM 107.5 ("Tejano 107," the most popular station in San Antonio), KEDA-AM 1540 ("Radio Jalapeño"), or KRIO-FM 94.1. For country your best frequency is usually KCYY-FM 100.3 ("Y-100"). Another good bet is KSYM-FM 90.1, which plays an eclectic mix of jazz, folk, new music, Texas artists, and other music not usually heard on the radio.

KSTX-FM 89.1, the local NPR affiliate, broadcasts 26 live jazz performances per year from The Landing on the River Walk. Call (210) 614-8982 for free tickets to the performances; call well in advance, as the tickets usually run out quickly.

The Alamo City recently became the setting for its own prime-time television series, *Heaven Help Us.* The 22-episode drama, starring Ricardo Montalban and produced by Branded Productions, was shot entirely on location in San Antonio.

IMAX Theatre

A special cinematic process uses 65 mm film and a print 10 times the size of ordinary 35 mm film to produce *Alamo: The Price of Freedom,* a 45-minute docudrama recounting the famous Alamo siege. The film was shot in 1987 at Alamo Village at Brackettville on the same set used for the original John Wayne version; in 1988 the Cowboy Hall of Fame presented the film with the Wrangler Award for "Best Historic Film." Other movies are occasionally shown on the huge 61-foot by 84-foot screen, backed by six-track stereo. At the Rivercenter Mall near the Marriott, street level (tel. 210-225-4629); open daily 10 a.m.-10 p.m. Admission is $5.25 adults, $3.95 ages 3-11.

Encountarium FX Theatre

IMAX's new competitor presents a 20-minute show using holographic images to re-create the battle of the Alamo (cannonballs seem to fly over the audience's heads) and other scenes from Texas history in *The Texas Adventure.* On the Paseo del Alamo, between the Hyatt and the Alamo. Three showings per hour 8 a.m.-10 p.m. daily during the summer, 8 a.m.-6 p.m. in winter. Admission is $6.25 adults, $4.25 children 3-11. For further information call (210) 227-8224.

EVENTS

January

River Bottom Festival and Mud Parade: On Saturday at the end of the first week of January, when the horseshoe bend extension of the river along the River Walk is drained for cleaning and maintenance, downtown San Antonio celebrates with live music, the coronation of a Mud King and Mud Queen, and a parade.

Los Pastores: Various Catholic churches throughout the city put on Christmas plays that tell the story of shepherds in search of the infant Jesus. The most elaborate is held at Mission San José (tel. 210-224-6163) on the first or second weekend of the month.

February

San Antonio Livestock Show and Rodeo: A 15-day event in mid-February with the usual rodeos, livestock judging, and carnival midway, plus auctions, Western art shows, parades, and country music concerts. At the Freeman Coliseum (tel. 210-225-5851), Houston St. and Coliseum Road.

Cine Festival: North America's oldest and largest Chicano/Latino film festival, sponsored by the Guadalupe Cultural Arts Center (tel. 271-3151). For 10 days in early February, the festival screens over 70 feature films, documentaries, and videos produced by and about Latinos in the U.S. and abroad.

Carnaval del Rio: A Texas music festival that covers the regional spectrum, including blues, country, jazz, rock 'n' roll, salsa, zydeco, and *conjunto*. Sponsored by the Paseo del Rio Association (tel. 227-4262), the three-day event takes place five days before Ash Wednesday in various venues along the river. In some years this falls in March rather than February.

March

Texas-Irish Festival: A St. Patrick's Day celebration held at La Villita. The city dyes the river green for the occasion (the river is even renamed "the River Shannon" for the weekend) and there's lots of beer, food, and music. On Saturday, events include a 10-kilometer run at Brackenridge Park and a street parade downtown. On the weekend nearest March 17.

Spring Renaissance Fair: A medieval Europe-style event held at Market Square the weekend after the St. Patrick's Day celebration. Features costumes, entertainment, arts and crafts, and food vendors.

Paseo de Marzo: A Mexican spring fair, with Mexican food, music, and dance at Market

Square, held the second or third weekend of the month.

April

Viva Botánica: Also called the Spring Flower Show, held the second weekend in April at the San Antonio Botanical Center (tel. 210-821-5115). Art show, food vendors, and lots of flowers.

Starving Artists Show: A large arts and crafts festival held along the River Walk and at La Villita. Part of the proceeds goes to the Little Church's program to feed the hungry. Some good bargains are usually available.

Fiesta San Antonio: This is the city's biggest annual festival, consisting of as many as 150 separate events over a 10-day period during the second and third weeks of the month. Parades, feasting, carnivals, *charreadas*, music, street dances, fireworks, and foot races are just a few of the festivities. Don't-miss events include the St. Mary's University oyster bake (first Saturday), A Day in Old Mexico Charreada (both Sundays at the San Antonio Charro Ranch), a march to the Alamo in commemoration of those who died there (Monday afternoon), the King's River Parade (river floats to celebrate the coronation of King Antonio), A Night in Old San Antonio (a huge, rollicking event at La Villita Tues.-Fri.), the Battle of Flowers Parade (downtown, Friday afternoon), the King William Fair (block party in the King William Historic District Saturday afternoon), the Fiesta Night Parade (downtown, Saturday evening), and the Fiesta Finale Street Dance (St. Luke's Catholic Church, 4603 Manitou, Sunday evening). For more information, call (210) 227-5191.

May

Cinco de Mayo: Two days of food, music, and dancing at Market Square to celebrate the Mexican defeat of the French at Puebla, Mexico, on May 5, 1862. Held the closest weekend to May 5.

Tejano Conjunto Festival: Spectators from as far away as Japan and Europe make pilgrimages to this five-day music festival that features the best *conjunto* performers from Texas and beyond. Most performances are held at Rosedale Park under a large dance shelter surrounded by picnic tables; Tex-Mex food, beer,

COURTESY GUADALUPE CULTURAL ARTS CENTER

and souvenirs are sold. Some events may also take place at Mission County Park and Guadalupe Theater. In 1995 the lineup included Mingo Saldívar, Rubén Naranjo y Los Gamblers, Valerio Longoria, Flaco Jiménez, La Tropa F, Eva Ybarra, Culturas, Los Dos Gilbertos, all Japanese Los Gatos, Grupo Mazz, Tony de La Rosa, and others. The festival is sponsored by the Guadalupe Cultural Arts Center (tel. 210-271-3151).

Return of the Chili Queens: On Memorial Day weekend (last weekend of the month) at Market Square, this two-day event celebrates the 19th-century chili queen tradition with lots of chili and other local foods, plus continuous live entertainment. Sponsored by El Mercado Merchants Association (tel. 299-8600).

May–September

Fiesta Noche del Rio: Every Thursday, Friday, and Saturday from Memorial Day weekend through Labor Day, the Alamo Kiwanis Club sponsors Latino music and dance performances at the Arneson River Theater. The quality of the lineup varies from year to year, but is usually quite good and includes both folk and classical elements. Another highlight is the Fiesta Flamenca, a series of flamenco concerts at the theater Sun.-Tues. evenings each week. Performances usually begin at 8:30 p.m. and admission is around $7 adult, $3 children under 14. The proceeds go to various charities.

Beethoven Hall Concerts: From Maifest through Oktoberfest, Beethoven Hall (tel. 210-222-1521), 422 Pereida, hosts Friday night outdoor concerts of German music; German food and beer/wine are served.

June-August
Ballet Folklórico de San Antonio: This professional Latino ballet troupe (tel. 210-733-3708) has been performing at the Arneson River Theater every Sunday during the summer since 1974. The rest of the year they tour the country. Polished and very colorful entertainment. Admission is $7 adults, $1 for children 6-12.

June
San Antonio Festival: A two-week international arts festival patterned after Europe's Salzburg Festival, featuring everything from Tokyo's Grand Kabuki to Steve Reich to the Bolshoi Ballet. Ticket prices and venues vary. For information, call (210) 226-1573.

July
Fourth of July: A five-day bash celebrated at several locations around the city, including La Villita, Market Square, Japanese Tea Gardens,

Sea World, and Fort Sam Houston. The celebrations at La Villita and Market Square emphasize *tejano* music, while at the Japanese Tea Gardens it's blues. There are evening fireworks displays at La Villita, Fort Sam Houston, Lackland AFB, and Sea World.

August
Texas Folklife Festival: A huge, four-day event (since 1972) that showcases some 30 different cultures and 64 countries with art and crafts shows, food, and entertainment at the Institute of Texan Cultures (tel. 210-226-7651). Usually the first weekend in August.

Semana de Las Misiones: Mission Week starts with *El Día de Las Misiones* on August 6 at Mission San José, then features celebrations at each of the city's five Spanish missions on the following five days.

September
Labor Day Festival: Three days of Mexican music and food at Market Square. Labor Day weekend.

Diez y Seis: Mexican Independence Day, with public celebrations at Market Square, La Villita, Guadalupe Plaza, and Arneson River Theater that include lots of food and music. Some of the battles for independence were actually fought in San Antonio, which at the time was part of Mexico. On the weekend nearest September 16.

Texas Folklife Festival

Great Country River Festival: Three days of free country and western music along the River Walk and at Arneson River Theater, co-sponsored by radio station KKYX and the San Antonio River Association. Usually the last weekend of September.

October

Greek Funstival: A weekend celebration of Greek culture, held at La Villita and at St. Sophia Greek Orthodox Church (tel. 210-735-5051), 2504 St. Mary's. Food, music, and folk dancing. Usually the first or second weekend in October.

Missionfest: Also called Feria de las Americas, this event is held at the missions and at La Villita around Columbus Day. Sponsored by Los Compadres de San Antonio Missions Historical Park, activities include food concessions, music, and dancing in the spirit of Renaissance Spain, complete with the coronation of King Ferdinand and Queen Isabella. Proceeds from the concessions go toward further restoration of the San Antonio missions.

Oktoberfest: Sausage, beer, and German music at Beethoven Hall (tel. 222-1521, 422 Pereida). Spirited performances by the Mænnerchor and Damenchor, men's and women's singing societies.

December

Festival Guadalupano: Our Lady of Guadalupe Church (tel. 210-226-4604) at 1321 El Paso St. is an official regional shrine for the feast day of the Virgin of Guadalupe, December 12, the anniversary of the New World's first miracle—the appearance of the Virgin before Indian peasant Juan Diego outside Mexico City in 1531. The festival is a 24-hour event that begins at midnight on the 12th and ends at midnight on the 13th, with over 20 local parishes participating. Many parishioners begin arriving around 3:30 a.m. for the *mañanitas* or morning serenades, and by dawn celebrations are in full swing. Ten special masses held at intervals throughout the day feature a different music and dance performances. Dancers wear satin robes emblazoned with the Virgin's image and imaginative headdresses. Between masses churchgoers help themselves to *champurrado* (hot chocolate), tacos, and *buñuelos* (sweet rolls). Visitors are welcome; the best time to come is 7 p.m., for

the colorful Children's Mass, followed by performances by the Ballet Folklórico de San Antonio.

Christmas: From mid-December through early January, San Antonio lights up for Christmas. On the first and second weekends, trees are strung with lights and thousands of candles are lit along the River Walk for the **Fiesta de Las Luminarias.** During the following week, the **Fiesta Navideña** is held at El Mercado and features mariachi music, piñata-breaking, and traditional Mexican holiday food like *pan dulce* (sweet pastries). On the second weekend, Joseph and Mary's search for lodging on the eve before Jesus' birth is reenacted in **Las Posadas,** a procession of candle-bearing singers along the River Walk. After Christmas, Catholic churches hold **Los Pastores** on various weekends through early February.

SPORTS AND RECREATION

Baseball
The city has a Texas League pro team, the San Antonio Missions, who are part of the L.A. Dodgers farm system. They play April-Aug. at Keefe Field, St. Mary's University (tel. 210-434-9311).

Basketball
The San Antonio Spurs are a winning NBA team, and the city's only national pro team of any kind. They play at the new Alamodome downtown between October and April.

Caving
Since San Antonio is right at the edge of the Hill Country, an area honeycombed with limestone caves, spelunking is a popular activity. The Alamo Regional Group of the Sierra Club (tel. 210-222-8195), P.O. Box 644, San Antonio, TX 78209, claims there are 172 caves worth exploring within a 70-mile radius of the city, and organizes group caving trips throughout the year. Hardcore spelunkers will want to contact the Bexar Grotto of the Speleological Society (tel. 699-1388 or 377-3948) for a schedule of weekend trips.

Cycling
Bicycle-riding is popular in and around San Antonio. The Alamo Regional Group of the Sierra

Club sells a guide called *Outdoor San Antonio and Vicinity* that contains several cycling maps for rides just outside the city. Another good source of information is the **San Antonio Wheelmen** (tel. 210-696-4204), P.O. Box 34208, San Antonio, TX 78265; the group meets monthly and organizes group rides almost daily throughout the year. **B&J Bike Shop** (tel. 826-0177), 2445 Nacogdoches, is well stocked with cycling gear and also offers repair service, as well as group cycle trips and instruction in bike repair. Need a house call? Call **Abel's Mobile Bicycle Shop** at 533-9927.

Golf

San Antonio's warm year round temperatures attract hordes of golfers, who may choose from over 20 private, public, and municipal courses in the immediate area. For those courses that admit the paying public, green fees typically run $13-14 weekdays, $14-16 weekends, exceptions noted below. Seniors usually receive a $2-4 discount.

The historic **Brackenridge Golf Course** (tel. 210-226-5612), 2315 Ave. B, constructed in 1915 and the oldest course in the state, offers an 18-hole, 6,490-yard run guarded by stately oak and pecan trees—very challenging. Critically acclaimed **The Quarry** (tel. 824-4500), 444 E. Base Rd., the city's newest public course, provides 18 holes/7,000 yards designed partially in the Scottish style (with links rather than fair-

ways) just 10 minutes from downtown. The back nine winds through a former rock quarry; duffers can practice on the adjacent driving range. $55 weekdays, $65 weekends, includes cart.

The 200-acre, 7,116-yard, 18-hole **Pecan Valley Golf Course** (tel. 333-9018 or 800-335-3418), 4700 Pecan Valley Dr., crosses Salado Creek seven times; the daily fee of $55 includes carts; $30-35 for San Antonio residents. **Cedar Creek Golf Course** (tel. 695-5050), 8250 Vista Colina, an 18-hole, 7,150-yard championship course, offers Hill Country views, triple-tiered greens, and an adjacent driving range.

Other public courses which promise to challenge golfers of all playing levels include **Olmos Basin** (tel. 826-4041), 7022 McCullough; **Mission del Lago** (tel. 627-2522), 1250 Mission Grande; **Riverside** (tel. 533-8371), 203 McDonald; and **Willow Springs** (tel. 226-6721), 202 Coliseum Road. Active and retired military can play at either of two 18-hole courses at **Fort Sam Houston** (tel. 222-9386); $5-10 for enlisted, $10-11 for officers, civilian guests $15-17.

Mexican Rodeo (*Charreada*)

Charreada, or Mexican-style rodeo, predates Western rodeo and in fact traces its roots back to Spain's *vaquero* tradition. The **San Antonio Charro Association** (tel. 210-532-0693) performs frequently for city festivals throughout the year, most notably April's Fiesta, and is one of the state's premier *charro* (Mexican cowboy)

COURTESY SAN ANTONIO CONVENTION AND VISITORS BUREAU

San Antonio charreada

organizations. The SACA practices most weekend afternoons at its *charro* ranch on Padre Drive, next to Mission County Park, and visitors are welcome to watch. During warm weather, attend full *charreadas* on Sunday afternoon for a small admission fee.

Volksmarches
Group walking as a sport started with the International Volkssport Association in Germany in the '60s; this organization in turn sanctioned the founding of the American Volkssport Association in Fredericksburg, Texas, in the late '70s. Volks of all ages walk in the volksmarches and receive a patch or other symbol for each walk they complete. There's a registration fee for every volksmarche; if you don't want the patch, it's free. In San Antonio, there are three AVS chapters: the Randolph Runners, the Selma Pathfinders, and the Texas Wanderers. For information and schedules, call the AVS at (210) 649-2112.

Parks and Gardens
Brackenridge Park (tel. 210-821-3000) off Broadway and Hildebrand is the city's largest and most varied park, founded in 1899. Besides the San Antonio Zoo, the park's former rock quarry is also the setting for the **Japanese Tea Gardens** (which were changed to the "Chinese Tea Gardens" during World War II, and later simply "Sunken Gardens"), a typical arrangement of paths, miniature bridges, and carp ponds.

Various paved roads traverse the 343-acre park, plus several hiking and equestrian trails, some along unspoiled sections of the San Antonio River. **Brackenridge Stables** (tel. 732-8881) offers horses for rent at $17.50 an hour. Two other modes of transport within the park are the **Skyride,** a cable-car system above the park that includes aerial views of the zoo and the Japanese Tea Gardens, and the **Brackenridge Eagle,** a 3.5-mile miniature railway. Hours of operation for both cable cars and trains are Mon.-Fri. 9:30 a.m.-6:30 p.m., Saturday and Sunday 9:30 a.m.-7:30 p.m.; fares for each are $2 adults, $1.50 children 3-12.

The 38-acre **San Antonio Botanical Center** (tel. 821-5115) at 555 Funston near Fort Sam Houston features a mixture of formal gardens and short bioregional trails. The trails emphasize three Texas biotic communities—the East Texas Piney Woods, the Hill Country, and the Southwest Texas plains—and display authentic early Texas houses appropriate to each region. Roughly a third of the area encompasses the formal gardens, including a section with medicinal and culinary herbs, a fragrance garden, and a biblical garden that features plants mentioned in the Bible.

In 1988 the center opened the $6.5-million **Lucile Halsell Conservatory,** which has since been cited for excellence by *Progressive Architecture* magazine. This 90,000-square-foot complex of underground and aboveground greenhouses is designed to work with the South Texas sun for the optimum benefit of the plantlife inside. Visitors enter the complex 16 feet below the ground, then are led through a series of conical pavilions climatically "tuned" to a variety of ecosystems, including a desert room, a palm room, a tropical room, and a citrus room (orangerie). The trapezoidal central pavilion forms a glass cone 100 feet wide and 55 feet high; a spiral ramp leads to a roof deck, with a view of the complex and surrounding area. Open Tues.-Sun. 9 a.m.-6 p.m. (conservatory closes at 5 p.m.); admission is $3 adults, $1.50 seniors, $1 children 3-13.

San Pedro Park (tel. 821-3000) at 1500 San Pedro, just north of downtown next to San Antonio College, is the oldest park in San Antonio and the second oldest in the U.S. after Boston Commons. When built in 1852, it featured a museum, zoo, tropical garden, pavilion, and bathhouse, but its history goes back further since the San Pedro Springs were an important water source for early Spanish settlers, who dug the first *acequias* here in 1716 to irrigate their farmlands. In 1859, Governor Sam Houston held an anti-secession rally at the park. The pavilion stills stands, but the other facilities have been replaced by the 22-court McFarlin Tennis Center (tel. 732-1223), a municipal pool, and the San Pedro Playhouse, a performance venue for the San Antonio Little Theatre (tel. 733-7258).

About 12 miles northwest of the city off I-10 and Milsa Rd. is **Friedrich Park,** over 200 acres of virgin Hill Country wilderness. Part of the municipal park system, Friedrich offers several hiking and nature trails of varying difficulty, including one that climbs a valley ridge for a San Antonio vista. The park is forested with plum, oak, walnut, and cedar, and there are a few stone ruins of early frontier settlements. During the week you'll practically have the place to yourself.

SHOPPING

Shopping Centers
San Antonio has the usual assortment of shopping malls, large and small, and like most American shopping centers, they're far from downtown (several are located along Loop 410, which encircles the city). But the jewel in the crown is the downtown **Rivercenter,** an attractively designed three-level mall at one end of the River Walk, next to the two Marriott hotels. The architects tried to make the mall the modern equivalent of a town square, and it almost succeeds. The three floors—river level, street level, and "fashion" level—feature some 125 shops and restaurants arranged in a "U" shape around a fountain plaza.

Other principal shopping centers include **North Star Mall** (tel. 342-2325), 2000 North Star Mall; **Ingram Park Mall** (tel. 684-9570), 6301 N.W. Loop 410; **South Park Mall** (tel. 921-0534), 2310 S.W. Military Dr.; and **Windsor Park Mall** (tel. 654-1760) 7900 I-35 N.

Mexican Goods
Many of the same crafts and souvenir items that you'd find in Mexico's tourist centers are also sold in San Antonio. Topping the list of places to shop for such merchandise is **El Mercado** at Market Square (514 W. Commerce)—basically a large warehouse divided into vendor stalls that carry everything from huaraches (Mexican leather sandals) to pottery and Mexican kitchen utensils. As in Mexico, bargaining is usually acceptable. Nearby **Nila's,** at 206 Produce Row, carries Mexican dresses for women and *guayabera* shirts for men. **Botica Guadalupaña** at 106 Produce Row, Market Square, is the oldest pharmacy in the city, and as the name suggests, it sells traditional Mexican herbal remedies. Also on Market Square is **La Villita Tortillería** (905 Dolorosa), where you can get fresh tortillas and other Mexican groceries. The **Farmers Market** (612 W. Commerce) has fresh produce, including an extensive selection of Mexican chilies, plus an assortment of arts and crafts vendors.

Along Commerce St. between Market Square and the River Walk are several Mexican-owned shops selling Spanish-language books and records. Down on the River Walk, **Mayan Tejidos de Guatemala** specializes in crafts from lower Mexico and Central America.

Up on street level near the Alamo, **Recuerdos de Mi Madre** (tel. 210-227-9001), 214 Losoya, carries the city's best selection of Mexican folk

crafting a bajo sexto

art. Nearby **Pinto Pony Art & Coffee Co.** (tel. 225-4175), 120 Losoya, also stocks Mexican handicrafts. **Santa Fe Collection** (tel. 224-5353), at 231 Losoya almost opposite Recuerdos de Mi Madre, purveys a variety of Mexican and Southwestern handicrafts and is generally less expensive than Recuerdos de Mi Madre.

If you're searching for a place that makes custom piñatas, look no further than **Sanchez Piñata Land** at 709 S. Alamo. Señor Sanchez will make a piñata in virtually any requested shape or size, and fill it with whatever you like. Or you can settle for a ready-made donkey or other animal stuffed with candy.

Dos Carolinas at 707 S. St. Mary's has handmade *guayaberas* (Yucatán-style shirts) in linen, silk, and lightweight wool, plus other Mexican classic and original Southwestern creations.

For the biggest selection of *tejano, conjunto,* and other Latin recordings, head for **Del Bravo Record Shop** (tel. 432-8351) at 554 Old US 90 W.

Produce

Looking for fresh figs, Mexican cheese, or yard eggs? **Farm To Market** purveys the largest selection of exotic produce in the state, along with a deli smorgasbord of fresh pastas, pestos, pastries, fresh fish, gourmet coffees and smoked meats, including andouille sausage and *chorizo.* Saturday, the most crowded day of the week, is practically a fiesta. Lots of free tasting samples. At 1133 Austin Hwy. (tel. 210-822-4450); open Mon.-Sat. 8:30 a.m.-8 p.m.

Antiques

Antique Conglomerate (tel. 210-494-7490) at 5525 Blanco, north of downtown, is a complex of around a dozen antique shops, the kind in which the word "antique" means almost anything used. **J. Adelman Antiques and Art** (tel. 225-5914) in the Menger Hotel offers high-quality antiques.

Bookstores

The city has a fair number of independent bookstores, something most Texas cities lack. The greatest selection overall is at the **Bookstop** stores; best of all, they sell at a discount to the public and at an even better discount if you buy a membership. There are now three Bookstops: 9985 I-10 W, Colonade shopping center (tel.

210-697-0588); 13415 San Pedro Ave. (tel. 496-2996); and 6496 N. New Braunfels, Sunset Ridge shopping center (tel. 828-9046). This last location, in Alamo Heights, is the best—an excellent magazine selection and books covering topics from computers to Texana. The **Book Worm** (tel. 342-4258), 4707 Blanco in northwest San Antonio, offers a mix of new and used books. Another independent bookshop with a carefully selected line is **The Twig** (tel. 826-6411) at 5005 Broadway in the northern part of the city. The **Antiquarian Book Mart** (tel. 828-4885), 3127 Broadway, and **Cheever Books** (tel. 824-2665), 140 Carnahan, carry only used and rare books.

Western Gear

Sheplers (tel. 210-681-8230) at 6201 N.W. Loop 410 at Ingram bills itself as the largest Western-wear store in the world, and it looks it. Sheplers carries all the standard boots, hats, jeans, and saddle tack, as well as piles of tacky pseudo-Western junk like ashtrays in the shape of a boot. Much more authentic is **Kallison's Farm and Ranch Store** (tel. 222-8411) at 1025 Nogalitos, which offers everything from fencing pliers to woodburning stoves. For custom saddles and other leather gear, trot over to **Lebman's Corral** (tel. 680-7117), at 6504 Bandera.

If you're making a tour of Texas bootmakers, check out **Little's Boots** (tel. 923-2221), 110 Division, where three generations of Littles have supplied San Antonians with custom boots for half a century. The best readymades in town are sold at **Lucchese Boot Co.** (tel. 828-9419) at 4025 Broadway near Alamo Heights in northern San Antonio. Lucchese, a San Antonio institution since 1883, made custom boots until the early '70s.

Paris Hatters (tel. 223-3453) at 119 Broadway carries a wide selection of hats, both western (Resistol, Stetson) and eastern (Dobbs, Kangol), plus name-brand Texas boots such as Justin, Tony Lama, and Nocona.

Flea Market

San Antonio's largest flea, the **Eisenhauer Road Flea Market** (tel. 210-653-7592), at 3903 Eisenhauer Rd. (between I-35 and Austin Hwy.), stays open daily year round. Food and beer sustain all-day shoppers, and on weekends live music adds to the festive atmosphere.

INFORMATION

Tourist Offices

The San Antonio Convention and Visitors Bureau maintains a **visitor information center** (tel. 210-299-8155) across from the Alamo on Alamo Plaza. It's open daily 8:30 a.m.-6 p.m. The mailing address for the CVB is P.O. Box 2277, San Antonio, TX 78298.

While not a tourist office per se, the San Antonio Conservation Society (tel. 224-6163) at 107 King William St. is a mine of information on historic sights in the city.

Mexico Information

San Antonio is a good starting place for a trip into Mexico. The office of the **Mexican Consulate General** (tel. 210-227-9145) is downtown at 127 Navarro, and can arrange visas and answer questions about customs regulations. **Sanborn's Mexican Insurance** (tel. 828-3587), 8107 Broadway, will arrange tourist cards, Mexican auto insurance, and currency exchange. Practically any travel agency in the city can take care of tourist cards.

Foreign Exchange

NationsBank (tel. 210-229-2600) at 112 E. Pecan has the most complete international exchange services of any San Antonio bank, including foreign currencies other than Mexican pesos—and no service charge. Another bank handling foreign exchange is **Frost Bank** (tel. 220-5651), 100 W. Houston.

Publications

The Paseo del Rio Association publishes the free monthly *Río,* which contains information on shops, services, and special events along the River Walk. Another tourist-oriented magazine is *Fiesta,* published monthly by the *San Antonio Light,* which features a dining guide, lists of museums and art galleries, an events calendar, and short descriptions of area attractions.

Current and *SA Weekly* are both free weeklies patterned after other American "free press" papers that contain a mixture of progressive politics, arts, and lifestyle features.

The Hispanic Chamber of Commerce of San Antonio publishes a free, bilingual tourist monthly called *Welcome/Bienvenidos,* in which all features and ads appear in Spanish and English.

Maps

The single best San Antonio map available is the AAA map. San Antonio's AAA office (tel. 210-736-4691) is at 323 Spencer Lane and is open Mon.-Fri. 8:30 a.m.-5 p.m., Sat. 9 a.m.-1 p.m. Continental Maps, Inc. publishes one of lesser quality, but it's adequate.

Telephone

The area code for San Antonio and vicinity is 210, unless otherwise noted.

SAN ANTONIO TELEPHONE INFORMATION

Emergency (police, fire, medical): 911
Telephone Directory Assistance: 411
Area Code: 210
National Weather Service: 828-3384
Time/Temperature: 844-4444
Highway Patrol: 533-9171
Bus Information: 227-2020
Amtrak: (800) 872-7245 or 223-3226
Mexican Consulate: 227-9145
Post Office Information: 657-8300
Western Union Telegraph: 227-8311

GETTING THERE AND AROUND

San Antonio International Airport

This airport is conveniently located only eight miles from downtown, about 20 minutes by car. It's also the state's best looking airport—Terminal 1, in fact, won a prestigious American Institute of Architects award. Ten U.S.-based airlines and three Mexico-based airlines provide service to over 50 cities in the U.S. and Mexico. **Panchito's Cantina,** just inside Terminal 1's security check, makes fresh tortillas daily to wrap around their respectable, inexpensive fajitas. **Star Shuttle** (tel. 210-366-3183) provides shuttle service between the airport and downtown hotels for $7 adults, $4 each additional passenger riding with one full-paying passenger.

A taxi downtown costs around $12 not including tip.

Train

San Antonio's Amtrak station (tel. 210-223-3226), at 1174 E. Commerce on St. Paul's Square, offers service three times weekly to/from New Orleans and Los Angeles and daily to/from Chicago.

Interstate and Regional Buses

The **Greyhound Bus Terminal** (tel. 210-270-5824) is at 500 N. St. Mary's. The **Kerrville Bus**

Co. (tel. 226-7371) runs a few buses back and forth between the city and the Hill Country.

City Buses and Streetcars

VIA Metropolitan Transit Service (tel. 210-227-2020) offers 94 bus routes plus four downtown streetcar routes. The streetcars are particularly convenient for downtown transportation since they stop at Market Square, the Alamo, the Spanish Governor's Palace, the King William Historic District, and other downtown attractions; they're also very inexpensive at only 10 cents. Actually built on regular bus chassis,

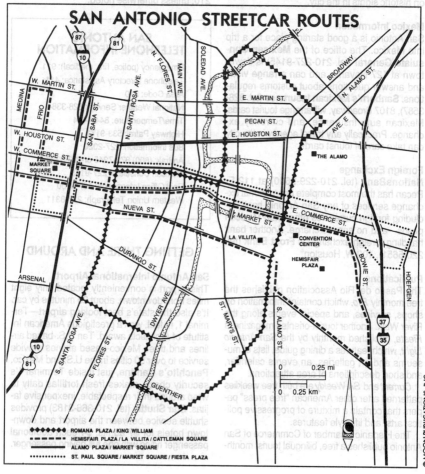

SAN ANTONIO STREETCAR ROUTES

◆◆◆◆◆◆◆ ROMANA PLAZA / KING WILLIAM

■ ■ ■ ■ ■ HEMISFAIR PLAZA / LA VILLITA / CATTLEMAN SQUARE

ALAMO PLAZA / MARKET SQUARE

•••••••••• ST. PAUL SQUARE / MARKET SQUARE / FIESTA PLAZA

© MOON PUBLICATIONS, INC.

the streetcars are replicas of the original railcars used in San Antonio until 1933, outfitted with authentic cast-iron and mahogany seats, brass railings, and leather grab-straps. Even the brass bells on top were cast from an original S.A. streetcar bell. All routes start at 7 a.m. Mon.-Fri. and 9 a.m. on weekends; service stops between 6:30 p.m. and 9 p.m. depending on the route. Houston St. is the best place to board the streetcars, since all four routes stop here and none of the buses do, so there's less room for confusion. Regular bus transfers are accepted on the streetcars.

Ordinary bus fare costs 40 cents each trip within a designated zone; crossing two zones costs 50 cents, three zones 60 cents. Express routes cost 75 cents, 85 cents, and $1 respectively across one, two, and three zones. Seniors, children ages 5-11, and disabled passengers pay half price. A $2 Day Tripper Pass allows unlimited rides on the system for one day; the pass can be purchased at the VIA Downtown Information Center at 112 Soledad and at certain stops along the VIA Vistas Cultural Route.

The very useful VIA Vistas Cultural Route (bus no. 7/40) operates daily 8:30 a.m.-6:30 p.m. between the McNay Art Museum and Mission San Juan south of the city, stopping along the way at San Antonio Botanical Gardens, San Antonio Zoo, Witte Museum, San Antonio Museum of Art, Alamo Plaza, La Villita, HemisFair Park, Buckhorn Museum and Bar, Mission San José, and Mission Espada. VIA also operates special express buses from the downtown area to Sea World (no. 63) and Fiesta Texas (no. 94).

River Taxis
Paseo del Rio Boats (tel. 210-222-1701) runs a fleet of flat-bottomed river taxis along the San Antonio River downtown. The main ticket office is under the Commerce St. Bridge at 430 E. Commerce, or you can purchase tickets at boat stops. Tickets are $3 adults, $1 children four feet tall and under. Hours are 9 a.m.-10:30 p.m. from April through October, 10 a.m.-8 p.m. from November through March.

Car Taxis
Call **B&B Cab** (tel. 210-225-3345) or **Checker Cab** (tel. 226-4242) for 24-hour taxi service.

Metered service starts at $2.80 for the first mile, $1.10 for each additional mile.

Tours
As befits the state's number-one tourist destination, the city supports a number of bus tour companies. **San Antonio City Tours** (tel. 210-225-8587 or 520-9687) has an office next to the Alamo where you can book a 90-minute city tour that includes Mission Concepción, the King William Historic District, and the Sunken Gardens at Brackenridge Park for $12 per person (ages 5-10 half price). The same company offers a half-day morning or afternoon "Highlights of San Antonio" tour for $24 per person and an all-day (9 a.m.-5 p.m.) "Grand Tour" of the city for $38.

Gray Line (tel. 226-1706) offers 10 different itineraries, like a two-hour "Mission Trail" tour for $16, children 5-11 $8. **Fiesta City Fun Tours** (tel. 533-5398) operates half-hour tours of historic San Antonio for $6 pp; $1 discount for anyone carrying *Texas Handbook*. The trolleys leave frequently from in front of the Alamo. Fiesta operates a three-hour tour of San Antonio, with visits to Mission San José and the Lone Star Brewery for $28 pp. All-day bus tours to the Hill Country, including a tour of the Texas Whitehouse, a stop in historic Fredericksburg, and lunch cost $69 pp. Fiesta also offers an all-day shopping tour of Nuevo Laredo for $79 pp; lunch $10. *Texas Handbook* readers receive a 10% discount on the above tours.

St. Anthony Tours (tel. 337-5017) and **Gray Line** feature one-day Hill Country trips for $38-45 each.

To Mexico: Alamo Coaches (tel. 271-0047) offers a convenient and economic three-day shopping/sightseeing tour of Monterrey and Saltillo. The tour departs San Antonio at 5:45 a.m. Friday morning and arrives just after noon in Monterrey for hotel check-in. In the afternoon the tour continues to Cañon de la Huasteca, the Basílica del Roble, and the Palacio Gobierno. On Saturday the tour moves on to Saltillo to see the Catedral de Saltillo and market square, and on Sunday returns to San Antonio with a shopping stop in Nuevo Laredo. The trip costs $99 per person including transport, tours, and lodging. All tour leaders are bilingual.

St. Anthony Tours and **Gray Line** offer one-day trips to Nuevo Laredo for $38-45 each.

VICINITY OF SAN ANTONIO

CASTROVILLE

This town of 1,900 has one of the most distinctive local cultures in the state and is only 25 miles west of San Antonio via US 90. Many of the residents are direct descendants of the original Alsatian colonists who settled the area and have preserved hallmarks of their mother culture. The architectural heritage of the town is also well preserved.

History

Henri Castro, a Portuguese Jew born in Alsace, France, first visited Texas in 1842 as the French consul general to the Republic of Texas; shortly thereafter he received a million-acre land grant under the Texas *empresario* program. After Stephen Austin, Castro was responsible for bringing more immigrants to Texas than any other single *empresario*—700 between 1842 and 1844. A number of the Alsatians he recruited (mostly from Mulhouse, France) founded Castroville on the banks of the Medina River, west of San Antonio, in 1844. They started small farms and ranches and built their houses of native limestone and cypress in the Alsatian style. This close-knit community handed down a modified Alsatian way of life from generation to generation.

Today, many Castrovillians born before the 1950s still speak Alsatian, an unwritten Germanic dialect, as a first language. Since Alsatian is not formally taught in any of the public or private schools in Medina County or Castroville (the county seat), the language will probably die out locally in another 25 or 30 years.

Economy

The local economy is still very much based on agriculture and ranching. Major farm products include corn, maize, wheat, oats, and vegetables. Much of the corn grown in the Castroville area is processed by the whole-kernel method for use in South Texas *tortillerías* and in the manufacture of corn chips. Beef cattle is the mainstay of livestock production, followed by dairy farming and sheep and goat ranching.

Historic Buildings

Castroville's unique architecture is based on Alsatian designs that have been adapted to local materials and Mexican building techniques.

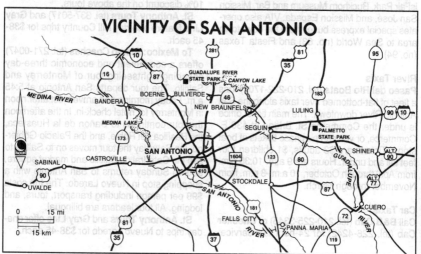

VICINITY OF SAN ANTONIO

© MOON PUBLICATIONS, INC.

Simple four-square walls of stone and wood predominate, with roofs that slope forward over house fronts. Nearly a hundred buildings in town bear state historical plaques. The **chamber of commerce** (tel. 210-538-3142) at London and Naples (many of the streets in Castroville are named after European cities) distributes a free *Visitor Guide* that contains a walking tour map that covers over 50 historic structures, including Henri Castro's house. The **Castro Garden Club** (tel. 538-2298), P.O. Box 10, Castroville, TX 78009, can arrange tours of restored historic homes, which otherwise aren't open to the public.

The oldest standing building is the **First St. Louis Baptist Church,** on the corner of Angelo and Moye. This small 1846 edifice was the first church built in Medina County. A second, larger St. Louis Church was completed in 1870 in the Gothic style, with a tall stone bell tower and 150-foot-long base. Some of the stained-glass windows were imported from Europe while others were made locally. The latter structure is on Angelo between Paris and Madrid.

Landmark Inn State Historic Site

One of the first town mayors, Cesar Monod, built a single-story, Alsatian-style stone building on the Medina River around 1850 that he used as a home and general store. An Irish immigrant bought the place in 1853, added a second story, and turned it into a travelers' inn. Castroville was on the San Antonio-El Paso Rd., and the California gold rush brought a steady stream of travelers. Local entrepreneurs built a stone grist mill and dam on the river next to the inn in 1854. After that, the property changed hands twice more until it was donated to the state park system by Ruth Curry Lawler, the last owner. As everyone in Castroville will tell you, Lawler is a significant figure in the preservation of local culture.

The state still runs the eight-room Landmark Inn as a country hotel. Ms. Lawler still lives on the property in a separate house, which is deeded to the state; the mill structures and inn are open to the public daily. Visitors may stay at the inn for a remarkably reasonable rate.

The site is just past the Medina River as you enter the city from the direction of San Antonio on US 90. For further information, contact the Park Manager (tel. 210-538-2133), P.O. Box 577, Castroville, TX 78009.

Accommodations

Rooms at the **Landmark Inn** (tel. 210-538-2133), off US 90, are furnished with 1930s antiques and cost $50 s, $55 d with private bath or $45 s, $50 d with shared bath; add $7 per each additional guest. Since there are only eight rooms, reservations are usually mandatory—made up to a year in advance. All but two of the rooms are air-conditioned.

The **Best Western Alsatian Inn** (tel. 538-2262 or 800-528-1234), about a half-mile west of the Landmark Inn off US 90, is nicely situated on a hill, so some rooms have a view of the Hill Country to the north. Rates are a reasonable $45-59.

Food

Traditional Alsatian cuisine lives on in a few dishes that all local restaurants or bakeries offer. *Parisa* is an appetizer of ground beef, onions, and herbs that's spread on crackers, a popular accompaniment for beer. French bread is common, as are a number of sausage, noodle, and pickled vegetable dishes. Anise cookies are a favorite coffee snack. The Alsatian Inn's **Britsch's Restaurant** (tel. 210-931-9451) specializes in Alsatian dishes and is open daily 7 a.m.-10 p.m. San Antonio visitors favor **The Alsatian Restaurant** (tel. 538-3260) on Houston Square (open daily lunch, dinner Wed.-Sun.), which also serves Alsatian food. The locals' favorite is **Sammy's** (tel. 538-2204), at 202 US 90, which has been operated by the Tschirhart family since 1948. Here you'll find a few Alsatian dishes, but the fortes are chicken-fried steak and Mexican.

Haby's Alsatian Bakery (tel. 931-2118) at 207 US 90 E is owned by the same family and features tasty apple fritters, strudel, *stollen,* homemade breads, pies, cookies, and coffee cakes; open Mon.-Sat. 5 a.m. to 7 p.m. Another early opener in town is **Margie's** (tel. 210-538-3087) at 1005 US 90 W. Mexican and American breakfasts are served beginning at 4 a.m.; the place closes at 2 p.m.

La Normandie (tel. 538-3070), in a quaint inn at 1302 Fiorella and Paris, emphasizes the French aspects of Alsatian cuisine; it's open for lunch Thurs.-Sun., dinner Wed.-Sunday. **Chan-**

tilly (tel. 538-9531), opposite September Square at 309 Lafayette, offers a moderately priced French, Cajun, and Creole menu; open Wed.-Sun. for lunch, Thurs.-Sat. for dinner.

Events

The Castroville event of the year is **St. Louis Day**, the feast day of the town's patron saint and a homecoming celebration for Castrovillians who have moved elsewhere. The main festivities are held on the Sunday nearest to August 25, St. Louis Day. A Sunday mass at St. Louis Catholic Church kicks things off, followed by a public feast at Koenig Park on the river. As many as 10,000 residents and visitors show up for the event, so book early if you plan to spend the night. The locals start preparing Alsatian-style sausage months in advance; in addition to eating, activities include an outdoor auction, arts and crafts exhibits, games, music, and dancing. The Alsatian Dancers of Castroville perform traditional Alsatian folk dances, an art that has been reestablished in recent years; a dancing instructor from Strasbourg visited the town in the early '80s and revived the custom.

Castroville Regional Park

This park in southwest Castroville covers 126 wooded acres along the Medina River. Facilities include an Olympic-size pool, picnic areas, tennis and volleyball courts, and camping areas. Bass fishing in the Medina River here is reputedly good. Day-use entry is $5 per vehicle. Tentsites cost $5 with water or $7.50 with w/e, while RV parking is $10 a night with weekly and monthly rates available. To reach the park take Athens St. south from US 90, then Lisbon St. west. For information or campsite reservations, contact Castroville Regional Park (tel. 210-538-2224), P.O. Box 479, Castroville, TX 78009.

NEW BRAUNFELS

During the 1840s, thousands of Germans immigrated to Texas in hopes of escaping political and economic hardships. A group of 10 German noblemen (Mainzer Adelsverein) formed the Society for the Protection of German Immigrants in Texas (Verein zum Schutze deutscher Einwanderer in Texas), whose purpose was to purchase large plots of Texas land for German colonization. Prince Carl of Solms-Braunfel (one of Queen Victoria's cousins) was the society's commissioner-general. He led several thousand Germans to the port of Indianola, Texas, in 1844, at which point the teamsters who were supposed to transport them to their land in South Central Texas broke their contract, choosing more lucrative deals with the U.S. Army at the outbreak of the War with Mexico. Disease and lack of food meant that only a few hundred survived the overland trek to New Braunfels (named after Prince Carl's hometown), and the commissioner-general himself returned to Germany in 1845 to marry his fiancée after less than a year at his newly founded colony.

The land the Germans had chosen at the intersection of the Comal and Guadalupe rivers was good to those who stayed, however, and by 1850 New Braunfels was one of the state's most prosperous farming towns. Today it's the Comal County seat and continues to capitalize on the raising of cattle, sheep, Angora goats, sorghum, wheat, and oats. Tourism is also an important part of the local economy—the major attractions are the historic nature of the town itself and recreation (fishing, tubing, and canoeing) in the two rivers.

Chili trivia: New Braunfels's Willie Gebhardt was the father of premixed chili powder and canned chili. He started with a small chili cafe in the back of the town's Phoenix Saloon in 1892, perfected the powder recipe by 1894, then moved to San Antonio and developed his infamous canned chili in 1908.

Museum of Texas Handmade Furniture

During the mid- to late 19th century, New Braunfels became a minor furniture and cabinet crafting center. The Breustedt House (tel. 210-629-6504) at 1370 Church Hill contains 75 exemplary works from this period, plus collections of pewter and stoneware. Open from Memorial Day to Labor Day, Tues.-Sat. 10 a.m.-4 p.m., Sunday 1-4 p.m., the remainder of the year Sat.-Sun. 1-4 p.m. Admission is $3 adults, $1 children 6-12.

Sophienburg Museum and Archives

This small museum (tel. 210-629-1572) is on the site that Prince Carl had chosen for his

Sophienburg castle (named for his fiancée Sophia), which was never built. Displays chronicle the history of local German immigration and include a replica bakery, barbershop, and pharmacy. At 401 W. Coll; open Mon.-Sat. 10 a.m.-5 p.m., Sunday 1-5 p.m. Admission is $1.50 adults, 50 cents 18 and under.

The Archives (tel. 629-1900) contain a collection of photographs, newspapers, oral history accounts, maps, and other written records of possible interest to scholars and researchers. Open Mon.-Fri. 10 a.m.-3 p.m.; admission $2.50.

Hummel Museum

You may not have heard the name, but you've probably seen the art of Sister Maria Innocentia Hummel, a German nun who created pastel, oil, and charcoal pictures of cherubic German children—usually shown dancing, hiking, or cavorting with cute farm animals—during the 1930s. She also inspired the "Hummel"-style figurines introduced to the U.S. by occupation forces returning from Germany after WW II. This museum (tel. 210-625-5635) at 199 Main Plaza contains the world's largest collection of original Hummel art—over 345 paintings and drawings by Sister Hummel herself as well as hundreds of Hummel figurines. The gift shop sells Hummel-inspired art.

Alamo Classic Car Museum

Just south of town on I-35 (between exits 180 and 182), this 35,000-square-foot museum showcases 150 restored antique, classic, sports, and utility vehicles, including a rare Amphicar, several makes of motorcycles, historic fire trucks, and other wheeled conveyances. Open 10 a.m.-6 p.m. daily; admission is $5 per adult male, $4 for women, $2.50 for children 11 and under. Call (210) 606-4311 for more details.

Conservation Plaza

This collection of seven early New Braunfels structures was moved to one spot and restored by the New Braunfels Conservation Society. They include an impressive *fachwerk* house of cedar, cypress, and adobe; a log barn; a couple of stores; a school; and a music studio. A Folklife Festival is held here in early May. At 1300 Church Hill. Only the Baetge House is open to

the oldest dance hall in Texas, Gruene Hall

public entry, Saturday and Sunday 2-5 p.m. (daily 10 a.m.-4 p.m. during Wurstfest).

Gruene Historic District

Pronounced "Green," this little ghost town four miles northwest of downtown New Braunfels was a cotton boomtown in the late 1800s and early 1900s. In 1925, boll weevils wiped the cotton business out and just about everyone left. In the 1970s, a few entrepreneurs from San Antonio and New Braunfels began moving and restoring the town for the burgeoning tourist trade. The main draw here is the 1878 **Gruene Hall,** the oldest continually running dance hall in Texas. There's usually live music Thurs.-Sun., featuring anything from folk to country to roots rock performers. Country phenom George Strait played here every Saturday night for six years as singer with the Ace in the Hole Band. A guide map of Gruene indicating shops, accommodations, and restaurants is available from the Greater New Braunfels Chamber of Commerce in New Braunfels.

A number of shops around town sell antiques and handicrafts, including **Dos Rios Pottery, Buck Pottery, Cactus Jack's Antiques, Gruene**

Antique Company, and **Gruene Marktplatz. Gruene Outfitters** specializes in outdoor wear and fly tackle.

To find Gruene, take FM 306 west off I-35 N to Hunter Rd., then turn left along Hunter to Gruene's main street.

Scenic Drive

Starting from Loop 337 at the north edge of New Braunfels, **River Road** heads north 15 miles to the town of Sattler just before Canyon Lake Dam. Along the way the road crosses the Guadalupe River four times and passes through charming cypress-and-oak, river-and-valley countryside.

Accommodations

The **Faust Hotel** (tel. 210-625-7791) at 240 S. Seguin is a nicely restored 1928 hotel with antique-furnished rooms. Rates are $70 s, $80 d. Even more historic is the restored 1898 **Prince Solms Inn** (tel. 625-9169), a bed and breakfast furnished with sumptuous antiques at 195 E. San Antonio, with eight rooms, three suites ranging $50 to $75 during the week, $65-110 on weekends. Prince Solms Inn requires a two-night minimum stay on May-Sept. weekends; children and pets are not accepted.

For something more modern, but with a lot less character, try the **Rodeway Inn** (tel. 629-6991), at 1209 I-35 S (exit 189), or **Hill Country Inn** (tel. 625-7373), at the junction of I-35 and FM 725 (exit 187), both of which have good rooms in the $40-75 range. In nearby Gruene, the **Gruene Mansion Inn** (tel. 629-2641), 1275 Gruene Rd., offers rooms in the main house, carriage house, and converted barns for rates starting at $75 a night including breakfast (best for small groups). At the 1860s adobe-and-cedar **Gruene Country Homestead** (tel. 606-0216), 832 Gruene Rd., antique-furnished rooms with private baths and full breakfast range from $95 to $115 a night.

If your visit to New Braunfels revolves around the amazing Schlitterbahn Waterpark, you can now stay in the park at the new 210-room **Schlitterbahn Resort at the Rapids** (tel. 625-2351), on the Comal River off Austin Street. The resort offers a wide range of accommodation possibilities, from simple motel rooms costing $56-97 a night to three-bedroom cottages with full

kitchens (plus sleeping arrangements for up to 12 persons) for $174-214.

Campgrounds and RV Parks

There are at least 15 campgrounds and RV parks in the New Braunfels vicinity. Rates are around $5-10 for tent sites, $10-15 for RV sites with full hookups. **Whitewater Sports Campground and Canoe Livery** (tel. 210-964-3800) has 500 acres of camping areas and hiking trails along the Guadalupe, off FM 306 just before it crosses the river north of New Braunfels. Others in the area include **River Rat's Place** (tel. 629-3009), 137 N. River Terrace; **Landa Trailer Park and Campground** (tel. 625-1222), 565 N. Market St.; **Hill Country RV Resort** (tel. 625-1919), 131 Ruekel Rd.; **Lakeside RV Park** (tel. 625-5494), 1671 Arndt Rd.; and **Stone Creek RV Park** (tel. 620-7759), 18905 I-35 N.

Food

Krause's Café (tel. 210-625-7581) at 148 S. Castell features inexpensive chili, stewed spareribs with dumplings and sauerkraut, various sausages, and other German-American fare (including *panna* and blood sausage in season—Nov.-March). Open Mon.-Sat. for breakfast, lunch, and dinner, except for the first three weeks in September when it's closed for a holiday. **Wolfgang's Keller** (tel. 625-9169) is in the cellar of the Prince Solms Inn and is a bit more formal, with American, German, and continental dishes. Open Tues.-Sun. 5-10 p.m. for dinner only.

The sprawling **New Braunfels Smokehouse** (tel. 625-2416) specializes in smoked meats of all kinds, including sausages, chicken, turkey, ham, beef brisket, and ribs. The Smokehouse also offers a few non-smoked dishes like chicken and dumplings. Huge breakfasts. At the junction of US 81 and State 46; open daily for breakfast, lunch, and dinner. There is a second branch at Mill Store Plaza on US 81 E.

Over in Gruene you might try **Adobe Verde** for Mexican, chicken-fried steak, and seafood, or the casual **Gristmill Restaurant** for grilled steaks, chicken, and fish served in a hundred-year-old cotton gin on the banks of the Guadalupe.

Guadalupe River State Park

Thirty miles west of New Braunfels off State 46 are 1,900 acres of unspoiled Guadalupe River and Hill Country terrain under state protection. The river flows through limestone cliffs and stands of bald cypress, pecan, sycamore, walnut, and willow. Higher park elevations feature oak and juniper woodlands. While not quite as rough as the Canyon Lake-New Braunfels run, canoeing is a popular activity here since there are four sets of rapids within the park boundaries.

Facilities include picnic areas, a playground, and camping areas. Campsites cost $12 with water only, $15 with w/e; if you stay six nights, the seventh is free. Dump stations are available. Reservations for overnight stays are highly recommended from March through November; call the TPWD's Central Reservations Center at (512) 389-8900. Park entry is $6 a day per vehicle, $2 for pedestrians, canoeists, and cyclists. For further information, contact the Park Superintendent (tel. 210-438-2656), Guadalupe River State Park, HC 54, Box 2087, Bulverde, TX 78163.

Natural Bridge
Caverns and Wildlife Ranch
This is one of the most popular series of limestone caves found throughout South Central Texas. The entrance to the caverns is spanned by a 60-foot length of limestone that forms a natural bridge, hence the name. Different rooms within the caverns are named for the predominant rock formations in each: the Castle of White Giants features imposing limestone columns; the Chandelier has a delicate, ribboned forma-

tion hanging from the ceiling; while the Sherwood Forest has tall, thin, tree-like formations. Guided tours take a leisurely hour and 15 minutes to complete the half-mile circuit through the various rooms open to the public.

Facilities outside the cave include a picnic area, snack bar, interpretive center, and gift shop. The caverns are located about halfway between San Antonio and New Braunfels, off FM 3009 (west off I-35, Garden Ridge-Schertz exit—you can't miss the signs).

The caverns open at 9 a.m. daily and tours leave every half-hour till 6 p.m. June-Aug., till 4 p.m. the rest of the year. Admission is $6.75 adults, $5 children. For further information, call (210) 657-6101.

Nearby **Natural Bridge Wildlife Ranch** (tel. 210-438-7400) raises exotic animals from around the world on 200 acres of Hill Country terrain. A paved, 3.5-mile "safari" drive-through allows visitors to view many of the animals, including ostrich, addax antelope, oryx, aoudad, llama, pygmy goat, monkey, bison, zebra, and giraffe. The ranch is open daily Sept.-May 9 a.m.-5 p.m., June-Aug. 9 a.m.-6:30 p.m. Admission costs $6.35 for adults, $5.50 ages 65 and over, $4 ages 3-11. The ranch entrance is on FM 3005 off I-35 (exit 175).

Events
The 10-day **Wurstfest,** billed as "the best of the *wurst*," is celebrated annually starting the

*babybaking
down on the ranch*

Friday before the first Monday in November. This is New Braunfels's own rendition of Germany's Oktoberfest, with the focus on sausage-eating as well as beer-drinking. Local men dress in lederhosen, the women in dirndl. It started as a local one-day affair in 1960 and now draws over 130,000 visitors a year. Don't go expecting an authentically German atmosphere, though, as it's really an ersatz American version—almost a self-parody at times. Most events are held at Landa Park and include arts shows, music and dancing, historical exhibits, food vendors, and the Tour de Gruene Bicycle Classic, a 26-mile road race. There is also an antique bike show attended by antique bicycle clubs from around the state and beyond. The antique bike riders wear period dress—quite a spectacle. Music and dance performances are held in the park's Wursthalle and in large outdoor tents.

Recreation

Landa Park: This 310-acre park (tel. 210-608-2165) on the Comal River features boat rentals and picnic areas. On weekends between Easter and Labor Day the park is closed to motor traffic, a brilliant policy that makes the park even more attractive. The park also has two large swimming pools, including one that's spring-fed, an 18-hole golf course, and a miniature train ride. Just below Landa Park on the river is **Prince Solms Park,** which offers the **Tube Chute,** a forced-water canal that shoots tubers into the Comal.

Schlitterbahn Waterpark: More whitewater excitement is available at the 15-year-old Schlitterbahn (German for "slippery road"), along the banks of the Comal across from Landa Park. The 65-acre park differs from the usual prefab water park in that the water used in the chutes and slides comes directly from the Comal and is recycled back into the river. Most of the rides were designed and constructed by the Henry family, who own and operate the park. Most involve ordinary inner tubes, rather than fake log-cars, so floaters exercise a degree of control over speed and trajectory. Probably the most exciting ride is the mile-long, 45-minute Raging River Tube Chute, which rockets tubers through 1,600 feet of banked turns, twists, and spins and into the river itself. Tubers then float down the river and arrive back at the park to start over.

Other highlights are the Schlittercoaster, a two-story raft slide, and the Dragon Blaster, in which streams of jetted water shoot tubers uphill into a system of tubes and dips. Several milder water rides are suitable for small children. In addition to nine tube chutes, extending two miles in all, and 17 water slides, the park offers five large hot tubs, five swimming pools, a playground, picnic area, miniature-golf course, two restaurants, 20 snack bars, and a hotel.

New to Schlitterbahn, the **Boogie Bahn** wave-pool manufactures nonstop, four-foot curls for boogie-boarders. Built by California's Flow Rider, the undisputed king of artificial wave environments, Boogie Bahn hosts the annual Flow Rider Bodyboarding Championships, an invitation-only international competition, in late May. For this event the waves are pumped up to eight feet. Schlitterbahn is open daily late May to late August, 10 a.m.-8 p.m., on weekends in May and September. The park is closed the remainder of the year except for special events like the Fourth of July Celebration (when the park is open late for fireworks) and the annual Texas Bikini Invitational, in which women from around the state compete for the "Miss Schlitterbahn" title. Admission, not including tax, is $18 for a full day, $13 after 2:30 p.m. Children 3-11 pay $15 for a full day, $11 after 2:30 p.m. Two-day passes are available for $29 adults, $23 children. Call (210) 625-2351 for further information.

Guadalupe River Running: The stretch of the Guadalupe River from Canyon Lake south to New Braunfels is the place for real whitewater canoeing, kayaking, and rafting. Most negotiable by novices when water levels are moderate, those rapids that are tricky, like Hueco Springs and Slumber Falls, offer easy portage along one side or the other. Trips can last anywhere from three to nine hours, depending on where you put in and what kind of craft you choose. Canoes typically rent for $30 a day, kayaks are $20, and rafts run from $30 for a two-person size to $120 for a raft that carries up to 10 people. Rates usually include paddles, life jackets, and river pick-up service. Some outfitters also rent large inner tubes for $4 a day, an economical way to shoot a few of the easier rapids. Because most of the land along the banks of the Guadalupe is privately owned, you can generally only put in or take out at designated points—many of the outfitters distribute maps. A map entitled *Guadalupe River Scenic Area,* available for free from the Greater New Braunfels Chamber of Commerce, shows the location of canoe/raft/tube vendors, food sources, campgrounds, and rapids along the popular Canyon Lake-New Braunfels stretch of the river.

Established outfitters include **Gruene River Co.** (tel. 625-2800), 1495 Gruene Loop Rd.; **Guadalupe River Station** (tel. 964-2850), River Rd.; **Rainbow River Trips** (tel. 964-2227), River Rd.; **Rockin' R River Rides** (tel. 629-9999 or 800-553-5628), 1498 Gruene Loop Rd.; **Texas Canoe Trails** (tel. 620-6503), 131 Ruekle Rd.; and **Texas Homegrown** (tel. 629-3176), 1641 Hunter Road.

Bungee Jumping: Bungy Over Texas (tel. 269-JUMP) has a crane set up over the Guadalupe River off River Road just north of New Braunfels; here you can take a flying leap for $30 a pop.

Shopping

Out on US 81, just off I-35 (exit 188), **Mill Store Plaza** (also known as New Braunfels Factory Stores) offers a collection of 50 factory outlets specializing in discounted clothing and housewares. Anchored by a huge WestPoint Pepperell bed-and-bath outlet, the center includes Corning, Oneida, Lenox, American Tourister, Reebok, Book Warehouse, Maidenform, Bugle Boy, Arrow, and Rawlings Sporting Goods stores. Discounts average 20-70%; about 80% of the merchandise is first quality, while the remainder consists of "seconds" with minor manufacturing flaws. Open Mon.-Sat. 9 a.m.-9 p.m., Sunday 10 a.m.-6 p.m.

In town, shops cater to out-of-towners looking for country or Victorian antiques and German souvenirs. **Opa's Haus** (tel. 629-1191) at 1600 River Rd. carries a large selection of merchandise imported from Germany, Austria, and Switzerland—everything from clocks to lederhosen. Along San Antonio and Seguin roads are several antique stores, including shops that carry furniture made by the 19th-century New Braunfels cabinetmakers. Opened since 1893, **Henne Hardware** continues to sell nails by the pound and other hardware stacked from wooden floor to pressed-tin ceiling.

Information

The **Greater New Braunfels Chamber of Commerce** (tel. 210-625-2385 or 800-572-2626) at the intersection of Coll St. and Seguin Ave. dispenses helpful tourist information on New Braunfels and Gruene.

CANYON LAKE

Formed by the impoundment of the Guadalupe River by the Canyon Dam and Reservoir, and completed by the U.S. Army Corps of Engineers in 1964, this is the major flood control facility in the San Antonio-New Braunfels area. It's also a major recreational spot, drawing a couple of million visitors a year who waterski, sail, windsurf, fish, swim, and scuba dive within its 8,231-acre surface area and 80-mile shoreline. As the lake is only 14 miles off I-35, it's a popular overnight stop for winter Texans with campers or RVs.

The U.S. Army operates eight recreation areas along the shoreline, six of which—North Park, Canyon Park, Potters Creek Park, Cranes Mill Park, Comal Park, and Overlook Park—are open to public use. Four of the latter parks feature campgrounds where basic tentsites cost $6 per night; sites with water and electricity are $8. All parks offer boat ramps; there are also two commercial marinas on the lake, Canyon Park Marina and Cranes Mill Park Marina, where you can rent motorboats.

The lake is 48 miles northeast of San Antonio or 16 miles northwest of New Braunfels via I-35 N and FM 306. For further information, contact the Project Manager, Canyon Lake, Fort Worth District, Corps of Engineers, HC 4, Box 400, Canyon Lake, TX 78133.

UVALDE

The Spanish tried to settle the area around Uvalde in the 18th century without success. The Spanish governor of Coahuila, Juan de Ugalde, won a famous battle here against the Mescalero Apaches in which he commanded a combined force of Comanches, Wichitas, Tawakonis, and Taovayas. The river valley where the 1890 engagement occurred was named Cañon de Ugalde, which later became Uvalde. The town was first established in

1855 by Reading Black, who moved to Mexico during the Civil War because of his opposition to the Confederacy. By the 1880s, Uvalde was a wild West town on the San Antonio-El Paso Trail (now US 90). Corrupt lawman Pat Garrett moved here after shooting Billy the Kid in New Mexico. Another Western legend, celluloid cowgirl Dale Evans, is a Uvalde native.

The town has calmed considerably since the turn of the century but is still primarily a ranching and farming community, with a 70% Hispanic majority.

Sights

The **Grand Opera House** (tel. 210-278-4184) on 100 W. North St. at US 83 was erected in 1891. After a brief opera career, this three-story brick edifice was used as an office building, but in recent years it's been restored to a 390-seat live performance venue. There's also a small museum in the building, open for free guided tours Mon.-Fri. 9 a.m.-3 p.m.

Franklin Delano Roosevelt's first- and second-term vice president, John Nance Garner, was born in Uvalde; after serving with FDR, he returned home and lived here until his death in 1967 at age 98. He also served as a congressman and speaker of the House. Texans nicknamed him "Cactus Jack" because of his unsuccessful campaign to make a cactus the state flower. When his wife died in 1948, he moved into a smaller house and presented the couple's old home to the city; it was made into the **Ettie R. Garner Museum** (tel. 278-5018), 333 N. Park, which contains memorabilia from Garner's political career. It's open Mon.-Sat. 9 a.m.-noon and 1-5 p.m.

For cowboy lore, gallop over to **Joe Peña Saddle Shop** (tel. 278-6531) at 2521 E. Main inside Uvalco Supply. Western saddle prices here start at a reasonable $800; many other hand-tooled leather items are available as well. Peña's customers have included John Wayne, Nick Nolte, and a number of Texas Rangers.

Fort Inge

Originally a U.S. Cavalry post (est. 1849), Fort Inge now serves as a regional park with hiking trails and facilities for Leona River fishing, camping, and picnicking. An extinct volcano cone within the park boundaries is considered one of the state's prime birding sites. The park lies 1.5 miles south of town on FM 140.

Accommodations and Food

Hotel rates in Uvalde are very economical. The **Inn of Uvalde** (tel. 210-278-9173 or 800-221-1391) at 810 E. Main has well-kept rooms for $26 s, $31 d, and a pool. Rooms at the newer **Holiday Inn** (tel. 278-4511) at E. Main cost $47 s, $55 d; the Holiday also has a pool. **Amber Sky Motel** (tel. 278-5602), 2005 E. Main St. is a classic Route 66-style motel with rooms for just $25 s, $28 d. There's also the **Best Western Continental Inn** (tel. 278-5671 or 800-528-1234) at 701 E. Main St., where rooms cost $30 s, $35 d.

South of town 1.5 miles via FM 140, at former Fort Inge, **Casa de Leona Bed and Breakfast** (tel. 210-278-8550), P.O. Box 1829, Uvalde, TX 78802, offers five rooms in a Spanish-style hacienda around a courtyard for $55-85 a night including full breakfast.

Friendly **Jerry's Restaurant** (tel. 278-7556) at 539 W. Main features a classic, small-town South Texas menu; house specialties include fajitas, migas, breakfast tacos, burgers with serrano chiles, hand-rolled tortillas, catfish, and oysters. It's open Mon.-Sat. 6 a.m.-10 p.m., Sunday 11 a.m.-2 p.m. Other small-town culinary sensations can be found at the old-fashioned soda fountain at **Uvalde Rexall Drug**, 201 N. Getty, which serves hand-dipped Blue Bell ice cream.

Fancier Mexican food and outdoor patio dining are available at **Cactus Jack Cafe and Tortilla Factory** at 2217 E. Main.

Entertainment and Events

A large dance hall, **The Purple Sage** (tel. 210-278-1006), is five miles west of town on US 90. There are two levels with bars, live music, and dance floors on each. It's open weekends only, and minors are admitted. The **Cactus Jack Festival** is held at the County Fairgrounds (on US 90 W) and other locations during the second weekend in October. Activities include a fiddler's contest, parade, barbecue cookoff, music and dancing, arts and crafts show, and an intercollegiate rodeo at Southwest Texas Junior College (FM 1023, off US 90E). Call the Uvalde Chamber of Commerce (tel. 278-3361) for information.

Palmetto State Park

BOB RACE

EAST OF SAN ANTONIO

The counties to the immediate east and southeast of San Antonio—Guadalupe, Gonzales, Karnes, DeWitt, and Lavaca—were mostly settled in the mid- to late 18th century by Germans, Czechs, and Poles who fled political and religious persecution in Central Europe (with Prussia, Russia, and Austria the main oppressors). Nearly all sailed to the port of Galveston, motivated by tales of Texas as a land of tolerance and opportunity. They were usually unprepared for the hardships they faced upon arrival, including lack of inland transport, hostile Indians, and disease in the low-lying coastal areas. Their common destination was South Central Texas, but many died between Galveston and San Antonio, while others gave up and settled in the most hospitable areas they found along the way.

Palmetto State Park

About 60 miles east of San Antonio near Luling is the Ottine Swamp, home to the dwarf palmetto (*Sabal minor*). Palmetto State Park protects 268 acres of wooded swamplands where the palmetto grows profusely. The swamp is fed by an artesian spring and by overflow from the San Marcos River, which passes through the park. The "oxbow" lake near the picnic area is a former San Marcos tributary and is now a popular local spot for swimming, fishing, and boating. Other facilities include hiking and nature trails, an interpretive center, and three camping areas.

Campsites with water only are $8; sites with w/e are $11. Admission to the park is $4 per vehicle, $2 cyclists and pedestrians. The park is located a couple of miles south of Luling (which is on I-10 E) off State 183. For further information contact the Park Superintendent (tel. 210-672-3266), Palmetto State Park, Route 5, Box 201, Gonzales, TX 78629.

Shiner

This Czech-German town of just over 2,000 residents is off the beaten path, well off I-10 between San Antonio and Houston. Out-of-towners visit to make a pilgrimage to the Spoetzl Brewery, home of Shiner beer. The town was founded in 1887 by a Luxembourgian named Henry Shiner as a trading center for local Czech and German farmers. In the late 1800s the town prospered from cotton grown in the sandy loam and black waxy soils of surrounding Lavaca County. The 1925 Central Texas boll weevil invasion forced the county to diversify, and ever since the economy has mostly rested upon livestock (cattle, chickens, and turkeys) and grain (hay, milo, and corn) production, although cotton remains an important crop.

Many of the older town residents still speak German or Czech as a first language. At the **Shiner Bar** on Ave. E (US 90 Alt.), in business since 1912, old-timers play dominoes and listen to polkas on the jukebox while drinking Shiner beer on tap. The interior of the bar is decorated with rococo tin panels in Old World patterns. **Patek's Market** on the same road sells home-made turkey sausage and polka records, some recorded by local bands.

Church: Saints Cyril and Methodius Catholic Church, built in 1922 in the majestic Romanesque Revival style, features a 142-foot domed tower with an octagonal, eight-story spire. Leaded-glass windows display saints above each side entrance and parts of the interior sport painted murals.

Brewery: Of the three major Texas beer labels, Shiner, Lone Star, and Pearl, Shiner is indisputably the best. The **Spoetzl Brewery** (tel. 512-594-3852) at 603 E. Brewery was founded in 1909 by Bavarian-born Kosmos Spoetzl, a graduate of the Augsburg Brewery Institute. After a career as a peripatetic brewmaster in Germany, Bohemia, Egypt, Canada, and California, Kosmos settled in Shiner and began producing only one beer, a dark malt lager called "Old World Bavarian Draft." It was sold only within a 70-mile radius of Shiner, in Czech- and German-dominated towns like Praha, Flatonia, Hochheim, Schulenburg, and Waelder. During Prohibition, he continued to make and distribute Shiner, reboiling the brew to remove the alcohol. After Prohibition, he changed the name of his beer to "Texas Special Export" and went after bigger markets like San Antonio and Austin, but even today Shiner beer is difficult to find outside Central Texas. When Kosmos died in 1950, his daughter Cecilie managed the business until she sold to New Braunfels investors in 1966. They unfortunately lightened the traditional recipe to follow the trend among American beers, which were becoming less and less flavorful in general, and this became the "Premium" label. Beer connoisseurs stick to the heavier "Shiner Bock," which uses toasted malt and is said to be closer to the original recipe. A third beer, "Kosmos Special Reserve," was recently established to compete with the state's increasing number of microbrewery products.

Although Shiner production is currently up to 70,000 barrels a year, it's still brewed by a staff of only 50 employees using an all-natural process that requires no additives. Kegs are still bunged by hand, and the tour guides boast they have the smallest commercial brewing kettle in the nation, with only a 75-barrel capacity. The brewery offers free half-hour tours Mon.-Fri. at 11 a.m. and 1:30 p.m. The hospitality room is open for free tasting Mon.-Fri. 9 a.m.-4:30 p.m.

Accommodations and Food: Stay at the **Shiner Country Inn** (tel. 512-594-3335), 1016 N. Ave. E (US 90 Alt.), for $32 s, $39 d a night, or **Old Kaspar House Bed & Breakfast** (tel. 594-4336), 219 Ave. C, for $45-60 a night including full breakfast.

The **Palace Cafe** on 7th St. has been in continuous operation since 1911. The menu includes burgers, stews, and chili, plus daily blue plate specials; it's open 9 a.m.-4 p.m. daily. The **Half-Moon Saloon & Restaurant** at 522 N. Ave. E (US 90 Alt.) is a full-service restaurant with Cajun chicken, Cantonese shrimp, and calorific desserts like pecan praline cheesecake and bread pudding with butter brandy sauce. Open Tues.-Thurs. for lunch and dinner, Fri.-Sat. for dinner only.

Events: If you happen to be in the Shiner vicinity on the Sunday before Labor Day, drop by the American Legion Park on Ave. G for the **Shiner Catholic Church Picnic,** an event that's been held annually since 1897. It runs from noon to midnight and features the famous Shiner Picnic Stew dinner, polka and country music, an auction, and a horseshoe-throwing tournament and other games.

Radio: In the Shiner area, radio stations KQRO-AM 1600/KQRO-FM 97.7, KRJH-AM 1520, and KYOC-FM 92.5 (from nearby Cuero, Hallettsville, and Yoakum, respectively) broadcast an intriguing mix of country and polka.

Getting There: Shiner can be hard to find on a Texas map. The quickest way to get there from San Antonio is to proceed east on I-10 about 28 miles, then take the US 90 Alternate exit for Seguin and continue east on US 90 Alt. via Belmont and Gonzales for another 58 miles to Shiner.

Panna Maria

In 1854 Father Leopold Moczygemba and 100 Catholic families fled religious persecution in

Catholic church, Panna Maria

Poland's Upper Silesia for brighter Texas horizons. On Christmas Eve of that year they arrived at the junction of the San Antonio River and Cibolo Creek after walking 200 miles from Galveston port, and named their new home Panna Maria, "Virgin Mary"—the first Polish settlement in the United States. The **Church of the Immaculate Conception,** built two years later, is still an active Polish Catholic church and stands in the center of the small village (less than a hundred current residents). Inside the church is a mosaic of the Black Madonna, a replica of the famous Black Madonna of Czestochowa, which President Lyndon Johnson presented to the town in 1966. Father Frank Kurzaj arrived from Poland to serve the parish in 1987, the same year Pope John Paul II proffered a gold, gem-studded com-

munion chalice to the people of Panna Maria during a special audience in San Antonio. The church is considered the mother parish of Polish-American Catholicism.

The first Polish school established in the U.S. (1868) now houses the **Panna Maria Historical Museum,** a modest collection of displays that chronicle local history. Panna Maria Elementary School is the successor to the original school and is operated by Felician Sisters. Many older town residents still speak a Silesian dialect. For local color, visit the **Snoga Store,** which was originally built as a barn in 1855.

Panna Maria is in Karnes County, about 55 miles southeast of San Antonio off US 181 and FM 81, about halfway between San Antonio and Goliad.

BOB RACE

SOUTH TEXAS

South Texas begins below the San Antonio River where the Coastal and Rio Grande plains meet. Spain founded many of its earliest Texas settlements in this area and introduced cattle ranching to North America here; some direct descendants of Spanish colonists still live on original colonial land grants. The first great cattle trail, the Shawnee Trail, stretched from Brownsville at the southernmost tip of South Texas to Kansas City in the 1840s.

Throughout early Texas history, Anglo and European immigrants were largely uninterested in South Texas, which remained a stronghold of Hispanic culture until well into the 20th century. Even today, most South Texas counties have Hispanic-majority populations. Ranching and agriculture are economic mainstays, along with winter tourism and hunting.

UPPER SOUTH TEXAS

GOLIAD

Founded in the early 1700s as Santa Dorotea, a colony of New Spain, Goliad has played a strategic role in the state's history. When a Spanish mission and presidio were moved here from the Gulf Coast in 1749, the name was changed to La Bahía; then, following the Mexican revolution of 1821, it was changed again to Goliad. Mission Espíritu Santo was the longest-running mission in Texas and during its 110-year tenure

was responsible for Goliad's development into a cattle ranching center. Because the settlement was between the early Texas port of Indianola and San Antonio, it also became an important trade center. When Galveston replaced Indianola as the coast's major port, Goliad trade declined and the area economy reverted to ranching and agriculture.

The main attractions here are the mission and the restored Spanish presidio—the oldest fort in the western United States. The **Courthouse Square Historic District** is also worth a tour—pick up a free walking-tour map at Goliad's Chamber of Commerce (tel. 512-645-3563), 205 Market at Franklin. In the same building is the **Market House Museum,** which features minor historical exhibits pertaining to Goliad history. The courthouse itself, designed by architect Alfred Giles in 1894, features limestone construction in the Second Empire style.

Presidio La Bahía

This fort was first established in 1721 among the ruins of France's Fort St. Louis on Matagorda Bay, hence the name La Bahía ("The Bay"). The full Spanish name for the fort was El Presidio Real de Nuestra Señora de Loreto de La Bahía del Espíritu Santo de Zúñiga; it was built to protect Mission Espíritu Santo de Zúñiga. Both mission and presidio were moved to their present location on the lower banks of the San Antonio River in 1749. Presidio La Bahía is said to be the only completely restored Spanish colonial fort in the Western Hemisphere and the most fought-over fort in American history. Over a hundred-year period, the presidio was involved in six separate independence wars and flew nine different flags.

Spanish soldiers stationed at La Bahía participated in the American Revolution of 1779-

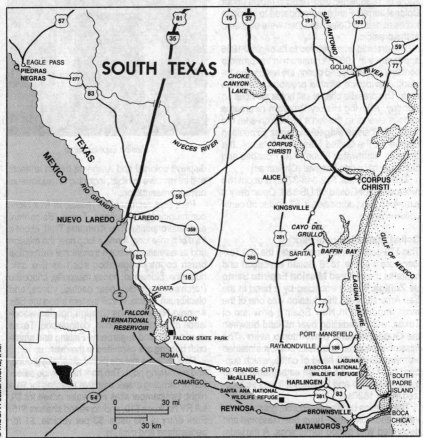

82 when they defeated the British colonial forces at Baton Rouge, Natchez, Mobile, and Pensacola. Three unsuccessful battles against Spanish rule were later fought here, in 1812, 1817, and 1821. Following Mexican independence, the fort was turned over to Mexican troops and became an important Mexican outpost. General Ignacio Zaragoza, born in Goliad and educated in Mexico, led the successful battle against the French invasion at Puebla, Mexico from the fort on May 5, 1862, an event now celebrated in Mexico and the American Southwest as Cinco de Mayo. For Texans, the most infamous incident here was the Goliad Massacre of 1836, when 300 Texican rebels under Colonel James Fannin surrendered to Mexican forces at nearby Coleto and then were executed at the presidio.

The presidio was restored to its original 1836 appearance in 1967. A museum in the presidio contains artifacts found during the restoration, including evidence of nine previous habitation eras. The presidio chapel still holds services on Sunday. A Living History Program re-creates various events in the fort's history on-site: the 1812-1813 siege/Magee-Gutierrez Expedition (January), the Goliad Massacre (March), the Spanish Nightwatch (June), Las Posadas and Our Lady of Loreto Festival (Christmas).

The presidio (tel. 512-645-3752) is about two miles south of Goliad off US 183. Open daily 9 a.m.-4:45 p.m.; admission is $2 adults, 50 cents children 6-12.

Goliad State Historical Park

This 178-acre park commemorates the 300 Texicans slain at the 1836 Goliad execution and contains the restored **Mission Espíritu Santo de Zúñiga.** Nearly encircled by a bend in the San Antonio River, this mission was one of the most important in New Spain's province of Texas, with jurisdiction over all land between the Guadalupe and San Antonio rivers. The mission prospered and, at its peak, maintained as many as 40,000 head of cattle, which supplied beef to other Spanish settlements as far away as Mexico and Louisiana. It was secularized in the 1820s.

The mission buildings—church, granary, *convento,* and workshop—have been restored and decorated with period furnishings. A museum

Mission Espíritu Santo

displays colonial and Aranama Indian artifacts and interpretive exhibits, including an audiovisual history presentation.

Park flora represents a mosaic of four biotic communities: Tamaulipan, Texan, Balconian, and Austroriparian. The **Aranama Trail,** about a third of a mile long, forms a loop near the mission and takes visitors through transitional subtropical brush country vegetation such as live oak, huisache, bluewood, honey mesquite, *chapotillo* (torchwood), prickly pear cactus, yucca, and blackbrush acacia. A trail system along the San Antonio River passes through riparian woodlands of sycamore, pecan, cottonwood, Texas persimmon, and sugarberry. Fishing and small-craft boating are permitted in the river.

Park facilities include picnic sites, playground, and swimming pool. The park has a wide selection of camping areas: primitive tentsites for $4 a night; tent/camper sites with water or w/e for $9, full RV hookups $10, and screened shelters $15. Park entry is the usual $3 per vehicle, $1 for pedestrians and cyclists.

For more information, contact Goliad State Historical Park (tel. 512-645-3405), P.O. Box 727, Goliad, TX 77963.

Accommodations and Food
The family-owned **Antlers Inn** (tel. 512-645-8215) on US 59 S is a standard-looking motel with rooms for $26-28 s, $31-33 d. Visitors may stay at 18th-century **The Quarters** (tel. 645-3752) in Presidio La Bahía for $150 a night; the unit contains two bedrooms, full kitchen, and bath. Bed-and-breakfast accommodations are available at **The Madison** (tel. 645-8693) at 736 N. Jefferson.

La Bahía Restaurant (tel. 645-3651), on US 77 at Refugio Rd., serves Mexican food daily for lunch and dinner. On Courthouse Square, **Empresario Restaurant** (tel. 645-2347) features soups, salads, sandwiches, daily specials, and homemade pies daily for lunch. **Hunter's Cafe** at the Antlers Inn is open daily 5 a.m.-10 p.m. and serves a variety of American standards.

RV Parks
Six miles west of Goliad on FM 1351, off US 59 W, is **Encino Grande RV Park** (tel. 512-645-3179), where full hookups are $10 a night. Senior discounts are available for stays of more than one night.

Entertainment and Events
For an authentic Texas roadhouse experience, seek out **Schroeder Dance Hall** on FM 622, about 15 miles northeast of Goliad off US 183. Schroeder's green-oak dance floor has been hosting country dances every weekend since 1949.

On the weekend closest to May 5 (Cinco de Mayo), Goliad County hosts the **Fiesta Zaragoza** in honor of the Goliad-born Mexican general who defeated the French at Puebla in 1862. Festivities are held at the Goliad County Fairgrounds on US 183 about a mile south of town and include a barbecue, music, dancing, arts and crafts, and a carnival midway. A field mass is held at the Presidio La Bahía amphitheater on May 5.

Goliad Market Days, held at Courthouse Square on the second Saturday of each month from March to December, features food, handicrafts, and live entertainment.

Coleto Creek Reservoir Park
Operated by the Guadalupe-Blanco River Authority (GBRA), this 3,100-acre reservoir 10 miles northeast of Goliad off US 59 is stocked with largemouth, Florida, and hybrid-striped bass, as well as crappie, catfish, and bluegill. In addition to a 200-foot lighted fishing pier, the park features a four-lane boat ramp, buoyed swimming area, picnic facilities, playground, nature trail, campgrounds, and park store.

Multi-use campsites with w/e, grills, picnic tables, and nearby trailer dump station cost $11 a night; discounts for long-term stays available. For reservations or further information, call or write the GBRA (tel. 512-575-6366), P.O. Drawer 58, Fannin, TX 77960.

CHOKE CANYON STATE PARK

This 385-acre park straddles a peninsula in Choke Canyon Lake, a 26,000-acre reservoir created by the impoundment of the Frio River. The rest of the shoreline—approximately 8,700 acres—comprises the James E. Daugherty Wildlife Management Area. Choke Canyon is the westernmost habitat for the American alligator.

Facilities
Park facilities are distributed among two recreational areas, the South Shore Unit and the Calliham Unit, and include swimming beaches, picnic pavilions, nature trails, boat ramps, bait and tackle concession, gym, baseball field, park store, and tennis courts—in short, everything needed for a long vacation. The plentiful campsites include water-only sites for $8, w/e for $11, and screened shelters for $18; trailer dump sites are also available.

Park entry is $3 weekdays, $5 weekends per vehicle, $1 for bicyclists and pedestrians. For further information, contact the Park Superintendent (tel. 512-786-3868), Choke Canyon State Park, P.O. Box 2, Calliham, TX 78007.

Getting There
Choke Canyon Lake is about 80 miles southeast of San Antonio off I-37, a little less than halfway to Corpus Christi on the Gulf Coast.

KINGSVILLE

What began as a ranch developed into a one-town county, with Kingsville (pop. 25,700) as the county seat of Kleberg County (pop. 30,500). Former Rio Grande riverboat captain Richard King stopped off at the abandoned Santa Gertrudis land grant in the Wild Horse Desert en route to the 1853 Lone Star Fair in Corpus Christi. He'd made a fortune supplying the U.S. Army during the War with Mexico and was seeking acreage for a cattle ranch. That same year he bought the Santa Gertrudis tract and eventually turned it into the largest ranch in the world. After his death, King's widow, Henrietta, together with son-in-law Robert Kleberg, established the town of Kingsville in 1904 as a railhead for the newly founded St. Louis, Brownsville, and Mexico railroad.

Today, Kingsville is still mainly a ranching center that services the huge King Ranch, and is also the home of Texas A & I University and the Kingsville U.S. Naval Air Station. Except for the ranch and the university's Conner Museum, however, there's little of interest in town. The **Sellers Market** is an arts and crafts cooperative housed in a hundred-year-old building at 205 E. Kleberg. The co-op sells its wares to the public Wed.-Fri. 10 a.m.-5:30 p.m.

King Ranch

The largest privately owned ranch in the world covers over 1.2 million acres in four Texas counties, with the main tract of 825,000 acres—larger than the state of Rhode Island—in Kleberg County. The ranch employs over 500 people to watch over the 2,000 miles of fences, 500 miles of roads, 60,000 head of cattle, and 300 registered quarter horses. The ranch's multinational corporate extension controls over four million acres worldwide for the production of cattle, sugarcane, sorghum, rice, hay, and corn.

The King family has not only been skilled in multiplying ranch acreage, but in animal breeding as well. In seeking to produce a cattle breed that could thrive in the harsh South Texas climate, they came up with the highly successful Santa Gertrudis, a cross between the Indian Brahman and the British shorthorn—the first new cattle breed in the Western Hemisphere.

They've also had luck with breeding champion quarter horses; when the American Quarter Horse Association was founded in Fort Worth in 1941, the number-one entry in the stud book was a King horse, Wimpy. The ranch has since produced several Derby winners among its world-class cutting horse stallions.

The **King Ranch Visitor Center** (tel. 512-592-8055) is off Hwy. 141 two miles west of US 77 in Kingsville. A small museum with modest displays and a video history of the ranch is open daily 9 a.m.-4 p.m.

Tours: Guided van tours along a 12-mile road through the Santa Gertrudis division are sometimes available from the center Mon.-Sat. 10 a.m.-3 p.m., Sunday 1-4 p.m. The cost is $6 per person for adults, $5 seniors, $2.50 children 5-12. The tour takes in cattle and horse pastures, feedlots, show pens, an auction ring, and various ranch buildings.

A new three-hour, 50-mile guided wildlife tour along ranch pastures and stock ponds, starting and ending at the Borregos gate west of the main headquarters, began in 1995. Among the 30-50 bird varieties you may spot on a typical day are great blue heron, crested caracara, double-crested cormorant, red-headed duck, snowy egret, ladder-backed and golden-fronted woodpecker, Harris and red-tailed hawk, phoebe, and green-winged teal. The ranch ecologist may point out whitetailed deer, alligators, coyotes, and javelinas. Call the ranch for tour prices.

In May, when King Ranch stockholders descend on the ranch for their annual meeting, the tour operation is temporarily suspended; the visitor center remains open.

For further information on visitor operations contact the King Ranch (tel. 512-592-8055), P.O. Box 1090, Kingsville, TX 78364.

Downtown Museum and Saddle Shop

If pressed for time, you can skip the ranch itself and go straight to the **King Ranch Museum** (tel. 592-0408), in the Henrietta Memorial Center at 6th and Lee streets. On display are photos documenting King Ranch life in the '30s and '40s as well as several vintage automobiles. One of the more amazing exhibits is the custom-built 1949 Buick Straight Eight hunting car, with triple rifle scabbards mounted on each fender and a

MODERN SPUR

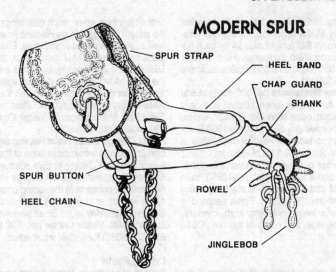

SPUR STRAP

HEEL BAND

CHAP GUARD

SHANK

SPUR BUTTON

ROWEL

HEEL CHAIN

JINGLEBOB

LOUISE FOOTE

bar in the rear. The museum is open Mon.-Sat. 10 a.m.-2 p.m., Sunday 1-5 p.m. Admission $4 adults, $3 seniors, $2.50 children 5-12.

Robert Salas, the skilled saddlemaker for the ranch, has recently opened the **King Ranch Saddle Shop** (tel. 800-282-KING) at 6th and Kleberg in the restored 1909 Ragland Building. In addition to 100% handmade saddles, Salas and his assistants fashion gun cases, purses, briefcases, and other leather items, each emblazoned with the running-W ranch logo. The saddle shop is open Mon.-Fri. 9 a.m.-6 p.m., Saturday 10 a.m.-2 p.m. The wait time for a custom saddle is about six weeks.

Texas A & I University

Founded in 1925 as South Texas State Teachers College, the school became the Texas College of Arts and Industries in 1929 and assumed its current name and university status in 1967. The enrollment of 5,400 is 53% Hispanic; a strong program in bilingual education is offered through the doctoral level. Other large programs include animal science and engineering. Majors are divided into five colleges: Agriculture and Home Economics, Arts and Sciences, Business Administration, Education, and Engineering.

The **John E. Conner Museum** (tel. 512-595-2819) at Armstrong and Santa Gertrudis on

campus features exhibits on the area's bicultural heritage, South Texas and northern Mexico natural history, and ranching history. The museum is open to the public Tues.-Sat. 9 a.m.-5 p.m.; admission is free.

Kaufer-Hubert Memorial Park

This county park is about 25 miles south of Kingsville on Baffin Bay, a huge brackish lagoon off the Gulf of Mexico 16 miles south on US 77, then another nine miles east on FM 771. Facilities include two freshwater lakes, boat ramps, picnic areas, bait/tackle concessions, restaurant, grocery, laundromat, bird-observation tower, horseshoe pits, soccer/softball fields, beach, jogging trail, and 12-station senior fitness course—everything for the winter Texan. The **Seawind RV Resort** (tel. 512-297-5738) operates in conjunction with the park and offers 134 RV sites with full hookups, including telephone. Post office boxes available. For further information, contact Kaufer-Hubert Memorial Park and Seawind RV Resort, Route 1, Box 67-D, Riviera, TX 78379.

Accommodations and Food

The **Best Western Kingsville Inn** (tel. 512-595-5657), on King Rd. at the US 77 bypass, has good rooms for $43-55 a night; pool, too.

Hojo Inn (tel. 592-6471) at 105 US 77 is similar. The nearby **Motel 6** (tel. 592-5106) has adequate rooms for $25 a night, plus $4 for each additional person. Also inexpensive is the **Sage Motel** (tel. 592-4331) on US 77 Business, where rooms are $30 s/d.

Monterrey Restaurant (tel. 595-1308) at 609 E. King is famous for its enchiladas and daily Mexican buffet; open Mon.-Sat. 11 a.m.-9 p.m. **Sirloin Stockade** (tel. 595-1182) at 1500 Brahma Blvd. reportedly serves the best steak in town and is open daily 11 a.m.-10 p.m.

At the edge of Cayo del Gruyo (a finger of Baffin Bay about 10 miles south on US 77, then east on FM 628 nine miles) is the **King's Inn Restaurant** (tel. 297-5265). Fresh seafood is the specialty here, including crab, oysters, shrimp, frog legs, and catch of the day. Open daily 11 a.m.-10:30 p.m.

Events

During the last weekend of February, the Kingsville campus of Texas A&M University hosts the annual **South Texas Ranching Heritage Festival,** an authentic display of ranching skills such as horsehair ropemaking, blacksmithing, chuckwagon cooking, and ranch rodeo. This fes-

tival differs from other ranch gatherings around the state in its emphasis on Hispanic American as well as Anglo American ranchcraft. Events take place on the Texas A&M campus and at nearby Dick Kleberg Park; admission is free except for the ranch rodeo, which costs $2 for ages 12 and above. For further information call the Texas A&M-Kingsville Public Affairs Office (tel. 512-595-3901) or the Kingsville Visitor Center (tel. 592-6438 or 800-333-5032).

The **George Strait Team Roping and Concert** is held one weekend in June at the Northway Exposition Center in Dick Kleberg Park. Country singer/native Texan George Strait and his brothers compete in the roping competition along with other U.S. teams on Saturday and Sunday. Saturday night Strait performs. Call the Kingsville Visitor Center (tel. 592-6438 or 800-333-5032) for further information.

Driving South

A word of caution to those driving south from Kingsville on US 77: for the 73-mile stretch between Kingsville and Raymondville, there are no gas stations. This is ranch country, most of it belonging to the King Ranch. Be sure to fill up before you leave town.

RIO GRANDE VALLEY

THE LAND AND WILDLIFE

Three counties—Willacy, Cameron, and Hidalgo—make up the "Rio Grande Valley," which is not really a valley but a river delta. In spite of the fact there are no nearby mountains to make it a valley, it's often referred to simply as "the Valley," a name that goes back to the last century. The topography represents a cross-section of Gulf Coastal Plains and North Mexico Plains—a unique blend of humid, subtropical conditions and brush country. Ten biotic communities have been identified in the area: Chihuahuan thorn forest, upper valley flood forest, barretal, upland thorn scrub (*matorral*), mid-delta thorn forest, mid-valley riparian woodland, woodland potholes and basins, coastal brushland potholes, Sabal palm forest, and loma (coastal clay) tidal flats.

These habitats together support over 115 unique vertebrate species, including four of the five remaining wild cats in the U.S.—cougars, bobcats, and the endangered ocelot and jaguarundi. Fifty years ago the Valley was also home to the jaguar and the margay cat, but these have since disappeared. These habitats also provide important nesting and migratory grounds for several hundred bird species, more birdlife than anywhere else in the United States.

The rich alluvial soils of the Rio Grande Plain were virtually ignored until the turn of the century, when river levees and underground irrigation systems were developed. Before that, periodic floods made farming along the Rio Grande a risky proposition. Also, although the soils were intrinsically rich, the naturally high evaporation rate made it almost impossible to farm the Valley without irrigation. As a result of controlled watering and mild year round temperatures, the area now enjoys a 330-day growing season and is an important truck-farming center. The land produces 56 varieties of fruits and vegetables, including citrus, sugarcane, onions, cucumbers,

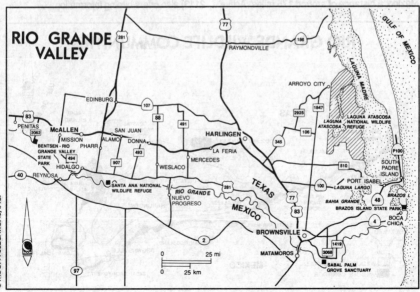

tomatoes, cabbage, and 99% of the aloe vera grown in the United States.

Farming has brought a measure of prosperity to planters, landowners, and trucking companies but little to the Chicano- and Mexican-majority workers who pick and process Valley produce. To get a feel for the Rio Grande Valley not described in the tourist brochures, take a drive along the area's back roads, off the palm-lined main highways; the fields of citrus, aloe, and sugarcane are beautiful, but the poverty of La Frontera, "The Borderland," is all too apparent.

Wildlife Corridor

Because local farming contributes to ever-increasing habitat loss, there are current local, state, and national efforts to create a "Wildlife Corridor" that would link several already existing state parks and national wildlife refuges throughout the 10 identified habitats. Some of the lands included in the proposal are under private ownership while others are public; the plan is to allow these "missing links" in the corridor to return to their natural state, thus establishing a 107,000-acre protected strip extending from the Falcon Dam in Zapata County to the Gulf of Mexico, a distance of around 175 miles. Active

participation in the lobbying and public education effort for the proposed corridor has become a favored activity for a small number of winter Texans, since habitat loss eventually affects everyone. For information on the project, contact the Wildlife Corridor Task Force (tel. 210-968-3275) or the Santa Ana/Lower Rio Grande Valley National Wildlife Refuges (tel. 787-7861), Route 2, Box 202A, Alamo, TX 78516. The staff at the Valley Nature Center (tel. 969-2475) at 301 S. Border Ave. in Weslaco are also involved in the Corridor project and are always looking for volunteers.

Birding

Up to 400 species of birds can be seen in the Valley throughout the year, especially during the fall and winter. Here, two North American migratory paths—the Central and Mississippi flyways—converge. Several local associations organize birding trips and distribute free information on Valley birdlife. To find out more about Valley birding groups, contact one of the local chapters of the National Audubon Society: the **Frontera Audubon Society** (tel. 210-968-3257) or the **Rio Grande Audubon Society** (tel. 464-3029). The **Lower Rio Grande Sierra Club** (tel. 969-2113) also offers birding information.

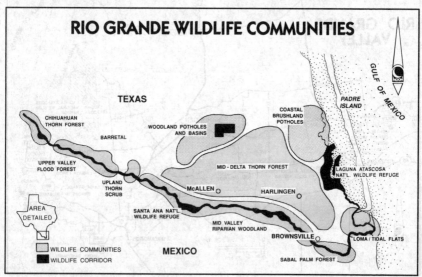

RIO GRANDE WILDLIFE COMMUNITIES

GULF OF MEXICO

TEXAS

PADRE ISLAND

CHIHUAHUAN THORN FOREST

BARRETAL

WOODLAND POTHOLES AND BASINS

COASTAL BRUSHLAND POTHOLES

UPPER VALLEY FLOOD FOREST

MID - DELTA THORN FOREST

UPLAND THORN SCRUB

McALLEN

HARLINGEN

LAGUNA ATASCOSA NAT'L. WILDLIFE REFUGE

AREA DETAILED

SANTA ANA NAT'L. WILDLIFE REFUGE

MID VALLEY RIPARIAN WOODLAND

BROWNSVILLE

LOMA / TIDAL FLATS

☐ WILDLIFE COMMUNITIES
■ WILDLIFE CORRIDOR

MEXICO

SABAL PALM FOREST

© MOON PUBLICATIONS, INC.

The Valley is famed for such species as pauraque, chachalaca, nightjar, green jay, white-tipped dove, Altamira oriole, hook-billed kite, tropical parula, buff-bellied hummingbird, collared falcon, and masked tityras.

The best written reference available is James Lane's *A Birder's Guide to the Rio Grande Valley of Texas,* available from L&P Press, P.O. Box 21604, Denver, CO 80221.

TODD CLARK

black-bellied whistling duck

and April—as many as 125,000 people. They're drawn primarily by climate—the average year round temperature is 76° F—and by the low cost of living, several points below the national average. Another major attraction is the Valley's unique position between the barrier islands of the Gulf of Mexico and Old Mexico itself. The vast majority of out-of-staters who winter in the Valley are retirees with time on their hands; the recreational opportunities provided by nearby South Padre Island, two national wildlife refuges, a state park, and the Mexican border towns of Matamoros and Reynosa add variety to what might otherwise be a mere escape from cold weather.

The average winter Texan spends up to three months in the Valley, which has made it the number-one destination in the state for visits of longer than 30 days.

CLIMATE

Most of the Rio Grande Valley lies at the same latitude as the Florida Keys, which means mild winter temperatures. The average low temperature in Brownsville for January is 51° F, while the average high for the same month is 70°. In general, summer highs in the Valley are several degrees lower than in San Antonio or Austin. In July, for example, Brownsville temperatures range from 76° to 93° F due to the cooling influences of the Gulf breezes reaching inland along the Rio Grande. Other communities further inland may top 100° F.

Annual precipitation in the Valley averages around 25 inches, about half the average rainfall in Miami. September is by far the wettest month, averaging around five inches. The hurricane season begins in May, peaks in August and September, and fades out by the end of October, but most of the Valley suffers little or no damage during tropical storms or hurricanes—just rain and high winds. There's only a one in seven chance of a hurricane striking this far south in any given year. With an eye to the weather, the best time of year for a visit is between October and May.

WINTER TEXANS

Winter Texans, or "snowbirds," are residents of snowy states in the upper midwestern and northeastern U.S. who spend their winters in South Texas; in the Valley, they comprise nearly a seventh of the population between November

Activities and Information

The main centers for winter tourism are Harlingen, Brownsville, and McAllen, followed by the smaller communities of Mission, San Juan, Pharr, Weslaco, Mercedes, and San Benito. During the winter the average age of the local population climbs, with as many as 20% over 55 years. Most Valley towns feature special centers providing services for seniors and retirees, such as health screening and social events. Common organized activities include square, tap, clogging, and jazz dancing; arts and crafts classes; photography clubs; card games such as bridge, poker; woodcarving; sewing; quilting; shopping trips to Mexico; and tennis, fishing, and golf. The larger RV parks also offer group activities—some even have their own dance halls, shuffleboard, golf courses, or tennis courts.

Square and round dancing are particularly popular, and the Valley deservedly calls itself the square dance capital of the United States. Dances are announced weekly in Harlingen's *Valley Morning Star* (Monday), McAllen's *The Monitor* (Saturday), and Brownsville's *The Herald* (Saturday). The *Magic Valley Square and*

Round Dance Directory is published twice per season (November-January, February-April) and provides information on dance locations, a caller and cuer directory, a list of dance clubs affiliated with the Magic Valley Square and Round Dance Association, a schedule of classes and workshops, and festival listings. Copies are freely distributed year round (many clubs maintain a year round schedule) throughout the Valley or are available by contacting the Magic Valley Square and Round Dance Directory (tel. 210-687-3931), 313 Nolan, McAllen, TX 78504.

A large number of out-of-state residents organize their own state-oriented picnics and potlucks in the Valley. Kansas, Minnesota, Oklahoma, Nebraska, Illinois, North Dakota, South Dakota, and Iowa are among the most active. The Rio Grande Valley Chamber of Commerce issues a seasonal schedule of events that includes listings for state-oriented activities. It's distributed free throughout the Valley or is available by mail for $1 from P.O. Box 1499, Weslaco, TX 78596.

Several educational institutions in the Valley offer adult or continuing education programs for winter Texans: **University of Texas-Pan American** in Brownsville and Edinburg, **University of Texas at Brownsville** in Brownsville, **South Texas Community College** in McAllen, and **Texas State Technical College** in McAllen and Harlingen. Non-degree program offerings are diverse, ranging from Spanish language to local ecological studies. See individual destinations for addresses and phone numbers.

The State Highway Department maintains one of its 12 state tourist bureaus on the outskirts of Harlingen, at the junction of US 77 and US 83. This office (tel. 428-4477) distributes free printed information on statewide travel with an emphasis on Rio Grande Valley material. The staff can answer just about any question regarding Valley tourism. It's open daily 8 a.m.-5 p.m.

RV Parks

This is big-time RV country: over 500 RV parks are scattered throughout the valley, comprising as many as 66,000 RV sites. Rates are low, especially for long-term stays. The average monthly rate is $90-100, three months $200-225, six months as low as $420. A listing of all the RV facilities in the Valley is beyond the scope of this book, but Data File's *The Park*

Book is available free at any state or town tourist office and contains up to date listings of all parks and RV dealers. It's revised annually and is also available by mail (include $1 for postage and handling) from Data File, Route 7, Box 508, Harlingen, TX 78552.

HARLINGEN

This town of approximately 55,000 is the unofficial capital of the Rio Grande Valley, mainly because Harlingen International Airport, also called Valley International, is the air transport hub for the entire area. Harlingen was the second major settlement in the area after Brownsville. Founder Lon C. Hill developed the levee and irrigation systems that brought fertility to the Valley and a resultant influx of settlers. During the early 1900s it was dubbed "Six-Shooter Junction" because a large contingent of Texas Rangers and Border Patrolmen were headquartered here to quell Mexican bandit activity.

Harlingen straddles the intersection of two main Valley thoroughfares, US 77 and US 83. Although the downtown area is quite compact, the town spreads in all directions for several miles.

Rio Grande Valley
Historical Museum Complex

Several buildings at the intersection of Boxwood and Raintree in the Harlingen Industrial Air Park (three miles north of town) comprise the museum. The main building contains exhibits that interpret the history of the Valley from the time of the Karankawa and Coahuiltecan Indians onward. Other buildings include the 19th-century Paseo Real Stagecoach Inn and the 1923 Harlingen Hospital, both moved here from their original locations and restored with period furnishings. A fourth building is the relocated Lon C. Hill home, built in 1905. Admission to all buildings is free (donations requested); open Tues.-Fri. 9 a.m.-noon and 2-5 p.m., Sunday 2-5 p.m. For further information, call (210) 423-3979.

Iwo Jima Memorial

Near the Rio Grande Valley Historical Museum stands the original sculpture that served as the model for the famous bronze statue of the flag-

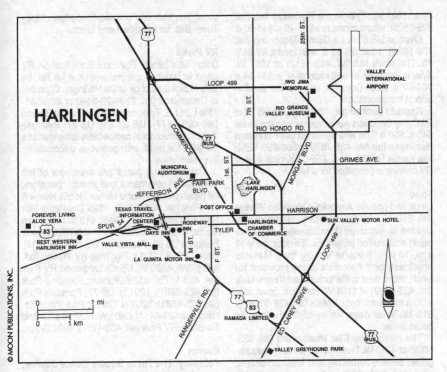

HARLINGEN

raising Marines. The sculpture itself was inspired by the Pulitzer Prize-winning photo of the pivotal WW II event by Joe Rosenthal. Sculptor Felix de Weldon spent over nine years fashioning the plaster statue, which stands 32 feet high, with a 78-foot steel flagpole. The three survivors of the Iwo Jima flag-raising posed for the sculptor, while the remaining three figures were sculpted using photos. The soldier placing the bottom of the flagpole into the ground was a Valley native, Corporal Harlon H. Block.

An adjacent visitors center is open Mon.-Sat. 10 a.m.-4 p.m., Sunday 1-4 p.m. The memorial is on Iwo Jima Dr., off FM 507 near the Marine Military Academy and airport.

Aloe Vera Information Center
The naturally formed gel inside aloe vera is valued for its astringent, antibiotic, and coagulating properties. Virtually all of this subtropical succulent grown in the U.S. comes from the Valley,

and 75% of it is cultivated by one enterprise, Harlingen's Forever Living Products. The company has established an information center to educate Valley visitors about aloe vera, and, less obviously, to expand sales. Admission is free, however, along with a video tour of the facilities and a 25-minute film that presents aloe's cultural and medicinal history. The center lies a few miles west of Harlingen at US 83 and Altas Palmas Rd.; hours are Mon.-Fri. 9 a.m.-4 p.m. Call (210) 425-2585 for information.

Accommodations
Sun Valley Motor Hotel (tel. 210-423-7222) is well located at the south edge of town (easy access to Brownsville and South Padre) at 1900 S. 77 Sunshine Strip. It offers separate duplexes from $35 a night, with senior and long-term discounts available. **Motel 6** (tel. 421-4200) is at 224 S. US 77 near the Tyler exit; rooms are $28.95 s plus $6 for each additional adult. Near-

by at 1821 W. Tyler is the **Rodeway Inn** (tel. 425-1525), where rooms are $39-45 s, $44-50 d.

Over on US 83 is **La Quinta Motor Inn** (tel. 428-6888), 1002 US 83 S, with rooms for $53-70. The **Days Inn** (tel. 425-1810) at 1901 W. Tyler is Harlingen's most expensive, at $54-64 s, $61-87 d. Both Days Inn and La Quinta offer airport transportation.

Ramada Limited (tel. 425-1333), on US 77 at Ed Carey Dr., offers newer rooms for a moderate $45 s, $50 d. The well-operated **Best Western Harlingen Inn** (tel. 425-7070 or 800-528-1234) has rooms for $50-52 s, $55-57 d, plus a pool; RV parking is permitted for a fee.

Food

Large and popular **Antonio's Mexican Village** (tel. 210-421-2106) at 2323 E. Harrison specializes in *alambres* (Mexican-style shish kebabs) and stuffed jalapeños. It's open daily 11 a.m.-10 p.m. If you're looking for a Mexican breakfast, or if Antonio's is too crowded for lunch, move over to the funkier **Las Vegas Cafe** (tel. 423-6749) at 1101 W. Harrison; open daily 6:30 a.m.-4 p.m. only. **Vela's** (tel. 428-9116) at 613 W. Tyler does Valley-style Mexican 24 hours a day.

The rustic **Lone Star Restaurant** (tel. 423-8002) at 4210 W. Business 83 serves mesquite-grilled steaks, barbecue, and Mexican dishes; open daily for lunch and dinner.

The popular **China Star Restaurant** (tel. 425-2991) at 1801 S. 77 Sunshine Strip offers an extensive Chinese menu and inexpensive weekday lunch specials; open daily for lunch and dinner. There are many other restaurants along 77 Sunshine Strip, including the usual fast-food chains.

The **Vannie Tilden Bakery** (tel. 423-4062), at 202 E. Harrison downtown, is a good place for breakfast—pastries, coffee, and full country breakfasts. For lunch there's chili, chicken and dumplings, sandwiches, and salads. Open Monday through Saturday.

If you happen to be passing through Raymondville on the way into the Valley and are looking for a food stop, consider the **Valley Bakery & Restaurant** at 383 E. Hidalgo. The Mexican family that owns and operates the restaurant serves acclaimed *caldo de res* or beef soup, *migas,* and fajitas, as well as tradi-tional Tex-Mex and chicken-fried steak. Open Tues.-Sat. for breakfast and lunch.

RV Parks

Data File's handy *The Park Book* lists 54 RV parks in Harlingen; if you want the full list, be sure to pick up a copy at the Harlingen Chamber of Commerce (tel. 210-423-5440 or 800-531-7346), 311 E. Tyler, or the Texas Tourist Bureau (tel. 428-4477), US 83 and US 77. Because there's so much local competition, rates start at a low $8-11 a night, with generous discounts for long-term stays.

The following parks are members of the chamber of commerce and should, therefore, be reputable: Dixieland Manor Mobile Home & RV Park (tel. 425-6707), 1325 Dixieland; Fair Park Estates (tel. 423-1948), 613 N. I St.; Palm Gardens Mobile Estates (tel. 423-7670), 3401 Business US 83; Posada del Sol (tel. 423-3534), Palm Dr. off US 83; Fig Tree RV Resort (tel. 423-6699), 8820 W. US 83; Lakewood RV Park (tel. 423-1170), 4525 Graham; Paradise Park (tel. 425-6881), 1201 N. US 77; Paradise Park (tel. 425-6881), 1201 N. US 77; Park Place Estates (tel. 428-4414), 5401 W. Business 83; and Sunshine RV Park (tel. 428-4137), 1900 Grace.

Events

February: The **Texas Square Dance Jubilee,** one of the Valley's largest square and round dance events, is held in mid-February at Lakewood RV Park (tel. 210-423-1170), 4525 Graham, and Fun 'N Sun RV Park (tel. 399-5125), Helen Moore Rd. off US 83, San Benito.

Los Fresnos PRCA Rodeo is held over the first weekend in February in nearby Los Fresnos; this pro rodeo features bullriding, saddle broncriding, bull-dogging, team roping, tie-down calf roping, and women's barrel racing.

April: **Riofest** is held for three days in mid-April at the Fair Park, Valley Fair Boulevard. A tent city is erected that features arts and crafts exhibits, music, dancing, and food.

Recreation

Harlingen Parks and Recreation (tel. 210-427-8870) sponsors a **Harlingen Tourist Club** at the Community Center, 201 E. Madison, between November and April. For a flat fee of $25 per season, winter Texans can avail themselves of the 14,000-square-foot, air-conditioned tourist center, 25 outdoor and 10 indoor shuffleboard courts, pool hall, and lawn bowling green. Other activities at the tourist center include arts and crafts classes, dancing, potluck dinners, card games, and various social events. The club is open Mon.-Sat. 9 a.m. to 10 p.m.

Golf: Harlingen has several golf courses, most of them private clubs. The municipal **Tony Butler Golf Course** (tel. 423-9913) is a 27-hole, par-70 course with a USGA rating of 69.6. It's located off M St., a half-mile south of US 77. The **Fairway Golf Course and Driving Range** (tel. 423-9098), at 2524 W. Spur 54 off US 77 N, has a municipal nine-hole course.

Tennis: H.E.B. Tennis Center (tel. 428-8889) in Pendleton Park (take 77 Sunshine Strip north to Morgan Blvd. at Grimes) features 12 lighted municipal courts where reservations aren't necessary—it's first-come, first-served. You can pay by the hour or buy a six- to 12-month pass that allows unlimited play. Resident pros offer tennis lessons, and ball machines are available. **Victor Park** at M St. and US 77 has eight lighted tennis courts that are free.

Greyhound Racing: The **Valley Greyhound Park** on south Ed Carey Dr. just south of town off US 77/83 offers greyhound races and pari-mutuel betting year round; highest payoffs run $20,000-30,000. The 80,000-square-foot, state-of-the-art spectator facility is fully air-conditioned and contains a clubhouse, several bars, and three restaurants. Races are held daily except Tuesday and admission is $1 general, $2 clubhouse, plus $1-3 for parking. Call 412-RACE for further information.

Shopping

In addition to a small downtown shopping area centered around Jackson Ave. and 2nd St., **Valle Vista Mall** near the junction of US 77 and US 83 offers the usual assortment of department and specialty stores.

For custom boots, it's worth making the 23-mile trip north along US 77 to **Raymondville**. Local history goes back to a 1790 Spanish land grant, and the town has been a bootmaking center since at least the turn of the century. Leo Torres's famous Rios Boot Co. has closed, but two heirs to his bootmaking prowess are **Armando's Boot Co.** (tel. 210-689-3521) at 169

N. 7th St. and **Torres Custom Boots** (tel. 689-3171) at 246 S. 7th Street. Both places offer just about the best prices for custom-made boots in the state, starting at around $250 for plain cowhide—similar boots in Austin or Dallas would fetch as much as $500-600.

Closer to Harlingen in the town of Mercedes (about 12 miles east on US 83) is **Amado's Boot Co.** (tel. 565-9641), 710 2nd Street. Boots here cost about the same as in Raymondville, but aren't quite as fine.

Information

The **Texas Travel Information Center** (tel. 210-428-4477), at the intersection of US 83 and US 77, contains a huge selection of brochures and maps detailing attractions, accommodations, and restaurants in South Texas. It's open 8 a.m.-5 p.m. daily. For more localized information, visit the **Harlingen Chamber of Commerce** (tel. 423-5440) on the 300 block of E. Tyler; open weekdays 8:30 a.m.-5 p.m.

Getting There and Around

Valley International Airport: Located on the northeast edge of Harlingen, this airport hosts American, Continental, and Southwest airlines, with daily flights to over 80 domestic and international destinations. The airport has a restaurant, five auto rental services, and taxi/limousine services.

Bus: **Valley Transit Company** (tel. 210-423-4710) at 219 North A St. operates regularly scheduled bus services throughout the Valley and to the larger Mexican border cities. The **Greyhound Bus Terminal** (tel. 423-1061) at 518 S. Commerce handles bus travel northward.

Rental Car: Advantage Rent-A-Car (tel. 421-5878 or 1-800-777-5500) at Valley International Airport offers good local rental rates.

LAGUNA ATASCOSA NATIONAL WILDLIFE REFUGE

Laguna Atascosa (Spanish for "Muddy Lagoon") is the southernmost wildlife refuge in the United States. It preserves a 45,000-acre chunk of the Rio Grande Valley as it was before farming and human habitation altered the topography, representing a transitional zone between semiarid brush country and subtropical wetlands. The terrain consists mostly of a series of estuaries, marshes, salt flats, and *resacas,* ox-bow lakes that were once tributaries of the Rio Grande.

Over 390 bird species visit the refuge during the year, attracted by mild temperatures, an abundance of food and water, and the protection from Gulf of Mexico tempests provided by South Padre Island and Laguna Madre. Fall and winter are the best times for waterfowl sighting, spring for songbirds. Among the commonly sighted species are loons, grebes, gannets, pelicans, cormorants, bitterns, herons, ibis, spoonbills, swans, ducks, geese, hawks, falcons, chachalacas, piping plover, great kiskadee, wild turkeys, pheasants, bobwhites, cranes, roadrunners, warblers, and pipits. The most common waterfowl is the redhead duck; 80% of the continent's population spends winters here.

Mammals inhabiting the refuge include various bats (cave myotis, Brazilian freetail), armadillos, cottontail rabbits, Mexican ground squirrels, coyotes, gray fox, raccoons, weasels, mountain lions, ocelots, jaguarundis, bobcats, javelinas, wild boar, white-tailed deer, and the occasional non-native nilgai (a short-horned antelope from India that escaped from nearby game ranches).

Facilities

Two tour roads are open to the public: Bayside Dr. passes through dense brush, coastal prairie, and along Laguna Madre; Lakeside Drive winds through farm fields and over a *resaca* to the banks of 3,100-acre Laguna Atascosa.

You're more likely to see native wildlife if you hike one or more of the six self-guided nature trails within the refuge. The best hiking times are around dawn or dusk, just after the refuge opens for public visitation or just before it closes. The 1.5-mile **Mesquite Trail** leaves from the visitor center parking lot and runs through a marsh area—good for watching waterfowl. The 1.5-mile **Lakeside Trail** starts at the Osprey Overlook and passes through dense brush along Laguna Atascosa—look for chachalacas, turkey, and bobwhites. There are also a couple of short side trails that lead away from the lagoon. The **Paisano Trail** forms a one-mile loop off Bayside Dr. through dense brush.

The 2.2-mile **Moranco Blanco Trail** also starts off Bayside Drive. Part of it proceeds along a service road through cord grass flats next to a *resaca;* then it leaves the service road and continues through brush to the Laguna Madre. The **Gunnery Range Trail** is a half-mile walk along an old railbed where WW II gunner trainees once practiced shooting. They fired at targets carried by a small automatic train that once ran along the rails here. The best place to see larger mammals is along the **White-tailed Trail,** which begins six miles from the visitor center off FM 106. It forms a 4.5-mile loop along Cayo Atascoso and winds through seven ponds among brush and grassland.

The visitor center features interpretive exhibits on natural history and standard national wildlife refuge literature. The NWR staff also lead occasional refuge tours; during the winter, local bird authority Father Tom Pincelli leads special monthly birding tours—highly recommended. The center is open daily 10 a.m.-4 p.m. from October to April, Saturday and Sunday 10 a.m.-4 p.m. in September and May, closed June-August. The trails and tour roads are open daily 7 a.m.-7 p.m. year round.

Getting There

From Harlingen, take State 345 north off US 77/83 S to FM 106, then east to the refuge entrance—a total trip of around 26 miles.

From Brownsville, take FM 1847 north till it meets FM 106 and then proceed east to the refuge, about 30 miles total.

BROWNSVILLE

The Rio Grande Valley's oldest town offers much to both short- and long-term visitors, including a mild year round climate, one of the nation's best zoos, and proximity to both South Padre Island and Mexico.

History

Sixteenth-Nineteenth Centuries: Along with San Antonio and Goliad, Brownsville is one of the most historic cities in Texas. In 1519, Spanish explorer Alonso Alvarez de Piñeda spent 40 days exploring the section of the Rio Grande that now passes between Brownsville and its

Mexican counterpart Matamoros; he named it "Rio de las Palmas" because it was lined with native Sabal palms. Piñeda and company were thus the first Europeans to reach the Texas coast. The fierce Karankawa Indians who inhabited the area weren't amenable to Spanish settlement, however. It wasn't until 1748 that another Spaniard, Don José de Escandón, was able to establish communities along the river's southern banks—by this time the nomadic Karankawas had left the area. One of the villages grew into a regional trade center known as Congregación de Nuestra Señora del Refugio, or simply Villa del Refugio. The name was later changed to Matamoros in honor of Mariano Matamoros, a priest executed during the Mexican war of independence in 1821.

The northern bank of the lower Rio Grande remained largely undeveloped until the Republic of Texas was annexed to the U.S. in 1845. The U.S. and Mexico disputed the border between the two countries—Mexico claimed it was the Nueces River while the U.S. claimed it was the Rio Grande—and this led to the establishment of Fort Taylor (also known as Fort Texas) across the river from Matamoros, thus sparking the Mexican-American War. After Mexican troops attacked the post and killed its commander, Major Jacob Brown, it was renamed Fort Brown. Several other battles in this brief war were fought in the area, until Mexico surrendered its border claim a few months after the establishment of the fort.

A New England businessman, Charles Stillman, planned the original town site that became Brownsville, also named for Major Brown. Because it was protected by Fort Brown, many residents who'd been living in Matamoros relocated across the river. They were joined by gold prospectors who arrived in Brownsville by boat via the Gulf of Mexico and who decided not to continue on to California.

During the Civil War, Brownsville-Matamoros made out very well by supplying Texas cotton to Europe via the Mexican Gulf port of Bagdad, southeast of Matamoros, thus avoiding the Union stockade along the Texas coast. Five weeks after Robert E. Lee's surrender at Appomattox, the last battle of the Civil War was fought at Palmito Ranch, east of town, when Union troops attacked from Brazos Island. They were defeated by Confederate soldiers under the command of Colonel Rip Ford.

Twentieth Century: Around the turn of the century the town became embroiled in the Bandit Wars that plagued the Rio Grande Valley, as Texas Rangers and U.S. National Guardsmen struggled to bring a measure of law and order to the vicinity. In 1904 the St. Louis, Brownsville, and Mexico railhead was established at Brownsville and the town's importance as a trade center increased. The Brownsville-Matamoros area now supports over 80 *maquilas.* A Union Pacific rail terminus connects with Mexico's national railway via the B&M Bridge over the Rio Grande; a 17-mile deep-sea channel in the Brownsville Navigation District links the area with the U.S. Inland Waterway System and the Gulf of Mexico. These transport systems allow Brownsville to act as a major shipping point for Valley agricultural products as well as Mexican and *maquila*-manufactured goods.

Winter tourism is also an important source of municipal income, and the local Convention and Visitors Bureau goes all out to make winter Texans feel welcome. For many Valley visitors, Brownsville is becoming a preferred destination because of its proximity to South Padre Island and Matamoros. It also has more of intrinsic interest than other Valley towns, with the Gladys Porter Zoo, a historic downtown, a strongly bicultural, bilingual community, a university and college, and the Sabal Palm Grove Sanctuary.

Downtown

Driving through Brownsville's downtown district, you might think you'd inadvertently crossed the border into Mexico—most signs are in Spanish or both English and Spanish. The town's original main avenue, Elizabeth St., has become a modern boulevard, but still runs through the town center; the most historic buildings are found along a street grid that straddles Elizabeth between Palm Blvd. to the west, E. Jackson St. to the north, International Blvd. to the east, and E. Fronton St. to the south. Common architectural styles include: Spanish Colonial, e.g., the 1897 El Globo Nuevo, 1502 E. Madison, or the 1928 Southern Pacific Depot, 601-641 E. Madison; Gothic, the 1859 Immaculate Conception Cathedral, 1218 E. Jefferson; Renaissance Revival, the 1883 Old

Cameron County Courthouse, 1131 E. Jefferson; and simple frame houses with double gables and decorative fascia, the 1887 El Globo Chiquito, 1059 E. Monroe.

The Brownsville Convention and Visitors Bureau's detailed city map contains a list of 44 historic structures in town and is available free from their information center (tel. 210-546-3721 or 800-626-2639) at the junction of US 77/83 and FM 802. The CVB also operates two-hour, narrated trolley tours of historic Brownsville for $6 adults, $3.50 children. The tours depart from the CVB office at 10 a.m. and 1 p.m. Wed.-Sunday.

Museums
The **Historic Brownsville Museum** (tel. 210-548-1313) is housed in the restored Southern Pacific Railroad Depot at 641 E. Madison. Various exhibits provide a detailed account of early Spanish exploration, with lots of old maps and blow-by-blow descriptions of historic battles—including the Battle of Resaca de la Palma, the Battle of Palmito Hill, and the Bandit Wars of the early 1900s. Features of the restored depot itself form part of the display, including segregated water fountains. Also on display is a huge portable altar that was once carried on a wagon for traveling Catholic masses. Outside the depot is an old Rio Grande Railroad steam engine and a caboose. The museum is open Mon.-Sat. 10 a.m.-4:30 p.m., and Sunday 2-5 p.m.; admission is $2 adults, 50 cents children.

The **Brownsville Art Museum** (tel. 542-0941) at 230 Neale Dr. is operated by the privately supported Brownsville Art League, headquartered next door in the historic 1850 Neal House. This is the center for the town's culture vultures and a host to traveling art exhibits, lectures, workshops, art classes, and films. A small permanent collection displays mostly Southwestern works. Open Mon.-Fri. 9:30 a.m.-3 p.m.; admission is free (donations accepted).

The **Stillman House** (tel. 542-3929) at 1305 E. Washington was built in 1850 by town founder Charles Stillman. It's been restored and turned into a museum that displays period furnishings and Brownsville memorabilia. Open Mon.-Fri. 10 a.m.-noon and 2-5 p.m., Sunday 3-5 p.m.; admission is $1 adults, 15 cents students, children under 12 free.

Gladys Porter Zoo
Zoo professionals named this zoo one of the country's 10 best in a recent poll. The considerable funds for the facility, which opened in 1971, were provided by the estate of Earl Sams, president and board chairman of the JC Penney Co. for 33 years. His daughter Gladys Porter oversaw the zoo design and selection of animals and is largely responsible for the resulting high quality. The zoo's 31 acres are divided into four zoogeographic areas: Tropical America (which exhibits many local species as well as species from Central and South America), Indo-Australia, Asia, and

Gladys Porter Zoo

Africa. Ancillary to the main design are a herpetarium, aquatic wing, children's zoo and nursery, bear grottoes, and a free-flight aviary. Some of the more rare creatures on display include Przewalski's horse, the jaguarundi, the Madagascan radiated tortoise, spectacled bears, and various rare African and Asian deer, oryx, bushbuck, bongos, bonteboks, and duikers. There's also a good collection of monkeys, baboons, crocodiles, elephants, and giraffes; the mountain gorillas are particularly healthy-looking specimens.

The main walking path through the zoo is a one-mile circuit around the center; shorter paths branch out from the circle, like wheel spokes. A tour train runs through the zoo on Sunday 1:30-3:30 p.m. ($1 adults, 50 cents children under 14). Zoo facilities include a couple of snack bars and restaurants, plus tables and benches. One of the nicest things about this zoo is that it never seems to get crowded, even in the peak winter Texan season.

The zoo (tel. 210-546-7187) is located at Ringgold and 6th, between International and Palm. It's open daily 9 a.m.-5 p.m., with extended weekend and summer hours (till sunset). Admission is $5.50 adults, $2.75 children 2-13. Wheelchairs and strollers are available for rent.

Fort Brown/University of Texas-Pan American

All that remains of the 1846 fort that sparked the War with Mexico is the post hospital, now the administration building for the University of Texas at Brownsville (tel. 210-544-8200); the post headquarters; and the guard house, now a fine arts center. At different times during the Civil War, both Union and Confederate troops used the fort. Just below the fort buildings is the curved Fort Brown Resaca.

The upper-division branch of **University of Texas-Pan American** (tel. 982-8230) is adjacent to Fort Brown and the University of Texas at Brownsville. Both schools offer special continuing education and adult education classes specially oriented toward winter Texans.

Access to the fort/college/university complex is via International Blvd. off E. Elizabeth.

Sabal Palm Grove Sanctuary

To see what the environment along the Rio Grande looked like before it was under heavy cultivation, pay a visit to this National Audubon Society-sponsored preserve. Formerly part of the Rabb Plantation, the sanctuary protects the last remaining Sabal palm grove in the delta. The *Sabal texana*, which reaches heights of 20-48 feet and is topped by a featherduster-like crown, is the state's only native palm. Once prolific in the area (hence, the early Spanish name for the Rio Grande—Rio de las Palmas), it's now considered an endangered species. It's also found several hundred miles south in certain Mexican valleys but is fast being eliminated there, too. *Micharos,* the fruit of the Sabal palm, is sometimes found in Matamoros markets and is considered a local delicacy.

Of the 172 acres protected by the sanctuary, only about 32 acres comprise a true *boscaje con las palmas* or palm grove. A walk along the trail leading through this dense forest conjures up visions of West Africa; in 1930 *Life Along the Delta,* an African hunting epic inspired by Frank Buck's *Bring 'Em Back Alive,* was filmed here. The tallest palm in the sanctuary, a national champion, extends 49 feet high, with a crown 12 feet across and a trunk 41 inches in diameter. The sanctuary consists of much more than the palm grove, however, and in fact preserves a unique ecosystem that includes coastal clay dunes (loma), wetlands, and old farm fields allowed to return to their natural state. Other protected vegetation include Texas ebony, tepeguaje, anacua (anaqua), brasil, colima, granjeño or spiny hackberry, manzanita or Barbados cherry, and two other endangered species, David's milkberry and Palmer's bloodleaf.

Birdwatchers flock to the sanctuary to catch glimpses of the rare green jay, as well as the chachalaca (sometimes called "Mexican pheasant"), white-tipped dove, olive sparrow, green and red-crowned parakeets, buff-bellied hummingbird, least grebe, kiskadee flycatcher, and black-bellied whistling duck. Most of these birds are easily seen by the patient eye. The sanctuary is also one of the few spots in South Texas still inhabited by ocelots and jaguarundi, though these nocturnal animals are very seldom seen by visitors.

The **Sabal Palm Grove Nature Trail** starts and ends at the visitor center near the entrance, making a half-mile loop to a *resaca* and back. A newer, second trail completes a separate half-mile loop to the river. A trail guide is available at the center, with plant and animal descriptions that correspond to numbered posts along the trail. It's a good idea to bring insect repellent along, as bugs occur in some abundance year round.

The sanctuary is open Thurs.-Mon. 8 a.m.-5 p.m. year round. Admission is $2 adults, $1 children. For further information, contact the Refuge Manager (tel. 210-541-8034), Sabal Palm Grove Sanctuary, P.O. Box 5052, Brownsville, TX 78523.

Getting There: The sanctuary is located right on the Rio Grande off FM 1419. Probably the easiest way to find it is to take Boca Chica Blvd. (State 4) east from Brownsville, then turn right (south) on FM 3068 till it ends at FM 1419. Turn right on FM 1419 and you'll come to a marked road on the left that leads down to the sanctuary. You can also get there by taking Southmost Rd. southeast off International Blvd. in town and following it through several twists and turns till it becomes FM 1419; the access road to the sanctuary will be on the right, about five miles from International Boulevard.

Accommodations

Motel 6 (tel. 210-546-4699), off US 77/83 at the FM 802 exit, has single rooms for $28 a night, plus $6 for each additional adult. The next least expensive motel is the new **Travelers Inn** (tel. 800-633-8300) at 2377 N. Expressway (US 77/83). Nearby **Best Western Rose Garden Inn** (tel. 546-5501), 845 US 77/83 N, has rooms for $48-70 s, $56-80 d. Just south of the Best Western, **Days Inn** (tel. 524-2201 or 800-325-2525) features similar rates. The well-appointed **Sheraton Plaza Royale** (tel. 350-9191 or 800-325-3535) is a bit farther north off US 77/83, near the tourist information center, and has rooms for $80 s, $91 d and two pools. The **Holiday Inn** (tel. 546-4591), near the convention and visitors bureau at 1945 N. Expressway (US 77/83), charges $50-90 a night. The Best Western, Sheraton, and Holiday Inn each provide airport transport.

Several resort hotels in town offer golf courses and tennis courts, and specialize in long-term room rentals—they're really more like resort condominiums. The **Fort Brown Hotel Resort** (tel. 546-2201 or 800-582-3333), at 1900 E.

Elizabeth near Fort Brown, has rooms for $70 s, $78 d per night, cheaper for stays of a week or more. Two lighted tennis courts, no golf. The upper-range **Ranch Viejo Resort** (tel. 350-4000), about 10 miles north of the town center off US 77/83, has one- to three-bedroom units ("villas") along a *resaca* and a 36-hole golf course. Nightly rates are $88-103 s/d plus $15 for each additional guest (up to six people), with discounts for longer stays.

There are also a couple dozen apartment complexes in town that take winter Texans for a few weeks or months at a time; rates are lower than at the resort hotels. The Brownsville Tourist Information Center (tel. 210-546-3721 or 800-626-2639) at US 77/83 and FM 802 maintains a list and can assist with reservations.

Camping and RV Parks

Like the rest of the Valley, Brownsville is well equipped for RV and mobile-home drivers. Most of the 41 area RV parks are scattered throughout an area east of town, off Boca Chica Blvd. and Minnesota Ave. (FM 313). Several reputable parks belonging to the Brownsville RV and MH Association include **Autumn Acres Trailer Park** (tel. 210-546-4979), 5034 Boca Chica; **Blue Bonnet Trailer Park** (tel. 546-0046), 2404 Las Casas; **Citrus Gardens Trailer Park** (tel. 546-0527), 2225 S. Dakota; **Crooked Tree Campland** (tel. 546-9617), 605 FM 802; **Four Seasons RV & MH Resort** (tel. 831-4918), 6900 Coffee Port; **Los Amigos Trailer Park** (tel. 542-8292), 3350 Boca Chica; **Paul's RV Park** (tel. 831-4852), 1129 N. Minnesota; **Rio RV & MH Park** (tel. 831-4653), 8801 Boca Chica; **Stagecoach RV Park** (tel. 542-8448), 325 FM 802; **Tip-O-Tex** (tel. 350-4031), 6676 N. Frontage; and **Trailer Village** (tel. 546-8350), 5107 Boca Chica. As elsewhere in the Valley, rates tend to be a uniform $10-12 nightly, $100 monthly, $200-225 for three months, $450 for six months.

The only tent-camping area in the Brownsville vicinity is **Brazos Island State Park** on the Gulf of Mexico, about 24 miles east of town via State 4. This park is completely undeveloped except for a few trash containers—you must bring in your own drinking water. On the plus side, you have the beach to yourself most of the time, the fishing's good, and there are no camping fees.

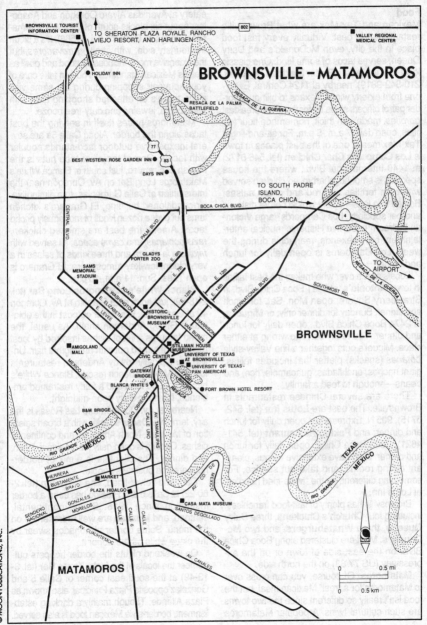

Food

Mexican and Tex-Mex are what Brownsville restaurants do best. Virtually every fast food place in the city, even McDonald's and Dairy Queen, serves tacos of some kind. One classic local joint is **Maria's Better Mexican Food** (tel. 210-542-9819), nearby at 1124 Central. Everyone from elderly winter Texans to bilingual border patrol officers stops by for the great breakfast *gorditas,* made with thick, homemade flour tortillas; open daily 7 a.m.-5 p.m. For sit-and-linger Tex-Mex meals, one of the best places in town is **Los Camperos Char Chicken** (tel. 546-8172) at 1440 International Blvd., where the house specialty is smoked, charbroiled chicken served with corn tortillas and red and green salsas. Broiled frog legs—a very typical border dish—is another specialty. Los Camperos' large Victorian ballroom hosts live Hispanic musical entertainment on weekends, mariachis during the week. Los Camperos is open daily for lunch and dinner.

Locals argue over who makes the best fajitas in town, **Antonio's,** at 2921 Boca Chica Blvd. in Strawberry Square, open Mon.-Sat. for lunch and dinner, Sunday for dinner only; or **Miguel's,** at 2474 Boca Chica Blvd., open daily for lunch and dinner. You really can't go wrong at either place. Miguel's puts together a fine Valley-style *botanas* (snacks) platter that includes fajitas, giant nachos, enchiladas, guacamole, rice, and beans—enough to feed a family.

There are several Chinese restaurants in Brownsville. The best are **Lotus Inn** (tel. 542-5715), 905 N. Expressway, open daily for lunch and dinner; and **Peking Restaurant** (tel. 541-4621), 3503 Boca Chica, open daily for lunch and dinner. Both have extensive menus, pleasant dining rooms, and take-out service. For something different, try the "twice-fried noodles" at Lotus Inn.

Brownsville has plenty of fast-food franchises, including four **Church's Chickens,** three **Dairy Queens,** three **Whataburgers,** and two **McDonald's.** Most are clustered along Boca Chica Blvd. on the east side of town or off the expressway (US 77/83) on the north side.

Matamoros: Of course, you can cross over to Matamoros for a "real" Mexican meal, but the food isn't really so different since the two towns are such cultural twins. A popular Matamoros eatery at Avenidas Alvaro Obregón and Anapolas, about six blocks south of Gateway International Bridge, is **García's** (tel. 31566). It's a bit on the touristy side, with strolling *trovadores,* but the extensive menu includes seafood and quail as well as Mexican standards. You can take care of your souvenir shopping during the same visit since there's an attached shopping area with handicrafts, jewelry, and duty-free booze.

Matamoros prides itself in serving the best tacos along the border. Along Calle 5a are several inexpensive outdoor taco stands popular with locals. One of the nicer taco huts is the newish **El Granero,** just south of Blanca White's Matamoros Long Bar on Av. Obregón near the intersection of Calle Gardenias. In a diminutive, air-conditioned building, El Granero's kitchen turns out over a dozen kinds of moderately priced tacos. Among the best are smoked chicken, *rajas poblanas,* and *carne asada,* all served with *frijoles a la charra* and three kinds of salsas in a very clean, low-key atmosphere. El Granero is open Tues.-Sun. 11 a.m.-10 p.m.

Blanca White's Matamoros Long Bar (tel. 2-18-59), just north of El Granero at Av. Obregón 49 at Gardenias, is another outpost in the ubiquitous Grupo Anderson chain. As usual, the menu features a list of dishes inspired by local recipes but turned out with an original flair. Unlike the typically rowdy Anderson restaurants found at Mexican beach resorts, Blanca White's has both good food and a fairly restrained ambience. It's open daily noon-midnight.

Nearby at Av. Obregón and Las Rosas is the airy, fern-style **Oscar's Café,** with a broad selection of Mexican, North American and continental dishes. Oscar's is open daily for breakfast, lunch, and dinner. The clientele is a mix of border-hoppers and business people.

Dark and velvet-lined, **The Drive Inn** (tel. 2-00-22) at Calle 6 and Hidalgo has been a border institution since 1916. Steak, continental, seafood, and Mexican are well represented on the menu. Some border aficionados swear by the place while others abhor it.

On weekend nights the border-hoppers outnumber the locals at the funky **Texas Bar** (tel. 3-13-49) at the southeast corner of Calle 5 and Gonzalez opposite Plaza Principal, also known as Plaza Allende. Though mainly a drinking establishment, border-style Mexican food is also served.

Brownsville Winter Residents Club

This city-sponsored service for winter Texans issues a weekly schedule of organized events, including dancing (square, round, ballroom, and pattern), golf, bowling, arts and crafts workshops, cards, films, shuffleboard, and state-oriented picnics. Most indoor activities take place at the New Pavilion at Dean Porter Park on Camille Drive. The club is open October to April; seasonal dues are $8.50. For more information, call Brownsville Parks and Recreation at (210) 542-2064.

Entertainment

Brownsville has a pretty quiet nightlife. Turn on the TV and you'll find that most stations broadcast in Spanish or in a mixture of English and Spanish. Mexican television station XHAB broadcasts Spanish-language films and MTV Internacional. Bilingual DJs at radio station KIWW-FM 96.1 play a hot selection of Tex-Mex and *onda-chicana* music.

Events

Charro Days is the Brownsville-Matamoros version of a pre-Lenten festival (à la Mardi Gras), held for three days in late February at various venues in each city. It's the area's oldest and biggest annual event and includes parades, costume balls, food, music and dancing.

Diez y Seis or Mexican Independence Day (September 16) is also big in both cities; on the nearest weekend to the 16th they cooperate for **Fiesta International,** a bicultural weekend of fireworks, parades, and *mucho* celebration. For scheduling details on either event, call the Brownsville Convention and Visitors Bureau (tel. 210-546-3721 or 800-626-2639).

Information

Tourist Office: The **Brownsville Information Center** (tel. 210-596-3721 or 800-626-2639 outside Texas), at the junction of FM 802 and US 77/83, has a very helpful staff and loads of free literature. It's open Mon.-Fri. 8:30 a.m.-5 p.m., Saturday 8 a.m.-5 p.m., Sunday 9 a.m.-4 p.m.

Mexican Consulate: Visas, tourist cards, and other international documentation for Mexico can be arranged at Brownsville's Mexican consulate (tel. 541-7601 or 542-4431) at 724 Elizabeth St. (at 7th Street).

Telephone: The area code for Brownsville is 210. To call a Matamoros number from Brownsville (or anywhere else in the Rio Grande Valley), dial 011-52-891 before the local five-digit number.

Getting There and Around

Brownsville has two downtown bus terminals: the **Trailways** station (tel. 512-546-7171) at 1134 E. St. Charles at 12th, and the **Greyhound/Valley Transit Co.** (VTC) station (tel. 546-2264) at 1305 E. Adams. Greyhound and Trailways buses ply long-distance intra- and interstate routes, while VTC handles Rio Grande Valley, South Texas, and northern Mexico routes.

City buses run hourly between Brownsville International Airport and the city terminal on 12th St.; the fare is 50 cents.

Across the Border to Matamoros

Of the larger Mexican towns along the Texas-Mexico border, Matamoros (pop. 350,000) is the most "Mexican," probably because its counterpart, Brownsville, is the least "American." Its history goes back to 1765, when it was settled as Congregación de Nuestra Señora del Refugio and laid out it in the traditional Spanish colonial grid along the Santa Cruz bend of the Rio Grande. Many of the older buildings feature 18th- and 19th-century Spanish Creole architecture, with inner patios, ironwork balconies on the second floor, shuttered doors and windows framed by pilasters, and molded brick cornices. Later renamed Matamoros in commemoration of Mexican independence hero Mariano Matamoros, it's one of only four cities in Mexico with a name preceded by the honorific "H.," which stands for the English equivalent of "Heroic, Loyal, and Unconquered" (this is why Mexican traffic signs in the area read "H. Matamoros").

The Gateway International Bridge joins Brownsville and Matamoros and leads to the clean and well-lit main tourist strip, Avenida Alvaro Obregón, which is lined with bars, restaurants, and souvenir shops. To get a feel for nontourist Matamoros, walk a few blocks down the Avenida and make a left at Calle 5 (Carranza) or 6, which lead to the **Plaza Hidalgo,** the main public square. As is typical for former colonial towns in Mexico, a Spanish cathedral (Nuestra Señora del Refugio, originally built in 1831, then

LA FRONTERA

Texas and Mexico share a thousand-mile border that has become more than just a political boundary. When residents on either side of the border refer to "La Frontera," they're talking about an area that extends as far as a hundred miles north and south from the Rio Grande, the center of a hybrid culture that's neither American nor Mexican. Here First World meets Third World, and north European, Protestant capitalism meets south European, Catholic feudalism. Despite the fact that Mexico is the U.S.'s third-largest trading partner, La Frontera is one of the poorest areas in either country.

The burgeoning twin-plant (*maquila* or *maquiladora*) industry along the border, in which American technology and management exploit cheap Mexican labor, was once trumpeted as the hope of the borderland. Goods produced at the plants were granted special trade status since they were established in "export-processing zones" using U.S. capital. As the number of *maquilas* increased, more unemployed Mexicans migrated to northern Mexico in hopes of landing steady, low-paying jobs. Once on the border, the migrants encountered the imminent attraction of higher-paying work just over the river. Today, human taxis wade across carrying passengers on their backs for 25 cents a trip during "commute" hours. In spite of a multimillion-dollar U.S. Border Patrol budget, the border will probably remain fluid far into the future.

The 1994 passage of the North American Free Trade Agreement (NAFTA) means all taxes and tariffs on goods exchanged between the U.S., Canada, and Mexico will eventually be eliminated, thus ending the demand for *maquilas* and, according to treaty supporters, reducing immigration and environmental pressure at the border. The agreement initially provides US$60 million in U.S. foreign aid for construction of sewage treatment plants in transborder metropolitan areas like Juárez-El Paso, Laredo-Nuevo Laredo, and Brownsville-Matamoros—a cleanup long overdue. In the 1983 La Paz Agreement, both the U.S. and Mexican governments pledged to cooperate in addressing problems of air, water, and soil pollution in a "Border Area" extending 100 km on either side of the international boundary, but little was accomplished due to a general lack of funds. This time around there will be little excuse; eventually the binational Border Environmental Cooperation Commission is expected to spend US$8 billion on border cleanup.

Rolando Hinojosa, a Chicano writer born in Mercedes, Texas, has captured La Frontera spirit in his well-written, humorous book *The Valley* (Tempe, AZ: Bilingual Press), a fictional narrative obviously inspired by the lower Rio Grande Valley. An imaginary "Jonesville-On-The-Rio" stands in for Brownsville.

rebuilt after a 1933 storm) faces the plaza. Day or night, this is the city's downtown heart.

Sights: The top cultural attraction in Matamoros is the **Museo del Maíz** or Museum of Maize, also called the Casa de Cultura. It's a short walk from the bridge at the corner of Calle 5 (Calle Carranza) and Av. Constituyentes, a block from the Gran Hotel Residencial. Exhibits detail the history of maize cultivation in Mexico from pre-Cortesian times through the present, as well as traditional folkloric and medicinal uses of the maize plant. There's a strong underlying political message accompanying some of the displays, focusing on criticism of national land distribution policies (Mexico was self-sufficient in corn until 1965 and is now a net importer). The exhibits are fairly easy to follow even if you can't understand the Spanish-only labels. Open

Tues.-Fri. 9:30 a.m.-5 p.m. and Sat.-Sun. 9:30 a.m.-3 p.m.; admission is free.

Another place of interest is **Casa Mata,** a fort that played a strategic role in the Mexican-American War. A museum at the fort displays Mexican revolution memorabilia and Indian artifacts, but very little concerning the Mexican-American War. It's located at the corner of Santos Degollado and Guatemala—take Calle 1 south to Santos Degollado and make a left. Usually open Tues.-Sun. 10 a.m.-5 p.m.; admission is free.

Bullfights and *Charreadas:* Matamoros has a Plaza de Toros at the southern outskirts of town off Av. Reforma. Local *charro* associations practice and compete at the **Lienzo Charro La Costeña,** also south of town on the highway. Check with the Matamoros tourist office at the international bridge or with the Brownsville

Convention and Visitors Bureau in Brownsville for scheduling information. Bullfight season generally runs May through September while *chairreadas* are held year round.

Shopping: Though not as popular a shopping venue as Nuevo Laredo, many Texans come to Matamoros for quick south-of-the-border bargains. The shops along Avenida Alvaro Obregón are not the cheapest, since they cater to day tourists who don't venture very far into town, but some of their folk art is decent. **Bárbara de Matamoros** at no. 40 is one of the better shops. Two large markets in town carry a wide selection of Mexican arts and crafts and are more susceptible to negotiation. **Mercado Juárez**, stretching across Abasolo and Matamoros between Calles 9 and 10 (about three blocks east of the plaza), is the biggest; a smaller version is on Bravo between Calles 8 and 9. The **Centro de Artesanías** on Av. Obregón near the Gran Hotel Residencial contains several shops selling glassware, boots, clothing, and other handicrafts.

Liquor is much cheaper in Matamoros than on the U.S. side, about 50% lower. It's also duty-free, as long as you don't bring back more than a quart within a 30-day period.

Crossing the Border: Buses to Matamoros from Brownsville leave frequently throughout the day from the **Greyhound/Valley Transit Co. (VTC)** station (tel. 210-546-2264), at 1305 E. Adams. The fare is US$3. You can also walk across the bridge into Matamoros from International Blvd. on the Brownsville side in 15-20 minutes. The Mexican government has a small tourist office at the end of the bridge on the Matamoros side, but there's very little printed information available. The staff at the customs and immigration post, also at the bridge, are very quick to let visitors in for stays of under 72 hours. If you're planning to continue deeper into Mexico (or look like you are), you need a tourist card.

Tours: Gray Line (tel. 542-8962) maintains a Brownsville/South Padre Island service that leads five-hour sightseeing/shopping tours of Matamoros for $15 per person. A local operation, **Bro-Mat** (tel. 544-6292), also offers Matamoros tours for $15 per person.

Train to Monterrey: Mexico's national rail system operates a first-class rail service (*primera especial*) between Matamoros and Monterrey, oriented toward overnight gringo shopping trips. The service, called *El Tamaulipeco,* features air-conditioned cars with reclining seats you can reserve in advance through most Brownsville travel agencies. The train leaves the Matamoros station (tel. 6-67-06) at Av. Hidalgo and Calle 10 daily in the midafternoon, arriving in Monterrey in the evening. In the reverse direction, it leaves Monterrey in the morning and arrives in Matamoros in the mid-afternoon. If you purchase your tickets at the Matamoros station, reserved first-class fares for the journey are US$19 Matamoros-Monterrey; second-class fares are US$2.50, US$3, and US$5.50 respectively. Travel agencies in Brownsville charge more—sometimes twice the standard fare. The train stops in Reynosa along the way.

Driving: Matamoros is one of the easier border cities to drive through because of its wide, well-planned avenues, which link the border crossing directly with Mexico 2 and Mexico 180.

SANTA ANA NATIONAL WILDLIFE REFUGE

This 2,000-acre refuge is one of the smallest in the national wildlife refuge system, yet it contains one of the nation's most diverse biomes. Similar to the Sabal Palm Grove Sanctuary outside Brownsville, it preserves a chunk of the Rio Grande delta as it appeared before the land was cleared for cultivation.

A cross-section of temperate, tropical, desert, and coastal elements attracts over 380 bird species, including a number of Mexican species rarely seen north of the border, including black-bellied tree duck, chachalaca, jacana, red-billed pigeon, crested caracara, groove-billed ani, pauraque, rose-throated becard, and green jay. The densely forested interior of the refuge supports cedar elm, Texas ebony, anaqua, granjeño or spiny hackberry, *tepeguaje* or leadtree, huisache, guayacan, retama or Jerusalem thorn, and mesquite. In patches of forest near Santa Ana Lake, the trees are thick with Spanish moss.

Mammals that inhabit the refuge include the endangered ocelot, a spotted cat around 30 inches long up to 45 inches with tail; and the jaguarundi, which reaches 20-30 inches in length—up to 50 inches with tail—and has short reddish or gray-blue fur.

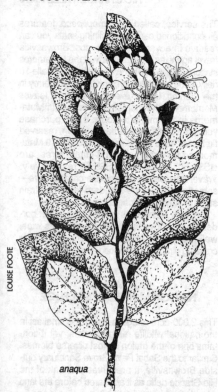

LOUISE FOOTE

anaqua

Facilities

The visitor center contains excellent interpretive displays describing lower Rio Grande habitats and the flora and fauna that thrive here. It's open Mon.-Fri. 8 a.m.-4:30 p.m., Saturday and Sunday 9 a.m.-4:30 p.m. A seven-mile paved road (Refuge Dr.) bisects the refuge and passes trailheads to 12 miles of foot trails. To really experience the biological diversity offered here, you have to get out on the trails, which wind past three lakes (always full of diverse waterfowl species) and through various vegetational zones. Permanent photo blinds are situated at bird concentration points and are good places to watch birdlife even if you don't have a camera. The trails are open daily from sunrise to sunset.

Between late November and the end of April, the refuge offers an interpretive tram tour along Refuge Dr. that costs $2.50 for adults, $1 for children under 12. On certain days during the tram season, the tours are available only to environmental education groups. Refuge Dr. is closed to private vehicles from mid-January through mid-April.

Admission to the refuge is free. For further information, call or write the Santa Ana National Wildlife Refuge (tel. 210-787-7861), Route 2, Box 202A, Alamo, TX 78516.

Getting There

The refuge is about 12 miles south of Alamo (a small town between Harlingen and McAllen on US 83) via FM 907, at US 281. Instead of taking US 83 to FM 907, you can get here by following US 281 west from Brownsville along the border, an interesting drive that passes citrus groves, sugarcane fields, and small border towns. The vertical concrete pipes in the fields act as vents for the underground irrigation system.

McALLEN

This town of around 90,000 was originally settled by Scotsman John McAllen in the mid-1800s but has a fairly undistinguished history. In 1904 a railway line parallel to the Mexican border led to further development and the addition of nearby towns Pharr, San Juan, Alamo, and San Benito. McAllen is the center for the Valley's citrus industry, and has been dubbed "The City of Palms" because of the non-native Egyptian palm trees planted in and around the city. It's third behind Harlingen and Brownsville in the number of RV parks in the immediate vicinity (around 37), but the nearby towns of Mission, San Juan, Pharr, Edinburg, Alamo, and Palmview are also popular with RVers, so McAllen has become a winter-Texan hub for this end of the Valley.

Eight miles from the center of McAllen across the Rio Grande is the Mexican city of Reynosa (pop. 375,000), a somewhat popular tourist destination for west Valley visitors. McAllen in return receives many Mexican visitors, who seem to favor the town over any other in "El Valle."

McAllen International Museum

This is the only museum in the Valley accredited by the American Association of Museums.

Galleries feature rotating exhibits of Mexican and American art (especially folk art), as well as exhibits on geology, archaeology, and natural history. A new meteorological exhibit contains a working weather station. There is also an on-going schedule of special programs, including seminars, workshops, and cinema. At 1900 Nolana at Bicentennial (tel. 210-682-1564); open Tues.-Sat. 9 a.m.-5 p.m., Sunday 1-5 p.m. Admission is $1 for adults, 25 cents for students, free on Sunday.

McAllen Botanical Gardens and Nature Center

This 20-acre park (tel. 210-682-1517) features nature trails through various landscapes planted with South Texas flora. It's off US 83 about 2.5 miles west of town, past Ware Road. Open daily sunrise to sunset; admission free.

Los Ebanos Ferry

The ferry at Los Ebanos has been running since 1954 and is the last hand-pulled ferry (called *chalón* on the Mexican side) on the Rio Grande. To get here, drive west from McAllen on US 83 to FM 886, between Havana and Sullivan City; then turn left (south) and follow the maze-like road until you hit the river. In service 7 a.m.-3 p.m. daily, the ferry works by a system of cables and pulleys pulled by hand; it can carry three cars and a small number of pedestrians on each crossing. The fare is US$1 per auto; pedestrians may ride for25 cents per person. There are immigration checks on both sides of the river. On the Mexican side, it's two miles to the nearest village, Díaz Ordaz, a small cotton- and sorghum-farming center. A new bridge is in the planning stages; the ferry may be kept as a tourist attraction.

Accommodations

Room rates at McAllen's **Motel 6** (tel. 210-687-3700), 700 US 83 (2nd or 10th St. exit), are among the highest Motel 6 rates in Texas: $33.95, plus $6 for each additional adult—but then hotel/motel accommodations in McAllen tend to run the highest in the Valley. Near McAllen's main shopping and restaurant area at 601 S. 10th, the **Imperial Motor Hotel** (tel. 686-0281) has decent rooms for $36 s, $40-43 d; airport transport is free. Also in this vicinity is the **El**

Matador Motor Inn (tel. 682-6171), 501 S. 10th St., where rooms cost $30-50. Out on US 83 east of 10th St., **Thrifty Inn** (tel. 631-6700) has simple rooms for $40-54.

In the mid-range category is the **Holiday Inn Civic Center** (tel. 686-2471), 200 US 83 (2nd St. exit), where rooms are $58-78 s, $66-86 d. There are a number of other motels along nearby S. 10th St., including the **McAllen Airport Hilton** (tel. 687-1161), 2721 S.10th St., $64-70 s, $76-78 d; and the **Quality Inn McAllen** (tel. 682-8301), 1401 S. 10th St., $53 s, $58 d. Both offer guests complimentary breakfast every morning. The **Best Western Rose Garden Suites** (tel. 630-3333 or 800-528-1234) at 300 E. US 83 offers good rooms for $51-54 s, $58-61 d including complimentary breakfast.

For a few dollars more, the best choice is the restored **Doubletree Casa de Palmas Hotel** (tel. 631-1101 or 800-274-1102), a Spanish Colonial-style inn built in 1918 at 100 N. Main downtown. Nicely appointed rooms are $65-85 s, $75-95 d; during the summer these rates drop $5. McAllen's Mexican consulate is next door.

Another atmospheric—but much less expensive—place is the **San Juan Hotel** (tel. 781-5339) at 125 Business 83 in nearby San Juan, east of McAllen, just west of FM 1426. Built in the Mission style in the 1800s, it was restored by the Sigle family in 1983 and now offers simple rooms for $22-25 s, $28-40 d, more elaborate rooms for more. A disadvantage to the San Juan Hotel is that it's a bit far from the McAllen action, though close to Garza's Café.

RV Parks

RV sites in and around McAllen run about the same as in Harlingen and Brownsville: approximately $10-15 nightly, $100-120 a month, $250-300 for three months, as low as $450 for six months. A few listed with the McAllen Chamber of Commerce include **Baldwin Mobile Home Manor** (tel. 210-682-0454), 400 Date Palm; **Citrus Valley RV Park** (tel. 383-8189), State 107 and Rooth; **Lake Tejano RV & MH Resort** (tel. 843-8435), 824 S. 11th St., Hidalgo; **McAllen Mobile Park** (tel. 682-3304), 4900 N. McColl; **Paradise Park** (tel. 682-9091), 100 E. Hackberry; **Tropic Star Park** (tel. 787-7957), 1401 S. Cage, Pharr; **VIP Motel & RV Park** (tel. 682-8384), 3501 US 83; and **Westway Mobile**

Home Park (tel. 687-4642), 1300 S. Ware. There are dozens more RV parks in the nearby communities of San Juan, Mission, Pharr, Alamo, and Penitas—many with the lowest rates in the Valley.

Food

We're still in the Valley, where Mexican food rules. A McAllen budget classic is **La Casa del Taco** (tel. 631-8193), 1100 Houston, where you make your own tacos from "the Sombrero," a stack of homemade tortillas under a straw hat, surrounded by fajitas (or *arracheras*), *frijoles a la charra*, grilled onions, and peppers; open daily for breakfast, lunch, and dinner. Cheap and tasty breakfast tacos (called *patos* here) are served in over a dozen combinations at three branches of **El Pato:** 2263 Pecan, 3019 N. 10th, and 1123 W. US 83. All are open from early in the morning till late at night. Old standby **Taco Cabana** at 1010 S. 10th St. is open 24 hours.

Popular **Alonso's Escorial** (tel. 686-1160) at 4501 N. 10th impresses visiting Mexicans as well as locals with its huge *botanas* platter piled with chicken and beef fajitas and the *parillada* of three grilled meats and quail. Alonso's is open daily for lunch and dinner.

If you happen to be in nearby San Juan and are looking for Tex-Mex, funky **Garza's Café** (tel. 787-9051) at 308 N. Nebraska (the main drag) is the place. The enchiladas with homemade sauce, *chalupas, carne guisada*, and Mexican breakfasts are known throughout the west end of the Valley and are quite inexpensive. Open Tues.-Thurs. 11 a.m.-3 p.m. and 4:30-8 p.m., Friday 11 a.m.-3 p.m. and 4:30-8:30 p.m., Saturday 10 a.m.-9 p.m., Sunday 8 a.m.-8 p.m.

Another San Juan draw is **Don Pancho's** (tel. 781-3601), at 104 N. Raul Longoria Rd. opposite the Virgen de San Juan del Valle shrine. A recent *Texas Monthly* report on Valley Mexican cuisine claimed Don Pancho's prepares the Valley's best fajita dinners. Delicious french-fried squash is another house specialty. In Pharr, **Armando's Taco Hut** at 106 N. Cage has good, inexpensive Tex-Mex food, a great Tex-Mex jukebox, and occasional live *conjunto* music; open daily 7 a.m.-3 a.m.

For Italian, try McAllen's **Ianelli** (tel. 631-0666) at 321 S. Main, which serves pasta, pizza, chicken, and seafood; open Mon.-Sat. for lunch and dinner. Texas chain restaurant **The Olive Garden** (tel. 618-1188), at 222 US 83 between 2nd and 10th, is also quite reliable, especially for fresh pastas and salads; it's open daily for lunch and dinner. McAllen has a branch of the **Lotus Inn** (tel. 631-2693) at 1120 N. 10th St., which has a mixed Chinese menu. Also good for Chinese are the **Chinese Inn North** (tel. 631-4705), 4000 N. 10th, and the **Chinese Inn South** (tel. 686-2328), 2001 S. 10th. All three Chinese restaurants are open daily for lunch and dinner.

Pepe's River Fiesta and **Rio's on the Rio Grande,** off FM 1016 just south of Mission, are built over the Rio Grande. Boaters can tie up at the restaurants' floating docks—the only such facilities anywhere along the Rio Grande from El Paso to the Gulf of Mexico. Pepe's is a favorite with winter Texans from November to March, when the restaurant features live music in the afternoons. During the summer the restaurant hosts live bands on weekend evenings.

Reynosa: Reynosa bears the distinction of having the largest number of restaurants per capita in the State of Tamaulipas, many along parallel Calles Zaragoza, Aldama, and Allende in the town's *zona rosa,* or tourist district. **Sam's** (tel. 2-00-34) at Allende and Ocampo is famous throughout the area for its inexpensive steak dinners, Mexican platters, and border specialties such as quail. Open daily 11 a.m.-midnight. Other *zona rosa* restaurants catering to gringos include **La Cucaracha,** 1000 Aldama at Campo, lunch and dinner daily; and **Meson del Colorado,** 1105 Alemán near the bridge, with breakfast, lunch and dinner daily. **Tupinamba** on Plaza Principal, several blocks uphill from the bridge, is good for *cabrito* and is open for lunch and dinner daily. For the best *norteña* cuisine (*carne asada, arracheras,* etc.) in Reynosa, head for **La Fogata** on Calle Matamoros off the Plaza Principal.

Entertainment

Hillbilly Heaven (tel. 210-687-1106), at 3509 N. 10th St. in McAllen, and **John Henry's** (tel. 383-8381), at 3915 S. US 281 in nearby Edinburg, are the main country dance halls in the area; live music is limited to weekend nights. **South Dallas** (tel. 682-4133) at 500 Hackberry in town hosts urban, top-40/country bands several nights a week.

Live jazz and blues can be heard on weekends at **JT's Restaurant & Lounge** (tel. 631-4561), 1005 Nolana.

Of the Valley's 22 radio stations, 12 broadcast a portion or all of their programming in Spanish. Radio station KIWW-FM 96.1 broadcasts *tejano* music from nearby Harlingen. For country and western, tune in KFRQ-FM 94.5.

Events

In nearby Mission, the **Texas Citrus Fiesta** is celebrated during the last two weeks of January with parades, arts and crafts shows, barbecues, costume shows, and the coronation of King Citrus and Queen Citrianna. All events feature citrus themes.

The **Texas Square Dance Jamboree**, possibly the largest square-dance festival in the state, is held the first Saturday in February at the McAllen Civic Center, junction of US 83 and S. 10th.

For further information on these annual events, contact the McAllen Chamber of Commerce at (210) 682-2871.

Shopping

For the most part McAllen, as a shopping destination, is oriented toward Mexican visitors. Bargain stores for inexpensive clothing and housewares line Main St. north of US 83. More upscale stores and shopping centers are found along 10th St. north of US Business 83 and in various malls around the city. One of the largest is **La Plaza Mall** on S. 10th St south of US 83.

Britton's Photo Supply (tel. 210-686-8332), at 208 S. Main (and at a second location in the Main Place shopping center, 1800 S. Main), carries the Valley's most complete line of films and photographic supplies.

Information

The **McAllen Convention and Visitors Bureau** (tel. 210-682-2871), at 10 N. Broadway, has printed information on local attractions in McAllen and Reynosa and can answer tourist-oriented questions. *McAllen: The Texas Tropics,* the bureau's annual magazine guide, is loaded with tips on things to see and do in the area. For Spanish-speaking visitors, the bureau publishes the similar *McNífico Guía Turística.* The

chamber's *Map of McAllen and Lower Río Grande Valley* contains a very detailed map of the city and border area.

To call Reynosa from McAllen, dial 011-52-892 before the local five-digit number.

McAllen has a **Mexican consulate** (tel. 210-78501) at 1418 Beech St., Suites 102-104.

Getting There and Around

Miller International Airport (tel. 210-682-9101), south of US 83 via Main St. or 10th St., is steadily catching up with Valley International in Harlingen; Miller now fields flights for Continental, Conquest, American Airlines, and Aerolitoral. The latter recently moved service from Harlingen.

Valley Transit Company (tel. 686-5479) at 129 S. 16th St. operates bus service around the Valley and to nearby Mexican border towns.

Tours

Mario's Tours (tel. 210-632-7834) offers day excursions to Reynosa for $14 per person; stops include the market, main square, cemetery, PEMEX oil refinery, residential areas, and a *maquiladora.* Mario's also runs three-day tours to Monterrey ($109) and Real de Catorce ($119), a former mining town on the Altiplano of San Luis Potosí.

Three local clubs lead bass fishing and hunting (dove, duck, geese, quail, deer) tours to the nearby Mexican state of Tamaulipas: **Antlers, Fur, and Feather Guide Service** (tel. 210-687-8188), Star R. Box 71, McAllen, TX 78503; **Club Exclusive/Big Bass Tours** (tel. 687-8513), 1418 Beech, Suite 122, McAllen, TX 78501; and **Mexico Whitewings Unlimited** (tel. 631-7286 or 687-3548), 1113 Upas, McAllen, TX 78501.

Across the Border to Reynosa

The second Escandón settlement on the Río Grande, Reynosa began in 1749 as Nuestra Señora de Guadalupe de Reynosa. The town eventually became an important post for the salt trade in early Nuevo Santander. A flood in 1800 destroyed the town and forced the residents to move to the current site.

Reynosa's main square, market, and cathedral sit atop a small hill about a half mile from the bridge via Calle Zaragoza at Juárez. Between the bridge and the square along Virreyes and Allende is a *zona rosa,* or "pink zone," of tourist-oriented shops, restaurants, *casas de cambio,* bars, discos, and hotels. The bar with the windmill out front on Zaragoza is **Dutch's,** an old gringo standby. Along the same strip, the **Alaskan** and **La Concha** discos are popular with young residents and visitors. The **Imperial** hosts live music.

Calle Hidalgo off the Plaza Principal (also known as Plaza Hidalgo) is closed to vehicular traffic so pedestrians can stroll amongst street vendors, itinerant mariachis, and shops. At the end of Hidalgo is **Mercado Zaragoza,** a large market with handicrafts.

For restaurant information, see the previous "Food" section.

Bullfights: Though Reynosa is not a big town for the *fiesta brava,* the Plaza de Toros off Matamoros and Zapata, about 10 blocks west of the main plaza, hosts occasional *corridas.* Check with the Mexican tourist office next to the international bridge for scheduling.

Events: On December 12 every year, the city celebrates the feast day of its patron saint, Our Lady of Guadalupe. Pilgrim processions begin the week before and folk dancers perform in front of the cathedral every afternoon.

Getting There: The Texas town directly across the river is Hidalgo, which is about eight miles south of McAllen via S. 23rd St./State 115. There's a cheap parking lot here where you can leave your car and walk over the bridge to Reynosa. **Valley Transit Co.** and **Transportes Monterrey-Cadereyta-Reynosa** buses direct to Reynosa leave from the McAllen VTC terminal at 129 S. 16th St. every 20-30 minutes till 11 p.m. for $3; get off at the bridge for the *zona rosa* or stay on till you reach the new bus terminal if you plan to connect with buses to other destinations in Mexico.

The *El Tamaulipeco* train runs between Reynosa and Monterrey for US$8 first class, US$2.50 second class.

Mexican Insurance: If you're heading toward Reynosa from the U.S. and need Mexican vehicle insurance, one of the oldest and most reliable agencies along the entire border is **Sanborn's Mexican Insurance** in McAllen (tel. 210-686-0711, fax 686-0732), 2009 S. 10th. In Hidalgo you can also arrange a Sanborn's insurance policy at **Patty's Insurance** (tel. 843-2863), 309 S. Bridge.

BENTSEN-RIO GRANDE VALLEY STATE PARK

This protected 588-acre section of Rio Grande delta riparian woodlands and *matorral* (thorn scrub) is the second-largest such preserve on either side of the border. Much of the flora is similar, including cedar elm, retama, huisache, guayacan, the rare (for the U.S.) manzanita or Barbados cherry, Texas ebony, honey mesquite, granjeño, colima, anaqua, and Spanish moss, plus coyotillo, lotebush, old man's beard, and desert olive. Overnight facilities provide opportunities for experiencing both diurnal and nocturnal wildlife.

As with parks and refuges farther southwest along the river, the Bentsen-Rio Grande Valley State Park is a mecca for birders, with hundreds of species either permanently residing or passing through in the spring and fall. This is the northern limit of the habitat range for many bird species: the green jay, chachalaca, groove-billed ani, pauraque, and Lichtenstein's oriole. Other com-

Bentsen-Rio Grande Valley State Park

monly seen winged residents are the great blue heron, snowy heron, turkey vulture, long-billed curlew, cactus wren, tropical parula, eight species of warblers, 16 species of duck, kites, six species of owl, hawks, falcons, and flycatchers.

Mammal residents are the same as for the Santa Ana National Wildlife Refuge: the nine-banded armadillo, coyote, cottontail rabbit, bobcat, ocelot, jaguarundi, javelina, seven species of bats, weasel, and badger. Two amphibians unique to the area are the Rio Grande siren, an eel-like salamander with two small front legs only, and the Rio Grande leopard frog. Both are found in the shallows of the Rio Grande bordering the south edge of the park and in the two *resacas* on either side. About a dozen snake species normally live in the park, including the colorful Texas indigo snake and the sometimes quite large bullsnake—both are nonvenomous. The only poisonous reptile in the area is the coral snake, which is rarely seen.

Facilities

The park has two hiking trails. The **Rio Grande**

Hiking Trail forms a two-mile loop from the camping area to the river and back, passing *matorral,* marshy areas next to the eastern *resaca,* and riverbanks festooned with willow and cattails. Numbered markers along the trail correspond to brief descriptions in a free trail guide available at park headquarters. The **Singing Chaparral Nature Trail** is a 1.5-mile loop that starts from the road between park headquarters and the camping area and leads to a wildlife waterhole. As with the Rio Grande Hiking Trail, there's a free interpretive booklet that identifies numbered areas along the way.

The camping area has tent/camper sites with water for $6 a night and full RV hookups for $10. Daily admission is $3 per vehicle, $1 for pedestrians or cyclists.

For further information, contact the Park Superintendent (tel. 210-585-1107), P.O. Box 988, Mission, TX 78572.

Getting There

The park is about five miles southwest of Mission via Loop 374 (west) and FM 2062 (south).

spotted bass

LOUISE FOOTE

LAREDO

Los Dos Laredos, "The Two Laredos" (Laredo on the U.S. side of the Rio Grande, Nuevo Laredo on the Mexico side), form one of the region's most historic and culturally intriguing municipalities. Founded as the first nonmissionary, nonmilitary Spanish settlement in North America, Laredo today has a population of about 155,000 that is 90% Hispanic. Most Laredoans are bilingual, and they take great pride in the ways local culture, cuisine, and language distinguish Laredo from Texas-Mexico border areas to the east and west. This is also the most festive area along the border, where holidays as culturally distinct as Washington's Birthday and Mexican Independence Day are celebrated with equal fervor on both sides of the river.

Laredo is the main business center of South Texas and Nuevo Laredo is the largest port of entry anywhere on the U.S.-Mexico border. Currently around 67% of all U.S. trade with Mexico passes through Laredo; consequently, tariff and customs revenues here are greater than at any other customs office in Mexico. The *maquiladora* industry that plays such an important economic role in other large border towns is here integrated into a more diverse area economy that includes import-export operations, transportation, oil production, cotton farming, ranching, and tourism. Banking is also an important industry—Mexicans keep billions of U.S. dollars on deposit in Laredo banks to escape the Mexican peso's downward-spiraling value relative to other world currencies. Because of this diversity, Laredo was one of the state's first cities to pull out of the oil-glut-induced slump of the early to mid-1980s. Since the passing of NAFTA, Laredo has become the second fastest growing city in the nation (after Las Vegas).

History

In 1755, Spanish *empresario* Don Tomás Sánchez established a settlement on the north banks of the Rio Grande and named it Villa de San Agustín de Laredo—the hometown of his sponsor José de Escandón was Laredo, Spain. Founded without either military or missionary aid, it became the center of the Spanish colonial province of Nuevo Santander, which included parts of what are now South Texas and northern Mexico. San Agustín Plaza, now part of restored downtown Laredo, was the heart of the new settlement.

Laredo was caught between two wars of national liberation in the early 1800s: Mexican independence from Spain, throughout which most Laredo residents remained Spanish loyalists, and then Texan independence from Mexico. When neither of the newly formed republics of Mexico and Texas would provide them with protection against marauding bandits and Indians, Laredo joined the north Mexican states of Tamaulipas, Nuevo León, and Coahuila in declaring the Republic of the Rio Grande in 1840. Laredo was made the capital of the new republic, which only lasted 10 months before Mexican troops brought the area back under *centralista* rule.

In 1845, when the Republic of Texas was annexed to the U.S., Laredo was again abandoned in a no-man's land between two countries, since the U.S. and Mexico disagreed over the boundary line between Texas and Mexico. The Treaty of Guadalupe Hidalgo, signed at the end of the Mexican-American War, established the Rio Grande as the boundary; those Laredoans who wanted to remain Mexican citizens moved across the river and established Nuevo Laredo in 1848.

During the American Civil War in the 1860s, Laredo prospered as a relay point for transshipment between the Confederate states and Europe. In the late 1880s, the founding of two new railroads made Laredo a major transportation link between the reunited U.S. and Mexico—the Texas-Mexican Railway connected the city with the deep-water port of Corpus Christi on the Texas Gulf Coast, while the Missouri Pacific joined the midwestern U.S. with Mexico's national railway and Mexico City. In 1935 the Pan-American Highway was completed, establishing a continuous roadway between Laredo and the Panama Canal via Mexico and Central America. Tourism first came to the area during the U.S. Prohibition years, when Texas residents would slip over the border to the Cadillac Bar and other Nuevo Laredo watering holes for a legal drink.

The Land and Climate
The terrain around Laredo is mostly lowland *monte* or *matorral,* characterized by flat plains covered with dense scrub—mesquite, prickly pear, dwarf oak, huisache, huajillo, blackbrush, catclaw, and cenizo. Sparse willow woodlands are found along the Rio Grande in places, but most trees in Laredo are non-native, planted species.

Average temperatures in the Laredo area range from a pleasant 45-68° F in January to a stifling 76-99° F in July. It's not unusual for the thermometer to break 100° F on a typical July afternoon. Annual average precipitation is a moderate 20 inches, with May and September receiving slightly more rainfall than other months. Any time besides June through August is good for a Laredo visit. If you come in the summer, it's best to stay indoors during the afternoon hours, as heatstroke is a very real threat to travelers who aren't used to temperatures in the high 90s and low 100s. The only town of any size in Texas that's hotter than Laredo in the summer is Presidio.

SIGHTS

Villa de San Agustín Historical District
San Agustín Plaza, bounded by Zaragoza, Flores, San Agustín, and Grant streets, is the site of the original 1755 Spanish settlement of Villa de San Agustín. At the east end of the plaza is **San Agustín Church,** built in 1872 on the foundation of two earlier churches. At the south end on Zaragoza sits the **Ortiz House,** begun in the 1700s and modified as late as 1870.

The small stone building on the plaza next to La Posada Hotel was built in 1830 and served as the capitol of the short-lived Republic of the Rio Grande. It now houses the **Republic of the Rio Grande Museum,** which displays memorabilia from the separatist movement of 1840, which went so far as to elect a president, appoint a presidential cabinet, and design its own flag. There are also three rooms decorated in period

style. Open Tues.-Sun. 10 a.m.-noon and 1-5 p.m.; admission is free.

Walking Tour: A map brochure outlining a suggested walking tour through the historic downtown area is available from the Laredo Chamber of Commerce. Street parking in the area can be difficult, but you can park in the large Riverdrive Mall parking lot near the International Bridge and walk downtown.

El Mercado/Laredo Center for the Arts
This old market building, constructed in 1883, has recently been partially restored to its original function as a public marketplace and headquarters for the Laredo Philharmonic Symphony, Laredo Art League, and Webb County Heritage Foundation. The surrounding city blocks, bounded by Flores, San Agustín, Hidalgo, and Lincoln streets, are also undergoing historic restoration so that the original cobblestone streets and Victorian buildings can join San Agustín Plaza in bringing a turn-of-the-century feel to downtown Laredo.

Texas A&M International University/ Laredo Community College
Formerly Laredo State University (tel. 210-722-8001), Texas A&M shares a 196-acre campus with Laredo Community College (tel. 722-0521) in West Laredo and is the most important institute of higher education in South Texas. Originally established as Texas A & I University in 1969, it was upgraded to state university status in 1977, and in 1989 became part of the Texas A&M University system. The total enrollment of 1,400 is about half graduate, half undergraduate. Many of the students hail from Mexico and Latin America.

The most acclaimed TA&MIU degree program is the MBA program in international trade, with an emphasis on Latin American trade; the bilingual education program is also highly reputable. The university's Acculturation Project provides a unique community service by introducing Los Dos Laredos newcomers to the local bilingual-bicultural milieu.

In the near future the university will be moving to a new campus near Macpherson and Del Mar in the northeastern sector of the city. Laredo Junior College will take over the former west campus.

ACCOMMODATIONS

Hotels and Motels

The most conveniently located hotel for Rio Grande crossings and downtown exploration is **La Posada** (tel. 210-722-1701 or 800-444-2099), on Zaragoza St. at San Agustín Plaza. Built in 1917 as Laredo High School, it's laid out in the classic Mexican colonial style around a courtyard and is a short walk from El Mercado, International Bridge no. 1, and downtown restaurants. Recently renovated rooms cost $75 s, $85 d, plus more expensive suites. Facilities in-

clude two swimming pools and three restaurants; airport transport is available for a fee.

Five blocks west of International Bridge no. 1 on S. Main Ave. stands the round tower of the **Holiday Inn on the Rio Grande** (tel. 722-2411 or 800-HOLIDAY), where rooms go for $59-69 s, $69-110 d (senior discount available). The Holiday Inn provides a shuttle to the International Bridge and the airport (for a fee).

Most other hotels and motels in town are located in North Laredo off I-35. The well-kept **Fiesta Inn** (tel. 723-3603 or 800-460-1176) is at the north end of San Bernardo Ave., just west of I-35; room rates are $54 s, $64 d during the week, $5

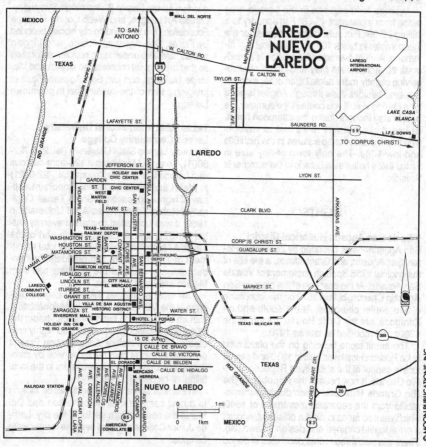

MEXICO
TO SAN ANTONIO
TEXAS
W. CALTON RD.
MALL DEL NORTE
McPHERSON AVE.

LAREDO-NUEVO LAREDO

LAREDO INTERNATIONAL AIRPORT

35
83
TAYLOR ST.
E. CALTON RD.
MCLELLAN AVE.
LAFAYETTE ST.
SAUNDERS RD.
59
LAKE CASA BLANCA
L.I.F.E. DOWNS
TO CORPUS CHRISTI
LAREDO
JEFFERSON ST.
LYON ST.
HOLIDAY INN
CIVIC CENTER
GARDEN ST.
WEST MARTIN FIELD
CLARK BLVD.
ARKANSAS AVE.
PARK ST.
SANTA URSULA AVE.
VIDAURRI AVE.
TEXAS-MEXICAN RAILWAY DEPOT
WASHINGTON ST.
HOUSTON ST.
MATAMOROS ST.
SAN AGUSTÍN
CORPUS CHRISTI ST.
GUADALUPE ST.
SANTA MARIA AVE.
CONVENT AVE.
FLORES AVE.
SAN BERNARDO AVE.
GREYHOUND DEPOT
HAMILTON HOTEL
HIDALGO ST.
LINCOLN ST.
ITURBIDE ST.
GRANT ST.
LAREDO COMMUNITY COLLEGE
CITY HALL/ EL MERCADO
MARKET ST.
VILLA DE SAN AGUSTÍN HISTORIC DISTRICT
ZARAGOZA ST.
RIVERDRIVE MALL
HOLIDAY INN ON THE RIO GRANDE
HOTEL LA POSADA
WATER ST.
TEXAS-MEXICAN RR
15 DE JUNIO
CALLE DE BRAVO
CALLE DE VICTORIA
CALLE DE BELDEN
EL DORADO
CALLE DE HIDALGO
MERCADO M. HERRERA
RAILROAD STATION
85
AMERICAN CONSULATE
NUEVO LAREDO
AVE. GRAL CESAR LOPEZ DE LARA
AVE. OBREGON
AVE. ALLENDE
AVE. JUAREZ
AVE. MORELOS
AVE. MATAMOROS
AVE. CAMARGO
AVE. OCAMPO
RIO GRANDE
TEXAS
359
20
83
SACRED HEART DR.
MOON
MEXICO
LAMAR RD.
RIO GRANDE
MISSOURI PACIFIC RR
TEXAS
MEXICO
0   1 mi
0   1km

© MOON PUBLICATIONS, INC.

lower on weekends. Senior and weekly discounts available. Also in this area is the **Holiday Inn Civic Center** (tel. 727-5800 or 900-HOLIDAY), at 800 Garden St. (exit 59 off I-35), where rooms are $71-120 s, $86-130 d; senior discount and airport transport available. A bit farther north off I-35 near the junction of US 59, the recently renovated **La Quinta Inn** (tel. 722-0511 or 800-531-5900) at 3600 Santa Ursula offers well-appointed rooms for $58-65 s, $68-77 d.

Less expensive motels include the **Monterrey Inn** (tel. 722-7631), 4820 San Bernardo Ave., $30 s, $35-37 d; and the **Siesta Motel** (tel. 723-3661), 4109 San Bernardo Ave., $32-36 s, $36-46 d. **Motel 6** has two Laredo locations, one at 5310 San Bernardo Ave. (tel. 725-8187) and one at 5920 San Bernardo Ave. (tel. 722-8133); rates are $30 and $31 respectively for singles, plus $6 for each additional adult.

Downtown near the bus terminal, the historic 13-story **Hotel Hamilton** (tel. 723-7421) at 815 Salinas and Matamoros still displays the original Southwest deco tilework inlaid during its 1923-28 construction. Although nothing special, large rooms cost $40-55.

La Conexión Bed & Breakfast (tel. 725-7563), a block east of La Posada at 907 Zaragoza, is a new boarding house with rooms for $40 s, $48 d including a full breakfast. Two of the rooms have private baths and two rooms share a bathroom; all come with telephone and TV.

Camping and RV Parks

Lake Casa Blanca State Park (tel. 210-725-3826), just east of Laredo International Airport off US 59, has primitive campsites for $6 a night, sites with water for $8, and screened shelters for $16. The next nearest campground is at Falcon State Recreation Area, about 80 miles south of Laredo off US 83 (see "Vicinity of Laredo" below).

Casa Norte Mobile Home and RV Park (tel. 722-3913), off I-35 N between Del Mar Blvd. and Mann Rd. (exit 3B), rents pull-through RV sites with full hookups for $11 a night, $60 weekly, $220 monthly. Facilities include pool, convenience store, laundry, and free cable TV. Also off I-35 at International Dr. is **Towne North Mobile Home & RV Park** (tel. 727-1222), with some overnight spaces with full hookups for $12 a night.

FOOD

Laredo has its own style of Tex-Mex cuisine that distinguishes it from San Antonio, El Paso, or even other border areas to the east and west. For one thing, they call Laredo-style breakfast tacos *mariachis;* local legend has it the name, and style, originated at **Las Cazuelas** (tel. 210-723-3693), 303 Market St., after a railroad worker in the 1930s made daily requests for a spicy breakfast taco that would make him shout like a mariachi. The recipe that finally satisfied his bent for chiles came to be called the *mariachi.* Practically every restaurant in the city that's open for breakfast features *mariachis* on the menu. Since this is cattle country, beef is a popular item on all menus. Another regional variation on a familiar Tex-Mex theme is *panchos,* which are nachos loaded down with beef, cheese, and jalapeños. A strictly local specialty you might come across is *machito,* goat-tripe sausage. Fajitas—which originated in this area—are also very popular, especially across the border in Nuevo Laredo.

With your Laredo menu vocabulary in hand, you might try some of the following Tex-Mex restaurants. **Cotulla Style Pit Bar-B-Q** (tel. 724-5747), at 4502 McPherson, specializes in a South Texas barbecue style that was created in the small town of Cotulla nearby and based on Mexican *carne asada* recipes. It's also well known locally for its *mariachis* and fajitas, served with fresh, homemade tortillas; open Tues.-Sat. 6:30 a.m.-5:45 p.m., Sunday 6:30 a.m.-2:45 p.m. A second location (tel. 725-5830) at 2201 Laredo St. is open Tues.-Thurs. 6:30 a.m.-4 p.m., Fri.-Sat. 6:30 a.m.-5:45 p.m., Sunday 6:30 a.m.-2:45 p.m. Note the early closing times of both locations.

Closing time is one thing you never have to worry about at **Taco Palenque** (tel. 725-9898), 4515 San Bernardo Ave., which serves fajitas, *mariachis, barbacoa,* menudo, *caldo de res,* and more—24 hours a day, dine-in or takeout. **Taquería Tlaquepaque** (tel. 726-6173) at 115 W. Hillside makes very good *migas* and huge breakfast tacos; it's open daily 7 a.m.-3 p.m. If you can't make it across the border, **Los Generales** (tel. 725-1797) at 3310 Santa Maria offers a reasonably authentic *norteña* menu, including *mari-*

achis, barbacoa, and tacos stuffed with *picadillo.* Open daily Mon.-Sat. 7 a.m.-11 p.m.

The popular **Unicorn Restaurant and Pegasus Bar** offers a mixed menu of mesquite-grilled steaks, chicken-fried steak, *carne asada,* seafood, salads, soups, and appetizers that ought to satisfy small groups who can't agree on what kind of food to eat. It's at 3810 San Bernardo (tel. 727-4663) and is open daily for lunch and dinner.

La Posada Hotel's **Main Dining Room** (tel. 722-1701) features different specialties every evening, as well as lunchtime buffets during the week that change daily and a Sunday brunch buffet. The regular menu offers a wide variety of Mexican and American dishes; open daily for breakfast, lunch, and dinner. The hotel's **Tack Room Restaurant & Bar** (same phone number as above) has character and style and prices to match; it's situated upstairs in a 1916 building that served as a home, high school, and telephone exchange before the hotel acquired it. Open Mon.-Sat. for dinner only; the bar features happy hour Mon.-Fri. 5-8 p.m.

For a change of pace from Tex-Mex and steak, try tiny **Chez Mauricette** (tel. 726-9453) at the northwest corner of Lincoln and San Agustín (part of El Mercado complex). The seven-table dining room serves simple country French cuisine, including traditional quiche lorraine, coq au vin, and inexpensive lunch specials Mon.-Fri. 11 a.m.-2:30 p.m.

Seasoned Mexico travelers may revel in the *paletas* (Mexican popsicles) and fresh *licuados* (blended fruit drinks) available at **Paletería La Playa** at 500 Flores in El Mercado; open daily 10 a.m.-6 p.m.

Nuevo Laredo has some excellent restaurants too—see "Across the Border to Nuevo Laredo," below.

ENTERTAINMENT

Music Halls

Along with San Antonio and Corpus Christi, Laredo is one of Texas's three main centers for *tejano* music—the other two are San Antonio and Corpus Christi. Most weekends the Civic Center (tel. 210-722-8143) at 2400 San Bernardo hosts live Latino, *tejano,* and *conjunto* performances. **Roli's Music Hall** (tel. 722-2453), at 100 E. Taylor near McClellan, also frequently features *tejano* and *conjunto.*

A mix of country and *tejano* bands play weekend nights at **Kikker's** (tel. 791-7019), 5100 Santa Maria, and **The Roundup Lounge** (tel. 726-4347), 5924 San Bernardo.

During the Jalapeño Festival in February, Laredo hosts a *tejano* music festival. A local *tejano/* country group to watch for is Kaktus.

Hotel Clubs

Ordinarily I wouldn't recommend hotels for local entertainment, since most hotel/motel clubs across the U.S. offer the same sort of mainstream pop. In Laredo, however, several hotels support local sounds. The **Crystal Palace** (tel. 210-722-2441), in La Hacienda Hotel at 4914 San Bernardo, features live *tejano* bands Tues.-Sun. nights until 2 a.m. Holiday Inn's **The Covey** also presents occasional *tejano* music, either live or on disc. **Rio's Coyote Grill & Saloon** in the Holiday Inn on the Rio Grande offers good views of the river and Nuevo Laredo.

EVENTS

February

George Washington's Birthday: In spite of the fact that George's birthday has been subsumed under "Presidents' Day" on a national level, it's a 10-day festival in Laredo-Nuevo Laredo that's been celebrated since 1898. In these twin cities, it really combines the traditional Mexican pre-Lenten festival of Carnaval with a commemoration of the signing of the U.S. Constitution. The schedule varies from year to year, but usually kicks off on the second Friday in February with a tejano music presentation at the Civic Center Auditorium, followed by the Princess Pocahontas Pageant on Saturday, also at the Civic Center. On Sunday there are fireworks and a band concert at Casa Blanca Lake, and during the week are more parades, a masquerade ball, and various smaller events.

On the second weekend, the festival divides in two: for the older, society-oriented population, there's the Colonial Pageant, which features the Society of Martha Washington Debutante Presentation and Ball, which reenacts the signing of the Constitution with two members of the community portraying George and Martha Washington. For the younger, *tejano*-oriented crowd, there's the **Jalapeño Festival,** which used to be held separately but has been combined with the George Washington's Birthday schedule. The Society of Martha Washington events are held at the Civic Center. Activities for the Jalapeño Festival take place at various venues around town and include the coronation of Miss Jalapeño, a jalapeño-eating contest (the winner is crowned "King Chile"), *tejano* music, and a water race on the Rio Grande.

On the final Saturday, there's a binational friendship ceremony on International Bridge no. 2, followed by a parade across the bridge. On the last day of the festival, Sunday, a "Farewell Fiesta" takes place in San Agustín Plaza with plenty of food, music, and dancing.

March
The event of the month is the **Laredo International Fair and Exposition,** held at the L.I.F.E. grounds on US 59, east of the airport, around the third weekend of the month. The show includes a rodeo, livestock exhibits, music and dancing, food booths, and quarter horse racing.

April
The week preceding Easter Sunday is **Semana Santa** or Holy Week for Catholics on both sides of the river. Religious events center around Holy Redeemer Church on Main Ave., but you'll also notice that cafes and bakeries offer special *buñuelos* (fried sweet bread) and *capirotada* (Mexican bread pudding with raisins and papayas) for the occasion.

May
The May 3 is **Day of the Holy Cross** in Mexico and is celebrated in Laredo with a *matachine* procession.

Cinco de Mayo is a Chicano-Mexican cultural festival that commemorates the Battle of Puebla in 1862. Events include a special bullfight and *charreada* at the bullring in Nuevo Laredo.

July
Borderfest is a folklife festival held Fourth of July weekend at the Laredo Civic Center grounds. The three-day event features arts and crafts exhibits, local music and dancing, and food vendors.

December
The 12th of the month is the feast day of the Virgin of Guadalupe, which in Laredo is celebrated by a unique *matachine* procession to Holy Redeemer Church on Main Avenue. *Matachine* is an inherited local variation of an ancient pre-Cortesian Indian folk dance (the word comes from the Aztec for dance, *matlaxin*) that fulfills a variety of religious, social, and cultural functions. The musical ensemble that accompanies the dancers includes a drum, violin, accordion, and sometimes guitar, while the dancers dress in velveteen coats hung with reed ornaments and bells. Someone at the head of the procession carries a flower-decorated eight-foot cross and small altars are erected along the procession route.

The *matachine* tradition is said to be stronger in Laredo than anywhere in Mexico or the Southwest and preserves *la flecha* ("arrow") style movements lost elsewhere. Several local groups practice throughout the year; the most authentic is said to be Los Matachines de la Santa Cruz de Ladrillera, while the most visually striking is Aztecas Matachines. Many Mexican observers visit Laredo to view this rare Guadalupe Day procession.

SPORTS AND RECREATION

Lake Casa Blanca State Park
This 1,600-acre impoundment of San Ygnacio and Chacon creeks has facilities for water recreation (swimming, boating, fishing, and water-skiing), picnicking, and camping. Just east of Laredo International Airport off US 59 E. Entrance to the park is $3 per vehicle, $1 for pedestrians and cyclists. Nearby is the 18-hole **Casa Blanca Golf Course** (tel. 210-727-9218), off Casa Blanca Lake Rd., which is open to the public.

L.I.F.E. Downs
This horse-racing track and rodeo arena is on the Laredo International Fair and Exposition grounds east of Casa Blanca Lake, off US 59. Quarter horse races, livestock shows, and

rodeos are held here during the yearly L.I.F.E. schedule and occasionally during other times of the year; call (210) 722-9948 for information.

Baseball
The **Tecolotes de Los Dos Laredos** ("Tecos" for short) is the only professional (AAA) baseball team in Mexico or the U.S. that regularly plays on both sides of the border. Member of the Béisbol Liga Mexicana (Mexican Baseball League), the Tecolotes alternate their home games between Parque La Junta in Nuevo Laredo and West Martin Field (tel. 210-722-8143), 2200 Santa Maria in Laredo; the season runs March through July. For ticket and schedule information, call 722-8143.

SHOPPING

Laredo's **Mall del Norte,** off I-35 N between Mann and Hillside, claims to be the largest shopping center on the U.S.-Mexico border; it even has its own 5,000-square-foot Catholic church, decorated in the Spanish colonial style, for Sunday visitors. Over 130 stores in the mall attract Mexican as well as local shoppers. The smaller **Riverdrive Mall** is off Zaragoza St. three blocks west of International Bridge no. 1. **El Mercado** at Hidalgo and Flores downtown has a few specialty and craft shops. **Oscar's Antiques** (tel. 210-723-0765) at 1002 Guadalupe carries Mexican, European, and American antique furniture, including salvaged architectural items like Spanish colonial doors. **Blue Gate Antiques** (tel. 727-4127) at 719 Corpus Christi specializes in antique china, silver, jewelry, and crystal.

LAREDO TELEPHONE INFORMATION

Emergency (police, fire, medical): 911
Telephone Directory Assistance: 411
Area Code: 210
National Weather Service: 722-8119
Highway Patrol: 727-2145
Post Office Information: 723-2043
Western Union Telegraph: 722-4321

Near the International Bridge along Zaragoza and Convent Streets are clusters of wholesale and discount shops selling name-brand U.S. products at rock-bottom prices. Similar shops selling discounted Mexican and Central American goods can be found along San Bernardo Ave. between Hidalgo and Matamoros.

INFORMATION

Tourist Offices
The main office of the **Laredo Convention and Visitors Bureau** (tel. 210-722-9895 or 800-292-2122) is located in the Laredo Civic Center at 2310 San Bernardo Avenue. The Bureau produces and distributes printed material on Laredo and Nuevo Laredo sights and can answer questions on area travel; open Mon.-Fri. 8:30 a.m.-5:30 p.m., Saturday 9 a.m.-1 p.m. There's also a subsidiary information center in El Mercado at Flores and Hidalgo, near San Agustín Plaza.

The State Highway Department operates one of its Texas Travel Information Centers (tel. 722-8119) off I-35, six miles north of town. Here you can receive free maps and tourist literature for the entire state, as well as for Laredo and South Texas; open daily 8 a.m.-5 p.m.

Telephone
The area code for Laredo is 210. To call numbers in Nuevo Laredo from Laredo, dial 011-52-871 before the local five-digit number.

Money
If you're heading for Mexico and need pesos, the best place to buy them is **Imperio Money Exchange** at the corner of Santa Ursula and Houston. The drive-in moneychanging window is easily approached via Santa Ursula Ave., which connects a few blocks farther south with the International Bridge; it's open 24 hours and the exchange rate is the best around.

Mexican Consulate
Paperwork for short- and long-term Mexico visits can be handled at the Mexican Consulate General (tel. 210-723-6360), 1612 Farragut Street.

GETTING THERE AND AROUND

Air

Laredo International Airport (tel. 210-722-4933) fields flights by: Continental Express (tel. 723-3402), direct service to/from Houston; American Eagle (tel. 722-8686), direct service to/from Dallas; Conquest (tel. 725-5500), McAllen and San Antonio; and TAESA (tel. 725-8414), Mexico City.

Intercity and International Buses

The **Greyhound Bus Depot** (tel. 210-723-4324) is at Matamoros and San Bernardo Ave. in downtown Laredo. Greyhound operates buses to other major cities in Texas (San Antonio $10, Dallas $36) as well as to Chicago and Los Angeles. Valley Transit Co. also operates bus lines to Zapata, McAllen, and Brownsville from this depot.

You can catch buses from this station to cities in interior Mexico. Servicio Turistar Ejecutivo runs 11 buses daily to Monterrey for $19 and four buses daily to San Luis Potosí for $52, plus routes to Mexico City, Guadalajara, Torreón, Durango, Aguascalientes, and Querétaro.

City Buses

Laredo's municipal transit system is called "El Metro," but for getting around downtown walking is easiest. El Metro does have special shuttle services, however, between most hotels and the Mall del Norte or Nuevo Laredo Downs.

City Taxis

Garza's Taxi (tel. 210-723-5313) and other companies charge around $15 from downtown Laredo to downtown Nuevo Laredo, $30 to/from the airport to Nuevo Laredo.

Tours

Olé Tours (tel. 210-726-4290) provides half-day van or bus tours of Laredo and Nuevo Laredo for around $12 per person, $6 children under 12. Olé also offers overnight tours to Monterrey and, during bullfighting season, special Nuevo Laredo bullfight tours.

The **Webb County Heritage Foundation** (tel. 727-0977) arranges walking and bus tours of Laredo's historic downtown, by appointment only.

ACROSS THE BORDER TO NUEVO LAREDO

This is the quintessential Texas-Mexico border town, since more tourists enter Mexico via this city of 300,000 than any other place along Mexico's entire frontier with the United States. The city offers a well-developed downtown with everything from elegant dining to street vendors to cut-rate liquor stores, plus two leafy public plazas, all within walking distance of the International Bridge. For Laredo residents and nearby South Texans, it's a place to shop and party on weekends or holidays. Most foreign visitors never get farther than a few blocks down Avenida Guerrero, the main tourist strip running directly south from the bridge.

If you're just going for the day, it's easiest to walk over International Bridge no. 1 from downtown Laredo, near La Posada Hotel—you can park your car in the free lots off Zaragoza St., below Riverdrive Mall. If you must drive across—and be aware finding parking in downtown Nuevo Laredo can be very difficult—you can use either International Bridge no. 2, which crosses the river from the south end of I-35 and joins Mexico 85 in downtown Nuevo Laredo, or bypass Nuevo Laredo altogether by crossing at the Colombia Bridge north of Laredo. Bridge tolls are $1 for cars, 25 cents for pedestrians.

Sights

Parque Arqueológico Morelos, three blocks east of International Bridge no. 1 between Calles Bravo and 15 de Junio, exhibits 50 replicas of historical artwork from Mexico City's famous Museum of Anthropology, as well as the Mayan ruins of Chichen Itza and Teotihuacán. The works represent seven pre-Hispanic cultures in Mexico and Central America. Seven blocks down Avenida Guerrero is the **main plaza** and municipal palace, a popular outdoor gathering place.

Three plazas strung out north to south along Avenida Guerrero are the focus of public life in Nuevo Laredo—**Plaza Juárez,** two blocks from the bridge at Calles Victoria and Galeana, **Plaza Hidalgo** at Av. Guerrero and Calle González, and **Plaza México** at Guerrero and Independencia. Plaza Hidalgo is the largest of the three and serves as city center, flanked by the Palacio

Federal on the east and various restaurants and hotels to the west.

Restaurants and Bars

Nuevo Laredo has been a favorite eating and drinking spot for South Texans since Prohibition in the 1920s. The most famous border joint of all is alive and well under its latest moniker, **El Dorado Bar & Grill** (tel. 2-00-15). Originally founded as a casino and restaurant named El Caballo Blanco in 1922, the restaurant became the Cadillac Bar in 1926 after its purchase by New Orleans native Mayo Bassan. The bar has since changed hands several times but is still a favorite gringo rendezvous. While it may have seen better days, you can order a tasty Ramos gin fizz (invented here and listed as "New Orleans gin fizz" on the current menu) and classic border/gulf cuisine like *cabrito,* braised frog legs, roast quail, and red snapper papillote, plus Tex-Mex standards like huevos rancheros. Another specialty drink here is the "popper," a savory tequila concoction served in a large shot glass with a loud flourish—a white-jacketed waiter slams the glass onto the bar. Somehow, the drink's name has been transformed to "slammer" in the Austin, Houston, San Antonio, and San Francisco franchise versions of the Cadillac Bar. El Dorado is located at the corner of Ocampo and Belden—walk two blocks south of the bridge and make a left on Belden. Open daily 10 a.m.-11 p.m.

Around the intersection of Victoria and Matamoros, only a block from the bridge, is a cluster of more upscale, tourist-oriented restaurants with international menus. Seafood fans swear by **Mariscos Mandinga** (tel. 3-12-05) at 1307 Obregón. Billing itself as "a little corner of Veracruz in Nuevo Laredo," Mandinga specializes in fresh *huachinango* (red snapper) as well as other fish and shellfish from the Gulf. The **Winery Pub and Grill** (tel. 2-88-95) at Matamoros 308 is quite popular also, and features live Latin music nightly after 9 p.m. Both are open daily for lunch and dinner.

Northern Tamaulipas food specialties include a dish whose fame has spread from the border and across Texas throughout the U.S., Canada, and even Europe: fajitas, marinated and mesquite-grilled skirt steak served with flour tortillas, grilled onions, salsas, and various other condiments. The moderately priced **Restaurant La Palapa**

(tel. 4-00-69) at 3301 Reforma (Mexico 85) specializes in mesquite-grilled fajitas, sold by the kilo. Open daily for dinner only. Another good place for fajitas, as well as *queso flameado,* a Mexican cheese fondue, is **Las Tablitas** (tel. 2-16-90) at H. de Nacataz and Degollado, east of Plaza Hidalgo downtown near the Nuevo Laredo City Hall; open daily noon-midnight.

For tacos of all kinds, Nuevo Laredo's most renowned restaurant is **Restaurant El Rancho** (tel. 4-87-53), also known as **Su Majestad El Taco** ("His Majesty the Taco"), at Av. Guerrero 2134 just north of Av. Lincoln. In addition to a huge selection of tacos, El Rancho specializes in *carnitas, pozole, birria estilo Jalisco* (Jalisco-style stew), *carne asada,* and a better than average selection of Mexican beers. It's open 11 a.m.-midnight daily.

Goat is also popular in the Nuevo Laredo area. The original source of the northern tradition of naming at least one goat eatery "Principal" in every town is the Cantú family-owned **Restaurant Principal** (tel. 2-13-01) at Av. Guerrero 624, just north of Calle Dr. Mier—look for the skewered *cabritos* roasting *al pastor* in the window. This clean, inexpensive restaurant also serves *pollo asado, carne asada,* and *machitos* (goat-tripe burritos), with *frijoles rancheros* (ranch-style beans) on the side. The Principal is open daily for lunch and dinner. The nearby **Restaurant Nuevo León,** at Av. Guerrero 508 just north of Calle Pino Suárez, is another authentic *norteña* place with *cabrito al pastor,* fajitas, and *machitos.*

Entertainment

Bullfighting: The new, 9,000-seat **Plaza de Toros Lauro Luis Longoria,** off Mexico 85 just past the Nuevo Laredo airport at 4111 Av. Monterrey, presents Sunday bullfights once a month between Washington's Birthday and mid-July. Tickets cost from US$5 for general admission on the sunny side of the ring to US$19 for first row reserved seats on the shady side. In Nuevo Laredo, you can purchase tickets at the Tecolotes de Los Dos Laredos office (tel. 12-71-02), Calles Obregón and Gutiérrez, and at Restaurant El Rancho. On the Laredo side they can be purchased at Narvaez Beef Store and Talamas Music Hall. Or you can buy them the day of the *corrida* at the Plaza de Toros; the box office opens at 10 a.m. Call the Laredo Chamber of Commerce for the latest schedule (tel. 210-722-9895).

Nuevo Laredo's discos are crowded with bouncing bodies on weekends. A few blocks down Guerrero and over one street, on parallel Matamoros next to The Winery Pub and Grill, is the **Lion's Den,** a disco popular with tourists. **Vivant's,** across from the El Rio Motel on Mexico 85, and **Firenze's,** two blocks down from Vivant's, attract a mix of young people from both sides of the border. All three are open Wed.-Sun. till 2 a.m.

Shopping
One of Nuevo Laredo's major tourist draws—for Mexicans as well as foreigners—is the fact it offers the best shopping anywhere along the U.S.-Mexico border. In large part this is due to its position at the head of the Pan-American Highway; all cargo heading north or south passes through Nuevo Laredo, a major convenience for wholesale buyers and sellers.

Tourist-oriented gift shops line the north end of Av. Guerrero near the bridge. Unless you're buying liquor and cigarettes, which cost about the same everywhere in Nuevo Laredo, the prices aren't always that good, so it pays to shop around. Overall the best selection and prices are at the **Nuevo Mercado de la Reforma,** a collection of around 100 shops occupying an entire block on the west side of Av. Guerrero. Look for a red sign reading "MERCADO."

The **New Juárez Market,** a small mall at Av. Guerrero and Calle Bravo with around ten shops, is also good. Most of the shops in both these malls accept credit cards.

For handicrafts alone, your best bet is the **Mercado M. Herrera,** a collection of 50 shops 1.5 blocks east of Av. Guerrero at Calles Ocampo and Hidalgo. The **Centro Artesanal,** at Av. Guerrero and M. Herrera a few blocks farther south, also offers arts and crafts for sale.

La Mansión, at Av. Guerrero 206, features very good prices on picture frames, whether readymade or custom. Including glazing and matting, prices run as much as 80% lower than in the United States or Canada. La Mansión also sells handicrafts, patio furniture, and planters.

Marti's, Calle Victoria 2923 at Av. Guerrero, is a boutique specializing in custom-designed clothes as well as high-end furniture and handicrafts—with boutique prices to match.

Reyes, on the east side of Av. Guerrero just south of Calle Hidalgo, offers boots, saddles, and other handmade leather goods at decent prices. **La Casa del Café** at Matamoros and Hidalgo sells whole or fresh-ground coffee beans by the kilo at excellent prices.

Information
The Mexican tourist office (tel. 2-01-04), just west of the end of International Bridge no. 1, distributes tourist brochures on Nuevo Laredo and Mexico; it's usually open Mon.-Sat. 9 a.m.-3 p.m. There's

souvenir shop,
Nuevo Laredo

CHIEF QUANAH PARKER AND THE TEXAS PEYOTEROS

The hallucinogenic cactus peyote (*Lophophora williamsii*) contains several psychoactive alkaloids, the most powerful of which is mescaline, a substance that affects the mind much like the synthetic drug LSD. The use of the plant to induce visionary experiences among Native American Church adherents dates to a cross-cultural series of events that occurred in 19th- and 20th-century Texas. Peyote's utilization in Mexico goes back several centuries, but north of the Rio Grande its history began in 1836, when a group of Comanches took nine-year-old Cynthia Ann Parker captive during a raid on Fort Parker, Texas, near present-day Mexia, about 40 miles east of Waco. Nine years later, fully integrated into the Comanche culture, Cynthia married Chief Peta Nocona, with whom she had two sons, Quanah and Pecos, and daughter Topsannah.

Texas Rangers re-took Parker during an attack on a Comanche camp of women and children. Quanah and Pecos were away at the time, but the Rangers brought Cynthia and her daughter back to Fort Parker, where all attempts to re-introduce them into Anglo-American ways failed. Mother and daughter repeatedly tried to escape; Topsannah died within four years of their capture, and Cynthia starved herself to death shortly thereafter.

Following her death, Cynthia's son Quanah Parker—half Comanche, half Anglo—became a famous Comanche chief on the Oklahoma Territory Indian reservations. For a time, Quanah's apparent skill in manipulating the reservation system allowed him special status among the Oklahoma and Texas chiefs, but he eventually rebelled against state and federal authority and led several historic battles against Anglo forces in the canyons of the Texas Panhandle.

Around 1875, Quanah visited an uncle in northern Mexico and while there fell seriously ill. When all other remedies failed to cure him, a *curandera* (traditional healer) restored his health using psycho-spiritual methods, including the ritual ingestion of peyote. Quanah returned to the Comanche reservation at Fort Sill, Oklahoma armed with peyote, and propagated its use.

The Comanches at Fort Sill—who, like the rest of the Amerindians in the U.S. territories, had never experienced peyote—were the first to follow Quanah's

Quanah Parker

an American consulate (tel. 4-05-12, after hours 210-727-9661 in Laredo) at Av. Galeana (one block east of Av. Ocampo) and Calle de Madero, about 12 blocks south of the bridge.

Getting There and Around

Most day visitors park their vehicles in the large, free lot just south of Riverdrive Mall along Water St. in Laredo, then walk across the bridge. If you want to drive across, park in one of the pay lots behind Marti's and behind El Dorado Bar & Grill. At the latter you can park free all day for the price of a single drink or meal. There's also a convenient parking garage in the same building as The Winery Pub and Grill at Matamoros and Belden near the bridge; rates are

lead. From Fort Sill the custom quickly passed to other North American tribes. In 1918, seven years after Quanah's death, cross-tribal groups formed the Native American Church and codified the peyote ceremony, using a portion of the Wichita Deer Dance combined with Christian elements.

Revered as "the Flesh of God" by many Amerindians, the spineless, blue-green cacti grow only in parts of South Texas and northern Mexico. In Mexico its use is most prominent among the Huicholes of Nayarit, Durango, and Jalisco, who gather the plant in annual pilgrimages to the high Chihuahuan Desert plains of San Luis Potosí. In the U.S. and Canada, its use is widespread among Native American Church members, who are the only citizens of either country exempt from state and province laws prohibiting possession of the drug. In the U.S. only 28 states recognize the NAC's special status with regard to peyote, a situation that creates a unique set of transportation problems when moving the cacti from source to worshipper.

Today only eight people in the U.S. are legally permitted to harvest peyote and sell it to the NAC. All eight *peyoteros* live and work in Webb, Zapata, and Starr counties in the upper Rio Grande Valley, where they slice the mescaline-filled cactus tops from wild peyote cacti growing in hot, dry, desolate areas. Thus sliced, the cacti will grow more "buttons" (cactus tops) within a month of receiving sufficient rainfall. The peyoteros dry the buttons on long wooden tables in well-fenced backyards; even the racks themselves require a federal permit. In 1993 Texas *peyoteros* sold 1.9 million dried buttons to the NAC at a price of around $150 per thousand.

It's ironic—if perhaps entirely logical—that peyote's use took root in the U.S. and Canada in the late 1800s, when large numbers of Amerindians were being herded onto reservations. Denied the physical freedom to enjoy their homelands, the disenfranchised tribes perhaps rediscovered an interior life where they could roam freely, unhampered by borders and government persecution.

85 cents an hour. Traffic in Nuevo Laredo isn't that bad as long as you avoid the bridge on Sunday afternoons and during ordinary commute hours. The bridges are open 24 hours.

For US$3 you can take a Transportes del Norte or Transportes Frontera bus from the Greyhound bus depot at Matamoros and San Bernardo Ave. in downtown Laredo. You can also buy through-fares for buses to/from other U.S. cities as well as into Mexico.

Onward to Monterrey: A new 53-mile, four-lane toll highway from Nuevo Laredo to Monterrey is only nine miles shorter than the old road but shortens the drive from an hour and a half to about an hour. The speed limit is 68 mph, one of the highest in Mexico. The toll is also a record-breaker—$11.50 each way.

Tours
You can arrange Nuevo Laredo city tours in Laredo through **Olé Tours** (tel. 210-726-4290) or in Nuevo Laredo through **City Tours** (tel. 14-38-40)—look for the old yellow school bus parked between the second and third block of Av. Guerrero. City Tours charges US$8 per person for an hour-long tour.

VICINITY OF LAREDO

Laredo is really in the middle of nowhere, so "in the vicinity" means within a 150-mile radius. Zapata is 49 miles southeast along US 83, followed by Roma (89 miles) and Rio Grande City (109 miles). This stretch of Texas border towns is held together by a common historical and cultural thread—all were settled by Spanish colonists in the mid-18th century as part of the famous José de Escandón land grant.

The area between Falcon and Rio Grande City makes an especially interesting road trip if you zigzag back and forth across the border at various small crossings: US 83 and Mexico 2 run parallel on either side of the border here. In a project called Los Caminos del Rio, state governments on both sides of the border are working together to restore historical architecture in the small towns along these two highways.

Eagle Pass is 126 miles in the opposite direction, almost as far northeast as Del Rio, where South Texas meets West Texas.

Zapata

The original settlement that became Zapata was founded in 1750 by Spaniard José Vasquez Borrego. It was later renamed for legendary Indian fighter Antonia Zapata. When the Rio Grande was dammed to create Falcon International Reservoir, old Zapata was completely submerged and a new Zapata was built on higher ground. To see what old Zapata looked like, visit the **La Paz Museum** in a 200-year-old house near Benavides Elementary School in San Ygnacio, about 25 miles northwest on US 83. The museum contains old photos of the original Zapata, local ranch and farm implements, and antiques. It's open from September to May, Mon.-Fri. 8 a.m.-3 p.m.; admission is free.

The folks at **Murray Leather Goods** (tel. 210-765-5654), off US 83 in Zapata, handcut and handstitch custom saddles, chaps, and other leather articles for ranching and horseback riding. Chaps are Murray's mainstay; he's made them for celebrities like Chuck Norris, Billy Joel, Ben Johnson, and Randy White.

Falcon State Park

Falcon Dam was constructed across the Rio Grande in 1953 to create the 87,210-acre Falcon International Reservoir. Both the U.S. and Mexico utilize the dam and reservoir for hydroelectric power, flood control, and recreation. Falcon State Park is at the southeast shore of the lake, off US 83 north of Roma via FM 2098 and Park Rd. 46. The fishing is said to be outstanding here, particularly for black and white bass, stripers, catfish, and crappie.

Approximately 572 acres of typical Rio Grande brush country are protected by the park along the lakeshores. Facilities include shaded picnic area, boat ramp, fish-cleaning shelter, and four camping areas. Tent/camper sites with water are $6 a night, with w/e $9. Full hookup RV sites are $10 a night; screened shelters are available for $15. Park entry is $3 per vehicle, $1 for pedestrians and cyclists. For further information, contact the Park Superintendent (tel. 210-848-5327), Falcon State Park, P.O. Box 2, Falcon Heights, TX 78545.

Other RV Parks: The **Oso Blanco RV Park** (tel. 765-4339) lies about 10 miles north of Falcon State Park off US 83; full hookups are $10-12 a night; facilities include boat ramp and docks. Thirty miles farther north off US 83 in Zapata is the larger **Bass Lake RV Park** (tel. 765-4961), with the same rates as Oso Blanco; facilities include boat ramps, docks, and spa.

Paddling the Rio Grande: Experienced canoeists and kayakers might enjoy the pristine 20-mile reach from Falcon Dam to Roma, a scenic paddle past semitropical islands verdant with anaqua, cypress, ebony, hackberry, Brazil, mesquite, and river cane. Prominent birdlife in the area includes brown jays, hook-billed kites, black-bellied whistling ducks, green jays, and the crested caracara, Mexico's national bird. White-tailed deer are also occasionally spotted on the islands.

Depending on the strength of upriver Gulf breezes and counteracting currents from dam releases, this can be either a fairly easy or very challenging paddle—either way count on a full day on the water.

Guerrero Viejo

Opposite Zapata on the Mexican shore of Falcon International Reservoir lie the partially submerged ruins of Guerrero Viejo, a town founded in 1750 under the Spanish *empresario* plan. Native son José Bernardo Gutierrez de Lara (1774-1841) served as the first Tamaulipas state governor and later as the first Mexican ambassador to the United States. Virtually the whole town of 4,000 packed up and relocated in 1953 when the Falcon Dam flooded the town with the impounded waters of the Rio Grande.

Many of the original buildings in Guerrero Viejo ("Old Guerrero") can be seen when the lake level drops. Guerrero Viejo is 32 km (20 miles) north of Nuevo Guerrero in the Mexican state of Coahuila. Along Mexico 2 parallel to the river, watch for a small Guerrero Viejo sign on the east side of the road at about Km 163, then drive 30 km east on a rocky road through several open gates. What can be seen of the old town, when the lake level permits, are the tops of several sandstone buildings, including the 1750-vintage **Nuestra Señora del Refugio** parish church, the outlines of the plaza and remains of the plaza *kiosko,* cobblestone streets, and the walls of the former Hotel Flores. The plaster from these buildings has washed away to reveal the masterful masonry beneath.

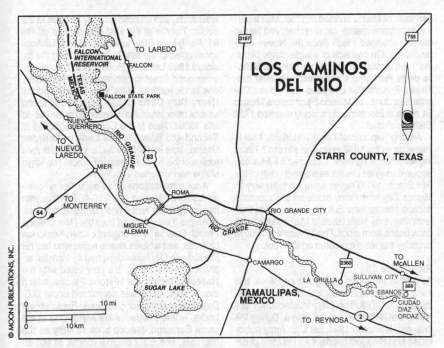

LOS CAMINOS DEL RIO

STARR COUNTY, TEXAS

TAMAULIPAS, MEXICO

Near Nuevo Guerrero, on the southwest edge of the 87,000-acre lake, is a *parque turístico* with facilities for camping, boating, picknicing (grills, tables, and trash receptacles), and fishing for black, white, and striped bass, crappie, and catfish.

Roma

This atmospheric little town was founded under a Spanish land grant in 1765. Before the railways arrived in South Texas in the late 1800s, it served as an important riverboat terminal on the Rio Grande for transshipment to and from the Gulf of Mexico. Unlike most Rio Grande border towns, Roma is situated in hilly terrain, a setting which shows off its historic buildings to good advantage. To see these mostly unrestored buildings, walk or drive through the streets on the river (west) side of town.

German architect Heinrich Portscheller built some of the more impressive structures around the *placita* in the late 19th century. His trademark building design includes double doors and

high windows with wrought-iron grillwork—a blend of Spanish and French Creole influences. The bell tower of Our Lady of Refuge Church, at Convent and Estrella, was erected in 1854 by Father Pierre Keralum. The *convento* across the street is a Portscheller design, as is the Manuel Guerra Store at Convent and Portscheller streets. The **Roma Historical Museum** (tel. 210-849-1535), at Estrella and Lincoln, contains exhibits chronicling local history; open Mon.-Fri. 9 a.m.-4 p.m. or by appointment.

Of further historical note: Roma was chosen as an outdoor set for the 1952 film *Viva Zapata* (directed by Elia Kazan and starring Marlon Brando and Anthony Quinn) because it so perfectly resembles a turn-of-the-century Mexican town. Roma was recently granted National Historic Landmark status.

Mier: A suspension bridge (the only one over the Rio Grande) built in 1927 links Roma with the small Mexican town of **Miguel Alemán**. There's nothing much to see in Miguel Alemán, but 11 miles northwest via Mexico 2 is the historic Mexican town of Mier. Founded in 1752, Mier's narrow sandstone streets, old churches, and plazas haven't changed much since the Nuevo Santander era. On one side of a large shady plaza, the 1798-vintage parish church **Nuestra Señora de la Purísima Concepción de Mier** features a Portscheller-designed clock tower. **Capilla San Juan,** off Mexico 2 just before Mexico 54 south to Monterrey, is a nicely restored 1752 Catholic chapel.

Among Republic of Texas historians, Mier is infamous as the 1842 execution site of 17 Texas independence fighters. Captured by Mexican troops during an unsuccessful raid north of the Río Bravo, 176 Texans were on their way to Mexico City when they made an unsuccessful escape attempt near Salado, Texas. Upon their recapture, they were taken to Mier and forced to draw beans from a pot. The 17 rebels who drew black beans were executed on the spot.

Rio Grande City

As part of the same land grant as Roma, this early Spanish town was founded as Carnestolendas in 1768. The hilly, brush-country terrain is similar to that around Roma. During the War with Mexico in 1848, the U.S. Army established Fort Ringgold nearby as a front line of defense, and it became an important steamboat terminal for supplying the fort. In the early 1850s, after the Rio Grande was designated as the U.S.-Mexico border, the town was made the new Starr County seat and renamed Rio Grande City. An army of Mexicans and Americans dissatisfied with both national governments convened in Rio Grande City in 1852 and led an unsuccessful attack against Mexican troops in nearby Camargo in an attempt to establish a "Republic of the Sierra Madre" in northern Mexico.

Like Roma, Rio Grande City's importance as a trade center lessened considerably when the railroads entered South Texas in the last half of the 19th century. An international bridge links the city with Camargo, a Mexican town with a population of around 10,000, so import-export still plays a role in the local economy, along with Starr County farming and ranching.

Sights: The remaining **Fort Ringgold** buildings—barracks, officers quarters, storerooms, stables, and bakery—are now used by the local school district. During after-school hours, on weekends, and on holidays they're open to the public. They're at the east end of town off US 83. Along Main St. in town are several buildings constructed in the late 1800s, including the restored 1899 **LaBorde House,** now a hotel. Another good street for sightseeing is Mirasoles, one block south of Main, where you'll find the **Henry Clay Davis House,** built in 1848, and several other structures constructed in the mid- to late 1800s. Next to the County Courthouse at Second and Britton is **Our Lady of Lourdes Grotto,** built in 1928 by a German priest as a replica of the famous shrine in France. The Virgin statue was imported from Paris.

Accommodations and Food: The renovated **LaBorde House** (tel. 210-487-5101), with its wrought-iron fence and hurricane shutters, looks like it was plucked from the New Orleans French Quarter. The original owner, Francoise LaBorde, was a New Orleans native who had his Rio Grande City home designed by Parisian architects in the 1890s. It's now listed with the National Register of Historic Places, which means restoration was completed under U.S. Department of Interior guidelines. Replacement bricks, where needed, were handmade at the same Camargo, Mexico brick foundry as the originals. The eight original rooms, at 601 E. Main, are furnished with Victorian antiques and cost $59; modern rooms in back of the historic building are $40.

The newer **Fort Ringgold Motor Inn** (tel. 487-5666) at 4350 US has 83 rooms for $50-55 s, $55-65 d. The family-run **Caro's** (tel. 487-2255), at 205 N. Garcia, is an inexpensive northern Mexican-style cafe with a statewide reputation; the corn for their tortillas is ground fresh daily, as are the Mexican spices. Open daily for lunch and dinner. **Che's Restaurant and Bar** (tel. 487-5101) in LaBorde House also offers good border cooking, plus fresh Rio Grande catfish. Open daily for breakfast, lunch, and dinner.

Ciudad Camargo: Across the river from Rio Grande City is the small Mexican town of Camargo (pop. 7,000). This was José de Escandón's first Nuevo Santander settlement, dating from 1749. The oldest building in town is a Catholic church with one bell tower on Calle Libertad, built in the early 1750s. A local quarry, the source for the molded bricks used in Portscheller buildings throughout the lower Rio

THE KIKAPU

Originally hailing from Wisconsin and Michigan, the Kikapu ("Kickapoo") Indians were driven south in the 18th and 19th centuries by westward-moving Europeans. In 1775, Spain's Charles III gave them permission to settle in the colonial province of Coahuila y Texas in return for defending the area against Comanche and Apache raids. By the late 1800s, many of those on the Texas side were banished to Oklahoma reservations. Some were able to flee to northern Mexico and were given land by the Mexican government; like the Seminoles, a number of Kikapus came north again to serve as scouts with the U.S. Cavalry in Texas.

Today a core of around 500 Kikapu choose to live together and follow a semi-traditional lifestyle at two seasonal settlements on either side of the Texas-Coahuila border. They speak an Algonquin dialect as their first language, pidgin (or "broken") Spanish as a second. Those who read and write Kikapu use a syllabary devised by the Cherokee Sequoyah. Their oval-shaped, windowless winter homes in Mexico are built of hackberry, bald cypress, or sycamore wood, with low, dome-shaped roofs. Summer houses feature a rectangular plan with wooden posts supporting airy walls of sotol.

For the most part the Kikapu dress in a style similar to that of other Mexican peasants. The main difference is the way females wear their hair; young girls plait their hair in three braids, often joined on top of the head in a topknot. After puberty women switch to one long braid.

The Kikapu belief system revolves around nature spirits presided over by Kitzihiat, the "Great Spirit." Subordinate to Kitzihiat is Wisaka, the creator of the cosmos. The most common regular religious practice among the Kikapu is the preparation and possession of *misami* or medicine bundles which serve as sacred talismans for warding off evil. *Misami* contents are closely guarded secrets although they usually include a variety of dried plants, roots, and herbs, plus occasional human and animal parts. Wrapped in white cloth and covered by the skin of a two-point buck, the bundles are usually around two feet long and six inches wide.

Although the Kikapu employ peyote for medicinal, non-ritual purposes only, they sometimes gather a surplus of the cactus to sell to the Oklahoma Kikapu and other Amerindians who use the hallucinogenic substance ritually. Northwestern Coahuila is a primary source of the plant.

Grande corridor, still supports local brickmasons. Camargo is also the birthplace of Texas *cumbia* king Fito Olivares.

The oldest section of the tidy downtown near the main plaza, **Plaza Hidalgo,** offers charming, narrow streets. Tall Washington palms surround the plaza, where a block of three 18th-century buildings has been nicely restored for use as local government offices. On another side of the plaza is **Parroquia de Nuestra Señora de Santa Anna,** a small, single-towered, 18th-century church. During local festivals, musical groups and dancers perform at the *kiosco* or gazebo on the town square.

Sixteen miles southwest of Camargo via Mexico 2 is **Presa Marte R. Gómez,** part of Parque Nacional Camargo (Camargo National Park). Also known as Presa del Azúcar ("Sugar Lake"), this impoundment of the Río San Juan lies 15 miles southwest of Camargo via a paved road. An old favorite with Texan anglers, Gómez still produces a fair number of largemouth bass as

well as crappie, dagger, and catfish. The lake has facilities for fishing, boating, and camping, plus a restaurant that serves Mexican food and freshwater fish under outdoor *palapas* (thatched umbrellas).

Eagle Pass

Few tourists ever make it to Eagle Pass, a sleepy Tex-Mex town of 24,000 on an isolated section of the Texas-Mexico border. During the 1849 California Gold Rush, a popular route between Texas and the U.S. West Coast forded the Rio Grande here and continued through Mexico to the Pacific Coast. A tent camp called "Camp California" quickly developed near the crossing. San Antonio banker John Twohig laid out a proper town in 1850 and named it for the river ford, which local Mexicans called El Paso del Aguila ("Eagle Pass").

The town became the Maverick County seat in 1856, named for rancher Sam Maverick, a signatory to the 1836 Texas Declaration of Independence. His name also has a permanent place in American vocabulary: so that he could say that any unbranded cattle on the range belonged to him, he didn't brand his cattle. This was such a unique scheme that the word "maverick" came to refer to any person with especially new, independent ideas. In ranching, it still refers to unbranded stock.

During the Civil War, Confederate forces garrisoned the town to protect the supply of cotton flowing in from Mexico. In 1865, Confederate General Joseph Shelby led his 500-soldier division across the Rio Grande into Mexico rather than surrender to Union troops; Shelby and his men sank their battle regalia—including the flag and Shelby's colorful hat plume—into the river to prevent it from being captured by the Yankees.

About the only reason to come to Eagle Pass is to visit **Piedras Negras** (pop. 120,000) on the other side of the Rio Grande, the closest border town to San Antonio—142 miles away via US 57/I-35, about two to three hours by car. It's really only 10 miles closer to San Antonio than Laredo, but the town is much less touristed. Eagle Pass is in many ways a "suburb" of Piedras Negras; the main newspaper in the area is the *Zócalo,* published in Spanish on the Mexican side of the border but containing an Eagle Pass section.

Based on a novel by Laura Esquivel and directed by her husband Alfonso Arau, the popular 1992 Mexican film *Like Water for Chocolate (Como Agua Para Chocolate)* was shot on location in Piedras Negras and Eagle Pass.

The Kikapus: About eight miles south of Eagle Pass off FM 1021 is a small Kikapu (Kickapoo) Indian reservation, for the most part used during the summer months only. The rest of the year the tribe resides at El Nacimiento, Mexico, about 90 miles southwest of Piedras Negras off Mexico 57 S and 53 N. The Kikapus originally hailed from Wisconsin and Michigan, but were driven south in the 18th and 19th centuries. In 1775, Spain's Charles III gave them permission to settle in the Mexican colonial province of Coahuila y Texas in return for defending the area against Comanche and Apache raids. By the late 1800s, many of those on the Texas side were banished to Oklahoma reservations. Some were able to flee to northern Mexico and were given land by the Mexican government; like the Seminoles, a number of Kikapus came north again to serve as scouts with the U.S. Cavalry in Texas. The Kikapus have maintained a strong sense of cultural identity and have preserved their language, religion, and many of their traditional customs, such as keeping a sacred fire burning year round in each home. Both the U.S. and Mexican governments have given them special permission to cross the border at will and reside in either country.

Accommodations: The **Eagle Pass Inn** (tel. 210-773-9531), four miles north of town on US 277, has rooms for $28-35 s, $35-45 d; senior discount and weekly rates available. **La Quinta Motor Inn** (tel. 773-7000), 2525 Main St., has slightly larger rooms for $47-54 s, $55-65 d; senior discount available.

Insurance: If you're planning to drive into Piedras Negras or beyond, Mexican vehicle insurance can be arranged at **Capitol Insurance** (tel. 773-2341) at 1115 Main.

Piedras Negras, Coahuila

Piedras Negras, or "Black Rocks," refers to a stratum of coal exposed by erosion in the area. Nearly five times the size of Eagle Pass, this is the main border crossing into the Mexican state of Coahuila. Cattle ranching and twin-plant manufacturing—around 35 *maquilas* at last count—support the local economy; the town is also an important transport junction because of the railway running south to Saltillo.

Although Piedras Negras is the closest border town to San Antonio, Texas, the town gets far fewer tourists than Nuevo Laredo. The international bridge is a short walk from downtown Eagle Pass; the chamber of commerce parking lot at 400 Garrison offers free parking for Piedras Negras day visitors. The many shops in the plaza area near the bridge are not particularly tourist-oriented so bargains are plentiful. The **Mercado Municipal** on Calle Zaragoza, one block west and two blocks south of the bridge, is full of handicrafts and housewares.

The **Plaza de Toros Monumental Arizpe,** on the north side of Av. López Mateos between Calles Mexicali and Tepic, about two km from the bridge, features bullfights on Sundays between June and September.

Small game hunting (rabbit, hare, quail, dove, duck, geese, javelina) and fishing are very popular area pastimes. Sports enthusiasts congregate at the local **Club de Caza, Tiro y Pesca** (Hunting, Shooting, and Fishing Club) on Calle Ocampo between Calles Mina and Dr. Coss. Local residents picnic, hunt, and fish at the nearby San Diego, Santo Domingo, San Rodrigo, San Antonio and Escondido rivers. **Río Grande Rancho Hunting Resort** (tel. 210-773-4444), P.O. Box 1143, Eagle Pass, TX 78853, off Mexico 2 between Piedras Negras and Nuevo Laredo, offers hunting vacations for dove, quail, duck, geese, sandhill crane, and Rio Grande wild turkey.

Food: The most famous institution ine Piedras Negras is the **Restaurant Bar Moderno,** three blocks west and two blocks south of the International Bridge on Calle Morelos between Calle Terán and Allende. Established in 1934 and originally called the Victory Club, the Moderno is purportedly the spot where cook Ignacio "Nacho" Anaya searched a near-empty pantry for something to feed a late-night party of hunters and came up with tortillas chips topped with melted cheese and sliced jalapeños—the birth of nachos.

You know you're in for something different when you walk in and find a large green Buddha statue at the end of the entrance hallway. Though the Moderno remains a citadel of Tex-Mex cuisine, the dining room and adjacent bar are actually quite elegant, with uniformed, starched-shirt waiters and clean white tablecloths. Nachos and other border dishes, including frog legs, *chalupas,* and *arracheras* (called "fajitas" on the English side of the menu), are prominently featured, along with steak, Mexican standards, and seafood. The waiters all speak English but at least half the clientele on any given night is Mexican. If nothing else, stop in for a drink in the attached bar; you haven't done the Tex-Mex border if you haven't been to the Moderno. Open Mon.-Fri. 11 a.m.-midnight, Saturday till 1 a.m.; live music and dancing most nights after 9 p.m.

Next to the plaza is the clean and inexpensive **El Oscar Drive Inn,** a classic take-out (or eat-in) joint with burgers and Tex-Mex.

crested caracara

BOB RACE

GULF COAST

America's "third coast" stretches along the Gulf of Mexico for over 360 miles—over 600 if you count the ins and outs of every bay and inlet—and offers an unparalleled variety of beaches, dunes, islands, lagoons, and saltwater marshes. Flashy tourist brochures call it the "Texas Riviera" or the "Texas Gold Coast," but the truth is you won't find anyplace comparable to St. Tropez or Miami Beach here. Instead, you'll find a rich mixture of laid-back fishing towns, seashore parks, wildlife refuges, a smattering of high-rise condo developments, and one sizable city—Corpus Christi, which barely disturbs the coast as it's set on an inland bay.

THE LAND AND SEA

A basic topographic pattern repeats itself along the coast's full length. Long, narrow barrier islands and peninsulas are separated from an inner shoreline by a series of wide, shallow lagoons. Fed by a mixture of saltwater from the Gulf and freshwater from inland rivers, these lagoons wash against saltmarshes and other coastal wetlands. Farther inland, the marshes and wetlands blend with coastal grasses to form the Gulf Coast Plains. This layered coastal barrier not only protects inland Texas from the full force of tropical cyclones and hurricanes originating in the Gulf, but also provides an unusually diverse concentration of habitats supporting wildlife of all kinds, from tiny fawn-breasted hummingbirds to giant manta rays. The Gulf itself contributes some $200 million to the state's economy annually in harvested seafood—shrimp, crab, oysters, flounder, red snapper, and a variety of other shell- and finfish.

The entire shoreline can be divided into three sections, according to the climate and terrain typical to each. The upper coast, extending from the northern end of the Bolivar Peninsula to Matagorda Island, is the most humid and receives the greatest precipitation; the inner shoreline is thick with salt grass. This is also the state's main rice-producing region. The central coast, from Matagorda Island to Corpus Christi, is a transition zone between the upper and lower coasts, with a mixture of grasslands, marshes, live oak, and scrub vegetation. The lower coast, from Corpus

Christi to the Mexican border, is much more arid, with fewer marshes and grasslands, more scrub country and sand dunes. This last section of Texas shoreline, which includes North and South Padre Island, has been designated one of the country's 10 most ecologically pristine coastal areas by the Coast Alliance and the University of Maryland's Coastal Research Laboratory.

Preservation Versus Development

The most developed areas of the Texas shoreline are along the upper coast between Galveston and Port Arthur, where inland oil refineries are located near large ports that ship petroleum products out of state. The central and lower coasts have, for the most part, been spared this intensive assault on coastal resources, but contend instead with the slow-growing menace of urbanization. One aspect of human intervention that affects all parts of the coast is the Gulf Intracoastal Waterway, a series of channels connecting lagoons and bays so that boats can navigate the Gulf Coast's entire length from Brownsville, Texas, to St. Marks, Florida. It's difficult to predict the long-term effects of these channels (except where they have obviously cut through wetlands and saltmarshes); for the moment, only the waterways around Galveston, Port Arthur, and Corpus Christi are

heavily trafficked. From Corpus Christi south, the Gulf Intracoastal Waterway is mainly used by pleasure craft and the occasional Brownsville ship. Total tonnage shipped between Corpus Christi and the Mexican border represents only about two percent of that shipped between Port Arthur and Galveston.

State and federal authorities have set aside 10 undeveloped coastal areas as wildlife refuges; the Coastal Barrier Resources System Act of 1982 protects another 200,000 acres of Texas coast. These lands are extremely important to the ecological health of not only the coastal system but the entire Gulf of Mexico; over 90% of all fish species found in the Gulf spend at least part of their life cycle in estuary systems along the Gulf Coast.

Many Texans are actively involved in ongoing efforts to preserve what remains of the unprotected virgin dunes, beaches, islands, wetlands, and saltmarshes between Galveston and Boca Chica, the southernmost beach in Texas. If you'd like to join them in their mission, contact one of these organizations: Coast Alliance (tel. 202-265-5518), 1536 16th St. NW, Washington, D.C. 20036; Lone Star Chapter of the Sierra Club (tel. 512-476-6962), 1104 Nueces, Suite 2, Austin, TX 78702; South Bay Taskforce (tel. 512-943-5571), 300 Garcia St., Port Isabel, TX 78578.

GALVESTON ISLAND

It's amazing how many Texans don't know Galveston is an island town. "Galveston Island? Never heard of it. Is it somewhere near Galveston?" To set the record straight: the city of Galveston (pop. 60,500) lies at the northern tip of Galveston Island, which is separated from the Texas mainland by Galveston Bay. It's also the seat of Galveston County, which encompasses the island plus a wedge of mainland around Texas City, southeast of Houston and Pasadena, and the Bolivar Peninsula, just northeast of Galveston across the mouth of Galveston Bay.

Galveston was once the state's largest city, and the first to establish a national bank, post of-

fice, telephone service, hospital, public library, streetcar system, and electric lighting. Today, the island is mostly a vacation spot that draws weekend, holiday, and summer tourists to its 19th-century historic districts and 32 miles of beaches. The beaches aren't the state's best, but they're very accessible—only 51 miles from Houston—and the county does an admirable job of keeping them clean. The historic districts are splendid, encompassing over 1,500 19th-century structures, 550 of which are listed on the National Register of Historic Places. The restored buildings of The Strand and East End districts are among the finest examples of Victorian architecture in North America.

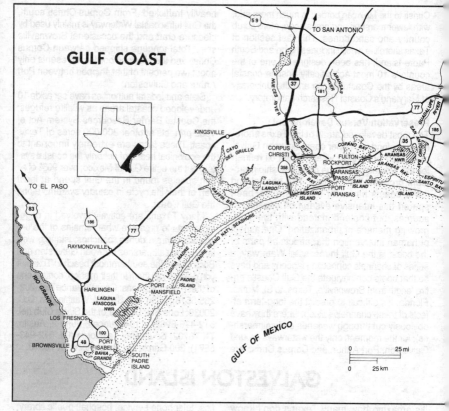

GULF COAST

TO SAN ANTONIO

TO EL PASO

0   25 mi

0   25 km

HISTORY

Pirates and Indians

Not much is known about the early history of human habitation on Galveston Island, mainly because periodic hurricanes have made it difficult to obtain reliable evidence from archaeological excavations. At one time the Karankawa Indians, who had a reputation for fierceness (some histories claim they practiced ritual cannibalism), held domain over the region. When famous Spanish explorer Alvar Nuñez Cabeza de Vaca was shipwrecked here in 1528, he and his crew were rescued and taken prisoner by the Karankawas, with whom they lived for several years. De Vaca finally made it to Mexico

City in 1536 after a series of adventures among Texas and Southwest Indian tribes, who tended to regard him as a great medicine man.

The Spanish returned in the mid-18th century and set up a short-lived presidio named for the Spanish governor of Louisiana, Bernardo de Galvez. They left the island to the French after Franco-Spanish relations in East Texas grew tense; by the end of the century, the French had abandoned their American colonies, too. Mexican revolutionaries stationed themselves here for a short time in the early 1800s, then left.

In 1817, buccaneer Jean Lafitte established a pirate colony called Campeachy on the island. After a run-in with an American gunboat, Lafitte was forced to leave in 1821, but he left behind a small but growing community that Anglicized the

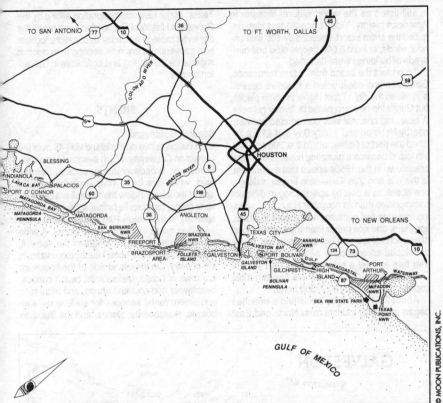

TO SAN ANTONIO 77 10

TO FT. WORTH, DALLAS 45

36

59

COLORADO RIVER

5

HOUSTON

BLESSING

BRAZOS RIVER

6

INDIANOLA
LAVACA BAY
PORT O'CONNOR
PALACIOS

MATAGORDA BAY
MATAGORDA
PENINSULA

60

35

36

288

SAN BERNARD NWR

MATAGORDA

ANGLETON

45

TEXAS CITY

BRAZORIA NWR

FREEPORT
BRAZOSPORT AREA

FOLLETS ISLAND

GALVESTON BAY

GALVESTON

PORT BOLIVAR

ANAHUAC NWR

GALVESTON ISLAND

GILCHRIST

BOLIVAR PENINSULA

GULF

INTRACOASTAL WATERWAY

HIGH ISLAND

87

McFADDIN NWR

SEA RIM STATE PARK

124

73

PORT ARTHUR

WATERWAY

TO NEW ORLEANS

10

TEXAS POINT NWR

GULF OF MEXICO

© MOON PUBLICATIONS, INC.

original Spanish name as "Galveston." Treasure-hunters still speculate about the likelihood of buried loot somewhere on the island.

Galveston banker Samuel May Williams poured loot of his own into the Texas revolution against Mexican rule in the late 1830s. Texas Navy ships stationed at Galveston held off a Mexican blockade of the coast and the town was made a temporary capital of the aspiring republic. Once independence was won, plans for a new town were laid as Galveston geared up to become the new republic's chief port.

Civil War, the 1900
Hurricane, and Renewal

During the state's 10-year status as a sovereign nation, the port of Galveston grew slowly as the Texan economy started and sputtered. Once Texas was annexed to the U.S., things looked rosy for the town—until its strategic position made it a focus for the Civil War in the 1860s. Union troops were able to capture the port in 1862, but the Confederates soon regained control and kept it till the end of the war. A Union naval blockade prevented any goods from coming in or out of the port, however, so the local economy stagnated along with the rest of the state.

After the war ended, Galveston prospered. By the late 1800s, it was the biggest and most modern city in the state, the third-largest port in the nation, and a banking center for the Southwest. The island town's destiny was forever altered, however, by the hurricane of 1900, which is still listed as the worst natural disaster in American history. Tides up to 20 feet high engulfed the entire island, speeded by 100-mile-an-hour winds; at least 6,000 people died and hundreds of buildings were flattened.

To protect the island from future hurricanes, Galvestonians constructed a massive seawall and raised the city 17 feet higher in some places, but Galveston never regained its former glamour. A new ship channel was constructed between nearby Houston and Trinity Bay that all but finished the port of Galveston. In the '30s and '40s the island became a gambling haven, but a legal crackdown in the 1950s ended that experiment. In the '60s and '70s, Galveston began making a comeback as a port by specializing in different commodities than its neighbor Houston, importing bananas and plantains and exporting wheat, sorghum, and rice rather than the import/export of petrochemicals and building materials. It also developed an especially efficient port system that has earned a reputation as the "Port of Quickest Dispatch"; it's now the seventh-most important of the state's 27 Gulf ports.

About 25 years ago, the island's beaches began attracting tourists from North and East Texas. Major historical restoration efforts by the Galveston Historical Foundation have made the city even more of a holiday destination; tourism and conventions are now second in economic importance to shipping and agriculture in Galveston county.

SIGHTS

Seawall Boulevard

Most visitors arrive on the island via I-45 over the Galveston Causeway, which eventually becomes Broadway. Broadway in turn ends at Seawall Blvd., which runs for 10 miles along the seaward side of the island. Below the seawall is a beach of sorts (better beaches lie farther south beyond the seawall), and between 10th and 61st streets are 14 jetties made of huge granite blocks. A wide sidewalk runs the entire length of the seawall, making it one of the longest beach promenades in the country. On the inland side of the boulevard are rows of hotels, restaurants, beach condos, beachwear and souvenir shops, and recreation equipment rental services for surfboards, sailboards, skateboards, skates, and the like. See

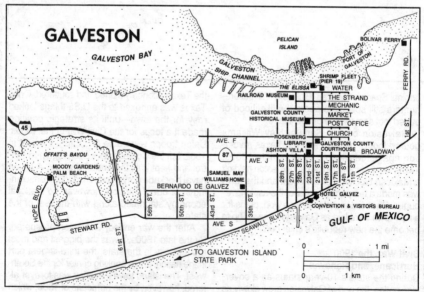

"Recreation," below, for descriptions of specific beaches and beach activities.

Museums

The **Galveston County Historical Museum** (tel. 409-766-2340), jointly sponsored by the county and the Galveston Historical Foundation, is housed in a 1919-vintage bank building at 2219 Market (Ave. D). Permanent exhibits on the first floor recount Galveston history, including early Karankawa Indian habitation, the exploits of pirate Jean Lafitte, and the 1900 hurricane. The mezzanine floor features rotating exhibits dealing with more arcane facets of local history. The museum also offers a lecture series. Open Memorial Day to Labor Day Mon.-Sat. 10 a.m.-5 p.m., Sunday noon-5 p.m.; the remainder of the year closed on Sunday. Admission is free; donations accepted.

The **Railroad Museum** (tel. 765-5700) is appropriately located in the old Galveston Railway Station, an art deco structure that's been restored to its original 1932 condition. Thirty-nine life-size plaster sculptures of "passengers" sit and stand in the former waiting room; headphone stations near each group of sculptures allow visitors to listen in on dramatized conversations. Other rooms in the station feature a working HO-scale model of the Port of Galveston and audiovisual displays that explain Texas rail development. Out on the tracks are collections of restored steam locomotives and passenger cars,

including 1920s-era Pullman sleepers and a 1922 Santa Fe engine (#555).

Two restored 1940s dining cars contain a full-service restaurant, Santa Fe Chew Chew. The station also serves as a terminus for the *Texas Limited* excursion train. The station/museum is at 25th and The Strand, at the west end of The Strand historic district. It's open daily 10 a.m.-5 p.m.; admission is $5 adults, $4.50 seniors, $2.50 children 4-12.

Historic Buildings

Galveston is full of late-19th-century homes built in the Victorian and Greek Revival styles. The most impressive is undoubtedly the **Bishop's Palace** (tel. 409-762-2475) at 1402 Broadway. It was designed for Colonel Walter Gresham by renowned Galveston architect Nicholas Clayton and completed in 1886 for a cost of $250,000; current appraisals estimate its value at $5.5 million. The local Catholic Diocese purchased it in 1923 for Bishop Byrne, who lived here until 1950. The 24-room mansion is listed with the Library of Congress as one of 14 structures in the U.S. most representative of the Victorian age of architecture, while the American Institute of Architects counts it as one of the 100 most significant buildings in the country.

The exterior is constructed of red sandstone, white limestone, and pink granite. Inside are 14 magnificent fireplaces, plus wood paneling and archways of black walnut burl. One of the most

Bishop's Palace

stunning interior features is a spiral staircase that took 61 craftsmen three years to build, using oak, maple, white mahogany, rosewood, satinwood, and other fine hardwoods. All rooms are fully restored and furnished in period antiques. It's open Memorial Day to Labor Day daily 10 a.m.-5 p.m., the remainder of the year Wed.-Sun. noon-4 p.m. Tours leave every 30 minutes; admission is $4 adults, $3 seniors, $2.50 children 13-18, $1 children under 13.

The **Ashton Villa** (tel. 762-3933), at 24th and Broadway, is a three-story, Victorian Italianate brick villa built in 1859 for Colonel James M. Brown. It was restored by the Galveston Historical Society, which offers a one-hour tour of the mansion and carriage house that includes an audiovisual presentation on the 1900 hurricane. It's open Memorial Day to Labor Day daily 10 a.m.-4 p.m.; Sunday noon-4 p.m.; admission is $4 adults, $3.50 seniors and children 7-18, free under seven. Families of two adults and two children receive a family admission fee of $14.

One restored example of Greek Revival architecture in Galveston is open to the public year round. **John Sydnor's 1847 Powhatan House** (tel. 763-0077) is a two-story mansion with 24-foot-high Doric columns and period furnishings at 3427 Ave. O. It's maintained by the Galveston Garden Club, which opens it to self-guiding tours Fri.-Mon. 1-5 p.m. Admission is $2 adults, $1 for students and seniors.

The **Samuel May Williams Home** (tel. 765-1839), at 3601 Bernardo de Galvez (Ave. P), is considered the town's oldest residence. A modest New England-style house crowned by a widow's walk, it was originally built in Maine, then disassembled and moved to Galveston, where it was reassembled piece by piece. Williams was an important local figure who started Texas banking, recruited volunteers for the Texas revolution, and built ships for the Texas Navy. The Galveston Historical Society leads tours of the home Memorial Day to Labor Day Mon.-Sat. 10 a.m.-5 p.m., Sunday noon-5 p.m.; the remainder of the year it closes at 4 p.m. on the same days. Admission is $4 adults, $3.50 children and seniors.

At the well-restored, Victorian-era **Grand 1894 Opera House** (tel. 765-1894) at 2020 Post Office, every visual detail recalls the turn of the century and no seat is more than 70 feet from the stage. Such artists as Anna Pavlova, Al Jolson, Sarah Bernhardt, John Philip Sousa, and the Marx Brothers performed here in the theater's heyday. Today it serves as a venue for everything from opera and symphony to rock and jazz concerts. It's also open to the public for self-guided tours Mon.-Sat. 9 a.m.-5 p.m., Sunday noon-5 p.m.; admission is $2 adults, children under six free.

The **Tremont House** (tel. 763-0300), 2300 Mechanic St. (Ship Mechanic's Row), is Galves-

Ashton Villa

GALVESTON CONVENTION AND VISITORS BUREAU

ton's most historic hotel. The original, built in 1839, hosted such famous guests as Sam Houston, Ulysses S. Grant, Clara Barton, and Anna Pavlova, but burned down in 1865. A replacement was erected in 1872, but was abandoned and leveled 56 years later. The latest incarnation, near the original site, is housed in a huge 1879 building that has been totally renovated and outfitted with Victorian-era furnishings. Wrought-iron bridges connect the upper floors, which are reached by old-fashioned birdcage elevators; most of the 117 guest rooms have 14-foot ceilings and 12-foot windows. Even if you can't afford to stay here, drop by the **Toujouse Bar** for a drink at the 1860s rosewood bar or traditional English afternoon tea.

Established in 1902, the **Rosenberg Library** (tel. 763-8854) at 23rd and Sealy (Ave. I) is the oldest continually operating public library in Texas. Besides offering the usual book collection and lending services, the library houses the Galveston Art League Gallery and several historical displays that recount different aspects of local and state history. It's open to the public Mon.-Thurs. 9 a.m.-9 p.m., Friday and Saturday 9 a.m.-6 p.m.

Moody Gardens

Galveston's biggest tourist attraction is Moody Gardens' 10-story, $130-million, glass Rainforest Pyramid containing 2,000 species of flora and fauna from the rainforests of Asia, Africa, and the Americas. Part of a 142-acre garden complex devoted to education and research, Moody Gardens harbors such exotica as red ginger, pygmy goats, poison arrow frogs, and rare species of Asian bamboo. Multimedia presentations—videos detailing rainforest functions and IMAX films on natural history—supplement the floral displays.

Outside the glass pyramid, flamingos cavort in a wading pool and trails lead through the Hope Rose Garden, Horticulture Terraces, the Japanese Garden of Life, and a Vietnam Memorial. Adjacent **Palm Beach** offers walking trails and an artificial white-sand beach with volleyball courts. The *Colonel* paddlewheeler cruises Offatt's Bayou daily.

A portion of the grounds is set aside for special therapy programs designed to treat or habilitate injured, disabled, and mentally challenged persons through interaction with plants and animals.

To reach Moody Gardens, take I-45 south to the 61st St. exit, then turn right on Seawall Blvd. and right again at 81st St.; turn left at Hope Blvd. and continue to the entrance. The facility is open daily 10 a.m.-10 p.m. Separate admission prices for each attractions—the pyramid, IMAX, Palm Beach, and the *Colonel*—are $6 per person. Package deals are available: any two attractions for $11, any three for $16, and all four for $20. For further information call (409) 744-1745 or (800) 582-4673.

Elissa: A Tall Ship for Texas

This 150-foot, square-rigged iron barque is the third-oldest ship afloat and possibly the only fully operational 19th-century vessel in the world. First launched in Scotland in 1877, the *Elissa* made calls at Galveston in 1883 and 1886, exchanging South American bananas for Texas cotton. When the Galveston Historical Foundation sought a 19th-century sailing ship connected with Galveston history, it found the *Elissa* rusting in a Piraeus, Greece, shipyard in 1974. The ship has since been fully restored to form and function and makes yearly voyages along the Gulf Coast and beyond. In 1986, the *Elissa* sailed up the Atlantic coast to participate in the Parade of Sail in New York Harbor.

Most of the year, the ship is moored at Pier 21, near 22nd and Water on the Galveston Ship Channel, an easy stroll from The Strand Historic District. Visitors are welcome to tour the ship and the various seafaring exhibits on board. When in port, the *Elissa* is open daily 10 a.m.-5 p.m.; admission is $4 adults, $3.50 for students and seniors, $3 for children 6-12.

The entry fee includes admission to the **Texas Seaport Museum,** an exhibit of Galveston's 19th-century maritime history at Pier 21. Among the displays are a small-scale model of the 1883 port, historical photos, period artifacts, and a tribute to turn-of-the-century immigrants who made Galveston the "Ellis Island of the West." Computer terminals allow access to a database listing over 117,000 immigrants who landed at the port, including names, occupations, countries of origin, ports of departure, and ship names. A multiscreen slide presentation chronicles the seafaring life of the *Elissa.* The museum is open daily 9:30

a.m.-5:30 p.m. Memorial Day through Labor Day, 10 a.m.-5 p.m. the remainder of the year.

For further information on the ship and museum, call (409) 763-1877.

Historic Districts

The Strand Historic District, a 12-block area along Water, Mechanic, and The Strand between 20th and 25th streets, represents one of the finest collections of iron-front Victorians in the country. The centerpiece of the district is The Strand, modeled after London's street of the same name in the late 1800s. During the late 19th century, when it served as the most important financial center between San Francisco and St. Louis, The Strand was known as "the Wall Street of the Southwest"; although the buildings survived the 1900 hurricane, the port's general decline thereafter led to the district's virtual abandonment. Fortunately, the city chose to preserve the old storefronts rather than tear them down or alter their appearance, and today the buildings are owned or leased by restaurants, shops, and other small businesses, most tourist-oriented. A few iron-fronts have been turned into residential apartments and lofts. Galveston's two biggest annual events are held on The Strand—Mardi Gras in February and Dickens on The Strand in December.

The **East End Historic District** is a 40-block area bounded by 11th, 19th, Market, and Broadway. Most of the homes here were built between 1875 and 1900, when this was an upscale residential district. The entire district is listed on the National Register of Historic Places. A driving and walking tour map of the district is available from The Strand Visitors Center, 2016 The Strand.

Several homes in the smaller **Silk Stocking Historic District,** along 24th and 25th between avenues L and O, are listed with the National Register of Historic Places or the Texas Historical Commission. The district's name is an early political label that referred to the fact only ladies living in this part of town could afford silk stockings. Nicholas Clayton, the architect of the Bishop's Palace, also designed the **Sweeney-Royston House** at Ave. L and 24th. It's closed to the public except during the Historic Homes Tour in May.

Lone Star Flight Museum

Housed in a custom-designed hangar at Scholes Field, 2002 Terminal Dr. (south of Galveston Municipal Airport and Offatt's Bayou), this is a prime attraction for air force buffs. The museum's collection of 32 historic planes includes a number of WW II-vintage military aircraft, a Vietnam-era A-37 Dragonfly, one of only six operational Republic P-47 Thunderbolts in existence, an F7F Tigercat, the best surviving example of a P-38 Lightning in the world, a 1836 Beech Staggerwing, and a Boeing B-17G. The museum (tel. 409-740-7722) is open daily 10 a.m.-5 p.m.; admission is $5 adults, $2.50 for seniors and children 2-13.

American National Tower Observation Area

A windowed observation room on the 20th floor of Galveston's tallest building, the American National Tower at 20th and Market, offers sweeping panoramas of the surrounding cityscape, port, and beach areas. Period photos and other displays chronicle the city's history.

The Strand

Open Mon.-Sat. 10 a.m.-5 p.m., Sunday noon-5 p.m. from Memorial Day through Labor Day, closing an hour earlier the rest of the year. Admission is $2 for people ages seven and older, free for children six and under. Call (409) 766-6642 for further information.

ACCOMMODATIONS

Hotels, Motels, and Condominiums

Galveston has a large selection of places to stay, most along Seawall Blvd. or farther down the southwest beaches. Naturally, the cheapest hotels and motels are those without a sea view, though most places on Seawall Blvd. are constructed so that all rooms face the Gulf. If you want a sea view, be sure to request one when making reservations.

Beach condos in Galveston usually cost between $65 and $200 a night, depending on the number of bedrooms. Since they're equipped with full kitchens, it's generally less expensive to stay in condos than in hotels or motels if you'll be there for several days or more. A few offer weekly or monthly rates, though beach home rentals are a better bargain for stays of a week or longer. For further details, see the "Galveston Hotels, Motels, and Condominiums" chart.

Beach and Bay Homes

Several local real estate agencies handle beachfront and bayfront home rentals, which start at around $300-500 a week—$150 and up for a weekend—for a basic one- or two-bedroom place. Most are located west of 100th St. and provide maid and linen service. Contact one of these realtors for further information: **Century 21 Bay Reef Realty** (tel. 409-737-2300 or 800-527-7333), 16708-C San Luis Pass Rd., Galveston, TX 77554; **Galveston Realty** (tel. 737-2663), Rte. 1, Box 162, Galveston, TX 77551; **Galveston Rentals and Management** (tel. 765-8600 or 800-742-5837), 201 Seawall Blvd., Galveston, TX 77550; **Menotti Properties** (tel. 737-4700), Rte. 1, Box 150-A1, Galveston, TX 77554; **Sand 'N Sea Properties** (tel. 737-2556), P.O. Box 5165, Galveston, TX 77554; or **Wolverton & Associates** (tel. 737-1430), P.O. Box 5255, Galveston, TX 77554.

Pirates' Beach & Cove (tel. 713-280-3973 or 409-737-4044) rents resort homes on the west side of Galveston Island overlooking West Bay by the week or weekend.

Bed and Breakfasts

Galveston has around a dozen bed-and-breakfast inns, most in restored Victorian homes. The Strand Visitors Center distributes brochures from local B&Bs, and **Bed & Breakfast Reservations** (tel. 409-762-1668 or 800-628-4644), P.O. Box 1326, Galveston, TX 77551, can assist with bookings. Rates are in the $65-150 range.

Several places will take reservations directly, including **The Gilded Thistle** (tel. 763-0194 or 800-654-9380) at 1805 Broadway, an elegant 1893 house with three rooms for $135-175 a night, including full breakfast and complimentary wine and cheese in the evening. The **Inn on The Strand** (tel. 763-0806), at 2021 The Strand, has four large rooms and two suites in a restored 1856 warehouse. Rates are $115-150 a night with continental breakfast and evening champagne.

Michael's (tel. 763-3760 or 800-776-8302), a 1916 brick house at 1715 35th, has rooms for $85 a night (shared bath only) including full breakfast. Galveston's first B&B was the **The Victorian Inn** (tel. 762-3235), a massive colonial-style home at 511 17th, within walking distance of The Strand. The four rooms cost $85-175 a night (only the most expensive has a private bath), including continental breakfast and evening hors d'oeuvres.

The 1817-vintage two-story Queen Anne-style **Coopersmith Inn** (tel. 409-763-7004 or 713-965-7273), at 1914 Ave. M between 19th and 20th streets roughly midway between The Strand and the beach, is notable for its well-restored winding teak staircase, turret corners, and gingerbread trim. Room rates vary from $85 to $135 (plus tax) a night, including a full breakfast and afternoon wine and hors d'oeuvres.

Under the same management as Galveston's historic Tremont House, **Harbor House** (tel. 763-0300 or 800-874-2300) sits adjacent to Pier 21 on the waterfront, close to the Texas Seaport Museum, the *Elissa*, and The Strand. Built to resemble a waterfront warehouse, the well-appointed 42-room inn charges $138 per night with full breakfast at Mallory's Wharf Cafe.

GALVESTON HOTELS, MOTELS, AND CONDOMINIUMS

Prices quoted are for the peak season of spring-summer and reflect both weekday (less expensive) and weekend (more expensive) rates. Fall and winter rates are generally less. Add 11% tax to all hotel rates. Area code: 409.

Best Western Beachfront Inn; 5914 Seawall; tel. 740-1261 or (800) 528-1234; $49-119; pool

By the Sea Condominiums; 7310 Seawall; tel. 744-0905 or (800) 666-0905 (outside TX); $100-135; pool, tennis court; weekly and monthly rates available

Casa del Mar Condominiums on the Beach; 6102 Seawall; tel. 740-2431 or (800) 392-1205 (in TX); $59-124; 1 bedroom suites with kitchens, sea view, pool, coin laundry; weekly and monthly rates available

Comfort Inn; 2300 Seawall; tel. 762-1166 or (800) 232-2476; $49-99; pool

Commodore on the Beach; 3618 Seawall; tel. 763-2375, (800) 231-9921 (outside TX), or (800) 543-0074; $64-90; all rooms with sea view, pool, airport shuttle

Crockett Motel; 4214 Ave. U; tel. 763-4385; $25-40

Days Inn; 6107 Broadway; tel. 740-2491 or (800) 325-2525 (outside TX); $35-80; pool, weekly rates

Econo Lodge; 2825 61st; tel. 744-7133 or (800) 424-4777 (outside TX); $60-90; pool

The Flagship Hotel; 2501 Seawall; tel. 762-9000 or (800) 392-6542 (outside TX); $89-389; on private pier, pool, fishing, weekly rates

Gaido's Seaside Inn; 3828 Seawall; tel. 762-9625 or (800) 525-0064 (outside TX); $40-90; pool, sea view, weekly rates

Galleon Suites Resort Hotel; 9520 Seawall; tel. 744-2244; $115-175; 1-2 bedroom suites with kitchen, pool, fitness center, complimentary continental breakfast

The Galvestonian Condominiums; 1401 East Beach; tel. 765-6161; $135-340; sea views, lighted tennis courts, heated pool, jacuzzi

Harbor House; Pier 21; tel. 763-0300 or (800) 874-2300; $85-105; next to Texas Seaport Museum

Harbor View Inn; 928 Ferry; tel. 762-3311 or (800) 892-0175; $39-75; adjacent to ferry, pool

Holiday Inn on the Beach; 5002 Seawall; tel. 740-3581 or (800) HOLIDAY; $85-119; sea view, pool, coin laundry

Hotel Galvez; 2024 Seawall; tel. 765-7721 or (800) 392-4285; $105-135; historic (established 1911), sea view, pool, sauna, whirlpool, senior discount

The Inn at San Luis; 5400 Seawall; tel. 744-5000 or (800) 833-0120; $69-129; sea view, pool, whirlpool

Islander East Condominiums; 415 East Beach; tel. 765-9301; $70-205; pool, tennis courts

La Quinta Galveston Motor Inn; 1402 Seawall; tel. 763-1224 or (800) 531-5900 (outside TX); $73-150; sea view, pool, senior discount

Manor House; 2300 Seawall; tel. 762-1166; $59-85; sea view, pool

Motel 6; 7404 Ave. J (Broadway); tel. 740-3794; $26-48; pool

Ocean Vue Motel; 3008 Seawall; tel. 762-0664; $20-70

Ramada Inn Resort; 600 The Strand; tel. 765-5544 or (800) 222-2244; $39-99; next to Galveston Yacht Basin, pool, sauna, whirlpool, weekly rates

Sandpiper Motel; 2nd and Seawall; tel. 765-9431; $40-100; pool

The San Luis Resort; 5222 Seawall; tel. 744-1500, (800) 445-0090, or (800) 392-5937 (outside TX); $55-166; sea views, pool, sauna, tennis courts

Seahorse Inn; 3402 Seawall; tel. 763-2433; $30-70

Seascape Condominiums; 10811 San Luis Pass; tel. 740-1245; $89-185; beach, heated pool, spa, tennis court

The Tremont House; 2300 Ships Mechanic Row; tel. 763-0300 or (800) 874-2300; $130-170; historic, near The Strand, senior discount, special midweek rates

Treasure Isle Motel; 1002 Seawall; tel. 763-8561; $29-69

The Victorian Condo Hotel; 6300 Seawall; tel. 740-3555 or (800) 231-6363 (outside TX); $109-189; 1-2 bedroom suites with sea views, kitchens, heated pool, whirlpools, tennis courts, weekly and monthly rates

Camping and RV Parks

Tent camping and RV parking are permitted at **Galveston Island State Park** at Seawall and 13 Mile Road. **Dellanera RV Park** (tel. 409-740-0390), at 10901 San Luis Pass just west of Sea-Arama and Six Mile Rd. off Seawall, is a city-operated facility with 50 full hookups, showers, laundry, grocery store, and beach area. Sites are $15-18 nightly, $84 weekly, and $300 monthly during the spring and summer, somewhat less during the fall and winter. Rates are similar at **Bayou Heaven** (tel. 744-2837), 6310 Heards Lane, and **Galveston Island R.V. Resort** (tel. 744-5464), 2323 Skymaster.

FOOD

The highest concentration of restaurants in Galveston stretches along Seawall Boulevard. Another restaurant area occupies The Strand Historic District, where meals are generally more expensive. You'll find several grocery stores along Seawall; if you're staying at the west-end beaches (Dellanera RV Park or Galveston Island State Park), the nearest grocery store is **Seven Seas Grocery** (tel. 409-737-1152), also known as Red's. Besides groceries, gas, and fishing tackle, Red's also offers a video rental service.

American

$$$ Santa Fe Chew Chew: Two restored dining cars at the Railroad Museum offer fixed-price menus with choice of beef or veal, seafood, and fowl entrees. At 25th and The Strand (tel. 409-763-4759); open Mon.-Sat. for lunch and dinner, Sunday for brunch.

$ to $$ Phoenix Bakery and Coffee Shop: This is a great place to start off the morning with good coffee and fresh-baked pastries, French toast, or breakfast burritos. At 2228 Ship's Mechanic Row just off The Strand (tel. 763-4611); open Sun.-Thurs. 7:30 a.m.-6 p.m., Friday and Saturday 7:30 a.m.-8 p.m.

$ Sonny's Place: Burgers, chili, fried shrimp, barbecue, and muffalettas (Tuesday and Saturday only) have kept a mostly local crowd satisfied for 50 years. At 1206 19th (tel. 763-9602); open Tues.-Fri. 11 a.m.-2 p.m. and 4:30-10 p.m., Saturday 11 a.m.-10 p.m.

$$ Yaga's: A Tropical Cafe: The Caribbean theme here carries over to the menu, which features tropical drinks and tasty "Rasta Pasta"— shrimp, crab, and pasta in a mildly spiced mayonnaise—as well as burgers, chicken, and fresh seafood. On weekends there's live music, usually reggae. At 2314 The Strand (tel. 762-6676); open Mon.-Thurs. 11:30 a.m.-10 p.m., Friday and Saturday 11:30 a.m.-2 a.m., Sunday noon-10 p.m.

$ Star Drug Store: The oldest continually operating drugstore in the state; the neon Coca-Cola sign out front is said to be the oldest in existence. The antique soda fountain offers sandwiches, ice cream, fountain drinks, and phosphates. At 510-512 23rd (tel. 762-8658); open 7 a.m. till sunset.

Continental

$$$ Nash D'Amico's Pasta and Clam Bar: This casual-but-classy restaurant on The Strand (in the 1895 Hutchings-Sealy Building) is a branch of the well-known Houston eatery. The menu's primary focus is Italian, and the clams are flown in fresh daily from Boston. At 24th and The Strand (tel. 409-763-6500); open daily for lunch and dinner.

$$$+   The Wentletrap: Named for a rare Texas seashell, Galveston's most elegant restaurant is housed in the restored 1871 League Building on The Strand, with a three-story atrium in the center. The menu changes periodically, usually featuring a short but varied selection of beef, seafood, and fowl. Men are required to wear coats after 6 p.m. At The Strand and Tremont (tel. 765-5545); open Mon.-Sat. for lunch and dinner, Sunday for brunch and dinner.

Mexican

Galveston has several funky Tex-Mex places that offer a cheap and tasty alternative to seafood.

$ Apache Tortilla Factory & Mexican Food: Good Mexican breakfasts and Tex-Mex standards, along with daily specials. At 511 20th (tel. 409-765-5646); open Tues.-Sat. for breakfast, lunch, and dinner, Sunday breakfast and lunch only.

$ El Nopalito: This family-run cafe is another classic Tex-Mex breakfast-and-lunch place. At 614 42nd (tel. 763-9815); closed Wednesday.

$ The Original Mexican Café: Claims to be Galveston's first; similar to El Nopalito. At 1401 Market (tel. 762-6001); open daily for lunch and dinner.

Seafood

Seafood is naturally Galveston's specialty. Many Cajuns have settled on the island over the years, so there's a strong Cajun influence in the way seafood is prepared locally. The "Mosquito Fleet," the island's shrimp boats, is anchored at Pier 19; you can sometimes buy fresh shrimp direct from the boats.

$ Benno's: One of several casual seafood places at the east end of Seawall. They're experts at preparing tasty Cajun-style shrimp, oysters, crab, and crawfish, plus Cajun standards like gumbo and red beans and rice—all at great prices, eat in or take out. At 12th and Seawall (tel. 409-762-4621); open daily from 11 a.m. till late.

$$ Christie's Beachcomber: Very popular, with inside and outside seating. At 4th and Seawall (tel. 762-8648); open daily 11 a.m.-9 p.m.

$$ to $$$ Clary's: Located on Offatt's Bayou, this is one of the better choices for more formal seafood dining. Besides a variety of fresh seafood specials, Clary's serves steak. At 8509 Teichman, off I-45 (tel. 740-0771); open Mon.-Fri. for lunch and dinner, Saturday dinner only; closed the last two weeks of November. Reservations suggested.

$$$ Gaido's Seafood Restaurant: This family-owned and operated place has been a local favorite for over 70 years. The menu features catch-of-the-day and there's usually a choice between grilled, fried, or broiled entrees. Deep-fried softshell crab is a house specialty. At 39th and Seawall (tel. 762-9625); open daily for lunch and dinner.

$$ to $$$ Landry's: A branch of a famous Corpus Christi restaurant that specializes in fresh seafood specials and large combo seafood platters. At 1502 Seawall (tel. 762-4261); open daily for lunch and dinner.

ENTERTAINMENT

Live Music

The majority of Galveston visitors are interested in sun, sand, and sea rather than late-night entertainment, so the island usually closes down early. The major exception is during spring break in March, when hundreds of college students flock here for round-the-clock partying.

During the summer, the **Beach Club** (tel. 409-765-5922) at Stewart Beach Park offers live music on weekends and DJs during the week, and it's open till 2 a.m. **Cafe Torrefie** and **Yaga's,** both on The Strand, have live bands year round on weekends, sometimes during the week. The larger hotels also often feature live music on weekends.

On Sunday 1-5 p.m., **Club 23** (tel. 763-9393), at 2009 23rd St., features live Cajun music. The show is always broadcast on local radio station KGBC-AM 1540, so if you can't make the club, tune in.

Galveston Island Outdoor Musicals

The 1,800-seat Mary Moody Northern Amphitheater (tel. 409-737-3440 or 800-54-SHOWS), at Galveston Island State Park, features up to five alternating musicals throughout the summer. One of them is always *The Lone Star,* a musical dramatization of the Texas revolution with a 100-person cast; others have been *Hello Dolly!, South Pacific,* and *Oklahoma!,* but they change from year to year. Tickets are usually around $20-24 for adults, $10-12 for children. Seniors receive a $2 discount.

The Grand 1894 Opera House

The "official opera house of the State of Texas" hosts a full schedule of variety, dance, and music performances, along with occasional Broadway-style musicals, most of which are oriented toward an older audience. Acts during the 1994-95 season included Mitzi Gaynor, the Smothers Brothers, Mark Russell, Ballet Folklorico, *Guys and Dolls, Oliver!,* Shirley Valentine, and Mel Torme. At 2020 Post Office, between 20th and 21st (tel. 409-765-1894).

The Strand Street Theatre

This 110-seat theater at 2317 Ships Mechanic Row hosts the island's only professional theater group for seven or eight shows a year. Performances are on weekends only, including a Sunday matinee. Call (409) 763-4591 for further information.

EVENTS

January-February

Mardi Gras: This pre-Lenten festival has been celebrated in Galveston since the mid-1800s, although until recently it had all but died out. It's now on its way to becoming the island's biggest annual celebration, drawing around 200,000 party-goers during the week before Ash Wednesday in February. Local events start in early January with a Miss Mardi Gras pageant, followed by mask-making workshops and parties later in the month at Galveston Arts Center, 2127 The Strand. During Mardi Gras week, there's a Mardi Gras Ball at the Grand 1894 Opera House (2020 Post Office), the arrival of King Neptune at the tall ship *Elissa*, and six parades. The final Grand Night Parade is held on the Saturday before Ash Wednesday and proceeds from Seawall Blvd. to The Strand. New Orleans celebrities like Fats Domino, Pete Fountain, and Al Hirt occasionally join the parade. If you plan to arrive in Galveston during Mardi Gras week, you'd better book your accommodations at least a month or two in advance. For scheduling information, call the Galveston Convention and Visitors Bureau (tel. 409-763-4311).

March

The four-day **Galveston Film Festival** is sponsored by the Motion Picture Producers of Texas, the Texas Film Commission, and the Houston Film Commission. Texas film screenings and panel discussions are held at the Galveston Arts Center (tel. 409-763-2403), 2127 The Strand.

April

A **Blessing of the Shrimp Fleet** is usually held on the first weekend following Easter. This two-day festival centers on the Cajun shrimper tradition of calling in Catholic priests to bless the trawlers for the spring harvest. As part of the celebration, the shrimper crews decorate their boats with streamers and flowers and cruise up and down the Galveston Ship Channel. On the waterfront near Pier 19 are arts and crafts exhibits, food vendors, and entertainment.

May

Historic Homes Tour: During the first two weekends of May, around 10 historic Galveston homes that aren't usually open to the public offer guided tours Saturday 10 a.m.-6 p.m. and Sunday noon-6 p.m. The Galveston Historical Foundation (tel. 409-762-TOUR) sells tickets for the tours.

June

A **Crawfish Fest** is usually held on the first or second weekend of the month. It's a serious crawfish cookoff in which such celebrated Louisiana Cajun/Creole chefs as Alex Patout and Enola Prudhomme compete against their Texas counterparts. Prizes are awarded for best-tasting crawfish dish, best presentation, and most original recipe, as well as biggest, fastest, and longest "bugs" (Cajun slang for crawfish). Check with the Galveston Convention and Visitors Bureau (tel. 409-763-4311) for the latest schedule and venue.

November

At the **Galveston Island Jazz Festival,** local, state, and national jazz acts convene for a weekend of free afternoon concerts, music cruises, and night performances at the Grand 1894 Opera House. It's usually held on the second weekend of the month. For further information, call the Galveston Convention and Visitors Bureau (tel. 409-763-4311).

December

Dickens on The Strand: The Strand Historic District is the perfect setting for this Victorian-style Christmas celebration on the first weekend of December. This annual event, sponsored by the Galveston Historical Foundation, began in 1974 and emphasizes a Charles Dickens theme, avowedly because of the town's historic maritime ties with England and London's own Strand. The entire district comes alive with Victorian-costumed entertainers—jugglers, musicians, magicians, carolers, handbell choristers, dancers, and mimes—who perform on street corners and on six stages placed throughout the 12-block area. Restaurants and street vendors along The Strand serve roasted chestnuts, bangers (British sausages), baked oysters, plum pudding, hot cider, and other evocative food and drink. For sauntering around The Strand during the weekend festivities, many citizens dress in Victorian clothing available new, used, or custom-made at **The Old Peanut Butter Warehouse** (tel. 409-925-4551), 100 39th Street.

In recent years, Dickens's great-great-grandson Gerald Charles Dickens has made public appearances at the event, reading from his own writings and those of his great-great-grandfather. Dickens's *A Christmas Carol* is also performed several times at the Grand 1894 Opera House during the weekend. One event held outside of The Strand district is the **Morning Tea at Ashton Villa,** 2328 Broadway (Sat.-Sun. at 9, 10, and 11 a.m.), which features tea, scones, fresh fruit, and a tour of the historic mansion. At 7 p.m. on both evenings, the Ashton Villa hosts a candlelight **Dickens Feast** of English-style roast turkey with all the trimmings.

As with Mardi Gras, it's a good idea to book accommodations well in advance if you plan to attend the festivities. For further information, contact the Galveston Historical Foundation at (409) 765-7834.

RECREATION

Beaches
Finding a spit of sand to call your own for the day isn't difficult—just drive, bike, or hike the 32 miles along the seaward side of the island till you find something that suits you. All beaches on the island are open to beach driving except between March 15 and September 15, when you must park along the road or in designated lots.

The city of Galveston operates four public beaches along FM 3005 (Seawall Blvd.). The most popular—and most crowded during the summer—is **Stewart Beach Park** (tel. 409-765-5023), which is right in front of the intersection of Broadway and Seawall. Facilities include a bathhouse, restaurant and food concessions, nightclub, roller skate rentals, and a small amusement park. Farther east near the intersection of Seawall and Boddecker is the **R.A. Apffel Park** (tel. 763-0166), with 800 acres of wide, sandy, dune-backed beach, plus a boat launch, fishing jetty, and an 11,000-square-foot recreation center with bathhouse and concessions. **Seven Mile Park** is at Seven Mile Rd. and has restrooms and a boardwalk only. The fourth is the much less frequented **Dellanera RV Park** (tel. 740-0390), west off Seawall near San Luis Pass Rd., which is open for day use as well as to RVers. There is no entry fee for use of these parks, although the parking lots closest to Apffel and Stewart charge parking fees.

The county operates three "pocket parks," one off Seawall at 7 Mile Rd., one at 9 Mile Rd.,

and one at 11 Mile Road. Each has a bathhouse, food concession, and beach boardwalk, and they're all closed October 15 to March 15; when they're open, there's a $3 entry fee per vehicle.

Palm Beach at Moody Gardens (tel. 744-PALM) is a pre-fab beach made of imported white sand that overlooks Offatt's Bayou at the end of Hope Blvd., not far from the airport. Two artificial freshwater lagoons provide a faux-tropical atmosphere; recreational facilities include volleyball courts, whirlpools, water slides, paddleboats, and a 30-foot submarine. Admission is $6 per person, free for seniors and the disabled.

Galveston Island State Park
This 2,000-acre park spans the island from the Gulf of Mexico to West Galveston Bay, about six miles southwest of the city of Galveston. The Gulf side of the park features a 1.6-mile sandy beach; the inland section has coastal prairie, saltmarshes, bayous, and tidal flats. Four miles of nature trails lead through coastal dunes and along the Jenkins and Butterowe bayous to observation platforms, bird blinds, and boardwalks over wetland areas. Fishing is permitted anywhere there's water, including the bayous and bay (for seatrout) and the Gulf (for flounder and red drum).

Park facilities include bathhouses, fish-cleaning shelters, picnic areas, campgrounds, and the Mary Moody Northern Amphitheater. Multi-use campsites with w/e cost $10 weekdays, $12 weekends, while screened shelters are $15/18. Admission to the park is $3-5 per vehicle, $1 for cyclists or pedestrians. For further information or campsite reservations, contact Galveston Island State Park (tel. 409-737-1222), Route 1, Box 156-A, Galveston, TX 77554.

Fishing and Boating
Anglers have a choice of surf, bay, freshwater, or deep-sea fishing, plus crabbing, gigging, and seining. A state fishing license is required and is available from most bait and tackle shops on the island or from the Galveston County Courthouse (tel. 409-762-8621), 722 Moody. Several free public piers extend into the Gulf from the seawall. Commercial fishing piers, which charge a user fee of around $2, include the **Flagship Pier** at 25th and Seawall, the **61st Street Pier** at

61st and Seawall, the **Gulf Coast Fishing Pier** at 90th and Seawall, and **San Luis Pass Fishing Pier** at FM 3005 and San Luis Pass.

Fishing boats can be chartered at Pier 19 on the ship channel or at the Galveston Yacht Basin, Holiday Dr. and Wharf St. near the Port of Galveston. Fishing trips start at around $15 per person for a four-hour trip and go up to $85 for a deluxe all-day affair. You can charter pleasure boats at Pier 19 and the Yacht Basin.

Surfing

Galveston is popular among Texas surfers for its seawall breaks; surfing is permitted wherever there are signs that read No Swimming. The best surf generally breaks along the granite jetties. Experienced hodads say the 61st St. jetty usually gets the top waves, but it varies from day to day. Shops along the east end of Seawall Blvd. rent boards by the hour or day.

Scuba Diving

Galveston Island and the immediate vicinity offer little of interest for divers but within a 50-mile radius is a collection of abandoned oil rigs and sunken tankers that present challenging dive possibilities. **The Deep** (tel. 409-765-9746), a dive shop at 4104 Seawall, offers one-day diving trips in the late spring and summer for $85-100 a day. The shop also provides diving instruction and equipment sales/rentals.

Reef Dives: About 110 miles southeast of the island are two huge, pristine reef communities known as the **Flower Garden Banks.** The **East Flower Garden Bank** is three miles in diameter and rises within 52 feet of the Gulf surface. At its crest, the total area is an incredible 400 acres. Twelve miles west is the **West Flower Garden Bank,** which is about seven by five miles in diameter and crests 66 feet below the water surface with an area of approximately 100 acres. The Flower Gardens are unique—more than 300 miles from the tropics and 500 miles from the next nearest major reef system in Tampico, Mexico.

A designated national marine sanctuary, this is the most ecologically complex area of the Texas-Louisiana continental shelf, with 253 macro-invertebrate species, 175 fish species, and 21 coral species—including mountainous star, smooth brain, cavernous star, giant brain, mustard hill, blushing star, stinging millepora, knobby brain, large flower, and solitary disk corals. Manta rays (*Manta birostris*) that measure up to 20 feet across and weigh 3,500 pounds are commonly seen; the mantas like to be stroked and even allow divers to hitch rides by holding onto their horn-like pectoral fins.

Because these reefs are so remote and so few divers visit them, they're among the healthiest in the entire Gulf of Mexico or Caribbean. Visibility extends up to 125 feet (100 feet is average) since the area is far from shore debris and suspended sedimentation. The U.S. Department of the Interior has enacted a "zone of no activity" over the reef system to protect it from Gulf oil and gas exploration and has placed it on an evaluation list for possible designation as a national marine sanctuary.

In the meantime, two 100-foot dive boats docked in Freeport—about 35 miles southeast of downtown Galveston via FM 3005—run regular trips to the Flower Garden: *M/V Fling* and *M/V Spree* (tel. 265-3366). The boat proprietors operate two- and three-day trips to the reefs from late June to late October. All trips offer four or five dives, including one night dive, visiting the East Flower Garden Bank, an abandoned oil rig, and the separate Stetson Bank, a massive brain coral formation; the three-day trip includes four or five dives at the West Flower Garden Bank as well. Rates are $275 ($295 weekends) and $395 respectively and include all meals and accommodations aboard the boat, plus unlimited air refills. Divers must bring full tanks at the beginning of the trip.

The *Colonel*

This restored paddlewheeler and floating museum (tel. 409-747-7797), docked at Moody Gardens, offers one-hour scenic cruises of Offatt's Bayou and Galveston Bay at noon, 2 p.m., and 4 p.m. daily weather permitting from Memorial Day through Labor Day. From Labor Day to Memorial Day cruises depart at 2 p.m. only on weekdays and at noon, 2, and 4 p.m. on weekends. The fare is $6 per person.

The paddlewheeler also hosts a two-hour buffet dinner/dance cruise that leaves Fri.-Sat. nights at 8 p.m.; the fare is $27.50 per adult, $15 children 4-12, including dinner.

Gulf Greyhound Park

The world's largest dog track, opened in 1992 at La Marque, off FM 2004 between Galveston and Houston, boasts 318 teller windows, 750 closed-circuit TVs, and 12 races per day Tues.-Sun. year round. Admission is $1 general admission, $4 clubhouse admission; all the usual wagers, such as trifecta, pick six, and quiniela are available. For further information call (800) ASK-2WIN.

SHOPPING

Shops in The Strand Historic District offer everything from cheap beach souvenirs to expensive designer clothing. Of special note is the **Hendley Market** (tel. 409-762-2610), at 2010 The Strand, which sells antiques and folk art. Another antique place is the **Peanut Butter Warehouse** (tel. 762-8358), at 20th and The Strand, which also sells homemade peanut butter, cookies, and candy. **Col. Bubbie's Strand Surplus Senter** (tel. 762-7397), at 2202 The Strand, features a huge selection of military surplus items from around the world.

INFORMATION

Tourist Offices

The **Galveston Convention and Visitors Bureau** (tel. 409-763-4311, 800-351-4236 in Texas, 800-351-4237 outside Texas) is on the ground floor of Moody Civic Center, 2106 Seawall. The staff are knowledgeable and helpful, with loads of brochures and information handouts, including a list of accommodations with current rates. It's open daily 9 a.m.-5:30 p.m. The Galveston His-

---

GALVESTON TELEPHONE INFORMATION

Emergency (police, fire, medical): 911
Telephone Directory Assistance: 411
Area Code: 409
National Weather Service: 763-4681
Local Weather: 765-9479
Department of Public Safety: 740-3239
Coast Guard: 766-3687

---

torical Foundation operates **The Strand Visitors Center** (tel. 765-7834) at 21st and The Strand. It's open daily for roughly the same hours and has a lot of the same information, plus historical displays and a free 11-minute island orientation film.

Telephone

The area code for Galveston Island and vicinity is 409.

Publications

The *Galveston Daily News,* the only daily newspaper published on the island, offers up-to-the-minute information on local activities and events.

GETTING THERE AND AROUND

Galveston Island Trolley

Galveston's original trolley system ran between 1866 and 1938. A new system has partially revived the service, with 4.7 miles of track between the east beachfront and downtown areas, including The Strand and Silk Stocking Historic Districts. Along the new track run four trolley cars, vintage replicas with interiors of solid cherry, oak, and mahogany that cost $495,000 each to build.

There are 25 stops along the route and two terminals, one on The Strand and one on Seawall, where full trolley information is available. Operating hours are 10 a.m.-4 p.m., extended during special events like Mardi Gras and Dickens on The Strand. Trolleys usually pass about once every 30 minutes; a round-circuit trip takes about an hour. The city plans to add more cars to the system as ridership increases, so waits may become shorter in the future. Fares are $2 roundtrip for adults, $1 for seniors and children 6-12. Discounted frequent rider and one-day passes are available.

The trolley connects with the **Island Transit** city bus system on 20th between Market and Post Office. Free transfers are available.

Texas Limited

This lovingly restored steam train runs between Houston and Galveston on weekends from the end of April though Labor Day. See "Getting There and Around" under "Houston" in the East Texas chapter for description, schedules, and fares.

Airport Limousine
Galveston Limousine (tel. 409-765-5288 or 744-0563) operates a shuttle service between Galveston hotels and Houston's Hobby (one hour, $15) and Intercontinental airports (two hours, $18). Door-to-door service from the airports to beach homes or condos is an additional $3.

Tours
The *Treasure Island Tour Train* (tel. 409-765-9564) makes a 1.5-hour, 17-mile auto-train tour of the town that leaves from Moody Center at 21st and Seawall. The number of tours per day varies, from two departures a day March to May to nine tours a day in the summer; no tours are given in January and February. The fare is $4.30 for adults, $3.75 for seniors, $2.50 for children 3-12.

Classic Carriage Tours (tel. 762-1260) operates horse-drawn carriage rides through The Strand and other historic districts. The rates depend on departure, destination, and the number of passengers. You can contact the carriage drivers directly on The Strand (in front of the visitor center) or in the parking lot of the Hotel Galvez on Seawall Boulevard.

VICINITY OF GALVESTON

BOLIVAR PENINSULA

This 50-mile-long strip of sparsely populated beaches, marshes, lagoons, and bayous lies northeast of Galveston Island, across the mouth of Galveston Bay. Many who find Galveston too touristed these days find that the Bolivar (locally they say "BALL-i-ver") Peninsula is just their cup of tea. Fishing (seatrout, redfish, croaker, flounder, and a variety of shellfish) and hunting (duck and goose) are the main local attractions, though many Texans have built beach houses along the southern end of the peninsula near the small town of **Crystal Beach,** where the beaches are widest.

The best fishing is usually found at **Port Bolivar** and at **Rollover Pass,** a narrow canal that cuts across the peninsula near Gilchrist, joining East Galveston Bay and the Gulf of Mexico. Rollover Pass is the narrowest section of the peninsula; it was named thus because Jean Lafitte and his pirates would roll supply barrels across the peninsula to and from boats anchored in the Gulf. Near Port Bolivar on the southern tip of the peninsula is the **Bolivar Point Lighthouse,** first erected of cast iron in 1852; the Confederates disassembled it for scrap during the Civil War but it was rebuilt in 1872 and remained in service till 1933. The only other towns on the peninsula include the equally minuscule fishing villages of **Gilchrist** and **High Island.** North of Crystal Beach the beaches are more narrow, virtually disappearing with high tides.

State 87 runs the entire length of the peninsula, eventually leading to Port Arthur at Sabine Pass.

Galveston-Port Bolivar Ferry
A free 24-hour ferry service (tel. 409-763-2386) carries vehicles and passengers across the bay mouth in about 15 minutes. The Galveston ferry pier is at the end of Ferry Rd., off the east end of Seawall Blvd.; on the other side of the channel the pier is at Bolivar Point, the end of State 87. On summer weekends and holidays the wait at either end can be as long as an hour; at other times there's a wait of up to 20 minutes or so (or no wait if you happen to drive up to the pier right when they're loading).

Wildlife Refuges
The Texas Point and McFaddin national wildlife refuges straddle the peninsula, while Anahuac National Wildlife Refuge lies just opposite Gilchrist across East Galveston Bay on the Chambers County line. All three permit waterfowl hunting in season, as well as fishing and crabbing.

McFaddin NWR is the largest of the three, covering 41,682 acres of beach, saltmarshes, and coastal prairie, and is a major winter habitat for migratory waterfowl, including the mottled duck, wood stork, least tern, roseate spoonbill, pelicans, herons, egrets, and several varieties of geese. Small fur-bearing animals—mink, raccoon, nutria, river otter, muskrat, gray fox, and bobcat—inhabit the refuge year round. American alligators are also abundant here in the marshes and bayous, though they're hard to see unless you hike or boat well into the refuge. Bayous feed into two small lakes, Clam Lake and Star Lake. Free camping is permitted along the 12-mile beach facing the Gulf at the edge of the refuge; for day visitors, the refuge is only open weekdays 7 a.m.-3:30 p.m. Other facilities include eight miles of interior roads, three boat ramps, nature trails, and a beach picnic area. Access is via State 87. For further information, contact McFaddin National Wildlife Refuge (tel.

409-971-2909), P.O. Box 609, Sabine Pass, TX 77655.

Anahuac NWR is the second largest, with 28,240 acres of fresh- and saltwater marshes, bayous, and rolling coastal prairie along the shore of East Galveston Bay. It's the most visited of the three refuges because it's open 24 hours and has easy road access deep into the center via 12 miles of shelled and gravel roads. From the Bolivar Peninsula, take State 124 north off

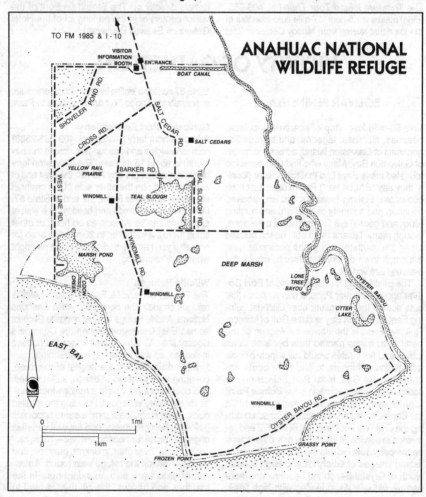

ANAHUAC NATIONAL WILDLIFE REFUGE

TO FM 1985 & I-10

VISITOR INFORMATION BOOTH — ENTRANCE

BOAT CANAL

SHOVELER POND RD.

CROSS RD.

SALT CEDAR RD.

SALT CEDARS

WEST LINE RD.

YELLOW RAIL PRAIRIE

BARKER RD.

WINDMILL

TEAL SLOUGH

TEAL SLOUGH RD.

MARSH POND

COON CREEK

WINDMILL RD.

WINDMILL

DEEP MARSH

LONE TREE BAYOU

OTTER LAKE

OYSTER BAYOU

EAST BAY

WINDMILL

OYSTER BAYOU RD.

GRASSY POINT

FROZEN POINT

0   1mi
0   1km

© MOON PUBLICATIONS, INC.

State 87 at High Island to FM 1985, then proceed west to the refuge entrance. Anahuac shelters many of the same wildlife species as McFaddin, plus the endangered southern bald eagle and peregrine falcon. Snow geese concentrations run to 50,000 between October and March. Alligators are easily viewed at Shoveler Pond in the northwest corner of the refuge, especially in the spring. The only facilities here are a refuge office, restrooms, and a few trails. Primitive camping (bring your own water) is permitted along the bayshore; three-day limit, no charge. Boating is allowed only on the designated boat canal (which feeds into Oyster Bayou); you can launch boats from the bayshore or at the ramp near the refuge office. For further information, contact Anahuac National Wildlife Refuge (tel. 267-3337), P.O. Box 278, Anahuac, TX 77514.

Texas Point NWR preserves 8,952 acres and protects many of the same species as McFaddin. Although it's located just off State 87 near Sabine Pass, there are no parking facilities here; access is by foot or boat via private launch at Texas Bayou in Sabine Pass. Texas Point is visited mostly by anglers and hunters—birdwatchers find either McFaddin or Anahuac much more to their liking. Like McFaddin, it's only open weekdays 7 a.m.-3:30 p.m. For more information, contact **Texas Point National Wildlife Refuge** (tel. 409-971-2909), P.O. Box 609, Sabine Pass, TX 77655.

Sea Rim State Park

This is one of the state's most unique parks, with 15,109 acres of beach, saltmarshes, sloughs, bayous, dunes, and lakes. The park is divided into two sections, the huge Marshlands Unit north of State 87 and the smaller D. Roy Harrington Beach Unit south of this road. The park shares a boundary with McFaddin National Wildlife Refuge, at the northern end of Bolivar Peninsula near Sabine Pass.

Beach Unit: The park's shoreline extends for 5.2 miles along the gulf; three miles is sandy beach separated from the marshlands by small dunes, while 2.2 miles is rare "sea rim marsh" where marshlands meet Gulf waters. The **Gambusia Trail** is a 3,640-foot boardwalk nature trail that winds through the sea rim marsh about two feet above the surface. Cord grass and salt grass comprise the marsh's primary vegetation. Several ponds in the marsh attract small mammals, including fur-bearing nutria, muskrat, mink, and raccoon; waterfowl; and various smaller reptiles and amphibians. In the spring and fall, birds are abundant and birdwatchers enjoy an opportunity to view some 289 winged species, including the great blue heron, the American bittern (which camouflages itself by sticking its beak straight up and swaying with the grass), American coot, and a wide variety of loons, grebes, ducks, geese, terns, cormorants, egrets, hawks, gulls, ibis, and songbirds. To see the greatest variety you must venture into the park's

campground,
Sea Rim State Park

marshlands unit. Facilities at the beach unit include a visitor center with excellent interpretive exhibits, first-aid station, observation deck, food concessions, bathhouse, and camping area.

Marshlands Unit: This section of the park is for visitors who want a more in-depth experience of these extraordinary coastal marshlands. Alligators one to 14 feet in length are a common sight along the unit's shallow lakes, sloughs, and bayous, especially in the summer when they sun themselves. The best way to explore the area is by boat along these waterways. Some routes are navigable only by airboat or mudboat, others only by pirogue or canoe. Between March and October, park rangers operate half-hour airboat tours for around $8 per person. Canoes can be rented year round at a store called **Breeze Inn Again** on State 87 just east of the park.

Crabbing is excellent throughout the marshlands, but especially in the lakes and ponds. The tasty blue crab is the most common and reaches about nine inches across its body shell. Crawfish are also abundant. Five camping platforms and four observation platforms with blinds are located throughout the marshes and are accessible only by boat.

Camping: The beach unit has 20 tent/camper sites with w/e (dump station available) for $9 a night. Tent camping is permitted on the beach for $4 a night. The camping platforms in the marshlands are suitable for tent camping only and are $4 a night on weekdays, $6 on weekends. The park entry fee is $3 per vehicle or $1 per person for cyclists and pedestrians. Be sure to bring plenty of insect repellent. For further information or campsite reservations, contact the Park Superintendent (tel. 409-971-2559), Sea Rim State Park, P.O. Box 1066, Sabine Pass, TX 77655.

Fort Travis Seashore Park
About a mile from the ferry landing, on the south side of State 87 near Port Bolivar, an abandoned army fort has been converted into a seaside park with camping, fishing, and picnicking facilities. The site's strategic location served as a naval lookout for Mexican, Confederate, and U.S. soldiers between 1852 and 1941; all that remain of the fortifications are four concrete batteries. Climb to the top of 1917-vintage Battery

Kimble for a view of ship traffic on the Gulf.

Campsites cost $10 a night; six screened cabanas with sink and electricity are also available for rent for $15 a night. Outdoor restrooms, grills, and showers serve both. For more information, call (409) 766-2411.

Motels
Two motels off State 87 in Crystal Beach—**Crystal Palace Resort Motel** (tel. 409-684-6554) and **Joy Sands Motel** (tel. 684-6152)—offer rooms for around $30-40 a night, some with kitchenettes. Rates are lower for stays of a week or more. A bit farther north in Gilchrist is the similarly priced **Ocean View Motel** (tel. 286-5864), also with kitchenettes. In Port Bolivar, **Fisherman's Cove Motel** (tel. 684-8567) offers yet another option in the same range.

Beach Home Rentals
The following realtors can arrange weekend, weekly, and monthly beach-home rentals in Crystal Beach: **Cobb Real Estate** (tel. 409-684-3790), **Hamilton Real Estate** (tel. 684-3792), **Mike Olsten Real Estate** (tel. 684-0012), and **Thompson Real Estate** (tel. 684-0363). Rates start at around $150 a weekend for a basic one- or two-bedroom home.

RV Parks
Gilchrist has two RV parks, both on State 87: **Hazel's** (tel. 409-286-5228) and **Las Palmas** (tel. 286-5612). Crystal Beach offers one, the **Crystal Beach Drive Through and RV Park** (tel. 684-4929), also on State 87. All three parks charge around $13 a night for full hookups and offer discounted weekly and monthly rates.

Food
The **Stingaree Restaurant** (tel. 409-684-2731) in Crystal Beach on the south side of State 87 is one of the better seafood places on the peninsula and is open daily for lunch and dinner. The specialty of the house is crab cooked Cajun-style, broiled, batter-fried, boiled, or barbecued. **Zev's Seafood and Crab House** (no phone), also in the Crystal Beach area, is a reasonable alternative if Stingaree is closed or crowded. Also off State 87 in Crystal Beach is **Mama Theresa's Flying Pizza** (tel. 684-3507), with pizza and Italian food; open Tues.-Sun. for lunch

and dinner. The **Corner Cafe** (tel. 286-5683) in Gilchrist serves simple American fare, including homemade bread, Mon.-Sat. for breakfast, lunch, and dinner. **Shirley's Bait Camp** (tel. 684-9251) in Port Bolivar offers seafood and plate lunches to take out and eat on picnic tables on the grass.

Three wholesale/retail seafood stores in Crystal Beach sell fresh fish, shrimp, crab, and oysters to the general public: **Falcon Seafood** (tel. 684-3838), **J. B.'s Seafood** (tel. 684-6464), and **Seafood Warehouse** (tel. 684-6270).

Information
The **Bolivar Peninsula Chamber of Commerce,** P.O. Box 1421, Crystal Beach, TX 77650, sends information brochures on request and can answer specific questions about Bolivar visits.

BRAZOSPORT

"Brazosport" is not a town name but rather a chamber of commerce term for the loose conglomeration of Brazoria County communities south of Galveston Island, including the beach towns of Surfside and Quintana as well as the industrial town/fishing port of Freeport and its satellites Clute, Oyster Creek, Lake Jackson, Richwood, and Jones Creek. The name means "Port of Brazos" and refers to the Brazos River. The beaches are few and they aren't great; chemical manufacturing plants provide an unsightly nine-mile backdrop.

Beauty is in the eye of the beholder, however, and inside the Dow Chemical-owned facility some of the most technically sophisticated research in the world is conducted on products people use everyday. Dow (tel. 409-238-9222) offers free tours of the facility each Wednesday at 2 p.m. for those interested in seeing the largest chemical facility in the country.

The 60-foot, 40-ton shrimp trawler *The Mystery* is enshrined on Brazosport Boulevard in Freeport. In her day she was the undisputed champion of Gulf shrimping, having netted an estimated 3.5 million pounds of pink crustaceans before retirement. The **Bridge Harbor Yacht Club** at the west end of Surfside Bridge is a sailing resort with over 300 deep-water slips. About the only other sight of renown is **Girouard's Gen-**

eral Store, said to be the only grocery store in the country that's also a certified government agent for marine charts. The store slogan is "If we don't have it, you don't need it," and it proffers everything from fresh meat to passport photos.

Center for the Arts and Sciences
The **Museum of Natural Science** (tel. 409-265-7831) at Lake Jackson's Center for the Arts and Sciences, 400 College Dr., houses the Hall of Malacology with one of the finest seashell collections in the country. The museum also contains exhibits on archaeology, mineralogy, and wildlife. Hours are Tues.-Sat. 10 a.m.-5 p.m. and Sunday 2-5 p.m.; admission is free.

The center also serves as a meeting place for the Brazosport Birders, a group of avid local birdwatchers. Year after year, Freeport's Christmas Count leads the U.S. in numbers of bird species identified within a 24-hour interval. For information on the club's year round activities, call the Museum of Natural History.

A self-guided nature trail along Oyster Creek, adjacent to the Center, introduces visitors to over 200 species of Texas river-bottom vegetation.

Beaches
The next link in the barrier island chain moving down the Texas coast is **Follets Island,** where Brazosport's Gulf beaches are located. Farm-to-Market 3005's south terminal is at **Surfside Beach,** a favorite among young Texans who come here to swim, surf, and party on summer weekends—Houston is only 60 miles away. At one time Surfside had a reputation for attracting rowdy crowds, but since the summer of 1982, when the small town instituted roadblocks to flush out drunk drivers, the scene has calmed down somewhat. Driving is still permitted on the beach, but you must purchase a beach driving permit, available at most local stores. The beachfront is lined with small shops offering fast food, beachwear, and surfboard rentals.

Farther south is the small **Quintana Beach,** which has a bathhouse, boardwalk, fishing pier, and camping facilities. At the south end of the island (which would be a peninsula if it weren't for the cut made by the Brazos River as it meets the Gulf) is the 878-acre **Bryan Beach State Recreation Area.** Since the road south from Quintana (FM 1495) ends well before the park, the only way to get here is to drive along the beach, walk, or take a boat in. Driving and walking along the beach can be tricky because of incoming tides. Bryan Beach is undeveloped except for a few trash receptacles. Primitive camping is permitted; no fee; bring your own water. The surf fishing here is good, as the Brazos River mouth is a feeding grounds for native fish. Birders can view a wide variety of shorebirds.

Wildlife Refuges

Freeport usually ranks first in the National Audubon Society's annual winter bird census and holds the all-time U.S. record for number of species counted in 24 hours within a 7.5-mile radius: 226. Freeport is such a good birding area because it's between two national wildlife refuges established as winter habitats for migratory birds: **Brazoria National Wildlife Refuge** (12,000 acres) to the north and **San Bernard National Wildlife Refuge** (24,500 acres) to the south. Among the more notable common birds at both are great blue herons, white ibis, mottled ducks, snow geese, sandhill cranes, and roseate spoonbills.

Access to marshy Brazoria for fishing and waterfowl hunting is by boat only (via Big Bayou or the Gulf Intracoastal Waterway). During the first weekend of every month, the refuge is open to daytime drive-through visitors. For information, contact the Refuge Manager (tel. 409-849-6062), Brazoria National Wildlife Refuge, P.O. Box 1088, Angleton, TX 77515.

The much larger San Bernard covers a wide range of habitats, including coastal prairies, salt flats, potholes, and both fresh- and saltwater ponds. Access is via State 36 west from Freeport to FM 2611, then south to FM 2918, and east to the refuge entrance. For information, contact the Refuge Manager (tel. 409-849-6062), San Bernard National Wildlife Refuge, P.O. Box 1088, Angleton, TX 77515.

Guided Fishing Trips

Several charter boats operate fishing trips out of Freeport, including deep-sea trips. **Captain El-**

liot's (tel. 409-233-1811) at 1010 W. 2nd in Freeport offers group deep-sea trips for around $55 per day.

Scuba Diving

The Fling, a 100-foot boat docked in Freeport, offers two- and three-day diving trips to the magnificent Flower Garden Banks reef system, 110 miles east in the Gulf. For details, see "Scuba Diving" under "Recreation" in the "Galveston Island" section.

Hotels and Motels

Most of the chain accommodations are concentrated a few miles inland along State 332 in Clute and Lake Jackson. The **Motel 6** (tel. 409-265-4764) at 1000 State 332 in Clute has rooms for $24-28. Nearby is **La Quinta Inn** (tel. 265-7461) at 1126 State 332, where rooms are $47-58. Farther west at 925 State 332 in Lake Jackson is the **Ramada Inn** (tel. 297-1161) with rooms for $55-75. The **Best Western Lake Jackson Inn** (tel. 297-3031) at 915 State 332 has rooms for $45-50.

Beach Home Rentals

A couple of hundred beach homes in the Surfside Beach area are available for rent year round. Most rates are based on weekly rentals, with an average of $450-800 a week for two or three bedrooms during the summer. You can rent a very basic one-bedroom place for as low as $200 a week in the winter. The following realtors handle beach home rentals: **Resort Rentals** (tel. 409-233-6734), Box 1195; **Sand Castle Rentals** (tel. 233-7879), Box 1155; **Brannan Realty** (tel. 233-1812), Box 1115; and **Haygood Properties** (tel. 233-6734), Box 1087. All box numbers are followed by Route 2, Surfside Beach, TX 77541.

Information

The **Brazosport Visitors and Convention Council** (tel. 409-265-2505) is at 420 State 332 in Clute. Staff will handle all queries on attractions in the Brazosport area.

CENTRAL COAST

The state's earliest ports were in the central coast area between Freeport to the north and Corpus Christi to the south, clustered around Matagorda and Lavaca bays. They included Indianola, Matagorda, Port Lavaca, Palacios, Point Comfort, and Port O'Connor. Because of their vulnerability to tropical storms and hurricanes, however, none grew into a major port like Corpus Christi or Galveston. Today they are for the most part sleepy backwaters supported by a combination of fishing, light industry, and agriculture, primarily rice-growing. Except for the gulfward side of Matagorda Island, the beaches along the central coast are unmemorable, though some Texans favor the area because of the laid-back and uncrowded atmosphere.

MATAGORDA BAY

Matagorda

The name "Matagorda" (Spanish for "Dense Cane") is attached to a town, county, bay, island, and peninsula. The town itself (pop. 700) was founded in 1829 as a port for Stephen Austin's colony because of its strategic location at the junction of three waterways: the mouth of the Colorado River, Matagorda Bay, and East Matagorda Bay (Matagorda Peninsula separates the two bays).

Of historical interest in Matagorda is **Christ Episcopal Church** at Cypress and Lewis, which was built in 1841, destroyed by an 1854 hurricane, and rebuilt in 1856 using salvaged cypress timbers. It's the state's oldest Episcopal church and services are still held regularly. Several other buildings in town date to the late 1800s.

Palacios

This town of around 4,000 inhabitants is on a smaller bay off Matagorda called Tres Palacios Bay. The bay and town were named after José Felix Trespalacios, the local governor when Stephen Austin established his first colony in the early 1800s. Fishing, both commercial and sport, is the main local source of livelihood. The

largest blue crab processing plant in the country has its home here, as well as a 300-boat shrimp fleet. Guided fishing trips can be arranged at the Palacios waterfront. At the nearby public beach are two lighted, no-fee fishing piers and a boat ramp.

The stately **Luther Hotel** (tel. 512-972-2312) at 408 S. Bay Blvd., between 4th and 5th, was built in 1903 entirely of cypress wood in the Greek Revival style. Commanding a view of Tres Palacios Bay, this classic Gulf Coast hotel has the feel of an antebellum mansion, the very epitome of Southern indolence. Many of the rooms have been converted to apartments that rent by the month or week; around 15 rooms are available on a nightly basis for $45-55. Some of the $55 rooms have kitchenettes; suites with full kitchens are available for $70 a night. There are no telephones or TVs in the guest rooms—proprietor Mrs. Luther says, "I don't want people to come here to watch television." There is, however, a TV in the lobby.

The most popular eating place in town is **Petersen's Restaurant** (tel. 972-2413) at 416 Main, which has been serving fresh seafood, burgers, steaks, chicken, and homemade pies since 1944. Open daily for breakfast, lunch, and dinner.

Blessing

About 11 miles north of Palacios via State 35 is this small town of 600 with no beach and nothing else to recommend it except for another Gulf Coast accommodation classic, the **Hotel Blessing** (tel. 512-588-9579) at 10th and Ave. B (FM 616). Built in 1906 by Jonathan Pierce, brother of famous cattle baron "Shanghai" Pierce, the hotel is constructed in the Spanish mission style of wood and is listed with the National Register of Historic Places. Rooms cost only $25 a night, whether or not they come with private or shared baths; discounted weekly and monthly rates are available. Locally, the hotel is known for its downhome coffee shop (tel. 588-6623), which is open daily for breakfast and lunch. During lunch, diners help themselves from pots of food in the kitchen—specialties include barbecued chicken, cream gravy, cornbread, vegetables, and lots of rice. On Sunday, turkey and ham are served.

LAVACA BAY

Port Lavaca

The largest Calhoun County town (pop. 12,000) and county seat is named for *la vaca*, "the cow" in Spanish, because at one time it was a major shipping point for exported cattle and cattle products. The current town was founded in 1840. Commercial and sport fishing are the main local industries; many Port Lavaca residents also work in the Alcoa bauxite refinery, the country's largest, in nearby **Point Comfort**.

Nearby **Indianola**, about 10 miles southeast of Port Lavaca at the end of State 316, was once the chief Texas port—everything from African slaves to camels to European immigrants arrived by ship in the early 1800s. Three major hurricanes between 1866 and 1886 turned the prospering port into a virtual ghost town. A 22-foot-high granite monument alongside State 316 commemorates French explorer LaSalle (René Robert Cavalier), who landed here in 1685 and established Fort Saint Louis nearby. LaSalle was killed by one of his men two years later, and Karankawa Indians burned the settlement. A cluster of fishermen's houses, an old courthouse foundation, and a 22-foot granite statue of LaSalle comprise what remains of Indianola.

The most popular local recreation spot is undoubtedly the **Port Lavaca State Fishing Pier** at the west end of the Lavaca Bay Causeway (State 35 N). The 3,200-foot pier is open 6 a.m. to midnight—it's lit at night—and is a good place to drop a line or two during redfish, flounder, or speckled trout runs. The pier bait shop issues daily fishing permits for $1.50 per fishing device. At the base of the pier is **Port Lavaca City Park,** with a boat ramp, picnic area, swimming pool, and waterfront RV park with two-way hookups, $8 a night with picnic tables, $7 without.

Accommodations and Food: The **Days Inn** (tel. 512-552-4511) at 2100 State 35 N Bypass has rooms for $46-52 s, $52-58 d, with weekly and monthly rates. Rental refrigerators available. Right at the start of the State 35 causeway,

facing the bay, is the **Shell Fish Inn** (tel. 552-3393), with rooms for $30 s, $34-37 d; refrigerators available on request, as are weekly and monthly rates. For fresh seafood, your best bet is the **Ocean Inn** at 116 Commerce, where portions are generous and not everything comes fried. Open daily for breakfast, lunch, and dinner; oyster bar open in the evenings only. **El Patio** (tel. 552-6316) at 534 W. Main serves standard Tex-Mex daily for breakfast, lunch, and dinner.

Port O'Connor–Seadrift

This area was first mapped by Spaniard Alonso Alvarez de Piñeda in 1519, when he named the mainland "Amichel." Today it's mostly a home port for commercial fishing boats and shrimp trawlers, as well as charter boats for deep-sea fishing trips and shuttle service to nearby Matagorda Island. Strategically situated at the intersection of Matagorda Bay, Espiritu Santo Bay, and the Gulf of Mexico, Port O'Connor has some of the best saltwater fishing on the coast, with redfish, drum, flounder, speckled trout, pompano, bonito, croakers, tarpon, and others in abundance.

The Matagorda Island State Park and Wildlife Management Area headquarters (tel. 512-983-2215) is in Port O'Connor at S. 16th and Maple. Ferry transport to the island and permits for camping are available here.

Accommodations and Food: The **Tarpon Motel** (tel. 983-2606) at 14th and Maple offers rooms for $40-50 a night, apartments for $50-65 a night (less for stays of a week or more), and RV sites with full hookups for $12 a night. A pool and grocery store are on the premises as well. There are also a few beach homes for rent through the Port O'Connor Chamber of Commerce (tel. 983-2898). **Port Motel** (tel. 983-2724) and **Verna's Motel** (tel. 983-2395) have rooms in the $25-30 range, $35 with kitchenette. In addition to the park adjacent to the Tarpon Motel, three other RV parks offer full hookups for $10-12 a night: **Lots O Luck** (tel. 983-2869), **Canal** (tel. 983-2621) and **Sea Isle** (tel. 983-2305).

In the small port town of Seadrift, at the west end of the peninsula on San Antonio Bay, is the historic **Hotel Lafitte** (tel. 785-2319), 302 Bay Avenue. Originally built as a railroad hotel in 1909, the restored three-story inn offers a range of rooms for $60-115 a night including a full breakfast for two, plus complimentary wine in the afternoons. For more information, call or write Hotel Lafitte, P.O. Box 489, Seadrift, TX 77983.

In Port O'Connor, **Stryker's Cafe** (tel. 983-2880) serves daily fresh seafood specials. If you have the use of a kitchen, you can buy fresh fish from several local seafood dealers who sell direct to the public, including **Clark's, Raby's,** and **Shotsie's.** Mexican food is available at **Josie's** (tel. 983-4720).

Matagorda Island State Park and Wildlife Management Area

Once a haven for 18th-century freebooters and smugglers, including pirate Jean Lafitte, 38-mile-long Matagorda Island preserves 56,669-acres of sand beaches, dune ridges, barrier flats, and coastal wetlands. Besides the occasional park staff, the only inhabitants are white-tailed deer, coyote, feral hogs, jackrabbits, waterfowl, and other wildlife, including at least 19 state or federally listed endangered animal species. Among these are American alligators, Texas horned lizards, Kemp's ridley, hawksbill, loggerhead, and green sea turtles, brown pelicans, peregrine falcons, piping plovers, and whooping cranes. Bottle-nosed dolphins are common along the gulf and bay shores of the island.

Birders can spot over 300 aviary species, including herons, egrets, ibis, gulls, terns, plovers, and roseate spoonbills; fall and spring are the best seasons for birding. When the Gulf surf is pumping, Matagorda provides surfers with unparalleled Gulf Coast wave action. Fishing is also excellent on both sides of the island, and off-road cyclists and hikers can make use of 80 miles of beach and island trails. Hardy local surf anglers combine fishing with cycling, pedaling around the island with rod and tackle in backpacks or panniers. Common gamefish include red drum (redfish), spotted seatrout, tarpon, shark, flounder, and mackerel.

Holders of the Texas Conservation Passport can sign up for birdwatching, beachcombing, and natural/cultural history tours with park staff for nominal fees; write park headquarters for a schedule.

Camping: Overnight visitors may stay at two primitive camping areas or in a park bunkhouse. The Army Hole Campground near the island dock offers shaded picnic tables, cold outdoor showers, fire rings, and pit toilets. On the other side of the island, about 3.5 miles from the dock via the island road, the Beach Campground stretches along two miles of sand beach; two shaded picnic tables and pit toilets are the only facilities. No open fires are permitted on the island except at the Army Hole Campground fire rings. Camping costs $4 per four-person site, with a 14-day limit. A new 12-bed bunkhouse near the dock area offers beds for $12 per person. You must bring your own food and water; no drinking water is available on the island.

Getting There: The state park headquarters in Port O'Connor on the mainland offers a regular ferry service to the island Thurs.-Sun. year round. Ferries leave from the park pier at 16th and Maple Thurs.-Fri. at 9 a.m. and Sat.-Sun. at 8 a.m., 10 a.m., and 3 p.m. The ferry takes about an hour to complete the 11-mile crossing. In the return direction, ferries leave the island dock Thurs.-Fri. at 4 p.m., Sat.-Sun. at 9 a.m., 2 p.m., and 4 p.m. The roundtrip fare is $10 for adults, $5 for children 12 and under. Reservations are required. Bicycles and surfboards are permitted on the ferry; pets are not.

On the island itself, the park service also operates a shuttle between the park pier and the beach. The shuttle service is free for those who have used the park ferry service to reach the island. For visitors arriving by private boat, the shuttle costs $2 roundtrip for adults, $1 for children under 12.

A few fishing boats in Port O'Connor also offer drop-off and pick-up service to the island; call **Red's Coastal Charter** (tel. 512-983-2937), Robby Gregory (tel. 983-2862), or Jimmy Crouch (tel. 983-2897) for arrangements or the chamber of commerce (tel. 983-2898) for other possibilities. The standard rates are $90 roundtrip for one to three people, plus $30 for each additional person.

You can also pilot your own boat from public boat ramps in Port O'Connor to finger piers at the island's park dock. The channel between Port O'Connor and the island is 11 miles long and only 5.5 to six feet deep. Charts are available in Port O'Connor. The coast guard station at Port O'Connor monitors marine band radio channel 16 around the clock; weather forecasts are transmitted on marine channel 2.

MATAGORDA ISLAND STATE PARK AND WILDLIFE MANAGEMENT AREA

© MOON PUBLICATIONS, INC.

Information: For further information and for campsite or shuttle reservations, contact the park staff at their Port O'Connor office (tel. 983-2215), 16th and Maple; mailing address is Matagorda Island State Park, P.O. Box 117, Port O'Connor, TX 77982-0117.

CORPUS CHRISTI

The Corpus Christi area is the closest the Gulf Coast comes to living up to the fanciful "Texas Riviera" image marketed so widely. Day or night, a drive south over the Harbor Bridge reveals a sparkling city and bay vista, where sailboat masts mix with downtown skyscrapers. Although central Corpus itself—Texans usually dispense with "Christi"—has only a few shelly bay beaches, nearby Mustang and Padre islands offer well over a hundred miles of sandy Gulf beaches, the best anywhere along the Texas coast. Parts of North Padre actually fall within the Corpus Christi city limits.

Although the main attractions are sun, sky, sea, and sand, Corpus doesn't go to sleep as soon as the sun goes down. The old adage about "a big city with a small town feel" should really be modified in this case; with a population of just over a quarter million, Corpus is a medium-sized port town with urban pretensions, perfect for visitors who want to do more than just fish and lie on the beach. As a prominent corner of the "South Texas Triangle," including San Antonio and Laredo, it also reflects the Hispanic-majority nature of the regional culture, which sets it apart from coastal towns farther north.

Land and Climate

Corpus Christi lies in a transition zone between the central coast and lower coast, which means that the usual Gulf Coast characteristics are somewhat tempered by Rio Grande Plain influences. Humid coastal plains meet arid northern Mexico plains to form a semiarid, subtropical zone producing a wide variety of dense scrub intermixed with coastal grasses. The Nueces River feeds into the Gulf here, providing a riparian habitat that further contributes to geographical and biological diversity.

The average temperature range in January is 46° to 67° F, while in July it's 76° to 94° F. Average annual precipitation is a moderate 27 inches, just two inches more than the Rio Grande Valley. September is by far the wettest month, generally speaking, logging an average of six inches of rain; the next wettest month is August, with 3.5 inches, followed by May, June, and October, each receiving a little over three inches per month on average. The average relative humidity in July at 6 p.m. is 63%.

The Corpus Christi area is one of the most consistently windy areas in the country, with an average year round wind speed of 12 miles per hour. Winds are highest in April when the average is 14 miles per hour, classified on the Beaufort wind scale as a "moderate breeze." Because of the abundance of water and wind, windsurfing magazines often rate Corpus Christi Bay and the nearby Laguna Madre among the top-10 windsurfing spots in the world.

Over the last 90 years only two hurricanes have struck Corpus, one in 1919 and one in 1970. The latter was Hurricane Celia, which reached maximum wind velocities of 130 mph and caused 11 deaths and an estimated $453 million in damages. In any given year, the odds of a tropical cyclone (hurricane or tropical storm) striking the Coastal Bend area from Baffin Bay to Aransas Bay, including Corpus are one in eight.

History

As with other points along the central and lower coasts, Corpus Christi was first mapped in 1519 by Spanish explorer Alonso Alvarez de Piñeda, who named the bay in honor of the feast day of the body of Christ—the day his ship landed here. A statue of Piñeda now stands at the corner of Laredo and Agnes streets in downtown Corpus Christi.

For the next three centuries, the area lay undeveloped; in 1839 U.S. Colonel Henry Kinney established a trading post on the bay. Until the War with Mexico, Kinney's settlement prospered on contraband trade between Texas and Mexico, since Corpus Christi was just below the Nueces River, which Mexico recognized as its northern border, yet above the Rio Grande, which the Republic of Texas, and later the United States, recognized as its southern border.

During the War with Mexico, the town further developed as a supply post for the U.S. Army. After 1848, when Mexico and the U.S. agreed that henceforth the Rio Grande would serve as the undisputed border, the town's fortunes waned until the 1920s, when the federal government authorized the dredging of the bay and ship channel, thus turning Corpus into a deep-water port. This attracted industry to the area almost immediately, followed by the military, which established a naval air station and Army depot at the bay's east end.

Economy

In terms of tonnage handled, the Port of Corpus Christi is now the sixth-largest in the country and the second largest in Texas after Houston. Other major economic contributors in surrounding Nueces County include the petrochemical industry, tourism, military bases, ranching, and agriculture—cotton, corn, wheat, and grain sorghum. Nearby Ingleside, in San Patricio County on the north side of Corpus Christi Bay, has recently been made a home port for several U.S. Navy reserve vessels and minesweepers. Though not all Corpus residents condone the city's dependence on military-industrial revenues, such diversity has given Corpus a higher overall growth rate than most other Texas cities in recent years.

The downtown area underwent a micro-depression in the '60s and '70s, however, as retail businesses moved out of central Corpus to sub-urban malls and business parks. The Downtown Management District (formerly the Heart of Corpus Christi), an urban revitalization group, has made great strides in bringing businesses back downtown, which, along with new office buildings, high-rise hotels, and a thriving marina, have made the Corpus waterfront the most visually striking city profile in the South Texas triangle.

Attracted by Corpus Christi's overall cultural appeal and mild climate, increasing numbers of "snowbirds" settle in the area for the winter as an alternative to the Rio Grande Valley. Corpus has welcomed them with open arms, responding quickly to the need for more RV parks and other facilities that cater to winter Texans. Retirement magazines unanimously cite the Corpus Christi area as one of the best places in the U.S. to spend the winter vis à vis climate and cost of living.

SIGHTS

Downtown Waterfront

Mount Rushmore sculptor Gutzon Borglum designed the two-mile downtown seawall that runs along Shoreline Blvd., with a walkway and benches along the top and wide steps leading down to the water. Convenient *miradores del*

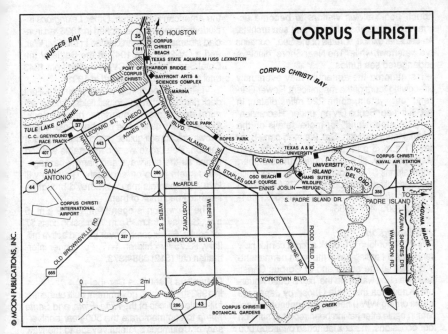

mar, attractive seawall gazebos, were recently added to offer shaded rest areas along the promenade.

The adjacent marina consists of three man-made peninsulas named for their shapes and for the downtown streets that meet them. The **Peoples Street T-Head** is the farthest north and is reserved for working boats including charter and party boats, cruise boats, and shrimpers, and recreational equipment rental—water trikes, sailboats, paddleboats, sailboards, and Jet Skis.

The **Lawrence Street T-Head** and **Cooper's Alley L Head** (usually just called "the L Head," since there's only one) are reserved for privately owned pleasure craft. Visiting boats are welcome; see "Recreation," below, for details on slip rental and transient use facilities. Every Wednesday at 5:30 p.m., local sailors compete in informal sailing regattas. Both T-heads feature restaurants open to the public.

As you drive east, Shoreline Blvd. eventually becomes **Ocean Drive,** a long bayfront residential avenue of large, older homes with the best views in town.

Harbor Bridge

Spanning the ship channel between the downtown area and Corpus Christi, this immense cantilever bridge is 620 feet long and 250 feet high. It was built in 1959 at a cost of $20 million, and features a pedestrian walkway with good views of Corpus Christi Beach, the marina, and the city skyline.

Texas State Aquarium

Opened in 1990, this expanding attraction at Corpus Christi Beach will be the largest seashore aquarium in the country when all four phases are completed, sometime before 2000. Together with other underwater habitat exhibits, the aquarium currently displays over 2,000 marine animals in 350,000 gallons of seawater. The biggest tank is the 132,500-gallon "Islands of Steel," which replicates the type of Gulf of Mexico reef habitat created by huge steel-legged oil rigs. A six-foot inset in the Lucite walls allows visitors a 180-degree wraparound view of the fish. The focus is on marinelife native to the Gulf of Mexico and the Caribbean; a unique "touch pool" allows visitors to become acquainted with crabs, starfish, and sea urchins. An estuarial exhibit, "Cradle of the Sea," contains live waterfowl, while "The Near Shore" displays endangered sea turtles.

It's rumored the aquarium may eventually offer diving tours of the magnificent Flower Gardens reef system, some 220 miles distant in the Gulf (see "Scuba Diving" under "Recreation" in "Galveston Island" for more details on the reefs). Hours are Mon.-Sat. 9 a.m.-5 p.m., Sunday 11 a.m.-5 p.m. from Labor Day through Memorial Day, till 6 p.m. during the summer. Admission is $7 for adults, $5 for seniors, military, and college students, and $3.75 for children 4-17. For further information, call (512) 881-1200 or (800) 477-4853.

USS *Lexington*

This 910-foot-long, 16-deck aircraft carrier now serves as a floating naval museum permanently docked at the south end of Corpus Christi Beach, a short walk from the Texas State Aquarium. Known as the "Blue Ghost" by Japanese forces during WW II because it continued to appear in battle after having been reported sunk on four occasions, the *Lex* launched over 300,000 planes, served longer than any carrier in U.S. naval history, and was the first U.S. carrier to sail with women among the crew. The ship is actually fifth in a line of U.S. military craft named *Lexington*, dating back to an armed brig used in

the American Revolution. Other *Lexington*s include a sloop-of-war launched in 1826, an ironclad steamer which participated in the Civil War, and a CV-2 sunk in 1942 at the Battle of the Coral Sea. The current CV-16 served from 1943 until it was decommissioned in 1991.

Visitors are permitted to tour the main flight deck (larger than three football fields), bridge, admiral and captain's quarters, hangar deck, foc'sle, crew's galley, and sick bay. Color-coded arrows indicate self-guided touring routes for each section. Be sure to wear comfortable walking shoes as the stairways and narrow passageways seem to go on endlessly. Children will love it but parents may wish they'd brought a leash to keep track of them.

The *Lexington* is open Mon.-Sat. 9 a.m.-5 p.m., Sunday 11 a.m.-5 p.m. Admission costs $7 for adults, $6 for seniors over 60 and active military, $3.75 for children 4-17. For further information call (512) 888-4873.

Columbus Fleet (Las Carabelas)

In 1992 the Spanish government built authentic, full-scale replicas of the *Niña, Pinta,* and *Santa María* to commemorate the 500-year anniversary of Columbus's fateful voyage to the New World. Until well into the next century, the ships will be moored alongside Cargo Dock One at the Port of Corpus Christi and open to public touring. Hours are 10 a.m.-5 p.m. daily Labor Day through Memorial Day, 10 a.m.-6 p.m. the

approaching the Lexington

remainder of the year. Admission costs $5 for adults, $2.50 children for under 12, $2 for students. For further information call (512) 883-4118 or 883-2863.

Bayfront Arts and Sciences Park

This complex on the bay, at the north end of Shoreline Blvd., serves as a combination arts and museum district, municipal park, and convention center. The park is roughly equivalent in area to eight city blocks, so all attractions are within walking distance of one another.

The **Art Museum of South Texas** (tel. 512-884-3844) at 1902 N. Shoreline hosts traveling exhibits of painting, sculpture, photography, and folk art, and is also developing a small permanent collection. The stark white, cast-concrete museum building was designed by renowned New York architect Philip Johnson. It's open Tues.-Fri. 10 a.m.-5 p.m., Saturday and Sunday noon-5 p.m.; admission free, donations appreciated.

The **Corpus Christi Museum of Science and History** (tel. 883-2862) at 1900 Chaparral is primarily devoted to natural history exhibits, along with some local history. A new wing houses an exhibit of artifacts from three Spanish galleons that wrecked on nearby Padre Island in 1554, including a replica of one of the ships. It's open Mon.-Sat. 10 a.m.-5 p.m., Sunday 1-5 p.m.; admission is $3 adults, $1 children ages 6-12.

Also in the park complex are a community theater, water gardens (with 150 four-foot fountains), municipal auditorium, and convention center.

Heritage Park

Various nonprofit organizations in Corpus Christi have brought a collection of eight historic local homes together into one area along N. Chaparral between Fitzgerald and Hughes near the Bayfront complex. Each organization has taken responsibility for restoring one structure for historical and educational purposes; in return, they're allowed to use the homes for group functions. Four of the homes, including one owned by the city, are open to public tours.

The most spectacular restoration is the **Sidbury House** (tel. 512-883-9351), built in 1893 in the Queen Anne (or High Victorian) style and listed with the National Register of Historic Places. The first floor is furnished in period style,

including hand-printed European wallpaper. It's open Tues.-Thurs. 9:30 a.m.-12:30 p.m. The two-story, Colonial Revival-style **Galvan House** (tel. 883-0639) was built in 1908 and houses the city-sponsored Multicultural Center (no period furnishings); open to the public Mon.-Fri. 10 a.m.-4 p.m., Saturday 10 a.m.-2 p.m. The smaller 1873 **Lichtenstein House** (tel. 888-5692), also designed in the Colonial Revival style and listed with the NRHP, is sponsored by the Creative Arts Center, which offers various community programs in the arts; open Mon.-Fri. noon-4 p.m. The front rooms of the 1882 Late Victorian-style, NRHP-listed **Guggenheim House** (tel. 887-1601) are furnished in period fashion; open Mon.-Fri. 10 a.m.-4 p.m. Admission to all Heritage Park homes is free.

Centennial House

The oldest existing house in Corpus Christi (tel. 512-992-6003), at 411 N. Upper Broadway, was built in 1849 and used as a hospital by both Union and Confederate forces in the Civil War. Its name comes from the fact it was awarded a Texas Historical Commission plaque during the Texas Centennial; it's now listed with the National Register of Historic Places. Restored and furnished in early American Empire style, it's open to visitors Wednesday 2-5 p.m.; admission is $2 adults, $1 students.

International Kite Museum

There's always a kite or two flying somewhere in Corpus. This unique little museum at the Best Western Sandy Shores Resort (tel. 512-883-7456) on Corpus Christi Beach (at the north end of the Harbor Bridge) celebrates the kite; exhibits trace the history of the device from its invention in China to its use in experiments conducted by Alexander Graham Bell, Benjamin Franklin, and the Wright Brothers. Naturally, an attached shop sells a variety of new kites. The museum is open daily 10 a.m.-5 p.m. and is free.

Museum of Oriental Cultures

Exhibits in this small museum at 418 Peoples St. (tel. 512-883-1303) focus mainly on East Asian (Chinese, Japanese, and Korean) arts and culture. The Japanese *hakata* doll collection is one of the largest in the United States and a diorama presents 20 scale-model scenes

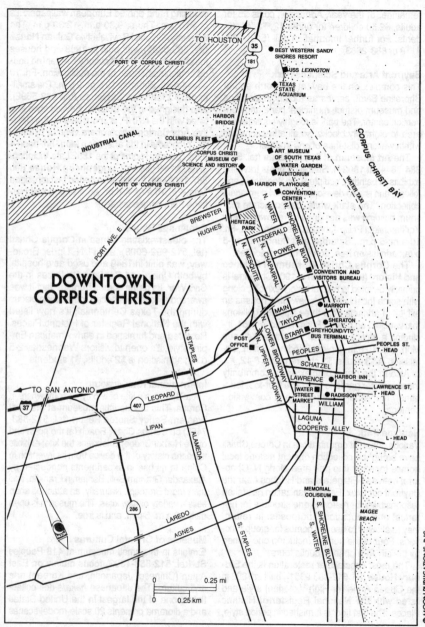

TO HOUSTON

PORT OF CORPUS CHRISTI

INDUSTRIAL CANAL

HARBOR BRIDGE

COLUMBUS FLEET

CORPUS CHRISTI MUSEUM OF SCIENCE AND HISTORY

PORT OF CORPUS CHRISTI

PORT AVE. E.

BREWSTER

HUGHES

HERITAGE PARK

FITZGERALD

POWER

N. MESQUITE

N. CHAPARRAL

N. WATER

N. SHORELINE BLVD.

ART MUSEUM OF SOUTH TEXAS

WATER GARDEN

AUDITORIUM

HARBOR PLAYHOUSE

CONVENTION CENTER

CORPUS CHRISTI BAY

WATER TAXI

DOWNTOWN CORPUS CHRISTI

CONVENTION AND VISITORS BUREAU

N. STAPLES

N. LOWER BROADWAY

N. UPPER BROADWAY

MAIN

TAYLOR

STARR

POST OFFICE

PEOPLES

SCHATZEL

LAWRENCE

WATER STREET MARKET

WILLIAM

LAGUNA

COOPER'S ALLEY

MARRIOTT

SHERATON

GREYHOUND/VTC BUS TERMINAL

PEOPLES ST. T-HEAD

LAWRENCE ST. T-HEAD

HARBOR INN

RADISSON

L-HEAD

TO SAN ANTONIO

37

LEOPARD

407

LIPAN

ALAMEDA

286

LAREDO

AGNES

MEMORIAL COLISEUM

S. SHORELINE BLVD.

S. WATER

S. STAPLES

MAGEE BEACH

0   0.25 mi
0   0.25 km

© MOON PUBLICATIONS, INC.

from traditional Japanese life. Occasional traveling exhibits are on display as well, such as the recent "Talismans of the Far East," a collection of 60 framed folk and religious talismans—woodblock prints, temple rubbings, small sculpture—from Japan, Taiwan, Korea, and Southeast Asia. Open Mon.-Fri. 10 a.m.-4 p.m.; admission is $1 for adults, 50 cents for seniors and children 5-12.

Colleges and Universities
Del Mar College (tel. 512-886-1200) is a two-year community college with an approximate enrollment of 10,000 and a broad range of academic and technical study programs. There are two campuses, the East Campus on Old Brownsville and Airport, and the West Campus at Baldwin and Ayers.

Texas A&M University of Corpus Christi (tel. 991-6810), formerly Corpus Christi State University, is smaller in enrollment (3,700) but much larger in physical size—it occupies an entire 250-acre island near the east end of Ocean Dr., with Corpus Christi Bay on one side and Cayo del Oso on the other. One of the more unusual program offerings is the National Spill Control School, which teaches techniques for handling hazardous material spills. The physical education department features sailing and windsurfing classes. The university also has music, film, and lecture series open to the public.

Corpus Christi Naval Air Station
This is the headquarters for the U.S. Naval Air Training Command, the next step for multi-engine pilots who've graduated from primary naval flight training in Pensacola, Florida. Also on base are the largest Army helicopter repair depot in the country and a Coast Guard search-and-rescue unit. The air station is closed to the non-military public except on Wednesday at 1 p.m., when free tours are given from the north gate at the east end of Ocean Drive. For further information, call (512) 939-2568.

ACCOMMODATIONS

Hotels, Motels, and Beach Condominiums
Corpus has just about every kind of accommodation except a youth hostel. They're clustered in four areas: downtown along Shoreline Blvd.

facing the marina (or one block back on Water St.), to the west of town near the airport, on Corpus Christi Beach at the north end of the Harbor Bridge, and on the Gulf side of North Padre Island. See "Corpus Christi Hotels, Motels, and Condominiums" chart for details.

Bed and Breakfasts
Sand Dollar Hospitality Bed & Breakfast (tel. 512-853-1222 or 800-264-7782), 3605 Mendenhall, Corpus Christi, TX 78415, maintains a register of around 15 bed-and-breakfast homes in Corpus Christi. Rates are $51-87 s, $54-90 d per night including full breakfasts. Weekly and monthly rates available.

Campgrounds and RV Parks
The nearest public campground is located at the county-operated **Padre Balli Park** (tel. 512-949-8121) on North Padre Island off Padre Island Drive. Beach or hardtop camping is $4 a night, $10 with w/e, and there's a three-day limit. You can also camp at Padre Island National Seashore.

Although Corpus Christi doesn't have nearly as many RV parks as the Rio Grande Valley farther south, there are enough spaces to meet the current demand. Rates are similar among all the Corpus Christi area facilities: around $10-12 nightly, $55-60 weekly, and $125-150 monthly ($90 a month at places where RVers pay for their own electricity). **Puerto del Sol RV Park** (tel. 882-5373), at 5100 Timon Blvd., is the only RV facility on Corpus Christi Beach, about 1.5 miles from the USS *Lexington* and Texas State Aquarium. In addition to 53 pull-through lots, Puerto del Sol offers picnic tables, rec room, laundry, and showers; propane nearby.

Most of the city's RV facilities are located in the southeast section of the city toward the naval air station and causeway to Padre Island. Among the largest parks is **Colonia Del Rey RV Park** (tel. 512-937-2435 or 800-966-2435), at 1717 Waldron off Padre Island Dr. between Cayo del Oso and Laguna Madre. Colonia Del Ray features a swimming pool, horseshoe pit, rec hall, showers, LP gas delivery, laundromat, and storage facilities. Farther south on the same road is the smaller **Shady Grove Mobile Home and RV Park** (tel. 937-1314) at 2919 Waldron, which boasts large

CORPUS CHRISTI HOTELS, MOTELS, AND CONDOMINIUMS

Prices quoted are for the peak season of spring-summer and reflect both weekday and weekend rates. Fall and winter rates are generally less. Add 11% hotel tax to all rates. Area code: 512.

CORPUS CHRISTI BEACH

Best Western Sandy Shores; 3200 Surfside; tel. 833-7456 or (800) 528-1234; $54-119; rooms with bay view available, heated pool, saunas, coin laundry

Gulf Beach II; 3500 Surfside; tel. 882-3500 or (800) 882-3502; $45-70; rooms with bay view, coin laundry, weekly rates

Koronado Motel; 3615 Timon; tel. 883-4411; $35-68; rooms with bay view available, pool, coin laundry, kitchens available (add $10)

Sea Shell Inn; 202 Kleberg; tel. 888-5391; $53-72; rooms with bay view available, heated pool, coin laundry, weekly and monthly rates (off season only)

Villa Del Sol Condos; 3839 Surfside; tel. 883-9748 or (800) 242-3291; $90-120; all rooms with bay view, kitchenettes available, heated pool, coin laundry, weekly rates, senior discount, weekend discount

DOWNTOWN (SHORELINE BOULEVARD)

Bayfront Inn; 601 N. Shoreline; tel. 883-7271; $59; pool, senior discount

Corpus Christi Marriott Bayfront; 900 N. Shoreline; tel. 887-1600 or (800) 874-4585; $99-109; bay views, heated pool, saunas, racquetball courts, airport shuttle

Holiday Inn Emerald Beach; 1102 S. Shoreline; tel. 883-5731 or (800) HOLIDAY; $83-115; private beach, pool, heated sauna, airport shuttle

Harbor Inn Bayfront; 411 N. Shoreline; tel. 884-4815; $54-64; rooms with bay view available, pool

Quality Hotel Bayfront Royal Nueces; 601 N. Water; tel. 882-8100 or (800) 688-0334; $59-79; 1 block from marina, atrium, pool, airport shuttle; complimentary continental breakfast

lots and storage space along with the usual amenities. A bit farther north, near the Naval Air Station, is the 200-site **Marina Village RV and Mobile Home Park** (tel. 937-2560) at 229 N.A.S. Dr.; facilities include laundromat, pool, and rec hall. **Padre Palms Travel Park** (tel. 937-2125) is in the same area, at 131 Skipper Lane off N.A.S. Dr.—a fishing pier and boat ramp are nearby. Also in the southeast part of the city, not far from Cayo del Oso at 7436 S. Padre Island Dr., **Gulfway RV-MH Park** (tel. 991-0106) has pull-through sites with full hookups, showers, rec room, and coin laundry. One of the major attractions at nearby **Misty Winds RV and MH Community** (tel. 853-7648), at 5902 Ayers St. off S. Padre Island Dr., is its swimming pool and jacuzzi. Call ahead to make sure vacancies are available.

Over on the west side of town is the conveniently located **Hatch RV Park** (tel. 883-9781 or 800-332-4509) at 3101 Up River Rd. (exit 2 off I-

37), just a couple of miles from downtown. Facilities include pull-throughs, showers, rec room, and coin laundry. **Gulley's RV Park** (tel. 241-4122) at 8225 Leopard is farther out I-37 off the Tuloso Rd. exit (#7).

About eight miles south of the city on US 77 in Robstown, **Highway 77 RV Park** (tel. 387-9850) offers full hookups for just $10 a night. Off US 77, on Country Road 48, is the somewhat quieter **Evelyn's RV & Mobile Home Park** (tel. 387-3777) for $12 a night. Both places also have discounted weekly and monthly rates.

FOOD

With Corpus Christi Bay, Cayo del Oso, Laguna Madre, and the Gulf of Mexico nearby, you'd better enjoy fresh seafood. Virtually every restaurant in town, outside of the chain burger joints, offers seafood specials. You can buy your own

Radisson Marina Hotel; 300 N. Shoreline; tel. 883-5111 or (800) 333-3333; $89-109; bay views, pool, sauna, tennis courts, airport shuttle, two RV spaces

Sheraton Corpus Christi Bayfront; 707 N. Shoreline; tel. 882-1700; $110-117; marina views, heated pool, sauna, airport shuttle

Summer Place; 4310 Ocean Dr.; tel. 853-4411; cottages with kitchenettes, fishing pier; call for rates

I-37/AIRPORT/GREYHOUND TRACK

Best Western Garden Inn; 11217 I-37 (exit 11B): tel. 241-6675 or (800) 528-1234; $49-65; pool, sauna, whirlpool, coin laundry, data ports

Comfort Inn Airport; 6301 I-37 (exit 5); tel. 289-6925; $42-52; pool, coin laundry, airport shuttle

Days Inn; 901 Navigation (I-37 exit 3A); tel. 888-8599 or (800) 325-2525; $39-67; pool, coin laundry, weekly rates, airport shuttle

Drury Inn; 2021 N. Padre Island (I-37 exit 4A); tel. 289-8200 or (800) 325-8300; $52-59; pool, senior discount, complimentary evening beverage; data ports

Eco Motel; 6033 Leopard; tel. 289-1116; $32-36; pool, coin laundry

Holiday Inn Airport; 5549 Leopard; tel. 289-5100 or (800) HOLIDAY; $69-75; heated pool, saunas, airport shuttle, weekend discount

La Quinta Motor Inn North; 5155 I-37 N (exit 3A); tel. 888-5721 or (800) 531-5900; $54-55; pool, senior discount, airport shuttle

Motel 6; 845 Lantana (I-37 exits 3B/4B); tel. 289-9397; $24-32; pool

NORTH PADRE ISLAND

Holiday Inn North Padre Island Resort; 15202 Windward; tel. 949-8041 or (800) HOLIDAY; $66-135; beach, pool, weekly rates (off season only)

Island House Condos; 15340 Leeward Dr.; tel. 949-8166; $90-150; 2- and 3-bedroom units with full kitchens, beach, pools, boat slips, weekly and monthly rates

Puente Vista Condominium Apartments; 14300 Aloha; tel. 949-7081; $105-130; 2-3 bedroom units with full kitchens, beach, pool, coin laundry, sauna, boat dock, weekly rates

Surfside Condo; 15005 Windward; tel. 949-8128 or (800) 548-4585; $85-100; 2-bedroom units w/full kitchens, beach, pool, coin laundry, weekly and monthly rates

---

fresh shrimp and fish directly from the commercial boats docked at the Peoples Street T-Head at the marina.

American

$ to $$ Black-Eyed Pea: Downhome food including chicken-fried steak. At 4833 S. Padre Island Dr. (tel. 512-993-4588); open daily for lunch and dinner.

$ to $$ Elmo's City Diner and Oyster Bar: A '50s diner-style decor with excellent Cajun, Texan, "blue plate specials," and fresh seafood dishes. At 622 N. Water (tel. 883-1643); open daily for lunch and dinner.

Barbecue

$ to $$ County Line: Another branch of the state's best barbecue franchise, with the usual brisket, links, and ribs, plus chicken, duck, and turkey. At 6102 Ocean Dr. (tel. 512-991-7427); open Wed.-Sun. for lunch and dinner.

$ Joe Cotten's Barbecue: Actually in Robs-

town, about eight miles southeast of the city limits on US 77. Barbecue aficionados swear this is the best in South Texas—and they crowd the place to prove it. On US 77 business (tel. 767-9973); open Mon.-Sat. for lunch and dinner.

European

$ to $$ Che Bello: A downtown eatery that may appease homesick New Yorkers or San Franciscans with its espressos, pastries, sandwiches, and gelatos. At 320-C William, Water Street Market (tel. 512-882-8832); open Mon.-Thurs. 7:30 a.m.-10 p.m., Friday 7:30 a.m.-midnight, Saturday 10 a.m.-midnight, Sunday 10 a.m.-10 p.m.

$$ The Italian Tomato: Despite the corny name, this spacious restaurant in the same building with La Pesca serves excellent woodfired pizza, fresh pastas, rotisserie-style meats, and Italian-style seafood. At 701 N. Water St. (tel. 887-4550); open daily for lunch and dinner.

Mexican

$ to $$ Kiko's Mexican Food: A Tex-Mex place located in the Mercado, a local Mexican curios market. The menu features fajitas, taquitos, enchiladas, *almuerzo,* and other South Texas favorites. At 5514 Everhart (tel. 512-991-1211); open Mon.-Sat. for breakfast, lunch, and dinner, Sunday for breakfast and lunch only.

$$ Ninfa's: The 24th link in the famous Houston Tex-Mex restaurant chain, packing them in with a boldly flavored menu. Particularly good are the *quesadillas compuestas,* flour tortillas stuffed with shrimp, cheese, and vegetables. Open daily for lunch and dinner.

$ to $$ Old Mexico: The same family has run this simple restaurant for the last 35 years. Often cited as the city's best all-around Mexican restaurant, it offers an especially good puff taco. At 3329 Leopard at Nueces Bay Blvd. (tel. 883-6461); open Tues.-Sat. for lunch and dinner.

$$ La Pesca: Corpus Christi's newest Mexican eatery, housed in a restored brick building with a funky warehouse-style atmosphere, is a welcome addition to the downtown scene. Gulf Coast-style seafood is the house specialty, along with innovatively prepared border standards such as fajitas, quail, and enchiladas. Weekdays, the "Taste of Mexico" buffet is a steal at $5.95. At 701 N. Water St. (tel. 887-4558); open daily for lunch and dinner.

Seafood

$$ Elmo's Boathouse Restaurant: Traditional Texas Gulf Coast-style seafood served with views of bay and beach. Expect long waits on summer and weekend evenings. At 2802 N. Shoreline, near the Texas State Aquarium and USS *Lexington* (tel. 512-887-6780); open daily for lunch and dinner.

$$ Elmo's Staples St. Seafood and Oyster Bar: Elmo again! The menu is similar to that at Elmo's City Diner but with a heavier emphasis on seafood and steaks. At 5253 S. Staples (tel. 992-3474); open daily for lunch and dinner.

$ to $$ Catfish Charlie's: Although the only seafood on the menu is shrimp, oysters, and catfish, low prices and Cajun cooking make this restaurant noteworthy. An all-you-can-eat platter of catfish fillets, hush puppies, cole slaw, and country-fried potatoes is $7.95. Gumbo, shrimp creole, frog legs, and red beans and rice are also served. At McArdle and Airline, Crossroads Center (tel. 993-0363); open daily for lunch and dinner.

$$ to $$$ Landry's Seafood: A restored 1939 barge is the setting for this floating restaurant at the city marina, which serves steak, smoked chicken, and fresh Gulf seafood. Monday-Sat. 5-7 p.m. and all day Sunday it offers economical "early-bird" specials; during the week there's a "Chill Out Hour" 4:30-7:30 p.m. when beer and margaritas are $1, oysters on the half-shell are 25 cents each, and a half-pound of boiled shrimp is $6. At the end of the Peoples Street T-Head (tel. 882-6666); open daily for lunch and dinner.

$$ to $$$ The Lighthouse Restaurant and Oyster Bar: Another marina restaurant, this one built on solid ground with the best bay view. The menu features fresh seafood, beef, and chicken. It can get crowded on Wednesday early in the evening when people come to watch the sailboat races. At the end of the Lawrence Street T-Head (tel. 883-3982); open daily for lunch and dinner.

$ to $$ Snoopy's: One of two popular seafood places located under the JFK Causeway between Corpus and Padre Island (the other, **Frenchy's,** is also good). Snoopy's serves only locally caught fish and shellfish, fried or broiled to order. At 13313 South Padre Island Dr. (tel. 949-8815); open daily for lunch and dinner.

$$ Water Street Oyster Bar: Specializes in mesquite-grilled and Cajun-style seafood, including blackened redfish and blackened shark. At 309 N. Water St. (tel. 881-9448); open daily for lunch and dinner.

$$ Water Street Seafood Company: A larger version of the above, with a more extensive menu. Same address (tel. 882-8684); open daily for lunch and dinner.

$$ to $$$ The Yardarm: French-influenced seafood (*coquilles St. Jacques,* red snapper papillote, sautéed frog legs) served in one of Ocean Drive's stately bayfront homes. At 4310 Ocean Dr. (tel. 855-8157); open Wed.-Sun. for dinner only, closed Nov.-February.

ENTERTAINMENT

Live Music

Urban kickers fill **Midnight Rodeo** (tel. 512-852-8088) at 24 Parkdale Plaza for the daily happy hour specials and live country bands later in the evening; K99 radio does live broadcasts from the club on Friday night. **Booters** (tel. 991-6091) at 5700 S. Staples is also popular for live C&W.

Still the city's premier live house, **Cantina Santa Fe** (tel. 888-8769) at 1011 Santa Fe St. hosts reggae, funk, rock, and alternative bands Wed.-Sun. each week. **Executive Surf Club** (tel. 884-7873), in the Water Street Market complex at 309 N. Water, features live blues, folk, and R&B Wed.-Saturday. **Doctor Rockit's Blues Bar** (tel. 884-7634) at 709 N. Chaparral is a strictly blues and R&B scene, with big regional names like Gatemouth Brown, Delbert McClinton, and Marcia Ball appearing nightly.

Comedy
Corpus has one comedy club, **High Tides** (tel. 887-1600), in the Corpus Christi Marriott, 1900 Shoreline. Comedians perform Tues.-Sun.; there's a cover charge and reservations are accepted.

Radio
Radio station KKED-FM 90, the local National Public Radio affiliate, broadcasts a variety of locally produced jazz and classical music shows. "Magic 105" (105.1 FM) is a good bilingual *tejano* radio station that plays an upbeat mix of local and international styles.

EVENTS

April
Buccaneer Days, a 10-day festival commemorating the 1519 European "discovery" of Corpus Christi Bay, is usually held the last two weeks of the month. Festivities include a beauty pageant, bayfront fireworks, downtown parades, music, sailing regattas, and a carnival.

July
The **Texas Jazz Festival** is a growing festival held around July 4 featuring three days of jazz performances, including concerts, cruises, jam sessions, and free workshops. The artists who appear are a mixture of state, local, and national names.

September-October
Bayfest, originally held for the Bicentennial, has become an annual fall festival at the Bayfront Arts and Science Park and is usually scheduled for the last weekend in September or first weekend in October. Activities include music, food vendors, arts and crafts, shows, and boat races.

December
On the first Saturday of the month, **Harbor Lights** celebrates Christmas Corpus Christi-style with a bayfront parade and the lighting of boats moored at the marina.

RECREATION

Beaches
Corpus Christi has five beaches within or contiguous with the city limits—three on Corpus Christi Bay and two on the Gulf. The oldest and most popular with tourists is **Corpus Christi Beach** at the north end of the Harbor Bridge. In the '30s casinos were lined up along the 1.5-mile beach (it was called "North Beach" then), and it carried an unsavory reputation for a long time thereafter. The U.S. Army Corps of Engineers restored the beach in the '70s and it's now chockablock with motels and beach condos. The USS *Lexington* and the Texas State Aquarium are situated at the south end of the beach.

Magee Beach, though only 250 yards long, is close to the city marina, across from the coliseum off Shoreline Boulevard. Besides the beach, there's a pier, a quarter-mile-long breakwater, food concession (open Memorial Day to Labor Day), and showers.

Farther east, off Ocean Dr. (2000 block), is **Cole Park,** which features a small beach, fishing pier, picnic area, and restrooms. This is a favorite local windsurfing spot. During the summer, the amphitheater here hosts Sunday evening concerts.

Padre Balli County Park is on the Gulf of Mexico, about 15 miles from downtown Corpus via Padre Island Dr. across the JFK Causeway. It's the closest Gulf beach to the city, so it gets crowded on summer weekends. Facilities include a 1,200-foot-long lighted fishing pier, picnic areas, bathhouse, and a campground.

Just north of North Padre's condo strip is the **J.P. Luby Surf Park,** a beach developed especially for surfers. See "Windsurfing and Surfing," below, for more details.

Parks and Gardens

Corpus Christi Botanical Gardens (tel. 512-993-7551) covers 290 acres along Oso Creek, at Staples and Yorktown in the southwest part of the city. A nature trail leads through virgin mesquite brush and small native subtropical gardens featuring such exotic flora as bottlebrush, pineapple guava, rubber plant, and hibiscus. Deer, raccoons, coyote, bobcat, javelinas, and roadrunners can occasionally be spotted. A guided sunset stroll through the gardens departs each Thursday evening at 7 p.m. Facilities include an information center, greenhouses, gift shop, and picnic area. Open Tues.-Sun. 9 a.m.-5 p.m.; admission is $2 adults, $1.50 seniors, 75 cents for children 12 and under.

Hans Suter Wildlife Refuge, a 22-acre park on Cayo del Oso (Oso Bay) off Ennis Joplin Rd., is the best birding spot within the city limits. Look for white pelicans, roseate spoonbills, egrets, herons, terns, and other shorebirds year round, as well as groove-billed anis and other migratory varieties during the winter. Facilities include an 800-foot boardwalk across a preserved saltmarsh, an observation tower, and hiking trails. It's open dawn to dusk and admission is free.

Birding the Corpus Christi Area, a brochure published by the Audubon Outdoor Club of Corpus Christi, contains an up-to-date bird checklist and map showing prime birding sites. It's available free from the Corpus Christi Convention and Visitors Bureau.

Boating

Launching/Berthing: The downtown marina/yacht basin is the city's pleasure-boat center, offering boat-launching facilities, slip rentals, boat rentals, charter boats, and excursion boats. If you plan to sail into the bay on your own craft, call ahead to the marina office (tel. 512-882-7333, or fax 883-4778) to reserve a guest slip. Guest sailors pay a daily rate of 50 cents per foot per boat or, for longer stays, flat rates of $89 a week, $330 a month. Permanent slips are $2.65 per foot per month. Marina facilities include restrooms, laundry, and hot showers.

Smaller boat launching facilities are available at the end of Ocean Dr. on Oso Bay and at the end of Rincon Road beneath the Nueces Bay Causeway.

Sailing Instructions and Charters: Corpus Christi Bay and Laguna Madre are excellent places to learn how to sail. The **International School of Sailing & Charters** (tel. 512-881-8503), P.O. Box 995, Corpus Christi, TX 78403, on the marina's L-Head offers a weekend sailing school (all day Saturday and Sunday) for $135. For more intensive instruction, consider the three-day or five-day "live-aboard" courses for $425 and $775 respectively, which include all boat accommodations on 25- to 38-foot yachts,

city marina

meals, and instruction. More advanced courses include coastal navigation, bareboat chartering, and offshore passagemaking.

The school can also arrange yacht charters ranging from $140 for an eight-hour bareboat 25-foot Columbia charter to $1900 for a week-long captained 38-foot Irwin trip.

Sightseeing Boats: The *Flagship* and the *Gulf Clipper,* both docked at the Peoples T-Head (tel. 512-884-1693), take passengers on one-hour harbor tours for $6 adults, $3.50 children 11 and under. During the summer, the tours leave three times a day; the rest of the year, they only leave once a day (except Tuesday, when they're closed). On Friday and Saturday nights night tours of the harbor and bay, with live music, are offered for $6.75 (7:30-9 p.m.) and $7.50 (9:30-11 p.m., summer only).

Dolphin Viewing

One of the more unique charter-boat operations, **Dolphin Connection** (tel. 512-776-2887), makes boat trips from Ingleside at the north end of Corpus Christi Bay to visit four pods of Atlantic bottlenose dolphins. The boat leaves two or three times daily year round, depending on weather conditions, and the trip lasts an hour and 15 minutes. Reservations are required; the cost is $15 per adults, $10 for children 12 and under.

Fishing

Anglers can choose among several fishing options in Corpus Christi Bay, Cayo del Oso (Oso Bay), Laguna Madre, and the Gulf of Mexico. Shore fishing is possible just about anywhere there's water, since there always seems to be a pier, breakwater, or wharf nearby. In the bays you can fish for speckled trout, redfish, sand trout, sheepshead, golden croakers, skipjack, drum, and flounder. In the Gulf inshore areas there are also tarpon, mackerel, ling, pompano, jackfish, jewfish, and blue runner.

Farther out in the Gulf is almost everything previously listed, plus kingfish, dolphin, bonito, sailfish, marlin, and barracuda. Deep-sea an-

LOUISE FOOTE

glers who make it to Snapper Banks, 40-60 miles out, have a shot at red snapper, grouper, amberjack, and warsaw. The Corpus Christi Area Convention and Visitors Bureau (tel. 512-882-5603) issues an excellent fishing calendar that lists the best seasons for each species.

Piers and Jetties: Fishing is allowed at the **marina** from the T-heads or from the seawall. The lighted breakwater jetty between the marina and Magee Park is open for fishing 24 hours. The pier at **Cole Park,** 2000 block of Ocean Dr., is also lighted and open 24 hours. All the foregoing piers and jetties are free. The lighted, 24-hour **Nueces Bay Pier** at Corpus Christi Beach (Hull St.) charges a small daily fee for fishing, as does the long **Bob Hall Pier** at Padre Balli Park on North Padre Island. **Trainer's** (tel. 937-5347), at 11801 S. Padre Island Dr., on the east side of Humble Channel, has its own lighted fishing pier, fish-packing services, bait and tackle, and—in case you don't catch anything— a fresh seafood market.

Fishing Boats: Several boats docked at the marina's Peoples Street T-Head offer bay fishing trips (for Gulf fishing trips, Port Aransas is a better choice; see "Vicinity of Corpus Christi" below). The 65-foot *Captain Clark* (tel. 884-4369) takes visiting anglers on two four-hour trips per day (7:30 a.m. and 2 p.m.), plus an extra night trip Fri.-Sat. at 8 p.m. The fee is $14 for adults, $6 for children 11 and under, and includes bait. Bring your own rod and reel or rent them for $3. Food and beverages are sold onboard. The *Star Trek* (tel. 883-5031) offers the same arrangements and departures.

Windsurfing and Surfing

Because of the steady breezes and long expanses of open water in the bay and in Laguna Madre (sheltered from high winds by barrier islands), Corpus is consistently rated among the world's top-10 windsurfing centers. The U.S. Open Pro Am windsurfing tournament is held annually on Corpus Christi Bay, and the Mistral World Championship also sets up here on occasion.

The semicircular geography of the "Coastal Bend" means the wind is always blowing somewhere around the bay—usually everywhere. The most popular windsurfing spot within the city limits is **Oleander Point** at the southern end of Cole Park (2000 block of Ocean Dr.). Farther east along Ocean Dr. are **Ropes Park** (3500 block) and **Poenisch Park** (5000 block), also good places to launch a sailboard. **Corpus Christi Beach**, at the north end of Harbor Bridge, gets its share of windsurfers, too, both novice and experienced.

You can rent windsurfing equipment at the Peoples Street T-Head, at Corpus Christi Beach, and at **M.D. Surf-N-Skate** (tel. 512-854-SURF) at 3821 S. Staples. Surf-N-Skate also offers windsurfing equipment sales, service, and instruction. Other shops in town offering instruction, rentals, and sales include **Mastercraft of Corpus Christi** (tel. 992-4459), 6425 S. Padre Island Dr., and **Wind & Wave Watersports** (tel. 937-9283), 10721 S. Padre Island Drive.

The nearest surfing spot is **J.P. Luby Surf Park** on North Padre Island. The main feature here is a 600-foot row of pier pilings that extend into the surf to enhance wave action for surfing. M.D. Surf-N-Skate and Wind & Wave Watersports provide sales and rental of surfboards and surfing gear.

Scuba Diving

Various jetty complexes in Aransas Bay and farther south at Port Mansfield offer artificial reef viewing, as do offshore oil rigs. For information on guided trips or equipment rental/service, contact **Copeland Dive Shop** (tel. 512-854-1135), 6341 S. Padre Island Dr., or **ARC** (tel. 949-9491), 14225 Park Rd. 22 (Big Shell Plaza #3), North Padre Island. It's possible to arrange overnight dive trips to the magnificent Flower Gardens reef system, 220 miles northeast in the Gulf, but Freeport is a much more convenient departure point since it cuts the total mileage in half. The Texas State Aquarium (tel. 881-1300) may begin offering dive trips to the Flower Gardens in the near future.

Golf

The city-operated **Oso Beach Golf Course** (tel. 512-991-5351), at 5600 S. Alameda at Glenmore, is an 18-hole, par-70 course near Oso Bay.

Greens fees are $9 on weekdays, $11 weekends. **Gabe Lozano Sr. Golf Center** (tel. 883-3696) is an 18-hole, par-72 public course with the same greens fees as the Oso Beach course.

Tennis

Corpus Christi operates two municipal tennis centers: **H.E.B. Tennis Center** (tel. 512-888-5681) at 1520 Shely (H.E.B. Butt Park) and **Al Kruse Center** (tel. 888-6942) at 502 King. At either, court fees (hour-and-a-half limit) are $2.25.

INFORMATION

Tourist Offices

The **Corpus Christi Area Convention and Visitors Bureau** (tel. 512-882-5603) at 1201 Shoreline is open Mon.-Fri. 8:30 a.m.-5 p.m. The staff is very helpful and has tons of free brochures on local attractions, accommodations, and recreation. The CCACVB also maintains a 24-hour toll-free line visitors can call to order a free packet of information through the mail (800-678-OCEAN). Similar information, though not as extensive, is available at the **Corpus Christi Tourist Information Center** (tel. 241-1464), at Nueces River Park (junction of US 77 and I-37), and at the **Corpus Christi Visitor Bureau** (tel. 937-6711), 9405 S. Padre Island Drive.

Publications

The Convention and Visitors Bureau publishes an annual *Beach & Bay Guide* in pocket format that contains a variety of short features on local attractions, recreation, and events. The Miller Publications *Visitors Guide* is somewhat similar but focuses more on dining, shopping, and cultural events. The *Island Sun* is a free weekly newspaper with up-to-date information on fishing, tides, and TV listings that cover the entire Coastal Bend from Padre Island to Rockport. Winter Texans and retirees may find useful the free "Senior Resource Directory," available as a supplement to the *Corpus Christi Caller-Times* or from the Convention and Visitors Bureau. The directory focuses on health care and senior services.

Maps

A good Corpus Christi area map is crucial for exploring the area, with all its bays, ship channels, and lagoons. The best all-around map is the one published by the city's own **Zdansky Map Store** (tel. 512-855-9226), 5230 Kostoryz, available throughout the city at shops carrying maps. In addition to a large city map, it features inset maps for downtown, North Padre Island, Robstown, Portland, Mustang Island, Port Aransas, and Nueces County. Runners-up in the map category include the Rand McNally and AAA efforts.

Telephone

The area code for Corpus Christi and vicinity is 512.

GETTING THERE AND AROUND

Corpus Christi International Airport

This airport is conveniently located about 15 minutes southwest of downtown Corpus via Agnes Street. Five commercial airlines (American, Conquest, Continental, Delta, and Southwest) operate daily flights to six other Texas cities as well as 18 destinations in the U.S. and Mexico. The terminal's one restaurant, **Riviera Red's** (tel. 512-289-5418), serves decent seafood.

Taxis from the airport to downtown Corpus Christi cost $7-13 depending on distance.

Intercity Buses

The **Greyhound Bus Terminal** (tel. 512-882-2516), downtown at 702 N. Chaparral near Starr, handles buses to points north such as Dallas, Houston, and San Antonio. **Valley Transit Company** (same phone number) in the same terminal operates buses to points south such as Port Isabel, Brownsville, and other towns in the Rio Grande Valley.

City Buses

The **Regional Transportation Authority** (tel. 512-289-2600) operates the city bus and water taxi system. Visitors will probably be most interested in the RTA's no. 73 "Trolley Scenic Trail" line, which uses buses modified to look like trolley cars. The line runs along Water St. and Shoreline Blvd. between Corpus Christi Museum and Buford St., passing a number of prominent bayfront hotels and restaurants as well as Heritage Park, the Convention Center/Bayfront Plaza, and the marina T-heads. Approximate hours of operation are 10 a.m.-8 p.m. These buses come by roughly every half-hour during the week, every 15 minutes on Saturday; a roundtrip circuit only takes 30 minutes. The basic fare is 50 cents, 25 cents for seniors, students, and disabled. Children under six accompanied by an adult ride free.

Other buses of interest to visitors include the no. 2 Hillcrest (downtown to Greyhound Race Track) and the no. 78 Beach Connector (downtown to Corpus Christi Beach/Texas State Aquarium).

The no. 77 Water Taxi is a RTA-operated passenger ferry that runs from the Peoples St. T-Head to Corpus Christi Beach, with a side route to the Columbus Fleet on request. Fares are $1 each way. The ferry runs Sat.-Sun. only from mid-September through the end of October and from mid-March through the end of May, then daily June-September.

Taxis

Call **Star Cab** (tel. 512-884-9451) for 24-hour taxi service.

VICINITY OF CORPUS CHRISTI

East of Corpus Christi are the barrier islands of Mustang and Padre, which really function as one island since the narrow channel that once separated them has silted up on the Gulf side. Padre Island runs 113 miles from its north end at Corpus Christi Pass to the south end at the Mansfield Cut (Mansfield Channel), while Mustang Island is only 18 miles long. To the north of Mustang Island are the Rockport-Fulton Peninsula, Aransas Bay, Copano Bay, St. Charles Bay, and the Aransas National Wildlife Refuge.

PORT ARANSAS

Perched at the northern tip of Mustang Island, this is one of America's few remaining old-fashioned beach towns, the kind with funky motel courts instead of Holiday Inns. Until the 1950s, it was rather difficult to reach Port Aransas; two ferry crossings were necessary, one from the mainland to Harbor Island, then another from Harbor Island to Mustang Island. There wasn't even a road leading to the mainland ferry terminal; you had to take a train from Aransas Pass. As the Port of Corpus Christi superseded Port Aransas, no one seemed to be in any hurry to improve island access. But finally in 1954 the Mustang Island Highway (State 361) and south causeway were built to connect the south part of the island with Corpus Christi, and in 1960 another causeway linked the mainland with Harbor Island. The ferry service between Harbor Island and Port A (as it's known locally) is still the only way to avoid coming through Corpus Christi.

State 361 leads, via the north causeway, to the Harbor Island ferry landing. The ferry service to Port A operates 24 hours a day, takes about five minutes to complete the crossing, and is free of charge. The usual waiting time to get on the ferry is five to 15 minutes. During summer weekends and spring break, however, the wait can last 45 minutes or more; when it's that backed up, it's best to drive around through Corpus to Padre Island, and from there north to Port A—a trip of about 60-80 minutes in normal traffic conditions. Along this route, a low bridge carries drivers over the silted Corpus Christi Pass that once separated Padre from Mustang.

Whichever way you choose to come to Port A, the accessibility issue tends to deter the average weekend beachgoer, a situation that's a major plus for those seeking a more tranquil seaside setting than is available in Galveston or Corpus Christi. In spite of the condo developments at the south edge of the city limits, the permanent population here is still just over 2,000 and the atmosphere remains that of a 1950s fishing village. From here all the way down to just above the Mexican border, where Padre Island is separated from South Padre Island by an artificial channel, the beaches are wide open.

The one time of year to avoid Port Aransas, unless you know what you're in for, is "spring break," a period stretching from the end of February to the beginning of April. Spring break brings thousands of college and university students to the island and town facilities are taxed almost to the breaking point. During this period, spring-breakers can outnumber locals 50 to one. Many locals clear out of town till it's over.

Port A's popularity among winter Texans has reached the point that winter visitors are advised to make reservations well in advance.

History
The first known Mustang Island inhabitants, the Karankawa Indians, were wiped out by Comanches, disease, and European colonists by the 1800s. Gulf pirates visited the area regularly, but the first European settler was Englishman R.L. Mercer, who brought his family to Mustang Island (named for the wild horses that once roamed here) in the 1850s to fish and raise cattle. The town that grew up around the Mercer settlement became known as Tarpon, after the fish of the same name that were once plentiful in nearby Gulf waters. As it developed into a ship-service stop for Aransas Pass, the name was changed to Port Aransas.

Economy
Commercial and sport fishing have kept Port Aransas alive over the years. As in Corpus

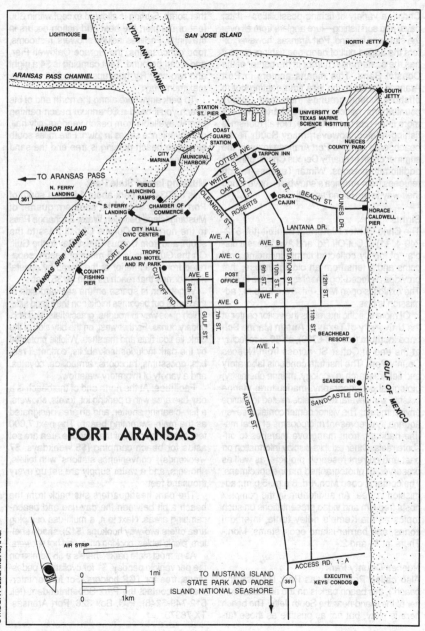

PORT ARANSAS

TO MUSTANG ISLAND
STATE PARK AND PADRE
ISLAND NATIONAL SEASHORE

Christi, a variety of fishing possibilities—flats, bays, and surf fishing—lure anglers from all over the state and beyond. Port Aransas, however, offers the added pull of deep-sea fishing, since it has the easternmost harbor in the center of the Coastal Bend. This means anglers in Port Aransas spend much less time boating out to offshore fishing grounds than their Corpus counterparts, hence deep-sea charter trips are more time- and cost-effective. Not all tourism is fishing-related, however; many South Texas beachgoers come to Port Aransas to avoid the summer crush in nearby Corpus Christi, bringing additional revenues. Winter Texans—retired refugees from America's snowbelt—have found their way to the island as well.

Sights
The **Civic Center Historical Exhibit** (tel. 512-749-4111) at Cut-Off Rd. and Ave. A has a display of locally collected items, including gold coins and a lens from an old lighthouse, that provides a pieced-together history of the island. The exhibit is open Mon.-Fri. 8 a.m.-5 p.m.; admission is free.

Of more specific interest is the visitor center at the **University of Texas at Austin Marine Science Institute** (tel. 749-6729), an 80-acre facility at the end of Cotter St. across from Nueces County Park. The institute conducts laboratory and field research in ecology, marine chemistry, biological oceanography, mariculture, marine botany, and several other fields related to marine environments. The visitor center contains seven aquaria that represent microcosms of local marine habitats, from mangrove marshes to offshore reefs. Other exhibits display information on past and current research projects, as well as preserved or photographed marine specimens. The center is open Mon.-Fri. 8 a.m.-5 p.m.; admission is free. An auditorium in the complex hosts free film and video presentations on such topics as the Kemp's ridley turtle, intertidal zones, and barrier-island ecosystems, Mon.-Thurs. at 11 and 2.

Nueces County Park
Also called Port Aransas Park (or just "the beach"), this beach park is on the northeast corner of the island near the South Jetty. The beach here is okay, but not as pristine as those farther south. Surfing is allowed except within 300 feet of the pier; the best surf action occurs in the winter. Facilities include showers, restrooms, food concessions, the Horace Caldwell Pier, and a campground. Tent camping is $4 a night and two-way RV hookups costs $10; 14-day maximum stay.

To park anywhere along the north end of the beach you'll need a $6 annual beach parking permit, available from beach vendors, city hall, or convenience stores in town. Five miles south along the beach parking is free and the sand is cleaner.

Mustang Island State Park
This 3,703-acre park about 14 miles south of Port Aransas spans the southern quarter of Mustang Island between Water Exchange Pass to the north and Corpus Christi Pass to the south, and from Corpus Christi Bay to the Gulf. On the Gulf side is 5.5 miles of beach, separated from the interior of the island by coastal ridge dunes that reach as high as 35 feet.

Vegetation is sparse on the seaward side of the dunes but becomes thicker on the inland side, which gives way to troughs, grassy flats, and secondary dunes. Farther west, on the bay side of the park, lie tidal flats and marshes. Wildlife protected by the park includes jackrabbits, cottontail rabbits, opossums, raccoons, armadillos, coyotes, and a variety of migratory waterfowl.

Facilities: At the north end of the beach is a day-use area with a parking lot, toilets, showers, a fish-cleaning shelter, and an area designated as the main swimming beach. The next 7,000 feet of beach south of the day-use area are set aside for beach camping ($5 weekdays, $7 weekends); "convenience stations" with toilets, showers, and a water supply are set up every thousand feet.

The park headquarters sits back from the beach a bit between the day-use and beach-camping areas. Next to it, a multi-use camping area offers two-way hookups ($12), shade shelters, picnic tables, cooking grills, and hot showers.

As at most state parks, there's a $5 admission fee per vehicle per day, $1 for cyclists or pedestrians, free for TCP holders. For further information, contact the Park Superintendent (tel. 512-749-5246), P.O. Box 326, Port Aransas, TX 78373.

San José Island

"Saint Joe," as locals call the island, lies just across the Aransas Pass Channel to the north of Port Aransas. The island is privately owned and has no facilities whatsoever except for the North Jetty—perfect for anglers and beachcombers who find even Port Aransas too civilized. Beach camping is permitted at the south end near the jetty, but you must bring all your own food and water by boat or ferry. The only public ferry is from **Woody's Boat Basin** (tel. 512-749-5252), off Cotter St. near the Station St. Pier. There are 10 departures a day between 6:30 a.m. and 6 p.m.; the crossing takes 15 minutes and costs a whopping $7.95 for adults, $4.50 for children ages 2-10.

Accommodations

Cottages and Motel Courts: The Port Aransas Chamber of Commerce reports 26 different places in this classification. Most are a few blocks off the beach along Station, Alister, Cotter, 9th, 10th, 11th, or Avenue G. The typical cottage (or motel court—more than two or three cottages in a group) has two or three bedrooms with air conditioning, kitchenette, and TV, but little else. They're great values, however; a two-bedroom place averages around $40-45 while a three-bedroom goes for about $50, not including 12% state and local tax. A complete list is available at the tourist information center at 421 W. Cotter. A few established cottages/motel courts include: **Anchor Courts** (tel. 512-749-5340), 403 S. 10th; **Angler's Courts** (tel. 749-5327), 403 N. Alister; **Captain Dan Motel** (tel. 749-6577), S. Station; **Double Barr Cottages** (tel. 749-5582), 415 Ave. G; **Gibbs Cottages** (tel. 749-5452), 400 N. Alister; **Gulf Beach Courts** (tel. 749-5416), 506 E. Ave. G; **Haney's Cottages** (tel. 749-5792), 225 E. Oaks; **Harbor View Motel** (tel. 749-6391), 111 W. Cotter; **King Fish Courts** (tel. 749-5527), 1648 E. 11th; **Lone Palm Motel** (tel. 749-5450), 316 S. Alister; **Malibu Motel & Cottages** (tel. 749-5531), 803 S. 9th; **Marine Courts** (tel. 749-5509), 411 N. Alister; **Paradise Isle Motel** (tel. 749-6993), 330 Cut-Off Rd.; **Seahawk Motel** (tel. 749-5572), 105 N. Alister; **Rock Cottages** (tel. 749-6360), 603 Ave. G; **Sunrise Courts** (tel. 749-5366), 302 E. Ave. C; and **Tropic Island Motel & Apartments** (tel. 749-6128), 303 Cut-Off Road.

Hotels and Motels: The **Tarpon Inn** (tel. 749-5555) at 200 E. Cotter is the oldest place to stay on Mustang Island and is listed with the National Register of Historic Places. It was first built in 1886 by an assistant lighthouse keeper who used surplus lumber from a Civil War barracks. It burned down in 1900 and was replaced by two inn buildings in 1904; a 1919 hurricane destroyed one of the buildings and damaged the other. The damaged building was repaired and reinforced with pier pilings, set in concrete, that extend from the ground through the attic. Over 7,000 tarpon scales, each signed and dated by an angler, decorate the lobby walls, including one signed by President Franklin Delano Roosevelt, who stayed here in 1937. All rooms open onto a shaded terrace and have private baths, but none offer TVs or telephones. There's a phone in the lobby, however. Rooms cost $40-55 Oct.-Feb., $45-75 March-September.

The **Seaside Inn** (tel. 749-4105) at Sand Castle and 11th has standard rooms for $35-40 s, $40-45 d, $65-75 for suites. **Port Aransas Inn** (tel. 749-5937) at 1500 11th St. costs a bit more and has a pool.

Bed and Breakfasts: Port Aransas Inn Bed & Breakfast (tel. 749-5937), at 1500 11th St., and **Harbor View Bed & Breakfast** (tel. 749-4294), on the ship channel near the charter boats, offer comfortable rooms with full breakfasts starting at $70 a night.

Condominiums: Port Aransas has nearly as many condo developments as motel courts, but they're spread thinly toward the south edge of town and just south of the city limits, off the Gulf side of Mustang Island Highway. Condo units are more spacious and modern than Port Aransas cottages and common facilities include swimming pools, spas, and tennis courts. Average nightly rates range from as low as $45 for a studio or one-bedroom condo during the fall to $200 for a two-bedroom in the summer (utilities included). Weekly and monthly rates are always available; some condos have a two-night minimum. Reserve at least several weeks in advance for summer weekends, when condo units tend to book up quickly. Rates are lowest during the fall months.

The chamber of commerce lists 22 condo developments, each with up to 100 units or more. One of the best-run and -located is the

Aransas Princess (tel. 749-5118) on Access Rd. 1A, off the highway close to town. Two-bedroom units here start at $145 in the winter and run to $305 for a three-bedroom penthouse in the summer. At the least expensive end of the spectrum, **The Courtyard Condominiums** (tel. 749-5243) advertises studio condos starting at $40 s, $50 d in the fall season. Other possibilities in the same vicinity off Mustang Island Hwy. with similar or lower rates include: **Bay Tree** (tel. 749-5859); **Beachhead** (tel. 749-6261); **Channelview** (tel. 749-6649); **Coral Cay** (tel. 749-5111); **The Courtyard** (tel. 749-6257); **Executive Keys** (tel. 749-6272); **El Cortes Villas** (tel. 749-6206); **Gulf Shores** (tel. 749-6257); **Mayan Princess** (tel. 749-5183); **Mustang Towers** (tel. 749-6212); **Port Royal By The Sea** (tel. 749-5011); and **Sandpiper Condominiums** (tel. 749-6251).

RV Parks

Around 18 RV parks are sprinkled throughout the town. Facilities at most are limited to three-way hookups; a few have LP gas and most feature fish-cleaning facilities. Rates are generally a little lower than elsewhere on the Texas coast: around $8-10 nightly, with weekly rates of $40 and monthly rates of $90-100, if RVers pay for electricity.

Two have swimming pools—**Tropic Island Motel & RV Park** (tel. 512-749-6128) at 303 Cut-Off and **Island RV Resort** (tel. 749-5600), 700 6th at Cut-Off Road. Several centrally located places include **Beachway RV** (tel. 749-6351), 223 N. Station; **Bomarito's RV Park** (tel. 749-5447, 312 S. 10th); **Bonar's** (tel. 749-6598), 315 S. 9th; **Buccaneer Courts RV Park** (tel. 749-5566), 715 Mustang Island Rd.; **Gulf Breeze** (tel. 749-5691), 319 Trojan; **Mayfield Trailer Park** (tel. 749-5505), 300 E. Ave. M; **Mustang Trailer Park** (tel. 749-5343), 300 E. Cotter; and **Texsun Cottages/RV** (tel. 749-5304), 107 E. Ave. G. **On the Beach RV Park** (tel. 749-4909 or 800-932-6337) sits on a nice stretch of Gulf beach off Beach Access Road 1-A.

Nueces County Park and Mustang Island State Park also have RV parking facilities—see separate entries above.

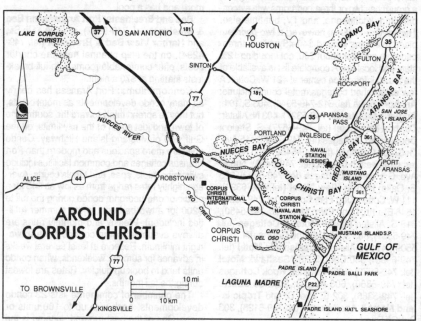

AROUND CORPUS CHRISTI

© MOON PUBLICATIONS, INC.

Food

The emphasis in Port A restaurants is naturally on fresh seafood. Business hours vary throughout the year; in the summer most are open every day, while during the winter they may close down for a day or two each week or even take several weeks off. At the north end of Alister St. near the marina are three waterfront restaurants quite popular with tourists: **Tortuga Flats Oyster Bar** (tel. 512-749-5255), **Dockside** (tel. 749-4322), and **Quarterdeck** (tel. 749-4449). All three specialize in fresh, locally caught fish and are open daily for lunch and dinner. Dockside also serves breakfast.

Yankee's and Betty's Seafood Galley (tel. 749-4869) at 417 Alister also serves local fish—baked, broiled, or grilled to order—with an added twist: the kitchen will cook fish you bring in for $3.50 a pound. You have to clean and fillet them first, though. Betty's also has a selection of Gulf fish, shrimp, oysters, and "Alaskan white" on hand for those who don't bring their own, as well as pizza. **Pelican's Landing** (tel. 749-6405) at 437 Cotter is popular among locals as well as tourists. The extensive menu includes steak and beef teriyaki in addition to a complete selection of fresh seafood. **Ocean Ranch Saloon** (tel. 749-5603) at 417 E. Alister, opposite the IGA supermarket, specializes in Kansas beef, baby back ribs, chicken kebabs, frog legs, and fresh seafood.

For something different, try the **Crazy Cajun** (tel. 749-5069) at Beach St. and Station. Here you'll find crawfish (in season), plus delicious seafood gumbo, jambalaya, Dixie beer, and a $7.95 "Hungry Cajun" platter that includes shrimp, crab, and gumbo, all served on butcher paper. Open Tues.-Sun. 5-9 p.m. Another good value is the **Island Cafe & Smokehouse** (tel. 749-6602) at 224 W. Cotter, which serves steak, seafood, and a few Tex-Mex dishes. Open daily for a la carte breakfast, lunch, and dinner, the Island Cafe also has lunch specials Mon.-Friday. **Rosita's Taco Beach** (tel. 749-6937), Port A's only Tex-Mex cafe, sits at the corner of 11th and Ave. G, opposite the Rock Cottages. It's open for breakfast 9 a.m.-noon on weekends, for lunch and dinner only the rest of the week; authentic menudo and *caldos* (soups) are available.

The **Village Bake Shoppe** serves coffee, donuts, pastries, and other baked goods daily except Tuesday from 5:30 a.m. to 1:30 p.m.

The only place open earlier, the Ocean Ranch, starts serving breakfast at 5 a.m. daily.

Across from the Village Bake Shoppe is an **IGA** grocery store that's open daily. You can buy fresh fish and shrimp from the docks off W. Cotter Street.

Entertainment and Events

Tortuga Flats Oyster Bar (tel. 512-749-5255), at the end of Alister on the harbor, has live rock and R&B on weekends. **Bobby Ray's Spring Creek Saloon** (tel. 749-8098) at 503 S. Alister features country and western bands on weekends. **Shorty's** (tel. 749-5966) on Tarpon St., between the Tarpon Inn and the harbor, is the island's oldest watering hole; the dart boards and pool tables attract a mostly local crowd. **Sharkey's** nearby has DJ rock on weekends and daily during spring break.

Most annual events in Port Aransas are centered around fishing tournaments—the chamber of commerce lists five in June, five in July, three in August, and two in October. The oldest and biggest is the **Deep-Sea Roundup,** held the first full week of July. It's the state's oldest fishing competition, having begun as the "Tarpon Roundup" in 1932.

Recreation

Fishing: This is what most people come to Port A for. Depending on the time of year, bay and pier anglers may hook redfish, flounder, speckled trout, or black drum, while surfcasters can pull in these same species plus sand shark, pompano, croaker, and mackerel. The more challenging sport fish are found in offshore Gulf waters, including the popular kingfish, red snapper, amberjack, barracuda, yellowfin and blackfin tuna, bonito, jackfish, ling, blue and white marlin, sailfish, wahoo, and several varieties of shark. The mighty tarpon, which reaches up to seven feet in length, has schooled one to five miles offshore since the late '80s—good news for anglers who'd resigned themselves to the silver king's virtual extinction. The tarpon season runs June-Oct., with peaks in mid- to late summer.

Popular free onshore fishing spots include the **North Jetty** at the entrance to the Aransas Pass Channel, **J.P. Luby Fishing Pier** at Roberts Point Park across from the municipal marina, **Ancel Brundrett Pier** (also called Station St. Pier) at the north end of Station St., and the **Nueces County Pier** at the end of Port St. across from Harbor Island. **Horace Caldwell Pier** at Nueces County Park is lighted, open 24 hours, and costs $1.50.

Party and charter boats for offshore bay and deep-sea fishing trips are docked at the harbor area along W. Cotter. Half-day party-boat trips start at around $20 per person for bay fishing, $40 for Gulf trips. Longer trips—six to 12 hours—are charter only and start at $300 for one to six persons. Tarpon excursions typically cost $450. Rates always include bait and tackle but not food and beverages. One of the larger operations, **Dolphin Docks** (tel. 512-749-6624), also offers 40-hour "snapper safaris." Other Cotter St. operations include **Fisherman's Wharf** (tel. 749-5448 or 749-5760), **Deep Sea Headquarters** (tel. 749-5597), **Island Sea Sports** (tel. 749-4167), and **Woody's** (tel. 749-5271). Also here is the **Sportsplex** (tel. 749-4088), which sells bait and tackle in additional to arranging fishing charters. An association of local fishing guides, **Port Aransas Boatmen** (tel. 749-6339), has its own dock at the municipal marina east of the ferry landing, where custom fishing trips can be arranged.

Boating: For sailboat or powerboat charters, go to the **Island Moorings Marina** (tel. 749-4983) south of town off State 361, near the airfield. Both crewed and bareboat charters are available.

Surfing: The best surf action is usually near the jetties on either side of the channel—the South Jetty on the Mustang side, or the North Jetty on the San José Island side—although surfing is allowed anywhere along Mustang Island's Gulf shore except within 300 feet of Horace Caldwell Pier. The beach off Ave. G is also decent in the winter. Tropical depressions coupled with hard south winds mean big surf anytime of year. Beach shops along Alister in Port A rent surfboards and boogie boards.

Horseback Riding: Mustang Riding Stables (tel. 512-749-5055) rents horses for beach riding at $20 an hour. The stables are located on the Gulf side of Mustang Island Hwy. just north of Mustang Island State Park, about 12 miles south of Port Aransas.

Information

The **Port Aransas Chamber of Commerce** (tel. 512-749-5919 or 800-452-6278) at 421 W. Cotter distributes free information on Port A accommodations and recreation. The office is open Mon.-Sat. 9 a.m.-5 p.m.

The weekly *Port Aransas South Jetty* newspaper covers local events and produces a free semi-annual *Port Aransas/Mustang Island Visitors Guide* that's packed with information, including extensive tips on local fishing.

ROCKPORT-FULTON

These adjacent towns on Aransas Bay, with a combined population of around 6,000, are protected from Gulf tempests by San José Island.

Port Aransas surfers

PORT ARANSAS CHAMBER OF COMMERCE

Rockport is the older of the two, having been founded in 1867 by New York's Morgan Steamship Co. as a transshipment point for cattle products destined for the eastern United States. Fulton developed next, as a cattle-processing town. Both towns almost died with the 1880s arrival of Texas railroads, which established faster and less expensive means of overland transport. But the area was too scenic and the fishing too good for people to abandon it completely, and Rockport-Fulton eventually evolved into a sportfishing and resort center.

Today Rockport-Fulton is mostly residential, with small beach homes mingling with thickets of windswept live oaks. It's also something of an art center and claims the highest per-capita concentration of artists in the state.

Sights

Displays at the **Texas Maritime Museum** (tel. 512-729-1271) provide an overview of Texas maritime history through a variety of photographic and hands-on exhibits. Souvenirs and books on the Texas coast are available in the gift shop. At Rockport Harbor next to the Rockport Center for the Arts, the museum is open Wed.-Sat. 10 a.m.-4 p.m., Sunday 1-4 p.m.; admission is $2.50 adults, $1 children 4-12.

The **Fulton Mansion State Historical Structure** (tel. 729-0386), on Fulton Beach Rd. at Henderson in Fulton, was built in the 1870s by cattle baron George Fulton. The three-story, French Second Empire house was considered state-of-the-art architecture in its time, since it was equipped with a water-cooled larder, central heat, shellcrete (crushed-shell concrete) insulation, gas lights, and flush toilets. To withstand hurricane-force gales, the upper walls were built of one- by five-inch pinewood planks, stacked horizontally and spiked together. Rooms are trimmed in walnut and cypress paneling, with English-tile floors in the halls and dining room. The Texas Parks and Wildlife Department has restored the mansion and furnished it in period style. Guided tours are given every half-hour Wed.-Sun. 9 a.m.-noon and 1-4 p.m. Admission is $4 adults, $2 for children 6-12.

To see some of the art Rockport's known for, visit the **Rockport Art Center** (tel. 729-5519) on Broadway at Rockport Harbor. Housed in the 19th-century Bruhl-O'Connor home, it features four galleries with rotating exhibits and three art studios. Art classes are open to public enrollment. The galleries are open Tues.-Sat. 10 a.m.-5 p.m., Sunday 2-5 p.m.; admission is free.

Rockport Beach Park

This artificial beach park lies on a small peninsula extending from Rockport Harbor. The beach itself stretches about a mile and a quarter and includes a bay swimming area as well as a saltwater pool. One end of the beach side of the peninsula is reserved for waterskiing, another for sailboats. The opposite side has a Jet Ski/waverunner area, boat-launch ramps, and a paddleboat area; equipment is available for rent in the park. Other facilities include an 800-foot lighted fishing pier, two small islands with bird sanctuaries, an observation tower, picnic cabanas, and a park store with refreshments and beach supplies. The park store is open Memorial Day through Labor Day only. Park hours are daily 5 a.m.-11 p.m. Admission is free but there's a nominal parking fee for vehicles.

Accommodations

Cottages and Motel Courts: Like Port Aransas, many of the accommodations here come in the form of inexpensive cottages and motel courts. An added advantage is that many of the Rockport motels and cottages have their own private piers (however rickety) over Aransas Bay. Rates run a little higher than in Port A: around $35-45 a night for a basic two-bedroom cottage with kitchenette, $45-55 for a three-bedroom. In Rockport are **Anchor Motel** (tel. 512-729-3249), 1114 E. Market; **Balboa Courts** (tel. 729-2517), 1408 Church; **Bayfront Cottages** (tel. 729-6693), next to Fulton Mansion; **Days Inn** (tel. 729-6379), 1212 Laurel; **Del Camino Apartments** (tel. 729-6379), 1023 State 35 N; **Holiday Lodge Motel** (tel. 729-3433), 1406 Raht; **Hunt's Courts** (tel. 729-2273), 901 S. Water; **Rockporter Inn** (tel. 729-9591), 813 S. Church; **Surf Court Motel** (tel. 729-3249), 1204 Market; and **Surfside Motel** (tel. 729-2348), 1809 Broadway.

Houses and Condominiums: Condos are springing up like toadstools in Rockport. One of the more interesting developments is **Key Allegro Island,** a complex of streets and canals opposite Rockport Harbor. Virtually every unit is situated either on a canal or on Aransas Bay. Many are privately owned and available only when the owners aren't in town, which is most of the year for many owners. **Key Allegro Condos & Home Rental** (tel. 729-2333 or 800-348-1627) at 1809 Bayshore handles island rentals. Rates range from $65 a night in the winter for a one-bedroom unit with kitchen and living room to $90 a night in the summer for a two-bedroom unit with kitchen and living room. Weekly rates start at $425, monthly at $630-1035. For the names of other condo developments in the area, contact the Rockport-Fulton Area Chamber of Commerce (tel. 729-6445 or 800-826-6441) at 404 Broadway.

Bed and Breakfasts: The **Blue Heron Inn** (tel. 729-7526), at 801 Patton St., offers four spacious rooms in an 1890s-vintage, two-story home surrounded by live oaks near the bay for $80-90 a night including full, homemade breakfasts. **Anthony's by the Sea** (tel. 729-6100), at 732 S. Pearl, boasts a similarly wooded setting along with a pool and spa for $55 d with shared bath, $65 in a huge suite with private bath, or $75 in a separate guest cottage with full kitchen; all rates include full breakfast. Anthony's is a short walk from the main strip and only four blocks from the beach.

RV Parks: Rockport features several RV parks within the city limits. All run about $10 a day for a three-way hookup, $40-60 weekly, $90-100 monthly. A few convenient to the harbor and Rockport Beach include **Ancient Oaks Campground** (tel. 729-5051 or 800-962-6134), 1222 State 35 S; **The Quiet One Travel Trailer Park** (tel. 729-2668), 500 W. James; **Woody Acres RV Park** (tel. 729-5636), off State 35 N at Mesquite; **Anderson Trailer & RV Park** (tel. 729-9651), FM 1781 at FM 2165; **Rockport 35 RV Park** (tel. 729-2307 or 800-392-2930), 4851 State 35 N; and **Trailer Inn by the Bay** (tel. 729-5608), State 35 and Fulton Beach Road.

Food

The Rockport-Fulton area has a nice variety of restaurants and cafes to choose from. Right in downtown Rockport is the **Austin St. Pub & Eatery** (tel. 512-729-4050), at 415 S. Austin, which offers a reasonably priced selection of sandwiches, chicken-fried steak, seafood, fajitas (beef, chicken, and shrimp), and daily specials like taco salad, meatloaf, and lasagna, plus homemade pies. It's open for lunch Mon.-Sat., for dinner Monday, Tuesday, and Thurs.-Saturday. **The Boiling Pot** (tel. 729-6972) on Fulton Beach Rd. specializes in Cajun-style blue crab, crawfish (in season), shrimp, and gumbo, and is open Mon.-Thurs. for dinner, Fri.-Sun. for lunch and dinner.

In spite of the name, seafood is the specialty at the **Duck Inn** (tel. 729-6663) at 705 Broadway; open Tues.-Sun. for breakfast (starting at 5 a.m.), lunch, and dinner. The only seafood place in town that overlooks the water is the **Sandollar Pavilion** (tel. 729-9589) at Fulton Beach Rd.; open daily 7 a.m.-10 p.m. If you're hankering for some barbecue, there's **Max's BBQ** (tel. 729-9388) at 815 E. Market; open Mon.-Sat. for lunch and dinner. For coffee-and-pastry breakfast, **Rockport Bakery** (tel. 729-5044) at State 35 N and Broadway is a good choice; open Mon.-Sat. 7 a.m.-5 p.m.

Events

March: The **Fulton Oysterfest** is held the first weekend of the month at Fulton Navigation Park, Fulton Beach Road. The two-day festival features a raw oyster-eating contest, oyster-shucking contest, seafood vendors, and outdoor concerts.

July: Sponsored by the Rockport Art Association, the **Rockport Art Festival** is held the nearest weekend to the Fourth of July at the festival grounds near the Rockport Center for the Arts. A tent village displays paintings, sculpture, woodwork, pottery, and other artwork by Rockport-Fulton artists as well as by other artists from throughout the Southwest. Most work is for sale.

October: The **Rockport Seafair,** held on the weekend preceding Columbus Day at the Rockport Harbor, features sailing regattas, arts and crafts shows, crab races, a gumbo cookoff, beauty pageant, parades, music, and lots of seafood booths.

Fishing

Sportfishing in the Rockport-Fulton area is not quite as serious an undertaking as in Port Aransas, but plenty of fishing opportunities are available. In Rockport, many motels have their own private fishing piers; ask if you're in doubt.

One of the best public spots in the area is the **Copano Bay Causeway State Park Fishing**

Pier, a 2.5-mile-long abandoned bridge that's been converted to a pier. A section in the middle is missing, so there's actually only about 1.5 pier miles. It's parallel to the Copano Bay Causeway (which joins the Rockport-Fulton Peninsula with the Lamar Peninsula to the north) and allows anglers to dangle their lines into the intersection of Copano and Aransas bays. At either end of the pier is a bait and tackle shop, snack bar, and restrooms. There's an entry fee of $1 per rod and reel.

You can also fish from the public pier at Fulton Navigation Harbor or join a party or charter boat from the same harbor for trips out into one of the bays; $18-25 for a half-day trip.

Another good fishing spot is the pier at Goose Island State Recreation Area.

Goose Island State Recreation Area

This 314-acre park encompasses the southernmost tip of the Lamar Peninsula, at the junction of the Aransas, Copano, and St. Charles bays, about 12 miles northeast of Rockport via the Copano Bay Causeway. The 174-acre mainland section of the park consists of live oak and redbay woodlands, coastal prairies, and wet inland meadows. Goose Island, just offshore, is 140 acres of tidal saltmarsh, salt flats, and grasslands. This is one of the lower coast's prime spots for viewing waterfowl, including great blue and Louisiana herons, common and snow egrets, killdeer, sandpipers, willets, terns, blue-winged teals, and many other species.

Facilities: The park has a 1,620-foot-long lighted fishing pier, boat launch, picnic areas, nature trails, bathhouses, and camping areas. Open shade shelters along the south shore of Goose Island, equipped with w/e, picnic tables, and cooking grills, cost $11. In the mainland park unit, in wooded areas, are tentsites with water nearby for $8 and tent/camper sites with w/e for $9. The entry fee for day use only is $3 per vehicle Mon.-Thurs., $4 Fri.-Sunday. For further information, contact the Park Superintendent (tel. 512-729-2858), Goose Island State Recreation Area, Star Route 1, Box 105, Rockport, TX 78382.

The Big Tree: Also known as the Lamar Oak, Bishop's Oak, and Goose Island Oak, this state-champion live oak grows just north of the park. Over a thousand years old, the tree is thought to have been used as a council tree by the Karankawa Indians and as a hanging tree around the turn of the century. Its venerable trunk measures 35 feet in circumference, the total height is 44 feet, and the crown has a spread of 89 feet. Take Palmetto Rd. north off Park 13 and follow the signs.

Bait and fishing tackle are readily available in Fulton.

Information

The **Rockport-Fulton Area Chamber of Commerce** (tel. 512-729-6445 or 800-826-6441), next to Rockport Harbor off Broadway, is open Mon.-Fri. 9 a.m.-5 p.m., Sat. 11 a.m.-4 p.m. Here you can pick up an excellent map of the area for $1.50 that includes a nautical map of Aransas and Copano bays. For birders, another worthwhile $1 chamber investment at the is the *Birder's Guide to Rockport-Fulton,* a full-color booklet featuring a driving guide to the area, bird sketches for identification, a bird checklist, and a comprehensive list of birding references and local resources. Also available for $1 is the 20-page *Fishing Guide to Rockport-Fulton,* which contains names of local fishing guides, tide tables, and pier and marina locations.

Twice a year the daily *Rockport Pilot* newspaper issues a *Visitor's Guide* supplement that contains comprehensive information on attractions, accommodations, fishing, and dining in Rockport-Fulton. Available free at the chamber of commerce.

ARANSAS NATIONAL WILDLIFE REFUGE

This is one of the crown jewels of the U.S. national wildlife refuge system. Founded in 1937 by President Franklin Delano Roosevelt as a refuge for the dwindling whooping crane population, it now protects over a dozen other endangered species as well, including the brown pelican, least tern, Attwater's prairie chicken, bald eagle, peregrine and aplomado falcons, Eskimo curlew, gray wolf, red wolf, jaguarundi, and coati.

Geography

The refuge covers 54,829 acres of the Blackjack Peninsula (named for the native blackjack oak), which is surrounded by the Aransas, San Antonio, and Mesquite bays. Habitats encompassed by the refuge include wooded sand dunes, brushland, live oak and redbay oak motts, cord grass prairies, tidal marshes, freshwater ponds, and marine bays.

Whooping Cranes

This is the refuge's most famous seasonal resident. The largest bird in North America, an adult whooper stands five feet tall with a 7.5-foot wingspread. Its name comes from the loud whooping call produced by its long, convoluted windpipe—John James Audubon claimed he could hear a whooper's call from three miles away. The bird's mating ritual is equally impressive, consisting of whooping, wing-flapping, head-bobbing, and huge leaps through the air. Whoopers mate for life and migrate in family groups of two to seven.

Whooping cranes were once prolific in North American skies, but hunting and human-induced habitat loss reduced the population by 1938 to only 10 adult whoopers and four youths on the entire continent. Through the dual efforts of U.S. and Canadian wildlife authorities (the bird's summer home is Woods Buffalo National Park in Alberta, Canada), Aransas whooper sightings in 1989 reached a record 146, a tenfold increase since the refuge was established.

Whooping cranes inhabit the refuge between November and March, after completing the 2,500-mile, 30-day journey from Canada. They can sometimes be seen at Mustang Lake from the observation tower (equipped with telescopes), about 4.5 miles from the refuge entrance, or you might glimpse a few flying overhead elsewhere in the park. Visitors often mistake other birds for the whooper, including sandhill cranes, snow geese, white pelicans, swans, and assorted herons. When these birds are standing in the water at some distance, the lighter-feathered species can be very difficult to tell apart. In flight, however, the whooper is easily distinguished by its black wing tips, long, straight neck, slow wing beat, and, most significantly, by the fact that its feet extend well beyond the tail. The sandhill crane also has feet that extend beyond its tail but lacks black wing tips and often flies alone or in larger flocks, rather than in the two-to-seven group.

The best way to see whooping cranes (as well as other waterfowl) during this time of year is to sign up with one of the several tour boats that cruise from Rockport-Fulton across Aransas Bay to San Antonio Bay along the refuge shores. **Captain Ted's Whooping Crane Tours** (tel. 512-729-9589 or 800-338-4551) is the oldest operation, guaranteeing whooper sightings or your money back. Captain Ted's MV *Skimmer* is docked next to the Sandollar Pavilion in Fulton and makes two trips daily, 7:45-11 a.m. and

12:45-4 p.m. The cost is $25 per adult, $15 per child under 12. The Sandollar Pavilion is open for breakfast at 7 a.m. for those who choose the early tour. At Rockport Harbor, the MV *Pisces* (tel. 729-7525 or 800-245-9324) and MV *Pelican* (tel. 729-8448) offer similar birding tours for $22 per adult, $14 under 12.

Other Wildlife

Birds: Aransas NWR attracts over 350 known bird species simply because its mild winters and tidal marshes produce an abundant, varied supply of food (vegetation, insects, fish, and shellfish) and water. Besides the magnificent whooping crane, the refuge is a temporary or permanent home for a variety of loons, grebes, pelicans, cormorants, frigate birds, bitterns, herons, ibis, spoonbills, storks, ducks, swans, geese, vultures, kites, hawks, falcons, the crested caracara (Mexico's national bird), wild turkey, plovers, sandpipers, gulls, terns, skimmers, doves, owls, goatsuckers, hummingbirds, woodpeckers, flycatchers, larks, swallows, jays, titmice, wrens, vireos, thrushes, thrashers, warblers, tanagers, sparrows, blackbirds, finches, and many other related species. A complete bird list is available at the refuge visitor center.

During the late spring, summer, and early fall, tour boats take visitors past various rookeries (bird colonies) along Aransas and Mesquite bay shores, including Blackjack Peninsula, San José ("St. Joe") Island, Matagorda Island, and a number of smaller isles. Times and rates are the same as for the whooping crane tours.

Mammals: Among the 80 mammalian species in the refuge, the largest are white-tailed deer, feral hogs (descendants of domesticated American hogs and European wild boar introduced to the area in the '30s and '40s), javelinas, the occasional axis deer who wander in from nearby game ranches, coyotes, red wolves (usually part coyote rather than purebred), and gray fox. Smaller mammals include ringtails, raccoons, coatis (rare), mink, long-tailed weasels, badgers, bobcats, cougars, three species of skunk, five species of bat, armadillos, blacktail rabbits, cotton-tailed rabbits, swamp rabbits, and opossums. Atlantic bottlenose dolphins are also common in the surrounding Aransas, Mesquite, and San Antonio bays.

Reptiles: The most popular reptile in the refuge is the American alligator, which is commonly seen in the lakes, sloughs, rivers, and marshes of the refuge. There are usually several loafing in Thomas Slough near the visitor center. Annual counts indicate there are about 250 gators living in the refuge, most in the four- to 10-foot-long range, with several individuals reaching 12-13 feet long. You can estimate a gator's length even if all you can see above water are its eyes and nostrils. Gauge the distance in inches between its eyes and nostrils, then transpose inches to feet and you'll know its approximate length. When provoked, gators make a hissing

Aransas alligator

sound. During mating season bull gators utter a loud roar and females reply with a groaning sound; baby gators make amusing burping and chirping sounds.

Though you're not very likely to see them, the refuge harbors at least 31 species of snakes. Six are venomous: the Texas coral snake, broad-banded copperhead, western cottonmouth, western massasauga, western pygmy rattlesnake, and western diamondback rattlesnake. Take care when walking in grassy areas.

Most of the sea turtles that turn up on the refuge shores are dead, killed by Gulf fishing nets. Live hawksbill sea turtles visit occasionally, and there are five other turtle species in the marshes and freshwater ponds farther inland.

Facilities

The **Wildlife Interpretive Center** near the refuge entrance is open daily 8 a.m.-4:30 p.m. and features a variety of displays, including taxidermic exhibits and an audiovisual program about the whooping crane. A 16-mile paved road makes a loop through the refuge and passes six different trailheads for nature trails of 0.2 to two miles in length. An observation tower overlooks Mustang Lake at the loop's 4.5-mile mark.

If you have a boat and want to navigate San Antonio Bay along the refuge shores on your own, you can use the private boat ramp at Harper's Landing, about two miles from the refuge entrance off FM 2040.

Practicalities: No camping is allowed in the refuge, but there's a picnic area near the Bay Overlook, about two miles from the entrance. No food or gas are available at the refuge; the nearest service stations are in Austwell (seven miles) and Tivoli (14 miles). Insect repellent is recommended year round for hikers.

Visiting hours are sunrise to sunset; admission is free.

Getting There

From the Rockport-Fulton area, take State 35 north to FM 774, then zigzag east on FM 774 (watch the curves—they're only slightly banked) to FM 2040, which leads southeast to the refuge entrance. Driving time from Rockport is 40-50 minutes. No public transport is available.

For further information, contact the Refuge Manager (tel. 512-286-3559), Aransas National Wildlife Refuge, P.O. Box 100, Austwell, TX 77950.

PADRE ISLAND NATIONAL SEASHORE

Padre Island, the longest coastal-barrier island in the world, extends 113 miles from Corpus Christi Pass, which once separated it from Mustang Island to the north, to Mansfield Channel, which separates it from South Padre Island to the south. Eighty miles of its length are under the protection of the National Park Service; the remaining portions (North Padre) belong to Corpus Christi, Nueces, or Kleberg counties.

Geography

The Island: The entire length of the Gulf side of Padre Island is sandy beach—one of the longest undeveloped beaches in North America. The beach is backed by a coastal dune ridge, held in place by salt-tolerant vegetation. On the Laguna Madre side of the dunes is a section of coastal grasslands that vary in width; in some places, the dunes extend all the way across the island. In other places, the land behind the dune ridge is submerged by washover channels. Beyond the grasslands, marshy tidal flats extend from the island's east edge into Laguna Madre.

Laguna Madre: Separating Padre Island from the mainland, this shallow, salty body of water covers an area of 609 square miles; the national seashore boundary runs well into the lagoon, protecting around 20,000 surface acres. The average natural depth is about 2.5 to three feet; in some places it's only a few inches deep. The Gulf Intracoastal Waterway at the lagoon's midline, however, reaches a depth of 14 feet, with a width of around 225 feet. The waterway was constructed in 1949 and forms a 1,116-mile link between Brownsville, Texas, and St. Marks, Florida. The sand and silt ("spoil") dredged during construction of the waterway have been allowed to form islands called "spoil banks"; these have since taken on local vegetation, and some have even become bird nesting grounds.

No major rivers flow into Laguna Madre, so salinity is quite high. Tides are largely wind-con-

PADRE ISLAND JELLYFISH

Seven species of jellyfish are commonly seen near the shores of Padre Island. Only two pack a sting powerful enough to bother humans. The Portuguese man-of-war (*Physalia physalia*) is a pretty, translucent blue blob with see-through tentacles up to 40 feet long; the tentacles are loaded with a venom that can cause a severe stinging sensation upon contact, even when the man-of-war is shriveling on the beach. The venom is actually 75% as strong as cobra venom, but humans rarely receive a dose high enough to cause serious injury or death. The man-of-war is a hydrozoan, meaning it doesn't move laterally under its own power but merely drifts with sea currents, so if you see one in the water, don't assume it's coming for you. They can turn up anytime of year but are most common in the spring when Gulf currents are changing directions.

The other jellyfish to avoid is the sea nettle (*Chrysaora quinquecirrha*), a bell-shaped creature with long tentacles around the bell's edge and four very long oral arms extending from the center underside of the bell. The tentacles vary in color from clear to pink to rust-brown. They're most commonly encountered in Laguna Madre during the summer.

The park staff at Malaquite Beach Visitor Center and at the ranger station a mile north of Malaquite Beach are adept at treating jellyfish stings. If you plan to visit a remote part of the park, especially in the spring, bring along a supply of unseasoned meat tenderizer; make sure it contains papain, an enzyme derived from papaya. To treat a sting, rub the affected area with alcohol, then make a paste of tenderizer and alcohol and rub it gently into the area. Papain neutralizes the proteins in jellyfish venom almost immediately on application, bringing welcome relief.

Not all jellyfish that end up at Padre Island are bothersome. One intriguing hydrozoan, the by-the-wind sailor (*Velella velella*), looks like a frisbee with a miniature sail on top. The plastic-like disk floats on the water surface and the little sail helps to speed it on its way. Polyps along the edge of the disk specialize in reproduction, feeding, and stinging. Look for them in spring when they're blown onto the beach, usually minus their polyps.

---

trolled. Because of the lack of riverine (and Gulf) interference and the absence of human population centers, the middle and lower sections of the lagoon, between Baffin Bay and Port Mansfield, are virtually free of pollution.

Wildlife

Fish, Mollusks, and Crustaceans: The aquatic interplay of lagoon, tidal flats, washover channels, and gulf waters produces a perfect environment for the spawning, foraging, and nursing of fish and shellfish species. Many local species spawn in one area, nurse in another, and forage in yet another, participating in a cycle that wouldn't be viable anywhere else. Redfish, for example, spawn in the gulf but spend most of their lives in Laguna Madre; young shrimp nurse in the laguna but move to the gulf as adults.

Fishing, within state legal limits, is permitted in the park. On the lagoon side, flounder, sheepshead, black drum, redfish, skipjack, striped mullet, and speckled trout are common; on the gulf side are sand trout, pompano, mackerel, tarpon, and, farther offshore, grouper, bonito, kingfish, red snapper, marlin, and sailfish. Commercial harvesting of gamefish in the Laguna Madre has been banned since 1981; as of 1994 the bay's finfish population registered the highest levels since the Texas Parks and Wildlife Department began counting in 1975.

A variety of oysters and crabs make their home among the island's intertidal zones. Crabs are especially plentiful; over 20 species are commonly seen, including the blue crab, the hermit crab, and a type of sand crab called "ghost shrimp" for its resemblance to shrimp.

Mammals: The most common mammals on Padre Island are rodents—squirrels, gophers, and moles—including one species that evolved here, the Padre Island kangaroo rat. Black-tailed jackrabbits, raccoons, and coyotes are also common. White-tailed deer, javelina, and nilgai (an African antelope introduced to nearby game ranches) occasionally visit from the mainland, wading across tidal flats. Three species of dolphin frequent nearby waters: the Atlantic bottlenose dolphin, the Atlantic spotted dolphin, and the bridled dolphin.

Reptiles: Five sea turtle species occasionally turn up on Padre beaches: Kemp's ridley, loggerhead, hawksbill, Atlantic green, and leatherback. All five are threatened or endangered, but the most endangered is the Kemp's ridley. In 1947, its numbers were estimated at 162,000; now there are fewer than 2,000 adults left in the world. Their main hatching ground is a 16-mile beach at Rancho Nuevo, Tamaulipas, Mexico; international efforts are underway to induce younger turtles to use Padre Island for nesting, since the Mexican market for sea turtle eggs, meat, skin, and shells makes protection at Rancho Nuevo very difficult. In the U.S., taking any sea turtle into possession is a felony punishable by fines up to $20,000.

Approximately 32 species of snake are known to inhabit the island; the most commonly seen are the western coachwhip, Mexican milk snake, Gulf Coast ribbon snake, and checkered garter snake—all harmless to humans. Two venomous species, the western diamondback and western massasauga, have been sighted but are considered uncommon.

Birds: Shorebirds and waterfowl are seen in abundant numbers on the island. Resident species include laughing, ring-billed, and herring gulls; royal, forester's and Caspian terns; black skimmers; brown and white pelicans; reddish and great blue herons; black-necked stilts, willets, long-billed curlews; American avocets; piping and black-bellied plovers; ruddy turnstones, and killdeer.

Facilities

Malaquite Beach Visitor Center: About a mile past the national seashore entrance is Malaquite Beach, the only beach area on the island with lifeguards on duty. Swimming is permitted anywhere along the Gulf shoreline, however. Next to the beach is the recently reconstructed visitor center, comprised of an interpretive center, observation deck, snack bar, gift shop, and bathhouse. The interpretive center has numerous books, brochures, and handouts on Padre Island attractions and activities. Most are distributed free, but one worth purchasing is *Padre Island National Seashore: A Guide to the Geology, Natural Environments, and History of a Texas Barrier Island,* published by the University of Texas. The staff is also quite knowledgeable. The visitor center is open 9 a.m.-6 p.m.

during the summer, 9 a.m.-4 p.m. the rest of the year.

Camping: A paved campground is situated a half mile north of Malaquite Beach and provides a supply of fresh water, cold showers, restrooms, picnic tables, and a dump station. No RV hookups are available. Cooking grills aren't provided, but campfires are allowed anywhere on the beach between the dunes and the water. This policy is the same for the entire island, except that no fires are allowed on Malaquite Beach. Camping fees are $5 a night, $2.50 for seniors. During the summer, park rangers present campfire programs at Malaquite Campground every evening; during the winter (Jan.-May), the programs are held on Friday and Saturday nights only. Rangers also lead seashore walks on weekends. A schedule of topics is available at the center.

About a mile south of the Visitor Center, the **South Beach** campground features no-fee primitive camping for tents and campers; chemical toilets are the only facilities. At **Bird Island Basin,** opposite Malaquite Beach on the Laguna Madre side of the island, is a no-fee primitive camping area suitable for tents or campers; chemical toilets are provided. Farther south at **Yarborough Pass** (Milepost 15), also on the Laguna Madre side, is another no-fee primitive camping area with chemical toilets (this one also has tables); to reach the area, however, you must hike or drive a four-wheel-drive vehicle.

No-fee primitive camping is also permitted anywhere on the Gulf side of the island. Camping is allowed on the beaches only, not on the dunes or in the grasslands.

Wherever you camp on the island, the NPS enforces a 14-day limit.

Beach Driving

The paved road into the park ends just after the visitor center. Beyond this point, driving is permitted on the beach only. For the first five miles, beach conditions are usually suitable for any kind of vehicle; after that, a four-wheel-drive or other off-road vehicle is necessary because the sand becomes too loose and full of shells. Four-wheel-drive vehicles are sometimes available for rent in Corpus Christi for around $75 for 24 hours; try **Advantage Car Rental** (tel. 512-289-5364) at Corpus Christi International Airport.

Even with a powerful four-by-four, careful preparation is necessary if you want to proceed beyond Milepost 5. The National Park Service recommends drivers carry extra fuel, extra water, car jack, basic tool kit, long-handled shovel, tow rope, and a few loose boards for traction if your vehicle gets stuck. To this list, add extra food, tent, and a flashlight with extra batteries if you plan to camp overnight.

Just past Milepost 5 is Little Shell Beach, named for the shell types commonly found here—mostly coquina clams. The shells pile up to one side of the beach to form shell banks. The trick in driving through here and across the next stretch (Big Shell Beach) is finding the right driving line between the deepest shell banks on the right and the softest sand on the left—it's very easy to get bogged down in either. Follow other vehicle tracks when they're visible. Big Shell Beach has coarse sand mixed with shells that makes it even more difficult to navigate without getting stuck.

After 10-15 miles, Big Shell Beach gives way to conditions similar to Little Shell Beach, which continue to the island's end at Mansfield Channel—a distance of about 60 miles from the Malaquite Beach Visitor Center.

Backpacking

Only the very hardy should attempt to hike the seashore's entire length. There is no fresh water and no shade available along the way. Hiking is only allowed on the beach, and progress is slow—10 miles a day maximum, which means six days to reach Mansfield Channel. A more reasonable goal might be to hike to Yarborough Pass at Milepost 15, where there's a primitive campsite with toilets, or to Cuba Island, a small offshore island on the Laguna Madre side at Milepost 21. Backpacking prerequisites for Padre Island include plenty of sunscreen, insect repellent, a broad-brimmed hat, sunglasses, a backpacking stove, tent, food, and at least a gallon of water per person per day. A rod and reel might make a handy addition, too—you can catch sand crabs to use as bait along the way. The most popular backpacking season on the island is winter, since the weather's cooler.

Boating and Windsurfing

The park has one boat launch at Bird Island Basin on Laguna Madre. This is also a popular spot for dedicated windsurfers looking to avoid the crowds in Corpus Christi.

Entry Fee

A seven-day pass into Padre Island National Seashore costs $5 per vehicle or $2 per person for pedestrians and cyclists. A year's pass is also available for just $10.

Information

For further information, contact the Park Superintendent (tel. 512-937-2621), Padre Island National Seashore, 9405 S. Padre Island Dr., Corpus Christi, TX 78418.

SOUTH PADRE ISLAND AND PORT ISABEL

If the Mansfield Channel hadn't been constructed in 1964, 34-mile South Padre Island would still be attached to Padre Island. It has most of the same geographic features as its progenitor, but since it's not part of the national seashore, it has all the amenities of a modern beach resort. Although I've placed it under "Vicinity of Corpus Christi" for convenience, South Padre is over 150 miles by road from Corpus and might best be combined with a visit to Brownsville in the Rio Grande Valley.

Port Isabel sits on the mainland just across Laguna Madre from South Padre. Linked by a causeway, the two communities function together as a sort of twin-tourist destination—Port Isabel provides history while South Padre has the beaches. The twin towns sit at the same latitude as Fort Lauderdale, Florida, and Loreto, Baja California Sur.

History

In the 16th and 17th centuries, Spanish colonists called what is now Padre (and South Padre) Island a variety of names, including Isla Santiago, Isla Corpus Christi, and Isla Blanca. They largely ignored the island, however, since it had a bad reputation among ship captains. At least 20 Spanish galleons ran aground here in the 16th century; it was also an area frequented by pirates who raided Spanish ships. In 1800, Catholic priest Padre Nicolas Balli applied for and received a Spanish land grant to establish

Rancho Santa Cruz about 26 miles from the island's southern end. He raised cattle, sheep, and horses here until his death in 1829, and the island was afterward renamed in his honor.

The island remained abandoned until John Singer, of sewing machine fame, and his wife built a driftwood home on the site of Balli's ranch in 1847. When the Civil War broke out, they buried $62,000 in jewelry and gold coins among the sand dunes and fled. When they returned after the war to retrieve their treasure trove, the dunes had shifted; they never found it and the loot remains undiscovered to this day.

Throughout the remainder of the 1800s and most of the 1900s, Padre Island remained virtually untouched. The nearest mainland point, Port Isabel, was originally named El Frontón de Santa Isabela by Mexican settlers in the 1830s. It became an important transshipment port during the mid-1800s, but with the arrival of the railroads in South Texas, it quickly declined into a small fishing port. The only access to Padre Island was by boat until a causeway was built from Port Isabel in 1954. In 1964, South Padre was lopped from Padre Island 34 miles from the southern end to form the Mansfield Channel, also called the Mansfield Cut. By this time, South Padre was beginning to attract a small contingent of avid anglers and nature lovers, but there were few facilities available for long-term stays. The hotel-motel industry wasn't anxious to build on the island because very few insurance companies would insure property in the hurricane zone.

Things changed in the '70s when a state law was passed that required insurance companies to provide hurricane coverage. Motels and condominiums began appearing one by one, and in 1974 a 2.6-mile, four-lane bridge (the Queen Isabella Causeway, the state's longest) was built to replace the earlier span. Today, only the southernmost five miles or so of the island are developed. Padre Blvd. (Park 100) runs up the center of the island another 10 miles; beyond this, the northern 20 miles remain completely undeveloped. The barrier island's average width is only a half mile.

Port Isabel Sights

Point Isabel Lighthouse State Historic Structure: This Parks and Wildlife-administered lighthouse at the intersection of State 100 and Tar-

avana (at the causeway) is the only one of 16 such structures along the Texas coast open to the public. Because Port Isabel had become an important port for vessels coming through the Brazos Santiago Pass (which links the Gulf of Mexico and Laguna Madre between South Padre Island and Brazos Island to the south), the U.S. government funded the construction of the lighthouse in 1851-53. It was originally crowned with a light that could be seen 16 miles away. During the Civil War, the beacon was extinguished and both Confederate and Union troops used it as an observation tower. After the war, it was relit and continued to operate as a lighthouse intermittently until 1905, when it was abandoned.

The State Parks and Wildlife Department acquired the structure in 1950 and had it restored by 1970, when it was opened to the public. Although the current mercury-vapor light is not as powerful as the original beacon, the tower is still marked on nautical charts as a navigation aid.

At the top of the 53-foot-high lighthouse is a rewarding view of Port Isabel, South Padre Island, Laguna Madre, and the Gulf. It's open daily 10 a.m.-5 p.m.; admission is $1 adults, 50 cents children 6-12.

The *Lady Bea* Shrimp Boat: Near the lighthouse in Beulah Lee Park, this restored trawler provides a close-up look at the outriggers, nets, and winches that are used in the shrimping industry. It's open 24 hours a day and is a first phase in the Laguna Madre Museum Foundation's effort to establish a permanent maritime museum in the park. When the museum facility is complete, it will contain photos, artifacts, and memorabilia related to local history, plus a souvenir shop. Free admission.

South Padre Island Sights

Pan American University Coastal Studies Laboratory: This university research facility, located in Isla Blanca Park at the south end of the island, focuses on the coastal ecosystems of South Texas and North Mexico, particularly the marine biology of Laguna Madre and the Gulf. It's also an important participant in the Texas Marine Mammal and Sea Turtle Stranding and Salvaging Network, which works to save whales, dolphins, and sea turtles that become stranded along the coast. A public education area features aquarium exhibits and displays of local flora. Open Sun.-Fri. 1:30-4:30 p.m.; admission to the lab is free, but Isla Blanca Park charges a $1.50 vehicle fee. For further information, call (210) 761-2644.

Isla Blanca Park: Though the northernmost 20 miles of South Padre offer acre after acre of virtually deserted beaches, this park at the southern tip of the island has the most popular beach. That's because it's the only beach on the island with a bathhouse, food concession, equipment rental, and other beach-going amenities, as well as a marina, campground, RV park, fishing jetty, cabins, shaded pavilion, and various civic facilities. Admission to the park is $1.50 per vehicle per day.

Sea Turtles, Inc. ("The Turtle Lady"): Ila Loetscher, known as "The Turtle Lady," is the founder of a nonprofit organization whose main purpose is the preservation of the endangered Kemp's ridley sea turtle. Ila's home at 5805 Gulf Blvd. has been turned into a sea turtle rehabili-

dunes, Padre Island

BILL REAVES, TEXAS HIGHWAYS

tation center where people bring stranded turtles. Ila and her assistants care for them until they can be released again into the open sea.

To support the organization, Ila offers "Meet the Turtles" programs Tues. and Sat. at 10 a.m. (Sept.-April) or 9 a.m. (May-August). Visitors are shown turtles in rehabilitation, including the Kemp's ridley; she sometimes offers performing turtles in costume. She asks for a donation of $2 (or more) per person at the door.

Hotels, Motels, Condominiums, and Beach Houses

The South Padre Island Convention and Visitors Bureau lists 55 places to stay along the gulf shore, 14 along Laguna Madre ("the bay"), and 28 in the middle of the island ("inner island"). Gulf hotels, motels, and condos generally cost more than inner island and bay locations.

See the "South Padre Island Hotels, Motels, and Condominiums" chart for information on selected locations. Rental agencies that handle reservations for condos not listed include **Island Services** (tel. 210-761-2649 or 800-426-6530), **Sand Dollar Realty and Management** (tel. 761-7857 or 800-527-0294), and **Padre Rentals** (tel. 761-5100 or 800-292-7518). Condos and beach houses start at around $80 a night for a one-bedroom place with a kitchen; discounts for weekly and monthly rentals.

Campgrounds and RV Parks

No-fee primitive camping is permitted at county-operated **Andy Bowie Park,** 3.5 miles north of the causeway on the gulf beach. An open pavilion and trash receptacles are the only facilities; no stay limit.

The only other legal place to camp on the island is **Isla Blanca Park** (tel. 210-761-5493) at the south end of Park 100. Tent camping is $8.50 a night. Two-way hookups are $11 a day, $50 a week, $165 a month, and $900 for six months; three-way hookups are $12 a night, $60 a week, $180 a month, and $1,000 for six months. There are also 18 screened cabins available, each with two double bunk beds (no linens), refrigerator, and stove for $25 a night. Other facilities at the park include a marina with 65 slips ($6-12 per day) and two boat ramps, restrooms and showers, grocery store, laundry, dump station, nondenominational chapel, and

SOUTH PADRE HOTELS, MOTELS, AND CONDOMINIUMS

Prices quoted are for the peak season, Memorial Day to Labor Day. Spring, fall, and winter rates are typically 30-60% less and discounts are usually offered for two-night and weekly stays. All condominiums listed have kitchens. Unless otherwise noted, accommodations face the Gulf of Mexico. Add 13% hotel tax to all rates. Area code: 210.

Bahia Mar Resort; 6300 Padre; tel. 761-1343 or (800) 292-7502; $140-175; pool, tennis courts

Bay Breeze Condominiums; 201 W. Red Snapper; tel. 761-7281; $75-85; inner island

Best Western Fiesta Isles Hotel; 5701 Padre; tel. 761-4913; $84-108; inner island, pool, kitchenettes available

The Breakers; 708 Padre Blvd.; tel. 761-2606 or (800) 447-4753; indoor pool, tennis, no springbreakers

Castaways Condominiums; 3700 Gulf; tel. 761-1903 or (800) 221-5218; $90-125; pool, no spring-breakers

Continental Condominiums; 4908 Gulf; tel. 761-1306; $105; pool

Days Inn South Padre; 3913 Padre; tel. 761-7831 or (800) 325-2525; $80; inner island, pool

Fisherman's Lodge; 214 West Saturn; tel. 761-2303; $45-65; bay, one-bedroom efficiencies with kitchenettes, fishing pier

Fisherman's Wharf; 211 W. Swordfish; tel. 761-7818 or (800) 752-9889; $55-65; bay

Gulfview I & II Condominiums; 250-260 Padre; tel. 761-5910; $90-190; inner island, pool, tennis courts

Holiday Inn SunSpree Resort; 100 Padre; tel. 761-5401 or (800) 531-7405; $75-95; pool, tennis courts

Island Inn; 5100 Gulf; tel. 761-7677; $65-180; pool

Laguna Motel; 201 W. Swordfish; tel. 761-2550 or (800) 647-2550; $45-65; inner island, no spring-breakers

La Internacional Condominiums; 5008 Gulf; tel. 761-1306 or (800) 221-5218 (in TX); $75; pool

Landfall Tower Resort Condominiums; 6402 Padre; tel. 761-4909 or (800) 683-1930; $82-160; bay, pool, tennis courts

Las Brisas Condominiums; 227 W. Morningside; tel. 761-5111 or (800) 241-5111; $85-145; bay, pool, tennis courts

Padre South Resort; 1500 Gulf; tel. 761-4951; $120; pool

Radisson Resort South Padre Island; 500 Padre; tel. 761-6511 or (800) 333-3333 (outside TX); $129-240; pool, tennis courts

Sand Castle Condominiums; 200 W. Kingfish; tel. (800) 221-5218 (in TX); $48-68; bay, pool

Sea Grape Motel; 120 E. Jupiter; tel. 761-2471; $55; inner island, pool

Seaside Apartments; 3201 Gulf Blvd.; tel. 761-7035; $65-85; inner island

Sheraton Fiesta South Padre Island Resort; 310 Padre; tel. 761-6551; $140; large pool, tennis courts

South Padre Marina Condominiums; 6201 Padre; tel. 761-7476 or (800) 637-9365; $95-120; bay, pool, tennis courts

Surf Motel; 2612 Gulf; tel. 761-2831 or (800) 723-6519; $65; pool

Tiki Condominium Hotel; 6608 Padre; tel. 761-2694 or (800) 879-8454; $98-125; pool, tennis courts, kitchens available, no spring-breakers

Vista Del Mar Condominiums; 102 E. Pompano; tel. 761-2766; $83; inner island, no spring-breakers

civic center. For cabin or campsite reservations, contact Isla Blanca Park (tel. 761-5493), P.O. Box 2106, South Padre Island, TX 78597.

Port Isabel Food

Port Isabel restaurants enjoy a better overall reputation, perhaps because they're more es-

tablished and less tourist-oriented than those on South Padre Island. They're also more expensive. The town's most renowned restaurant is the **Yacht Club** (tel. 210-943-1301) at 700 Yturria. First opened in 1929 as a private club, the restaurant has been public for many years now and serves excellent seafood, including blue crab-stuffed jalapeños, ceviche, and various combination platters, plus a few beef and chicken dishes. You can order red snapper broiled, blackened, meunière, and "Amsterdam-style," topped with shrimp, *beurre blanc*, and caviar. The wine list is extensive. It's open Thurs.-Tues. for dinner only and is moderately expensive.

A less expensive seafood place here is **Cross-Eyed Pelican** (tel. 943-8923) at 823 Garcia. It's open Mon.-Fri. for lunch and dinner, Saturday for dinner only; the menu features all-you-can-eat lunch buffets Mon.-Fri. and dinner specials Mon.-Saturday. **Pirate's Landing** (tel. 943-3663) at 100 N. Garcia, between the lighthouse and the water, also offers inexpensive all-you-can-eat seafood specials and is open daily for lunch and dinner.

For Mexican-style seafood, try the inexpensive **Mexquito** (tel. 943-6106) at 802 S. Garcia; open daily for lunch and dinner (all-you-can-eat dinner specials on Wednesday and Friday evenings). Good Mexican breakfasts and lunches are available at **Lupita's Cafe** (tel. 943-89-7) at 103 State 100; open Mon.-Sat. 7 a.m.-3 p.m., Sunday 7 a.m.-1 p.m.

You can buy fresh seafood to cook yourself at Port Isabel's **B&A Seafood Market** (tel. 943-2461) or **Quik Stop** (tel. 943-1159), both on State 100. The **IGA Val-U-Fest** at Las Palmas Plaza on State 100 is Port Isabel's only full-service grocery. At **Gulf Seafood & Mini Mart** (tel. 943-4501), at 207 Maxan St., you can buy seafood to go 8 a.m.-9 p.m. or sit on the patio 11 a.m.-6 p.m. and eat boiled shrimp, oysters, or fried fish.

South Padre Food

For such a small community, South Padre has loads of restaurants and cafes. This means business competition is keen, so prices stay at very reasonable levels.

Rossi's Italian Ristorante (tel. 210-761-9361), 2412 Padre Blvd., is one of the better bargains. The menu includes seafood and Italian standards such as eggplant parmigiana, fried oysters, manicotti, and flounder primavera. Dinner specials are under $6, lunch specials are under $4, breakfast specials are as low as $1.50 (two eggs, hash browns, grits or beans, and toast or tortilla) or $4.99 for all you can eat.

Jake's (tel. 761-5012), 2400 Padre Blvd., has good, moderately priced seafood, steak, and Mexican; open daily for lunch and dinner. A more extensive Tex-Mex menu is available at **Jesse's Cantina & Restaurant** (tel. 761-4500), 2700 Padre Blvd., including fajitas, *carnitas, camarones rancheros, pollo guisada, picadillo,* enchiladas, flautas, fresh-made corn and flour tortillas, and potent margaritas; open daily for lunch and dinner. **Peso's** (tel. 761-7890) at 4001 Padre Blvd. specializes in buckets of fajitas with all the trimmings (*pico de gallo,* sour cream, rice, beans, and tortillas) to go; open 11 a.m.-11 p.m. daily.

The most popular restaurant on the island these days, **Sea Ranch** (tel. 761-1314), opposite Charlie's Paradise at 1 Padre Blvd., serves well-prepared fresh seafood in a pleasant, Cape Cod-style setting with one of the island's better sunset views. It's open daily for lunch and dinner; long waits are the norm on summer evenings. If you can't get into Sea Ranch, the outdoor section of **Louie's Backyard** (tel. 761-6406) at Laguna and Ling is also good for sunsets, though the food is definitely second- or third-place. Louie's is popular with the eat-till-you-bust crowd for its generous nightly buffet.

La Jaiba (tel. 761-9878), 2001 Padre Blvd., specializes in fresh Gulf seafood only, at reasonable prices; open Tues.-Sun. for lunch and dinner. **Dolphin Cove Oyster Bar** (tel. 761-2850), a grass shack overlooking Brazos Santiago Pass in Isla Blanca Park, serves only fresh-shucked oyster and you-peel-'em shrimp. On Tuesday and Thursday beers cost just 50 cents each.

If you're looking for an early breakfast, **Rovan's Bakery, Restaurant & BBQ** (tel. 761-6872) at 5300 Padre Blvd. opens at 6 a.m. In addition to a variety of breakfasts and baked goods, Rovan's does mesquite-barbecued brisket, chicken, ribs, and sausage—but don't dally because the place closes at 6 p.m.

The **Oasis Cafe** (tel. 761-5332), in Naturally's Health Food Store at 3112-A Padre Blvd., serves healthy, homemade soups, sandwiches, salads, stir-fry, and juices. Open Mon.-Sat. 10 a.m.-5:30 p.m.

The **IGA Blue Marlin Supermarket** at 2216 Padre Blvd. sells fresh seafood, produce, and other groceries; open daily.

Entertainment

The larger South Padre hotels have clubs with live music, but it's pretty middle-of-the-road stuff. The island's biggest live music venue is **Charlie's Paradise** (tel. 210-761-9409), opposite Sea Ranch on the Gulf side of Padre Boulevard. Charlie's hosts a mixture of local and national touring acts in a casual warehouse-style room; outside are a guitar-shaped pool, bar, and the Skycoaster, a variation on bungee-jumping in which up to three persons bundled together trace a long, high arc through the air while dangling from an A-shaped scaffold.

The **Third Coast** (tel. 210-761-6192), 5908 Padre Blvd., features live country music most nights and has a few pool tables. **Coconuts Bar & Grill** (tel. 761-4218), Marlin and Laguna, plays recorded rock and reggae during the week and occasionally hosts live bands on weekends. The **Island Pub** (tel. 761-1734) at 2300 Padre Blvd. offers DJ dancing, an outside bar, and an extended noon-9 p.m. happy hour that includes free munchies.

During the summer, open-air bars are popular, including **Parrot Eyes Island** (tel. 761-9457), 6101 Padre Blvd., and **Tequila Sunset** (tel. 761-6198), 2300 W. Pike.

Events

College/university **spring break** brings over 100,000 youthful revelers to the island starting around the second or third week in March; the stragglers are usually gone by the end of the first week in April.

A variety of sailing regattas and fishing tournaments are held on the island from June to August. The biggest event, held the first week of August at various South Padre and Port Isabel locations, is the **Texas International Fishing Tournament,** the state's second-oldest state fishing event. Trophies and cash prizes are awarded in a variety of categories, including both bay and offshore fishing.

Windsurfing competitions take place around the beginning of May, including the **South Padre Island Windsurfing Blowout.** During June's **Windjammer Regatta,** 70-80 Hobie catamarans compete in two days of races near the beach in front of Sunchase III Condominiums. Call the South Padre Island Convention and Visitors Bureau (tel. 210-761-6433 or 800-343-2368) for the latest schedule information.

In early October the Rio Grande Valley Vegetarian Society holds its annual **Lone Star Vegetarian Chili Cookoff** at the South Padre Island Convention Center. Don't knock it till you've tried it—some of the recipes combine chiles and fresh vegetables in ways that would make any meat-eating chili cook sit up and take notes. Call 831-0698 for more information.

Fishing

Piers and Jetties: Captain Murphy's Fishing Pier (tel. 210-943-7437) at Purdy's Point, just north of the foot of Queen Isabella Causeway in Port Isabel, is a lighted pier open 24 hours. The pier store offers snacks, tackle, fishing licenses, and bait; rental tackle is also available. The fee for using the pier is $2.25 per rod for a 12-hour period; non-fishing spectators pay 75 cents. A variety of Laguna Madre fish take the hook here, including flounder and redfish.

The jetties at Isla Blanca Park are also suitable for fishing ($1.50 vehicle entry fee).

Bay and Surf: Wade-fishing in the Laguna Madre "flats" (shallow sand flats) is popular and free—look for flounder, sheepshead, and croaker, plus occasional redfish and speckled trout. Surfcasting on the Gulf side is a bit more difficult but offers a wider variety of redfish, speckled trout, black drum, whiting, and sand trout.

Crabbing: Laguna Madre is full of crabs. The hunting's best in shallow areas, from piers or flatbottom boats. All you need for a crabbing expedition is a length of twine equal to the water's depth, crab bait (chicken meat is recommended), and a handnet; net the crab *before* you pull it from the water or it'll let go of the bait.

Fishing Boats: Rates are virtually the same among all outfitters. **Jim's Pier** (tel. 761-2865) at 209 S. Whiting (north of the causeway, Laguna Madre side) operates party and charter boats for both bay and deep-sea fishing. A four-hour bay trip is $14 per person, bait included. All-day red snapper expeditions cost $60 per person including all tackle and bait. Deep-sea trolling for kingfish, wahoo, ling, dolphinfish, and yellowfin tuna runs $350 for a five-hour trip for up to four anglers; add $25 for each additional person. Marlin and sailfish charters are also available starting at $900 a day for up to four people. Jim's also has a boat launching facility for privately owned boats, a bait and tackle shop, and a Shamrock gas station.

One block up, off Swordfish St., is **Fisherman's Wharf** (tel. 761-7818) with similar facilities and rates. South of the causeway near the entrance to Isla Blanca Park, at Sea Ranch Marina, is **Captain Murphy's Charter Services** (tel. 761-2764), which specializes in deep-sea red snapper expeditions.

Beach Activities

Sonny's Beach Service at the Sheraton Fiesta Resort offers banana boat, sailboat, and parasailing rides, and also rents waverunners, boogie boards, flotation rafts and tubes, beach umbrellas and beach chairs. **Water Sport Center** (tel. 210-761-1060), next to Louie's Backyard on the Laguna Madre, offers a similar array of activities on the bay side at lower rates.

Horseback riding along the beach can be arranged at **Island Equestrian** (tel. 761-HOSS), a half mile north of the convention center.

Windsurfing and Sailing: Windsurf the Boatyard (tel. 761-5061) at 212 W. Dolphin rents catamarans, sailboards, and kayaks by the hour or day. Staff also offer instruction for each craft. **Windsurf on the Bay** (tel. 761-1434) at 224 W. Carolyn on South Padre Island specializes in boardsailing equipment, rentals, and instruction. Padre's best windsurfing months are Sept.-May, when winds on the bay side average a steady 18 miles per hour.

Scuba Diving

American Diving (tel. 210-761-2030), at 401 State 100 in Port Isabel and 1807 Padre Blvd. on South Padre, has a 60-foot boat that takes divers out for offshore oil rig and shipwreck exploration. American also offers NAUI-certified instruction and equipment rental. Non-divers may be interested in the shop's "Dolphin Watch," a two-hour tour aboard the MV *Diver 1* to see bottlenose and spinner dolphins.

Ocean Quest Dive Center (tel. 761-5003), at 5009 Padre Blvd., also offers scuba equipment, rental, and instruction.

Information

Tourist Offices: The **South Padre Island Convention and Visitors Bureau** (tel. 210-761-6433 or 800-343-2368 in the U.S. and Canada), at 600 Padre Blvd. across from the causeway, has a full-service information desk that's open Mon.-Fri. 9 a.m.-6 p.m., Saturday and Sunday 10 a.m.-5 p.m. The **Port Isabel Chamber of Commerce** (tel. 943-2262 or 800-527-6102 in TX), at 213 Yturria, also has information on the area; the office is open Mon.-Fri. 9 a.m.-4 p.m.

Publications: The free monthly *South Padre Parade* newspaper is full of information on attractions and activities in the Port Isabel-South Padre area, plus the latest restaurant and happy-hour specials. You can pick it up at the Convention and Visitors Bureau or at any one of 150 other locations around the island and in Port Isabel. Other similar freebies include the weekly *Coastal Current* and *The Island Times*.

Telephone: The area code for the South Padre and Port Isabel area is 210.

Transportation: The nearest full-service airport to South Padre/Port Isabel is **Valley International** in Harlingen, 40 minutes away by car or taxi. Nearby Brownsville has a smaller but expanding airport, **Brownsville/South Padre Island International,** with direct daily flights from Houston. This airport is only 20 minutes by car from South Padre. **B.B.'s Taxi** (tel. 761-2851) operates a 24-hour taxi service, including transport to Valley International Airport and Matamoros, Mexico.

You can rent bicycles and cars at **American Auto Rental** (tel. 761-5000), 4812 Padre Boulevard.

"The Wave," a motorized trolley, picks up passengers along Padre Blvd. for 50 cents per ride or $1 for unlimited rides all day.

Port Mansfield

This town didn't exist until the 1940s when Willacy County officials convinced the King Ranch to sell them 2,500 acres of coastal ranchland to build a fishing port. It's still surrounded by ranches; the nearest town of any substance is Raymondville, 24 miles west. The port is opposite the Mansfield Channel, which severs South Padre Island from Padre Island proper. Because of the co-mingling of Gulf and Laguna Madre fish at this point and the area's isolation from large human populations, the fishing here is some of the best along the Texas coast. Port Mansfield is also the only "wet" town—where mixed drinks can be sold—in an otherwise dry Willacy County.

Fishing: This is Port Mansfield's solitary attraction. At **Fred Stone County Park** at the north end of town is a lighted public pier open 24 hours. Onshore facilities include a fish-cleaning station and restrooms. Many of the local beach houses also have private piers. If you can get there (you need a boat), the jetties on either side of the channel are good fishing spots.

The **Port Mansfield Guides Association** (tel. 210-844-2528), P.O. Box 148, Port Mansfield, TX 78598, maintains a roster of experienced fishing guides for bay or Gulf trips. Besides the usual party and charter fishing boats offered in other coastal towns, the association maintains fishing barges anchored in Laguna Madre near prime fishing grounds. The barges are equipped with bunkhouses; the owners ferry their clients out to the platforms for overnight fishing trips at about $30 per person per night.

The association can also arrange boat transport to Padre Island National Seashore, directly opposite, for about $40 roundtrip.

Accommodations: Beach houses rent for $35-100 a night. The **Port Mansfield Chamber of Commerce** (tel. 944-2354), P.O. Box O, Port Mansfield, TX 78598, or **Glaze Realty** (tel. 944-2355), 701 Bayshore, can assist with reservations.

Fisherman's Inn (tel. 944-2882), **Casa de Pescadores** (tel. 944-2333), and **Harbor House Inn** (tel. 944-2888) rent rooms and efficiency apartments for $30-75 a night. The **Bay-View RV Park** (tel. 944-2253) and **R&R RV Park** (tel. 944-2253) have full hookups and other amenities for $10 a night.

BOB RACE

EAST TEXAS

Culturally and geographically, this part of the state is linked more to the American Southeast than the American Southwest. On a languid summer day in green East Texas, you could easily think you're in Louisiana or Mississippi. It's more than geographic appearance; lifestyles in rural East Texas are similar to those in other states of the Collard-Green Belt. The locals here speak more slowly than their counterparts elsewhere in Texas—if you stop to ask directions, a little patience is in order. East Texans like to sit and chat for a spell when they get the chance, unlike the average tight-lipped West Texan.

THE LAND

East Texas is so much greener than the rest of the state because it rains more here, from 43 inches a year in Tyler to 59 inches a year in Orange. The heart of the region is the "Piney Woods," a western extension of the Pine Belt that stretches from here to Georgia. The pine forests are interspersed with various hardwoods, and the lumber industry is the main economic staple for many

East Texas counties. Vast oil fields, another regional economic resource, lie beneath Gregg, Rusk, and Smith counties. Morris County harbors significant iron deposits, adding to the area's array of marketable natural resources.

Parts of East Texas are also in the Post Oak and Blackland belts, where the pine forests thin out and the sandy, black-clay alluvial soils are especially well suited to farming. Cotton is the traditional crop in these sections, along with a variety of grains, fruits, and vegetables.

The southern extremes of East Texas, including Houston, Port Arthur, and Beaumont, belong to the state's coastal prairies. Grasslands are plentiful from the coast to as far as 30-60 miles inland, so cattle ranching is one of the principal economic activities. In irrigated areas, rice is the principal crop, followed by grain sorghum and various truck crops.

THE PEOPLE

East Texas is the most polyglot, multicultural area of the state, though this is a relatively recent

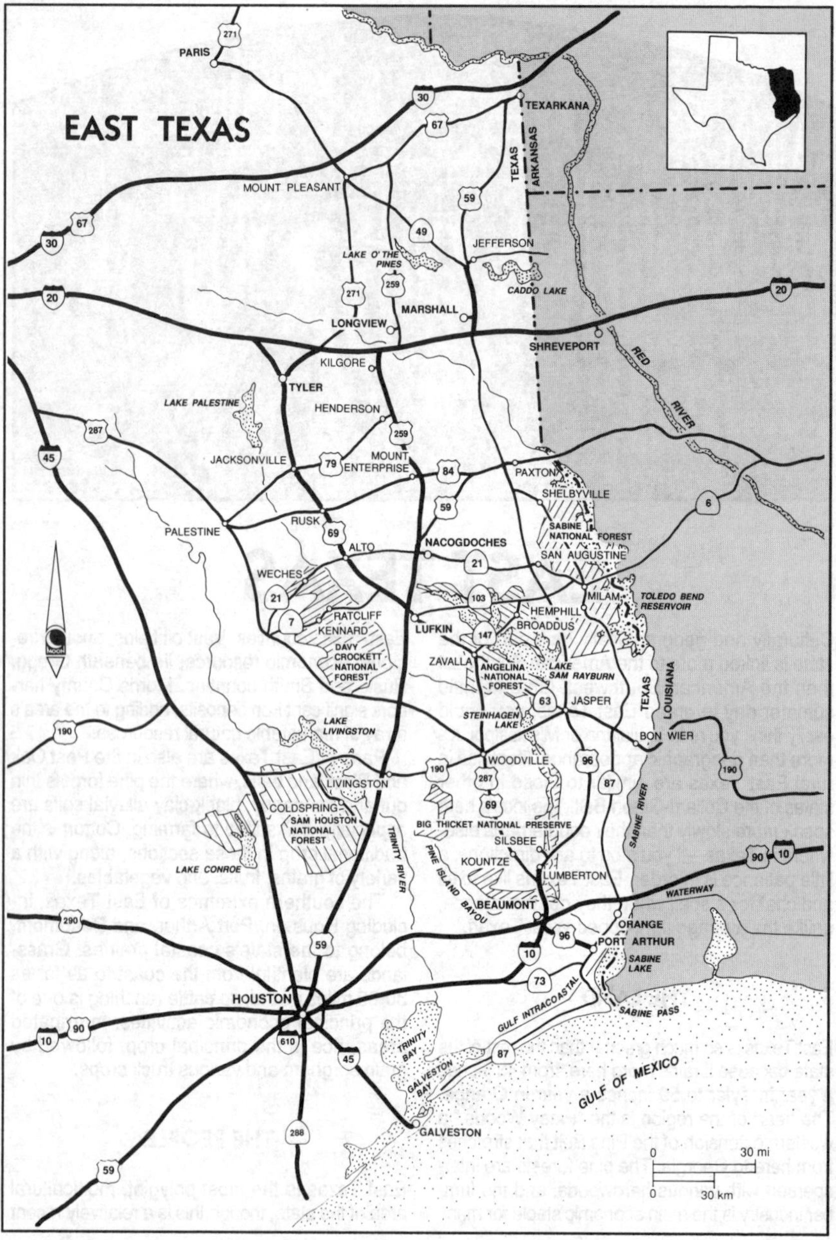

EAST TEXAS

PARIS
TEXARKANA
TEXAS
ARKANSAS
MOUNT PLEASANT
JEFFERSON
LAKE O' THE PINES
CADDO LAKE
MARSHALL
SHREVEPORT
LONGVIEW
RED RIVER
KILGORE
TYLER
LAKE PALESTINE
HENDERSON
JACKSONVILLE
PAXTON
SHELBYVILLE
MOUNT ENTERPRISE
SABINE NATIONAL FOREST
SAN AUGUSTINE
PALESTINE
RUSK
ALTO
NACOGDOCHES
WECHES
MILAM
TOLEDO BEND RESERVOIR
RATCLIFF
KENNARD
DAVY CROCKETT NATIONAL FOREST
HEMPHILL
BROADDUS
LUFKIN
ZAVALLA
ANGELINA NATIONAL FOREST
LAKE SAM RAYBURN
JASPER
LAKE LIVINGSTON
STEINHAGEN LAKE
BON WIER
LOUISIANA
TEXAS
LIVINGSTON
WOODVILLE
COLDSPRING
SAM HOUSTON NATIONAL FOREST
BIG THICKET NATIONAL PRESERVE
SABINE RIVER
LAKE CONROE
TRINITY RIVER
PINE ISLAND BAYOU
SILSBEE
KOUNTZE
LUMBERTON
BEAUMONT
WATERWAY
HOUSTON
ORANGE
PORT ARTHUR
SABINE LAKE
GULF INTRACOASTAL
SABINE PASS
TRINITY BAY
GALVESTON BAY
GULF OF MEXICO
GALVESTON

0   30 mi
0   30 km

© MOON PUBLICATIONS, INC.

development. The original French and Spanish dalliances with East Texas were brief and inconclusive due to the area's relative remoteness from colonial centers. Significant colonizing of the territory didn't begin until the Anglo-American immigration of the 19th century. It's often said this part of the state attracted the less adventurous American settlers who crossed the Mississippi in search of cheap land—dirt farmers from Tennessee, Kentucky, Louisiana, Mississippi, and Georgia. But it also brought woodsmen who wouldn't dream of advancing beyond the western treeline to the god-forsaken open prairies and plains of Central and West Texas—not because they were afraid of new frontiers but because they viewed cattle-ranching as a lazy, undignified occupation. In less than half a century, American pioneers established what the Europeans couldn't achieve for over 200 years—permanent settlements.

As East Texas farmers prospered, they began to develop a plantation economy based on models in Southeastern states and sustained on the backs of slave labor. East Texan slaveholders were the primary supporters of Texas secession in the 1860s. When the Civil War ended and slavery was outlawed, freed blacks became part of the civil population at large. They were followed by more African-Americans who migrated to Texas in search of jobs around the turn of the century, when the state economy began to surge.

When oil was discovered in the 1930s, a new type of Texan began to emerge in East Texas—the wildcatter and the investor. Get-rich-quick schemes proliferated and many farmers sold out to the highest bidder. As the petrochemical industry expanded in the 1940s and '50s, East Texas received another large influx of non-Anglos—Cajuns and Creoles from Louisiana.

The population became further diversified with the growing Asian immigration of the late 20th century. Southeast Asians in particular have discovered a familiar climate in the coastal areas of East Texas, concentrating here in large numbers. In general, the communities nearest Houston and the Gulf Coast are the most ethnically diverse, while those farthest north around historic Longview and Marshall are more homogeneously Anglo and European. In spite of the relative plurality of East Texas, it has never exhibited as much Hispanic influence as South, Central, and West Texas.

HOUSTON

Chamber of commerce publications often boast that Houston is the state's largest city and the fourth-largest city in the United States. But with city limits encompassing over 500 square miles, a numerical comparison based on strict municipal boundaries in a city notoriously lacking in city regulation hardly provides an accurate picture. Actually, when compared with other consolidated metropolitan statistical areas, Houston ranks ninth in the U.S. with a total population 3.7 million.

What really distinguishes Houston from Dallas (eighth) and San Antonio (10th) is not its size but its atmosphere of relative newness and lack of tradition. Houston has been a maverick town since brothers John and Augustus Allen first set up a trading post on the Buffalo Bayou in 1836 to capitalize on Texas's new status as a republic, boasting that Houston would become the next New Orleans.

When cotton was king, Houston did very well trading with the eastern U.S. and abroad. The Civil War slowed growth, though, and the Allen prediction rang hollow until the coming of the railroads in the late 1800s. When oil was discovered at nearby Spindletop in 1901, entrepreneurs moved in to make the most of the new commodity. During WW II Houston received another large boost when it became a wartime center for steel manufacturing, shipbuilding, and petrochemical production.

By the 1970s, Houston had become a national capital for the nouveau riche, but the wealth was still about 35% oil-dependent. In the '80s, following the drastic decline in world oil prices, downtown Houston threatened to become the country's largest ghost town. The local economy has since turned itself around primarily due to other industries—medical research, aerospace technology, education, shipping, international banking, and high-tech manufacturing. The city's traditional theme of boom/bust cycles dependent on local commodities is steadily giving way to an expanded international role. Today Houston is home to a consular corps of over 50 nations—the largest in the South or Southwest—and the country's largest multisite foreign-trade zone. As befits its maverick reputation, Houston remains a relatively young city with a median age of 29. The city plays host to over 260 academic and government research centers. In 1994 *Fortune* magazine ranked Houston number seven on its list of the top 10 best cities for business.

You won't find many Texans without an opinion of Houston. Some love the city for all it has to offer—museums and galleries, first-class ballet, symphony, and opera companies, a variety of exotic cuisines. Others hate it for what it lacks—reasonable zoning laws, traffic control, clean air, a pleasant climate. Both sides are right, and both sides exaggerate. Neither the traffic nor the pollution are as bad as in Los Angeles, for example. Nor are the museums and restaurants on a par with New York's or Washington's. Houston is still Texas, but at the same time, Houston is its own city.

CLIMATE

Among the state's large cities, Houston vies with Amarillo for worst climate. Whereas Amarillo is dry, windy, and cold much of the year, Houston is largely humid and hot. It's also given to torrential downpours, with an average annual precipitation of 45-50 inches. At an elevation of only 49 feet above sea level, this means occasional flooding, usually in May and September when rainfall is heaviest. The months with the highest probability for sunshine are June and July, when two of every three days are clear. The humidity is highest in October (93% at 6 a.m.) and lowest in July (58% at midnight).

On the plus side, temperatures rarely reach freezing in the winter, and at the height of the summer, temperatures don't often climb above the 90-95° F range. Of course at 70% relative humidity, even 90° F can be pretty miserable. When President Jimmy Carter tried to require all federal offices nationwide to set summer thermostats at 80° F during his administration, federal employees in Houston protested and an exception was made for that city. In the summer,

HOUSTON TEMPERATURES

MONTH	MAX. (° F)	MIN. (° F)
January	62	41
March	72	50
May	85	65
July	94	73
September	89	68
November	72	49

expect air-conditioned buildings in Houston to be cooler than average—even cold.

SIGHTS

Art Museums

Houston has nearly 20 major museums and galleries, plus over 200 minor museums and cultural institutes. The principal ones are centrally located in the Museum District near the intersection of Montrose Blvd. and Bissonnet Street. The **Museum of Fine Arts** (tel. 713-639-7300) at 1001 Bissonnet between Montrose and S. Main, established in 1924, houses the city's most comprehensive art collection: some 27,000 works of American, European, Latin American, North American Indian, African, and Asian/Pacific origin. The Renaissance and impressionist collections are among the more noteworthy. The museum's Hirsch Library has an extensive collection of books on art history. Across the street, the affiliated Glassell School of Art, 5101 Montrose, offers a full range of art classes. Along one side of the school, the Cullen Sculpture Garden features works by Henri Matisse, Alberto Giacometti, Auguste Rodin, and many other 19th- and 20th-century sculptors; it's open 9 a.m.-10 p.m. daily, admission free.

The MFA also sponsors an ongoing film and lecture series, and runs a museum store and cafe. Museum hours are Tues.-Sat. 10 a.m.-5 p.m. (Thursday till 9 p.m.), Sunday 12:15-6 p.m.; admission $3 adults, $1.50 seniors and children (under 6 free). On Thursday admission is free. Special exhibition prices vary.

The Menil Collection (tel. 525-9400) at 1515 Sul Ross between Mandel and Mulberry, the legacy of John and Dominique de Menil, features rotating displays from their 10,000-piece collection and occasional traveling exhibits. The cypress-wood building was designed by architect Renzo Piano, co-creator of Pompidou Art Center in Paris, and usually contains a compelling mix of African, Oceanic, Byzantine, Coptic, surrealist, and contemporary works. Open Wed.-Sun. 11 a.m.-7 p.m.; free admission.

One block east is the **Rothko Chapel** (tel. 524-9839), 3900 Yupon at Sul Ross, an octagonal brick structure built to house 14 paintings by abstract expressionist Mark Rothko commissioned by the de Menils. The Menil Foundation-sponsored facility hosts a variety of ecumenical colloquia on religion, human rights, and cross-cultural studies. Any religious group can book the chapel for services; it's also open to individuals who want to pray or meditate independently. Open to the public daily 10 a.m.-6 p.m.; admission free.

The city's boldest museum is undoubtedly the **Contemporary Art Museum** (tel. 526-3129) at 5216 Montrose, across from the Museum of Fine Arts. Inspired by the European art-hall (Kunsthalle) tradition, the emphasis is on art presentation rather than collection and maintenance. There are two galleries, a large upstairs space for "pivotal" one-person or group exhibitions, and a smaller downstairs space for mixed presentations by emerging artists. Only art created since 1945 is displayed. The museum has no permanent collection; new shows open approx-

imately every six weeks year round. CAM also hosts a series of films and lectures, with informal gallery talks each Thursday at noon. Open Tues.-Fri. 10 a.m.-5 p.m., Sat.-Sun. noon-5 p.m.; admission $3 adults, $1 seniors and students, children under 12 free. Free admission Thursday.

Bayou Bend (tel. 520-2600), a 28-room, copper-roofed, Latin Colonial-style mansion surrounded by 14 acres of gardens along Buffalo Bayou at 1 Westcott St., was built in the 1920s by the late Ima Hogg, daughter of former Governor Jim Hogg. In 1966 it was converted into an American decorative-arts museum under the auspices of the Museum of Fine Arts. Miss Hogg's extensive private collection, expanded by the MFA, includes 18th- and 19th-century furniture, paintings, silverwork, textiles, ceramics, glass, and folk art.

A two-year, $7.5 million renovation completed in 1993 added new lighting to better display the collection. Guided tours provide great detail on the history of American decorative arts and the life of Miss Hogg. Sixty-minute tours cost $7.50 adults, $5 seniors and students, $3.75 children 10-18; 90-minute tours run $10/$8.50/$5. Call ahead for times and reservations. Admission is free from 1-5 p.m. on Family Day, the third Sunday of each month from September to May. Admission to the collection covers self-guided tours of the 14-acre gardens surrounding the mansion. Visitors may tour the gardens for $3; free for those 10 and under.

Bayou Bend, Houston

Houston's commitment to art is perhaps most visible in the dozens of outdoor sculptures and murals around the city, commissioned by various private and public organizations. The greatest proliferation of outdoor artwork is found in the downtown area, with some 28 pieces at last count. Another 25 or so are in the Museum District and around Rice University; 14 more are scattered around the University of Houston.

Science Museums
The **Museum of Natural Science** (tel. 713-639-4600), at 1 Hermann Circle in Hermann Park (opposite Rice University), opened in 1909 and moved to its present location twenty years later. It contains exhibits pertaining to several scientific disciplines relevant to Houston's high-tech history, from astronomy to petroleum science. A $23 million expansion completed in 1994 doubled the size of the paleontology hall, provided funding for a high-tech, interactive chemistry lab, and added the Wortham IMAX Theater, the Weiss Energy Hall (focusing on oil and gas), and the pièce de résistance, the 25,000-square-foot **Cockrell Butterfly Center.** This impressive glass cone displays species from Asia, Mexico, Central America, and South America cavorting in a lush Mayan rainforest setting. Museum hours are Mon.-Sat. 9 a.m.-6 p.m., Sunday noon-6 p.m. General admission is $3 adults, $2 seniors and children under 12. Additional fees are collected for IMAX shows and entry to the butterfly center.

HOUSTON MUSEUM OF NATURAL SCIENCE

Bones are plentiful in the recently expanded paleontology hall at the Museum of Natural Science.

The park also contains the domed **Burke Baker Planetarium,** offering multimedia and laser shows. Themes and times vary seasonally, so call ahead to check the schedule. Fees are generally $2-5 adults, $1.50-5 seniors and children.

Historic Spots
Sam Houston Park (tel. 713-655-1912), downtown at 1100 Bagby, is Houston's oldest park. It's sponsored by the Harris County Heritage Society, which maintains eight restored historic structures built in the mid-1800s. Guided tours are conducted hourly Mon.-Sat. 10 a.m.-4 p.m., Sunday 1-5 p.m.; admission is $6 for adults, $4 for students, and $2 for children 6-11.

The **Market Square Historic District,** bounded by Congress, Preston, Travis, and Milam downtown, is flanked by 53 historic buildings—Houston's original business district. For a taste of old Houston, step into **Le Carafe,** a wine bar just off the Square in the city's oldest building.

The small **Allen's Landing Park,** at Main and Commerce on Buffalo Bayou, is the site where the Allen brothers first stepped off their boat and started their trading post in 1836.

San Jacinto Battleground State Historical Park (tel. 479-2421), 15 miles east of the city via State 225 and State 134, commemorates the 1836 battle in which Texan revolutionary forces defeated Santa Anna's Mexican army and secured independence. The **San Jacinto Monument** marks the battle site itself; the 570-foot obelisk is said to be the tallest masonry monument in the world. An elevator takes visitors to the top for a bird's-eye view of the Gulf Coast, ship channel, and Houston skyline—if the haze isn't too thick. The monument is open daily 9 a.m.-6 p.m.; the elevator ride costs $2.50 for adults, $1 for children.

The **San Jacinto Museum of History** (tel. 479-2421) contains exhibits chronicling regional history from Indian habitation through statehood. A theater in the battleground's museum presents *Texas Forever!,* a 35-minute, multimedia documentary of the Battle of San Jacinto narrated by Charlton Heston. Admission is $3.50 for adults, $2 seniors and children. Shows are presented on the hour, 10 a.m.-5 p.m. daily.

On the ship channel near San Jacinto Battleground Historical Park is the battleship *Texas,* a veteran of both World Wars. The ship is permanently moored here to serve as a naval museum, containing exhibits recounting the ship's wartime involvement. Open Wed.-Sun. 10 a.m.-5 p.m.; admission is $4 adults, $2 children, under six free.

Houston Zoological Gardens

The recently upgraded 50-acre zoo (tel. 713-525-3300) in Hermann Park now charges admission. It's very well kept throughout and features a mammal marina, education center, tropical bird house, deep-sea aquarium, and reptile house, the latter housing a rare 17.5-foot Burmese python. A new $6.7 million primate center houses 40 of the zoo's primates in a tropical rainforest setting; a seven-foot elevated pathway gives visitors a tree-top view of spectacled langurs and other arboreal monkeys. Open daily 10 a.m.-6 p.m.; admission is $2.50 for adults, $2 for seniors, 50 cents for children.

NASA-Johnson Space Center and Space Center Houston

Operated by the National Aeronautics and Space Administration (NASA) as the center for the country's manned spaceflight program, this is the number-three tourist destination in the state, averaging 1.5 million visitors a year. Space Center Houston (tel. 800-972-0369 or 713-244-2100), a 183,000-square-foot, $70 million educational and entertainment facility designed by NASA and Walt Disney Imagineering, was completed in 1992 to serve as the new visitor center for Johnson Space Center. Together these centers employ 20,000 scientists and researchers.

The new complex provides a fascinating look at the manned spaceflight program through interactive exhibits—shuttle and space-module mockups, shuttle-landing simulators, maneuvering units that teach low-gravity movement, a walk-in vault housing lunar rocks. Large-format films like the 70 mm To Be an Astronaut are projected on a five-story screen. Forty- and 75-minute behind-the-scenes, guided tram tours visit Mission Control Center, the Skylab/Space Shuttle Training Facility, Rocket Park, and other areas of Johnson Space Center that were previously off-limits. Mercury, Gemini, and Apollo spacecraft and a complete collection of NASA spacesuits are also on display.

spacesuit inspection

Allow a full day to take in all the various tours, films, and educational exhibits. The new center houses two dining outlets—the Silver Moon Cafe and the Zero-G Diner; visit the Space-Trader shop for souvenirs. Tram tours are included in the general admission of $11.95 adults, $10.75 seniors, and $8.50 for children under 12; under three free. Open weekdays 10 a.m.-6 p.m., weekends and holidays 9 a.m.-7 p.m.

Johnson Space Center is 25 miles southeast of Houston via I-45 S, on NASA Road.

Astrodome

This 76,000-seat sports facility (tel. 713-799-9544) at 8400 Kirby (at Loop 610 S) is home to the Houston Astros pro baseball and Houston Oilers pro football teams, as well as the Houston Livestock Show and Rodeo and other large-scale events. Tours of the stadium are conducted daily at 11 a.m., 1 p.m., and 3 p.m., except when preempted by scheduled events. The tours take visitors onto the Astroturf field, to the owner's lounge, and to the radio/TV broadcasting areas. Prices are $4 for adults, $3 for seniors and children 4-11.

The Orange Show

The brainchild of Jeff McKissack, a former postman, this urban folk-art park must be seen to be believed. For 25 years, McKissack assembled a collection of found objects to create a fanciful monument to the orange. The part-Alexander Caldwell, part-Rube Goldberg design represents his personal testament to wisdom and good health. When McKissack died in 1980 at the age of 77, a group of Houston artists and city arts representatives formed The Orange Show Foundation to preserve the complex, which consists of several enclosed rooms, two small arenas, and two rooftop observation areas, all bedecked with hardy orange displays. The dominant motif is the wheel—many sculptures consist of iron buggy wheels and tractor seats. Nearly every wall, pillar, and door is inlaid with tile messages like "Oranges for energy," "Love me, orange please love me," or "Be alert." Beneath a huge circular clown face is a sign that reads "The clown said I am alert. I take care of myself every hour every minute of every day. You can too if you will. Clowns never lie."

The Orange Show is located at 2401 Munger St., southeast of central Houston off the Gulf Freeway. Take I-45 S to the Telephone Rd. exit, then follow the access road to Munger. The complex is open to visitors Mon.-Fri. 9 a.m.-1 p.m. and on weekends noon-5 p.m. Admission is $1 adults, free for children under 12. The Orange Show Foundation also uses the exhibit as a venue for community children's theater, poetry workshops, art shows, and musical performances. Call (713) 926-6368 for more information.

Colleges and Universities

The city's two major universities are the **University of Houston** and **Rice University**. The state-supported University of Houston (tel. 713-749-1000) has a total enrollment of 31,000, which includes an open-admissions undergraduate division; graduate schools in engineering, pharmacology, and optometry; the Bates College of Law; and the Hilton School of Hotel and Restaurant Management. The central campus is south of the downtown area off I-45,

Calhoun exit; the downtown campus is on Main. The **Blaffer Gallery** (tel. 743-9430) on the central campus and the **O'Kane Gallery** (tel. 221-8042) downtown feature changing local and national art exhibits.

Rice University (tel. 520-6022) is a private liberal arts school with a scenic campus southwest of downtown and a total enrollment of approximately 4,000. The **Rice Media Center** (tel. 527-4894) hosts local, national, and international photography exhibitions and also screens classic and contemporary cinema. The university's **Farish Gallery** (tel. 527-4870) in the School of Architecture is devoted to changing architectural exhibits.

Other tertiary schools include the sectarian **Houston Baptist University** (tel. 774-7661), at 7502 Fondren; **University of St. Thomas** (tel. 525-3500), at 3800 Montrose; and the state-supported **Texas Southern University** (tel. 527-7011), at 3100 Cleburne. Two major medical schools, **Baylor College of Medicine** and the **University of Texas Medical School at Houston,** are located at the Texas Medical Center.

Texas Medical Center

The TMC is a conglomerate of 40 member institutions—hospitals, research institutes, nursing and medical schools—covering a 580-acre area adjacent to Hermann Park. As a group, they comprise the city's largest employer. Among the care facilities is the Versailles of free-enterprise heart surgery, Michael DeBakey's Methodist Hospital, where incisions start at $25,000 and patients in luxury suites receive catered meals from Jamail & Sons, a highbrow Houston deli.

Free tours of the grounds and some facilities are conducted Mon.-Fri. at 10 a.m. from the TMC Assistance Center (tel. 713-790-1136), on the first floor of TMC parking garage no. 2, at Bertner and Holcombe. Call ahead for reservations—these tours fill quickly.

Port of Houston

This port is the eighth largest in the U.S.—over 4,800 ships a year call here—and a linchpin of the local economy. The inspection boat *Sam Houston* (tel. 713-670-2416) takes visitors on free tours of the ship channel Tuesday, Wednesday, Friday, and Saturday at 10 a.m. and 2:30

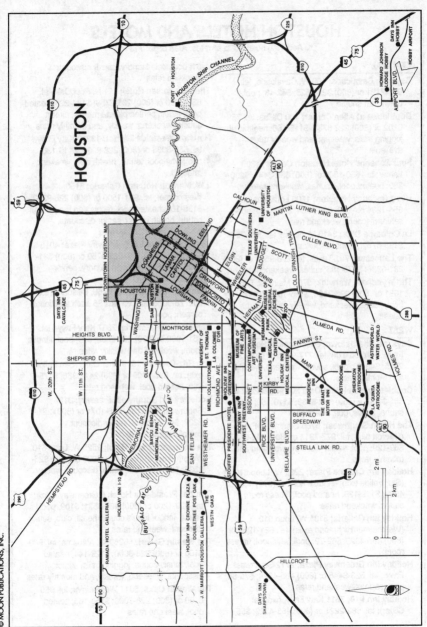

HOUSTON HOTELS AND MOTELS

Add 15% hotel tax to all rates. Area code: 713

CENTRAL

Days Inn Cavalcade; 100 W. Cavalcade; tel. 869-7121 or (800) 325-2525; $42-48; pool, downtown shuttle

Doubletree at Allen Center; 400 Dallas; tel. 759-0202 or (800) 222-8733; $115-160; health club, jogging trails, weekend and weekly rates available

Four Seasons Hotel Houston Center; 1300 Lamar; tel. 650-1300 or (800) 332-3442; $200-280; heated pool, saunas, weekend rates

Hyatt Regency Houston; 1200 Louisiana; tel. 654-1234 or (800) 233-1234; $145-185; pool, senior discount, weekend rates

La Colombe D'Or; 3410 Montrose; tel. 524-7999; $195-575; historic, all suites

The Lancaster; 701 Texas; tel. 228-9500 or (800) 231-0336; $175-195; suites, weekend rates

The Wyndham Warwick; 5701 Main; tel. 526-1991 or (800) 996-3426; $165-185; historic, pool, sauna, weekend, weekly, and monthly rates

WEST

Days Inn Sharpstown; 6060 Hooton (Southwest Frwy., Hillcroft exit); tel. 777-9955 or (800) 325-2525; $43-60; pool, sauna, weekend, weekly, and monthly rates

Doubletree Hotel Post Oak; 2001 Post Oak; tel. 961-9300 or (800) 222-8733; $110-150; pool, sauna, tennis, golf, health club

The Hilton Southwest; 6780 Southwest Frwy. (Hillcroft exit); tel. 977-7911 or (800) 445-8667; $69-129; pool, senior discount, weekend and monthly rates

Holiday Inn Crowne Plaza; 2222 W. Loop 610 (San Felipe exit); tel. 961-7272 or (800) 465-4329; $119-129; heated pool, fitness room, sauna, weekend rates

Holiday Inn Galleria; 3131 W. Loop 610 (Westheimer/Richmond exits); tel. 621-1900 or (800) 465-4329; $69-79; pool, whirlpool, fitness room

Holiday Inn Greenway Plaza; 2712 Southwest Frwy.; tel. 523-8448 or (800) 465-4329; $76-86; pool, saunas, weekend rates

Holiday Inn I-10; 7611 Katy Frwy. (west at Silber); tel. 688-2221 or (800) 465-4329; $55-61; pool, coin laundry, senior discount, weekend rates

The Houstonian Hotel; 111 N. Post Oak; tel. 680-2626 or (800) 231-2759; $134-225; heated pool, health center, bicycle rentals, airport shuttle, weekend, weekly, and monthly rates

Houston Westside Marriot; 13210 Katy Frwy.; tel. 558-8338 or (800) 228-9290; $119-130; pool, whirlpool, tennis, health club, weekend rates

J.W. Marriott Houston Galleria; 5150 Westheimer; tel. 961-1500 or (800) 228-9290; $135-165; heated pool, tennis and racquetball courts, health center, senior discounts, weekend and monthly rates

La Quinta Motor Inn Greenway Plaza; 4015 Southeast Frwy.; tel. 623-4750 or (800) 531-5900; $59-65; pool, coin laundry, senior discount

Motel 6; 9638 Plainfield (US 59, Bissonnet exit); tel. 778-0008; $29.95 plus $6 each additional person; pool

Ramada Hotel Galleria; 7887 Katy Frwy.; tel. 681-5000 or (800) 272-6232; $79; pool, fitness room, weekend and weekly rates

The Ritz-Carlton; 1919 Briar Oaks (San Felipe exit); tel. 840-7600 or (800) 241-3333; $175-280; heated pool, weekend rates

Rodeway Inn Southwest Freeway; 3135 Southwest Frwy.; tel. 526-1071 or (800) 221-2222; $41-47; pool, senior discount, complimentary breakfast

The Sheraton Grand Hotel; 2525 W. Loop 610 (Westheimer exit); tel. 961-3000 or (800) 325-3535; $89-109; pool, senior discount, weekly rates

Stouffer Presidente Hotel; 6 Greenway Plaza; tel. 629-1200 or (800) 469-3571; $109; pool, sauna, indoor tennis courts, health club, senior discount, weekend rates

The Westin Galleria; 5060 W. Alabama; tel. 960-8100 or (800) 228-3000; $129-144; heated pool, tennis courts, jogging trails, senior discounts, weekend, weekly, and monthly rates

The Westin Oaks; 5011 Westheimer; tel. 960-8100 or (800) 228-3000; $150-165; heated pool, weekend rates

SOUTH MAIN (NEAR TEXAS MEDICAL CENTER AND ASTRODOME)

Econo Lodge 7905 S. Main; tel. 667-8200; $44-49; pool, senior discount

The Grant Motor Inn; 8200 S. Main; tel. 668-8000 or (800) 255-8904; $31-38; pool, coin laundry, senior discount, weekly rates

Holiday Inn Medical Center; 6701 S. Main; tel. 797-1110 or (800) 465-4329; $78-93; pool, medical center, shuttle, weekend rates

Houston Marriott Medical Center; 6580 Fannin; tel. 796-0080 or (800) 228-9290; $99-129; heated pool, saunas, health center, senior discount, weekend rates

Houston Plaza Hilton; 6633 Travis; tel. 524-6633 or (800) 445-8667; $89-140; heated pool, saunas, health center

Houston Villa Motor Hotel; 9604 S. Main; tel. 666-1411; $27-37; pool

La Quinta Astrodome; 9911 Buffalo Speedway; tel. 668-8082 or (800) 531-5900; $59-66; pool, coin laundry, airport shuttle

Radisson Suite Hotel; 1400 Old Spanish Trail; tel. 796-1000 or (800) 333-3333; $83-119; kitchenettes in all units, pool, sauna, coin laundry, senior discount, complimentary breakfast

Ramada Astrodome; 2100 S. Braeswood; tel. 797-9000; $69-109; pool, coin laundry

Residence Inn Astrodome; 7710 S. Main; tel. 660-9993 or (800) 228-9290; $79; pool, tennis, complimentary breakfast

Sheraton Astrodome; 8686 Kirby; 748-3221. 800-325-3535; $74-84; pools, sauna, health center, complimentary full breakfast on weekends, weekend rates

HOUSTON INTERCONTINENTAL AIRPORT

Best Western Greenspoint Inn; 11211 I-45 N (exit 60); tel. 447-6311 or (800) 528-1234; $39-44; pool, airport shuttle

Comfort Inn Greenspoint; 12500 I-45 N (exit 61); tel. 876-3888 or (800) 221-2222; $37-45; pool, coin laundry, senior discount, airport shuttle

Days Inn Airport; 17607 Eastex Frwy.; tel. 446-4611 or (800) 325-2525; $44-49; pool, coin laundry, airport shuttle

Doubletree Hotel; 15747 JFK Blvd.; tel. 442-8000 or (800) 222-8733; $95-123; pool, refrigerators available, sauna, fitness center, airport shuttle, weekend rates

Holiday Inn Houston Intercontinental; 3702 N. Sam Houston Parkway E; tel. 999-9492 or (800) 465-4329; $54-60; pool, saunas, tennis courts, coin laundry, airport shuttle

Houston Airport Marriott; Airport Terminal; tel. 443-2310 or (800) 228-9290; $99-135; suites, pool, coin laundry, airport shuttle, weekend rates

Houston Marriott North; 255 Sam Houston Parkway E; tel. 875-4000 or (800) 228-9290; $109-129; suites, heated pool, saunas, airport shuttle, weekend rates

La Quinta Inn Intercontinental Hotel; 6 N. Belt E; tel. 447-6888 or (800) 531-5900; $52-65; pool, airport shuttle, senior discount

Rodeway Inn North; 13611 N. Rankin Cr.; tel. 821-0410 or (800) 221-2222; $39-45; pool, sauna, fitness room, airport shuttle, complimentary breakfast

Sheraton Crown Hotel; 15700 JFK; tel. 442-5100 or (800) 325-3535; $85-110; suites, heated pool, coin laundry, airport shuttle, complimentary breakfast

Super 8 Motel; 15350 JFK Blvd.; tel. 442-1830 or (800) 800-8000; $40-55; pool, sauna, airport shuttle, senior discount, weekly rates

Wyndham Greenspoint; 12400 Greenspoint; tel. 875-2222; $129-179; pool, sauna, racquetball courts, airport shuttle, monthly rates

HOBBY AIRPORT

Days Inn Hobby Airport; 8611 Airport; tel. 947-0000 or (800) 325-2525; $60-67; pool, airport shuttle

Hobby Airport Hilton; 8181 Airport; tel. 645-3000 or (800) 445-8667; $65-122; pool, airport shuttle, weekend rates

Holiday Inn Hobby Airport; 9100 Gulf Frwy.; tel. 934-7979 or (800) 465-4329; $98-112; heated pool, sauna, health center, airport shuttle

Howard Johnson Lodge Hobby Airport; 7777 Airport; tel. 644-1261 or (800) 446-4656; $39-43; pool, airport shuttle, weekly rates

La Quinta Motor Inn Hobby Airport; 9902 Gulf Frwy.; tel. 941-0900 or (800) 531-5900; $60-67; pool, airport shuttle, senior discount

Rodeway Inn Hobby Airport; 1505 College; tel. 946-5900 or (800) 221-2222; $39-44; pool, airport shuttle, weekend and weekly rates

p.m., Thursday and Sunday at 2:30 only. The tour is free but you usually must make reservations at least a month in advance. Reservations are accepted by phone Mon.-Fri. 8:30 a.m.-12:30 p.m. only. The boat docks at Gate 8, 7300 Clinton Drive.

Texas Limited

You can relive a little of the Golden Age of Rail on this passenger excursion train that runs between Houston and Galveston, April 30-Labor Day and every weekend in December. Among the train's eight refurbished coaches from railroad yesteryear are the *Chimayo,* a 1938 Pullman originally built for Santa Fe's famous Super Chief; the *Hawkeye,* a 1941 car from the Chicago, Rock Island, and Pacific Railroad's Rocket streamliners; the 1948 *Silver Stirrup,* formerly in service for the California Zephyr; and the *Silver Queen,* an old Minneapolis & St. Louis coach with an interior restoration inspired by the famed *Orient Express.*

Trains depart the Houston station at 567 T.C. Jester (off Loop 610) Wed.-Fri. and Sunday at 9:30 a.m. and start the return trip from the Galveston railway station (25th and The Strand) at 4 p.m. On Saturday the train makes two round trips, leaving Houston at 8 a.m. and 5:30 p.m., and leaving Galveston for the return trip at 1:45 p.m. and 10:45 p.m., respectively. The 50-mile trip takes two hours and 20 minutes each way. Roundtrip fares are $40 first class, $26 children 3-12, $38 seniors 65 and over; and $30 excursion class, $16 children 3-12, $28 seniors 65 and over. All fares include admission to Galveston's Railroad Museum.

Advance ticket purchase is required; tickets are available at any Ticketmaster outlet in Houston or in Galveston at the Railroad Museum (25th and The Strand). Special Murder Mystery tours are occasionally held. For more information, call (713) 522-0574 or (800) 374-7475.

ACCOMMODATIONS

Hotels and Motels

Hotel and motel accommodations are concentrated in five major areas: central Houston, including downtown; the west side, near the junction of US 59 and Loop 610; the S. Main/Astrodome area; near Houston Intercontinental Airport; and near Hobby Airport. See the "Houston Hotels and Motels" chart for details.

Bed and Breakfasts

Houston's **Bed & Breakfast Society of Texas** (tel. 713-523-1114), 1200 Southmore Ave., Houston, TX 77004, maintains a registry of 24 B&Bs in Houston, many in the historic Heights district. Rooms with private baths start at $45 s, $60 d.

Houses that accept direct bookings include **Durham House Bed & Breakfast** (tel. 868-4654) at 921 Heights, a large Victorian listed with the National Register of Historic Places. All rooms are furnished with antiques and most have private baths; rates are $50-75 s, $60-85 d. **Sara's Bed & Breakfast Inn** (tel. 868-1130) at 941 Heights is a Victorian with double rooms (all with shared bath) at $50-75; one private suite with private bath goes for $120. Weekly rates available.

The Downtown YMCA Residence

The conveniently located downtown Y (tel. 713-659-8501) at 1600 Louisiana welcomes men and women for an unbeatable $17 in the older rooms, $21 for new rooms (available only in the men's section). All rooms have air-conditioning, TV, and shared bath. Weekly rates are $72-110.

Hostels

Houston International Youth Hostel, also called Perry House (tel. 713-523-1009, fax 526-8618), 5302 Crawford St., is a large converted home in a residential area of the Museum District, about three miles southwest of downtown Houston. Dorm beds rent for $11.39 a night for AYH cardholders, $14.25 for nonmembers. Hermann Park—where you'll find the Museum of Natural Science, Burke Baker Planetarium, and Houston Zoo—is just four blocks from the hostel. Metro buses nos. 2, 4, 8 and 9 stop at the nearby intersection of Main and Southmore, from there it's a six-block walk east to Crawford, then one more block right (south) to the hostel. **Cyclists note:** Next door is Daniel Boone Cycles, one of the city's best bike shops.

Space City AYH Hostel (tel. 996-0323) at 2242 W. Bay Area Blvd. in Friendswood offers similar fa-

Perry House

cilities for $11.25 a night; just two miles from NASA's Space Center Houston. Call for a shuttle bus ($15) from either of Houston's airports.

Campgrounds and RV Parks
All Star RV Resort (tel. 713-981-6814) at 10515 Southwest Freeway, US 59 near Beltway 8, is the closest RV park to the downtown area (just 10 miles southwest) and offers full hookups with cable TV for $16-22 per night.

Alexander Deussen County Park (tel. 454-7057), a 309-acre wooded park about 20 miles northeast of the city on Lake Houston's southwest side, has camper sites with w/e for $5 a day with a 14-day limit. Tent camping is permitted only on weekends, no charge. Facilities include bicycle trails, boat ramps, dump station, restrooms, picnic shelters, cooking grills, snack bar, and grocery shop.

Another camping area is at **Spring Creek Park** (tel. 353-4196), 12 miles northwest of FM 1960 off FM 149, on Spring Creek. Tent/camper sites with w/e are free, and there's a three-day limit. Call in advance to see if there are sites available.

KOA offers two campgrounds on the city outskirts. The **KOA Houston Central** (tel. 442-3700) is at 1620 Peachleaf, 12 miles north of downtown via US 59 N and Beltway 8 (west to Aldine-Westfield, south to Peachleaf). Tentsites are $16, two-way hookups $18, and three-ways $20. **KOA Houston East/Baytown** (tel. 383-3618) is 33 miles east in Baytown off I-10 (exit 798); rates are $16-24.

Houston Leisure Park (tel. 426-3576) is a huge RV facility 19 miles east of the city off I-10 (exit 787) near San Jacinto State Park; rates are $12 for tents, $17-19 for full hookups, with weekly and monthly rates available. **Red Dot RV Park** (tel. 448-3438) lies 12 miles north off I-45 (Aldine-Bender exit) at 15014 Sellers. Rates are $14.50 for full hookups, weekly and monthly rates available.

Traders Village RV Park (tel. 890-5500) offers four wooded acres and 200 sites at 7979 N. Eldridge off US 290 northwest of Houston; full hookups cost $14-18 a night. Facilities include a mini-mart, laundromat, air-conditioned rec hall, and ATM machine.

FOOD

San Antonio for Tex-Mex, Dallas for Southwestern, and Houston for Cajun is the usual refrain, but Houston's reputation really ought to be broadened to include Asian cuisine as well. With a large Asian population and the state's only "Chinatown," Houston has more Chinese, Japanese, Thai, Vietnamese, Indian, and Indonesian restaurants than any other city in Texas.

To judge from the variety and depth of the city's cuisines, Houstonians seem to have the most sophisticated palates in the state. But unlike San Antonio and Dallas, you really have to be on wheels to dine out as there are no dining districts comparable to the River Walk or Deep Ellum.

DOWNTOWN HOUSTON

© MOON PUBLICATIONS, INC.

Most of the chain restaurants are located along Westheimer Rd. outside Loop 610, but a few independent gems are tucked away here and there in the endless series of shopping centers.

American

$$ Ashland House: This restaurant in a converted two-story Victorian cooks up traditional American entrees like pot roast served with fresh vegetables and homemade yeast rolls. At 1801 Ashland (tel. 713-863-7613); open Mon.-Sat. 11 a.m.-3 p.m. only.

$$$+   Café Annie: A chi-chi joint considered one of the state's foremost exponents of Southwestern/new-American cuisine. The menu varies but is guaranteed to impress (e.g., cream of mussel soup seasoned with serrano chiles and cilantro, crabmeat tostadas). At 1728 Post Oak (tel. 840-1111); open Mon.-Fri. for lunch and dinner, Saturday dinner only.

$$ Hard Rock Cafe: Part of a chain with outlets around the world. The main attraction here is the decor—electric guitars, gold records, a Harley, a T-Bird, and other symbols of rock 'n' roll culture—but the burgers aren't bad either. At 2801 Kirby (tel. 520-1134); open daily for lunch and dinner.

$ One's A Meal: If you're stuck for a place to nosh after midnight, try this reliable and inexpensive, round-the-clock diner in the River Oaks-Memorial Park area. Typical diner fare, including waffles, biscuits and gravy, and corned-beef hash. At 2019 W. Gray (tel. 523-8432); open 24 hours.

$$$+   Tony's: One of the hubs of Houston's social scene for over a decade now. This red-walled eatery is usually classified "continental," but entrees like veal medallions in a pecan-bourbon sauce, red snapper in walnut-herb sauce, and chicken breast over grilled mangoes with chile sauce make it hybrid nouvelle American. Men must wear jackets for lunch, coat and tie for dinner—even in July. At 1801 Post Oak (tel. 622-6778); open Mon.-Fri. for lunch and dinner, Saturday dinner only.

Barbecue

$ to $$ Goode Company Bar-B-Q: Often cited as the best barbecue place in the city. Jim Goode's original restaurant (he also has seafood and burger spinoffs) features a menu that goes beyond the standard brisket and links to include crisp-skinned duck, Czech sausage-and-ribs with "dirty rice," and jalapeño-cheese bread. At 5109 Kirby (tel. 713-522-2530); open daily for lunch and dinner.

$ to $$ County Line Barbeque: Yet another in the statewide chain that started in Austin, this '40s-style roadhouse is located in a pleasant pinewood setting in northwest Houston; menu includes smoked duck and chicken. At 13850 Cutten, a mile north of FM 1960 (tel. 537-2454); open daily for lunch and dinner.

$ to $$ Luther's Bar-B-Q: A very popular Houston-based chain specializing in slow-smoked barbecue brisket, pork ribs, links, and chicken. At 8777 S. Main (tel. 432-1107) and 11 other locations; open daily for lunch and dinner.

Cajun/Creole

Houston shines in this category, thanks to a substantial number of Cajuns and Creoles among the local population. You might find more authentic cooking in Port Arthur or Beaumont, but you'd be hard-pressed to find this much variety. Crawfish are in season late October to May.

$$ to $$$ Pappadeaux Seafood Kitchen: The *Houston Chronicle* voted Pappadeaux Houston's number one restaurant, though it didn't specify which of the six locations was best. Dixieland decor complements the consistently fresh seafood served blackened, charbroiled, or mesquite grilled. At 6015 Westheimer (tel. 713-782-6310) and 10499 Katy Frwy. (tel. 722-0221); open daily for lunch and dinner.

$$$+   Brennan's: A branch of the famed New Orleans Brennan's, this one has a few Texas/Southwestern dishes, such as oysters in a chile-corn salsa, sprinkled into its mostly Creole menu. As in New Orleans, men are required to wear jackets for dinner. At 3300 Smith (tel. 522-9711); open Mon.-Fri. for lunch, daily for dinner, Saturday and Sunday for brunch.

$$ Louisiana Don's: A long-established restaurant, originally started in Lafayette, Louisiana, in 1934. It specializes in Cajun seafood—gumbos, bisques, jambalaya, stuffed red snapper, fried oysters, soft-shell crab, and frog legs. On Friday nights the eatery presents live Cajun and zydeco bands. At 3009 Post Oak (tel. 629-5380); open daily for lunch and dinner.

$$ to $$$ Magnolia Bar & Grill: Patterns itself after the new "serious" Creole restaurants in New Orleans, with such haute dishes as Opelousas duck and crawfish bisque. At 6000 Richmond (tel. 781-6207); open Mon.-Sat. for lunch and dinner.

$ to $$ Pe-Te's Cajun Barbecue House: This honky-tonk restaurant is a few miles southeast of town on Old Galveston Rd. (State 3) toward the NASA center. It's worth the drive on Saturday afternoon (2-6 p.m.) when you can listen to Cajun or zydeco bands while you savor gumbo, boudin (rice and pork sausage), alligator stew, red beans and rice, hog cracklins, and other down-home Cajun dishes. At 11902 Old Galveston Rd. (tel. 481-8736); open Mon.-Thurs. 9 a.m.-7 p.m., Friday 9 a.m.-8 p.m., Saturday 10:30 a.m.-6:30 p.m. except the third Saturday of the month when they're open till midnight for "double dances."

$ to $$ Ragin' Cajun: Despite the lame name, this funky cafe offers some of the best Cajun cooking in the city. Dishes include crawfish pie, fried rabbit, and étouffée. At 4302 Richmond (tel. 623-6321); open Mon.-Sat. for lunch and dinner. If Ragin' Cajun is packed, try **Bayou Seafood and Pasta** a couple of blocks west at 4730 Richmond Ave.

$$ Treebeard's: The place to go if you're looking for a downtown lunch spot for Cajun/Creole. Great jalapeño cornbread, red beans and rice. At 315 Travis (tel. 225-2160); open Mon.-Fri. for lunch.

$ Zydeco Diner: Oyster po'boys, blue-plate specials, vegetable plates, and other Cajun dishes served cafeteria style. During crawfish season the diner hosts crawfish boils, accompanied by live Cajun and Zydeco music, Tuesday and Thursday nights. At 1119 Pease (tel. 759-2001); open Mon.-Fri. 11 a.m.-2 p.m. only, except for Tuesday/Thursday crawfish boils in season. Second location at 9741 Westheimer, West Chase Shopping Center (tel. 781-4586); open Mon.-Sat. for lunch and dinner.

Caribbean

$$ Calypso: This place covers the territory with everything from Jamaican curries to Cuban black-bean soup, in a '50s-Miami setting. Live music on some evenings. At 5555 Morningside (tel. 713-524-8571); open Mon.-Sat. for lunch and dinner.

$$ Caribbean Cuisine: Mostly Jamaican dishes, including chicken curry and oxtail stew. At 7433 Bissonnet (tel. 774-7428); open Mon.-Sat. for lunch and dinner.

Chinese

Houston's many Chinese restaurants seem to come in two varieties—flashy, expensive places full of *gwailos* (non-Asians), usually set in shopping centers or malls, and inexpensive, no-interior-design places in Chinatown (mostly along St. Emanual and Chartres, east of downtown), where the local Chinese tend to eat.

$ Chinese Cafe: Bold flavors in all directions—hot, salty, tart, bitter—but well-balanced. Prices are very reasonable, starting at $1 for a plate of anise-steamed peanuts, to $4.95 for the house special "Chinese Cafe bean curd," tofu slabs cooked with shredded pork and spicy black-bean sauce. Less than $9 for a whole fish. At 5092 Richmond (tel. 713-621-2888); open daily for lunch and dinner.

$$ to $$$ Dong Ting: It's owned by a native of China's Hunan Province, so spicy Hunan cuisine is the focus, along with a mix of other regional dishes. House specialties include smoked duck and crab in black-bean sauce. *USA Today* once named this one of the best nine Chinese restaurants in the country. At 611 Stuart (tel. 527-0005); open Mon.-Sat. for lunch and dinner.

$$ East Ocean Chinese Seafood Restaurant: Prospective seafood dinners swim in aquarium displays while dim sum carts roll among the tables at this large, very authentic Hong Kong-style restaurant in the Bellaire/Gessner district—the city's "New Chinatown." Around 25 species of fresh fish and shellfish flown in daily. At 9399 S. Gessner (tel. 271-6668); open daily 11 a.m.-10 p.m.

$$ Golden China: Another good place for dim sum; weekend afternoons are boisterous (to say the least) when the place is packed to capacity with Chinese families and rolling carts of dumplings, pot stickers, sticky rice, and barbecued pork buns. Dim sum is available 10 a.m.-3 p.m. daily; much calmer on weekdays. A menu of standard Cantonese dishes available as well. At 7668 DeMoss (tel. 774-6688); open daily for lunch and dinner.

$ Hung Kee Restaurant: In the heart of Chinatown, specializing in fresh egg noodles and

Mandarin cuisine. At 902 St. Emanuel (tel. 225-9401); open daily 11 a.m.-10 p.m.

$$$+ Uncle Tai's Hunan Yuan: A branch of the New York Uncle Tai's and arguably the best (inarguably, the most expensive) Chinese restaurant in the city. The menu is extensive, with a preponderance of Hunan dishes. At 1980 Post Oak (tel. 960-8000); open daily for lunch and dinner.

Downhome

This is East Texas, state stronghold of "downhome" or Southern cooking. Then again, this is Houston, so expect some urban variations.

$$ The Black-Eyed Pea: Specialties here include pot roast, meatloaf, and fresh catfish, along with fried okra, baked squash, and cornbread. At 14 locations throughout the city, including 4729 Calhoun, near the University of Houston (tel. 713-748-0471); open daily for lunch and dinner.

$$ to $$$ Norris: Upscale downhome may seem oxymoronic, but this Astrodome-area eatery packs them in for Louisiana-style soul food—fried chicken, crawfish étouffée, grilled catfish, fried boudin balls, and sweet potato pie. At 2491 S. Braeswood (tel. 664-9447); open daily for lunch and dinner.

$ to $$ This Is It: An independent, funky place that's been serving soul food for over 25 years. Depending on what's in the steam table, you might find ham hocks, chitlins, smothered steak, cabbage, cornbread, rice, sweet potatoes, pinto beans, or other classics. At 239 W. Gray at Genessee (tel. 523-5319); open Mon.-Sat. for breakfast, lunch, and dinner (till 3 a.m. Friday and Saturday).

Health Food and Vegetarian

$$ Heaven on Earth: The vegetarian Thai portions of the menu seemed uncannily similar to the menu at a place I know in Bangkok. As it turns out, this place—like Bangkok's Whole Earth—is run by Transcendental Meditation adherents. In addition to vegetarian versions of Thailand's *mee krop* (thin, crispy noodles in coconut sauce) and *yam wun sen* (spicy cellophane noodle salad), the menu selections feature a few Indian dishes. Attached to the Heaven on Earth Hotel, 801 Calhoun (tel. 713-659-2222); open daily for lunch and dinner.

$$ Rich's Café: Conveniently located in Ye Seekers Natural Foods and Supermarket (tel. 461-0858), 9336 Westview; open Mon.-Sat. for lunch and dinner, Sat.-Sun. for breakfast.

$-$$ Wonderful Vegetarian: The unique menu combines tofu, black mushrooms, wheat gluten, beans, and nuts to produce delightful Chinese/kosher/vegetarian dishes. Specially prepared brown rice accompanies most entrees. At 7549 Westheimer (tel. 977-3137). Open Tues.-Sun. 11 a.m.-9:30 p.m.

Indian

The city has several good Indian restaurants, most serving similar North Indian, tandoor-based cuisines. The muggy, almost equatorial climate has long begged for a good South Indian place, a couple of which have finally arrived since the last edition of this guidebook.

Houston's Indian restaurants—especially the South Indian ones—feature plenty of vegetarian dishes, so if you can't find what you like at the "Health Food and Vegetarian" places listed previously, try one of these.

$ Annapurna: Very inexpensive Indian vegetarian food is served in a fast-food style atmosphere. Probably the only Indian restaurant in town where you can regularly get *paan,* ground betel nut and spices wrapped in betel leaf and eaten as a "digestive." At 5827 Hillcroft (tel. 713-780-4453); open daily for lunch and dinner.

$ Anand Bhavan: Typical South Indian snacks like *masala dosa,* vegetable stuffed, rice-and-lentil-flour crepe, and *sambar,* a thin incendiary soup made with red lentils, coconut, and vegetables. All vegetarian menu. At 6662 Southwest Freeway in southwest Houston (tel. 977-0150); open daily for lunch and dinner.

$ to $$ Bombay Palace: This restaurant is easy to find and has an all-you-can-eat lunch buffet Mon.-Friday. All the usual chicken, lamb, and beef dishes, grilled or in curries. At 3901 Westheimer (tel. 960-8472); open daily for lunch and dinner.

$$ India's Restaurant: One of the few North Indian restaurants in the city that isn't afraid to bring dishes more in line with authentic recipes by adding a little chile. At 5704 Richmond (tel. 266-0131); open daily for lunch and dinner.

$ Madras Cafe: Another vegetarian South Indian spot in southwest Houston; similar menu to

Anand Bhavan's. At 9725 Bissonnet (tel. 772-1002); open daily for lunch and dinner.

$$ Shiva: North Indian again, focusing on tandoori, with some interesting daily specials like potatoes stuffed with *paneer* (Indian cheese), raisins, and nuts. At 2514 Times (tel. 523-4753); open daily for lunch and dinner.

Italian and Pizza

$$ to $$$ Damian's Cucina Italiana: A city favorite, with standard pasta dishes as well as more trendy entrees like grilled chicken with sun-dried tomatoes and goat cheese. At 3011 Smith (tel. 713-522-0439); open Mon.-Fri. for lunch and dinner, Saturday dinner only.

$$ Carrabba's: The woodburning oven turns out some of the best and most popular pizza in town. The fun trattoria serves homemade pasta, too. At 1399 S. Voss (tel. 468-0868) and 3115 Kirby (tel. 522-3131); open daily for lunch and dinner.

$$ Nash D'Amico's Pasta & Clam Bar: As the name suggests, clams and pasta are the focus here; other fresh seafood is available as well. The menu was created with the help of the American Heart Association and a registered nutritionist, to make the choices as guilt-free as possible. At 2421 Times Blvd. in the Village (tel. 521-3010) and 5640 Westheimer (tel. 960-1230); open Mon.-Fri. for lunch and dinner, Saturday and Sunday for dinner only.

$$ to $$$ Rao's: Another Italian place with a light, low-calorie touch. One of the house specialties is *ossobuco* with risotto, along with grilled seafood and pastas. At 3700 Richmond (tel. 622-8245); open Mon.-Fri. for lunch and dinner, Saturday for dinner only.

$$ Pizzeria Uno: A branch of the famous Chicago pizza parlor, known for its deep-dish-style pizzas. At 7531 Westheimer (tel. 780-8866) and 3401 Kirby (tel. 520-0040); open daily for lunch and dinner.

$ to $$ Star Pizza: A favorite among Houston students because the pizza is quick, tasty, and inexpensive. At 2111 Norfolk, off Montrose (tel. 523-0800) and 140 S. Heights Blvd. (tel. 869-1241); open daily for lunch and dinner.

Japanese

$$ Tokyo Gardens: Houston's longest-running Japanese restaurant and sushi bar; classical Japanese dancing nightly. At 4701 Westheimer (tel. 713-622-7886); open Mon.-Fri. for lunch and dinner, Saturday and Sunday for dinner only.

$$ Miyako Japanese Restaurant & Sushi Bar: Extensive sashimi selection, tatami dining rooms. At 6345 Westheimer (tel. 781-6300) and 3910 Kirby (tel. 520-9797); open daily for lunch and dinner.

$$ Yoshida-Ya: The blond-wood paneling brings a reasonable facsimile of modern Tokyo to Houston; the sushi and traditional Japanese dishes are also authentic. At 855 Frostwood (tel. 464-3449); open Mon.-Sat. for lunch and dinner, Sunday dinner only.

Mexican and Latin American

Mexican food in Houston is better than in Dallas, but not quite as good as in San Antonio, Austin, or El Paso. And there's a definite lack of places with Mexican breakfasts.

$ to $$ Amalia's: Some Houstonians say Amalia's serves the city's best chicken and beef fajitas. The salsas—an avocado-based green and a garlic-infused red—also get raves. At 6892 Southwest Freeway, between Hillcroft and Bellaire Blvd. (tel. 713-785-4533); open daily for lunch and dinner.

$$$+ Américas: The menu of this ultra-classy eatery in the Saks Pavilion is far reaching to say the least, covering the foods of North, Central, and South America. Black bean soup, pork tenderloin on roasted red peppers, quail taquitos, shrimp over corn fettucine, and chicken breast roasted in coconut milk and pineapple are samples of what's available. At 1800 Post Oak Blvd. (tel. 961-1492); open Mon.-Fri. for lunch and dinner, Saturday for dinner only.

$$ to $$$ Armando's: The city's most upscale Mexican place and one of the most authentic—e.g., it uses white Mexican cheese rather than orange American. At 1811 S. Shepherd (tel. 521-9757); open daily for lunch and dinner.

$$ Cadillac Bar: Yet another clone of Nuevo Laredo's 1920s border classic. Some of the menu items, like *cabrito*, roast quail, and frog legs, are the same as the south-of-the-border Cadillac; others are Houston additions. At 1802 Shepherd (tel. 862-2020); open daily for lunch and dinner.

$$ to $$$ **Cafe Noche:** Innovative interior cooking produces dishes such as walnut-laced *chile en nogada,* Portobello mushroom fajitas (no meat, just huge mushrooms), and chicken cooked in *hoja santa* ("holy leaf"). Great Sunday brunch buffet. At 2409 Montrose (tel. 529-2409); open Mon.-Sat. for lunch and dinner, Sunday for brunch and dinner.

$ **Cortés Meat Market & Deli:** A homey hole-in-the-wall recommended for aficionados of bean-and-cheese and bean-and-rice tacos. Available enhancers include a mind-bending green salsa, fresh guacamole, and *pico de gallo.* Also serves fajitas rancheras, ceviche, and Mexican breakfasts. At 2404 W. Alabama (tel. 522-7771); open daily for breakfast and lunch.

$$ **Cyclone Anaya:** Very popular for its giant frozen margaritas. The food is classic Tex-Mex, with fajitas and soft tacos prominently featured. Named for a pro wrestler. At 1015 Durham (tel. 862-3209); open daily for lunch and dinner.

$ to $$ **Doneraki's:** A Greek family owns this authentic Tex-Mex restaurant that features Laredo-style *machitos* (goat-tripe sausage), *tacos al carbón, molcajete,* and fajitas. At 2836 Fulton (tel. 224-2509); open daily for lunch and dinner, weekends till 3 a.m.

$$ **Merida Restaurant:** Great Yucatecan specialties, including *cochinita pibil,* marinated, pit-cooked pork which can be ordered in *panuchos,* Yucatecan-style tacos with extra-thick corn tortillas and black beans. At 2509 Navigation (tel. 227-0260); open daily for lunch and dinner.

$ **Taquería Mexico:** A good selection of fillings for its tacos, including *milanesa, pollo guisada,* and *barbacoa.* Wash it down with *horchata,* a traditional Mexican beverage not commonly found in Texas. At 7626 Clarewood (tel. 271-0174); open daily 8:30 a.m.-3 p.m.

$ **La Victoria Bakery:** Very good Tex-Mex specialties like *carne guisada,* as well as South Texas-style breakfast tacos, gorditas, and *pan dulce* (Mexican pastries and sweets). At 7138 Lawndale in east Houston (tel. 921-0861); open daily 6 a.m.-9 p.m.

Seafood

$ **Captain Benny's:** Four locations, all small and designed to look like boats. The oysters, crab, catfish, shrimp, and gumbo are quick, fresh, cheap, and tasty. One is at 8018 Katy Freeway (tel. 713-683-1042); open Mon.-Sat. for lunch and dinner.

$$ **Christie's:** A Houston institution since 1917, Christie's features a friendly, family atmosphere and no-frills, simply prepared seafood mostly fresh from the Gulf. At four locations, including 6029 Westheimer (tel. 978-6563) and 3512 S. Main (tel. 522-5041); open daily for lunch and dinner.

$$ **Goode Company Texas Seafood:** A successful spinoff of Goode's barbecue restaurant specializing in mesquite-grilled seafood. At 2621 Westpark (tel. 523-7154); open daily for lunch and dinner.

$$ **Pappas Seafood House & Oyster Bar:** Probably the most popular seafood restaurant in the city, Pappas serves fresh Gulf fish and shellfish fried, blackened, or pan-broiled. At five locations, including 6894 Southwest Freeway (tel. 784-4729) and 12010 I-10 E (tel. 453-3265); open daily for lunch and dinner.

$$ to $$$ **Shanghai Red's:** People come here for the nighttime view of the Houston Ship Channel. Offers a variety of fresh seafood. At 8501 Cypress (tel. 926-6666); open daily for lunch and dinner.

$$ **Tony Mandola's:** Fresh seafood with an Italian slant, including crawfish ravioli (in season). At 1962 W. Gray (tel. 528-3474); open Mon.-Sat. for lunch and dinner, Sunday for dinner only.

Steak

$$ **Cattleguard:** A macho, ranch-style steakhouse that serves large portions of Mexican and Cajun food as well as steak. At 2800 Milam (tel. 713-520-5400); open daily for lunch and dinner.

$$$ **Lynn's Steakhouse:** Prime beef—filet, strip, ribeye, and porterhouse—cut to order. At 955 Dairy Ashford (tel. 870-0807); open Mon.-Sat. for lunch and dinner.

$$$ **Ruth's Chris Steak House:** A transplant from the Panhandle (Amarillo and Lubbock) that serves only USDA prime beef, plus lamb, veal, and seafood. At 6213 Richmond (tel. 789-2333); open daily for lunch and dinner.

Thai

$$ **Nit Noi Thai Cafe:** This tiny place in Rice Village is often overcrowded, but the excellent

© MOON PUBLICATIONS, INC.

Thai fare makes it worth the hassle. At 2426 Bolsover (tel. 713-524-8114); open daily for lunch and dinner.

$$ Paddy Thai Cuisine: A small, intimate restaurant where the Thai menu changes nightly. At 6018 Westheimer (tel. 782-4849); open Mon.-Fri. for lunch and dinner, Saturday for dinner only.

$$ Patu Thai: Houston's oldest Thai restaurant. Good bets on the menu include *yam makheua* (roasted eggplant salad), chicken *panang* (a savory curry), and *pad voon sen* (spicy bean thread noodles with chicken and shrimp). At 2420B Rice Blvd. (tel. 528-6998).

Open Tues.-Sun. for lunch and dinner; good-value lunch buffet Tues.-Friday.

$$ Thai Pepper: Houston's most authentic Thai restaurant uses fresh herbs and spices and no MSG. The *yam* ("lime salads" on the menu) are especially good. At 2120 Post Oak (tel. 963-0341) and 2049 W. Alabama (tel. 520-8225); open Mon.-Fri. for lunch and dinner, Saturday for dinner only.

Vietnamese

$ Kim Son: The daily lunch buffet at this cavernous restaurant features at least 15 dishes and is backed by an a la carte menu with a mind-boggling 235 entries. Decorated with Vietnamese folk instruments, costumes, art, and other cultural artifacts. At 2001 Jefferson (tel. 713-222-2461); second branch at 8200 Wilcrest (tel. 498-7841). Open daily for lunch and dinner.

$ **Pho Cong Ly** and **Pho Tau Bay:** These two unassuming noodle houses in Houston's Little Saigon serve splendid *pho*, wide rice noodles in a huge bowl of broth with bean sprouts and various meats. Open daily 11 a.m.-8 p.m.

$ to $$ **Van Loc Restaurant:** The menu here encompasses 140 reasonably priced Vietnamese and Chinese dishes. At 3010 Milam (tel. 528-6441) and 825 Travis St. (tel. 236-0542); open daily for lunch and dinner till midnight, on weekends till 3 a.m.

$ to $$ **Vietnam Restaurant:** Standard Vietnamese specialties; lunch buffet weekdays. At 3215 Main at Elgin (tel. 526-0917); open daily for lunch and dinner.

ENTERTAINMENT

Live Music

Houston's black wards, especially the 4th and 5th, were very influential in the early Texas blues scene, and the city remains very much a blues and R&B town, with a little zydeco and country thrown in. The *Houston Chronicle* carries a relatively complete listing of the more popular clubs. Even more thorough is the one compiled weekly by *Coors Light Music News* and distributed at local clubs and music shops.

Blues: A number of clubs feature blues on weekends only; look for performances by local blues legends Pete Mayes, Joe Hughes, Texas Johnny Brown, Big Roger Collins, and I.J. Gosey. **Evening Shadows** (tel. 713-748-7683), 5665 Old Spanish Trail, hosts blues or R&B performers every night of the week. **Etta's Lounge** (tel. 528-2611), 5120 Scott, south of downtown, features mostly blues—one of the last of the city's great blues bars that were so common in the '30s and '40s. One of the regular acts here is Grady Gaines, tenor saxman during Little Richard's glory days, and his Texas Upsetters. Gaines also books one-nighters at several other spots around town. **Mr. Blues** (tel. 644-8118), 4937 Martin Luther King, lives up to its name, as does **Billy Blues** (tel. 266-9294),

6025 Richmond. At some places blues gigs are traditionally limited to Sunday afternoon jam sessions. Among these are **Mr. Gino's Lounge** (tel. 738-0555), 7318 Cullen, a neighborhood bar off South Loop; **Club Success** (tel. 694-8143), 5710 Wheatley in northwest Houston, where if you're lucky you'll catch Clarence Green and the Rhythmaires, featuring Guitar Slim; and **Mingo's** (tel. 520-6750), 2541 MacGregor Way.

Zydeco: Houston is one of the best places in the U.S. to hear zydeco; this is where it was created. Probably the best place to hear zydeco in Houston is at Catholic church dances—there's usually at least one Creole parish holding a zydeco dance on any given weekend. Twelve or 13 rotate by month, including St. Nicholas, St. Francis, St. Peter the Apostle, Our Lady Star of the Sea, St. Anne, and St. Gregory the Great. Three clubs book zydeco acts on weekend nights as well: **Continental Zydeco Ballroom** (tel. 229-8624), 3103 Collingsworth; **Silver Slipper Club** (tel. 673-9004), 3717 Crane; and **Mr. Gino's** (tel. 738-0555), 7318 Cullen.None of these clubs are in so-called "good" neighborhoods, so it's best to check them out in the daytime first to see if they're your cup of tea or not. Somewhat tamer are the several Cajun restaurants featuring Cajun and zydeco bands on the weekends, including **Pe-Te's Cajun Barbecue House.** Stay on the lookout for these zydeco artists who perform frequently in the Houston area: Buckwheat Zydeco, Lonnie Mitchell, Wilfred Chavis, Fernest Arceneaux, L. C. Donatello, Anderson Moss, Boozoo Chavis, Paul Richard, Jabo, and Vincent Frank.

Jazz: Cody's (tel. 522-9747), 3400 Montrose, is a longtime Houston favorite for jazz and also has a nighttime view of the city. **Cody's in the Village** (tel. 520-5660), 2540 University, and **Dizzy's** (tel. 520-7221), 1336 Westheimer, are also good options, with the latter fast becoming the city's jazz-talent headquarters. Most other jazz in the city is of the piano-bar variety.

Folk and Singer-Songwriters: Oddly enough, considering the setting, British-style pubs are fashionable in Houston. Several book local rock and folk bands; try **The Pig Live** (tel. 524-0696), 2150 Richmond; the **Ale House** (tel. 521-2333), 2425 Alabama; the **Red Lion** (tel. 795-5000), 7315 S. Main; **Sherlock's Baker**

St. Pub (tel. 977-1857), 10001 Westheimer, in Carillon Center; **Munchies** (tel. 528-3545), 1617 Richmond; and the **Black Labrador Pub** (tel. 529-1199), 4100 Montrose. For low-key, singer-songwriter-type gigs, check out the established **Anderson Fair** (tel. 528-8576), 2007 Grant St.; **Ovations** (tel. 522-9801), 2536B Times Blvd. at Kirby; and **Wunsche Bros. Cafe** (tel. 350-2777), 103 Midway in Old Town Spring.

Eclectic: Several clubs in the Heights district, north of Buffalo Bayou, book a mix of local, regional, and national acts, mostly (but not limited to) roots rock, blues, and R&B. These clubs include **Bon Ton Room** (tel. 863-0001), 4216 Washington; **Fitzgerald's** (tel. 862-3838), 2706 White Oak; **Reddi Room** (tel. 868-6188), 2626 White Oak; **Fabulous Satellite Lounge** (tel. 869-COOL), 3616 Washington Ave.; **The Outback Pub** (tel. 780-2323), 3100 Fountainview; and **Rockefeller's** (tel. 861-9365), 3620 Washington. In a similar vein but just northeast of downtown is the **Last Concert Cafe** (tel. 226-8563), 1403 Nance. **Zelda's** (tel. 862-7469), 2706 White Oak the Heights, features pop and modern-rock bands. North of the Heights just inside the loop is **Dan Electro's Guitar Bar** (tel. 862-8707), 1031 E. 24th, where Monday night is blues night, Tuesday and Wednesday are open-mike nights, and Thurs.-Sat. mostly rock 'n' roll. The bar's name comes from the decor—on the walls hang a number of guitars, including some rare Danelectros. **McGonigel's Mucky Duck** (tel. 528-5999), 2425 Norwalk, is probably the best acoustic venue in town, featuring a range of C&W, Latino, R&B, and folk performers.

Country: Of the many country-music venues in and around the city, the most popular are the **Pecos Grill** (tel. 861-0180), 2400 East T.C. Jester; the **Post Oak Ranch** (tel. 627-2624), 1625 W. Loop South; and **Eddie's Country Ballroom** (tel. 489-8181), State 288, Manvel. **Blanco's Bar & Grill** (tel. 439-0072), 3406 W. Alabama, specializes in Austin artists like Gary P. Nunn and Alvin Crow on Thursday and Friday nights only. Other spots in town with occasional live country music include **Cattle Kings Grill** (tel. 623-6000), 5430 Westheimer; and **The Swingin' Door** (tel. 342-4758), FM 359. In nearby Pasadena, just east of the city limits, the **SPJST Ballroom** (tel. 487-3297), 3609 Preston Rd., hosts Czech and Western swing bands—look for one-time Bob Wills sideman Clyde Brewer and the Original River Road Boys.

Discos

Houston's best dance clubs are in the Montrose area, the city's well-known gay district, just southwest of downtown. The dance floors at **Heaven** (tel. 713-521-9123), 925 Hyde Park, and **Pacific Street** (tel. 523-0213), 710 Pacific, are jumping most of the week, but especially Thurs.-Sunday. Both attract a mixed straight and gay crowd. Two-story **Rich's** (tel. 759-9606), at 2401 San Jacinto on the edge of downtown, is also popular.

Comedy and Magic

Houston's comedy clubs continue to grow in number, with the addition of the **Hip Hop Comedy Stop** (tel. 713-437-8444), 4816 Main; **The Laugh Spot** (tel. 955-9200), FM 1960 and 249 behind TGI Friday; and **Spellbinders** (tel. 266-2525). Performances are usually Tues.-Sun. nights, with two shows on weekend evenings. **The Comedy Showcase** (tel. 481-1188), 12547 Gulf Frwy. at Fuqua, and **The Laff Stop** (tel. 524-2333), 1952 W. Gray, book touring as well as local acts, Wed.-Sunday.

The **Radio Music Theater** (tel. 522-7722) at 2623 Colquitt is a unique comedy repertory group that performs skits inspired by different radio-show styles. Performances—some recorded for a nationally syndicated radio broadcast—are offered Thurs.-Sat. nights.

Magic Island (tel. 526-2442), 2215 Southwest Frwy., features a nightly dinner show of magic, comedy, and dancing.

Other Bars

Although it doesn't offer live music, the friendly, British-style **Richmond Arms Pub** (tel. 713-784-7722) at 5920 Richmond Ave. offers an amazing 69 different beers on tap. A fireplace and wood accents provide just the right atmosphere. Open 11 a.m.-2 a.m. daily.

Wortham Center

This 437,000-square-foot, $70.5 million performing arts center at the corner of Smith and Texas is a city showpiece. A variety of events are scheduled here throughout the year, but the center's main function is as home for the **Houston Ballet** and the **Houston Grand Opera.** Each is housed in a separate theater within the center. The Houston Ballet (tel. 713-523-6300) is a first-rate company that tours the U.S. and abroad regularly.

The Wortham Center is open for free public tours by appointment only; call 237-1439 for reservations.

Radio

Houston has radio stations for practically every taste. Rockers listen to KLOL-FM 101.1, kickers (country music fans) to KIKK-FM 95.7; for public radio fans it's KTSU-FM 90.9, broadcasting a broad variety of jazz, blues, and gospel, with an all-night blues show every Monday. KMJQ-FM 102 plays jazz and R&B while KCOH-AM 1430 offers straight R&B. KYST-AM 920 serves up a mix of rock, dance tunes, and *tejano* music; KLAT-AM 1010 plays Latin and *tejano* music 24 hours a day. The only station that spins discs by local bands is KRBE-AM 1070.

EVENTS

February
Chinese New Year Festival: The timing for this festival varies according to the Chinese lunar calendar; call 713-780-8112 for current scheduling. Activities include fireworks, lion parades, food vendors, and music. At McKinney and St. Emanuel in Chinatown.

February-March
Houston Livestock Show and Rodeo: Usually held the last 10 days in February and first week of March at the Astrodome (Kirby and S. Loop 610) and adjacent Astrohall and Astroarena. The rodeo ranks as a top-five event, with a payout of over $325,000.

April
Houston International Festival: An arts and culture festival that celebrates Houston's ethnic diversity and brings in artists and performers from abroad as well. Events include outdoor music, dance, and theater performances, arts and crafts shows, food presentations, and the Houston International Film Festival. Held for 10

days beginning the third week of the month at various locations throughout the city.

May
Cinco de Mayo: A celebration of Mexico's victory over the French navy in 1862, featuring food vendors, music, and dancing. At the Brown Convention Center on the nearest weekend to May 5.

Heights Home Tour: During Mother's Day weekend several historic homes in the Heights district are open for tours. Call (713) 868-0120 for information.

June
Juneteenth: Houston's biggest annual celebration commemorates the June 19, 1865, announcement in Galveston of the abolition of slavery. Activities are mostly based around music, starting with the Juneteenth USA Gospel Festival and the Juneteenth Blues Festival at Miller Outdoor Theater on the weekend before Juneteenth weekend. Then, on the weekend nearest to June 19, the National Emancipation Association sponsors a Juneteenth Freedom Festival, also at Miller Outdoor Theater. In between the two weekends are various other cultural events celebrating Houston's African-American heritage.

September
Fiestas Patrias: A celebration of Mexican Independence Day (September 16) that features a downtown parade, beauty pageant, ball, music and dance festivals, and civic awards ceremonies. Held at various locations throughout the city.

October
Italian Parade and Festival: Three days of food, music, and parades, on the nearest weekend to Columbus Day at St. Anne's Catholic Church on Westheimer.

Alamo Challenge Bike Trek: A two-day, 160-mile bicycle race between Houston and San Antonio, sponsored by the American Lung Association and run on the second weekend of the month. Call (800) 252-5864 for information.

Asian-American Festival: A weekend of Asian arts, music, dance, food, and cultural exhibits at Miller Outdoor Theater, on the third weekend of the month.

October-November

Texas Renaissance Festival: This popular theme festival is staged 45 miles northwest of the city off FM 1774 between Plantersville and Magnolia every weekend between October 1 and November 15. The food, entertainment, costumes, arts and crafts, and setting attempt to re-create the atmosphere of Renaissance England. Call (800) 458-3435 for details.

November

Foley's Thanksgiving Day Parade: A classic American-style parade that starts downtown in front of Foley's department store at 1110 Main.

SPORTS AND RECREATION

Professional Team Sports

The hometown pro **baseball** team is the **Houston Astros** (tel. 713-799-9555 for tickets), who play home games April-Oct. at the Astrodome. The **Houston Rockets** (tel. 627-0600 for tickets) play pro **basketball** Oct.-April at The Summit (Greenway Plaza, Southwest Freeway), while die-hard fans of American **football** can watch the underdog **Houston Oilers** (tel. 797-1000 for tickets) play Sept.-Dec. at the Astrodome.

Bicycling

Houston has a very active cycling community, perhaps because the city and surrounding areas are so flat. The **Houston Bicycle Club** (tel. 713-729-9333), P.O. Box 52752, Houston, TX 77052, has information on local cycling events. Alexander Deussen County Park has several miles of bicycle trails, as does Brazos Bend State Park southwest of Houston.

Alkek Velodrome (tel. 578-0858) is a unique facility operated by the city Parks and Recreation Department in Cullen Park, 19008 Saums Road. This Olympic-standard bike arena (333 meters long with a 33° bank) is open for general recreational use as well as serious training. Races are held on Saturday evenings; racing instruction is available.

Golf

Seven municipal 18-hole golf courses are open to the public: **Brock** (tel. 713-458-1350), 8201 John Ralston Rd.; **Glenbrook** (tel. 649-8089), 8101 Bayou Dr.; **Hermann** (tel. 526-0077), 6201 Golf Course Dr.; **Memorial** (tel. 862-4033), 1001 Memorial Park Loop E; **Sharpstown** (tel. 988-2099), 6600 Harbor Town; and **Wortham** (tel. 921-3227), 311 S. Wayside Drive. Hours are daily 6 a.m.-6 p.m. in the winter, 7 a.m.-8:30 p.m. in the summer.

Tennis

Many of the public parks in Houston have tennis courts where facilities are available on a first-come, first-served basis. The city also operates three tennis centers that take reservations: **Homer L. Ford Center** (tel. 713-747-5466), 5225 Calhoun, 16 lighted courts; **Memorial Tennis Center** (tel. 861-3765), 1500 Memorial Loop Dr., Memorial Park, 18 lighted courts; and **Southwest Tennis Center** (tel. 772-0296), 9506 Gessner, 26 lighted courts. Rates are the same at all three: $4 per hour-and-a-half before 5:30 p.m. on weekdays, $6 per hour-and-a-half after 5:30 and on weekends.

Horse Racing

The **Sam Houston Race Park** (tel. 713-807-8700) opened in early 1994 for thoroughbred and quarter horse racing. The 200,000 square-foot, enclosed and air-conditioned grandstand contains concessions for drinks and dining, and a members-only Jockey Club. Post times vary from meet to meet, but races typically begin at 7 p.m. Wed.-Sat., 1 p.m. Sunday and holidays. Admission is $3-5 unreserved seating (Pavilion Level), $7-8 reserved (Club Level); children under 12 free. On the south side of Sam Houston Tollway between the Fallbrook/Windfern and 249/Tomball exits.

Parks and Gardens

The **Armand Bayou Nature Center** (tel. 713-474-2551), off I-45 S at 8600 Bay Area, is an 1,800-acre preserve with woodland, marsh, and prairie nature trails, plus a turn-of-the-century farm. The bayou, which feeds into Clear Lake, is popular for boating. Free guided tours on weekends. Open Wed.-Sat. 9 a.m.-5 p.m., Sunday noon to dusk; admission $2.50 for adults, $1 for seniors and children 5-17.

Mercer Arboretum and Botanic Gardens (tel. 443-9731), off Aldine-Westfield Rd. in Humble (a small township next to Houston Intercontinental Airport), features 214 acres of formal gardens displaying local flora, five miles of nature trails, and a Big Thicket-style arboretum with a picnic area. Open daily 8 a.m.-7 p.m. during daylight saving time, 8 a.m.-5 p.m. standard time; free admission. **Houston Arboretum and Nature Center** (tel. 681-8433) in Memorial Park (off I-10 at Woodway) is similar but smaller, though there are five miles of trails through native woods and prairies. Open dawn to dusk; free admission.

Buffalo Bayou

Houston got its start as a trading post on Buffalo Bayou and owes its preeminence as a port to the dredging of the bayou to create the Houston Ship Channel and Port of Houston. There's still a lot of bayou left, however; it bisects the city, beginning in rural west Harris County at Barker Reservoir, an impoundment of the bayou for flood control, and meanders 50 miles east through suburbs, downtown business districts, and parks to the ship channel. The most scenic section is in lush Memorial Park, where the bayou's banks are lined with black willow, sycamore, box elder, ash, and river birch, with an undergrowth of moss, ferns, verbena, dwarf palmetto, muscodyne vine, and mustang grape. Fauna sightings include the occasional alligator, opossum, or armadillo.

Canoeing is permitted along the bayou within Memorial Park and farther east in Cleveland Park; canoe equipment can be rented or purchased from Canoesport (tel. 713-660-7000), 5630 Bellaire Boulevard. Plans are underway to extend greenbelt areas along the bayou all the way from Cleveland Park to the ship channel.

The 14-acre gardens at **Bayou Bend** (tel. 529-8773), 1 Westcott St. off Memorial Dr., are open for self-guided touring Wed.-Sat. 10 a.m.-5 p.m., Sunday 1-5 p.m. Admission is $3 for adults, free for children under 10. On the third Sunday of each month (March and August excepted) admission to the gardens is free for everyone.

Brazos Bend State Park

Less than 50 miles from the city is one of the state park system's largest parks, covering 4,897 acres of bayous, creeks, lakes, wetlands, coastal prairies, and hardwood forests. Migrating waterfowl, including ibis, grebes, egrets, and herons, are numerous here, as are white-tailed deer, feral hogs, Russian boars, gray foxes, bobcats, coyotes, and alligators.

The **George Observatory,** operated by Houston's Museum of Natural Science, is another park attraction. This working research facility is open to the public each Saturday from dusk to 10 p.m. A $1 viewing fee is charged for a peek through the 36-inch, 10-ton telescope, but there are usually smaller, privately owned telescopes set up for viewing at no charge.

Facilities: The 15 miles of hike-and-bike trails at Brazos Bend are some of the system's best maintained. Fishing is permitted on all of the park's six lakes; Elm Lake has seven piers, while both Forty Acre and Hale lakes feature lighted piers for night fishing. Fish-cleaning tables are close at hand. Camping areas include tent/camper sites with water ($6 on weekdays, $9 weekends), multi-use sites with w/e ($10/15), and screened shelters ($18/20). For further information or campsite reservations, contact the Park Superintendent (tel. 409-553-3243), Brazos Bend State Park, 21901 FM 762, Needville, TX 77461. The park charges an entry fee of $5 per car; free with the Texas Conservation Passport.

Getting There: Brazos Bend State Park is 55 minutes from downtown on US 59 S (exit Crabb River Road). There are two routes from Houston, both about the same distance, 45-50 miles. The scenic, and shorter, route is via State 288 south to Rosharon, then west on FM 1462. Slightly quicker because of the higher speed limit is US 59 south to Richmond, then east on FM 762.

Amusement Parks

Six Flags AstroWorld (tel. 713-799-1234), opposite the Astrodome off Loop 610, covers 75 acres of concrete and landscaping with over a hundred rides. Thillseekers head straight for the Viper, a rollercoaster with a 360° loop inside the pitch-black "Viper Pit." "Batman The Escape" is another rollercoaster—riders make a similar loop standing up. The new "Mayan Mindbender," an indoor coaster ride similar in concept to Disneyland's "Space Mountain," cannons passengers through a Mayan-inspired pyramid. The park is open at 10 a.m.-dusk weekends only from mid-March to late May and mid-Sept.

to October, and daily during spring break and from late May to early September. All-inclusive admission is $27 for adults, $18.35 for children two years to 48 inches, $14 for seniors.

Next door is **WaterWorld** (tel. 794-3221), with various water rides and a wave pool. Open the same hours as AstroWorld except the season is May-September. Admission is $14 adult, $11.95 children, under three free.

The complex also includes the **Southern Star Amphitheater** (tel. 799-1234), one of the city's main venues for large-scale concerts. The reserved area has 3,000 seats; beyond that it's general-admission grass seating.

SHOPPING

Shopping Areas
The Galleria, at 5075 Westheimer, is the city's premier mall. A three-level extravaganza centered around a skating rink with a vaulted-glass ceiling, its department store pillars are Macy's, Marshall Fields, Neiman-Marcus, and Lord & Taylor. The nearby **Post Oak** area is thick with other high-end department stores and smaller boutiques.

Rice Village, near Rice University between Morningside, Kirby, University, and Bolsover, is a public-square-style shopping area frequented by students, faculty, medical-center staff, tourists, and European expatriates. Clothing stores, arts and crafts shops, and bookstores sit side by side with bistros and neighborhood pubs. Even more idiosyncratic is the **Montrose** district, centered on Montrose Boulevard. This ever-changing area of small specialty stores near the museum district features designer clothing, jewelry, cards, and various art-oriented items.

Chinatown, bounded by St. Emanuel, Chartres, Lamar, and Rush in the downtown area, offers a selection of shops dealing in Orientalia, including foods, jewelry, herbs, furniture, and clothing.

Antique Districts, Auction Houses, and Flea Markets
Junk and antiquity hunters will love Houston, which has more than its share due to its huge port status. The **River Oaks Antiques Center** (tel. 713-520-8238), 2119 Westheimer, is comprised of 25 antique dealers who mostly handle furniture, crystal, china, and jewelry. There are several other antique shops along Westheimer, from the 300 block out to Shepherd. Roughly parallel strips run along Washington and W. Gray farther north. **Norbert Antiques** (tel. 522-7300), 3607-3617 Main, specializes in French and English antiques, primarily furniture and objets d'art.

Kuehnert's Antique Center and Auction Gallery (tel. 827-7835), 8719 Katy Frwy., sells consignment antiques Mon.-Sat. and frequently holds estate auctions. **Webster's Auction Palace** (tel. 442-2351), 14463 Luthe Rd., holds auctions of American antiques on Friday and Sunday.

There are at least six flea markets in the city, all open on weekends only. The busiest is the outdoor **Houston Flea Market** (tel. 782-0391), also known as the Southwest Common Market, at 6616 Southwest Frwy. (Westpark exit). Booths cover 14 acres of pavement—very hot in the summertime. The **Coles Antique Village/ Flea Market** (tel. 485-2277) at 1014 N. Main off State 35 in Pearland features 600 dealers in a 70,000-square-foot air-conditioned facility. Two more indoor places that beat the heat include the equally huge **Trade Mart** (tel. 467-2506) at 2121 Sam Houston Tollway N, and **Trading Fair II** (tel. 731-1111) at 5515 S. Loop 610 near the Astrodome. The 100-acre, outdoor **Trader's Village** (tel. 890-5500) at 7979 N. Eldridge Pkwy. features over 600 flea-market dealers.

Western Wear
Several of Houston's Western-wear stores have been around since the turn of the century. The city's oldest is **Stelzig's** (tel. 713-629-7779) at 3123 Post Oak, which has been a purveyor of boots, hats, saddles, and ranching supplies since 1870. The venerable **Shudde Bros. Hatters** at 905 Trinity (est. 1907) specializes in hats, both new and reconditioned. For custom-made boots, try the **Palace Boot Shop** (tel. 224-1411) at 1212 Prairie, which also carries factory-made boots. **Boot Town** (tel. 627-2668) at 2335 Post Oak sells several brands of Texas boots from a total stock of over 100,000, and offers hats at discount prices. **Wild West Outfitters** (tel. 621-1212) at 3115 W. Loop 610

South carries all the big names in boots and Western attire.

INFORMATION

Tourist Offices

The **Greater Houston Convention and Visitors Bureau** (tel. 713-227-3100 or 800-365-7575) at 801 Congress has a wealth of free printed material on area attractions, services, and accommodations as well as a staffed information counter. French-, Spanish-, and German-speaking specialists are available. Open Mon.-Fri. 8:30 a.m.-5 p.m.

Houston is the only Texas city outside Laredo that has a **Mexican Government Tourist Office** (tel. 880-5153), at 2707 N. Loop 610 W, Suite 450.

Consulates

Houston has more foreign consulates than any other city in the state. If you're planning a trip outside the U.S. in the near future, this is a good place to collect the necessary visas. Most of the consulates are located in the city's west end. See the "Houston Consulates" chart.

Telephone

The area code for Houston is 713.

Foreign Exchange

With all the international trade centered here, Houston is a good place to change foreign currency. **Thomas Cook Foreign Exchange** (tel. 713-782-8091) at 10777 Westheimer, Suite 105, is a full-service moneychanging agency with good rates; it also sells traveler's checks. **Valuta Corp.** (tel. 975-9517) at 3760 S. Gessner provides 24-hour money-exchange services every day, including holidays.

Some of the major banks offer foreign-exchange services for a limited number of currencies—Canadian dollars, German marks, Japanese yen, Mexican pesos. Try **First Bank of Houston** (2824 Hillcroft), **First City Bancorporation of Texas** (1001 Main), and **Texas Commerce Bank** (712 Main).

HOUSTON CONSULATES

Argentina: 2000 Post Oak, Ste. 1810; tel. 871-8935
Australia: 1990 Post Oak, Ste. 800; tel. 629-9131
Austria: 7887 Katy Frwy.; tel. 623-2233
Belgium: 2929 Allen Pkwy., Ste. 2222; tel. 529-0775
Brazil: 1700 W. Loop 610 S; tel. 961-3063
Chile: 1360 Post Oak, Ste. 2300; tel. 621-5853
China: 3417 Montrose; tel. 524-0778
Colombia: 2990 Richmond, Ste. 544; tel. 527-8919
Denmark: 5 Post Oak, Ste. 2180; tel. 622-7514
Ecuador: 4200 Westheimer; tel. 622-1787
Egypt: 2000 W. Loop 610 S., Ste.1750; tel. 961-4915
El Salvador: 6420 Hillcroft; tel. 270-6239
Finland: 1300 Post Oak, Ste. 1990; tel. 627-9700
France: 2727 Allen Pkwy., Ste. 976; tel. 528-2181
Germany: 1330 Post Oak, Ste. 1850; tel. 627-7770
Indonesia: 5633 Richmond; tel. 785-1691
Israel: 1 Greenway Plaza, Ste. 722; tel. 627-3780
Italy: 1300 Post Oak, Ste. 660; tel. 850-7520
Japan: 1000 Louisiana; tel. 652-2977
Korea: 1990 Post Oak, Ste. 745; tel. 961-0186
Mexico: 4200 Montrose, Ste. 120; tel. 524-2300
Netherlands: 2200 Post Oak, Ste. 610; tel. 622-8000
Norway: 2777 Allen Pkwy., Ste. 1185; tel. 521-2900
Peru: 5847 San Felipe, Ste. 1481; tel. 781-5000
Philippines: 5177 Richmond, Ste. 1100; tel. 621-8618
Spain: 1800 Bering Dr.; tel. 783-6200
Switzerland: 1000 Louisiana, Ste. 5670; tel. 650-0000
Turkey: 1990 Post Oak, Ste. 1300; tel. 622-5849
United Kingdom: 2250 Dresser Tower, 601 Jefferson; tel. 659-6270
Venezuela: 2700 Post Oak, Ste. 1500; tel. 961-5141

GETTING THERE AND AROUND

Airports

Houston Intercontinental Airport (tel. 713-230-3000), 22 miles north of the city via Eastex Frwy. (US 59), is Houston's main air hub, with daily service to 101 U.S. destinations and 26 international destinations. Its four terminals and Marriott Hotel are connected by an efficient subway system, but the airport is miserably lacking in decent dining opportunities. Driving to the airport from the city takes a half hour when the traffic's light, at least 45 minutes during rush hours. **Airport Express** (tel. 523-8888) operates a shuttle between the airport and three city terminals—the Hyatt Regency downtown, the Texas Medical Center, and the Galleria/Post Oaks/Greenway area (5000 Richmond). The shuttle runs every half hour, $13 per person one-way. A taxi from Intercontinental to downtown Houston costs a flat rate of $29.

Hobby Airport (tel. 643-4597) was the city's first commercial airport but is now relegated to secondary status, with daily flights to 72 U.S. cities. The food selection here is better than at Intercontinental; the **Food Court** allows travelers to choose from several fast-food outlets, including **Por-ras Mexican Food,** where a vegetarian burrito costs less than $2.

Hobby is only seven miles southeast of town, about 15-20 minutes during off-peak traffic periods, up to 45 minutes in rush hours. Airport Express also runs shuttles between Hobby and several city terminals.

Taxi service between Hobby and downtown is $16-18.

Train

The Amtrak passenger station is at 902 Washington downtown. The *Sunset Limited* has thrice-weekly service, west to Los Angeles, east to New Orleans. Call (713) 224-1577 or 800-USA-RAIL for schedule information.

For information on excursion train travel to Galveston, see "Texas Limited" under "Sights."

Intercity Buses

The **Greyhound Bus Terminal** (tel. 713-759-6565 or 800-231-2222) is at 2121 Main downtown, where buses are available to most major towns in the state and beyond. **Texas Bus Lines** (tel. 523-5694) departs from the same terminal to various regional destinations, including Galveston (five departures a day, $11 one-way).

HOUSTON TELEPHONE INFORMATION

Emergency (police, fire, medical): 911

Telephone Directory Assistance: 411

Area Code: 713

Time/Temperature: 222-8463

Highway Conditions: 869-4571

Travelers Aid: 668-0911 or 228-8703

Coast Guard Air and Sea Rescue: 481-0657

Passport Office: 653-3153 or 653-3159

Downtown Tunnel/Skywalk System

Dozens of buildings downtown are linked by a system of underground tunnels and suspended skywalks, open Mon.-Fri. year round. Maps are available at several system junctions, or you can purchase the TunnelWalks *Shop 'N Walk* and *Taste of the Tunnel Map and Restaurant Guide* self-guided tour brochures for under $2.

City Buses

The **Metropolitan Transit Authority** (tel. 713-635-4000), called Metro for short, operates more than 100 bus routes in the city and parts of surrounding Harris County, including the NASA/Clear Lake area. The basic fare is 85 cents. Two of the downtown routes are only 30 cents; the Texas Special Red runs along Lamar, McKinney, Smith, and Louisiana, while the Texas Special Blue runs on Franklin, Main, Travis, and short sections of Calhoun and Pierce.

On all routes, free transfers are available for bus changes and short stopovers. A free *Transit Map of Greater Houston* is available from the Greater Houston Convention and Visitors Bureau at 801 Congress.

Taxis

Houston has around 20 taxi companies. **Yellow Cab** (tel. 713-236-1111) is the largest; others include **United Cab** (tel. 699-0000) and **Liberty Cab** (tel. 999-0088). **Fiesta Cab** (tel. 225-2666) employs Spanish bilingual drivers.

Tours

Gray Line (tel. 713-223-8800) offers a 4.5-hour tour of the city for $20 per person that covers the downtown area, the Texas Medical Center, Hermann Park, the Galleria, and the Astrodome. The company also offers a 5.5-hour tour of NASA's Space Center Houston for $29 per person.

BEAUMONT-PORT ARTHUR-ORANGE

Beaumont (pop. 116,000), Port Arthur (pop. 59,600), and Orange (pop. 19,700) form a triangle that encompasses two counties in the southeastern corner of the state. This area borders southwestern Louisiana and is sometimes called the Cajun Triangle because of the predominance of Cajun culture on either side of the state boundaries here. It's also been called the "Golden Triangle" for the abundance of oil that brought wealth to these communities during the 20th century.

All three cities have deep-water ports and oil refineries, though the surrounding counties are very rural; shipping, marine construction/repair, petrochemical production, agriculture (primarily rice cultivation), and crawfish farming are the primary sources of income. This variety of economic opportunities has drawn a multicultural melange of people from far and wide. In terms of regional culture, this is one of the richest areas in the state.

The area code for all telephone numbers in the triangle area is 409.

BEAUMONT

History

The lower Neches River area was first settled by Spanish and French fur trappers in the early 1800s; the original Beaumont city charter was issued by the Republic of Texas in 1838. For the next six decades, the town supported itself almost exclusively by cutting the abundant local timber for lumber mills and growing and milling rice. The Neches River provided a convenient outlet to the Gulf of Mexico via Sabine Pass, so Beaumont products were able to reach a wide market.

Beaumont would probably have remained a sleepy agricultural town if it hadn't been for the gusher that blew on January 10, 1901 at Spindletop, a salt-dome hill just south of town. It was the richest oil field in America at the time and ushered in an era of cheap liquid fuel that ignited the world's petrochemical industry. Six hundred oil companies sprang up over the next

year or two, including a few that became industry giants: the Texas Company (Texaco), Guffey Petroleum Company (Gulf, now Chevron), Magnolia Petroleum Company (Mobil), and Standard Oil (Exxon).

Today Beaumont is the state's fourth-largest port and the county seat for Jefferson County, which has one of the highest percentages (32%) of African-American residents in the state. Black culture has exercised a strong influence on Beaumont's cultural identity, from arts and music to cuisine. Beaumont is also known for its small, offbeat museums.

Sights

Spindletop/Gladys City Boomtown and Lucas Gusher Monument is a reproduction of the small boomtowns that grew up practically overnight in the Spindletop area in 1901 and '02. Located on the Lamar University campus (tel. 409-835-0823), at University Dr. and US 69/96/287, the exhibit consists of 15 clapboard buildings around a square. Among them are replicas of oil company offices, a general store, post office, barbershop, saloon, and livery. The complex is open Tues.-Sun. 1-5 p.m.; admission is $2 adults, $1 children.

Nearby is a 58-foot granite monument to the gusher that changed East Texas history. It's named for Anthony Lucas, the Austrian engineer who drilled the first Spindletop well.

The well-designed **Art Museum of Southeast Texas** (tel. 832-3432) at 500 Main St. houses permanent and traveling art exhibits by Texas artists. Besides the galleries, the museum has a sculpture courtyard and several rooms that host films, lectures, musical performances, and art classes. A tea room is open for lunch Mon.-Fri. 11:30 a.m.-1:30. The galleries are open Mon.-Sat. 9 a.m.-5 p.m., Sunday noon-5 p.m.; free admission.

Edison Plaza Museum: The chief executive officer for Gulf States Utilities Co. from 1979 to 1982 donated the funds to restore the 1920s-vintage Travis St. Power Substation and convert it into this museum celebrating the achievements of inventor Thomas Edison. Displays include

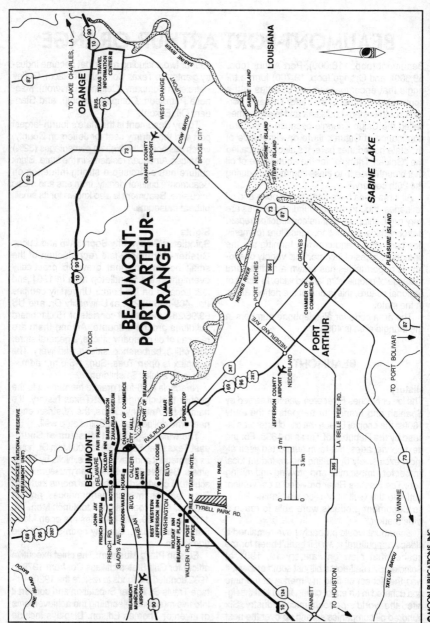

BEAUMONT-PORT ARTHUR-ORANGE

© MOON PUBLICATIONS, INC.

several of Edison's original inventions, including an 1890s cylinder phonograph, the 1880 Mimeograph, the Ediphone, and "The Master Violet Ray Machine," which was once used to treat a wide variety of ailments. Other exhibits explain present energy technology and anticipate future developments. The museum (tel. 839-3089) is at 350 Pine, behind the Gulf State Utilities Building. Hours are Mon.-Fri. 8 a.m.-4:30 p.m.; free admission.

Cattail Marsh: When it came time for Beaumont to upgrade the city's water treatment facilities, the city opted to let nature do the work through constructed wetlands that cover eight miles of levees on 900 acres. Since its opening in 1993, the $12.5 million artificial marsh, planted with over 375,000 plants—including cattails, yellow canna, bullrush, and blue flag iris—has become a favorable habitat for ducks, egrets, herons, cranes, ibis, cormorants, small fish, snakes, and turtles. Two observation towers will allow a broader view of the wetlands. The marsh is in Tyrell Park off I-10 and Walden Rd. Open 6 a.m.-7 p.m. Oct.-March, 6 a.m.-9 p.m. the rest of the year; free admission.

The **Fire Museum of Texas** (tel. 880-3927), is housed in the 1927 Beaumont Fire Department headquarters at 440 Walnut. Among the collection of antique firefighting equipment are a 1779 Chinese hand pump, a horse-drawn fire wagon, an 1856 hand-drawn tub pumper, an 1879 steamer, and the country's first searchlight truck, developed in Beaumont in 1931. Also on display are collections of photos, newspaper clippings, and other memorabilia from famous fires. The museum is open Mon.-Fri. 8 a.m.-4:30 p.m.; free admission.

Texas Energy Museum: Exhibits relating to energy and the petroleum industry are narrated by fancy cinematic robots at this high-tech, multimedia museum. Among the collection portraying the evolution of the Age of Energy are early gas trucks and a mockup of the Spindletop rig complete with "oil" running down the sides and gushing sound effects. The museum (tel. 833-5100), at 600 Main St., is open Tues.-Sat. 9 a.m.-5 p.m., Sunday 1-5 p.m.; admission is $2 adults, $1 seniors and children six to 12.

Babe Didrikson Zaharias Museum and Visitors Information Center commemorates Beaumont native Zaharias, who was considered the greatest female athlete of the first half of the century. The Associated Press named her Woman Athlete of the Year six times—1931, 1945, 1946, 1947, 1950, and 1954. In track and field sports, she held or tied world records for four events and also gained All-American status in basketball. Later in her career she took up golf and eventually won every major golf championship at least once—most of them several times. In 1950 alone she won the All-American Open, World Championship, U.S. Women's Open, Titleholders, 144-hole Weathervane, and the Women's Western Open.

The round memorial building, located off I-10 at the Gulf St. exit (#854), contains a collection of trophies, awards, and other memorabilia tracing "The Babe's" career. Open daily 9 a.m.-5 p.m.; free admission. Travel info on the Beaumont area and Texas is available in the attached Visitor Information Center.

The **John Jay French Museum** occupies a simple Greek Revival-style house (tel. 898-3267) at 2985 French Rd. (Delaware exit, US 69/96/287 N). The structure was the city's first two-story house and the first constructed of lumber rather than logs. Built in 1845 by merchant John Jay French, it is now operated as a museum by the Beaumont Heritage Society and has been refurbished in period style. Open Tues.-Sat. 10 a.m.-4 p.m., Sunday 1-4 p.m.; admission is $2 adults, 50 cents children under 18.

The 1906 **McFaddin-Ward House** (tel. 832-2134), a magnificent example of Beaux Arts Colonial architecture, stayed in the McFaddin family until the 1982 death of Mamie McFaddin Ward, who established a foundation before she died to provide for the preservation of the house as a museum. The rooms are decorated with antiques collected over a 75-year period, including noteworthy silver, porcelain, and Persian rug collections. The house is at 1906 McFaddin Avenue. From I-10 E exit at Calder, turn right to 3rd, then left to McFaddin. It's open Tues.-Sat. 10 a.m.-4 p.m., Sunday 1-4 p.m. for one-hour guided tours; reservations suggested. Admission is $3; children under eight aren't admitted.

Old Town is a 36-block area between Laurel, Harrison, 2nd, and 10th is noted for historic houses, many converted to shops selling jewelry, antiques, and clothing. The Babe Didrikson Za-

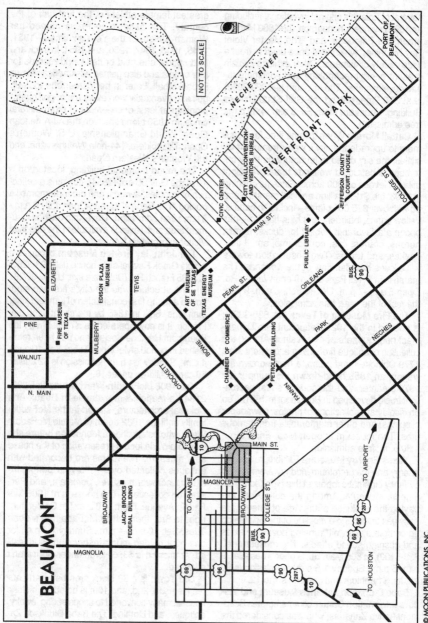

BEAUMONT

FIRE MUSEUM OF TEXAS
EDISON PLAZA MUSEUM
ART MUSEUM OF SE TEXAS
TEXAS ENERGY MUSEUM
CHAMBER OF COMMERCE
PETROLEUM BUILDING
JACK BROOKS FEDERAL BUILDING
CIVIC CENTER
CITY HALL/CONVENTION AND VISITORS BUREAU
PUBLIC LIBRARY
JEFFERSON COUNTY COURT HOUSE
PORT OF BEAUMONT

RIVERFRONT PARK

NECHES RIVER

NOT TO SCALE

PINE
WALNUT
N. MAIN
BROADWAY
MAGNOLIA
ELIZABETH
MULBERRY
TEVIS
CROCKETT
BOWIE
MAIN ST.
PEARL ST.
ORLEANS
PARK
NECHES
FANNIN
COLLEGE ST.
BUS. 90

TO ORANGE
TO AIRPORT
TO HOUSTON
MAIN ST.
MAGNOLIA
BROADWAY
COLLEGE ST.
10
69
96
287
90
BUS. 90

© MOON PUBLICATIONS, INC.

harias Museum and Visitors Information Center at I-10 W and Martin Luther King Pkwy. (exit 854) distributes a free map brochure of Old Town that lists all the shops and their locations.

Lamar University: This medium-sized university of 11,000 students offers a full range of undergraduate and graduate programs but is strongest in health sciences, engineering, and computer science. The Fine Arts and Theater departments are also quite active. The central campus is off Martin Luther King Pkwy. in the southeast corner of town. Lamar has smaller branches in Port Arthur and Orange as well. For further information, call 880-7011.

Port of Beaumont, at the east edge of town (end of Milam) on the Neches River, is the state's fourth largest port (four million cargo tons per year) even though it's 40 miles from the Gulf of Mexico. You can get a good view of the port from the observation deck atop the Harbor Island Transit Warehouse, about a thousand feet from the main gate. The deck (tel. 832-1546) is open daily 8 a.m.-5 p.m.; free tours of the port are available during these hours as well. Ask at the gate.

Crawfish and Alligator Farms

Near the small town of China, about 16 miles west of Beaumont via US 90, **Doguet's Crawfish Farm** (tel. 409-752-5105), 1801 US 90 E, and **H&L Crawfish Farm** (tel. 752-5514 or 835-1017), S. China Rd., offer free 30- to 60-minute tours daily during the Jan.-June crawfish season.

Alligator Island is the largest gator-breeding farm in the state and home to "Big Al," the largest gator in captivity. The farm is 10 miles southwest of the city at the junction of State 365 and I-10, near Fannett. Open Tues.-Sat. 10 a.m.-5 p.m., Sunday 1-4 p.m. from March to October only. Admission is $3 adults, $2 children, three and under free.

Hotels and Motels

See the "Beaumont Hotels and Motels" chart.

Bed and Breakfasts

Grand Duerr Manor (tel. 409-833-9600) at 2298 McFaddin is Beaumont's first bed and breakfast. The New Orleans-style southern mansion has three themed rooms—Victorian romance, bluebonnet, and silver-screen—with private bath

---

BEAUMONT HOTELS AND MOTELS

Add 13% hotel tax to all rates. Area code: 409.

Beaumont Hilton; 2355 I-10 S (Washington Ave. exit); tel. 842-3600 or (800) 445-8667; $89-119; pool, airport shuttle, weekly and monthly rates

Best Western Beaumont Inn; 2155 N. 11th; tel. 898-8150; $38-44; pool, coin laundry

Best Western Jefferson Inn; 1610 I-10 S (exit 851); tel. 842-0037; $38-44; pool, continental breakfast, coin laundry

Days Inn; 30 I-10 N (Clader/Harrison exit); tel. 838-0581 or (800) 325-2525; $33-36; pool, coin laundry

Econo Lodge; 1155 I-10 S (College/US 90 exit); 835-5913; $30-38; pool, weekend discount

Holiday Inn Beaumont Plaza; 3950 I-10 S (College St. exit); tel. 842-5995 or (800) 465-4329; $84-88; heated pool, airport shuttle, weekly rates

Holiday Inn Midtown; 2095 N. 11th; tel. 892-2222 or (800) 465-4329; $60; pool, YMCA privileges, airport shuttle, weekly rates

La Quinta Motor Inn; 220 I-10 N (exit 852A/B); tel. 838-9991 or (800) 531-5900; $46-64; pool, senior discount, continental breakfast

Motel 6; 2640 I-10 E (exit 853B/C); tel. 898-7190; $22 plus $4 each additional person; pool

Quality Inn; 1295 N. 11th; tel. 892-7722 or (800) 221-2222; $45-50; pool, senior discount

Ramada Hotel; 2525 N. 11th; tel. 898-2111 or (800) 272-6232; $45; pool

Red Carpet Inn; I-10 and 11th; tel. 892-8111; $22-28; pool

Relay Station Motel; 4085 I-10 S (exit 848); tel. 842-9341; $30-35; coin laundry, continental breakfast

Roadrunner Inn; 3985 College at I-10; tel. 842-4420; $34-37; pool, 24-hour restaurant

Super 8; I-10 and 11th; tel. 899-3040; $30-37; pool

for $79-99 s or d; generous continental breakfast included in the tariff.

Campgrounds and RV Parks

Tyrell Park, operated by Beaumont's City Park Department (tel. 409-838-3648), offers 46 camper/ RV sites with full hookups, 18 sites with sewer only, and 64 sites for self-contained rigs only. Slots are allotted on a first-come, first-served basis and cost $9 per rig per day ($7 if the driver is 55 or older). No tent camping and no reservations. From I-10 take the Walden Rd. exit (#848) and follow Walden Rd. south a half mile to Tyrell Park Road. Other facilities include a golf course, playground, riding stables, and botanical gardens.

East Lucas RV Park (tel. 899-9209), at 2590 E. Lucas Dr. 1.4 miles off US 69 N, has RV slots on shaded grounds for $15, tent camping for $12.

Village Creek State Park (tel. 755-7322), off State 96/287 in Lumberton, 12 miles north of Beaumont, opened in 1994 and has 25 RV sites with w/e for $9-12 and 35 tentsites with water for $4-6, with w/e for $6-8, primitive sites $3. The 942-acre park also has a popular flat-water canoe stream, 10 miles of hiking trails, playground, and canoe launch. Village Creek is one of the few undammed streams in East Texas. Admission to the park is $3 per car; free with a Texas Conservation Passport.

Food

The Golden Triangle is a great area for travelers seeking to taste authentic regional cuisines. Beaumont is particularly strong in downhome cooking and barbecue. Many restaurants will have a few Cajun or Creole dishes on the menu, or a Cajun touch to the cooking.

If you're on a food pilgrimage or just want some of the best barbecue in the state, don't miss **Patillo's BBQ,** an informal over-the-counter place with two locations: 2775 Washington (tel. 409-833-3154) and 610 N. 11th (tel. 832-2572). The standard platter—choice of brisket, homemade links, or chicken—comes with extra southeast-Texas-style sauce, beans, coleslaw, potato salad, and dirty rice (the Cajun touch). Another local favorite is **Dean's Bar-B-Que** (tel. 835-7956) at 805 Magnolia.

Don's Seafood (tel. 842-0686), at I-10 and Washington, specializes in Cajun and Creole seafood. The **Texas Crawfish Co. & Seafood Restaurant** (tel. 866-1625) on US 90 just west of I-10 also has a few Cajun dishes, plus all-you-can-eat buffets daily for lunch (boiled crawfish, barbecue crabs, fried shrimp, and étouffée) and dinner (the same, plus gumbo, frog legs, and oysters). Another good spot for seafood is **Sartin's** (tel. 892-6771), a branch of the famous barbecued-crab specialists in Sabine Pass near Port Arthur. It's at 6725 Eastex Frwy. (US 69 N).

For downhome cooking, you have several choices: **The Black-Eyed Pea** (tel. 866-2617) at 6455 Phelan, **Shilo's Restaurant** (tel. 835-5153) at 2999 Goliad at Washington, and **Texas Pig Stand** at 612 Washington (tel. 835-5753) or 1595 Calder in Old Town (tel. 835-9702); both Texas Pig Stands are open 24 hours.

David's Upstairs (tel. 898-0214), above the cinema in Gaylynn Center at 11th and Calder, is a bit tricky to find, but serves imaginative continental fare in a romantic setting; the inexpensive "early bird special" (5-6:30 p.m.) includes soup or salad, choice of entree, vegetables, and dessert. Live jazz and cabaret Mon.-Saturday.

For lighter fare, the **Green Beanery Café** (tel. 833-5913) at 2121 McFaddin in Old Town is a good alternative; the menu here includes salads, soups, sandwiches, crepes, and pasta. The **House of Chee** (tel. 898-8783) at 4414 Dowlen in the Crossroads Shopping Center and **The Mandarin** (tel. 899-4344) at 4415 Calder are reputed to have the best Chinese food in town. If you're looking for Mexican, an interesting choice is **Chula Vista** (tel. 898-8855) at 1135 N. 11th, just off I-10, where Sonoran dishes are the specialty. You know exactly what's on the menu at **Robert's Fajitas and Tamales** (tel. 866-3503), housed in a former burger joint at 6096 College. If you can't decide between Mexican and Cajun, **The Tamale Co.** (tel. 866-8033) at 6025 Phelan (behind Fertita's Grocery) offers both homemade tamales and chicken gumbo.

Entertainment

Beaumont has been fertile territory for roots music ever since local-boy Moon Mullican perfected the piano style later popularized by Jerry Lee Lewis; Mullican also wrote the song "Jambalaya", a hit for country singer Hank Williams. Civic pride is currently focused on country singer-picker Mark Chestnutt, who's had 11 consecutive top-ten country singles. A billboard on I-10 outside Beaumont reads Welcome To Beaumont, Home Of Mark Chestnutt.

Due to Chestnutt's success, Beaumont's most notorious club at the moment is **Cutter's** (tel. 409-842-3840), a 10,000-square-foot, prefabricated steel dance hall at 4120 College Street where Chestnutt got his start. This classic honkytonk roadhouse has a pool and blackjack tables in the back—just in case you can't two-step. Check out Cutter's regular George Dearborne before he rockets to stardom.

Boulevard (tel. 833-3271) at 3965 Phelan features live bands (usually R&B) Mon.-Sat. until 2 a.m. **Get Down Brown's** (tel. 892-1931) in the Holiday Inn Midtown on N. 11th is a change from the usual Holiday Inn disco-lounge; the DJs play a gnarly mix of R&B, old rock 'n' roll, Cajun, and country. On Wednesday evening the club offers free barbecue buffets; in season, Brown's boils up crawfish for $3 a pound. The original Get Down Brown's was on State 347 near Port Arthur, where the DJ/owner invented the dance known as the "funky chicken."

If you happen to be passing through the Beaumont area on a Sunday morning between 6 and 10:30 a.m., tune in *Tee Bruce's Cajun Jamboree* radio show on KLVI-AM 560. Listening to Tee Bruce take requests and dedicate songs is as much fun as listening to the Cajun music; the show has been a Golden Triangle

tradition for 25 years now. During the rest of the week the station plays country. The station's signal is so strong that on a clear day it can be heard all the way to Austin.

Tucked away in the town of Anahuac, slightly less than halfway back to Houston off I-10, the **Double Bayou Dance Hall** has served as East Texas blues headquarters since the 1950s. Texas blues legends T-Bone Walker, Clarence "Gatemouth" Brown, Joe Hughes, Pete Mayes, and many others have performed here; guitarist Mayes and his Texas Houserockers still headline on occasion. To reach Anahuac from Beaumont, drive 39 miles west along I-10 to the State 61 junction, then turn south on State 61 and follow the road four miles to the State 65 junction and turn west. This road terminates after three miles in Anahuac, which sits on the northeast edge of Galveston Bay—often called Trinity Bay from this end. From Houston it's 48 miles to the State 61 junction along I-10 east. For Double Bayou information call (713) 961-0970.

Events

The city's biggest annual celebration is the **Neches River Festival,** held for 10 days near the end of April. Activities include a ball, parade, concerts, arts and crafts shows, flower shows, and boat races.

On Mother's Day weekend in May is **Kaleidoscope,** a juried art show staged outdoors in tents at the Art Museum of South Texas (tel.

at the Bill Pickett Invitational Rodeo, Beaumont

409-832-3432). Entries from all over the U.S. are accepted and all the art is for sale at the close of the show. Entertainment and food available; the whole shebang culminates in a Saturday night dance.

Juneteenth (June 19th, the date that news of the Emancipation Proclamation reached Texas) is celebrated with fervor by Beaumont's black population. On the nearest weekend to the 19th, at Riverfront Park near the junction of Main and Cypress, the city sponsors an outdoor program of gospel, R&B, rap, and zydeco music. The food booths focus on Cajun and Creole food, including crawfish and boudin. This last is rice-pork sausage, in this area spelled and pronounced "boudain."

For 10 days in the middle of October, the **South Texas State Fair** packs them in at Fair Park. Participants come from all over the Golden Triangle area and beyond to take part in rodeos, livestock shows, auctions, and music.

Information

The **Beaumont Convention and Visitors Bureau** (tel. 409-880-3749 or 800-392-4401) is located in the city hall at 801 Main; open Mon.-Fri. 8 a.m.-5 p.m. It offers stacks of information on attractions, accommodations, and dining, and the staff can answer other questions about the city. A visitor information center at the Babe Didrikson Zaharias Museum (tel. 833-4622), I-10 W and Martin Luther King Pkwy. (exit 854), also dis-

tributes information on the Beaumont area. Open daily 9 a.m.-5 p.m.

PORT ARTHUR

The city began in 1895 when Arthur Stilwell selected Sabine Lake as the terminal for his Kansas City, Pacific, and Gulf Railroad. He modestly called the town Port Arthur and set about looking for investors and settlers. One of the investors was John "Bet-A-Million" Gates, who gained control of the railroad and changed the name to Kansas City and Southern. Also among the investors was a group of Dutch settlers who bought 42,000 acres of prairie from the Port Arthur Land Co. in 1897 and named it Nederland; there are now some 500 families in Nederland and Port Arthur descended from the original 51 settlers. The late country music star Tex Ritter was a Nederland descendant.

When the oil business took off following the Spindletop discovery of 1901, thousands of Cajuns from southwest Louisiana began migrating to Port Arthur to take jobs in oil exploration and, later, at the city's huge refineries. Port Arthur, or "Port Ar-tour" as it's pronounced by Cajuns, now has the largest concentration of Acadian descendants in Texas.

During the late 1970s Southeast Asian immigrants, particularly Vietnamese, began arriving in Port Arthur in some numbers. Many

Buddhism and Catholicism coexist peacefully in Port Arthur's Asian community.

PHYLLIS STAFF

Vietnamese took jobs on shrimp boats and later started their own shrimping enterprises. They were so successful—many families had fished the South China Sea for generations—that at first there was some friction between the locals and the immigrants. Lately, though, the warring groups seem to have worked things out and the Vietnamese have been accepted as part of the community.

Riverboat gambling is a future possibility on Lake Sabine, and the renovation of Old Town is well underway. Many abandoned warehouses and buildings will get a new lease on life when new boutiques, clubs, and restaurants move in. Several historic homes around town are slated to become bed and breakfasts.

Sights
Museum of the Gulf Coast: This expanding museum moved into a three-story, white marble, former bank at 700 Proctor and Beaumont in 1994. The new facility contains exhibits chronicling the history and cultural diversity of the southeast Texas and southwest Louisiana Gulf Coast. An impressive 125-foot mural illustrates the development of the region from the Pleistocene epoc through the 20th century. A hands-on archaeological exhibit on the first floor lets children dig into the more distant Paleozoic era for trilobytes while adults mill through the various displays on the geology, flora, and fauna of the region. A navigation beacon retired from duty in the Gulf blinks continuously from the second floor balcony; rooms beyond are filled with memorabilia of such Golden Triangle sports legends as Babe Zaharias, Bubba Busheme, Little Joe Walsh, and Jimmy Johnson.

Perhaps because of all the cross-cultural influences—Cajun, Dutch, Anglo, Hispanic, African-American—the triangle area has been an unusually fertile ground for American music. The area's most famous musical native is undoubtedly Janis Joplin. Born in Port Arthur in 1943, she shot to stardom in the late '60s as a blues and rock singer, dying of a drug overdose in 1970. Part of the exhibit is devoted to Janis and includes photos, paintings, album covers, early childhood memorabilia donated by the Joplin family, and a large five-headed sculpture by Doug Clark. New to the collection is a replica of Joplin's psychedelic Porsche, revolving on a gold record platform.

Other exhibits chronicle the lives and music of Gene Joseph Bourgeois, born in Port Arthur in 1940 and known as Jivin' Gene, a pioneer of "swamp music"; Harry Choates, the "godfather of Cajun music"; country singer George Jones, born in nearby Saratoga in 1931; blues singer Ivory Joe Hunter, born in nearby Kirbyville in 1911; Jerry LaCroix, a singer and saxophonist for the influential jazz/rock/R&B band Blood, Sweat, and Tears who still lives and performs in Port Arthur; mandolin and fiddle player Tiny Moore, a Port Arthur native who played with Bob Wills and Merle Haggard; R&B singer Barbara Lynn, born in Beaumont in 1942; the Big Bopper, born Jules Richardson in Sabine Pass in 1930; Nederland native Tex Ritter; and the Winter brothers, Johnny and Edgar, Beaumont-born practitioners of blues, R&B, and rock. A bank of six antique Wurlitzers provides audio-video images of these local stars who hit it big.

The museum is open Mon.-Sat. 9 a.m.-5 p.m., Sunday 1-5 p.m.; admission is $3.50 adults, $1.50 children, preschoolers 50 cents. Call (409) 982-7000 for more information.

Historic Buildings: Several of the homes along Lakeshore Dr. were built in the early 1900s as winter resorts for wealthy businessmen from the Midwest. They once commanded a view of Sabine Lake, but dredging of the Gulf Intracoastal Waterway and the construction of levees for hurricane protection have obstructed the view. Still, the district retains a quiet, antebellum atmosphere. The most unusual building in the district is the **Pompeiian Villa** (tel. 983-5977) at 1953 Lakeshore, constructed in 1900 as an architectural replica of an A.D. 79 Pompeiian home. The house is built around a three-sided courtyard, with a Roman fountain in the center; each room opens onto the courtyard. The house is painted according to Pompeiian color schemes—cerulean blue, pink, ivory, gray, almond green, and peach—and is furnished with 18th-century antiques, the preference of original owner Isaac Ellwood. The house is listed with the National Register of Historic Places and maintained by the Port Arthur Historical Society. It's open to the public Mon.-Fri. 9 a.m.-4 p.m. or by appointment; admission is $2 adults, $1 children.

Pompeiian Villa,
Port Arthur

White Haven (tel. 982-3068) at 2545 Lakeshore is a large Greek Revival-style home built in 1915 and furnished with Victorian antiques. Tours are conducted by a local chapter of the Daughters of the American Revolution on Monday, Wednesday, and Friday 10 a.m.-1 p.m. or by appointment; admission is $2 per person. Similar in style but larger is **Rose Hill Manor** (tel. 985-7292) at 100 Woodworth at the east end of Lakeshore. Built in 1906, it's listed with the NRHP and maintained by the Port Arthur Federated Women's Club. Open for guided tours Tues.-Fri. 9 a.m.-5 p.m., Saturday 9 a.m.-noon; free admission. During the summer, lemonade is sometimes served on the front lawn.

Area of Peace: This district along 9th Ave. (700-900 block) is occupied mostly by the residences and businesses of local Vietnamese, who've designated it Khu Vuc Hoa Binh or "Area of Peace." The center of the district is the **Queen of Peace Park** at 801 9th, which consists of flower gardens surrounding a huge statue of the Virgin Mary, built by the parishioners of the Queen of Vietnamese Martyrs' Catholic Church. About 10% of Port Arthur's current population is Vietnamese.

Buu Mon Buddhist Temple: Not all the Vietnamese in Port Arthur are Catholics. An old Baptist church at 2701 Proctor has been converted into a Buddhist temple, complete with a four-tiered pagoda outside and a seven-foot bronze Thai Buddha inside. The temple is open to nonworshippers Sat.-Sun. 11 a.m.-4 p.m. or any time by appointment. Buddhist meditation

classes, open to all, are usually held once a week in the evening; call 982-9319 for schedule.

Seawall Drive: Along the top of the levee between the Gulf Intracoastal Waterway (here called the Sabine-Neches Canal) and Lakeshore Dr. is a one-way street and walkway for sightseeing purposes. When ships pass, you can almost reach out and touch them.

Tex Ritter Park in the little town of Nederland on Port Arthur's northern city limits commemorates hometown boy and country singer Tex Ritter. To make the most of this piece of real estate, the town added the **Dutch Windmill Museum,** which contains Ritter mementos as well as artifacts pertaining to the original 1890s Dutch settlement. There's also **La Maison Acadienne Museum,** a replica of an early southern Louisiana Cajun home. The park is located at 1500 Boston, west of Twin Cities Hwy. (State 347) and is open Tues.-Sun. 1-5 p.m. between March 1 and Labor Day, Thurs.-Sun. 1-5 p.m. the rest of the year; free admission.

Port of Port Arthur: It sounds redundant but that's what it's called. Although not as large as the ports of Houston, Beaumont, or Galveston, this harbor (tel. 983-2011) at West Lakeshore and Houston can handle ships with a 40-foot draft and lengths up to a thousand feet. The port authorities offer free guided tours Mon.-Fri. 8 a.m.-5 p.m.

Rainbow Bridge: This amazing two-lane bridge was built over the Neches River between the Gulf and the Port of Beaumont in 1938 and arches to a height of 177 feet above the water. The bridge was originally built to accommodate the USS *Patoka,* a U.S. Navy dirigible tender which sported an extremely tall mast for dirigible moorings. But before the bridge was even completed, the Navy quit using dirigibles. Nothing that passes beneath the bridge these days requires such clearance. To drive over the bridge, an uplifting experience to say the least, take State 87 east out of town. A new, lower bridge parallels Rainbow Bridge; each carries traffic in different directions.

The **Martin Luther King Jr. Memorial Bridge,** at a height of 138 feet above the water, is just about as impressive as the Rainbow Bridge. Constructed in 1970, it connects the city with Pleasure Island, a narrow barrier island on the south side of the Gulf Intracoastal Waterway.

Touted as the world's largest petrochemical complex, the adjacent Texaco and Chevron **refineries** at the junction of State 82 and State 87 at the southwest end of town look like somebody's version of technological hell. Then again, the many Port Arthurians who rely on them for their livelihoods may find them beautiful. You have to drive right through these monsters to get to Sabine Pass and the Bolivar Peninsula.

Hotels and Motels
If you're on a budget, Port Arthur is a good base from which to explore the Triangle area—hotel/motel rates are very reasonable. The basic

Sea Gull Motel (tel. 409-962-4437) at 6828 Gulfway has rooms for $25 s, $35 d. At the **Seashell Motel** (tel. 736-1589), 2811 State 73, rooms are $25 s or $27 d, with kitchenettes available on request. **Cajun Cabins on Pleasure Island** (tel. 982-6050 or 800-554-3169) at 1900 State 82 S (Martin Luther King Blvd.) rents cabins with kitchenettes for $55-65 s or d; the rate includes a continental breakfast.

In nearby Sabine Pass, the **Sabine Pass Motel** (tel. 971-2156) at 5623 Greenwich (first street past Broadway from Port Arthur) has rooms for $23-32. Other economical hotels include the **Holiday Motor Hotel** (tel. 985-2538) at 3889 Gulfway, $28 s or d; the **Imperial Inn** (tel. 985-9316) at 2811 Memorial, $33 s, $35 d; and **Percy's Motel** (tel. 736-1554) at State 73 and Jade, in the west end of town, $31-35. Percy's has the distinct advantage of being near Percy's Cafe.

For more spacious rooms and lobbies, you can spend a bit more for the **Holiday Inn Park Central** (tel. 724-5000) at 2929 75th, where rooms run $52-58 s, $55-64 d; or the **Ramada Inn of Port Arthur** (tel. 962-9858) at 3801 State 73, $50-53 s, $50-61 d.

Campgrounds and RV Parks
The nearest public campground is at Sea Rim State Park on the Bolivar Peninsula, about nine miles southwest of Port Arthur via State 87. The **Lazy L Campground** (tel. 409-794-2985) at

Rose Hill Manor,
Port Arthur

FM 365 at I-10, 18 miles west of Port Arthur in Fannett, has tent/camper sites with w/e for $10 a night and RV sites with full hookups for $15.

Pleasure Island, the thin barrier island just across the Gulf Intracoastal Waterway, features two RV facilities. **Jep's RV Park** (tel. 983-3822) at 1900 Martin Luther King charges $15 a day, $65 on weekends. On the same road is **J&C RV Park** (tel. 985-3638) with similar rates.

Oak Leaf Park KOA (tel. 886-4082), off I-10 in Orange (exit 87-A, Oak Leaf Dr.), offers RV sites in the $15 range, plus prefab cabins for $21 a night. Facilities include pool, laundry, store, and snack bar.

Food

If you like Cajun, you'll like eating in Port Arthur. **Farm Royal** (tel. 409-982-6483) at 2701 Memorial specializes in Cajun-style seafood, including gumbo and étouffée. If the food at this old stand-by isn't soulful enough for you, head for **Charlie's** (tel. 722-5639) at 8901 US 69, which serves up "boudain balls" and live music at dinner. Another downhome joint is **Percy's Cafe** (tel. 736-3573) at 5891 Jade, just off State 73 W. House specialties include shrimp gumbo and chicken-fried steak, and the decor features John Wayne collectibles. **Southern Kitchen** (tel. 983-2115) at 2749 Memorial is similar but with a heavier emphasis on Cajun dishes.

Cajun-owned **Esther's Seafood and Oyster Bar** (tel. 962-6268), at 9902 Gulfway Dr. on a barge at the foot of the Rainbow Bridge (off State 87), does shrimp creole, gumbo, étouffée, and other Cajun and Creole dishes. The Lighthouse (tel. 985-3535) on Pleasure Island specializes in crab cakes and fried alligator, plus daily seafood specials, all with Sabine Lake views.

A little hard to find but worth the trip for the Cajun-style catfish is **Boondocks** (tel. 794-2769). To get there, take State 73 13 miles west to Jap Rd., then head right about 1.3 miles; it's on the left, on Taylor Bayou near Fannett. A window table will give you a view of the picturesque bayou, including alligators and raccoons who gather near the restaurant hoping for handouts.

Locals say the best downhome seafood in the area is at two restaurants in nearby Sabine Pass, a small fishing town about nine miles southwest of town via State 87. Both specialize

---

PORT ARTHUR GUMBO

Recipe:
1 cup cooking oil
1 cup flour
2 yellow onions, chopped
1 cup green onions, chopped
2 ribs celery, chopped
1 cup green pepper, chopped
2 lbs. shrimp, chicken, crawfish, or duck (or any combination)
4 quarts water
$1/2$ tablespoon red pepper (or more to taste)
1 tablespoon black pepper
2 tablespoons salt
1 teaspoon gumbo filé

Heat oil in heavy skillet with flour to make a roux. Cook until it turns medium brown, stirring constantly, about 4-5 minutes.

When roux is done, add to four quarts of water in saucepan on medium heat; stir until the roux is dissolved. Add yellow onions, celery, and green pepper; bring to a boil, reduce heat, and simmer for an hour.

Add seasonings, green onions, and shrimp (or chicken, etc.) and cook on medium heat until the shrimp (or chicken, etc.) is done. Serves at least six.

---

in "barbecue crabs," which aren't really barbecued but deep-fried in Cajun spices. They also serve catfish, frog legs, shrimp, stuffed crab, crab claws, oysters, and other fresh seafood broiled or fried. The advertised "platter service" means seafood is served family-style (three-person minimum)—a platter of barbecue crabs, a platter of fried shrimp, etc.—and the platters are refilled until you've had enough. Of the two, **Sartin's** (tel. 892-6771) is the oldest and most well known—it's also the most crowded. The **Channel Inn** (tel. 971-2400) across the road is often a better choice, since the staff tries harder and it's usually emptier. Both restaurants are on State 87 at the entrance to Sabine Pass (the channel, not the town). Both are open every day from around 11 a.m. to 9 or 10 p.m.

The Schooner (tel. 722-2323) at 1508 US 69/96/287, just north of Port Arthur in Nederland, has been in business for nearly 50 years, serving steak and a dependable variety of seafood dishes. The house specialty is red snapper Alexander—snapper stuffed with crab and shrimp and smothered in onions and artichoke hearts. Hours are Mon.-Sat. 11 a.m.-10 p.m.

The Port Arthur branch of **Robert's Fajitas and Tamales** (tel. 724-1410) at 7628 Twin City has Beaumont's beat for atmosphere, and serves the same no-nonsense Tex-Mex daily for lunch and dinner.

Entertainment

Live Music: Charlie's (see "Food") features live C&W or Cajun bands every night but Monday. The long-established **Rodair Club** (tel. 409-736-9001) on FM 365, about four miles west of US 69/96/287, holds Cajun dances Friday and Saturday nights and Sunday afternoon.

For a break from Cajun entertainment, try **The Lighthouse** (see "Food"), where live contemporary pop and light rock is showcased on weekends, or **Foc'sle** (tel. 983-5050), 416 Proctor, an Irish pub and piano bar with frequent singalongs.

Radio: Local station KOLE-AM 1340 broadcasts zydeco music Mon.-Fri. noon-3 p.m., Cajun music Mon.-Fri. 3-6 p.m. and Saturday 7 a.m.-noon. KQHN-AM 1510 from nearby Nederland also broadcasts the occasional Cajun music program. For a wide selection of gospel, R&B, and blues, tune in KALO-AM 1250.

Events

January: Janis Joplin's birthday (January 19), an on-again, off-again event, is usually celebrated with a concert featuring local performers as well as original members of Joplin's band Big Brother and the Holding Company. In previous years the concert has been held at the Port Arthur Civic Center; contact the Port Arthur Convention and Visitors Bureau (tel. 409-985-7822) for the latest information.

February: The weekend before Ash Wednesday is the time for **Mardi Gras** festivities, which in Port Arthur include grand balls, art exhibits, parades, and plenty of live entertainment. The Saturday highlight is the Aurora Parade, when the Majestic Grande Krewe throw strings of beads into the cheering crowds a la New Orleans.

March: On a weekend in mid-March, over a dozen Port Arthur restaurants compete in the **Taste of Gumbo** at the Port Arthur Civic Center

on Cultural Center Dr., off 9th, just north of the State 73 junction. Sponsored by the Rotary Club (tel. 724-7663 or 962-8448).

May: The **Pleasure Island Music Festival,** held the first weekend of the month at the Logan Music Park on Pleasure Island (off T.B. Ellison Pkwy.), brings together the best of the local music talent and a few national acts for three days of blues, gospel, jazz, country, Cajun, rock, and R&B music, plus food vendors, arts and crafts, and various family-oriented games. For information, call the Port Arthur Convention and Visitors Bureau at 985-7822.

September: The **Cayman Island Fest** is a joint effort with Port Arthur's sister community in the Caribbean, the Cayman Islands. A planeload of Cayman Islanders fly in for the festival, which features a soccer match between the Cayman national team and the Southeast Texas All-Stars as well as Caribbean music and plenty of Cajun and Caribbean food. Held at the Civic Center on the second weekend of the month. For further information, call the Convention and Visitors Bureau at 985-7822.

On either the last weekend of September or the first weekend of October, the small town of Winnie (30 miles west via State 73) hosts the **Texas Rice Festival,** featuring a beauty pageant, parade, carnival, music, farm equipment displays, and food booths emphasizing rice dishes.

October: Shrimpfest occupies the Pleasure Island Concert Park during the last weekend of the month; a gumbo cookoff and "shrimp calling" contest are part of the fun. Call 962-1107 for further details.

December: Christmas Reflections fills the month with elaborate lighting displays in the Area of Peace and on Pleasure Island, where the lights seem to dance off the Intracoastal Waterway.

Fishing

The Port Arthur area offers a combination of freshwater and saltwater fishing opportunities unparalleled along the Texas coast. Freshwater anglers have a choice of Taylor and Cow bayous, several smaller bayous, and the Neches and Sabine rivers for bass, bream, crappie, catfish, and gar. Saltwater fishing spots include the Sabine Ship Channel, Sabine Lake, the lower

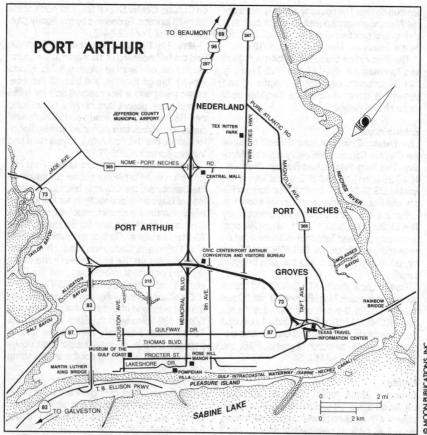

PORT ARTHUR

TO BEAUMONT

NEDERLAND

JEFFERSON COUNTY
MUNICIPAL AIRPORT

TEX RITTER
PARK

PURE ATLANTIC RD.

TWIN CITIES HWY.

MAGNOLIA AVE.

NECHES RIVER

NOME - PORT NECHES RD.

CENTRAL MALL

JADE AVE.

PORT   NECHES

PORT ARTHUR

CIVIC CENTER/PORT ARTHUR
CONVENTION AND VISITORS BUREAU

GROVES

MOLASSES
BAYOU

TAYLOR BAYOU

ALLIGATOR
BAYOU

SALT BAYOU

HOUSTON AVE.

MEMORIAL BLVD.

9th AVE.

TAFT AVE.

RAINBOW
BRIDGE

GULFWAY DR.

THOMAS BLVD.

TEXAS TRAVEL
INFORMATION CENTER

MUSEUM OF THE
GULF COAST

PROCTER ST.

ROSE HILL
MANOR

MARTIN LUTHER
KING BRIDGE

LAKESHORE DR.

POMPEIIAN
VILLA

GULF INTRACOASTAL WATERWAY (SABINE - NECHES CANAL)

PLEASURE ISLAND

T. B. ELLISON PKWY.

TO GALVESTON

SABINE LAKE

0   2 mi

0   2 km

© MOON PUBLICATIONS, INC.

reaches of the Neches River east of Rainbow Bridge, the Taylor Bayou Outfall where Taylor Bayou joins the Gulf Intracoastal Waterway, and Cow Bayou south of I-10. Saltwater catches include speckled trout, drum, flounder, croaker, redfish, and sheepshead. Crabbing is excellent in the latter areas, too. The Gulf of Mexico is easily reached from Sabine Pass or the Bolivar Peninsula for offshore and deep-sea fishing.

Boat-launching facilities are available at the Pleasure Island Marina on Sabine Lake and at the Rainbow Marina on the Neches River. Taylor Bayou offers a few private landings on the west side of the State 73 bridge and one public

landing on the east. For Cow Bayou, there's LeBlanc's Landing on the east side of the State 87 bridge at Round Bunch Road. In those sections of the bayous where saltwater fish can be caught, anglers must possess saltwater fishing permits, available at most bait shops or marinas.

Information

The **Port Arthur Convention and Visitors Bureau** (tel. 409-985-7822 or 800-235-7822), in the Civic Center at 3401 Cultural Center Drive (off 9th and State 73), distributes printed information on Port Arthur and the vicinity and a free street map of the city, including the nearby towns of

Nederland, Groves, and Port Neches. The helpful *Easy Driving Tour* pamphlet outlines an auto route for seeing the city's main attractions, providing a description of each and a simplified route map. A brochure of discount coupons valid for local lodging and dining is also available by request.

ORANGE

Orange, the eastern point of the Cajun Triangle, is just across the Sabine River from Louisiana. Pirate Jean Lafitte reportedly used the Sabine Rive mouth as a haven for ship repairs in the early 1800s. French traders and fur trappers settled along the river in the 18th century but it wasn't until the 1850s that the county was established. No one's quite sure whether the town and county's name originally referred to a small grove of wild orange trees on the river or was a reference to Holland's House of Orange—some of the 19th-century settlers in the area were Dutch.

Originally a lumber and rice town like Beaumont, Orange eventually became prominent in the marine construction and petrochemical industries. Rice and timber, however, still play a role in the local economy.

Stark Museum of Art
The collection in this imposing marble structure focuses on traditional American art, including works by Frederic Remington, Charles Russell, and the Taos Society of Artists, as well as Audubon prints, Steuben glass, and Amerindian art from the Plains and Southwest. The museum (tel. 409-993-6661) is at 712 Green Ave., on the Civic Plaza. Open Wed.-Sat. 10 a.m.-5 p.m., Sunday 1-5 p.m.; free admission.

W.H. Stark House
Another legacy of the wealthy Stark family, this three-story Queen Anne-style Victorian (tel. 409-883-0871) at 610 W. Main was built in 1894 and has been restored and furnished to serve as a museum. It's open for one-hour guided tours Tues.-Sat. 10 a.m.-3 p.m.; admission $2, no one under 14 admitted. Reservations required.

Heritage House Museum
This two-story colonial-style home at 905 Division St. was built in 1902 and now serves as a his-torical museum for Orange County. Like the Stark House, it's listed on the National Register of Historic Places; part of the house has been restored and furnished in period style. Admission $1.

Lutcher Memorial Church Building (First Presbyterian)
Begun in 1908 and completed in 1912, this monumental church was financed by Frances Ann Lutcher in memory of her husband. Kansas City architect James Hogg used Texas granite and Italian marble for the walls and floor of the church, topping the center of the ceiling with the nation's only opalescent glass dome. The outside of the dome is protected by a copper outer dome; light fixtures throughout the building are bronze, other metalwork is brass, and the pews and paneling in the organ loft are mahogany. When the church opened in 1912, it required a private power plant to provide sufficient current to operate the lighting, cooling, and heating systems. The church is located at 902 W. Green Ave.; free tours can be arranged by calling (409) 883-2097.

Piney Woods Country Wines
One of the only wineries in East Texas, Piney Woods specializes in award-winning muscadine and fruit wines, including plum, pear, peach, mayberry, strawberry, and orange. This boutique winery is at 3408 Willow Dr. off I-10 east (exit 875 and 876) and is usually open for tasting and sales Mon.-Sat. 8:30 a.m.-5:30 p.m., Sunday 12:30-5:30 p.m. Call (409) 883-5408 before visiting to be sure it's open.

Super Gator Tours
Super Gator (tel. 409-883-7725) at 108 E. Lutcher Dr. (exit 878 off I-10) leads swamp-boat tours of Cypress Lake and vicinity to view waterfowl, alligators, and other wildlife native to East Texas swamps, lakes, and bayous. The hour-long tours cost $15 per adult, $10 for children under 12.

Delta Downs
Ten miles east of Orange via I-10 is this Louisiana horse track where pari-mutuel betting is legal; thoroughbred and quarter-horse races are held year round. Post times are usually 6:15 p.m. Fri.-Sat., 1 p.m. Sunday. General admission tickets cost $1.25 per person, plus $1 for

parking; more expensive clubhouse seats are available for $4.50 and $8.

Events

During the first weekend in May, the **International Gumbo Cookoff** takes over downtown Orange. Cajun chefs from Texas, Louisiana, and beyond square off to see who can screw the best roux into a gumbo. Besides all the gumbo permutations available—which, as in chili cookoffs, may contain just about anything—the celebration includes country and Cajun music, dancing, and a parade. Call the Orange Convention and Visitors Bureau at (409) 883-3536 for further information.

Accommodations

The **Best Western Inn** (tel. 409-883-6616 or 800-528-1234) at 2630 I-10 (exit 877) and **Red Carpet Inn** (tel. 883-9981) at 2900 I-10 (exit 876) each have rooms for $35-40 s, $45-50 d. Slightly more expensive is the **Ramada Inn** (tel. 883-0231 or 800-228-2828) at 2600 I-10 (exit 877), with room rates around $50 s, $60 d.

Information

The **Orange Convention and Visitors Bureau** (tel. 409-883-3536 or 800-528-4906) at 1012 Green Ave. can provide an informative walking tour map as well as a dining guide to the city.

PINEY WOODS

The vast Piney Woods form the heart of East Texas and have provided shelter and livelihood for its inhabitants for centuries. The name is a loose term for the various forest communities stretching from Beaumont in the southeast all the way to the Texas-Arkansas border in the northeast. To the west, the pine-predominant forests give way to the Post Oak Belt and blackland prairies after a couple of hundred miles. The forests are bordered on the east by Louisiana—they continue past the state line, of course, but "Piney Woods" is primarily a Texas term.

The East Texas timber industry got its start in the 19th century and has grown steadily ever since, threatening to defoliate the entire region. Much has been lost forever, or at least for the foreseeable future; fortunately, the federal government has taken measures to preserve at least some portions of the Piney Woods by creating the Sabine, Davy Crockett, Angelina, and Sam Houston national forests and Big Thicket National Preserve—a combined total of about 750,000 acres. Only Big Thicket National Preserve is completely protected, however, since the U.S. National Forest Service practices "timber management" in the four national forests, allowing planned felling of trees by the lumber industry. You can tell how important the industry is to the area by the town names—Woodville, Wildwood, Bleakwood, Lumberton, Forest, Pineland.

Along the Neches River in the Big Thicket area a local dialect similar to that spoken in isolated parts of Virginia and Maryland survives. A dead giveaway is the word "usen" for "used."

BIG THICKET NATIONAL PRESERVE

American Indians knew it as "the Big Woods," the Spanish called it "impenetrable," and to the Anglo-Americans who settled here in the early 1800s, it was "the Big Thicket." Nowadays, as complex forest environments are disappearing from the planet at an ever-increasing rate, it's called "America's ark" and "the best-equipped ecological laboratory in North America."

Before the early 19th century, the Big Thicket covered an area of over 3.5 million acres and successfully resisted all but the most tentative of human intrusion. Draft dodgers and runaway slaves hid here during the Civil War. Since the arrival of the lumber and petroleum industries, human intervention has whittled Big Thicket's domain to approximately 300,000 acres, a figure undergoing further reduction at a current rate of about 50 acres a day. Congress established Big Thicket National Preserve in 1974 to protect 86,000 acres. In 1982, the United Nations added Big Thicket National Preserve to its select list of 250 International Biosphere Reserves worth protecting worldwide. In 1993 the U.S. legislature passed a bill expanding Big Thicket to 100,000 acres. The Alabama-Coushatta Indians also act as guardians over about 4,000 acres of Big Thicket.

The preserve currently encompasses 15 separate units, consisting of six waterway corridors and nine land tracts ranging in size from the 550-acre Loblolly Unit to the 25,000-acre Lance Rosier Unit. Four units are connected by a 54-mile stretch of the Neches River, which in turn is linked to the Lance Rosier Unit via the Little Pine Island Bayou Corridor.

The Land

One of the main features giving the Big Thicket its character is the Neches River, together with the bayous, creeks, and sloughs that feed into it and the swamps that form in its floodplains during rainy periods. Historically, this thickly forested, watery environment made it difficult for even the indigenous Caddo and Atakapa Indians to navigate the interior of the Big Thicket.

Five basic North American environments—Eastern and Appalachian forests, Southeastern swamps, Midwestern prairies, and Southwestern desert—meet here to produce an unusually high number of "ecotones," or ecological meeting zones. The result of this interweaving of ecotones is a mosaic of nearly a hundred different soil types, which, coupled with the abundant rainfall (55-60 inches a year), produce more plant communities than any other area of comparable size on the continent.

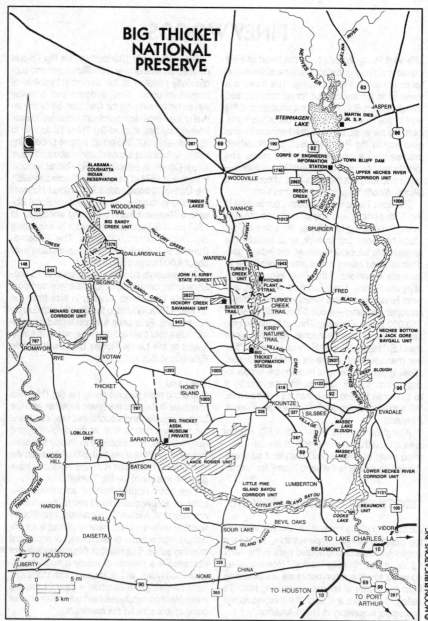

BIG THICKET
NATIONAL
PRESERVE

© MOON PUBLICATIONS, INC.

Climate

Because the forest environment acts as a natural insulator, temperatures are moderate throughout the year. The average temperature range in January is 42-61° F; in July it's 73-92° F. Rain and humidity are the key to this climate. The relative humidity reaches as high as 94% in July. You can expect rain at any time of year, an average of 4.5 inches a month. The driest months are usually February, March, and October. During the late spring and summer, mosquitoes can be a problem; any time of year, be sure to bring insect repellent.

Flora

There are eight vegetational zones within the preserve: palmetto-hardwood flatlands, wetland savannahs, dry savannahs, pine uplands, sandhills or sandyland, mixed pine-hardwood slope forests, baygalls, and stream flood plains. These harbor 85 tree species, over 60 shrubs, and nearly a thousand flowering plants, including rare ferns, orchids, and carnivorous plants.

In places, Big Thicket forests are comprised of a six-layer canopy of trees. Dominant trees across several of the drier plant communities include beech, magnolia, and shortleaf, longleaf, and loblolly pine; in the sandylands grow post oak, bluejack oak, and black hickory. Two trees—bald cypress and tupelo—predominate in the scenic cypress sloughs along the floodplains; both feature swollen bases, but cypress trunks are reddish and the base is fluted, while the tupelo has a grayish trunk and smooth base. Sweetbay and gallberry holly trees thrive in baygalls or acid bogs, perpetually wet depressions where decaying vegetation creates tea-colored, highly acidic pools of water.

The nine carnivorous plant species that grow in the preserve fall into four of the five known types found in the U.S.: pitcher plants, bladderworts, butterworts, and sundew. The pitcher plant is the largest and most common and grows mostly in wet savannahs. Like all carnivorous plants, it needs animal matter to supplement the low mineral content of its native soil.

Fauna

The black bear, black panther, and red wolf who once roamed the Big Thicket haven't been sighted for years. Still present in varying numbers are deer, coyotes, bobcats, raccoons, beavers, otters, gray foxes, armadillos, feral hogs, squirrels, rabbits, alligators, turtles, and snakes. Over 300 bird species are permanent or migrating residents, including the endangered red-cockaded woodpecker and the large, very rare pileated woodpecker. The ivory-bill woodpecker, once the largest woodpecker existent, hasn't been sighted since 1904.

Visiting the Preserve

The **Big Thicket Information Station** is located at the southern end of the Turkey Creek Unit, off FM 420 about 30 miles north of Beaumont via US 69/287 N. The information station is open daily 9 a.m.-5 p.m. except Christmas Day. It's staffed by a park ranger and stocked with free printed information on the preserve. Park Service rangers offer a range of free lectures, seminars, guided hikes, and canoe trips. If you're new to the Big Thicket, participating in one or more of these activities is an excellent way to introduce yourself to the preserve's complexities. In the Big Thicket, more than at any other national park facility in Texas, it pays to enter the area with a guide the first time out. All ranger-guided programs require reservations; call (409) 246-2337.

The Park Service has plans to open a new visitor center at the US 69/FM 420 junction within two or three years.

Hiking

The preserve maintains eight established hiking trails, ranging from less than a mile to 18 miles in length. No permits are required for hiking these trails, but the Park Service asks that you register at the trailhead; upon registering, you'll receive a detailed trail map or trail guide booklet.

Besides the usual preparations—wearing comfortable shoes, carrying plenty of drinking water—Big Thicket hikers should bring along a good insect repellent, preferably one containing a high percentage of DEET (N,N-diethylmetatoluamide), the most effective synthetic repellent. People wishing to avoid synthetics should use lemongrass oil or citronella. For maximum protection, spread repellent on exposed skin and clothes. During the warmer, wetter months, mosquitoes can be ferocious—without some kind of protection, most people can't walk 10 yards before they're forced to run for shelter.

It's also important to consider the weather. During periods of heavy rain, trails may be flooded—always inquire at the information station about trail conditions before setting out.

Trails: The **Kirby Nature Trail** begins at the Big Thicket Visitor Information Station and forms a 4.1-mile double loop through a mixture of hardwood and pine stands, cypress sloughs, and floodplains.

The 15-mile **Turkey Creek Trail** winds through the most diverse vegetation in the preserve. The main trailhead is 3.5 miles east of Warren on FM 1943, about 18 miles north-northeast of the information station; two other trailheads begin at the south end of the trail and toward the middle of the trail via unnumbered gravel roads. Inquire at the information station for exact directions to these trailheads. Starting from the north end, the trail passes through a pine-hardwood forest interspersed with sandy knolls, then into a forest of loblolly and short-leaf pines, red and white oak, beech, and magnolia. Next comes a floodplain forest of sweetgum, beech, and water and basket oak, with occasional sloughs supporting bald cypress and tupelo. Near the south end of the trail, a boardwalk leads across a baygall where sweetbay and gallberry predominate, along with black titi, red and white bay, blackgum, and azalea.

Running east off the Turkey Creek Trail, near its north end, is the quarter-mile-long **Pitcher Plant Trail.** You can choose to take this trail as an adjunct to the Turkey Creek Trail or drive 4.3 miles east of Warren on FM 1943, then 1.9 miles south along the east boundary road to the trailhead. From the trailhead, a surfaced trail leads through a mixed pine forest to the edge of a wetland savanna, where a boardwalk allows hikers to view a number of carnivorous plants (predominantly the pitcher plant) and wild orchids.

For a look at a wetland savannah containing the more delicate sundew take the **Sundew Trail** in the **Hickory Creek Savannah Unit,** a half mile south of FM 2827, off US 69/287 10 miles north of the road that leads to the information station. A one-mile loop leads through a longleaf pine wetland savannah full of perennial flowers, including the sundew. The sundew is a carnivorous plant that looks deceptively like a common wildflower. Sticky globules at the base of the plant attract and trap insects until the plant can digest them.

The **Beech Woods Trail,** a one-mile loop in the southwest corner of the **Beech Creek Unit,** winds through one of the preserve's best examples of a beech/loblolly/magnolia forest. To reach the trailhead, go 4.3 miles north of Warren on US 69/287 to Hillister, then east 10.2 miles on FM 1013 to FM 2992. The trail starts at the parking lot about two miles north off FM 2992.

The **Woodland Trail,** at the northwest edge of the **Big Sandy Creek Unit,** is a 5.4-mile loop through upland pine forests, overgrown pastures, and mature floodplain forests. This unit is 21 miles east of Woodville via US 190, then 3.3 miles south on FM 1276. From the information station, a quicker way is to take FM 1003 1.8 miles east off US 69/287, then FM 943 north 18.5 miles to the FM 1276 junction; from there it's about 10 miles to the trailhead.

In 1991 the NPS added two new trails to the preserve. The **Beaver Slide Trail** is in the southeast corner of the **Big Sandy Creek Unit,** off FM 943 about a quarter mile west of the FM 1276/943 intersection. This 1.5-mile loop trail winds around a series of ponds formed by beaver dams. In the same vicinity is the new **Big Sandy Horse Trail,** an 18-mile roundtrip trail designed for horseback riding, hiking, and all-terrain bicycling. The trail is reached by proceeding west on Sunflower Rd. off FM 1276 a half mile north of Dallardsville; the trailhead is three miles west of this intersection.

Canoeing

The Big Thicket looks its best from water level and is a favorite destination for savvy canoeists. Even novices can easily handle most preserve watercourses since there are no rapids or strong currents to contend with. The main requirement is a good map; purchase detailed topographical maps at the Turkey Creek Unit Information Station. Without a map, first-timers can easily lose their way in the dense array of rivers, sloughs, creeks, and bayous.

The main navigable watercourses in the preserve are the Neches River, 93 miles from Steinhagen Lake near Woodville to Cooks Lake in the Beaumont Unit; Pine Island Bayou, 49 miles from Saratoga to Beaumont; and Village Creek, 37 miles from Village Mills to the Neches River below Silsbee. Detailed maps of each of these watercourses, showing put-in/take-out locations, are available at the information station.

Canoe Camping: Camping along riverbanks or on sandbars is permitted in designated back-country camping areas within the preserve boundaries as long as you possess a back-country use permit. The land along sections located between preserve units—much of Pine Island Bayou and almost all of Village Creek—is privately owned, but camping is usually permitted on banks or sandbars only unless otherwise posted. Open fires are not permitted within the preserve except on Neches River sandbars, so overnight canoeists should bring campstoves for cooking.

Overnight backcountry trips are limited to five days. During hunting season (October to mid-January), backcountry camping is suspended in all units of the preserve except the Turkey Creek, Upper and Lower Neches, and Loblolly units.

Backcountry use permits are issued free at three locations: the Turkey Creek Unit Information Station; the preserve headquarters at 3785 Milam, Beaumont (Mon.-Fri. 8 a.m.-4:30 p.m.); and the North District Ranger Office on US 287 in Woodville, open whenever a ranger is there.

Canoe Rentals: Several local businesses rent canoe equipment by the day; most provide drop-off and pick-up services to renters as well. Contact **Eastex Canoe Rentals** (tel. 409-892-3600), 5865 Cole, Beaumont, $15 per day, shuttle service available; **H&H Boat Dock and Marina** (tel. 283-3257), US 190 near State 92 junction, Steinhagen Lake, $10 per day, no shuttle service; **Piney Woods Canoe Rental** (tel. 246-4481), FM 418, Kountze, $17 per day, shuttle service available; or **Canoe Rentals Silsbee** (tel. 385-6241), Old Beaumont Hwy., Silsbee, shuttle service available.

Tours: In addition to canoe rentals, **Timber Ridge Tours** (tel. 246-3107) in Kountze operates guided pontoon boat tours of the area during the summer months.

Camping outside the Preserve

Big Thicket RV Park & Campground (tel. 409-246-3759 May-Aug. or 246-4488 Sept.-April), about nine miles west of Kountze on FM 1003 three miles south of Honey Island, is a 12-acre facility with tent and RV sites (two-way hookups only) for $8 and $10. **Chain-O-Lakes Campground** (tel. 592-2150), farther northwest off FM 787 near Romayor, is a 271-acre area with tent facilities for $12, full RV hookups $15, cabins for $45-130 a night.

The U.S. Army Corps of Engineers (tel. 429-3491 or 800-284-2267) maintains two campgrounds along the east side of Steinhagen Lake, **Sandy Park** and **East End Park,** and one on the west, **Magnolia Ridge Park;** rates are $6 for tent/camper sites without utilities, $8 with electricity. Also on the east side of Steinhagen Lake is **Martin Dies, Jr. State Park** (tel. 384-5231), a 705-acre park with tentsites for $6 off season, $8 high season (Memorial Day-Oct.), tent/camper sites with w/e for $9/12, and screened shelters for $15/20.

The Alabama-Coushatta Indian Reservation, just north of the Big Sandy Creek Unit, operates a full-service campground. You can also camp at **Village Creek State Park** in Lumberton, 12 miles north of Beaumont.

Food: There are grocery stores in Woodville and Beaumont, but not much in between. **Rice Grocery,** on the left side of US 69/287 a few miles north of the FM 420 junction, sells groceries and gas. **Homestead Restaurant** (tel. 283-7324), off US 69/287 at Hillister north toward Woodville, serves homestyle fare (salads, soups, fried chicken, chicken and dumplings) Fri.-Sat. 5-10 p.m. and Sunday 11 a.m.-3 p.m. only; the menu usually includes an all-you-can-eat special.

Information

Further information can be obtained by contacting the Superintendent (tel. 409-839-2689), Big Thicket National Preserve, 3785 Milam, Beaumont, TX 77701.

ALABAMA-COUSHATTA INDIAN RESERVATION

The Alabama-Coushatta Indian tribe lives on 4,800 acres adjacent to Big Thicket National Preserve's Big Sandy Creek Unit. Had it not been for the tenacity and self-determination of this Amerindian group, they would probably have been run out of Texas and all but dispersed by now. This is one of America's few remaining forest Indian reservations; the Alabama-Coushattas have resisted all attempts by loggers and oil interests to buy them off, preferring to maintain their given homeland in its natural state.

History

Little is known of the Alabama-Coushattas' prehistoric past. Anthropologists surmise they're descendants of the Mississippian Temple-Mound Culture that flourished in the southeastern U.S. between A.D. 700 and 1300 and disappeared by 1700. By the early 18th century, there were two tribes left, the Alabama (Alibamo) clans who lived along the Alabama, lower Coosa, and Tallapoosa rivers, and the Coushatta (Koasati), who lived along the Tennessee River; both groups are members of the Muskogean Nation. Traditionally, their tribal economies were based on hunting and subsistence farming. Europeans who came into contact with them in their native lands called them "Creek" Indians because their villages were built along rivers and creeks.

In the late 1700s the Alabamas and Coushattas began migrating westward into East Texas from Alabama to escape pressure from European immigrants. When English and French colonists competed for their political affiliation, they decided to side with the French; when England gained control of French territories, their fear of Anglo vengeance hastened their migra-

tion. By 1809, the two tribes occupied several villages in the Big Thicket area with a combined population of around 1,650. During the Texan struggle for independence from Mexico, the tribes adopted a neutral position but harbored Texans who passed through their village in flight. In 1839, the Coushattas successfully turned back a Comanche raid at Long King Creek, a decisive event in the struggle to hold onto their adopted homelands.

The future seemed fairly secure when Republic of Texas President Sam Houston granted two leagues of East Texas land to each tribe in 1840. But they never received title to the designated real estate—it was occupied instead by white settlers. After Texas became a state, the state legislators purchased 1,110 acres in Polk County for the Alabamas and approved a 640-acre land grant for the Coushattas; because the Coushattas never received their land, they moved onto the Alabama land in 1858. This same year, however, Governor H.R. Runnels tried to persuade both tribes to move to another reservation in Young County northeast of Fort Worth, probably acquiescing to pressure from the timber industry, but the tribes refused to move. As a gesture of solidarity, the two tribes elected one common chief in 1871. In 1873, the U.S. Congress approved a plan to move the tribes to Oklahoma together with many other Texas tribes, but the Alabama-Coushattas again stood fast.

*Alabama-Coushatta
pine needle baskets*

In a last attempt to shake their stance, the state abolished the post of Indian agent for Polk County Indians in 1879. After this, political conditions began improving; in 1928, following a lobbying trip to Washington, D.C. by Alabama-Coushatta Chief Charles Thompson and Second Chief McConnico Battise, the U.S. government purchased 3,701 Polk County acres to add to the Alabamas' original 1,110 acres.

Culture and Customs

Well before they left Alabama for Texas, the Alabama-Coushattas had replaced their stone implements with tools of steel as a result of contact with Europeans; they also began wearing European-style clothing. Today they dress like just about anyone else in this part of the state, except during Indian ceremonies when they may wear traditional clothing. The traditional homes of the Alabama-Coushatta Indians were made of logs and branches but the people now live in wood-frame or brick homes. Alabama-Coushatta children attend public schools in nearby Woodville, Livingston, and Big Sandy, a right granted them only in 1942.

Around 500 people currently live on the reservation. The tribal government is organized around a first chief, second chief, and tribal council. The chiefs are elected for a lifetime term; the second chief takes over in the event of the first's death, in which case a new second chief is elected. The seven tribal council members are elected for three-year terms. Meetings of the council are conducted in the Alabama-Coushatta language—the separate Alabama and Coushatta dialects were always very close and have emerged as one language.

The tribe supports itself by employment outside the reservation, often with lumber mills and a multifaceted visitor program that includes the sale of traditional arts and crafts. Many feature a circular symbol with two waterfowl (head and stylized wings) facing in opposite directions. These are said to represent the dual aspects of day and night, earth and sky, life and death, male and female, strength and vulnerability, and the two voluntarily affiliated tribes. The waterfowl are joined at the center by a smaller circle representing the cell, egg, or seed of creation. The wing feathers feature seven points symbolizing the seven members of the tribal council, the seven sacred ceremonial fires, and the seven sacred pipes. There are two sets of feathers—seven times seven equals the age at which the tribe recognizes a member has embarked on the final stage of wisdom and spiritual power, as proven through various deeds and tests.

One of the most outstanding examples of Alabama-Coushatta craftwork is pine-needle basketry. Since they're handwoven, no two baskets are alike; most are bowl-shaped but some are formed into animal shapes. The first step in the basket-weaving process is collecting longleaf pine needles and drying them for several weeks. When the needles are ready, the basketmakers weave them into coils and bind them with fibers from the raffia palm. Rainy or humid days, when the needles are more pliant, are preferred workdays. The amount of time it takes to finish a basket depends on the size—a few hours for a smaller basket, a few days for a large one. A few pine-needle baskets are sometimes available for sale in the reservation gift shop, but demand often exceeds supply.

Visitor Programs

A single admission price to the tourist complex covers a Big Thicket nature bus tour, Indian country historical tour, living Indian village tour, narrow-gauge train ride, and tribal dance performance. The reservation also operates a gift shop and the **Inn of the Twelve Clans** restaurant, which serves burgers, burritos, frybread, Indian tacos, beverages, and snacks.

The tourist complex is open Mon.-Sat. 10 a.m.-6 p.m., Sunday 12:30-6 p.m. between June and August. From mid-March to May and September to late November, it's open Friday and Saturday 10 a.m.-5 p.m., Sunday 12:30-5 p.m. The gift shop stays open year round. Prices: $11 adults, $9 children 4-10 on weekdays in the spring and fall, $11 adults, $9 children on weekends and during the summer; senior, military, and AAA discounts available.

Camping

The campgrounds are situated around 26-acre Lake Tombigbee a bit beyond the tourist complex. Tentsites are $6 a night and trailer sites with w/e are $10, with full hookups $12. Fishing in the lake is permitted.

Information

For further information or campsite reservations, contact the Alabama-Coushatta Indian Reservation (tel. 409-563-4391 or 800-444-3507), Route 3, Box 640, Livingston, TX 77351.

Getting There

The main entrance to the reservation is about 17 miles west of Woodville via US 190.

NATIONAL FORESTS

The U.S. Forest Service administers 665,729 acres of the Piney Woods timberlands as national forests. This administration differs from U.S. Park Service efforts to preserve Texas woodlands in that it follows a "multiple-use" practice in which timber, wildlife, recreation, and other forest resources are consumed according to a master plan that accounts for replenishment rates. In other words, they're trying for the best of both worlds, preservation *and* consumption. Outside opinions differ as to how prudent and effective such management is, but it's definitely a compromise. Without the Forest Service presence, however, these forests would probably disappear by the end of the century.

Each of the four Piney Woods national forests features designated recreation areas with varying facilities. Many have tent and trailer camping facilities; only Ratcliff Lake Recreation Area in Davy Crockett National Forest, Red Hills Lake in the Sabine National Forest, and Double Lake Recreation Area in the Sam Houston National Forest feature electrical hookups. Rates vary from $3 to $10 a night. Primitive camping is allowed anywhere within national forest boundaries except during hunting season (October to mid-January); no charge. There are also designated wilderness areas where only primitive camping is allowed. It would require a hundred-page book to describe in detail all the features of each of the 26 recreational areas in the national forests; contact the relevant office for further information.

Angelina National Forest

This forest covers 156,153 acres surrounding Lake Sam Rayburn in Angelina, Jasper, Nacogdoches, and Augustine counties. Contact U.S.

Forest Service (tel. 409-639-8620), P.O. Box 756, Lufkin, TX 75901.

Bouton Lake Recreation Area: Picnicking, camping, boating (no motors), hiking trails; 15 miles southeast of Zavalla via State 63 and Forest Service Road (FSR) 303.

Boykin Springs Recreation Area: Picnicking, camping, swimming, boating (no motors), hiking trails; 14 miles southeast of Zavalla via State 63 and FSR 313.

Caney Creek Recreation Area: Picnicking, camping, swimming, boating, fishing, food concessions; on Lake Sam Rayburn 14 miles southeast of Zavalla via State 63 and FM 2390.

Harvey Creek Recreation Area: Picnicking, camping, boating, fishing, hiking trails; on Lake Sam Rayburn, east and south of Broaddus via FM 83 and FM 2390.

Sandy Creek Recreation Area: Picnicking, camping, swimming, boating, fishing, food concessions; on Lake Sam Rayburn, 21 miles southeast of Zavalla via State 63 and FSR 333.

Townsend Recreation Area: Picnicking, camping, swimming, boating, fishing, hiking trails; on Lake Sam Rayburn five miles northwest of Broaddus via State 147, FM 255, and FSR 335.

Sawmill Hiking Trail: Connects Boykin Springs Recreation Area and Bouton Lake Recreation Area; 5.5 miles.

Turkey Hill Wilderness Area: Primitive camping only; five miles north of Broaddus via State 147 and east on FSR 300.

Upland Island Wilderness Area: Primitive camping only; 1.5 miles north of the Neches River via US 60 and east on FSR 314.

Davy Crockett National Forest

Covers 161,478 acres in Houston and Trinity counties. There are two ranger offices: Neches Ranger District (tel. 409-544-2046), 1240 E. Loop 304, Crockett, TX 75835; and Trinity Ranger District (tel. 831-2246), P.O. Box 130, Apple Springs, TX 75926.

Big Slough Canoe Trail: Canoeing on Big Slough and the Neches River, primitive camping; two miles north of Ratcliff on FM 227, then east five miles on FSR 314.

Ratcliff Lake Recreation Area: Picnicking, camping (including electrical hookups), swimming, boating (no motors), food concessions, hiking trails; between Kennard and Ratcliff on FSR 520.

4-Cs Hiking Trail: Twenty-mile trail from Ratcliff Lake to the Neches Overlook; primitive camping.

Kickapoo Recreation Area: Picnicking, hiking trails; three miles southeast of Groveton via US 287.

Neches Bluff Recreation Area: Picnicking, hiking trails; on Neches River, seven miles southwest of Alto via State 21 and FSR 511.

Sabine National Forest
Covers 189,451 acres along Toledo Bend Reservoir in Jasper, Sabine, Newton, and Shelby counties. Two ranger offices: Tenaha Ranger District (tel. 409-275-2632), 101 S. Bolivar, San Augustine, TX 75972; and Yellowpine Ranger District (tel. 787-2791), Box F, Hemphill, TX 75948.

Indian Mounds Recreation Site and Wilderness Area: Picnicking, camping, boating, fishing, hiking trails; on Toledo Bend Reservoir, five miles east of Hemphill via FM 93, then seven miles southeast on FSR 115 and FSR 115A.

Lakeview Recreation Area: Picnicking, camping; on Toledo Bend Reservoir, 16 miles southeast of Hemphill via State 87 and access road.

Ragtown Recreation Area: Picnicking, camping, boating, fishing, food concessions, hiking trails; on Toledo Bend Reservoir, 15 miles southeast of Shelbyville via State 87, FM 139, FSR 101, and FSR 1262.

Red Hills Lake Recreation Area: Picnicking, camping, swimming, boating (no motors), food concessions, hiking trails; on Toledo Bend Reservoir, three miles north of Milam via State 87.

Willow Oak Recreation Area: Picnicking, camping, boating, fishing; on Toledo Bend Reservoir, 14 miles southeast of Hemphill via State 87 and FSR 117.

Sam Houston National Forest
Covers 160,443 acres in Montgomery, San Jacinto, and Walker counties. Two ranger offices: Raven Ranger District (tel. 409-344-6205), P.O. Box 393, New Waverly, TX 77358; and San Jacinto Ranger District (tel. 592-6462), P.O. Box 1818, Cleveland, TX 77327.

Double Lake Recreation Area: Picnicking, camping, swimming, boating (no motors), food concessions, hiking trails; four miles south of Coldspring via State 150 and FM 2025.

Kelley Pond Recreation Area: Primitive camping, chemical toilets; 11 miles west of New Waverly via FM 1375, then one mile south on FSR 204 and FSR 271.

Little Lake Creek Wilderness Area: Primitive camping; 14 miles east of New Waverly via FM 1375, then four miles south on FM 149.

Lone Star Hiking Trail: A 126-mile trail that starts west of Lake Conroe off FM 149, then proceeds to Kelly Pond, Stubblefield Lake, Huntsville State Park, Double Lake, and finally ends at FM 1725 in Cleveland; primitive camping along the trail, drinking water at established campgrounds.

Stubblefield Lake Recreation Area: Picnicking, camping, boating, fishing, hiking trails; on the West Fork of the San Jacinto River, about 12 miles northwest of New Waverly via FM 1375 and FSR 208.

NACOGDOCHES

Touted as the oldest city in Texas—an honor contested by Ysleta and San Angelo in West Texas—Nacogdoches (pronounced "Nack-a-DOE-chez") was once an important settlement of the Caddo Indian confederacy, which spread from here east into Louisiana. It later became a center for the Texas independence movement and the site of the first two newspapers printed in the state.

Today Nacogdoches is a mixture of early and modern East Texas. A number of older homes in town date back to the 19th and early 20th centuries; many of the historical sites are marked only by historical plaques.

History
Caddo legend says an early Caddo chief who lived on the Sabine River had twin sons, one with fair hair and skin, the other with dark hair and skin. When they were old enough to lead their own clans, he sent one son east and one west, both with orders to stop after a three day journey and start a village. The light-haired son established Nacogdoches, the other Natchitoches

NACOGDOCHES

MILLARD'S CROSSING

LOOP 224

© MOON PUBLICATIONS, INC.

NACOGDOCHES COUNTY
EXPOSITION CENTER

OLD TYLER RD.

NORTH ST.

PARKER RD.

LAKEWOOD

PEARL

E. AUSTIN

RAGUET

BOWIE

E. COLLEGE

STALLINGS DR.

UNIVERSITY DR.

LOGANSPORT RD.

CHAMBER OF COMMERCE
(EUGENE BLOUNT HOUSE)

STEPHEN F.
AUSTIN STATE
UNIVERSITY

RUSK

POWERS

KING

HOUSTON

MOUND

LANANA

PARK

DURST

VIRGINIA AVE.

FREDONIA ST.

STERNE - HOYA HOUSE

UNIVERSITY DR.

SAN AUGUSTINE RD.

TO LAKE
NACOGDOCHES

LOOP 224

MOON

NOT TO SCALE

in Louisiana, each about 50 miles as the crow flies from the Sabine River in opposite directions.

The first Europeans probably came upon the village around 1541, when De Soto's men stopped here on their way to Mexico following their leader's death. In 1716, Spain's Padre Margil established Misión de Nuestra Señora de Guadalupe de Nacogdoches as a counter to French claims on the area. Pressure from French colonists to the east and the dissolution of the Caddo confederacy, caused by disease and social decline under missionary influence, forced the missionaries to leave around 1720; later in the century, when the French were no longer in the picture, Spain ordered all Spanish colonists to move from East Texas to San Antonio. Some of the colonists negotiated for permission to resettle along East Texas's Trinity River, 60-70 miles west of Nacogdoches, but they weren't happy here, hampered by flooding and Comanche raids. A few began moving back to Nacogdoches in 1770. One of the leaders of this movement was Gil Antonio Ybarbo (Ibarvo), who built a stone house considered the town's first permanent structure.

By the early 19th century, Anglo-Americans were migrating into East Texas as the territory was transformed from a Spanish colony into part of the Republic of Mexico. Nacogdoches was an important way station along the migration route and many Anglo-American immigrants settled down here. Perhaps because the area was so far removed from the Coahuila y Texas state government in San Antonio, the growing dissatisfaction with Mexican authority was particularly intense. In 1819 a group of Anglo-Americans tried unsuccessfully to claim Texas as part of the Louisiana Purchase, using Ybarbo's stone fort as a headquarters. The following year Haden Edwards, a man who had a grievance against the Mexican government over a land grant (he hadn't thoroughly understood the contract, which was of course in Spanish), gathered a group of sympathizers who raised a flag at the old stone fort and declared an independent "Republic of Fredonia." They were immediately dispersed by Mexican troops and Fredonia was never heard from again.

When Texas independence was finally declared in 1836, four of the signers were from Nacogdoches, which became one of the original counties (established 1836) with U.S. annexation in 1846. The state's first oil well was drilled a few miles from here by Lyne Tol Barret in 1866, but oil was not an important economic consideration in Nacogdoches County until the early 1900s. Timber, poultry, and cattle were the traditional livelihoods for the county until manufacturing, education (Stephen F. Austin State University), and tourism flourished in the latter half of this century.

Sights

Walking Tour: The Nacogdoches Chamber of Commerce distributes the free, tourist-oriented *Nacogdoches Sampler* newspaper, which contains a map of the historic central part of town. Over 25 points of historic interest are marked on the map.

Old Stone Fort: This reconstruction of Gil Ybarbo's 1779 house, at Griffith and Clark on the Stephen F. Austin State University campus, originally stood at the corner of Main and Fredonia. In 1936 it was rebuilt using the original stones for the Texas centennial. Over its long history, the building has been used as trading post, jail, fort, the state's first newspaper office, the first district court in the state, the home of a judge and district attorney, and now a muse-

um. Displays include guns, tools, Indian artifacts, and other early Nacogdoches memorabilia. Open Tues.-Sat. 9 a.m.-5 p.m., Sunday 1-5 p.m.; free admission. Call (409) 568-2408 for more information.

Sterne-Hoya House: This East Texas colonial-style house (tel. 409-560-5426) at Pilar and Lanana is the oldest surviving, unreconstructed home in Nacogdoches. It was built around 1830 by German immigrant Nicolas Adolphus Sterne, who participated in the 1820 Fredonia episode and invested in the Texas revolution in 1836. Many early Texas dignitaries visited the Sterne house; Sam Houston was baptized into the Catholic church here. After Sterne died, his widow sold the house to Prussian immigrant Joseph von der Hoya; it stayed in the Hoya family until the city acquired it in 1958. It now serves as a museum (a few of the rooms are furnished in period style) and historical library. Open Mon.-Sat. 9 a.m.-noon and 2-5 p.m.; free admission.

Millard's Crossing: Lera Millard Thomas, the first woman from Texas to serve in the U.S. House of Representatives, has moved a number of early East Texas structures to Millard's Crossing for historical preservation. Included are an 1830 double corncrib, 1843 Methodist church, 1830 log cabin, 1837 two-story house containing a collection of early Texas maps and other historic documents, and several other 19th-century buildings. All are furnished with period antiques. Millard's Crossing (tel. 564-6631) is at 6020 North St. (US 59 Business), on the north edge of town. Open Mon.-Sat. 9 a.m.-4 p.m., Sunday 1-4 p.m.; admission is $3 adults, $2 children 6-12.

Stephen F. Austin State University: This tertiary institution with an enrollment of around 13,000 (nearly half the Nacogdoches population of 32,000) offers a wide variety of baccalaureate and master's degree programs, plus a doctoral program in forestry. The 400-acre campus is in the center of town off North St. at Griffith. A number of university film, theater, and musical events are open to the public. For information, call 568-2011.

Hotels and Motels

Most of the city's hotels and motels are found along State 21 (San Augustine Rd.), US 59 Business (North or South streets), or Loop 224.

Millard's Crossing

Less expensive places include the **Nacog-doches Continental Inn** (tel. 409-564-3726) at 2728 North, where rooms are $30 s, and $36 d; and the **Heritage Motor Inn** (tel. 560-1906) at 4809 N.W. Stallings (Loop 224), $33 s or d. The **Econo Lodge** (tel. 569-0880) at 2020 N.W. Stallings and the **La Quinta Motor Inn** (tel. 560-5453 or 800-531-5900) at 3215 South are both in the $35-50 range. Better in this range is the **Stratford House Inn** (tel. 560-6038) at 3612 North St., where rooms are $35-45 s, $40-50 d. The **Holiday Inn** (tel. 569-8100) at 3400 South costs $53 s, $65 d and is also a good choice.

Centrally located for downtown exploration is the newly restored **Fredonia Hotel and Convention Center** (tel. 564-1234), 200 N. Fredonia. Rooms range from $53 s and $63 d to $135 for a suite.

Bed and Breakfasts

The **Haden-Edwards Inn** (tel. 409-564-9999) is an 1860 house within walking distance of the downtown area at 106 N. Lanana; rooms with private bath are $65, while rooms with shared bath are $50. All rates include a full breakfast. The **Little House** (tel. 564-2735) is a country cottage behind the 1880 Raguet House at 110 Sanders, within walking distance of downtown. The cottage accommodates two guests for $55 a night with continental breakfast.

True Texas decor and a fine sense of style mark the **Mound Street Bed and Breakfast** (tel.

569-2211), a graceful 1899 Victorian at 408 N. Mound St. in the downtown area. Rates, which include a continental breakfast, run $75-80 for rooms with bath, $65 for rooms that share a bath.

The **Llano Grande Plantation** (tel. 569-1249), three miles south of Loop 224 on FM 2863, has three separate houses with B&B accommodations. The 1848 East Texas-style **Tol Barret House,** listed with the National Register of Historic Places, is $70 for the first night, $60 each additional night, including a generous continental breakfast. The proprietors live in the **Sparks House** and offer the second floor at the same rates. The **Gate House,** a 50-year-old ranch-style farmhouse, is also available. The plantation's mailing address is Route 4, Box 9400, Nacogdoches, TX 75961.

Campgrounds and RV Parks

The new **Piney Woods RV Park** (tel. 409-560-1287), 5001 N.W. Stallings Dr., offers the only campground in Nacogdoches. Sites run $9 per night or $45 per week. **Mission San Francisco de los Tejas State Historical Park** (tel. 687-2394), mailing address Route 2, Box 108, Grapeland, TX 75844, about 37 miles southwest of the city off State 21 just past Weches, offers tent/camper sites with water for $6, with w/e $9, with full hookups $10.

The **Ratcliff Lake Recreation Area** (Neches Ranger District, tel. 544-2046) in Davy Crockett National Forest is 36 miles southwest of Nacogdoches via State 7; rates are $5 for tent/camper sites, $8 with electricity.

Food

Fried alligator, blackened catfish, gumbo, étouffée and other Cajun standards are served at **Bayou Tesh** (tel. 409-568-9588) at 2215 N. W. Stallings. **Catfish King of Nacogdoches** (tel. 560-9470) at 3120 North is part of an East Texas chain that specializes in fresh catfish and other seafood at moderate prices.

Casa Tomas Mexican Restaurant (tel. 560-2403) at 1514 North serves a variety of Tex-Mex, including fajitas and *pollo al carbón*. More upscale is **La Hacienda** (tel. 564-6450), a Mexican, steak, and seafood restaurant in a large converted house at 1411 North.

Events

The week-long **Heritage Festival** is held in early June to celebrate the city's glorious history and features an old-fashioned "barn dance," antique show and sale, "Tastes of Nacogdoches" restaurant sampler, beauty pageant and coronation of Heritage Queen, chili cookoff, old-timers hall of fame breakfast, and a charity ball. The chili cookoff and barn dance are held at the Nacogdoches County Exposition Center on US 59, north of State 21 near the Old Tyler Rd. (FM 1638) junction.

The Expo Center is also the venue for October's **Piney Woods Fair,** which features agricultural and livestock exhibits, a carnival, music, arts and crafts, and food booths, and for the **Nacogdoches County Championship Rodeo** in March.

Lake Nacogdoches

This 2,210-acre impoundment of Bayo Loco Creek, 12 miles southwest via FM 225, has two municipal parks with facilities for picnicking, boating, fishing, swimming, waterskiing, and hiking.

Caddoan Mounds State Historic Site

Known to archaeologists as the George C. Davis site, Caddoan Mounds was the westernmost center of the Mississippian Temple-Mound Culture that spanned the southeastern woodlands of North America from approximately 1000 B.C. to A.D. 1500. This particular site, known as "Kee-nuk" to the Caddos, was inhabited by the most sophisticated of the Indian mound-builder tribes, the Early Caddos. The Caddos (short for Kadohadacho or "Real Chiefs") traded in stone, flint, quartz, and tobacco all over what is now the southeastern United States. Chosen for its fertile alluvial soil and proximity to the Neches River, Kee-nuk remained active for over 500 years beginning around A.D. 700.

The Caddos constructed earthen mounds for religious and civil rites. Modern anthropologists have surmised that whenever a great Caddo chief died, several family members and followers were sacrificed and buried in the mound with the chief, and a new temple erected on the burial mound. The Caddos mysteriously abandoned the site in the late 13th or early 14th century; contemporary theory has it the ruling elite here lost influence over outlying Caddo villages, so its members left. Drought or other natural disasters may also have played a role. A community of 3,300 remaining Caddos live near Binger, Oklahoma.

Current exhibits consist of two temple mounds, a burial mound, and some village remnants. A visitor center offers interpretive exhibits and an audiovisual presentation about Caddo history and culture; a three-quarter-mile self-guided trail leads visitors through the mound and village area. The facilities are open for day use only, Fri.-Mon. 10 a.m.-6 p.m.; admission is $2 adult, $1 seniors and children. Guided tours are available by appointment.

The site is located on State 21, six miles west of Alto and about 30 miles west of Nacogdoches. For more information, contact Caddoan Mounds State Historic Site (tel. 409-858-3218), Route 2, Box 85C, Alto, TX 75925.

Information

The **Nacogdoches Chamber of Commerce** (tel. 409-564-7351), housed in the historic Eugene Blount House at 1801 North, distributes the *Nacogdoches Sampler,* maps, and brochures containing information on attractions, dining, and accommodations in and around Nacogdoches.

KSAU-FM 90.1 radio station, sponsored by Stephen F. Austin University, plays an eclectic mix of jazz, classical, blues, world beat, and alternative.

The area code for Nacogdoches and vicinity is 409 unless otherwise noted.

TEXAS STATE RAILROAD
STATE HISTORICAL PARK

The only railroad park in the state system began in 1896 as a prison railroad serving an iron plant in Rusk. By 1913 the penitentiary and iron plant had closed and the line was operated by Southern Pacific until the Parks and Wildlife Department acquired it in 1969. Missouri Pacific Railroad still leases a 3.7-mile stretch to serve a local meat-packing plant.

The 25-mile stretch between Rusk and Palestine farther west is dedicated to the preservation and exhibition of steam locomotives. Steam trains take passengers on a four-hour, 50-mile roundtrip excursion through pine and hardwood forests, including Fairchild State Forest, and across 30 bridges, including a 1,100-foot span across the Neches River. The six locomotives in use were built between 1896 and 1927 and range in weight from 71 to 224 tons each. Park facilities at Rusk include a small film theater and various exhibits recounting the railroad's history. Facilities at both ends include picnic grounds.

Trains run Thurs.-Mon. from May 30 to July 31, Saturday and Sunday only the rest of the year. A train departs from each end of the line at 11 a.m.; return trips are at 3 p.m. Two hours each way, with a two-hour break between—time enough for a picnic. The fare is $10 one-way, $15 roundtrip for adults, $6 and $9 for children 3-12.

Camping
The park in Rusk offers tent/camper sites with w/e for $9, full hookups for $10.

Information
Contact Texas State Railroad State Historical Park (tel. 903-683-2561 or 800-442-8951 in TX), P.O. Box 39, Rusk, TX 75785. Rusk is 40 miles northwest of Nacogdoches via State 21 W and US 175 N.

TYLER

Named for John Tyler, the 10th U.S. president and signer of the agreement by which the Republic of Texas was admitted to the Union, Tyler began as a pioneer trading post nestled in the rolling hills of East Texas. Some of the well-preserved historic homes date to the 1850s, and the brick streets of downtown serve as a reminder of earlier times. The city made its leap to prominence during the 1930s oil boom when several major oil companies set up headquarters here due to the town's strategic location between Dallas and the East Texas oil fields. Tyler has since grown to become the largest urban center

Tyler Rose

TYLER AREA CHAMBER OF COMMERCE

of the area, with a current population of approximately 80,000.

With an average temperature of 45° in January and 82° in July, Tyler's mild climate is ideal for plants, and the area seems to be in bloom almost year round. Known as the "Rose Capital of America," Tyler now markets 20% of the rose bushes produced in the United States. The city takes its roses very seriously indeed; the Tyler Municipal Rose Garden, Tyler Rose Museum, and Texas Rose Festival draw hundreds of thousands of visitors each year, pouring stacks of dollars into local coffers. The locals even go so far as to compose odes to the fragrant blossoms:

Where the air is full of fragrance
From the lovely blooming rose
And the city gets a blessing
From each rippling breeze that blows . . .
That's Tyler Texas.

—TOMMIE GODFREY

Tyler Municipal Rose Garden and Museum

The nation's largest municipal rose garden contains over 30,000 bushes and 400 varieties spread over 14 meticulously landscaped acres. Within the compound are test gardens where new varieties are studied for vigor, disease resistance, and floral characteristics; a Heritage Rose and Sensory Garden with antique varieties dating back to the mid-1800s; and the Vance Burke Memorial Garden of camellias and day lilies.

During the annual Rose Festival in mid-October, the Municipal Garden is the focal point of many events, including the Queen's Tea, when thousands turn out to see the pretty white festival pavilions, meet the current festival queen, and enjoy refreshments. The peak blooming period is between May and early October.

The garden (tel. 903-531-1212) is at 1900 W. Front and is open daily 8 a.m.-midnight, except on days they spray for rose diseases and pests. Admission is free.

Within the Tyler Rose Garden Center, a 30,000-square-foot structure bordering the west side of the rose garden, is a visitor center, gift shop, and the **Tyler Rose Museum** (tel. 597-3130). This spacious new museum chronicles Tyler's rose-growing history from the turn of the century to the present and contains the jeweled gowns and other memorabilia of past Texas Rose Festival Queens. Multimedia exhibits include films on the rose industry and the Rose Festival, and a computerized catalog of roses. At 420 S. Rose Park Drive. Open Tues.-Fri. 9 a.m.-4 p.m., Saturday 10 a.m.-4 p.m., and Sunday 1:30-4 p.m.; admission is $3.50 adults, $2 children 3-11. Admission is higher ($4.50-5) during the Rose Festival when the museum is decorated with fresh roses.

Caldwell Zoo

What started in 1937 as a backyard menagerie at the Caldwell Playschool has grown into one of the best little zoos in Texas. Divided into sections covering North America, South America, Africa, and the Texas Farm, this 50-acre facility houses buffalo, rhinos, elephants, giraffes, mountain lions, cheetahs, monkeys, alligators, sloths, flamingos, and macaws, all in natural environments. Amazingly, admission to the park is free year round. At 2203 Martin Luther King, Jr. Blvd., tel. (903) 593-0121; open April-Sept. 9:30 a.m.-6 p.m. and Oct.-March 9:30 a.m.-4:30 p.m.

Goodman-LeGrand Home and Museum

Antique lovers and Texas history buffs will enjoy this 1859 antebellum home furnished with original furniture, rare china, period photographs, Civil War memorabilia, antique medical tools, and Indian artifacts. Thirty-minute guided tours afford a good introduction to Tyler history. At 624 N. Broadway (tel. 903-597-5304). Open Nov.-Feb., Mon.-Fri. 1-5 p.m.; March-Oct., Wed.-Sun. 1-5 p.m.

Accommodations

Motel 6 (tel. 903-595-6691) at 3236 Gentry Pkwy. has rooms for $27 s and $32 d, while the **Coachlight Inn** (tel. 882-6145) at 13629 I-20 W and the **Econo Lodge** (tel. 593-0103) at 3209 W. Gentry Pkwy. both charge $28-30 s, $32-36 d. Next up in price is the **Tyler Inn** (tel. 597-1301) at 2843 North NW Loop 323, where rooms are $45 s, $50 d. Rates at the **Residence Inn by Marriott** (tel. 595-5188 or 800-331-3131) at 3303 Troup Hwy. are $59-86 s, $69-114 d and include complimentary evening cocktails and continental breakfast.

Of numerous bed and breakfasts in historic homes around town, two of the most popular are the **Azalea Inn** (tel. 595-3610) at 313 E. Charnwood and the **Charnwood Hill** (tel. 597-3980) next door at 223 E. Charnwood. Rates at these graceful, antique-filled inns start at $95 s or d; children and pets are not welcome.

Camping
Whispering Pines Resort and Campground (tel. 903-858-2405) at 5583 Farm Rd. offers tent spaces for $12, drive-in sites with w/e for $13.50, full hookups for $15, and rental trailers that sleep 4-8 for $35-50. On the premises are a pool, tennis and volleyball courts, mini-golf, nature trails, and a dump station.

Food
For lunch on the lighter side, **The Potpourri House** (tel. 903-592-4171) at 2301 S. Broadway is hard to beat. Homemade soups, salads, sandwiches, and desserts fill the menu of this quaint tea room open Mon.-Sat. 11 a.m.-3 p.m. only. **Rick's** (tel. 531-2415) on the square downtown at 104 W. Erwin is a good alternative, serving similar light fare for lunch and dinner and providing entertainment in the evenings.

Armadillo Willy's Cafe (tel. 509-0122) at 215 West SW Loop 323 serves up live blues on the weekends along with a mix of burgers and Tex-Mex fare. **Giuseppe's** (tel. 534-0265) at 212 Grande Blvd. is the choice for fine dining; the menu is continental with a strong Italian emphasis. For the best seafood and steaks in town, choose **Cace's Seafood** (tel. 581-0744) at 7011 S. Broadway, a branch of the famous Longview restaurant.

Events
The event of events in Tyler is the internationally famous **Texas Rose Festival,** an annual shindig since 1933. Held in mid-October, the festival includes a rose show, coronation of the Rose Queen and her court, a Queen's Tea in the Municipal Rose Garden, and a grand floral parade. The Rose Museum (tel. 903-597-3130) can provide details.

Tyler residents love to celebrate their green thumbs, and do so with panache during the **Azalea and Spring Flower Trail,** a two-week event in late March and early April that focuses on the vibrant azaleas, dogwood, redbuds, and other colorful blooms that coat the city each spring. The event culminates with Heritage on Tour, an open house tour of several historic homes graced by young women in antebellum gowns. Call 592-0837 for more information and tour reservations.

Information
The **Tyler Convention and Visitors Bureau** (tel. 903-592-1661 or 800-235-5712) at 407 N. Broadway distributes brochures and maps of the city.

KILGORE

Kilgore was named after its founder, C.B. "Buck" Kilgore, who started businesses here in 1871 to serve lumberjacks and sawmill workers. Cotton was the only other game in town until the massive East Texas Oil Field was discovered eight miles south of Kilgore in December 1930. By August 1931 the National Guard had to be called in to restore law and order among the wildcatters, drillers, roughnecks, and camp followers that had descended on the little town. Since then, petroleum deposits have produced 4.5 billion barrels of crude oil.

The city leadership had enough foresight to begin diversifying the economy before the bottom dropped out of the oil market in the 1980s. Kilgore is no longer solely reliant on local commodities; numerous manufacturing companies here produce everything from fiberglass fishing boats to communication satellite dishes.

Sights
Architecture: You can tell that the '30s were Kilgore's glory days by all the leftover art deco buildings in the downtown area. A few brick structures from the late 1800s are also still standing. The Kilgore Chamber of Commerce (tel. 903-984-5022), 1100 Stone, distributes two informative pamphlets for those interested in historic buildings: *Downtown Walking Tour: Historic Sites & Art Deco Architecture* and *Driving Tour of Historic Sites.*

East Texas Oil Museum: On the campus of Kilgore College at Henderson (US 59) and Ross, this museum (tel. 983-8295) features handpainted murals depicting early oil production, films on the Texas oil boom, and an indoor replica of an oil boomtown in the '30s, with vintage cars and horse-drawn carriages stuck in the mud street, a general store, barbershop, post office, feed store, and other boomtown businesses, all furnished with original period artifacts. Open Tues.-Sat. 9 a.m.-4 p.m., Sunday 2-5 p.m.; admission is $3.50 adults, $3 children under 12.

Rangerette Showcase: The Kilgore College Rangerettes were organized in 1940 to "bring show business to the gridiron" and were the first to develop precision dancing for sports events. Today they're much in demand for halftime shows at national football bowls. The Rangerette Showcase (tel. 984-8531), at Broadway and Ross on the Kilgore College campus, displays a collection of Rangerette props, photos, newspaper clippings, and such costumes as stylized white cowboy hats, white boots, blue skirts, and red blouses or jackets. The facility also includes a theater showing a 20-minute film about the Rangerettes. Open Tues.-Fri. 10 a.m.-noon and 1-4:30 p.m., Saturday and Sunday 2-5 p.m.; free admission.

Accommodations

With a population of 12,000, Kilgore only has a few motels. The **Kilgore Community Inn** (tel. 903-984-5501) is well located at 801 US 259 N near Kilgore College and the downtown area. Rooms are $35 s, $42 d.

The **Ramada Inn** (tel. 983-3456 or 800-228-2228) at 3501 US 259 N has rooms for $42-52. Nearby, the **Budget Inn** (tel. 983-2975) at 3505 US 259 N has economical rooms for $25 s, $35 d.

The **Hidden Valley Mobile Home & RV Park** (tel. 983-2760) is about two miles south of I-20 off FM 1249 at 1803 Roberts. Full hookups are $12 a night—lower for longer stays.

Food

The hickory-smoked barbecue—beef, ham, sausage, and turkey—at **Bodacious Bar-B-Q** (tel. 903-983-1421), State 42 N near I-20, is very popular. The wood is stacked out back and the meat is served on butcher paper, always a good sign. Locals claim the **Country Tavern**, on State 31 about six miles west of Kilgore, is the most famous barbecue establishment in East

Texas. Their advice: "You can't go wrong with the rib plate." Even Tyler residents, who have plenty of barbecue joints of their own, drive 30 miles to eat at the Country Tavern.

The most authentic Tex-Mex in town is at **Los Dos Mexican Restaurant** (tel. 984-4790) at 2612 US 259 N. Farther north in a huge 1935 mansion is the more upscale **La Hacienda** (tel. 983-1629). The inexpensive breakfast buffet at the Kilgore Community Inn is a favorite local meeting spot.

Events

Kilgore College hosts the **Texas Shakespeare Festival** in its Van Cliburn Auditorium during the last week in June and first two weeks of July. Four Shakespeare plays are performed on an alternating basis. Ticket prices range $12-15; season tickets are available for $40. Call (903) 983-8601 for more information.

Information

Contact the **Kilgore Chamber of Commerce** (tel. 903-984-5022) at 1100 Stone Road. The area code for Kilgore is 903.

LONGVIEW

Established as a rail terminal for the regional cotton and timber trade in 1870, Longview mushroomed overnight with the East Texas oil boom of the 1930s, centered at nearby Kilgore. It's now the Gregg County seat with a population of approximately 75,000 and is a headquarters for such diverse manufacturing interests as Resistol Hats, the Stroh Brewery, Continental Can, and various oil-field equipment manufacturers.

Gregg County Historical Museum

This small museum, housed in a restored 1910 bank at 214 N. Fredonia, chronicles the county history with exhibits on early oil industry, lumber, farming, printing, and railroads. It also makes the most of its setting with a refurbished teller's cage, bank president's office, and bank vault. Other period rooms include a dentist's office, schoolroom, and log cabin interior. Open Tues.-Sat. 10 a.m.-4 p.m.; admission is $2 adults, $1 seniors and people under 18.

Longview Museum and Arts Center

The permanent collection in this museum (tel. 903-753-8103) at 102 W. College focuses on contemporary Texan artists. Temporary exhibits change six to eight times a year and feature a range of work by Texas and Southwestern artists, including occasional East Texas folk art. Open Tues.-Sat. 10 a.m.-4 p.m.; free admission.

The Stroh Brewery Company

This is one of seven breweries operated by Stroh nationwide and is the largest brewery in Texas. On-line since 1966, this one produces Stroh's, Old Milwaukee, Schaefer, and Schlitz, plus "light" and malt liquor variations of these labels.

Visitors may join guided 40-minute tours of the brewing and packaging facilities that end in the Strohaus hospitality room for free samples. Tours are conducted Mon.-Fri. at 10 a.m., 11 a.m., 1 p.m., 2 p.m., and 3 p.m.; free admission. The bad news is that tours are off-again, on-again, so call first to check that a tour will be available before you go. At 1400 W. Cotton St. (tel. 903-753-0371).

Accommodations

Motel 6 (tel. 903-758-5256) at 110 I-20 W (exits 595/595A) has rooms for $28, plus $6 for each additional adult. Next up in price is the **Ramada Inn** (tel. 758-0711 or 800-222-2244) at 3304 S. Eastman (I-20 and State 149), where rooms are $35 s, $50 d. In the same range is the **Comfort Inn** (tel. 757-7858 or 800-221-2222) at 203 N. Spur 63, one block north of US 80.

La Quinta Motor Inn (tel. 757-3663) at Estes Pkwy. and I-20 has rooms for $46-53 s, $52-59 d; senior discount available. The nearby **Longview Inn** (tel. 753-0350) has rooms for $36 s, $44 d. Also at Estes Pkwy. and I-20 is the **Holiday Inn** (tel. 758-0500), where rooms are $50-60 s, $57-89 d. **Stratford House Inn** (tel. 758-4322) at 3100 Estes Pkwy. has more in-room amenities than most; rooms range between $46 s and $60 d and include continental breakfast.

Annie's Bed & Breakfast (tel. 636-4355) is a three-story Queen Anne Victorian 23 miles west of Longview (via US 80 W and State 155 N) in the small town of Big Sandy; rates range from $50 for a cozy second-floor room with shared bath to $115 for a spacious, elegant third-floor room with private balcony. All 13 rooms are furnished with country antiques; a full breakfast is served in Annie's Tea Room, which is also open to nonguests.

Closer to the heart of Longview but still in the woodlands is **Fisher Farm Bed & Breakfast** (tel. 660-2978), where rooms with private baths run $89 s or d. On the grounds are an orchard, nature trail, and hot tub; carriage and wagon rides can be arranged. Take US 80 east to State 450 south, then head west on Country Club Road.

Food

They say you haven't been to Longview if you haven't dined at friendly **Johnny Cace's Seafood and Steak House** (tel. 903-753-7691) at 1501 E. Marshall (US 80 E), which has been serving Creole-style seafood since 1949. According to the menu, "The oysters you eat here today slept in their shells last night."

The original **Bodacious Bar-B-Q** (tel. 753-8409) at 2227 S. Mobberly staked its claim to fame with hickory-smoked ribs, brisket, ham, sausage, and turkey. **Armadillo Willy's** (tel. 236-4970) at 102 E. Tyler serves standard burgers and steaks along with unusual selections like fried jalapeños and "dillo eggs."

Lupe's is a local Tex-Mex chain specializing in *tacos al carbón, flautas,* fajitas, and *carne asada.* In Longview, there are two locations: 809 Pine Tree (tel. 297-6916) and 1015 E. Marshall (tel. 757-5940).

US 80 (Marshall Ave.) is good hunting grounds for fast-food outlets like Dairy Queen, Pizza Hut, and the like.

Entertainment

Longview has the oldest continually operating dance hall in the state, the **Reo Palm Isle Ballroom** (tel. 903-753-4440) at the junction of State 31 and FM 1845 between I-20 and US 80. Originally established as Mattie's Ballroom in the 1930s, the hall features a hardwood dance floor and serves only beer and setups; until recently men were required to check their hats at the door. Elvis performed here during the rockabilly phase of his career. Live country bands generally appear Tues.-Sun. nights.

Annie's Tea Room hosts occasional art shows, dinner theaters, and small country fairs.

Events

On the second or third weekend in July, the **Great Texas Balloon Race** is held at nearby Gregg County Airport. In this 16-year-old event nearly a hundred top-ranking hot-air balloon pilots compete for $80,000 in prize money. Prizes are also awarded for "specials shapes"; some of the custom balloons have to be seen to be believed. For information, call (903) 237-4000.

The **Old Country School of East Mountain** (tel. 297-7854), a renovated 1930s schoolhouse on the northern edge of Longview, has been converted into a festival facility and now hosts numerous music/food/crafts festivals throughout the year, including **Mountaineer Days** in April, **Celtic Heritage Festival** in May, October's **Harvest Moon Festival,** and **Country Christmas Extravaganza** in late November.

Information

The **Longview Convention and Visitors Bureau** (tel. 903-753-3281 or 800-234-7794) at 410 N. Center has printed information on the city and area, as does the larger **East Texas Tourism Association** (tel. 757-4444 or 800-766-3349) at 400 N. Center.

The area code for Longview is 903.

JEFFERSON

This little town on Big Cypress Bayou between Lake O' The Pines and Caddo Lake is well worth visiting for those with an interest in Texas history. At one time it was the westernmost terminus for Mississippi, Ohio, and Tennessee river steamboats, which reached Jefferson via the Red River, Caddo Lake, and the bayou. Second in importance only to the Port of Galveston, the docks in Jefferson offloaded westward passengers arriving from New Orleans—800 miles away, via the joined Red and Mississippi rivers—and shipped cotton and timber east.

During the Civil War, Trans-Mississippi Confederate troops were stationed here and the port served as an important supply point for textiles and munitions. After the war, the port continued to grow; in 1872, over 200 sternwheelers, each with a cargo capacity of 225 to 700 tons, called at Jefferson. The first refrigerator in the state arrived here in 1873, followed by the first ice factory and brewery. Later that same year, the U.S. Army Corps of Engineers irrevocably reversed the town's fortunes when they dynamited a 170-mile-long logjam in the Red River (the infamous "Red River Raft") which had diverted a great deal of water into Big Cypress Bayou. Once the logjam was cleared, the water level in Caddo Lake and Big Cypress Bayou lowered to such an extent that riverboat travel was no longer feasible; within a very short time the population dropped from 30,000 to 2,000.

Jefferson's loss was the historian's gain. "Progress" bypassed the little town in this forgotten corner of the state and instead of being torn down and replaced by glass-and-concrete blocks, old buildings were left standing. Today Jefferson has no skyscrapers, Holiday Inns, apartment buildings, or supermarkets, and in fact almost no modern buildings of any kind. Except for improved roads, it looks very much like it must have looked in the steamboat era. Nearly a hundred structures in a 20-block radius of downtown bear historical plaques of one kind or another.

The town's population hasn't increased much since the blasting of the Red River Raft and is now only about 2,500 (though around 10,000 are buried in the cemetery). Tourism keeps the town alive; nearly 25 local structures have been restored and converted into bed-and-breakfast inns while dozens of others have become antique shops, art studios, restaurants, and cafes. Some residents are employed in Marshall, a manufacturing and petroleum center of 27,000 people, 16 miles south of Jefferson.

Historic Buildings

Many Jefferson buildings are made of cypress heartwood gathered from the floodplains of Big Cypress Bayou or Caddo Lake. Such wood is well suited to construction since it's straight, strong, and impervious to termites; only cypress trees over 300 years old contain heartwood, and very few are left today. Several homes are open year round for public tours while others are open only during the annual Spring Pilgrimage. For a complete list of historic buildings, contact the Marion County Chamber of Commerce (tel. 903-665-2672) at 115 W. Austin near Excelsior House.

House of the Seasons

The second-oldest hotel in Texas, the **Excelsior House** (tel. 665-2513) at 211 W. Austin, was built in 1858 in the New Orleans style and hosted such luminaries as railroad tycoon Jay Gould, Ulysses S. Grant, Rutherford B. Hayes, and Oscar Wilde. It was eventually purchased and restored by the local Jessie Allen Wise Garden Club, responsible for a number of restoration projects in town. Inside, the ballroom and dining room are crowned by two French Sevres chandeliers; walls and ceilings are of pressed tin and all rooms are furnished in period antiques. A French cast-iron fountain sits in the center of the New Orleans-style courtyard in back and original guest registers are on view in the lobby. Tours of the building are conducted daily at 1 p.m. and 2 p.m.; admission is $2 adults, $1 children under 12.

The **House of the Seasons** (tel. 665-1218), at 409 S. Alley, was built at the peak of Jefferson's early glory in 1872 by Benjamin H. Epperson, a prominent lawyer and Sam Houston confidante. The two-story house shows a transition between Greek Revival and Victorian styles, with Italianate details superimposed on the basic colonial design. It's crowned by a four-sided cupola with stained-glass windows; each side represents a different season with a different color. Inside, a dome lined with frescoes can be viewed from the first floor through a banistered opening in the second floor. Guided tours are conducted Mon.-Thurs. and Sunday at 10:30

a.m. and 1:30 p.m., Saturday at 10:30 a.m., 1:30, 3:30, and 5:30 p.m., or by appointment; admission is $5 adults, $3 students, $1 children under 12.

The **Freeman Plantation** (tel. 665-2320), about a mile west of town on State 49, was built in 1850, in the middle of a thousand-acre sugarcane plantation. The design is typical Louisiana/Greek Revival-style, with the main body of the house raised seven feet above the ground. The 14-inch-thick walls of the lower floor are made of clay brick handmolded by slave labor; the upper walls are cypress, with framing timbers notched and pegged rather than nailed. Listed with the National Register of Historic Places, the restoration and period furnishings are first rate. Guided tours are given Thurs.-Tues. at 3:30 p.m.; admission is $3 adults, $1 children 6-12.

The **Atalanta**, a private railcar opposite Excelsior House, once belonged to financier Jay Gould. Gould had asked for right of way to lay a railroad through Jefferson, promising increased prosperity for a town with an economy based on the transportation industry. At the time, Jefferson was riding high as a riverboat port, so the city leadership declined. Gould is reputed to have written in the Excelsior House guest register, "The end of Jefferson." But the town's still around, he's not, and now they've got his plushly appointed private railcar on display, purchased by the historically minded Jessie Allen Wise Gar-

JEFFERSON AREA

TEXAS

LOUISIANA

CEDAR SPRINGS

ORE CITY

LAKE O' THE PINES

CYPRESS CREEK

JEFFERSON

CLINTON LAKE

UNCERTAIN

CADDO LAKE

WOODLAWN

KARNACK

TO MARSHALL

TO MARSHALL

© MOON PUBLICATIONS, INC.

0   5mi
0   5km

den Club in 1953. Built in 1890, the mahogany- and curly maple-paneled car contains four state-rooms, a lounge, dining room, kitchen, butler's pantry, and bathroom. Open for tours daily 9:30 a.m.-noon and 2:30-4:30 p.m.; admission is $1 adults, 50 cents children under 12.

Jefferson Historical Society Museum

Housed in the 1888 Federal Building at 223 W. Austin (tel. 903-665-8880), this four-story museum contains 3,000 items pertaining to Jefferson history. Some of the more notable exhibits are the Caddo Indian artifacts, gun collection, and antique furniture on the second floor. Historic documents are displayed on the main floor. Open daily 9:30 a.m.-5 p.m.; admission is $1 adults, 50 cents children under 12.

Hotels and Motels

The historic **Excelsior House** (tel. 903-665-2513) at 211 Austin has 13 rooms and one two-bedroom suite furnished with antiques. Rates range $45-90; advance booking is a necessity, especially for weekend stays.

Across the street at 124 W. Austin is the **Hotel Jefferson** (tel. 665-2631), which started out as a cotton warehouse in 1851. Rooms are $65 s or d, $75-85 for four people.

The only other regular hotels/motels in town are the **Best Western Inn** (tel. 665-3983 or 800-528-1234), at 400 S. Walcott ($46-56 s, $50-60 d), and the **Budget Inn** (tel. 665-2581), 1.5 miles south of town on US 59 ($34-36 s, $35-38 d).

Bed and Breakfasts

Over 40 historic Jefferson homes have been converted to bed-and-breakfast inns, ranging in price from $35 to $115 a night including breakfast—sometimes "continental" (coffee, juice, and bread or pastries), sometimes "plantation" (eggs, sausage or bacon, rolls or cornbread, coffee, and juice). Top choices include the **Steamboat Inn** (tel. 903-665-8946), a handsome Greek Revival at 114 N. Marshall just a block from all the Austin St. sights, where rooms with private bath run $95. Just behind the House of the Seasons, the **Seasons Guest House** (tel. 665-1218) offers comparable rates that include a tour of the House.

The Marion County Chamber of Commerce (tel. 665-2672), 115 W. Austin, Jefferson, TX 75657, can furnish visitors with a complete list of bed and breakfasts.

Campgrounds and RV Parks

Jefferson sits between two of the state's most attractive waterways, Lake O' The Pines and Caddo Lake. Plenty of camping and RV facilities are available at each.

Food

Probably the top restaurant in town is **The Black Swan** (tel. 903-665-8922) at 210 Austin, which specializes in Cajun and Creole dishes. It's open Thurs.-Tues. for lunch and dinner; prices are moderate. Also competing for top slots are two converted homes with creative daily continental menus, **The Grove** (tel. 665-2638), 405 Moseley, open Thurs.-Mon. for dinner only; and the **Stillwater Inn** (tel. 665-8415), 203 E. Broadway, open Tues.-Sun. for dinner, brunch the last Sunday of the month.

The Bakery (tel. 665-2253) at 201 W. Austin is a casual sit-down/takeout place that will please just about anybody, with a menu that includes gumbo, red beans and rice, dressed baked potatoes, Italian pasta, chili, and chicken-fried steak, plus assorted fresh-baked goods. Another fine choice for a casual lunch is the **Cotton Gin** (tel. 665-1153) at 123 W. Austin, serving soups, salads, hamburgers, gyros, and tasty New Orleans-style muffalettas. Hot dogs, root beer, milkshakes, and nickel coffee are available at the **Jefferson General Store & Soda Fountain** (tel. 665-8481) at 113 E. Austin.

Downhome or Southern-style cooking is available at the **Club Cafe** (tel. 665-2881), 109 N. Polk, for breakfast and lunch, and the **Galley Pub** (tel. 665-3641), 121 W. Austin, for lunch and dinner. **Auntie Skinner's Riverboat Club** (tel. 665-7121) at 107 W. Austin serves Mexican and downhome lunch and dinner, Wednesday through Sunday.

The Jefferson Fudge Co. serves up true homestyle fudge, rich with real cream, butter, and chocolate, at the **Old Store,** 123 Walnut Street.

Entertainment

Most of Jefferson seems to be asleep by 9 p.m. However, on weekends the **Galley Theater** (tel. 903-665-8929) at 121 W. Austin hosts live 1890s melodramas in a cozy theater above the Galley Pub. On occasional weekend nights, Auntie Skinner's Riverboat Club (see "Food") features live music.

Events

On the first weekend of May, the Jessie Allen Wise Garden Club sponsors the **Spring Pilgrimage** in which many historic homes closed to the public most of the year are open for tours.

Another feature of this celebration is the annual performance of *The Diamond Bessie Murder Trial* at the Jefferson Playhouse, Delta and Henderson. Every year since 1955, local residents have presented this reenactment of an actual 1887 trial in which diamond heir Abe Rothschild was charged with the murder of his wife, an ex-prostitute called "Diamond Bessie" because of the abundance of diamonds she wore.

During the second weekend in June, the streets of downtown Jefferson are filled with live country music, dancing, clogging, a talent show, and arts and crafts exhibits celebrating **Vernon Dalhart Days.** This festival also includes a talent show, arm-wrestling contest, an anything-that-floats race, and a "roadkill" cookoff, all in honor of local boy Vernon Dalhart. Dalhart, an opera-turned-hillbilly singer, recorded on Edison cylinders in the early 1900s, selling millions of copies and becoming country music's first international star.

The **Jefferson Christmas Candlelight Tour** is held the first weekend of December and is the town's most popular event. Four historic homes are selected and bedecked with 19th-century Christmas decorations (lots of candles); hostesses in Victorian gowns receive visitors and conduct tours. Carolers and handbell choirs roam the streets; there are Christmas music concerts at the Jefferson Playhouse and the First United Methodist Church, 305 W. Henderson.

Canoeing the Bayou

Paddler's Post (tel. 903-665-3251 or 938-3334), 101 Market St., and **Big Cypress Canoe Rental** (tel. 665-7163 or 665-7288), 502 E. Watson, rent equipment for canoeing on Big Cypress Bayou, which runs along the southeast edge of town. Standard rates are around $5 an hour or $20 a day. These rental facilities can also provide shuttle service to a more remote seven-mile upper section of the bayou popular for fishing and primitive camping—ask for maps and information. Put-in points are below Lake O' The Pines or closer to Jefferson just east of French Creek; popular takeouts are in Jefferson itself, farther east at Black Cypress Bayou, or at Long's Camp.

Lake O' The Pines

This 18,700-acre reservoir, an impoundment of Cypress Creek set among pine forests, is one of the most scenic lakes in the state and very popular for fishing, swimming, and boating. During most times of year, the best fishing (bass, bream, crappie, catfish) is at the north end of the lake near Willow Point and Cedar Springs. A wide variety of facilities—campgrounds, marinas, picnic areas, and boat ramps—encircle the lake, most administered by the Army Corps of Engineers. **Alley Creek** (open March-September only), **Buckhorn Creek** (March-September only), **Brushy Creek,** and **Johnson Creek** each have tent/camper sites with w/e for $8-12 a night. The **Cedar Springs, Hurricane Creek,** and **Oak Valley** areas have no-fee primitive campsites with pit toilets and cooking grills only. The stay limit for all Corps-operated camping areas is 14 days.

Several commercial concessions operate campgrounds on the lake as well, including **Big Cypress Marina** (tel. 903-665-8582), **Island View Landing** (tel. 777-4161), **Sunrise Cove** (tel. 968-4017), and **Willow Point** (tel. 755-2912). All offer two-way hookups, but only Willow Point has a trailer dump station. Rates are about the same as at the Corps facilities. Willow Point also rents cabins for around $25 a night.

For further information, contact the Corps of Engineers (tel. 665-2336), Lake O' The Pines, Drawer W, Jefferson, TX 75657. For reservations call (800) 284-2267.

Caddo Lake

Before the 1873 blasting of the Red River Raft near Shreveport, Caddo Lake was an important waterway for steamboat traffic between New Orleans and Jefferson. Caddo Indian legend says the 26,000-acre lake was created by powerful earthshaking spirits who were angry with a Caddo chief.

Even before the rise and fall of the Red River Raft, a bayou was present on the Texas-Louisiana border; the logjam enlarged and deepened the bayou by many times its original size. The lake owes its current volume to a U.S. Army Corps-built weir placed upstream on the Sabine River in 1914 to raise the water level high enough to float heavy machinery to Louisiana oil-drilling sites. Hence when Texans argue over whether Caddo is a natural or "artificial" lake, both sides are right to a certain degree.

Today the lake straddles the Texas-Louisiana border and is one of the most atmospheric lakes

in either state, bending around coves and islands and fringed by lush floodplain forests. Cypress trees and tupelo, hung with Spanish moss, dot the lake's surface and add to the primeval effect.

Eager to meddle in the waterway's destiny yet a third time, the U.S. Army Corps of Engineers has proposed the construction of an 80-mile barge canal through the heart of the lake to link northeast Texas and the Red River at Shreveport—in essence reinstating the Red River Raft the same Corps destroyed in 1873. Many folks living around the lake are dead set against the proposal, though of course Jefferson developers envision a boost in tourism with the return of steamboats to Shreveport.

Meanwhile in 1992 the park and wildlife management area placed an additional 7,000 acres under TPWD/WMA protection. Park supporters hope an increase in ecotourism will replace the canal proposal as a potential source of regional revenue. In 1993 the international Ramsar Convention designated Caddo Lake a "Wetland of International Importance" at about the same time the U.S. Fish and Wildlife Service granted the lake "Priority One," its highest classification for wetlands. Music celebrity Don Henley, formerly of the pop group the Eagles and a native of nearby Linden, Texas, recently established the Caddo Lake Scholars Program to focus research attention on the lake and surrounding area. In light of these events, the canal construction proposal has been permanently tabled.

The only Texas town on the lake is Uncertain (pop. 194), situated on the southwestern shore. Just north of town along the lake are several fishing camps where bait, tackle, and boats are available. Some of the townspeople have decided the town's name sounds negative and are trying to change it to Certain, so it reads differently on some maps. You might say they're uncertain about the name.

Canoeing and Tours: The lake and its adjoining bayous and creeks are a favorite destination among canoeists since they offer so many possibilities for exploration. The lake has only two public boat ramps, one at Caddo Lake State Park, the other next to the Morringsport Dam in Louisiana.

Several private concessions along the lakeshore offer canoe rentals for around $20 a day. If you're new to the lake, be sure to get a map that shows the 40 miles of established boat lanes; channel markers on the lake help, but it's easy to get lost. Several bait and tackle shops, lodges, and campgrounds can also arrange for boating/fishing guides at a rate of approximately $55 per half day, $75 for a full day.

A portion of the lake belongs to the **Caddo Lake Wildlife Management Area,** where occasional naturalist-guided boat tours are arranged for those with Texas Conservation Passport cards. Call (903) 679-3743 for information.

Fishing: Caddo Lake is one of the region's top warm-water fly-fishing spots, home to the hard-fighting chain pickerel, a type of muskellunge. Other gamefish include paddlefish, alligator gar, crappie, catfish, and bass. A double-T fishing pier and concrete boat ramp in the park zone on Saw Mill Pond provide public access for anglers and boaters.

Cabins: Johnson's Ranch (tel. 789-3213) and **Pine Needle Lodge** (tel. 665-2911) offer cabins for rent along the south and southwest shores of the lake. Rates start at $30-45 a night for a one-bedroom cabin (two beds) with kitchenette and reach as high as $100 for a three-bedroom cabin (six beds) with a large kitchen; most cabins are air-conditioned. Caddo Lake State Park also has cabins.

Camping: Caddo Lake State Park is on Big Cypress Bayou where it feeds into the lake's west end, just off FM 134 from Jefferson. Day-use facilities include picnic areas, a boat launch, fishing pier, boat rentals, and hiking trails. Camping facilities include tent/camper sites with water only ($8), with w/e ($11), RV sites with full hookups ($16), screened shelters ($16-20), and cabins ($40 for one to two people, plus $5 for each additional adult, $2 for children 6-12). For information or reservations, contact Caddo Lake State Park (tel. 679-3351), Route 2, Box 15, Karnack, TX 75661.

Private camping areas are available at Uncertain's **Crip's Camp** (tel. 789-3233), northwest of Caddo Lake State Park near Baldwin (off FM 134) on Big Cypress Bayou. Tentsites run around $5 with water only, $10 with w/e. Also in this area is **Shady Glade** (tel. 789-3295), where RV sites with full hookups are $11 and you can pitch a tent for $5, and **Big Cypress** (tel. 665-8582), where hookups run $8-12.

Shopping

Jefferson has over 30 antique and collectibles shops, most along Polk, Austin, Lafayette, and Walnut. A map/brochure listing them all is available from the chamber of commerce (tel. 903-665-2672) at 115 W. Austin. **Old Mill Antiques** (tel. 665-8601) houses 10 dealers under one roof at 210 E. Austin. **Three Rivers Antiques & Collectors Mall** (tel. 665-8721) at 116 Walnut also has several dealers. The **Bazaar Mall** (tel. 665-7271) at 211 N. Polk offers a wide selection of goods including antiques, Victorian collectibles, woodcrafts, ceramics, and folk art.

Getting Around

Jefferson Narrated Tours (tel. 903-665-1122) offers half-hour tours by mule-drawn surrey, departing from 302 Dallas; $5 adults, $3 children under 12. **Pols Street Trolley** (tel. 665-1665) operates a one-hour narrated tour by open-air trolley-style bus, departing from tour headquarters at 102-B S. Polk St.; $5 adults, 50 cents seniors, $3.50 children under 12.

The same family operates one-hour boat tours of Big Cypress Bayou aboard the *Bayou Queen,* passing abandoned mills and a Confederate gunpowder magazine along the old steamboat route. Focusing on the history, flora, and fauna of the area, this tour departs from **Jefferson Landing;** from Austin St., go north to Polk, then south across the bridge and follow the sign to the landing. An easy walk. Fares are the same as for the trolley tour.

In addition to surrey, bus, and boat tours, you can take a ride on the **Jefferson and Cypress Bayou Railroad** (tel. 665-8400), a narrow-gauge steam train that runs along Big Cypress Bayou. The five-mile, hour-long trip runs through stands of cypress, pine, and dogwood to the Confederate powder magazine, then on to "Hang Town" where riders might experience a train robbery, Indian attack, shootout, or hanging before returning to the station. The depot is at the end of E. Austin; June-Sept. departures are Monday at 1:30 p.m., Thursday, Friday, and Sunday at 1:30 p.m. and 3:30 p.m., Saturday at 1:30 p.m., 3 p.m., and 4:30 p.m. During the remainder of the year the train runs Fri.-Sun. only. The fare is $7.89 adults, $4.89 children 3-12.

Information
The **Marion County Chamber of Commerce** (tel. 903-665-2672) at 115 W. Austin distributes free information on Jefferson and vicinity; staff can also arrange bed and breakfast bookings. Open Mon.-Sat. 9 a.m.-5 p.m.

The area code for Jefferson and vicinity is 903.

BOOKLIST

DESCRIPTION AND TRAVEL

American Automobile Association. *Texas Tour Book*. Published annually. A slim summary of things to see in the more popular tourist areas, including up-to-date hotel, motel, and restaurant information.

Brook, Stephen. *Honkytonk Gelato: Travels Through Texas*. Paragon House, 1988; 283 pages. Brook is an Englishman who brings insight and humor to bear on his Texas travels; probably the best travelogue yet written about the state.

Cummings, Joe. *Northern Mexico Handbook*. Moon Publications, 1994. A new guidebook, the first ever published in English, to a largely undiscovered region that shares many geographical and cultural characteristics with West and South Texas. The book covers mainland Mexico's nine northernmost states—Sonora, Sinaloa, Chihuahua, Durango, Coahuila, Nuevo León, Tamaulipas, Zacatecas, and San Luis Potosí—and provides in-depth information on every Texas-Mexico border town.

Rafferty, Robert R. *Texas*. The Texas Monthly Guidebooks series, Texas Monthly Press, 1989. Ambitious guide covering a large number of Texas towns by region, in alphabetical order. Despite some organizational problems (Beaumont is placed in South Texas while Houston—in reality farther south—is put under East Texas), the completeness of the coverage is exemplary.

Ruff, Ann. *A Guide to Historic Texas Inns and Hotels*. Houston: Lone Star Books, 1985. A survey of hotels and inns built mostly between 1880 and 1950. Worth reading for the historical background, but out of date for practical information.

State Department of Highways and Public Transportation. *Texas Public Campgrounds*. Published annually. A free publication that lists the facilities and locations of virtually every city, county, state, Corps of Engineers, or National Park Service campground in the state. Keyed to the State Department of Highways' *Official Highway Travel Map*. **

State Department of Highways and Public Transportation. *Texas State Travel Guide*. Published annually. Another free publication; contains capsule descriptions of a wide range of state destinations, in alphabetical order. **

Texas Almanac. Dallas Morning News. Published annually. Contains a wealth of information in the areas of politics, government, geography, culture, business, transportation, and education. Each year the book concentrates on the history of a different part of the state.

Works Projects Administration. *Texas: A Guide to the Lone Star State*. American Guide Series, 1940, reprinted by Texas Monthly Press, 1986; 718 pages. Part of the classic guide series that employed writers during the New Deal era. Contains some interesting historical tidbits.

NATURE

Bomar, George W. *Texas Weather*. University of Texas Press, 1985; 265 pages. An excellent summary of weather patterns throughout the state, including the physics of hurricanes and tornadoes. Contains charts with average temperatures, relative humidity, precipitation, and wind velocities for various points in all Texas regions.

Kutac, Ed. *Birder's Guide to Texas*. Gulf Publications, 1989. The best general guide to Texas birding; contains a complete list of bird clubs in the state.

Lane, James A., and John L. Tveten. *A Birder's Guide to the Texas Coast.* American Birding Association, 1993. Detailed and comprehensive, covering the coastal area from Beaumont to Brownsville; includes sections on indigenous mammals, amphibians, and reptiles.

McAlister, Wayne H., and Martha K. McAlister. *Matagorda Island: A Naturalist's Guide.* University of Texas Press, 1993. The copious information on Gulf Coast wildlife contained in this book would be useful anywhere along the barrier islands.

Peterson, Roger Tory. *Field Guide to the Birds of Texas.* Peterson Field Guide Series, 1979. While not as up to date as Kutac's book, the Peterson standard in color illustrations has a strong appeal.

Phelan, Richard. *Texas Wild: The Land, Plants, and Animals of the Lone Star State.* This out-of-print book offers a wonderful synthesis of the state's geography and natural history. Instead of isolating the animate and the inanimate, Phelan demonstrates their intricate connections; along the way he takes a few jabs at local, regional, and state environmental policies. Includes color plates and maps.

Tennant, Alan. *A Field Guide to Texas Snakes.* Texas Monthly Field Guide Series, Texas Monthly Press, 1985; 260 pages. A well-researched, well-written guide; includes an identification key, color plates, and a useful section on venom poisoning.

Texas Parks & Wildlife. *A Checklist of Texas Birds.* Technical Series No. 32; 1989; 33 pages. A complete birder's checklist categorized by bird family, including extinct, hypothetical, accidental, introduced, historical, and extirpated species. Available free at many state parks. *

Wauer, Roland H. *Naturalist's Big Bend.* Texas A&M University Press, 1980; 149 pages. A good introduction of the flora and fauna of the Big Bend area.

CULTURE

Govenar, Alan. *Meeting the Blues: The Rise of the Texas Sound.* Taylor Publishing Co., 1988; 239 pages. An excellent combination of interviews, photos, and historical descriptions tracing the development of Texas musical styles (including R&B, swamp music, Cajun, and zydeco as well as blues) from the late 19th century to the present.

Hall, Douglas Kent. *The Border: Life on the Line.* Abbeville Press; 1988; 251 pages. Part photo essay, part narrative, successfully evoking life along the Texas-Mexican border.

Linck, Ernestine Sewell, and Joyce Gibson Roach. *Eats: A Folk History of Texas Foods.* Texas Christian University Press, 1989; 257 pages. A montage of recipes, history, regional food classification, and anecdotes.

Porterfield, Bill. *The Greatest Honky-Tonks in Texas.* Taylor Publishing Co., 1981; 148 pages. Indispensable reading for anyone contemplating a serious journey along the honky-tonk circuit; not as out of date as its 1981 publication date might indicate, since the author attempted to select the tried and true. Humorously written, it includes charts and instructions for learning the dance hall waltz, polka, cotton-eyed Joe, sweetheart schottische, and two-step.

Shank, Barry. *Dissonant Identities: The Rock-'n' Roll Scene in Austin, Texas.* Wesleyan University Press of New England, 1994. This heavy academic analysis examines the development of Austin's musical milieu from the city's cattle kingdom days (termed a "homosocial utopia") through the post-punk era. The author suggests Austin's rebel music image dates from WW II-era honky-tonks, concluding, "The performance of identity in the practice of popular music involves a constant renegotiation of the relationships between Imaginary sincerity and a commodified Symbolic."

Smith, Erwin E., and Haley, J. Evetts. *Life on the Texas Range*. University of Texas Press, 1994. First published in 1952, this classic photographic work contains a striking visual record of cowboy life in early 20th-century Texas, as interpreted through the camera of Erwin E. Smith.

Stewart, Rick. *Lone Star Regionalism: The Dallas Nine and Their Circle*. Texas Monthly Press, 1985. Examines the work of a group of young Dallas artists (around 25 in all, led by an influential nine) who achieved nationwide recognition in the 1930s for their strong regional style, which combined elements of surrealism, American Indian design, and Italian quattrocento painting. Contains many color plates.

HISTORY

A Concise History of Texas. Dallas Morning News, 1988; 157 pages; formerly part of the *Texas Almanac*. Exactly what it claims to be; remarkably comprehensive and accurate.

Fehrenbach, T.R. *Lone Star*. American Legacy Press, 1988; 761 pages. This thick tome is considered the best history of the state available, but is sadly lacking in proportion and style.

Newcombe, W.W. Jr. *The Indians of Texas*. University of Texas Press, 1961. The definitive work on Texas Indians; well balanced.

RECREATION

Dunn, Barbara, and Stephan Myers. *Diving and Snorkeling Guide to Texas*. Pisces Books (Gulf Publishing), 1991. Contains maps and useful information on dive sites along the Texas Gulf Coast.

Parent, Laurence. *The Hiker's Guide to Texas*. Falcon Press, 1991; 200 pages. Contains up-to-date descriptions of 75 trails throughout the state, noting length, elevation, difficulty, water availability, and special features of each.

Swan, Ed et al. *Cycling Texas*. Dallas: Taylor Publshing Co., 1993. This guide to Texas bicycle touring contains detailed itineraries and route maps for Big Bend Country, the Hill Country, North Texas backroads, Panhandle canyons and plains, and the South Texas plains and coast. Also included are general tips on Texas cycling and a list of over 90 cycling clubs in the state.

Texas Music Office. *Texas Music Industry Directory*. Issued annually. A 300-page sourcebook listing everything from recording services to live music venues to musical instrument dealers statewide. Available from Texas Music Office, P.O. Box 13246, Austin, TX 78711, for $16.50.

Texas Parks & Wildlife. *Texas Hunting Guide*. Published annually; page count varies. A free publication that contains a thorough listing of state hunting regulations. *

Texas Parks & Wildlife. *Texas Recreational Fresh & Saltwater Fishing Guide*. Published annually; page count varies. A free, complete account of all state fishing regulations, including those for shellfish. *

* Can be ordered by writing the Texas Parks & Wildlife Dept., 4200 Smith School Rd., Austin, TX 78744.

** Can be ordered by writing the Texas Department of Highways and Public Transportation, Travel and Information Division, P.O. Box 5064, Austin TX 78763.

INDEX

Page numbers in **boldface** indicate the primary reference. *Italicized* page numbers indicate information in maps, charts, or special topics.

ABOUT THE AUTHOR

THE GREAT-GREAT-GREAT GRANDFATHER *of author Joe Cummings emigrated to the state from "up north" in the 1840s. Another relative, David Lawhon, published the state's first bilingual newspaper,* The Texian and Emigrant's Guide, *printed in both Spanish and English and praised by the* New York Courier *as a publication "edited with intelligence and success." Lawhon was later appointed chief justice of Jefferson County.*

With his Panhandle-born father in the Army, Joe moved in and out of Texas, California, Washington D.C., and France before attending college and university in North Carolina and California. Attracted to geological extremes—a probable Texas legacy—his first in-depth journeys after college involved the river deltas and rainforests of Southeast Asia, where he worked as a Peace Corps volunteer in Thailand and a university lecturer in Malaysia. He later authored or co-authored popular guidebooks to Thailand, Laos, Malaysia, Singapore, Burma, Indonesia, and China. He has since penned Moon guides to Northern Mexico, Baja, and Cabo, and is co-author of Mexico Handbook.

Joe crisscrosses Texas freeways, ranch roads, plains, forests, mountains, and canyons for every edition of Texas Handbook.

ARIZONA TRAVELER'S HANDBOOK
by Bill Weir and Robert Blake, 500 pages, **$16.95**
"This is the best book ever published with practical travel
information about the state." —*Arizona Republic*

ATLANTIC CANADA HANDBOOK
by Nan Drosdick and Mark Morris, 450 pages, **$17.95**
Like a corner of Europe, Canada's Atantic provincs harbor a
multicultural melange where Irish brogue and Scottish kilts
can be found along with historic French forts and deserted
Viking villages. *Atlantic Canada Handbook* provides extensive
coverage of this region, including New Brunswick, Nova
Scotia, Newfoundland, and Prince Edward Island. While there
are many guides to Canada, none offers the detailed regional
coverage of this comprehensive handbook.

BIG ISLAND OF HAWAII HANDBOOK
by J.D. Bisignani, 347 pages, **$13.95**
"The best general guidebooks available." —*Hawaii Magazine*

BRITISH COLUMBIA HANDBOOK
by Jane King, 381 pages, **$15.95**
"Deftly balances the conventional and the unconventional, for both
city lovers and nature lovers."
—*Reference and Research Book News*

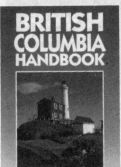

CATALINA ISLAND HANDBOOK
by Chicki Mallan, 299 pages, **$10.95**
"*Catalina Handbook* should be aboard any vessel venturing to the
fabled recreation spot." —*Sea Magazine*

COLORADO HANDBOOK
by Stephen Metzger, 418 pages, **$17.95**
"Hotel rooms in the Aspen area, in the height of winter sports
season, for $20-$30? . . . who but a relentless researcher from
Moon could find it?" —*The New York Daily News*

GEORGIA HANDBOOK by Kap Stann, 350 pages, **$16.95**
". . . everything you need to know to enjoy a journey through
Georgia." —*Southern Book Trade*

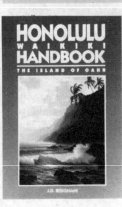

HAWAII HANDBOOK by J.D. Bisignani, 1000 pages, **$19.95**
"No one since Michener has told us so much about our 50th
state." —*Playboy*

HONOLULU-WAIKIKI HANDBOOK
by J.D. Bisignani, 365 pages, **$14.95**
"The best general guidebooks available." —*Hawaii Magazine*

IDAHO HANDBOOK by Bill Loftus, 310 pages, **$14.95**
"Well-organized, engagingly written, tightly edited, and chock-full
of interesting facts about localities, backcountry destinations,
traveler accommodations, and cultural and natural history."
—*Sierra Magazine*

KAUAI HANDBOOK by J.D. Bisignani, 228 pages, **$13.95**
"This slender guide is tightly crammed. . . . The information
provided is staggering." —*Hawaii Magazine*

MAUI HANDBOOK by J.D. Bisignani, 370 pages, **$14.95**
"*Maui Handbook* should be in every couple's suitcase. It
intelligently discusses Maui's history and culture, and you can
trust the author's recommendations for best beaches, restaurants,
and excursions." —*Bride's Magazine*

MONTANA HANDBOOK
by W.C. McRae and Judy Jewell, 400 pages, **$15.95**
"Well-organized, engagingly written, tightly edited, and chock-full
of interesting facts about localities, backcountry destinations,
traveler accommodations, and cultural and natural history."
—*Sierra Magazine*

NEVADA HANDBOOK by Deke Castleman, 450 pages, **$16.95**
"Veteran travel writer Deke Castleman says he covered more
than 10,000 miles in his research for this book and it shows."
—*Nevada Magazine*

NEW MEXICO HANDBOOK
by Stephen Metzger, 329 pages, **$14.95**
"The best current guide and travel book to all of New Mexico"
—New Mexico Book League

NORTHERN CALIFORNIA HANDBOOK
by Kim Weir, 775 pages, **$19.95**
"That rarest of travel books–both a practical guide to the region
and a map of its soul." —*San Francisco Chronicle*

OREGON HANDBOOK
by Stuart Warren and Ted Long Ishikawa, 450 pages, **$16.95**

TEXAS HANDBOOK by Joe Cummings, 598 pages, **$17.95**
"Reveals a Texas with a diversity of people and culture that is as
breathtaking as that of the land itself."
—*Planet Newspaper*, Australia

"I've read a bunch of Texas guidebooks, and this is the best one."
–Joe Bob Briggs

UTAH HANDBOOK by Bill Weir and Robert Blake, 445 pages, $16.95

"What Moon Publications has given us—at long last—is a one-volume, easy to digest, up-to-date, practical, factual guide to all things Utahan. . . . This is the best handbook of its kind I've yet encountered." —*The Salt Lake Tribune*

WASHINGTON HANDBOOK
by Dianne J. Boulerice Lyons and Archie Satterfiled, 443 pages, $15.95

"Departs from the general guidebook format by offering information on how to cope with the rainy days and where to take the children. . . . This is a great little book, informational, fun to read, and a good one to keep." —*Travel Publishing News*

WYOMING HANDBOOK by Don Pitcher, 495 pages, $14.95

"Wanna know the real dirt on Calamity Jane, white Indians, and the tacky Cheyenne gunslingers? All here. And all fun."
—*The New York Daily News*

". . . perhaps the most definitive tourist guide to the state ever published." —*The Oregonian*

MOONBELT

A new concept in moneybelts. Made of heavy-duty Cordura nylon, the Moonbelt offers maximum protection for your money and important papers. This pouch, designed for all-weather comfort, slips under your shirt or waistband, rendering it virtually undetectable and inaccessible to pickpockets. It features a one-inch high-test quick-release buckle so there's no more fumbling around for the strap or repeated adjustments. This handy plastic buckle opens and closes with a touch, but won't come undone until you want it to. Moonbelts accommodate traveler's checks, passports, cash, photos, etc. Size 5 x 9 inches. Available in black only. **$8.95**

MOON TRAVEL HANDBOOKS

NORTH AMERICA AND HAWAII

Alaska-Yukon Handbook (0161)	$14.95
Alberta and the Northwest Territories Handbook (0676)	$17.95
Arizona Traveler's Handbook (0536)	$16.95
Atlantic Canada Handbook (0072)	$17.95
Big Island of Hawaii Handbook (0064)	$13.95
British Columbia Handbook (0145)	$15.95
Catalina Island Handbook (3751)	$10.95
Colorado Handbook (0137)	$17.95
Georgia Handbook (0609)	$16.95
Hawaii Handbook (0005)	$19.95
Honolulu-Waikiki Handbook (0587)	$14.95
Idaho Handbook (0617)	$14.95
Kauai Handbook (0013)	$13.95
Maui Handbook (0579)	$14.95
Montana Handbook (0544)	$15.95
Nevada Handbook (0641)	$16.95
New Mexico Handbook (0153)	$14.95
Northern California Handbook (3840)	$19.95
Oregon Handbook (0102)	$16.95
Texas Handbook (0633)	$17.95
Utah Handbook (0684)	$16.95
Washington Handbook (0552)	$15.95
Wyoming Handbook (3980)	$14.95

ASIA AND THE PACIFIC

Bali Handbook (3379)	$12.95
Bangkok Handbook (0595)	$13.95
Fiji Islands Handbook (0382)	$13.95
Hong Kong Handbook (0560)	$15.95
Indonesia Handbook (0625)	$25.00
Japan Handbook (3700)	$22.50
Micronesia Handbook (3808)	$11.95
Nepal Handbook (3646)	$12.95
New Zealand Handbook (3883)	$18.95
Outback Australia Handbook (3794)	$15.95
Philippines Handbook (0048)	$17.95
Southeast Asia Handbook (0021)	$21.95

South Pacific Handbook (3999) $19.95
Tahiti-Polynesia Handbook (0374) $13.95
Thailand Handbook (3824) $16.95
Tibet Handbook (3905) $30.00
*Vietnam, Cambodia & Laos Handbook (0293) $18.95

MEXICO

Baja Handbook (0528). $15.95
Cabo Handbook (0285) $14.95
Cancún Handbook (0501). $13.95
Central Mexico Handbook (0234) $15.95
*Mexico Handbook (0315) $21.95
Northern Mexico Handbook (0226) $16.95
Pacific Mexico Handbook (0323) $16.95
Puerto Vallarta Handbook (0250) $14.95
Yucatán Peninsula Handbook (0242). $15.95

CENTRAL AMERICA AND THE CARIBBEAN

Belize Handbook (0370). $15.95
Caribbean Handbook (0277) $16.95
Costa Rica Handbook (0358). $18.95
Jamaica Handbook (0129) $14.95

INTERNATIONAL

Egypt Handbook (3891). $18.95
Moon Handbook (0668) $10.00
Moscow-St. Petersburg Handbook (3913) $13.95
Staying Healthy in Asia, Africa, and Latin America (0269) . . $11.95

* New title, please call for availability

PERIPLUS TRAVEL MAPS
All maps $7.95 each

Bali	Hong Kong	Singapore
Bandung/W. Java	Java	Vietnam
Bangkok/C. Thailand	Ko Samui/S. Thailand	Yogyakarta/C. Java
Batam/Bintan	Penang	
Cambodia	Phuket/S. Thailand	

WHERE TO BUY MOON TRAVEL HANDBOOKS

BOOKSTORES AND LIBRARIES: Moon Travel Handbooks are sold worldwide. Please write to our sales manager for a list of wholesalers and distributors in your area.

TRAVELERS: We would like to have Moon Travel Handbooks available throughout the world. Please ask your bookstore to write or call us for ordering information. If your bookstore will not order our guides for you, please contact us for a free title listing.

> Moon Publications, Inc.
> P.O. Box 3040
> Chico, CA 95927-3040 U.S.A.
> Tel: (800) 345-5473
> Fax: (916) 345-6751
> E-mail: travel@moon.com

IMPORTANT ORDERING INFORMATION

PRICES: All prices are subject to change. We always ship the most current edition. We will let you know if there is a price increase on the book you order.

SHIPPING AND HANDLING OPTIONS: Domestic UPS or USPS first class (allow 10 working days for delivery): $3.50 for the first item, 50 cents for each additional item.

EXCEPTIONS:

Tibet Handbook and *Indonesia Handbook* shipping $4.50; $1.00 for each additional *Tibet Handbook* or *Indonesia Handbook.*

Moonbelt shipping is $1.50 for one, 50 cents for each additional belt.

Add $2.00 for same-day handling.

UPS 2nd Day Air or Printed Airmail requires a special quote.

International Surface Bookrate 8-12 weeks delivery: $3.00 for the first item, $1.00 for each additional item. Note: Moon Publications cannot guarantee international surface bookrate shipping. Moon recommends sending international orders via air mail, which requires a special quote.

FOREIGN ORDERS: Orders that originate outside the U.S.A. must be paid for with either an international money order or a check in U.S. currency drawn on a major U.S. bank based in the U.S.A.

TELEPHONE ORDERS: We accept Visa or MasterCard payments. Minimum order is US$15.00. Call in your order: (800) 345-5473, 8 a.m.-5 p.m. Pacific Standard Time.

ORDER FORM

Be sure to call (800) 345-5473 for current prices and editions or for the name of the bookstore nearest you that carries Moon Travel Handbooks • 8 a.m.–5 p.m. PST.
(See important ordering information on preceding page.)

Name: _____ Date: _____

Street: _____

City: _____ Daytime Phone: _____

State or Country: _____ Zip Code: _____

QUANTITY	TITLE	PRICE

Taxable Total _____

Sales Tax (7.25%) for California Residents _____

Shipping & Handling _____

TOTAL _____

Ship: ☐ UPS (no P.O. Boxes) ☐ 1st class ☐ International surface mail
Ship to: ☐ address above ☐ other _____
_____

Make checks payable to: **MOON PUBLICATIONS, INC.** P.O. Box 3040, Chico, CA 95927-3040 U.S.A. We accept Visa and MasterCard. **To Order:** Call in your Visa or MasterCard number, or send a written order with your Visa or MasterCard number and expiration date clearly written.

Card Number: ☐ **Visa**   ☐ **MasterCard**

☐ ☐ ☐ ☐ ☐ ☐ ☐ ☐ ☐ ☐ ☐ ☐ ☐ ☐ ☐ ☐

Exact Name on Card: _____

Expiration date: _____

Signature: _____

F/95–AH

THE METRIC SYSTEM

1 inch = 2.54 centimeters (cm)
1 foot = .304 meters (m)
1 mile = 1.6093 kilometers (km)
1 km = .6124 miles
1 fathom = 1.8288 m
1 chain = 20.1168 m
1 furlong = 201.168 m
1 acre = .4047 hectares
1 sq km = 100 hectares
1 sq mile = 2.59 square km
1 ounce = 28.35 grams
1 pound = .4536 kilograms
1 short ton = .90718 metric ton
1 short ton = 2000 pounds
1 long ton = 1.016 metric tons
1 long ton = 2240 pounds
1 metric ton = 1000 kilograms
1 quart = .94635 liters
1 US gallon = 3.7854 liters
1 Imperial gallon = 4.5459 liters
1 nautical mile = 1.852 km

To compute celsius temperatures, subtract 32 from Fahrenheit and divide by 1.8. To go the other way, multiply celsius by 1.8 and add 32.

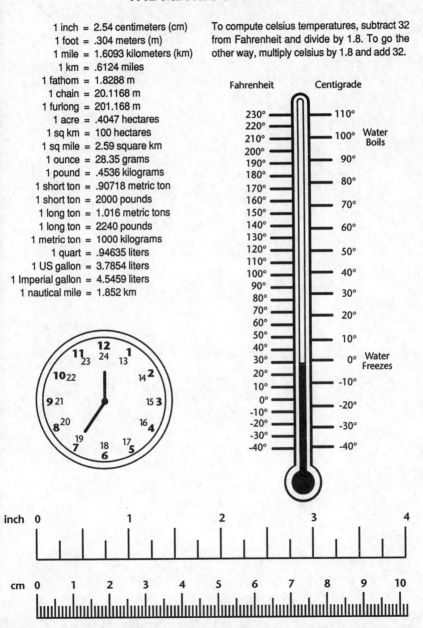